CLYMER®

MERCURY/MARINER

OUTBOARD SHOP MANUAL
75-275 HP • 1994-1997 (Includes Jet Drive Models)

The world's finest publisher of mechanical how-to manuals

PRIMEDIA
Business Directories & Books

P.O. Box 12901, Overland Park, KS 66282-2901

Copyright ©1998 PRIMEDIA Business Magazines and Media Inc.

FIRST EDITION
First Printing August, 1998
Second Printing January, 2002
Third Printing June, 2003

Printed in U.S.A.

CLYMER and colophon are registered trademarks of PRIMEDIA Business Magazines and Media Inc.

This book was printed at Von Hoffmann an ISO certified company.

ISBN: 0-89287-707-3

Library of Congress: 98-72837

Tools shown in Chapter Two courtesy of Thorsen Tool, Dallas, Texas. Test equipment shown in Chapter Two courtesy of Dixson, Inc., Grand Junction, Colorado.

Technical assistance provided by Mike Burleson, Burleson Marine, Garland, Texas.

Technical illustrations by Steve Amos, Bob Caldwell, Michael St. Clair and Donald Oberdoester.

Technical photography by Scott Johnson

COVER: Photo courtesy of Mercury Marine, a Brunswick Company.

PRODUCTION: Dylan Goodwin.

Contents

Quick Reference Data

RECOMMENDED SPARK PLUGS

Model	NGK spark plug number (RFI)*	Gap in. (mm)
75, 90 hp and 65 Jet	BUHW-2 (BUZHW-2)	NA
100, 115, 125 hp and 80 Jet	BP8H-N-10 (BPZ8H-N-10)	.040 (1.02)
135-200 hp, 105 and 140 Jet	BU8H (BUZ8H)	NA
200 DFI (direct fuel injected)	Champion RC10ECC	.040 (1.02)
225 hp		
(carbureted 1994-1996)	Use resistor (BPZ8H-N-10)	.040 (1.02)
225 hp (carbureted 1997)	Champion QL77CC	.035 (0.89)
225-250 hp EFI		
(electronic fuel injection)	Champion QL77CC	.035 (0.89)
275 hp	BU8H (BUZ8H)	NA

*Use resistor or suppression spark plugs if radio frequency interference (RFI) suppression is required.

GEARCASE GEAR RATIO AND APPROXIMATE LUBRICANT CAPACITY

Model	Gear ratio	Tooth count	Lubricant capacity
75 and 90 hp	2.3:1	13:30	22.5 oz. (665 ml)
100, 115 and 125 hp	2.07:1	14:29	22.5 oz. (665 ml)
135 and 150 hp	2.00:1	14:28	22.5 oz. (665 ml)
XR6 and Magnum III			
(small gearcase)	1.78:1	14:25	21.0 oz. (621 ml)
XR6 and Magnum III			
(large gearcase)	1.87:1	15:28	22.5 oz. (665 ml)
150-200 XRI, 175-200 hp	1.87:1	15:28	22.5 oz. (665 ml)
200 DFI			
(direct fuel injection)	1.75:1	12:21	28.0 oz. (828 ml)
225-250 hp (1994)	1.64:1	17:28	28.0 oz. (828 ml)
225-250 hp (1995-1997)	1.75:1	12:21	28.0 oz. (828 ml)
275 hp	1.64:1	17:28	29.0 oz. (858 ml)

RECOMMENDED LUBRICANTS, SEALANTS AND ADHESIVES

	Part No.
Lubricants	
Quicksilver 2-Cycle TC-W3 outboard oil	(dealer stock item)
Quicksilver Special Lubricant 101	92-13872A-1
Quicksilver 2-4-C Multi-Lube	(dealer stock item)
Quicksilver Anti-Corrosion Grease	92-78376A-6
Quicksilver Needle Bearing Grease	92-825265A-1
Quicksilver Power Trim and Steering Fluid	92-90100A12
Quicksilver Premium Blend Gear Lube	(dealer stock item)
Quicksilver High Performance Gear Lube	(dealer stock item)
	(continued)

RECOMMENDED LUBRICANTS, SEALANTS AND ADHESIVES (continued)

	Part No.
Sealants	
Quicksilver Perfect Seal	92-34227-1
Loctite 5900 Ultra black RTV sealant	92-809826
Sealer (crankcase halves)	92-90113-2
Loctite Master Gasket Sealer	92-12564-2
Quicksilver Liquid Neoprene	92-25711-2
Loctite 567 PST pipe sealant	92-809822
Quicksilver Bellows Adhesive	92-86166-1
Quicksilver Ignition Coil Insulation Compound	92-41669-1
Adhesives	
Locquic Primer	92-809824
Loctite 271 threadlocking sealant (high strength)	92-809819
Loctite 242 threadlocking sealant (medium strength)	92-809821
Loctite RC680 high strength retaining compound	92-809833
Miscellaneous	
Quicksilver Power Tune Engine Cleaner	92-15104A12
Quicksilver Corrosion Guard	92-815869A12
Quicksilver Storage Seal Rust Inhibitor	92-86145A12
Quicksilver Dielectric silicone grease	92-823506-1

STARTING SERIAL NUMBER LISTING

	1994	1995	1996	1997
Mercury outboard models				
75 hp	0D283222	0G077367	0G301751	0G438000
90 hp	0D283222	0G077369	0G301751	0G438000
100 hp	0D283222	0G090125	0G301751	0G438000
115 hp	0D283222	0G127522	0G301751	0G438000
125 hp	0D283222	0G090127	0G301751	0G438000
135 hp	0D284788	0G127861	0G303046	0G438000
150 hp	0D284788	0G129272	0G303046	0G438000
175 hp	0D284788	0G129337	0G303046	0G438000
200 hp	0D284788	0G077376	0G303046	0G438000
200 DFI	–	–	0G386496	0G438000
225 hp	0D280813	0G077384	0G303046	0G438000
250 EFI	–	–	0G303046	0G438000
275 hp	0D280900	–	–	–
Mercury Jet models				
Jet 65 hp	0G052651	0G077369	0G301804	0G438000
Jet 80 hp	0G052652	0G127529	0G302040	0G438000
Jet 105 hp	0G052656	0G129884	0G304512	0G438000
Jet 140 hp	0G052657	0G129601	0G304134	0G438000
Mariner outboard models				
75 hp	0D283222	0G127540	0G301751	0G438000
90 hp	0D283222	0G127561	0G301751	0G438000
100 hp	0D283222	0G127812	0G302262	0G438000
115 hp	0D283222	0G127500	0G301751	0G438000

(continued)

STARTING SERIAL NUMBER LISTING (continued)

	1994	1995	1996	1997
Mariner outboard models (continued)				
125 hp	0D283222	0G127766	0G301751	0G438000
135 hp	0D284788	0G129222	0G303046	0G438000
150 hp	0D284788	0G129477	0G303046	0G438000
175 hp	0D284788	0G129394	0G303046	0G438000
200 hp	0D284788	0G129303	0G303046	0G438000
200 DFI	–	–	0G386496	0G438000
225 hp	0D280813	0G106786	0G303046	0G438000
250 EFI	–	–	0G303046	0G438000
275 hp	0D280900	–	–	–
Mariner Jet models				
Jet 65 HP	0G052651	0G127642	0G302037	0G438000
Jet 80 HP	0G052652	0G127629	0G301751	0G438000
Jet 105 HP	0G052656	0G129872	0G325593	0G438000
Jet 140 HP	0G052657	0G129675	0G303046	0G438000

CLYMER®

MERCURY/MARINER

OUTBOARD SHOP MANUAL

75-275 HP • 1994-1997 (Includes Jet Drive Models)

Introduction

This Clymer shop manual covers service and repair of 75-275 hp Mercury and Mariner outboard motors, designed for recreational use, during the years 1994-1997. Coverage is also provided for 65-140 jet drive models and outboards equipped with electronic fuel injection (EFI) and direct fuel injection (DFI). Commercial, high-performance, Sail and 4-stroke models are not covered in this manual.

Refer to the QRD (quick reference data) section for commonly needed specifications and service information.

Step-by-step instructions and hundreds of illustrations guide you through tasks ranging from routine maintenance to complete overhaul.

This manual can be used by anyone from a first time owner to a professional technician. Easy-to-read type, detailed drawings and clear photographs give you all the information needed to do the procedure correctly.

Having a well-maintained outboard engine will increase your enjoyment of your boat as well as ensuring your safety offshore. Keep this shop manual handy and use it often. Performing routine, preventive maintenance will save you time and money by helping to prevent premature failure and unnecessary repairs.

Chapter One

General Information

This detailed, comprehensive manual contains complete information covering maintenance, repair and overhaul. Hundreds of photos and drawings guide you throughout every procedure.

Troubleshooting, tune-up, maintenance and repair are not difficult if you know what tools and equipment to use and what to do. Anyone not afraid to get their hands dirty, of average intelligence and with some mechanical ability can perform most of the procedures in this manual. See Chapter Two for more information on tools and techniques.

A shop manual is a reference. You want to be able to find information quickly. Clymer books are designed with you in mind. All chapters are thumb tabbed and important items are indexed at the end of the manual. All procedures, tables, photos and instructions in this manual assume the reader may be working on the machine or using the manual for the first time.

Keep the manual in a handy place in your toolbox or boat. It will help you to better understand how your boat runs, lower repair and maintenance costs and generally increase your enjoyment of your boat.

MANUAL ORGANIZATION

This chapter provides general information useful to boat owners and marine mechanics.

Chapter Two discusses the tools and techniques for preventative maintenance, troubleshooting and repair.

Chapter Three provides troubleshooting and testing procedures for all systems and individual components.

Following chapters describe specific systems, providing disassembly, inspection, assembly and adjustment procedures in simple step-by-step form. Specifications concerning a specific system are included at the end of the appropriate chapter.

NOTES, CAUTIONS AND WARNINGS

The terms NOTE, CAUTION and WARNING have specific meanings in this manual. A NOTE provides additional information to make a step or procedure easier or more clear. Disregarding a NOTE could cause inconvenience, but would not cause damage or personal injury.

A CAUTION emphasizes areas where equipment damage could cause permanent mechanical damage; however, personal injury is unlikely.

A WARNING emphasizes areas where personal injury or even death could result from negligence. Mechanical damage may also occur. WARNINGS *must* be taken seriously. In some cases, serious injury or death has resulted from disregarding similar warnings.

TORQUE SPECIFICATIONS

Torque specifications throughout this manual are given in foot-pounds (ft.-lb.), inch-pounds (in.-lb.) and newton meters (N•m.). Newton meters are being adopted in place of meter-kilograms (mkg) in accordance with the International Modernized Metric System. Existing torque wrenches calibrated in meter-kilograms can be used by performing a simple conversion: move the decimal point one place to the right. For example, 4.7 mkg = 47 N•m. This conversion is accurate enough for most mechanical operations even though the exact mathematical conversion is 3.5 mkg = 34.3 N•m.

ENGINE OPERATION

All marine engines, whether two or four-stroke, gasoline or diesel, operate on the Otto cycle of intake, compression, power and exhaust phases.

Two-Stroke Cycle

A two-stroke engine requires one crankshaft revolution (two strokes of the piston) to complete the Otto cycle. All engines covered in this manual are a two-stroke design. **Figure 1** shows gasoline two-stroke engine operation.

Four-Stroke Cycle

A four-stroke engine requires two crankshaft revolutions (four strokes of the piston) to complete the Otto cycle. **Figure 2** shows gasoline four-stroke engine operation.

FASTENERS

The material and design of the various fasteners used on marine equipment are carefully thought out and designed. Fastener design determines the type of tool required to work with the fastener. Fastener material is carefully selected to decrease the possibility of physical failure or corrosion. See *Galvanic Corrosion* in this chapter for information on marine materials.

Nuts, bolts and screws are manufactured in a wide range of thread patterns. To join a nut and bolt, the diameter of the bolt and the diameter of the hole in the nut must be the same. It is just as important that the threads are compatible.

The easiest way to determine if fastener threads are compatible is to turn the nut on the bolt, or bolt into its threaded opening, using fingers only. Be sure both pieces are clean. If much force is required, check the thread condition on each fastener. If the thread condition is good but the fasteners jam, the threads are not compatible.

Four important specifications describe the thread:
1. Diameter.
2. Threads per inch.
3. Thread pattern.

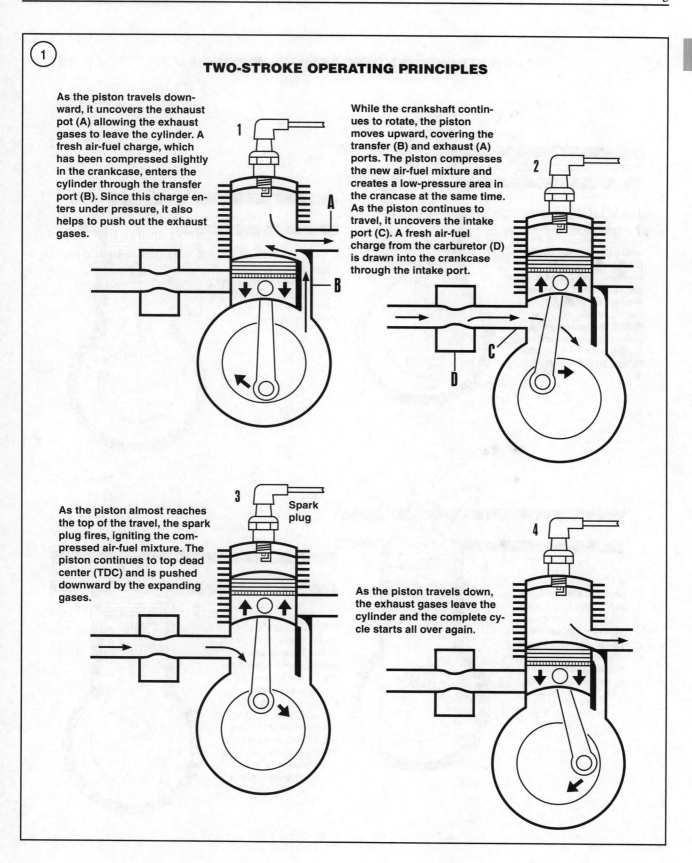

①

TWO-STROKE OPERATING PRINCIPLES

1

As the piston travels down-ward, it uncovers the exhaust pot (A) allowing the exhaust gases to leave the cylinder. A fresh air-fuel charge, which has been compressed slightly in the crankcase, enters the cylinder through the transfer port (B). Since this charge enters under pressure, it also helps to push out the exhaust gases.

While the crankshaft contin-ues to rotate, the piston moves upward, covering the transfer (B) and exhaust (A) ports. The piston compresses the new air-fuel mixture and creates a low-pressure area in the crancase at the same time. As the piston continues to travel, it uncovers the intake port (C). A fresh air-fuel charge from the carburetor (D) is drawn into the crankcase through the intake port.

As the piston almost reaches the top of the travel, the spark plug fires, igniting the com-pressed air-fuel mixture. The piston continues to top dead center (TDC) and is pushed downward by the expanding gases.

As the piston travels down, the exhaust gases leave the cylinder and the complete cy-cle starts all over again.

Spark plug

② **FOUR-STROKE GASOLINE OPERATING PRINCIPLES**

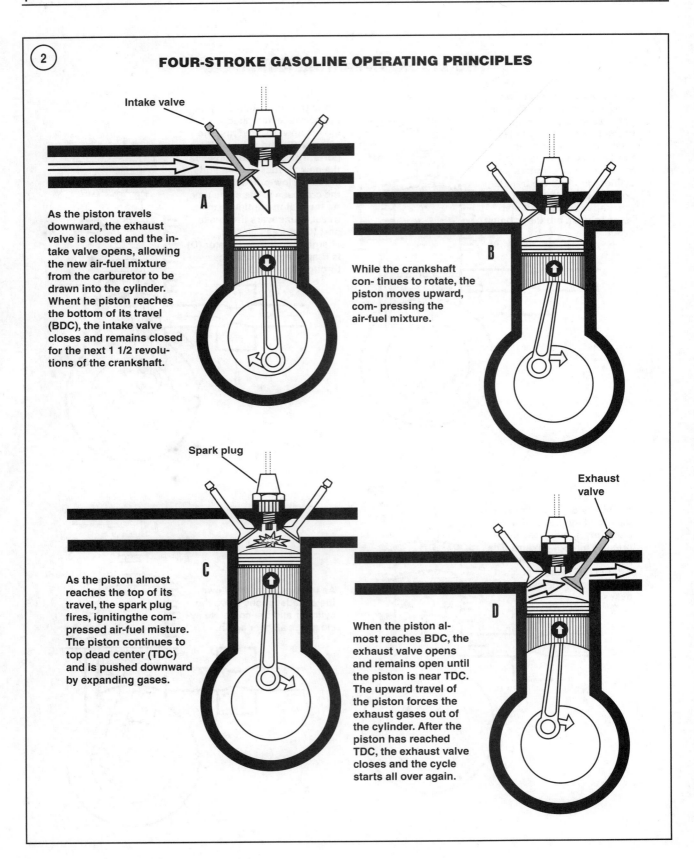

Intake valve

As the piston travels downward, the exhaust valve is closed and the intake valve opens, allowing the new air-fuel mixture from the carburetor to be drawn into the cylinder. Whent he piston reaches the bottom of its travel (BDC), the intake valve closes and remains closed for the next 1 1/2 revolutions of the crankshaft.

A

While the crankshaft con- tinues to rotate, the piston moves upward, com- pressing the air-fuel mixture.

B

Spark plug

As the piston almost reaches the top of its travel, the spark plug fires, ignitingthe compressed air-fuel misture. The piston continues to top dead center (TDC) and is pushed downward by expanding gases.

C

Exhaust valve

When the piston almost reaches BDC, the exhaust valve opens and remains open until the piston is near TDC. The upward travel of the piston forces the exhaust gases out of the cylinder. After the piston has reached TDC, the exhaust valve closes and the cycle starts all over again.

D

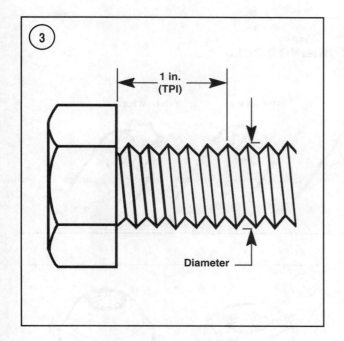

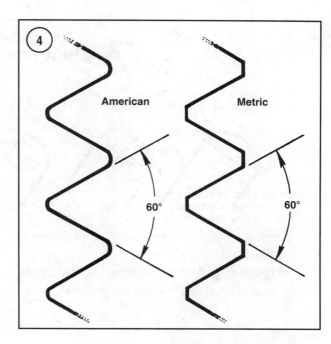

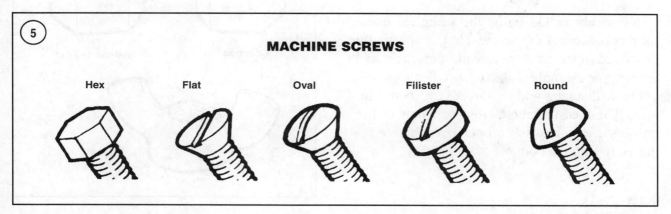

MACHINE SCREWS

Hex   Flat   Oval   Filister   Round

4. Thread direction

Figure 3 shows the first two specifications. Thread pattern is more subtle. Italian and British standards exist, but the most commonly used by marine equipment manufactures are American standard and metric standard. The root and top of the thread are cut differently as shown in **Figure 4**.

Most threads are cut so the fastener must be turned clockwise to tighten it. These are called right-hand threads. Some fasteners have left-hand threads; they must be turned counterclockwise to tighten. Left-hand threads are used in locations where normal rotation of the equipment would tend to loosen a right-hand threaded fastener. Assume all fasteners use right-hand threads unless the instructions specify otherwise.

Machine Screws

There are many different types of machine screws (**Figure 5**). Most are designed to protrude above the secured surface (rounded head) or be slightly recessed below the surface (flat head). In some applications the screw head is recessed well below the fastened sur-

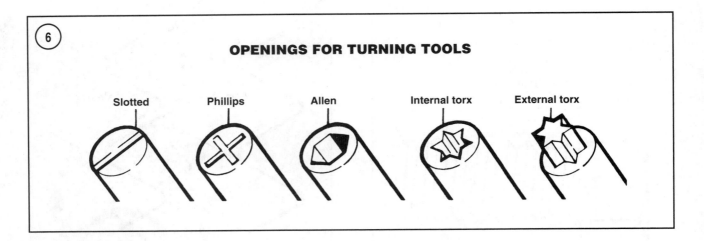

OPENINGS FOR TURNING TOOLS

Slotted   Phillips   Allen   Internal torx   External torx

face. **Figure 6** shows a number of screw heads requiring different types of turning tools.

Bolts

Commonly called bolts, the technical name for this fastener is cap screw. They are normally described by diameter, threads per inch and length. For example, 1/4-20 × 1 indicates a bolt 1/4 in. in diameter with 20 threads per inch, 1 in. long. The measurement across two flats of the bolt head indicates the proper wrench size required to turn the bolt.

Nuts

Nuts are manufactured in a variety of types and sizes. Most are hexagonal (six-sides) and fit on bolts, screws and studs with the same diameter and threads per inch.

Figure 7 shows several types of nuts. The common nut is usually used with some type of lockwasher. Self-locking nuts have a nylon insert that helps prevent the nut from loosening; no lockwasher is required. Wing nuts are designed for fast removal by hand. Wing nuts are used for convenience in non-critical locations.

To indicate the size of a nut, manufactures specify the diameter of the opening and the threads per inch. This is similar to a bolt specifi-

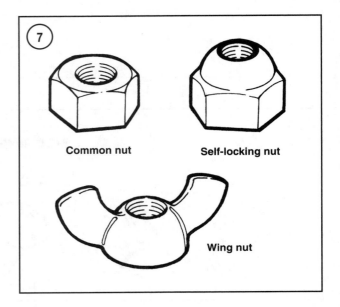

Common nut   Self-locking nut

Wing nut

cation, but without the length dimension. The measurement across two flats of the nut indicates the wrench size required to turn the nut.

Washers

There are two basic types of washers: flat washers and lockwashers. A flat washer is a simple disc with a hole that fits the screw or bolt. Lockwashers are designed to prevent a fastener from working loose due to vibration, expansion and contraction. **Figure 8** shows several types of lockwashers. Note that flat washers are often

1

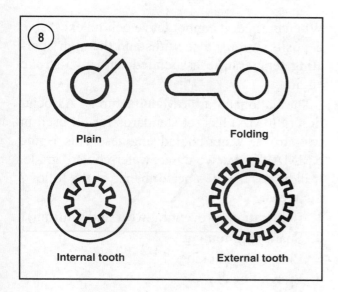

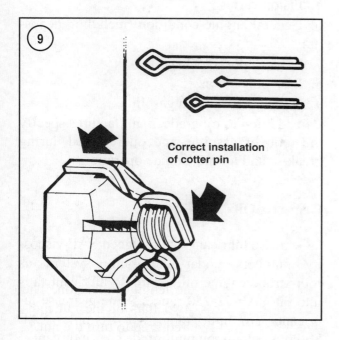

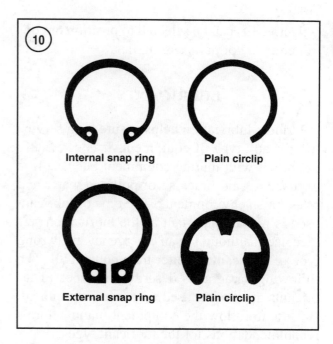

used between a lockwasher and a fastener to provide a smooth bearing surface. This allows the fastener to be turned easily with a tool.

Cotter Pins

In certain applications, a fastener must be secured so it cannot possibly loosen. The propeller nut on some marine drive systems is one such ap-

plication. For this purpose, a cotter pin (**Figure 9**) and slotted or castellated nut is often used. To use a cotter pin, first make sure the pin fits snugly, but not too tight. Then, align a slot in the fastener with the hole in the bolt or axle. Insert the cotter pin through the nut and bolt or propeller shaft and bend the ends over to secure the cotter pin tightly. If the holes do not align, tighten the nut just enough to obtain the proper alignment. Unless specifically instructed to do so, never loosen the fastener to align the slot and hole. Because the cotter pin is weakened after installation and removal, never reuse a cotter pin. Cotter pins are available in several styles, lengths and diameters. Measure cotter pin length from the bottom of its head to the tip of its shortest prong.

Snap Rings

Snap rings (**Figure 10**) can be an internal or external design. They are used to retain components on shafts (external type) or inside openings (internal type). Snap rings can be reused if they are not distorted during removal. In some applications, snap rings of varying thickness (selective fit) can be selected to position or control end play of parts assemblies.

LUBRICANTS

Periodic lubrication helps ensure long service life for any type of equipment. It is especially important with marine equipment because it is exposed to salt, brackish or polluted water and other harsh environments. The type of lubricant used is just as important as the lubrication service itself, although in an emergency, the wrong type of lubricant is better than none at all. The following paragraphs describe the types of lubricants most often used on marine equipment. Be sure to follow the equipment manufacture's recommendations for the lubricant types.

Generally, all liquid lubricants are called *oil*. They may be mineral-based (including petroleum bases), natural-based (vegetable and animal bases), synthetic-based or emulsions (mixtures). *Grease* is lubricating oil that has a thickening compound added. The resulting material then usually enhanced with anticorrosion, antioxidant and extreme pressure (EP) additives. Grease is often classified by the type of thickener added; lithium and calcium soap are the most commonly used.

Two-stroke Engine Oil

Lubrication for a two-stroke engine is provided by oil mixed with the incoming air/fuel mixture. Some of the oil mist settles out in the crankcase, lubricating the crankshaft, bearings and lower end of the connecting rod. The rest of the oil enters the combustion chamber to lubricate the piston, rings and the cylinder wall. This oil is then burned along with the air/fuel mixture during the combustion process.

Engine oil must have several special qualities to work well in a two-stroke engine. It must mix easily and stay in suspension in gasoline.

When burned, it cannot leave behind excessive deposits. It must also withstand the high operating temperature associated with two-stroke engines.

The National Marine Manufacturer's Association (NMMA) has set standards for oil used in two-stroke, water-cooled engines. This is the NMMA TC-W (two-cycle, water-cooled) grade. It indicates the oil's performance in the following areas:

1. Lubrication (preventing wear and scuffing).
2. Spark plug fouling.
3. Piston ring sticking.
4. Preignition.
5. Piston varnish.
6. General engine condition (including deposits).
7. Exhaust port blockage.
8. Rust prevention.
9. Mixing ability with gasoline.

In addition to oil grade, manufactures specify the ratio of gasoline and oil required during break-in and normal engine operation.

Gearcase Oil

Gearcase lubricants are assigned SAE viscosity numbers under the same system as four-stroke engine oil. Gearcase lubricant falls into the SAE 72-250 range. Some gearcase lubricants are multigrade. For example, SAE 80-90 is a common multigrade gear lubricant.

Three types of marine gearcase lubricants are generally available; SAE 90 hypoid gearcase lubricant is designed for older manual-shift units; type C gearcase lubricant contains additives designed for the electric shift mechanisms; high-viscosity gearcase lubricant is a heavier oil designed to withstand the shock loads of high performance engines or units subjected to severe duty use. Always use the gearcase lubricant specified by the manufacturer.

1

Grease

Greases are graded by the National Lubricating Grease Institute (NLGI). Greases are graded by number according to the consistency of the grease. These ratings range from No. 000 to No. 6, with No. 6 being the most solid. A typical multipurpose grease is NLGI No. 2. For specific applications, equipment manufactures may require grease with an additive such as molybdenum disulfide (MOS^2).

GASKET SEALANT

Gasket sealant is used instead of preformed gaskets on some applications, or as a gasket dressing on others. Three types of gasket sealant are commonly used: gasket sealing compound, room temperature vulcanizing (RTV) and anaerobic. Because these materials have different sealing properties, they cannot be used interchangeably.

Gasket Sealing Compound

This nonhardening liquid is used primarily as a gasket dressing. Gasket sealing compound is available in tubes or brush top containers. When exposed to air or heat it forms a rubber-like coating. The coating fills in small imperfections in gasket and sealing surfaces. Do not use gasket sealing compound that is old, has began to solidify or has darkened in color.

Applying Gasket Sealing Compound

Carefully scrape residual gasket material, corrosion deposits or paint from the mating surfaces. Use a blunt scraper and work carefully to avoid damaging the mating surfaces. Use quick drying solvent and a clean shop towel and wipe oil or other contaminants from the surfaces. Wipe or blow loose material or contaminants from the gasket. Brush a light coating on the mating surfaces and both sides of the gasket. Do not apply more compound than needed. Excess compound will be squeezed out as the surfaces mate and may contaminate other components. Do not allow compound into bolt or alignment pin holes

A hydraulic lock can occur as the bolt or pin compresses the compound, resulting in incorrect bolt torque.

RTV Sealant

This is a silicone gel supplied in tubes. Moisture in the air causes RTV to cure. Always place the cap on the tube as soon as possible if using RTV. RTV has a shelf life of approximately one year and will not cure properly after the shelf life expires. Check the expiration date on the tube and keep partially used tubes tightly sealed. RTV can generally fill gaps up to 1/4 in. (6.3 mm) and works well on slightly flexible surfaces.

Applying RTV Sealant

Carefully scrape all residual sealant and paint from the mating surfaces. Use a blunt scraper and work carefully to avoid damaging the mating surfaces. The mating surfaces must be absolutely free of gasket material, sealant, dirt, oil grease or other contamination. Lacquer thinner, acetone, isopropyl alcohol or similar solvents work well to clean the surfaces. Avoid using solvents with on oil, wax or petroleum base as they are not compatible with RTV compounds. Remove all sealant from bolt or alignment pin holes.

Apply RTV sealant in a continuous bead 0.08-0.12 in. (2-3 mm) thick. Circle all mounting bolt or alignment pin holes unless otherwise specified. Do not allow RTV sealant into bolt holes or other openings. A hydraulic lock can

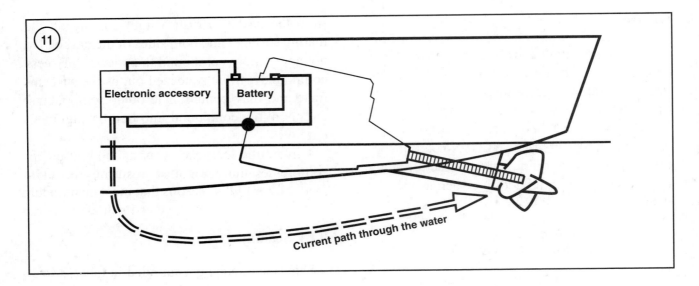

Current path through the water

occur as the bolt or pin compresses the sealant, resulting in incorrect bolt torque. Tighten the mounting fasteners within 10 minutes after application.

Anaerobic Sealant

This is a gel supplied in tubes. It cures only in the absence of air, as when squeezed tightly between two machined mating surfaces. For this reason, it will not spoil if the cap is left off the tube. Do not use anaerobic sealant if one of the surfaces is flexible. Anaerobic sealant is able to fill gaps up to 0.030 in. (0.8 mm) and generally works best on rigid, machined flanges or surfaces.

Applying Anaerobic Sealant

Carefully scrape all residual sealant from the mating surfaces. Use a blunt scraper and work carefully to avoid damaging the mating surfaces. The mating surfaces must be absolutely free of gasket material, sealant, dirt, oil grease or other contamination. Lacquer thinner, acetone, isopropyl alcohol or similar solvents work well to clean the surfaces. Avoid using solvents with

on oil, wax or petroleum base as they are not compatible with anaerobic compounds. Clean a sealant from the bolt or alignment pin holes. Apply anaerobic sealant in a 0.04 in. (1 mm) thick continuous bead onto one of the surfaces. Circle all bolt and alignment pin opening. Do not apply sealant into bolt holes or other openings. A hydraulic lock can occur as the bolt or pin compresses the sealant, resulting in incorrect bolt torque. Tighten the mounting fasteners within 10 minutes after application.

GALVANIC CORROSION

A chemical reaction occurs whenever two different types of metal are joined by an electrical conductor and immersed in an electrolytic solution such as water. Electrons transfer from one metal to the other through the electrolyte and return through the conductor.

The hardware on a boat is made of many different types of metal. The boat hull acts as a conductor between the metals. Even if the hull is wooden or fiberglass, the slightest film of water (electrolyte) on the hull provides conductivity. This combination creates a good environment for electron flow (**Figure 11**). Unfortunately, this electron flow results in galvanic corrosion of the metal involved, causing one of the metals to be corroded or eroded away. The amount of electron flow, and therefore the amount of corrosion, depends on several factors:

1. The types of metal involved.
2. The efficiency of the conductor.
3. The strength of the electrolyte.

Metals

The chemical composition of the metal used in marine equipment has a significant effect on the amount and speed of galvanic corrosion. Certain metals are more resistant to corrosion than others. These electrically negative metals are commonly called *noble*; they act as the cathode in any reaction. Metals that are more subject to corrosion are electrically positive; they act as the anode in a reaction. The more *noble* metals include titanium, 18-8 stainless steel and nickel. Less *noble* metals include zinc, aluminum and magnesium. Galvanic corrosion becomes more severe as the difference in electrical potential between the two metals increases.

In some cases, galvanic corrosion can occur within a single piece of metal. For example, brass is a mixture of zinc and copper, and, when immersed in an electrolyte, the zinc portion of the mixture will corrode away as a galvanic reaction occurs between the zinc and copper particles.

Conductors

The hull of the boat often acts as the conductor between different types of metal. Marine equipment, such as the drive unit can act as the conductor. Large masses of metal, firmly connected together, are more efficient conductors than water. Rubber mountings and vinyl-based paint can act as insulators between pieces of metal.

Electrolyte

The water in which a boat operates acts as the electrolyte for the corrosion process. The more efficient a conductor is, the more severe and rapid the corrosion will be.

Cold, clean freshwater is the poorest electrolyte. Pollutants increase conductivity; therefore, brackish or saltwater is an efficient electrolyte. This is one of the reasons that most manufacturers recommend a freshwater flush after operating in polluted, brackish or saltwater.

Protection From Galvanic Corrosion

Because of the environment in which marine equipment must operate, it is practically impossible to totally prevent galvanic corrosion. However, there are several ways in which the process can be slowed. After taking these precautions, the next step is to *fool* the process into occurring only where you want it to occur. This is the role of sacrificial anodes and impressed current systems.

Slowing Corrosion

Some simple precautions can help reduce the amount of corrosion taking place outside the hull. These precautions are not substitutes for the corrosion protection methods discussed under *Sacrificial Anodes* and *Impressed Current Systems* in this chapter, but they can help these methods reduce corrosion.

Use fasteners made of metal more noble than the parts they secure. If corrosion occurs, the parts they secure may suffer but the fasteners are protected. The larger secured parts are more able to withstand the loss of material. Also major problems could arise if the fasteners corrode to the point of failure.

Keep all painted surfaces in good condition. If paint is scraped off and bare metal exposed, corrosion rapidly increases. Use a vinyl- or plastic-based paint, which acts as an electrical insulator.

Be careful when applying metal-based antifouling paint to the boat. Do not apply antifouling paint to metal parts of the boat or the drive unit. If applied to metal surfaces, this type of paint reacts with the metal and results in corrosion between the metal and the layer of paint. Maintain a minimum 1 in. (25 mm) border between the painted surface and any metal parts. Organic-based paints are available for use on metal surfaces.

Where a corrosion protection device is used, remember that it must be immersed in the electrolyte along with the boat to provide any protection. If you raise the gearcase out of the water with the boat docked, any anodes on the gearcase may be removed from the corrosion process rendering them ineffective. Never paint or apply any coating to anodes or other protection devices. Paint or other coatings insulate them from the corrosion process.

Any change in the boat's equipment, such as the installation of a new stainless steel propeller, changes the electrical potential and may cause increased corrosion. Always consider this when adding equipment or changing exposed materials. Install additional anodes or other protection equipment as required ensuring the corrosion protection system is up to the task. The expense to repair corrosion damage usually far exceeds that of additional corrosion protection.

Sacrificial Anodes

Sacrificial anodes are specially designed to do nothing but corrode. Properly fastening such pieces to the boat causes them to act as the anode in any galvanic reaction that occurs; any other metal in the reaction acts as the cathode and is not damaged.

Anodes are usually made or zinc, a far from a noble material. Some anodes are manufactured of an aluminum and indium alloy. This alloy is less noble than the aluminum alloy in drive system components, providing the desired sacrificial properties. The aluminum and indium alloy is more resistant to oxide coating than zinc anodes. Oxide coating occurs as the anode material reacts with oxygen in the water. An oxide coating will insulate the anode, dramatically reducing corrosion protection.

Anodes must be used properly to be effective. Simply fastening anodes to the boat in random locations will not do the job.

First determine how much anode surface is required to adequately protect the equipment's surface area. A good starting point is provided by the Military Specification MIL-A-818001, which states that one square inch of new anode protects either:
1. 800 square inches of freshly painted steel.
2. 250 square inches of bare steel or bare aluminum alloy.
3. 100 square inches of copper or copper alloy.

This rule is valid for a boat at rest. If underway, additional anode area is required to protect the same surface area.

The anode must be in good electrical contact with the metal that it protects. If possible, attach an anode to all metal surfaces requiring protection.

Good quality anodes have inserts around the fastener holes that are made of a more noble material. Otherwise, the anode could erode away around the fastener hole, allowing the anode to loosen or possibly fall off, thereby loosing needed protection.

Impressed Current System

An impressed current system can be added to any boat. The system generally consists of the anode, controller and reference electrode. The anode in this system is coated with a very noble

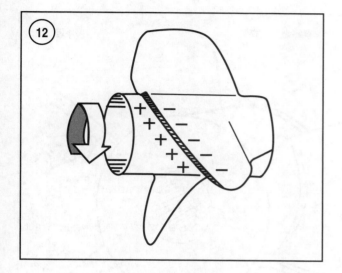

metal, such as platinum, so that it is almost corrosion-free and can last almost indefinitely. The reference electrode, under the boat's waterline, allows the control module to monitor the potential for corrosion. If the module senses that corrosion is occurring, it applies positive battery voltage to the anode. Current then flows from the anode to all other metal component, regardless of how noble or non-noble these components may be. Essentially, the electrical current from the battery counteracts the galvanic reaction to dramatically reduce corrosion damage.

Only a small amount of current is needed to counteract corrosion. Using input from the sensor, the control module provides only the amount of current needed to suppress galvanic corrosion. Most systems consume a maximum of 0.2 Ah at full demand. Under normal conditions, these systems can provide protection for 8-12 weeks without recharging the battery. Remember that this system must have constant connection to the battery. Often the battery supply to the system is connected to a battery switching device causing the operator to inadvertently shut off the system while docked.

An impressed current system is more expensive to install than sacrificial anodes but, considering it low maintenance requirements and the superior protection it provides, the long term cost may be lower.

PROPELLERS

The propeller is the final link between the boat's drive system and the water. A perfectly maintained engine and hull are useless if the propeller is the wrong type, is damaged or is deteriorated. Although propeller selection for a specific application is beyond the scope of this manual, the following provides the basic information needed to make an informed decision. The professional at a reputable marine dealership is the best source for a propeller recommendation.

How a Propeller Works

As the curved blades of a propeller rotate through the water, a high-pressure area forms on one side of the blade and a low-pressure area forms on the other side of the blade (**Figure 12**). The propeller moves toward the low-pressure area, carrying the boat with it.

Propeller Parts

Although a propeller is usually a one-piece unit, it is made of several different parts (**Figure 13**). Variations in the design of these parts make different propellers suitable for different applications.

The blade tip is the point of the blade furthest from the center of the propeller hub or propeller shaft bore. The blade tip separates the leading edge from the trailing edge.

The leading edge is the edge of the blade nearest the boat. During forward operation, this is the area of the blade that first cuts through the water.

The trailing edge is the surface of the blade furthest from the boat. During reverse operation,

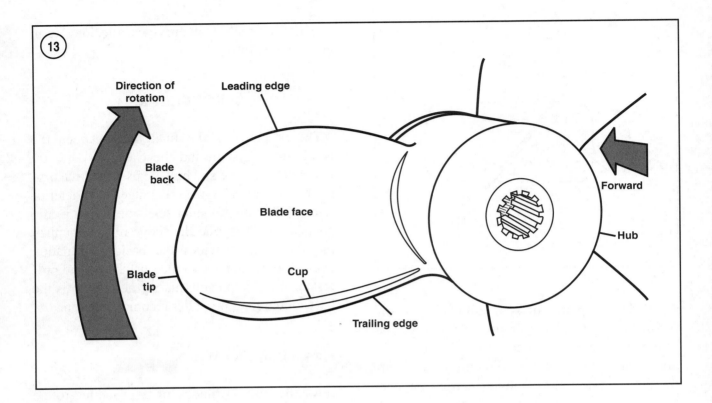

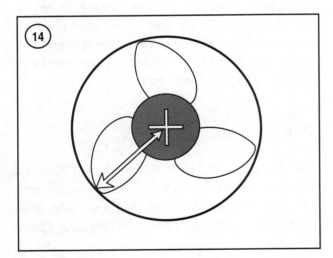

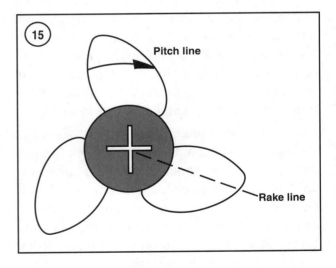

this is the area of the blade that first cuts through the water.

The blade face is the surface of the blade that faces away from the boat. During forward operation, high-pressure forms on this side of the blade.

The blade back is the surface of the blade that faces toward the boat. During forward gear operation, low-pressure forms on this side of the blade.

The cup is a small curve or lip on the trailing edge of the blade. Cupped propeller blades generally perform better than non-cupped propeller blades.

The hub is the center portion of the propeller. It connects the blades to the propeller shaft. On most drive systems, engine exhaust is routed through the hub; in this case, the hub is made up of an outer and inner portion, connected by ribs.

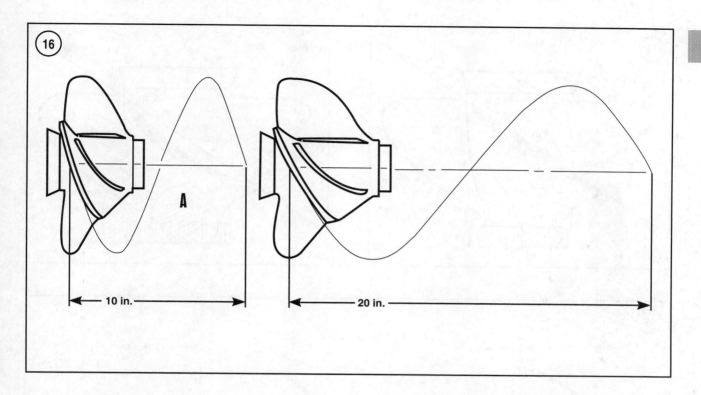

16

A

— 10 in. —

— 20 in. —

The diffuser ring is used on though- hub exhaust models to prevent exhaust gasses from entering the blade area.

Propeller Design

Changes in length, angle, thickness and material of propeller parts make different propellers suitable for different applications.

Diameter

Propeller diameter is the distance from the center of the hub to the blade tip, multiplied by two. Essentially it is the diameter of the circle formed by the blade tips during propeller rotation (**Figure 14**).

Pitch and rake

Propeller pitch and rake describe the placement of the blades in relation to the hub (**Figure 15**).

Pitch describes the theoretical distance the propeller would travel in one revolution. In A, **Figure 16**, the propeller would travel 10 inches in one revolution. In B, **Figure 16**, the propeller would travel 20 inches in one revolution. This distance is only theoretical; during operation, the propeller achieves only 75-85% of its pitch. Slip rate describes the difference in actual travel relative to the pitch. Lighter, faster boats typically achieve a lower slip rate than heavier, slower boats.

Propeller blades can be constructed with constant pitch (**Figure 17**) or progressive pitch (**Figure 18**). On a progressive propeller, the pitch starts low at the leading edge and increases toward the trailing edge. The propeller pitch specification is the average of the pitch across the entire blade. Propellers with progressive pitch usually provide better overall performance than constant pitch propellers.

Blade rake is specified in degrees and is measured along a line from the center of the hub to the blade tip. A blade that is perpendicular to the

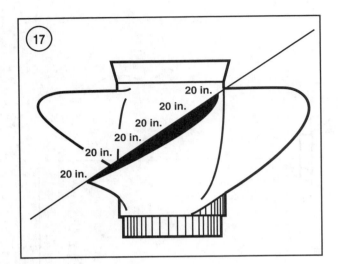

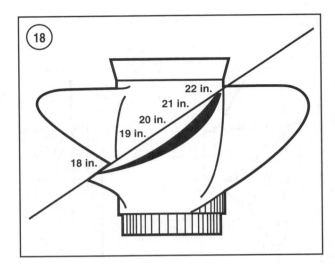

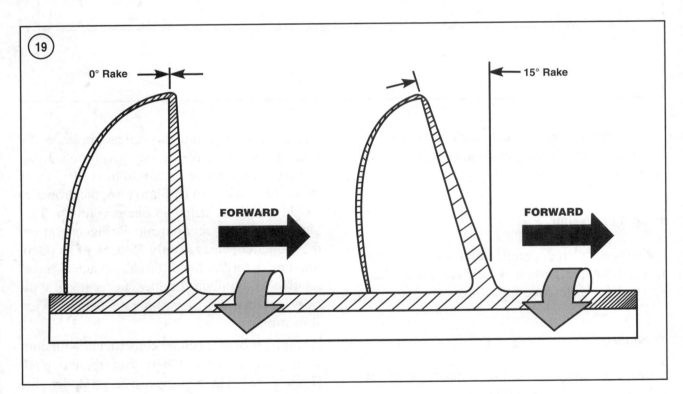

hub (**Figure 19**) has 0° rake. A blade that is angled from perpendicular (**Figure 19**) has a rake expressed by its difference from perpendicular. Most propellers have rakes ranging from 0-20°. Lighter faster boats generally perform better with propeller with a greater amount of rake. Heavier, slower boats generally perform better using a propeller with less rake.

Blade thickness

Blade thickness in not uniform at all points along the blade. For efficiency, blades are as thin a possible at all points while retaining enough strength to move the boat. Blades are thicker where they meet the hub and thinner at the blade tips (**Figure 20**). This is necessary to support the

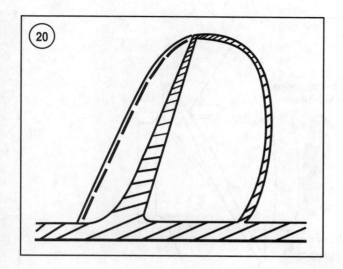

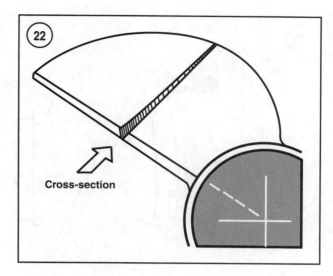

Cross-section

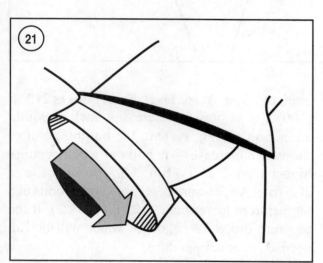

heavier loads at the hub section of the blade. Overall blade thickness is dependent on the strength of the material used.

When cut along a line from the leading edge to the trailing edge in the central portion of the blade (**Figure 21**), the propeller blade resembles and airplane wing. The blade face, where high-pressure exists during forward rotation, is almost flat. The blade back, where low-pressure exists during forward rotation, is curved, with the thinnest portions at the edges and the thickest portion at the center.

Propellers that run only partially submerged, as in racing applications, may have a wedge shaped cross-section (**Figure 22**). The leading edge is very thin and the blade thickness increases toward the trailing edge, where it is thickest. If a propeller such as this is run totally submerged, it is very inefficient.

Number of blades

The number of blades used on a propeller is a compromise between efficiency and vibration. A one-bladed propeller would the most efficient, but it would create an unacceptable amount of vibration. As blades are added, efficiency decreases, but so does vibration. Most propellers have three or four blades, representing the most practical trade-off between efficiency and vibration.

Material

Propeller materials are chosen for strength, corrosion resistance and economy. Stainless steel, aluminum, plastic and bronze are the most commonly used materials. Bronze is quite strong but rather expensive. Stainless steel is more common than bronze because of its combination of strength and lower cost. Aluminum alloy and plastic materials are the least expensive

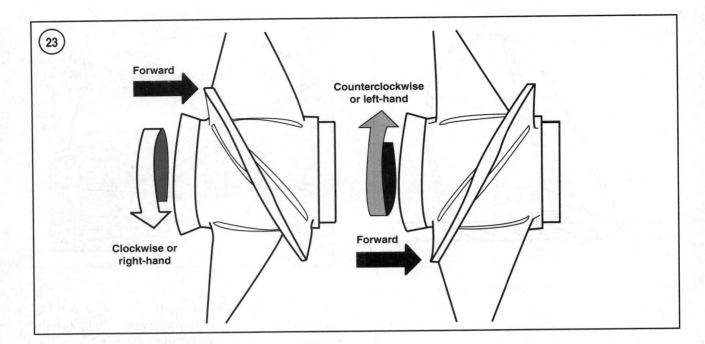

Forward

Counterclockwise or left-hand

Clockwise or right-hand

Forward

but usually lack the strength of stainless steel. Plastic propellers are more suited for lower horsepower applications.

Direction of rotation

Propellers are made for both right-hand and left hand rotations although right-hand is the most commonly used. As viewed from the rear of the boat while in forward gear, a right-hand propeller turns clockwise and a left-hand propeller turns counterclockwise. Off the boat, the direction of rotation is determined by observing the angle of the blades (**Figure 23**). A right-hand propeller's blade slant from the upper left to the lower right; a left-hand propeller's blades are opposite.

Cavitation and Ventilation

Cavitation and ventilation are *not* interchangeable terms; they refer to two distinct problems encountered during propeller operation.

To help understand cavitation, consider the relationship between pressure and the boiling point of water. At sea level, water boils at 212° F (100° C). As pressure increases, such as within an engine cooling system, the boiling point of the water increases—it boils at a temperature higher than 212° F (100° C). The opposite is also true. As pressure decreases, water boils at a temperature lower than 212° F (100° C). It the pressure drops low enough, water will boil at normal room temperature.

During normal propeller operation, low pressure forms on the blade back. Normally the pressure does not drop low enough for boiling to occur. However, poor propeller design, damaged blades or using the wrong propeller can cause unusually low pressure on the blade surface (**Figure 24**). If the pressure drops low enough, boiling occurs and bubbles form on the blade surfaces. As the boiling water moves to a higher pressure area of the blade, the boiling ceases and the bubbles collapse. The collapsing bubbles release energy that erodes the surface of the propeller blade.

Corroded surfaces, physical damage or even marine growth combined with high-speed operation can cause low pressure and cavitation on gearcase surfaces. In such cases, low pressure

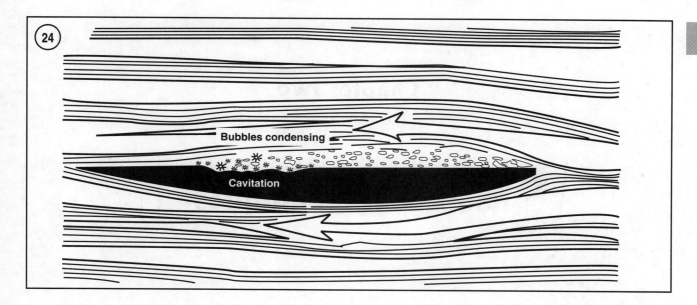

Bubbles condensing

Cavitation

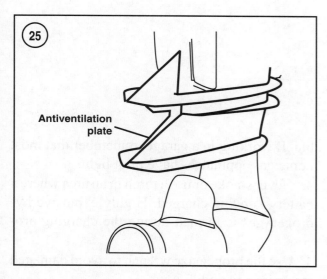

Antiventilation plate

forms as water flows over a protrusion or rough surface. The boiling water forms bubbles that collapse as they move to a higher pressure area toward the rear of the surface imperfection.

This entire process of pressure drop, boiling and bubble collapse is called *cavitation*. The ensuing damage is called *cavitation burn*. Cavitation is caused by a decrease in pressure, not an increase in temperature.

Ventilation is not as complex a process as cavitation. Ventilation refers to air entering the blade area, either from above the water surface or from a though-hub exhaust system. As the blades meet the air, the propeller momentarily looses it bite with the water and subsequently loses most of its thrust. An added complication is that the propeller and engine over-rev, causing very low pressure on the blade back and massive cavitation.

Most marine drive systems have a plate (**Figure 25**) above the propeller designed to prevent surface air from entering the blade area. This plate is correctly called an *anti-ventilation plate*, although it is often incorrectly called an *anticavitation plate*.

Most propellers have a flared section at the rear of the propeller called a diffuser ring. This feature forms a barrier, and extends the exhaust passage far enough aft to prevent the exhaust gases from ventilating the propeller.

A close fit of the propeller to the gearcase is necessary to keep exhaust gasses from exiting and ventilating the propeller. Using the wrong propeller attaching hardware can position the propeller too far aft, preventing a close fit. The wrong hardware can also allow the propeller to rub heavily against the gearcase, causing rapid wear to both components. Wear or damage to these surfaces will allow the propeller to ventilate.

Chapter Two

Tools and Techniques

This chapter describes the common tools required for marine engine repair and troubleshooting. Techniques that make the work easier and more effective are also described. Some of the procedures in this book require special skills or expertise; in some cases it is better to entrust the job to a specialist or qualified dealership.

SAFETY FIRST

Professional mechanics can work for years and never suffer a serious injury. Avoiding injury is as simple as following a few rules and using common sense. Ignoring the rules can and often does lead to physical injury and/or damaged equipment.

1. Never use gasoline as a cleaning solvent.
2. Never smoke or use a torch near flammable liquids, such as cleaning solvent. Dirty or solvent soaked shop towels are extremely flammable. If working in a garage, remember that most home gas appliances have pilot lights.
3. Never smoke or use a torch in an area where a battery is being charged. Highly explosive hydrogen gas is formed during the charging process.
4. Use the proper size wrench to avoid damaged fasteners and bodily injury.
5. If loosening a tight or stuck fastener, consider what could happen if the wrench slips. Protect yourself accordingly.
6. Keep the work area clean, uncluttered and well lighted.
7. Wear safety goggles while using any type of tool. This is especially important when drilling, grinding or using a cold chisel.
8. Never use worn or damaged tools.
9. Keep a Coast Guard approved fire extinguisher handy. Ensure it is rated for gasoline (Class B) and electrical (Class C) fires.

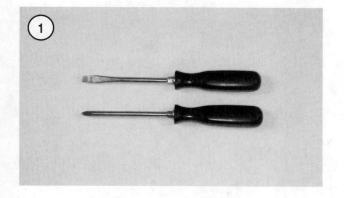

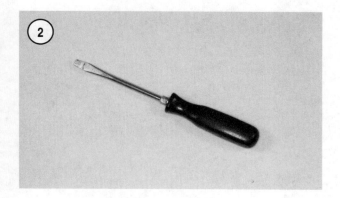

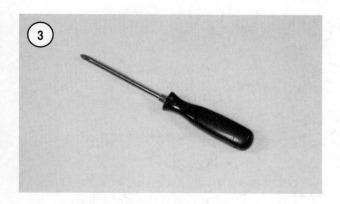

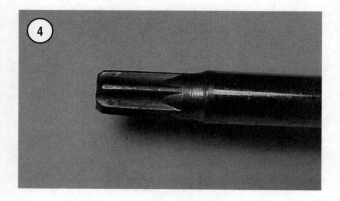

BASIC HAND TOOLS

A number of tools are required to maintain and repair a marine engine. Most of these tools are also used for home and automobile repair. Some tools are made especially for working on marine engines; these tools can be purchased from a marine dealership. Having the required tools always makes the job easier and more effective.

Keep the tools clean and in a suitable box. Keep them organized with related tools stored together. After using a tool, wipe it clean using a shop towel.

The following tools are required to perform virtually any repair job. Each tool is described and the recommended size given for starting a tool collection. Additional tools and some duplication may be added as you become more familiar with the equipment. You may need all U.S. standard tools, all metric size tools or a mixture of both.

Screwdrivers

A screwdriver (**Figure 1**) is a very basic tool, but if used improperly can do more damage than good. The slot on a screw has a definite dimension and shape. Always select a screwdriver that conforms to the shape of the screw. Use a small screwdriver for small screws and a large one for large screws or the screw head are damaged.

Three types of screwdrivers are commonly required: a slotted (flat-blade) screwdriver (**Figure 2**), Phillips screwdriver (**Figure 3**) and Torx screwdriver (**Figure 4**).

Screwdrivers are available in sets, which often include an assortment of slotted Phillips and Torx blades. If you buy them individually, buy at least the following:

    a. Slotted screwdriver—5/16 × 6 in. blade.

    b. Slotted screwdriver—3/8 × 12 in. blade.

    c. Phillips screwdriver—No. 2 tip, 6 in. blade.

d. Phillips screwdriver—No. 3 tip, 6 in. blade.

e. Torx screwdriver—T15 tip, 6 in. blade.

f. Torx screwdriver—T20 tip, 6 in. blade.

g. Torx screwdriver—T25 tip, 6 in. blade.

Use screwdrivers only for driving screws. Never use a screwdriver for prying or chiseling. Do not attempt to remove a Phillips, Torx or Allen head screw with a slotted screwdriver; you can damage the screw head so that even the proper tool is unable to remove it.

Keep the tip of a slotted screwdriver in good condition. Carefully grind the tip to the proper size and taper if it is worn or damaged. The sides of the blade must be parallel and the blade tip must be flat. Replace a Phillips or Torx screwdriver if its tip is worn or damaged.

Pliers

Pliers come in a wide range of types and sizes. Pliers are useful for cutting, gripping, bending and crimping. Never use pliers to cut hardened objects or turn bolts or nuts. **Figure 5** shows several types of pliers.

Each type of pliers has a specialized function. General-purpose pliers are mainly used for gripping and bending. Locking pliers are used for gripping objects very tightly, like a vise. Use needlenose pliers to grip or bend small objects. Adjustable or slip-joint pliers (**Figure 6**) can be adjusted to grip various sized objects; the jaws remain parallel for gripping objects such as pipe or tubing. There are many more types of pliers. The ones described here are the most common.

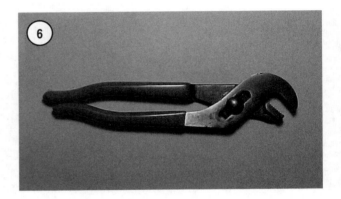

Box-end and Open-end Wrenches

Box-end and open-end wrenches (**Figure 7**) are available in sets in a variety of sizes. The number stamped near the end of the wrench refers to the distance between two parallel flats on the hex head bolt or nut.

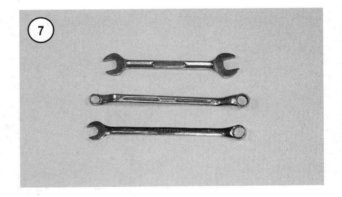

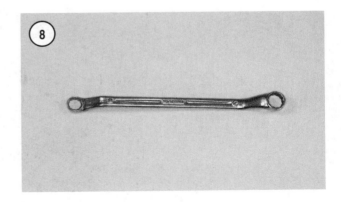

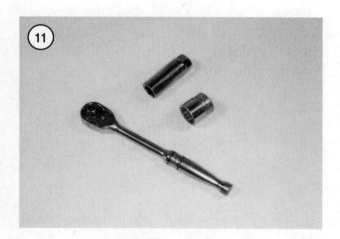

Box-end wrenches (**Figure 8**) provide a better grip on the nut and are stronger than open end wrenches. An open-end wrench (**Figure 9**) grips the nut on only two flats. Unless it fits well, it may slip and round off the points on the nut. A box-end wrench grips all six flats. Box-end wrenches are available with six-point or 12 point openings. The six-point opening provides

superior holding power; the 12-point allow a shorter swing if working in tight quarters.

Use an open-end wrench if a box-end wrench cannot be positioned over the nut or bolt. To prevent damage to the fastener, avoid using and open-end wrench if a large amount of tightening or loosening toque is required.

A combination wrench has both a box-end and open- end. Both ends are the same size.

Adjustable Wrenches

An adjustable wrench (**Figure 10**) can be adjusted to fit virtually any nut or bolt head. However, it can loosen and slip from the nut or bolt, causing damage to the nut and possible physical injury. Use an adjustable wrench only if a proper size open-emd or box-end wrench in not available. Avoid using an adjustable wrench if a large amount of tightening or loosening torque is required.

Adjustable wrenches come in sized ranging from 4-18 in. overall length. A 6 or 8 in. size is recommended as an all-purpose wrench.

Socket Wrenches

A socket wrench (**Figure 11**) is generally faster, safer and more convenient to use than a common wrench. Sockets, which attach to a suitable handle, are available with six-point or 12-point openings and use 1/4, 3/8, and 1/2 in. drive sizes. The drive size corresponds to the square hole that mates with the ratchet or flex handle.

Torque Wrench

A torque wrench (**Figure 12**) is used with a socket to measure how tight a nut or bolt is installed. They come in a wide price range and in 1/4, 3/8, and 1/2 in. drive sizes. The drive size

2

corresponds to the square hole that mates with the socket.

A typical 1/4 in. drive torque wrench measures in in.-lb. increments, and has a range of 20-150 in.-lb. (2.2-17 Nm,). A typical 3/8 or ½ in. torque measures in ft.-lb. increments, and has a range of 10-150 ft.-lb. (14-203 Nm.).

Impact Driver

An impact driver (**Figure 13**) makes removal of tight fasteners easy and reduces damage to bolts and screws. Interchangeable bits allow use on a variety of fasteners.

Circlip Pliers

Circlip (snap ring) pliers are required to remove circlips. Circlip pliers (**Figure 14**) usually come with different size tips; many designs can be switched to handle internal or external type circlips.

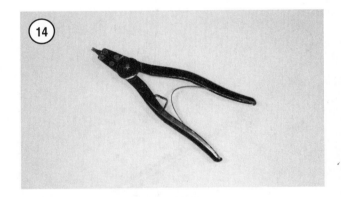

Hammers

Various types of hammers (**Figure 15**) are available to accommodate a number of applications. Use a ball-peen hammer to strike another tool, such as a punch or chisel. Use a soft-face hammer to strike a metal object without damaging it.

Never use a metal-faced hammer on engine and drive system components as severe damage will occur. You can always produce the same amount of force with a soft-faced hammer.

Always wear eye protection when using hammers. Make sure the hammer is in good condition and that the handle is not cracked. Select the correct hammer for the job and always strike the object squarely. Do not use the handle or the side of the hammer head to stroke an object.

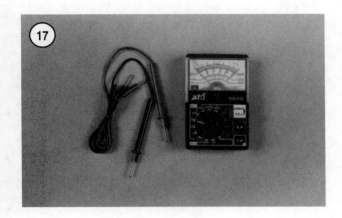

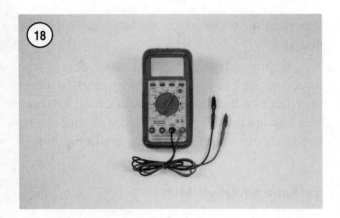

Feeler Gauges

This tool has either flat or wire measuring gauges (**Figure 16**). Use wire gauges to measure spark plug gap; use flat gauges for other measurements. A nonmagnetic (brass) gauge may be specified if working around magnetized components.

Other Special Tools

Many of the maintenance and repair procedures require special tools. Most of the necessary tools are available from a marine dealership or from tool suppliers. Instructions for their use and the manufacture's part number are included in the appropriate chapter.

Purchase the required tools from a local marine dealership or tool supplier. A qualified machinist, often at a lower price, can make some tools locally. Many marine dealerships and rental outlets will rent some of the required tools. Avoid using makeshift tools. Their use may result in damaged parts that cost far more than the recommended tool.

TEST EQUIPMENT

This section describes equipment used to perform testing, adjustments and measurements on marine engines. Most of these tools are available from a local marine dealership or automotive parts store.

Multimeter

This instrument is invaluable for electrical troubleshooting and service. It combines a voltmeter, ohmmeter and an ammeter in one unit. It is often called a VOM.

Two types of mutimeter are available, analog and digital. Analog meters (**Figure 17**) have a moving needle with marked bands on the meter face indicating the volt, ohm and amperage scales. An analog meter must be calibrated each time the scale is changed.

A digital meter (**Figure 18**) is ideally suited for electrical troubleshooting because it is easy to read and more accurate than an analog meter. Most models are auto-ranging, have automatic polarity compensation and internal overload protection circuits.

Either type of meter is suitable for most electrical testing described in this manual. An analog meter is better suited for testing pulsing voltage signals such as those produced by the ignition system. A digital meter is better suited for testing very low resistance or voltage reading (less than 1 volt or 1 ohm). The test procedure will indicate if a specific type of meter is required.

The ignition system produces electrical pulses that are too short in duration for accurate measurement with a using a conventional multimeter. Use a meter with peak-volt reading capability to test the ignition system. This type of meter captures the peak voltage reached during an electrical pulse.

Scale selection, meter specifications and test connections vary by the manufacturer and model of the meter. Thoroughly read the instructions supplied with the meter before performing any test. The meter and certain electrical components on the engine can be damaged if tested incorrectly. Have the test performed by a qualified professional if you are unfamiliar with the testing or general meter usage. The expense to replace damaged equipment can far exceed the cost of having the test performed by a professional.

Strobe Timing Light

This instrument is necessary for dynamic tuning (setting ignition timing while the engine is running). By flashing a light at the precise instant the spark plug fires, the position of the timing mark can be seen. The flashing light makes a moving mark appear to stand still next to a stationary mark.

Timing lights (**Figure 19**) range from inexpensive models with a neon bulb to expensive models with a xenon bulb, built in tachometer and timing advance compensator. A built in tachometer is very useful as most ignition timing

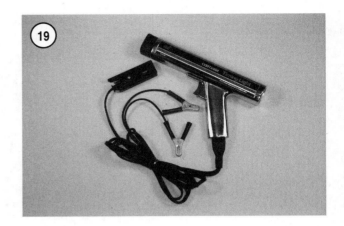

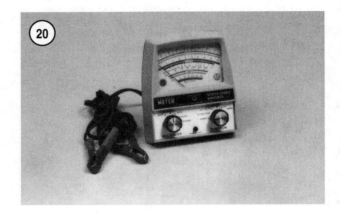

specifications are based on a specific engine speed.

A timing advance compensator delays the strobe enough to bring the timing mark to a certain place on the scale. Although useful for troubleshooting purposes, this feature should not be used to check or adjust the base ignition timing.

Tachometer/Dwell Meter

A portable tachometer (**Figure 20**) is needed to tune and test most marine engines. Ignition timing and carburetor adjustments must be performed at a specified engine speed. Tachometers are available with either an analog or digital display.

The fuel/air mixture must be adjusted with the engine running at idle speed. If using an analog

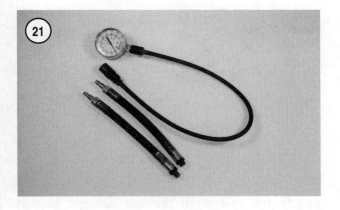

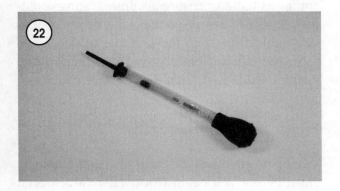

vide accurate measurement at all speeds without the need to change the range or scale. Many of these use an inductive pickup to receive the signal from the ignition system.

A dwell meter is often incorporated into the tachometer to allow testing and/or adjustments to engines with a breaker point ignition system.

Compression Gauge

This tool (**Figure 21**) measures the amount of pressure created in the combustion chamber during the compression stroke. Compression indicates the general engine condition making it one of the most useful troubleshooting tools.

The easiest type to use has screw-in adapters that fit the spark plug holes. Rubber tipped, press-in type gauges are also available. This type must be held firmly in the spark plug hole to prevent leakage and inaccurate test results..

Hydrometer

Use a hydrometer to measure specific gravity in the battery. Specific gravity is the density of the battery electrolyte as compared to pure water and indicates the battery's state of charge. Choose a hydrometer (**Figure 22**) with automatic temperature compensation; otherwise the electrolyte temperature must be measured during charging to determine the actual specific gravity.

Precision Measuring Tools

Various tools are required to make precision measurements. A dial indicator (**Figure 23**), for example, is used to determine piston position in the cylinder, runout and end play of shafts and assemblies. It is also used to measure free movement between the gear teeth (backlash) in the drive unit.

tachometer, choose one with a low range of 0-1000 rpm or 0-2000 rpm range and a high range of 0-6000 rpm. The high range setting is needed for testing purposes but lacks the accuracy needed at lower speeds. At lower speeds the meter must be capable of detecting changes of 25 rpm or less.

Digital tachometers are generally easier to use than most analog type tachometers. They pro-

Venier calipers (**Figure 24**), micrometers (**Figure 25**) and other precision tools are used to measure the size of parts, such as the piston.

Precision measuring equipment must be stored, handled and used carefully or it will not remain accurate.

SERVICE HINTS

Most of the service procedures in this manual are straightforward and can be performed by anyone reasonably handy with tools. It is suggested, however, that you consider your skills and available tools and equipment before attempting a repair involving major disassembly of the engine or drive unit.

Some operations, for example, require the use of a press. Other operations require precision measurement. Have the procedure or measurements performed by a professional if you do not have access to the correct equipment or are unfamiliar with its use.

Special Battery Precautions

Disconnecting or connecting the battery can create a spike or surge of current throughout the electrical system. This spike or surge can damage certain components of the charging system. Always verify the ignition switch is in the OFF position before connecting or disconnecting the battery or changing the selection on a battery switch.

Always disconnect both battery cables and remove the battery from the boat for charging. If the battery cables are connected, the charger may induce a damaging spike or surge of current into the electrical system. During charging, batteries produce explosive and corrosive gasses. These gases can cause corrosion in the battery compartment and creates an extremely hazardous condition.

Disconnect the cables from the battery prior to testing, adjusting or repairing many of the systems or components on the engine. This is nec-

essary for safety, to prevent damage to test equipment and to ensure accurate testing or adjustment. Always disconnect the negative battery cable first, then the positive cable. When reconnecting the battery, always connect the positive cable first, then the negative cable.

Preparation for Disassembly

Repairs go much faster if the equipment is clean before you begin work. There are special cleaners such as Gunk or Bel-Ray Degreaser, for cleaning the engine and related components. Just spray or brush on the cleaning solution, let it stand, then rinse with a garden hose.

Use pressurized water to remove marine growth and corrosion or mineral deposits from external components such as the gearcase, drive shaft housing and clamp brackets. Avoid directing pressurized water directly as seals or gaskets; pressurized water can flow past seal and gasket surfaces and contaminate lubricating fluids.

> *WARNING*
> *Never use gasoline as a cleaning agent. It presents an extreme fire hazard. Always work in a well-ventilated area if using cleaning solvent. Keep a coast Guard approved fire extinguisher, rated for gasoline fires, readily accessible in the work area.*

Much of the labor charged for a job performed at a dealership is usually for removal and disas-

sembly of other parts to access defective parts or assemblies. It is frequently possible to perform most of the disassembly then take the defective part or assembly to the dealership for repair.

If you decide to perform the job yourself, read the appropriate section in this manual, in its entirety. Study the illustrations and text until you fully understand what is involved to complete the job. Make arrangements to purchase or rent all required special tools and equipment before starting.

Disassembly Precautions

During disassembly, keep a few general precautions in mind. Force is rarely needed to get things apart. If parts fit tightly, such as a bearing on a shaft, there is usually a tool designed to separate them. Never use a screwdriver to separate parts with a machined mating surface, such as the cylinder head or manifold). The surfaces will be damaged and leak.

Make diagrams or take instant photographs wherever similar-appearing parts are found. Often, disassembled parts are left for several days or longer before resuming work. You may not remember where everything came from, or carefully arranged parts may become disturbed.

Cover all openings after removing parts to keep contamination or other parts from entering.

Tag all similar internal parts for location and mounting direction. Reinstall all internal components in the same location and mounting direction as removed. Record the thickness and mounting location of any shims as they are removed. Place small bolts and parts in plastic sandwich bags. Seal and label the bags with masking tape.

Tag all wires, hoses and connections and make a sketch of the routing. Never rely on memory alone; it may be several days or longer before you resume work.

Protect all painted surfaces from physical damage. Never allow gasoline or cleaning solvent on these surfaces.

Assembly Precautions

No parts, except those assembled with a press fit, require unusual force during assembly. If a part is hard to remove or install, find out why before proceeding.

When assembling parts, start all fasteners, then tighten evenly in an alternating or crossing pattern unless a specific tightening sequence or procedure is given.

When assembling parts, be sure all shims, spacers and washers are installed in the same position and location as removed.

Whenever a rotating part butts against a stationary part, look for a shim or washer. Use new gaskets, seals and O-rings if there is any doubt about the conditions of the used ones. Unless otherwise specified, a thin coating of oil on gaskets may help them seal more effectively. Use heavy grease to hold small parts in place if they tend to fall out during assembly.

Use emery cloth and oil to remove high spots from piston surfaces. Use a dull screwdriver to remove carbon deposits from the cylinder head, ports and piston crown. *Do not* scratch or gouge these surfaces. Wipe the surfaces clean with a *clean* shop towel when finished.

If the carburetor must be repaired, completely disassemble it and soak all metal parts in a commercial carburetor cleaner. Never soak gaskets and rubber or plastic parts in these cleaners.

Clean rubber or plastic parts in warm soapy water. Never use a wire to clean jets and small passages because they are easily damaged. Use compressed air to blow debris from all passages in the carburetor body.

Take your time and do the job right. Break-in procedure for a newly rebuilt engine or drive is the same as for a new one. Use the recommended break-in oil and follow the instructions provided in the appropriate chapter.

SPECIAL TIPS

Because of the extreme demands placed on marine equipment, several points must be kept in mind when performing service and repair. The following are general suggestions that may improve the overall life of the machine and help avoid costly failure.

1. Unless otherwise specified, apply a threadlocking compound, such as Loctite Threadlocker, to all bolts and nuts, even if secured with a lockwasher. Use only the specified grade of threadlocking compound. A screw or bolt lost from an engine cover or bearing retainer could easily cause serious and expensive damage before the loss is noticed. When applying threadlocking compound, use only enough to lightly coat the threads. If too much is used, it can work its way down the threads and contaminate seals or bearings.

2. If self-locking fasteners are used, replace them with new ones. Do not install standard fasteners in place of self-locking ones.

3. Use caution when using air tools to remove stainless steel nuts or bolts. The heat generated during rapid spinning easily damages the threads of stainless steel fasteners. To prevent thread damage, apply penetrating oil as a cooling agent and loosen or tighten them slowly.

4. Use a wide chisel to straighten the tab of a fold-over type lockwasher. Such a tool provides a better contact surface than a screwdriver or pry bar, making straightening easier. During installa-

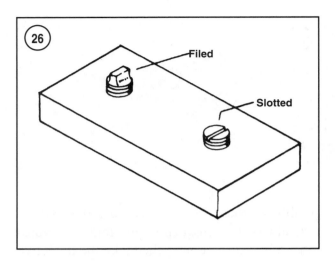

tion, use a new fold-over type lockwasher. If a new lockwasher is not available, fold over a tab on the washer that has not been previously used. Reusing the same tab may cause the washer to break, resulting in a loss of locking ability and a loose piece of metal adrift in the engine. When folding the tab into position, carefully pry it toward the flat on the bolt or nut. Use a pair or plies to bend the tab against the fastener. Do not use a punch and hammer to drive the tab into position. The resulting fold may be too sharp, weakening the washer and increasing its chance of failure.

5. Use only the specified replacement parts if replacing a missing or damaged bolt, screw or nut. Many fasteners are specially hardened for the application.

6. Install only the specified gaskets. Unless specified otherwise, install them without sealant. Many gaskets are made with a material that swells when it contacts oil. Gasket sealer prevents them from swelling as intended and can result in oil leakage. Most gaskets must be a specific thickness. Installing a gasket that is too thin or too thick in a critical area could cause expensive damage.

7. Make sure all shims and washers are reinstalled in the same location and position. Whenever a rotating part contacts a stationary part, look for a shim or washer.

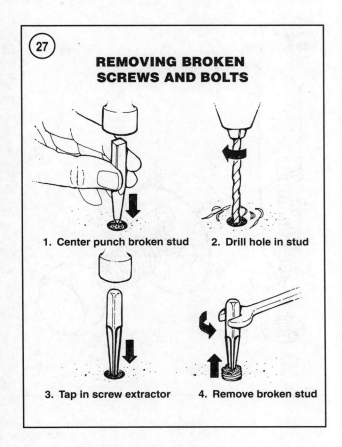

**REMOVING BROKEN
SCREWS AND BOLTS**

1. Center punch broken stud

2. Drill hole in stud

3. Tap in screw extractor

4. Remove broken stud

MECHANICS TECHNIQUES

Marine engines are subjected to conditions very different from most engines. They are repeatedly subjected to a corrosive environment followed by periods of non-use for weeks or longer. Such use invites corrosion damage to fasteners, causing difficulty or breakage during removal. This section provides information that is useful for removing stuck or broken fasteners and repairing damaged threads.

Removing Stuck Fasteners

When a nut or bolt corrodes and cannot be removed, several methods may be used to loosen it. First, apply penetrating oil, such as Liquid Wrench or WD-40. Apply it liberally to the threads and allow it to penetrate for 10-15 minutes. Tap the fastener several times with a small

hammer; however, do not hit it hard enough to cause damage. Reapply the penetrating oil if necessary.

For stuck screws, apply penetrating oil as described, then insert a screwdriver in the slot. Tap the top of the screwdriver with a hammer. This looses the corrosion in the threads allowing it to turn. If the screw head is too damaged to use a screwdriver, grip the head with locking pliers and twist the screw from the assembly.

A Phillips, Allen or Torx screwdriver may start to slip in the screw during removal. If slippage occurs, stop immediately and apply a dab of course valve lapping compound onto the tip of the screwdriver. Valve lapping compound or a special screw removal compound is available from most hardware and automotive parts stores. Insert the driver into the screw and apply downward pressure while turning. The gritty material in the compound improves the grip on the screw, allowing more rotational force before slippage occurs. Keep the compound away from any other engine components. It is very abrasive and can cause rapid wear if applied onto moving or sliding surfaces.

Avoid applying heat unless specifically instructed because it may melt, warp or remove the temper from parts.

Removing Broken Bolts or Screws

The head of bolt or screw may unexpectedly twist off during removal. Several methods are available for removing the remaining portion of the bolt or screw.

If a large portion of the bolt or screw projects out, try gripping it with locking pliers. If the projecting portion is too small, file it to fit a wrench or cut a slot in it to fit a screwdriver (**Figure 26**). If the head breaks off flush or cannot be turned with a screwdriver or wrench, use a screw extractor (**Figure 27**). To do this, center punch the remaining portion of the screw or bolt. Select the proper size of extractor for the size of the fastener. Using the drill size specified on the extractor, drill a hole into the fastener. Do not drill deeper than the remaining fastener. Carefully tap the extractor into the hole and back the remnant out using a wrench on the extractor.

Remedying Stripped Threads

Occasionally, threads are stripped through carelessness or impact damage. Often the threads can be repaired by running a tap (for internal threads on nuts) or die (for external threads on bolts) through threads (**Figure 28**).

To clean or repair spark plug threads, use a spark plug tap. If an internal thread is damaged, it may be necessary to install a Helicoil or some other type of thread insert. Follow the manufacturer's instructions when installing their insert.

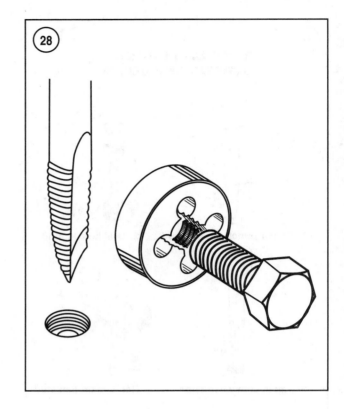

Chapter Three

Troubleshooting

Troubleshooting is the simple process of testing individual systems for the express purpose of quickly isolating good systems from the defective or inoperative system(s). When a system is identified as defective, troubleshooting continues with testing of the individual components from the suspect system. It is very important to perform only one test procedure at a time, otherwise it will be difficult, if not impossible, to determine the condition of each component. Occasionally a component in a system cannot be stand-alone tested. In this case, other components are tested and eliminated until the suspect component is identified as defective by the process of elimination. The most important rules of troubleshooting are to test systems before components and to be methodical. Haphazardly jumping from one system or component to another may eventually solve the problem, but time and effort will be wasted. Use the various system diagrams provided in this manual to identify all components in a system. Test each component in a rational order to determine which component has caused the system's failure.

The process generally begins with the operator noticing a symptom (a noticeable decrease in performance or unsatisfactory operating characteristic). Key questions to consider are as follows:

a. Did the problem occur all at once (suddenly) or was its onset gradual?

b. Is there a specific rpm or load at which the problem occurs?

c. Does the weather (extreme cold or heat) affect the symptom?

d. Has any recent service work been performed?

e. Has the engine recently come out of storage?

f. Have you changed fuel suppliers or fuel grades recently?

g. Is the manufacturer's recommended oil being used?

h. Have any accessories been added to the boat or motor recently?

Simple things like failing to prime the fuel system, attach the safety lanyard and incorrect starting procedures have caused untold grief to boat operators.

Before beginning any troubleshooting procedure, perform a thorough visual inspection of the unit. Pay special attention to the condition of the battery cable connections (at both ends), all electrical harness connectors and terminals, fuel quantity, quality and supply, indications of engine overheat, evidence of leaks (fuel, oil and water) and mechanical integrity (loose fasteners, cracked or broken castings). Learning to recognize visual defects is a skill that comes from self-discipline and patience. Take your time and look closely. Use your hands to touch, feel and wiggle components.

If you are not a professional technician, be realistic about your capabilities, especially when working from a home garage or driveway. Avoid situations where a major disassembly has been hastily performed and you feel compelled to continue in a predicament that is well beyond your qualifications. Service departments tend to charge heavily to reassemble an engine that comes into the shop in several boxes, while some will refuse to take on such a job.

Proper lubrication, maintenance and engine tune-up as described in Chapter Four will reduce the necessity for troubleshooting. However, because of the harsh and demanding environment in which the outboard motor operates, troubleshooting at some point in the motors serviceable life is inevitable.

This chapter concentrates on the actual troubleshooting procedures. Once the defective component is identified, refer to appropriate chapter for the applicable removal and installation procedure. **Tables 1-3** list recommended test equipment and tools, wire color code and battery cable recommendations. **Tables 4-10** cover typical symptoms and solutions for the starting, charging, ignition and fuel systems. **Tables 11-18** list specifications for the starting, charging and ignition systems. **Table 19** provides ignition system identification. **Table 20** lists Quicksilver DDT (digital diagnostic terminal) data, **Table 21** lists ECT (engine coolant temperature) and IAT (intake air temperature) sensor data, **Table 22** provides fuel pump specifications and **Table 23** lists

EFI multimeter specifications. **Tables 1-23** are located at the end of this chapter.

SAFETY PRECAUTIONS

Wear approved eye protection at all times (**Figure 1**), especially when machinery is in operation and hammers are being used. Wear approved ear protection during all running tests and in the presence of noisy machinery. Keep loose clothing tucked in and long hair tied back and secured. Refer to Chapter 2, *Safety First* for additional safety guidelines.

When making or breaking any electrical connection, always disconnect the negative battery cable first. When performing tests that require cranking the engine without starting, disconnect and ground the spark plug leads to prevent accidental starts and sparks.

Securely cap or plug all disconnected fuel lines to prevent fuel discharge when the motor is cranked or the primer bulb is squeezed.

Thoroughly read all manufacturer's instructions and safety sheets for test equipment and special tools being used.

Do not substitute parts unless you know they meet or exceed the original manufacturer's specifications.

Never run an outboard motor without an adequate water supply. Never run an outboard motor at wide-open throttle without an adequate load. Do not exceed 3000 rpm in neutral (no load).

Safely performing on-water tests requires 2 people. One person to operate the boat, the other to monitor the gauges or test instruments. All personnel must remain seated inside the boat at all times. It is not acceptable to lean over the transom while the boat is under way. Use extensions to allow all gauges and meters to be located in the normal seating area.

A test propeller is an economical alternative to the dynometer. A test propeller is also a convenient alternative to on-water testing. Test pro-

pellers are made by modifying (turning down) the diameter of a standard low pitch aluminum propeller until the recommended wide-open throttle engine speed can be obtained with the motor in a test tank or on the trailer, when backed into the water. Be careful of tying the boat to a dock as considerable thrust is developed by the test propeller. Some docks may not be able to withstand the load.

Propeller repair stations can provide the modification service. Normally, approximately 1/3 to 1/2 of the blades will be removed. However, it is far better to remove too little, than too much. It may take several tries to achieve the correct full throttle speed, but once achieved, no further modifications will be required. Many propeller repair stations have experience with this type of modification and may be able to recommend a starting point.

Test propellers also allow simple tracking of engine performance. The full throttle test speed of an engine fitted with a correctly modified test wheel can be tracked (recorded) from season to season. It is not unusual for a new or rebuilt engine to show a slight increase in test propeller engine speed as complete break-in is achieved. The engine will generally hold this speed over the normal service life of the engine. As the engine begins to wear out, the test propeller engine speed will show a gradual decrease that deteriorates to a marked or drastic decrease, as the point of engine failure is reached.

OPERATING REQUIREMENTS

All 2-stroke engines require 3 basic conditions to run properly: The correct air and fuel mixture from the carburetor, crankcase and combustion chamber compression and adequate spark delivered to the spark plug at the correct time. When troubleshooting, it is helpful to remember: fuel, compression and spark (**Figure 2**). If any of these are lacking, the motor will not run. First, verify the mechanical integrity of the engine by per-

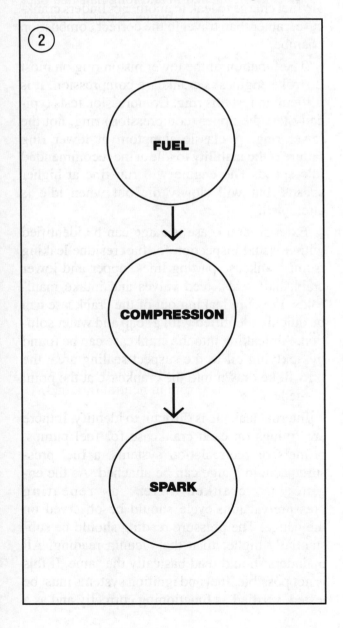

3

forming a compression test (Chapter Four). Once compression has been verified, test the ignition system with an air gap spark tester and then finally focus your attention on the fuel system. Troubleshooting in this order will provide the quickest results.

If the motor has been sitting for any length of time and refuses to start, check the condition of the battery first to make sure it is adequately charged, then inspect the battery cable connections at the battery and the engine. Examine the fuel delivery system. This includes the fuel tank, fuel pump, fuel lines, fuel filters and carburetor(s). Rust or corrosion may have formed in the tank, restricting fuel flow. Gasoline deposits may have gummed up carburetor jets and air passages. Gasoline tends to lose its potency after standing for long periods. Condensation may contaminate the fuel with water. Connect a portable tank containing fresh fuel mix to help isolate the problem. Do not drain the old gasoline unless you are sure it is at fault. Always dispose of old gasoline in accordance with EPA regulations.

Starting Difficulties

Occasionally, an outboard motor will be plagued by hard starting and generally poor performance (especially at low speeds) for which there seems to be no good cause. Fuel and ignition systems test satisfactorily and a compression test indicates that the combustion chamber (piston, rings, cylinder walls and head gasket) is in good condition.

What has not been tested is crankcase sealing. A 2-stroke engine cannot function unless the crankcase is adequately sealed. As the piston travels downward, the crankcase must pressurize and push the air/fuel mixture into the combustion chamber as the intake ports are uncovered. Conversely, as the piston travels upward, the crankcase must create a vacuum to pull the air/fuel mixture into the crankcase from the carburetor in preparation for the next cycle. Refer to Chap-

ter Two for operational diagrams of a typical 2-stroke engine.

Leaks in the crankcase cause the air/fuel charge to leak into the atmosphere under crankcase compression. During the intake stroke, crankcase leakage will cause air from the atmosphere to be drawn into the crankcase, diluting the air/fuel charge. The net result is inadequate fuel in the combustion chamber. On multiple cylinder engines, each crankcase must be sealed from all other crankcases. Internal leakage will allow the air/fuel charge to leak to another cylinders crankcase, rather than travel to the correct combustion chamber.

The function of the lower piston ring on most 2-stroke engines is crankcase compression. It is difficult to test this ring. Compression tests typically test the upper (compression) ring, not the lower ring. A classic symptom of lower ring failure is the inability to idle at the recommended idle speed. The engine will run fine at higher speeds, but will slowly die out when idle is attempted.

External crankcase leakage can be identified with a visual inspection for fuel residue leaking from: crankcase parting lines, upper and lower crankshaft seals, reed valves and intake manifolds. Pressure leaking out of the crankcase can be quickly identified with a soap and water solution. Air leaking into the crankcase can be found by applying oil to the suspect sealing area, the oil will be drawn into the crankcase at the point of the leak.

Internal leakage is difficult to identify. If there are fittings on each crankcase for fuel pumps, primers or recirculation systems, a fuel pressure/vacuum gauge can be attached. As the engine is cranked over, a repeating pressure/vacuum cycle should be observed on the gauge. The pressure reading should be substantially higher than the vacuum reading. All cylinders should read basically the same. If this is not possible, fuel and ignition systems must be tested, verified as functioning correctly and as a final resort, the engine disassembled and internally inspected.

TEST AND REPAIR EQUIPMENT

Terminology

Voltage

Voltage is the pressure in an electrical circuit, the more pressure, the more work that can be done. Voltage can be visualized as water pressure in a garden hose. The more pressure, the further the water can be sprayed. You can have water present in the hose, but without pressure, you cannot accomplish anything. If the water pressure is too high, the hose will burst. When voltage is excessive it will leak past insulation and arc to ground. Voltage is always measured with a voltmeter in a simple parallel connection. The connection of a voltmeter directly to the negative and positive terminals of a battery is an example of a parallel connection (**Figure 3**). Nothing has to be disconnected to make a parallel connection.

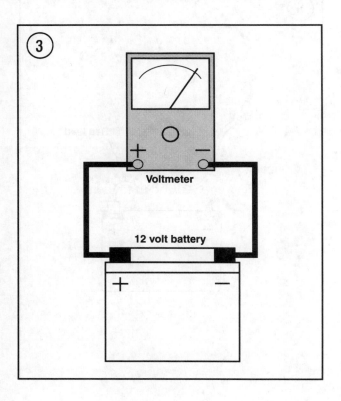

Just as a water pressure gauge simply taps into a hose or pipe, a voltmeter is an electrical pressure gauge that taps into the electrical circuit.

DC voltage

DC voltage is direct current voltage, meaning that the electricity always flows in one direction only. All circuits associated with the battery are DC circuits.

AC voltage

AC voltage is alternating current, which means that the current flows in one direction momentarily and then switches to the opposite direction. The frequency at which AC voltage changes direction is referred to as Hertz. Household wiring is 115 volts AC and typically 60 hertz (the average value of electrical pressure is 115 volts and the electricity changes direction 60 times per second). In typical outboard motor applications, the charging system's stator output is AC voltage. In larger, inboard powered applications, AC voltage is typically created by a dedicated AC generator (genset) that powers high load devices such as air-conditioning and appliances. Shore power is also AC voltage. Standard AC voltmeters take an average reading of the fluctuating voltage signal. RMS (root mean square) AC voltmeters use a different mathematical formula to come up with a value of the voltage signal. RMS meters should only be used where specified, since the difference in readings between a standard AC meter and a RMS AC meter will be significant.

DVA voltage

DVA stands for direct voltage adapter which is used to measure peak AC voltage. This type of measurement of AC voltage takes the absolute peak or highest value of the fluctuating AC voltage signal. Peak readings will be substantially higher than standard or RMS AC values and are typically used when testing marine CD (capacitor discharge) ignition systems. Failure to use a meter with a DVA (peak) scale can cause good ignition components to be incorrectly diagnosed as bad. See **Figure 4** for a typical multimeter with a DVA scale.

Amperes

Amperes (amps) are referred to as current. Current is the actual flow of electricity in a circuit. Current can be visualized as water flowing from a garden hose. There can be pressure in the hose, but if we do not let it flow, no work can be done. The higher the flow of current the more work that can be done. However, when too much current flows through a wire, the wire will overheat and melt. Melted wires are caused by excessive current, not excessive volts. Amps are measured with an ammeter in a simple series connection. The connection of an ammeter requires the disconnection of a circuit and the splicing of the ammeter into the circuit. Just as a water flow-meter must have the water flow through it in order to measure the flow, an ammeter is an electrical flow-meter that must have all of the current flow through it. Always use an ammeter that can read higher than the anticipated current flow. Always connect the red lead of the ammeter to where the electricity is coming from (electrical source) and the black lead of the ammeter to where the electricity is going (electrical load). See **Figure 5**.

Many digital multimeters can use inductive or clamp-on ammeter probes (**Figure 6**). These probes read the magnetic field strength created from current flowing through a wire. No electrical connection is required, simply slip the probe over the lead.

A simple form of ammeter is the direct reading inductive ammeter (**Figure 7**). These meters directly read the magnetic field strength created

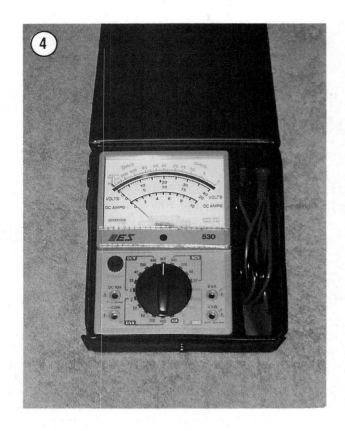

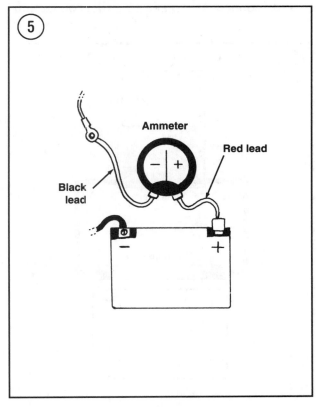

from current flowing through a wire. No electrical connection is required, simply slip the meter over the lead so that the lead is located in the channel or groove located on the rear of the meter. See **Figure 7**.

Watts

Watts (W) is the measurement unit for power in an electrical circuit. Watts rate the ability to do electrical work. The easiest for-

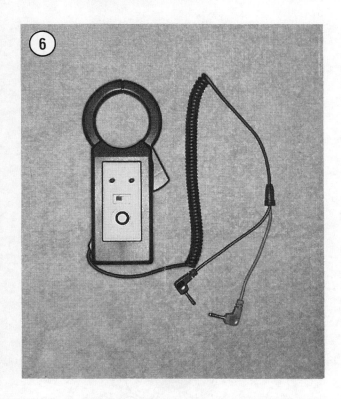

mula for calculating watts is to take the system voltage times the amps flowing (12 volts system times 10 amp alternator = 120 watt maximum load). You can easily reverse calculate amp load by dividing watts by voltage (12 watt radio divided by 12 volt system uses 1 amp of current). When calculating load on a charging system, remember that you cannot carry more load than the system is rated for or the battery will constantly discharge.

Ohms

Ohms is the measurement unit for resistance in an electrical circuit. Resistance will cause a reduction in current flow and a reduction (or drop) in voltage. Visualized as a kink in a garden hose, which would cause less water (current) to flow, it would also cause less pressure (volts) to be available downstream from the kink. Resistance is measured with ohmmeters that are self-powered. Ohmmeters send a small amount of electricity into a circuit and measure how hard they have to push to return the electricity to the meter. An ohmmeter must only be used on a circuit or component that is isolated (disconnected from any other circuit or component) and has no voltage present. Ohmmeters are technically connected in series.

Voltage drop test

Since resistance causes voltage to drop, resistance can be measured on an active circuit with a voltmeter. This is the voltage drop test. Basically, a voltage drop test measures the difference in voltage from the beginning of the tested circuit to the end of the tested circuit, *while* the circuit is being operated. If the circuit has no resistance, there will be no voltage drop (the meter will read zero volts). The more resistance the circuit has, the higher the voltmeter reading will be. Generally, voltage drop readings of 1 or more volts are considered unsatisfactory. The chief advantage to the voltage drop test over an ohmmeter resistance test is that the circuit is tested while under operation. It is important to remember that a zero reading on a voltage drop test is good, while a battery voltage reading would signify an open circuit.

The voltage drop test provides an excellent means of testing solenoids (relays), battery cables and high current electrical leads (both positive and negative). As with the ammeter, always connect the red lead of the voltmeter to where the electricity is coming from (electrical source) and the black lead of the voltmeter to where the electricity is going (electrical load).

Multipliers

When using an analog multimeter to measure ohms, the scale choices will typically be labeled R × 1, R × 10, R × 100 and so on. These are resistance scale multipliers. R × 100 means to multiply the meter reading by 100. If the needle indicated a reading of 75 ohms while set to the R x100 scale, the actual resistance reading would be 75 × 100 or 7500 ohms. It is important to note and remember the scale multiplier when using an analog ohmmeter.

Other multipliers commonly used for volts, ohms and amps scales are: mega- (M), kilo- (k), milli- (m) and micro-(%). Mega (M) is a 1,000,000 multiplier, 75 mega-ohms (or 75 M-ohms) would be 75 million ohms. Kilo (k) is a 1,000 multiplier, 75 kilo-volts (or 75 k-volts) would be 75 thousand volts. Milli (m) is a 0.001 multiplier, 75 milli-volts (or 75 m-volts) would be 0.075 volts or 75 thousandths of a volt. Micro (%) is a 0.000001 multiplier, 75 micro-amps (or 75 %-amps) would be 0.000075 amps or 75 millionths of an amp.

Diodes

Diodes are one-way electrical check valves. A series of diodes used to change AC current to DC

current is called a rectifier. Single diodes used to prevent reverse flow of electricity are typically called blocking diodes. Diodes can be tested with an analog meter set to any ohmmeter scale other than *low* or with a digital multimeter set to the diode test scale. A diode tested with an analog ohmmeter will indicate a relatively low reading in one polarity and a relatively high reading in the opposite polarity. A diode tested with a digital multimeter will read a voltage drop of approximately 0.4-0.9 volts in one polarity and an open circuit (OL or OUCH) in the opposite polarity.

Analog Multimeter

A highly recommended analog multimeter is the Electro-Specialities model No.530, available from Quicksilver parts and accessories as part No. 91-99750 (**Figure 8**). This economical meter features AC and DC volt, DVA, 10 amp DC and four ohmmeter ranges. When using an analog meter to read ohms, the meter must be re-calibrated (zeroed) each time the scale or range is changed. Normally the ohmmeter leads are

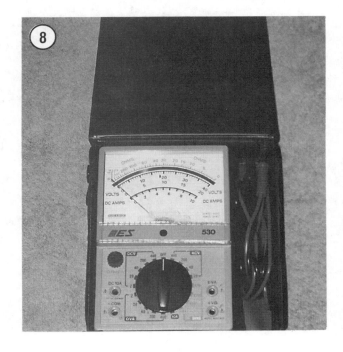

connected for calibration, however some meters require the leads to be apart for calibration when using the low ohms scale. Always follow the manufacturer's instructions for calibration. When checking for *shorts to ground* calibrate on the highest scale available. When checking diodes, calibrate on the R × 10 scale or higher. If the ohmmeter is so equipped, never use the *low* scale to test a diode or short to ground. When checking for a specific ohm value, calibrate the ohmmeter on a scale that allows reading the specification as near the middle of the meter movement as possible. Analog meters allow easy visual identification of erratic or fluctuating readings.

Digital Multimeter

The digital multimeter is rapidly gaining popularity in the marine industry after many years of acceptance in the automotive industry.

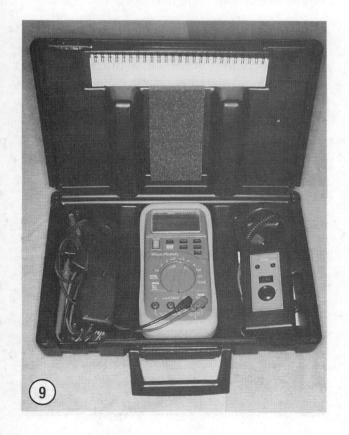

Digital displays are easy and clear to read. Most digital meters are auto-ranging, which means that they automatically shift to the scale most appropriate for displaying the value being read. However, the technician must be careful to read the scale correctly. Fluctuating readings can be frustrating to read as the display will change several times a second. Quality digital multimeters typically have a bar graph located below the digital number display. The bar graph allows easy interpretation of fluctuating readings, similar to an analog meter. The scale range and multiplier (if applicable) will be displayed alongside the actual reading. Most quality digital meters will have a special diode test scale that measures the voltage drop of the diode, instead of the resistance. Do not attempt to use the digital multimeter's ohms scale to test diodes, as the readings will be inconsistent. The digital multimeter is protected by internal fuses that are usually uncommon sizes. Buy several spare fuses at the time of purchase.

Adapters are available for temperature readings, inductive ammeter readings and many other functions. **Figure 9** shows a digital multimeter in a protective case with several adapters.

Test Light

The test light is a useful tool for simple troubleshooting, such as starter circuits. A test light should not be used on electronic circuits, such as modern ignition and fuel injection circuits. The current draw of the test lamp can damage delicate electronic circuits. A test light should also not be used where specific voltage values are being sought. Before beginning any troubleshooting with a test lamp, connect the test lamp directly to the battery and observe the brightness of the bulb. You must reference the rest of your readings against this test. If the bulb does not glow as brightly as when it was hooked directly to the battery, a problem is indicated.

A test lamp can be used to check ground circuits by connecting the test lamp lead directly to the positive (+) battery terminal. When the test lamp probe is connected to any ground circuit, the light should glow brightly.

Electrical Repairs

Check all electrical connections for corrosion, mechanical damage, heat damage and loose connections. Clean and repair all connections as necessary. All wire splices or connector repairs must be made with waterproof marine grade connectors and heat shrink tubing. An electrical hardware repair kit and crimping pliers are available from Quicksilver to repair the serviceable connectors and make wire splices on the engine. The Quicksilver dealer catalog also lists heat shrink connectors and heat shrink tubing for making other waterproof connections and repairs. Marine and industrial suppliers are other good sources for quality electrical repair equipment.

NOTE
On engines equipped with an ECM (electronic control module), any electrical connection or repair that does not have perfect continuity will affect the signal being sent to or from the ECM, effectively throwing the system out of calibration. This will always have a detrimental effect on engine operating quality and performance.

STARTING SYSTEM

Description

All models covered in this manual are equipped with electric start systems. The starter motor is mounted vertically on the engine. When battery current is supplied to the starter motor, its pinion gear is thrust upward to engage the teeth on the engine flywheel (**Figure 10**, typical). Once the engine starts, the pinion gear disen-

gages from the flywheel. This process is similar to that used to crank an automotive engine.

The starting system requires a fully charged battery to provide the large amount of electrical current necessary to operate the starter motor. Electric start models are equipped with an alternator to charge the battery during operation.

The electric starting system consists of the battery, starter switch, neutral safety switch, starter solenoid, starter motor (and starter drive) and related wiring. See **Figure 11**. The neutral safety switch allows starter engagement only when the gear shift is in the NEUTRAL position. Tiller handle models have the neutral safety switch mounted on the engine. Remote control models have the neutral safety switch mounted in the remote control box. Remote control models incorporate a 20 amp fuse to protect the remote control key switch circuits. The fuse is located on the engine, between the starter solenoid and the boat main harness connector.

Engaging the starter switch allows current to flow to the starter solenoid coil windings. The neutral safety switch will be on the positive side of the solenoid on remote control models and the negative side of the solenoid on tiller handle models. In either case, when the current path is complete, the solenoid contacts close, allowing current to flow from the battery through the solenoid to the starter motor.

Solenoid design will vary, but all solenoids use 2 large terminal studs (battery positive and starter cables) and 2 small terminal studs (black and yellow/red primary leads).

NOTE
The cable connecting the battery to the starter solenoid is red or black with red sleeved ends. The cable connecting the starter solenoid to the starter motor is yellow/black with yellow sleeved ends or black with red sleeved ends.

CAUTION
To prevent starter damage from over-heating, do not operate the starter motor continuously for more than 30 seconds. Allow the motor to cool for at least 2 minutes between attempts to start the engine.

3

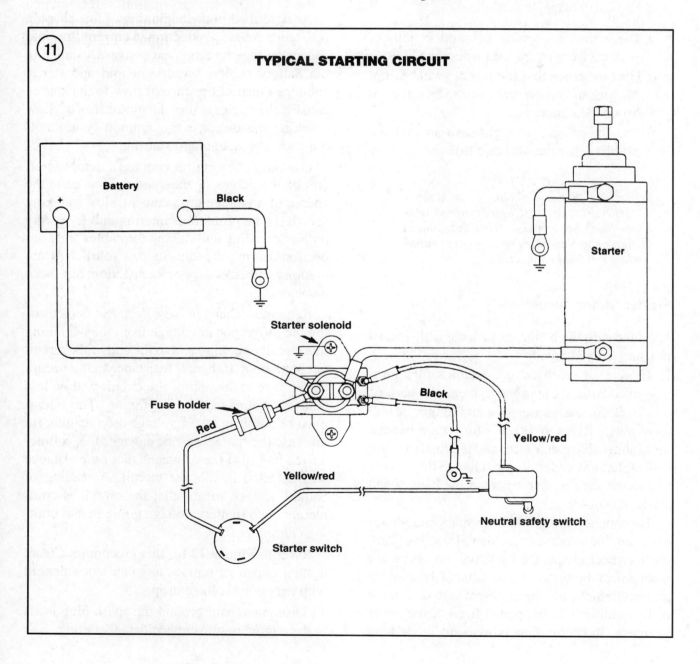

⑪ **TYPICAL STARTING CIRCUIT**

Battery

Black

Starter

Starter solenoid

Fuse holder

Red

Black

Yellow/red

Yellow/red

Neutral safety switch

Starter switch

Troubleshooting Preparation

If the following procedures do not locate the problem, refer to **Table 4** for additional information. Before troubleshooting the starting circuit, be sure of the following:

a. The battery is fully charged.

b. The shift control lever is in the NEUTRAL position.

c. All electrical connections are clean and tight.

d. The wiring harness is in good condition, with no worn or frayed insulation.

e. The fuse protecting the starter switch is not blown (all remote control models and 30 hp-up tiller models).

f. The power head and gearcase are not the problem (mechanical failure).

CAUTION
Unless otherwise noted, all voltage or test light tests must be performed with the leads connected, but with the connection or terminals exposed to accommodate test lead connection.

Starter Motor Turns Slowly

1. Make sure the battery is in acceptable condition and fully charged.

2. Inspect all electrical connections for looseness or corrosion. Clean and tighten as necessary.

3. Check for the proper size and length of battery cables. Refer to **Table 3** for recommended minimum cable gauge sizes and lengths. Replace cables that are undersize or relocate the battery to shorten the distance between the battery and starter solenoid.

4. Disconnect and ground the spark plug leads to the engine to prevent accidental starting. Turn the flywheel clockwise by hand and check for mechanical binding. If mechanical binding is evident, remove the lower gearcase to determine if the binding is in the power head or the lower gearcase. If no binding is evident, other than

normal compression and water pump impeller drag, continue to Step 5.

5. Perform the starting system voltage drop test as described in the next section.

6. Check the starter motor current draw as described in this chapter.

Starting system voltage drop test

As described in the beginning of this chapter, resistance causes a reduction in current flow and causes voltage to drop. Excessive resistance in the battery cables, starter solenoid and starter cable can restrict the current flow to the starter, causing the starter to turn the motor slowly. Slow cranking speeds cause low ignition system output and subsequent hard starting.

Use the following procedure to determine if any of the cables or the starter solenoid is the source of a voltage drop causing slow cranking speeds. If the problem is intermittent, try gently pulling, bending and flexing the cables and connections during the test. Sudden voltmeter fluctuations indicate a poor connection has been located.

Remember that a voltage drop test is measuring the difference in voltage from the beginning of a circuit or component to the end of the circuit or component. If there is resistance in the circuit, the voltage at the end of the circuit will be less than the voltage at the beginning. The circuit must be active to take a voltage drop reading (in this case the starter must be engaged). A voltmeter reading of 0 (zero) means that no resistance was detected in the test circuit. A reading of battery voltage means that the circuit is completely open (battery voltage going in and nothing coming out).

Refer to **Figure 12** for this procedure. Clean, tighten, repair or replace any cable or solenoid with excessive voltage drop.

1. Disconnect and ground the spark plug leads to the engine to prevent accidental starting.

2. Connect the positive (red) voltmeter lead to the positive battery terminal (1, **Figure 12**). Connect the negative (black) voltmeter lead to the positive solenoid terminal (2, **Figure 12**).

3. Engage the electric starter and observe the meter. If the meter indicates more than 0.3 volts, excessive resistance is present in the positive battery cable. Clean the connections, repair the terminal ends or replace the positive battery cable.

CAUTION
Do not connect the positive voltmeter lead in Step 4 until after the engine begins cranking. The open solenoid will read battery voltage and could damage a voltmeter set to a very low volts scale. In addition, disconnect the voltmeter before stopping cranking.

4. Connect the negative voltmeter lead to the starter side of the solenoid (3, **Figure 12**). Engage the electric starter. While the engine is

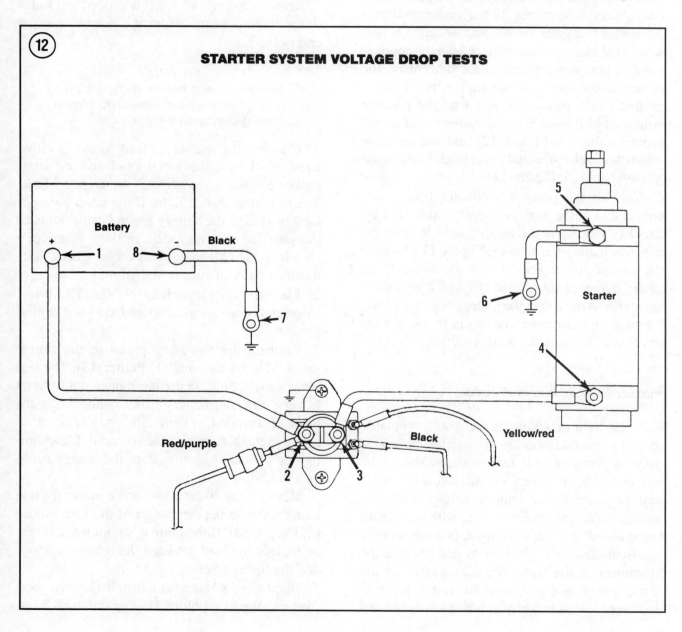

STARTER SYSTEM VOLTAGE DROP TESTS

cranking, touch the positive voltmeter lead to the battery cable positive solenoid terminal (2, **Figure 12**). Note the meter reading, remove the positive voltmeter lead and discontinue cranking. If the meter indicates more than 0.2 volts, the starter solenoid has excessive internal resistance and should be replaced.

5. Connect the positive voltmeter lead to the starter side of the solenoid (3, **Figure 12**) and the negative voltmeter lead to the starter motor terminal (4, **Figure 12**). Engage the electric starter and observe the meter. If the meter indicates more than 0.2 volts, excessive resistance is present in the starter motor cable. Clean the connections, repair the terminal ends or replace the starter motor cable. If the starter motor has a ground cable, repeat this test with the positive voltmeter lead hooked to the starter end of starter ground cable (5, **Figure 12**) and the negative voltmeter lead connected to the engine end of the ground cable (6, **Figure 12**).

6. Connect the positive voltmeter lead to the engine end of the negative battery cable (7, **Figure 12**) and the negative voltmeter lead to the negative battery terminal (8, **Figure 12**). Engage the electric starter and observe the meter. If the meter indicates more than 0.3 volts, excessive resistance is present in the battery negative cable. Clean the connections, repair the terminal ends or replace the negative battery cable.

Starter Motor Does Not Turn

A test light or voltmeter are both acceptable tools for troubleshooting the starter circuit. If using a voltmeter, all test readings should be within 1 volt of battery voltage. Readings of 1 volt or more below battery voltage indicates problems (excessive resistance) with the circuit being tested. If using a test light, first connect the test light directly to the battery and observe the brightness of the bulb. You must reference the rest of your readings against this test. If the bulb does not glow as brightly as when it was hooked

directly to the battery, a problem (excessive resistance) is indicated.

> *CAUTION*
> *Disconnect and ground the spark plug leads to the engine to prevent accidental starting during all test procedures.*

Remote control models and 50-60 hp tiller handle models

Refer to **Figure 13** for this procedure. Refer to the individual model wiring diagrams at the end of the book.

> *CAUTION*
> *Disconnect and ground the spark plug leads to the engine to prevent accidental starting during all test procedures.*

1. Connect the test lamp lead to the positive terminal of the battery and touch the test lamp probe to metal anywhere on the engine block. The test lamp should light. If the lamp does not light or is dim, the battery ground cable connections are loose or corroded, or there is an open circuit in the battery ground cable. Check connections on both ends of the ground cable.

2. Place the shift lever into the NEUTRAL position and connect test lamp lead to a good engine ground.

3. Connect the test lamp probe to the starter solenoid input terminal (1, **Figure 13**). The test lamp should light. If the lamp does not light or is very dim, the battery cable connections are loose or corroded, or there is an open in the cable between the battery and the solenoid. Clean and tighten connections or replace the battery cable as required.

4. Remove the 20 amp fuse and connect the test lamp probe to the input side of the fuse holder (2, **Figure 13**). If the lamp does not light, repair or replace the lead between the starter solenoid and the fuse holder.

5. Inspect the 20 amp fuse. Install a known good fuse into the fuse holder. Unplug the main 8-pin

connector and connect the test light probe to pin No.8 of the main engine harness connector. If the test lamp does not light, repair or replace the lead between the fuse holder and the main engine harness connector.

6A. *Remote models*—Reconnect the main harness connector and gain access to the key switch on the dash or in the remote control box. Connect the test lamp probe to terminal B on the key switch (3, **Figure 13**). If the lamp does not light, repair or replace the lead between pin No.8 of the main boat harness connector and the key switch terminal B.

6B. *50-60 hp tiller models*—Reconnect the main harness connector. Connect the test lamp probe to terminal B on the key switch (3, **Figure 13**). If the lamp does not light, repair or replace

the lead between pin No.8 of the main harness connector and the key switch terminal B.

7. Connect the test lamp probe to the key switch terminal S (4, **Figure 13**). With the key switch turned to the START position observe the test lamp. If the test lamp does not light, replace the key switch.

8A. *Remote control models*—Remove the cover from the remote control box and connect the test lamp probe to the key switch side of the neutral safety switch (5, **Figure 13**). With the key switch turned to the START position observe the test lamp. If the test lamp does not light, repair or replace the lead between the neutral safety switch and the key switch.

8B. *50-60 hp tiller models*—Connect the test lamp probe to the key switch side of the neutral

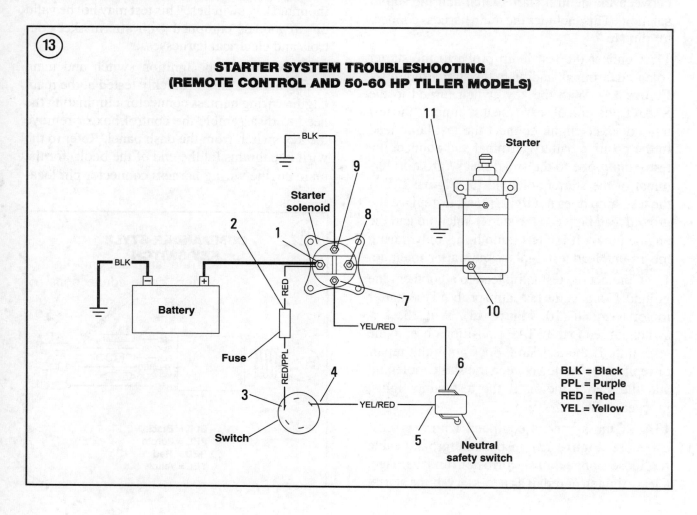

(13) **STARTER SYSTEM TROUBLESHOOTING (REMOTE CONTROL AND 50-60 HP TILLER MODELS)**

BLK = Black
PPL = Purple
RED = Red
YEL = Yellow

safety switch (5, **Figure 13**). With the key switch turned to the START position observe the test lamp. If the test lamp does not light, repair or replace the lead between the neutral safety switch and the starter switch.

9. Move the test lamp probe to the solenoid side of the neutral safety witch (6, **Figure 13**). With the key switch turned to the START position observe the test lamp. If the test lamp does not light, make sure the shift control is still in neutral and retest. Replace the neutral safety switch if the lamp does not light.

10. Connect the test lamp probe to the yellow/red terminal on the starter solenoid (7, **Figure 13**). With the key switch turned to the START position observe the test lamp. If the test lamp does not light, repair or replace the lead between the neutral start switch and the starter solenoid. This includes the main harness connector pin No.7.

11. Connect the test lamp probe to the starter solenoid terminal leading to the starter motor (8, **Figure 13**). With the key switch turned to the START position observe the test lamp. If the test lamp does not light, connect the test lamp lead to the positive battery terminal and connect the test lamp probe to the small black (ground) terminal of the starter solenoid (9, **Figure 13**). If the test lamp does not light, repair or replace the ground lead between the starter solenoid and the engine block. If the test lamp lights only during the ground lead test, replace the starter solenoid.

12. Connect the test lamp lead to a good engine ground. Connect the test lamp probe to the starter motor terminal (10, **Figure 13**). With the key switch turned to the START position observe the test lamp. If the test lamp does not light, repair or replace the cable between the starter solenoid and the starter motor. If the test lamp lights, proceed to Step 13.

13A. If the starter is equipped with a ground cable (11, **Figure 13**), inspect the ground cable for loose connections, corrosion and damage. Clean, tighten or repair as necessary. If the starter

still will not engage, remove the starter for replacement or repair.

13B. If the starter is not equipped with a ground cable, remove the starter and inspect for paint or corrosion on the mounting bolts and bosses. If paint or corrosion is found, clean the mounting bolts and bosses and reinstall the starter and test starter engagement. If the starter still will not engage, remove the starter for replacement or repair.

Key (Ignition) Switch Test

The following procedure tests the ignition switch on models equipped with Quicksilver Commander style remote control assemblies and standard aftermarket remote controls or dash-mounted key switches. This test may not be valid on *all* models equipped with aftermarket controls and electrical harnesses.

If so desired, the ignition switch and main wiring harness can be quickly tested at the main engine wiring harness connector, eliminating the need to disassemble the control box or remove the key switch from the dash panel. Refer to the wiring diagrams (at the end of the book) for the main engine wiring harness connector pin loca-

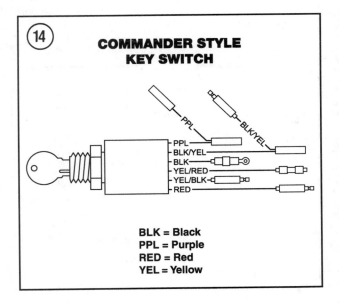

(14)   **COMMANDER STYLE
         KEY SWITCH**

    BLK = Black
    PPL = Purple
    RED = Red
    YEL = Yellow

tion and wire color code identification. If testing at the main engine harness connector, connect the ohmmeter to the appropriate pins based on the wire color codes called out in the following text. Testing at the main engine harness connector will **not** isolate a bad wiring harness from the key switch. If the switch and harness fails the test procedure (at the main harness connector), the key switch must be disconnected and retested to verify that the main harness is not the problem. To test the key switch by itself, follow the procedure as written.

Use an ohmmeter calibrated on the R × 1 scale to test the key switch circuits. Refer to **Figure 14** for Mercury/Mariner factory switches or **Figure 15** for typical after-market switches. Refer to **Table 3** for ohmmeter guidelines.

1. Disconnect the negative battery cable from the battery.

NOTE
Mercury/Mariner factory switches typically use short color-coded leads with bullet connectors. Aftermarket switches typically use screw terminals that are labeled with abbreviations. If testing at the main harness connector, consult the wiring diagrams at the end of the book

for pin locations at the main engine harness connector.

2. Gain access to the key switch and disconnect the leads from the bullet connectors or key switch terminals. Note the color code and terminal markings of aftermarket switches.

3. Connect one lead of the ohmmeter to the switch red/purple lead (BAT, B or B+ terminal) and the other ohmmeter lead to the purple lead (A, ACC or IGN terminal). When the switch is in the OFF position, no continuity should be noted.

4. Turn the switch to the ON or RUN position. The ohmmeter should indicate continuity.

5. Turn the switch to the START or CRANK position. The ohmmeter should indicate continuity.

6. Turn the switch to the OFF or STOP position. Connect one ohmmeter lead to black/yellow lead (first M terminal) and the other ohmmeter lead to the black lead (second M terminal). The ohmmeter should indicate continuity.

7. While noting the meter, turn the switch to the ON (RUN) and START (CRANK) positions. The ohmmeter should read no continuity in both positions.

8. Turn the switch to the OFF or STOP position. Connect one ohmmeter lead to the red/purple lead (BAT, B or B+ terminal) and the other ohmmeter lead to the yellow/black lead (C terminal). The ohmmeter should read no continuity.

9. Turn the switch to the ON or RUN position. The ohmmeter should read no continuity. Press in on the key to engage the CHOKE or PRIME position. The ohmmeter should read continuity in the CHOKE or PRIME position.

10. Turn the switch to the START or CRANK position. The ohmmeter should read no continuity. Press in on the key to engage the CHOKE or PRIME position. The ohmmeter should read continuity in the CHOKE or PRIME position.

11. Replace the key switch if it does not perform as specified.

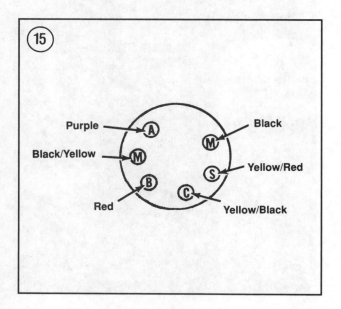

Starter Solenoid Bench Test

> *NOTE*
> *All engine wiring harness leads must be disconnected from the solenoid for this test.*

Solenoid style varies from engine to engine, but all solenoids have 2 large terminal studs and 2 small terminal studs. Refer to **Figure 16** for this procedure.

1. Disconnect the negative battery cable from the battery.

2. Disconnect all leads from the solenoid terminal studs. If necessary, remove the solenoid from the engine.

3. Connect an ohmmeter (calibrated on the R × 1 scale) to the 2 large terminal studs (1 and 2, **Figure 16**). The ohmmeter must indicate no continuity. Replace the solenoid if any other reading is noted.

4. Attach a 12-volt battery (with suitable jumper leads) to the 2 small terminal studs (3 and 4, **Figure 16**). Polarity is not important. An audible click should be heard as (if) the solenoid engages. The ohmmeter must now indicate continuity. Replace the solenoid if any other reading is noted.

5. Reconnect all leads when finished. Connect the negative battery cable last.

**Starter Motor
Current Draw Tests**

Load test

A clamp-on or inductive ammeter, if available, is simplest to use as no electrical connections are required. Make sure that the ammeter being used can read higher than the anticipated highest amp reading (**Table 8**). The spark plugs must be installed for the load test.

1. If using a conventional ammeter, disconnect the negative battery cable from the battery.

2. Disconnect the starter motor lead from the starter motor (**Figure 17**, typical) and securely

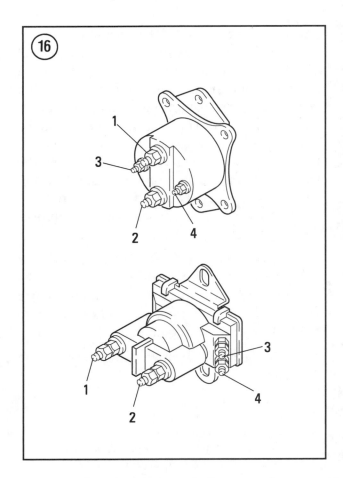

connect the ammeter red lead to the starter motor lead. Insulate the connection with electrical tape to prevent accidental arcing.

3. Securely connect the ammeter black lead to the starter motor terminal. Disconnect and ground the spark plug leads to the engine to prevent accidental starting.

4. Reconnect the negative battery cable.

5. Crank the engine to check the current draw. If excessive current draw is indicated (**Table 8**), repair or replace the starter motor.

No-load test

If starter system troubleshooting indicates that additional starter motor tests are necessary, use the starter no-load current draw test as an indicator of internal starter condition. A clamp-on or inductive ammeter, if available, is simplest to use as no electrical connections are required. Make sure that the ammeter being used can read higher

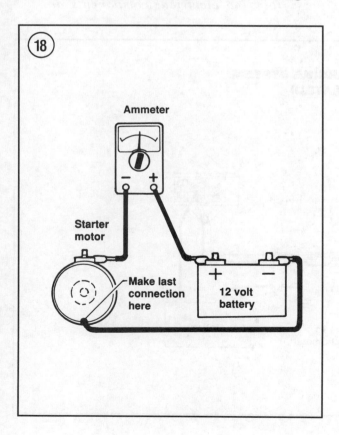

than the anticipated highest amp reading (**Table 9**).

1. Remove the starter motor assembly from the power head. Securely fasten the starter motor in a vise or other suitable holding fixture. Do not damage the starter motor by crushing it in the vise.

2. Obtain a fully charged battery that meets the requirements for the engine being tested.

3. Using heavy gauge jumper cable, connect a conventional ammeter in series with the positive battery cable and the starter motor terminal. Connect another heavy gauge jumper cable to the negative battery terminal. See **Figure 18**.

> *WARNING*
> *Make the last battery connection to the starter frame in Step 4. DO NOT create any sparks at or near the battery or a serious explosion could occur.*

4. When ready to perform the no-load test, quickly and firmly connect the remaining connection to the starter motor frame (**Figure 18**). Observe the amperage reading, then disconnect the jumper cable from the starter motor frame.

5. If the motor does not perform to specifications (**Table 8**), repair or replace the motor. See Chapter Seven. Refer to **Table 4** for additional starter motor symptoms and remedies.

BATTERY CHARGING SYSTEM

Description

An alternator charging system is used on all electric start models. The job of the charging system is to keep the battery fully charged and supply current to run accessories. Charging systems can be divided into 2 basic designs: integral regulated and external (belt driven) regulated. Refer to **Table 9** and **Table 10** for charging system specifications and applications.

Integral systems use permanent magnets mounted in the flywheel and a stator coil winding mounted to the power head. As the flywheel rotates, the magnetic fields in the flywheel pass through the stator coil windings, inducing AC (alternating current).

Integral regulated systems use the same type flywheel magnets and stator coil windings as the non-regulated system, with the rectifier being replaced with a rectifier/regulator. The rectifier portion of the rectifier/regulator changes the AC current to DC current, while the regulator portion monitors system voltage and controls the charging system output accordingly. Batteries that are maintained at 13-15 volts will stay fully charged without excessive venting. The regulator controls the output of the charging system to keep system voltage at approximately 14.5 volts. The large red lead of the rectifier/regulator is DC output. The small red lead is the sense terminal which allows the regulator portion to monitor system voltage. See **Figure 20**.

Another function of the integral charging system is to provide the signal for the tachometer.

The tachometer simply counts AC voltage pulses coming out of the stator before the AC voltage is rectified to DC. Tachometer failure on models with integral charging systems is related to the charging system, not the ignition system. The tachometer connects to one of the stator yellow leads on unregulated systems and connects to the rectifier/regulator gray lead (**Figure 20**) on regulated models.

Refer to **Table 9** and **Table 10** for charging system specifications. Refer to **Table 5** for typical charging system problems and solutions. Refer to the wiring diagrams at the end of the book.

NOTE
On 75-125 hp and 65-80 Jet models with the original black stator, a terminal block that looks similar to a standard rectifier is used, except that it is gray colored. This terminal block has the 2 yellow stator leads and the gray tachometer lead connected to it. It contains no electrical components or

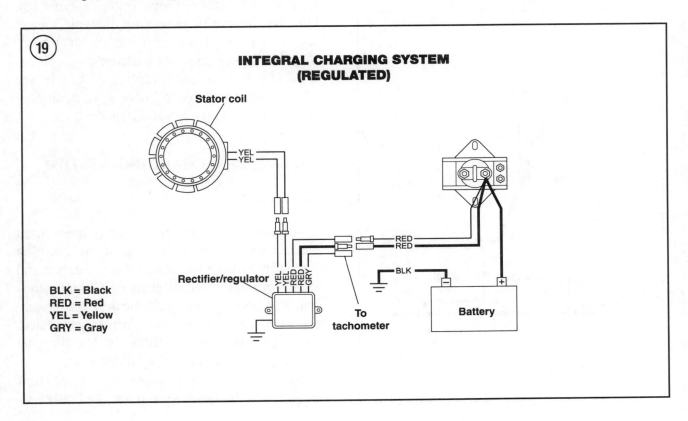

19

INTEGRAL CHARGING SYSTEM (REGULATED)

Stator coil

YEL
YEL

Rectifier/regulator

YEL
YEL
RED
RED
GRY

RED
RED

BLK

To tachometer

Battery

BLK = Black
RED = Red
YEL = Yellow
GRY = Gray

circuitry. *It is simply a junction point.*
See **Figure 20.**

External (belt-driven) regulated systems use a belt-driven, excited rotor, internally regulated 60

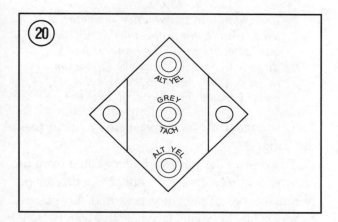

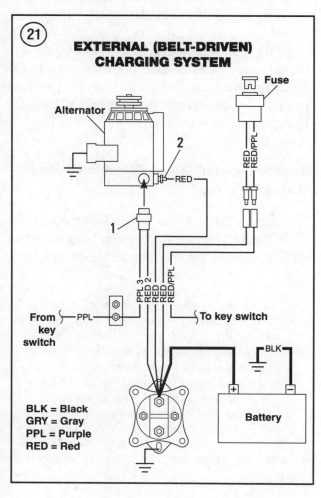

amp alternator, similar to many automotive designs. See **Figure 21**. The alternator has no permanent magnets. The voltage regulator sends current through the rotor windings to create an electromagnetic field. The output of the alternator can be controlled by changing the strength of the rotor magnetic field. The alternator is not serviceable and is sold only as an assembly. This system is used on the 200 DFI, 225 and 250 hp models. The tachometer signal on these models is produced by the ECM (electronic control module).

Malfunctions in the charging system generally cause the battery to be undercharged and on integral systems, the tachometer to read erratically or totally fail. The following conditions will result in rectifier, rectifier/regulator or alternator failure.

a. Reversing the battery leads.
b. Disconnecting the battery leads while the engine is running.
c. Loose connections in the charging system circuits, including battery connections and ground circuits.

NOTE
The 40 amp charging system is basically 2 separate 20 amp charging systems. Half of the stator windings are connected to the upper regulator/rectifier assembly and the remaining stator windings are connected to the lower regulator/rectifier. Should one regulator/rectifier fail, the charging system will still function, but at only one half of its rated output. Note that each regulator/rectifier assembly should be tested separately from the other.

CAUTION
If an integral unregulated or integral regulated charging system equipped outboard motor must be operated with the battery removed or disconnected, both stator yellow (or 1 yellow and 1 gray) leads must be disconnected and insulated (taped or sleeved) on both ends of the connection. It is not recommended to attempt to operate external (belt-driven)

regulated charging system outboard motors without a battery connected. ECM (electronic control module) equipped engines, such as EFI (electronic fuel injection) models, 225 and 250 hp models (carbureted and injected) and 200 DFI (direct fuel injection) models cannot be started without battery voltage.

System Inspection (All Models)

Before performing the troubleshooting procedure, check the following.

1. Make sure the battery is properly connected. If the battery polarity is reversed, the rectifier or voltage regulator will be damaged.

2. Check for loose or corroded connections. Clean and tighten as necessary.

3. Check the battery condition. Recharge or replace the battery as necessary.

4. Check the wiring harness between the stator and battery for cut, chafed or deteriorated insulation and corroded, loose or disconnected connections. Repair or replace the wiring harness as necessary.

5. *Integral systems*—Visually inspect the stator windings for discoloration and burned windings. Replace any stator that shows evidence of overheating.

6. *External models*—Check belt tension and adjust as necessary. See Chapter Four.

CAUTION
Unless otherwise noted, perform all voltage tests with the leads connected, but with the terminals exposed to accommodate test lead connection. All electrical components must be securely grounded to the power head any time the engine is cranked or started or the components will be damaged.

Current Draw Test

Use this test to determine if the total load of the engine electrical system and boat accessories exceeds the capacity of the charging system.

NOTE
If a clamp-on or inductive ammeter is used, install the probe on the positive battery cable (near the battery) and go directly to Step 3. If a conventional ammeter is being used, make sure the ammeter is rated for at least 50 amps.

1. Disconnect the negative battery cable from the battery.
2. Disconnect the positive battery cable from the battery. Securely connect a suitable ammeter between the positive battery post and the positive battery cable. Reconnect the negative battery cable.
3. Turn the ignition switch ON (RUN) and turn on all accessories. Note the ammeter reading. Turn the ignition switch OFF (STOP) and turn off all accessories. If the ammeter reading exceeds the rated capacity of the charging system, reduce the accessory load connected to the charging system.

Troubleshooting Integral Regulated Models (Except 40 Amp)

Refer to **Table 9** and **Table 10** for specifications, **Table 2** for ohmmeter guidelines and to the end of the book for specific wiring diagrams.

NOTE
A regulated charging system only puts out the current necessary to maintain 14.5 volts at the battery. If the battery is fully charged, the alternator will not produce its rated output unless enough accessory demand is present. If a clamp-on or inductive ammeter is being used, install the probe on the rectifier/regulator large red lead and go directly to Step 4.

1. Disconnect the negative battery cable from the battery.

2. Connect an ammeter of sufficient size to measure the maximum rated output of the charging system in SERIES between the large red positive (+) output lead of the rectifier/regulator and the lead that was hooked to the large red positive (+) output lead of the rectifier/regulator (**Figure 19**). Hook the red lead of the ammeter to the rectifier/regulator lead (male bullet connector) and the black lead of the ammeter to the rectifier/regulator engine harness lead (female bullet connector). Make sure the connections are secure and insulated from any other leads or grounds.

3. Reconnect the negative battery cable.

4. Install a shop tachometer according to its manufacturer's instructions.

5. Connect a voltmeter to the battery terminals.

CAUTION
*Do not run the engine without an adequate water supply and do not exceed 3000 rpm without an adequate load. Refer to **Safety Precautions** at the beginning of this chapter.*

6. Start the engine and run it at the engine speed specified in **Table 9** and **Table 10** while noting both the ammeter and voltmeter readings. If the voltage exceeds 12.5 volts, turn on accessories or attach accessories to the battery to maintain battery voltage at 12.5 volts or less. If amperage output is less than specified, continue to Step 7. If amperage output is within specification, turn

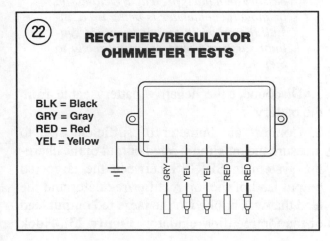

RECTIFIER/REGULATOR OHMMETER TESTS

BLK = Black
GRY = Gray
RED = Red
YEL = Yellow

GRY YEL YEL RED RED

off or disconnect the accessories and run the engine at approximately 3000 rpm while observing the voltmeter. As the battery approaches full charge, the voltage should rise to approximately 14.5 volts and stabilize. If the voltage stabilizes at approximately 14.5 volts, the voltage regulator is functioning correctly. If the voltage exceeds 15 volts, go to Step 7 and check the rectifier/regulator sense circuit voltage.

7. To test the rectifier/regulator sense circuit, disconnect the rectifier/regulator small red lead from the engine harness. Connect the red lead of a voltmeter to the engine harness side of the small red lead (male bullet connector) and the black lead of the voltmeter to the negative battery terminal. The voltmeter must read battery voltage. If the voltage is more than 0.5 volt below battery voltage, clean and tighten the connections or repair or replace the lead between the regulator small red lead and the battery. If the voltage is within 0.5 volt of battery voltage, go to Step 9 and check the stator for shorts to ground. If the stator tests good, replace the rectifier/regulator.

8. To check the resistance of the stator, disconnect the negative battery cable. Disconnect the 2 yellow stator leads from the rectifier/regulator. Calibrate an ohmmeter on the appropriate scale to read the stator resistance specification (**Table 9** or **Table 10**). Connect one lead of the ohmmeter to each of the stator leads. Note the reading. Replace the stator if its resistance is out of the specification range.

9. To check the stator for shorts to ground, calibrate the ohmmeter on its highest scale. Connect one lead of the ohmmeter to a clean engine ground. Connect the other lead alternately to each of the 2 yellow stator leads. The ohmmeter must read *no continuity*. Any reading other than no continuity means the stator is shorted to ground and must be replaced.

10. To check the diodes in the rectifier/regulator, disconnect the negative battery cable. Disconnect the 2 red, 2 yellow and 1 gray rectifier/regulator leads (**Figure 22**). Connect the ohmmeter

positive (red) lead, calibrated on the appropriate scale to read 100-400 ohms, to the rectifier/regulator large red lead and the ohmmeter negative (black) lead to one of the rectifier/regulator yellow AC leads. Note the ohmmeter reading. The reading should be very low (100-400 ohms). Replace the rectifier/regulator if the reading is not as specified. Repeat the test for the other yellow AC lead.

11. Connect the ohmmeter negative (black) lead, calibrated on the appropriate scale to read 40,000 ohms or greater, to the rectifier regulator large red lead and the ohmmeter positive (red) lead to one of the rectifier/regulator yellow AC leads (**Figure 22**). Note the meter reading. Repeat the test for the other yellow AC lead. One yellow lead should read no continuity, while the other lead should read 40,000 ohms or more. Replace the rectifier/regulator if the readings are not as specified.

12. To check the rectifier/regulator SCR (silicon controlled rectifier) in each yellow lead, calibrate an ohmmeter on the highest ohms scale. Connect the ohmmeter negative (black) lead to one of the rectifier/regulator yellow AC leads. Connect the ohmmeter positive (red) lead to the rectifier/regulator metal case (**Figure 22**). The ohmmeter must read 10,000 ohms or more. Replace the rectifier/regulator if a lower reading is obtained. Repeat the test for the other yellow AC lead.

13. To check the rectifier/regulator tachometer circuit, calibrate an ohmmeter on the high-ohms scale. Connect the ohmmeter negative (black) lead to the rectifier/regulator metal case (**Figure 23**). Connect the ohmmeter positive (red) lead to the rectifier/regulator tachometer (gray) lead. The ohmmeter must read 10,000-50,000 ohms. Replace the rectifier/regulator if any other reading is obtained.

14. To check the continuity of the rectifier/regulator positive (+) lead back to the battery, make sure the negative lead of the battery is disconnected. Make sure the rectifier/regulator large

red lead is disconnected from the rectifier/regulator. Calibrate an ohmmeter on a high-ohms scale. Connect one lead of the ohmmeter to the battery positive terminal, connect the other lead of the ohmmeter to the rectifier/regulator end of the lead that connects to the rectifier/regulator large red lead. Note the ohmmeter reading. A good circuit will have a zero or very low resistance reading. If the reading is not very low, repair or replace the lead, connections and fuse between the rectifier/regulator and the battery.

15. Reconnect all leads when finished.

Troubleshooting Integral Regulated 40 Amp Models

The 40 amp system is 2 separate 20 amp systems in parallel. Each must be tested individually. The 2 short yellow stator leads and the upper regulator make up one 20 amp system. The 2 long yellow stator leads and the lower regulator make up the second 20 amp system. Refer to **Table 9** for specifications and to the end of the book for individual wiring diagrams.

> *NOTE*
> *A regulated charging system only puts out the current necessary to maintain 14.5 volts at the battery. If the battery is fully charged the alternator will not produce its rated output unless enough accessory demand is present. If a clamp-on or inductive ammeter is being used, install the probe on the top rectifier/regulator large red lead and go directly to Step 4.*

1. Disconnect the negative battery cable from the battery.

2. Connect an ammeter of sufficient size to measure the maximum rated output of the charging system in SERIES between the large red output lead of the top rectifier/regulator and the lead that was hooked to the large red output lead of the top rectifier/regulator (**Figure 23**). Hook

the red lead of the ammeter to the rectifier/regulator lead and the black lead of the ammeter to the rectifier/regulator engine harness lead. Make sure the connections are secure and insulated from any other leads or grounds.

3. Disconnect the 2 long yellow stator leads from the lower voltage regulator. Insulate (tape or sleeve) both ends of the leads from each other and from ground.

4. Reconnect the negative battery cable.

5. Install a shop tachometer according to the manufacturer's instructions.

6. Connect a voltmeter to the battery terminals.

CAUTION
Do not run the engine without an adequate water supply and do not exceed

*3000 rpm without an adequate load. Refer to **Safety Precautions** at the beginning of this chapter.*

7. Start the engine and run it to the rpm specified in **Table 9** while noting both the ammeter and voltmeter readings. If the voltage exceeds 12.5 volts, turn on accessories or attach accessories to the battery to maintain battery voltage at 12.5 volts or less. If amperage output is less than specified, continue to Step 9. If amperage output is within specification, turn off or disconnect the accessories and run the engine at approximately 3000 rpm while observing the voltmeter. As the battery approaches full charge the voltage should rise to approximately 14.5 volts and stabilize. If the voltage stabilizes at approximately 14.5

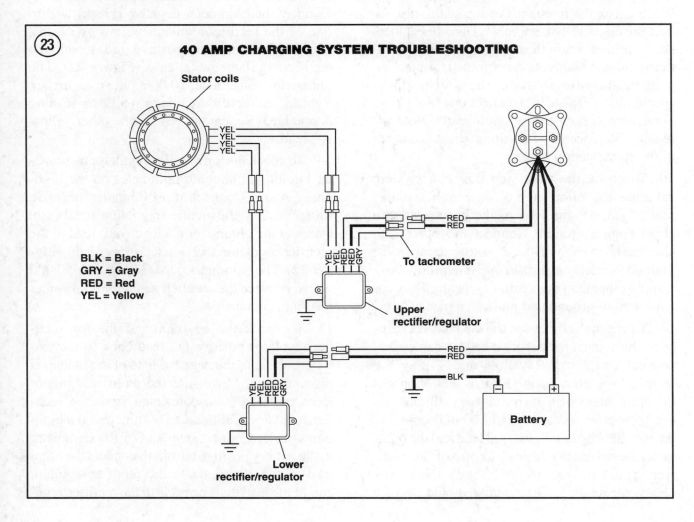

40 AMP CHARGING SYSTEM TROUBLESHOOTING

Stator coils

YEL
YEL
YEL
YEL

BLK = Black
GRY = Gray
RED = Red
YEL = Yellow

YEL
YEL
RED
RED
GRY

RED
RED

To tachometer

Upper rectifier/regulator

RED
RED

BLK

Battery

YEL
YEL
RED
RED
GRY

Lower rectifier/regulator

volts, the voltage regulator is functioning correctly. If the voltage exceeds 15 volts, go to Step 8 and test the top rectifier/regulator sense circuit.

8. To test the rectifier/regulator sense circuit, disconnect the top rectifier/regulator small red lead from the engine harness. Connect the red lead of a voltmeter to the engine harness side of the small red lead and the black lead of the voltmeter to the negative battery terminal. The voltmeter must read battery voltage. If the voltage is more than 0.5 volts below battery voltage, clean and tighten the connections or repair or replace the lead between the regulator small red lead and the battery. If the voltage is within 0.5 volts of battery voltage, go to Step 10 and check the stator for shorts to ground. If the stator tests good, replace the rectifier/regulator.

9. To check the resistance of the stator, disconnect the negative battery cable. Disconnect the 2 short yellow stator leads from the top rectifier/regulator. Calibrate an ohmmeter on the appropriate scale to read the stator ohms specification (**Table 9**). Connect one lead of the ohmmeter to each of the stator leads. Note the reading. Replace the stator if its resistance is out of the specification range.

10. To check the stator for shorts to ground, calibrate the ohmmeter on the highest ohms scale. Connect one lead of the ohmmeter to a clean engine ground. Connect the other lead alternately to each of the 2 yellow stator leads. The ohmmeter must read *no continuity*. Any reading other than no continuity means the stator is shorted to ground and must be replaced.

11. To check the diodes in the top rectifier/regulator, disconnect the negative battery cable. Disconnect the 2 red, 2 yellow and 1 gray top rectifier/regulator leads (**Figure 22**). Connect the ohmmeter positive (red) lead, calibrated on the appropriate scale to read 100-400 ohms, to the rectifier/regulator large red lead and the ohmmeter negative (black) lead to one of the rectifier/regulator yellow AC leads. Note the ohmmeter reading. The reading should be very

low (100-400 ohms). Replace the rectifier/regulator if the reading is not as specified. Repeat the test for the other yellow AC lead.

12. Connect the ohmmeter negative (black) lead, calibrated on the appropriate scale to read 40,000 ohms or greater, to the top rectifier regulator large red lead and the ohmmeter positive (red) lead to one of the top rectifier/regulator yellow AC leads (**Figure 22**). Note the meter reading. Repeat the test for the other yellow AC lead. One yellow lead should read no continuity, while the other lead should read 40,000 ohms or greater. Replace the rectifier/regulator if the readings are not as specified.

13. To check the top rectifier/regulator SCR (silicon controlled rectifier) in each yellow lead, calibrate an ohmmeter on the highest ohms scale. Connect the ohmmeter negative (black) lead to one of the rectifier/regulator yellow AC leads. Connect the ohmmeter positive (red) lead to the rectifier/regulator metal case (**Figure 22**). The ohmmeter must read 10,000 ohms or higher. Replace the rectifier/regulator if a lower reading is obtained. Repeat the test for the other yellow AC lead.

14. To check the top rectifier/regulator tachometer circuit, calibrate an ohmmeter on the high-ohms scale. Connect the ohmmeter negative (black) lead to the rectifier/regulator metal case. Connect the ohmmeter positive (red) lead to the rectifier/regulator tachometer (gray) lead (**Figure 22**). The ohmmeter must read 10,000-50,000 ohms. Replace the rectifier/regulator if any other reading is obtained.

15. To check the continuity of the top rectifier/regulator positive (+) lead back to the battery, make sure the negative lead of the battery is disconnected. Make sure the rectifier/regulator large red lead is disconnected from the rectifier/regulator. Calibrate an ohmmeter on a high-ohms scale. Connect one lead of the ohmmeter to the battery positive terminal, connect the other lead of the ohmmeter to the rectifier/regulator end of the lead that connects to the rectifier/regu-

lator large red lead. Note the ohmmeter reading. A good circuit will have a zero or very low resistance reading. If the reading is not very low, repair or replace the lead, connections and fuse between the top rectifier/regulator and the battery.

16. Repeat this procedure for the 2 long yellow stator leads and the lower voltage regulator. Disconnect and insulate (tape or sleeve) both ends of the 2 short yellow stator leads from the upper voltage regulator before beginning. If both upper and lower regulators output 19-21 amps at 5000 rpm and voltage is regulated to approximately 14.5 volts, the system is functioning correctly.

17. Reconnect all leads when finished.

Stator Ohmmeter Tests (Integral Models)

NOTE
The 40 amp charging system has 2 separate stator windings and 2 sets of stator leads. Be sure that both sets of leads are tested.

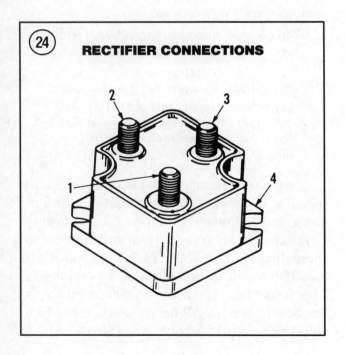

(24) **RECTIFIER CONNECTIONS**

1. To check the resistance of the stator, disconnect the negative battery cable. Disconnect the 2 yellow (or 1 yellow and 1 gray) stator leads connected to the terminal block, rectifier or rectifier/regulator. Calibrate an ohmmeter on the appropriate scale to read the stator ohms specification (**Table 9** or **Table 10**). Connect one lead of the ohmmeter to each of the stator leads. Note the reading. Replace the stator if the resistance is out of specification.

2. To check the stator for shorts to ground, calibrate the ohmmeter on the high ohms scale. Connect one lead of the ohmmeter to a clean engine ground. Connect the other lead alternately to each of the 2 stator leads. The ohmmeter must read *no continuity*. Any reading other than no continuity means the stator is shorted to ground and must be replaced.

3. *40 amp charging systems*—Repeat Steps 1 and 2 for the second set of stator leads. See **Figure 23**.

4. Reconnect all leads when finished.

Rectifier Ohmmeter Tests (Integral Models)

1. To check the diodes in the rectifier, disconnect the negative battery cable. Then disconnect all of the leads from the rectifier terminal studs.

2. Calibrate the ohmmeter on the appropriate scale to test diodes. Connect one ohmmeter lead to the rectifier mounting base (4, **Figure 24**) and the other lead to one of the AC terminals (2, **Figure 24**). Note the ohmmeter reading. Reverse the ohmmeter leads and note the reading. The reading should be high in one polarity and low in the other. If the reading was high in both polarities or low in both polarities replace the rectifier. Repeat the test for the other AC terminal (3, **Figure 24**).

3. Connect one lead of the ohmmeter, still calibrated to test diodes, to the rectifier positive (+) terminal (1, **Figure 24**) and the other lead to one of the AC terminals (2, **Figure 24**). Note the

ohmmeter reading. Reverse the ohmmeter leads and note the reading. The reading should be high in one polarity and low in the other. If the reading is high in both polarities or low in both polarities replace the rectifier. Repeat the test for the other AC terminal (3, **Figure 24**).

4. Reconnect all leads when finished.

Rectifier/Regulator Ohmmeter Tests (Integral Models)

1. Disconnect the negative battery cable. Disconnect the 2 yellow, 2 red and 1 gray rectifier/regulator leads from the engine harness. See **Figure 22**.

2. To check the diodes in the rectifier/regulator, disconnect the negative battery cable. Disconnect the 2 red, 2 yellow and 1 gray rectifier/regulator leads (**Figure 22**). Connect the ohmmeter positive (red) lead, calibrated on the appropriate scale to read 100-400 ohms, to the rectifier/regulator large red lead and the ohmmeter negative (black) lead to one of the rectifier/regulator yellow AC leads. Note the ohmmeter reading. The reading should be very low (100-400 ohms). Replace the rectifier/regulator if the reading is not as specified. Repeat the test for the other yellow AC lead.

3. Connect the ohmmeter negative (black) lead, calibrated on the appropriate scale to read 40,000 ohms or greater, to the rectifier regulator large red lead and the ohmmeter positive (red) lead to one of the rectifier/regulator yellow AC leads (**Figure 22**). Note the meter reading. Repeat the test for the other yellow AC lead. One yellow lead should read no continuity, while the other lead should read 40,000 ohms or greater. Replace the rectifier/regulator if the readings are not as specified.

4. To check the rectifier/regulator SCR (silicon controlled rectifier) in each yellow lead, calibrate an ohmmeter on the highest ohms scale. Connect the ohmmeter negative (black) lead to one of the rectifier/regulator yellow AC leads. Connect the

ohmmeter positive (red) lead to the rectifier/regulator metal case (**Figure 22**). The ohmmeter must read 10,000 ohms or higher. Replace the rectifier/regulator if a lower reading is obtained. Repeat the test for the other yellow AC lead.

5. To check the rectifier/regulator tachometer circuit, calibrate an ohmmeter on the high ohms scale. Connect the ohmmeter negative (black) lead to the rectifier/regulator metal case (**Figure 22**). Connect the ohmmeter positive (red) lead to the rectifier/regulator tachometer (gray) lead. The ohmmeter must read 10,000-50,000 ohms. Replace the rectifier/regulator if any other reading is obtained.

6. Reconnect all leads when finished.

Troubleshooting External 60 Amp Models

Refer to **Table 9** for specifications and to the end of the book for individual wiring diagrams.

1. Check and adjust belt tension as specified in Chapter Four.

2. Install a shop tachometer according to the manufacturer's instructions.

3. Connect a voltmeter to the battery terminals.

> *CAUTION*
> *Do not run the engine without an adequate water supply and do not exceed 3000 rpm without an adequate load. Refer to **Safety Precautions** at the beginning of this chapter.*

4. Start the engine and run it to the engine speed specified in **Table 9** while noting both the ammeter and voltmeter readings. As the battery approaches full charge the voltage should rise to approximately 14.5 volts (13.5-15.1) and stabilize. If the voltage stabilizes at approximately 14.5 volts (13.5-15.1), the voltage regulator is functioning correctly. If the voltage is below 13.5 volts or exceeds 15.1 volts, go to Step 5.

5. To test the alternator sense circuit, disconnect the alternator 2-lead (red and purple) plug in from the alternator. Connect the red lead of a voltmeter to the plug in (1, **Figure 21**) red lead (pin No. 2) and the black lead of the voltmeter to the negative battery terminal. The voltmeter must read battery voltage. If the voltage is more than 0.5 volts below battery voltage, clean and tighten the connections or repair or replace the red lead between the alternator 2-lead plug in and the battery. If the voltage is within 0.5 volts of battery voltage, go to Step 6.

6. To test the alternator excite circuit, disconnect the alternator 2-lead (red and purple) plug from the alternator. Connect the red lead of a voltmeter to the plug (1, **Figure 21**) purple lead (pin No. 3) and the black lead of the voltmeter to the negative battery terminal. Turn the ignition switch to the ON or RUN position. The voltmeter must read battery voltage. Turn the ignition switch to the OFF or STOP position. If the voltage is more than 1 volt below battery voltage, clean and tighten the connections or repair or replace the circuit between the alternator 2-lead plug and the battery (this includes the key switch and 20 amp fuse). If the voltage is within 1 volt of battery voltage, go to Step 7.

7. To test the alternator output circuit, connect the red lead of a voltmeter to the alternator output (B) terminal (2, **Figure 21**) and the black lead of the voltmeter to the negative battery terminal. The voltmeter must read battery voltage. If the voltage is more than 0.5 volts below battery voltage, clean and tighten the connections or repair or replace the lead between the alternator output (B) terminal and the battery. If the voltage is within 0.5 volts of battery voltage, go to Step 8 and test the amperage output.

NOTE
If a clamp-on or inductive ammeter is being used, install the probe on the alternator output large red lead (terminal B) and go directly to Step 9.

8. Disconnect the negative battery cable from the battery

9. Connect an ammeter of sufficient size to measure the maximum rated output of the charging system (60 amps) in SERIES between the output terminal of the alternator and the large red engine harness output lead (2, **Figure 21**). Hook the red lead of the ammeter to the alternator output terminal and the black lead of the ammeter to the engine harness lead. Make sure the connections are secure and insulated from any other leads or grounds.

10. Reconnect the negative battery cable.

NOTE
Due to the high output of this alternator, the regulator must be bypassed to check the rated output of the alternator. Bypass the regulator by grounding terminal F (field) on the lower end frame of the alternator. Do not keep terminal F grounded longer than necessary or the battery will be overcharged and damaged.

11. Fashion a tool from a stiff piece of wire as shown in **Figure 25**. Insert the tool through the

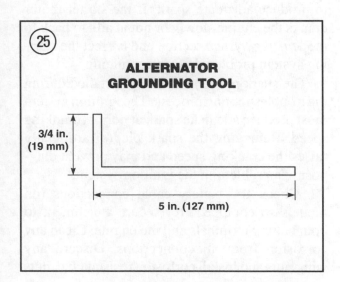

㉕

ALTERNATOR GROUNDING TOOL

3/4 in. (19 mm)

5 in. (127 mm)

access hole (**Figure 26**) located in the lower end cover of the alternator and ground the terminal F. A jumper wire may be used to ensure that the tool is securely grounded to the power head.

12. Start the engine and run it at the speed specified in **Table 9** while observing the ammeter. If the alternator output is as specified, the charging system is working correctly. If the output is less than specified, remove the alternator and check for paint and corrosion on the mounting brackets. Reinstall the alternator and retest the output. If the output is still unsatisfactory, replace the alternator.

ELECTRICAL ACCESSORIES

The wiring harness used between the ignition switch and outboard motor is adequate to handle the electrical requirements of the outboard motor. It *will not* handle the electrical requirements of accessories. Whenever an accessory is added, run new wiring between the battery and the accessory, installing a separate fuse panel on the instrument panel.

If the ignition switch requires replacement, *never* install an automotive-type switch. Use only a switch approved for marine use.

IGNITION SYSTEM

This section deals with troubleshooting the various ignition systems used on Mercury and Mariner outboard motors. Once the defective component has been identified, refer to Chapter Seven for component removal and replacement procedures.

Troubleshooting Notes and Precautions (All Models)

Several troubleshooting precautions must be strictly observed to avoid damaging the ignition system or injuring yourself.

1. Do not reverse the battery connections. Reverse battery polarity will damage electronic components.

2. Do not *spark* the battery terminals with the battery cable connections to determine polarity.

3. Do not disconnect the battery cables while the engine is running.

4. Do not crank or run the outboard if any electrical components are not grounded to the power head.

5. Do not touch or disconnect any ignition components while the outboard is running, while the ignition switch is ON or while the battery cables are connected.

6. Do not rotate the flywheel when performing ohmmeter tests. The meter will be damaged.

7. If a sudden unexplained timing change is noted:

    a. Check the trigger magnets in the hub of the flywheel (if so equipped) for damage or a possible shift in magnet position. If the magnets are cracked, damaged or have shifted position, replace the flywheel. See Chapter Seven.

    b. Check the flywheel key for a sheared condition. See Chapter Seven.

8. The ignition system on electric start models requires that the electric starter crank the engine at normal speed in order for the ignition system to produce adequate spark. If the starter motor cranks the engine slowly or not at all, go back to the *Starting System* section and correct the starting system problem before continuing.

9. The spark plug(s) should be installed during the troubleshooting process. The ignition system must produce adequate spark at normal cranking speed. Removing the spark plug(s) artificially raises the cranking speed and may prevent diagnosing a problem in the ignition system.

10. Check the battery cable connections (on models so equipped) for secure attachment to both battery terminals and the engine. Clean any corrosion from all connections. Discard any wing nuts and install corrosion resistant hex nuts

at all battery cable connections. Place a corrosion resistant locking washer between the battery terminal stud and battery cable terminal end to ensure a positive connection. Loose battery connections can cause every symptom imaginable.

11. Check all ignition component ground leads for secure attachment to the power head. Clean and tighten all ground leads, connections and fasteners as necessary. Loose ground connections and loose component mounting hardware can cause every symptom imaginable.

CAUTION
If an integral unregulated or integral regulated charging system equipped outboard motor must be operated with the battery removed or disconnected, both stator yellow (or 1 yellow and 1 gray) leads must be disconnected and insulated (taped or sleeved) on both ends of the connection. It is not recommended to attempt to operate external (belt-driven) regulated charging system outboard motors without a battery connected. ECM (electronic control module) equipped engines, such as EFI (electronic fuel injection) models, 225 and 250 hp models (carbureted and injected) and 200 DFI

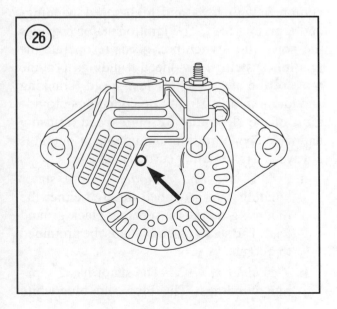

(direct fuel injection) models cannot be started without battery voltage.

Resistance (Ohmmeter) Tests

The resistance values specified in the following test procedures are based on tests performed at room temperature. Actual resistance readings obtained during testing will generally be slightly higher if checked on hot components. In addition, resistance readings may vary depending on the manufacturer of the ohmmeter. Therefore, use discretion when failing any component that is only slightly out of specification. Many ohmmeters have difficulty reading less than 1 ohm accurately. If this is the case, specifications of less than 1 ohm generally appear as a very low (continuity) reading.

NOTE
Terminal stud style switch boxes have the lead color code abbreviations embossed into the switch box at each lead terminal stud. To remove the switch box leads, unsnap the rubber cap and remove the nut holding each lead to be removed. Reinstall the nut on the terminal to prevent its loss.

Direct Voltage Tests

Direct voltage tests are designed to check the voltage output of the ignition stator and the switch box (CD module). The test procedures check voltage output at normal cranking speed. If an ignition misfire or failure occurs only when the engine is running and cranking speed tests do not show any defects, perform the output tests at the engine speed at which the ignition symptom or failure occurs. **Table 11** lists the cranking and high-speed running voltages for all applicable tests. When checking the DVA voltage output of a component, observe the meter needle for fluctuations, which indicates erratic voltage output.

The voltage output of the ignition stator and switch box (CD module) will change with engine speed, but should not be erratic.

CAUTION
*Do not run the engine without an adequate water supply and do not exceed 3000 rpm without an adequate load. Refer to **Safety Precautions** at the beginning of this chapter.*

The term *Peak Volts* is used interchangeably with *DVA (Direct Volts Adapter)*. The Mercury Marine 91-99750 multimeter has a *DVA* scale that should be used whenever the specification is in *Peak Volts* or listed as *DVA*. A DVA adapter is available (part No. 91-98045) to adapt any analog voltmeter that is capable of reading at least 400 DC volts. If the *DVA or Peak Volts* specification is listed as polarity sensitive, reverse your meter test leads and retest if the initial reading is unsatisfactory.

CAUTION
Unless otherwise noted, all direct voltage tests must be performed with the leads connected, but with the terminals exposed to accommodate test lead connection. All electrical components must be securely grounded to the power head any time the engine is cranked or started or the components will be damaged.

WARNING
High voltage is present during ignition system operation. Do not touch ignition components, leads or test leads while cranking or running the engine.

ALTERNATOR DRIVEN IGNITION (MECHANICAL ADVANCE [75-125 HP AND 65-80 JET])

Description

This AD-CDI ignition is an alternator driven, capacitor discharge ignition system with mechanical spark advance. It is used on 1994-1996 75-125 hp and 65-80 Jet models. CDM (capacitor discharge module) ignition is used on 75-125 hp and 65-80 Jet models manufactured for 1997 (serial No. 0G438000-on).

Refer to **Figure 27** and **Figure 28** for operational diagrams of typical 3- and 4-cylinder AD-CDI ignition systems.

The firing order (and trigger coil and ignition coil wire color codes) of 3-cylinder AD-CDI models vary with model and year of manufacture. Consult the appropriate wiring diagram at the end of the book.

NOTE
*A red stator and adapter module upgrade kit is available for 75-125 hp and 65-80 Jet models. If the original equipment stator is encased in black plastic, use the following troubleshooting procedure. If the stator is encased in red plastic, continue to **Red Stator Upgraded Models** for troubleshooting and functional description.*

The major components are the:
1. *Flywheel*—The flywheel inner magnets are for the trigger coil (timing information). The outer magnets are for the ignition stator and battery charging stator (if equipped).
2. *Ignition stator (charge) coils*—The stator is equipped with low- and high-speed windings and a ground lead. The ignition stator provides the power the switch box needs to operate the ignition system. Low-speed windings provide most of the electricity for low-speed (cranking and idle) running. High-speed windings provide most of the electricity for high-speed (cruising and wide open throttle) running. Stator output is always AC (alternating current) voltage.
   a. *2- and 3-cylinder models*—Both stator windings are grounded through either the mounting bolts or a separate black ground lead. The stator assembly must be grounded to operate.
   b. *4-cylinder models*—The stator has 2 separate windings. The blue and blue/white

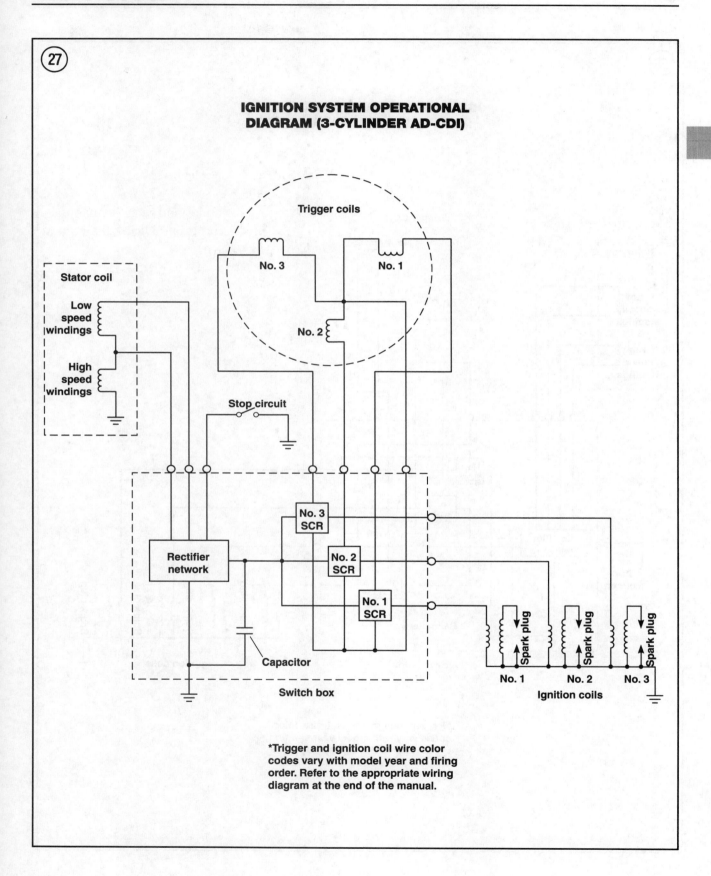

IGNITION SYSTEM OPERATIONAL DIAGRAM (3-CYLINDER AD-CDI)

*Trigger and ignition coil wire color codes vary with model year and firing order. Refer to the appropriate wiring diagram at the end of the manual.

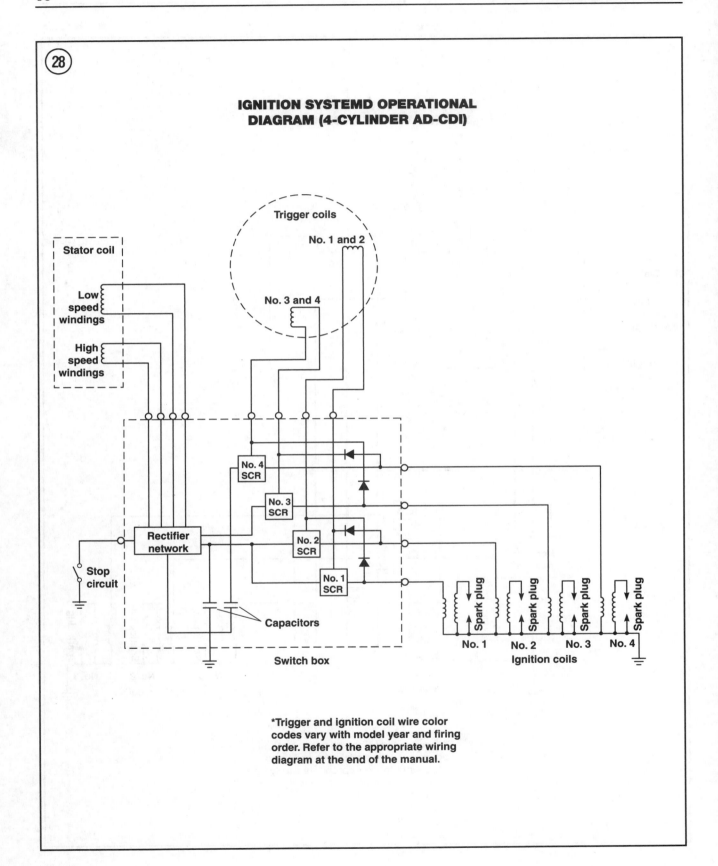

(28)

**IGNITION SYSTEMD OPERATIONAL
DIAGRAM (4-CYLINDER AD-CDI)**

Trigger coils

No. 1 and 2

No. 3 and 4

Stator coil

Low
speed
windings

High
speed
windings

No. 4
SCR

No. 3
SCR

No. 2
SCR

No. 1
SCR

Rectifier
network

Stop
circuit

Capacitors

Switch box

Spark plug
Spark plug
Spark plug
Spark plug

No. 1   No. 2   No. 3   No. 4

Ignition coils

*Trigger and ignition coil wire color
codes vary with model year and firing
order. Refer to the appropriate wiring
diagram at the end of the manual.

leads are both ends of the low speed windings. The red and red/white leads are both ends of the high speed winding. The stator assembly has no separate ground.

3. *Trigger coil*—The trigger coil tells the switch box when to fire the ignition coils. The trigger coil is rotated by mechanical linkage to change the trigger's position relative to the flywheel. This movement advances or retards the ignition spark timing.

   a. *2-cylinder models*—The trigger coil has one winding with 2 leads (brown/white and brown/yellow). A trigger failure will cause no spark on both cylinders.

   b. *3-cylinder models*—The trigger coil has three windings grounded by a common lead (white/black). The 3 individual trigger leads are brown, white and purple. Failure of the common (white/black) lead can cause erratic spark on all cylinders. Failure of a single trigger lead will cause the loss of spark on one cylinder.

   c. *4-cylinder models*—The trigger coil has 2 separate windings. The brown and black leads are both ends of one winding and trigger 2 cylinders. The white and purple leads are both ends of the second winding and trigger the other 2 cylinders. Trigger failure will always affect 2 or 4 cylinders.

4. *Switch box*—The switch box stores the electricity from the ignition stator until the trigger coil(s) tells it to send the electricity to the ignition coils. The switch box uses an internal rectifier to change the ignition stator AC voltage to DC (direct current) voltage. The DC voltage is stored in a capacitor (an electrical storage tank), until it is released by a SCR (silicon controlled rectifier), which is simply an electronic switch. There is one SCR for each cylinder. The SCR is controlled by the trigger coil. Three-cylinder and V6 models incorporate a bias circuit in the switch box. A separate test is necessary to make sure the bias circuit is functioning properly. On 4-cylin-der models, the switch box is equipped with 2 capacitors; each capacitor powers 2 cylinders.

NOTE
The 100-125 hp and 80 Jet are equipped with a switch box that uses terminal studs. All other switch boxes use bullet connectors.

5. *Ignition coils*—There is one ignition coil for each cylinder. The ignition coil transforms the relatively low voltage from the switch box into voltage high enough (35,000 volts) to jump the spark plug gap and ignite the air/fuel mixture.

6. *Spark plugs*—There is one spark plug for each cylinder. Use only the recommended spark plugs or catastrophic engine damage may result. Resistor or suppressor plugs are designed to reduce RFI (radio frequency interference) emissions that can cause interference with electrical accessories. Use the recommended RFI spark plug if RFI interference is suspected of causing interference or malfunction of electrical accessories.

7. *Stop circuit*—The stop circuit is connected to one end of the capacitor in the switch box. Whenever the stop circuit is connected to ground, the capacitor is shorted to ground and cannot store electricity. At this point there is no voltage available to send to the ignition coil and the ignition system ceases producing spark. The stop circuit must have an open circuit (to ground) for the engine to run.

NOTE
The 100-125 hp and 65-80 Jet models are equipped with a rpm limit module. The rpm limit module is connected to the switch box stop circuit (black/yellow). When engine speed exceeds the preprogrammed limit, the rpm limit module momentarily shorts the black/yellow lead to ground, limiting engine speed.

Troubleshooting

Refer to **Table 11** for specifications and the back of the manual for individual wiring diagrams. Read *Troubleshooting Notes And Precautions (All Models)* at the beginning of the ignition section before continuing. The recommended troubleshooting procedure is listed below.

1. Preliminary checks.
    a. Spark test.
    b. Stop circuit isolation.
2. Switch box stop circuit test.
3. Ignition stator output test.
4. Ignition stator resistance test.
5. Switch box bias test (3-cylinder models).
6. Trigger resistance test.
7. Switch box output test.
8. Ignition coil ohmmeter test.

> *CAUTION*
> *Do not run the engine without an adequate water supply and do not exceed 3000 rpm without an adequate load. Refer to **Safety Precautions** at the beginning of this chapter.*

> *WARNING*
> *High voltage is present in the ignition system. **Do not** touch or disconnect ignition components while the engine is running.*

Preliminary checks

1. Disconnect the spark plug leads from the spark plugs and install an air gap spark tester (FT-11295 or equivalent) to the spark plug leads. Connect the alligator clip of the spark tester to a clean engine ground. Set the spark tester air gap to 7/16 in. (11.1 mm).
2. Make sure the safety lanyard is installed on the safety lanyard switch and the ignition switch (remote models) is in the RUN position.
3. Crank the engine while observing the tester. If a crisp, blue spark is noted at each air gap, the ignition system is functioning correctly. If the engine will not start or does not run correctly, check the spark plugs and ignition timing. If the engine backfires or pops when attempting to start, remove the flywheel and check for a

sheared flywheel key. If no spark, weak spark or erratic spark is noted, continue with Step 4.

4. Disconnect the stop circuit black/yellow lead from the switch box bullet connector or the switch box terminal stud. Crank the engine while observing the spark tester. If good spark is now noted, the stop circuit is shorted to ground.
    a. On tiller models, a short to ground is present in the push button stop switch, safety lanyard switch or rpm limit module (if equipped). Test the push button stop switch, safety lanyard switch and rpm limit module as described in this chapter. Replace the defective component and retest spark output.
    b. On remote control models, a short to ground is present in the key switch, safety lanyard switch, rpm limit module (if equipped) or the main engine harness black/yellow lead. Test, repair or replace the circuit or component as necessary.

Switch box stop circuit test

> *WARNING*
> *To prevent accidental starting, remove the spark plug leads from the spark plugs and install the spark gap tester (FT-11295) to the spark plug leads. Connect the alligator clip of the spark tester to a clean engine ground.*

1. Connect the meter black lead to a good engine ground and the meter red lead to the black/yellow lead bullet connector nearest the switch box or the black/yellow terminal stud at the switch box.
2. Set the meter selector switch to 400 DVA.
3. Crank the engine while noting the test meter.
4. If the stop circuit voltage is within specification (**Table 11**), continue at *Ignition stator output tests* in this section.
5. If the stop circuit voltage is above specification, either the switch box or the trigger coil is defective. Test the trigger coil(s) as described in *Trigger coil ohmmeter tests* in this section. If the

trigger coil(s) is within specification, replace the switch box.

6. If the stop circuit voltage is below specifications, disconnect the black/yellow stop circuit lead from the switch box bullet connector or the switch box terminal stud.

7. Repeat Step 3. If the stop circuit voltage is now within the specified range, the stop circuit is defective (partially shorted to ground) and must be repaired. If the stop switch voltage is still below specification, continue at *Ignition stator output tests* in this section.

Ignition stator output tests

> *WARNING*
> *To prevent accidental starting, remove the spark plug leads from the spark plugs and install the spark gap tester (FT-11295) to the spark plug leads. Connect the alligator clip of the spark tester to a clean engine ground.*

1. *3 and 4-cylinder models*—To test the ignition stator low- speed winding output, connect the meter black lead to a good engine ground and the meter red lead to the blue ignition stator lead bullet connector or switch box terminal stud.

2. Set the meter selector switch to 400 DVA.

3. Crank the engine and note the meter.

4. If the reading is not within specification (**Table 11**), test the resistance of the ignition stator low-speed windings as described in the next section.

5. *4-cylinder models*—Repeat the low-speed output test for the blue/white ignition stator lead.

6. *3 and 4-cylinder models*—To test the stator high-speed winding output, connect the meter black lead to a good engine ground and the meter red lead to the red ignition stator lead bullet connector or switch box terminal stud.

7. Verify the meter is still set to the 400 DVA scale.

8. Crank the engine and note the meter.

9. If the reading is not within specification (**Table 11**), test the resistance of the ignition stator high-speed windings as described in the next section.

10. *4-cylinder models*—Repeat the high-speed output test for the red/white ignition stator lead.

Ignition stator resistance tests

1A. *3-cylinder models*—Disconnect the ignition stator blue and red leads from the switch box bullet connectors.

1B. *4-cylinder models*—Disconnect the ignition stator blue, blue/white, red and red/white leads from the switch box terminal studs.

2. To check the resistance of the ignition stator low-speed windings, calibrate an ohmmeter on the appropriate scale to read the specification listed in **Table 12**.

3A. *3-cylinder models*—Connect the ohmmeter black lead to blue ignition stator lead bullet connector and the ohmmeter red lead to the red ignition stator lead bullet connector.

3B. *4-cylinder models*—Connect the ohmmeter black lead to the ignition stator blue lead and the ohmmeter red lead to the ignition stator blue/white lead.

4. If the reading is not within the low speed winding specification (**Table 12**), replace the stator coil assembly and retest spark output.

5. To check the resistance of the ignition stator high-speed windings, calibrate an ohmmeter on the appropriate scale to read the high speed winding specification listed in **Table 12**.

6A. *3-cylinder models*—Connect the ohmmeter black lead to a good engine ground and the ohmmeter red lead to the red ignition stator lead bullet connector.

6B. *4-cylinder models*—Connect the ohmmeter black lead to the red ignition stator lead and the ohmmeter red lead to the red/white ignition stator lead.

7. If the reading is not within the high-speed winding specification (**Table 12**), replace the stator coil assembly and retest spark output.

8. *4-cylinder models*—To check the ignition stator windings for shorts to ground, calibrate an ohmmeter on the highest scale available. Connect one ohmmeter lead to a good engine ground and the other ohmmeter lead alternately to the ignition stator blue, blue/white, red and red/white leads while noting the meter. The meter should indicate no continuity. If continuity is noted at any connection, replace the stator coil assembly and retest spark output.

Switch box bias test (3-cylinder models)

WARNING
To prevent accidental starting, remove the spark plug leads from the spark plugs and install the spark gap tester (FT-11295) to the spark plug leads. Connect the alligator clip of the spark tester to a clean engine ground.

CAUTION
The switch box bias circuit voltage output is DC (direct current). Do not use the DVA scale or adaptor for this test.

1. To check the switch box bias circuit output, connect the red lead of a DC voltmeter, set to the 20 VDC scale, to a clean engine ground. Connect the black lead of the DC voltmeter to the switch box white/black lead bullet connector.

2. Crank the engine while observing the meter. The meter should indicate 2-10 volts DC. If the reading is not 2-10 volts DC, replace the switch box and retest spark output.

Trigger coil resistance test

1A. *3-cylinder models*—Disconnect the brown, white, purple and white/black trigger coil leads from the switch box bullet connectors.

1B. *4-cylinder models*—Disconnect the brown, black, white and purple trigger coil leads from the switch box terminal studs.

2. Calibrate an ohmmeter on the appropriate scale to read the specification listed in **Table 12**.

3A. *3-cylinder models*—Connect one ohmmeter lead to the trigger coil white/black lead and the other ohmmeter lead to the trigger coil brown lead.

3B. *4-cylinder models*—Connect one ohmmeter lead to the trigger coil brown lead and the other ohmmeter lead to the trigger coil black lead.

4. If the reading is not within specification, replace the trigger coil and retest spark output.

5A. *3-cylinder models*—Repeat the test for the next (second) trigger coil winding. Leave the one ohmmeter lead connected to the trigger coil white/black lead. Connect the other ohmmeter lead to the trigger coil white lead.

5B. *4-cylinder models*—Repeat the test for the final (second) trigger coil winding. Connect one lead of the ohmmeter to the trigger coil white lead and the other ohmmeter lead to the trigger coil purple lead.

6. If the reading is not within specification, replace the trigger coil and retest spark output.

7. *3-cylinder models*—Repeat the test for the final (third) trigger coil winding. Leave the one ohmmeter lead connected to the trigger coil white/black lead. Connect the other ohmmeter lead to the trigger coil purple lead.

8. If the reading is not within specification, replace the trigger coil assembly and retest spark output.

Switch box output tests

WARNING
To prevent accidental starting, remove the spark plugs and install the spark gap tester (FT-11295 or equivalent) to the spark plug leads. Connect the alligator clip of the spark tester to a clean engine ground.

1. To check the switch box voltage output to the ignition coils, connect the meter red lead to the cylinder No.1 ignition coil positive (+) primary terminal. Connect the meter black lead to the cylinder No. 1 ignition coil negative (–) primary terminal (black lead). See **Figure 29**.

2. Set the meter selector switch to 400 DVA.

3. Crank the engine while noting the meter reading.

4. If the meter reading is below specification (**Table 11**), continue to *Ignition coil ohmmeter tests*. If the ignition coil ohmmeter tests are within specifications, replace the switch box and retest spark output. If the ignition coil tests are not within specification, replace the ignition coil(s) and retest spark output. If the meter reading is within specification, but no spark, weak spark or erratic spark is still noted, continue to *Ignition coil ohmmeter tests*.

5. Repeat the test procedure for the remaining ignition coil(s).

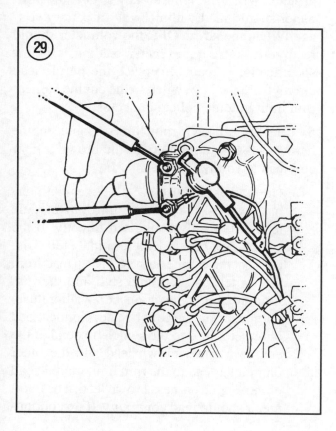

Ignition coil ohmmeter tests

1. To check the ignition coil primary resistance, calibrate an ohmmeter on the appropriate scale to read the primary resistance specification listed in **Table 12**.

2. Disconnect the spark plug leads. Carefully remove the spark plug leads from the ignition coils. Disconnect the switch box primary lead from each ignition coil positive (+) primary terminal stud.

3. Connect the ohmmeter black lead to the cylinder No. 1 ignition coil negative (–) terminal. Connect the ohmmeter red lead to the cylinder No. 1 ignition coil positive (+) terminal stud.

4. If the meter reading is within specification, go to Step 5. If the meter reading is not within specifications, replace the ignition coil and retest spark output. Repeat the test for the remaining ignition coils.

5. To check the ignition coil secondary resistance, calibrate the ohmmeter on the appropriate scale to read the specification listed in **Table 12**.

6. Connect the ohmmeter red lead to the cylinder No. 1 ignition coil spark plug tower. Connect the ohmmeter black lead to the cylinder No.1 ignition coil primary positive (+) terminal stud.

7. If the meter reading is not within specification, replace the ignition coil and retest spark output. If the meter reading is within specification and all other ignition components are within specification, but no spark, weak spark or erratic spark is still noted, replace the ignition coil(s) and retest spark output. Repeat the test for the remaining ignition coils.

8. To check the ignition coil spark plug leads for continuity, calibrate an ohmmeter on the R × 1 scale. Connect one ohmmeter lead to each end of the spark plug lead. Gently twist and flex the spark plug lead while observing the meter. The meter should indicate a very low reading. If the meter indicates a high reading or fluctuates when the lead is flexed, replace the spark plug lead.

Repeat the test for the remaining spark plug leads.

RPM Limit Module

Description

The 100-125 hp and 65 and 80 Jet models are equipped with a rpm limit module. The rpm limit module is connected to the switch box stop circuit (black/yellow). When engine rpm exceeds the preprogrammed limit, the rpm limit module momentarily shorts the black/yellow lead to ground, limiting engine speed. There are 4 leads on the rpm limit module. The purple lead is power for the module from the key switch. The brown lead is connected to the brown trigger coil lead and is an rpm signal for the module. The black/yellow lead is connected to the switch box stop circuit and is shorted to ground by the module to control engine speed by switching the ignition system on and off. The black lead is the ground path for the module.

Troubleshooting the rpm limit module

Refer to the end of the book for individual wiring diagrams.

> *CAUTION*
> *Do not run the engine without an adequate water supply and do not exceed 3000 rpm without an adequate load. Refer to **Safety Precautions** at the beginning of this chapter.*

> *NOTE*
> *If the rpm limit module is suspected of causing a high-speed misfire, make sure that the correct operating speed of the engine is verified using a shop tachometer and that the boat's tachometer (if equipped) is correctly set. The high-speed misfire may be caused by the engine over-speeding without the operator's knowledge.*

1. If the rpm limit module is suspected of causing a no-spark, weak spark, erratic spark or misfire while running, disconnect the rpm limit module black/yellow and brown engine harness bullet connectors from the rpm limit module.

2. Retest spark output or run the engine at the speed at which the misfire occurs. If the spark output is now satisfactory or the misfire is no longer present, the rpm limit module is defective and must be replaced.

3. If the rpm limit module is suspected of not functioning when needed, check the ground lead for secure attachment to the power head. Clean and tighten the connection as necessary to assure a good ground path.

4. Disconnect the purple lead bullet connector from the rpm limit module. Connect the red lead of a voltmeter set to read 20 volts DC, to the engine harness purple lead connector. Connect the black lead of the voltmeter to a good engine ground. When the ignition key is ON, the voltmeter should read within 1 volt of battery voltage. When the key is OFF, the voltmeter should read zero volts. If the meter reading is below specification, repair or replace the purple lead circuit from the key switch to the engine harness rpm limit module bullet connector.

5. Check the brown rpm limit module engine harness lead for continuity to the brown trigger coil lead as follows:

   a. On models that use switch boxes with terminal studs, the brown rpm limit module lead is typically connected directly to the switch box brown lead terminal stud. Disconnect the engine harness brown lead from the switch box terminal stud and the rpm limit module bullet connector. Calibrate an ohmmeter on the R × 1 scale. Connect one ohmmeter lead to the switch box end of the engine harness brown lead and the other ohmmeter lead to the rpm limit module end of the engine harness brown lead. The ohmmeter should read continuity. If no continuity is noted, repair or replace the engine harness brown lead.

b. On models that use switch boxes with bullet connectors, the brown rpm limit module is connected to the engine harness at the brown or purple trigger coil lead bullet connector. Disconnect the engine harness brown lead from the brown or purple trigger coil bullet connector and the rpm limit module bullet connector. Calibrate an ohmmeter on the R × 1 scale. Connect one ohmmeter lead to the trigger coil end of the engine harness brown lead and the other ohmmeter lead to the rpm limit module end of the engine harness brown lead. The ohmmeter should read continuity. If no continuity is noted, repair or replace the engine harness brown lead.

6. Check the black/yellow rpm limit module engine harness lead for continuity to the switch box. Disconnect the engine harness black/yellow lead at the rpm limit module bullet connector. Disconnect the engine harness black/yellow lead at the switch box bullet connector or terminal stud. Calibrate an ohmmeter on the R × 1 scale. Connect one ohmmeter lead to the switch box end of the engine harness black/yellow lead and the other ohmmeter lead to the rpm limit module end of the engine harness black/yellow lead. The ohmmeter should read continuity. If any other reading is noted, repair or replace the engine harness black/yellow lead.

7. Reconnect all leads when finished.

Red Stator Upgraded Models

NOTE
Red stator and adapter module upgrade kits are available for 75-125 hp and 65 and 80 Jet models. If the stator on your engine is encased in red plastic, use the following troubleshooting procedure. If the stator on your engine is encased in black plastic, go back to Alternator

Driven Ignition—Capacitor Discharge (Mechanical Advance [75-125 hp and 65-80 Jet]) for troubleshooting and functional description.

Description

Red stator upgraded models are standard ADI-CD models that have had the black stator removed and a red stator and adapter module installed. The new stator has a single winding around 3 bobbins with 2 ignition leads (white/green and green/white) exiting the stator assembly. There are no separate low- and high-speed windings. There are 2 different adapter modules available, 1 for the 3-cylinder models and 1 for 4-cylinder models. Voltage regulation is incorporated into both adaptor modules to keep the increased output of the red stator from damaging the switch box internal components.

Manual start models may use a separate stator winding (blue/white and black) for powering the warning circuits and rpm limit modules on models so equipped.

Red stator upgrade kits also incorporate improved charging system stator windings. The output is increased to 9 or 16 amps, depending on model and an upgraded charging system rectifier/regulator is included (where required).

Troubleshooting procedures require new specifications for checking ignition and charging system stator output and stator resistance tests. New specifications are also required for switch box stop circuit tests and switch box output tests. No changes are required for trigger resistance tests, ignition coil resistance tests and rpm limit module troubleshooting (if equipped). All specifications for red stator models are listed in **Table 10** (charging system) and **Table 13** (ignition system) under *Red stator upgraded models*.

3

3-cylinder adaptor

The 3-cylinder adapter module uses 4 leads (**Figure 30**). The green/white and white/green leads (C, **Figure 30**) are connected to the same colored ignition stator leads. The black lead (B, **Figure 30**) is connected to ground and the blue lead (A, **Figure 30**) is connected to the switch box low-speed ignition stator terminal or bullet connector. The switch box high-speed (red lead) terminal or bullet connector is not used. The adapter module incorporates a full wave rectifier and a shunt voltage regulator. The rectifier changes the ignition stator AC voltage to DC voltage and the voltage regulator limits the voltage entering the switch box to 300 volts. The regulator and rectifier are necessary because the high-speed winding (red lead) is no longer used and the red stator is not grounded to the engine block.

4-cylinder adaptor

The 4-cylinder adapter module uses 5 leads (**Figure 31**). The green/white and white/green leads (C, **Figure 31**) are connected to the same colored ignition stator leads. The black lead (B, **Figure 31**) is connected to ground. The blue and blue/white leads (A, **Figure 31**) are connected to the switch box low-speed ignition stator terminals or bullet connectors. The switch box high-speed (red and red/white leads) terminals or bullet connectors are not used. The adapter module incorporates 2 shunt voltage regulators. Each voltage regulator limits the voltage entering the switch box (from the green/white or white/green) to 300 volts. Two regulators are necessary because of the 2 (blue and blue/white) leads entering the switch box. One regulator controls the voltage on the green/white lead and the other regulator controls the voltage on the white/green lead. The rectifier is not needed because the switch box rectifier network has a complete current path between the blue and blue/white leads.

Troubleshooting (75-125 hp, 65 and 80 Jet Equipped With Red Stator Upgrade)

1. Perform the preliminary spark test, stop circuit isolation and mercury switch test (if so equipped) as described under *Alternator Driven Ignition (Mechanical Advance [75-125 Hp And 65—80 Jet])* in this chapter.

2. Perform the switch box stop circuit test as described in this chapter. Make sure to reference the specifications for the *Red Stator Upgraded Models* in **Table 13**.

3. Perform the ignition stator and adaptor module output tests as described under the *Ignition stator and module output tests (red stator models)* in the following section (this chapter).

4. Perform the ignition stator resistance tests as described under *Ignition stator and adaptor module resistance tests (red stator models)* in the following section (this chapter).

5. *3-cylinder models*—Perform the switch box bias test as described in this chapter. Be sure to reference the specifications (**Table 13**) for *Red Stator Upgraded Models*.

6. Perform the trigger resistance test as described in this chapter.

7. Perform the switch box output test as described in this chapter. Be sure to reference the

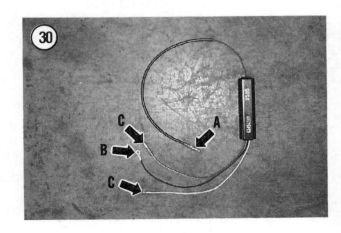

specifications for *Red Stator Upgraded Models* in **Table 13**.

8. Perform the ignition coil ohmmeter test as described in this chapter.

Ignition stator and adaptor module output tests (red stator models)

> WARNING
> *To prevent accidental starting, remove the spark plug leads from the spark plugs and install the spark gap tester (FT-11295 or equivalent) to the spark plug leads. Connect the alligator clip of the spark tester to a clean engine ground.*

1. To test the ignition stator and adapter module output, connect the meter red lead to a good engine ground and the meter black lead to the blue ignition stator lead bullet connector or switch box terminal stud.

2. Set the meter selector switch to 400 DVA.

3. Crank the engine and note the meter.

4. If the reading is not within specification (**Table 13**, red stator upgraded models), test the resistance of the ignition stator windings as described in the next section. If the resistance is within specification, replace the adapter module and retest spark output.

5. *4-cylinder models*—Repeat the output test for the blue/white adaptor module lead at the switch box.

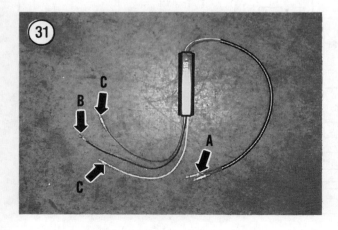

Ignition stator resistance test (red stator models)

1. Disconnect the ignition stator green/white and white/green leads from the adaptor module bullet connectors.

2. To check the resistance of the ignition stator windings, calibrate an ohmmeter on the appropriate scale to read the specification listed in **Table 13** (red stator upgraded models).

3. Connect the ohmmeter black lead to the ignition stator green/white lead bullet connector and the ohmmeter red lead to the ignition stator white/green lead bullet connector.

4. If the reading is not within specification (**Table 13**), replace the stator coil assembly and retest spark output.

5. To check the ignition stator windings for shorts to ground, calibrate an ohmmeter on the highest scale available.

6. Connect one ohmmeter lead to a good engine ground and the other ohmmeter lead alternately to the ignition stator green/white and white/green leads while noting the meter. The meter should indicate no continuity. If any continuity is noted, replace the stator coil assembly and retest spark output.

ALTERNATOR DRIVEN IGNITION (135-200 HP, 275 HP, 105 AND 140 JET [V6])

Description

This AD-CDI ignition is an alternator driven, capacitor discharge ignition system with mechanical spark advance. It is used on 135-200, 275 hp and 105-140 Jet (V-6) models. It is important to note that on EFI (electronic fuel injection) models, the ignition system operates independently of the fuel injection system. However, the fuel injection ECM (electronic control module) requires input from the inner switch box primary ignition coil leads for cylinders No. 1,

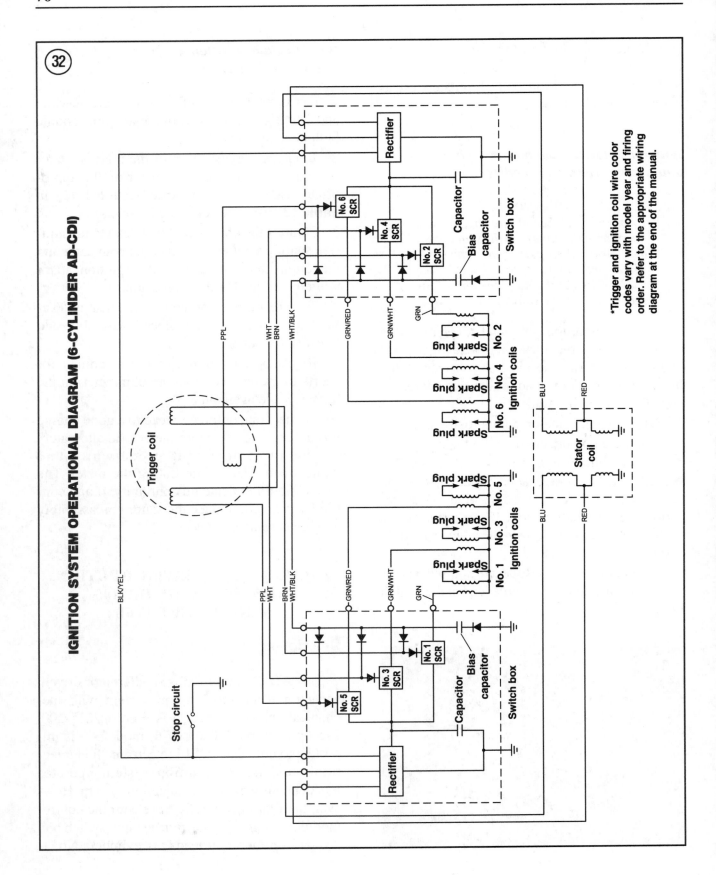

IGNITION SYSTEM OPERATIONAL DIAGRAM (6-CYLINDER AD-CDI)

*Trigger and ignition coil wire color codes vary with model year and firing order. Refer to the appropriate wiring diagram at the end of the manual.

No. 3 and No. 5. An ignition failure on any one of these cylinders will cause 2 cylinders not to receive fuel, since the ECM will not receive a fuel injector trigger signal from the ignition system.

Refer to **Figure 32** for an operational diagram of the AD-CDI 6-cylinder ignition system. The major components are the:

1. *Flywheel*—The flywheel inner magnets are for the trigger coil (timing information). The outer magnets are for the ignition stator and battery charging stator.

2. *Ignition stator (charge) coils*—The stator is equipped with 2 low- and 2 high-speed windings and a ground lead. The ignition stator provides the power the 2 switch boxes need to operate the ignition system. Low-speed windings provide most of the electricity for low-speed (cranking and idle) running. High-speed windings provide most of the electricity for high speed (cruising and wide open throttle) running. Stator output is always AC (alternating current) voltage. The ignition stator has one set of leads banded with a yellow sleeve for identification. The yellow banded ignition stator leads must be connected to the same switch box as the yellow banded trigger coil leads. The non-yellow banded ignition stator leads must be connected to the same switch box as the non-yellow banded trigger coil leads. Normally the yellow banded leads go to the outer (or upper on 275 hp) switch box.

3. *Trigger coil*—The trigger coil tells the switch box when to fire the ignition coils. The trigger

coil is rotated by mechanical linkage to change the trigger's position relative to the flywheel. This movement advances or retards the ignition spark timing. The trigger coil has 3 windings. Each winding has 2 leads. One lead from each winding goes to each switch box. The trigger coil has 3 leads banded with a yellow sleeve for identification. The yellow banded trigger coil leads must connect to the same switch box as the yellow banded ignition stator leads. The non-yellow banded trigger coil leads must connect to the same switch box as the non-yellow banded stator leads. Normally the yellow banded leads go to the outer (or upper on 275 hp) switch box. The 3 individual trigger leads on each switch box are brown, white and purple. Failure of a single trigger winding or lead will cause the loss of spark on 2 cylinders on opposing cylinder banks.

4. *Switch boxes*—V-6 models use 2 switch boxes with terminal stud connectors. The switch boxes store the electricity from the ignition stator windings until the trigger coils tell them to send the electricity to the ignition coils. The switch box uses an internal rectifier to change the ignition stator AC voltage to DC (direct current) voltage. The DC voltage is stored in a capacitor (an electrical storage tank), until it is released by a SCR (silicon controlled rectifier), which is simply an electronic switch. There is one SCR for each cylinder. The SCR is controlled by the trigger coil.

All V-6 model switch boxes incorporate a bias circuit that is primarily used to control (stabilize) ignition spark advance and to keep the 2 switch boxes from interfering with each other. A separate test is conducted to make sure the bias circuit is functioning correctly on each switch box. V-6 switch boxes must be grounded to each other and the engine block anytime the engine is cranked or run.

5A. *Idle stabilizer module*—All V-6 models (except the 275 hp) use an idle stabilizer module connected to the switch box bias circuit. See **Figure 33**. When idle speed drops below a pre-

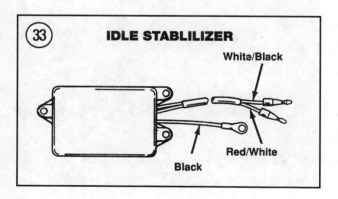

(33) IDLE STABLILIZER

White/Black

Red/White

Black

programmed value, additional spark advance is added (through the bias circuit) to stabilize engine speed.

5B. *Detonation sensor and module*—The 200 XRI and 200 Magnum EFI models are also equipped with a detonation sensor (A, **Figure 34**) and module (B, **Figure 34**) which detects potentially damaging spark knock (abnormal combustion) and retards ignition spark advance up to 8°. The detonation module also signals the fuel system ECM (electronic control module) to enrichen fuel flow up to 15 percent. The reduction of spark advance and enrichment of fuel will stop spark knock under all reasonable operating conditions.

6. *Ignition coils*—There is one ignition coil for each cylinder. The ignition coil transforms the relatively low voltage from the switch box into voltage high enough (35,000 volts) to jump the spark plug gap and ignite the air/fuel mixture.

7. *Spark plugs*—There is one spark plug for each cylinder. Use only the recommended spark plugs or catastrophic engine damage may result. Resistor or suppressor plugs are designed to reduce RFI (radio frequency interference) emissions that can cause interference with electrical accessories. Use the recommended RFI spark plug if RFI interference is suspected of causing interference or malfunction of electrical accessories.

NOTE
The 275 hp is equipped with a mercury tilt switch that is connected to the switch box stop circuit (black/yellow). Refer to **Mercury (tilt) switch test** *in this section for troubleshooting procedures and functional description.*

8. *Stop circuit*—The stop circuit is connected to one end of the capacitor in each switch box. Whenever the stop circuit is connected to ground, the capacitors are shorted to ground and cannot store electricity. At this point, there is no voltage available to send to the ignition coils and the ignition system ceases producing spark. The

stop circuit must have an open circuit (to ground) for the engine to run.

NOTE
The 275 hp and 105 and 140 Jet models are equipped with an rpm limit module. The rpm limit module is connected to the switch box stop circuit (black/yellow). When engine speed exceeds the preprogrammed limit, the rpm limit module momentarily shorts the black/yellow lead to ground, limiting engine speed.

Troubleshooting

Refer to **Table 11** for specifications and the end of the book for wiring diagrams. Read *Troubleshooting Notes and Precautions (All Models)* at the beginning of the ignition section before continuing. Test harness part No. 91-1443A1 has a 6 position rotary switch and 6 long test leads that allow connection to 6 different test points. The purpose of the harness is to allow testing on a running motor while safely seated in the passenger compartment. A typical use of the harness is to check quickly all 6 switch box outputs at the engine speed that the ignition symptom is occurring.

The recommended troubleshooting procedure is listed below.

1. Preliminary checks.
   a. Spark test.
   b. Stop circuit isolation.

c. Mercury switch test (275 hp).

d. Idle stabilizer module isolation test (except 275 hp).

e. Detonation sensor module isolation test (200 EFI models).

2. Switch box stop circuit test.

3. Ignition stator output test.

4. Ignition stator resistance test.

5. Switch box bias test.

6. Trigger resistance test.

7. Switch box output test.

8. Ignition coil ohmmeter test.

CAUTION
Do not run the engine without an adequate water supply and do not exceed 3000 rpm without an adequate load. Refer to Safety Precautions at the beginning of this chapter.

WARNING
High voltage is present in the ignition system. Do not touch or disconnect ignition components while the engine is running.

Preliminary checks

NOTE
Weak, intermittent or no spark at 2 cylinders (1 cylinder on each bank) usually indicates a defective trigger coil. Weak, intermittent or no spark at 3 cylinders (1

complete bank) usually indicates a defective stator assembly or switch box. Weak, intermittent or no spark at any 1 cylinder usually indicates a defective spark plug, ignition coil or switch box.

1. Disconnect the spark plug leads from the spark plugs and install an air gap spark tester (part No. 91-850439 or equivalent) to the spark plug leads. Connect the alligator clip of the spark tester to a clean engine ground. Set the spark tester air gap to 7/16 in. (11.1 mm).

2. Make sure the safety lanyard is installed on the safety lanyard switch and the ignition switch is in the RUN position.

3. Crank the engine while observing the tester. If a crisp, blue spark is noted at each air gap, the ignition system is functioning correctly. If the engine will not start or does not run correctly, check the spark plugs and ignition timing. If ignition timing is unstable at cranking speed and idle speed, go to *Switch box bias test* in this section. If the engine backfires or pops when attempting to start, remove the flywheel and check for a sheared flywheel key. If no spark, weak spark or erratic spark is noted, continue at Step 4.

CAUTION
The switch boxes on V6 models (except 275 hp) must be removed from the power head to gain access to the inner switch box lead terminals. The switch boxes must be grounded to the power head when cranking or starting the engine, or the switch boxes may be damaged. Be sure to connect a suitable jumper lead securely between BOTH switch boxes and a good engine ground before cranking the engine in the following tests.

4. *135-200 hp and 105 and 140 Jet*—Remove the 2 screws securing the switch boxes to the power head (**Figure 35**). Without disconnecting any switch box leads, separate the inner and outer switch boxes, being careful not to lose the spacers located between switch boxes at each mounting screw.

5. Disconnect the stop circuit black/yellow leads from *both* switch box terminal studs. Crank the engine while observing the spark tester. If good spark is now noted, a short to ground is present in the key switch, safety lanyard switch, rpm limit module (if equipped) or the main engine harness black/yellow lead. Test, repair or replace the circuit or component as necessary. On 275 hp models test the mercury switch as described in the next section.

6. *135-200 hp and 105 and 140 Jet*—To isolate the idle stabilizer module from the ignition system, disconnect the white/black and red/white leads from the idle stabilizer module bullet connectors (**Figure 33**). Crank the engine while observing the spark tester. If good spark is now noted, replace the idle stabilizer and retest spark output.

> *CAUTION*
> *The switch boxes on 200 XRI and 200 Magnum EFI models must be removed from the power head to gain access to the inner switch box lead terminals. The switch boxes must be grounded to the power head when cranking or starting the engine or the switch boxes may be damaged. Be sure to connect a suitable jumper lead securely between **BOTH** switch boxes and a good engine ground before cranking the engine in the following tests.*

7. *200 XRI and 200 Magnum EFI*—To isolate the detonation sensor module from the ignition system, remove the 2 screws securing the switch boxes to the power head (**Figure 35**). Without disconnecting any switch box leads, separate the inner and outer switch boxes, being careful not to lose the spacers located between switch boxes at each mounting screw. Disconnect the detonation module white/black leads from each switch box. Crank the engine while observing the spark tester. If good spark is now noted, replace the detonation sensor module and retest spark output.

Mercury (tilt) switch test

Early model 275 hp outboards may be equipped with a mercury switch. The mercury switch is designed to short the switch box stop circuit (black/yellow) to ground, stopping the engine, if the motor exceeds a specific angle of tilt. This reduces the risk of injury (and mechanical damage) if an impact should drive the gearcase (and propeller) from the water. The mercury switch on 275 hp models is mounted just above the upper switch box.

1. Remove the mercury switch black/yellow lead, mounting screw and black ground lead.
2. Connect an ohmmeter, calibrated on the R × 1 scale, between the black ground lead and the terminal stud on the switch.
3. Hold the mercury switch as it would be positioned with the outboard motor in the fully DOWN position. The meter should indicate no continuity.
4. Hold the mercury switch as it would be positioned with the outboard motor in the fully UP position. The meter should now indicate continuity.
5. Replace the mercury switch if it does not perform as specified.

Switch box stop circuit tests

> *WARNING*
> *To prevent accidental starting, remove the spark plug leads from the spark plugs and install the spark gap tester (91-850439) to the spark plug leads. Connect the alligator clip of the spark tester to a clean engine ground.*

> *CAUTION*
> *The switch boxes on V6 models (except 275 hp) must be removed from the power head to gain access to the inner switch box lead terminals. The switch boxes must be grounded to the power head when cranking or starting the engine, or the switch boxes may be damaged. Be sure to connect a suitable jumper lead*

*securely between **BOTH** switch boxes and a good engine ground before cranking the engine in the following tests.*

1. Remove the 2 screws securing the switch boxes to the power head (**Figure 35**). Without disconnecting any switch box leads, separate the inner and outer switch boxes, being careful not to lose the spacers located between switch boxes at each mounting screw.

2. Connect the meter black lead to a good engine ground and the meter red lead to the black/yellow terminal stud on the outer (upper on 275 hp) switch box.

3. Set the meter selector switch to 400 DVA.

4. Crank the engine while noting the test meter.

5. Move the meter red lead to the black/yellow terminal stud on the inner (lower on 275 hp) switch box.

6. Crank the engine while noting the test meter.

7. If the stop circuit voltage is within specification (**Table 11**) at both switch boxes, continue at *Ignition stator output test* in this section.

8. If the stop circuit voltage is above specifications at one or both switch boxes, either the switch box(es) or the trigger coil assembly is defective. Test the trigger coils as described under *Trigger coil ohmmeter tests* in this section. If the trigger coils are within specification, replace the switch box(es) that exhibits high stop circuit voltage and retest.

9. If the stop circuit voltage is below specification at one or both switch boxes, disconnect the black/yellow stop circuit lead from both switch box terminal studs.

10. Recheck the stop circuit voltage at both switch boxes (Steps 2-6). If the stop circuit voltages are now within the specified range, the stop circuit is defective (partially shorted to ground) and must be repaired. If the stop switch voltage is still below specification, continue at *Ignition stator output tests* in this section.

Ignition stator output tests

WARNING
To prevent accidental starting, remove the spark plug leads from the spark plugs and install the spark gap tester (part No. 91-850439) to the spark plug leads. Connect the alligator clip of the spark tester to a clean engine ground.

CAUTION
*The switch boxes on V6 models (except 275 hp) must be removed from the power head to gain access to the inner switch box lead terminals. The switch boxes must be grounded to the power head when cranking or starting the engine, or the switch boxes may be damaged. Be sure to connect a suitable jumper lead securely between **BOTH** switch boxes and a good engine ground before cranking the engine in the following tests.*

NOTE
*A malfunctioning idle speed stabilizer module may cause the following test results to be inaccurate. If so equipped, disconnect the red/white bullet connector from the idle speed stabilizer module before performing the ignition stator output test. See **Figure 33**.*

1. To test the ignition stator low-speed winding output, connect the meter black lead to a good engine ground and the meter red lead to the inner (or upper on 275 hp) switch box blue ignition stator lead terminal stud.

2. Set the meter selector switch to 400 DVA.

3. Crank the engine and note the meter.

4. If the reading is not within specification (**Table 11**), test the resistance of the ignition stator low-speed windings as described in the next section.

5. Repeat the low-speed output test for outer (or lower on 275 hp) switch box blue/white ignition stator lead.

6. To test the stator high-speed winding output, connect the meter black lead to a good engine ground and the meter red lead to the inner (or

upper on 275 hp) red ignition stator lead terminal stud on the switch box.

7. Verify the meter is still set to the 400 DVA scale.

8. Crank the engine and note the meter.

9. If the reading is not within specification (**Table 11**), test the resistance of the ignition stator high-speed windings as described in the next section.

10. Repeat the high-speed output test for the outer (or lower on 275 hp) switch box red/white ignition stator lead.

Ignition stator resistance tests

1. Disconnect the ignition stator blue and red leads from the inner (or upper on 275 hp) switch box and the blue/white and red/white leads from the outer (or lower on 275 hp) switch box terminal studs.

2. To check the resistance of the ignition stator low-speed windings, calibrate an ohmmeter on the appropriate scale to read the low speed specification listed in **Table 12**.

3. Connect the ohmmeter black lead to the ignition stator blue lead and the ohmmeter red lead to the ignition stator red lead.

4. If the reading is not within the low speed winding specification (**Table 12**), replace the stator coil assembly and retest spark output.

5. Repeat the test (Steps 2-4) for the ignition stator blue/white and red/white leads.

6. To check the resistance of the ignition stator high-speed windings, calibrate an ohmmeter on the appropriate scale to read the high-speed winding specification listed in **Table 12**.

7. Connect the ohmmeter black lead to a good engine ground and the ohmmeter red lead to the red ignition stator lead.

8. If the reading is not within the high speed winding specifications (**Table 12**), replace the stator coil assembly and retest spark output.

9. Repeat the test (Steps 6-8) for the ignition stator red/white lead.

Switch box bias test

> *WARNING*
> *To prevent accidental starting, remove the spark plug leads from the spark plugs and install the spark gap tester (part No. 91-850439) to the spark plug leads. Connect the alligator clip of the spark tester to a clean engine ground.*

> *CAUTION*
> *The switch box bias circuit voltage output is DC (direct current). Do not use the DVA scale or adaptor for this test.*

> *NOTE*
> *A malfunctioning idle speed stabilizer or detonation sensor module may cause the following test results to be inaccurate. On all models except the 275 hp, disconnect the white/black lead from the idle speed stabilizer bullet connector (**Figure 33**). On 200 EFI models, also disconnect the white/black detonation sensor module leads from both switch boxes before proceeding.*

1. To check the switch box bias circuit output, connect the red lead of a DC voltmeter, set to the 20 VDC scale, to a clean engine ground. Connect the black lead of the DC voltmeter to the outer (or lower on 275 hp) switch box white/black lead terminal stud.

2. Crank the engine while observing the meter. The meter should indicate 2-10 volts DC.

> *NOTE*
> *The detonation sensor module on 200 EFI models completes the bias circuit between the 2 switch boxes. It is necessary to check the bias circuit voltage on both switch boxes.*

3. *200 XRI and 200 Magnum EFI models*—Repeat Steps 1-2 for the inner switch box white/black terminal stud.

4. If switch box bias is below the specified voltage, one or both switch boxes are defective. Disconnect all leads from both switch box white/black terminal studs. Calibrate an ohmme-

ter on the appropriate scale to read 1300-1500 ohms.

5. Connect one ohmmeter lead to the inner (or upper on 275 hp) switch box white/black terminal stud. Connect the other ohmmeter lead to the inner switch box case ground.

6. The ohmmeter should read 1300-1500 ohms. If the reading is not within specification, replace the switch box and retest the switch box bias circuit voltage.

7. Repeat the test (Steps 4-6) for the outer (or lower on 275 hp) switch box.

8A. *200 XRI and 200 Magnum EFI models*—If the ohmmeter tests are within specification, but the bias circuit voltage is still below specification for both switch boxes, replace both switch boxes and retest switch box bias circuit voltage. If the bias circuit voltage is below specification on one switch box, replace the suspect switch box and retest switch box bias circuit voltage.

8B. *All other models*—If the ohmmeter tests are within specification, but the bias circuit voltage is below specification, one or both switch boxes are defective. Replace the outer (or lower on 275 hp) switch box and retest switch box bias circuit voltage. If the reading is still below specification, replace the inner (or upper on 275 hp) switch box and retest switch box bias circuit voltage.

> *NOTE*
> *A frequent cause of switch box bias failure is a poor ground to the adjacent switch box. If repeated bias failure occurs in the same switch box, the other switch box ground should be closely inspected. If the ground is clean, tight and appears to be in acceptable condition, the manufacturer recommends replacing **both** switch boxes.*

Trigger coil resistance test

> *NOTE*
> *Ohmmeter tests require connection to one lead from the yellow banded trigger*

harness and one lead from the non-yellow banded trigger coil harness.

1. Disconnect the brown, white and purple trigger coil leads from the terminal studs of both switch boxes.

2. Calibrate an ohmmeter on the appropriate scale to read the specification listed in **Table 11**.

3. Connect one ohmmeter lead to the trigger coil brown lead (without yellow sleeve) and the other ohmmeter lead to the trigger coil white lead (with yellow sleeve).

4. If the reading is not within specification, replace the trigger coil and retest spark output.

5. Repeat the test for the next (second) trigger coil winding. Connect one ohmmeter lead to the white trigger coil lead (without yellow sleeve) and the other ohmmeter lead to the purple trigger coil lead (with yellow sleeve).

6. If the reading is not within specification, replace the trigger coil and retest spark output.

7. Repeat the test for the final (third) trigger coil winding. Connect one ohmmeter lead to the trigger coil purple lead (without yellow sleeve) and the other ohmmeter lead to the trigger coil brown lead (with yellow sleeve).

8. If the reading is not within specification, replace the trigger coil assembly and retest spark output.

Switch box output test

> *WARNING*
> *To prevent accidental starting, remove the spark plug leads from the spark plugs and install the spark gap tester (part No. 91-850439) to the spark plug leads. Connect the alligator clip of the spark tester to a clean engine ground.*

> *NOTE*
> *The inner (or upper on 275 hp) switch box controls the ignition coils for cylinder No. 1, No. 3 and No. 5. The outer (or lower on 275 hp) switch box controls the ignition coils for cylinder No. 2, No. 4 and No. 6.*

1. To check the switch box voltage output to the ignition coils, connect the meter red lead to the cylinder No. 1 ignition coil positive (+) primary terminal. Connect the meter black lead to the cylinder No. 1 ignition coil negative (–) primary terminal (black lead).

2. Set the meter selector switch to 400 DVA.

3. Crank the engine while noting the meter reading.

4. If the meter reading is below specification (**Table 11**), continue to *Ignition coil ohmmeter test*. If the ignition coil ohmmeter tests are within specification, replace the switch box and retest spark output. If the ignition coil tests are not within specification, replace the ignition coil(s) and retest spark output. If the meter reading is within specification, but no spark, weak spark or erratic spark is still noted, continue to *Ignition coil ohmmeter test*.

5. Repeat the test procedure for the remaining ignition coil(s).

Ignition coil ohmmeter test

1. To check the ignition coil primary resistance, calibrate an ohmmeter on the appropriate scale to read the primary resistance specification listed in **Table 12**.

2. Disconnect the spark plug leads. Carefully remove the spark plug leads from the ignition coils. Disconnect the switch box primary lead from each ignition coil positive (+) primary terminal stud.

3. Connect the ohmmeter black lead to the cylinder No. 1 ignition coil negative (–) terminal. Connect the ohmmeter red lead to the cylinder No.1 ignition coil positive (+) terminal stud.

4. If the meter reading is within specification, go to Step 5. If the meter reading is not within specification, replace the ignition coil and retest spark output. Repeat the test for the remaining ignition coils.

5. To check the ignition coil secondary resistance, calibrate the ohmmeter on the appropriate scale to read the specification listed in **Table 12**.

6. Connect the ohmmeter red lead to the cylinder No. 1 ignition coil spark plug tower. Connect the ohmmeter black lead to the cylinder No. 1 ignition coil primary positive (+) terminal stud.

7. If the meter reading is not within specification, replace the ignition coil and retest spark output. If the meter reading is within specification and all other ignition components are within specification, but no spark, weak spark or erratic spark is still noted, replace the ignition coil(s) and retest spark output. Repeat the test for the remaining ignition coils.

8. To check the ignition coil spark plug leads for continuity, calibrate an ohmmeter on the R × 1 scale. Connect one ohmmeter lead to each end of the spark plug lead. Gently twist and flex the spark plug lead while observing the meter. The meter should indicate a very low reading. If the meter indicates a high reading or fluctuates when the lead is flexed, replace the spark plug lead. Repeat the test for the remaining spark plug leads.

RPM Limit Module

Description

The 275 hp and 105-140 Jet models are equipped with a rpm limit module. The rpm limit module is connected to the switch box stop circuits (black/yellow). If engine speed exceeds the preprogrammed limit, the rpm limit module momentarily shorts the black/yellow lead to ground, limiting engine speed. There are 4 leads on the rpm limit module. The purple (red on 275 hp) lead is power for the module from the key switch (starter solenoid battery positive terminal on 275 hp). The brown (gray on 275 hp) lead is connected to the brown trigger coil lead (gray voltage regulator lead on 275 hp) and is an rpm signal for the module. The black/yellow lead is connected to the switch box stop circuits and is shorted to ground by the module to control engine rpm by switching the ignition system on and off. The black lead is the ground path for the module.

The 275 hp incorporates a diode in the rpm limit module black/yellow circuit to prevent the rpm limit module from shorting all 6 cylinders (both switch boxes). When the diode is working correctly, only the lower switch box (cylinder No. 2, No. 4 and No. 6) is affected by the rpm limit module. If diode failure is suspected, refer to *Troubleshooting the rpm limit harness diode* in this section.

Troubleshooting the rpm limit module

Refer to the end of the book for wiring diagrams.

> *CAUTION*
> *Do not run the engine without an adequate water supply and do not exceed 3000 rpm without an adequate load. Refer to **Safety Precautions** at the beginning of this chapter.*

> *NOTE*
> *If the rpm limit module is suspected of causing a high-speed misfire, make sure the correct operating speed of the engine is verified with a shop tachometer and that the boat's tachometer (if equipped) is correctly set. The high-speed misfire may be due to the engine over-speeding without the operator's knowledge.*

1. If the rpm limit module is suspected of causing a no spark, weak spark, erratic spark or misfire while running, disconnect the rpm limit module black/yellow leads from the engine harness or outer (lower on 275 hp) switch box.

2A. *105-140 Jet*—Disconnect the brown rpm limit module lead from the outer switch box.

2B. *275 hp*—Disconnect the gray lead from the lower voltage regulator bullet connector.

3. Retest spark output or run the engine to the speed at which the misfire occurs. If the spark output is now satisfactory or the misfire is no longer present, the rpm limit module is defective and must be replaced.

4. If the rpm limit module is suspected of not functioning when needed, check the ground lead for secure attachment to the power head. Clean and tighten the connection as necessary to ensure a good ground path.

5A. *105-140 Jet*—Disconnect the purple lead bullet connector at the rpm limit module. Connect the red lead of a voltmeter set to read 20 VDC, to the engine harness purple lead bullet connector. Connect the black lead of the voltmeter to a good engine ground. When the ignition key is ON, the voltmeter should read within 1 volt of battery voltage. When the key is OFF, the voltmeter should read zero volts. If the meter reading is below specification, repair or replace the purple lead circuit from the key switch to the engine harness rpm limit module bullet connector.

5B. *275 hp*—Check the red rpm limit module lead for secure attachment to the starter solenoid positive terminal. Clean and tighten the connections as necessary to ensure a good connection.

6A. *105-140 Jet*—Check the brown rpm limit module engine harness lead for continuity to the brown trigger coil lead. Disconnect the engine harness brown lead from the switch box terminal stud and the rpm limit module bullet connector. Calibrate an ohmmeter on the R × 1 scale. Connect one ohmmeter lead to the switch box end of the engine harness brown lead and the other ohmmeter lead to the rpm limit module end of the engine harness brown lead. The ohmmeter should read continuity. If no continuity is noted, repair or replace the engine harness brown lead.

6B. *275 hp*—Check the gray rpm limit module engine harness lead for continuity to the lower voltage regulator gray lead. Disconnect the engine harness gray lead from the lower voltage regulator and the rpm limit module bullet connector. Calibrate an ohmmeter on the R × 1 scale. Connect one ohmmeter lead to the voltage regulator end of the engine harness gray lead and the other ohmmeter lead to the rpm limit module end of the engine harness gray lead. The ohmmeter should read continuity. If no continuity is noted, repair or replace the engine harness gray lead.

7A. *105-140 Jet*—Check the black/yellow rpm limit module engine harness lead for continuity to the switch box. Disconnect the engine harness black/yellow lead at the rpm limit module bullet connector. Disconnect the engine harness black/yellow lead at the switch box terminal stud. Calibrate an ohmmeter on the R × 1 scale. Connect one ohmmeter lead to the switch box end of the engine harness black/yellow lead and the other ohmmeter lead to the rpm limit module end of the engine harness black/yellow lead. The ohmmeter should read continuity. If no continuity is noted, repair or replace the engine harness black/yellow lead.

7B. *275 hp*—Check the black/yellow rpm limit module lead for secure attachment to the lower switch box terminal stud. Clean and tighten the connection as necessary to ensure a good connection. Test the harness diode as described in the next section.

8. Reconnect all leads when finished.

Troubleshooting the rpm limit harness diode (275 hp)

If the rpm limit harness diode fails in an open circuit, the engine will continue to run on 3 cylinders after the ignition switch is turned OFF. If the diode is incorrectly installed (electrically backward) the engine may continue to run on all 6 cylinders after the ignition switch is turned off. If the diode is shorted in a closed circuit, all 6 cylinders will misfire when the rpm limit module activates. The diode is connected to the black/yellow terminal of the lower switch box.

Refer to the end of the book for wiring diagrams. To test the diode, proceed as follows:

1. Disconnect the diode leads from the lower switch box and the engine harness bullet connector.

2. Calibrate an ohmmeter on the appropriate scale to test a diode. Connect the ohmmeter red lead to the diode ring terminal and the ohmmeter black lead to the diode bullet connector. Note the reading. Reverse the ohmmeter lead and again note the reading.

3. The meter should indicate continuity in one polarity and no continuity in the other. If the diode shows continuity in both directions or no continuity in both directions, replace the diode assembly.

Idle Stabilizer Module Troubleshooting (All Models Except 275 hp)

All V6 models (except 275 hp) are equipped with an idle stabilizer module. The module is a solid-state, nonserviceable device that must be replaced if not functioning correctly. Whenever engine speed drops below approximately 550 rpm, the idle stabilizer electronically advances ignition timing (through the switch box bias circuit). The idle stabilizer can advance ignition timing a maximum of 9° above normal base timing. The additional timing advance raises the engine speed to 550 rpm, at which time the module returns ignition timing to normal operation. The idle stabilizer module has 3 leads. The red/white lead provides power to the module from the ignition stator high-speed winding, the white/black lead is connected to the switch box bias circuit to allow the idle stabilizer module to control ignition timing and the black lead is ground. See **Figure 33**. To test the idle stabilizer, proceed as follows:

CAUTION
Do not run the engine without an adequate water supply and do not exceed 3000 rpm without an adequate load. Re-

*fer to **Safety Precautions** at the beginning of this chapter.*

Refer to the end of the book for wiring diagrams.

1. Remove the engine cover and connect a timing light to the No. 1 (top starboard) spark plug lead. Connect an accurate tachometer to the engine following its manufacturer's instructions.

2. Start the engine and allow it to warm to operating temperature. Reduce the engine speed to approximately 600-650 rpm.

3. Slowly, pull forward on the spark advance lever to retard the timing (and reduce the engine speed). Using the timing light, observe the timing as the spark advance lever is moved.

NOTE
Due to variations in individual idle stabilizer modules and in tachometers from different manufacturers, the engine speed at which timing advance occurs may vary slightly.

4. If the ignition timing rapidly advances (as much as 9°) as the engine speed falls below

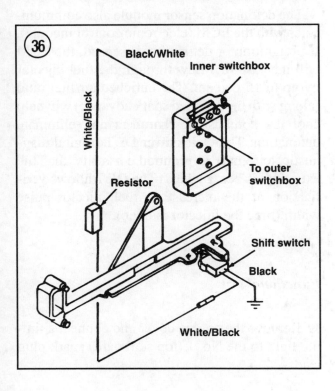

36
Black/White
Inner switchbox
White/Black
Resistor
To outer switchbox
Shift switch
Black
White/Black

approximately 550 rpm, the idle stabilizer is operating properly. If timing advance is not noted, replace the idle stabilizer module.

Idle Stabilizer Shift System (XR6, Magnum III, 175 hp Carbureted, 150 and 175 XRI and Magnum [EFI] Models)

Description

The idle stabilizer shift system is designed to prevent stalling by advancing the ignition timing 3° when the outboard is shifted into forward gear.

When the outboard motor is running at idle speed in neutral, the shift switch (**Figure 36**) is open. When shifted into gear, the shift switch closes and completes the switch box bias circuit from each switch box to ground through a 6800 ohm resistor, resulting in a 3° timing advance. If the 6800 ohm resistor (**Figure 36**) is open, or the shift switch remains open, the timing advance will not occur. In addition, full-throttle timing will be 3° retarded. Should the resistor or the white/black lead between the resistor and the outer switch box short to ground, the timing will be excessively advanced and could cause engine damage from detonation.

CAUTION
If the idle stabilizer shift system is installed on models other than XR6, Magnum III, 175 hp carbureted, 150 and 175 XRI and Magnum [EFI] models (as an accessory), the maximum ignition timing must be retarded 3°. Refer to Chapter Five for the timing procedure.

Idle stabilizer shift system troubleshooting

CAUTION
*Do not run the engine without an adequate water supply and do not exceed 3000 rpm without an adequate load. Refer to **Safety Precautions** at the beginning of this chapter.*

1. Remove the engine cover and connect a timing light to the No. 1 (top starboard) spark plug lead.

2. Start the engine and allow it to reach operating temperature. Reduce the engine speed to idle.

3. While observing the ignition timing, shift into forward gear. The idle stabilizer shift system is functioning properly if the timing advances 3° upon shifting into gear.

4. If the timing does not advance 3° upon shifting into gear, shut the engine off. Disconnect the white/black resistor lead from the shift switch bullet connector and the outer switch box white/black terminal stud.

5. Calibrate an ohmmeter on the appropriate scale to read 6800-7140 ohms. Connect one ohmmeter lead to each end of the resistor. If the reading is not within 6800-7140 ohms, replace the resistor and lead assembly. If the reading is within 6800-7140 ohms, go to Step 6.

6. Calibrate an ohmmeter on the R × 1 scale. Disconnect the shift switch lead from the white/black resistor lead bullet connector. Connect one ohmmeter lead to the shift switch ground lead terminal and the other ohmmeter lead to the shift switch bullet connector.

7. Position the gear shift mechanism in the NEUTRAL position. The ohmmeter should read no continuity. Position the gear shift mechanism in the FORWARD gear position. The ohmmeter should read continuity. Replace the shift switch if the readings are not as specified. If the shift switch and resistor test satisfactorily and the timing is still not advancing 3° when shifting into gear, test the switch box bias circuit as previously described in this section.

Detonation Sensor and Module (200 EFI Models)

Description

The 200 XRI and 200 Magnum III EFI (electronic fuel injection) models are equipped with a detonation sensor (A, **Figure 34**) and detonation sensor module (B, **Figure 34**). The detonation sensor is designed to detect the high-frequency vibration caused by abnormal combustion (pre-ignition or detonation). The detonation sensor creates a small voltage signal anytime the engine is running (from normal engine vibration), but increases the voltage signal dramatically if abnormal combustion (preignition or detonation) is present. When the module detects the correct voltage signal (from normal engine vibration at approximately 2500-3500 rpm), the module adds 6° spark advance. The module holds this advance as long as the voltage signal is in the normal range. If the module detects a voltage signal higher than normal, (from preignition or detonation) it removes timing advance as necessary, up to the 6° and if necessary, an additional 2° (total of 8° retard). The detonation module is basically a high-speed advance module that advances timing as long as the correct detonation sensor voltage signal is present. If the detonation sensor sends no voltage signal, the 6° timing advance will not be added.

The detonation sensor module also communicates with the ECM (electronic control module). If preignition or detonation is sensed, the ECM will increase fuel flow through the fuel injector by up to 15 percent. The enriched air/fuel ratio (along with the retarded spark advance) will help cool the combustion chambers and eliminate detonation. The Quicksilver DDT (digital diagnostic terminal) is required to verify that the extra fuel is being added. The DDT allows verification of the increase in fuel injector pulse width (time the injector is open).

Functional test

1. Remove the engine cover and connect a timing light to the No. 1 (top starboard) spark plug lead.

WARNING
To prevent accidental starting, remove the spark plug leads from the spark plugs and install the spark gap tester (part No. 91-850439) to the spark plug leads. Connect the alligator clip of the spark tester to a clean engine ground.

2. Check the maximum timing at cranking speed as described in Chapter 5. Adjust the timing as necessary.

3. Remove the spark gap tester and reconnect the spark plug leads to the spark plugs.

CAUTION
*Do not run the engine without an adequate water supply and do not exceed 3000 rpm without an adequate load. Refer to **Safety Precautions** at the beginning of this chapter.*

4. Start the engine and allow it to reach operating temperature. Run the engine at 3500 rpm or higher in FORWARD gear. Note the timing.

5. If the timing at 3500 rpm or higher is 6° more than the timing at cranking speed, the detonation sensor and detonation module are functioning correctly. If timing advance is not noted, continue to *Troubleshooting* in the next section.

Troubleshooting

Refer to the end of the book for wiring diagrams.

1. If the detonation sensor and module are not functioning as described, check the ground lead for secure attachment to the power head. Clean and tighten the connection as necessary to assure a good ground path.

2. Set the voltmeter on the 20 volt DC scale. Connect the red voltmeter lead to the detonation sensor purple lead terminal at the power head terminal strip. Connect the black voltmeter lead to a good engine ground. When the ignition key is ON, the voltmeter should read within 1 volt of battery voltage. When the key is OFF, the voltmeter should read zero volts. If the meter reading is below specification, repair or replace the purple lead circuit from the key switch to the 2 terminal, power head terminal strip.

3. Check the green detonation sensor module engine harness lead for continuity to the cylinder No. 2 ignition coil primary positive (+) terminal stud. Disconnect the engine harness green lead from the cylinder No. 2 ignition coil positive (+) terminal stud and the detonation sensor module bullet connector. Calibrate an ohmmeter on the R × 1 scale. Connect one ohmmeter lead to the ignition coil end of the engine harness green lead and the other ohmmeter lead to the detonation sensor module end of the engine harness green lead. The ohmmeter should read continuity. If no continuity is noted, repair or replace the engine harness green lead.

4. Check the detonation sensor module gray/white lead and bullet connector for secure attachment to the ECM gray/white lead and bullet connector. Repair or replace the gray/white lead and connectors as necessary.

5. Check both white/black detonation sensor module leads for secure attachment to each switch box bias terminal stud.

6. If corrosion or sealant is evident around the base of the sensor (**Figure 37**), remove the sensor and clean the threads of the sensor and cylinder head. Do not install any sealant on the threads of the sensor. Reinstall the sensor and torque it to 144 in.-lb. (16.2 N•m). Check the blue/white

sensor lead for secure attachment. Clean and tighten the connection as necessary.

NOTE
A digital voltmeter with an input imped-ance of 10 mega-ohms per volt is re-quired for the following Step. Using an incorrect meter could give inaccurate results and possibly damage electronic components.

7. Set a digital multimeter to the correct scale to read AC voltage in the 200 milli-volt range. Connect the meter black lead to the detonation sensor housing (ground). Connect the meter red lead to the detonation sensor terminal (white/blue lead).

CAUTION
*Do not run the engine without an ade-quate water supply and do not exceed 3000 rpm without an adequate load. Re-fer to **Safety Precautions** at the begin-ning of this chapter.*

8. Start the engine and allow it to reach operat-ing temperature. Reduce the engine speed to idle.
9. Note the meter reading. The meter should read approximately 75-120 milli-volts AC (0.075-0.120 VAC) at idle speed. As engine speed is increased, the voltage output will also increase.
10. Replace the sensor if the voltage readings are not within specification.
11. To check the detonation sensor module volt-age signal to the ECM, set the digital multimeter to the correct scale to read 0-8 volts DC. Connect the meter black lead to a good engine ground. Connect the meter read lead to the gray/white lead bullet connector between the ECM and detonation sensor module. Do not disconnect the bullet connector.

CAUTION
Do not run the engine without an ade-quate water supply and do not exceed 3000 rpm without an adequate load. Re-

*fer to **Safety Precautions** at the begin-ning of this chapter.*

12. Start the engine and allow it to reach oper-ating temperature. Reduce the engine speed to idle. Note the meter reading. The meter should read 300-700 millivolts DC (0.30 to 0.70 VDC) at idle speed.
13. Increase engine speed to 3000-4000 rpm (in gear) while noting the meter. The meter reading should be approximately 10 millivolts DC (0.01 volt DC).
14. If the readings are within specification the detonation sensor and module are functioning correctly. If the readings are higher than specifi-cation, preignition or detonation is occurring. Refer to **Table 6** to check for causes of preigni-tion and detonation. If the reading stays constant at approximately 6.6 volts DC at all engine speeds, replace the detonation sensor module.

CAPACITOR DISCHARGE MODULE (CDM) IGNITION (75-125 HP AND 65-80 JET [SERIAL NO. 0G438000-ON])

Description

This CDM ignition is an alternator driven, capacitor discharge module system with me-chanical spark advance. It is used on 75-125 hp and 65-80 Jet (serial No. 0G438000-on). Igni-

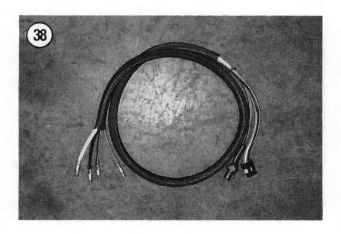

tion test harness part No. 84-825207A2 (**Figure 38**) is required to test the CDM system without damaging the wiring harness and connectors.

The major components (**Figure 39**) are the:

1. *Flywheel*—The flywheel inner magnet is for the trigger coil (timing information). The outer magnets are for the ignition stator and battery charging stator.

2. *Ignition stator (charge) coils*—The stator consists of one winding around 3 bobbins. The ignition stator is not grounded to the power head. The ignition stator provides power to the CDM modules. Stator output is always AC (alternating current) voltage.

NOTE
The ignition stator circuit must be complete from the stator to a CDM module and back to the stator through a different CDM module in order for the system to function.

a. *3-cylinder models*—The voltage return path for cylinder No. 1 CDM module is *either* cylinder No. 2 or No. 3 CDM module. The voltage return path for cylinder No. 2 and No. 3 CDM modules is through cylinder No. 1 CDM module. See **Figure 40**.

b. *4-cylinder models*—The voltage return path for cylinder No. 1 and No. 2 CDM modules is through *either* cylinder No. 3 or

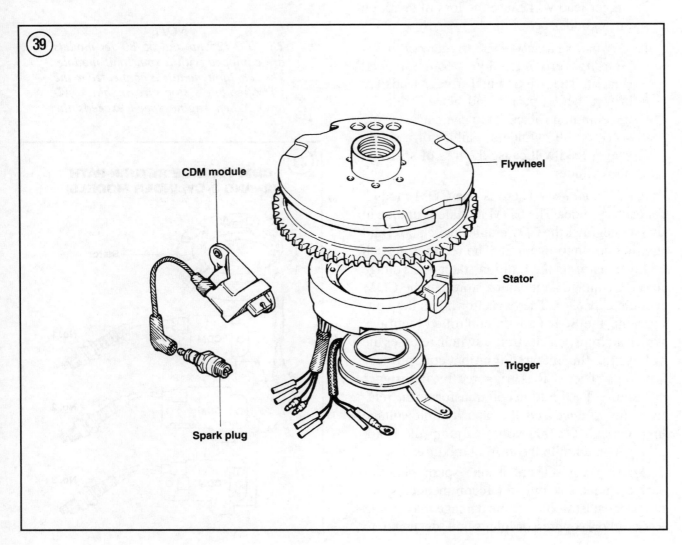

39

CDM module

Flywheel

Stator

Trigger

Spark plug

No. 4 CDM module. The voltage return path for cylinder No. 3 and No. 4 CDM modules is through *either* cylinder No. 1 or No. 2 CDM module. See **Figure 41**.

3. *Trigger coil*—The trigger coil tells the CDM modules when to fire. The trigger coil is rotated by mechanical linkage to change the trigger's position relative to the flywheel. This movement advances or retards the ignition spark timing.

   a. *3-cylinder models*—The trigger coil has 3 windings grounded by a common lead (black). The 3 individual trigger leads are brown, white and purple. Failure of the common (black) lead can cause erratic spark on all cylinders. Failure of a single trigger lead will cause the loss of spark on one cylinder.

   b. *4-cylinder models*—The trigger coil has 4 windings grounded by a common lead (black). The 4 individual trigger leads are brown, white, purple and blue. Failure of the common (black) lead can cause erratic spark on all cylinders. Failure of a single trigger lead will cause the loss of spark on one cylinder.

4. *CDM modules*—There is one CDM module for each cylinder. The CDM module is unique in that it integrates the CD module (switch box) and ignition coil into one unit. The rectifier in each CDM transforms the ignition stator AC voltage into DC voltage so it can be stored in the CDM module capacitor. The capacitor holds the voltage until the SCR (silicon controlled rectifier), which is simply an electronic switch, releases the voltage to the integral ignition coil primary windings. The SCR is triggered by the trigger coil signal. The ignition coil transforms the relatively low voltage from the capacitor into voltage high enough (45,000 volts) to jump the spark plug gap and ignite the air/fuel mixture.

5. *Spark plugs*—There is one spark plug for each cylinder. Use only the recommended spark plugs or catastrophic engine damage may result. Resistor or suppressor plugs are designed to reduce RFI (radio frequency interference) emissions that can cause interference with electrical accessories. Use the recommended RFI spark plug if RFI interference is suspected of causing interference or malfunction of electrical accessories.

6. *Stop circuit*—The stop circuit is connected to one end of the capacitor in each CDM module. Whenever the stop circuit is connected to ground the capacitor is shorted out and cannot store electricity. At this point there is no voltage available to send to the ignition coil windings and the ignition system ceases producing spark. The stop circuit must have an open circuit (to ground) in order for the engine to run.

NOTE
The 100-125 hp and 65-80 Jet models are equipped with a rpm limit module. The rpm limit module is connected to the CDM module's stop circuit (black/yellow). When engine speed exceeds the

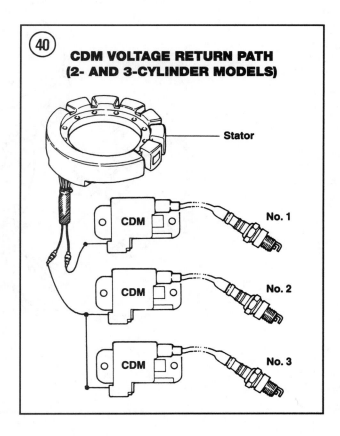

40 **CDM VOLTAGE RETURN PATH (2- AND 3-CYLINDER MODELS)**

Stator

CDM   No. 1

CDM   No. 2

CDM   No. 3

preprogrammed limit, the rpm limit module momentarily shorts the black/yellow lead to ground, limiting engine speed.

Troubleshooting

Refer to **Tables 16-18** for specifications and to the end of the book for wiring diagrams. Read *Troubleshooting Notes and Precautions (All Models)* at the beginning of the ignition section before continuing.

The recommended troubleshooting procedure is listed below.
1. Preliminary checks.
2. Ground circuit verification test.
3. Stop circuit isolation test.

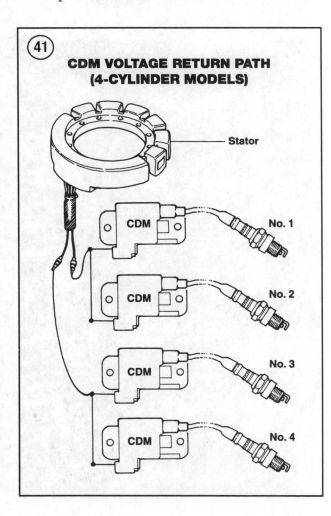

4. Ignition stator output test.
5. Ignition stator resistance test.
6. Trigger output test.
7. Stop circuit output test.
8. CDM module resistance test (optional).

CAUTION
Do not run the engine without an adequate water supply and do not exceed 3000 rpm without an adequate load. Refer to Safety Precautions at the beginning of this chapter.

WARNING
High voltage is present in the ignition system. Do not touch or disconnect ignition components while the engine is running.

NOTE
All CDM modules must be connected when troubleshooting the system. On 3-cylinder models, disconnecting cylinder No. 1 CDM module will cause a loss of spark on all cylinders. On 4-cylinder models, disconnecting any CDM module will cause a loss of spark on 2 of the remaining cylinders. Disconnecting either stator lead will always cause a loss of spark on all cylinders on all models.

Preliminary checks

1. Disconnect the spark plug leads from the spark plugs and install an air gap spark tester (part No. FT-11295 or equivalent) to the spark plug leads. Connect the alligator clip of the spark tester to a clean engine ground. Set the spark tester air gap to 7/16 in. (11.1 mm).
2. Make sure the safety lanyard is installed on the safety lanyard switch and the ignition switch is in the RUN position.
3. Crank the engine while observing the tester. If a crisp, blue spark is noted at each air gap, the ignition system is functioning correctly. If the engine will not start or does not run correctly, check the spark plugs and ignition timing. If the engine backfires or pops when attempting to

start, remove the flywheel and check for a sheared flywheel key. If no spark, weak spark or erratic spark is noted, continue with *Ground circuit verification* in the next section.

Ground circuit verification test

NOTE
*To prevent damage to the connector pins, use test harness adapter (part No. 84-825207A2) for all tests involving connection to the CDM modules and engine harness connectors (**Figure 42**, typical).*

1. Disconnect all of the CDM module plugs and connect the test harness adapter to the ignition wiring harness connector of the cylinder No. 1 CDM module. Do not connect the test harness to the CDM module. Calibrate an ohmmeter on the highest scale available. Connect one lead of the ohmmeter to a clean engine ground and connect the other ohmmeter lead to the black lead of the test harness. The ohmmeter must indicate continuity. If high resistance or no continuity is shown, repair or replace the engine harness black lead or CDM module connector as necessary.

2. Repeat Step 1 for each of the remaining CDM module harness connectors. Continue to Step 3 once all CDM module grounds are verified.

3. Verify the grounding of the ignition component mounting plate by connecting the one lead of an ohmmeter (calibrated on the highest scale) to a clean engine ground and the other lead to the ground lead terminal(s) (A, **Figure 43**, typical) on the ignition component mounting plate. The ohmmeter must indicate continuity. If high resistance or no continuity is shown, tighten, repair or replace the ground path(s) (leads and ground stud) as required.

Stop circuit isolation test

WARNING
To prevent accidental starting, remove the spark plug leads from the spark plugs

and install the spark gap tester (part No. FT-11295 or equivalent) to the spark plug leads. Connect the alligator clip of the spark tester to a clean engine ground.

1. Isolate the stop circuit from the CDM ignition system by disconnecting the black/yellow bullet connector. This connector is located in the tie-strapped bundle of leads near the voltage regulator (B, **Figure 43**, typical). Make sure that the black/yellow lead is not touching any other lead or ground.

2. Crank the motor and observe the spark tester. If good spark is now noted, a short to ground is present in the key switch, safety lanyard switch, rpm limit module (if equipped) or main engine harness black/yellow lead. Test, repair or replace the circuit or component as necessary.

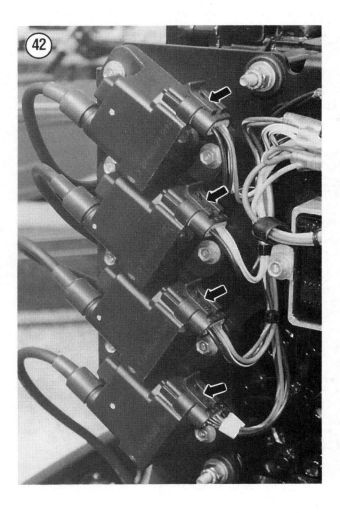

Ignition stator output test

> *WARNING*
> *To prevent accidental starting, remove the spark plug leads from the spark plugs and install the spark gap tester (part No. FT-11295 or equivalent) to the spark plug leads. Connect the alligator clip of the spark tester to a clean engine ground.*

1. Install the test harness (part No. 84-825207A2) between the cylinder No. 1 CDM module and the ignition harness. Set the multimeter to the 400 DVA scale, connect the meter red lead to the test harness green lead and the meter black lead to the test harness black lead.

2. Crank the engine while noting the meter reading. Refer to **Table 18** for specifications. The meter must indicate at least 100 DVA. Repeat the test for each remaining CDM module. If only one CDM module is below specification, replace that CDM module and retest. If all stator voltage readings are below 100 DVA, go to *Ignition stator resistance test*.

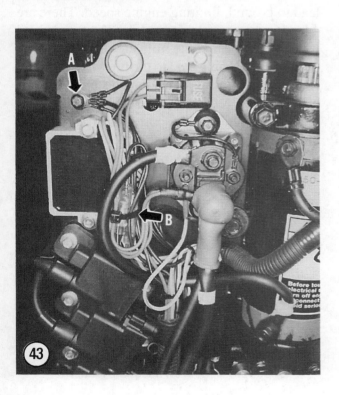

> *NOTE*
> *If all CDM ignition stator voltages are below specification **and** stator resistance tests are within specification, perform the **Stop circuit output test** in this section or replace each CDM module (one at a time) with a known good CDM module until the defective CDM module is located.*

Ignition stator resistance test

1. To check the resistance of the stator windings, disconnect the green/white and white/green stator lead bullet connectors. Calibrate an ohmmeter on the appropriate scale to read 660-710 ohms. Connect the red ohmmeter lead to the stator assembly white/green lead and the black ohmmeter lead to the stator assembly green/white lead. Note the meter reading. Resistance should be 660-710 ohms. If the resistance is not within 660-710 ohms, replace the stator. If the resistance is within specification, continue to Step 2.

2. To check the ignition stator windings for shorts to ground, calibrate an ohmmeter on the highest scale available. Connect one ohmmeter lead to a good engine ground and the other ohmmeter lead alternately to the ignition stator green/white and white/green leads while noting the meter. The meter must indicate no continuity. If continuity is noted, replace the stator coil assembly and retest spark output.

Trigger output test

> *NOTE*
> *Pin C of the CDM module connector is the trigger lead. The trigger leads on the ignition harness are color coded for each cylinder. Cylinder No. 1 uses a purple trigger lead, cylinder No. 2 uses a white trigger lead, cylinder No. 3 uses a brown trigger lead and cylinder No.4 uses a dark blue trigger lead. Connecting the wrong trigger lead to the wrong*

CDM module will cause the engine to fire out of time.

WARNING
To prevent accidental starting, remove the spark plug leads from the spark plugs and install the spark gap tester (part No. FT-11295 or equivalent) to the spark plug leads. Connect the alligator clip of the spark tester to a clean engine ground.

1. Install the test harness part No. 84-825207A2 between the cylinder No. 1 CDM module and the ignition harness.

2. Set the multimeter to the lowest DVA scale. Connect the meter red lead to the test harness white lead and the meter black lead to the test harness black lead. Crank the engine while noting the meter reading. The meter should indicate 0.2-2.0 DVA. If trigger voltage is below specification, replace the trigger and retest. If trigger voltage is above specification, replace the cylinder No. 1 CDM module. Repeat the test for each remaining CDM module.

NOTE
If a trigger voltage remains low after installing a new trigger, replace the CDM module that the low reading trigger lead is connected to.

Stop circuit output test

This procedure checks the internal stop circuit of each CDM module. Perform this test only after all of the preceding tests have been completed.

WARNING
To prevent accidental starting, remove the spark plug leads from the spark plugs and install the spark gap tester (part No. FT-11295 or equivalent) to the spark plug leads. Connect the alligator clip of the spark tester to a clean engine ground.

1. Install the test harness (part No. 84-825207A2) between the cylinder No. 1 CDM module and the ignition harness. Set the multimeter to the 400 DVA scale, connect the meter red lead to the test harness black/yellow lead and the meter black lead to the test harness black lead.

2. Crank the engine while noting the meter reading. Refer to **Table 18** for specifications. Each CDM module must show at least 100 DVA. Repeat the test for each remaining CDM module. Replace any CDM module with stop circuit output below 100 DVA and retest.

RPM Limit Module

Description

The 100-125 hp and 65-80 Jet models are equipped with a rpm limit module. The rpm limit module is connected to the CDM module's stop circuits (black/yellow). When engine speed exceeds the preprogrammed limit, the rpm limit module momentarily shorts the black/yellow lead to ground, limiting engine speed. There are 4 leads on the rpm limit module. The purple lead is power for the module from the key switch. The brown lead is connected to the brown trigger coil lead and is an rpm signal for the module. The black/yellow lead is connected to the CDM module's stop circuit and is shorted to ground by the module to control engine speed by switching the ignition system on and off. The black lead is the ground path for the module.

Troubleshooting the rpm limit module

Refer to the end of the book for wiring diagrams.

CAUTION
Do not run the engine without an adequate water supply and do not exceed 3000 rpm without an adequate load. Re-

fer to **Safety Precautions** at the beginning of this chapter.

NOTE
If the rpm limit module is suspected of causing a high speed misfire, first verify the operating speed of the engine using a shop tachometer. Also, make sure the boat's tachometer (if equipped) is correctly set. The high speed misfire may be due to the engine is over-speeding without the operators knowledge.

1. If the rpm limit module is suspected of causing a no-spark, weak spark, erratic spark or misfire while running, disconnect the rpm limit module black/yellow and brown engine harness bullet connectors at the rpm limit module.

2. Retest spark output or run the engine to the speed at which the misfire occurs. If the spark output is now satisfactory or the misfire is no longer present, the rpm limit module is defective and must be replaced.

3. If the rpm limit module is suspected of not functioning when needed, check the ground lead for secure attachment to the power head. Clean and tighten the connection as necessary to ensure a good ground path.

4. Disconnect the purple lead bullet connector from the rpm limit module. Connect the red lead of a voltmeter set to read 20 volts DC, to the engine harness purple lead bullet connector. Connect the black lead of the voltmeter to a good engine ground. When the ignition key is ON, the voltmeter should read within 1 volt of battery voltage. When the key is OFF, the voltmeter should read zero volts. If the meter reading is below specification (key ON), repair or replace the purple lead circuit from the key switch to the engine harness rpm limit module bullet connector.

5. Check the brown rpm limit module engine harness lead for continuity to the brown trigger coil lead by disconnecting the engine harness brown lead from the trigger coil bullet connector and the rpm limit module bullet

connector. Calibrate an ohmmeter on the R × 1 scale. Connect one ohmmeter lead to the trigger coil end of the engine harness brown lead and the other ohmmeter lead to the rpm limit module end of the engine harness brown lead. The ohmmeter should read continuity. If no continuity is noted, repair or replace the engine harness brown lead.

6. Check the black/yellow rpm limit module engine harness lead for continuity to each CDM module. Disconnect the engine harness black/yellow lead from the rpm limit module bullet connector. Disconnect the engine harness 4-pin connector at each CDM module. Connect the CDM test harness (part No. 84-825207A-2) to the cylinder No. 1 CDM module engine harness connector. Calibrate an ohmmeter on the R × 1 scale. Connect one ohmmeter lead to the rpm limit module end of the engine harness black/yellow lead and the other end to the CDM test harness black/yellow bullet connector. The ohmmeter should read continuity. If no continuity is noted, repair or replace the engine harness black/yellow lead between the rpm limit module and the cylinder No. 1 CDM module engine harness connector.

7. Repeat Step 6 for each CDM module engine harness connector.

8. Reconnect all leads when finished.

CAPACITOR DISCHARGE MODULE (CDM) IGNITION (225 AND 250 HP)

Description

This CDM ignition is an alternator driven, capacitor discharge module system with electronic spark advance. It is used on 1994-1997, 225 hp (carbureted and EFI [electronic fuel injection] models) and 250 hp EFI models. There are 2 versions of this system. Early model (1994-1995) CDM modules have a 3-pin connector (A,

Figure 44) and a separate ground lead (B, **Figure 44**). Later model (1996-1997) CDM modules have a 4-pin connector with an integrated ground (**Figure 45**). Ignition test harness part No. 84-825207A1 (3-pin models [**Figure 46**]) or part No. 84-825207A2 (4-pin models [**Figure 47**]) is required to test the CDM system without damaging the wiring harness and connectors.

This ignition system was designed to be most easily diagnosed with the Quicksilver DDT (digital diagnostic terminal). The DDT (**Figure 48**) is normally found only in Mercury or Mariner dealerships, where the investment can be justified. The DDT displays sensor input values and actuator output values as the ECM (electronic control module) sees them. The DDT and required adapter cables are listed in **Table 1**. If using the DDT for troubleshooting, refer to the manual included with the DDT software cartridge for troubleshooting procedures. DDT displayed sensor and actuator values are listed in **Table 20**. The troubleshooting procedure outlined in the following section requires only a multimeter and 1 or 2 adapter cables.

The major components are the:

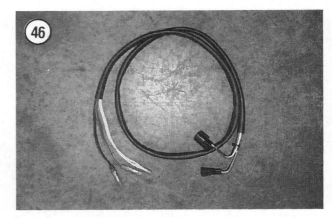

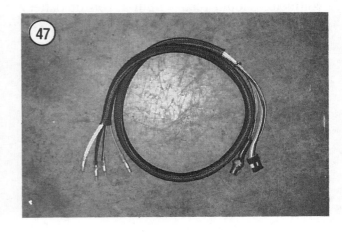

1. *Flywheel*—The magnets are for the ignition stator. The outer diameter, lower edge of the flywheel contains cast in encoding ribs (A, **Figure 49**) for the crankshaft position sensor (B, **Figure 49**).

2. *Crankshaft position sensor*—The crankshaft position sensor (CPS) detects the presence of the encoding ribs on the flywheel and sends a signal to the electronic control module (ECM). This signal tells the ECM crankshaft position and engine rpm. The air gap between the flywheel encoding ribs and the CPS must be set to 0.020-0.060 in. (0.51-1.52 mm).

3. *Ignition stator (charge) coils*—The stator consists of 6 windings around 6 bobbins. The ignition stator provides power to the CDM modules. Stator output is always AC (alternating current) voltage.

   a. *1994 models*—The 2 leads from each bobbin (12 total) are individually wired through a quick-disconnect connector to the main engine harness. One lead from each bobbin provides CDM module power, the other lead provides a backup trigger signal. The ignition stator is not grounded to the power head. This stator and ignition system features *Limp home mode*. If the ignition ECM should fail, the timing will be fixed at approximately 9° BTDC by the back-up trigger signal leads.

   b. *1995-1997 models*—One lead from each bobbin (6 total) is connected to engine ground (A, **Figure 50**). The 6 individual bobbin leads are connected to the main engine harness through a quick-disconnect connector (B, **Figure 50**). This stator does not feature a *Limp home mode*. If the ignition ECM fails, there will be no spark.

4. *CDM modules*—There is one CDM module for each cylinder. The CDM module is unique in that it integrates the CD module (switch box) and ignition coil into one unit. The rectifier in each CDM transforms the ignition stator AC voltage into DC voltage so it can be stored in the CDM

module capacitor. The capacitor holds the voltage until the SCR (silicon controlled rectifier), which is simply an electronic switch, releases the voltage to the integral ignition coil primary windings. The SCR is triggered by the ignition ECM. The ignition coil transforms the relatively low voltage from the capacitor into voltage high enough (45,000 volts) to jump the spark plug gap and ignite the air/fuel mixture.

5. *Spark plugs*—There is one spark plug for each cylinder. Use only the recommended spark plugs or catastrophic engine damage may result. Resistor or suppressor plugs are designed to reduce RFI (radio frequency interference) emissions that can cause interference with electrical accessories. Use the recommended RFI spark plug if RFI interference is suspected of causing interference or malfunction of electrical accessories.

6. *Stop circuit*—The stop circuit is connected to one end of the capacitor in each CDM module. Whenever the stop circuit is connected to ground the capacitor is shorted and cannot store electricity. At this point there is no voltage available to send to the ignition coil windings and the ignition system ceases producing spark. The stop circuit must have an open circuit (to ground) for the engine to run.

7. *Ignition ECM*—The ignition ECM (electronic control module) is the heart of the ignition system. The ignition ECM (**Figure 51**, typical) monitors input from the crankshaft position sensor (CPS), Throttle position sensor (TPS) and engine coolant temperature sensor (ECT). The ECM then calculates the correct timing for each cylinder. On EFI models, the ignition ECM interfaces with the fuel ECM to coordinate the firing of the fuel injectors. The ignition ECM contains a cold engine start, idle stabilizer, rpm limit, overheat protection, low oil level (carbureted models) and sensor failure warning programs.

> *NOTE*
> *EFI models incorporate the low-oil level and the water-in-fuel warning programs into the fuel ECM.*

a. *Cold start program*—The cold engine start program advances the ignition timing anytime the engine is below operating temperature and below 3000 rpm. The amount of timing advance is proportional to engine temperature and is in addition to normal spark advance. Once the engine reaches 146° Fahrenheit (60° Celsius) or 3000 rpm, all cold start timing advance is removed. On carbureted models, the fuel primer valve is also activated by the ECM during warm-up. On EFI models, all fuel injector pulse widths are increased (by the fuel ECM) to enrichen the air/fuel mixture during warm-up.

b. *Idle stabilizer program*—The idle stabilizer program advances the ignition timing anytime the idle speed drops to 475 rpm or lower. At 475 rpm, 3° advance is added. If the idle speed drops below 450 rpm, 6° advance is added. This advance is in addi-

tion to the normal spark advance. Once idle speed exceeds 475 rpm, all idle stabilizer advance is removed.

c. *Rpm limit program*—The rpm limit program retards ignition timing anytime engine speed exceeds 6000 rpm (carbureted models) or 6100 rpm (EFI models). Timing retard is gradual unless engine speed exceeds 6400 (carbureted models) or 6500 rpm (EFI models). If this occurs, timing is immediately retarded to 2° ATDC. When engine speed drops below the preprogrammed limit, timing advance returns to normal. The low-oil and overheat lamps will alternately flash and the warning horn will sound any time the rpm limit program is activated.

d. *Overheat warning program*—The overheat warning program retards ignition timing anytime the ECT (engine coolant temperature sensor) indicates 200° Fahrenheit (93° Celsius). Timing is retarded until engine speed is reduced (and limited) to approximately 3000 rpm. Timing advance will return to normal when the ECT indicates 190° Fahrenheit (88° Celsius). The overheat lamp will flash and the warning horn will sound continuously anytime the overheat warning program is activated.

e. *Low-oil warning program (carbureted models)*—The low oil warning program sounds the warning horn and illuminates the low-oil warning light anytime the switch in the engine mounted oil tank closes. When the oil switch closes, the horn will beep 4 times (at 1 second intervals), shut off for 2 minutes, then begin the warning cycle again. The warning light illuminates continuously until the ignition switch is turned off. This program does not affect ignition system operation.

f. *Sensor failure warning program*—The sensor warning program is designed to alert the boat operator to a TPS (throttle position sensor) or ECT (engine coolant temperature) sensor failure. This is very similar to the check engine light on a modern fuel injected car. If the ECM detects a failure in the TPS or ECT circuits, the low oil and overheat lamps (of the dash-mounted warning panel) will flash alternately and the warning horn will be activated. The warning will continue until the failed sensor is corrected or the ignition switch is turned off. The TPS and ECT sensors can be tested with a digital multimeter.

The ignition ECM on 1996-1997 EFI models incorporates the MAP (manifold absolute pressure) and IAT (intake air temperature) sensors into the sensor failure warning program. The IAT sensor can be tested with a digital multimeter; however, the MAP sensor can only be tested with the Quicksilver DDT (digital diagnostic terminal). If the fuel ECM is disconnected, the warning horn will be activated and the low-oil and overheat warning lamps will flash alternately (the engine will not run).

8. *Warning panel*—A multifunction warning panel is recommended for all models. The EFI model has 3 lights that allow easy identification of low oil tank level, engine overheat, engine over-speed, sensor malfunction or water in fuel situations. The carbureted model does not include the water in fuel light. See **Figure 52**.

The 1994 225 hp carbureted engine uses a shift interrupt circuit connected to the black/yellow stop circuit of the port bank of cylinders (No. 2, No. 4 and No. 6). A diode is used to separate the stop circuit from the starboard cylinder bank. When shift loads exceed the spring force of the shift interrupt switch, the diode protected black/yellow circuit is shorted to ground, shorting out the port bank of cylinders. The resultant drop in engine speed reduces shift effort. As soon as the shift is completed, the shift interrupt switch opens and all cylinders resume normal operation. The shift switch is mounted underneath the shift cable on the PORT side of the engine. See **Figure 53**.

Newer models (1995-on) use a shift interrupt circuit connected to the ignition ECM. When shift loads exceed the spring force of the shift interrupt switch, the ignition ECM green/yellow lead is shorted to ground. The ignition ECM then retards spark advance to 20° ATDC. The retarded timing reduces engine speed, reducing shift effort. As soon as the shift is completed, the shift interrupt switch opens and the ignition ECM returns spark advance to normal. If for some reason the shift interrupt switch stays closed for more than 2 seconds, the ignition ECM automatically returns spark advance to normal.

Troubleshooting

Refer to **Table 14** and **Table 15** for specifications and to the end of the book for wiring diagrams. Read *Troubleshooting Notes and Precautions (All Models)* at the beginning of the ignition section before continuing. If troubleshooting a timing control problem, go directly to the crankshaft position sensor tests and throttle position sensor tests. The recommended general troubleshooting procedure is listed below.

1. Preliminary checks.
2. Ground circuit verification test.
3. Stop circuit verification test.
4. Ignition ECM power test.
5. Tachometer circuit verification test.
6. Ignition stator output test.
7. Ignition stator resistance test.
8. ECM trigger signal output test.
9. Crankshaft position sensor test.
10. Throttle position sensor test.
11. CDM module resistance test (optional).

CAUTION
*Do not run the engine without an adequate water supply and do not exceed 3000 rpm without an adequate load. Refer to **Safety Precautions** at the beginning of this chapter.*

WARNING
*High voltage is present in the ignition system. **Do not** touch or disconnect ignition components while the engine is running.*

NOTE
Due to the ECM's idle stabilizer program, it is normal for timing to fluctuate

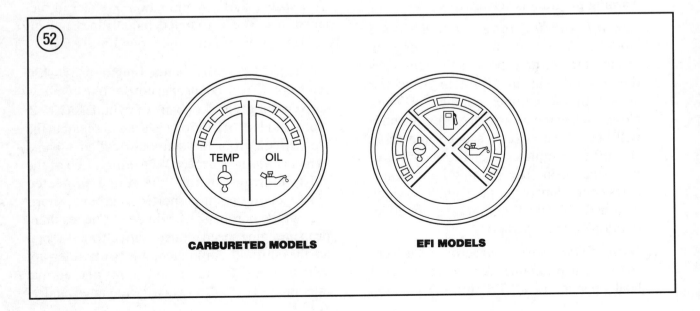

CARBURETED MODELS   EFI MODELS

several degrees at idle speed. Timing fluctuations at high speed could be caused by activation of the engine over-heat or rpm limit programs. Verify that engine temperature is normal and wide-open throttle speed does not exceeded the recommended range before attempting to troubleshoot a timing control problem.

Preliminary checks

1. Disconnect the spark plug leads from the spark plugs and install an air gap spark tester (part No. FT-11295 or equivalent) to the spark plug leads. Connect the alligator clip of the spark tester to a clean engine ground. Set the spark tester air gap to 3/8 in. (9.5 mm).

2. Make sure the safety lanyard is installed on the safety lanyard switch and the ignition switch is in the RUN position.

3. Crank the engine while observing the tester. If a crisp, blue spark is noted at each air gap, the ignition system is functioning correctly. If the engine will not start or does not run correctly, first make sure the correct spark plugs are installed and that they are in good condition. If the engine backfires or pops when attempting to start, remove the flywheel and check for a sheared flywheel key. If no spark, weak spark or

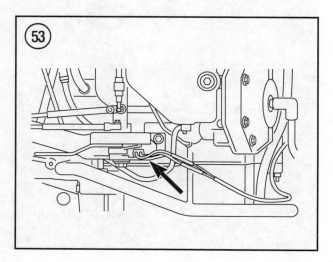

erratic spark is noted, continue with *Ground circuit verification* in the next section.

1994 models—If no spark is present on the PORT cylinder bank (No. 2, No. 4 and No. 6), go to *Troubleshooting the shift interrupter switch* and *Troubleshooting the shift interrupter switch harness diode* later in this section.

> *NOTE*
> *A CDM module that has a failed stop circuit (internally shorted to ground), will disable all of the remaining CDM modules. Disconnect each CDM module one at a time and retest spark output. When a CDM is disconnected and the other CDM modules start firing, the dis-connected CDM module is defective.*

Ground circuit verification test

1. *1994-1995 models*—Inspect each CDM module ground (black) lead (B, **Figure 44**) for a secure connection. Clean and tighten as necessary.

2A. *1996-1997 models*—Disconnect all of the CDM module plugs (**Figure 45**) and connect the test harness adapter (part No. 84-825207A2 [**Figure 47**]) to the ignition wiring harness connector of the cylinder No. 1 CDM module. Do not connect the test harness to the CDM module. Calibrate an ohmmeter on the highest scale available. Connect one lead of the ohmmeter to a clean engine ground, connect the other ohmmeter lead to the black lead of the test harness. The ohmmeter must indicate continuity. If high resistance or no continuity is shown, repair or replace the engine harness black lead or CDM module connector as necessary.

2B. *1996-1997 models*—Repeat Step 2A for each of the remaining CDM module harness connectors. Continue to Step 3 once all CDM module grounds have been verified.

3. Trace the black ground lead from the ignition ECM main plug-in connector to its power head ground. Inspect all ground leads at this point for

a secure connection. Clean and tighten as necessary.

4. Inspect all ignition ECM ground connections (A, **Figure 54**) on the ECM mounting plate. Clean and tighten as necessary. *EFI models—* Additionally check the fuel ECM ground (B, **Figure 54**).

Stop circuit verification test

1. Isolate the stop circuit from the CDM ignition modules by disconnecting all 6 CDM module connectors. Connect the appropriate test harness (**Table 1**) to the cylinder No. 1 CDM module engine wiring harness connector. Do not connect the test harness to the CDM module.

2. Calibrate an ohmmeter on the highest scale available. Connect one ohmmeter lead to a good engine ground and the other ohmmeter lead to the test harness stop circuit lead. The stop circuit lead is black on the 3-pin test harness and black/yellow on the 4-pin test harness.

3. Make sure the safety lanyard is installed on the safety lanyard switch and the ignition switch is in the RUN position. Note the meter reading.

4. The meter should indicate no continuity. If any other reading is noted, a short to ground is present in the key switch, safety lanyard switch or the main engine harness black/yellow lead. Test, repair or replace the circuit or component as necessary.

5. Turn the ignition switch to the OFF position or pull the lanyard from the safety lanyard switch. Note the meter reading.

6. The meter should indicate continuity. If no continuity is noted, an open circuit or high resistance is present in the key switch, safety lanyard switch or the main engine harness black/yellow lead. Test, repair or replace the circuit or component as necessary.

7. Repeat the test for the remaining CDM module engine wiring harness connectors.

Ignition ECM power test

The ignition ECM needs key-switched, battery positive voltage to operate. The ignition ECM receives power through the purple lead connected to the power head mounted single (or double) terminal block. To check that the ignition ECM is receiving voltage, proceed as follows:

1. Set a multimeter to the 20 volts DC scale. Connect the meter black lead to a good engine ground. Connect the meter red lead to the purple lead stud of the single (or double) terminal block.

2. Turn the ignition switch to the ON or RUN position. The meter should indicate within 1 volt of battery voltage. If the meter shows less voltage, an open circuit or high resistance is present in the circuit from the ignition switch, boat wiring harness purple lead or the engine wiring harness purple lead. Isolate and repair or replace the defective circuit.

> *NOTE*
> *The 1994 model year ignition ECM has electrical connectors at the end of each of the 2 ECM harness bundled leads. The*

1995-1997 model year ignition ECM has 1 main harness electrical connector mounted directly to the ignition ECM.

3. If the voltage reading is within 1 volt of battery voltage in Step 2, turn the ignition switch OFF and disconnect the engine wiring harness connector(s) from the ignition ECM.

4. Set the multimeter to the 20 volts DC scale. Connect the black lead to a good engine ground. Connect the red lead to the purple lead pin of the ignition ECM engine harness connector. Be careful not to damage the connector pin.

5. Turn the ignition switch to the ON or RUN position. The meter should indicate within 1 volt of battery voltage. If the meter shows less voltage, an open circuit or high resistance is present in the circuit from the purple lead stud of the single (or double) terminal block and the ignition ECM engine wiring harness connector. Repair or replace the circuit as necessary.

Tachometer circuit verification test

The tachometer signal is produced by the ignition ECM based on the crankshaft position sensor input. The tachometer signal is sent through the engine wiring harness to the main harness plug-in, through the boat wiring harness and finally into the dash mounted tachometer. On EFI models the engine wiring harness also sends the tachometer signal to the fuel ECM. If the tachometer signal lead (gray lead) is shorted to ground at any point, the engine will not run. To check the tachometer lead for continuity and short to ground, proceed as follows:

1. To check the engine wiring harness tachometer lead for continuity, disconnect the remote control harness from the main engine harness connector. Disconnect the main harness plug-in from the ignition ECM. On EFI models, also disconnect the main harness plug-in from the fuel ECM.

2. Calibrate an ohmmeter on the highest scale available. Connect one ohmmeter lead to the ignition ECM main harness connector gray lead. Connect the other ohmmeter lead to pin No. 5 of the main engine harness connector. The meter should indicate continuity. If no continuity is obtained, an open circuit or high resistance is present in the engine wiring harness gray lead. Isolate and repair or replace the circuit as necessary.

3. *EFI models*—Repeat Step 2 for the fuel ECM gray lead.

4. To check the engine wiring harness tachometer lead for a short to ground, calibrate an ohmmeter on the highest scale available. Connect one ohmmeter lead to a good engine ground. Connect the other ohmmeter lead to pin No. 5 of the main engine harness connector. The meter should indicate no continuity. If continuity is obtained, a short to ground is present in the engine wiring harness gray lead. Isolate and repair or replace the circuit as necessary.

5. To check the boat wiring harness for a short to ground, disconnect the remote control harness from the main engine harness connector.

6. Disconnect and insulate the gray lead from the tachometer. If the gray lead is connected to any accessories, disconnect and insulate the gray lead from all accessories.

7. Calibrate an ohmmeter on the highest scale available. Connect one ohmmeter lead to pin No. 5 of the boat wiring harness main plug in connector. Connect the other ohmmeter lead alternately to each of the remaining connector pins. The meter should indicate no continuity at each connector pin. If continuity is present at any pin, a short is present between the tachometer gray lead and the tested pin. Isolate, repair or replace the circuit or harness as necessary.

Ignition stator output test

WARNING
To prevent accidental starting, remove the spark plug leads from the spark plugs and install the spark gap tester (part No. FT-11295 or equivalent) to the spark

plug leads. *Connect the alligator clip of the spark tester to a clean engine ground.*

NOTE
*To prevent damage to the connector pins, use the appropriate test harness adapter (**Table 1**) for all tests involving connection to the CDM modules and engine harness connectors.*

1. Install the appropriate test harness (**Table 1**) between the cylinder No. 1 CDM module and the ignition harness. Set the multimeter to the 400 DVA scale.

2A. *1994-1995 models*—Connect the meter red lead to the test harness red lead and the meter black lead to the CDM module ground lead terminal at the power head.

2B. *1996-1997 models*—Connect the meter red lead to the test harness green lead and the meter black lead to the test harness black lead.

3. Crank the engine while noting the meter reading. Refer to **Table 15** for specifications. The meter must indicate at least 100 DVA. Repeat the test for each remaining CDM module. If any or all ignition stator voltage readings (at the CDM module) are below 100 DVA, go to *Ignition stator resistance test.*

NOTE
If one or more voltages in the preceding Step are below 100 DVA and all of the ignition stator resistance tests are satisfactory, replace the CDM module(s) on the low reading ignition stator circuit(s). Retest ignition stator output after replacing the module.

Ignition stator resistance test (1994 models)

1. To check the resistance of the ignition stator windings, disconnect the ignition stator to engine wiring harness quick-disconnect connector.

2. Calibrate an ohmmeter on the appropriate scale to read 990-1210 ohms.

NOTE
The 2 leads from each of the ignition stators' 6 bobbins must be tested in the following Step. Visually attempt to identify the color codes of each pair of leads from each of the 6 bobbins before proceeding.

3. Connect one ohmmeter lead to the ignition stator connector white/orange lead and the other ohmmeter lead to the ignition stator connector white/green lead. Note the meter reading. Resistance should be 990-1210 ohms. If the resistance is not within 990-1210 ohms, replace the stator. If the resistance is within 990-1210 ohms, continue to Step 4.

4. Repeat Step 3 for each of the following pairs of leads: White/red and green/red, white/green and green, white/blue and green/blue, white/black and green/black, white/yellow and green/yellow.

5. To check the ignition stator windings for a short to ground, calibrate an ohmmeter on the highest scale available. Connect one ohmmeter lead to a good engine ground and the other ohmmeter lead alternately to each of the ignition stator quick-disconnect connector pins while noting the meter. The meter must indicate no continuity at each pin. If continuity is noted, replace the ignition stator coil assembly and retest spark output.

Ignition stator resistance test (1995-1997 models)

1. To check the resistance of the ignition stator windings, disconnect the ignition stator-to-engine wiring harness connector (B, **Figure 50**).

2. Calibrate an ohmmeter on the appropriate scale to read 990-1210 ohms.

NOTE
One lead from each of the ignition stators' 6 bobbins is connected to engine ground. The other lead from each of the ignition stators' 6 bobbins is connected

to the ignition stator quick-disconnect connector. Each of the 6 bobbins must be tested in the following Step.

3. Connect one ohmmeter lead to a good engine ground and the other ohmmeter lead to the ignition stator connector green lead. Note the meter reading. Resistance should be 990-1210 ohms. If the resistance is not within 990-1210 ohms, replace the stator. If the resistance is within 990-1210 ohms, continue to Step 4.

4. Repeat Step 3 for each of the following ignition stator connector leads: Green/red, green/orange, green/blue, green/black and green/yellow.

ECM trigger output test

NOTE
The trigger leads on the engine harness are color coded for each cylinder. Cylinder No. 1 uses a white/blue trigger lead, cylinder No. 2 uses a white/orange trigger lead, cylinder No. 3 uses a white/black trigger lead, cylinder No. 4 uses a white/red trigger lead, cylinder No. 5 uses a white/yellow trigger lead and cylinder No. 6 uses a white/green trigger lead. Connecting the wrong trigger lead to the wrong CDM module will cause the engine to fire out of time.

WARNING
To prevent accidental starting, remove the spark plug leads from the spark plugs and install the spark gap tester (part No. FT-11295 or equivalent) to the spark plug leads. Connect the alligator clip of the spark tester to a clean engine ground.

1. Install the appropriate test harness (**Table 1**) between the cylinder No. 1 CDM module and the ignition harness. Set the multimeter to the 20 DVA scale.

2A. *1994-1995 models*—Connect the meter red lead to the test harness white lead and the meter black lead to a good engine ground.

2B. *1996-1997 models*—Connect the meter red lead to the test harness white lead and the meter black lead to the test harness black lead.

3. Make sure the safety lanyard is installed on the safety lanyard switch and the ignition switch is in the RUN position.

4. Crank the engine while noting the meter reading. The meter should indicate 2-10 DVA. If trigger voltage is below specification, note the cylinder number and voltage reading. Repeat the test for each remaining CDM module.

If trigger voltage is below specification on one CDM module, swap the leads with an adjoining CDM module and retest. If the low voltage reading follows the CDM module, replace that CDM module. If the low voltage reading does not follow the CDM module, verify the continuity of the trigger lead from the ECM to the suspect CDM module connector. If the trigger lead is good, replace the ECM.

If the trigger voltage is low or 0 on all CDM modules, go to *Crankshaft position sensor test* in the next section. If the crankshaft position sensor tests satisfactorily, replace the ECM.

Crankshaft position sensor test

The crankshaft position sensor provides the ignition ECM with engine speed and crankshaft position information. Its function is similar to trigger coil of other ignition systems. The ignition ECM must know the precise position of all the pistons and how fast the engine is running in order to fire the CDM modules accurately. The crankshaft position sensor can cause erratic spark, erratic timing or no spark at all if it is incorrectly adjusted or failed. If the boat's tachometer is operating normally, the crankshaft position sensor is functioning.

WARNING
To prevent accidental starting, remove the spark plug leads from the spark plugs and install the spark gap tester (part No. FT-11295 or equivalent) to the spark

plug leads. Connect the alligator clip of the spark tester to a clean engine ground.

1. Disconnect the negative battery cable and remove the flywheel cover.

2. Slightly rotate the flywheel to align an encoder rib (A, **Figure 49**) with the crankshaft position sensor (B, **Figure 49**).

3. Measure the gap between the flywheel encoder rib and the crankshaft position sensor with a feeler gauge. The gap should be 0.020-0.060 in. (0.51-1.52 mm). If the gap is not within specification, loosen the 2 sensor mounting screws (A, **Figure 55**) slightly and reset the gap to specification. Tighten the screws to 100 in.-lb. (11.3 N•m) and recheck the sensor air gap.

4. If the air gap was out of specification, recheck the ignition system for spark output after the air gap is correctly set. If the air gap was correct, continue to Step 4.

5. Disconnect the 2-pin crankshaft position sensor wiring harness connector (B, **Figure 55**). Calibrate an ohmmeter on the appropriate scale to read 900-1300 ohms. Connect one ohmmeter lead to each of the crankshaft position sensor leads. Replace the crankshaft position sensor if the reading is not within 900-1300 ohms.

6. Reinstall the flywheel cover. Reconnect the negative battery cable.

Throttle position sensor (TPS) test

Correct adjustment and function of the TPS (throttle position sensor) is critical to correct ignition system operation. The TPS adjustment is made with the throttle at the idle position. The wide-open throttle TPS specification is not adjustable. If the wide-open throttle stop is correctly set, the TPS idle voltage reading (setting) is correct, but the TPS wide-open throttle voltage reading is incorrect, replace the TPS. To prevent damage to the throttle position sensor and wiring harness, test harness part No. 84-825207A1 (**Figure 46**) is required. A digital multimeter is

recommended for this procedure, as most analog meters will not accurately read the low voltages specified. To test and adjust the TPS, proceed as follows:

> *NOTE*
> *On EFI models, any change to the idle speed air flow screw will require the TPS setting to be rechecked and adjusted as necessary. On carbureted models, the TPS setting has a direct effect on idle timing (and idle speed). On carbureted models, the TPS setting is changed (within the specified range) to obtain the specified idle speed.*

1. Disconnect the throttle cable from the engine throttle linkage.

2. Disconnect the engine wiring harness from the TPS. Connect test harness part No. 84-825207A1 (1, **Figure 56**) to the TPS and the engine wiring harness.

3A. *1994-1995 models*—Set the multimeter to the 20 volt DC scale. Connect the meter black lead to the test harness black lead. Connect the meter red lead to the white test harness lead.

3B. *1996-1997 models*—Set the multimeter to the 20 volt DC scale. Connect the meter black lead to the test harness white lead. Connect the meter red lead to the red test harness lead.

4. Verify that the throttle linkage is against the idle stop screw.

5. Turn the ignition switch to the ON or RUN position. The voltmeter should indicate 0.90-1.00 volts. If the reading is not as specified,

loosen the 2 adjustment screws (2, **Figure 56**) slightly and rotate the sensor to obtain 0.90-1.00 volt DC. Tighten the screws while holding the sensor in position. Recheck the meter reading. The meter must indicate 0.90-1.00 volts with the throttle at the idle stop position.

6. Slowly advance the throttle lever until it is against the wide-open throttle stop while noting the meter. The meter should indicate a smooth increase in voltage, without any sudden fluctuations. With the throttle lever held against the wide-open throttle stop, the meter should indicate 3.70-3.80 volts on carbureted models and 3.55-4.05 volts on EFI models. If the meter reading is not within specification, verify that the wide-open throttle stop is correctly set (Chapter 5). If the wide-open throttle stop is correctly set, but the wide-open throttle voltage is not correct, replace the throttle position sensor. If the meter shows voltage fluctuations instead of a smooth voltage transition as the sensor is rotated, replace the throttle position sensor.

Troubleshooting the shift interrupt switch (all models)

The 1994 225 hp carbureted engine uses a shift interrupt circuit connected to the black/yellow

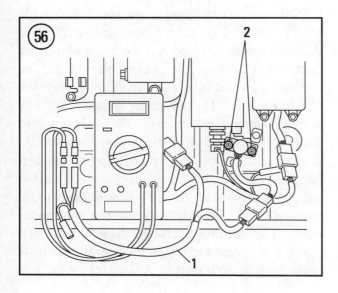

stop circuit of the port bank of cylinders (No. 2, No. 4 and No. 6). A diode is used to separate the stop circuit from the starboard cylinder bank. When shift load exceeds the spring force of the shift interrupt switch, the diode protected black/yellow circuit is shorted to ground, disabling ignition to the port bank of cylinders. The resultant drop in engine speed reduces shift effort. As soon as the shift is completed, the shift interrupt switch opens and all cylinders resume normal operation. The shift switch is mounted underneath the shift cable on the PORT side of the engine. On 1995 and later models, the shift switches are connected to the ignition ECM. When the shift switch activates, the ignition ECM green/yellow lead is shorted to ground. The ignition ECM then retards spark advance to 20° ATDC. The retarded timing reduces engine speed, reducing shift effort. As soon as the switch opens, the ignition ECM returns spark advance to normal. If the shift interrupt switch stays closed for more than 2 seconds, the ignition ECM automatically returns spark advance to normal. To test the shift interrupt switch, proceed as follows:

1. Calibrate an ohmmeter on the R × 1 scale. Disconnect both shift interrupt switch lead's bullet connectors (**Figure 53**) from the engine harness black and black/yellow (1994 models) or green/yellow (1995-1997 models) leads. Connect one ohmmeter lead to each of the shift interrupt switch leads.

2. Position the shift mechanism in the NEUTRAL position. The ohmmeter should read no continuity. Position the shift mechanism in the FORWARD gear position. The ohmmeter should read continuity. Replace the shift switch if the readings are not as specified.

Troubleshooting the shift interrupt switch harness diode (1994 models)

The shift interrupt switch harness diode, when failed in an open circuit, can cause the engine to continue to run on 3 cylinders after the ignition switch is turned OFF. If the diode fails shorted (in a closed circuit), the engine may stall when shifting out of gear as all six cylinders will quit sparking when the shift interrupt switch activates. If the diode or shift switch circuit is shorted to ground, the PORT bank of CDM modules will have no spark. If the diode is incorrectly installed (electrically backward) the engine may continue to run on 3 cylinders after the ignition switch is turned off.

The diode is connected to the black/yellow stop circuit leads of the PORT bank (No. 2, No. 4 and No. 6) CDM modules. Refer to the end of the book for wiring diagrams and **Table 3** for ohmmeter guidelines. To test the diode, proceed as follows:

1. Disconnect the black/yellow engine harness lead female bullet connector from the shift interrupt switch black lead. Disconnect the remote control main engine harness from the main engine harness connector.

2. Calibrate an ohmmeter on the appropriate scale to test a diode. Connect the ohmmeter red lead to the black/yellow engine harness lead female bullet connector and the ohmmeter black lead to pin No. 1 of the engine main harness connector plug. Note the reading. Reverse the ohmmeter lead and again note the reading.

3. The meter should indicate continuity in one polarity and no continuity in the other. If the diode shows continuity in both directions or no continuity in both directions, replace the diode with diode replacement kit, part No. 17461A5.

CDM MODULE
RESISTANCE TESTS (OPTIONAL)

Refer to **Table 14** for specifications.

Early model CDM modules (part No. 822779) use a 3-pin connector and a separate ground lead. Early modules use test harness part No. 84-825207A1. Late model CDM modules (part No. 827509) integrate the ground terminal into a new

4 pin connector. Late model CDM modules use test harness part No. 84-825207A2.

NOTE
*Specifications for each test vary depending on whether an analog or digital meter is used. Refer to **Table 11** for specifications.*

Testing Part No. 822779 CDM Module

1. Connect the test harness (part No. 84-825207A1) to the CDM, but **do not** connect the test harness to the ignition harness. This test is for the CDM module only. Calibrate the ohmmeter on an appropriate scale to read the specification (**Table 11**) for CDM ground lead to the white test lead. Connect the ohmmeter red lead to the CDM module ground (black) lead and the ohmmeter black lead to the white test harness lead. Note meter reading. Replace the CDM module if the resistance is out of specification.

NOTE
*The following 2 Steps are diode tests. The ohmmeter readings may be reversed depending on the polarity of the ohmmeter being used. As long as the first part of the test is opposite of the second part of the test, the test can be considered successful. Refer to **Table 14** for specifications.*

2. Calibrate an ohmmeter on the appropriate scale to test a diode. Connect the ohmmeter red lead to the test harness red lead and the black ohmmeter lead to the CDM module ground (black) lead. The ohmmeter should show a low reading. Reverse the ohmmeter leads. The ohmmeter should now show a high reading. Replace the CDM module if both tests show high or both tests show low readings.

3. Connect the ohmmeter red lead to the test harness red lead and the ohmmeter black lead to the test harness black lead. The ohmmeter should show a high reading. Reverse the ohmmeter leads. The ohmmeter should now show a low reading. Replace the CDM module if both tests show high or both tests show low readings.

4. Calibrate an ohmmeter on an appropriate scale to read the specification (**Table 14**) for the spark plug terminal to the CDM module ground. Connect the ohmmeter red lead to the spark plug lead (terminal inside spark plug boot) and connect the ohmmeter black lead to the CDM module ground (black) lead. Note the meter reading. Replace the CDM module if the resistance is out of specification.

Testing Part No. 827509 CDM Module

1. Connect the test harness (part No. 84-825207A2) to the CDM, but **do not** connect the test harness to the ignition harness. This test is for the CDM module only. Calibrate the ohmmeter on an appropriate scale to read the specification (**Table 14**) for pin A to pin C. Connect the ohmmeter red lead to the test harness black lead and the ohmmeter black lead to the test harness white lead. Note meter reading. Replace the CDM module if the resistance is out of specification.

NOTE
The following 2 Steps are diode tests. The ohmmeter readings may be reversed de-

*pending on the polarity of the ohmmeter being used. As long as the first part of the test is opposite of the second part of the test, the test can be considered successful. Refer to **Table 14** for specification.*

2. Calibrate the ohmmeter on the appropriate scale to test a diode. Connect the ohmmeter red lead to the test harness green lead and the black ohmmeter lead to the test harness black lead. The ohmmeter should show a low reading. Reverse the ohmmeter leads. The ohmmeter should now show a high reading. Replace the CDM module if both tests show high or both tests show low readings.

3. Connect the ohmmeter red lead to the test harness black/yellow lead and the ohmmeter black lead to the test harness green lead. The ohmmeter should show a low reading. Reverse the ohmmeter leads. The ohmmeter should now show a high reading. Replace the CDM module if both tests show high or both tests show low readings.

4. Calibrate an ohmmeter on an appropriate scale to read the specification (**Table 14**) for pin A to the spark plug lead. Connect the ohmmeter red lead to the test harness black lead and connect the ohmmeter black lead to the spark plug lead (terminal inside spark plug boot). Note the meter reading. Replace the CDM module if the resistance is out of specification.

DI (DIGITAL INDUCTIVE [200 DFI])

Description

The digital inductive ignition system is a battery driven, ECM (electronic control module) controlled system with electronic spark advance. Once the engine starts, a 60 amp belt-driven alternator provides all operating voltage for the system. This system is used exclusively on the 1997 model year 200 hp DFI (direct fuel injection).

This ignition system was designed to be diagnosed with the Quicksilver DDT (digital diagnostic terminal). The DDT (**Figure 57**) is

57

normally found only in Mercury or Mariner dealerships, where the investment can be justified. The DDT displays sensor input values and actuator output values as the ECM (electronic control module) sees them. The DDT and required adapter cables are listed in **Table 1**. If using the DDT for troubleshooting, refer to the manual included with the DDT software cartridge for troubleshooting procedures. DDT displayed sensor and actuator values are listed in **Table 20**.

Troubleshooting without the DDT extremely limits the components and systems that can be tested. If the procedure outlined in the following section does not isolate the failed component or system, a DDT will have to be obtained or the motor taken to a Mercury/Mariner dealership for diagnosis.

The major components are the:

1. *Flywheel*—The outer diameter, lower edge of the flywheel (A, **Figure 58**) contains cast-in encoding ribs for the crankshaft position sensor (B, **Figure 58**).

2. *Crankshaft position sensor*—The crankshaft position sensor (CPS) detects the presence of the encoding ribs on the flywheel and sends a signal to the electronic control module (ECM). This signal tells the ECM crankshaft position and engine rpm. The air gap between the flywheel encoding ribs and the CPS must be set to 0.030 in. (0.76 mm).

3. *Ignition coils*—There is one ignition coil (**Figure 59**) for each cylinder. The ignition coil transforms the relatively low voltage from the battery into voltage high enough (50,000 volts) to jump the spark plug gap and ignite the air/fuel mixture. The ignition coil positive (+) terminal has battery voltage present any time the ignition switch is on. The ECM opens the ignition coil negative (–) terminal to create spark.

4. *Spark plugs*—There is one spark plug for each cylinder. Use only the recommended spark plugs or catastrophic engine damage may result. The only recommended spark plug for the 200 DFI is the Champion RC10ECC.

5. *Stop circuit*—The stop circuit is connected to the ECM. Whenever the stop circuit is connected to ground, the ECM shuts off the ignition coils. The stop circuit must have an open circuit (to ground) for the engine to run.

6. *ECM*—The ECM (electronic control module) is the heart of the electrical, ignition and fuel systems. The ECM (C, **Figure 58**) monitors input from all of the sensors. The ECM then calculates the correct spark timing, fuel injector timing and direct injector timing for each cylinder. The ECM contains a cold engine start, idle stabilizer, rpm limit, overheat protection, water in fuel, low oil level, no oil flow and sensor failure warning programs. The ECM receives power from a main power relay. The main power relay is activated by the ignition switch.

   a. *Cold start program*—The cold engine start program increases all fuel injector pulse widths any time the engine is below operating temperature. The amount of fuel injec-

tor pulse width increase is proportional to engine temperature.

b. *Idle stabilizer program*—The idle stabilizer program controls the idle speed by advancing or retarding spark advance to maintain 625-675 rpm any time the TPS (throttle position sensor) indicates that the throttle control is in the idle position. Idle speed is not adjustable.

c. *Rpm limit program*—The rpm limit program is activated anytime engine speed exceeds 5800 rpm. If engine speed exceeds 6050 rpm, the ECM shuts the engine systems off until engine speed drops below the preprogrammed rpm limit, at which point engine operation returns to normal. The warning horn will sound continuously any time the rpm limit program is activated.

d. *Overheat warning program*—The overheat warning program retards ignition timing any time the ECT (engine coolant tempera-

ture sensor) indicates 221° Fahrenheit (105° Celsius). Timing is retarded until engine speed is reduced (and limited) to approximately 3000 rpm. Timing advance will return to normal when the ECT indicates normal temperature. The overheat lamp will flash and the warning horn will sound continuously anytime the overheat warning program is activated.

e. *Water-in-fuel warning program*—The water-in-fuel warning program sounds the warning horn and illuminates the water-in-fuel warning light anytime the water separating fuel filter accumulates enough water to short the sensor to ground. If the water sensor shorts to ground, the horn will beep 4 times (at 1 second intervals), shut off for 2 minutes, then begin the warning cycle again. The warning light illuminates continuously until the ignition switch is turned off. This program does not affect ignition system operation.

f. *Low-oil warning program*—The low oil warning program sounds the warning horn and illuminates the oil warning light anytime the switch in the engine mounted oil tank closes. When the oil switch closes, the horn will beep 4 times (at 1 second intervals), then shutoff for 2 minutes, then begin the warning cycle again. The warning light illuminates continuously until the ignition switch is turned off. This program does not affect ignition system operation.

g. *No-oil flow warning program*—The no-oil flow warning program sounds the warning horn and illuminates the oil light and check engine light. Engine speed will be reduced and limited to 3000 rpm. The ignition switch must be turned off to reset the warning program. If the no-oil flow warning program is activated, the motor should be stopped as soon as possible and the defect corrected. Operating the motor without oil flow will result in catastrophic engine failure.

h. *Sensor failure warning program*—The sensor warning program is designed to alert the boat operator to a sensor (such as TPS [throttle position sensor]), ignition coil or injector failure. This is very similar to the check engine light on a modern fuel injected car. If the ECM detects a failure in any of the sensor, ignition coil or injector circuits, the check engine lamp will illuminate. If one of the 2 throttle position sensors has failed, the warning horn will also sound. If both sensors fail, the engine will not run above idle speed. The ignition coils, injectors and the ECT (engine coolant temperature) sensor can be tested with an ohmmeter. All other sensors require the DDT to determine if they are functioning correctly.

NOTE
The MAP (manifold absolute pressure), IAT (intake air temperature) and knock sensor are installed and wired to the ECM, but are not used by the 1997 model ECM internal programming.

7. *Warning panel*—A multifunction warning panel is recommended for this model. The warning panel has 4 lights that allow easy identification of low oil tank level, no oil flow, engine overheat, sensor malfunction, ignition coil or injector malfunction and water in fuel situations. See **Figure 60**.

The 200 hp DFI models use a shift interrupt circuit connected to the ECM. When shift loads exceed the spring force of the shift interrupt switch, the ECM black/red lead is shorted to ground. The ECM then reduces engine speed by shutting off fuel to 3 cylinders, reducing shift effort. As soon as the shift is completed, the shift interrupt switch (**Figure 53**) opens and the ECM returns fuel delivery and engine speed to normal.

Troubleshooting

Refer to **Table 14** and **Table 15** for specifications and to the end of the book for wiring diagrams. Read *Troubleshooting Notes and Precautions (All Models)* at the beginning of the ignition section before continuing. The recommended general troubleshooting procedure is listed below.
1. Preliminary check.
2. Ground circuit verification test.
3. Stop circuit verification test.
4. ECM power test.
5. Ignition coil power test.
6. Ignition coil resistance test.
7. Crankshaft position sensor check.
8. ECT sensor resistance test.

CAUTION
*Do not run the engine without an adequate water supply and do not exceed 3000 rpm without an adequate load. Refer to **Safety Precautions** at the beginning of this chapter.*

WARNING
*High voltage is present in the ignition system. **Do not** touch or disconnect igni-*

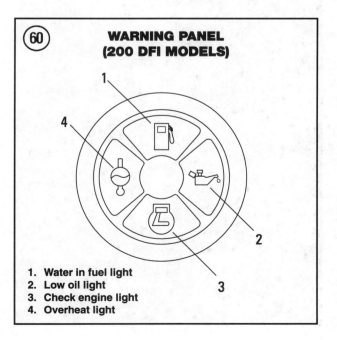

60 **WARNING PANEL (200 DFI MODELS)**

1. Water in fuel light
2. Low oil light
3. Check engine light
4. Overheat light

tion components while the engine is running.

Preliminary checks

> *NOTE*
> *Air gap spark testers are not recommended as the resultant RFI (radio frequency interference) can cause the ECM to malfunction and produce erroneous results.*

1. Install an inductive (clamp-on) timing light to the cylinder No. 1 (top starboard) spark plug lead.
2. Make sure the safety lanyard is installed on the safety lanyard switch and the ignition switch is in the RUN position.
3. Crank the engine while observing the timing light. If the timing light flashes brightly and consistently the ignition coil is firing correctly. Repeat the test for each remaining ignition coil. If all ignition coils are firing correctly but the engine will not start or does not run correctly, first make sure the correct spark plugs are installed and that they are in good condition. If the engine backfires or pops when attempting to start, remove the flywheel and check for a sheared flywheel key. If the timing light does not flash, flashes weakly or erratically, continue with *Ground circuit verification* in the next section.

Ground circuit verification test

Trace the black and black/tan ground leads from each of the 3 ECM plug-in connectors (1-3, **Figure 61**) to the power head. Inspect all ground

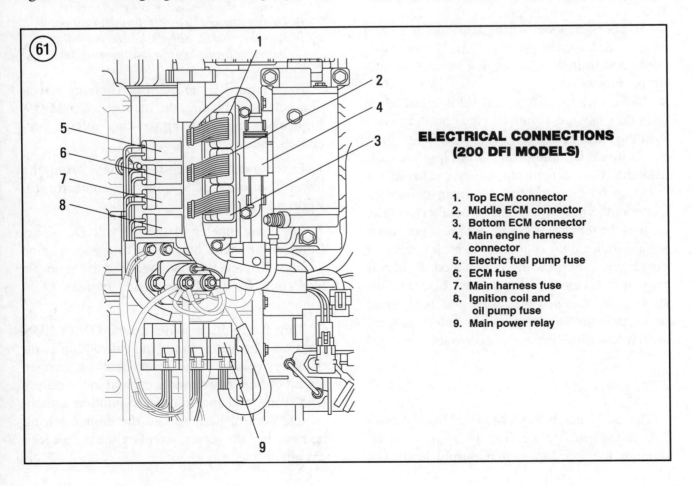

ELECTRICAL CONNECTIONS (200 DFI MODELS)

1. Top ECM connector
2. Middle ECM connector
3. Bottom ECM connector
4. Main engine harness connector
5. Electric fuel pump fuse
6. ECM fuse
7. Main harness fuse
8. Ignition coil and oil pump fuse
9. Main power relay

leads at these attachment points for a secure connection. Clean and tighten as necessary.

Stop circuit verification test

1. To check the engine wiring harness stop circuit lead for a short to ground, disconnect the remote control harness from the main engine harness connector (4, **Figure 61**). Then, disconnect the engine harness plug-in from the lowest (bottom) ECM plug-in connector (3, **Figure 61**).
2. Calibrate an ohmmeter on the highest scale available. Connect one ohmmeter lead to a good engine ground. Connect the other ohmmeter lead to pin No. 1 of the main engine harness connector. The meter should indicate no continuity. If any other reading is obtained, a short to ground is present in the engine wiring harness black/yellow lead. Repair or replace the circuit as necessary.
3. To check the boat wiring harness for a short to ground, leave the remote control harness disconnected from the main engine harness connector (4, **Figure 61**).
4. Make sure the safety lanyard is installed on the safety lanyard switch and the ignition switch is in the RUN position.
5. Calibrate an ohmmeter on the highest scale available. Connect one ohmmeter lead to pin No. 1 of the boat wiring harness main connector. Connect the other ohmmeter lead alternately to each of the remaining connector pins. The meter should indicate no continuity at each connector pin. If any other reading is obtained, a short is present between the boat harness black/yellow stop circuit lead and the tested pin. Test, repair or replace the ignition switch, safety lanyard switch or wiring harness as necessary.

ECM power test

The ECM needs key-switched, battery positive voltage to operate. The ECM is activated through the ignition switch purple lead. The ECM then controls the main power relay by grounding the main power relay yellow/purple lead. When the main power relay is activated, battery voltage from the starter solenoid positive terminal is relayed to the ignition coil (and oil pump) and fuel pump fuses. Power is also relayed back to the ECM through the ECM driver fuse. This fuse supplies protected working voltage and current to the ECM. The ECM will shut off the main power relay after 3 seconds if the engine is not cranked or started. The ECM (when activated) continuously monitors the crankshaft position sensor signal to determine if main power relay should be engaged. See **Figure 61** for fuse identification and function.

CAUTION
When measuring voltage or resistance at the ECM connectors, be careful not to damage the connector pins or sockets. Do not attempt to insert the meter probe into the socket. Simply touch and hold the meter probe against the pin or socket.

To determine if the ECM is receiving activation voltage, engaging the main power relay (9, **Figure 61**) and receiving working voltage, proceed as follows:

1. Disconnect the engine harness from the lower (bottom) ECM plug-in connector (3, **Figure 61**).

2. Set a multimeter to the 20 volt DC scale. Connect the meter black lead to a good engine ground. Connect the meter red lead to the purple lead (pin No. 1) of the engine harness ECM connector.

3. Turn the ignition switch to the ON or RUN position. The meter should indicate within 1 volt of battery voltage. If the meter reads less, an open circuit or high resistance is present in the purple lead from (and including) the ignition switch, remote control harness and the engine wiring harness. Isolate, repair or replace the purple lead circuit.

4. Reconnect the engine harness to the lower (bottom) ECM connector.

5. Remove the ECM fuse (6, **Figure 61**) from its protective cover and disconnect the fuse from the fuse holder. Inspect the fuse for evidence of failure. Replace the fuse if there is any question of its integrity.

6. Set a multimeter to the 20 volt DC scale. Connect the meter black lead to a good engine ground. Connect the meter red lead to the ECM fuse holder red/white lead.

NOTE
If the engine is not cranked or started, the ECM will turn the main power relay off after 3 seconds. The meter reading must be noted before this time elapses.

7. Turn the ignition switch to the ON or RUN position. The meter should indicate within 0.5 volt of battery voltage. If the meter reading is as specified, proceed to Step 12. If the meter reading is less than specified, proceed to Step 8.

8. Unplug the main power relay (9, **Figure 61**) from the engine wiring harness. Set a multimeter to the 20 volt DC scale. Connect the meter black lead to a good engine ground. Connect the meter red lead to the red lead of the engine wiring harness main power relay connector. The meter should indicate within 0.5 volt of battery voltage. If the meter shows less voltage, an open circuit or high resistance is present in the red lead from the starter solenoid battery positive terminal to the main power relay connector. If the meter shows the specified voltage, proceed with Step 9.

9. Move the meter red lead to the purple lead terminal of the engine wiring harness main power relay connector. Turn the ignition switch to the ON or RUN position. The meter should indicate within 1 volt of battery voltage. If the meter shows less voltage, an open circuit or high resistance is present in the purple lead from (and including) the ignition switch to the main power relay connector. Isolate, repair or replace the

circuit or component as necessary. If the meter shows the specified voltage, replace the main power relay and repeat Steps 5-7. If after replacing the main power relay, voltage is still below specification, continue with Step 10.

10. Unplug the main power relay (9, **Figure 61**) from the main engine wiring harness. Calibrate an ohmmeter on the R × 1 scale. Connect one ohmmeter lead to the red/white lead of the ECM fuse holder (6, **Figure 61**) and the other ohmmeter lead to the red/white lead of the main power relay connector. The meter should indicate continuity. If no continuity is noted, repair or replace the red/white lead from the main power relay connector to the ECM fuse holder.

11. If the voltage at the ECM fuse holder red/white lead is still not within specification, test the yellow/purple lead from the main power relay connector to the lower (bottom) ECM connector (3, **Figure 61**) for continuity with an ohmmeter. If the lead has no continuity, repair or replace the yellow/purple lead and repeat Steps 1-3. If the yellow/purple lead has continuity, the ECM has an internal defect and must be replaced. Consult a Mercury/Mariner dealer for ECM replacement policies and procedures. It is extremely rare for an ECM to fail. Repeat Steps 5-7 after ECM replacement.

12. To verify the continuity of the red/blue leads from the ECM fuse holder to the ECM connector, unplug the engine wiring harness from the lower (bottom) ECM connector. Unplug the ECM fuse from the fuse holder. Calibrate an ohmmeter on the R × 1 scale.

13. Connect one ohmmeter lead to the red/blue lead of the ECM fuse holder and the other lead alternately to the ECM connector pin No. 1 and pin No. 2 (red/blue leads). The meter should show continuity for both leads. If no continuity is noted, repair or replace the circuit between the ECM fuse holder red/blue lead and the middle (center) ECM plug-in connector pins No. 1 and No. 2.

3

Ignition coil power test

The ignition coils receive power from the main power relay (9, **Figure 61**) and the ignition coil (and oil pump) fuse (8, **Figure 61**). This circuit is composed of a red/yellow lead for each ignition coil. Any time the ignition switch is on, battery voltage should be present at the red/yellow lead of each ignition coil connector. Do not test the ignition coil power unless the ECM power tests have been successfully completed.

To test the ignition coil power, proceed as follows:

1. Set a multimeter to the 20 volt DC scale. Connect the meter black lead to a good engine ground.

2. Disconnect the cylinder No. 1 ignition coil wiring harness connector by pressing in on the metal clip (**Figure 62**) while gently pulling the connector from the ignition coil. Connect the meter red lead to the red/yellow pin of the ignition coil lead harness connector. Be careful not to damage the wiring harness connector or pins.

3. Turn the ignition switch to the ON or RUN position. The meter should indicate within 1 volt of battery voltage. If the meter indicates less voltage, an open circuit or high resistance is present in the circuit from the main power relay red/white lead to the ignition coil (and oil pump) fuse, the ignition coil (and oil pump) fuse or the red/yellow lead from the fuse to the ignition coil connector. Proceed with Step 4 to isolate the defect. If the meter indicates the specified voltage, repeat the test for the remaining ignition coils.

4. Turn the ignition switch to the OFF or STOP position. Unplug the main power relay (9, **Figure 61**) and the ignition (and oil pump) fuse (8, **Figure 61**). Inspect the fuse for evidence of failure. Replace the fuse if there is any question of its integrity.

5. Calibrate an ohmmeter on the R × 1 scale. Connect one ohmmeter lead to the red/white lead of the main power relay connector and the other

ohmmeter lead to the red/white lead of the ignition coil (and oil pump) fuse holder. The meter should indicate continuity. If no continuity is noted, repair or replace the red/white lead between the main power relay connector and the ignition coil fuse holder. Repeat Steps 1-3. If the meter indicates continuity, proceed with Step 6.

6. Connect one lead of the ohmmeter, still calibrated on the R × 1 scale, to the red/yellow lead of the ignition coil (and oil pump) fuse holder. Connect the other ohmmeter lead to the red/yellow lead of the ignition coil connector being tested. The meter should indicate continuity. If no continuity is noted, repair or replace the red/yellow lead between the ignition coil (and oil pump) fuse holder and the ignition coil connector being tested.

Ignition coil resistance test

The ignition coil primary resistance can be tested with an ohmmeter. However, there are no

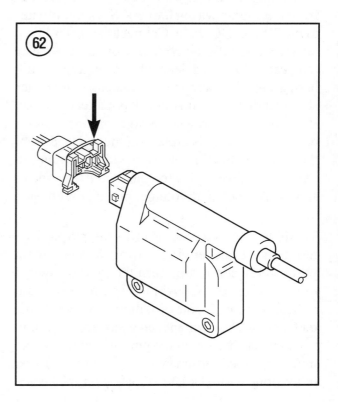

specifications for secondary resistance. If an ignition coil is not firing, swap the ignition coil with an ignition coil that is firing. If the problem follows the ignition coil, the coil is defective and must be replaced. If the problem stays at the original location, the problem is in the ECM or wiring harness. To test the ignition coil primary resistance, proceed as follows:

1. Disconnect the suspect ignition coil from the wiring harness connector by pressing in on the metal clip (**Figure 62**) while gently pulling the connector from the ignition coil.

2. Calibrate an ohmmeter on the lowest scale available. Connect one ohmmeter lead to each of the ignition coil connector terminals. The meter should indicate 0.66-0.68 ohms. Replace the ignition coil if any other reading is obtained.

3. Repeat the test for the remaining suspect ignition coils.

Crankshaft position sensor check

The crankshaft position sensor provides the ECM with engine speed and crankshaft position information. Its function is similar to a trigger coil of other ignition systems. The ECM must know the precise position of all the pistons and how fast the engine is running to fire the ignition coils accurately. The crankshaft position sensor can cause erratic spark, erratic timing or no spark at all if it has failed or is incorrectly adjusted. The DDT (Digital Diagnostic Terminal) will indicate

if the crankshaft position sensor is functioning correctly. If the boat's tachometer is operating normally, the crankshaft position sensor is functioning.

1. Disconnect the negative battery cable and remove the flywheel cover.

2. Slightly rotate the flywheel to align an encoder rib (A, **Figure 63**) with the crankshaft position sensor (B, **Figure 63**).

3. Measure the gap between the flywheel encoder rib and the crankshaft position sensor with a feeler gauge. The gap should be 0.030 in. (0.76 mm). If the gap is not within specification, loosen the 2 sensor mounting screws slightly and reset the gap to specifications. Tighten the screws to 100 in.-lb. (11.3 N•m) and recheck the sensor air gap.

4. Recheck the ignition system for spark output after the air gap is correctly set.

5. Reinstall the flywheel cover. Reconnect the negative battery cable.

ECT sensor resistance test

The ECT (engine coolant temperature) sensor provides the ECM with engine (coolant) temperature data. If the ECT reads above 221° Fahrenheit (105° Celsius), the ECM will retard ignition timing to limit engine speed to approximately 3000 rpm. Refer to **Table 20** for ECT sensor resistance values. The ECT sensor (A, **Figure 64**) is located on the top of the starboard cylinder head. To test the ECT sensor, proceed as follows:

1. Disconnect the two tan/black ECT sensor leads (B, **Figure 64**) from the wiring harness. Calibrate an ohmmeter on the appropriate scale to read the engine temperature as listed in **Table 20**.

NOTE
The temperature of the engine must be accurately determined before the ECT sensor can be tested.

2. Measure the temperature of the cylinder head with a pyrometer or allow the engine to cool to ambient temperature. Connect one ohmmeter lead to each of the tan/black ECT sensor leads. Note the meter reading and compare to specification. If the reading is not within specification, the ECT sensor must be replaced. If the reading is within specification, continue to Step 3.

3. Remove the sensor from the cylinder head (with ohmmeter still connected) and immerse the sensing element into a glass of crushed ice and water while noting the meter reading. The reading should smoothly increase as the sensing element cools. If the reading does not increase to specification (**Table 20**), replace the ECT sensor. If the reading is within specification, continue to Step 4.

4. Calibrate an ohmmeter on the ohms scale available. Connect one ohmmeter lead to the black ECT sensor lead. Connect the other ohmmeter lead alternately to each of the tan/black ECT sensor leads. The meter must indicate no continuity at each lead. If continuity is noted, replace the ECT sensor.

FUEL SYSTEM

Outboard owners often assume the carburetor(s) is(are) at fault when the engine does not run properly. While fuel system problems are not uncommon, carburetor adjustment is seldom the solution. In many cases, adjusting the carburetor only compounds the problem by making the engine run worse.

Never attempt to adjust the carburetor(s) idle speed and idle mixture until the following conditions are ensured:

a. The ignition timing is correctly adjusted.

b. The engine throttle and ignition linkage is correctly synchronized and adjusted.

c. The engine is running at normal operating temperature.

d. The outboard is in the water, running in FORWARD gear with the correct propeller installed.

If the engine appears to be running lean or starving for fuel, fuel system troubleshooting should be divided into determining whether the boat fuel system or the engine fuel system is causing the problem. Engines that appear to be running rich or receiving excessive fuel, usually have a problem located in the engine fuel system, not the boat fuel system.

The boat fuel system consists of the fuel tank, fuel vent line and vent fitting, the fuel pickup tube and antisiphon valve, the fuel distribution lines, boat mounted water separating fuel filter (recommended) and the primer bulb.

The typical carbureted engine fuel system consists of an engine fuel filter, crankcase pulse driven fuel pump, carburetor(s), primer valve and the necessary lines and fittings.

An EFI (electronic fuel injection) engine's fuel system consists of a crankcase pulse driven fuel pump, a water separating fuel filter (with

water sensor), a vapor separator tank with integral final fuel filter and high pressure electric fuel pump, fuel rail(s) that house the 6 fuel injectors, a fuel pressure regulator on the return line to the vapor separator and the necessary high and low pressure lines and fittings. Fuel flow diagrams are located later in this chapter.

The 200 hp DFI (direct fuel injection) fuel system consists of a crankcase driven fuel pump, a water separating fuel filter (with water sensor), a vapor separator tank with integral final fuel filter and high-pressure electric fuel pump, 2 air/fuel rails that house the 6 fuel injectors, a fuel pressure regulator in the port rail, a fuel cooler and the necessary high- and low-pressure lines and fittings. A water screen is installed in the water outlet fitting at the power head adapter plate to filter the water going to the fuel cooler. The screen should be removed and cleaned every 100 hours of operation or once a season. Air and fuel flow diagrams are located later in this chapter.

The 200 hp DFI (direct fuel injection) air system consists of a belt driven, water cooled air compressor with an air inlet filter in the flywheel cover, an air restrictor in the air compressor inlet line (must be installed at altitudes below 5000 feet), the same air/fuel rails mentioned in the previous paragraph (that also house the 6 DFI injectors), an air pressure regulator in port rail, a tracker diaphragm in the starboard rail (dampens pressure pulses between the air and fuel chambers) and the necessary hoses, high-pressure lines and fittings. The excess air from the air pressure regulator is dumped into the exhaust at the power head adapter plate. The compressor air inlet filter should be replaced every 100 hours or once a season; the filter cannot be cleaned. Air and fuel flow diagrams are located later in this chapter.

Troubleshooting

The first step is to make sure that fresh fuel is present in the fuel tank. If the fuel is stale or sour, drain the fuel tank and dispose of the fuel in an

approved manner. Clean all fuel filters and flush all fuel lines to remove all traces of the stale or sour fuel. Inspect all fuel lines for evidence of leakage or deterioration. Replace any suspect components. Make sure the fuel tank vent is open and not restricted. Refer to Chapter Six for component removal, rebuild and replacement procedures and component illustrations.

NOTE
When troubleshooting the fuel system, connect a substitute fuel tank (and fuel line) filled with fresh fuel to the engine. If the symptom is eliminated, the problem is in the original fuel tank and lines. If the symptom is still present, the problem is located on the engine.

All models use a mechanical fuel pump (or 2) driven by crankcase pressure and vacuum pulses. If the cylinder(s) that drives the fuel pump(s) fails, the fuel pump(s) cannot operate. Check the cranking compression before continuing. If the boat is equipped with a permanent fuel system make sure the fuel tank vent line is not kinked or obstructed. If all visual checks are satisfactory continue with the mechanical fuel pump pressure and vacuum tests.

Mechanical fuel pump pressure and vacuum tests

CAUTION
*Do not run the engine without an adequate water supply and do not exceed 3000 rpm without an adequate load. Refer to **Safety Precautions** at the beginning of this chapter.*

NOTE
The 275 hp is equipped with 2 mechanical fuel pumps connected in series. Check the vacuum into the first pump and the pressure out of the second pump. Rebuild both pumps if the pressure output is not within specification.

1A. *Permanent fuel tank*—Make sure the fuel vent fitting and vent line are not obstructed.

1B. *Portable fuel tank*—Open the fuel tank vent to relieve any pressure that may be present and verify that the tank is no more than 24 in. (61 cm) below the level of the fuel pump.

2. Disconnect the fuel inlet hose from the fuel pump. See **Figure 65**.

3. Connect a combination vacuum and fuel pressure gauge between the fuel pump and the inlet line using a T-fitting, a short piece of clear vinyl hose and the appropriate fittings and clamps. See **Figure 66**.

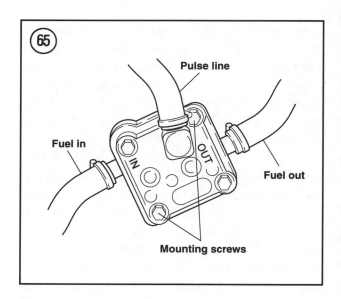

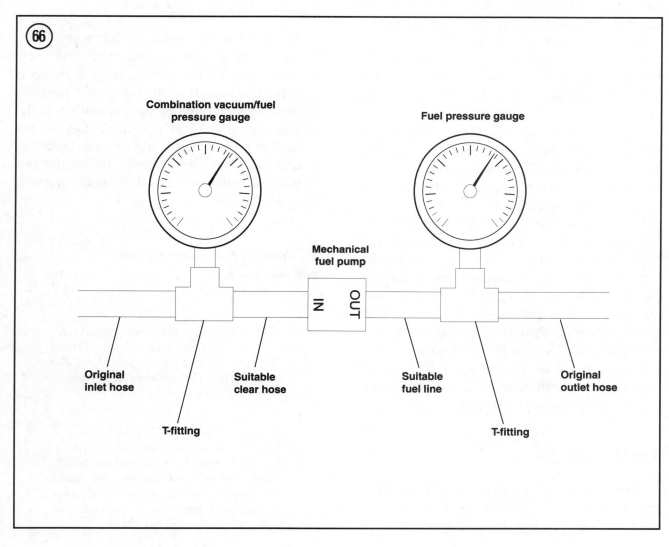

4A. *Carbureted models*—Disconnect the fuel pump output hose that leads to the carburetor(s). See **Figure 65**.

4B. *EFI and DFI models*—Disconnect the fuel pump output hose that leads to engine mounted water separating fuel filter. See **Figure 65**.

5. Connect a fuel pressure gauge between the fuel pump and the output line using a T-fitting and appropriate fuel line and clamps. See **Figure 66**. Squeeze the primer bulb and check for leaks.

> *CAUTION*
> *Do not run the engine without an adequate water supply and do not exceed 3000 rpm without an adequate load. Refer to **Safety Precautions** at the beginning of this chapter.*

6. Start the motor and allow it to reach operating temperature. Refer to **Table 22** for fuel pump specifications. Run the engine in FORWARD gear to the speed listed in **Table 22**. Observe the fuel pressure gauge, vacuum gauge and clear hose at each engine speed.

7. If air bubbles are visible in the clear hose at any of the test speeds, check the fuel supply line back to the pickup tube in the fuel tank for loose fittings, loose clamps, defective primer bulb, damaged filters or any problems that would allow air to leak into the fuel line. The fuel pump cannot develop the specified pressure if air is present. Correct any problems and retest.

8. If no air bubbles are visible in the clear hose and the vacuum gauge reading does not exceed 4 in. Hg (13.5 kPa), the fuel supply system is in satisfactory condition. If the fuel pressure is below specification, repair or replace the fuel pump(s) as necessary.

9. If no air bubbles are visible in the clear hose and the vacuum did not exceed 4 in. Hg (13.5 kPa) and fuel pressure is within specification, the mechanical fuel pump and fuel supply system are not the problem.

10A. *Carbureted models*—Inspect the fuel lines and fittings from the fuel pump(s) to the carburetor(s) for leaks, deterioration, kinks and blockages. Correct any problems found. If the lines and fittings are in satisfactory condition and the problem is still believed to be fuel related, the carburetor(s) must be rebuilt and adjusted. On multi-carburetor engines, it is recommended that all carburetors be serviced, even if only one is malfunctioning at this time.

10B. *EFI models*—Go to *EFI fuel system troubleshooting* in this chapter.

10C. *200 DFI models*—Go to *DFI air/fuel system troubleshooting* in this chapter.

FUEL PRIMER AND ENRICHMENT SYSTEMS

Fuel Primer Valve (75-200 and 275 hp Carbureted Models)

Fuel primer valves (**Figure 67**) have replaced choke valves as the primary means of enrichening the air/fuel mixture for cold starting. The fuel primer valve typically enrichens the air/fuel mixture by flowing fuel directly into the intake manifold or carburetor(s). If the fuel is injected into the carburetor(s), it is injected on the intake manifold side of the throttle plate(s). The fuel primer valve is an electrical solenoid valve that simply opens and closes. The fuel primer valve does not pump fuel; fuel must be supplied by the primer bulb or engine fuel pump. When electricity is applied to the yellow/black lead, the solenoid is energized and the fuel valve opens. An internal spring forces the valve closed when the solenoid is not energized. The fuel primer valve is equipped with a button to allow manual operation of the valve if the electrical circuit fails. Pressing the button allows fuel to flow as long as the button is depressed.

Refer to Chapter Six for fuel primer valve hose routing diagrams and to the end of the book for wiring diagrams.

Troubleshooting

> *NOTE*
> *The ignition switch must be held in the CHOKE or PRIME position for all of the following tests.*

1. Check the fuel lines going to and from the fuel primer valve for deterioration and obstructions. Correct any problems found.
2. Check that the black lead coming out of the fuel primer valve is connected to a clean ground. Clean and tighten the connection as necessary.
3. Connect the test lamp lead to a good engine ground.
4. Gain access to the ignition switch yellow/black lead (terminal C). Connect the test lamp probe to this lead. With the ignition switch in the CHOKE or PRIME position the test lamp should light. If the test lamp lights, go to Step 6, if the test lamp does not light, go to Step 5.
5. Connect the test lamp probe to the ignition switch red/purple lead (terminal B or BAT). The test lamp should light regardless of the ignition switch position. If the test lamp lights, replace the ignition switch and retest Step 4. If the test lamp does not light, repair or replace the red or red/purple lead from terminal B of the ignition switch back through the main 20 amp fuse to the starter solenoid.
6. Disconnect the yellow/black lead at the fuel primer valve. Connect the test lamp probe to the yellow/black lead on the engine harness side.

With the ignition switch in the CHOKE or PRIME position the test lamp should light. If the test lamp does not light, repair or replace the yellow/black lead from the fuel primer valve to the ignition switch.
7. Disconnect the yellow/black and black leads from the fuel primer valve. Connect an ohmmeter, calibrated on the appropriate scale to read 10-12 ohms. Connect one meter lead to the fuel primer valve yellow/black lead and the other meter lead to the fuel primer valve black lead. Replace the solenoid if the resistance is not within specifications.
8. Disconnect the fuel hoses from the fuel primer valve and connect a short length of hose to one of the valve ports. Blow into the hose while depressing the manual valve button on top of the valve. Air should flow through the valve with the button depressed, but not when the button is released. Replace the valve if it does not perform as specified.

Thermal Enrichment Air Valve (135-200 hp Carbureted Models)

The thermal air valve (**Figure 68**) is designed to enrich the idle circuits of the WMH and WMV

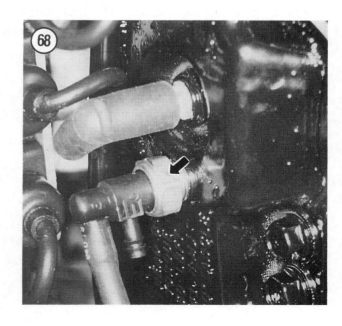

series of V-6 carburetors by restricting air flow to the idle circuits whenever the engine temperature is below 100° F (38° C). The thermal valve is mounted in the starboard cylinder head just below the No. 3 spark plug. The valve has 2 ports.

One is connected to each carburetor through a series of fittings on the carburetor bodies. The other port is open to the atmosphere (6, **Figure 69**). When the engine temperature is below 100° Fahrenheit (38° Celsius), the valve is closed,

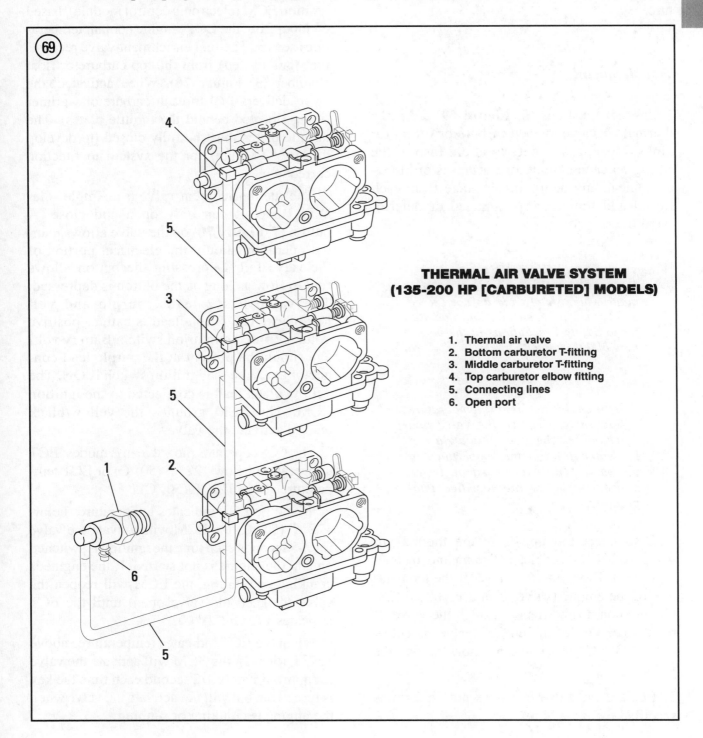

**THERMAL AIR VALVE SYSTEM
(135-200 HP [CARBURETED] MODELS)**

1. Thermal air valve
2. Bottom carburetor T-fitting
3. Middle carburetor T-fitting
4. Top carburetor elbow fitting
5. Connecting lines
6. Open port

preventing air from entering the idle circuits, causing a richer air/fuel mixture. When the temperature is above 100° F (38° C), the valve will be open, allowing air to enter the idle circuits, providing the normally calibrated air/fuel mixture.

Troubleshooting

1. Inspect the lines (5, **Figure 69**) from the thermal air valve to each carburetor fitting for kinks, blockages or deterioration. Inspect the fitting on each carburetor for debris or blockage. Clean any debris or blockage from each fitting and replace any damaged or deteriorated lines.

> *CAUTION*
> *Do not run the engine without an adequate water supply and do not exceed 3000 rpm without an adequate load. Refer to **Safety Precautions** at the beginning of this chapter.*

> *NOTE*
> *Run the engine to raise the temperature of the valve. Remove the valve and place the sensing element in a glass of ice water to lower the temperature of the valve. The valve must be tested above and below the specified temperature.*

2. Disconnect the line from the thermal air valve. Attach a short piece of scrap line to either valve port. Blow into the valve. If the temperature of the engine (valve) is above 100° F (38° C), air should flow freely through the valve. If the temperature of the engine (valve) is below 100° F (38° C), air should not flow through the valve.

3. Replace the valve if it does not perform as specified.

Fuel Enrichment Valve (225 hp Carbureted Models)

The fuel enrichment valve (1, **Figure 70**) on the 225 hp carbureted models is controlled by the ignition ECM (electronic control module), based on input from the ECT (engine coolant temperature) sensor. The fuel enrichment valve receives fuel (gravity fed) from the top carburetor float chamber (3, **Figure 70**). When activated, the valve delivers fuel to each carburetor's primer fitting (located behind the throttle plates). The throttle plates must be fully closed (to develop the most vacuum) for the system to function correctly.

The fuel enrichment valve is a simple solenoid valve. It can only open and close. A button (7, **Figure 70**) on the valve allows manual operation should the electrical portion of the valve fail. Depressing the button allows fuel to flow as long as the button is depressed. The valve has 2 leads, purple and yellow/black. The purple lead is battery positive voltage from the ignition switch. Battery voltage should be present at the purple lead connector any time the ignition switch is ON. The yellow/black lead is connected to the ignition ECM. The ECM grounds the yellow/black lead to activate the valve.

The ECM operates the valve in 2 modes: ECT temperature below 122° F (50° C) or ECT temperature above 122° F (50° C).

When the ECT indicates temperatures below 122° F (50° C) the ECM will activate the valve for 2-3 seconds each time the ignition is switched on and the engine is not started. If the engine is cranking or running, the ECM will reopen the valve (or keep the valve open) until the ECT indicates 122° F (50° C).

When the ECT indicates temperatures above 122° F (50° C), the ECM will activate the valve for approximately 1/2 second each time the key is turned on, but will not activate the valve when the engine is cranking or running.

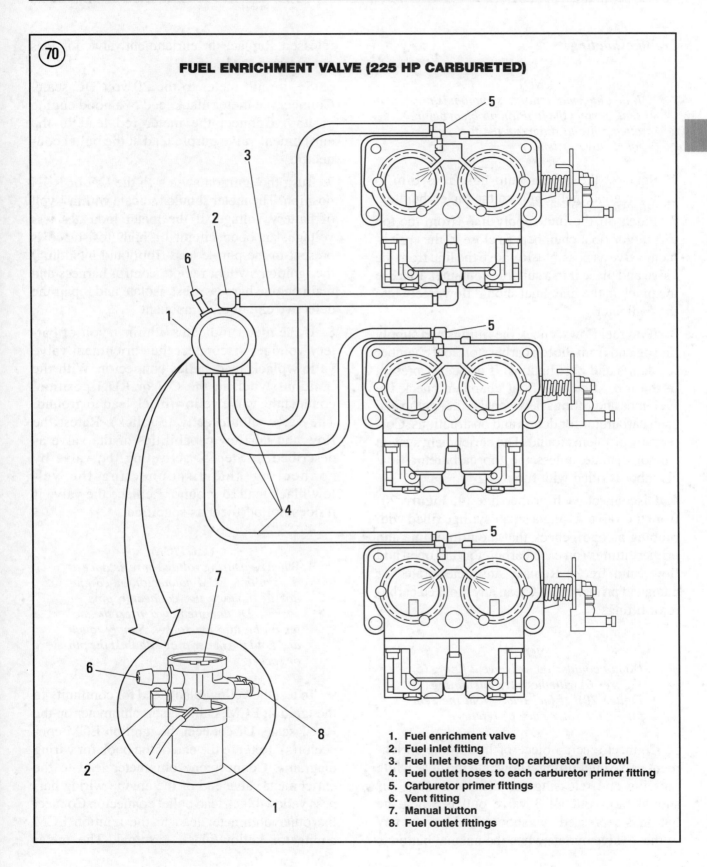

⑦⓪ **FUEL ENRICHMENT VALVE (225 HP CARBURETED)**

1. Fuel enrichment valve
2. Fuel inlet fitting
3. Fuel inlet hose from top carburetor fuel bowl
4. Fuel outlet hoses to each carburetor primer fitting
5. Carburetor primer fittings
6. Vent fitting
7. Manual button
8. Fuel outlet fittings

3

Troubleshooting

> *NOTE*
> *If an abnormal ignition symptom is present, correct the ignition problem before attempting to diagnose the fuel enrichment valve system.*

1. Squeeze the primer bulb until it is firm to ensure a good fuel supply to the top carburetor.

2. Pinch off the fuel supply line (from the top carburetor float chamber) as close to the enrichment valve as possible. Remove the line from the valve and place it in a suitable container. Release the pinch in the line. Fuel should flow freely into the container.

3. If no fuel flows, check the fittings and supply line on and from the top carburetor float chamber for debris and obstructions. If no fuel is present in the top carburetor float chamber, check the fuel lines and fittings between the fuel pump and each carburetor for debris and obstructions. Correct any problems found. The enrichment system cannot operate unless the top carburetor float chamber is filled with fuel.

4. Disconnect each primer line (4, **Figure 70**) from the valve. Using a small syringe filled with rubbing alcohol, check that the primer line and primer fittings (on each carburetor) are open and flow fluid freely. Replace any deteriorated or damaged primer lines. Clean any blocked carburetor fittings.

> *NOTE*
> *Do not confuse the valve vent fitting (6, **Figure 70**) with the valve inlet fitting (2, **Figure 70**). If fuel leaks from the vent fitting, the valve must be replaced.*

5. Connect a scrap piece of line to the enrichment valve inlet fitting. Blow into the hose while pressing and releasing the manual button. Air should blow out all 3 valve outlets when the button is depressed. Air should not blow out any of the 3 valve outlets when the manual button is

released. Replace the enrichment valve if it does not perform as specified.

6. Set a multimeter to the 20 volt DC scale. Connect the meter black lead to a good engine ground. Connect the meter red lead to the enrichment valve purple lead at the bullet connector.

7. Turn the ignition switch to the ON or RUN position. The meter should indicate within 1 volt of battery voltage. If the meter indicates less voltage, an open circuit or high resistance is present in the purple lead from (and including) the ignition switch, remote control harness and main engine harness. Test, isolate and repair the defective circuit or component.

8. If the meter indicates within 1 volt of battery voltage, disconnect the enrichment valve yellow/black lead bullet connector. With the ignition switch in the ON or RUN position, connect the valve yellow/black lead to ground. The valve should activate (click). Retest the flow and no-flow capabilities of the valve as described in Step 5, activating the valve by connecting and disconnecting the yellow/black lead to ground. Replace the valve if it does not perform as specified.

> *CAUTION*
> *When measuring voltage or resistance at the ignition ECM connector, be careful not to damage the connector pins or sockets. Do not attempt to insert the meter probe into the socket. Simply touch and hold the meter probe against the pin or socket.*

9. To test the yellow/black lead for continuity to the ignition ECM, calibrate an ohmmeter on the R × 1 scale. Disconnect the ignition ECM connector(s). Refer to the end of the book for wiring diagrams. Connect one ohmmeter lead to the enrichment valve end of the engine wiring harness yellow/black lead bullet connector. Connect the other ohmmeter lead to the ignition ECM connector yellow/black terminal. The meter

should indicate continuity. Repair or replace the wiring harness if any other reading is obtained.

10. If all tests are satisfactory to this point, test the ECT sensor as described in the *Capacitor Discharge Module Ignition (225 and 250 hp)*.

11. Test the ECT sensor tan/black engine harness leads for continuity. Refer to the end of the book for wiring diagrams. One tan/black lead should have continuity to the ignition ECM connector. The other tan/black lead should have continuity to ground. If the ECT sensor and leads test satisfactorily, the ignition ECM is defective and must be replaced.

EFI FUEL SYSTEM TROUBLESHOOTING

This section deals with troubleshooting the various EFI (electronic fuel injection) fuel systems used on the larger Mercury and Mariner outboard motors. Once the defective component is identified, refer to appropriate chapter for component removal and replacement procedures.

Troubleshooting Notes and Precautions (All Models)

Several troubleshooting precautions must be strictly observed to avoid damaging the ignition system or injuring yourself.

1. Do not reverse the battery connections. Reverse battery polarity will damage electronic components.

2. Do not *spark* the battery terminals with the battery cable connections to determine polarity.

3. Do not disconnect the battery cables with the engine running.

4. Do not crank or run the outboard if any electrical components are not grounded to the power head.

5. Do not disconnect the ECM (electronic control module) when the outboard is running, while the ignition switch is ON or while the battery cables are connected.

6. The EFI fuel system requires that the electric starter crank the engine at normal speed in order for ignition system to produce adequate spark. All EFI fuel systems are triggered by the ignition system. If the starter motor cranks the engine slowly or not at all, go back to the *STARTING SYSTEM* section and correct the starting system problem before continuing.

7. Check the battery cable connections for secure attachment to both battery terminals and the engine. Clean any corrosion from all connections. Discard any wing nuts and install corrosion resistant hex nuts at all battery cable connections. Place a corrosion resistant locking washer between the battery terminal stud and battery cable terminal end to ensure a positive connection. Loose battery connections can cause every symptom imaginable.

8. Check all ECM and EFI component ground leads for secure attachment to the power head. Clean and tighten all ground leads, connections and fasteners as necessary. Loose ground connections and loose component mounting hardware can cause every symptom imaginable.

NOTE
All EFI engines are equipped with at least one ECM (electronic control module). EFI models cannot be started or operated without battery voltage.

Resistance (Ohmmeter) Tests

The resistance values specified in the following test procedures are based on tests performed at room temperature. Actual resistance readings obtained during testing will generally be slightly higher if checked on hot components. In addition, resistance readings may vary depending on the manufacturer of the ohmmeter. Therefore, use discretion when failing any component that is only slightly out of specification. Many ohmmeters have difficulty reading less than 1 ohm

3

accurately. If this is the case, specifications of less than 1 ohm generally appear as a very low (continuity) reading.

System Description (150-200 hp Models)

The 150-200 hp EFI (electronic fuel injection) fuel system is dependent on the mechanical fuel pump to provide fuel to the vapor separator (and high pressure electric fuel pump). The system is also dependent on the ignition system inner switch box primary circuit output (to cylinders No. 1, No. 3 and No. 5 ignition coils) to provide tachometer signals to the ECM (electronic control module) so the ECM can calculate and fire the 6 fuel injectors at the correct time. The fuel injectors are fired in pairs. Cylinder No. 1 primary ignition circuit triggers cylinder No. 3 and No. 4 injectors, cylinder No. 3 primary ignition circuit triggers cylinder No. 5 and No. 6 injectors, cylinder No. 5 primary ignition circuit triggers cylinder No. 1 and No. 2 injectors.

An ignition system failure that eliminates the switch box primary ignition voltage output to cylinders No. 1, No. 3 or No. 5 will *always* prevent the ECM from firing the 2 fuel injectors triggered by that primary circuit.

The major components of the EFI fuel system are the:

1. *ECM*—Two distinct versions of ECMs are used. Early 1994 ECMs (14632AXX series) are analog. Analog ECMs cannot be diagnosed with the Quicksilver DDT (digital diagnostic terminal). 1994-1/2 and newer ECMs (824003-XX

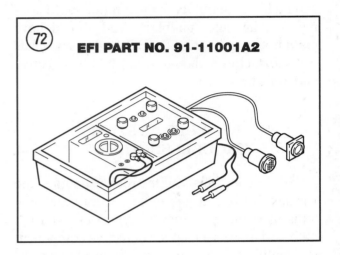

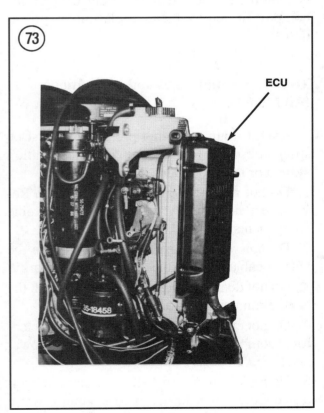

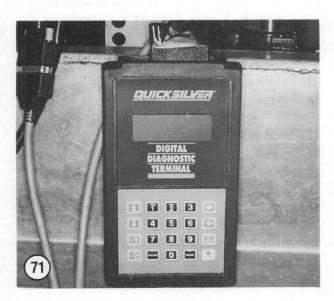

series) are digital. Digital ECMs are best diagnosed with the DDT (**Figure 71**). Analog ECMs are replaced with digital ECMs if update is desired or a failure occurs. Both digital and analog ECMs can be diagnosed with the EFI tester part No. 91-11001A2 (**Figure 72**).

The ECM monitors engine coolant temperature, throttle plate position, intake air tempera-

ture, manifold absolute pressure, barometric pressure and engine speed data based on signals from the various sensors and the ignition system. The ECM processes this information and determines the pulse width and injector timing necessary for optimum performance during all engine operating conditions. The ECM is mounted to the induction manifold assembly as shown in **Figure 73**.

> *NOTE*
> *Early model (1994-1995) vapor separators use an externally mounted electric fuel pump and final fuel filter. Late model (1996-1997) vapor separators use an internally mounted electric fuel pump and final fuel filter.*

2. *Vapor separator, final filter and high pressure fuel pump*—The vapor separator (**Figure 74**, early models or **Figure 75**, late models) is mounted on the induction manifold and serves as a reservoir where fuel from the diaphragm fuel pump and oil from the oil pump are blended and circulated. Unused fuel from the fuel rail bleed system is also returned to the vapor separator for recirculation. The fuel level in the vapor separator is regulated by a float and needle and seat valve assembly. If the float should become stuck in the up position, fuel flow into the vapor separator will be restricted. If the float should become stuck in the down position, fuel will overflow the vapor separator resulting in an excessively rich mixture. The electric fuel pump (2, **Figure 74** or

74 **VAPOR SEPARATOR (1994-1995 150-200 HP EFI MODELS)**

1. Vapor separator body
2. Electric fuel pump cover
3. Oil inlet check valve
4. Fuel outlet check valve
5. Hat filter inside line
6. Final fuel filter
7. High-pressure test point
8. Regulator vacuum line
9. Fuel pressure regulator
10. Vent and bleed line fittings

A, **Figure 75**) delivers fuel under pressure to the fuel rail. Any unused fuel is returned to the vapor separator. When the ignition switch is in the ON position (engine not running), the ECM activates the pump for approximately 30 seconds to pressurize the fuel system.

The ECM has an internal fuel pump driver circuit that controls the pump. Battery voltage is always present at the pump positive (red) terminal. The ECM internally grounds the red/purple lead to activate the pump. The pump operates at 2 speeds, both controlled by the ECM. The pump generally runs at the low speed below 2000 rpm.

There is a final fuel filter (6, **Figure 74**) that is mounted above the fuel pump (early models) and prevents contamination from entering the fuel rail. Later models have the fuel filter mounted on the bottom of the fuel pump, inside the vapor separator. See Chapter Six.

3. *Fuel pressure regulator*—The electric fuel pump is capable of developing approximately 90 psi (621 kPa) fuel pressure. The fuel pressure regulator (9, **Figure 74**) or (B, **Figure 75**) is mounted on top of the vapor separator and regu-

lates the pressure to the fuel injectors to approximately 36 psi (248 kPa). The regulator has a vacuum line (8, **Figure 74**, typical) that goes to the induction manifold assembly. Fuel pressure will vary as manifold vacuum changes. Complete pressure specifications are listed in **Table 22**. If fuel pressure is too low, the engine will run lean. If fuel pressure is too high, the engine will run rich.

4. *Fuel filter, water sensor and module*—The water separating filter (**Figure 76**) is provided to prevent water contamination from damaging the fuel injection components. The water separating

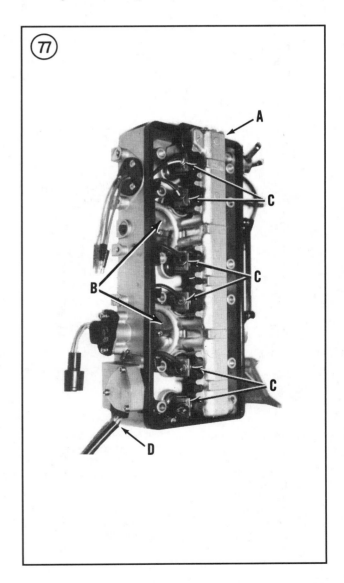

filter assembly is equipped with a sensor that activates a warning light (**Figure 76**) and horn should the water level in the filter canister reach the level of the sensor probe.

To determine if the water sensing system is functioning properly, place the ignition switch in the ON position, disconnect the tan lead from the sensor probe (**Figure 76**) and connect it to a good engine ground for 10 seconds. The warning light should glow and the horn should sound if the system is functioning properly.

5. *Induction manifold assembly*—The induction manifold assembly (A, **Figure 77**) contains 4 throttle valves (B, **Figure 77**) mounted on 2 throttle shafts. The manifold assembly contains the fuel rail, fuel injectors, throttle position sensor and intake air temperature sensor. A fuel rail service port (early models) is located on the lower port side of the manifold and is used to measure fuel pressure inside the rail.

The fuel injectors (C, **Figure 77**) are connected to the fuel rail and are located inside the induction manifold assembly. Each injector con-

sists of an electric solenoid that actuates a pintle valve assembly. The ECM determines when to fire the injectors by referencing the primary ignition circuits.

The injectors are connected to the ECM by a 4-lead harness (D, **Figure 77**). The red lead provides battery voltage (at all times) to the injectors. The ECM actuates the injectors by grounding either the white (cylinders No. 1 and No. 2), blue (cylinders No. 3 and No. 4) or yellow (cylinders No. 5 and No. 6) leads.

NOTE
The fuel injectors have a serviceable fuel filter in the inlet fitting of each injector. Any time the injector is removed, the filter should be cleaned or replaced. See Chapter Six.

6. *TPS*—The throttle position sensor (TPS) is a variable resistor that provides throttle position information to the ECM. The TPS (**Figure 78**) is mounted to the side of the induction manifold and is engaged with the lower throttle valve shaft. The sensor inputs throttle position information to the ECM as a voltage signal and has a direct effect on the air/fuel ratio at all engine speeds. The air/fuel mixture becomes richer as TPS resistance increases.

7. *MAP*—The manifold absolute pressure (MAP) sensor detects changes in manifold pressure and is connected to the intake manifold by a vacuum hose. The sensor is mounted inside the ECM and is non-serviceable. The ECM uses manifold pressure information from the MAP sensor to compensate for engine load conditions and changes in barometric pressure (altitude). When the ECM is first turned on, a barometric pressure reading is taken before the engine starts.

8. *ECT*—The engine coolant temperature (ECT) sensor provides the ECM with engine temperature information. The ECM uses this information to calculate the correct air/fuel enrichment during cold starts and engine warm up. The ECM stops the enrichment process when the engine temperature reaches 90° F (32° C).

The sensor is located directly below the No. 2 (top port) spark plug. See **Figure 79**. The sensor must make clean, positive contact with the cylinder head or an overly-rich air/fuel mixture can occur.

9. *IAT*—The intake air temperature (IAT) sensor (**Figure 80**) provides air temperature information to the ECM. As air temperature increases, the sensor resistance decreases, causing the ECM to lean the air/fuel mixture. If the sensor is disconnected (open circuit), the air/fuel mixture will enrichen by up to 10 percent. If the sensor is grounded (short circuit), the air/fuel mixture will lean by up to 10 percent.

10. *Detonation sensor and module*—This system is used only on the 200 XRI and 200 Magnum III models. System operation and troubleshooting are covered in the *ADI-CD, 135-200 hp Ignition System Troubleshooting* section located previously in this chapter. When detonation (abnormal combustion) occurs, the detonation sensor module sends signals to the ignition system bias circuit (to retard spark timing) and to the ECM (to enrich the air/fuel mixture up to 15 percent). The detonation module gray/white lead transmits the signal to the ECM. Retarding ignition timing and enriching the air/fuel ratio are effective means of eliminating detonation.

11. *Bleed system*—At idle speed, some of the fuel discharged by the fuel injectors puddles in the crankcase. The bleed system, through a series of check valves and hoses, collects and pumps this unburned fuel from the crankcase to the vapor separator for recirculation. On 1994-1995 models the bleed system flow to the vapor separator is shut off by a throttle linkage actuated, bleed system shutoff valve, whenever engine speed is above approximately 2000 rpm. The valve is mounted on the port side of the induction manifold as shown in **Figure 81**.

An inline bleed system filter (all models) prevents contamination from entering the vapor separator assembly (**Figure 82**). A plugged bleed system filter will cause an excessively rich mix-

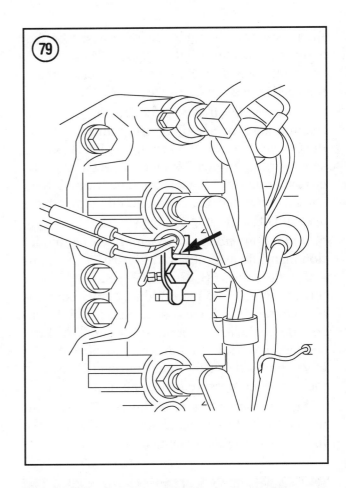

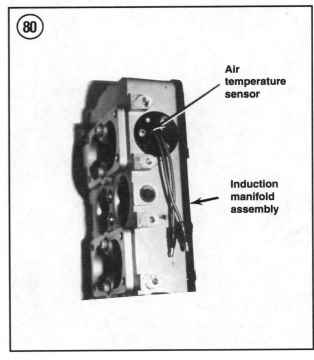

Air temperature sensor

Induction manifold assembly

ture at idle and hesitation during acceleration. Refer to Chapter Six for bleed line routing and service. Refer to Chapter Four for filter service.

Troubleshooting (150-200 hp EFI Models)

All synchronization and linkage adjustments (Chapter Five) must be verified before beginning

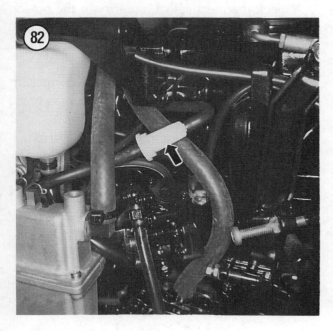

any EFI fuel system troubleshooting. Maximum effort must be made to correct all ignition system problems before attempting fuel system diagnosis.

Current EFI fuel systems use fully digital electronics and are designed to be diagnosed by either the Quicksilver EFI tester or the DDT (digital diagnostic terminal). The EFI tester (**Figure 72**) and DDT (**Figure 71**) are normally found only in Mercury or Mariner dealerships, where the investment can be justified.

NOTE
The DDT cannot be used on early (analog) ECMs. Analog ECMs are identified with a 14632A(XX) series part number. All part No. 824003-(XX) series ECMs are digital. Digital ECMs can also be quickly identified by the presence of the DDT terminal harness and plug-in. See **Figure 83.**

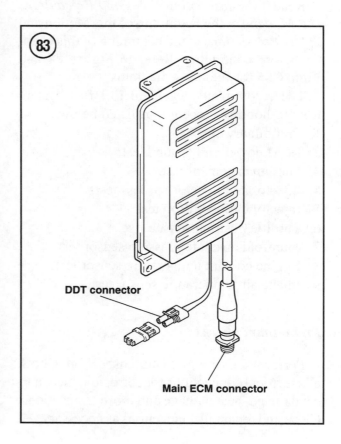

The DDT displays sensor input values and actuator output values as the ECM (electronic control module) sees them. The DDT and required adapter cables are listed in **Table 1**. If using the DDT for troubleshooting, refer to the manual included with the DDT software cartridge for troubleshooting procedures. DDT displayed sensor and actuator values are listed in **Table 20**.

The EFI tester allows testing of the ECM and all wiring circuits. A digital multimeter is provided for use with the EFI tester. Refer to the manual included with the EFI tester for troubleshooting procedures.

Troubleshooting without the EFI tester or DDT extremely limits the components and systems that can be tested. If the procedure outlined in the following section does not isolate the failed component or system, an EFI tester or DDT will have to be obtained or the motor taken to a Mercury/Mariner dealership for diagnosis.

Read *Troubleshooting Notes and Precautions (All Models)* at the beginning of this section and *Safety Precautions* at the beginning of this chapter before continuing. Refer to **Figure 84** and **Figure 85** for fuel flow diagrams.

The recommended general EFI fuel system troubleshooting procedure is listed below.
1. Preliminary checks.
2. ECM power and ground test.
3. Fuel management test.
4. Injector and injector harness test.
5. Injector cylinder drop test.
6. Throttle position sensor test.
7. Manifold absolute pressure sensor test.
8. Engine coolant temperature sensor test.
9. Intake air temperature sensor test.

Preliminary checks

Perform a thorough visual inspection. Check all electrical connections for corrosion, mechanical damage, heat damage and loose connections. Clean and repair all connections as necessary. All lead splices or connector repairs must be made with waterproof marine grade connectors and heat shrink tubing. An electrical hardware repair kit and crimping pliers (**Table 1**) are available from Quicksilver to repair the serviceable connectors and make lead splices on the engine. The Quicksilver dealer catalog also lists heat shrink connectors and heat shrink tubing for making other waterproof connections and repairs. Marine and industrial suppliers are other good sources for quality electrical repair equipment.

> *NOTE*
> *Any electrical connection or repair that does not have perfect continuity will affect the signal sent to or from the ECM, effectively throwing the system out of calibration. This will always have a detrimental effect on engine operating quality and performance.*

1. Check both battery cable connections at the battery and engine. Clean, tighten and repair the connections and terminals as necessary. Any loose connections will cause erratic and intermittent symptoms. If the cranking speed is slower than normal, perform the *voltage drop tests* in the starting system troubleshooting section. The engine must crank at normal speed in order to start.
2. Check the mechanical integrity of the power head by performing a cranking compression test (Chapter Four). Correct any mechanical deficiencies before proceeding.
3. Inspect the spark plugs for fouling, correct air gap and correct application. Replace any suspect spark plugs.
4. Perform an air gap spark test to verify that the ignition system is operating correctly. Refer to *preliminary checks* in the ADI-CD 135-200 hp ignition system section of this chapter.

ECM power and ground test

The ECM must receive power (battery voltage through the red and purple leads) and have good ground continuity (through all black leads) in

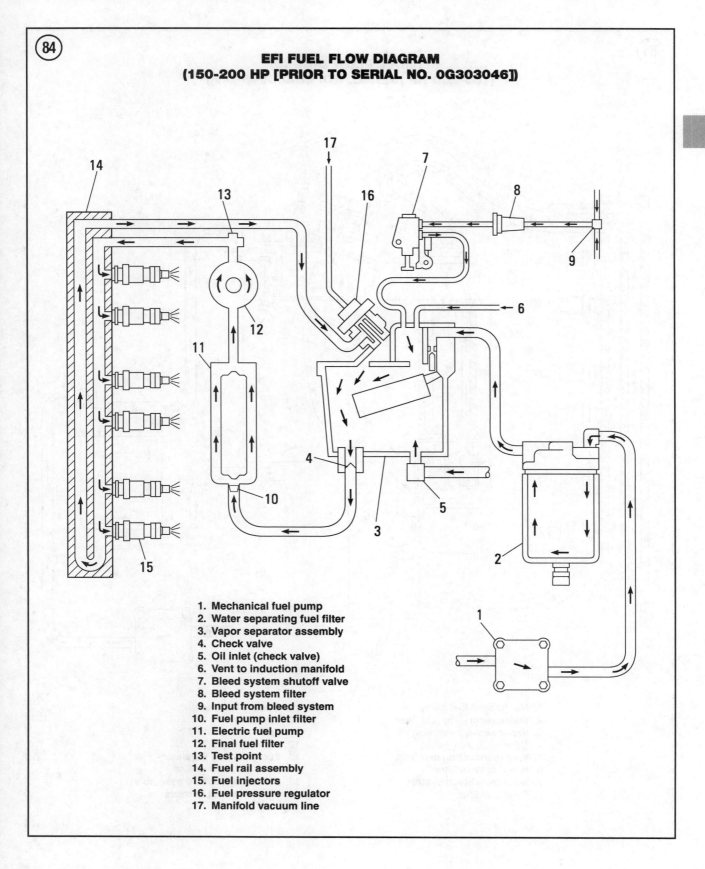

84

**EFI FUEL FLOW DIAGRAM
(150-200 HP [PRIOR TO SERIAL NO. 0G303046])**

3

1. Mechanical fuel pump
2. Water separating fuel filter
3. Vapor separator assembly
4. Check valve
5. Oil inlet (check valve)
6. Vent to induction manifold
7. Bleed system shutoff valve
8. Bleed system filter
9. Input from bleed system
10. Fuel pump inlet filter
11. Electric fuel pump
12. Final fuel filter
13. Test point
14. Fuel rail assembly
15. Fuel injectors
16. Fuel pressure regulator
17. Manifold vacuum line

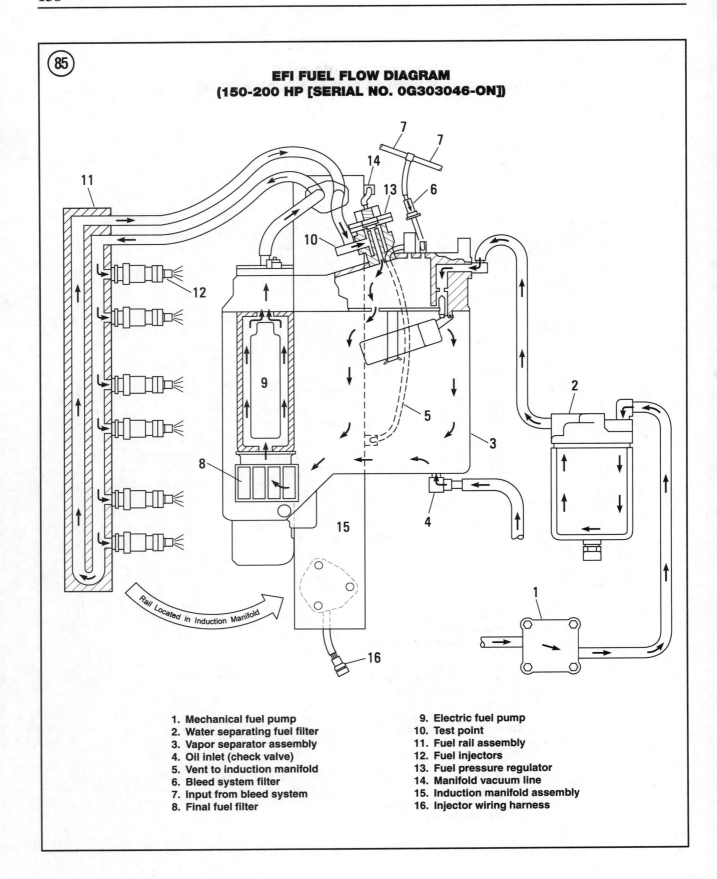

**EFI FUEL FLOW DIAGRAM
(150-200 HP [SERIAL NO. 0G303046-ON])**

1. Mechanical fuel pump
2. Water separating fuel filter
3. Vapor separator assembly
4. Oil inlet (check valve)
5. Vent to induction manifold
6. Bleed system filter
7. Input from bleed system
8. Final fuel filter
9. Electric fuel pump
10. Test point
11. Fuel rail assembly
12. Fuel injectors
13. Fuel pressure regulator
14. Manifold vacuum line
15. Induction manifold assembly
16. Injector wiring harness

order to function correctly. Refer to the end of the book for wiring diagrams.

CAUTION
When measuring voltage or resistance at the ECM connectors, be careful not to damage the connector pins or sockets. Do not attempt to insert the meter probe into the socket. Simply touch and hold the meter probe against the pin or socket.

1. To check the ECM ground circuits, disconnect the main ECM engine wiring harness connector from the engine wiring harness. See **Figure 83**.

2. Calibrate an ohmmeter on the R × 1 scale. Connect one ohmmeter lead to a good engine ground. Connect the other ohmmeter lead to pin No. 16 of the *engine* wiring harness ECM connector. The meter should indicate continuity. If no continuity is noted, a high resistance or open circuit is present in the black lead between pin No. 16 of the engine wiring harness ECM connector and engine ground. Repair or replace the black lead as necessary.

3. Inspect all ground leads coming from the ECM and ECM mounting brackets that are directly connected to ground. Clean, tighten or repair all connections and fasteners as necessary to ensure a good ground. Verify that all ECM mounting hardware is tightened securely.

4. To check the ECM power circuits, set a multimeter to the 20 volt DC scale. Connect the meter black lead to a good engine ground. Connect the meter red lead to pin No. 6 of the *engine* wiring harness ECM connector. The meter should indicate within 0.5 volt of battery voltage.

5. If the meter reads less, an open circuit or high resistance is present in the red lead from the starter solenoid battery positive terminal and pin No. 6 of the engine wiring harness ECM connector. Repair or replace the red lead as necessary.

6. Move the meter red lead to pin No. 7 of the engine wiring harness ECM connector. Turn the ignition switch to the ON or RUN position. The

meter should indicate within 1.0 volt of battery voltage.

7. If the meter reads less, an open circuit or high resistance is present in the purple lead from (and including) the ignition switch, remote control wiring harness, main engine harness connector, main engine wiring harness and the ECM connector. Isolate, repair or replace the purple lead or electrical components as necessary.

8. Reconnect all connectors and leads when finished.

Fuel management test (1994-1995 models)

NOTE
The fuel pressure at the high-pressure test point must be within specification at all engine speeds. If the symptom occurs only at a certain engine speed, perform the test at the speed the symptom occurs.

CAUTION
*Do not run the engine without an adequate water supply and do not exceed 3000 rpm without an adequate load. Refer to **Safety Precautions** at the beginning of this chapter.*

1. Connect the fuel pressure test gauge (**Table 1**) to the test port located at the top of the final filter assembly above the electric fuel pump. Make sure the gauge connections are secure. See **Figure 86**.

2. Squeeze the primer bulb to ensure the fuel system is primed.

NOTE
If the engine is not cranked or started, the ECM will turn the fuel pump off after 30 seconds.

3. Turn the ignition switch to the ON or RUN position and observe the fuel pressure gauge. Fuel pressure should be 36-39 psi (248.2-268.9kPa).

4. If the pressure is above specification, replace the fuel pressure regulator and retest.

3

5. If the fuel pressure is below specification, determine if the electric fuel pump is running or not. Turn the ignition switch to the ON or RUN position while listening for pump operation. The pump should operate for approximately 30 seconds and then shut off. A mechanic's stethoscope can be used to better hear the pump. If the electric fuel pump does not operate, proceed to Step 12. If the electric fuel pump operates correctly, proceed to Step 6.

6. To make sure the vapor separator is receiving fuel, place a suitable container under the vapor separator drain plug. Remove the plug. Fuel should flow freely from the vapor separator. If fuel flows, proceed with Step 8. If fuel does not flow, check the engine mounted water separating fuel filter for water, debris or blockage. Check the fuel lines and fittings from the mechanical fuel pump to the vapor separator (including the vapor separator float and valve) for deterioration, debris or blockage. Clean, repair or replace components as necessary. If no defects are noted, proceed with Step 7.

7. Test the mechanical fuel pump and boat fuel system for pressure and vacuum as described previously in this chapter.

8. If the electric fuel pump runs and the vapor separator is receiving fuel, but fuel pressure is still below specification, disconnect the fuel pump inlet hose from the bottom of the electric fuel pump. Remove and inspect the fuel filter inside the fuel line (**Figure 87**). Replace the filter if it is damaged or obstructed. Retest fuel pressure if the filter is obstructed. If the filter is clean, either the electric fuel pump or fuel pressure regulator is defective. Proceed with Step 9.

9. Remove the fuel pressure regulator from the vapor separator without disconnecting any vacuum or fuel lines. See Chapter Six. Hold the fuel pressure regulator over a suitable container. Turn the ignition switch to the ON or RUN position and note the fuel flow from the regulator.

10. If fuel flows freely from the regulator discharge port, but fuel pressure is below specifica-

tion, replace the fuel pressure regulator. If little or no fuel flows from the regulator discharge port, inspect the final filter at the top of the electric fuel pump. Replace the final filter (Chapter Four) if it is dirty or clogged and retest fuel pressure. If the final filter is clean, leave the fuel filter disassembled and continue to Step 11.

CAUTION
EFI systems operate under high pressure. Do not remove the crimped stainless steel clamps unless absolutely necessary. Do not disconnect the rubber lines from the electric fuel pump, fuel pressure regulator and fuel management

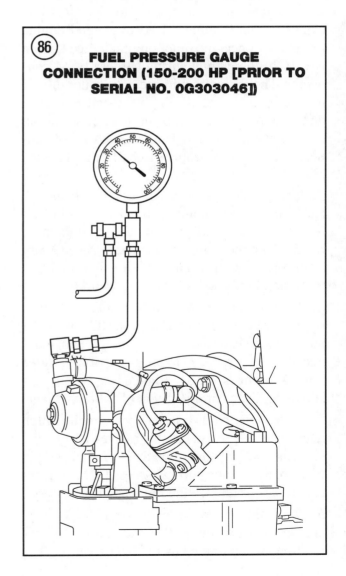

(86)

FUEL PRESSURE GAUGE CONNECTION (150-200 HP [PRIOR TO SERIAL NO. 0G303046])

adaptor unless new hoses and clamps are to be installed.

11. Disconnect the return line from the induction manifold fuel management (1, **Figure 88**) adaptor going to the fuel pressure regulator, *or* remove the 2 screws securing the regulator return fitting (3, **Figure 88**) to the regulator (Chapter 6). Place a shop rag over the regulator line (or fitting) to catch any fuel that may be present in

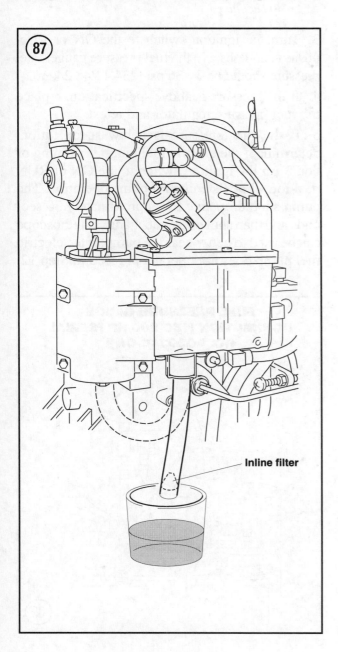

Inline filter

the lines. Blow into the final fuel filter output port (2, **Figure 88**) with low pressure air. Air (or fuel) should exit freely from the regulator line (1, **Figure 88**). If the flow is restricted, the induction manifold and fuel rail must be disassembled and cleaned. If air flows freely, replace the electric fuel pump, inlet filter (in the fuel line) and final filter (on top of the fuel pump) and retest fuel pressure.

12. To check the electric fuel pump for power, set a multimeter to the 20 volt DC scale. Connect the black lead to a good engine ground and the red lead to the electric fuel pump positive (+) terminal. The meter should indicate within 0.5 volt of battery voltage.

13. If the reading is less, check the red lead from the fuel pump positive terminal to the starter

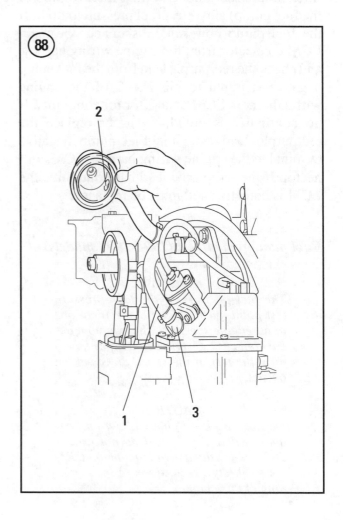

solenoid battery positive terminal for continuity. If no continuity is noted, repair or replace the red lead as necessary.

> *CAUTION*
> *When measuring voltage or resistance at the ECM connectors, be careful not to damage the connector pins or sockets. Do not attempt to insert the meter probe into the socket. Simply touch and hold the meter probe against the pin or socket.*

14. To check the electric fuel pump ground, disconnect the red/purple lead from the negative (–) fuel pump terminal. Connect a suitable jumper lead to the fuel pump negative (–) terminal and a good engine ground. If the fuel pump does not run, replace the electric fuel pump, inlet filter (in the fuel line) and final filter (on top of the fuel pump) and retest fuel pressure output. If the fuel pump now runs, disconnect the main ECM connector from the engine wiring harness and check the red/purple lead from the fuel pump negative terminal to pin No. 2 of the engine wiring harness ECM connector for continuity. If no continuity is noted, repair or replace the red/purple lead from the fuel pump negative terminal to the engine wiring harness ECM connector. If the red/purple lead has continuity, the ECM is defective and must be replaced.

Fuel management test (1996-1997 models)

> *NOTE*
> *The fuel pressure at the high-pressure test point must be within specifications at all engine speeds. If the symptom occurs only at a certain engine speed, perform the test at the speed the symptom occurs.*

> *CAUTION*
> *Do not run the engine without an adequate water supply and do not exceed 3000 rpm without an adequate load. Refer to Safety Precautions at the beginning of this chapter.*

1. Connect the fuel pressure test gauge (**Table 1**) to the test port at the top of the induction manifold, near the fuel pressure regulator. See **Figure 89**. Make sure the gauge connections are secure.

2. Squeeze the primer bulb to ensure the fuel system is primed.

> *NOTE*
> *If the engine is not cranked or started, the ECM will turn the fuel pump off after 30 seconds.*

3. Turn the ignition switch to the ON or RUN position and observe the fuel pressure gauge. Fuel pressure should be 34-36 psi (234.4-248.2 kPa).

4. If the pressure is above specification, replace the fuel pressure regulator and retest.

5. If the fuel pressure is below specification, determine if the electric fuel pump is running or not. Turn the ignition switch to the ON or RUN position while listening for pump operation. The pump should operate for approximately 30 seconds and then shut off. A mechanic's stethoscope can be used to better hear the pump. If the electric fuel pump does not operate, proceed to Step 12.

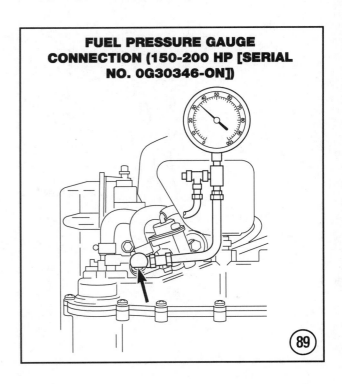

FUEL PRESSURE GAUGE CONNECTION (150-200 HP [SERIAL NO. 0G30346-ON])

(89)

If the electric fuel pump operates correctly, proceed to Step 6.

6. To make sure the electric fuel pump and vapor separator are receiving fuel, place a suitable container under the vapor separator drain plug. Remove the plug. Fuel should flow freely from the vapor separator. See **Figure 90**. If fuel flows, proceed with Step 8. If fuel does not flow, check the engine mounted water separating fuel filter for water, debris or blockage. Check the fuel lines and fittings from the mechanical fuel pump to the vapor separator (including the vapor separator float and valve assembly) for deterioration, debris or blockage. Clean, repair or replace components as necessary. If no defects are noted, proceed with Step 7.

7. Test the mechanical fuel pump and boat fuel system for pressure and vacuum as described previously in this chapter.

8. If the electric fuel pump runs and the vapor separator is receiving fuel, but fuel pressure is

still below specification, either the electric fuel pump or fuel pressure regulator is defective. Proceed with Step 9.

9. Remove the fuel pressure regulator from the vapor separator without disconnecting any vacuum or fuel lines. See Chapter Six. Hold the fuel pressure regulator over a suitable container. Turn the ignition switch to the ON or RUN position and note the fuel flow from the regulator.

10. If fuel flows freely from the regulator discharge port and fuel pressure is below specification, replace the fuel pressure regulator. If little or no fuel flows from the regulator discharge port, remove the vapor separator cover and inspect the final filter. Replace the final filter if it is dirty or clogged and retest fuel pressure. If the final filter is clean, continue to Step 11.

CAUTION
EFI systems operate under high pressure. Do not remove the crimped stainless steel clamps unless absolutely necessary. Do not disconnect the rubber lines from the electric fuel pump, fuel pressure regulator and fuel management adaptor unless new hoses and clamps are to be installed.

11. Disconnect the electric fuel pump output line (1, **Figure 91**) to the induction manifold fuel management adaptor and the fuel rail return line

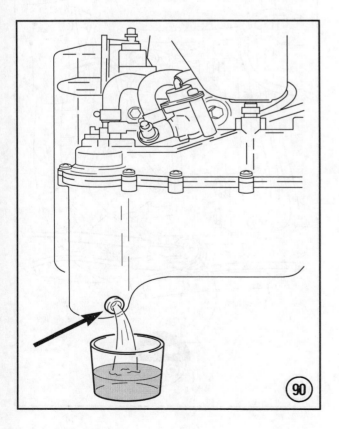

90

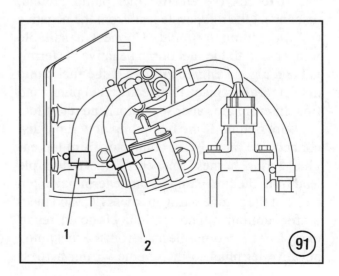

91

(2, **Figure 91**) from the fuel pressure regulator. Place a shop rag over the regulator line to catch any fuel that may be present in the lines. Blow into the fuel pump output line with low pressure air. Air (or fuel) should exit freely from the regulator line. If the air flow is restricted, the induction manifold and fuel rail must be disassembled and cleaned. If air flows freely, replace the electric fuel pump and final filter (in the vapor separator) and retest fuel pressure.

12. To check the electric fuel pump for power, set a multimeter to the 20 volt DC scale. Connect the black lead to a good engine ground and the red lead to the electric fuel pump positive (+) terminal. The meter should indicate within 0.5 volt of battery voltage.

13. If the reading is less, check the red lead from the fuel pump positive terminal to the starter solenoid battery positive terminal for continuity. If no continuity is noted, repair or replace the red lead as necessary.

> *CAUTION*
> *When measuring voltage or resistance at the ECM connectors, be careful not to damage the connector pins or sockets. Do not attempt to insert the meter probe into the socket. Simply touch and hold the meter probe against the pin or socket.*

14. To check the electric fuel pump ground, disconnect the red/purple lead from the negative (–) fuel pump terminal. Connect a suitable jumper lead to the fuel pump negative (–) terminal and a good engine ground. If the fuel pump does not run, replace the electric fuel pump and final filter (in the vapor separator) and retest fuel pressure output. If the fuel pump now runs, disconnect the main ECM connector from the engine wiring harness and check the red/purple lead from the fuel pump negative terminal to pin No. 2 of the engine wiring harness ECM connector for continuity. If no continuity is noted, repair or replace the red/purple lead from the fuel pump negative terminal to the engine wiring harness

ECM connector. If the red/purple lead has continuity, the ECM is defective and must be replaced.

Injector and injector harness test

This test will determine if the fuel injectors are receiving battery voltage and if any open circuits are present in the injector wiring harness. Use only a digital multimeter for the following tests. Refer to **Figure 92** for this procedure.

1. To check the battery voltage to the injectors, disconnect the injector harness 4-pin connector.

2. Set a digital multimeter to the 20 VDC scale. Connect the meter black lead to a good engine ground. Connect the meter red lead to pin No. 2 (red lead) of the engine harness side of the injec-

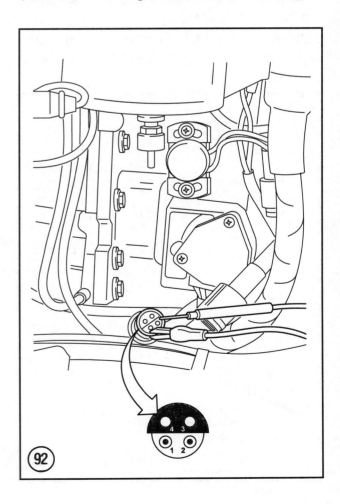

tor harness 4-pin connector. The meter should indicate within 0.5 volt of battery voltage.

3. If the meter reads less, a high resistance or open circuit is present in the red lead from the starter solenoid battery positive terminal and pin No. 2 of the injector harness 4-pin connector. Repair or replace the red lead as necessary.

4. To check the injector and injector harness resistance, set the digital ohmmeter to the 200 ohm scale.

5. Connect the red ohmmeter lead to pin No. 2 of the injector harness side of the injector harness 4-pin connector. Connect the black ohmmeter lead alternately to each of the following pins on the injector harness side of the 4-pin injector harness connector:

   a. Pin No. 4 (white lead) for cylinders No. 1 and No. 2 injectors.

   b. Pin No. 3 (blue lead) for cylinders No. 3 and No. 4 injectors.

   c. Pin No. 1 (yellow lead) for cylinders No. 5 and No. 6 injectors.

6. The reading at each connection should be 0.9-1.3 ohms. If the resistance is not as specified, the induction manifold will have to be disassembled and the resistance of each injector tested and the continuity of each injector harness lead verified. If the measured resistance is 2.0-2.4 ohms at any one connection, one injector or injector circuit has an open circuit.

Injector cylinder drop test

If the engine appears to be misfiring on 1 or more cylinders, perform a cylinder drop test to determine if each cylinder is firing normally. Before performing a cylinder drop test, however, make sure all previous tests have been performed with satisfactory results. Also make sure compression is acceptable and that the ignition system is functioning properly.

CAUTION
Do not run the engine without an adequate water supply and do not exceed

*3000 rpm without an adequate load. Refer to **Safety Precautions** at the beginning of this chapter.*

1. Start the engine and allow it to warm to operating temperature.

2. Adjust engine speed to approximately 1000-1500 rpm in neutral.

WARNING
High voltage is present during ignition system operation. Do not touch ignition components, leads or test leads while cranking or running the engine.

3. Using insulated spark plug pliers, disconnect the spark plug lead from each spark plug (one at a time) and note the resulting change in engine operation.

4. The engine speed should drop approximately the same amount as each spark plug lead is individually disconnected. If any cylinders do not produce a noticeable rpm drop or the same rpm drop as the majority of the cylinders, record the suspect cylinder numbers.

5. Remove the induction manifold and fuel rail. Remove the suspect injector(s) and inspect the injector inlet filter. If the filter is clean, replace the suspect injector. If the filter was dirty or clogged, clean or replace the filter and reassemble the induction manifold and retest the cylinder drop. If the cylinder drop is still unsatisfactory, replace the suspect injector.

Throttle position sensor test

The correct operation and setting of the TPS (throttle position sensor) is critical to achieving the correct air/fuel ratio. High TPS voltages provide a richer air/fuel ratio. Low TPS voltages provide a leaner air/fuel ratio. Adjustments (within specifications) to the TPS may be used to fine tune the idle air/fuel mixture. Never adjust the TPS out of the specified range. Use only a digital multimeter for the following test. Test

3

harness part No. 91-816085 (1, **Figure 93**) is required for this procedure.

> *NOTE*
> *Make sure the correct idle speed has been verified before adjusting the TPS. If idle speed is changed, the TPS setting must be readjusted.*

1. Disconnect the TPS from the engine wiring harness. Connect the test harness (part No. 91-816085) to the TPS and engine wiring harness. Connect the test harness meter leads to a digital multimeter. Set the multimeter to the 20 volt DC scale.

2. Disconnect both engine wiring harness tan/black leads from the ECT (engine coolant temperature) sensor.

> *NOTE*
> *If the TPS cannot be correctly set or reads zero, check the continuity of the sensor leads from the TPS connector to the ECM connector. The orange lead goes to ECM connector pin No. 1, the light blue lead goes to pin ECM connector pin No. 15 and the tan/black lead goes to ECM connector pin No. 14.*

3. Turn the ignition switch to the ON or RUN position. Make sure the throttle plates are against the idle stop. Note the meter reading and compare to specification (**Table 20**). If the reading is within specification, continue to Step 5. If the reading is not within specification, loosen the 2 screws (2, **Figure 93**) securing the TPS to the induction manifold.

4. With the throttle shaft held against the idle stop screw, rotate the TPS to obtain the desired specification (**Table 20**). While holding the TPS at the correct setting, tighten the screws securely. Recheck the voltage reading.

5. Disconnect the throttle cable and slowly move the throttle linkage to the full throttle position while noting the meter reading. The voltage should increase smoothly to 7.00-7.46 volts DC. If the meter reading fluctuates or is erratic

as the throttle was advanced, replace the TPS sensor. If the meter reading is not within 7.00-7.46 volts DC at wide-open throttle, check the wide-open throttle stop (Chapter Five) for correct adjustment.

MAP sensor test

The MAP (manifold absolute pressure) sensor provides engine load and barometric pressure data to the ECM. The MAP sensor is mounted inside the ECM case and is not serviceable. The MAP sensor is best tested with the EFI tester or DDT (**Table 1**).

1. Inspect the MAP sensor vacuum line (from the ECM to the induction manifold) for secure attachment, kinks, deterioration or leakage. The line can be repaired up to the point that it enters the ECM. Use a plastic line fitting (such as a speedometer hose coupler) and repair or replace portions of the vacuum line as necessary.

> *CAUTION*
> *Do not run the engine without an adequate water supply and do not exceed 3000 rpm without an adequate load. Refer to **Safety Precautions** at the beginning of this chapter.*

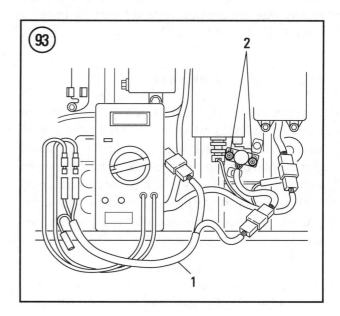

2. Start the engine and let it warm to operating temperature.

3. Stop the engine and disconnect the MAP sensor line from the induction manifold.

4. Attach a hand vacuum pump to the MAP sensor line.

5. Run the engine at idle speed. Vary the vacuum applied to the MAP sensor line from zero to 10 in. Hg (34 kPa) of vacuum as the engine idles. A noticeable change in engine running quality should be noticed. If no change in running quality occurs, the MAP sensor is defective and the ECM will have to replaced.

Engine coolant temperature sensor test

The ECT (engine coolant temperature) sensor provides the ECM with engine (coolant) temperature data. The ECT sensor has 4 leads. The 2 tan/black leads are used by the ECM to sense

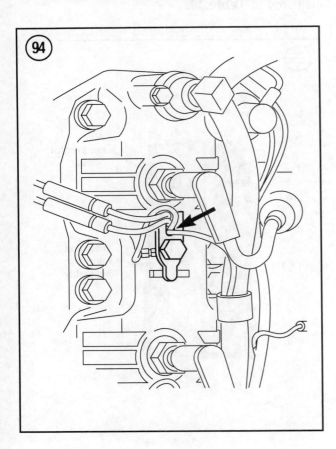

engine temperature. The tan/blue and black leads are the temperature switch portion of the ECT sensor and are used to sound the warning horn whenever the temperature of the engine exceeds the switch rating. Refer to **Table 21** for ECT sensor resistance values and to the end of the book for wiring diagrams. To test the ECT sensor and switch, refer to **Figure 94** and proceed as follows:

1. Disconnect the ECT sensor tan/blue and 2 tan/black leads from the engine wiring harness.

2. Calibrate an ohmmeter on the highest scale available. Connect one meter lead to the black sensor lead (ground) and the other meter lead to the tan/blue sensor lead. The ohmmeter should read no continuity. Replace the sensor assembly if continuity is noted.

> *CAUTION*
> *Do not run the engine without an adequate water supply and do not exceed 3000 rpm without an adequate load. Refer to* **Safety Precautions** *at the beginning of this chapter.*

3. Run the engine up to operating temperature as described in *Engine temperature check* in this chapter. The ohmmeter should continue to indicate no continuity when the engine is at normal operating temperature. Replace the sensor assembly if continuity is noted. The only time the sensor should indicate continuity is if the engine is actually overheating (exceeding normal operating temperature).

4. Calibrate the ohmmeter on the appropriate scale to read the ECT sensor engine temperature data as listed in **Table 20**.

> *NOTE*
> *The temperature of the engine must be accurately determined before the ECT sensor can be tested.*

5. Measure the temperature of the cylinder head with a pyrometer or allow the engine to cool to ambient temperature. Connect one ohmmeter lead to each of the tan/black ECT sensor leads.

Note the meter reading and compare to specification. If the reading is not within specification, the ECT sensor must be replaced. If the reading is within specification, continue to Step 6.

6. Remove the sensor from the cylinder head (with ohmmeter still connected) and immerse the sensing element into a container of crushed ice and water while noting the meter reading. The reading should smoothly increase as the sensing element cools. If the reading does not increase to specification (**Table 20**), replace the ECT sensor. If the reading is within specification, continue to Step 7.

7. Calibrate an ohmmeter on the highest scale available. Connect one ohmmeter lead to the black ECT sensor lead. Connect the other ohmmeter lead alternately to each of the tan/black ECT sensor leads. The meter must indicate no continuity. If continuity is noted, replace the ECT sensor.

8. Disconnect the ECM connector from the engine wiring harness. Calibrate an ohmmeter on the R × 1 scale. Connect one ohmmeter lead to the engine wiring harness ECM connector pin No. 13 (orange lead) and the other ohmmeter lead to the engine wiring harness orange lead bullet connector at the ECT sensor. The meter should indicate continuity. If any other reading is noted, an open circuit or high resistance is present in the engine wiring harness orange lead. Repair or replace the orange lead as necessary.

9. Connect one ohmmeter lead, still calibrated on the R × 1 scale, to the engine wiring harness ECM connector pin No. 14 (tan/black lead). Connect the other ohmmeter lead to the engine wiring harness tan/black lead bullet connector at the ECT sensor. The meter should indicate continuity. If no continuity is noted, an open circuit or high resistance is present in the engine wiring harness tan/black lead. Repair or replace the tan/black lead as necessary.

Intake air temperature sensor test

The IAT (intake air temperature) sensor provides the ECM with ambient temperature infor-

mation. Cold air, being more dense and containing more oxygen, requires a richer fuel delivery. Warm air is less dense and contains less oxygen, requiring a leaner fuel delivery. The ECM can compensate the normal air/fuel ratio a maximum of 10 percent richer or leaner. IAT sensor failure would generally cause a running quality problem, but it will not normally cause a no-start condition. There are 2 brown leads coming from the IAT sensor. One lead is connected to engine ground and the other lead is connected to the ECM connector pin No. 12. Refer to the end of the book for wiring diagrams and **Table 20** for IAT sensor ohmmeter values. To test the IAT sensor, refer to **Figure 95** and proceed as follows:

1. Disconnect the IAT sensor brown leads from the engine wiring harness.

2. Calibrate the ohmmeter on the appropriate scale to read the IAT sensor temperature value as listed in **Table 20**.

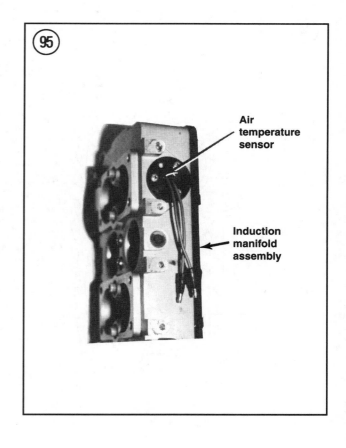

(95)

Air temperature sensor

Induction manifold assembly

NOTE
The ambient temperature must be accurately determined before the IAT sensor can be tested.

3. Allow the engine to cool to ambient temperature. Connect one ohmmeter lead to each of the brown IAT sensor leads. Note the meter reading and compare to specification. If the reading is not within specification, the IAT sensor must be replaced. If the reading is within specification, continue to Step 6.

4. Remove the sensor from the induction manifold (with ohmmeter still connected) and immerse the sensing element into a container of crushed ice and water while noting the meter reading. The reading should smoothly increase as the sensing element cools. If the reading does not increase to specification (**Table 20**), replace the IAT sensor. If the reading is within specification, continue to Step 7.

5. Disconnect the ECM connector from the engine wiring harness. Calibrate an ohmmeter on the R × 1 scale. Connect one ohmmeter lead to the engine wiring harness ECM connector pin No. 12 (brown lead) and the other ohmmeter lead to the engine wiring harness brown lead bullet connector at the IAT sensor. The meter should indicate continuity. If no continuity is noted, an open circuit or high resistance is present in the engine wiring harness brown lead. Repair or replace the brown lead as necessary.

6. Connect one ohmmeter lead, still calibrated on the R × 1 scale, to the engine wiring harness ECM connector pin No. 16 (black lead). Connect the other ohmmeter lead to the engine wiring harness black lead bullet connector at the IAT sensor. The meter should indicate continuity. If no continuity is noted, an open circuit or high resistance is present in the engine wiring harness black lead. Repair or replace the black lead as necessary.

Water sensor and module test

The water sensor and module are designed to alert the boat operator to a buildup of water in the engine mounted water separating fuel filter. If the water level in the filter reaches potentially damaging levels, the LED (light emitting diode) on the warning module will illuminate and the warning horn will sound intermittently. There is a 5-10 second delay built into the warning module.

There are 4 leads used in the system. The purple lead should indicate battery voltage any time the ignition switch is in the ON or RUN position. The black lead should have continuity to ground at all times. The light blue lead should have continuity to the lube alert module. The lube alert module sounds the warning horn when it receives a signal from the water sensor module. The tan lead is connected to the sensing probe in the water separating fuel filter. When water contacts (submerges) the sensing element, the tan lead is shorted to ground. After a 5-10 second delay the LED illuminates and the signal is sent to the lube alert module to sound the warning horn.

Refer to the end of the book for wiring diagrams. To test the water sensor and module, refer to **Figures 96** and **Figure 97** and proceed as follows.

1. Disconnect the tan lead from the water sensor at the base of the water separating fuel filter (**Figure 97**).

2. Turn the ignition switch to the ON or RUN position.

3. Connect the tan lead to a good engine ground.

4. After approximately 10 seconds, the LED (**Figure 96**) should illuminate and the warning horn should sound. If the LED illuminates, but the warning horn does not sound, verify the continuity of the light blue lead to the lube alert module. Repair or replace the light blue lead as necessary. If the light blue lead has continuity to the lube alert module, test the lube alert module as described in Chapter Eleven.

5. If the LED does not illuminate, test the power and ground to the water sensor module. If the water sensor module is receiving power and ground, but the LED does not illuminate when the tan lead is connected to ground for approximately 10 seconds, replace the water sensor module.

System Description (225-250 hp Models)

The 225-250 hp EFI fuel system is dependent on the mechanical fuel pump to provide fuel to the vapor separator and dependent on the igni-

tion ECM to provide a reference tachometer signal to the Fuel ECM.

Since the fuel and ignition ECMs are electrically connected (**Figure 98** [port side of engine]) and share many of the same sensors, refer to the *Capacitor Discharge Module Ignition (225 and 250 hp)* section of this chapter for an operational explanation and troubleshooting procedures on this ignition system.

The major components of the EFI fuel system are:

1. *Fuel ECM*—The fuel ECM monitors engine coolant temperature, throttle plate position, intake air temperature, manifold absolute pressure, barometric pressure and engine speed data based on signals from the various sensors and the ignition ECM. The fuel ECM processes this information and determines the pulse width and injector timing necessary for optimum performance during all engine operating conditions. The

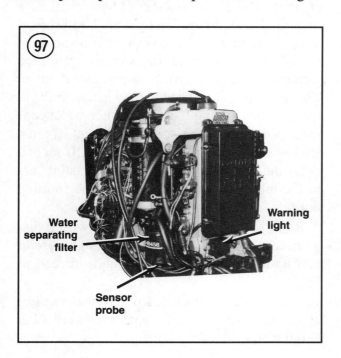

Water separating filter

Warning light

Sensor probe

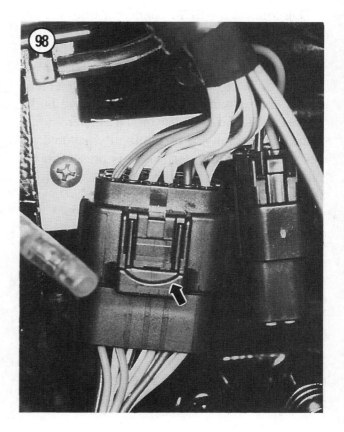

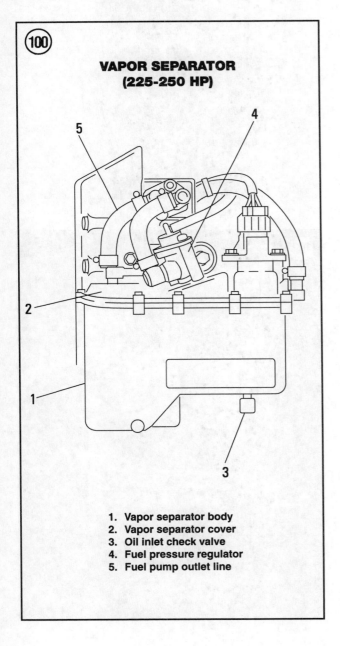

**VAPOR SEPARATOR
(225-250 HP)**

1. Vapor separator body
2. Vapor separator cover
3. Oil inlet check valve
4. Fuel pressure regulator
5. Fuel pump outlet line

fuel ECM is mounted at the rear of the engine, below the ignition ECM as shown in **Figure 99**.

The fuel ECM incorporates a warning program for low-oil tank level and water-in-fuel situations. The fuel ECM will sound the warning horn and illuminate the appropriate warning panel light should the oil tank level become too low or the water separating fuel filter accumulate too much water.

2. *Vapor separator, final filter and high pressure fuel pump*—The vapor separator (1, **Figure 100**) is mounted on the induction manifold and serves as a reservoir where fuel from the diaphragm fuel pump and oil from the oil pump are blended and circulated. Unused fuel from the fuel rail bleed system is also returned to the vapor separator for recirculation. The fuel level in the vapor separator is regulated by a float and needle and seat valve assembly. If the float should become stuck in the up position, fuel flow into the vapor separator will be restricted. If the float should become stuck in the down position, fuel will overflow the vapor separator resulting in an excessively rich mixture. The internal electric fuel pump delivers fuel (5, **Figure 100**) under pressure to the fuel rail. Any unused fuel is returned to the vapor separator. When the ignition switch is in the ON position (engine not running), the fuel ECM activates the pump for approximately 30 seconds to pressurize the fuel system.

The fuel ECM has an internal fuel pump driver circuit that controls the pump. Battery voltage is always present at the pump positive (red) terminal. The fuel ECM internally grounds the red/purple lead to activate the pump. The pump operates at variable speeds, controlled by the fuel ECM. The pump generally runs at full speed above 3000 rpm.

There is an internal final fuel filter that is mounted at the bottom of the fuel pump to prevent contamination from entering the fuel rail.

3. *Fuel pressure regulator*—The electric fuel pump is capable of developing approximately 90 psi (621 kPa) fuel pressure. The fuel pressure

regulator (4, **Figure 100**) is mounted on top of the vapor separator and regulates the pressure to the fuel injectors to approximately 36 psi (248 kPa). The regulator has a vacuum line that goes to the induction manifold assembly. Fuel pressure will vary as manifold vacuum changes. Complete pressure specifications are listed in **Table 22**. If fuel pressure is too low, the engine will run lean. If fuel pressure is too high, the engine will run rich.

4. *Fuel filter and water sensor*—The water separating filter (A, **Figure 101**) is provided to prevent water contamination from damaging the fuel injection components. The water separating filter assembly is equipped with a sensor (B, **Figure 101**) that activates a warning light and horn (at the control station) should the water level in the filter canister reach the level of the sensor probe.

5. *Induction manifold assembly*—There are 2 different induction manifold assemblies. The 225 hp uses 2 throttle valves mounted on 1 throttle shaft. The 250 hp induction manifold uses 4 throttle valves mounted on 2 throttle shafts (**Figure 102**). The manifold assembly contains the fuel rail, fuel injectors, throttle position sensor and intake air temperature sensor.

The fuel injectors (A, **Figure 103**) are connected to the fuel rail (B, **Figure 103**) and are located inside the induction manifold assembly. Each injector consists of an electric solenoid that actuates a pintle valve assembly. The fuel ECM determines when to fire the injectors (in pairs) by referencing the primary ignition circuits.

The injectors are connected to the fuel ECM by a 4-lead harness (C, **Figure 103**). The red lead provides battery voltage (at all times) to the injectors. The fuel ECM actuates the injectors by grounding either the white (cylinders No. 1 and No. 2), blue (cylinders No. 3 and No. 4) or yellow (cylinders No. 5 and No. 6) leads.

6. *Sensor input*—The fuel ECM relies on sensor input from the throttle position, manifold absolute pressure, engine coolant temperature, intake

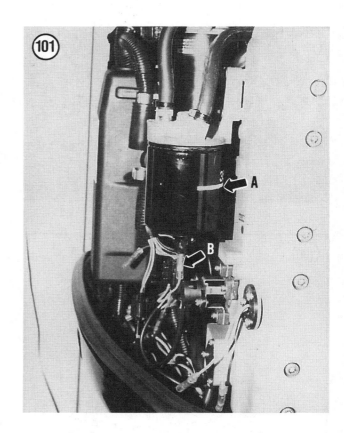

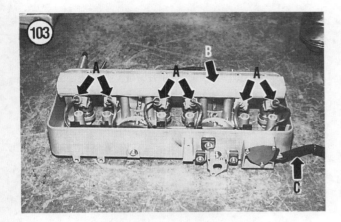

air temperature and the ignition ECM to provide detailed information about the engine operating conditions. Refer to *Capacitor Discharge Module Ignition System (225-250 hp)* for more information about the ignition ECM and ignition sensors.

a. *Throttle position sensor*—The throttle position sensor (TPS) is a variable resistor that provides throttle position information to the fuel and ignition ECMs. The TPS (**Figure 104**) is mounted to the side of the induction manifold and is engaged with the lower throttle valve shaft. The sensor inputs throttle position information to the ECM as a voltage signal and has a direct effect on the air/fuel ratio and ignition timing at all engine speeds. The TPS adjustment is a critical engine adjustment.

b. *Manifold absolute pressure*—The manifold absolute pressure (MAP) sensor detects changes in manifold pressure and is connected to the intake manifold by a vacuum hose. The sensor (**Figure 105**) is mounted on top of the vapor separator. The fuel ECM uses manifold pressure information from the MAP sensor to compensate for engine load conditions and changes in barometric pressure (altitude). When the fuel ECM is first turned on, a barometric pressure reading is taken before the engine starts.

c. *Engine coolant temperature*—The engine coolant temperature (ECT) sensor provides the fuel and ignition ECMs with engine temperature information. The fuel ECM uses this information to calculate the correct air/fuel enrichment during cold starts and engine warm up. The fuel ECM stops the enrichment process when the engine temperature reaches 110° F (43° C). The sensor is located directly below the No. 1 (top, starboard) spark plug. The sensor must make clean, positive contact with the cylinder head or an overly-rich air/fuel mixture can occur.

    d. *Intake air temperature*—The intake air temperature (IAT) sensor (**Figure 106**) provides air temperature information to the ECM. As air temperature increases, the sensor resistance decreases, causing the ECM to lean the air/fuel mixture.

7. *Bleed system*—At idle speed, some of the fuel discharged by the fuel injectors puddles in the crankcase. The 1995-1996 bleed system, through a series of check valves and hoses, collects and pumps this unburned fuel from the crankcase to the vapor separator for recirculation. An inline bleed system filter (**Figure 107**) prevents contamination from entering the vapor separator assembly. A plugged bleed system filter will cause an excessively rich mixture at idle and hesitation during acceleration. The 1997 bleed system collects the unburned fuel and returns it to a different cylinder's intake system for recirculation. The 1997 system does not return any fuel to the vapor separator. Refer to Chapter 6 for bleed system troubleshooting and hose routing diagrams.

8. *Warning panel*—A multifunction warning panel is recommended. The warning panel has 3 lights (**Figure 108**) that allow easy identification of low oil tank level, engine overheat, engine over-speed, sensor malfunction or water in fuel situations.

Troubleshooting (225-250 hp EFI Models)

All synchronization and linkage adjustments (Chapter Five) must be verified before beginning any EFI fuel system troubleshooting. Maximum effort must be made to correct all ignition system problems before attempting fuel system diagnosis.

Current EFI fuel and ignition systems use fully digital electronics and are designed to be diagnosed with the Quicksilver DDT (digital diagnostic terminal). The DDT (**Figure 109**) is normally found only in Mercury or Mariner dealerships, where the investment can be justified.

The DDT displays sensor input values and actuator output values as the ECM (electronic control module) sees them. The DDT and required adapter cables are listed in **Table 1**. If using the DDT for troubleshooting, refer to the manual included with the DDT software cartridge for troubleshooting procedures. DDT displayed sensor and actuator values are listed in **Table 20** and **Table 21**.

Troubleshooting without the DDT extremely limits the components and systems that can be tested. If the procedure outlined in the following

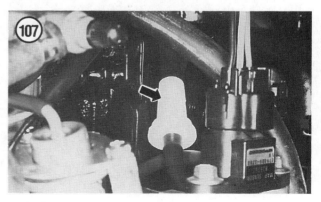

section does not isolate the failed component or system, a DDT must be obtained or the motor taken to a Mercury/Mariner dealership for diagnosis.

Read *Troubleshooting Notes and Precautions (All Models)* at the beginning of this section and *Safety Precautions* at the beginning of this chapter before continuing. Refer to **Figure 110** for a fuel flow diagram.

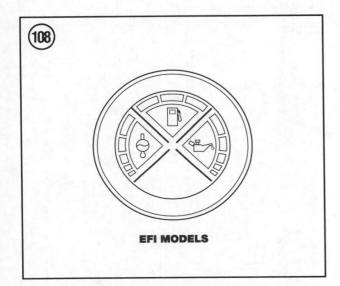

EFI MODELS

The recommended general EFI fuel system troubleshooting procedure is listed below.
1. Preliminary checks.
2. Fuel ECM power and ground test.
3. Fuel management test.
4. Injector and injector harness test.
5. Injector cylinder drop test.
6. Throttle position sensor test.
7. Manifold absolute pressure sensor test.
8. Engine coolant temperature sensor test.
9. Intake air temperature sensor test.

Preliminary checks

Perform a thorough visual inspection. Check all electrical connections for corrosion, mechanical damage, heat damage and loose connections. Clean and repair all connections as necessary. All lead splices or connector repairs must be made with waterproof marine grade connectors and heat shrink tubing. An electrical hardware repair kit and crimping pliers (**Table 1**) are available from Quicksilver to repair the serviceable connectors and make lead splices on the engine. The Quicksilver dealer catalog also lists heat shrink connectors and heat shrink tubing for making other waterproof connections and repairs. Marine and industrial suppliers are other good sources for quality electrical repair equipment.

> *NOTE*
> *Any electrical connection or repair that does not have perfect continuity will affect the signal being sent to or from the ECM, effectively throwing the system out of calibration. This will always have a detrimental effect on engine operating quality and performance.*

1. Check both battery cable connections at the battery and engine. Clean, tighten and repair the connections and terminals as necessary. Any loose connections will cause erratic and intermittent symptoms. If the cranking speed is slower than normal, perform the *Voltage drop tests* in the starting system troubleshooting section. The

3

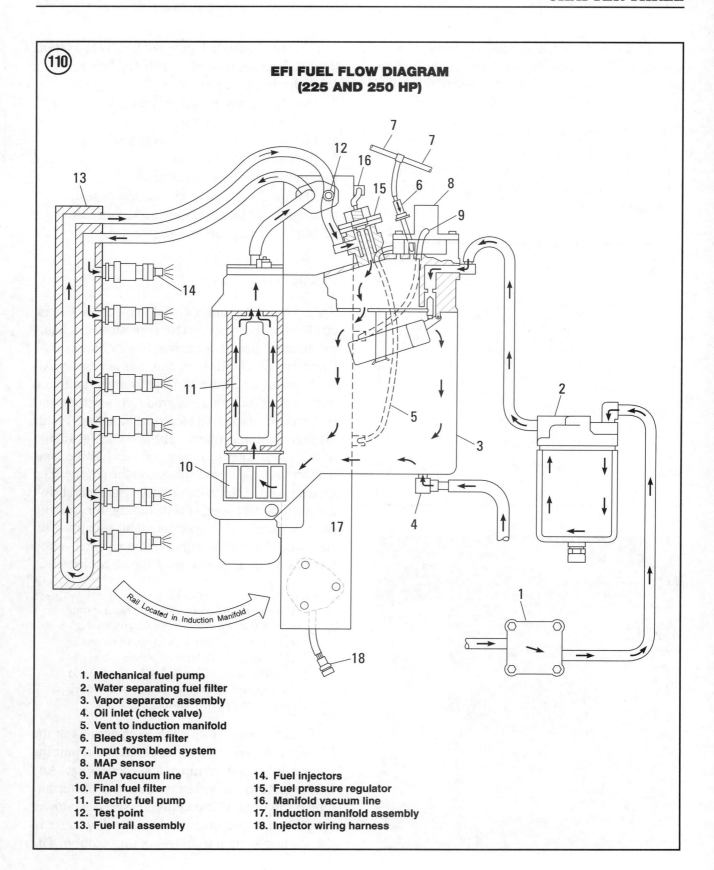

⑾⓪

**EFI FUEL FLOW DIAGRAM
(225 AND 250 HP)**

Rail Located in Induction Manifold

1. Mechanical fuel pump
2. Water separating fuel filter
3. Vapor separator assembly
4. Oil inlet (check valve)
5. Vent to induction manifold
6. Bleed system filter
7. Input from bleed system
8. MAP sensor
9. MAP vacuum line
10. Final fuel filter
11. Electric fuel pump
12. Test point
13. Fuel rail assembly
14. Fuel injectors
15. Fuel pressure regulator
16. Manifold vacuum line
17. Induction manifold assembly
18. Injector wiring harness

engine must crank at normal speed in order to start.

2. Check the mechanical integrity of the power head by performing a cranking compression test (Chapter Four). Correct any mechanical deficiencies before proceeding.

3. Inspect the spark plugs for fouling, correct air gap and correct application. The Champion QL77CC spark plug gapped at .035 in. (0.89 mm) is the only recommended spark plug for this system. Replace any suspect spark plugs.

4. Perform an air gap spark test to verify that the ignition system is operating correctly. Refer to *preliminary checks* in the *Capacitor Discharge Module Ignition (225-250 hp)* section of this chapter. Any ignition system deficiencies must be corrected before attempting to troubleshoot the EFI fuel system.

Fuel ECM power and ground tests

The fuel ECM must receive power (battery voltage through the red and purple leads) and have good ground continuity (through all black leads) in order to function correctly. On 1996-1997 models, if the fuel ECM is disconnected and the ignition ECM is functioning, the warning horn will activate intermittently and the low oil level and overheat lights will alternately flash on the warning panel.

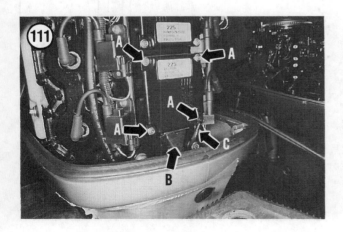

CAUTION
When measuring voltage or resistance at the ECM connectors, be careful not to damage the connector pins or sockets. Do not attempt to insert the meter probe into the socket. Simply touch and hold the meter probe against the pin or socket.

1. To check the fuel ECM ground circuits, disconnect the main fuel ECM engine wiring harness connector (B, **Figure 111**) from the fuel ECM.

2. Calibrate an ohmmeter on the R × 1 scale. Connect one ohmmeter lead to a good engine ground. Connect the other ohmmeter lead alternately to pin No. 1 (black/white) and pin No. 17 (black/white) of the engine wiring harness fuel ECM connector. The meter should indicate continuity. If no continuity is noted, a high resistance or open circuit is present in the black/white leads between pins No. 1 and No. 17 of the engine wiring harness fuel ECM connector and engine ground. Repair or replace the black/white leads as necessary.

3. Connect one ohmmeter lead (still calibrated on the R × 1 scale) to a good engine ground. Connect the other ohmmeter lead alternately to pin No. 6 (black) and pin No. 21 (black) of the engine wiring harness fuel ECM connector. The meter should indicate continuity. If no continuity is noted, a high resistance or open circuit is present in the black leads between pins No. 6 and No. 21 of the engine wiring harness fuel ECM connector and engine ground. Repair or replace the black leads as necessary.

4. Inspect any other ground leads coming from the fuel ECM and fuel ECM mounting brackets that are directly connected to ground (C, **Figure 111**). Clean, tighten or repair all connections and fasteners as necessary to ensure a good ground. Verify that all ECM mounting hardware (A and C, **Figure 111**) is tightened securely.

5. To check the fuel ECM power circuits, set a multimeter to the 20 volt DC scale. Connect the meter black lead to a good engine ground. Con-

nect the meter red lead to pin No.4 (purple) of the engine wiring harness fuel ECM connector (B, **Figure 111**). The meter should indicate within 1.0 volt of battery voltage.

6. If the meter reads less, an open circuit or high resistance is present in the purple lead from (and including) the ignition switch, remote control wiring harness, main engine harness connector, main engine wiring harness, engine mounted terminal block and the fuel ECM connector. Isolate, repair or replace the purple lead or electrical components as necessary.

7. Reconnect all connectors and leads when finished.

Fuel management test

> *NOTE*
> *The fuel pressure at the high-pressure test point must be within specification at all engine speeds. If malfunction occurs only at a certain engine speed, perform the test at the speed the symptom occurs.*

> *CAUTION*
> *Do not run the engine without an adequate water supply and do not exceed 3000 rpm without an adequate load. Refer to **Safety Precautions** at the beginning of this chapter.*

1. Connect the fuel pressure test gauge (**Table 1**) to the test port at the top of the induction manifold, near the fuel pressure regulator. See **Figure 112**. Make sure the gauge connections are secure.

2. Squeeze the primer bulb to ensure the fuel system is primed.

> *NOTE*
> *If the engine is not cranked or started, the ECM will turn the fuel pump off after 30 seconds.*

3. Turn the ignition switch to the ON or RUN position and observe the fuel pressure gauge.

Fuel pressure should be 34-36 psi (234.4-248.2 kPa).

4. If the pressure is above specification, replace the fuel pressure regulator and retest.

5. If the fuel pressure is below specification, determine if the electric fuel pump is running or not. Turn the ignition switch to the ON or RUN position while listening for pump operation. The pump should operate for approximately 30 seconds and then shut off. A mechanic's stethoscope can be used to better hear the pump. If the electric fuel pump does not operate, proceed to Step 12. If the electric fuel pump operates correctly, proceed to Step 6.

6. To make sure the electric fuel pump and vapor separator are receiving fuel, place a suitable container under the vapor separator drain plug (**Figure 113**). Remove the plug. Fuel should flow freely from the vapor separator. If fuel flows,

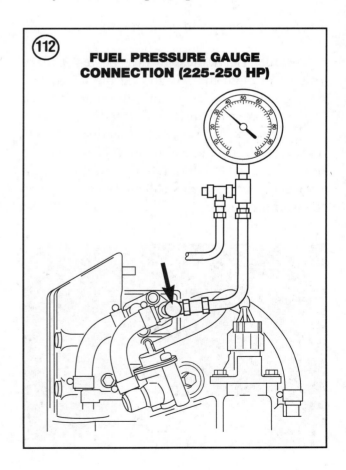

(112) **FUEL PRESSURE GAUGE CONNECTION (225-250 HP)**

proceed with Step 8. If fuel does not flow, check the engine mounted water separating fuel filter for water, debris or blockage (Chapter Four). Check the fuel lines and fittings from the mechanical fuel pump to the vapor separator (including the vapor separator float and valve assembly) for deterioration, debris or blockage. Clean, repair or replace components as necessary. If no defects are noted, proceed with Step 7.

7. Test the mechanical fuel pump and boat fuel system for pressure and vacuum as described in this chapter.

8. If the electric fuel pump runs and the vapor separator is receiving fuel, but fuel pressure is still below specification, either the electric fuel pump or fuel pressure regulator is defective. Proceed with Step 9.

9. Remove the fuel pressure regulator from the vapor separator without disconnecting any vacuum or fuel lines (Chapter Six). Hold the fuel pressure regulator over a suitable container. Turn the ignition switch to the ON or RUN position and note the fuel flow from the regulator.

10. If fuel flows freely from the regulator discharge port but fuel pressure is below specification, replace the fuel pressure regulator. If little or no fuel flows from the regulator discharge port, remove the vapor separator cover and inspect the final filter (Chapter Four). Replace the final filter if it is dirty or clogged and retest fuel pressure. If the final filter is clean, continue to Step 11.

CAUTION
EFI systems operate under high pressure. Do not remove the crimped stainless steel clamps unless absolutely necessary. Do not disconnect the rubber lines from the electric fuel pump, fuel pressure regulator and fuel management adaptor unless new hoses and clamps are to be installed.

11. Disconnect the electric fuel pump output line (1, **Figure 114**) to the induction manifold fuel management adaptor and the fuel rail return line (2, **Figure 114**) from the fuel pressure regulator. Place a shop rag over the regulator line to catch any fuel that may be present in the lines. Blow into the fuel pump output line with low pressure air. Air (or fuel) should exit freely from

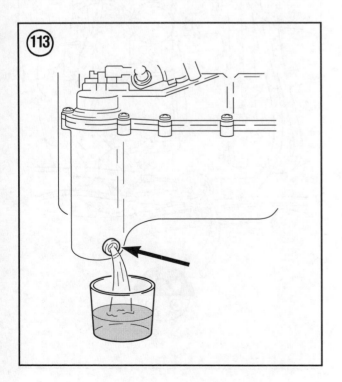

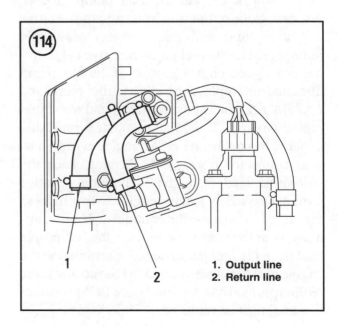

1. Output line
2. Return line

the regulator line. If the air flow is restricted, the induction manifold and fuel rail must be disassembled and cleaned. If air flows freely, replace the electric fuel pump and final filter (in the vapor separator) and retest fuel pressure.

12. To check the electric fuel pump for power, set a multimeter to the 20 volt DC scale. Connect the black lead to a good engine ground and the red lead to the electric fuel pump positive (+) terminal. The meter should indicate within 0.5 volt of battery voltage.

13. If the reading is less, check the red lead from the fuel pump positive terminal to the starter solenoid battery positive terminal for continuity. If no continuity is noted, repair or replace the red lead as necessary.

> *CAUTION*
> *When measuring voltage or resistance at the ECM connectors, be careful not to damage the connector pins or sockets. Do not attempt to insert the meter probe into the socket. Simply touch and hold the meter probe against the pin or socket.*

14. To check the electric fuel pump ground, disconnect the red/purple lead from the negative (–) fuel pump terminal. Connect a suitable jumper lead to the fuel pump negative (–) terminal and a good engine ground. If the fuel pump does not run, replace the electric fuel pump and final filter (in the vapor separator) and retest fuel pressure output. If the fuel pump now runs, disconnect the main fuel ECM engine wiring harness connector from the ECM and check the red/purple lead from the fuel pump negative terminal to pin No. 9 of the engine wiring harness fuel ECM connector for continuity. If no continuity is noted, repair or replace the red/purple lead from the fuel pump negative terminal to the engine wiring harness fuel ECM connector. If the red/purple lead has continuity, the ECM is defective and must be replaced.

Injector and injector harness test

This test will determine if the fuel injectors are receiving battery voltage and if any open circuits are present in the injector wiring harness. Use only a digital multimeter for the following tests. Refer to **Figure 115** and proceed as follows:

1. To check the battery voltage to the injectors, disconnect the injector harness 4-pin connector.

2. Set a digital multimeter to the 20 volt DC scale. Connect the meter black lead to a good engine ground. Connect the meter red lead to pin No. 2 (red lead) of the engine harness side of the

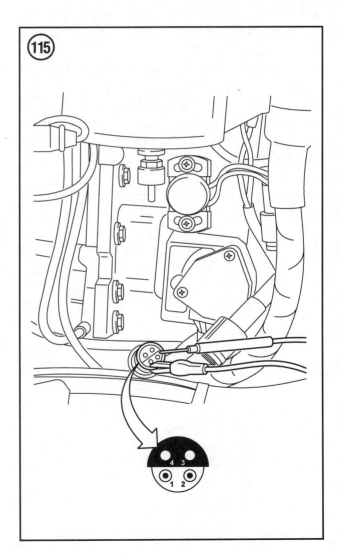

injector harness 4-pin connector. The meter should indicate within 0.5 volt of battery voltage.

3. If the meter reads less, a high resistance or open circuit is present in the red lead from the starter solenoid battery positive terminal and pin No. 2 of the injector harness 4-pin connector. Repair or replace the red lead as necessary.

4. To check the injector and injector harness resistance, set the digital ohmmeter to the 200 ohm scale.

5. Connect the red ohmmeter lead to pin No. 2 of the injector harness side of the injector harness 4-pin connector. Connect the black ohmmeter lead alternately to each of the following pins on the injector harness side of the 4-pin injector harness connector:

   a. Pin No. 4 (white lead) for cylinders No. 1 and No. 2 injectors.

   b. Pin No. 3 (blue lead) for cylinders No. 3 and No. 4 injectors.

   c. Pin No. 1 (yellow lead) for cylinders No. 5 and No. 6 injectors.

6. The reading at each connection should be 5.0-7.0 ohms. If the resistance is not as specified, the induction manifold must be disassembled and the resistance of each injector tested and the continuity of each injector harness lead verified. If the measured resistance is 11.0-13.0 ohms at any one connection, one injector or injector circuit has an open circuit.

Injector cylinder drop test

If the engine appears to be misfiring on 1 or more cylinders, perform a cylinder drop test to determine if each cylinder is firing normally. Before performing a cylinder drop test, however, make sure all previous tests have been performed with satisfactory results. Also make sure compression is acceptable and that the ignition system is functioning properly.

CAUTION
*Do not run the engine without an adequate water supply and do not exceed 3000 rpm without an adequate load. Refer to **Safety Precautions** at the beginning of this chapter.*

1. Start the engine and allow it to warm to operating temperature.

2. Adjust engine speed to approximately 1000-1500 rpm in neutral.

WARNING
High voltage is present during ignition system operation. Do not touch ignition components, leads or test leads while cranking or running the engine.

3. Using insulated spark plug pliers, disconnect the spark plug lead from each spark plug (one at a time) and note the resulting change in engine speed.

4. The engine speed should drop approximately the same amount as each spark plug lead is individually disconnected. If any cylinders do not produce a noticeable rpm drop or the same rpm drop as the majority of the cylinders, record the suspect cylinder numbers.

5. Remove the induction manifold and fuel rail. Remove the suspect injector(s) and inspect the injector inlet filter. If the filter is clean, replace the suspect injector. If the filter is dirty or clogged, clean or replace the filter and reassemble the induction manifold and retest the cylinder drop. If the cylinder drop is still unsatisfactory, replace the suspect injector.

Throttle position sensor test

The correct operation and setting of the TPS (throttle position sensor) is critical to achieving the correct air/fuel ratio. High TPS voltages provide a richer air/fuel ratio. Low TPS voltages provide a leaner air/fuel ratio. Use only a digital multimeter for the following test. Test harness part No. 84-825207A-1 (A, **Figure 116**) is required for this procedure.

NOTE
Make sure the correct idle speed has been verified before adjusting the TPS sensor. If idle speed is changed, the TPS setting must be readjusted.

1. Disconnect the TPS from the engine wiring harness. Connect the test harness (part No. 84-825280A-1) to the TPS sensor and engine wiring harness. Connect the test harness red lead to the red meter lead. Connect the test harness white lead to the black meter lead. Set the multimeter to the 20 volt DC scale.

NOTE
If the TPS sensor cannot be correctly set or reads zero, check the continuity of the sensor leads from the TPS connector to both the ignition and fuel ECM connectors and engine ground. The blue/yellow lead goes to both the ignition and fuel ECM connector pins No. 14 and the blue/red lead goes to both the ignition and fuel ECM connector pins No. 15. The black lead goes directly to engine ground.

2. Turn the ignition switch to the ON or RUN position. Make sure the throttle plates are against the idle stop. Note the meter reading and compare to specification (**Table 20**). If the reading is within specification, continue to Step 4. If the reading is not within specification, loosen the 2 screws (B, **Figure 116**) securing the TPS to the induction manifold.

3. With the throttle shaft held against the idle stop screw, rotate the TPS to obtain the desired specification (**Table 20**). While holding the TPS at the correct setting, tighten the screws securely. Recheck the voltage reading.

4. Disconnect the throttle cable and slowly move the throttle linkage to the full-throttle position while noting the meter reading. The voltage should increase smoothly to specification (**Table 20**). If the meter reading fluctuates or is

erratic as the throttle is advanced, replace the TPS. If the meter reading is not within specification at wide-open throttle, check the wide-open throttle stop (Chapter Five) for correct adjustment.

MAP sensor tests

The MAP (manifold absolute pressure) sensor provides engine load and barometric pressure data to the ECM. The MAP sensor is mounted on top of the vapor separator. A vacuum line connects the MAP sensor to the induction manifold. The MAP sensor is best tested with the DDT (Digital Diagnostic Terminal [**Table 1**]). On 1996-1997 models, the warning horn will sound and the warning panel will alternately flash the low oil level and overheat lamps if a (any) sensor failure is detected.

1. Inspect the MAP sensor vacuum line to the induction manifold for secure attachment, kinks, deterioration or leakage. Replace the line as necessary.

CAUTION
*Do not run the engine without an adequate water supply and do not exceed 3000 rpm without an adequate load. Refer to **Safety Precautions** at the beginning of this chapter.*

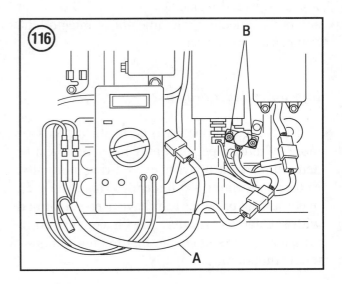

2. Start the engine and let it warm to operating temperature.

3. Stop the engine and disconnect the MAP sensor line from the induction manifold.

4. Attach a hand vacuum pump to the MAP sensor line.

5. Run the engine at idle speed. Vary the vacuum applied to the MAP sensor line from zero to 10 in. Hg (34 kPa) as the engine idles. A noticeable change in engine running quality should be noticed. If no change in running quality occurs, check the wiring harness leads for continuity to the ECMs and engine ground.

6. To check the MAP sensor blue/yellow lead for continuity to the ignition *and* fuel ECMs, disconnect the map sensor from the engine wiring harness. Disconnect the fuel and ignition ECM engine wiring harness connectors from the ECMs.

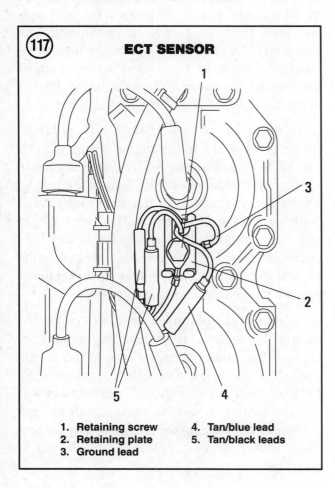

ECT SENSOR

1. Retaining screw
2. Retaining plate
3. Ground lead
4. Tan/blue lead
5. Tan/black leads

7. Calibrate an ohmmeter on the R × 1 scale. Connect one ohmmeter lead to the engine wiring harness blue/yellow lead at the MAP sensor. Connect the other ohmmeter lead alternately to the fuel *and* ignition ECM connector pins No. 14 (blue/yellow). The meter should indicate continuity. If no continuity is noted, an open circuit or high resistance is present in the engine wiring harness blue/yellow lead. Repair or replace the blue/yellow lead as necessary.

8. Connect one ohmmeter lead, still calibrated on the R × 1 scale, to the engine harness white/green lead at the MAP sensor connector. Connect the other ohmmeter lead to the fuel ECM connector pin No. 7 (white/green). The meter should indicate continuity. If no continuity is noted, an open circuit or high resistance is present in the engine wiring harness green/white lead. Repair or replace the green/white lead as necessary.

9. Connect one ohmmeter lead, still calibrated on the R × 1 scale, to a good engine ground. Connect the other ohmmeter lead to the engine wiring harness black lead at the MAP sensor. The meter should indicate continuity. If no continuity is noted, an open circuit or high resistance is present in the engine wiring harness black lead. Repair or replace the black lead as necessary.

Engine coolant temperature sensor test

The ECT (engine coolant temperature) sensor provides the ECM with engine (coolant) temperature data. The ECT data is primarily used for the cold start and engine overheat programs. The ECT sensor has four leads. The two tan/black leads are used by the ECM to sense engine temperature. The tan/blue and black leads are the temperature switch portion of the ECT sensor and are used to sound the warning horn whenever the temperature of the engine exceeds the switch rating. Refer to **Table 21** for ECT sensor resistance values and to the end of the book for wiring diagrams. To test the ECT sensor and switch, refer to **Figure 117** and proceed as follows:

1. Disconnect the ECT sensor tan/blue and 2 tan/black leads from the engine wiring harness.

2. Calibrate an ohmmeter on the highest scale available. Connect one meter lead to the black sensor lead (ground) and the other ohmmeter lead to the tan/blue sensor lead. The ohmmeter should read no continuity. Replace the sensor assembly if no continuity is noted.

CAUTION
*Do not run the engine without an adequate water supply and do not exceed 3000 rpm without an adequate load. Refer to **Safety Precautions** at the beginning of this chapter.*

3. Run the engine up to operating temperature as described in *Engine temperature check* in this chapter. The ohmmeter should continue to indicate no continuity when the engine is at normal operating temperature. Replace the sensor assembly if continuity is noted. The only time the sensor should indicate continuity is if the engine is actually overheating (exceeding normal operating temperature).

4. Calibrate the ohmmeter on the appropriate scale to read the ECT sensor engine temperature data as listed in **Table 21**.

NOTE
The temperature of the engine must be accurately determined before the ECT sensor can be tested.

5. Measure the temperature of the cylinder head with a pyrometer or allow the engine to cool to ambient temperature. Connect one ohmmeter lead to each of the tan/black ECT sensor leads. Note the meter reading and compare to specification. If the reading is not within specification, the ECT sensor must be replaced. If the reading is within specification, continue to Step 6.

6. Remove the sensor from the cylinder head (with ohmmeter still connected) and immerse the sensing element into a container of crushed ice and water while noting the meter reading. The reading should smoothly increase as the sensing

element cools. If the reading does not increase to specification (**Table 21**), replace the ECT sensor. If the reading is within specification, continue to Step 7.

7. Calibrate an ohmmeter on the highest scale available. Connect one ohmmeter lead to the black ECT sensor lead. Connect the other ohmmeter lead alternately to each of the tan/black ECT sensor leads. The meter must indicate no continuity. If continuity is noted, replace the ECT sensor.

8. Disconnect the ignition (upper) and fuel (lower) ECM engine wiring harness connectors from the ECMs. Calibrate an ohmmeter on the R × 1 scale. Connect one ohmmeter lead to the engine wiring harness ignition ECM connector pin No. 16 (brown lead) and the other ohmmeter lead to the engine wiring harness brown (or tan/black) lead bullet connector at the ECT sensor. The meter should indicate continuity. If no continuity is noted, an open circuit or high resistance is present in the engine wiring harness brown lead. Repair or replace the brown lead as necessary.

9. Connect one ohmmeter lead, still calibrated on the R × 1 scale, to the engine wiring harness fuel ECM connector pin No. 16 (tan/black lead). Connect the other ohmmeter lead to the engine wiring harness brown (or tan/black) lead bullet connector at the ECT sensor. The meter should indicate continuity. If no continuity is noted, an open circuit or high resistance is present in the engine wiring harness tan/black lead. Repair or replace the tan/black lead as necessary.

10. Connect one ohmmeter lead, still calibrated on the R × 1 scale, to a clean engine ground. Connect the other ohmmeter lead to the engine wiring harness black lead bullet connector at the ECT sensor. The meter should read continuity. If no continuity is noted, an open circuit or high resistance is present in the engine wiring harness black lead. Repair or replace the black lead as necessary.

Intake air temperature sensor test

The IAT (intake air temperature) sensor provides the ECM with ambient temperature information. Cold air, being more dense and containing more oxygen, requires a richer fuel delivery. Warm air, being less dense and containing less oxygen, requires a leaner fuel delivery. The ECM can compensate the normal air/fuel ratio richer or leaner as IAT sensor data dictates. IAT sensor failure will generally cause a running quality problem, but it will normally not cause a no-start condition. There are 2 brown leads coming from the IAT sensor. One lead is connected to engine ground and the other lead is connected to the fuel ECM connector pin No. 22. Refer to the end of the book for wiring diagrams and **Table 21** for IAT sensor ohmmeter values. To test the IAT sensor, refer to **Figure 118** and proceed as follows:

1. Disconnect the IAT sensor brown leads from the engine wiring harness.

2. Calibrate the ohmmeter on the appropriate scale to read the appropriate IAT sensor temperature value as listed in **Table 21**.

NOTE
The ambient temperature must be accurately determined before the IAT sensor can be tested.

3. Allow the engine to cool to ambient temperature. Connect one ohmmeter lead to each of the brown IAT sensor leads. Note the meter reading and compare to specifications. If the reading is not within specification, the IAT sensor must be replaced. If the reading is within specification, continue to Step 6.

4. Remove the sensor from the induction manifold (with ohmmeter still connected) and immerse the sensing element into a container of crushed ice and water while noting the meter reading. The reading should smoothly increase as the sensing element cools. If the reading does not increase to specification (**Table 21**), replace the IAT sensor. If the reading is within specification, continue to Step 7.

5. Disconnect the fuel ECM engine wiring harness connector from the fuel ECM. Calibrate an ohmmeter on the R × 1 scale. Connect one ohmmeter lead to the engine wiring harness fuel ECM connector pin No. 22 (tan lead) and the other ohmmeter lead to the engine wiring harness tan lead bullet connector at the IAT sensor. The meter should indicate continuity. If no continuity is noted, an open circuit or high resistance is present in the engine wiring harness brown lead. Repair or replace the tan lead as necessary.

6. Connect one ohmmeter lead, still calibrated on the R × 1 scale, to a good engine ground. Connect the other ohmmeter lead to the engine wiring harness black lead bullet connector at the IAT sensor. The meter should indicate continuity. If no continuity is noted, an open circuit or high resistance is present in the engine wiring harness black lead. Repair or replace the black lead as necessary.

3

Water sensor test

The water sensor is designed to alert the boat operator to a buildup of water in the engine mounted water separating fuel filter. When the water level in the filter reaches potentially damaging levels, the fuel ECM turns on the water in fuel light on the warning panel and activates the warning horn. The warning horn will sound 4 times and then be silent for 2 minutes. After 2 minutes the horn will repeat the cycle.

1. Disconnect the tan/blue lead (A, **Figure 119**) from the water sensor at the base of the water separating fuel filter (B, **Figure 119**).
2. Turn the ignition switch to the ON or RUN position.
3. Connect the tan/blue lead to a good engine ground.
4. The water in fuel light on the warning panel should illuminate and the warning horn should sound as described previously. If the lamp does not illuminate and the horn does not sound, check the tan/blue lead for continuity to the fuel ECM connector pin No. 12. Repair or replace the lead as necessary.

DFI AIR/FUEL SYSTEM TROUBLESHOOTING

This section deals with troubleshooting the DFI (direct fuel injection) air/fuel system used on the Mercury and Mariner 200 DFI outboard motors. Once the defective component is identified, refer to appropriate chapter for component removal and replacement procedures.

Troubleshooting Notes And Precautions

Several troubleshooting precautions must be strictly observed to avoid damaging the system or injuring yourself.

1. Do not reverse the battery connections. Reverse battery polarity will damage electronic components.

2. Do not *spark* the battery terminals with the battery cable connections to determine polarity.

3. Do not disconnect the battery cables with the engine running.

4. Do not crank or run the outboard if any electrical components are not grounded to the power head.

5. Do not disconnect the ECM (electronic control module) when the outboard is running, while the ignition switch is ON or while the battery cables are connected.

6. The DFI air/fuel system ON requires that the electric starter crank the engine at normal speed for the ignition system to produce adequate spark and the air system to produce adequate air rail pressure. If the starter motor cranks the engine slowly or not at all, go back to the *Starting System* section and correct the starting system problem before continuing.

7. Check the battery cable connections for secure attachment to both battery terminals and the engine. Clean any corrosion from all connections. Discard any wing nuts and install corrosion resistant hex nuts at all battery cable connections. Place a corrosion resistant locking

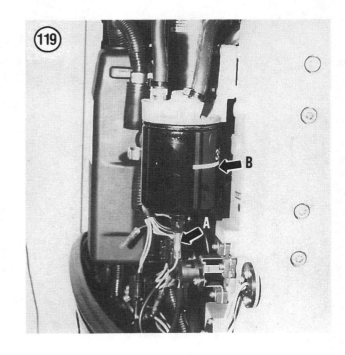

washer between the battery terminal stud and battery cable terminal end to ensure a positive connection. Loose battery connections can cause every symptom imaginable.

8. Check all ECM and DFI component ground leads for secure attachment to the power head. Clean and tighten all ground leads, connections and fasteners as necessary. Loose ground connections and loose component mounting hardware can cause every symptom imaginable.

> *CAUTION*
> *The 200 DFI (direct fuel injection) cannot be started or operated without battery voltage.*

Resistance (Ohmmeter) Tests

The resistance values specified in the following test procedures are based on tests performed at room temperature. Actual resistance readings obtained during testing will generally be slightly higher if checked on hot components. In addition, resistance readings may vary depending on the manufacturer of the ohmmeter. Therefore, use discretion when failing any component that is only slightly out of specification. Many ohmmeters have difficulty reading less than 1 ohm accurately. If this is the case, specifications of less than 1 ohm generally appear as a very low (continuity) reading.

System Description

The 200 DFI engine can best be described as an EFI engine with an air compressor. In addition to all of the normal EFI components, a belt-driven, water-cooled air compressor (with an intake air filter that must be serviced), port (A, **Figure 120**) and starboard (A, **Figure 121**) air/fuel rails, an air pressure regulator, 6 DFI (direct fuel injection) injectors, a tracker diaphragm in the starboard air/fuel rail and the necessary hoses, high pressure lines and fittings are required.

The air compressor (A, **Figure 120**) and air pressure regulator (C, **Figure 120**) work to maintain air pressure in the air portion of the air/fuel rails at approximately 80 psi (552 kPa). The fuel regulator (D, **Figure 120**) maintains fuel pressure at 10 psi (69 kPa) over air pressure. If this 10 psi (69 kPa) working differential is not maintained, the ECM (electronic control module) calibrations will be incorrect. Fuel rail and fuel injector working pressure is approximately 90 psi (621 kPa). The fuel injectors each fire into their individual air chambers (pressurized at 80 psi [552 kPa]) machined into the air/fuel rails. The DFI injectors (C, **Figure 121**) then fire this air/fuel mix directly into the combustion chamber at the precise time calculated by the ECM.

The tracker diaphragm (B, **Figure 121**) dampens pressure fluctuations between the air and fuel passages. The diaphragm is positioned between the air and fuel passages and flexes inward or outward depending on which chamber (air or fuel) has the highest pressure at the moment.

> *NOTE*
> *To help the motor start more quickly, the ECM opens the DFI injectors briefly during the first moments of cranking. This allows combustion chamber compression to help charge the air rail faster than the air compressor is able to alone.*

The object of the DFI system is to inject the air/fuel charge into the combustion chamber after the intake and exhaust ports have closed, preventing leakage or dilution of the air/fuel charge with exhaust gases. A dramatic increase in fuel economy and a reduction in exhaust emissions are obtained with the DFI system.

Current (1997) DFI models depend only on the following sensors for operation:

1. *Throttle position sensors*—Two throttle position sensors (TPS) are used on DFI models. This is done to improve reliability by adding redundancy. One sensor reads from low voltage to high voltage, the other sensor reads from high voltage to low voltage. If one sensor fails, the check engine light will illuminate and the warning horn will sound. If both sensors fail, the engine will not operate above idle speed. The sensors are mounted back to back and read off the bottom throttle shaft as shown in **Figure 122**.

2. *Crankshaft position sensor*—The crankshaft position sensor (CPS) detects the presence of the encoding ribs on the flywheel (A, **Figure 123**) and sends a signal to the electronic control module (ECM). This signal tells the ECM (C, **Figure 123**) crankshaft position and engine speed. The air gap between the flywheel encoding ribs and the CPS (B, **Figure 123**) must be set to 0.030 in. (0.76 mm). If the CPS fails, the motor will not run.

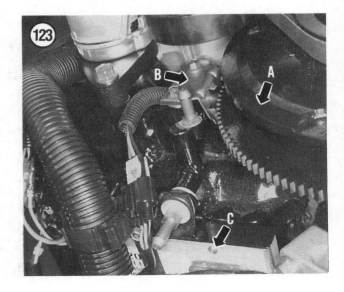

3. *Engine coolant temperature sensor*—The ECT (engine coolant temperature) sensor provides the ECM with engine (coolant) temperature data. See **Figure 124**. The ECM adjusts the fuel injector pulse width (on time) to compensate for different engine temperatures, such as cold

starts. If the ECT reads above 221° F (105° C), the ECM will retard ignition timing to limit engine speed to approximately 3000 rpm. Refer to **Table 21** for ECT sensor resistance values.

4. *Manifold absolute pressure sensor*—The MAP (manifold absolute pressure) sensor on 1997 models is only used for altitude compensation. When the key is turned on, the MAP sensor (**Figure 125**) immediately provides a barometric pressure reading to the ECM. The ECM then adjusts engine operation for the present altitude. The actual MAP function, when used, indicates engine load to the ECM. This allows for subtle adjustments to the spark advance and air/fuel mixture as engine load changes, maintaining maximum combustion efficiency and minimum exhaust emissions.

The following sensors are installed and wired to the ECM, but are not used by the 1997 model year ECM.

1. *Intake air temperature sensor*—The IAT (intake air temperature) sensor (**Figure 118**), when used, allows compensation for air temperature fluctuations. As air temperature changes, the density of the air changes, requiring subtle changes to the air/fuel ratio to maintain maximum combustion efficiency and minimum exhaust emissions.

2. *Knock sensor*—The KS (knock sensor), when used, allows the early detection and elimination of preignition and detonation. The KS (**Figure 126**) detects the high frequency vibration caused

by abnormal combustion. When the ECM receives the signal from the KS, the ECM retards ignition timing and increases fuel injector pulse width (within programmed limits) until the knock signal is eliminated or the preprogrammed limit is reached. The principle advantage of a knock sensor is the ability to run lower octane fuels without the need for recalibration or adjustments.

The DFI air/fuel system is integrated with the DI (digital inductive) ignition. Refer to the *DI (Digital Inductive [200 DFI])* section of this chapter for system description and components. If the ignition system is working correctly, it can be assumed that the CPS (crankshaft position sensor) is functional.

The DFI air/fuel system and DI ignition systems use fully digital electronics and are designed to be diagnosed by the Quicksilver DDT (digital diagnostic terminal). The DDT (**Figure 127**) is normally found only in Mercury or Mariner dealerships, where the investment can be justified. The DDT displays sensor input values and actuator output values as the ECM (electronic control module) sees them. The DDT and required adapter cables are listed in **Table 1**. If using the DDT for troubleshooting, refer to the manual included with the DDT software cartridge for troubleshooting procedures. DDT displayed sensor and actuator values are listed in **Table 20**.

Troubleshooting without the DDT extremely limits the components and systems that can be tested. If the procedure outlined in the following section does not isolate the failed component or system, a DDT will have to be obtained or the motor taken to a Mercury/Mariner dealership for diagnosis.

Troubleshooting

Refer to **Figure 128** for air/fuel components and flow diagrams. Refer to the end of the book for wiring diagrams. Read the *Troubleshooting*

Notes And Precautions at the beginning of this section and *Safety Precautions* at the beginning of this chapter before proceeding. Sensors and injectors can be disconnected and reconnected during engine operation without ECM damage. A noticeable change in engine performance will result if the sensor or injector is functioning. If substitute injectors (DFI and fuel) are available, they can be plugged into each wiring harness connector to verify circuit operation while the engine is being cranked or run. The injectors will audibly click when operating. A mechanic's stethoscope can also be used to listen for injector operation. If necessary, the other injectors (DFI and fuel) in close proximity can be disconnected to reduce background noise. Automotive *Noid Lites* or injector test lights with compatible connectors can also be used to check injector circuit operation. The recommended troubleshooting procedure is as follows:

1. Perform all of the ignition system checks (in DI [digital inductive] ignition section).

2. Preliminary checks.

3. Fuel rail pressure test.

4. Air rail pressure test.

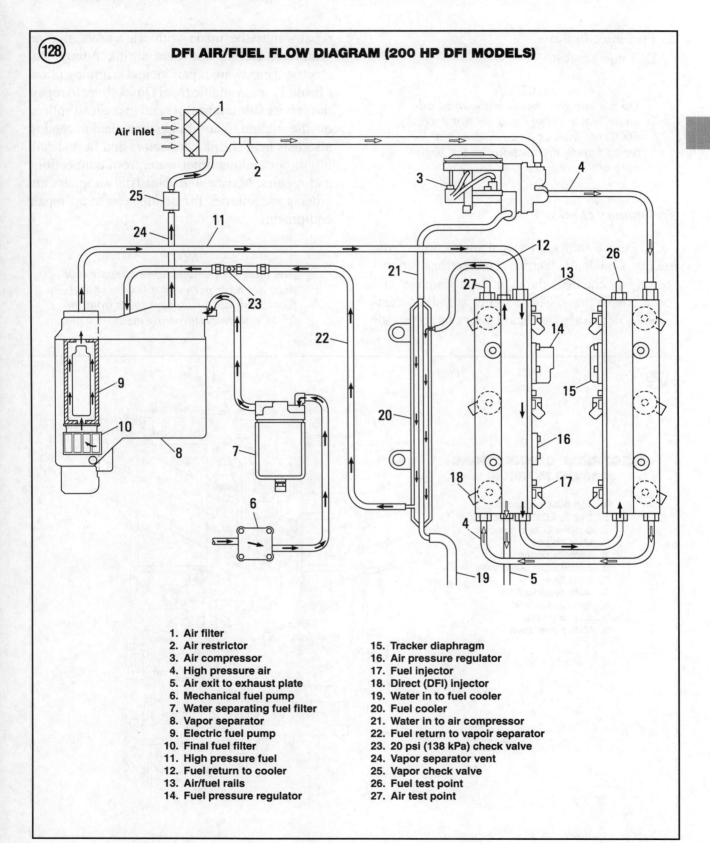

DFI AIR/FUEL FLOW DIAGRAM (200 HP DFI MODELS)

3

1. Air filter
2. Air restrictor
3. Air compressor
4. High pressure air
5. Air exit to exhaust plate
6. Mechanical fuel pump
7. Water separating fuel filter
8. Vapor separator
9. Electric fuel pump
10. Final fuel filter
11. High pressure fuel
12. Fuel return to cooler
13. Air/fuel rails
14. Fuel pressure regulator

15. Tracker diaphragm
16. Air pressure regulator
17. Fuel injector
18. Direct (DFI) injector
19. Water in to fuel cooler
20. Fuel cooler
21. Water in to air compressor
22. Fuel return to vapoir separator
23. 20 psi (138 kPa) check valve
24. Vapor separator vent
25. Vapor check valve
26. Fuel test point
27. Air test point

5. Fuel injector test.
6. DFI injector test.

CAUTION
*Do not run the engine without an adequate water supply and do not exceed 3000 rpm without an adequate load. Refer to **Safety Precautions** at the beginning of this chapter.*

Preliminary checks

Perform a thorough visual inspection of the engine. Check all electrical connections for corrosion, mechanical damage, heat damage and loose connections. Clean and repair all connections as necessary. All lead splices or connector

repairs must be made with waterproof marine grade connectors and heat shrink tubing. An electrical hardware repair kit and crimping pliers (**Table 1**) are available from Quicksilver to repair the serviceable connectors and make lead splices on the engine. The Quicksilver dealer catalog also lists heat shrink connectors and heat shrink tubing for making other waterproof connections and repairs. Marine and industrial suppliers are other good sources for quality electrical repair equipment.

NOTE
Any electrical connection or repair that does not have perfect continuity will affect the signal being sent to or from the ECM, effectively throwing the system out

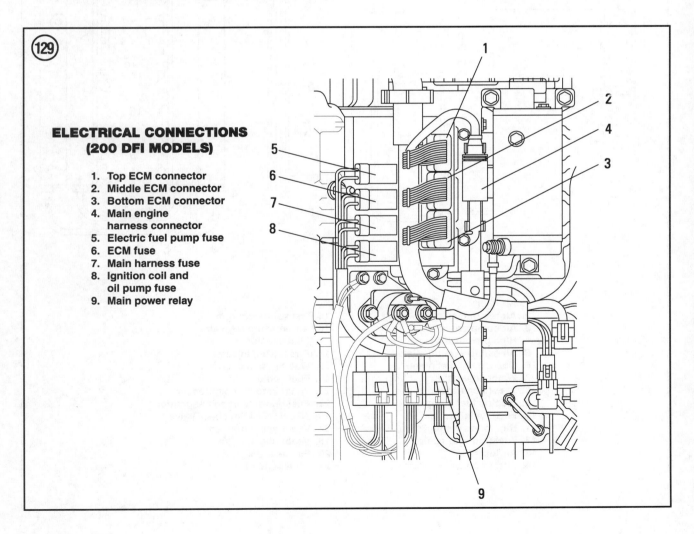

(129)

ELECTRICAL CONNECTIONS (200 DFI MODELS)

1. Top ECM connector
2. Middle ECM connector
3. Bottom ECM connector
4. Main engine harness connector
5. Electric fuel pump fuse
6. ECM fuse
7. Main harness fuse
8. Ignition coil and oil pump fuse
9. Main power relay

of calibration. This will always have a detrimental effect on engine operating quality and performance.

1. Inspect the battery. Make sure the battery rating is at least 750 CCA (cold cranking amps) or 1000 MCA (marine cranking amps). The 200 DFI has the highest battery rating requirements of any engine in the marine industry. A smaller battery will not provide consistent starts.

2. Check both battery cable connections at the battery and engine. Clean, tighten and repair the connections and terminals as necessary. Any loose connections will cause erratic and intermittent symptoms. If the cranking rpm is slower than normal, perform the *voltage drop tests* in the starting system troubleshooting section. The engine must crank at normal speed in order to start.

NOTE
If the recommended troubleshooting procedure is followed, the ECM and ignition coil (and oil pump) fuses and circuits have been tested in the DI ignition system section. If so, test only the remaining fuses (electric fuel pump and remote control harness) in the next section.

3. Check the four 20 amp fuses (**Figure 129**) on the starboard side of the power head. The top fuse is for the electric fuel pump, the second fuse from the top is the ECM main fuse, the third fuse from

the top is the standard remote control harness fuse and the bottom fuse is the oil pump and ignition coils fuse. Test the fuses with an ohmmeter set to the R × 1 scale. All fuses should read continuity. If no continuity is obtained, replace the suspect fuse.

4. Check the air compressor air filter. Replace the filter if debris is visible and if the filter is damaged or deteriorated. The white side of the filter must face out.

5. Check the air compressor and alternator belt. The belt is tensioned automatically by the floating idle pulley. Make sure the air compressor turns normally (without binding) and the alternator turns freely. Replace any damaged components.

6. Check the mechanical integrity of the power head by performing a cranking compression test (Chapter Four). Correct any mechanical deficiencies before proceeding.

7. Inspect the spark plugs for fouling, correct air gap and correct application. The only recommended spark plug for the 200 DFI is the Champion RC10ECC, gapped at .040 in. (1.02 mm). The use of any other spark plug will cause erratic operation and possible power head damage. Replace any suspect spark plugs.

Air rail pressure test

CAUTION
The 200 DFI uses a high-pressure air system to inject the air/fuel charge into the combustion chamber. Do not attempt to check the air rail pressure unless a liquid filled gauge assembly capable of reading a minimum of 160 psi (1103 kPa) is used. Quicksilver test gauge part No. 84-16850A-2 meets these requirements.

1. Connect the test gauge to the test port (**Figure 130**) at the top of the port air/fuel rail. Make sure the gauge connections are secure.

NOTE
Record the air pressure for later reference. The fuel pressure test results in the

next section are dependent on the air pressure in the system.

CAUTION
Do not run the engine without an adequate water supply and do not exceed 3000 rpm without an adequate load. Refer to Safety Precautions at the beginning of this chapter.

2. Crank (or start the engine, if possible) the engine for several seconds until air pressure stabilizes. Air pressure should be 77-81 psi (531-559 kPa). If the pressure is below 70 psi (483 kPa) the engine will not start. If the pressure is below specification, inspect all of the high-pressure air lines from the air compressor to the top of the starboard rail and high-pressure line from the bottom of the starboard rail to the bottom of the port rail. If no leaks are found, check the air compressor reed valves for failure. If the reed valves are in acceptable condition, the air pressure regulator or tracker diaphragm have failed.

The air pressure regulator (14, **Figure 128**) is located on the port air/fuel rail and the tracker diaphragm (15, **Figure 128**) is located in starboard air/fuel rail. The rails are not serviceable and are replaced individually if defective. If the tracker diaphragm fails, there should be fuel in the air passages of the air/fuel rails.

3. If the air pressure exceeds specification, check the air regulator exit hose at the bottom of the port fuel rail for blockage or kinks. This hose connects to the exhaust adapter plate. If the hose and fittings are not blocked or kinked, replace the port air/fuel rail.

Fuel rail pressure test

CAUTION
The 200 DFI uses a much higher fuel pressure system than traditional EFI engines. Do not attempt to check the fuel rail pressure unless a liquid filled gauge assembly capable of reading a minimum of 160 psi (1103 kPa) is used. Quicksil-

ver test gauge part No. 84-16850A-2 meets these requirements.

1. Connect the test gauge to the test port (**Figure 131**) at the top of the starboard air/fuel rail. Make sure the gauge connections are secure.

NOTE
The fuel pressure regulator (14, Figure 128) regulates fuel pressure at 10 psi (69 kPa) over air pressure. If there is zero air pressure, the fuel pressure should be 10 psi (69 kPa). No attempt should be made to check fuel pressure until air pressure is verified.

CAUTION
Do not run the engine without an adequate water supply and do not exceed 3000 rpm without an adequate load. Refer to Safety Precautions at the beginning of this chapter.

2. Crank (or start the engine, if possible) the engine for several seconds until fuel pressure stabilizes. Fuel pressure should be 10 psi (69 kPa) over the air rail test previously recorded. If the air pressure was within specification, fuel pressure should be 87-91 psi (600-627 kPa). If the fuel pressure is not 10 psi (69 kPa) over air pressure, the engine will be out of calibration and will operate poorly, if it all.

3. If the pressure is over specification, inspect the fuel return line and fittings from the port air/fuel rail to the fuel cooler assembly for obstructions and kinks. Inspect the fuel cooler fuel

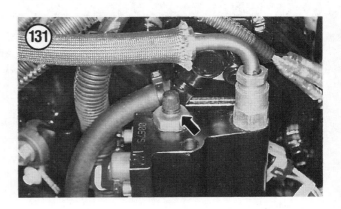

passageways and fittings for debris or blockage. Inspect the fuel line and fittings from the fuel cooler to the vapor separator for obstructions, kinks and blockages. If no restriction to the fuel flow from the port rail to the vapor separator is found, replace the port air/fuel rail.

NOTE
If the engine is not cranked or started, the ECM will turn the main power relay (and fuel pump) off after 3 seconds.

4. If the fuel pressure is below specification, determine if the electric fuel pump is running or not. Turn the ignition switch to the ON or RUN position while listening for pump operation. The pump should operate for approximately 3 seconds then shut off. A mechanic's stethoscope can be used to better hear the pump. If the electric fuel pump does not operate, proceed to Step 8. If

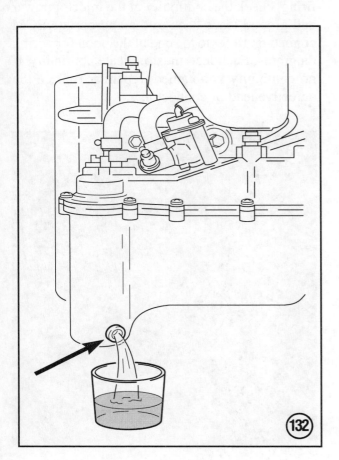

the electric fuel pump operates correctly, proceed to Step 5.

5. To make sure the electric fuel pump and vapor separator are receiving fuel, place a suitable container under the vapor separator drain plug (**Figure 132**). Remove the plug. Fuel should flow freely from the vapor separator. If fuel flows, proceed with Step 7. If fuel does not flow, check the engine mounted water separating fuel filter for water, debris or blockage. Check the fuel lines and fittings from the mechanical fuel pump to the vapor separator (including the vapor separator float and valve) for deterioration, debris or blockage. Clean, repair or replace components as necessary. If no defects are noted, proceed with Step 6.

6. Test the mechanical fuel pump and boat fuel system for pressure and vacuum as described previously in this chapter.

7. If the electric fuel pump runs and the vapor separator is receiving fuel, but fuel pressure is still below specifications, disconnect the air line (4, **Figure 128**) from the bottom of both air/fuel rails. If fuel is present in the air chamber of either air/fuel rail, the tracker diaphragm or fuel pressure regulator diaphragm have failed. Replace the suspect rail and retest fuel pressure. If no fuel flows from the air chamber of either air/fuel rail, either the electric fuel pump or fuel pressure regulator valve seat is defective. Replace the fuel pump or the port air/fuel rail and retest fuel pressure.

8. To check the electric fuel pump for power, set a multimeter to the 20 volt DC scale. Connect the black lead to a good engine ground and the red lead to the electric fuel pump positive (+) terminal.

NOTE
If the engine is not cranked or started, the ECM will turn the main power relay (and fuel pump) off after 3 seconds. The meter reading must be noted before this time elapses.

9. Turn the ignition switch to the ON or RUN position. The meter should indicate within 0.5 volt of battery voltage.

NOTE
If the recommended troubleshooting procedure is followed, the main power relay and associated circuits have been tested in the DI (digital inductive) ignition system section. If so, continue. If not, perform the ECM power tests in the DI ignition system section before continuing.

10. If the reading is less, check the red lead from the fuel pump to the fuel pump fuse holder and the red/white lead from the fuel pump fuse holder to the main power relay for continuity. If no continuity is noted, repair or replace the red and red/white leads as necessary.

11. To check the electric fuel pump ground, calibrate an ohmmeter on the R × 1 scale. Connect one ohmmeter lead to a good engine ground. Connect the other meter lead to the fuel pump negative (–) terminal. The meter should read continuity. If any other reading is noted, repair or replace the black ground lead as necessary.

12. If all Steps to this point have tested satisfactorily, but the fuel pump still does not run, replace the electric fuel pump and final fuel filter (in the vapor separator) and retest fuel pressure output.

Fuel injector test

The fuel injectors (**Figure 133**) are mounted in the air/fuel rails. There is one fuel injector for each cylinder. The fuel injectors are normally closed. The fuel injectors fire (open) and close under ECM control. The period of time that the injectors are open is referred to as *pulse width*. The longer the pulse width, the more fuel that is delivered to the direct injector air chamber. The 2 leads (power and ground) for each injector are individually wired back to the ECM (a total of 12 injector leads).

1. To test the resistance of the fuel injectors, disconnect each fuel injector wiring harness plug-in. Calibrate an ohmmeter on the appropriate scale to read 1.7-1.9 ohms. Connect one ohmmeter lead to each of the fuel injector terminals. If the reading is not 1.7-1.9 ohms, the fuel injector is defective.

2. Repeat Step 2 for the remaining fuel injectors.

CAUTION
When measuring voltage or resistance at the ECM connectors, be careful not to damage the connector pins or sockets. Do not attempt to insert the meter probe into the socket. Simply touch and hold the meter probe against the pin or socket.

3. If an injector with good resistance is not firing, check the continuity of the injector power and ground leads back to the appropriate ECM connector. Refer to the end of the book for wiring diagrams. Each lead must indicate continuity. If no continuity is obtained, repair or replace the defective lead or connector.

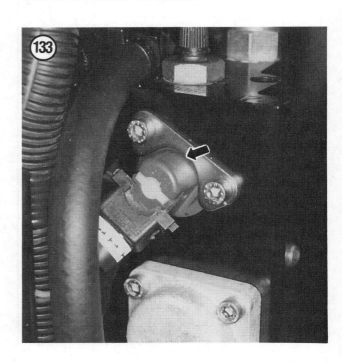

DFI injector tests

The DFI (direct fuel injection) injectors are mounted between the air/fuel rails and the cylinder heads. See **Figure 134**. The DFI injector releases the air/fuel charge into the combustion chamber from the air chamber of the air/fuel rail. There is one DFI injector for each cylinder. The DFI injectors are normally closed. The DFI injectors fire (open) and close under ECM control. The DFI injectors must be precisely timed in relation to piston position and ignition timing. Any miscalculations will result in a misfire. The 2 leads (power and ground) for each injector are individually wired back to the ECM (a total of 12 injector leads).

1. To test the resistance of the DFI injectors, disconnect each DFI injector wiring harness plug-in. Calibrate an ohmmeter on the appropriate scale to read 1.0-1.6 ohms. Connect one ohmmeter lead to each of the DFI injector terminals. If the reading is not within 1.0-1.6 ohms, the DFI injector is defective.

2. Repeat Step 2 for the remaining fuel injectors.

CAUTION
When measuring voltage or resistance at the ECM connectors, be careful not to damage the connector pins or sockets. Do not attempt to insert the meter probe into the socket. Simply touch and hold the meter probe against the pin or socket.

3. If an injector with good resistance is not firing, check the continuity of the injector power and ground leads back to the appropriate ECM connector. Refer to the end of the book for wiring diagrams. Each lead must indicate continuity. If any other reading is obtained, repair or replace the defective lead or connector.

ENGINE TEMPERATURE AND OVERHEATING

Proper temperature is critical to good engine operation. Internal engine damage will occur if the engine is operated in an overheat condition. Engines that are overcooling will experience fouled spark plugs, poor acceleration and idle quality, excessive carbon buildup in the combustion chamber and reduced fuel economy. V-6 models use one thermostat in each cylinder head, failure of a single thermostat would cause only one cylinder bank to overheat.

The thermostat(s) control the flow of water leaving the cylinder block. Many engines with thermostat(s) also incorporate a poppet (or pressure relief) valve. These valves may be mounted on the power head or in the power head adapter plate. These valves control the pressure in the cooling system. When water pressure exceeds the spring pressure of the valve, cooling water is bypassed out the water discharge, on some models, this will have the same effect as bypassing the thermostats. On these models, thermostats control the water temperature at idle and low speeds. Once the engine speed has increased to the point that water pressure overcomes the poppet valve, the thermostats are no longer in pri-

3

mary control of engine temperature. Since an engine at high power settings is producing a lot of combustion chamber heat, this system helps keep the combustion chambers cool enough to prevent preignition and detonation. There is only 1 poppet valve on engines so equipped. **Figure 135** shows a typical in-line engine thermostat (A) and poppet valve (B) cover.

It is important to note that on all thermostat equipped engines, the thermostat always controls the maximum temperature that the engine can reach. The number stamped on the thermostat is the initial opening or *cracking* temperature (Fahrenheit). The thermostat will not reach full opening (full water flow) until 15°-20° F above the thermostat rated temperature. If the engine temperature drops at high engine speeds, but returns to thermostat controlled temperature at idle and low speeds, the system is working correctly. In no case should engine temperature exceed the thermostat rated temperature by more than 20° F.

Troubleshooting

Engine temperature can be checked with the use of Markal Thermomelt Stiks available from Stevens Instrument Company, P.O. Box 193, Waukegan, Illinois 60079-0193. Thermomelt Stiks (**Figure 136**) come in 100, 125, 131, 163, and 175° F ratings. The Thermomelt Stik looks similar to a piece of chalk. When the engine is marked with the Thermomelt Stik, the mark will stay dull and chalky until the temperature of the engine exceeds the rating of the stik, at which point the mark will become liquid and glossy.

The preferred and most accurate way to check engine temperature is using a pyrometer. A pyrometer is an electronic thermometer. Pyrometers come as a single instrument or as an adapter module designed to fit a standard digital multimeter. When using a pyrometer, a dab of silicone grease on the end of the probe will help to create a good thermal bond between the probe and the power head.

The temperature check should be taken on the cylinder block side of the thermostat housing. Ideally the temperature is measured just before the water reaches the thermostat.

Engine temperature check

To be accurate, the cooling water inlet temperature should be within 60°-80° F (18-24° C). Extreme variation in water inlet temperature can affect engine operating temperature. Refer to engine specifications in Chapter Five for thermostat specifications. Engine temperature checks cannot be performed on an outboard running on a flushing device.

> *CAUTION*
> *Do not run the engine without an adequate water supply and do not exceed 3000 rpm without an adequate load. Refer to **Safety Precautions** at the beginning of this chapter.*

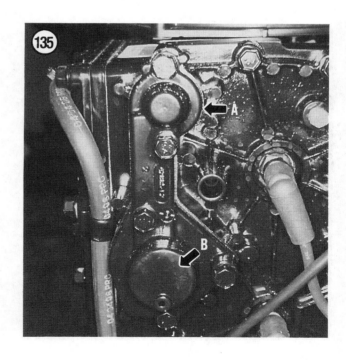

1. Start the engine and run it at 2000-3000 rpm in forward for 5-10 minutes to allow it to reach operating temperature.

2. Reduce the speed to the specified idle speed (or a maximum of 900 rpm) for 5 minutes.

3A. If using Thermomelt Stiks, mark the cylinder block (both banks on a V-6) with the 2 Thermomelt Stiks that are just above and just below the thermostat(s) rated temperature.

3B. If using a pyrometer, note the temperature of the cylinder block (both banks on a V-6) and compare to the thermostat rated temperature. The engine should operate within 5° F (plus or minus) of the thermostat rated temperature at idle.

4A. If the lower temperature Thermomelt Stik does not melt (remains dull and chalky) or the pyrometer reads more than 5° F below the thermostat rated temperature, the engine is over-cooling. Check the thermostat(s) and poppet valve (if so equipped) for debris preventing the thermostat and poppet valve from closing. If the thermostat and poppet valve pass a visual inspection, test the thermostat(s) as described in the following section.

4B. If the lower temperature Thermomelt Stik melts (turns liquid and glossy) or the pyrometer reads within 5° F of the thermostat rated temperature, the engine is at least reaching operating temperature and is not overcooling.

5A. If the higher temperature Thermomelt Stik does not melt (stays dull and chalky) or the

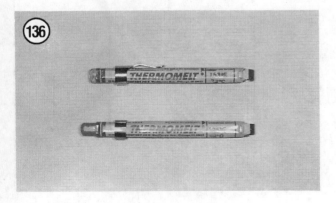

pyrometer does not read more than 5° F above the thermostat rated temperature, the engine is not overheating.

5B. If the higher temperature Thermomelt Stik melts (turns liquid and glossy), the engine is overheating. Test the thermostat(s) as described in the following section. Check the water inlet screens (or cast inlet holes) in the lower gearcase for blockage from debris or corrosion, clean as necessary. Remove the lower gearcase and inspect the water pump assembly. Inspect the water tube going from the water pump to the power head for damage or corrosion. If necessary remove the cylinder head(s) or cylinder cover and inspect for debris and corrosion in the water jackets surrounding the cylinder(s).

NOTE
It is normal for the engine to run cooler than thermostat rated temperature at higher speeds if the engine is equipped with a poppet valve. However, regardless of whether the engine is equipped with poppet valve or not, in no case should engine temperature exceed the thermostat rated temperature by more than 20° F.

6. Repeat the temperature test at 3000 rpm and wide-open throttle. It is acceptable for the pyrometer to read up to 15-20° F above the thermostat rated temperature during the higher speed tests.

CAUTION
If running the engine in a test tank, it may not be possible to perform the 3000 rpm and wide open throttle tests accurately due to the aeration of the test tank water and subsequent overheating.

Thermostat test

1. Remove the screws securing the thermostat cover to the cylinder block or cylinder head(s). Carefully remove the thermostat cover(s).

2. Clean all gasket material from the thermostat cover(s) and cylinder block or cylinder head(s).

3. Check thermostat covers for cracks or corrosion damage and replace as necessary.

4. Wash the thermostat (**Figure 137**) with clean water. Remove the thermostat grommet (if so equipped) and discard it. Read the thermostat rated opening temperature stamped on the thermostat.

5. Manually open the thermostat and insert a thread (or narrow feeler gauge) through the valve and seat. Let the thermostat shut, pinching the thread (or feeler gauge) in the valve.

6. Suspend the thermostat from the thread in a container of water that can be heated. Then suspend an accurate thermometer in the container of water. See **Figure 138**.

> *NOTE*
> *The thermostat and thermometer must not touch the sides or bottom of the container of water.*

7. Heat the water and note the temperature at which the thermostat falls free from the thread (or feeler gauge). The thermostat should begin to open within 5° F (plus or minus) of the rated temperature.

8. Continue to heat the water until the thermostat fully opens. The thermostat must fully open within 15-20° F above the rated temperature.

9. Replace the thermostat(s) if it fails to open at the specified temperature or if it does not open

completely. Install a new gasket and grommet (if so equipped).

> *NOTE*
> *If the engine is equipped with a poppet valve in the thermostat housing, make sure the poppet valve, spring and seat are correctly orientated and not damaged before reinstalling the thermostat cover. Replace any damaged or worn parts (Chapter Eight).*

Engine temperature switches and sensors

All models are equipped with a temperature switch and warning horn to alert the operator of an engine overheat. Temperature switches are normally open and close (short) to ground when the engine temperature exceeds the rated temperature of the switch. The temperature switch may or may not have a separate ground lead. If no separate ground lead is present, the switch grounds through direct contact with the cylinder head. **Figure 139** shows a typical temperature switch with a separate ground lead.

(137)

(138)

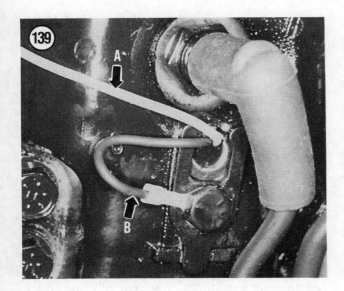

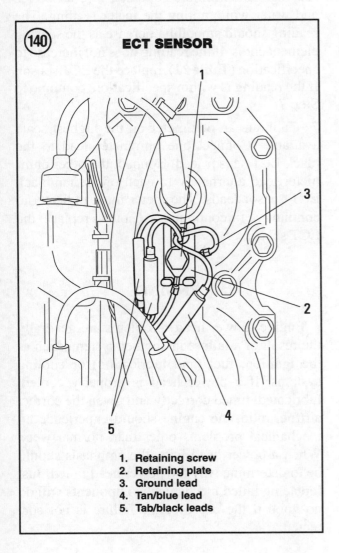

ECT SENSOR

1. Retaining screw
2. Retaining plate
3. Ground lead
4. Tan/blue lead
5. Tab/black leads

If the temperature switch has 4 leads, it provides an ECM (electronic control module) with precise engine temperature data and incorporates the temperature switch function. **Figure 139** shows a typical ECT (engine coolant temperature) sensor installation.

On 200 DFI and 225-250 hp (carbureted and EFI) models, the temperature switch will also activate an engine protection module or ECM program that will limit engine speed to approximately 3000 rpm when an overheat occurs.

Temperature switch test (single or double lead switch)

1. Disconnect the engine wiring harness tan/blue lead (4, **Figure 140**) from the temperature switch lead.

2. *Double lead switches*—Check the ground lead (3, **Figure 140**) for secure attachment to the cylinder head. Clean and tighten the connection as necessary.

3. Calibrate an ohmmeter on the highest ohms scale available. Connect one meter lead to a clean engine ground and the other ohmmeter lead to the temperature switch lead. The ohmmeter should read no continuity. Replace the temperature switch continuity is noted.

> *CAUTION*
> *Do not run the engine without an adequate water supply and do not exceed 3000 rpm without an adequate load. Refer to **Safety Precautions** at the beginning of this chapter.*

4. Warm the engine to operating temperature as described in *Engine temperature check* in this chapter. The ohmmeter should continue to indicate no continuity when the engine is at normal operating temperature. The only time the switch should indicate continuity is if the engine is actually overheating (exceeding normal operating temperature).

ECT sensor resistance tests(4-lead sensor)

The ECT (engine coolant temperature) sensor provides the ECM with engine (coolant) temperature data. On 200 DFI and 225-250 hp models, if the indicated ECT sensor temperature exceeds the preprogrammed ECM value, the ECM will retard ignition timing to limit engine speed to approximately 3000 rpm. The ECT sensor has 4 leads. The 2 tan/black leads are used by the ECM to sense engine temperature. The tan/blue and black leads are the temperature switch portion of the ECT sensor and are used to sound the warning horn whenever the temperature of the engine exceeds the switch rating. Refer to **Table 21** for ECT sensor resistance values. To test the ECT sensor and switch, refer to **Figure 139** and proceed as follows:

1. Disconnect the tan/blue and 2 tan/black leads from the temperature sensor switch.

2. Calibrate an ohmmeter on the highest scale available. Connect one meter lead to the black sensor lead (ground) and the other ohmmeter lead to the tan/blue sensor lead. The ohmmeter should read no continuity. Replace the sensor assembly if continuity is noted.

CAUTION
*Do not run the engine without an adequate water supply and do not exceed 3000 rpm without an adequate load. Refer to **Safety Precautions** at the beginning of this chapter.*

3. Warm the engine to operating temperature as described in *Engine temperature check* in this chapter. The ohmmeter should continue to indicate no continuity when the engine is at normal operating temperature. The only time the sensor should indicate continuity is if the engine is actually overheating (exceeding normal operating temperature).

4. Calibrate the ohmmeter on the appropriate scale to read the ECT sensor engine temperature data as listed in **Table 21**.

NOTE
The temperature of the engine must be accurately determined before the ECT sensor can be tested.

5. Measure the temperature of the cylinder head with a pyrometer or allow the engine to cool to ambient temperature. Connect one ohmmeter lead to each of the tan/black ECT sensor leads. Note the meter reading and compare to specifications. If the reading is not within specification, the ECT sensor must be replaced. If the reading is within specification, continue to Step 6.

6. Remove the sensor from the cylinder head (with ohmmeter still connected) and immerse the sensing element into a container of crushed ice and water while noting the meter reading. The reading should smoothly increase as the sensing element cools. If the reading does not increase to specification (**Table 21**), replace the ECT sensor. If the reading is within specification, continue to Step 7.

7. Calibrate an ohmmeter on the highest scale available. Connect one ohmmeter lead to the black ECT sensor lead. Connect the other ohmmeter lead alternately to each of the tan/black ECT sensor leads. The meter must indicate no continuity. If continuity is noted, replace the ECT sensor.

ENGINE

Engine (power head) problems are generally the result of a failure in another system, such as the ignition, fuel (and lubrication) or cooling systems. If a power head is properly cooled, lubricated, timed correctly and given the correct air/fuel ratio, the engine should experience no mechanical problems other than normal wear. When a power head fails, the emphasis should be to determine why the power head failed. Just replacing failed mechanical components will do no good if the cause of the failure is not corrected.

Overheating and Lack of Lubrication

Overheating and lack of lubrication cause the majority of engine mechanical problems. Anytime an outboard motor is to be run, adequate cooling water must be supplied by immersing the gearcase water inlets in the water (test tank or lake) or using an approved flushing device. The motor should only be run at low speeds when operating on a flushing device. The motor must *never* be started without a water supply. Irreparable water pump damage will occur in seconds.

Carbon buildup in a 2-stroke outboard motor *will* cause premature power head failure. Carbon buildup comes from 2 possible sources: the lubricating oil and the fuel. The use of a premium quality outboard motor power head lubricant cannot be overemphasized. The current TCW-3 specification for power head lubricants ensures that maximum lubrication is delivered with minimal carbon deposit buildup. Using gasoline from a major brand manufacturer ensures that the fuel contains the detergents necessary to minimize carbon build-up from the fuel. Fuels that contain alcohol tend to build carbon up at an accelerated rate. The manufacturer recommends avoiding alcohol blended fuels whenever possible. Refer to Chapter Four for additional fuel and oil recommendations.

Use Quicksilver Power Tune periodically to remove carbon deposits from the combustion chamber and piston rings before they can contribute to high combustion chamber temperatures.

Preignition

Preignition is the premature ignition of the air/fuel charge in the combustion chamber. Preignition is caused by hot spots in the combustion chamber. See **Figure 141**. Basically, anything in the combustion chamber that gets hot enough to light off the air/fuel charge will cause preignition. Glowing carbon deposits, inadequate cooling, improperly installed thread inserts, incorrect head gaskets, sloppy machine work, previous combustion chamber damage (nicks and scratches) or overheated (incorrect) spark plugs can all cause preignition. Preignition is usually first noticed in the form of a power loss, but will eventually result in extensive damage to the internal engine components (especially pistons) because of excessive combustion chamber pressure and temperature. Preignition damage typically looks like an acetylene torch was used to melt away the top of the piston, sometimes the piston will actually have a hole melted through the piston crown. It is important to remember that pre-ignition can lead to detonation and detonation can lead to pre-ignition. Both types of damage may be evident when the engine is disassembled.

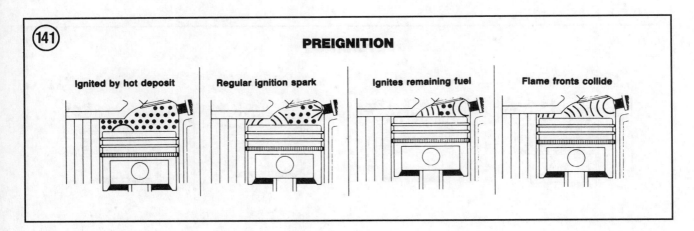

141 **PREIGNITION**

| Ignited by hot deposit | Regular ignition spark | Ignites remaining fuel | Flame fronts collide |

Detonation

Commonly referred to as *spark knock* or *fuel knock*, detonation is the violent, spontaneous explosion of fuel in the combustion chamber, as opposed to the smooth, progressive, even burning of the air/fuel mixture that occurs during normal combustion. See **Figure 142**. When detonation occurs, combustion chamber pressure and temperature rise dramatically, creating severe shock waves in the engine. This will cause severe engine damage. It is not unusual for detonation to break a connecting rod or crankshaft.

Detonation occurs when the octane requirements of the engine exceed the octane of the fuel being used. It does not necessarily mean that the wrong fuel is being used. It does mean that at the time of detonation, the engine needed higher octane fuel than was being used. All fuel will spontaneously explode if it is subjected to enough pressure and temperature.

The fuel octane requirements of an engine are generally determined by the:

a. *Compression ratio*—Higher compression ratios require higher octane fuel. It is important to note that carbon buildup raises compression ratios.

b. *Combustion chamber temperature*— Higher temperature requires higher octane fuel. Water pump and thermostat malfunctions typically raise the combustion chamber temperature.

c. *Air/fuel mixture*—Leaner mixtures require higher octane fuels. Richer mixtures require lower octane fuels.

d. *Spark advance*—Spark occurring too early causes excessive combustion chamber pressures. Spark occurring extremely late causes the combustion flame front to quench along a larger surface area of the cylinder walls, exceeding the cooling system capacity to remove the heat. Both of these situations raise the octane requirements.

e. *Operating speed*—Propping an engine so it cannot reach the recommended operating speed range is considered *lugging* or *overpropping* the engine. This is like trying to drive a manual shift car or truck in too high of gear. When an engine is overpropped to the point that it cannot reach its recommended speed, combustion chamber temperature will skyrocket, increasing the octane requirement.

Fuel degrades over time and storage causing the actual octane rating of the fuel to drop. Even though the fuel may have exceeded the manufacturer's recommendations when the fuel was fresh, it may have dropped well below recommendations over time. Use a fuel stabilizer, such as Quicksilver gasoline stabilizer to prevent octane deterioration. The fuel stabilizer must be added to fresh fuel. It will not raise the octane of stale or sour fuel.

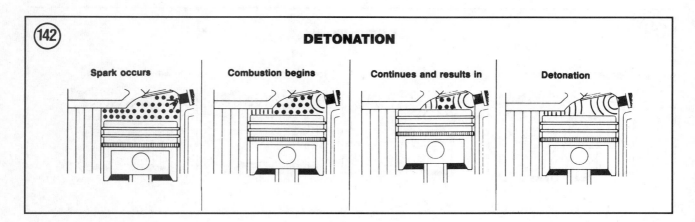

(142) **DETONATION**

| Spark occurs | Combustion begins | Continues and results in | Detonation |

It is better to properly and safely dispose of questionable fuel and start with a fresh tank, rather than risk a power head failure. Catastrophic failure typically occurs in a few seconds or less when an engine is detonating, so rarely can an operator detect detonation and reduce engine speed in time to save the power head. It is important to remember that detonation can lead to preignition and preignition can lead to detonation. Both types of damage may be evident when the engine is disassembled.

Poor Idle Quality

Poor idle quality can usually be attributed to one of the following conditions:

1. *Overcooling*—If the power head does not reach the recommended operating temperature, fuel tends to puddle in the crankcase, resulting in a lean air/fuel ratio in the combustion chamber. This tends to produce a lean spit or backfire through the carburetor at idle. Overheating is usually caused by debris caught in the thermostat(s) or poppet valve (if so equipped). A few selected models will not be equipped with thermostats. Refer to the *Engine Temperature and Overheating* section in this chapter for engine temperature checks.

2. *Crankcase seal failure*—A 2-stroke engine cannot function unless the crankcase is adequately sealed. As the piston travels downward, the crankcase must pressurize and push the air/fuel mixture into the combustion chamber as the intake ports are uncovered. Conversely, as the piston travels upward, the crankcase must create a vacuum to pull the air/fuel mixture into the crankcase from the carburetor in preparation for the next cycle.

Leaks in the crankcase cause the air/fuel charge to leak into the atmosphere under crankcase compression. During the intake cycle, crankcase leakage will cause air from the atmosphere to be drawn into the crankcase, diluting the air/fuel charge. The net result is inadequate fuel

in the combustion chamber. On multiple cylinder engines, each crankcase must be sealed from all other crankcases. Internal leakage will allow the air/fuel charge to leak to another cylinder crankcase, rather than travel to the correct combustion chamber. Refer to *Starting Difficulties* at the beginning of this chapter for additional information.

3. *Crankcase bleed system failure*—Multiple cylinder motors are equipped with a fuel recirculation system designed to collect unburned fuel and oil from the low spots of the crankcase. Since the intake system used by 2-stroke engines does not completely transfer all of the fuel sent through the crankcase to the combustion chamber (especially during low-speed operation), the recirculation system provides a method of collecting the fuel and oil pooled in the low spots of the crankcase and transferring it to the intake ports or intake manifold where it can be burned.

Correct recirculation system operation is vitally important to efficient engine operation. If the system fails, excessive amounts of fuel and oil will puddle in the crankcase and not reach the combustion chamber during low-speed operation, causing a lean mixture. When the engine is accelerated, the puddles of fuel and oil are quickly drawn into the engine causing a temporary excessively rich mixture. This will result in poor low speed performance, poor acceleration, spark plug fouling, stalling or spitting at idle and excessive smoke on acceleration. Refer to Chapter Six for bleed system service.

4. *Incorrect carburetor adjustments or carburetor malfunction*—The carburetor idle mixture screw must be correctly adjusted for the engine to idle and accelerate properly. An engine that is too lean at idle will spit or backfire through the carburetor at idle and hesitate on acceleration. Refer to Chapter Six for carburetor adjustments.

Misfiring

True misfiring is an ignition system malfunction, generally caused by weak (or erratic) spark

3

or defective spark plugs. The ignition system is simply not able to deliver enough spark energy to fire the spark plug at the time of the misfire.

Four-stroking is a form of misfire caused by an air/fuel ratio so rich that it cannot consistently ignite. The term 4-stroking comes from the fact that the engine is typically firing every other revolution (like a 4-stroke engine), instead of every revolution. Four-stroking is caused by a fuel system malfunction. Check for excessive fuel pump pressure, carburetor(s) with leaking inlet needle and seats or fuel primer systems stuck in the on position.

Mechanical failure (insufficient compression) can cause a misfire at all speeds, but will often cause a cylinder to not fire at idle and low speed, but begin firing at mid-range and high speed. Always perform a compression test to verify the mechanical integrity of the combustion chamber.

Flat Spots and Hesitation On Acceleration

If the engine seems to hesitate or bog down when the throttle is opened, and then recovers, check for a restricted main jet in the carburetor(s), water in the fuel, or an excessively lean fuel mixture. Faulty accelerator pump operation (on models so equipped) and incorrect synchronization of the spark advance to the throttle opening (on models with adjustments) can cause flat spots and hesitation on acceleration.

Water Leakage into Cylinder(s)

A simple method to check for water leakage into a cylinder is to check the spark plugs. Water in the combustion chamber tends to clean the spark plug. If one spark plug in a multi-cylinder engine is clean and the others have normal deposits, a water leak is likely in the cylinder with the clean spark plug. A compression test can also be performed to check the mechanical integrity of the combustion chamber. The piston crown can be visually inspected for the absence of

carbon deposits. A cylinder crown that looks steam cleaned, is a typical indication of water leakage into that combustion chamber. If the exhaust port area can be accessed, look for evidence of hard mineral deposits and the absence of soft, wet carbon deposits.

Water Damage in Power Head Lower Cylinder(s)

While water leakage into the combustion chambers is generally caused by defective or failed head gaskets (if so equipped), water can also enter the lower cylinder(s) of a power head through the exhaust ports and carburetor(s). When a steep unloading ramp or tilted trailer bed is used to launch the boat from a trailer and the boat enters the water too quickly, water can be forced into the drive shaft housing and up through the exhaust chamber into the cylinders if the pistons are not covering the exhaust ports.

Sudden deceleration, with the engine shut off, can cause a wave to swamp the engine and enter the exhaust ports or enter through the lower carburetor(s). This is most prevalent with stern heavy boats. Operating a boat with twin engines, with one engine shut off, is considered hazardous because there is no exhaust back pressure to keep water out of the engine that is not running. This is most likely when backing the boat up with one engine shut off. It is recommended that the engine that is not being used (for docking or low speed maneuvering) be left running at idle speed to reduce the risk of water entry.

Water entering a cylinder can result in a bent connecting rod, a broken piston and/or piston pin, a cracked cylinder and/or cylinder head or any combination of these conditions. Even if no immediate physical damage is done to the power head, the entry of water will result in rust and corrosion of all internal surfaces (bearings, crankshaft, cylinder walls, connecting rods and piston rings).

Power Loss

Several factors can cause a loss of power. Remember that an engine needs 3 things to run properly: compression, fuel and fire (ignition). Check the mechanical integrity of the combustion chamber by performing a cranking compression test. Test the ignition system with an air gap tester and verify ignition timing at wide open throttle. Check the fuel system for air leaks into the fuel lines and fittings and test the fuel pump for adequate output pressure at wide open throttle. Clean or replace all fuel filters. Remove a carburetor and inspect the float chamber for water in the fuel and gum or varnish buildup in the metering passages and jets. Clean all of the carburetors if any debris or buildup is found in any one carburetor.

If the compression test reveals a mechanical defect in a combustion chamber, treat the engine with Quicksilver Power Tune Engine Cleaner. Many times the piston rings are stuck to the piston and cannot adequately seal to the cylinder walls. Power Tune can free stuck piston rings and prevent unnecessary disassembly if no mechanical damage has yet occurred. Follow the instructions on the can and retest cranking compression after the treatment. If the compression is now within specification, consider changing lubricant and fuel to a higher quality brand. See Chapter Four.

If the compression is still not within specification after the Power Tune treatment, the motor must be disassembled and the defect located and repaired. After the power head rebuild, make sure the carburetors and fuel pump are rebuilt, a new water pump and thermostat(s) are installed and all synchronization and linkage adjustments are made (Chapter Five).

Marine growth on the bottom of the hull and lower gearcase will drastically reduce the top speed and fuel economy of any boat. If the motor is in a good state of tune and has no apparent malfunction, yet fuel economy and top speed have suffered, inspect the bottom of the hull and lower gearcase for marine growth and clean as necessary.

Piston Seizure

Piston seizure can be caused by insufficient piston-to-cylinder bore clearance, improper piston ring end gap, inadequate or inferior lubrication, cooling system failure (overheating), preignition or detonation.

Excessive Vibration

Excessive vibration can be caused by an engine misfiring on one or more cylinders, loose or broken motor mounts and worn or failed bearings. Gearcase problems that can cause excessive vibration are bent propeller shafts, damaged propellers, or propellers with marine growth on the blades. A propeller that is ventilating from damage or defects on the leading edge of the gearcase, an improperly mounted speedometer or depth finder sending unit, or any hull deformity that disturbs the water flow to the propeller can also cause excessive vibration.

Engine Noise

Experience is needed to diagnose engine noises accurately. Noises are difficult to differentiate and harder yet to describe. Even a properly assembled 2-stroke power head produces much more mechanical noise than its 4-stroke counterpart and a 2-stroke power head produces substantial intake (induction) noise. Deep knocking noises usually mean crankshaft main or rod bearing failure. A light slapping noise generally comes from a loose piston, however some piston noise is normal, especially during warm-up. Any knocking noise on acceleration or at high speed could be preignition or detonation and should be investigated immediately.

Table 1 TEST EQUIPMENT AND TOOLS

Description	Part No.
Electrical connector hardware kit	86-813937A-1
Crimping pliers	91-808696
Multimeter/DVA tester	91-99750
DVA adaptor (for analog multimeter)	91-89045
Spark tester (adjustable air gap, up to 6 cylinders)	FT-11295
Dial indicator set (for determining TDC)	91-58222A-1
Timing light	91-99379
Shop tachometer/dwell meter	91-59339
Digital shop tachometer	79-17391A-1
Interface module (spark plug wire)	825824A-2
AD-CDI ignition test harness (6-position switch)	91-14443A-1
CDM ignition test harness	
Part No. 822779 modules (3 pin connector)	84-825207A-1
Part No. 827509 modules (4-pin connector)	84-825207A-2
Digital Diagnostic Terminal (DDT)	91-823686A-2
DDT software cartridge	91-822608-2
225 hp carbureted (1994) adapter harness	84-822560A-1
225-250 hp (1995-on) adapter harnesses	84-822560A-6 and 84-822560A-7
150-200 hp (824003 digital ECM) adapter harness	84-822560A-5
150-200 hp (analog ECM) adapter harnesses	84-822560A-6 and 84-822560A-7
200 DFI (direct fuel injected) adapter harness	84-822560A-5
EFI 100 psi fuel pressure gauge	84-16850A-1
DFI 160 psi liquid filled air and fuel pressure gauge	84-16850A-2
Injector test harness (150-200 hp EFI models)	91-833169
TPS test harness (150-200 hp EFI models)	91-816085
EFI diagnostic tester (150-200 hp EFI models)	91-11001A2

Table 2 BOAT WIRING HARNESS STANDARD COLOR CODES

Main harness circuits	Color code	Trim/tilt circuits	Color code
Starter engagement	Yellow/red	Trim motor up	Blue
Tachometer	Gray	Trim motor down	Green
Stop 1 (ignition side)	Black/yellow	Switching circuit up	Blue/white
Stop 2 (ground side)	Black	Switching circuit down	Green/white
Choke or primer	Yellow/black	Switching circuit B+	Red/white
Overheat warning	Tan/blue	Trim trailer circuit	Purple/white
Switched B+	Purple	Trim sender circuit	Brown/white
Protected B+	Red/purple	Trim system grounds	Black
Temperature gauge	Tan	Ignition coil primary circuit	Green/(stripe)
Fuel sender circuit	Pink	Charging circuit	
Grounds	Black	Stator output (AC)	Yellow

Table 3 BATTERY CABLE RECOMMENDATIONS

Cable length	Minimum cable gauge size (AWG)
To 3-1/2 ft. (8.9 cm)	4
3-1/2 to 6 ft. (8.9-15.2 cm)	2
(continued)	

Table 3 BATTERY CABLE RECOMMENDATIONS (continued)

Cable length	Minimum cable gauge size (AWG)
6 to 7-1/2 ft. (15.2-19 cm)	1
7-1/2 to 9-1/2 ft. (19-24 cm)	0
9-1/2 to 12 ft. (24-30.5 cm)	00
12-15 ft. (30.5-38.1 cm)	000
15-19 ft. (38.1-48.3 cm)	0000

Table 4 STARTER SYSTEM TROUBLESHOOTING

Symptom	Probable cause	Remedy
Low no-load speed with high current draw.	Tight or dirty bushings. Shorted armature.	Clean and lubricate bushings. Test armature on growler.
Low no-load speed with low current draw.	High resistance in the armature circuit.	Check brushes and springs. Test armature on growler. Clean and inspect commutator.
High current draw with no rotation.	Stuck armature. Internal short to ground.	Clean and lubricate bushings, remove internal corrosion. Check brush leads for shorts.
No current draw with no rotation.	Open armature circuit.	Check brushes and springs. Test armature on growler. Clean and inspect commutator.
Starter continues running after key is released.	Solenoid stuck on. Key switch failure. Yellow or yellow/red wire circuit malfunction.	Replace solenoid. Test key switch. Remove yellow or yellow/red wire from solenoid. If starter now stops, repair or replace the yellow or yellow/red wire from the key switch to the starter solenoid.
Starter turns motor over too slowly.	Solenoid has high internal resistance.	Measure voltage drop across the solenoid while starter is engaged. 0.2 volts maximum drop allowed. Connect red voltmeter lead to battery side of solenoid and black voltmeter lead to the starter side. Measure voltage with starter engaged.
	Mechanical failure of power head or gearcase.	Turn flywheel by hand. If resistance is excessive, remove gearcase and recheck. Repair gearcase or power head.
	Battery cables too small or excessively long.	Do not use cables smaller than the manufacturer installed. If extending cable length, use larger diameter cables.

(continued)

Table 4 STARTER SYSTEM TROUBLESHOOTING (continued)

Symptom	Probable cause	Remedy
Starter spins but starter drive does not engage.	Starter drive is corroded or needs lubrication.	Clean thoroughly and lubricate the splines under the starter drive.
Starter spins but starter drive does not engage.	Starter is not producing necessary speed and torque to engage the drive.	Check the battery charge, battery cables and connections. Test the solenoid voltage drop (see Starter turns motor slowly). Disassemble the starter and: Clean and lubricate bushings Clean and inspect commutator. Check brushes and springs. Test armature on growler.

Table 5 CHARGING SYSTEM TROUBLESHOOTING

Symptom	Probable cause	Remedy
Battery overcharges Unregulated system	Extended high speed running	Turn on accessories during high speed runs.
Regulated system	Regulator failure	Test sense circuit, if good, replace regulator.
	Stator shorted to ground	Perform Stator Resistance Tests
Battery gasses excessively	Overcharging Defective battery (internally shorted)	See battery overcharges Substitute another battery and retest.
Battery loses charge with engine running	Alternator failure Excessive accessory load	Test system per text. Perform Current Draw Test.
Battery loses charge during storage	Current drain from engine components ohmmeter tests.	Perform rectifier or rectifier/regulator.
	Current drain from accessories left on Defective battery	Verify accessories off, consider installing battery switch. Disconnect battery cables. If battery still loses charge, battery is defective.

Table 6 IGNITION SYSTEM TROUBLESHOOTING

Symptom	Probable cause	Remedy
Engine fails to start (spark tests good)	Fouled spark plugs Incorrect timing from sheared flywheel key	Clean or replace spark plugs Check flywheel key.

(continued)

Table 6 IGNITION SYSTEM TROUBLESHOOTING (continued)

Symptom	Probable cause	Remedy
Engine backfire	Improper timing	Check timing.
	Incorrect firing order	Check primary and secondary wire routing and connections.
	Cracked spark plug insulator	Replace spark plugs.
High speed misfire	Insufficient spark	Perform air gap spark test.
	Incorrect spark plug gap	Gap spark plugs (if applicable).
	Loose electrical connections	Check battery connections, engine harness connections and terminals.
	Secondary spark leakage	Inspect ignition coils and spark plug leads for cracks, arcing and evidence of leakage.
Engine pre-ignition	Excessively high combustion chamber temperature.	Check for correct spark plugs. Check for excessive spark advance. Inspect cooling system. Check fuel system for restricted supply (lean mixture).
Spark plug failure	Incorrect spark plug	Use correct spark plug(s).
	Spark plugs not torqued	Torque spark plug(s).
	Air/fuel mixture incorrect	Check fuel supply and carburetor(s).
	Excessive carbon buildup	Use recommended fuel and oil.
	Engine overheat	Inspect cooling system.
Ignition component failure	Loose electrical connections	Clean and tighten all connections.
	Loose mounting (vibration)	Tighten mounting hardware.
	Overheating	Inspect cooling system.
	Corrosion (water damage)	Locate source of moisture.

Table 7 FUEL SYSTEM TROUBLESHOOTING

Symptom	Probable cause	Remedy
Engine fails to start	No fuel to carburetor	Verify gas in tank. Check gas tank air vents. Check gas tank pickup filter. Clean all fuel filters. Verify primer bulb operation.
	Carburetor failure	Rebuild and adjust carburetor.
Flooding at carburetor	Carburetor float malfunction	Disassemble suspect carburetor and replace inlet needle and seat. Adjust float level.

(continued)

3

Table 7 FUEL SYSTEM TROUBLESHOOTING (continued)

Symptom	Probable cause	Remedy
Flooding at carburetor	Excessive fuel pump pressure overcoming float system.	Check fuel pump pressure. Check for stuck piston rings.
Loss of power, hesitation on acceleration	Restricted fuel supply (lean air/fuel mixture)	Clean fuel filters, check fuel lines for kinks and restrictions. Check carburetor jets for obstructions.
	Air leaks into fuel supply	Check all connections and hoses between fuel pickup and fuel pump.
Engine backfire	Lean air/fuel ratio	Adjust idle mixture and speed.
Rough operation	Water or dirt in fuel	Clean fuel system.
	Broken or damaged reed valve(s)	Inspect reed valves.
Engine pre-ignition	Restricted fuel supply (lean air/fuel mixture)	Clean fuel filters, check fuel lines for kinks and restrictions. Check carburetor jets for obstructions.
	Low fuel pump pressure	Check fuel pump pressure
	Air leaks into fuel supply	Check all connections and hoses between fuel pickup and fuel pump.
Engine detonation	Fuel octane does not meet engine octane requirements	Use higher octane fuel. Check for excessive carbon buildup in combustion chamber. See pre-ignition.
Excessive fuel consumption	Carburetor float malfunction	Rebuild and adjust carburetor.
	Blocked air bleeds	Clean air bleeds.
	Gasket failure	Replace all gaskets.
	Cracked carburetor casting(s)	Replace castings as needed.
	Incorrect metering jets	Install correct jets.
	High fuel pump pressure	Test fuel pump pressure and check for stuck piston rings.
Spark plug fouling	Fuel mixture too rich	See excessive fuel consumption
	Excessive oil in fuel	Adjust oil injection pump. Mix fuel and oil at recommended ratio.

Table 8 STARTER SPECIFICATIONS

Model	Normal current draw	No load current draw
75, 90 hp and 65 Jet	120 amps	75 amps
100, 115, 125 hp and 80 Jet	150 amps	75 amps

(continued)

Table 8 STARTER SPECIFICATIONS (continued)

Model	Normal current draw	No-load current draw
135-200 hp and 275 hp	175 amps	40 amps
225-250 hp	165 amps	25 amps
*Spark plugs should be installed. No-load test is a bench test.		

Table 9 CHARGING SYSTEM SPECIFICATIONS

Model	Minimum output Amperage @ rpm	Stator ohms	Maximum output Amperage @ rpm	Regulated
75-125 hp, 65 and 80 Jet with AD-CDI ignition (serial No. 0D283222-0G437999)				
16 amp black stator	4.0 @ idle	0.1-0.5	18.0 @ 4000	yes
15 amp black stator	5.0 @ idle	0.1-0.5	14.0 @ 4000	yes
75-125 hp, 65 and 80 Jet with CDM ignition (serial No. 0G438000-on)				
16 amp red stator	2.8 @ idle	0.16-0.19	16.0 @ 2000	yes
135-200 hp, 105-140 Jet	N/A	0.25-0.45	38-42 @ 5000	yes
200 DFI	N/A	N/A	33-38 @ 2000	yes
225-250 hp	30 @ 750	N/A	60 @ 2000	yes
275 hp	N/A	0.25-0.45	38-42 @ 5000	yes

Table 10 CHARGING SYSTEM SPECIFICATIONS RED STATOR UPGRADE MODELS (75-125 HP AND 65-80 JET)

Model	Stator ohms	Rated output	Regulated
9 amp electric start	0.4-1.0	9 amps at wide-open throttle	no
16 amp electric start	0.16-0.19	16 amps by 3000 rpm	yes

Table 11 PEAK/DVA OUTPUT SPECIFICATIONS (AD-CDI)

Model	Low-speed stator	High-speed stator	Switch box stop circuit	Ignition coil primary input	Switch box bias
75, 90 hp & 65 Jet Serial No. 0D283222-0G280043					
Cranking speed	200-300	20-90	200-360	150-250	2-10 DC volts
At 4000 rpm	200-300	130-300	200-360	180-280	10-30 DC volts
Serial No. 0G280044-on					
Cranking speed	215-265	10-15	215-265	145-175	2-10 DC volts
At 4000 rpm	260-320	205-255	260-320	200-240	10-30 DC volts

(continued)

Table 11 PEAK/DVA OUTPUT SPECIFICATIONS (AD-CDI) (continued)

Model	Low-speed stator	High-speed stator	Switch box stop circuit	Ignition coil primary input	Switch box bias
100-125 hp & 80 Jet					
Serial No. 0D283222-0G301750					
Cranking speed	200-300	20-90	200-360	150-250	N/A
At 4000 rpm	190-310	140-310	200-360	180-280	N/A
Serial No. 0G301751-on					
Cranking speed	160-200	8-10	160-200	110-140	N/A
At 4000 rpm	270-330	165-205	270-330	215-265	N/A
135-200 hp					
Cranking speed	100-265	25-50	200-300	90-145	1-6 DC volts
At 4000 rpm	255-345	230-320	225-400	175-240	10-30 DC volts

Table 12 RESISTANCE SPECIFICATIONS

Ignition coil	
All AD-CDI models	
Primary	0.02-0.04 ohms
Secondary	800-1100 ohms
Trigger resistance	
All 4-cylinder models	700-1100 ohms
All 3 and 6-cylinder models	1100-1400 ohms
V-6 switch box bias circuit resistance	
White/black terminal stud to ground	1300-1500 ohms
Stator resistance	
75,90 hp and 65 Jet	
Serial No.0D283222-0G280043	
Low-speed	3600-4200 ohms
High-speed	90-140 ohms
Serial No.0G280044-on	
Low-speed	1100-1600 ohms
High-speed	30-35 ohms
100-125 hp and 80 Jet	
Serial No.0D283222-0G301750	
Low-speed	6800-7600 ohms
High-speed	90-140 ohms
Serial No.0G301751-on	
Low-speed	1000-1400 ohms
High-speed	15-30 ohms
135-200 hp	
Low-speed	3500-4200 ohms
High-speed	90-140 ohms

Table 13 IGNITION SPECIFICATIONS RED STATOR UPGRADED MODELS (75-125 HP AND 65-80 JET)

Peak/DVA output	
Cranking rpm	
Switch box	
Blue lead	190
Blue/white	190
Stop circuit	190
Ignition coil primary input	130
Running at 4000 rpm	
Switch box	
Blue lead	260-320
Blue/white	260-320
Stop circuit	260-320
Ignition coil primary input	195-275
Stator resistance values	
Green/white to white/green	
Electric start	660-710 ohms
Manual start	660-710 ohms
Blue/white to black	
Electric start	not applicable
Manual start	130-145 ohms

TABLE 14 IGNITION SPECIFICATIONS (225-250 HP MODELS)

Throttle position sensor voltage	
Carbureted models	
Idle position	0.90-1.00 DC volt
Wide-open throttle position	3.70-3.80 DC volts
EFI models	
Idle position	0.90-1.00 DC volt
Wide-open throttle position	3.55-4.05 DC volts
Crank position sensor resistance	900-1300 ohms
Crank position sensor air gap	0.020-0.060 in. (0.51-1.52 mm)
Stator resistance	990-1210 ohms (each bobbin)

Table 15 DVA OUTPUT (225-250 HP MODELS)

	Cranking rpm	Idle to 3000 rpm	Above 4000 rpm
Ignition stator	100-225	250-300	200-230
ECU trigger signal	2-10	2-10	2-10

Table 16 CDM RESISTANCE (3-PIN MODULE PART NO. 822779)

Meter red lead	Meter black lead	Analog meter	Digital multimeter
CDM ground	White test lead	30-50 ohms	30-50 ohms
Red test lead	CDM ground	Low reading	Open circuit
Red test lead	Black test lead	High reading	0.4-0.9 volts
Spark plug lead	CDM ground	700-1300 ohms	800-1200 ohms

Table 17 CDM RESISTANCE (4-PIN MODULE PART NO. 827509)

Meter red lead	Meter black lead	Analog meter	Digital multimeter
Pin A	Pin C	950-1550 ohms	1125-1375 ohms
Pin A	Pin D	High reading	Open circuit
Pin B	Pin D	Low reading	0.4-0.9 volts
Pin A	Spark plug lead	700-1300 ohms	950-1150 ohms

Table 18 DVA OUTPUT TESTS (CDM IGNITION)

Stator output	
At cranking speed	100-350 DVA
At idle speed	200-350 DVA
Trigger output	
At cranking speed	0.2-2.0 DVA
At idle speed	2-8 DVA
Stop circuit output	
At cranking speed	100-350 DVA
At idle speed	200-350 DVA

Table 19 IGNITION SYSTEM IDENTIFICATION

Model	System	Advance	Features
75-125 hp and 65-80 Jet (serial No. 0D283222-0G437999)			
75-90 hp	AD-CDI	Mechanical	–
100-125 hp and 65-80 Jet	AD-CDI	Mechanical	Rpm limit module
75-125 hp and 65-80 Jet (serial No. 0G438000-on)			
75-90 hp	CDM	Mechanical	–
100-125 hp and 65-80 Jet	CDM	Mechanical	Rpm limit module
105 and 140 Jet	AD-CDI	Mechanical	Idle stabilizer, rpm limit modules
135-200 hp	AD-CDI	Mechanical	Idle stabilizer module
XR6 and Magnum III	AD-CDI	Mechanical	Idle stabilizer module
200 DFI	DI	Electronic	ECM (integrated fuel and ignition)
225 and 250 hp	CDM	Electronic	Ignition ECM
275 hp	AD-CDI	mechanical	Rpm limit module

Table 20 DIGITAL DIAGNOSTIC TERMINAL DATA

Selected display	Normal reading (typical)
Engine rpm	
150-200 hp	650-5800
225 and 250 hp	650-5500 Carbureted, 650-5800 EFI
200 DFI	650-5800
	(continued)

3

Table 20 DIGITAL DIAGNOSTIC TERMINAL DATA (continued)

Selected display	Normal reading (typical)
Coolant temperature	
150-200 hp	143° F thermostat
225-250 hp	130-155° F at idle
200 DFI	130-155° F at idle
Throttle position sensor	
150-200 (digital ECM)	
Idle	0.240-0.260 DC volt
Wide-open throttle	7.00-7.46 DC volts
225 and 250 hp	
Idle	0.95 DC volt
Wide-open throttle (carbureted)	3.70-3.80 DC volts
Wide-open throttle (EFI)	3.55-4.05 DC volts
200 DFI	
Inner (No. 1) TPS	0.484-0.872 idle, 3.54-3.93 W.O.T.
Outer (No. 2) TPS	4.088-4.476 idle, 1.07-1.46 W.O.T.
Spark Angle (advance)	
150-200 hp	N/A
225 and 250 hp	20° ATDC-30° BTDC
Idle	4-9° ATDC
Wide-open throttle	Refer to Chapter 5
200 DFI	not displayed
Knock volts	
150-175 hp	not used
200 hp	7 volts maximum
225-250 hp	not used
200 DFI	not used
Battery volts	11-15 DC volts
Atmosphere PSI	11-16, varies with altitude
MAP PSI	
225 and 250 hp	9-16, varies with engine load and altitude
200 DFI	not used
Air temperature	
150-200 hp	Ambient temperature
225-250 hp	Ambient temperature
200 DFI	not used
Injector millisecond	
150-200 hp	
Injector set A	7 maximum
Injector set B	7 maximum
Injector set C	7 maximum
225 and 250 hp	3.5-8.0
Idle	4
3000 rpm	5.5
5000 rpm	6.5
200 DFI	not specified
Fuel pump amperage draw	
150-200 hp	8 amps maximum
Fuel pump % on	
225 and 250 hp	100% above 2500 rpm
200 DFI	100% at all engine speeds

Table 21 ENGINE COOLANT AND INTAKE AIR TEMPERATURE SENSOR DATA (EFI AND DFI MODELS)

Temperature (Fahrenheit)	Temperature (Celsius)	ECT sensor ohms range	IAT sensor ohms value*
14	-10	5073-6199	–
32	0	2959-3615	16500
50	10	1797-2195	12200
68	20	1125-1375	8800
86	30	725-885	6600
104	40	479-585	5000
122	50	324-396	3200
140	60	224-272	–
158	70	158-192	–
176	80	114-128	–
194	90	83-101	–
212	100	62-74	–
230	110	46-56	–
248	120	35-41	–

*IAT (intake air temperature) sensor values are approximate.

Table 22 FUEL PUMP SPECIFICATIONS

	psi (kPa)
Mechanical fuel pump models	
75-250 hp and 105-140 Jet	
Normal psi (kPa) at idle	1-3 (6.9-10.3)
Normal psi (kPa) at W.O.T.	6-8 (41.4-55.2)
275 hp (2 pumps)	
Normal psi (kPa) at idle	5 (34.5)
Normal psi (kPa) at W.O.T.	6-8 (41.4-55.2)
High pressure electric pumps	
Normal psi (kPa) at all engine speeds	
150-200 hp EFI at fuel rail	
1994-1995 models	36-39 (248.2-268.9)
1996-1997 models	34-36 (234.4-248.2)
225-250 hp EFI at fuel rail	34-36 (234.4-248.2)
200 DFI at air/fuel rail	87-91 (600-627.4), 10 psi (69 kPa) above air rail pressure.
Amperage draw	6-9 amps at all speeds

Table 23 EFI AND DFI MULTIMETER SPECIFICATIONS

150-200 hp models	
ECM part No.14632A13 and below	
Throttle position sensor	
Desired position	
Idle position	0.125-0.145 DC volt
Wide-open throttle position	7.00-7.46 DC volts
ECM part No.14632A15	
Throttle position sensor	
Desired position	
Idle position	0.24-0.26 DC volt
Wide-open throttle position	7.00-7.46 DC volts

(continued)

Table 23 EFI AND DFI MULTIMETER SPECIFICATIONS (continued)

150-200 hp models (continued)	
ECM part No.14632A16 or	
824003-1 and above	
Throttle position sensor	
Allowable range	
Idle position	0.20-0.30 DC volt
Wide-open throttle position	7.00-7.46 DC volts
Desired position	
Idle position	0.24-0.26 DC volt
Wide-open throttle position	7.00-7.46 DC volts
150-200 hp models	
Fuel injector resistance	
At individual injectors	2.0-2.4 ohms
At injector harness (pairs)	0.9-1.3 ohms
ECM amperage draw	60-90 milli-amps
225-250 hp models	
Throttle position sensor voltage	
Carbureted models	
Idle position	0.90-1.00 DC volt
Wide-open throttle position	3.70-3.80 DC volts
EFI models	
Idle position	0.90-1.00 DC volt
Wide-open throttle position	3.55-4.05 DC volts
Fuel injector resistance	
At individual injectors	11.0-13.0 ohms
At injector harness (pairs)	5.0-7.0 ohms
200 DFI	
Direct injector resistance	1.0-1.6 ohms (measured at each injector)
Fuel injector resistance	1.7-1.9 ohms (measured at each injector)
Crankshaft position sensor air gap	0.020-0.060 in. (0.51-1.52 mm)
Ignition coil primary resistance	0.66-0.68 ohms

Chapter Four

Lubrication, Maintenance and Tune-up

With higher compression ratios, improved electrical systems and other design advances, the modern outboard motor delivers more power and performance than ever before. Proper lubrication, maintenance and tune-ups are increasingly important to maintain a high level of performance, extend engine life and extract the maximum economy of operation.

The owner's operation and maintenance manual is helpful supplement to this service manual and valuable resource for anyone operating or maintaining the engine. If missing, an owners manual should be obtained through a Mercury or Mariner dealership. The complete serial number of the outboard motor is required to obtain the correct owners manual.

You can do your own lubrication, maintenance and tune-up if you follow the correct procedures and use common sense. The following information is based on recommendations from Mercury Marine that will help you maintain your Mercury or Mariner outboard motor operating at its peak performance level. **Table 1** provides the recommended preventive maintenance schedule. **Table 2** contains the recommended spark plugs. **Tables** 3-8 provide compression specifications, torque specifications, gearcase ratio and lubricant capacity. **Tables 1-8** are located at the end of this chapter.

HOUR METER

Since a boat is not equipped with an odometer, service schedules for outboard motors are based on hours of engine operation. An engine hour meter is highly recommended to help the owner keep track of the actual hours of engine operation. Many types of hour meters are available. The most accurate type (for maintenance purposes) is triggered by a spark plug lead. This makes sure that only actual running time is recorded. If an hour meter is operated by the key switch, any time the operator forgets to turn off the key, artificial running hours are recorded.

The Quicksilver Service Monitor (part No. 79-828010A-1) is a spark plug wire driven hour meter that can also be set to flash an alarm at any time interval set by the operator. Quicksilver also offers many models of ignition switch operated hour meters.

A sample service log is included in the back of this manual to help with record keeping purposes.

FUELS AND LUBRICATION

Proper Fuel Selection

Two-stroke engines are lubricated by mixing oil with the fuel. The oil is either premixed in the fuel tank (by the operator) or automatically mixed by an oil injection system. The various components of the engine are thus lubricated as the fuel/oil mixture passes through the crankcase and cylinders. Since 2-stroke fuel serves the dual function of producing combustion and distributing the lubrication, never use marine white gasoline or any other fuel that is not intended to be used in modern gasoline powered engines. Any substandard fuel (and lubricating oil) will aggravate combustion chamber deposits, which leads to piston ring sticking, exhaust port blockage and abnormal combustion (preignition and detonation).

> *NOTE*
> *The simplest way to reduce combustion chamber deposits and the resulting problems, is to use the highest quality fuel (without alcohol) and lubricating oil available.*

The *recommended* fuel is regular unleaded gasoline from a major supplier with a minimum pump posted octane rating of 87 with no alcohol. The *minimum* fuel requirements are regular unleaded gasoline with a minimum pump posted octane rating of 87 with no more than 10% ethanol. The use of methanol in any quantity is not recommended.

Recently, *reformulated* fuels have been introduced in parts of the United States that have not achieved federally mandated reductions in emissions. Reformulated fuels are specifically blended to reduce emissions. Reformulated fuels normally contain oxygenates, such as ethanol, methanol or MTBE (methyl tertiary butyl ether). Reformulated fuels may be used as long as they do not contain methanol and normal precautions for alcohol (ethanol) extended fuels are taken. See *Alcohol Extended Gasoline*.

If the engine is used for severe service, or if detonation is suspected to be caused by a poor grade gasoline, use mid-grade gasoline of 89-91 pump posted octane (with no alcohol) from a major supplier.

The installation of a Quicksilver Water Separating Fuel Filter is recommended as a preventive measure on all permanently installed fuel systems. The manufacturer specifically recommends the installation of the Quicksilver Water Separating Fuel Filter if any alcohol blended or alcohol extended gasoline is used.

Sour Fuel

Fuel should not be stored for more than 60 days (under ideal conditions). As gasoline ages, it forms gum and varnish deposits that restrict carburetor and fuel system passages, causing the engine to starve for fuel. The octane rating of the fuel also deteriorates over time, increasing the likelihood of preignition or detonation. Use a fuel additive such as Quicksilver Gasoline Stabilizer on a regular basis to stabilize the octane rating and prevent gum and varnish formation. All gasoline stabilizers must be added to fresh fuel. Gasoline stabilizers cannot rejuvenate fuel. If the fuel is known to be sour or stale, it must be drained and replaced with fresh gasoline. Dispose of the sour fuel in an approved manner. Always use fresh gasoline when mixing fuel for your outboard motor.

Alcohol Extended Gasoline

Although the manufacturer does not recommend the use of gasoline that contains alcohol, the minimum gasoline specification allows for a maximum of 10% ethanol to be used. Methanol is not recommended since the detrimental effects of methanol are more extreme than ethanol. If alcohol extended gasoline is being used, the following must be considered.

1. Alcohol extended gasoline promotes leaner air/fuel ratios, which can:
   a. Raise combustion chamber temperatures, leading to preignition and/or detonation.
   b. Cause hesitation or stumbling on acceleration.
   c. Cause hard starting, hot and cold.
   d. Cause the engine to produce slightly less horsepower.

2. Alcohol extended gasoline attracts moisture, which can:
   a. Cause a water buildup in the fuel system.
   b. Block fuel filters.
   c. Block fuel metering components.
   d. Cause corrosion of metallic components in the fuel system and power head.

3. Alcohol extended gasoline deteriorates non-metallic components, such as:
   a. Rubber fuel lines.
   b. Primer bulbs.
   c. Fuel pump internal components.
   d. Carburetor internal components.
   e. Fuel recirculation components.

4. Alcohol extended gasoline promotes vapor lock and hot soak problems.

5. Alcohol extended fuel tend to build up combustion chamber deposits more quickly, which leads to:
   a. Higher compression ratios, increasing the likelihood of preignition or detonation.
   b. Piston ring sticking, which causes elevated piston temperatures, loss of power and ultimately preignition or detonation.
   c. Exhaust port blockage or obstruction on engines with small or multiple exhaust ports.

NOTE
When the moisture content of the fuel reaches 0.5%, the water separates from the fuel and settles to the low points of the fuel system. This includes the fuel tank, fuel filters and carburetor float chambers. Alcohol extended fuels aggravate this situation.

If any or all of these symptoms are regularly occurring, consider testing the fuel for alcohol or simply changing to a different gasoline supplier. If the symptoms are no longer present after the change, continue using the gasoline from the new supplier.

If usage of alcohol extended fuel is unavoidable, perform regular maintenance and inspections more often than normal recommendations. Pay special attention to changing or cleaning the fuel filters, inspecting rubber fuel system components for deterioration, inspecting metallic fuel system components for corrosion and monitoring the power head for warning signs of preignition and/or detonation. It is sometimes necessary to enrich the carburetors metering circuits to compensate for the leaning effect of these gasolines.

Reformulated gasolines that contain MTBE (methyl tertiary butyl ether) in normal concentrations have no side effects other than those listed previously. This does not apply to reformulated gasoline that contains ethanol or methanol.

The following procedure is an accepted and widely used field procedure for detecting alcohol in gasoline. Note that the gasoline must be checked prior to mixing with oil. Use any small transparent bottle or tube that can be capped and provided with graduations or a mark at approximately 1/3 full. A pencil mark on a piece of adhesive tape is sufficient.

1. Fill the container with water to the 1/3 full mark.

2. Add gasoline until the container is almost full. Leave a small air space at the top.

3. Shake the container vigorously, then allow it to sit for 3-5 minutes. If the volume of water appears to have increased, alcohol is present. If the dividing line between the water and gasoline

becomes cloudy, reference from the center of the cloudy band.

This procedure can not differentiate between types of alcohol (ethanol or methanol), nor is it considered to be absolutely accurate from a scientific standpoint, but it is accurate enough to determine if sufficient alcohol is present to cause the user to take precautions.

Gasoline Additives

The only recommended fuel additives and the associated benefits from their use are:

a. *Quicksilver Fuel System Treatment and Stabilizer*—This additive, when added to *fresh* fuel, stabilizes the octane rating, preventing fuel degradation and oxidation, prevents the formation of gum and varnish in the fuel system components and prevents moisture buildup in the fuel tank, fuel system and carburetors.

b. *Quicksilver Gasoline Stabilizer*—Same benefits as Quicksilver Fuel System Treatment and Stabilizer, but much more concentrated (used to treat large quantities of fuel).

c. *Quicksilver QuicKleen Fuel Treatment*—QuicKleen is designed to help prevent combustion chamber deposits and protect the internal fuel system and power head mechanical surfaces against corrosion. Use QuicKleen if substandard or questionable fuels (or oils) are being used, or if combustion chamber deposits are a continual problem.

Unless the boat is consistently operated with fresh fuel in the fuel tank, the use of a fuel stabilizer on a continual basis is recommended.

CAUTION
Some marinas are blending valve recession additives into their fuel to accommodate owners of older 4-stroke marine engines. Valve recession additives are designed to help prevent premature valve seat wear on older 4-stroke en-

gines. The valve recession additives may react with some outboard motor oils causing certain 2-stroke oil additives to precipitate (gel). This precipitation can plug fuel system filters and smaller passages; therefore, avoid the use of any fuel containing valve recession additives in an outboard motor.

Recommended Fuel/Oil Mixtures

The recommended oil for all Mercury/Mariner outboard motors (except the 200 DFI) is Quicksilver Premium or Premium Plus, 2-Cycle Outboard Oil. This oil meets or exceeds TCW-3 (two-cycle, water cooled, 3rd revision) standards set by the NMMA (National Marine Manufacturers Association). If Quicksilver Premium Blend is not available, use a NMMA certified TCW-3 outboard oil from another engine manufacturer. The only recommended oil for the 200 DFI outboard motor is Quicksilver Premium Plus Outboard Oil.

TCW-3 oils are designed to improve lubrication over previous standards (TCW and TCW-II), as well as reduce combustion chamber deposits caused by the lubricating oil. Do not use any oil other than a NMMA approved TCW-3 outboard motor oil.

CAUTION
Do not, under any circumstances, use automotive crankcase oil or gear lubricant. These types of lubricants will cause a catastrophic power head failure. Use only a NMMA approved TCW-3 outboard oil.

The recommended fuel/oil ratio for normal operation in all models without oil injection is 50:1 (50 parts fuel to 1 part oil). This is the standard 6 gal. (22.7 L) of gasoline to 16 fl. oz. (473 mL) of oil.

The 75 hp and larger models are normally equipped with an engine mounted oil injection system. Oil injection equipped models can be readily identified by the presence of an engine mounted oil reservoir.

The 200 DFI (direct fuel injection) is equipped with an electric oil pump controlled by the ECM (electronic control module). The ECM controls the fuel/oil ratio for all operating modes, including break-in. Oil should never be mixed with the fuel on a 200 DFI engine.

Power head break-in procedure

A new outboard motor, rebuilt power head or replacement power head must be operated in accordance with the manufacturer's recommended break-in procedure. During the first hour of engine operation, change the engine speed frequently and avoid extended full-throttle operation. After the first hour of operation has been completed, the engine can be operated as desired within normal operating guidelines.

Mercury Marine also requires that a new motor, rebuilt power head or replacement power head be operated on a 25:1 fuel/oil mixture (often called double oiling), for the first tank of fuel or a calculated quantity of fuel based on the engine's horsepower.

The formula is 1 gal. (3.8 L) of 25:1 fuel/oil mix for every 10 hp, rounded to the nearest gallon (liter). For example, a 150 hp outboard motor should be operated on double oil (25:1) for the first 15 gal. (56.8 L) of fuel. It is perfectly acceptable to exceed the formula in order to accommodate the fuel tank size (especially on mid-size motors), but in no case should the amount of 25:1 fuel/oil mix be less than the formula recommends.

All models equipped with oil injection (except 200 DFI)

To provide the required 25:1 fuel/oil mixture during the engine break-in period, mix 8 fl. oz. (236.6 mL) of the recommended outboard oil for every 3 gal. (11.4 L) of the recommended fuel.

This will provide a 50:1 fuel/oil mixture in the fuel tank that will be supplemented by the engine mounted oil injection system. The final result will be a 25:1 fuel/oil mixture to the engine.

To provide the required fuel/oil mixture after break-in and for all normal operation, do not mix any oil in the fuel tank. The engine mounted oil injection system provides the engine with the required fuel/oil mixture. Monitor the engine mounted oil tank (reservoir) and the boat mounted oil tank (if so equipped) and keep the tank(s) filled with the recommended outboard oil.

> *CAUTION*
> *The 200 DFI uses an electric oil pump controlled by the ECM (electronic control module). The ECM controls the fuel/oil ratio for all operating modes, including break-in. Oil should never be mixed with the fuel on a 200 DFI engine.*

Fuel Mixing Procedure

> *WARNING*
> *Gasoline is an extreme fire hazard. Never use gasoline near heat, spark or flame. Do not smoke while mixing fuel.*

Mix the fuel and oil outside or in a well-ventilated area. Mix the fuel and oil to the recom-

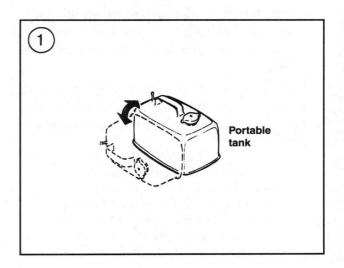

Portable tank

mended fuel/oil ratio. Using less than the specified amount of oil can result in insufficient lubrication and serious engine damage. Using more oil than specified causes spark plug fouling, erratic fuel metering, excessive smoke and accelerated carbon accumulation.

Cleanliness is of prime importance when mixing fuel. Even a very small particle of dirt can restrict fuel metering passages.

Use fresh fuel only. If the fuel is sour, dispose of the fuel in an approved manner and start over with fresh fuel. If the fuel mix is not going to be used immediately, add a fuel stabilizer to the fuel mix.

Above 32° F (0° C)

Measure the required amount of gasoline and recommended outboard oil accurately. Pour the oil into the remote tank and add the fuel. Install the tank fill cap and mix the fuel by tipping the tank from side-to-side several times. See **Figure 1**.

If a built-in tank is used, insert a large filter-type funnel into the tank fill neck. Carefully pour the specified oil and gasoline into the funnel at the same time. See **Figure 2**.

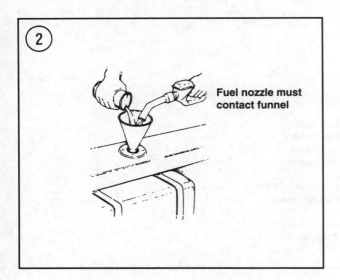

Fuel nozzle must contact funnel

Below 32° F (0° C)

Measure the required amount of gasoline and the recommended outboard oil accurately. Pour approximately 1 gal. (3.8 L) of gasoline into the tank and then add the required amount of oil. Install the tank fill cap and shake the tank vigorously to mix thoroughly the fuel and oil. Remove the cap, add the balance of the gasoline and shake the tank again.

If a built-in tank is used, insert a large filter-type funnel into the tank fill neck. Mix the required amount of oil with one gallon of gasoline in a separate container. Carefully pour the mixture into the funnel at the same time the tank is being filled with gasoline.

Consistent Fuel Mixtures (Carbureted Models)

The carburetor idle mixture adjustment is sensitive to fuel mixture variations which result from the use of different oils and gasolines or due to inaccurate measuring and mixing. This may require constant readjustment of the idle mixture screw(s). To prevent the necessity of carburetor readjustment or erratic running qualities from one fuel batch to another, always be consistent when mixing fuel. Prepare each batch of fuel exactly the same as previous ones.

Use caution if considering the use of premixed fuel sold at some on-water locations, such as marinas, since the quality and consistency of premixed fuel can vary greatly. The possibility of engine damage resulting from use of an incorrect or substandard fuel/oil mixture often outweighs the convenience of premixed fuel. Consult with the operator of the marina or fuel supply station as to the specifications for the oil and fuel being used in the advertised premix. Premixed fuel should not be used if there is any concern that the fuel does not meet or exceed the engine fuel and oil requirements as previously stated in this manual.

4

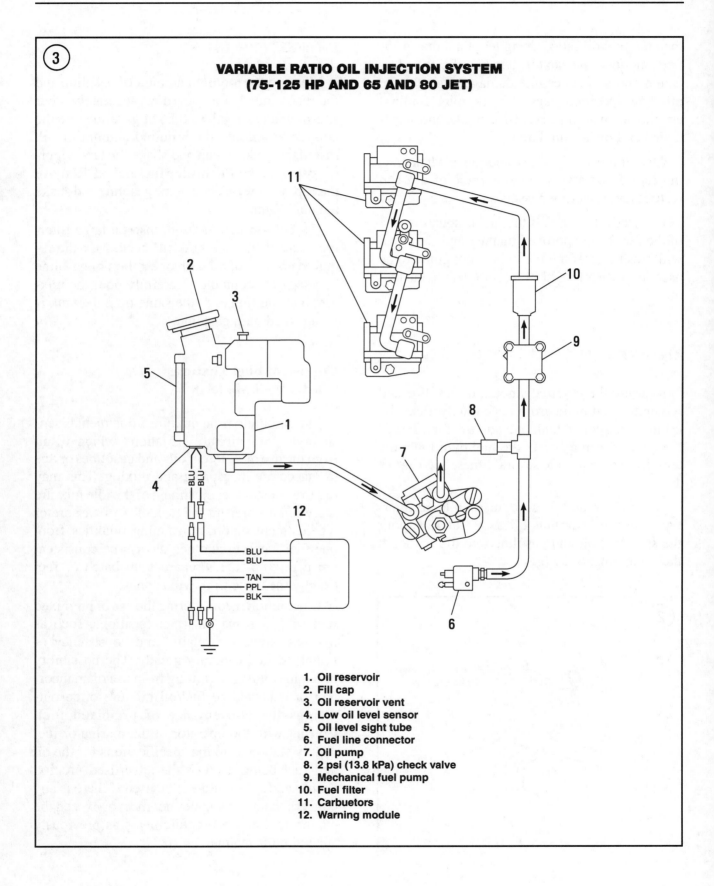

③

**VARIABLE RATIO OIL INJECTION SYSTEM
(75-125 HP AND 65 AND 80 JET)**

1. Oil reservoir
2. Fill cap
3. Oil reservoir vent
4. Low oil level sensor
5. Oil level sight tube
6. Fuel line connector
7. Oil pump
8. 2 psi (13.8 kPa) check valve
9. Mechanical fuel pump
10. Fuel filter
11. Carbuetors
12. Warning module

Variable Ratio Oil Injection (75-125 hp and 65-80 Jet Models)

> *CAUTION*
> *While it should not normally be necessary, if a boat mounted electric fuel supply pump is to be used, fuel pressure must not exceed 2 psi (13.8 kPa) at the engine fuel line connector. If necessary, install a fuel pressure regulator between the electric fuel pump and engine fuel line connector. Adjust the fuel pressure regulator to a maximum of 2 psi (13.8 kPa) fuel pressure. The electric fuel pump should also conform to all applicable Coast Guard safety standards for permanently installed fuel systems.*

The 75-125 hp and 65-80 Jet models are equipped with an oil injection system very similar to the one shown in **Figure 3**.

On 1994-1995 models, the engine-mounted oil reservoir capacity is 1 gal. (3.78 L) on 75-90 hp and 65 Jet models and 1.4 gal. (5.3 L) on 100-125 hp and 80 Jet models. This capacity provides sufficient oil for approximately 6 hours of operation at wide-open throttle. The reservoir is equipped with an oil level sight gauge (**Figure 4**), visible through an opening in the engine cowl. To fill the oil reservoir on 1994-1995 models, remove the engine cowl, remove the reservoir fill cap and fill with the recommended outboard oil.

On 1996-1997 models, the engine-mounted oil reservoir capacity is 3.2 qt. (3.0 L) on 75-90 hp and 65 Jet models and 5.13 qt. (4.9 L) on 100-125 hp and 80 Jet models. This capacity provides sufficient oil for approximately 5 hours of operation at wide-open throttle. The reservoir on 1996-1997 models is equipped with a dipstick to determine remaining oil level. To fill the reservoir on 1996-1997 models, it is not necessary to remove the engine cowl, simply remove the fill cap (and dipstick) and fill with recommended outboard oil.

An oil level sensor contained within the oil reservoir activates the low-oil warning module and warning horn when the oil level drops to 1 qt (0.95 L). When the low-oil warning horn sounds, enough oil for approximately 50-60 minutes of wide-open throttle operation remains. The warning module incorporates a self-test that sounds briefly each time the ignition switch is turned to the ON or RUN position to indicate the warning system is functioning.

The oil pump is driven by the engine crankshaft and injects oil into the fuel stream prior to the fuel pump as shown in **Figure 3**. The oil pump delivers oil relative to carburetor throttle valve opening and engine speed. The fuel-oil ratio is approximately 80:1 at idle and approximately 50:1 at wide-open throttle. Refer to Chapter Eleven for additional system information and service procedures.

Variable Ratio Oil Injection (135-200 hp, 275 hp and 105-140 Jet Models)

> *CAUTION*
> *While it should not normally be necessary, if a boat mounted electric fuel supply pump is to be used, fuel pressure must not exceed 4 psi (27.6 kPa) at the engine fuel line connector. If necessary, install a fuel pressure regulator between the electric fuel pump and engine fuel line connector. Adjust the fuel pressure regulator to a maximum of 4 psi (27.6 kPa) fuel pressure. The electric fuel pump must also conform to all applicable*

Coast Guard safety standards for permanently installed fuel systems.

A 3 gallon (11.4 L) remote oil tank supplies oil to the reservoir mounted under the engine cowl (**Figure 5**, typical). The reservoir oil capacity is 2.75 qt. (2.6 L) on 275 hp models and 0.94 qt. (0.89 L) on all other models. The engine mounted reservoir provides enough oil for approximately 1 hour (275 hp models) or 30 minutes (all other models) of wide-open throttle operation after the remote oil tank is empty.

The oil tank (1, **Figure 6**) is pressurized by crankcase pressure, causing oil to flow from the remote tank to the engine mounted reservoir (5). Should the oil line between the remote tank and engine mounted reservoir become restricted, the 4 psi (27.6 kPa) check valve (3, **Figure 6**) will unseat, allowing air to vent through the hose, allowing the injection pump to consume the oil in the engine mounted reservoir.

To refill the engine mounted oil tank, make sure the remote oil tank is full and the cap is securely attached. With the engine running at idle speed, loosen the engine oil tank filler cap to allow air to escape and oil to enter. Tighten the filler cap when the tank is full.

The injection pump is mounted to the engine block and is driven by a gear on the crankshaft. The pump is synchronized with throttle plate opening by mechanical linkage. The fuel/oil mixture is varied from approximately 100:1 (80:1 on the 275 hp) at idle to approximately 50:1 at wide-open throttle. On carbureted models, the oil pump injects the oil into the fuel stream prior to the mechanical fuel pump. On EFI models, the oil is injected into the fuel at the bottom of the vapor separator assembly.

A low-oil sensor (**Figure 7**) attached to the reservoir fill cap activates the warning module and warning horn if the oil level in the reservoir becomes low. If this occurs, the engine must be stopped immediately and both oil reservoirs refilled, or permanent power head damage will occur.

135-200 hp and 105-140 Jet models also incorporate a motion sensor (6, **Figure 6**) that detects movement of the oil pump shaft via a magnet inside the pump coupler. If the motor is running and the motion sensor detects no oil pump shaft movement, the warning module will pulse the warning horn intermittently. If this occurs, the engine must be stopped immediately and the cause of the failure determined and corrected, or permanent power head damage will occur.

The warning module incorporates a self test feature that sounds the warning horn briefly each time the ignition switch is turned to the ON or RUN position. This indicates that the warning module is functioning. If the self test does not occur, or if the horn sounds intermittently or continuously after the ignition is switched ON, do not attempt to start the engine. Refer to Chapter Eleven for additional system information and service procedures.

Variable Ratio Oil Injection (225 and 250 hp Models)

CAUTION
While it should not normally be necessary, if a boat mounted electric fuel supply pump is to be used, fuel pressure must not exceed 4 psi (27.6 kPa) at the engine fuel line connector. If necessary, install a fuel pressure regulator between the electric fuel pump and engine fuel line

6

OIL INJECTION SYSTEM (135-200 HP, 275 HP AND 105-140 JET [CARBURETED MODEL])

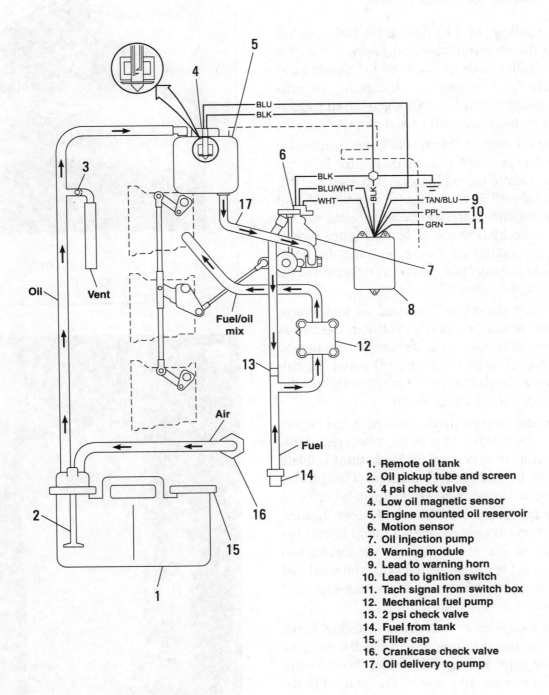

1. Remote oil tank
2. Oil pickup tube and screen
3. 4 psi check valve
4. Low oil magnetic sensor
5. Engine mounted oil reservoir
6. Motion sensor
7. Oil injection pump
8. Warning module
9. Lead to warning horn
10. Lead to ignition switch
11. Tach signal from switch box
12. Mechanical fuel pump
13. 2 psi check valve
14. Fuel from tank
15. Filler cap
16. Crankcase check valve
17. Oil delivery to pump

4

connector. Adjust the fuel pressure regulator to a maximum of 4 psi (27.6 kPa) fuel pressure. The electric fuel pump must also conform to all applicable Coast Guard safety standards for permanently installed fuel systems.

A 3 gallon (11.4 L) remote oil tank supplies oil to the reservoir mounted under the engine cowl on the starboard side of the power head (**Figure 8**). The reservoir oil capacity is sufficient for 30 minutes of wide-open throttle operation after the remote oil tank is empty.

The oil tank (1, **Figure 9**) is pressurized by crankcase pressure, causing oil to flow from the remote tank to the engine mounted reservoir (5). Should the oil line between the remote tank and engine mounted reservoir become restricted, the 4 psi (27.6 kPa) check valve (3, **Figure 9**) will unseat, allowing air to vent through the hose, allowing the injection pump to consume the oil in the engine mounted reservoir.

To refill the engine mounted oil tank, make sure the remote oil tank is full and the cap is securely attached. With the engine running at idle speed, loosen the engine oil tank filler cap to allow air to escape and oil to enter. Tighten the filler cap when the tank is full.

The injection pump is mounted to the engine block and is driven by a gear on the crankshaft. The pump is synchronized with throttle plate opening by mechanical linkage. The fuel/oil mixture is varied from approximately 100:1 at idle to approximately 50:1 at wide-open throttle. On carbureted models, the oil pump injects the oil into the fuel stream prior to the mechanical fuel pump. On EFI models, the oil is injected into the fuel at the bottom of the vapor separator assembly.

A low-oil sensor (4, **Figure 9**) attached to the engine mounted reservoir activates the warning program in the ignition ECM (electronic control module) and warning horn if the oil level in the reservoir becomes low. If this occurs, the engine must be stopped immediately and both oil reser-

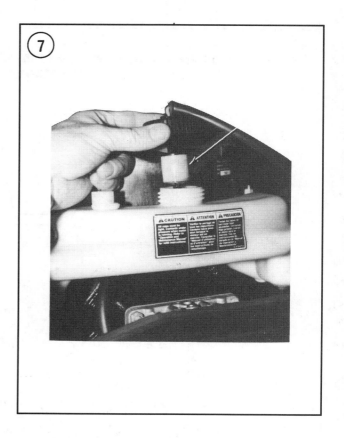

4

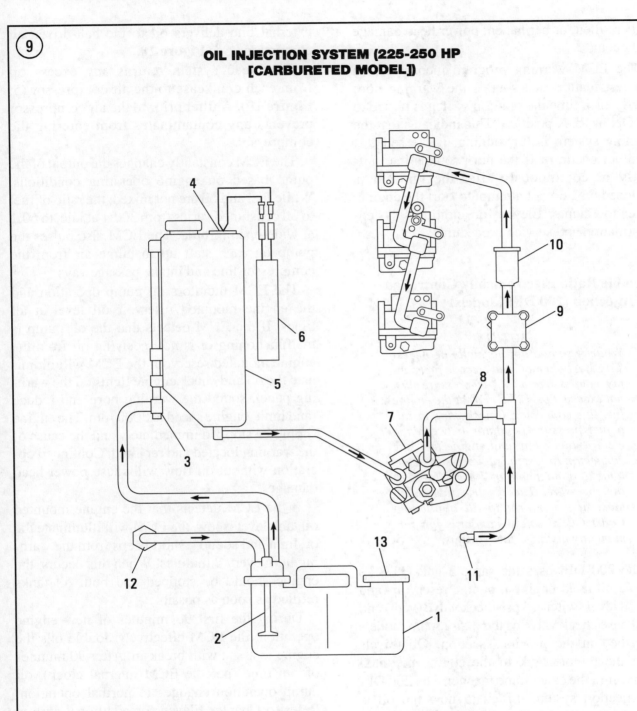

⑨

**OIL INJECTION SYSTEM (225-250 HP
[CARBURETED MODEL])**

1. Remote oil tank
2. Oil pickup tube and screen
3. 4 psi check valve (vent)
4. Low oil magnetic sensor
5. Engine mounted oil reservoir
6. Ignition ECM (electronic
   control module)
7. Oil injection pump
8. 2 psi check valve
9. Mechanical fuel pump
10. Fuel filter
11. Fuel in from tank
12. Crankcase check valve
13. Filler cap

voirs refilled, or permanent power head damage will occur.

The ECM warning program incorporates a self test feature that sounds the warning horn briefly each time the ignition switch is turned to the ON or RUN position. This indicates that the warning system is functioning. If the self test does not occur, or if the horn sounds intermittently or continuously after the ignition is switched ON, do not attempt to start the engine. Refer to Chapter Eleven for additional system information and service procedures.

Variable Ratio Electronically Controlled Oil Injection (200 DFI Models)

CAUTION
While it should not normally be necessary, if a boat mounted electric fuel supply pump is to be used, fuel pressure must not exceed 4 psi (27.6 kPa) at the engine fuel line connector. If necessary, install a fuel pressure regulator between the electric fuel pump and engine fuel line connector. Adjust the fuel pressure regulator to a maximum of 4 psi (27.6 kPa) fuel pressure. The electric fuel pump must also conform to all applicable Coast Guard safety standards for permanently installed fuel systems.

The 200 DFI uses the same 3 gal. (11.4 L) remote oil tank, engine mounted reservoir (and low oil level switch), 4 psi check valve (vent) and crankcase check valve as the 225-250 hp models described in the previous section. Oil travels from the remote tank to the engine mounted reservoir in the exact same manner. The 200 DFI oil injection system differs in how the oil is delivered to the engine. Oil is injected by an ECM (electronic control module) controlled, electric oil pump that is mounted directly to the intake manifold. Oil is not mixed with the fuel. Straight oil flows from the oil pump directly into machined passages in the intake manifold and is discharged in front of each reed block. A single

external line delivers oil to the belt-driven air compressor. See **Figure 10**.

The bleed system returns any excess oil from each crankcase to the air compressor (5, **Figure 10**). A filter prior to the air compressor prevents any contaminates from entering the compressor.

The ECM constantly changes the output of the pump based on engine operating conditions. While fuel and oil are not mixed, the ratio of fuel to oil consumed varies from 300:1 at idle, to 60:1 at wide-open throttle. The ECM also pulses the pump on each start up to purge air from the compressor line and intake passageways.

The ECM monitors oil pump operation and the engine mounted reservoir oil level at all times. If the ECM detects that the oil pump is malfunctioning or is not receiving oil from the engine mounted reservoir, the ECM will illuminate the oil and check engine lights on the warning panel, sound the warning horn and reduce (and limit) engine speed to 3000 rpm. The engine should be stopped immediately and the cause of the warning located and repaired. Continued operation without oil flow will cause power head damage.

If the ECM detects that the engine mounted oil tank level is low, the ECM will illuminate the oil light and sound 4 short beeps from the warning horn every 2 minutes. When this occurs, the engine should be stopped and both oil tanks refilled as soon as possible.

During the first 90 minutes of new engine operation, the ECM effectively double oils the engine to assist with break-in. After 90 minutes of run time (per the ECM internal clock), oil pump operation changes to normal operation. Refer to Chapter Eleven for additional system information and service procedures.

Checking Lower Gearcase Lubricant

After being refilled, check the lower gearcase lubricant level after 20 hours of operation or 10 days, then every 50 hours of operation or once a month thereafter. The recommended lubricant is Quicksilver Premium Blend Gear Lube. If the gearcase is subjected to severe duty, consider using Quicksilver High Performance Gear Lube.

CAUTION
Do not use regular automotive gear lubricant in the gear housing. The expan- *sion and foam characteristics and water tolerance of automotive gear lube are not suitable for marine use.*

1. Place the outboard motor in an upright (vertical) position. Place a suitable container under the gear housing. Loosen the gearcase drain/fill plug (**Figures 11-13**). Allow a small amount of lubricant to drain. If water is present inside the

4

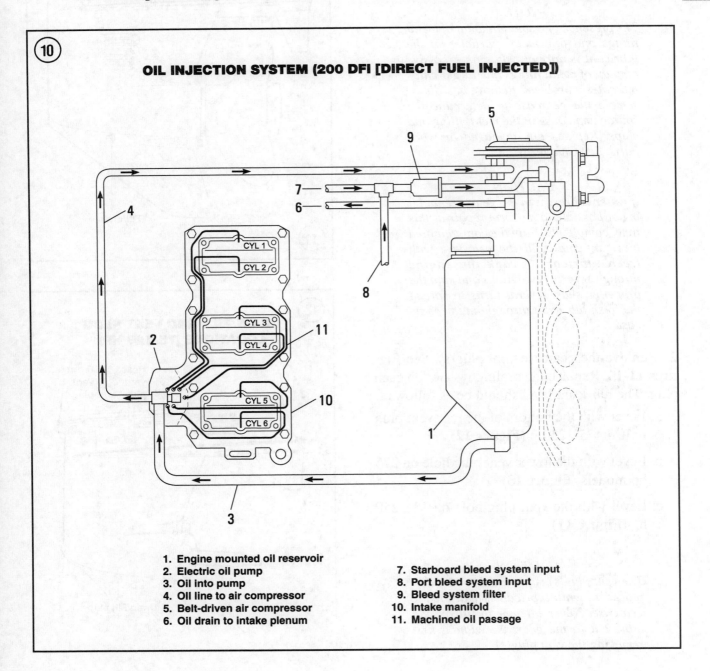

(10)

OIL INJECTION SYSTEM (200 DFI [DIRECT FUEL INJECTED])

1. Engine mounted oil reservoir
2. Electric oil pump
3. Oil into pump
4. Oil line to air compressor
5. Belt-driven air compressor
6. Oil drain to intake plenum
7. Starboard bleed system input
8. Port bleed system input
9. Bleed system filter
10. Intake manifold
11. Machined oil passage

gear housing, it will drain before the lubricant, or the lubricant will have a white or cream tint to the normal lubricant color. If the lubricant looks satisfactory, retighten the drain/fill plug securely. If water was present in the lubricant, or if the lubricant is dirty, fouled or contains substantial metal shavings, allow the remaining lubricant to drain completely from the gearcase.

NOTE
The presence of a small amount of metal filings and fine metal particles in the lubricant is normal, while an excessive amount of metal filings and larger chips indicates a problem. Remove and disassemble the gearcase to determine the source and cause of the metal filing and chips. Replace any damaged or worn parts. See Chapter Nine.

CAUTION
If water is present in the gearcase and it is not possible to perform repair at this time, completely drain the contaminated lubricant and refill the gearcase with fresh lubricant. Crank the engine through several revolutions and spin the propeller shaft several turns to spread the fresh lubricant throughout the gearcase.

2. Remove the gearcase vent plug(s). See **Figures 11-13**. Replace the sealing washer on each plug. The lubricant level should be as follows:

   a. Level with the bottom of the rear vent plug hole on 75-125 hp (**Figure 12**).

   b. Level with the lower vent plug hole on 275 hp models (**Figure 13**).

   c. Level with the vent plug hole on 135-250 hp (**Figure 11**).

CAUTION
The vent plug(s) is provided to vent displaced air while lubricant is added to the gearcase. Never attempt to fill or add lubricant to the gearcase without first removing the vent plug(s).

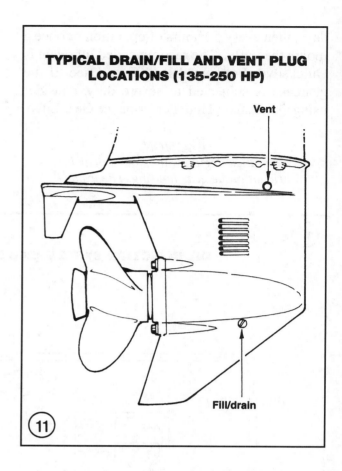

TYPICAL DRAIN/FILL AND VENT PLUG LOCATIONS (135-250 HP)

Vent

Fill/drain

(11)

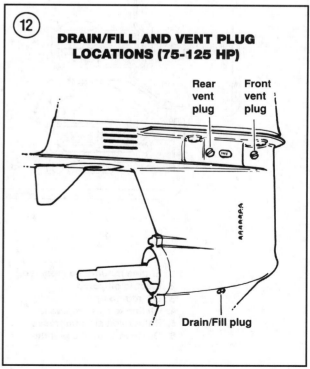

(12)

DRAIN/FILL AND VENT PLUG LOCATIONS (75-125 HP)

Rear vent plug

Front vent plug

Drain/Fill plug

3. If the lubricant level is low, temporarily reinstall the vent plug(s) and remove the drain/fill plug. Insert the gearcase filling tube into the drain/fill plug hole, then remove the vent plug(s) again.

4. Replace the sealing washer on the drain plug.

5A. *135-250 hp models*—Inject the recommended lubricant into the drain/fill plug hole until excess lubricant flows from the vent plug hole (**Figure 11**). Install and tighten the vent plug. Remove the gearcase filling tube and quickly install and tighten the drain/fill plug.

5B. *75-125 hp models*—Inject the recommended lubricant into the drain/fill plug hole until lubricant flows from the front vent plug hole (**Figure 12**). Install and tighten the front vent plug. Continue adding lubricant until the lubricant flows from the rear vent plug hole. Without removing the filling tube from the drain/fill plug hole, install and tighten the rear vent plug. Remove the gearcase filling tube and quickly install and tighten the drain/fill plug.

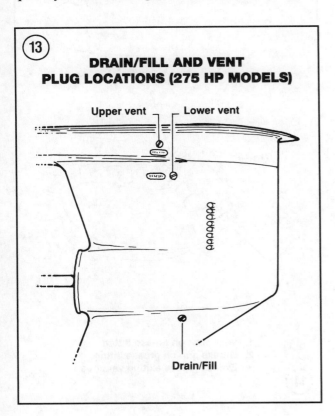

DRAIN/FILL AND VENT PLUG LOCATIONS (275 HP MODELS)

Upper vent Lower vent

Drain/Fill

NOTE
Due to the path the lubricant must travel to exit the vents on 275 hp models, lubricant will flow from the top vent plug hole first.

5C. *275 hp models*—Inject the recommended lubricant into the drain/fill plug hole, until lubricant flows from the upper vent plug hole (**Figure 13**). Install and tighten the top vent plug. Continue to add lubricant until the lubricant flows from the lower vent plug hole. Allow any excess lubricant to drain from the lower vent plug hole. When the lubricant stops draining from the lower vent, install and tighten the lower vent plug. Remove the gearcase filling tube and quickly install and tighten the drain/fill plug.

Changing Lower Gearcase Lubricant

Change the lower gearcase lubricant after the first 20 hours of operation and every 100 hours (or seasonally) thereafter. Refer to **Table 5** for gearcase capacities.

Refer to **Figure 11** for 135-250 hp, **Figure 12** for 75-125 hp and **Figure 13** for 275 hp models.

1. Remove the engine cover. Disconnect and ground the spark plug leads to the power head to prevent accidental starting.

2. Place the outboard motor in an upright (vertical) position. Place a suitable container under the lower gearcase.

3. Remove the drain/fill plug, then the vent plug(s). Allow the lubricant to drain fully into the container.

4. Inspect the drained lubricant. Lubricant that is contaminated with water will have a white or cream tint to the normal lubricant color. The presence of a small amount of metal filings and fine metal particles in the lubricant is normal, while an excessive amount of metal filings and larger chips indicates a problem.

NOTE
If excessive metal filings and larger chips are present, remove and disassem-

ble the gearcase to determine the cause of the metal filings and chips. Replace any damaged or worn parts. See Chapter Nine.

CAUTION
If water is present in the gearcase and it is not possible to perform repairs at this time, completely drain the contaminated lubricant and refill the gearcase with fresh lubricant. Crank the engine through several revolutions and spin the propeller shaft several turns to spread the fresh lubricant throughout the gearcase.

5. Refill the gearcase with the recommended lubricant as described under *Checking Lower Gearcase Lubricant* in this chapter. Refer to **Table 5** for lower gearcase lubricant capacities.

Jet Pump Maintenance

The Jet pump unit used on 65, 80, 105 and 140 Jet models requires that the drive shaft bearings be lubricated daily or every 10 hours of operation, whichever comes first. After every 30 hours of operation, extra lubricant must be pumped in to purge out the old grease and any moisture that may have accumulated.

The clearance of the jet pump impeller to the impeller liner should be 0.030 in, (0.8 mm). If the jet pump is operated consistently in silt laden or sandy waters, check the clearance frequently. There are shims located above and below the impeller that are repositioned to set the required clearance. Refer to Chapter Nine for Jet pump service procedures.

1. To lubricate the drive shaft bearings, disconnect the vent hose (1, **Figure 14**) from the grease fitting.

2. Connect a grease gun filled only with Quicksilver 2-4-C with Teflon (**Table 6**) or Lubriplate 630-AA lubricant to the grease fitting (2, **Figure 14**).

3. Pump in grease until grease exits the vent hose (3, **Figure 14**).

4. Reconnect the vent hose back onto the grease fitting.

NOTE
Every 30 days, pump in extra grease until all old grease is purged from the bearings and fresh grease exits the vent hose. If more than slight traces of water are present in the exiting grease, the drive shaft seals should be replaced. See Chapter Nine.

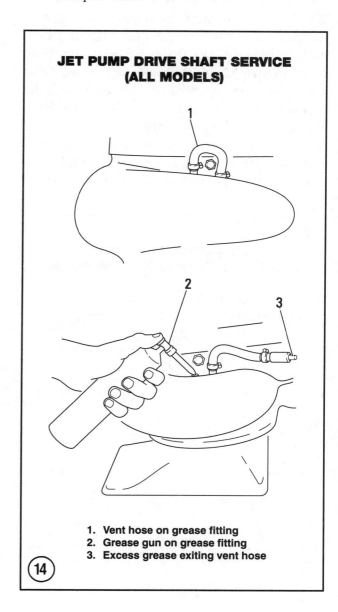

JET PUMP DRIVE SHAFT SERVICE (ALL MODELS)

1. Vent hose on grease fitting
2. Grease gun on grease fitting
3. Excess grease exiting vent hose

(14)

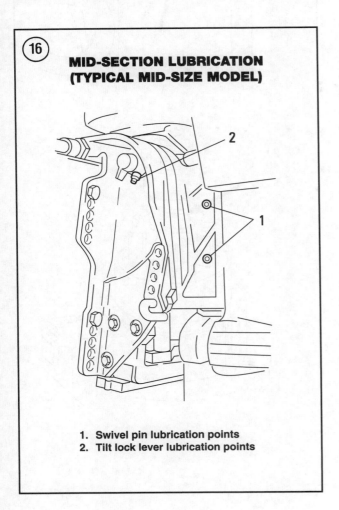

**LINKAGE LUBRICATION
(TYPICAL MID-SIZE MODEL)**

**MID-SECTION LUBRICATION
(TYPICAL MID-SIZE MODEL)**

1. Swivel pin lubrication points
2. Tilt lock lever lubrication points

Propeller Shaft

To prevent corrosion and to ease the future removal of the propeller, lubricate the propeller shaft at least once each season during freshwater operation or every 60 days of saltwater operation. Remove the propeller (Chapter Nine) and thoroughly clean any corrosion or dried grease, then coat the propeller shaft splines with Quicksilver Special Lubricant 101, Quicksilver 2-4-C Marine Lubricant or a suitable waterproof anti-corrosion grease.

Recommended Preventive Maintenance and Lubrication

Refer to **Table 1** for recommended preventive maintenance procedures. Since it would be futile to show every lubrication point for every 1994-1997 model year engine, the more common engines and their typical lubrication points have been selected and shown in **Figures 15-25**.

Basically, every grease fitting on the mid-section should be lubricated with 2-4-C grease (**Table 6**). Lubricate all pivoting or sliding throttle, shift and ignition linkages with 2-4-C grease. Lubricate the steering arm pivot points (remote control models) with SAE 30 engine oil. Lubricate the steering cable sliding surfaces with 2-4-C grease.

The factory supplied operation and maintenance manual that comes with each engine from Mercury Marine is an excellent source for detailed pictures of the lubrication points for a specific engine. If you do not have an operation and maintenance manual for your engine, one can be ordered from any Mercury/Mariner dealership. Make sure you have the complete engine serial number before attempting to order the manual.

*CAUTION
When lubricating the steering cable, make sure its core is fully retracted into the cable housing. Lubricating the cable*

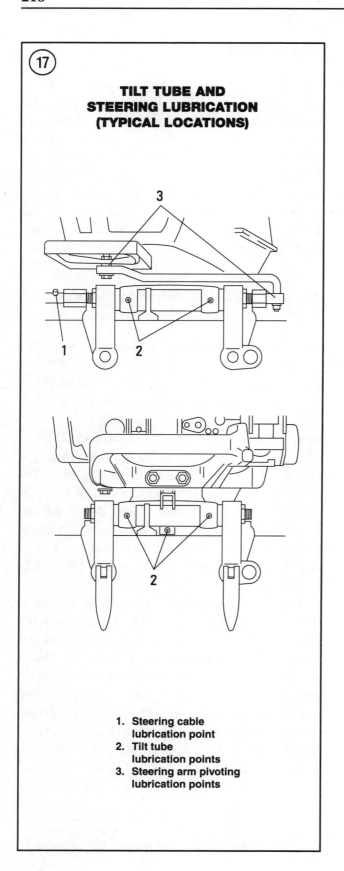

17

**TILT TUBE AND
STEERING LUBRICATION
(TYPICAL LOCATIONS)**

1. Steering cable
   lubrication point
2. Tilt tube
   lubrication points
3. Steering arm pivoting
   lubrication points

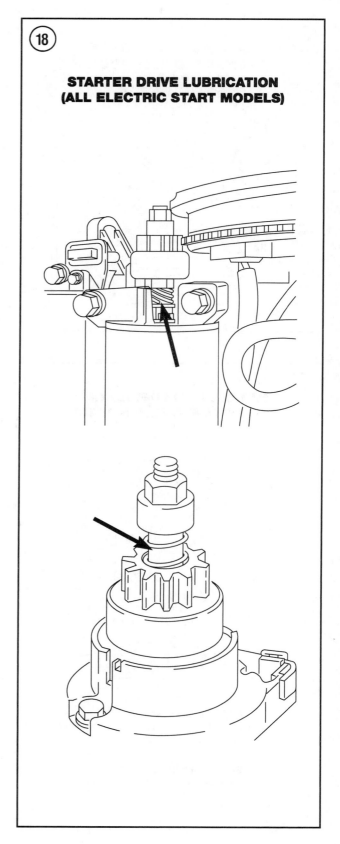

18

**STARTER DRIVE LUBRICATION
(ALL ELECTRIC START MODELS)**

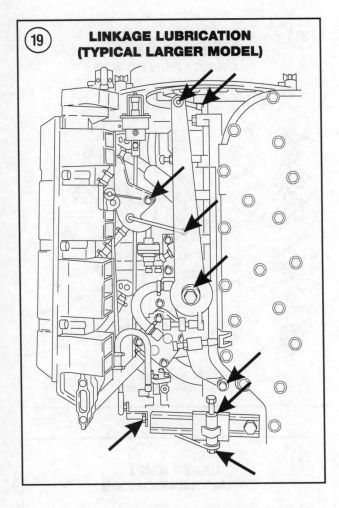

19 LINKAGE LUBRICATION (TYPICAL LARGER MODEL)

while extended can cause a hydraulic lock to occur that could result in hard turning or loss of steering control.

Corrosion of the Propeller Shaft Bearing Carrier

Saltwater corrosion that is allowed to accumulate between the propeller shaft bearing carrier

4

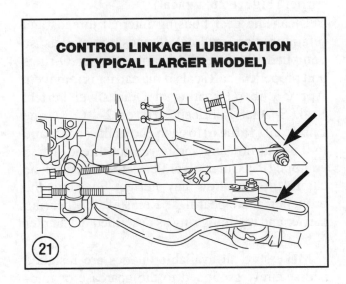

CONTROL LINKAGE LUBRICATION (TYPICAL LARGER MODEL)

21

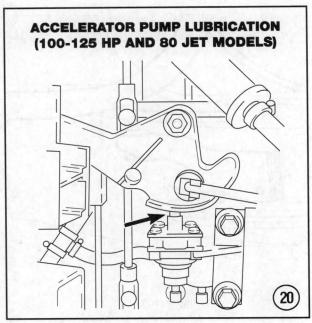

ACCELERATOR PUMP LUBRICATION (100-125 HP AND 80 JET MODELS)

20

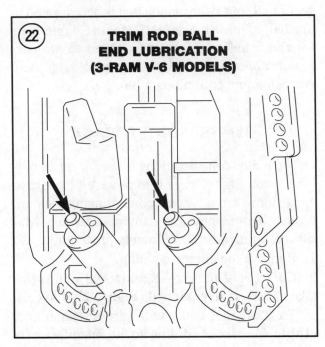

22 TRIM ROD BALL END LUBRICATION (3-RAM V-6 MODELS)

and gearcase housing can eventually split the housing and destroy the lower gearcase assembly. If the outboard motor is operated in saltwater, remove the bearing carrier retaining ring (or bearing carrier attachment hardware) and the propeller shaft bearing carrier at least once per season. Refer to Chapter Nine for bearing carrier removal procedures for all models.

Thoroughly clean all corrosion and dried lubricant from each end of the propshaft bearing carrier (**Figure 26**, typical).

Clean the gear housing internal threads and retaining ring external threads on models so equipped. Replace the bearing carrier O-rings and propeller shaft seals if the carrier is removed. Apply a liberal coating of Quicksilver Perfect Seal, Special Lubricant 101 or 2-4-C Marine Lubricant (**Table 6**) to each end of the carrier and to the gear housing and cover nut threads (if so equipped). If Quicksilver Perfect Seal is used, be careful not to allow any Perfect Seal into the propeller shaft bearings. Reinstall the bearing carrier and retaining ring as described in Chapter Nine.

Make sure all available anodes are installed and securely grounded to the gearcase or midsection. Replace any anode that is deteriorated to one half of its original size. Refer to Chapter One for anode theory information. Refer to *Anticorrosion maintenance* in this chapter for additional corrosion prevention procedures.

OFF-SEASON STORAGE

The major considerations in preparing an outboard motor for storage is to protect it from rust, corrosion, dirt or other contamination and to protect it from physical damage. Mercury Marine recommends the following procedure.

1. Remove the engine cowling.
2. *Carbureted models*—Remove the air box (intake cover), if so equipped (**Figure 27**, typical).
3. Treat all fuel tanks with gasoline stabilizer (**Table 6**). Mix according to its manufacturers

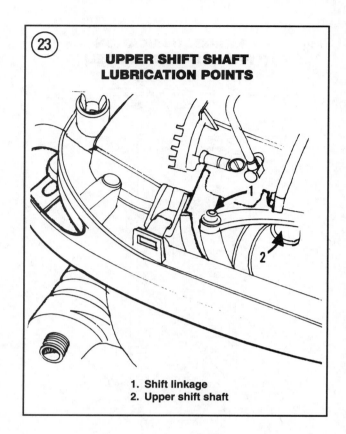

UPPER SHIFT SHAFT LUBRICATION POINTS

1. Shift linkage
2. Upper shift shaft

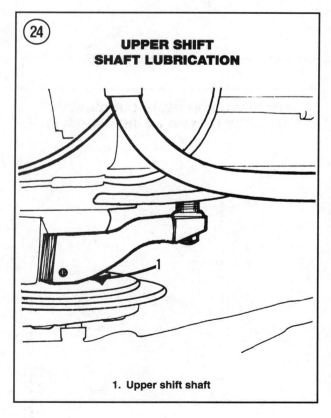

UPPER SHIFT SHAFT LUBRICATION

1. Upper shift shaft

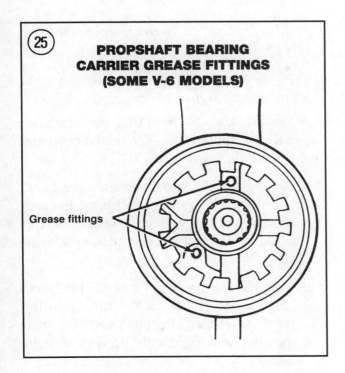

PROPSHAFT BEARING CARRIER GREASE FITTINGS (SOME V-6 MODELS)

Grease fittings

instructions for *storage*. Gasoline stabilizer, when added to fresh gasoline:

a. Prevents gum and varnish from forming in the fuel system.

b. Controls moisture in the fuel system.

c. Prevents modern fuels from reacting with brass and copper fuel system components.

d. Stabilizes the fuel to prevent octane loss and prevents the fuel from going sour.

CAUTION
*Do not run the engine without an adequate water supply and do not exceed 3000 rpm without an adequate load. Refer to **Safety Precautions** at the beginning of Chapter Three.*

4. Start the engine and run at fast idle until warmed up to operating temperature (at least 15 minutes). This ensures that the gasoline stabilizer has had time to reach the carburetor(s) or the fuel injection system.

NOTE
If the fuel in the fuel tank is fresh and properly stabilized, it is not necessary to run the engine fuel system dry. However, it may be desirable on small, portable engines that are going to be transported or stored in a position that could cause spillage. Engines permanently mounted to the transom and connected to permanently installed fuel tanks gain no benefit from running the engine fuel system dry.

5. *Carbureted models*—With the engine running at fast idle (and at operating temperature), spray the recommended quantity of Quicksilver Storage Seal or equivalent (**Table 1**) into each carburetor throat, following its manufacturers instructions. Remove the motor from the water supply when the application of Quicksilver Storage Seal is complete.

6. *EFI and DFI models*—Prepare a 50:1 fuel/oil mixture in a portable fuel tank using the recommended oil, fresh gasoline and a gasoline stabilizer (**Table 6**). Connect the portable fuel tank to the engine fuel inlet connector.

7. *EFI and DFI models*—Start the engine and allow to run at approximately 1000 rpm for 15 minutes. After 15 minutes, shut off the engine and disconnect the portable fuel tank from the engine. Remove the motor from the water supply when finished.

8. *All models*—Remove the spark plugs as described in this chapter. Spray about 1 oz. (30 mL) of Quicksilver Storage Seal into each spark plug hole. Crank the engine (clockwise) by hand several revolutions to distribute the Storage Seal throughout the cylinders. Reinstall the spark plugs.

9. *Portable fuel tanks*—service the portable fuel tank filter by detaching the fuel hose from the tank. Unthread the pickup tube assembly or pickup tube retaining ring from the tank. Remove the pickup tube assembly. Clean or replace the fine mesh filter as necessary. Replace any gaskets, seals or o-rings. Thread the pickup assembly into the tank and tighten it or the retaining ring securely.

NOTE
Carbureted models use either a sight bowl filter or an inline filter. EFI and DFI models all use a spin-on water separating filter and one of 2 types of a final filter. EFI models normally have a small inline fuel filter in the bleed system return to the vapor separator. DFI models have a small inline fuel

filter in the bleed system return to the belt-driven air compressor.

10. To service models equipped with a sight bowl fuel filter (**Figure 28**), proceed as follows:

   a. Unscrew the sight bowl from the filter base. Safely dispose of any fuel in the bowl and discard the bowl seal.

   b. Remove the filter element from the bowl. Clean the element and fuel bowl in clean solvent and dry with compressed air. Replace the element if it cannot be satisfactorily cleaned.

   c. Install a new bowl seal into the fuel bowl (**Figure 29**). Reinstall the filter into the bowl and reinstall the bowl assembly onto the filter base. Tighten the bowl securely *by hand*.

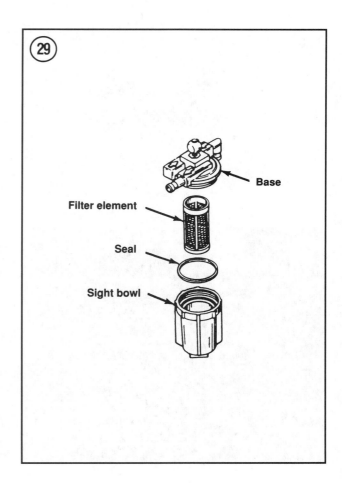

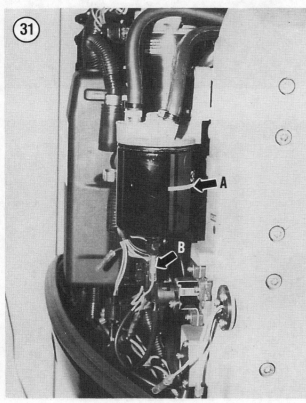

d. Test the installation by squeezing the primer bulb and checking for leaks.

11. On models equipped with an inline fuel filter (**Figure 30**), service the filter as follows:

    a. Carefully compress the spring clamps or cut the ty-strap clamps from each end of the filter.

    b. Disconnect the fuel lines from the filter. Discard the filter and replace any fuel lines damaged in the filter removal process.

    c. Connect the fuel lines to the new filter. Make sure the arrow is pointing in the direction of fuel flow (toward the carburetor). Fasten the hoses to the filter securely with new tie-straps.

    d. Test the installation by squeezing the primer bulb and checking for leaks.

13. To service the water separating fuel filter (**Figure 31**, typical) on EFI and DFI Models, proceed as follows:

    a. Disconnect the water sensor lead (B, **Figure 31**) from the bottom of the filter canister (A, **Figure 31**).

    b. Remove the water separating fuel filter by unscrewing the filter from the filter base. Empty the contents of the filter into a suitable container for inspection.

    c. If excessive debris or water accumulation are present, inspect the fuel tanks for water contamination and other debris.

    d. Remove the water sensing probe from the bottom of the filter and discard the filter.

    e. Install the water sensing probe into a new filter. Lubricate the filter seal with a light coat of outboard motor oil.

    f. Install the filter onto the filter base and tighten securely *by hand*. Reconnect the water sensor probe lead. Coat the sensor lead connection with Quicksilver Liquid Neoprene (**Table 6**).

    g. Test the installation by squeezing the primer bulb and checking for leaks.

14. To service the final fuel filter on EFI and DFI models, refer to Chapter Five. The final filter is

mounted between the electric fuel pump outlet and the fuel rail (**Figure 32**, typical) on 1994-1995, 150-200 hp EFI models. The final filter is mounted inside the vapor separator (**Figure 33**, typical) on all 225-250 EFI, 200 DFI and 1996-1997, 150-200 hp EFI models. Fuel rail pressure must be relieved before servicing the final fuel filter.

15. Replace the bleed system filter on 200 DFI models (**Figure 34**) and on EFI models so equipped (**Figure 35**).

16. Drain and refill the lower gearcase with the recommended lubricant as described in this chapter. Install new sealing washers on all drain and vent plugs.

17. *Jet pump models*—Refer to *Jet pump maintenance* for drive shaft bearing lubrication.

18. Refer to **Figures 15-25** and **Table 1** as appropriate, for preventive maintenance and general lubrication recommendations.

19. Clean all exterior areas of the outboard motor, including all accessible power head parts. Spray the entire power head, including all electrical connections with Quicksilver Corrosion Guard. Install the engine cowling and spray a thin film of Quicksilver Corrosion Guard on all remaining metal painted surfaces (midsection and lower gearcase).

20. Remove the propeller as described in Chapter Nine. Lubricate the propeller shaft with

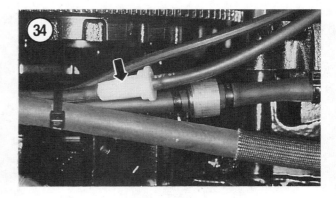

Quicksilver Special Lubricant 101 or Quicksilver 2-4-C Marine Lubricant and reinstall the propeller.

CAUTION
Make certain all water drain holes in the gear housing are open to allow water to drain. Water expands as it freezes and

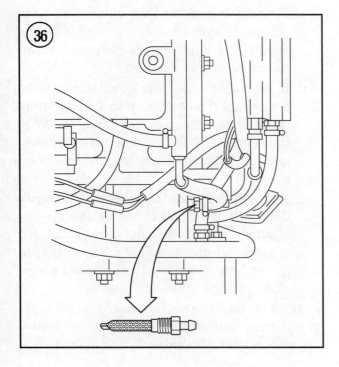

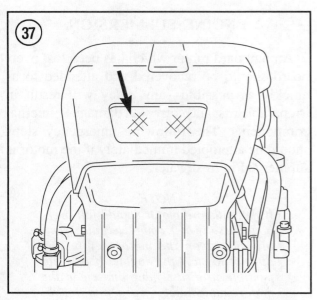

can crack the gear housing or water pump. If the boat is equipped with a speedometer, disconnect the pickup tube and allow it to drain completely, then reconnect the tube.

21. Drain the cooling system completely (to prevent freeze damage) by positioning the motor in a vertical position. Check all water drain holes for blockage.

22. *200 DFI models*—Remove the cooling water strainer (**Figure 36**) from the power head adapter plate. It will be necessary to remove the split lower cowl panels to gain access. Clean the strainer and allow any water to drain from the hose and adapter plate. Coat the threads of the water strainer with Loctite 567 PST pipe sealant (**Table 6**). Install and tighten the strainer securely.

23. *200 DFI models*—Inspect the air compressor inlet filter (**Figure 37**). Replace the filter if it is obstructed. It is recommended that the filter be replaced at least once a year. Simply pull the filter from the flywheel cover to inspect or change. The white side of the filter must face out.

24. Store the motor in a vertical position. In no case can an outboard motor be stored with the power head below the lower gearcase. The power head must be higher than the lower gearcase to prevent any water from entering the engine through the exhaust ports.

25. Prepare the battery for storage as follows:
    a. Disconnect the negative, then the positive battery cables.
    b. Clean all grease, sulfate or other contamination from the battery case and terminals.
    c. Remove the vent caps (if possible) and check the electrolyte level of each cell. Add distilled water to the level recommended by the battery manufacturer. Do not overfill.
    d. Lubricate the terminals and terminal fasteners with Quicksilver Corrosion Guard (**Table 6**).

CAUTION
A discharged battery can be damaged by freezing. Consider a battery float style

charger to maintain the battery charge indefinitely. A float charger is an inexpensive way to keep the battery at peak charge without causing excessive venting or gassing (and subsequent water loss). The Guest Battery Pal No. 2602 is available from any Mercury/Mariner dealership.

e. With the battery in a fully-charged condition (specific gravity at 1.260-1.280), store the battery in a *cool, dry* location where the temperature will not drop below freezing.

f. Recharge the battery every 45 days or whenever the specific gravity drops below 1.230. Maintain the recommended electrolyte level at all times. Add distilled water as necessary to maintain the level recommended by the battery manufacturer. For maximum battery life, avoid charge rates in excess of 6 amps. Discontinue charging when the specific gravity reaches 1.260 at 80° F (27° C).

g. Remove the grease on the battery terminals prior to returning the battery to service. Make sure the battery is installed in a fully-charged state.

ANTICORROSION MAINTENANCE

NOTE
Magnesium anodes are available for extra corrosion protection in freshwater. Do not use magnesium anodes in saltwater. The unit will be overprotected, causing the paint to blister and peel off.

1. Flush the cooling system with freshwater as described in this chapter after each outing in saltwater. Wash the exterior with freshwater.

2. Dry the exterior of the outboard and apply primer over any paint nicks and scratches. Use only Mercury Marine recommended touch-up paint. Do not use paints containing mercury or copper. Do not paint sacrificial anodes or the trim tab (if anodic).

3. Spray the power head and all electrical connections with Quicksilver Corrosion Guard.

4. Inspect all of the sacrificial anodes and trim tab (if anodic). Replace any that are deteriorated to less than one-half their original size.

a. To check for proper anode grounding, calibrate an ohmmeter on the highest scale available.

b. Connect one meter lead to a power head ground. Connect the other meter lead to the anode. The ohmmeter should indicate continuity (very low reading).

c. If any other reading is noted, remove the anode and thoroughly clean the mounting surfaces of the anode and the motor. Wire brush the threads of the mounting hardware and run a thread chaser into the mounting holes.

d. Reinstall the anode and retest as previously described. If the meter reading is still unsatisfactory, replace the anode and check the gearcase to midsection and midsection to power head mounting hardware for corrosion and high resistance.

5. If the outboard motor is operated consistently in saltwater, polluted or brackish water, reduce lubrication intervals (**Table 1**) by one-half.

ENGINE SUBMERSION

An outboard motor which has been lost overboard should be recovered and attended to as quickly as possible—any delay will result in irreparable rust and corrosion damage to internal components. The following emergency steps should be attempted immediately if the motor is submerged in freshwater.

NOTE
If the outboard motor should fall overboard in saltwater, completely disassemble and clean the motor before any attempt to start the engine. If it is not possible to disassemble and clean the motor immediately, flush and resub-

merge the outboard in freshwater to minimize rust and corrosion until it can be properly attended to.

1. Wash the outside of the motor with clean water to remove weeds, mud and other debris.

2. Remove the engine cowling.

3. Rinse the power head clean of all weeds, mud and other debris with freshwater.

4. Remove, clean and dry the spark plug(s).

5A. *EFI models*—Drain the vapor separator assembly, do not reinstall the drain plug. See Chapter Six.

5B. *Carbureted models*—Drain the carburetor float bowl(s), do not reinstall the float chamber plugs. See Chapter Six.

6. *Oil injected models*—drain and clean all oil tanks (reservoirs). Flush out all lines. Refill the system with the recommended oil. Bleed as much air out of the system as possible at this time.

7. Connect a clean fuel tank to the engine fuel line connector. Squeeze the primer bulb repeatedly to flush fresh fuel through the entire fuel system and purge the system of water.

NOTE
If a boat with a permanent fuel system and remote controls was involved in the submersion, the boat's fuel system and electrical system must be serviced in the same manner as the engine's fuel and electrical systems.

8. Replace *all* fuel filters.

9. Reinstall the carburetor (or vapor separator) drain plugs.

CAUTION
If there is a possibility that sand may have entered the power head, do not attempt to start the engine or severe internal damage could occur. If the outboard is lost overboard while running, internal engine damage is likely. Do not force the motor if it fails to turn over easily with the spark plug(s) removed. This is an indication of internal damage

such as a bent connecting rod or broken piston.

10. Drain as much water as possible from the power head by placing the motor in a horizontal position. Position the spark plugs facing downward and manually rotate the flywheel to expel water from the cylinder(s).

11. Pour liberal amounts of isopropyl (rubbing) alcohol into each carburetor or throttle body throat while rotating the flywheel to help absorb any remaining water or moisture.

12. Disconnect all electrical connectors and dry with electrical contact cleaner or isopropyl alcohol. Lubricate all electrical connectors with Quicksilver Dielectric silicone grease (**Table 6**).

13. Remove the electric starter motor. Disassemble the starter motor and dry all components with electrical contact cleaner or isopropyl alcohol. Reassemble and install the starter (Chapter Seven).

14. *225-250 hp and 200 DFI models*—If the alternator can be disassembled, cleaned and dried without damaging any parts, it is acceptable to do so. However, if any parts are damaged, the alternator is replaced as an assembly.

15. *150-200 hp EFI models:*

   a. Remove the electronic control unit (ECU) from the power head. Drain as much water as possible from the manifold absolute pressure (MAP) sensor tube. Do not attempt to remove the MAP sensor hose from the ECU.

   b. Place the ECU assembly in an oven and heat at 120° F (50° C) for approximately 2 hours to dry the ECU assembly. Remove the ECU from the oven and have it tested with the tester part No. 91-11011A2 EFI (Mercury Marine dealer item).

16. *225-250 EFI and 200 DFI models*—Remove and replace the MAP sensor. Make sure the map sensor vacuum line to the induction manifold is completely free of water and moisture before reconnection.

4

17. Pour approximately one teaspoon of engine oil into each cylinder through the spark plug hole(s). Rotate the flywheel by hand to distribute the oil.

18. Position the outboard with the induction system facing upward. Pour engine oil into each carburetor or throttle body throat while rotating the flywheel by hand to distribute the oil.

19. Reinstall the spark plug(s).

20. Attempt to start the engine using a fresh tank of 50:1 fuel/oil mixture (all models). If the outboard motor will start, allow it to run at least one hour to evaporate any remaining water inside the engine. Purge any remaining air from the oil injection system on models so equipped.

21. If the motor will not start, attempt to diagnose the cause as fuel, electrical or mechanical and repair as necessary. If the engine cannot be started within 2 hours, completely disassemble, clean and oil all internal components as soon as possible.

COOLING SYSTEM FLUSHING

Periodic flushing with clean freshwater will prevent salt or silt deposits from accumulating in the cooling system passageways. Perform the flushing procedure after each outing in saltwater, polluted or brackish water.

Keep the motor in an upright (vertical) position during and after flushing. This prevents water from passing into the power head through the drive shaft housing and exhaust ports during the flushing procedure. It also eliminates the possibility of residual water being trapped in the drive shaft housing or other passages.

75-200 hp (Except 200 DFI) and 275 hp Models

NOTE
Late model 135-200 hp outboards (serial No. 0G303046 and higher) are equipped with a built-in static flushing

*port. This port can only be used for static flushing. Any attempt to operate the engine will result in water pump failure and subsequent engine overheat. To use the static flush port, position the engine in a vertical position, remove the plug from the port and connect a garden hose to the port (**Figure 38**). Run water into the port for 3-5 minutes. Make sure to reinstall the plug when finished.*

The recommended flushing adapter is Quicksilver part No. 44357A-2 (**Figure 39**).

1. Remove the propeller as described in Chapter Nine.

2. Position the outboard in the vertical (normal operating) position.

3. Attach the flushing device to the lower gearcase as shown in **Figure 39**.

4. Connect a garden hose (1/2 in. or larger) between a water tap and the flushing device.

5. Open the water tap partially. Adjust the water pressure until a significant amount of water escapes from around the flushing cups, but do not apply full pressure.

6. Shift the outboard into NEUTRAL and start the engine. Adjust the engine speed to approximately 1000-1500 rpm.

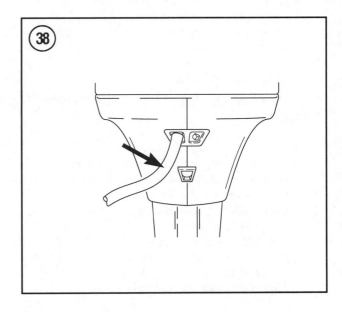

7. Adjust the water flow to maintain a slight loss of water around the rubber cups of the flushing device.

8. Check the motor to be certain that water is being discharged from the water pump indicator hose or fitting (tattle-tale). If not, stop the motor immediately and determine the cause of the problem.

9. Flush the motor for 5-10 minutes or until the discharged water is clear. If the outboard was last used in saltwater, flush for 10 minutes minimum.

10. Stop the engine, then shut off the water supply. Remove the flushing device from the outboard.

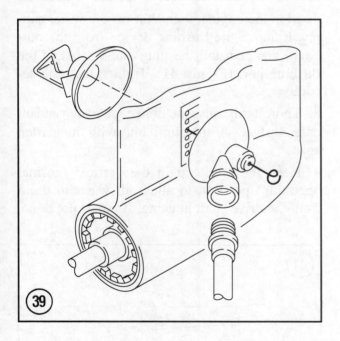

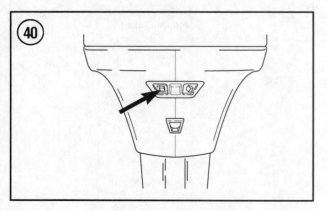

11. Keep the outboard in the vertical (normal operating) position to allow all water to drain from the drive shaft housing. If this is not done, water can enter the power head through the exhaust ports.

12. Reinstall the propeller as described in Chapter Nine.

200 DFI, 225 and 250 hp Outboard Models

These engines incorporate an integral flushing adaptor (**Figure 40**). The engine can be flushed statically or at idle speed (1500 rpm). To use the static flush port, position the engine in a vertical position, remove the plug from the port and connect a garden hose to the port (**Figure 38**). Run water into the port for 3-5 minutes. Make sure to reinstall the plug when finished.

If so desired, the Quicksilver part No. 44357A-2 flushing adaptor may be used as described in the previous section.

1. Remove the propeller as described in Chapter Nine.

2. Position the outboard in the vertical (normal operating) position.

3. Remove the integral flushing port plug and connect a 1/2 in. or larger garden hose to the flushing port (**Figure 38**).

4. Open the water tap approximately halfway. It is not necessary to use full water pressure.

5. Shift the outboard into NEUTRAL and start the engine. Adjust the engine speed to approximately 1000-1500 rpm.

6. Check the motor to be certain that water is being discharged from the water pump indicator hose or fitting (tattle-tale). Adjust the water tap as necessary. If no water is being discharged, stop the motor immediately and determine the cause of the problem.

7. Flush the motor for 5-10 minutes or until the discharged water is clear. If the outboard was last used in saltwater, flush for 10 minutes minimum.

8. Stop the engine, then shut off the water supply. Remove the flushing device from the outboard and reinstall the plug in the flushing port.

9. Keep the outboard in the vertical (normal operating) position to allow all water to drain from the drive shaft housing. If this is not done, water can enter the power head through the exhaust ports.

10. Reinstall the propeller as described in Chapter Nine.

65-140 Jet Models

The 65-140 Jet models have a flushing port built into the jet pump unit. A flushing adaptor is available from Quicksilver Parts and Accessories as part No. 24789A-1. The flushing procedure is outlined in the following procedure.

Rinse the water intake grate area, impeller and the entire outside surface of all jet pump units with freshwater. Direct a garden hose into the grate area and over the outer surfaces of the pump unit *after* the recommended flushing procedure has been completed.

> *CAUTION*
> *Late model 105-140 Jet models (serial No. 0G303046 and higher) are equipped with a built-in static flushing port. This port can only be used for static flushing. Any attempt to operate the engine will result in water pump failure and subsequent engine overheat. To use the static flush port, position the engine in a vertical position, remove the plug from the port and connect a garden hose to the port (Figure 38). Run water into the port for 3-5 minutes. Make sure to reinstall the plug when finished.*

1. Position the outboard in the vertical (normal operating) position.

2. Remove the flushing port plug and washer (**Figure 41**), install the flushing adapter and connect a 1/2 in. or larger garden hose to the flushing adapter.

3. Open the water tap approximately halfway. It is not necessary to use full water pressure.

4. Shift the outboard into NEUTRAL and start the engine. Adjust the engine speed to approximately 1000 rpm.

5. Check the motor to be certain that water is being discharged from the water pump indicator hose or fitting (tattle-tale). Adjust the water tap as necessary. If no water is being discharged, stop the motor immediately and determine the cause of the problem.

6. Flush the motor for 5-10 minutes or until the discharged water is clear. If the outboard was last used in saltwater, flush for 10 minutes minimum.

7. Stop the engine, then shut off the water supply. Remove the flushing device from the outboard and reinstall the plug and washer in the flushing port (**Figure 41**). Tighten the plug securely.

8. Thoroughly rinse the intake grate area and all outer surfaces of the pump unit with the garden hose.

9. Keep the outboard in the vertical (normal operating) position to allow all water to drain from the drive shaft housing. If this is not done,

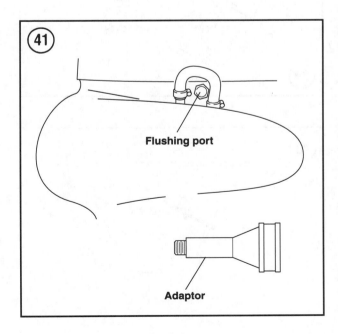

(41)

Flushing port

Adaptor

water can enter the power head through the exhaust ports.

TUNE-UP

A tune-up consists of a series of inspections, adjustments and parts replacement to compensate for normal wear and deterioration of the outboard motor components. Regular tune-ups are important to maintain the proper power, performance and economy. Mercury Marine recommends that tune-up procedures be performed at least once a season or every 100 hours of operation. Individual operating conditions may dictate that a tune-up be performed more often. A tune-up should also be performed any time the outboard exhibits a substantial performance loss.

Since proper outboard motor operation depends upon a number of interrelated system functions, a tune-up consisting of only one or two of the recommended procedures will seldom provide satisfactory results. For best results, a thorough and systematic procedure of analysis and correction is necessary.

Prior to performing a tune-up, flush the outboard cooling system as described in this chapter to check for proper water pump operation.

The recommended tune-up procedure is listed below. Any procedure not covered in this chapter or section is so identified.

1. Quicksilver Power Tune treatment—*Removing Combustion Chamber Deposits.*
2. Compression test.
3. Cylinder head bolt torque (**Table 5**).
4. Electrical wiring harness inspection.
5. Spark plug service.
6. Gearcase lubricant change and propshaft spline lubrication.
7. General engine lubrication (all applicable lubrication points). See **Table 1**.
8. Filter service (fuel, air, water and bleed filters, as applicable).
9. Lower gearcase water pump service.

10. Fuel system and oil injection system (if so equipped) service.
11. Ignition system service.
12. Charging system service (if so equipped).
13. Battery and starter system service (if so equipped).
14. All synchronization and linkage adjustments (Chapter Five).
15. On-water performance test.

Anytime the fuel or ignition system is adjusted or defective parts replaced, all engine synchronization and linkage adjustments *must* be verified. These procedures are described in Chapter Five. Perform all synchronization and linkage adjustments *before* running the on-water performance test.

Removing Combustion Chamber Deposits

During operation, carbon deposits will accumulate on the piston(s), rings, cylinder head(s) and exhaust ports. If the carbon is allowed to build up unchecked, the effective compression ratio will increase, raising the fuel octane requirements of the power head.

If the carbon builds up in the piston ring area, the piston rings will stick in the piston ring grooves causing a loss of compression and the loss of heat transfer to the cylinder walls (and water passages). When the piston rings stick, performance suffers and combustion chamber temperatures increase dramatically, leading to preignition and detonation. All of these situations will eventually lead to catastrophic power head failure.

Quicksilver Power Tune is designed to remove combustion chamber deposits and free stuck piston rings, restoring engine performance and lowering the risk of engine failure.

NOTE
Using quality gasoline and an NMMA approved TCW-3 outboard oil will minimize combustion chamber deposits and piston ring sticking. If the use of poor

*quality gasoline and outboard oil is unavoidable, or combustion chamber deposits are a continual problem, use Quicksilver QuicKleen Fuel Treatment regularly (**Table 1**).*

For effective preventive maintenance, all engines should have Quicksilver Power Tune Engine Cleaner (**Table 6**) applications performed every 100 hours of operation or as required. Follow the manufacturers instructions on the Quicksilver Power Tune container.

Compression Test

An accurate cylinder cranking compression check provides an indication of the mechanical condition of the combustion chamber. It is an important preliminary step in any tune-up as a motor with low or unequal compression between cylinders *cannot* be satisfactorily tuned. Any compression problem discovered during this test must be corrected before continuing with the tune-up procedure. A thread-in compression tester is recommended for best results.

A variation of more than 15 psi (103.4 kPa) between any 2 cylinders indicates a problem. If the compression is unacceptable, remove the cylinder head (if applicable) and inspect the cylinder wall(s), piston(s) and head gasket(s) condition. If the cylinder wall(s), piston(s) and head gasket show no evidence of damage or failure, the piston rings are stuck, worn or damaged and the power head will have to be repaired.

CAUTION
Do not run the engine without an adequate water supply and do not exceed 3000 rpm without an adequate load. Refer to Safety Precautions at the beginning of Chapter Three.

1. Run the engine up to operating temperature.
2. Remove the spark plug(s) as described in this chapter.

3. Securely ground the spark plug lead(s) to the engine to disable the ignition system, prevent accidental starting and possible ignition system damage.

4. Following the compression gauge manufacturer's instructions, connect the gauge to the No. 1 cylinder (top) spark plug hole (**Figure 42**, typical).

5. Manually hold the throttle plates in the wide-open throttle position. Crank the engine through at least 4 compression strokes and record the gauge reading.

6. Repeat Step 4 and Step 5 for all remaining cylinders. Refer to **Table 3** for compression specifications. A variation of more than 15 psi (103.4 kPa) between 2 cylinders indicates a problem with the lower reading cylinder, such as worn or sticking piston rings and/or scored pistons or cylinder walls. In such cases, pour a tablespoon of engine oil into the suspect cylinder and repeat Step 4 and Step 5. If the compression increases significantly (by 10 psi [69 kPa] or more) the rings are worn or damaged and the power head must be disassembled and repaired.

If the compression is within specification, but the outboard motor is difficult to start or has poor idle quality, refer to *Starting Difficulties* in Chapter Three.

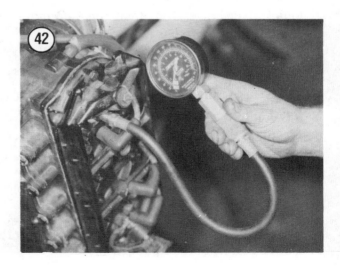

Cylinder Head
Bolt Torque

CAUTION
Excessive torque will distort the cylinder bore(s) or cylinder head(s). Insufficient torque will allow the cylinder head gaskets or seals to leak. The motor should be cool to the touch for this operation.

NOTE
*Do **not** retorque the cylinder head bolts on engines that use the **torque and turn** cylinder head tightening process. See **Table 4**.*

On models equipped with removable cylinder heads (that do not use the torque and turn tightening process), the cylinder head bolts should be retorqued during a tune-up. Loosen each bolt slightly and retorque to the specification listed in **Table 4**. Refer to Chapter Eight for cylinder head service procedures and tightening sequences if the cylinder head has been removed from the power head.

Electrical Wiring
Harness Inspection

Inspect all harnesses, leads, connectors and terminals for loose connection, corrosion, mechanical damage, damaged insulation and improper routing. Harnesses that are close to moving components should be checked for chafing or rubbing damage. Reroute, retape and secure harnesses as necessary. Inspect all harnesses, leads and components on or near the cylinder head and exhaust passages for heat damage. Repair any damage found. Refer to Chapter Three for recommended tools and repair kits.

Spark Plug Replacement

Improper installation and incorrect application are common causes of poor spark plug performance in outboard motors. The gasket on the plug must be fully compressed against a clean plug seat for heat transfer to take place effectively. If heat transfer cannot take place, the spark plug will overheat and fail. This may also lead to preignition and detonation. Make sure the spark plugs are correctly torqued.

Incorrect application can cause not only spark plug problems, but can also lead to ignition system symptoms or failure from RFI (radio frequency interference). Most engines with an ECM (electronic control module) require suppression or inductor spark plugs that reduce the RFI caused by the spark jumping the air gap of the spark plug. Always use the recommended spark plugs.

If the engine does not require inductor or suppression spark plugs, yet ignition interference with onboard accessories is noted, install the recommended inductor or suppression spark plug as recommended in **Table 2**.

CAUTION
When the spark plug(s) are removed, dirt or other foreign material surrounding the spark plug hole(s) can fall into the cylinder(s). Foreign material inside the cylinders can cause engine damage when the engine is started.

1. Clean the area around the spark plug(s) using compressed air or an appropriate brush.

2. Disconnect the spark plug lead(s) by twisting the boot back and forth on the spark plug insulator while pulling outward. Pulling on the lead instead of the boot can cause internal damage to the lead.

3. Remove the spark plugs using an appropriate size spark plug socket. Arrange the spark plugs in order of the cylinder from which they were removed.

4

4. Examine each spark plug. See **Figure 43** for surface gap plugs and **Figure 44** for conventional gap plugs. Compare spark plug condition to **Figure 45** (surface gap) or **Figure 46** (conventional gap). Spark plug condition is a good indicator of piston, rings and cylinder condition, and can provide a warning of developing trouble.

5. Check each plug for make and heat range. All spark plugs should be identical. Refer to **Table 2** and check that the spark plugs are correct for your application.

6. If the spark plugs are in good condition, they may be cleaned and regapped (if applicable).

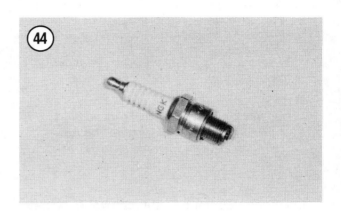

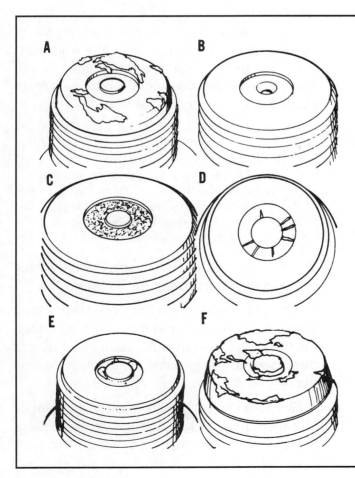

SPARK PLUG ANALYSIS (SURFACE GAP SPARK PLUGS)

A. Normal—Light tan or gray colored deposits indicate that the engine/ignition system condition is good. Electrode wear indicates normal spark rotation.
B. Worn out—Excessive electrode wear can cause hard starting or a misfire during acceleration.
C. Cold fouled—Wet oil or fuel deposits are caused by "drowning" the plug with raw fuel mix during cranking, overrich carburetion or an improper fuel:oil ratio. Weak ignition will also contribute to this condition.
D. Carbon tracking—Electrically conductive deposits on the firing end provide a low-resistance path for the voltage. Carbon tracks form and can cause misfires.
E. Concentrated arc—Multi-colored appearance is normal. It is caused by electricity consistently following the same firing path. Arc path changes with deposit conductivity and gap erosion.
F. Aluminum throw-off—Caused by preignition. This is not a plug problem but the result of engine damage. Check engine to determine cause and extent of damage.

④⑥

SPARK PLUG CONDITION

NORMAL
- Identified by light tan or gray deposits on the firing tip.
- Can be cleaned.

GAP BRIDGED
- Identified by deposit buildup closing gap between electrodes.
- Caused by oil or carbon fouling. If deposits are not excessive, the plug can be cleaned.

OIL FOULED
- Identified by wet black deposits on the insulator shell bore and electrodes.
- Caused by excessive oil entering combustion chamber through worn rings and pistons, excessive clearance between valve guides and stems or worn or loose bearings. Can be cleaned. If engine is not repaired, use a hotter plug.

CARBON FOULED
- Identified by black, dry fluffy carbon deposits on insulator tips, exposed shell surfaces and electrodes.
- Caused by too cold a plug, weak ignition, dirty air cleaner, too rich a fuel mixture or excessive idling. Can be cleaned.

LEAD FOULED
- Identified by dark gray, black, yellow or tan deposits or a fused glazed coating on the insulator tip.
- Caused by highly leaded gasoline. Can be cleaned.

WORN
- Identified by severely eroded or worn electrodes.
- Caused by normal wear. Should be replaced.

FUSED SPOT DEPOSIT
- Identified by melted or spotty deposits resembling bubbles or blisters.
- Caused by sudden acceleration. Can be cleaned.

OVERHEATING
- Identified by a white or light gray insulator with small black or gray brown spots and with bluish-burnt appearance of electrodes.
- Caused by engine overheating, wrong type of fuel, loose spark plugs, too hot a plug or incorrect ignition timing. Replace the plug.

PREIGNITION
- Identified by melted electrodes and possibly blistered insulator. Metallic deposits on insulator indicate engine damage.
- Caused by wrong type of fuel, incorrect ignition timing or advance, too hot a plug, burned valves or engine overheating. Replace the plug.

4

Install new spark plugs if there is any question as to the condition of the spark plugs.

7. Inspect the spark plug threads in the engine and clean them with a thread chaser (**Figure 47**) if necessary. Wipe the spark plug seats clean before installing new spark plugs.

8. Install the spark plugs with new gaskets and tighten to 20 ft.-lb. (27.1 N•m) on all models except the 275 hp. On 275 hp models tighten to 17 ft.-lb. (23.0 N•m). If a torque wrench is not available, seat the plugs finger tight, then tighten an additional 1/4 turn with a wrench.

9. Inspect each spark plug lead before reconnecting it to its spark plug. If the insulation is damaged or deteriorated, install a new plug lead. Push the boot onto the plug terminal making sure it is fully seated.

Spark Plug Gap Adjustment (Conventional Gap Only)

Carefully set the electrode gap on new spark plugs to ensure a reliable, consistent spark. Use a special spark plug gapping tool with wire gauges. **Figure 48** shows a common type of gapping tool.

1. Make sure the gaskets are installed on the spark plugs (except taper seat spark plugs).

NOTE
*Some spark plug brands require that the terminal end be screwed on the plug before installation. See **Figure 49**.*

2. Insert the appropriate size wire gauge (**Table 2**) between the electrodes. If the gap is correct, there will be a slight drag as the wire is pulled through. To adjust the gap, bend the side electrode with the gapping tool (**Figure 50**), then remeasure the gap.

CAUTION
Never attempt to close the gap by tapping the spark plug on a solid surface. This can damage the spark plug. Always

use the proper adjusting tool to open or close the gap.

Lower Gearcase (and Jet Pump Unit) Water Pump

Overheating and extensive power head damage can result from a faulty water pump. Therefore, the manufacturer recommends replacing the water pump impeller, seals and gaskets at the following intervals:

NOTE
Individual operating conditions may dictate that the pump be serviced more often. It is also recommended that the water pump be serviced anytime the

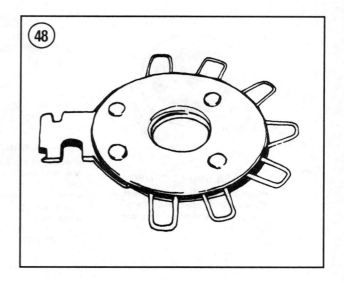

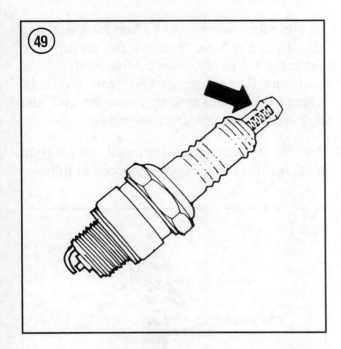

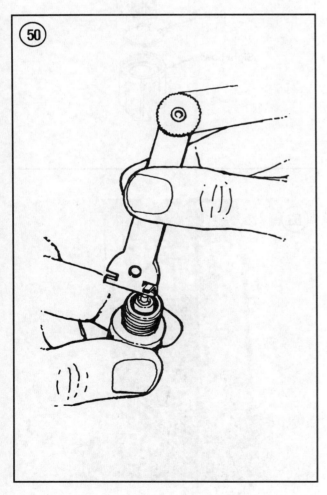

lower gearcase or jet pump assembly is removed for service.

1. *High-pressure pump*—Replace the water pump after every 100 hours of operation of once per year. Refer to Chapter Nine for pump identification and service procedures.

2. *High-volume pump*—Replace the water pump after every 300 hours of operation or every 3 years. Refer to Chapter Nine for pump identification and service procedures.

NOTE
*Anytime the lower gearcase is removed, clean and lubricate the drive shaft splines with 2-4-C or SP101 lubricant (**Table 6**). Do not apply any lubricant to the top drive shaft surface as this may prevent the drive shaft from fully seating into the crankshaft.*

Many outboard owners depend upon the visual indication provided by the water pump indicator hose or *tattle tale* as the sole indicator of water pump performance. While it is important to monitor the water pump indicator hose, the installation of a water pressure gauge kit (available from any Mercury/Mariner dealership) is a more effective method to ensure that the pump is actually operating correctly. The kit contains a fitting and hose that attaches to the power head and a water pressure gauge that is mounted in the boat.

Water pressure specifications are listed in the appropriate engine's general specification table at the end of Chapter Five. However, after installing the pressure gauge kit and every time the water pump is serviced, it is important to note the normal water pressure readings (at various speeds) for your motor. If the pressure readings show a gradual drop from the normal readings, impeller wear is indicated and impeller replacement should be planned in the near future. If the pressure readings show a sudden drop, water pump damage has occurred and the pump should be serviced immediately (Chapter Nine).

Fuel and Oil Injection Systems

During a tune-up, verify all synchronization and linkage adjustments as described in Chapter Five. Clean or replace all fuel, bleed and air filters. Inspect all fuel lines, fuel system components and all spring clamps, worm clamps or tie-straps for leaks, deterioration, mechanical damage and secure mounting. All replacement fuel lines must be alcohol resistant. If the fuel system is suspected of not functioning correctly, refer to Chapter Three for troubleshooting procedures.

Refer to *Fuel and Lubrication* in this chapter for basic oil injection system description and component function. Check the oil injection system (if so equipped) for leaks, loose lines and fittings and deterioration. Synchronize the oil pump linkage with the throttle linkage (Chapter Five). Inspect the warning module and sensor wiring (if so equipped) as described under *Electrical Wiring Harness Inspection* in this chapter. If the oil injection system is suspected of not functioning correctly, refer to Chapter Eleven for oil injection system troubleshooting and service procedures.

Fuel, bleed, air and water filters

1. Service the portable fuel tank filter by detaching the fuel hose from the tank. Unthread the

pickup tube assembly or pickup tube retaining ring from the tank. Remove the pickup tube assembly. Clean or replace the fine mesh filter as necessary. Replace any gaskets, seals or o-rings. Thread the pickup assembly into the tank and tighten it or the retaining ring securely.

2A. To service models equipped with a sight bowl fuel filter (**Figure 51**), proceed as follows:

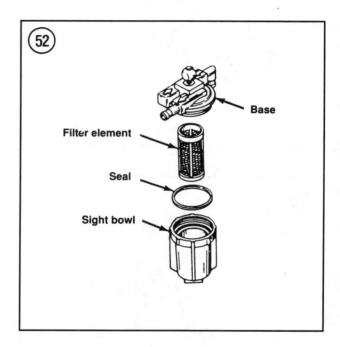

a. Unscrew the sight bowl from the filter base. Safely dispose of any fuel in the bowl and discard the bowl seal.

b. Remove the filter element from the bowl. Clean the element and fuel bowl in clean solvent and dry with compressed air. Replace the element if it cannot be satisfactorily cleaned.

c. Install a new bowl seal into the fuel bowl (**Figure 52**). Reinstall the filter into the bowl and reinstall the bowl assembly onto the filter base. Tighten the bowl securely *by hand*.

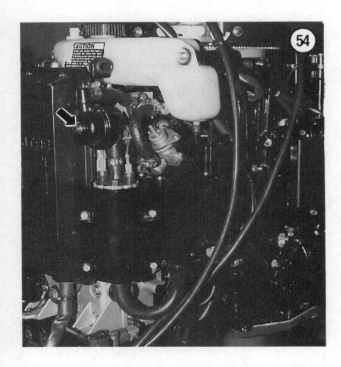

d. Test the installation by squeezing the primer bulb and checking for leaks.

2B. To service the water separating fuel filter (**Figure 53**, typical) on EFI and DFI models, proceed as follows:

a. Disconnect the water sensor lead (B, **Figure 53**) from the bottom of the filter canister (A, **Figure 53**).

b. Remove the water separating fuel filter by unscrewing the filter from the filter base. Empty the contents of the filter into a suitable container for inspection.

c. If excessive debris or water accumulation is present, inspect the fuel tank for water contamination and other debris.

d. Remove the water sensing probe from the bottom of the filter and discard the filter.

2C. To service the final fuel filter on EFI and DFI models, refer to Chapter Five. The final filter is mounted between the electric fuel pump outlet and the fuel rail (**Figure 54**, typical) on 1994-1995, 150-200 hp EFI models. The final filter is mounted inside the vapor separator (**Figure 55**, typical) on all 225-250 EFI, 200 DFI and 1996-1997, 150-200 hp EFI models. Fuel rail pressure must be relieved before servicing the final fuel filter.

2D. Replace the bleed system filter on 200DFI models (**Figure 56**) and on EFI models so equipped (**Figure 57**).

2E. *200 DFI models*—Remove the cooling water strainer (**Figure 58**) from the power head adapter plate. It is necessary to remove the split lower cowl panels to gain access. Clean the strainer and allow any water to drain from the hose and adapter plate. Coat the threads of the water strainer with Loctite 567 PST pipe sealant (**Table 6**). Install and tighten the strainer securely.

2F. *200 DFI models*—Inspect the air compressor inlet filter (**Figure 59**). Replace the filter if it is obstructed. Replace the filter at least once a year. Simply pull the filter from the flywheel cover to inspect or change. The white side of the filter must face out.

Fuel pump

The fuel pump does not generally require service during a tune-up. However, conduct a visual inspection of the fuel pump, pump mounting hardware, all fuel and crankcase pulse hoses and all spring clamps, worm clamps or tie-straps. Replace any damaged or deteriorated components. If the fuel pump or fuel system is sus-

pected of not functioning correctly, refer to Chapter Three for troubleshooting procedures.

Ignition System Service

Other than inspecting or replacing the spark plugs, the ignition system is relatively maintenance free. During a tune-up, verify all synchronization and linkage adjustments as described in Chapter Five. If the ignition system is suspected of not functioning correctly, refer to Chapter Three for troubleshooting procedures.

Charging System Service

Other than inspecting the belt and belt tension on 225-250 hp and 200 DFI models, no maintenance is required on the charging system. If the charging system is suspected of not functioning correctly, refer to Chapter Three for troubleshooting procedures.

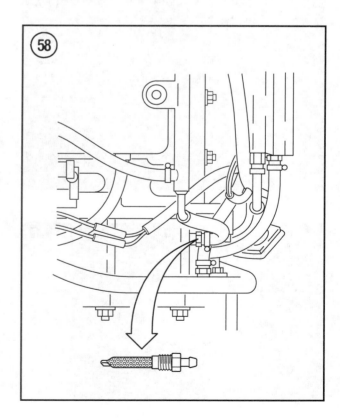

Alternator Belt (225 and 250 hp)

The 225 and 250 hp models use a V-belt to drive the alternator off of the crank pulley. Adjust belt tension by rotating the alternator away or toward the flywheel pulley. Belt tension should be 1/4-1/2 in. (6.3-12.7 mm) deflection under moderate thumb pressure at the point shown in **Figure 60**. Inspect the belt for deterioration, wear and fraying. To tension or replace the belt, proceed as follows.

1. Remove and ground the spark plug leads to the power head to prevent accidental starting.

2. Remove the flywheel cover.

3. Loosen the pivot bolt (**Figure 60**) and the tension bolt (**Figure 60**). Rotate the alternator toward the flywheel and slip the belt off of both pulleys.

4. Install a new belt over both pulleys. Rotate the alternator away from the flywheel until the belt is properly tensioned (1/4-1/2 in. [6.3-12.7 mm] deflection under moderate thumb pressure). Snug the tension bolt to hold the alternator in place.

5. Recheck belt tension, repeating Step 4 as necessary. When tension has been verified, tighten both the pivot bolt and tension bolt to 40 ft.-lb. (54 N.m).

6. Reinstall the flywheel cover.

7. Reconnect the spark plug leads to the spark plugs.

8. Recheck belt tension and condition after the first 10 hours of new belt operation and every 50 hours thereafter.

Alternator Belt (200 DFI)

The 200 DFI uses a serpentine belt and automatic tensioner system very similar to current automotive designs. While no adjustments are required with this system, the belt and belt tensioner assembly should be inspected for deterioration, wear, fraying and any mechanical damage or failure. To replace the belt, proceed as follows:

1. Remove and ground the spark plug leads to the power head to prevent accidental starting.

2. Remove the flywheel cover. Be careful to disconnect the air compressor inlet at the rear and the vent line at the front.

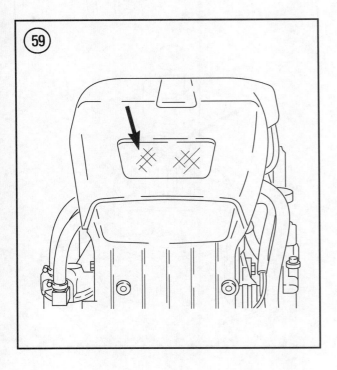

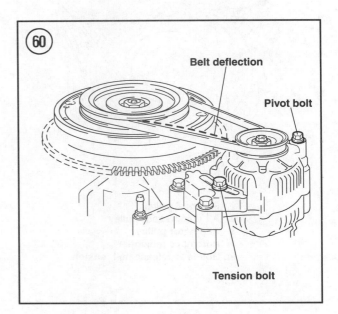

3. Manually rotate the tensioner (4, **Figure 61**) away from the belt (5, **Figure 61**) and slip the belt off of the pulleys.

4. Install a new belt while holding the tensioner fully open. Route the belt as shown in **Figure 61**.

5. Release the tensioner against the belt. Make sure the belt is tracking on each pulley correctly.

6. Reinstall the flywheel cover. Make sure the air compressor inlet is connected at the rear and the vent line is connected at the front.

7. Reconnect the spark plug leads to the spark plug.

Battery and Electric Starter System

During a tune-up, the electric starter system requires minimal maintenance. Clean and lubricate the starter motor shaft and starter drive *lightly* with SAE 30 engine oil as shown in **Figure 62**.

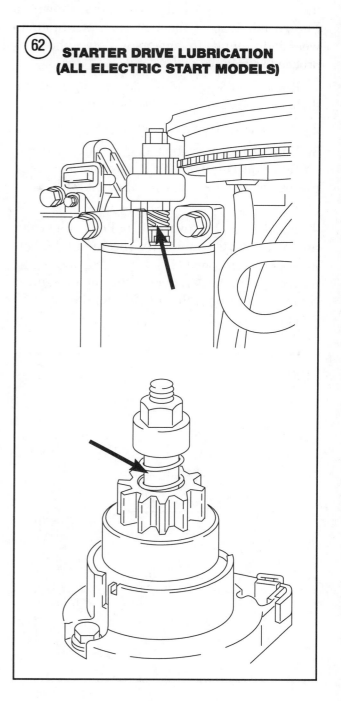

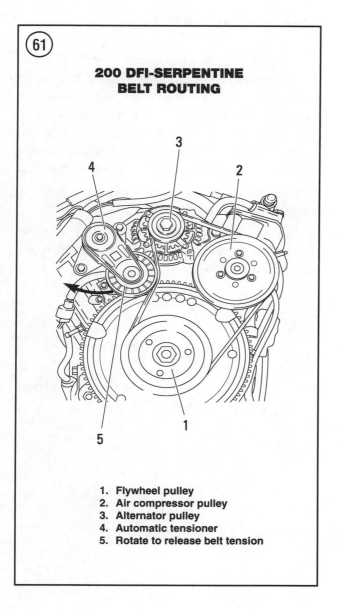

1. Flywheel pulley
2. Air compressor pulley
3. Alternator pulley
4. Automatic tensioner
5. Rotate to release belt tension

Inspect the battery cable connections for corrosion, loose connections or mechanical damage. If wing-nuts are present, discard them and replace them with corrosion resistant hex nuts and lock washers. Place a lock washer under each battery cable to ensure positive contact with the battery terminal. Tighten the battery connections securely. Loose battery connections can cause every imaginable symptom. To verify correct operation of the electric starter system, proceed as follows:

1. Check the battery state of charge. See Chapter Seven.

2. Disable the ignition system by removing the spark plug lead from each spark plug and securing the spark plug leads to the power head (electrical ground).

3. Connect a multimeter, set to the 20 volt DC scale, to the battery positive and negative terminals.

4. Turn the ignition switch to the START position and note the meter reading while the engine is cranking for several seconds.

a. If the voltage is 9.5 volts or higher and the cranking speed is normal, the starting system is functioning normally and the battery is of sufficient capacity for the engine.

b. If the voltage is below 9.5 volts and/or the cranking speed is below normal, the starting system is malfunctioning. Refer to Chapter Three for troubleshooting procedures.

5. Reconnect the spark plug leads when finished.

On Water Performance Testing

Before performance testing the outboard motor, make sure that the boat bottom is cleaned of all marine growth and that no *hook* or *rocker* is present in the boat bottom (**Figure 63**). Any of these conditions will reduce the boat performance considerably.

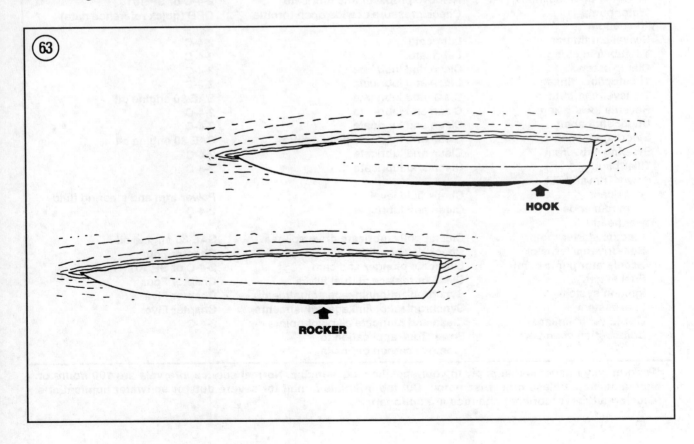

63

HOOK

ROCKER

The boat should be performance tested with an average load on board. Tilt or trim the outboard motor at an angle that will produce optimum performance and balanced steering control. If equipped with an adjustable trim tab, it should be properly adjusted to allow the boat to steer in either direction with equal ease at the boat's normal cruising speed.

CAUTION
Mercury/Mariner outboard motors tend to perform best when propped toward

the upper limit of the recommended rpm range. In no case should the engine be allowed to operate above or below the recommended speed range at wide-open throttle or catastrophic engine damage will occur.

Check the engine speed at wide-open throttle. If engine speed is not within the specified range (Chapter Five) and the engine is in a proper state of tune, change the propeller. Use a higher pitch propeller to reduce engine speed or a lower pitch propeller to increase engine speed.

Table 1 RECOMMENDED PREVENTIVE MAINTENANCE SCHEDULE*

Component or system	Recommended procedure	Quicksilver lubricant or service manual reference
Lower gearcase		
Lubricant level	Check lubricant level	Premium Blend Gear Lube
Gear lubricant	Change lubricant	Premium Blend Gear Lube
V-6 bearing carrier	Lubricate grease fittings	2-4-C or SP 101
Retaining ring	Remove, clean, lubricate and reinstall	2-4-C or SP 101
Drive shaft splines	Remove gearcase and lubricate	2-4-C or SP 101
Propeller shaft splines	Remove propeller and lubricate	2-4-C or SP 101
Water pump	Check pressure at wide open throttle	QRD (quick reference data)
Mid-section		
Swivel pin fittings	Lubricate	2-4-C
Tilt tube/pin fittings	Lubricate	2-4-C
Clamp screws	Clean and lubricate	2-4-C
Tilt stop/lock linkage	Clean and lubricate	2-4-C
Tilt lever shaft/brace	Clean and lubricate	SAE 30 engine oil
Reverse lock linkage	Clean and lubricate	2-4-C
Upper shift shaft	Clean and lubricate	2-4-C
Steering arm link	Clean and lubricate pivot points	SAE 30 engine oil
Steering cable/ram	Clean and lubricate	2-4-C
Tiller handle	Clean and lubricate	2-4-C
Power Trim and Tilt		
Lubricant	Check fluid level	Power trim and steering fluid
Trim ram ends	Clean and lubricate	2-4-C
Power head		
Electric starter motor	Clean/lightly lubricate drive splines	SAE 30 engine oil
Belt-driven alternator	Check belt condition and tension(er)	Chapter Four
Accelerator pump cam	Lubricate plunger and cam	2-4-C or SP 101
Fuel Filters	Clean or replace all fuel filters	Chapter Four
Ignition system	Synchronization/linkage adjustments	Chapter Five
Fuel system	Synchronization/linkage adjustments	Chapter Five
Throttle/shift linkage	Clean and lubricate all pivot points	2-4-C
Combustion chambers	Power Tune application to remove carbon deposits	–

*Perform only the items that apply to your specific model engine. Normal service intervals are 100 hours or once a season, unless otherwise noted. Cut the intervals in half for severe duty or saltwater applications (accelerated gear lubricant changes are optional).

Table 2 RECOMMENDED SPARK PLUGS

Model	NGK spark plug number (RFI)*	Gap in. (mm)
75, 90 hp and 65 Jet	BUHW-2 (BUZHW-2)	NA
100, 115, 125 hp and 80 Jet	BP8H-N-10 (BPZ8H-N-10)	.040 (1.02)
135-200 hp, 105 and 140 Jet	BU8H (BUZ8H)	NA
200 DFI (direct fuel injected)	Champion RC10ECC	.040 (1.02)
225 hp		
(carbureted 1994-1996)	Use resistor (BPZ8H-N-10)	.040 (1.02)
225 hp (carbureted 1997)	Champion QL77CC	.035 (0.89)
225-250 hp EFI		
(electronic fuel injection)	Champion QL77CC	.035 (0.89)
275 hp	BU8H (BUZ8H)	NA

*Use resistor or suppression spark plugs if radio frequency interference (RFI) suppression is required.

Table 3 POWER HEAD COMPRESSION SPECIFICATIONS

Model	Compression specification
75-200 hp and 275 hp	Maximum 15 psi (103.4 kPa) variation between cylinders
225 and 250 hp	110-120 psi (758.5-827.4 kPa) typical

Table 4 CYLINDER HEAD BOLT TORQUE SPECIFICATIONS

Model	Torque specification
75-125 hp and 30-80 Jet	not applicable
135-200 hp, 105 and 140 Jet	Torque and turn
225-250 hp	Torque and turn
275 hp	180 in.-lbs. (20.3 N.m)

Table 5 GEARCASE GEAR RATIO AND APPROXIMATE LUBRICANT CAPACITY

Model	Gear ratio	Tooth count	Lubricant capacity
75 and 90 hp	2.3:1	13:30	22.5 oz. (665 ml)
100, 115 and 125 hp	2.07:1	14:29	22.5 oz. (665 ml)
135 and 150 hp	2.00:1	14:28	22.5 oz. (665 ml)
XR6 and Magnum III			
(small gearcase)	1.78:1	14:25	21.0 oz. (621 ml)
XR6 and Magnum III			
(large gearcase)	1.87:1	15:28	22.5 oz. (665 ml)
150-200 XRI, 175-200 hp	1.87:1	15:28	22.5 oz. (665 ml)
200 DFI			
(direct fuel injection)	1.75:1	12:21	28.0 oz. (828 ml)
225-250 hp (1994)	1.64:1	17:28	28.0 oz. (828 ml)
225-250 hp (1995-1997)	1.75:1	12:21	28.0 oz. (828 ml)
275 hp	1.64:1	17:28	29.0 oz. (858 ml)

Table 6 RECOMMENDED LUBRICANTS, SEALANTS AND ADHESIVES

	Part No.
Lubricants	
Quicksilver 2-Cycle TC-W3 outboard oil	(dealer stock item)
Quicksilver Special Lubricant 101	92-13872A-1
Quicksilver 2-4-C Multi-Lube	(dealer stock item)
Quicksilver Anti-Corrosion Grease	92-78376A-6
Quicksilver Needle Bearing Grease	92-825265A-1
Quicksilver Power Trim and Steering Fluid	92-90100A12
Quicksilver Premium Blend Gear Lube	(dealer stock item)
Quicksilver High Performance Gear Lube	(dealer stock item)
Sealants	
Quicksilver Perfect Seal	92-34227-1
Loctite 5900 Ultra black RTV sealant	92-809826
Sealer (crankcase halves)	92-90113-2
Loctite Master Gasket Sealer	92-12564-2
Quicksilver Liquid Neoprene	92-25711-2
Loctite 567 PST pipe sealant	92-809822
Quicksilver Bellows Adhesive	92-86166-1
Quicksilver Ignition Coil Insulation Compound	92-41669-1
Adhesives	
Locquic Primer	92-809824
Loctite 271 threadlocking sealant (high strength)	92-809819
Loctite 242 threadlocking sealant (medium strength)	92-809821
Loctite RC680 high strength retaining compound	92-809833
Miscellaneous	
Quicksilver Power Tune Engine Cleaner	92-15104A12
Quicksilver Corrosion Guard	92-815869A12
Quicksilver Storage Seal Rust Inhibitor	92-86145A12
Quicksilver Dielectric silicone grease	92-823506-1

Table 7 STANDARD TORQUE VALUES—U.S. STANDARD FASTENERS

Screw or nut size	in.-lbs.	ft.-lbs.	N•m
6-32	9	—	1.0
8-32	20	—	2.3
10-24	30	—	3.4
10-32	35	—	4.0
12-24	45	—	5.1
1/4-20	70	6	7.9
1/4-28	84	7	9.5
5/16-18	160	13	18.1
5/16-24	168	14	19.0
3/8-16	270	23	30.5
3/8-24	300	25	33.9
7/16-14	—	36	48.8
7/16-20	—	40	54.2
1/2-13	—	50	67.8
1/2-20	—	60	81.3

Table 8 STANDARD TORQUE VALUES—METRIC FASTENERS

Screw or nut size	in.-lbs.	ft.-lbs.	N•m
M5	36	–	4.1
M6	70	6	8.1
M8	156	13	17.6
M10	312	26	35.3
M12	–	35	47.5
M14	–	60	81.3

4

Chapter Five

Synchronization and Linkage Adjustments

For an outboard motor to deliver maximum efficiency, performance and reliability, the engine must have both the ignition and fuel systems correctly adjusted. This adjustment procedure is referred to as *synch and link*.

Failure to properly *synch and link* an engine will not only result in a loss of engine performance and efficiency, but can lead to power head damage. All *synch and link* adjustments must be performed during a tune-up or whenever any ignition or fuel system components are replaced, serviced or adjusted.

On a typical larger engine, a *synch and link* procedure will generally involve the following:

a. Synchronizing and adjusting the ignition and fuel systems linkages.

b. Verifying that the fuel system throttle plate(s) fully open and close, and that all throttle plates are synchronized to open and close at exactly the same time.

c. Synchronizing the ignition system spark advance with throttle plate(s) operation to provide optimum off-idle acceleration and smooth part-throttle operation.

d. Adjusting the ignition timing at idle and wide-open throttle engine speeds.

e. Setting the idle speed correctly and verifying the wide-open throttle rpm.

Synch and link procedures for Mercury/Mariner outboard motors differ according to engine model and the specific ignition and fuel systems used. This chapter is divided into self-contained sections for fast and easy reference. Each section specifies the appropriate procedure and sequence to be followed. **Tables 1-6** provide the necessary general specifications. All tables are located at the end of the chapter.

Read the safety precaution and general information in the next two sections, then proceed directly to the section pertaining to your particular outboard motor.

SAFETY PRECAUTIONS

Wear approved eye protection at all times, especially when machinery is in operation. Wear approved ear protection during all running tests and in the presence of noisy machinery. Keep loose clothing tucked in and long hair tied back and secured. Refer to Chapter 2, *Safety First* for additional safety guidelines.

When making or breaking any electrical connection, always disconnect the negative battery cable. When performing tests that require cranking the engine without starting, disconnect and ground the spark plug leads to prevent accidental starts and sparks.

Securely cap or plug all disconnected fuel lines to prevent fuel discharge when the motor is cranked or the primer bulb is squeezed.

Thoroughly read all manufacturer's instructions and safety sheets for test equipment and special tools being used.

Do not substitute parts unless you know they meet or exceed the original manufacturer's specifications.

Never run an outboard motor without an adequate water supply. Never run an outboard motor at wide-open throttle without an adequate load. Do not exceed 3000 rpm in neutral (no load).

Safely performing on-water tests requires 2 people; one person to operate the boat, the other to monitor the gauges or test instruments. All personnel must remain seated inside the boat at all times. It is not acceptable to lean over the transom while the boat is under way. Use extensions to allow all gauges and meters to be located in the normal seating area.

A test propeller is an economical alternative to the dynometer. A test propeller is also a convenient alternative to on-water testing. Test propellers are made by modifying (turning down) the diameter of a standard low pitch aluminum propeller until the recommended wide-open throttle speed can be obtained with the motor in a test tank or on the trailer backed into the water. Be careful of tying the boat to a dock as considerable thrust is developed by the test propeller. Some docks may not be able to withstand the load.

Propeller repair stations can provide the modification service. Normally, approximately 1/3 to 1/2 of the outer blade surface is removed. However, it is far better to remove too little, than too much. It may take several tries to achieve the correct full throttle speed, but once achieved, no further modifications will be required. Many propeller repair stations have experience with this type of modification and may be able to recommend a starting point.

Test propellers also allow simple tracking of engine performance. The full-throttle test speed of an engine fitted with a correctly modified test wheel can be tracked from season to season. It is not unusual for a new or rebuilt engine to show a slight increase in test propeller speed as complete break-in is achieved and then to hold that speed over the normal service life of the engine. As the engine begins to wear out, the test propeller speed will show a gradual decrease that becomes a marked or drastic decrease as the point of engine failure is reached.

GENERAL INFORMATION

Perform synch and link adjustments with the engine running under actual operating conditions to be as accurate as possible. Carburetor idle mixture and idle speed adjustments are very sensitive to engine load and exhaust system back pressure. If the adjustments are made with the engine running on a flushing device, the adjustments will not be correct when the motor is operated in the water under load.

CAUTION
*Do not run the engine without an adequate water supply and do not exceed 3000 rpm without an adequate load. Refer to **Safety Precautions** at the beginning of this chapter.*

5

Ignition Timing

All models use some form of timing marks that allow the ignition timing to be checked using a suitable stroboscopic timing light. On models with adjustable timing, a linkage adjustment is made to bring the timing into specification. If the timing is not within specification on models with nonadjustable timing, either a mechanical or electrical defect is present in the system. Chapter Three covers ignition troubleshooting for all models.

The maximum timing specification is best checked at wide-open throttle. This method is not always practical, however, as the outboard must be operated at full throttle in forward gear (under load) to verify maximum timing advance. This requires the use of a test tank or test wheel, as timing an engine while speeding across open water is not safe and is not recommended. Refer to *Safety Precautions* in the previous section.

The maximum timing advance on some models can be set by holding the ignition linkage in the full-throttle position while the engine is being cranked. While acceptable (where noted), this procedure is not considered as accurate as the wide-open throttle check. Whenever possible, check the maximum timing specification at wide-open throttle with a test propeller.

High-Speed Air/Fuel Mixture (Carbureted Models)

CAUTION
Running a carbureted engine with too small (too lean) high-speed jets can cause catastrophic power head failure. It is better to have the high-speed air/fuel mixture slightly rich, rather than slightly lean. Lean air/fuel mixtures cause high combustion chamber temperature that leads to preignition and detonation (Chapter Three).

The high speed air/fuel ratio is controlled by a fixed high speed jet (main jet). Refer to Chapter

Six for standard main jet sizes. The standard main jet should only be changed to compensate for changes in elevation, fuel blends or unique operating conditions. Changing the high speed jet can affect the air/fuel ratio across the entire rpm range. If the engine runs satisfactorily, do not attempt to change the high speed jet size. If changes to the high speed jet sizes are warranted, see Chapter Six for additional information.

Wide-Open Throttle Speed Verification

All outboard motors have a specified wide-open throttle (W.O.T.) speed range (**Tables 2-6**). This means that when the engine is mounted on a boat and run at wide-open throttle, the engine speed must be within the specified range. If the engine speed is above or below the specified range, engine damage will result.

NOTE
Use an accurate shop tachometer for checking W.O.T. speed. Do not use the boat's tachometer for W.O.T. verification.

Operating an engine with a propeller that will not allow the engine to reach its specified range is called over-propping. This causes the combustion chamber temperature to rise dramatically, leading to preignition and detonation (Chapter Three).

Operating an engine with a propeller that allows an engine to exceed its specified range is called over-speeding. Over-speeding an engine will lead to mechanical failure of the reciprocating engine components. Some engines are equipped with an rpm limit module that shorts out the ignition system to limit engine speed. Over-speeding these engines can cause ignition misfire symptoms that can cause troubleshooting difficulty.

Changing propellers (pitch, diameter or style) changes the load on the engine and the resulting W.O.T. engine speed. If the W.O.T. engine speed exceeds the specified range, install a propeller with more pitch or a larger diameter and recheck engine speed. If the W.O.T. engine speed is below the specified range, install a propeller with less pitch or smaller diameter and retest engine speed.

Required Equipment

Static adjustment of the ignition timing and/or verification of the timing pointer requires the use of a suitable dial indicator to position the No. 1 piston at top dead center (TDC) accurately before making timing adjustments. TDC is determined by removing the No. 1 spark plug and installing the dial indicator in the spark plug hole. Refer to **Figure 1**.

All ignition timing checks and adjustments require the use of a stroboscopic timing light connected to the No. 1 spark plug lead. As the engine is cranked or operated, the light flashes each time the spark plug fires. When the light is pointed at the moving flywheel, the mark on the flywheel appears to stand still. The appropriate timing marks will be aligned if the timing is correctly adjusted.

NOTE
Timing lights with built-in features (such as a timing advance function) are not

recommended for use on outboard motors. A basic high-speed timing light with an inductive pickup is recommended. Mercury Marine timing light part No. 91-99379 fulfills these requirements.

CAUTION
*Factory timing specifications provided by Mercury Marine are given in the tables at the end of the chapter. However, Mercury Marine has occasionally found it necessary to modify their specifications during production. If your engine has a decal attached to the power head or air box, always follow the specification listed on the decal, instead of the specification in **Tables 2-6**.*

Use an accurate shop tachometer to determine engine speed during timing adjustment. Do not rely on the tachometer installed in a boat to provide accurate engine speed readings.

75, 90 HP AND 65 JET MODELS

The ignition timing is mechanically advanced and requires adjustment of the idle and maximum timing. Timing can be set at cranking speed or while running. Setting the timing while running is the most accurate.

Refer to **Table 2** for general specifications. The recommended synch and link procedure is as follows:

1. Preliminary adjustments.

2. Throttle plate synchronization.

3. Throttle cam adjustment.

4. Wide-open throttle stop adjustment.

5. Timing adjustments.

6. Idle speed and idle mixture adjustments.

7. Oil pump linkage adjustment.

8. Shift and throttle cable adjustments (remote control models).

9. Wide-open throttle speed verification.

Preliminary Adjustments

1. Disconnect the remote control throttle cable from the throttle lever arm.
2. Remove the screws from the carburetor air box cover. Remove the air box cover.
3. Turn the idle mixture screw (**Figure 2**) on each carburetor clockwise until each is lightly seated. Do not force the screws tightly into the carburetors or the tips of the screws and the carburetors will be damaged. Back out each mixture screw to specification (**Table 2**).

Throttle Plate Synchronization

1. Loosen the cam follower adjusting screw (**Figure 3**).
2. Loosen the 2 throttle shaft synchronizing screws on the upper and lower carburetor throttle shafts (5, **Figure 4**, similar).
3. Make sure the throttle valves in all 3 carburetors are fully closed, then retighten the screws (5, **Figure 4**). Do not tighten the cam follower screw at this time (**Figure 3**).
4. Verify that all throttle plates open and close together. Readjust as necessary.

Throttle Cam Adjustments

1. Hold the idle stop screw (1, **Figure 5**) against its stop.
2. Position the cam follower roller (2, **Figure 5**) against the throttle cam. Adjust the idle stop screw (1, **Figure 5**) to align the throttle cam mark (3, **Figure 5**) with the center of the follower roller (2, **Figure 5**), then tighten the idle stop screw locknut.
3. While holding the throttle arm in the idle position, adjust the cam follower to set a 0.005-0.020 in. (0.13-0.51 mm) clearance between the cam follower roller and throttle cam. See **Figure 3**. Make sure the throttle cam mark is aligned with the center of the roller, then securely tighten the cam follower screw (**Figure 5**).

4. Hold the throttle arm so the wide-open throttle stop screw (4, **Figure 5**) is against its stop. Adjust the wide-open throttle stop screw so the carburetor throttle valves are fully open (wide-open throttle) while allowing for approximately 0.015 in. (0.38 mm) play in the throttle linkage. Be certain the throttle valves do not bottom out (bind) at wide-open throttle.

CAUTION
The carburetors can be damaged if the throttle valves serve as throttle stops during full throttle operation.

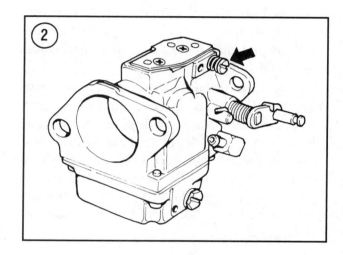

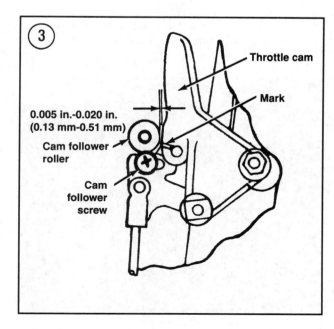

5. Reinstall the carburetor air box cover.

Timing Adjustments

Running adjustment

1. Connect a suitable timing light to the top (cylinder No. 1) spark plug lead.

CAUTION
Do not run the engine without an adequate water supply and do not exceed

3000 rpm without an adequate load. Refer to Safety Precautions at the beginning of this chapter.

2. Start the engine and allow it to warm to normal operating temperature.

3. Reduce the engine speed to idle and shift the gearcase into FORWARD gear.

4. Point the timing light at the flywheel and timing pointer. Note the reading. Timing should be 5° BTDC at idle speed, at this time.

5. While holding the idle stop screw (1, **Figure 5**) against the idle stop, adjust the idle *timing*

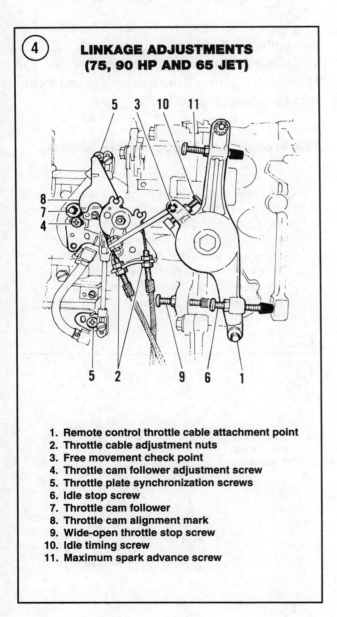

LINKAGE ADJUSTMENTS (75, 90 HP AND 65 JET)

1. Remote control throttle cable attachment point
2. Throttle cable adjustment nuts
3. Free movement check point
4. Throttle cam follower adjustment screw
5. Throttle plate synchronization screws
6. Idle stop screw
7. Throttle cam follower
8. Throttle cam alignment mark
9. Wide-open throttle stop screw
10. Idle timing screw
11. Maximum spark advance screw

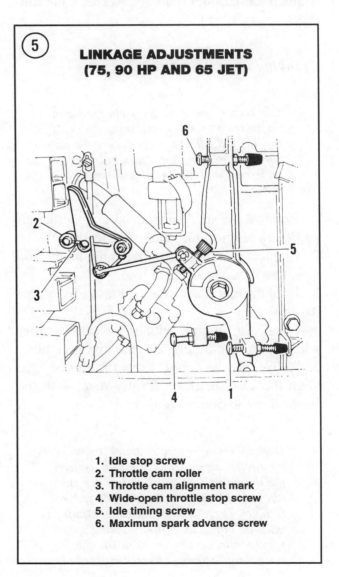

LINKAGE ADJUSTMENTS (75, 90 HP AND 65 JET)

1. Idle stop screw
2. Throttle cam roller
3. Throttle cam alignment mark
4. Wide-open throttle stop screw
5. Idle timing screw
6. Maximum spark advance screw

5

screw (5, **Figure 5**) to obtain a 5° BTDC timing reading.

6. Point the timing light at the flywheel and timing pointer.

7. Advance the throttle to position the maximum spark advance screw against its stop (6, **Figure 5**). Note the timing reading.

8. Refer to **Table 2** for maximum timing at 3000 rpm or higher. If adjustment is needed, stop the engine and loosen the maximum spark advance adjustment jam nut.

9. Turn the adjustment screw clockwise to retard timing or counterclockwise to advance timing. Tighten the jam nut securely. Recheck the timing.

Cranking speed adjustment

NOTE
The battery must be fully charged and the starting system functioning properly for this adjustment procedure to be accurate. Removing the spark plugs helps increase cranking speed and timing accuracy.

1. Remove the spark plugs and connect an air gap spark tester to the spark plug leads.

2. Connect a suitable timing light to the top (cylinder No.1) spark plug lead.

3. Hold the idle stop screw (1, **Figure 5**) against its stop.

4. Crank the engine with the electric starter while noting the timing with the timing light.

5. Adjust the idle *timing* screw (5, **Figure 5**) to align the TDC mark on the flywheel with the V-notch in the timing window.

NOTE
Due to the electronic spark advance characteristics of this ignition system, the timing will retard slightly when running at wide-open throttle (3000 rpm or higher). Therefore, the maximum timing must be adjusted to the cranking speed specification to obtain the desired wide-open throttle timing when running above

3000 rpm. Verify all timing adjustments made at cranking speed with the outboard running.

6. Hold the throttle arm so the maximum advance screw (6, **Figure 5**) is against its stop.

7. Crank the engine while noting the timing with the timing light. Refer to **Table 2** for maximum timing at cranking speed.

8. If adjustment is necessary, adjust maximum spark advance screw (6, **Figure 5**) to align the timing pointer with the specified timing mark on the flywheel.

9. Tighten the maximum spark advance screw jam nut when finished.

10. Remove the timing light and the air gap spark tester. Reinstall the spark plugs and reconnect the spark plug leads.

Idle Mixture and Idle Speed Adjustments

NOTE
The idle mixture must be properly set on all carburetors. Adjust the top carburetor first, the middle carburetor second and the bottom carburetor last. It may be necessary to switch back and forth between the carburetors several times to get the mixture correct. If necessary, reset the mixture screws to the initial settings and try again.

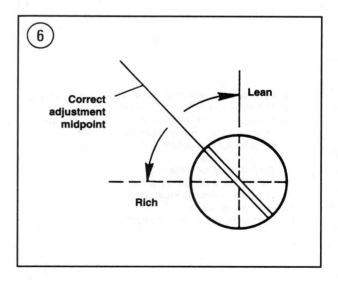

1. Connect an accurate shop tachometer to a spark plug lead.

2. Start the engine and run at 2000 rpm until warmed to normal operating temperature. Once operating temperature is reached, shift the gearcase into FORWARD gear and allow the motor to idle 1-2 minutes to stabilize and allow the fuel recirculation system to begin functioning.

3. Set the throttle lever control to the idle position. If necessary adjust the idle timing screw (5, **Figure 5**) temporarily to obtain 650-700 rpm in FORWARD gear.

NOTE
Idle mixture cannot be properly set unless the carburetors are operating on the idle circuit(s). Make sure the throttle plates are fully closed when making this adjustment.

4. Slowly turn the idle mixture screw counterclockwise in 1/8 turn increments, pausing at least 10 seconds between turns. Continue this step until the idle speed decreases and idle becomes rough due to an overly rich mixture. Note the position of the mixture screw slot.

5. Slowly turn the idle mixture screw clockwise in 1/8 turn increments, pausing at least 10 sec-

onds between turns. The idle speed will gradually become smooth and speed will increase. Continue this step until the engine speed begins to slow again and/or misfires due to the excessively lean mixture. Note the position of the mixture screw slot.

6. Position the mixture screw at a midpoint between the settings of Step 4 and Step 5. See **Figure 6**. Repeat Steps 4-6 for the remaining carburetors.

7. Quickly accelerate the engine to wide-open throttle then throttle back to idle. The engine will accelerate cleanly and without hesitation if the mixture is adjusted correctly. Readjust as necessary.

8. Remove the throttle cable barrel from the barrel retainer on the cable anchor bracket.

9. Adjust the idle timing screw (5, **Figure 5**) to obtain 650-700 rpm in FORWARD gear.

10. Hold the throttle lever against the idle stop. Adjust the cable barrel to slip into the retainer with a very light preload of the throttle lever against the idle stop. Fasten the barrel in the retainer.

NOTE
Excessive preload in Step 10 will result in difficult shifting from FORWARD or REVERSE gear into NEUTRAL.

11. Check the throttle cable preload by inserting a thin piece of paper (such as a matchbook cover) between the idle stop and stop screw. If the preload is correct, a slight drag (without tearing) will be noted when removing the paper. Readjust the cable as required to obtain the desired preload.

Oil Pump Linkage Adjustment

Any time the throttle linkage is adjusted, the oil pump linkage must be synchronized to the throttle linkage.

1. Hold the throttle arm against the idle stop.

2. The mark stamped in the oil pump control lever should be aligned with the mark stamped in the oil pump body. See A, **Figure 7**. A second mark (B, **Figure 7**) is stamped in the oil pump

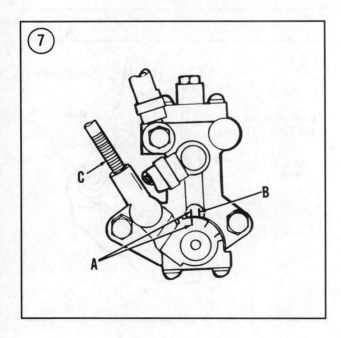

body on some models. *Do not* use this mark for oil pump synchronization.

3. If adjustment is necessary, disconnect the oil pump control rod (C, **Figure 7**) and adjust length of rod to align the marks.

Shift and Throttle Cable Adjustments (Remote Control Models)

Refer to Chapter Twelve for additional information on remote control cable adjustments.

Wide-Open Throttle Speed Verification

1. Connect an accurate shop tachometer to a spark plug lead.

2. With the engine mounted on a boat, the boat unrestrained in the water and the engine running at wide-open throttle in forward gear, record the maximum rpm noted on the tachometer.

3. If the maximum rpm exceeds the recommended speed range listed in **Table 2**, check the propeller for damage. Repair or replace the propeller as necessary. If the propeller is in good condition, a propeller with more pitch or larger diameter must be installed and the wide-open throttle speed rechecked.

4. If the maximum rpm does not reach the recommended speed range listed in **Table 2**, install a propeller with less pitch or smaller diameter and recheck the wide-open speed.

100-125 HP AND 80 JET MODELS

The ignition timing is mechanically advanced and requires adjustment of the idle and maximum timing. Timing can be set at cranking speed or while running. Setting the timing while running is the most accurate.

These engines idle on the top 2 cylinders only. The top 2 carburetors are different from the bottom 2 in that only the top 2 carburetors have idle mixture adjustment screws. These engines

are also equipped with a mechanical accelerator pump system that injects fuel into the bottom 2-cylinders on acceleration (as the throttle linkage is advanced).

Refer to **Table 2** for general specifications. The recommended synch and link procedure is as follows:

1. Preliminary adjustments.
2. Throttle plate synchronization.
3. Throttle cam adjustment.
4. Wide-open throttle stop adjustment.

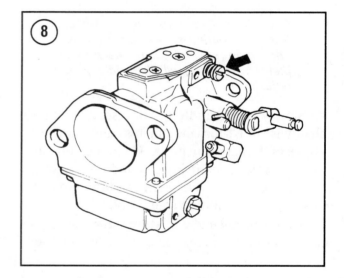

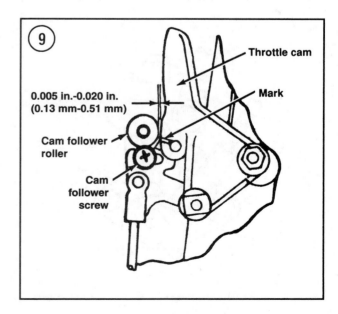

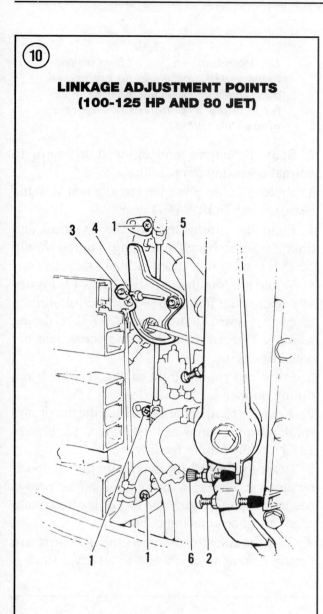

(10)

**LINKAGE ADJUSTMENT POINTS
(100-125 HP AND 80 JET)**

1. Throttle plate
   synchronization screws
2. Idle stop screw
3. Throttle cam follower
4. Throttle cam alignment mark
5. Wide-open throttle stop screw
6. Idle timing screw

5. Accelerator pump clearance adjustment.
6. Timing adjustments.
7. Idle speed and idle mixture adjustments.
8. Oil pump linkage adjustment.
9. Shift and throttle cable adjustments (remote control models).
10. Wide-open throttle verification.

Preliminary Adjustments

1. Disconnect the remote control throttle cable from the throttle lever arm.

2. Remove the screws from the carburetor air box cover. Remove the air box cover.

3. Turn the idle mixture screws (**Figure 8**) on the top two carburetors clockwise until each is lightly seated. Do not force the screws tightly into the carburetors or the tips of the screws and the carburetors will be damaged. Back out each mixture screw to specification (**Table 2**).

Throttle Plate Synchronization

1. Loosen the cam follower adjusting screw (**Figure 9**).

2. Loosen the 3 throttle shaft synchronizing screws (1, **Figure 10**) on the cylinder No. 1, 3 and 4 carburetor throttle shafts.

3. Make sure the throttle valves in all 4 carburetors are fully closed, then retighten the screws (1, **Figure 10**). Do not tighten the cam follower screw **Figure 9** at this time.

4. Verify that all throttle plates open and close together. Readjust as necessary.

Throttle Cam Adjustments

1. Hold the idle stop screw (2, **Figure 10**) against its stop.

2. Position the cam follower roller (3, **Figure 10**) against the throttle cam. Adjust the idle stop screw (2, **Figure 10**) to align the throttle cam mark (4, **Figure 10**) with the center of the fol-

lower roller (3, **Figure 10**), then tighten the idle stop screw locknut.

3. While holding the throttle arm in the idle position, adjust the cam follower to set a 0.005-0.020 in. (0.13-0.51 mm) clearance between the cam follower roller and throttle cam. See **Figure 9**. Make sure the throttle cam mark is aligned with the center of the roller, then securely tighten the cam follower screw (**Figure 9**).

4. Hold the throttle arm so the wide-open throttle stop screw (5, **Figure 10**) is against its stop. Adjust the wide-open throttle stop screw so the carburetor throttle valves are fully open (wide-open throttle) while allowing for approximately 0.015 in. (0.38 mm) play in the throttle linkage. Be certain the throttle valves do not bottom out (bind) at wide-open throttle.

CAUTION
The carburetors can be damaged if the throttle valves serve as throttle stops during full throttle operation.

5. Reinstall the carburetor air box cover.

Accelerator Pump Adjustment

1. Hold the throttle arm against the wide-open throttle stop (5, **Figure 10**).

2. Check for the specified clearance (0.030 in. [0.76 mm]) between the throttle cam and the top of the pump casting as shown in **Figure 11**.

3. If adjustment is required, loosen the 2 pump mounting screws (1, **Figure 12**) and adjust the pump position to obtain 0.030 in. (0.76 mm) clearance.

4. Tighten the pump mounting screws securely (1, **Figure 12**).

Timing Adjustments

Running adjustment

1. Connect a suitable timing light to the top (cylinder No. 1) spark plug lead.

CAUTION
*Do not run the engine without an adequate water supply and do not exceed 3000 rpm without an adequate load. Refer to **Safety Precautions** at the beginning of this chapter.*

2. Start the engine and allow it to warm to normal operating temperature.

3. Reduce the engine speed to idle and shift the gearcase into FORWARD gear.

4. Point the timing light at the flywheel and timing pointer. Note the reading. Timing should be 2° BTDC at idle speed, at this time.

5. While holding the idle stop screw (2, **Figure 10**) against the idle stop, adjust the idle timing screw (6, **Figure 10**) to obtain a 2° BTDC timing reading. Tighten the idle timing screw jam nut when finished.

6. Point the timing light at the flywheel and timing pointer.

7. Advance the throttle to position the maximum spark advance screw against its stop (2, **Figure 12**). Note the timing reading.

8. Refer to **Table 2** for maximum timing specifications at 3000 rpm or higher. If adjustment is needed, stop the engine and loosen the maximum spark advance adjustment jam nut.

9. Turn the adjustment screw clockwise to retard timing or counterclockwise to advance timing.

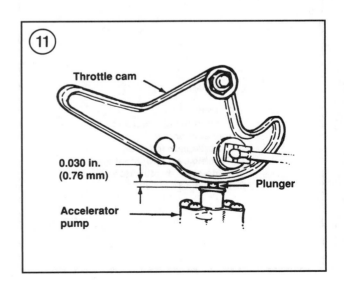

(11)

Throttle cam

0.030 in. (0.76 mm)

Plunger

Accelerator pump

Tighten the jam nut securely. Recheck the timing.

Cranking speed adjustment

> **NOTE**
> *The battery must be fully charged and the starting system functioning properly for this adjustment procedure to be accurate. Removing the spark plugs helps increase cranking speed and timing accuracy.*

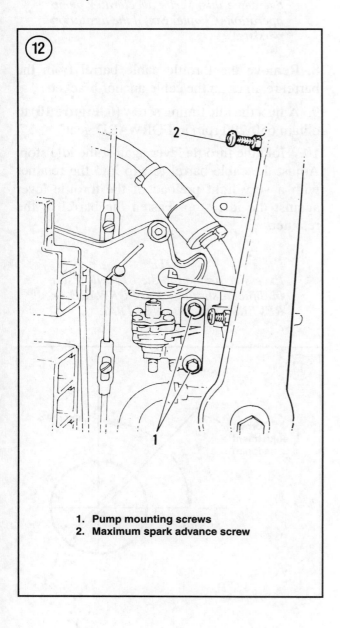

1. **Pump mounting screws**
2. **Maximum spark advance screw**

1. Remove the spark plugs and connect an air gap spark tester to the spark plug leads.
2. Connect a suitable timing light to the top (cylinder No. 1) spark plug lead.
3. Hold the idle stop screw against its stop (2, **Figure 10**).
4. Crank the engine with the electric starter while noting the timing with the timing light.
5. Adjust the idle timing screw (6, **Figure 10**) to align the TDC mark on the flywheel with the V-notch in the timing window.

> **NOTE**
> *Due to the electronic spark advance characteristics of this ignition system, the timing will retard slightly when running at wide-open throttle (3000 rpm or higher). Therefore, the maximum timing should be adjusted to the cranking speed specification to obtain the desired wide-open throttle timing when running above 3000 rpm. All timing adjustments made at cranking speed should be verified with the outboard running and readjusted if necessary.*

6. Hold the throttle arm so the maximum advance screw (2, **Figure 12**) is against its stop.
7. Crank the engine while noting the timing with the timing light. Refer to **Table 2** for the maximum timing specification at cranking speed.
8. If adjustment is necessary, adjust the maximum spark advance screw (2, **Figure 12**) to align the timing pointer with the specified timing mark on the flywheel.
9. Tighten the maximum spark advance screw jam nut when finished.
10. Remove the timing light and the air gap spark tester. Reinstall the spark plugs and reconnect the spark plug leads.

Idle Mixture and Idle Speed Adjustments

> **NOTE**
> *The idle mixture can only be set on the top two carburetors. Adjust the top carburetor first and the cylinder No. 2 car-*

buretor last. It may be necessary to switch back and forth between the carburetors several times to get the mixture correct. If necessary, reset the mixture screws to the initial settings and try again.

1. Connect an accurate shop tachometer to a spark plug lead.

2. Start the engine and run at 2000 rpm until warmed to normal operating temperature. Once operating temperature is reached, shift the gearcase into FORWARD gear and allow the motor to idle 1-2 minutes to stabilize the motor and allow the fuel recirculation system to begin functioning.

3. Set the throttle lever control to the idle position. If necessary adjust the idle timing screw (6, **Figure 10**) temporarily to obtain 650-700 rpm in FORWARD gear.

> *NOTE*
> *Idle mixture cannot be properly set unless the carburetors are operating on the idle circuit(s). Make sure the throttle plates are fully closed when making this adjustment.*

4. Slowly turn the idle mixture screw counterclockwise in 1/8 turn increments, pausing at least 10 seconds between turns. Continue this step until the idle speed decreases and becomes rough due to an overly rich mixture. Note the position of the mixture screw slot.

5. Slowly turn the idle mixture screw clockwise in 1/8 turn increments, pausing at least 10 seconds between turns. The idle speed will gradually become smooth and speed will increase. Continue this step until the engine speed begins to slow again and/or misfires due to the excessively lean mixture. Note the position of the mixture screw slot.

6. Position the mixture screw at a midpoint between the settings of Step 4 and Step 5. See **Figure 13**. Repeat Steps 4-6 for the remaining carburetor.

7. Quickly accelerate the engine to wide-open throttle, then throttle back to idle. The engine will accelerate cleanly and without hesitation if the mixture is adjusted correctly. Readjust as necessary.

> *NOTE*
> *If the accelerator pump circuit to cylinders No. 3 and No. 4 is malfunctioning, the engine will hesitate on acceleration. Adjustments to the idle mixture of cylinders No. 1 and No. 2 will not be able to overcome this. Verify accelerator pump operation (Chapter Six) if the hesitation persists.*

8. Remove the throttle cable barrel from the barrel retainer on the cable anchor bracket.

9. Adjust the idle timing screw (6, **Figure 10**) to obtain 650-700 rpm in FORWARD gear.

10. Hold the throttle lever against the idle stop. Adjust the cable barrel to slip into the retainer with a very light preload of the throttle lever against the idle stop. Fasten the barrel in the retainer.

> *NOTE*
> *Excessive preload in Step 10 will result in difficult shifting from FORWARD or REVERSE gear into NEUTRAL.*

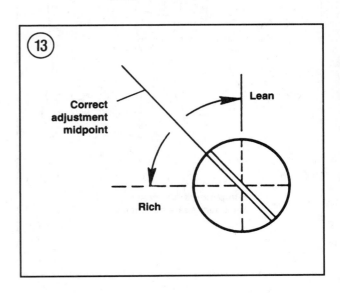

11. Check the throttle cable preload by inserting a thin piece of paper (such as a matchbook cover) between the idle stop and stop screw. If the preload is correct, a slight drag (without tearing) will be noted when removing the paper. Readjust the cable as required to obtain the desired preload.

Oil Pump Linkage Adjustment

Any time the throttle linkage is adjusted, the oil pump linkage must be synchronized to the throttle linkage.

1. Hold the throttle arm against the idle stop (2, **Figure 10**).

2. The mark stamped in the oil pump control lever should be aligned with the mark stamped in the oil pump body. See A, **Figure 14**. A second mark (B, **Figure 14**) is stamped in the oil pump body on some models. Do not(end) use this mark for oil pump synchronization.

3. If adjustment is necessary, disconnect the oil pump control rod (C, **Figure 14**) and adjust length of rod to align the marks.

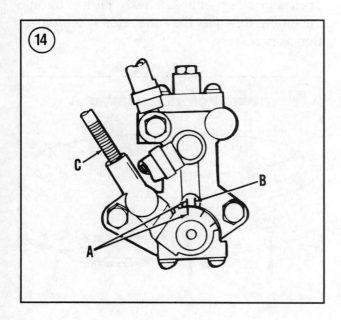

Shift and Throttle Cable Adjustments (Remote Control Models)

Refer to Chapter Twelve for additional information on remote control cable adjustments.

Wide-Open Throttle Verification

1. Connect an accurate shop tachometer to a spark plug lead.
2. With the engine mounted on a boat, the boat unrestrained in the water and the engine running at wide-open throttle in forward gear, record the maximum rpm noted on the tachometer.
3. If the maximum rpm exceeds the recommended speed range listed in **Table 2**, check the propeller for damage. Repair or replace the propeller as necessary. If the propeller is in good condition, a propeller with more pitch or larger diameter must be installed and the wide-open throttle rechecked.
4. If the maximum rpm does not reach the recommended speed range listed in **Table 2**, install a propeller with less pitch or smaller diameter and recheck the wide-open throttle.

135-200 HP CARBURETED MODELS

The ignition timing is mechanically advanced and requires adjustment of the idle (primary pickup) and maximum timing. Timing can be set at cranking speed or while running. Setting the timing while running is the most accurate.

CAUTION
Idle stabilizer modules must be disconnected during timing adjustments.

Refer to **Table 3** for general specifications. The recommended synch and link procedure is as follows:
1. Preliminary adjustments.
2. Timing pointer adjustment.
3. Throttle cam adjustment.
4. Throttle plate synchronization.

5. Wide-open throttle stop adjustment.

6. Oil pump linkage adjustment.

7. Timing adjustments.

8. Idle speed and idle mixture adjustments.

9. Shift and throttle cable adjustments.

10. Wide-open throttle speed verification.

Preliminary Adjustments

1. Disconnect the remote control throttle cable from the throttle lever arm.

2. Remove the screws from the carburetor air box cover. Remove the air box cover.

3. Remove the spark plugs and ground the spark plug leads to the power head to prevent accidental starting during the timing pointer adjustment.

Timing Pointer Adjustment

1. Install a dial indicator (part No. 91-58222A1 or equivalent) into the top starboard (cylinder No. 1) spark plug hole.

2. Rotate the flywheel clockwise until the top starboard (cylinder No. 1) piston is positioned at TDC, then zero the indicator.

3. Rotate the flywheel counterclockwise until the dial indicator needle is approximately 1/4 turn past the 0.462 in. (11.73 mm) BTDC reading on the indicator dial.

4. Rotate the flywheel clockwise until the dial indicator reads exactly 0.462 in. (11.73 mm) BTDC. The timing pointer should now be aligned with the .462 mark on the flywheel. If not, loosen the 2 timing pointer adjustment screws and reposition the timing pointer as required (**Figure 15**). Retighten the timing pointer screws securely.

5. Remove the dial indicator.

6. Reinstall the spark plugs if the timing adjustments are to be made with the engine running. If the timing adjustments are to be made with the engine cranking, leave the spark plugs removed.

Throttle Cam Adjustment

1. Loosen the throttle cam follower adjusting screw (1, **Figure 16**) on the lower carburetor to allow the cam follower to move freely.

2. With the cam follower roller resting on the throttle cam, adjust the idle stop screw (2, **Figure 16**) so the raised mark on the throttle cam (3, **Figure 16**) is aligned with the center of the cam follower roller. Do not tighten the cam follower screw at this point.

3. Tighten the idle stop screw jam nut when finished.

Throttle Plate Synchronization

1. Loosen the 2 carburetor synchronizing screws (4, **Figure 16**) on the middle and upper carburetors, allowing the carburetor throttle valves to close fully.

2. Position the throttle arm against the idle stop. Move the throttle cam follower so the follower roller just contacts the throttle cam. While holding the roller in this position, securely tighten the cam follower screw (1, **Figure 16**) and the 2 carburetor synchronizing screws (4, **Figure 16**).

3. Make sure that all carburetor throttle valves open and close simultaneously during throttle operation. Readjust the carburetor synchronization as necessary.

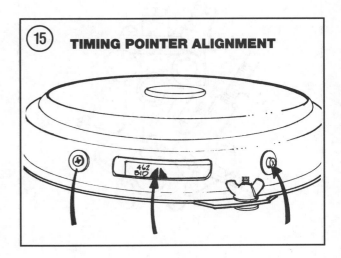

⑮ **TIMING POINTER ALIGNMENT**

Wide-Open Throttle Stop Adjustment

1. Hold the throttle arm in the wide-open throttle position.

2. Adjust the wide-open throttle stop screw (5, **Figure 16**) to position the carburetor throttle valves in the wide-open position while allowing for 0.010-0.015 in. (0.25-0.38 mm) free play between the throttle shaft arms and the cast-in stop (6, **Figure 16**) on the carburetor bodies.

3. Tighten the wide-open throttle stop screw jam nut securely.

CAUTION
The carburetors can be damaged if the throttle valves bottom out at wide-open throttle.

5

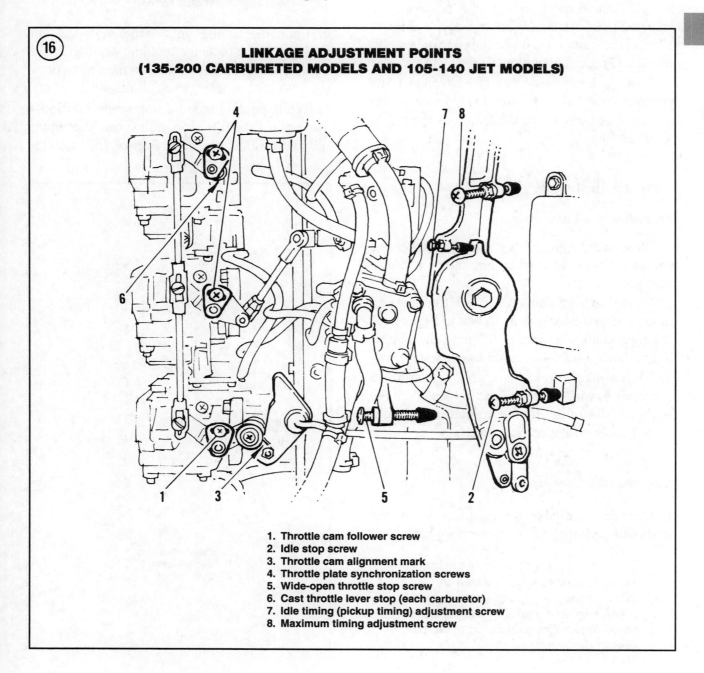

(16)

LINKAGE ADJUSTMENT POINTS
(135-200 CARBURETED MODELS AND 105-140 JET MODELS)

1. Throttle cam follower screw
2. Idle stop screw
3. Throttle cam alignment mark
4. Throttle plate synchronization screws
5. Wide-open throttle stop screw
6. Cast throttle lever stop (each carburetor)
7. Idle timing (pickup timing) adjustment screw
8. Maximum timing adjustment screw

4. Reinstall the carburetor air box cover.

Oil Pump Linkage Adjustment

Anytime the throttle linkage is adjusted, the oil pump linkage must be synchronized to the throttle linkage.

1. Place the throttle arm against the idle stop.

2. With the throttle in the idle position, the stamped mark on the oil pump body (1, **Figure 17**) and the stamped mark on the control lever (2, **Figure 17**) should be aligned.

3. If adjustment is necessary, disconnect the pump control rod (3, **Figure 17**) from the pump control lever and adjust the length of the rod to align the marks.

Timing Adjustments

Preliminary adjustments

These steps must be performed whether the engine is being timed while running or at cranking speed.

1. Verify the trigger link rod length from the end of the rod to the locknut as shown in **Figure 18**. If length is not 11/16 in. (17.5 mm), disconnect link rod and adjust the length as necessary.

2. Disconnect the idle stabilizer module white/black wire bullet connector located on the starboard side of the engine. Insulate the disconnected wires with electrical tape.

Running adjustment

1. Connect a suitable timing light to the top starboard (cylinder No. 1) spark plug lead.

CAUTION
*Do not run the engine without an adequate water supply and do not exceed 3000 rpm without an adequate load. Refer to **Safety Precautions** at the beginning of this chapter.*

2. Start the engine and allow it to warm to normal operating temperature.

3. Reduce the engine speed to idle and shift the gearcase into FORWARD gear.

NOTE
*If there is a timing specification decal on the engine, use the specifications on the decal if they differ from the specifications in the text and **Table 3**.*

4. Point the timing light at the flywheel and timing pointer. Note the reading. Timing should be within specification listed on the timing decal (or 4° ATDC at idle speed), at this time.

5. While holding the idle stop screw (2, **Figure 16**) against the idle stop, adjust the idle timing (pickup timing) screw (7, **Figure 16**) to obtain

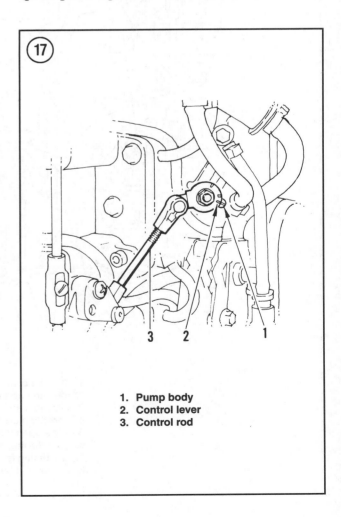

1. Pump body
2. Control lever
3. Control rod

the specified timing reading. Tighten the idle timing (pickup timing) screw jam nut when finished.

6. Point the timing light at the flywheel and timing pointer.

7. Advance the throttle to position the maximum spark advance screw (8, **Figure 16**) against its stop. Note the timing reading.

8. Refer to the engine timing decal or **Table 3** for the maximum timing specification at wide-open throttle. If adjustment is needed, stop the engine and loosen the maximum spark advance adjustment jam nut.

9. Turn the adjustment screw clockwise to retard timing or counterclockwise to advance timing. Tighten the jam nut securely. Recheck the timing and adjust as necessary.

10. When timing is correct, reconnect the idle stabilizer module white/black wire bullet connector located on the starboard side of the engine.

Cranking speed adjustment

NOTE
The battery must be fully charged and the starting system functioning properly for this adjustment procedure to be ac-

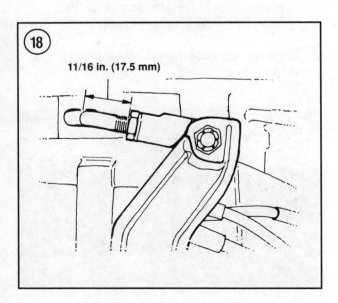

11/16 in. (17.5 mm)

curate. Removing the spark plugs helps increase cranking speed and timing accuracy.

CAUTION
Perform all cranking timing adjustments in NEUTRAL.

1. Remove the spark plugs and connect an air gap spark tester to the spark plug leads.

2. Connect a suitable timing light to the top starboard (cylinder No. 1) spark plug lead.

3. Hold the idle stop screw (2, **Figure 16**) against its stop.

4. Crank the engine with the electric starter while noting the timing with the timing light.

NOTE
If there is a timing specification decal on the engine, use the specifications on the decal if they differ from the specifications in the text and **Table 3**.

5. Timing should be within the specification listed on the timing decal (or 4° ATDC) at this time.

6. While holding the idle stop screw (2, **Figure 16**) against the idle stop, adjust the idle timing (pickup timing) screw (7, **Figure 16**) to obtain the specified timing reading. Tighten the idle timing (pickup timing) screw jam nut when finished.

NOTE
Due to the electronic spark advance characteristics of this ignition system, the timing will retard slightly when running at wide-open throttle. Therefore, the maximum timing should be adjusted to the cranking speed specification to obtain the desired wide-open throttle timing when running at wide-open throttle. Verify all timing adjustments made at cranking speed with the outboard running and readjusted if necessary.

CAUTION
On models (except 150XR6, Magnum III and 175 hp models) equipped with the idle stabilizer shift kit (part No. 87-

*814281A-1) installed as an accessory, the maximum ignition timing must be retarded 3° from the specification listed in **Table 3** or on the engine timing decal. On 150XR6, Magnum III and 175 hp models, the idle stabilizer shift kit is installed at the factory as standard equipment and the timing specification listed in **Table 3** (or the timing decal) is correct.*

7. Hold the throttle arm so the maximum advance screw (8, **Figure 16**) is against its stop.

8. Crank the engine while noting the timing with the timing light.

9. Refer to the engine timing decal or **Table 3** for the maximum timing specification at cranking speed. If adjustment is needed, stop the engine and loosen the maximum spark advance adjustment jam nut.

10. Adjust maximum spark advance screw (8, **Figure 16**) to align the timing pointer with the specified timing mark on the flywheel.

11. Tighten the maximum spark advance screw jam nut when finished.

12. Remove the timing light and the air gap spark tester. Reinstall the spark plugs and reconnect the spark plug leads.

13. Reconnect the idle stabilizer module white/black wire bullet connector located on the starboard side of the engine.

Idle Speed and Idle Mixture Adjustments

Each carburetor is equipped with 2 idle mixture screws. See **Figure 19**. The idle mixture screws are set at the factory and plastic limiter caps are installed on each screw to limit adjustment range. When adjusting the idle mixture, be certain that all mixture screws are turned equal amounts in the same direction; clockwise rotation leans the air/fuel mixture and counterclockwise rotation enrichens the air/fuel mixture. Do not remove the limiter caps to increase the adjustment range. If the limiter caps are missing,

refer to *Idle mixture adjustment—limiter caps missing*.

These engines are equipped with a thermal air valve enrichment system (**Figure 20**). The thermal valve is mounted in the starboard cylinder head near the No. 3 spark plug. The thermal air valve restricts air flow into the carburetors when the engine is cold, enrichening the air/fuel mixture. When the engine is warm, the valve opens, letting air flow into the carburetors and normalizing the air/fuel mixtures. The valve must be open in order to set the idle mixture properly.

To verify that the thermal air valve is open, warm the engine to operating temperature. Reduce the engine speed to idle and cover the valve's open port (**Figure 20**) with your finger. The engine should slow slightly and run rough as the air/fuel mixture is enriched. If no change to engine operation is noted, refer to Chapter Three for troubleshooting procedures. Carburetor idle mixture cannot be adjusted until the thermal air valve is open.

NOTE
The idle mixture must be properly set on all carburetors (total of 6 mixture screws). Note the original position of each mixture screw before starting. If the mixture adjustment procedure goes poorly, reposition the screws to their original position and try again.

1. Connect an accurate shop tachometer to a spark plug lead.

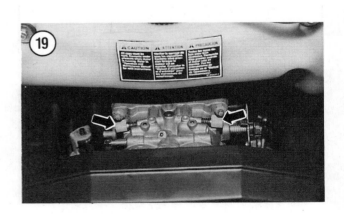

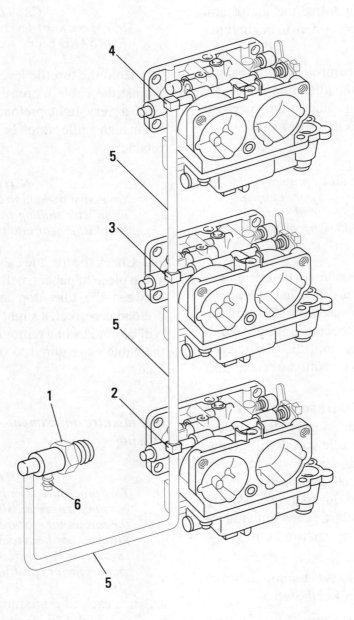

20

**THERMAL AIR VALVE SYSTEM
(135-200 HP [CARBURETED] MODELS)**

4

5

3

5

1

2

5

5

1. **Thermal air valve**
2. **Bottom carburetor T-fitting**
3. **Middle carburetor T-fitting**
4. **Top carburetor elbow fitting**
5. **Connecting lines**
6. **Open port**

5

2. Start the engine and run at 2000 rpm until warmed to normal operating temperature. Once operating temperature is reached, shift the gearcase into FORWARD gear and allow the motor to idle 1-2 minutes to stabilize the motor and allow the fuel recirculation system to begin functioning.

3. Set the throttle lever control to the idle position. If necessary adjust the idle timing screw (7, **Figure 16**) temporarily to obtain the specified idle speed (**Table 3**) in FORWARD gear.

NOTE
The idle mixture cannot be properly set unless the carburetors are operating on the idle circuit(s). Make sure the throttle plates are fully closed when making this adjustment.

4. Turn all idle mixture screws counterclockwise in 1/8 turn increments, pausing at least 10 seconds between turns. Repeat this step until the idle speed decreases and becomes rough due to an overly rich mixture or until the plastic caps limit movement. Note the position of each mixture screw limiting cap.

5. Turn all of the idle mixture screws clockwise in 1/8 turn increments, pausing at least 10 seconds between turns. The idle speed will gradually become smooth and speed will increase. Repeat this step until the engine speed begins to slow again and/or misfires due to the excessively lean mixture or until the plastic caps limit movement. Note the position of each mixture screw limiting cap.

6. Position the mixture screw at a midpoint between the settings of Step 4 and Step 5.

7. Quickly accelerate the engine to wide-open throttle, then throttle back to idle. The engine will accelerate cleanly without hesitation if the mixture is adjusted correctly. Readjust all mixture screws together as necessary.

8. Remove the throttle cable barrel from the barrel retainer on the cable anchor bracket.

9. Adjust the idle timing screw (7, **Figure 16**) to obtain the specified idle speed (**Table 3**) in FORWARD gear.

CAUTION
Idle speed must never exceed 750 rpm in FORWARD gear.

10. Hold the throttle lever against the idle stop. Adjust the cable barrel to slip into the retainer with a very light preload of the throttle lever against the idle stop. Fasten the barrel in the retainer.

NOTE
Excessive preload in Step 10 will result in difficult shifting from FORWARD or REVERSE gear into NEUTRAL.

11. Check the throttle cable preload by inserting a thin piece of paper (such as a matchbook cover) between the idle stop and stop screw. If the preload is correct, a slight drag (without tearing) will be noted when removing the paper. Readjust the cable as required to obtain the desired preload.

Idle mixture adjustment—limiter caps missing

NOTE
This procedure is only necessary if the carburetors are missing the limit caps, the carburetor mixture screw factory adjustment has been tampered with or the carburetor has been repaired or rebuilt and the factory position was not noted.

1. Turn each idle mixture screw on all the carburetors clockwise until each is lightly seated. Do not force the screws tightly into the carburetors or the tips of the screws and the carburetors will be damaged. Back out each mixture screw to specification (**Table 3**).

2. Connect an accurate shop tachometer to a spark plug lead.

3. Start the engine and run at 2000 rpm until warmed to normal operating temperature. Once operating temperature is reached, shift the gearcase into FORWARD gear and allow the motor to idle 1-2 minutes to stabilize the motor and allow the fuel recirculation system to begin functioning.

4. Set the throttle lever control to the idle position. If necessary, adjust the idle timing screw (7, **Figure 16**) temporarily to obtain 650-700 rpm in FORWARD gear.

NOTE
The idle mixture cannot be properly set unless the carburetors are operating on the idle circuit(s). Make sure the throttle plates are fully closed when making this adjustment. Each adjustment screw affects only one cylinder. Changes in the idle mixture on only 1 cylinder of a 6 cylinder engine will produce subtle changes to engine running quality. Take your time and listen to the engine carefully.

5. Slowly turn the first idle mixture screw counterclockwise in 1/8 turn increments, pausing at least 10 seconds between turns. Continue this step until the idle speed decreases and idle becomes rough due to an overly rich mixture. Note the position of the mixture screw slot.

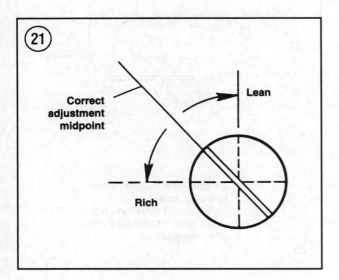

6. Slowly turn the idle mixture screw clockwise in 1/8 turn increments, pausing at least 10 seconds between turns. The idle speed will gradually become smooth and speed will increase. Continue this step until the engine speed begins to slow again and/or misfires due to the excessively lean mixture. Note the position of the mixture screw slot.

7. Position the mixture screw at a midpoint between the settings of Step 4 and Step 5. See **Figure 21**. Repeat Steps 5-7 for the remaining mixture screws.

8. Quickly accelerate the engine to wide open throttle and back to idle. The engine will accelerate cleanly without hesitation if the mixture is adjusted correctly. Readjust as necessary.

9. Continue at Step 8 in the preceding section for throttle cable and final idle speed adjustments.

Shift and Throttle Cable Adjustments

Refer to Chapter Twelve for additional information on remote control cable adjustments.

Wide-Open Throttle Speed Verification

1. Connect an accurate shop tachometer to a spark plug lead.

2. With the engine mounted on a boat, the boat unrestrained in the water and the engine running at wide-open throttle in forward gear, record the maximum rpm noted on the tachometer.

3. If the maximum rpm exceeds the recommended speed range listed in **Table 3**, check the propeller for damage. Repair or replace the propeller as necessary. If the propeller is in good condition, a propeller with more pitch or larger diameter must be installed and the wide-open throttle speed rechecked.

4. If the maximum rpm does not reach the recommended speed range listed in **Table 3**, install a propeller with less pitch or smaller diameter and recheck the wide-open throttle speed.

150-200 HP EFI (ELECTRONIC FUEL INJECTION) MODELS

The ignition timing is mechanically advanced and requires adjustment of the idle (primary pickup) and maximum timing. Timing can be set at cranking speed with the ECM (electronic control module) and idle stabilizer module disconnected or while the engine is running with only the idle stabilizer disconnected.

The 200 XRI and 200 Magnum models are equipped with a detonation sensor and module that advances the ignition timing 6° at high speed (beginning at approximately 2500-3000 rpm) if detonation is **not** present.

The setting of the TPS (throttle position sensor) has a direct effect on air/fuel mixture. Setting the TPS requires a test harness (part No. 91-816085) and a digital multimeter. The ECT (engine coolant temperature) sensor tan/black leads must also be disconnected during TPS adjustment.

Refer to **Table 3** for general specifications. The recommended synch and link procedure is as follows:

1. Preliminary adjustments.
2. Timing pointer adjustment.
3. Throttle cam adjustment.
4. Wide-open throttle stop adjustment.
5. Oil pump linkage adjustment.
6. Timing adjustments.
7. Idle speed adjustment.
8. Throttle position sensor adjustment.
9. Shift and Throttle cable adjustments.
10. Wide-open throttle speed verification.

Preliminary Adjustments

1. Disconnect the remote control throttle cable from the throttle lever arm.
2. Remove the spark plugs and ground the spark plug leads to the power head to prevent accidental starting during the timing pointer adjustment.

Timing Pointer Adjustment

1. Install a dial indicator (part No. 91-58222A1 or equivalent) into the top starboard (cylinder No. 1) spark plug hole.

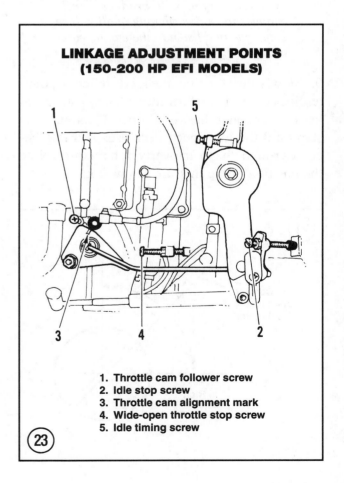

LINKAGE ADJUSTMENT POINTS (150-200 HP EFI MODELS)

1. Throttle cam follower screw
2. Idle stop screw
3. Throttle cam alignment mark
4. Wide-open throttle stop screw
5. Idle timing screw

23

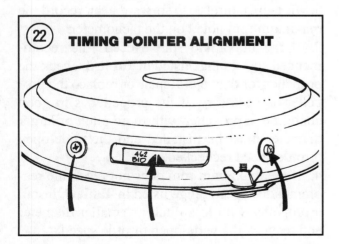

22 **TIMING POINTER ALIGNMENT**

2. Rotate the flywheel clockwise until the top starboard (cylinder No. 1) piston is positioned at TDC, then zero the indicator.

3. Rotate the flywheel counterclockwise until the dial indicator needle is approximately 1/4 turn past the 0.462 in. (11.73 mm) BTDC reading on the indicator dial.

4. Rotate the flywheel clockwise until the dial indicator reads exactly 0.462 in. (11.73 mm) BTDC. The timing pointer should now be aligned with the .462 mark on the flywheel. If not, loosen the 2 timing pointer adjustment screws and reposition the timing pointer as required (**Figure 22**). Retighten the timing pointer screws securely.

5. Remove the dial indicator.

6. Reinstall the spark plugs if the timing adjustments are to be made with the engine running. If the timing adjustments are to be made with the engine cranking, leave the spark plugs removed.

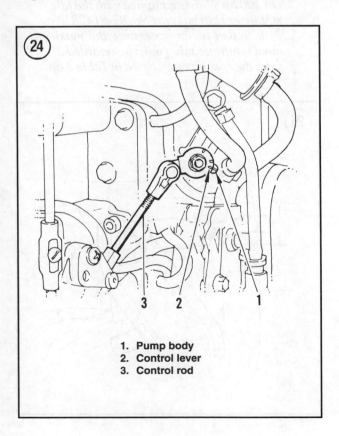

1. **Pump body**
2. **Control lever**
3. **Control rod**

Throttle Cam Adjustment

1. Loosen the throttle cam follower screw (1, **Figure 23**) and allow cam follower roller to rest against the throttle cam.

2. Adjust the idle stop screw (2, **Figure 23**) so the throttle cam mark (3, **Figure 23**) is aligned with the center of the cam follower roller. Tighten the idle stop jam nut securely.

3. Hold the throttle arm against the idle stop, then tighten the cam follower screw securely.

Wide-Open Throttle Stop Adjustment

1. Hold the throttle arm against the wide-open throttle stop screw (4, **Figure 23**).

2. Adjust the wide-open throttle stop screw so the induction chamber throttle valves are fully open, while allowing for slight free play in the throttle linkage between the throttle shaft arm and the stop on the induction chamber.

CAUTION
To prevent the throttle linkage from binding at full throttle, be sure 0.010-0.015 in. (0.25-0.38 mm) clearance is present between the throttle cam and cam follower roller at wide-open throttle. If necessary, readjust the wide-open throttle stop screw as necessary to provide clearance.

Oil Pump Linkage Adjustment

Any time the throttle linkage is adjusted, the oil pump linkage must be synchronized to the throttle linkage.

1. Hold the throttle arm against the idle stop.

2. With the throttle in the idle position, the stamped mark on the oil pump body (1, **Figure 24**) and the stamped mark on the control lever (2, **Figure 24**) should be aligned.

3. If adjustment is necessary, disconnect the pump control rod (3, **Figure 24**) from the pump control lever and adjust the length of the rod as required to align the marks.

5

Timing Adjustments

Preliminary adjustments

These steps must be performed whether the engine is being timed while running or at cranking speed.

1. Verify the trigger link rod length from the end of the rod to the locknut as shown in **Figure 25**. If length is not 11/16 in. (17.5 mm), disconnect link rod and adjust the length as necessary.

2. Disconnect the idle stabilizer module white/black wire bullet connector located on the starboard side of the engine. Insulate the disconnected wires with electrical tape.

Cranking speed adjustment

> *NOTE*
> *The battery must be fully charged and the starting system functioning properly for this adjustment procedure to be accurate. Removing the spark plugs helps increase cranking speed and timing accuracy.*

> *CAUTION*
> *Perform all cranking timing adjustments in NEUTRAL.*

1. Remove the spark plugs and connect an air gap spark tester (part No. FT-11295) to the spark plug leads.

2. Connect a suitable timing light (**Table 1**) to the top starboard (cylinder No. 1) spark plug lead.

3. Disconnect the electronic control module (ECM) from the wiring harness.

4. Hold the idle stop screw against its stop (2, **Figure 23**).

5. Crank the engine with the electric starter while noting the timing with the timing light.

> *NOTE*
> *If there is a timing specification decal on the engine, use the specifications on the decal if they differ from the specifications in the text and **Table 3**.*

6. Timing should be within the specification listed on the timing decal (or 4° ATDC) at this time.

7. While holding the idle stop screw (2, **Figure 23**) against the idle stop, adjust the idle timing screw (5, **Figure 23**) to obtain the specified timing reading. Tighten the idle timing screw jam nut when finished.

> *NOTE*
> *Due to the electronic spark advance characteristics of this ignition system, the timing will change slightly when running at wide-open throttle. Therefore, the maximum timing should be adjusted to the cranking speed specification to obtain the desired wide-open throttle timing when running at wide-open throttle. All timing adjustments made at cranking speed should be verified with the outboard running and readjusted if necessary.*

> *CAUTION*
> *On 200 hp models equipped with the idle stabilizer shift kit (part No. 87-814281A-1) installed as an accessory, the maximum ignition timing must be retarded 3° from the specification listed in **Table 3** or*

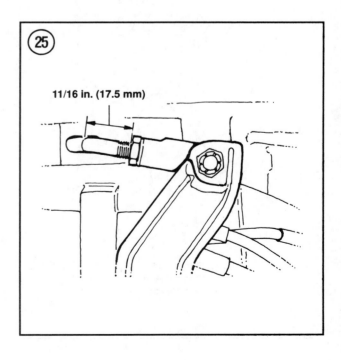

25

11/16 in. (17.5 mm)

on the engine timing decal. On 150 and 175 EFI models, the idle stabilizer shift kit is installed at the factory as standard equipment and the timing specification listed in **Table 3** *(or the timing decal) is correct.*

8. Hold the throttle arm so the maximum advance screw (**Figure 26**) is against its stop.

9. Crank the engine while noting the timing with the timing light.

10. Refer to the engine timing decal or **Table 3** for the maximum timing specification at cranking speed. If adjustment is needed, stop the engine and loosen the maximum spark advance adjustment jam nut.

11. Adjust maximum spark advance screw (**Figure 26**) to align the timing pointer with the specified timing mark on the flywheel.

12. Tighten the maximum spark advance screw jam nut when finished.

13. Remove the timing light and the air gap spark tester. Reinstall the spark plugs and reconnect the spark plug leads.

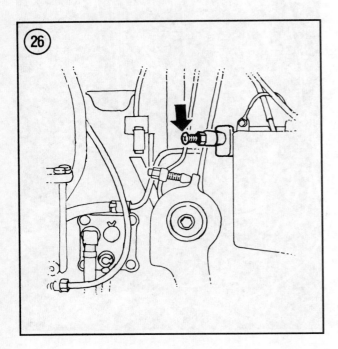

14. Reconnect the idle stabilizer module white/black wire bullet connector located on the starboard side of the engine.

15. Reconnect the ECM to the engine wiring harness.

Running adjustment

1. Connect a suitable timing light to the top starboard (cylinder No. 1) spark plug lead.

CAUTION
Do not run the engine without an adequate water supply and do not exceed 3000 rpm without an adequate load. Refer to **Safety Precautions** *at the beginning of this chapter.*

2. Start the engine and allow it to warm to normal operating temperature.

3. Reduce the engine speed to idle and shift the gearcase into FORWARD gear.

NOTE
If there is a timing specification decal on the engine, use the specifications on the decal if they differ from the specifications in the text and **Table 3***.*

4. Point the timing light at the flywheel and timing pointer. Note the reading. Timing should be within the specification listed on the timing decal (or 4° ATDC at idle speed), at this time.

5. While holding the idle stop screw (2, **Figure 23**) against the idle stop, adjust the idle timing screw (5, **Figure 23**) to obtain the specified timing reading. Tighten the idle timing screw jam nut when finished.

NOTE
The 200 XRI and 200 Magnum models are equipped with a detonation sensor and module that advances the ignition timing 6° at high speed (beginning at approximately 2500-3000 rpm) if detonation is **not** *present. If the maximum timing reading is approximately 6-8° out of specification, refer to Chapter Three*

5

*for detonation sensor and module trou-
bleshooting procedures.*

6. Point the timing light at the flywheel and timing pointer.

7. Advance the throttle to position the maximum spark advance screw against its stop (**Figure 26**). Note the timing reading.

8. Refer to the engine timing decal or **Table 3** for the maximum timing specification at the specified high speed. If adjustment is needed, stop the engine and loosen the maximum spark advance adjustment jam nut.

9. Turn the adjustment screw clockwise to retard timing or counterclockwise to advance timing. Tighten the jam nut securely. Recheck the timing and adjust as necessary.

10. When timing is correct, reconnect the idle stabilizer module white/black wire bullet connector located on the starboard side of the engine.

Idle Speed Adjustment

1. Connect an accurate shop tachometer to a spark plug lead.

2. Start the engine and warm it to normal operating temperature.

3. Position the throttle lever against the idle stop and shift the gearcase into FORWARD gear.

4. Loosen the throttle cam follower screw (1, **Figure 23**).

5. While holding the throttle arm against the idle stop, adjust the idle speed screw (**Figure 27**) to the specified idle speed (**Table 3**).

6. Retighten the cam follower screw.

7. Connect the throttle cable to the throttle arm.

8. While holding the throttle arm against the idle stop, adjust the throttle cable barrel to slip into the barrel retainer on the cable anchor bracket with a slight preload of the throttle arm against the idle stop.

9. Lock the throttle cable barrel in place.

NOTE
Excessive preload in Step 8 will result in difficult shifting from FORWARD and REVERSE gears into NEUTRAL.

10. Check the throttle cable preload by inserting a thin piece of paper (such as a matchbook cover) between the idle stop and stop screw. If the preload is correct, a slight drag (without tearing) will be noted when removing the paper. Readjust the cable as required to obtain the desired preload.

Throttle Position Sensor (TPS) Adjustment

The correct operation and setting of the TPS (throttle position sensor) is critical to achieving the correct air/fuel ratio. High TPS voltage provide a richer air/fuel ratio. Low TPS voltage provide a leaner air/fuel ratio. Adjustments (within specification) to the TPS may be used to fine tune the idle air/fuel mixture. Never adjust the TPS out of the specified range. Use only a digital multimeter for the following test. Test harness part No. 91-816085 is required for this procedure.

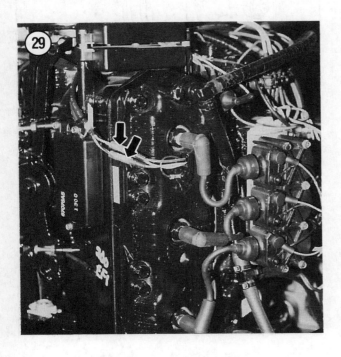

NOTE
Make sure the correct idle speed is verified before adjusting the TPS. If idle speed is changed, the TPS setting must be readjusted. It may be necessary to go back and forth between idle speed and TPS adjustment more than once to get both systems correctly adjusted.

1. Disconnect the TPS (A, **Figure 28**) from the engine wiring connector (B). Connect the test harness (91-816085) to the TPS and engine wiring harness. Connect the test harness meter leads to a digital multimeter. Set the multimeter to the DC voltage scale.

2. Disconnect both engine wiring harness tan/black leads from the ECT (engine coolant temperature) sensor (**Figure 29**).

NOTE
If the TPS cannot be correctly set or reads zero, refer to Chapter Three for troubleshooting procedures.

3. Turn the ignition switch to the ON or RUN position. Make sure the throttle plates are against the idle stop. Note the meter reading and compare to specification (**Table 3**). If the reading is within specification, continue to Step 5. If the reading is not within specification, loosen the 2 screws securing the TPS to the induction manifold.

4. With the throttle shaft held against the idle stop screw, rotate the TPS to obtain the desired specification (**Table 3**). While holding the TPS at the correct setting, tighten the screws securely. Recheck the voltage reading.

5. Slowly move the throttle linkage to the full-throttle position while noting the meter reading. The voltage should increase smoothly to 7.00-7.46 volts DC. If the meter reading fluctuates or is erratic as the throttle is advanced, replace the TPS. If the meter reading is not within 7.00-7.46 volts DC at wide-open throttle, recheck the wide-open throttle stop for correct adjustment.

5

6. Remove the TPS test harness. Reconnect the TPS lead to the wiring harness. Reconnect the ECT leads to the wiring harness.

Shift and Throttle Cable Adjustments

Refer to Chapter Twelve for additional information on remote control cable adjustments.

Wide-Open Throttle Speed Verification

1. Connect an accurate shop tachometer to a spark plug lead.

2. With the engine mounted on a boat, the boat unrestrained in the water and the engine running at wide-open throttle in forward gear, record the maximum rpm noted on the tachometer.

3. If the maximum speed exceeds the recommended range listed in **Table 3**, check the propeller for damage. Repair or replace the propeller as necessary. If the propeller is in good condition, a propeller with more pitch or larger diameter must be installed and the wide-open throttle speed rechecked.

4. If the maximum speed does not reach the recommended range listed in **Table 3**, install a propeller with less pitch or smaller diameter and recheck the wide-open throttle speed.

200 DFI (DIRECT FUEL INJECTION) MODELS

The ignition timing is controlled by the ECM (electronic control module) and is not adjustable. Refer to the timing decal on the engine for specifications, if timing verification is desired.

The oil injection system is controlled by the ECM and requires no adjustment.

CAUTION
The throttle plate stop screws (Figure 30) are preset at the factory and should not be adjusted. Tampering with these screws can cause a power head failure.

If the screws have been tampered with, contact a Mercury/Mariner dealership or Mercury Marine Customer Support for adjustment procedures.

Refer to **Table 4** for general specifications. The recommended synch and link procedure is as follows:
1. Preliminary adjustments.
2. Crankshaft position sensor adjustment.
3. Throttle cam adjustment.
4. Wide-open throttle stop screw adjustment.
5. Shift and throttle cable adjustments.

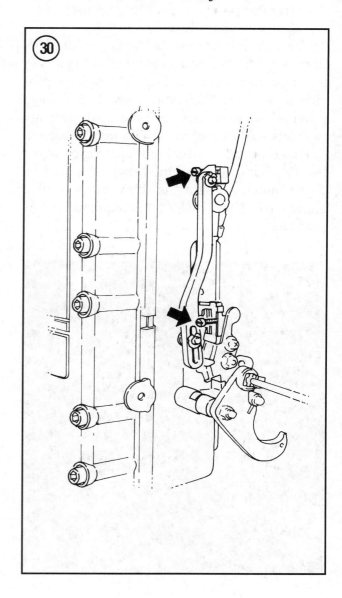

6. Wide-open throttle speed verification.

Preliminary Adjustments

1. Disconnect the negative battery cable and remove the flywheel cover.

2. Remove the spark plugs and ground the spark plug leads to the power head to prevent accidental starting during the following adjustments.

3. Disconnect the throttle cable from the throttle arm.

4. Refer to Chapter Four, *Tune-up Procedures, Charging System Service* and inspect the serpentine belt and tensioner that runs the air compressor and alternator.

Crankshaft Position Sensor Adjustment

The crankshaft position sensor (**Figure 31**) provides the ECM with engine speed and crank-

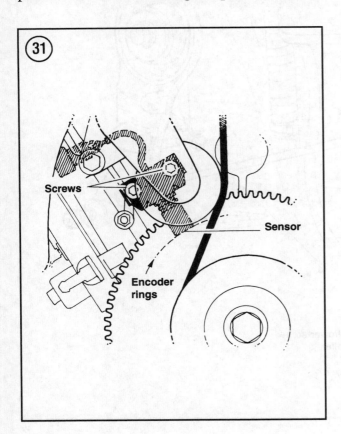

shaft position information. Its function is similar to the trigger coil used on a conventional CDI ignition system. The ECM must know the precise position of all the pistons and how fast the engine is running to fire the ignition coils accurately. If the crankshaft position sensor fails or is incorrectly adjusted, it can cause erratic spark, erratic timing or no spark at all.

1. Slightly rotate the flywheel to align an encoder rib with the crankshaft position sensor.

2. Measure the gap between the flywheel encoder rib and the crankshaft position sensor with a feeler gauge. The gap should be 0.030 in. (0.76 mm). If the gap is not within specification, loosen the 2 sensor mounting screws (**Figure 31**) slightly and reset the gap to specification. Tighten the screws to 100 in.-lb. (11.3 N•m) and recheck the sensor air gap.

3. Reinstall the flywheel cover.

Throttle Cam Adjustment

1. Loosen the throttle cam follower screw (1, **Figure 32**) and allow the cam follower roller (2, **Figure 32**) to rest against the throttle cam.

2. Adjust the idle stop screw (3, **Figure 32**) so the throttle cam mark (4, **Figure 32**) is aligned with the center of the cam follower roller. Tighten the idle stop jam nut securely.

3. Hold the throttle arm against the idle stop and the cam follower roller against the throttle cam, then tighten the cam follower screw securely.

Wide-Open Throttle
Stop Screw Adjustment

1. Hold the throttle arm against the wide-open throttle stop screw (1, **Figure 33**).

2. Adjust the wide-open throttle stop screw so the throttle cam mark (2, **Figure 33**) is aligned with the center of the cam follower roller (3, **Figure 33**). Tighten the wide-open throttle stop screw securely.

Shift and Throttle Cable Adjustments

Refer to Chapter Twelve for additional information on remote control cable adjustments.

1. Connect the throttle cable to the throttle arm.

2. While holding the throttle arm against the idle stop, adjust the throttle cable barrel to slip into the barrel retainer on the cable anchor bracket with a slight preload of the throttle arm against the idle stop.

3. Lock the throttle cable barrel in place.

NOTE
Excessive preload in Step 3 will result in difficult shifting from FORWARD and REVERSE gears into NEUTRAL.

4. Check the throttle cable preload by inserting a thin piece of paper (such as a matchbook cover) between the idle stop and stop screw. If the preload is correct, a slight drag (without tearing) will be noted when removing the paper. Readjust the cable as required to obtain the desired preload.

5. Reinstall the spark plugs and reconnect the spark plug leads.

6. Reconnect the negative battery cable.

Wide-Open Throttle Speed Verification

1. Connect an accurate shop tachometer to a spark plug lead.

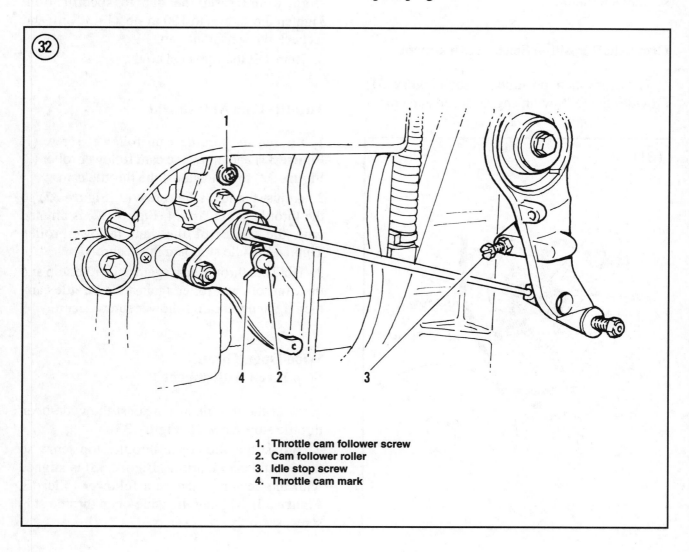

1. **Throttle cam follower screw**
2. **Cam follower roller**
3. **Idle stop screw**
4. **Throttle cam mark**

2. With the engine mounted on a boat, the boat unrestrained in the water and the engine running at wide-open throttle in forward gear, record the maximum rpm noted on the tachometer.

3. If the maximum rpm exceeds the recommended speed range listed in **Table 4**, check the propeller for damage. Repair or replace the propeller as necessary. If the propeller is in good condition, a propeller with more pitch or larger diameter must be installed and the wide-open throttle speed rechecked.

4. If the recorded maximum rpm does not reach the recommended speed range listed in **Table 4**, install a propeller with less pitch or smaller diameter and recheck the wide-open throttle speed.

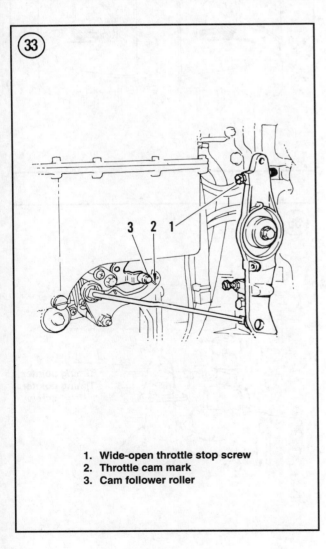

1. **Wide-open throttle stop screw**
2. **Throttle cam mark**
3. **Cam follower roller**

225 HP CARBURETED MODELS

The ignition timing is controlled by the ECM (electronic control module) and is not adjustable. Ignition timing is dependent on the crankshaft position sensor and throttle position sensor signals. As long as the crankshaft position sensor and throttle position sensor are correctly adjusted, the ECM will correctly calculate timing. If timing verification is desired, timing specifications are listed in **Table 5**.

The throttle position sensor is adjusted (within specification) to set the idle speed. A test harness (part No. 84-825207A1) and a digital multimeter are required for throttle position sensor adjustment.

The 1996-1997 models are not equipped with a throttle cam and as such, do not require throttle cam adjustment.

The oil pump linkage is not adjustable on 1994-1995 models. On 1996-1997 models, the shift rail assembly must be removed to see the oil pump alignment marks and adjust the oil pump linkage.

Refer to **Table 5** for general specifications. The recommended synch and link procedure is as follows:

1. Preliminary adjustments.
2. Timing pointer adjustment.
3. Throttle cam adjustment (1994-1995 models).
4. Throttle plate synchronization.
5. Oil pump linkage adjustment (1996-1997 models).
6. Crankshaft position sensor adjustment.
7. Throttle position sensor adjustment.
8. Idle mixture and idle speed adjustments.
9. Shift and throttle cable adjustments.
10. Wide-open throttle speed verification.

Preliminary Adjustments

1. Disconnect the negative battery cable and remove the flywheel cover.

2. Release the 2 carburetor air box latches (**Figure 34**) and remove the carburetor air box.

3. Remove the spark plugs and ground the spark plug leads to the power head to prevent accidental starting during the following adjustments.

4. Disconnect the throttle cable from the throttle arm.

5. Refer to Chapter Four, *Tune-up Procedures, Charging System Service* and inspect the alternator belt as instructed.

Timing Pointer Adjustment

The timing pointer must be adjusted before any timing checks are made.

1. Install a dial indicator (part No. 91-58222A1 or equivalent) into the top starboard (cylinder No.1) spark plug hole.

2. Rotate the flywheel clockwise until the top starboard (cylinder No. 1) piston is positioned at TDC, then zero the indicator.

3. Rotate the flywheel counterclockwise until the dial indicator needle is approximately 1/4 turn past the 0.526 in. (13.36 mm) BTDC reading on the indicator dial.

4. Rotate the flywheel clockwise until the dial indicator reads exactly 0.526 in. (13.36 mm) BTDC. The timing pointer should now be aligned with the .526 mark on the flywheel. If not, loosen the timing pointer adjustment screw and reposition the timing pointer as required (**Figure 35**). Retighten the timing pointer screw (**Figure 35**) to 105 in.-lb. (11.9 N•m).

5. Remove the dial indicator.

Throttle Cam Adjustment
(1994-1995 Models)

1. Loosen the throttle cam follower screw (1, **Figure 36**).

2. While holding the throttle cam follower lightly against the throttle cam and the throttle arm against the idle stop, adjust the idle stop screw (2, **Figure 36**) so the throttle cam mark (3,

Figure 36) is aligned with the center of the cam follower roller. Tighten the idle stop jam nut securely.

3. Do not tighten the throttle cam follower screw (1, **Figure 36**) at this time.

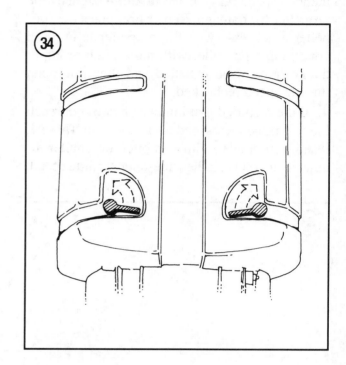

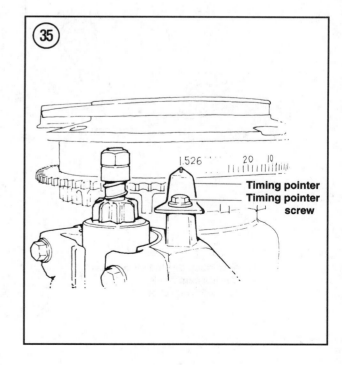

Throttle Plate Synchronization

1994-1995 models

1. Loosen the 2 carburetor synchronizing screws (4, **Figure 36**) on the upper and lower carburetors, allowing the carburetor throttle valves to close fully.

2. Position the throttle arm against the idle stop. Move the throttle cam follower so the follower roller just contacts the throttle cam. While holding the roller in this position, securely tighten the cam follower screw (1, **Figure 36**) and the 2 carburetor synchronizing screws (4, **Figure 36**).

3. Make sure that all carburetor throttle valves open and close simultaneously during throttle operation. Readjust the carburetor synchronization as necessary.

1996-1997 models

1. Hold the throttle arm against the idle stop (1, **Figure 37**).

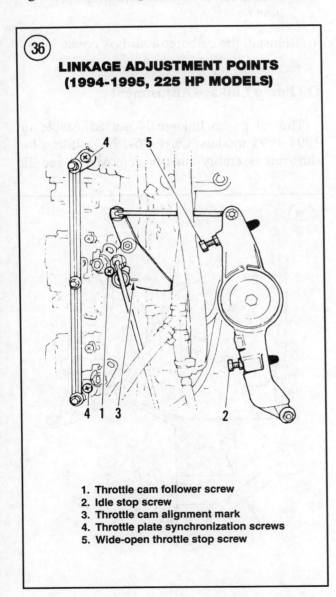

36

**LINKAGE ADJUSTMENT POINTS
(1994-1995, 225 HP MODELS)**

1. Throttle cam follower screw
2. Idle stop screw
3. Throttle cam alignment mark
4. Throttle plate synchronization screws
5. Wide-open throttle stop screw

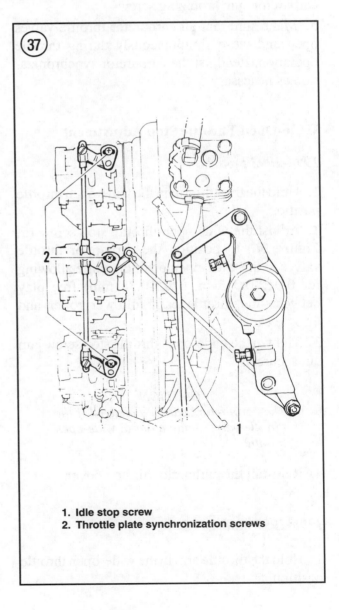

37

1. Idle stop screw
2. Throttle plate synchronization screws

5

2. Adjust the idle stop screw until the bend in the carburetor linkage (1, **Figure 38**) is 1/4 in. (6.3 mm) from the crankcase casting (2, **Figure 38**). The idle stop screw should be approximately in the middle of its adjustment range.

3. Loosen the 3 throttle plate synchronizing screws (2, **Figure 37**) on the carburetors, allowing the carburetor throttle valves to close fully.

4. Position the throttle arm against the idle stop. While holding the throttle arm in this position, securely tighten the center carburetor synchronizing screw first and then the upper and lower carburetor synchronizing screws.

5. Make sure that all carburetor throttle valves open and close simultaneously during throttle operation. Readjust the carburetor synchronization as necessary.

Wide-Open Throttle Stop Adjustment

1994-1995 models

1. Hold the throttle arm in the wide-open throttle position.

2. Adjust the wide-open throttle stop screw (5, **Figure 36**) to position the carburetor throttle valves in the wide-open position while allowing for 0.010-0.015 in. (0.25-0.38 mm) free play between the throttle cam follower roller and throttle cam.

3. Tighten the wide-open throttle stop screw jam nut securely.

> *CAUTION*
> *The carburetors can be damaged if the throttle valves bottom out at wide-open throttle.*

4. Reinstall the carburetor air box cover.

1996-1997 models

1. Hold the throttle arm in the wide-open throttle position.

2. Adjust the wide-open throttle stop screw (1, **Figure 39**) to position the carburetor throttle valves in the wide-open position while allowing for 0.010-0.015 in. (0.25-0.38 mm) free play between the carburetor throttle arms and the carburetor body cast throttle arm stops (2, **Figure 39**).

3. Tighten the wide-open throttle stop screw jam nut securely.

> *CAUTION*
> *The carburetors can be damaged if the throttle valves bottom out at wide-open throttle.*

4. Reinstall the carburetor air box cover.

Oil Pump Linkage Adjustment

The oil pump linkage is not adjustable on 1994-1995 models. On 1996-1997 models, the shift rail assembly must be removed to see the

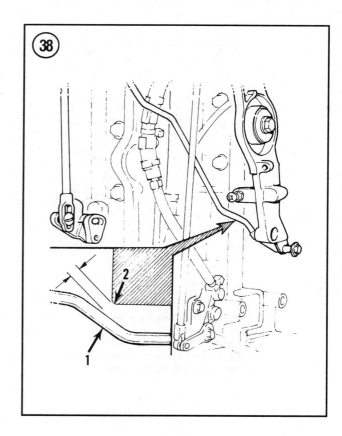

oil pump alignment marks and adjust the oil pump linkage. The pump must be adjusted any time the idle stop position is changed.

1. Hold the throttle arm against the idle stop.

2. With the throttle in the idle position, the stamped mark on the oil pump body (1, **Figure 40**) and the lower stamped mark on the control lever (2, **Figure 40**) should be aligned.

3. If adjustment is necessary, disconnect the pump control rod (3, **Figure 40**) from the pump control lever and adjust the length of the rod as required to align the marks.

Crankshaft Position Sensor Adjustment

The crankshaft position sensor provides the ignition ECM (electronic control module) with engine speed and crankshaft position information. Its function is similar to a trigger coil on a conventional CDI ignition system. The ignition ECM must know the precise position of all the pistons and how fast the engine is running in order to fire the CDM modules accurately.

1. Slightly rotate the flywheel to align an encoder rib (1, **Figure 41**) with the crankshaft position sensor (2, **Figure 41**).

2. Measure the gap (3, **Figure 41**) between the flywheel encoder rib and the crankshaft position sensor with a feeler gauge. The gap should be 0.020-0.060 in. (0.51-1.52 mm). If the gap is not within specification, loosen the 2 sensor mounting screws (4, **Figure 41**) slightly and reset the gap to specifications.

3. Tighten the screws to 100 in.-lb. (11.3 N•m) and recheck the sensor air gap.

4. Reinstall the flywheel cover. Reconnect the negative battery cable.

5

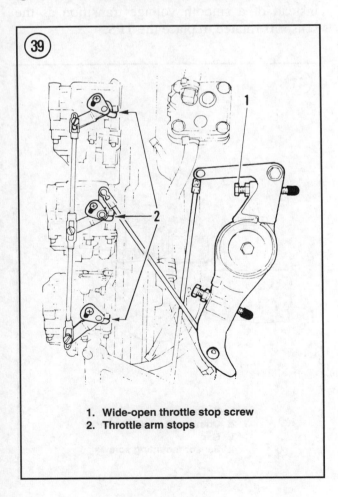

39

1. **Wide-open throttle stop screw**
2. **Throttle arm stops**

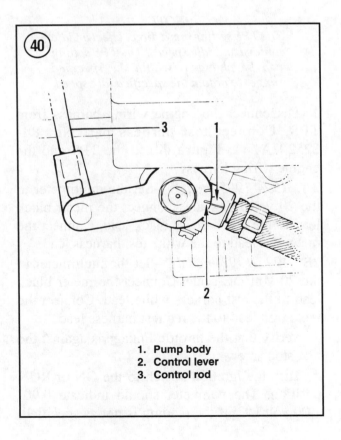

40

1. **Pump body**
2. **Control lever**
3. **Control rod**

5. Reinstall the spark plugs and reconnect the spark plug leads.

Throttle Position Sensor Adjustment

Correct adjustment and function of the TPS (throttle position sensor) is critical to correct ignition system operation. The TPS adjustment is made with the throttle against the idle stop. The wide-open throttle TPS specification is not adjustable. If the wide-open throttle stop is correctly set, the TPS idle voltage reading (setting) is correct, but the TPS wide-open throttle voltage reading is incorrect, replace the TPS sensor. To prevent damage to the throttle position sensor and wiring harness, test harness 84-825207A1 is required to adjust the TPS. A digital multimeter is recommended for this procedure, as most analog meters will not accurately read the low voltage specified. To adjust the TPS, proceed as follows:

> *NOTE*
> *The TPS setting has a direct effect on idle timing (and idle speed). The TPS setting can be changed (within the specified range) to obtain the specified idle speed.*

1. Disconnect the engine wiring harness from TPS. Connect test harness part No. 84-825207A1 (1, **Figure 42**) to the TPS and the engine wiring harness.

2A. *1994-1995 models*—Set the multimeter to the 20 volt DC scale. Connect the meter black lead to the test harness black lead. Connect the meter red lead to the white test harness lead.

2B. *1996-1997 models*—Set the multimeter to the 20 volt DC scale. Connect the meter black lead to the test harness white lead. Connect the meter red lead to the red test harness lead.

3. Verify that the throttle linkage is against the idle stop screw.

4. Turn the ignition switch to the ON or RUN position. The voltmeter should indicate 0.90-1.00 volt DC. If the reading is not as specified,

loosen the 2 adjustment screws (2, **Figure 42**) slightly and rotate the sensor to obtain 0.90-1.00 volt DC. Tighten the screws while holding the sensor in position. Recheck the meter reading. The meter must indicate 0.90-1.00 volt DC with the throttle lever held against the idle stop.

5. Slowly advance the throttle lever until it is against the wide-open throttle stop while noting the meter. The meter should indicate a smooth increase in voltage, without any sudden fluctuations. With the throttle lever held against the wide-open throttle stop, the meter should indicate 3.70-3.80 volts DC. If the meter reading is not within specification, verify that the wide-open throttle stop is correctly set. If the wide-open throttle stop is correctly set, but the wide-open throttle voltage is not correct, replace the TPS. If the meter shows voltage fluctuations, instead of a smooth voltage transition as the sensor is rotated, replace the TPS.

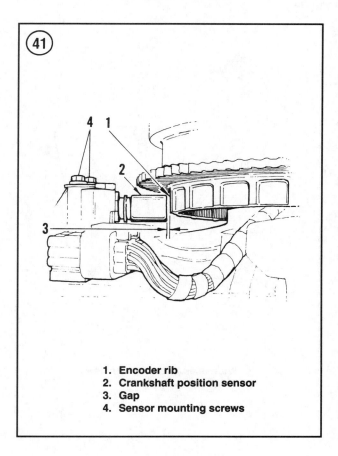

(41)

1. Encoder rib
2. Crankshaft position sensor
3. Gap
4. Sensor mounting screws

Idle Mixture and Idle Speed Adjustments

Each carburetor is equipped with 2 idle mixture screws, one on each side of the carburetor. See **Figure 43**. The idle mixture screws are set at the factory and plastic limiter caps are installed on each screw to limit adjustment range. When adjusting the idle mixture, be certain that all mixture screws are turned equal amounts in the same direction; clockwise rotation leans the air/fuel mixture and counterclockwise rotation enrichens the air/fuel mixture. Do not remove the limiter caps to increase the adjustment range. If the limiter caps are missing, refer to *Idle mixture adjustment—limiter caps missing*.

These engines are equipped with an electronic fuel enrichment valve. The ignition ECM (electronic control module) opens the enrichment valve for varying lengths of time based on the engine temperature signal from the ECT (engine coolant temperature) sensor. Refer to Chapter Three for a functional description and troubleshooting procedures. The carburetor idle mixture cannot be adjusted if the enrichment valve is open (enriching the air/fuel mixture).

> *NOTE*
> *The idle mixture must be properly set on all carburetors (total of 6 mixture screws). Note the original position of each mixture screw before starting. If the mixture adjustment procedure goes poorly, reposition the screws to their original position and try again.*

1. Connect an accurate shop tachometer to a spark plug lead.

2. Start the engine and run at 2000 rpm until warmed to normal operating temperature. Once operating temperature is reached, shift the gearcase into FORWARD gear and allow the motor to idle 1-2 minutes to stabilize the motor and allow the fuel recirculation system to begin functioning.

3. Set the throttle lever control to the idle position.

> *NOTE*
> *Idle mixture cannot be properly set unless the carburetors are operating on the idle circuit(s). Make sure the throttle plates are fully closed when making this adjustment.*

1. **Test harness**
2. **Adjusting screws**
3. **Throttle position sensor**

4. Turn all idle mixture screws counterclockwise in 1/8 turn increments, pausing at least 10 seconds between turns. Repeat this step until the idle speed decreases and becomes rough due to an overly rich mixture or until the plastic caps limit movement. Note the position of each mixture screw limiting cap.

5. Turn all of the idle mixture screws clockwise in 1/8 turn increments, pausing at least 10 seconds between turns. The idle speed will gradually become smooth and speed will increase. Repeat this step until the engine speed begins to slow again and/or misfires due to the excessively lean mixture or until the plastic caps limit movement. Note the position of each mixture screw limiting cap.

6. Position the mixture screw at a midpoint between the settings of Step 4 and Step 5.

7. Quickly accelerate the engine to wide-open throttle then throttle back to idle. The engine will accelerate cleanly without hesitation if the mixture is adjusted correctly. Readjust all mixture screws together as necessary.

8. Remove the throttle cable barrel from the barrel retainer on the cable anchor bracket.

9. Check the idle speed in FORWARD gear. Make sure the throttle lever is held against the idle stop. If necessary, adjust the throttle position sensor (within specification) to obtain 600-700 rpm in FORWARD gear.

CAUTION
Idle speed must never exceed 700 rpm in FORWARD gear.

10. Hold the throttle lever against the idle stop. Adjust the cable barrel to slip into the retainer with a very light preload of the throttle lever against the idle stop. Fasten the barrel in the retainer.

NOTE
Excessive preload in Step 10 will result in difficult shifting from FORWARD or REVERSE gear into NEUTRAL.

11. Check the throttle cable preload by inserting a thin piece of paper (such as a matchbook cover) between the idle stop and stop screw. If the preload is correct, a slight drag (without tearing) will be noted when removing the paper. Readjust the cable as required to obtain the desired preload.

Idle mixture adjustment—limiter caps missing

NOTE
This procedure is necessary only if the carburetors are missing the limit caps or if the carburetor mixture screw factory adjustment has been tampered with or the carburetor has been repaired or rebuilt and the factory position was not noted.

1. Turn each idle mixture screw on all of the carburetors clockwise until each is lightly seated. Do not force the screws tightly into the carburetors or the tips of the screws and the carburetors will be damaged. Back out each mixture screw to specification (**Table 5**).

2. Connect an accurate shop tachometer to a spark plug lead.

3. Start the engine and run at 2000 rpm until warmed to normal operating temperature. Once operating temperature is reached, shift the gearcase into FORWARD gear and allow the motor to idle 1-2 minutes to stabilize the motor and allow the fuel recirculation system to begin functioning.

4. Set the throttle lever control to the idle position.

NOTE
Idle mixture cannot be properly set unless the carburetors are operating on the idle circuit(s). Make sure the throttle plates are fully closed when making this adjustment. Each adjustment screw affects only one cylinder. Changes in the idle mixture on only 1 cylinder of a 6 cylinder engine will produce subtle

changes to engine running quality. Take your time and listen to the engine carefully.

5. Slowly turn the first idle mixture screw counterclockwise in 1/8 turn increments, pausing at least 10 seconds between turns. Continue this step until the idle speed decreases and idle becomes rough due to an overly rich mixture. Note the position of the mixture screw slot.

6. Slowly turn the idle mixture screw clockwise in 1/8 turn increments, pausing at least 10 seconds between turns. The idle speed will gradually become smooth and speed will increase. Continue this step until the engine speed begins to slow again and/or misfires due to the excessively lean mixture. Note the position of the mixture screw slot.

7. Position the mixture screw at a midpoint between the settings of Step 4 and Step 5. See **Figure 44**. Repeat Steps 5-7 for the remaining mixture screws.

8. Quickly accelerate the engine to wide-open throttle then throttle back to idle. The engine will accelerate cleanly without hesitation if the mixture is adjusted correctly. Readjust as necessary.

9. Continue at Step 8 in the preceding section for throttle cable and final idle speed adjustments.

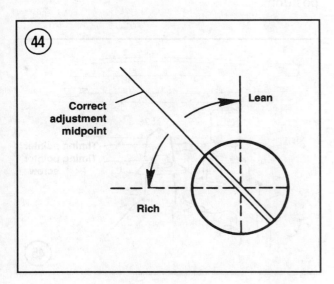

Shift and Throttle Cable Adjustments

Refer to Chapter Twelve for additional information on remote control cable adjustments.

Wide-Open Throttle Speed Verification

1. Connect an accurate shop tachometer to a spark plug lead.

2. With the engine mounted on a boat, the boat unrestrained in the water and the engine running at wide-open throttle in forward gear, record the maximum rpm noted on the tachometer.

3. If the maximum rpm exceeds the recommended speed range listed in **Table 5**, check the propeller for damage. Repair or replace the propeller as necessary. If the propeller is in good condition, a propeller with more pitch or larger diameter must be installed and the wide-open throttle speed.

4. If the recorded maximum rpm does not reach the recommended rpm range listed in **Table 5**, install a propeller with less pitch or smaller diameter and recheck the rpm.

225 AND 250 HP EFI MODELS

The ignition timing is controlled by the ECM (electronic control module) and is not adjustable. Ignition timing is dependent on the crankshaft position sensor and throttle position sensor signals. As long as the crankshaft position sensor and throttle position sensor are correctly adjusted, the ECM will correctly calculate timing. If timing verification is desired, timing specifications are listed in **Table 5**.

The throttle position sensor adjustment requires a test harness (part No. 84-825207A1) and a digital multimeter.

On 1996-1997 models, the shift rail assembly must be removed to see the oil pump alignment marks and adjust the oil pump linkage.

Refer to **Table 5** for general specifications. The recommended synch and link procedure is as follows:

1. Preliminary adjustments.
2. Timing pointer adjustment.
3. Throttle cam adjustment.
4. Wide-open throttle stop adjustment.
5. Oil pump linkage adjustment.
6. Crankshaft position sensor adjustment.
7. Throttle position sensor adjustment.
8. Idle speed adjustment.
9. Shift and throttle cable adjustments.
10. Wide-open throttle speed verification.

Preliminary Adjustments

1. Disconnect the negative battery cable and remove the flywheel cover.
2. Remove the spark plugs and ground the spark plug leads to the power head to prevent accidental starting during the following adjustments.
3. Disconnect the throttle cable from the throttle arm.
4. Refer to Chapter Four, *Tune-up Procedures, Charging System Service* and inspect the alternator belt.

Timing Pointer Adjustment

The timing pointer must be adjusted before any timing checks are made.

1. Install a dial indicator (part No. 91-58222A1 or equivalent) into the top starboard (cylinder No. 1) spark plug hole.
2. Rotate the flywheel clockwise until the top starboard (cylinder No. 1) piston is positioned at TDC, then zero the indicator.
3. Rotate the flywheel counterclockwise until the dial indicator needle is approximately 1/4 turn past the 0.526 in. (13.36 mm) BTDC reading on the indicator dial.
4. Rotate the flywheel clockwise until the dial indicator reads exactly 0.526 in. (13.36 mm) BTDC. The timing pointer should now be

aligned with the .526 mark on the flywheel. If not, loosen the timing pointer adjustment screw and reposition the timing pointer as required (**Figure 45**). Retighten the timing pointer screw (**Figure 45**) to 105 in.-lb. (11.9 N•m).

5. Remove the dial indicator.

Throttle Cam Adjustment

1. Loosen the throttle cam follower screw (1, **Figure 46**).
2. With the throttle cam follower resting on the throttle cam and the throttle arm against the idle stop, adjust the idle stop screw (2, **Figure 46**) so the throttle cam mark (3, **Figure 46**) is aligned with the center of the cam follower roller (4, **Figure 46**). Tighten the idle stop jam nut securely.
3. Hold the cam follower 0.000-0.010 in. (0.00-0.25 mm) from the throttle cam and tighten the cam follower screw securely. Make sure there is 0.000-0.010 in. (0.00-0.25 mm) clearance (5, **Figure 46**) between throttle cam and the throttle cam follower.

Wide-Open Throttle Stop Adjustment

1. Hold the throttle arm in the wide-open throttle position.

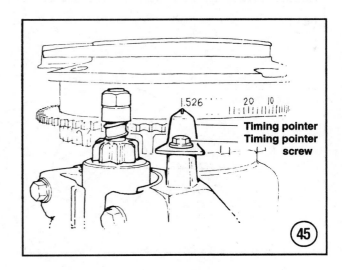

Timing pointer
Timing pointer screw

45

2. Adjust the wide-open throttle stop screw (6, **Figure 46**) to position the induction manifold throttle valves in the wide-open position while allowing for 0.010-0.015 in. (0.25-0.38 mm) free play between the throttle cam follower roller and throttle cam.

3. Tighten the wide-open throttle stop screw jam nut securely.

CAUTION
The induction manifold can be damaged if the throttle linkage bottoms out at wide-open throttle.

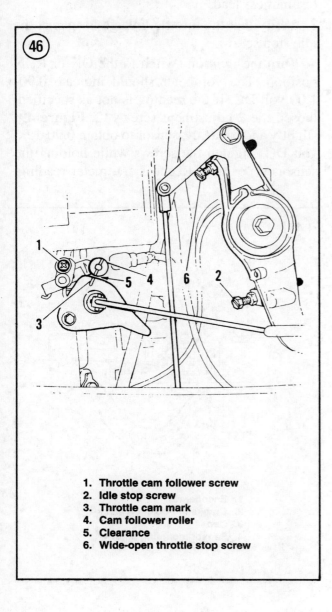

1. Throttle cam follower screw
2. Idle stop screw
3. Throttle cam mark
4. Cam follower roller
5. Clearance
6. Wide-open throttle stop screw

Oil Pump Linkage Adjustment.

The oil pump linkage may not be adjustable on 1995 models. On 1996-1997 models, the shift rail assembly must be removed to see the oil pump alignment marks and adjust the oil pump linkage. The pump must be adjusted (if adjustable) any time the idle stop position is changed.

1. Hold the throttle arm against the idle stop.
2. With the throttle in the idle position, the stamped mark on the oil pump body (1, **Figure 47**) and the lower stamped mark on the control lever (2, **Figure 47**) should be aligned.
3. If adjustment is necessary, disconnect the pump control rod (3, **Figure 47**) from the pump control lever and adjust the length of the rod as required to align the marks.

Crankshaft Position Sensor Adjustment

The crankshaft position sensor provides the ignition ECM (electronic control module) with

5

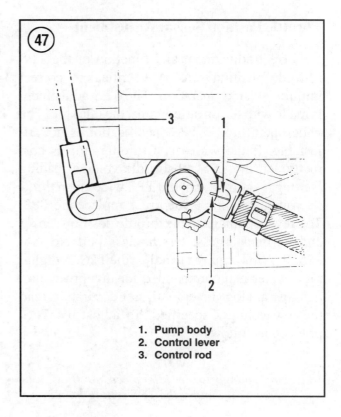

1. Pump body
2. Control lever
3. Control rod

engine speed and crankshaft position information. Its function is similar to a trigger coil used on a conventional CDI ignition system. The ignition ECM must know the precise position of all the pistons and how fast the engine is running in order to fire the CDM modules accurately.

1. Slightly rotate the flywheel to align an encoder rib (1, **Figure 48**) with the crankshaft position sensor (2, **Figure 48**).

2. Measure the gap (3, **Figure 48**) between the flywheel encoder rib and the crankshaft position sensor with a feeler gauge. The gap should be 0.020-0.060 in. (0.51-1.52 mm). If the gap is not within specification, loosen the 2 sensor mounting screws (4, **Figure 48**) slightly and reset the gap to specifications.

3. Tighten the screws to 100 in.-lb. (11.3 N•m) and recheck the sensor air gap.

4. Reinstall the flywheel cover. Reconnect the negative battery cable.

5. Reinstall the spark plugs and reconnect the spark plug leads.

Throttle Position Sensor Adjustment

Correct adjustment and function of the TPS (throttle position sensor) is critical to correct ignition system operation. The TPS adjustment is made with the throttle against the idle stop. The wide-open throttle TPS specification is not adjustable. If the wide-open throttle stop is correctly set, the TPS sensor idle voltage reading (setting) is correct, but the TPS wide-open throttle voltage reading is incorrect, replace the TPS. To prevent damage to the throttle position sensor and wiring harness, test harness part No. 84-825207A1 is required to adjust the TPS. A digital multimeter is recommended for this procedure, as most analog meters will not accurately read the low voltages specified. To adjust the TPS, proceed as follows:

NOTE
Any change to the idle speed air flow screw will require the TPS setting to be

rechecked and readjusted as necessary. It may be necessary to go back and forth between idle speed and TPS adjustment more than once to get both systems correctly adjusted.

1. Disconnect the engine wiring harness from TPS. Connect test harness part No. 84-825207A1 (1, **Figure 49**) to the TPS and the engine wiring harness.

2. Set the multimeter to the 20 volt DC scale. Connect the meter black lead to the test harness white lead. Connect the meter red lead to the red test harness lead.

3. Verify that the throttle linkage is against the idle stop screw.

4. Turn the ignition switch to the ON or RUN position. The voltmeter should indicate 0.90-1.00 volt DC. If the reading is not as specified, loosen the 2 adjustment screws (2, **Figure 49**) slightly and rotate the sensor to obtain 0.90-1.00 volt DC. Tighten the screws while holding the sensor in position. Recheck the meter reading.

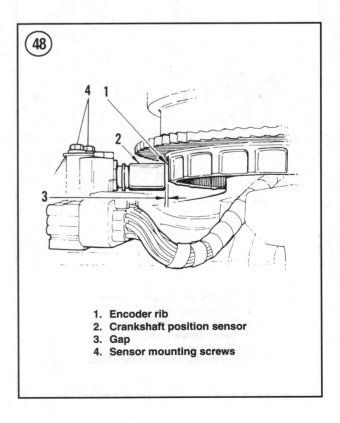

48

1. **Encoder rib**
2. **Crankshaft position sensor**
3. **Gap**
4. **Sensor mounting screws**

The meter must indicate 0.90-1.00 VDC with the throttle at the idle stop position.

5. Slowly advance the throttle lever until it is against the wide-open throttle stop while noting the meter. The meter should indicate a smooth increase in voltage, without any sudden fluctuations. With the throttle lever held against the wide-open throttle stop, the meter should indicate 3.55-4.05 volts. If the meter reading is not within specification, verify that the wide-open throttle stop is correctly set. If the wide-open throttle stop is correctly set, but the wide-open throttle voltage is not correct, replace the TPS. If the meter shows voltage fluctuations, instead of a smooth voltage transition as the sensor is rotated, replace the TPS.

Idle Speed Adjustment

1. Remove the throttle cable barrel from the barrel retainer on the cable anchor bracket.

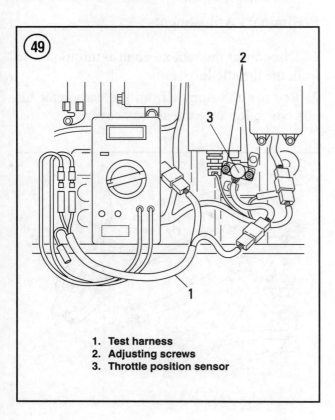

49

1. Test harness
2. Adjusting screws
3. Throttle position sensor

2. Check the idle speed in FORWARD gear. Make sure the throttle lever is held against the idle stop. The idle speed in FORWARD gear should be 600-700 rpm.

3. If necessary, adjust the idle air flow screw on the lower throttle shaft, on the port side of the induction manifold as shown in **Figure 50**. Tighten the idle air flow screw jam nut securely when finished.

4. Recheck the throttle position sensor setting and readjust as necessary as described in the previous section.

CAUTION
Idle speed must never exceed 700 rpm in FORWARD gear.

5. Attach the throttle cable to the throttle arm.

6. Hold the throttle lever against the idle stop. Adjust the cable barrel to slip into the retainer with a very light preload of the throttle lever against the idle stop. Fasten the barrel in the retainer.

NOTE
Excessive preload in Step 6 will result in difficult shifting from FORWARD or REVERSE gear into NEUTRAL.

5

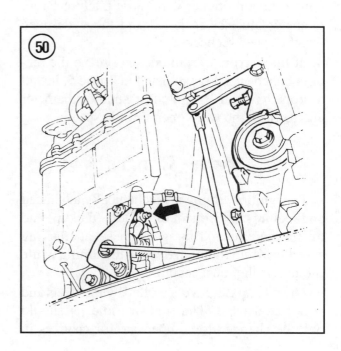

50

7. Check the throttle cable preload by inserting a thin piece of paper (such as a matchbook cover) between the idle stop and stop screw. If the preload is correct, a slight drag (without tearing) will be noted when removing the paper. Readjust the cable as required to obtain the desired preload.

Shift and Throttle Cable Adjustments

Refer to Chapter Twelve for additional information on remote control cable adjustments.

Wide-Open Throttle Speed Verification

1. Connect an accurate shop tachometer to a spark plug lead.
2. With the engine mounted on a boat, the boat unrestrained in the water and the engine running at wide-open throttle in forward gear, record the maximum rpm noted on the tachometer.
3. If the maximum rpm exceeds the recommended speed range listed in **Table 5**, check the propeller for damage. Repair or replace the propeller as necessary. If the propeller is in good condition, a propeller with more pitch or larger diameter must be installed and the wide-open throttle speed rechecked.
4. If the maximum rpm does not reach the recommended speed range listed in **Table 5**, install a propeller with less pitch or smaller diameter and recheck the wide-open throttle speed.

275 HP MODELS

The ignition timing is mechanically advanced and requires adjustment of the idle (pickup) and maximum timing. Timing can be set at cranking speed or while running. Setting the timing while running is the most accurate.

The idle mixture is controlled by fixed jets and is not adjustable. The standard idle jet should only be changed to compensate for changes in elevation, fuel blends or unique operating conditions. Changing the idle jet will only affect the air/fuel ratio at idle speed. If the engine runs satisfactorily, do not attempt to change the jet size. If changes to the idle jet sizes are warranted, see Chapter Six for additional information.

Refer to **Table 6** for general specifications. The recommended synch and link procedure is as follows:
1. Preliminary adjustments.
2. Timing pointer adjustment.
3. Throttle plate synchronization.
4. Throttle cam adjustment.
5. Wide-open throttle stop adjustment.
6. Timing adjustments.
7. Idle speed adjustment.
8. Oil pump linkage adjustment.
9. Shift and throttle cable adjustments.
10. Wide-open throttle speed verification.

Preliminary Adjustments

1. Disconnect the remote control throttle cable from the throttle lever arm.
2. Remove the screws from the carburetor air box cover. Remove the air box cover.

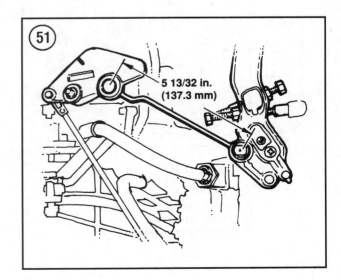

3. Remove the spark plugs and ground the spark plug leads to the power head to prevent accidental starting during the timing pointer adjustment.

Timing Pointer Adjustment

1. Install dial indicator (part No. 91-58222A1, or equivalent) into the top starboard (cylinder No. 1) spark plug hole.

2. Rotate the flywheel clockwise until the No. 1 piston is at TDC.

3. Rotate the flywheel counterclockwise until the dial indicator needle is approximately 1/4 turn past the 0.557 in. (14.15 mm) BTDC reading on the indicator dial.

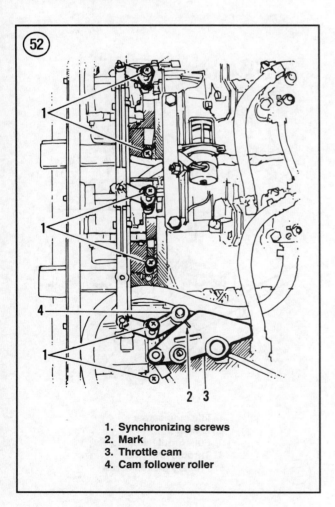

1. Synchronizing screws
2. Mark
3. Throttle cam
4. Cam follower roller

4. At this point, the timing pointer should be aligned with the *.557* mark on the flywheel. If not, loosen the 2 timing pointer screws and reposition the pointer as necessary. Securely retighten the pointer screws.

5. Remove the dial indicator from the No. 1 spark plug hole.

6. Reinstall the spark plugs if the timing adjustments are to be made with the engine running. If the timing adjustments are to be made with the engine cranking, leave the spark plugs removed.

5

Throttle Plate Synchronization

1. Measure the distance of the link rod between the throttle arm barrel and throttle cam at the points shown in **Figure 51**. The distance should be 5-13/32 in. (137.3 mm).

2. If adjustment is required, disconnect the link rod and adjust the distance.

3. Loosen the 6 carburetor synchronizing screws (1, **Figure 52**). Allow the carburetor throttle valves to close freely.

4. Position the throttle arm so the idle stop screw (1, **Figure 53**) is against its stop and the cam follower roller (4, **Figure 52**) is lightly contacting the throttle cam (3, **Figure 52**).

5. Adjust the idle stop screw (1, **Figure 53**) to align the throttle cam mark (2, **Figure 52**) with the center of the follower roller (4, **Figure 52**). Holding the follower roller in this position, tighten the carburetor synchronizing screws (1, **Figure 52**).

6. Make sure all carburetor throttle valves open and close simultaneously. Repeat Steps 3-5 as necessary. Reinstall the carburetor air box cover.

Wide-Open Throttle Stop Adjustment

1. Move the throttle arm so the full-throttle stop screw (3, **Figure 53**) is against its stop.

2. Adjust the full throttle stop screw so the carburetor throttle valves are in the fully open position while allowing 0.010-0.015 in. (0.25-0.38

mm) clearance between the throttle cam and cam follower roller.

CAUTION
The carburetors can be damaged if the throttle valves bottom out during wide-open throttle operation.

Timing Adjustments

Preliminary adjustments

Verify the trigger link rod length from the end of the rod to the locknut as shown in **Figure 54**. If length is not 11/16 in. (17.5 mm), disconnect the link rod and adjust its length as necessary.

Running adjustment

1. Connect a suitable timing light to the top starboard (cylinder No. 1) spark plug lead.

CAUTION
*Do not run the engine without an adequate water supply and do not exceed 3000 rpm without an adequate load. Refer to **Safety Precautions** at the beginning of this chapter.*

2. Start the engine and allow it to warm to normal operating temperature.
3. Reduce the engine speed to idle and shift the gearcase into FORWARD gear.

NOTE
*If there is a timing specification decal on the engine, use the specifications on the decal if they differ from the specifications in the text and **Table 6**.*

4. Point the timing light at the flywheel and timing pointer. Note the reading. Timing should be the specification listed on the timing decal (or 5° ATDC at idle speed), at this time.
5. While holding the idle stop screw (2, **Figure 53**) against the idle stop, adjust the idle timing (pickup timing) screw (5, **Figure 53**) to obtain the specified timing reading. Tighten the idle

timing (pickup timing) screw jam nut when finished.

6. Point the timing light at the flywheel and timing pointer.

7. Advance the throttle to position the maximum spark advance screw against its stop (**Figure 55**). Note the timing reading.

8. Refer to the engine timing decal or **Table 6** for the maximum timing specification at wide-open throttle. If adjustment is needed, stop the engine and loosen the maximum spark advance adjustment jam nut.

9. Turn the adjustment screw clockwise to retard timing or counterclockwise to advance timing. Tighten the jam nut securely. Recheck the timing and adjust as necessary.

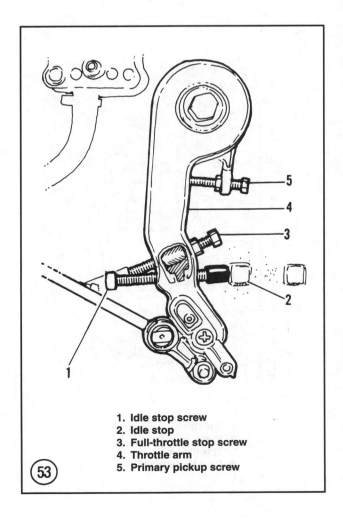

1. **Idle stop screw**
2. **Idle stop**
3. **Full-throttle stop screw**
4. **Throttle arm**
5. **Primary pickup screw**

(53)

Cranking speed adjustment

NOTE
The battery must be fully charged and the starting system functioning properly for this adjustment procedure to be accurate. Removing the spark plugs helps increase cranking speed and timing accuracy.

CAUTION
Perform all cranking timing adjustments in NEUTRAL.

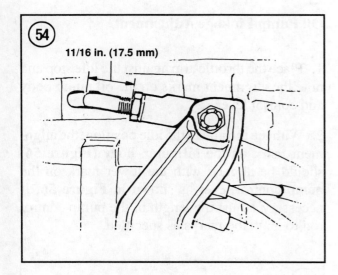

11/16 in. (17.5 mm)

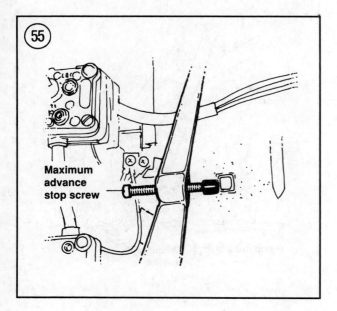

Maximum advance stop screw

1. Remove the spark plugs and connect an air gap spark tester (part No. FT-11295) to the spark plug leads.

2. Connect a suitable timing light (**Table 1**) to the top starboard (cylinder No. 1) spark plug lead.

3. Hold the idle stop screw against its stop (2, **Figure 53**).

4. Crank the engine with the electric starter while noting the timing with the timing light.

NOTE
*If there is a timing specification decal on the engine, use the specifications on the decal if they differ from the specifications in the text and **Table 6**.*

5. Timing should be within the specification listed on the timing decal (or 5° ATDC) at this time.

6. While holding the idle stop screw (2, **Figure 53**) against the idle stop, adjust the idle timing (pickup timing) screw (5, **Figure 53**) to obtain the specified timing reading. Tighten the idle timing (pickup timing) screw jam nut when finished.

NOTE
Due to the electronic spark advance characteristics of this ignition system, the timing will retard slightly when running at wide-open throttle. Therefore, the maximum timing should be adjusted to the cranking speed specification to obtain the desired wide-open throttle timing when running at wide-open throttle. Verify all timing adjustments made at cranking speed with the outboard running.

7. Hold the throttle arm so the maximum advance screw (**Figure 55**) is against its stop.

8. Crank the engine while noting the timing with the timing light.

9. Refer to the engine timing decal or **Table 6** for the maximum timing specification at cranking speed. If adjustment is needed, stop the en-

gine and loosen the maximum spark advance adjustment jam nut.

10. Adjust the maximum spark advance screw (**Figure 55**) to align the timing pointer with the specified timing mark on the flywheel if necessary.

11. Tighten the maximum spark advance screw jam nut when finished.

12. Remove the timing light and the air gap spark tester. Reinstall the spark plugs and reconnect the spark plug leads.

Idle Speed Adjustment

The idle mixture is controlled by fixed jets and is not adjustable. The standard idle jet should only be changed to compensate for changes in elevation, fuel blends or unique operating conditions. Changing the idle jet will only affect the air/fuel ratio at idle speed. If the engine runs satisfactorily, do not attempt to change the jet size. If changes to the idle jet sizes are warranted, see Chapter Six for additional information.

1. With the outboard motor in the water, start the engine and allow it to warm to normal operating temperature.

2. Shift outboard into FORWARD gear.

3. With the engine idling in forward gear, adjust the primary pickup screw (5, **Figure 53**) to obtain 650-700 rpm.

CAUTION
Idle speed must never exceed 750 rpm in gear.

4. Connect the throttle cable to the throttle arm.

5. While holding the throttle arm against the idle stop, adjust the throttle cable barrel to slip into the barrel retainer on the cable anchor bracket with a slight preload of the throttle arm against the idle stop.

6. Lock the throttle cable barrel in place.

NOTE
Excessive preload in Step 7 will result in difficult shifting from FORWARD gear to NEUTRAL.

7. Check the throttle cable preload by inserting a thin piece of paper between the idle stop and stop screw. If the preload is correct, a slight drag (without tearing) will be noted when removing the paper. Readjust the cable as required to obtain the desired preload.

Oil Pump Linkage Adjustment

1. Place the throttle arm against the idle stop and note the alignment marks on the oil pump body and control lever.

2. With the throttle in the idle position, the alignment mark on the oil pump body (**Figure 56**) should be aligned with the lower mark on the pump control lever as shown in **Figure 56**. If necessary, adjust the length of the pump control rod to align the marks as specified.

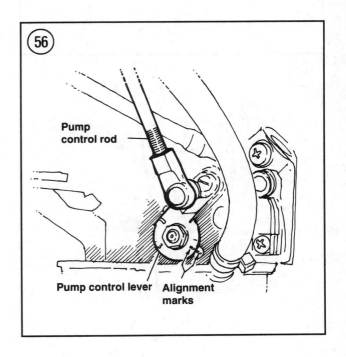

(56)

Pump control rod

Pump control lever   Alignment marks

Shift and Throttle Cable Adjustments

Refer to Chapter Twelve for additional information on remote control cable adjustments.

Wide-Open Throttle Speed Verification

1. Connect an accurate shop tachometer to a spark plug lead.
2. With the engine mounted on a boat, the boat unrestrained in the water and the engine running at wide-open throttle in forward gear, record the maximum rpm noted on the tachometer.
3. If the maximum rpm exceeds the recommended speed range listed in **Table 6**, check the propeller for damage. Repair or replace the propeller as necessary. If the propeller is in good condition, a propeller with more pitch or larger diameter must be installed and the wide-open throttle speed rechecked.
4. If the maximum rpm does not reach the recommended speed range listed in **Table 6**, install a propeller with less pitch or smaller diameter and recheck the wide-open throttle speed.

5

Table 1 TEST EQUIPMENT AND TOOLS

Description	Part No.
Electrical connector hardware kit	86-813937A-1
Crimping pliers	91-808696
Multimeter/DVA tester	91-99750
DVA adaptor (for analog multimeter)	91-89045
Spark tester (7/16 in. air gap, single cylinder)	91-63998A-1
Spark tester (adjustable air gap, up to 6 cylinders)	FT-11295
Dial indicator set (for determining TDC)	91-58222A-1
Timing light	91-99379
Shop tachometer/dwell meter	91-59339
Digital shop tachometer	79-17391A-1
Interface module (spark plug wire)	825824A-2
AD-CDI ignition test harness (6-position switch)	91-14443A-1
CDM ignition test harness	
Part No. 822779 modules (3 pin connector)	84-825207A-1
Part No. 827509 modules (4-pin connector)	84-825207A-2
Digital Diagnostic Terminal (DDT)	91-823686A-2
DDT software cartridge	91-822608-2
225 hp carbureted (1994) adapter harness	84-822560A-1
225-250 hp (1995-on) adapter harnesses	84-822560A-6 and 84-822560A-7
150-200 hp (824003 digital ECM) adapter harness	84-822560A-5
150-200 hp (analog ECM) adapter harnesses	84-822560A-6 and 84-822560A-7
200 DFI (direct fuel injected) adapter harness	84-822560A-5
EFI 100 psi fuel pressure gauge	84-16850A-1

(continued)

Table 1 TEST EQUIPMENT AND TOOLS (continued)

Description	Part No.
DFI 160 psi liquid filled air and fuel pressure gauge	84-16850A-2
Injector test harness (150-200 hp EFI models)	91-833169
TPS test harness (150-200 hp EFI models)	91-816085
EFI diagnostic tester (150-200 hp EFI models)	91-11001A2

Table 2 GENERAL SPECIFICATIONS: 75, 90, 100, 115, 125 HP, 65 AND 80 JET

Rated output	
75 hp	75 hp (56 kW) at 5000 rpm
90 hp and 65 Jet	90 hp (67.1 kW) at 5250 rpm
100 hp	100 hp (74.6 kW) at 5000 rpm
115 hp and 80 Jet	115 hp (85.8 kW) at 5000 rpm
125 hp	125 hp (93.3 kW) at 5000 rpm
Induction type	Loop-charged
Number of cylinders and configuration	
65 Jet, 75 and 90 hp	3, inline, cast-iron bore
80 Jet, 100, 115 and 125 hp	4, inline, cast-iron bore
Displacement	
3 cylinder models	84.6 cu. in. (1386 cc)
4 cylinder models	112.8 cu. in. (1848 cc)
Standard bore	3.50 in. (88.9 mm)
Stroke	2.93 in. (74.42 mm)
Recommended full-throttle operating range	
75, 100, 115, 125 hp and 80 Jet	4750-5250 rpm
90 hp and 65 Jet	5000-5500 rpm
Idle speed in forward gear	650-700 rpm
Cranking compression	15 psi (103.4 kPa) maximum variation
Oiling system	Variable ratio oil injection system
Initial idle mixture screw adjustment	
75 hp	1-1/8 turns from lightly seated position
90 hp and 65 Jet	1-1/4 turns from lightly seated position
100-125 hp and 80 Jet	1-1/2 turns from lightly seated position
Ignition system	
Serial No.0D283222-0G437999	AD-CDI (alternator driven ignition-capacitor discharge)
Serial No.0G438000-on	CDM (capacitor discharge module)
Idle timing	
75, 90 hp and 65 Jet	2° ATDC - 6° BTDC
100, 115, 125 hp and 80 Jet	4° ATDC - 2° BTDC
Maximum timing	Cranking speed (3000 rpm)
90 hp and 65 Jet	22° BTDC (20° BTDC)
75 hp	20° BTDC (18° BTDC)
100, 115, 125 hp and 80 Jet (1994-1995)	22° BTDC (20° BTDC)
100, 115, 125 hp and 80 Jet (1996-on)	25° BTDC (23° BTDC)
Ignition system firing order	
3 cylinder	
1994-1995	1-3-2
1996-on	1-2-3
4 cylinder	1-3-2-4

Table 3 GENERAL SPECIFICATIONS: 135-200 HP, 150-200 XRI AND MAGNUM, XR6 AND MAGNUM III, 105 AND 140 JET

Rated output	
135 hp	135 hp (100.7 kW) at 5300 rpm
150 hp, 150 XRI, 150 Magnum and 105 Jet	150 hp (111.9 kW) at 5300 rpm
XR6 and Magnum III	150 hp (111.9 kW) at 5250 rpm
175 hp, 175 XRI and 175 Magnum	175 hp (130.6 kW) at 5300 rpm
200 hp and 140 Jet	200 hp (149.2 kW) at 5300 rpm
200 XRI, 200 Magnum	200 hp (149.2 kW) at 5400 rpm
Induction type	Loop-charged
Number of cylinders and configuration	6, 60° V-6, cast-iron bore
Displacement	
135, 150 hp and 105 Jet	121.9 cu. in. (1998 cc)
All other models	153 cu. in. (2507 cc)
Standard bore	
135, 150 hp and 105 Jet	3.125 in. (79.38 mm)
All other models	3.500 in. (88.90 mm)
Stroke	2.650 in. (67.31 mm)
Recommended full-throttle operating range	
200 XRI	5000-5800 rpm
All other models	5000-5600 rpm
Idle speed in forward gear	
XR6 and Magnum III	625-725 rpm
All other models	600-700 rpm
Throttle position sensor voltage at	
closed throttle	
Prior to ECM No. 14632A14	0.125-0.145 volt
ECM No. 14632A15, 14632A16 and	
8240031-on	0.24-0.26 volt
Cranking compression	15 psi (103.4 kPa) maximum variation between cylinders
Oiling system	Variable ratio oil injection system
Carburetor identification	
1994-1995 models	
135 hp	WMH-30
150 hp and 105 Jet	WMH-31
XR6 and Magnum III	WMH-32
175 hp	WMH-33
200 hp and 140 Jet	WMH-34/39
1996-1997 models	
135 hp	WMV-1
150 hp and 105 Jet	WMV-2
XR6 and Magnum III	WMV-3
175 hp	WMV-4
200 hp and 140 Jet	WMV-5
Initial idle mixture screw adjustment	1-1/2 turns from lightly seated position
Ignition system	AD-CDI (alternator-driven capacitor discharge ignition)
Idle timing/pickup timing	
135, 150 hp and 105 Jet	2°-9° ATDC
All other models	0°-9° ATDC
Maximum timing*	Cranking speed (wide-open throttle)
135, 150 hp and 105 Jet	
carbureted models	21° BTDC (19° BTDC)
150-175 XRI and Magnum EFI models	20° BTDC (19° BTDC)
XR6, Magnum III and	
175 hp carbureted	20° BTDC (19° BTDC)

(continued)

Table 3 GENERAL SPECIFICATIONS: 135-200 HP, 150-200 XRI AND MAGNUM, XR6 AND MAGNUM III, 105 AND 140 JET (continued)

Ignition system (continued)	
200 hp and 140 Jet carbureted models	22° BTDC (20° BTDC)
200 XRI and 200 Magnum EFI models	16° BTDC (22° BTDC)
Ignition system firing order	1-2-3-4-5-6

*The timing decal on the engine takes precedence over service manual specifications. Due to the many different timing modules used on these engines, refer to Chapter 5 for exact timing procedures.

Table 4 GENERAL SPECIFICATIONS: 200 DFI (DIRECT FUEL INJECTED)

Rated output	200 hp (149.2 kW) at 5400 rpm
Induction type	Loop-charged
Number of cylinders and configuration	6, 60° V-6, cast-iron bore
Displacement	185 cu. in. (3032 cc)
Standard bore	3.6265 in. (92.11 mm)
Stroke	3.000 in. (76.2 mm)
Recommended full-throttle operating range	5000-5750 rpm
Idle speed in forward gear	625-650 rpm (not adjustable)
Cranking compression	15 psi (103.4 kPa) maximum variation between cylinders
Oiling system	Variable ratio oil injection system
Ignition system	Digital Inductive
Ignition timing	ECM controlled, not adjustable
Ignition system firing order	1-2-3-4-5-6

Table 5 GENERAL SPECIFICATIONS: 225 AND 250 HP

Rated output	
225 hp carbureted	225 hp (167.9 kW) at 5250 rpm
225 hp EFI (electronic fuel injection)	225 hp (167.9 kW) at 5400 rpm
250 hp EFI (electronic fuel injection)	250 hp (186.5 kW) at 5400 rpm
Induction type	Loop-charged
Number of cylinders and configuration	6, 60° V-6, cast-iron bore
Displacement	185 cu. in. (3032 cc)
Standard bore	3.6265 in. (92.11 mm)
Stroke	3.000 in. (76.2 mm)
Recommended full-throttle operating range	
Carbureted models	5000-5500 rpm
Electronic fuel injection models (EFI)	5000-5800 rpm
Idle speed in forward gear	600-700 rpm
Cranking compression	15 psi (103.4 kPa) maximum variation between cylinders
Typical results	100-110 psi (689.5-758.5 kPa)
Oiling system	Variable ratio oil injection system
Initial idle mixture screw adjustment	1-1/2 turns from lightly seated position

(continued)

Table 5 GENERAL SPECIFICATIONS: 225 AND 250 HP (continued)

Charging system	60 amp belt-driven alternator (regulated)
Ignition system	CDM (Capacitor Discharge Module)
Idle timing	4°-9° ATDC
Maximum timing	
225 hp (carbureted)	Timing at 5000 rpm (5500 rpm), or as specified
1994 models with 821717 ECU	22° BTDC at 5500 rpm
1994 models with 824866 ECU	25°-27° BTDC at 5500 rpm
1995 models	20° BTDC (23° BTDC)
1996-1997 models	19° BTDC (26° BTDC)
225 EFI (electronic fuel injection)	Timing at 5000 rpm (5800 rpm)
1995 models	20° BTDC (23° BTDC)
1996-1997 models	24° BTDC (24° BTDC)
250 EFI (electronic fuel injection)	24° BTDC (28° BTDC)
Ignition system firing order	1, 2, 3, 4, 5, 6

Table 6 GENERAL SPECIFICATIONS: 275 HP

Rated output	275 hp (205 kW) at 5250 rpm
Induction type	Loop-charged
Number of cylinders and configuration	6, 74° V-6, chrome bore
Displacement	207 cu. in. (3392 cc)
Standard bore	3.74 in. (95 mm)
Stroke	3.14 in. (79.76 mm)
Recommended full throttle operating range	5000-5500 rpm
Idle speed in forward gear	650-700 rpm
Cranking compression	15 psi (103.4 kPa) maximum variation between cylinders
Oiling system	Variable ratio oil injection system
Initial idle mixture screw adjustment	not applicable, fixed jet
Charging system	40 amp (regulated)
Ignition system	AD-CDI (alternator-driven capacitor discharge ignition)
Idle timing/Pickup timing	5° ATDC
Maximum timing	
Cranking speed (wide-open throttle)	22° BTDC (20° BTDC)
Ignition system firing order	1-2-3-4-5, 6

5

Chapter Six

Fuel System

This chapter contains removal, overhaul, installation and adjustment procedures for fuel pumps, carburetors, reed valves, fuel primer valves, thermal air valves and fuel enrichment valves, bleed (recirculation) systems, electronic fuel injection components, portable fuel tanks and connecting lines used with the Mercury/Mariner outboard motors covered in this manual.

Carburetor specifications are listed in **Tables 1-7**. EFI (electronic fuel injection) and DFI (direct fuel injection) specifications are listed in **Table 8**. Fuel pump specifications are listed in **Table 9** and **Table 10**. Reed valve specifications are listed in **Table 11**. Torque values are listed in **Tables 12-15**.

CAUTION
*Metric **and** U.S. standard fasteners are used on newer model outboards. Always match a replacement fastener to the original. Do not run a tap or thread chaser into a hole (or over a bolt) without first verifying the thread size and pitch. Newer manufacturer's parts catalogs list every standard fastener by di-ameter, length and pitch. Always have the engine model and serial numbers when ordering a parts catalog from a dealer.*

FUEL PUMP

All models are equipped with a diaphragm-type fuel pump operated by crankcase pressure and vacuum pulses. The 275 hp model is equipped with 2 remote-mounted fuel pumps, connected in series.

EFI and DFI models use a mechanical fuel pump to supply fuel to the vapor separator (fuel reservoir). An electric fuel pump in (or after) the vapor separator provides the high fuel pressure necessary for correct fuel injector operation.

These types of mechanical fuel pumps cannot move large quantities of fuel at cranking rpm, therefore, fuel must be transferred to the carburetor (or vapor separator) by manually operating the primer bulb installed in the fuel supply hose.

Mechanical fuel pumps are operated by crankcase pressure and vacuum pulses created by movement of the piston(s). The pulses reach the fuel pump through either an external hose or internal passages in the crankcase.

Upward piston movement creates a low pressure in the crankcase and against the pump diaphragm. This low pressure opens the inlet check valve in the pump, drawing fuel from the supply line into the pump.

Downward piston movement creates a high pressure in the crankcase and against the pump diaphragm. This pressure closes the inlet check valve and opens the outlet check valve, forcing the fuel out of the fuel pump and into the carburetor(s) (or vapor separator). **Figure 1** shows the general operating principles of a pulse driven, mechanical fuel pump.

Not all Mercury/Mariner mechanical fuel pumps use the pressure/vacuum pulses from 2-cylinders as shown in **Figure 1**. Many pumps will operate off one cylinder's pressure and vacuum pulses.

NOTE
If the cylinder(s) that supplies crankcase pressure and vacuum to a fuel pump mechanically fails, all of the cylinders will starve for fuel. Check the compression of the engine before failing the fuel pump. See Chapter Four.

Mercury/Mariner fuel pumps are extremely simple in design and reliable in operation. Diaphragm failures are the most common problem,

6

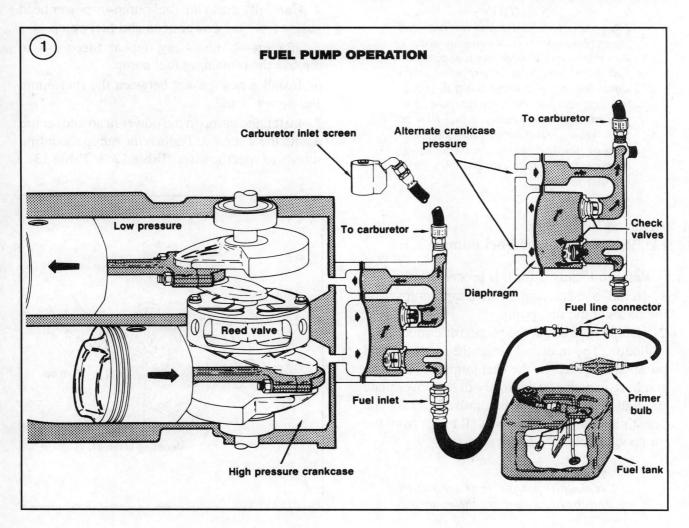

FUEL PUMP OPERATION

Carburetor inlet screen

Alternate crankcase pressure

To carburetor

Low pressure

To carburetor

Check valves

Reed valve

Diaphragm

Fuel line connector

Fuel inlet

Primer bulb

High pressure crankcase

Fuel tank

although the use of sour fuel or fuel with excessive alcohol or other additives can cause check valve failure. Refer to Chapter Four for fuel recommendations.

If the fuel pump is suspected of not functioning correctly, refer to Chapter Three for fuel system troubleshooting. For reference purposes, fuel pump specifications are listed in **Table 9** at the end of this chapter.

Test the remote fuel pump as described in Chapter Three. Also check the fuel delivery hose for restrictions and air leakage by connecting a vacuum gauge and a piece of clear hose to the fuel pump inlet using a T-fitting. Check fuel pump output using a pressure gauge connected to the fuel pump outlet using a T-fitting.

> *CAUTION*
> *Fuel pump assemblies and internal fuel pump components vary between models. Be certain that the correct fuel pump or fuel pump components are used when replacing or rebuilding the fuel pump. An incorrect fuel pump or internal components can cause reduced fuel flow to the engine, resulting in poor performance or power head failure. Never interchange fuel pump components from another model.*

Removal/Installation
(All Remote Mounted Fuel Pumps)

Refer to **Figure 2** for this procedure.

1. Remove and discard the tie-strap clamps from the hoses at the fuel pump.

2. Label the hoses at the pump for correct reinstallation. The inlet and outlet fitting of the fuel pump are marked on the fuel pump cover plate. If a hose is connected directly to the cover plate through a 90° fitting, it is a pulse hose for the boost diaphragm. Disconnect all hoses from the pump assembly. See **Figure 2**.

> *NOTE*
> *If 2 of the fuel pump screws are slotted or Phillips head, they are the mounting*

> *screws. The 2 screws that hold the fuel pump components together are always hex-head screws. If all 4 fuel pump screws are hex head, look at the rear of the pump to determine which 2 screws go through the mounting gasket and into the power head.*

3. Remove the 2 screws securing the fuel pump assembly to the power head and remove the pump.

> *NOTE*
> *On 275 hp models, 2 fuel pumps connected in series are used. The bottom fuel pump delivers fuel to the top pump and the top pump delivers fuel to the carburetors.*

4. Carefully clean the fuel pump-to-power head gasket from the power head and fuel pump.

5. *275 hp*—If necessary, repeat Steps 2-4 to remove the remaining fuel pump.

6. Install a new gasket between the fuel pump and power head.

7. Install the pump to the power head and secure it with the 2 screws. Tighten the pump mounting screws to specification (**Table 12** or **Table 13**).

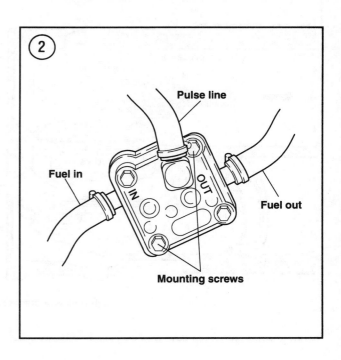

Pulse line

Fuel in

OUT

IN

Fuel out

Mounting screws

8. Reconnect the fuel inlet and outlet hoses. Secure the hoses with new tie-strap clamps.

9. On models so equipped, install and secure the pulse hose to the fuel pump cover fitting with a new tie-strap clamp.

10. *275 hp*—If removed, install the remaining pump.

Disassembly/Reassembly
Remote Fuel Pump

NOTE
Replace all fuel pump gaskets and diaphragms anytime the pump is disassembled. If the check valves are removed, they must be replaced. Refer to **Figure 3** *for the following procedures.*

Disassembly

1. Remove the hex-head screws holding the pump assembly together.

2. Separate the pump cover, gaskets and diaphragms from the pump body and base. Discard the gaskets and diaphragms.

3. Using needlenose pliers, remove the check valve retainers (4, **Figure 3**) from the pump body. Remove the plastic discs and check valves from the retainers.

4. Remove the cap (9, **Figure 3**) and spring (10) from the pump cover.

5. Remove the cap (5, **Figure 3**) and spring (6) from the pump body.

6. Using needle nose pliers remove the check valve retainers from the pump body. Remove the plastic discs and check valves from the retainers. Discard the check valves and check valve retainers. *Do not* discard the plastic discs.

Cleaning and inspection

1. Clean the pump components in a suitable solvent and dry with compressed air.

2. Inspect the plastic discs for cracks, holes or other damage. Replace as required.

3. Inspect the pump base, pump body and pump cover for cracks, distortion, deterioration or other damage. Replace as required.

Check valve installation

1. Insert a new check valve retainer into the plastic disc, then into a new check valve. See **Figure 4**. Repeat the step for the other check valve assembly.

2. Lubricate the check valve retainers with motor oil. Insert the check valve and retainer assemblies into the pump body. See **Figure 4**.

3. Bend the check valve retainer stem from side to side, until the stem breaks off flush with the retainer cap. See **Figure 5**. Repeat this step for the other retainer.

4. Insert the broken retainer stem into the retainer as shown in **Figure 6**. Using a small hammer and punch, tap the stem into the retainer until flush with the retainer cap.

Reassembly

NOTE
Fuel pump components have one or more V tabs on one side for directional reference during assembly. Be certain the V tabs on all components are aligned. To ensure the correct alignment of pump components, use 1/4-in. bolts or dowels as guides. Insert the guides through the pump mounting screw holes.

1. Referring to **Figure 3**, reassemble the pump. Do not use gasket sealer on the pump gaskets or diaphragms. Be sure that all pump components are properly aligned and that the springs and spring caps are properly assembled. Spring caps should always push against the diaphragm.

2. Remove one of the alignment bolts or dowels and install a hex-head screw finger-tight. Re-

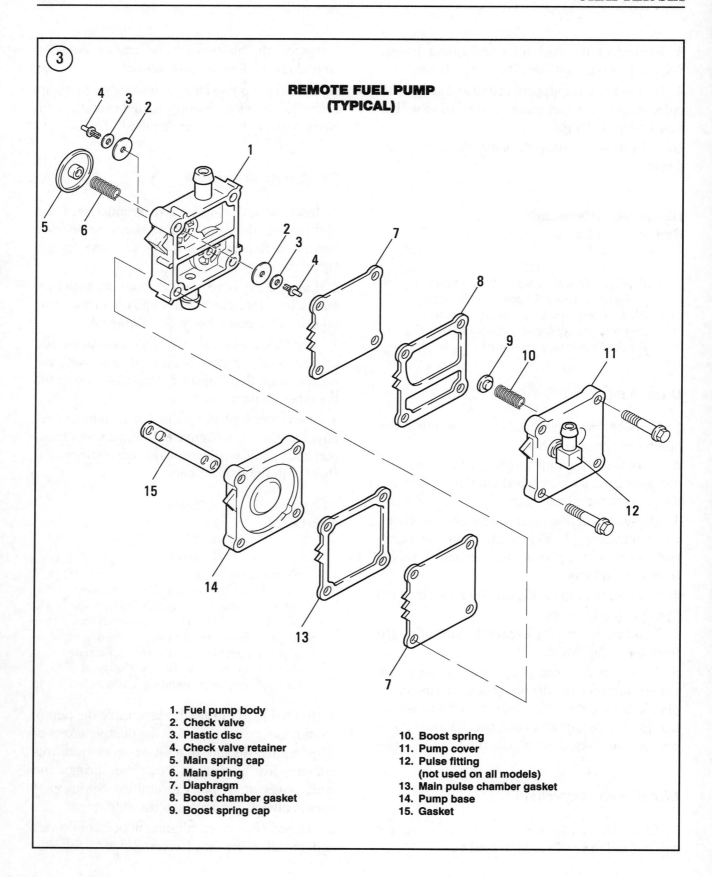

1. Fuel pump body
2. Check valve
3. Plastic disc
4. Check valve retainer
5. Main spring cap
6. Main spring
7. Diaphragm
8. Boost chamber gasket
9. Boost spring cap
10. Boost spring
11. Pump cover
12. Pulse fitting
   (not used on all models)
13. Main pulse chamber gasket
14. Pump base
15. Gasket

move the other alignment bolt or dowel and install the other hex-head screw finger-tight.

3. Tighten both hex-head screws to specification (**Table 12** or **Table 13**).

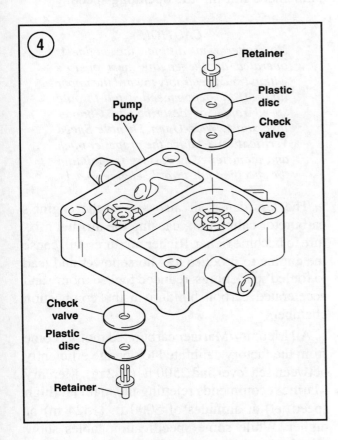

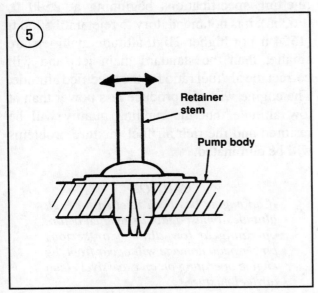

CARBURETORS

Carburetor Identification

All Mercury/Mariner carburetors have a carburetor series identification number cast into the carburetor body and a carburetor model identification number stamped into the front or rear flange. The stamped model identification number is in the following format: model number, carburetor location (on multi-carburetor models) and Julian date code.

For example, a WMV-7-3-3246 is a *WMV* series carburetor, model No. 7, mounted in the third carburetor location (third from top), built on the 324th day of 1996. Carburetor location refers to the position of the carburetor on the power head. This is not always the same as the cylinder number.

Current (1994-1997) model Mercury/Mariner outboard motors use the following carburetors:

1. *75-90 hp (3-cylinder)*—Three WME series carburetors.

2. *100-125 hp and 80 Jet*—Four WME series carburetors.

3. *135-225 hp and 105 and 140 Jet*—Three WMH or WMV series carburetors.

4. *275 hp*—Six WO series *MerCarb* carburetors.

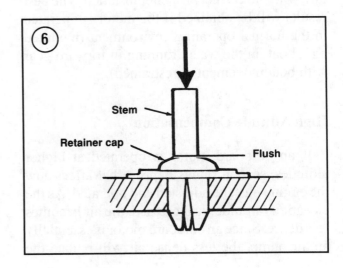

Carburetor Adjustments (Static)

Refer to **Tables 1-4** for carburetor specifications. Carburetor scale part No. 91-36392 is recommended for all float adjustments.

Carburetor Adjustments (Engine Running)

NOTE
Any time service or repair has been performed on the carburetor(s), **Synchronization and Linkage Adjustments** *must be performed as described in Chapter Five.*

All running adjustments are detailed in Chapter Five. The engine must be provided with an adequate supply of cooling water when performing any procedures that involve starting and running the engine. Refer to *Safety Precautions* at the beginning of Chapter Three or Chapter Four.

NOTE
Idle speed and idle mixture adjustments cannot be satisfactorily performed with the engine running on a cooling system flushing device.

When performing idle speed and idle mixture adjustments, the outboard must be running in FORWARD gear at normal operating temperature with the correct propeller installed. The best results will be obtained if the motor is operated in the normal operating environment (mounted on a boat, in the water, running in forward gear with boat movement unrestrained).

High Altitude Compensation

If an outboard motor is operated at higher altitudes, several things happen that affect how the engine must be adjusted and operated. As the elevation (altitude) is increased, the air becomes less dense. Since an outboard motor is essentially an air pump, the less dense air will reduce the efficiency of the engine, reducing the horsepower output proportionally to the air density. The loss of horsepower will require propeller pitch and diameter changes to maintain the recommended full-throttle operating speed.

CAUTION
No matter what altitude the engine is operated at, the engine must operate within (and preferably toward the upper limit of) the recommended full-throttle speed range as described in Chapter Five under, **Wide-Open Throttle Speed Verification**. *Change the propeller pitch and diameter as necessary to maintain the specified full-throttle engine speed.*

The less dense air also affects the engine's carburetor calibration, causing the air/fuel mixture to become richer. Richer mixtures will cause the engine to produce less horsepower and lead to fouled spark plugs, reduced fuel economy and accelerated carbon buildup in the combustion chamber.

All Mercury/Mariner carbureted motors come from the factory calibrated to operate efficiently between sea level and 2500 ft. (762 m). Mercury Marine recommends rejetting the main jet (high speed jet) at altitudes of 5000 ft. (1524 m) or higher. While some specification tables show rejetting specifications beginning at 2500 ft. (762 m), it is not mandatory to rejet until 5000 ft (1524 m) or higher. High altitude main jets are smaller than the standard main jets and will correct the air/fuel ratio for the specified altitude. The engine will still produce less power than at low altitude, but the running quality will be restored and the rich air/fuel mixture problems will be eliminated.

CAUTION
If an engine has been rejetted for high altitude, it must again be rejetted before operating at low altitude or serious power head damage will occur from the engine operating on an excessively lean air/fuel mixture.

Refer to **Table 2** and **Table 3** for carburetor main jet size recommendations for the altitude the motor will be operated at. The idle speed and idle mixture must also be reset at the new altitude as described in Chapter Five. Expect the new idle mixture screw position (at 5000 ft. [1524 m] or higher) to be 1/16 to 1/8 turn leaner (clockwise) than the original setting.

NOTE
The 275 hp models must have all of the fixed jets (main, vent and idle) compensated.

Mercury Marine also recommends regearing the lower gearcase on larger engines at altitudes of 5000 ft. (1524 m) or higher. The new gear ratio will be a higher number ratio that will allow more gear reduction between the power head and the propshaft. This increases the torque at the propeller shaft, increasing the engine's efficiency at high altitudes. Remember that the wide-open throttle speed must be verified as described in Chapter Five after any altitude or gear ratio change. Refer to Chapter Nine for gearcase and gear ratio information.

Cleaning and Inspection (All Models)

CAUTION
Do not remove the throttle plate(s) and throttle shaft unless absolutely necessary and parts are available. Be careful to reinstall each throttle plate in its original bore and orientation. Make sure the throttle plate(s) will open and close fully before torquing the screws. Use Loctite 271 threadlocking adhesive on the throttle plate screws. Throttle shafts and throttle plates are not serviceable on WMH and WMV series carburetors.

1. Thoroughly and carefully remove any gasket material from all mating surfaces. Do not nick, scratch or damage the mating surfaces.

2. Clean the carburetor body and metal parts using an aerosol carburetor and choke cleaning solvent (available at any auto parts store) to remove gum, dirt and varnish.

3. Rinse the carburetor components in clean solvent and dry with compressed air. Be sure to blow out all orifices, nozzles and passages thoroughly.

CAUTION
Do not use wire or drill bits to clean any carburetor passages. Doing so will alter calibration and ruin the carburetor.

4. Check the carburetor body casting for stripped threads, cracks or other damage.

5. Check the fuel bowl for distortion, corrosion, cracks, blocked passages or other damage.

6. Check the float for fuel absorption, deterioration or other damage. Check the float arm for wear in the hinge pin and inlet needle contact areas. Replace the float as necessary. If available, and if specifications are listed, weigh the float using a gram scale. If the float weighs more than specified, it has absorbed fuel and must be replaced.

7. Check the idle mixture screw(s) tip for grooving, nicks or other damage. Replace the idle mixture screw(s) as necessary.

8. Check the inlet needle and seat for excessive wear. Some carburetors do not have a replaceable inlet needle seat. Replace the needle and seat as an assembly if both parts are serviceable.

WME SERIES CARBURETOR (75-125 HP, 65 AND 80 JET)

Remote control models use an electric fuel primer valve to enrich the air/fuel mixture whenever the fuel primer valve is engaged by the operator. The throttle plate(s) must be fully closed (to develop the most vacuum) for the system to function correctly. Refer to Chapter Three for operational information and trou-

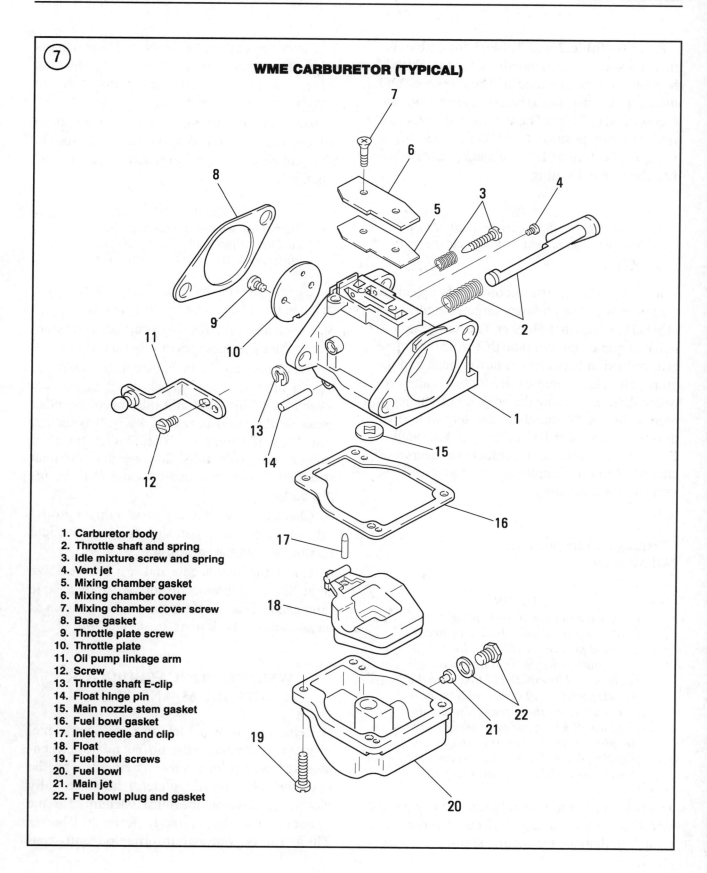

⑦

WME CARBURETOR (TYPICAL)

1. Carburetor body
2. Throttle shaft and spring
3. Idle mixture screw and spring
4. Vent jet
5. Mixing chamber gasket
6. Mixing chamber cover
7. Mixing chamber cover screw
8. Base gasket
9. Throttle plate screw
10. Throttle plate
11. Oil pump linkage arm
12. Screw
13. Throttle shaft E-clip
14. Float hinge pin
15. Main nozzle stem gasket
16. Fuel bowl gasket
17. Inlet needle and clip
18. Float
19. Fuel bowl screws
20. Fuel bowl
21. Main jet
22. Fuel bowl plug and gasket

bleshooting procedures on the electric fuel primer valve.

Manual start models use an engine mounted primer bulb. Depressing the primer bulb delivers fuel from the top carburetor's fuel bowl (or a T-fitting between the upper 2 carburetors) into one or more fittings on the intake manifold.

A vent jet (back draft) circuit is used on some early model 3-cylinder carburetors for improved mid-range fuel economy by controlling the pressure inside of the float chamber. **Table 4** lists which carburetors use vent jets and which carburetors do not. Carburetors without vent jets are still machined to accept vent jets. Removing the vent jet disables the back draft circuit and enriches the air/fuel mixture at mid-range speeds. Blocking the vent jet leans the air/fuel mixture at mid-range speeds and could cause power head failure.

NOTE
Each carburetor must be installed in the correct location according to its identi-

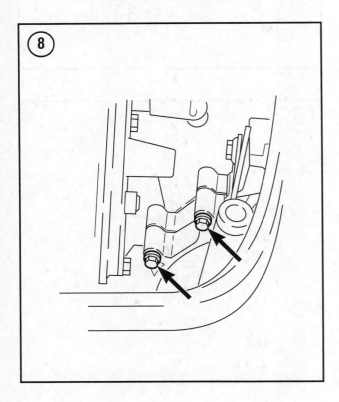

*fication number. See **Carburetor Identification** at the beginning of this section.*

On 4-cylinder models, the carburetors for cylinders 3 and 4 do not have an idle mixture adjustment screw. These engines idle on cylinders No. 1 and No. 2 only. The carburetors for cylinders No. 3 and No. 4 do not provide a combustible air/fuel mixture at engine speeds below approximately 1600-2000 rpm, due to the design of the idle and off-idle circuits. Cylinders No. 3 and No. 4 carburetors provide an air/fuel mixture at idle and off-idle speeds that is too lean for combustion to occur, yet adequate for proper engine lubrication. As the engine speed reaches approximately 1600-2000 rpm (depending on engine load), the air/fuel mixture to cylinders No. 3 and No. 4 becomes sufficient to support combustion and all 4 cylinders become operational.

An accelerator pump system injects fuel into the intake manifold of cylinders No. 3 and No. 4 during acceleration to prevent hesitation during the transition from 2-cylinder to 4-cylinder operation.

Figure 7 shows a typical WME carburetor.

Removal/Installation (75-125 hp and 65 and 80 Jet)

These models use 3 or 4 carburetors. Do not intermix components. Install each carburetor in its original location.

1. Disconnect the negative battery cable.
2. Disconnect and ground the spark plug leads to the power head.
3. Disconnect the lower cowl mounted trim and tilt switch bullet connectors.
4. Remove the water indicator (tattle-tale) hose from the top of the exhaust cover.
5. Remove the 2 inside lower cowl bolts from the rear of the engine (**Figure 8**) and the one outside cowl bolt from the port side of the engine just above the steering arm (**Figure 9**).

6. Loosen the port nut securing the front latch to the lower cowl (**Figure 10**). Remove both lower cowl halves from the engine.

7A. *3-cylinder models*—Remove 6 screws retaining the air intake cover. Remove the air intake cover.

7B. *4-cylinder models*—Remove the 8 screws retaining the air intake cover. Remove the air intake cover.

8. Remove the 2 bolts securing the voltage regulator to the top of the inner air intake plate. Do not disconnect the voltage regulator leads. Tape or tie-strap the voltage regulator out of the way.

9. Remove the upper and lower oil reservoir support bolts.

10. Disconnect the oil lines from the oil reservoir. Plug the lines and remove the reservoir.

11A. *3-cylinder models*—Remove the 2 air intake plate/carburetor mounting nuts and 4 bolts. Remove the air intake plate.

11B. *4-cylinder models*—Remove the 2 air intake plate/carburetor mounting nuts and 6 bolts. Remove the air intake plate.

12A. *3-cylinder models*—Disconnect the oil pump linkage from the center carburetor ball socket.

12B. *4-cylinder models*—Disconnect the oil pump linkage from the cylinder No. 2 carburetor ball socket.

13. Disconnect the fuel supply line from the top carburetor.

14. Disconnect the primer line from the top carburetor fuel bowl or T-fitting between the upper 2 carburetors.

15. *4-cylinder models*—Disconnect the accelerator pump fuel supply line from the T-fitting between the middle 2 carburetors.

16. Remove the carburetors as an assembly. Discard the carburetor base gaskets.

17. Separate the carburetors by disconnecting the fuel lines and throttle linkage from each carburetor.

18. To install the carburetors, connect the fuel lines and throttle linkages to each carburetor. Secure the fuel lines with new tie-straps.

19. Install new base gaskets over the carburetor mounting studs. The lowest cylinder uses bolts to secure the carburetor. The gasket must be inserted when the air intake plate and lower carburetor mounting bolts are installed.

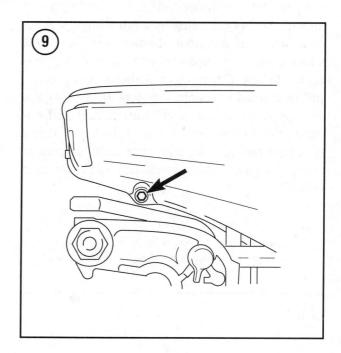

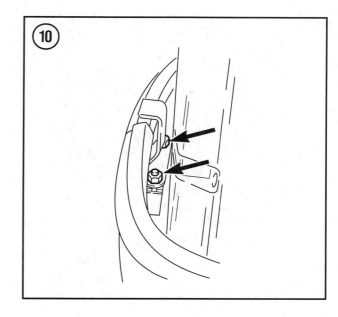

20. Install the carburetors as an assembly. Install the air intake plate. Install the 6 or 8 carburetor/air intake plate mounting nuts finger-tight.

21. Position the lower carburetor base gasket in place between the carburetor and intake manifold. Insert the lower carburetor mounting bolts through the air intake plate and lower carburetor making sure the bolts go through the gasket and the gasket is properly positioned.

22. Tighten the carburetor/air intake plate mounting hardware evenly to 100 in.-lb. (11.3 N.m).

23. Reconnect the fuel supply and primer lines. Secure the lines with new tie-straps.

24. *4-cylinder models*—Reconnect the accelerator pump fuel supply line. Secure the line with a new tie-strap.

25. Reconnect the oil pump linkage to the appropriate carburetor throttle arm.

26. Reinstall the oil reservoir and reconnect the oil lines. Refer to Chapter Eleven for bleeding procedures. All air must be bled from the system before restarting the engine.

27. Reinstall the voltage regulator. Make sure all ground leads are reconnected securely to ground.

28. Reinstall the air intake cover. Tighten the 6 or 8 screws securely.

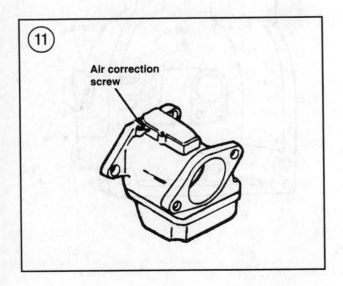

11

Air correction screw

29. Reinstall both lower cowls. Tighten the port nut securing the front latch to the lower cowl (**Figure 10**).

30. Install the 2 inside lower cowl bolts to the rear of the engine (**Figure 8**) and the one outside cowl bolt on the port side of the engine just above the steering arm (**Figure 9**). Tighten the bolts securely.

31. Install the water indicator (tattle-tale) hose to the top of the exhaust cover. Secure the hose with a new tie-strap.

32. Reconnect the lower cowl mounted trim and tilt switch bullet connectors.

33. Reconnect the spark plug leads to the spark plugs.

34. Reconnect the negative battery cable.

35. Refer to Chapter Five for carburetor and linkage adjustment procedures.

Disassembly

Refer to **Figure 7** for this procedure. On models with multiple carburetors, do not intermix components. Install each carburetor in its original location.

> *CAUTION*
> *Do not remove or attempt to adjust the air correction screw (**Figure 11**). This screw is preset by the manufacturer and never requires adjustment. Conventional carburetor cleaning solvents will not affect the sealant securing the screw adjustment. If the air correction screw has been tampered with, seal the threads with Loctite 271 threadlocking adhesive. Seat the screw lightly into the carburetor body, then back out the screw 1/4 turn.*

1. Remove the 4 screws securing the fuel bowl to the carburetor body. Remove the fuel bowl. Discard the fuel bowl gasket.

2. Remove the float pin, float and inlet needle.

3. Remove the main nozzle stem gasket (15, **Figure 7**).

6

4. Remove 2 screws securing the mixing chamber cover (**Figure 12**) to the carburetor body. Remove the cover and gasket. Discard the gasket.

NOTE
On 4-cylinder models, only the top carburetors (cylinders No. 1 and No. 2) are equipped with idle speed mixture screws. The bottom 2 carburetors have plugs installed in place of mixture screws. The plugs should be removed so the passages can be cleaned.

5. Remove the idle speed mixture screw and spring (**Figure 12**).

6. Remove the vent (back draft) jet, if so equipped (**Figure 12**).

7. Remove the main jet plug and gasket from the fuel bowl, then remove the main jet from the fuel bowl. Discard the gasket. See **Figure 13**.

CAUTION
Further disassembly is not necessary for normal cleaning and inspection. Proceed to Step 8 only if the throttle shaft or throttle valve requires replacement and parts are available. If the throttle shaft is not being removed, proceed directly to Step 10.

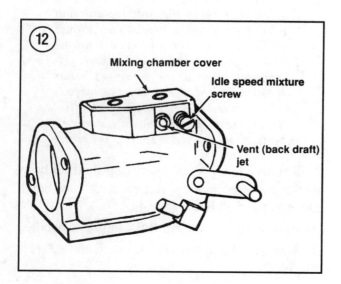

8. Inspect the throttle shaft and valve for excessive wear or damage. If throttle shaft or valve removal is necessary, remove the oil pump linkage arm on models so equipped.

9. Remove the E-clip from the end of the throttle shaft, then remove the 2 screws securing the throttle valve to the shaft. Remove the throttle valve, then pull the shaft from the carburetor body.

10. Refer to *Cleaning and Inspection—All Models* in this chapter.

Reassembly

Refer to **Figure 7** for this procedure. On models with multiple carburetors, do not intermix components. Install each carburetor in its original location.

1. If removed, insert the throttle shaft into the carburetor body. Make sure the throttle shaft

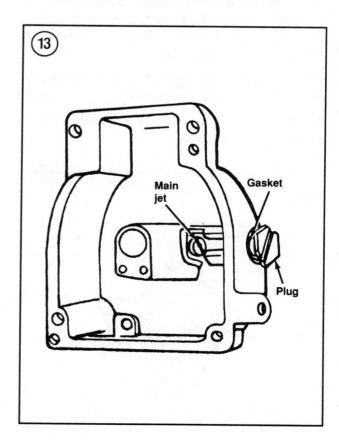

return spring is properly engaged with the throttle lever and the boss on the carburetor body. Position the throttle plate in its original orientation in the throttle bore.

2. Apply Loctite 271 threadlocking adhesive to the threads of the throttle valve screws, then install the screws finger-tight.

3. Install the E-clip onto the end of the throttle shaft. Check the alignment of the throttle plate. Make sure the throttle plate opens and closes fully without binding. Adjust throttle plate posi-

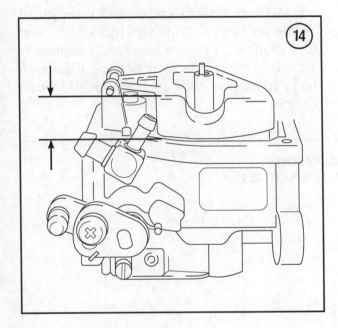

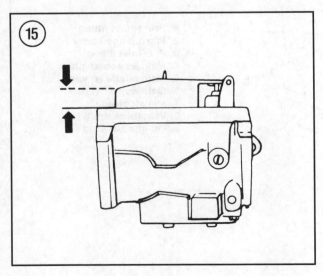

tion as necessary and tighten the throttle plate screws to 6 in.-lb. (0.7 N•m).

4. If so equipped, install the oil pump linkage arm. Tighten the retaining screw securely.

5. Install the main jet into the fuel bowl. Using a new gasket, install the fuel bowl plug (**Figure 13**). Tighten the fuel bowl plug to 33 in.-lb. (11.3 N•m).

6. Install the vent (back draft) jet on models so equipped (**Figure 12**).

NOTE
On 4-cylinder models, carburetors No. 3 and No. 4 do not have idle mixture screws. Make sure the plugs are installed in the idle mixture screw holes.

7. Install the idle speed mixture screw and spring. Turn the screw in until lightly seated, then back out to specification (**Table 1**).

8. Install the mixing chamber cover using a new gasket. Tighten the cover screws to 18 in.-lb. (2.0 N•m).

9. Install a new main nozzle stem gasket (15, **Figure 7**).

10. Attach the inlet needle wire clip over the float's metal tab. Install the float, making sure the inlet needle properly enters the inlet valve seat. Install the float pin.

11. With the float bowl removed and the carburetor inverted, measure the float height. Refer to **Table 1** for specifications. Refer to **Figure 14** for models requiring float levels of 35/64-37/64 in. (13.89-14.68 mm) and **Figure 15** for models requiring float levels of 27/64-29/64 in. (10.72-11.51 mm). If adjustment is necessary, carefully bend the float's metal tab as necessary.

12. Install the float bowl using a new gasket. Tighten the bowl screws evenly to 18 in.-lb. (2.0 N•m).

6

WMH AND WMV SERIES CARBURETORS (135-225 HP AND 105-140 JET MODELS)

WMH and WMV carburetors are 2-barrel, single fuel bowl carburetors used on all V6 models except the 275 hp. The intake manifolds on these engines *crosses* the air/fuel charge coming from the carburetor. The starboard side of the carburetor meters fuel to the port cylinders and the port side of the carburetor meters fuel to the starboard cylinders.

These carburetors are equipped with a vent (back draft) circuit designed to lean the air/fuel mixture at mid-range speeds for improved fuel economy. There is one vent jet per carburetor. Removing the vent jet disables the back draft circuit and enriches the air/fuel mixture at mid-range speeds. Blocking the vent jet leans the air/fuel mixture at mid-range speeds and could cause power head failure.

The throttle plates and the throttle shaft are not serviceable on WMH and WMV carburetors. Do not attempt to remove them.

NOTE
*Each carburetor must be installed in the correct location according to its identification number. See **Carburetor Identification** at the beginning of this section.*

WMH carburetors incorporate 2 main jets, 2 off-idle air bleeds, 2 off-idle fuel jets, 1 vent (back draft) jet, 1 idle air bleed and 2 adjustable idle mixture screws with limit caps. **Figure 16** shows an external view of a typical WMH carburetor.

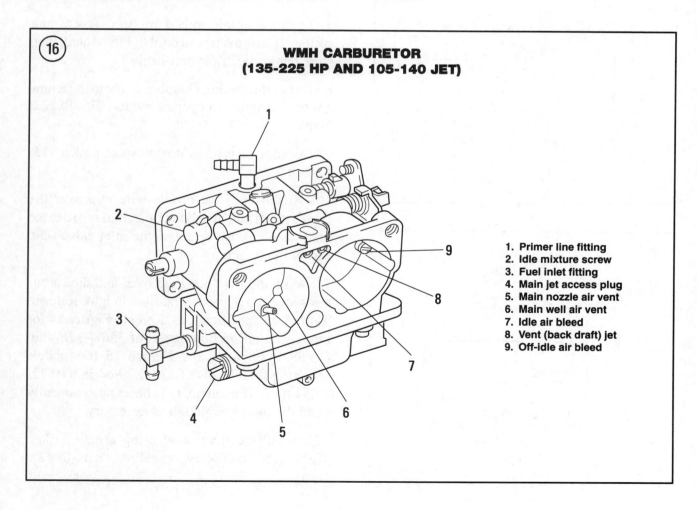

16

**WMH CARBURETOR
(135-225 HP AND 105-140 JET)**

1. Primer line fitting
2. Idle mixture screw
3. Fuel inlet fitting
4. Main jet access plug
5. Main nozzle air vent
6. Main well air vent
7. Idle air bleed
8. Vent (back draft) jet
9. Off-idle air bleed

WMV carburetors incorporate 2 main jets, 2 idle air bleeds, 1 vent (back draft) jet and 2 adjustable idle mixture screws with limit caps. WMV carburetors have removable top covers that allow easy cleaning and inspection of the metering circuits. **Figure 17** shows an external view of a typical WMV carburetor.

Main jets always meter fuel flow. Decreasing the main jet size will lean the air/fuel mixture and increasing the main jet size will enrichen the air/fuel mixture.

Off-idle fuel jets on the WMH series carburetors meter fuel flow. Decreasing the jet size will lean the off-idle air/fuel mixture and increasing the jet size will enrichen the off-idle air/fuel mixture. The off-idle fuel jets are not normally adjusted or changed in the field.

Air bleeds and vent (back draft) jets meter air flow. Decreasing the air bleed or vent jet size will enrichen the air/fuel mixture and increasing the air bleed or vent jet size will lean the air/fuel mixture (for the circuit the air bleed or vent is located on).

A thermal air valve is used on 135-200 hp and 105 and 140 Jet models to automatically enrichen the idle circuits of the carburetors whenever the engine temperature is below 100° F (38° C). The thermal valve is mounted in the starboard cylinder head just below the No. 3 spark plug. The valve has 2 ports. One is connected to each carburetor through a series of fittings on the carburetor bodies. The other port is open to the atmosphere. When the engine temperature is below 100° F (38° C), the valve will be closed, preventing air from entering the idle circuits and

6

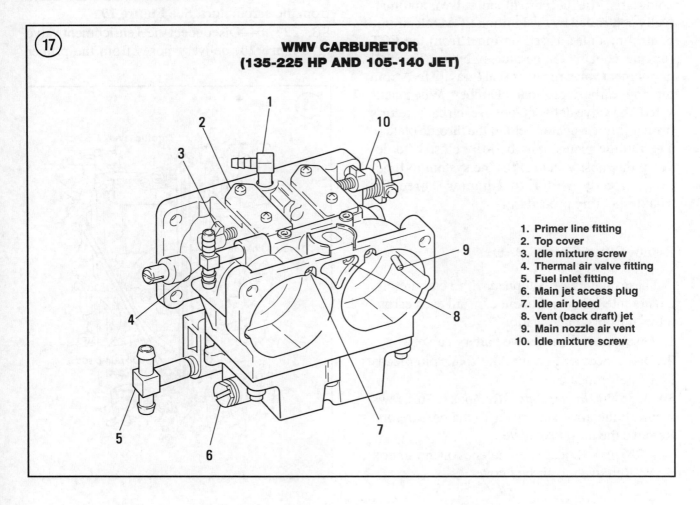

(17)
WMV CARBURETOR
(135-225 HP AND 105-140 JET)

1. Primer line fitting
2. Top cover
3. Idle mixture screw
4. Thermal air valve fitting
5. Fuel inlet fitting
6. Main jet access plug
7. Idle air bleed
8. Vent (back draft) jet
9. Main nozzle air vent
10. Idle mixture screw

causing a richer air/fuel mixture. When the temperature is above 100° F (38° C), the valve will be open, allowing air to enter the idle circuits, providing the normally calibrated air/fuel mixture. Refer to Chapter Three for troubleshooting procedures.

These models also use an electric fuel primer valve to enrichen the air/fuel mixture whenever the fuel primer valve is engaged by the operator. This system delivers fuel to the middle and lower carburetors only. The throttle plates must be fully closed (to develop the most vacuum) for the system to function correctly. Refer to Chapter Three for operational information and troubleshooting procedures on the electric fuel primer valve.

A fuel enrichment valve is used on 225 hp models to enrichen the air/fuel mixture during cold starts. The fuel enrichment valve is automatically controlled by the ignition ECM (electronic control module), based on input from the ECT (engine coolant temperature) sensor. The fuel enrichment valve receives fuel (gravity fed) from the top carburetor float chamber. When activated, the valve delivers fuel to each carburetor's primer fitting (located behind the throttle plates). The throttle plates must be fully closed (to develop the most vacuum) for the system to function correctly. Refer to Chapter Three for troubleshooting procedures.

Removal/Installation

These models are equipped with 3 carburetors. Do not intermix components. Install each carburetor in its original location.

1. Disconnect the negative battery cable.

2. Disconnect and ground the spark plug leads to the power head.

3A. *135-200 hp and Jets*—Remove the 6 screws securing the air intake cover to the carburetors. Remove the air intake cover.

3B. *225 hp*—Release the 2 latches on the air box cover. Remove the air box cover.

4. *225 hp*—Remove the 6 screws securing the air intake plate to the carburetors. Remove the air intake plate.

5. Carefully pry the throttle linkage away from the throttle lever at each carburetor (**Figure 18**, typical).

6A. *135-200 hp and Jets*—Disconnect the oil pump control rod (**Figure 18**) from the bottom carburetor throttle lever.

6B. *225 hp (1994-1995 models)*—If the oil pump control rod interferes with carburetor removal, disconnect the oil pump control rod from the throttle cam.

7. Disconnect the fuel supply hose from the top carburetor. Disconnect the upper and lower fuel supply hoses interconnecting all 3 carburetors.

8A. *135-200 hp and Jets*—Disconnect the fuel primer valve hose and thermal air valve hoses from the carburetors. See **Figure 19**.

8B. *225 hp*—Disconnect the 3 enrichment valve (1, **Figure 20**) delivery hoses from the primer

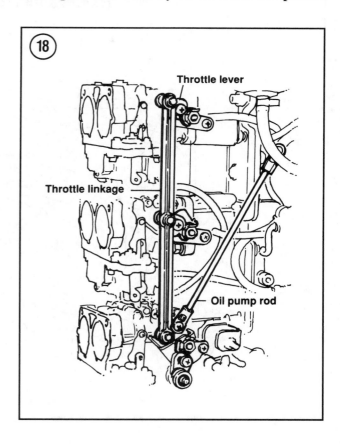

⑱

Throttle lever

Throttle linkage

Oil pump rod

fitting on the top of each carburetor mounting flange. Disconnect the enrichment valve supply hose (2, **Figure 20**) from the top carburetor's float chamber.

9. Remove 2 nuts and 2 Allen screws from each carburetor to be removed. Remove the carburetor(s). Remove and discard the carburetor base gasket(s).

10. To reinstall the carburetor(s), place new carburetor gaskets onto the mounting studs and install the carburetor(s) in their original locations.

11. Install the nuts and Allen screws and tighten evenly to 70 in.-lb. (8.0 N•m).

12. Reconnect the fuel supply hose to the top carburetor. Reconnect the upper and lower fuel supply hoses interconnecting all three carburetors. Secure all connections with new tie-straps.

13A. *135-200 hp and Jets*—Connect the fuel primer valve hose and thermal air valve hoses to

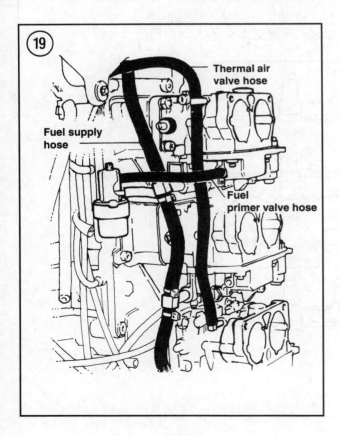

the carburetors as shown in **Figure 19**. Secure all connections with new tie-straps.

13B. *225 hp*—Connect the enrichment valve supply hose to the top carburetor's float chamber. Connect the 3 enrichment valve delivery hoses to the primer fittings on top of each carburetor mounting flange. See **Figure 20**. Secure the supply hose connection (2, **Figure 20**) with a new tie-strap.

14. Install the throttle linkage (**Figure 18**, typical).

15A. *135-200 hp and Jets*—Reconnect the oil pump control rod (**Figure 18**) to the bottom carburetor throttle lever.

15B. *225 hp (1994-1995 models)*—If the oil pump control rod was removed, reconnect the oil pump control rod to the throttle cam.

16A. *135-200 hp and Jets*—Install the air intake cover to the carburetors and secure the cover with 6 screws. Tighten the 6 screws securely.

16B. *225 hp*—Install the air intake plate to the carburetors and secure the plate with 6 screws. Tighten the screws to 70 in.-lb. (7.9 N•m).

17. *225 hp*—Install the air box cover. Secure the 2 latches on the air box cover.

18. Reconnect the spark plug leads to the spark plugs.

19. Reconnect the negative battery cable.

20. Refer to Chapter Five for carburetor and linkage adjustment procedures.

Disassembly

Refer to **Figure 21** for WMH models and **Figure 22** for WMV models. If disassembling 2 or more carburetors, be sure to keep individual components with their respective carburetors. Do not interchange parts between carburetor assemblies.

CAUTION
*Do not attempt to adjust the air trim (calibration) screws (**Figure 23**) on WMH carburetors. These screws are preset by the manufacturer and never*

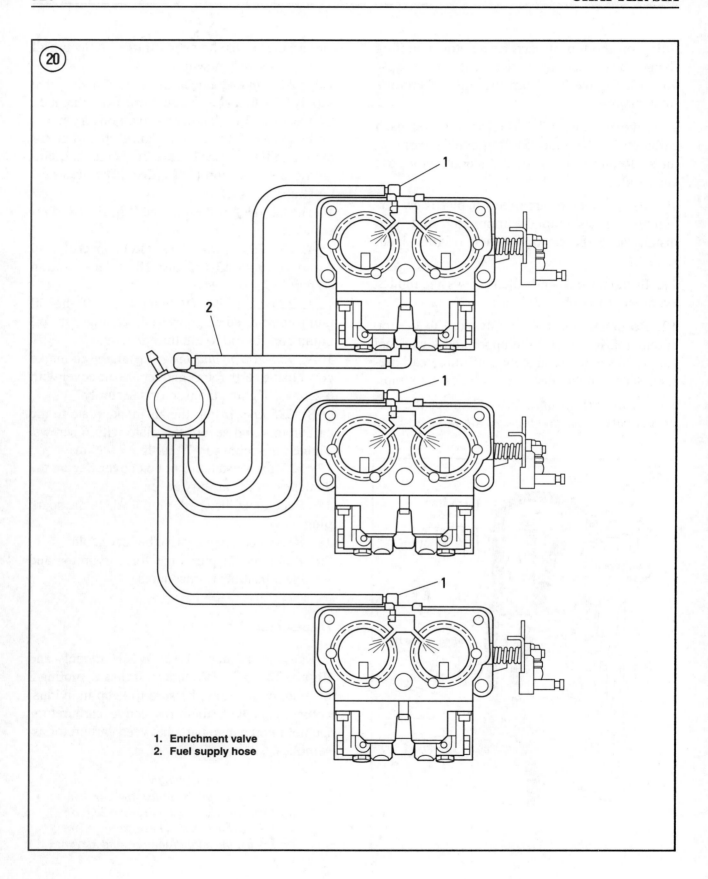

1. Enrichment valve
2. Fuel supply hose

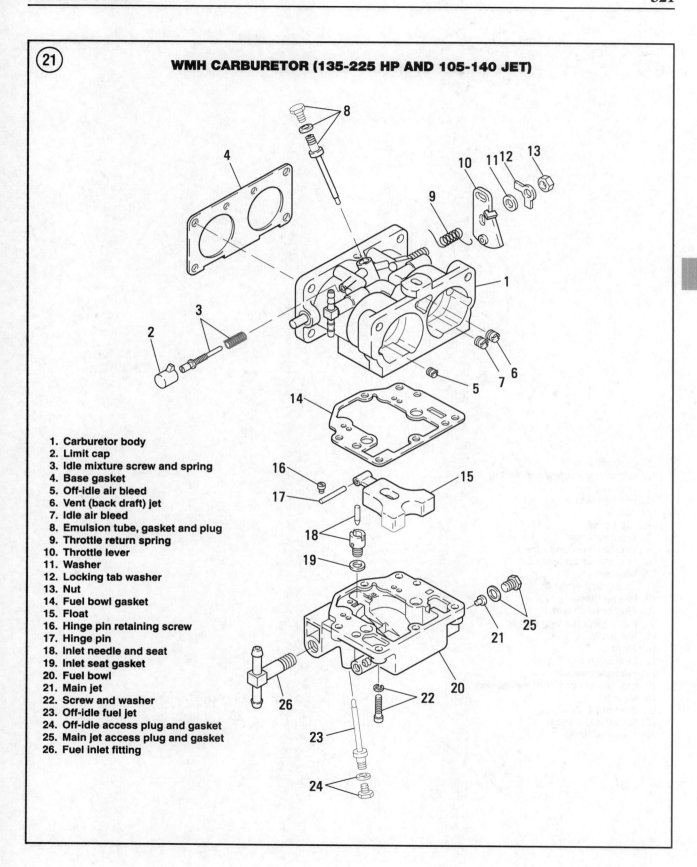

6

WMH CARBURETOR (135-225 HP AND 105-140 JET)

1. Carburetor body
2. Limit cap
3. Idle mixture screw and spring
4. Base gasket
5. Off-idle air bleed
6. Vent (back draft) jet
7. Idle air bleed
8. Emulsion tube, gasket and plug
9. Throttle return spring
10. Throttle lever
11. Washer
12. Locking tab washer
13. Nut
14. Fuel bowl gasket
15. Float
16. Hinge pin retaining screw
17. Hinge pin
18. Inlet needle and seat
19. Inlet seat gasket
20. Fuel bowl
21. Main jet
22. Screw and washer
23. Off-idle fuel jet
24. Off-idle access plug and gasket
25. Main jet access plug and gasket
26. Fuel inlet fitting

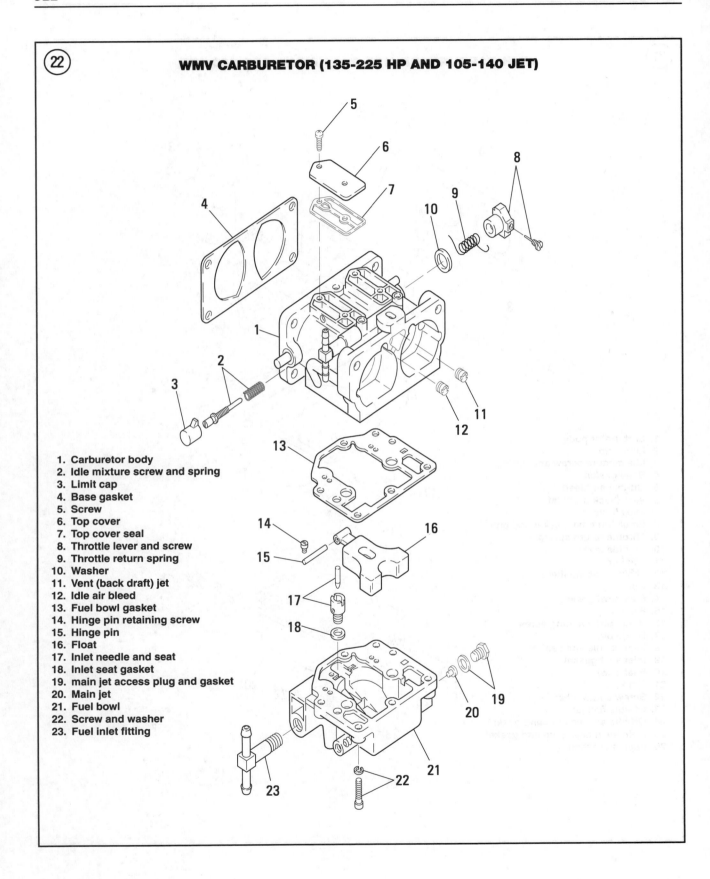

WMV CARBURETOR (135-225 HP AND 105-140 JET)

1. Carburetor body
2. Idle mixture screw and spring
3. Limit cap
4. Base gasket
5. Screw
6. Top cover
7. Top cover seal
8. Throttle lever and screw
9. Throttle return spring
10. Washer
11. Vent (back draft) jet
12. Idle air bleed
13. Fuel bowl gasket
14. Hinge pin retaining screw
15. Hinge pin
16. Float
17. Inlet needle and seat
18. Inlet seat gasket
19. main jet access plug and gasket
20. Main jet
21. Fuel bowl
22. Screw and washer
23. Fuel inlet fitting

require additional adjustment. Conventional carburetor cleaning solvents will not affect the sealant securing the screw adjustment. If the air trim screws have been tampered with, seal the threads with Loctite 271 threadlocking adhesive. Seat the screws lightly into the carburetor body, then back out the screws 1-1/4 turn. Install new welch plugs to cover the screws and prevent further tampering.

NOTE
The WMH carburetors used on 225 hp models are not equipped with a removable emulsion tube.

1A. *WMH models*—Remove the emulsion tube plug and gasket. Remove the emulsion tube (135-200 hp models).

1B. *WMV models*—Remove the 4 top cover screws. Remove both top covers and the seals. Discard both seals.

2. Carefully pry off the idle mixture limit caps. Count the turns required to seat each idle mixture needle lightly in the carburetor body. Record the figures for reassembly.

3. Remove the idle mixture screws and springs. Mark the components for reassembly in their original location.

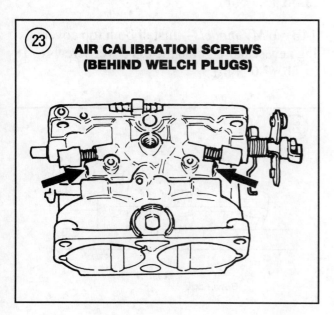

(23) **AIR CALIBRATION SCREWS (BEHIND WELCH PLUGS)**

4. Remove the main jet access plugs and gaskets, then remove the main jets. Discard the gaskets.

5. *WMH models*—Remove the off-idle access plugs and gaskets. Then remove the off idle jets (23, **Figure 21**). Discard the gaskets.

6A. *WMH models*—Remove the off-idle air bleeds, the idle air bleed and the vent jet. See **Figure 16**.

6B. *WMV models*—Remove the idle air bleeds and the vent jet. See **Figure 17**.

7. Remove 6 screws securing the fuel bowl to the carburetor body. Separate the fuel bowl from the body. Remove and discard the fuel bowl gasket.

8. Remove the hinge pin retaining screw. Lift the float and hinge pin out of the float bowl.

9. Remove the inlet needle. Remove the inlet valve seat using a wide-blade screwdriver. Remove and discard the seat gasket.

NOTE
Further disassembly is not required for normal cleaning and inspection. If the throttle shaft is excessively worn or damaged, the carburetor must be replaced. Should it become necessary to remove the air calibration screws for carburetor cleaning, continue at Step 10. If not, proceed directly to Step 12.

CAUTION
*The air calibration screws located behind the 2 welch plugs (**Figure 23**) are preset at the factory for optimum performance and efficiency. The screws do not require removal for normal cleaning and should not be tampered with or adjusted from the factory setting. However, if the screws **must** be removed for carburetor cleaning, turn the screws inward and record the number of turns required to seat the screws lightly **prior** to removal.*

10. If absolutely necessary, carefully drill a small hole into the center of the air trim screw welch plugs (**Figure 23**), then pry the welch plugs out using a small punch or similar tool.

11. Turn the air trim (calibration) screws inward, while counting the number of turns required to seat the screws lightly. Record the number of turns for reassembly, then remove the air trim screws. Mark the components for reassembly in their original location.

12. Refer to *Cleaning and Inspection—All Models* at the beginning of the carburetor section.

Reassembly

Refer to **Figure 21** for WMH models and **Figure 22** for WMV models.

1. *WMH models*—If the air trim screws were removed, coat the screw threads with Loctite 271 threadlocking adhesive. Install the screws and thread them inward until they are lightly seated in the carburetor body. Back the screws out to the setting noted on disassembly. If the setting was not noted or the screws have been tampered with, set the screws to 1-1/4 turns out from a lightly seated position.

2. Install new welch plugs to cover the air trim screws. Place new welch plugs into the screw bores (convex side facing outward). Using a hammer and an appropriately sized punch, carefully flatten the plugs to provide a tight seal. Seal the plug and area around the plug with a light coat of fingernail polish.

3. Using a new gasket, install the inlet valve seat into the float bowl with a wide blade screwdriver. Be careful not to damage the inlet valve seat.

4. Place the inlet valve needle into the valve seat.

5. Insert the hinge pin into the float. Install the float and hinge pin assembly into the float bowl and secure with the hinge pin retaining screw.

6. Invert the float bowl and place a machinist's scale or a straightedge across the float bowl as shown in **Figure 24**. The float should be flush with the float bowl mating surface.

7. If adjustment is necessary, carefully bend the float's metal tab as necessary.

8. Invert the carburetor body and place a new float bowl gasket onto the body. Install the fuel bowl and the 6 fuel bowl screws. Tighten the screws evenly to 26 in.-lb. (2.9 N•m).

9. Install the main jets. Install the main jet access plugs using new gaskets. Tighten the access plugs to 33 in.-lb. (3.7 N•m).

10. *WMH models*—Install the off-idle jets. Install the off-idle access plugs using new gaskets. Tighten the access plugs to 33 in.-lb. (3.7 N•m).

11A. *WMH models*—Install the off-idle air bleeds, the idle air bleed and the vent jet. See **Figure 16**.

11B. *WMV models*—Install the idle air bleeds and the vent jet. See **Figure 17**.

12. Install the idle mixture screws and springs. Turn the screws inward until lightly seated. Back out the screws to the setting noted on disassembly, or to specification listed in **Table 1**.

13. Install the idle mixture screw limit caps with tabs pointing straight up.

14A. *WMH models*—Install the emulsion tube (135-200 hp models). Install the emulsion tube plug using a new gasket. Tighten the plug to 33 in.-lb. (3.7 N•m).

14B. *WMV models*—Install both top covers using new seals. Tighten the top cover screws to 18 in.-lb. (2.0 N•m).

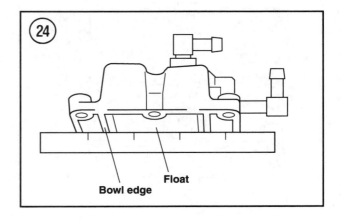

Float

Bowl edge

WO SERIES (MERCARB) CARBURETOR (275 HP)

Six MerCarb center bowl carburetors are used on 275 hp models. The induction system on these engines *crosses* the air/fuel charge coming from each carburetor. The starboard side of the carburetor meters fuel to the port cylinders and the port side of the carburetor meters fuel to the starboard cylinders. Idle, mid-range and high speed mixtures are controlled by fixed jets. There are no idle mixture adjustment screws.

These carburetors are equipped with a vent (back draft) circuit designed to lean the air/fuel mixture at mid-range speeds for improved fuel economy. There is one vent jet per carburetor. Removing the vent jet disables the back draft circuit and enrichens the air/fuel mixture at mid-range speeds. Blocking the vent jet leans the air/fuel mixture at mid-range speeds and could cause power head failure.

An electric fuel primer valve is used to enrichen the air/fuel mixture whenever the fuel primer valve is engaged by the operator. This system delivers fuel from carburetors No. 1 and No. 3 to all 6 intake manifold fittings. The throttle plates must be fully closed (to develop the most vacuum) for the system to function correctly. Refer to Chapter Three for operational information and troubleshooting procedures on the electric fuel primer valve.

NOTE
*Each carburetor must be installed in the correct location according to its identification number. See **Carburetor Identification** at the beginning of this section. The location number indicates the installed position of the carburetor on the power head (not the cylinder number), numbered from top (No. 1) to bottom (No. 6).*

Removal/Installation

1. Disconnect the negative battery cable.

2. Disconnect and ground the spark plug leads to the power head.

3. Remove the remote fuel tank connector from the lower cowl support bracket.

4. Remove the air intake cover. Replace the gasket if it is damaged or deteriorated.

5. Remove the 12 nuts securing the air intake plate to the carburetors. Remove the air intake plate and lower cowl support bracket as an assembly.

6. Disconnect the carburetors fuel supply hose from the upper fuel pump.

7. Disconnect the fuel primer valve hoses from the No. 1 and No. 3 carburetors.

8A. *Individual carburetors*—Disconnect the fuel hose(s) and throttle linkage from the carburetor(s) being removed. Remove the carburetor(s) from the power head.

8B. *All carburetors*—Remove the 6 carburetors along with the throttle linkage and fuel hoses as an assembly. Remove the throttle linkage and fuel hoses to separate carburetors.

9. Discard the base gaskets. Clean any old gasket material from the carburetors and intake manifolds.

10. To install the carburetors, begin by connecting the fuel lines and throttle linkages to the carburetors. Make sure each carburetor is in the correct position based on the carburetor identification number. Secure all fuel line connections with new tie-straps.

11. Place new carburetor base gaskets onto the carburetor mounting studs. Install the carburetor(s) as an assembly over the mounting studs. Seat the carburetors against the intake manifolds.

12. Connect the fuel supply hose to the upper fuel pump. Securely clamp the hose with a new tie-strap.

13. Connect the fuel primer valve supply hoses to the float bowl fittings on the No. 1 and No. 3 carburetors. Secure the hose connections with new tie-straps.

6

14. Reinstall the air intake plate. Install the 12 flat washers and nuts. Tighten the nuts evenly to 60 in.-lb. (6.8 N•m).

15. Install the air intake cover and gasket. Apply a suitable thread locking compound to the threads of the cover screws. Tighten the cover screws to 60 in.-lb. (6.8 N•m).

16. Apply Loctite 242 threadlocking adhesive to the remote fuel tank connector mounting screw. Install the connector to the lower cowl bracket and tighten the screw to 60 in.-lb. (6.8 N•m).

17. Reconnect the spark plug leads to the spark plugs.

18. Reconnect the negative battery cable.

19. Refer to Chapter Five for carburetor and linkage adjustment procedures.

Disassembly

Refer to **Figure 25** for this procedure. Be sure to note the size and location of each jet during disassembly. If disassembling 2 or more carburetors, keep all individual components with their respective carburetors. Do not interchange parts between carburetor assemblies.

1. Remove the 4 screws securing the top cover to the carburetor. Remove the top cover and gasket. Discard the gasket.

2. Remove the main jet carrier plug and gasket from the float bowl. Discard the gasket. Remove the main jet from the carrier plug.

3. Remove the idle jet access plug and gasket from the carburetor body. Discard the gasket. Remove the idle jet from the carburetor body.

4. Remove the 4 screws securing the fuel bowl to the carburetor body. Remove the fuel bowl and gasket. Discard the gasket.

5. Remove the float pin (1, **Figure 26**), then lift off the float (2, **Figure 26**).

6. Remove the float lever pin (3, **Figure 26**) and float lever.

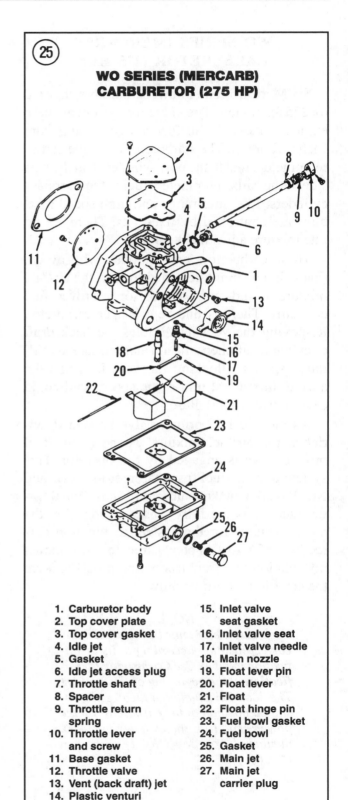

(25)

WO SERIES (MERCARB) CARBURETOR (275 HP)

1. Carburetor body
2. Top cover plate
3. Top cover gasket
4. Idle jet
5. Gasket
6. Idle jet access plug
7. Throttle shaft
8. Spacer
9. Throttle return spring
10. Throttle lever and screw
11. Base gasket
12. Throttle valve
13. Vent (back draft) jet
14. Plastic venturi
15. Inlet valve seat gasket
16. Inlet valve seat
17. Inlet valve needle
18. Main nozzle
19. Float lever pin
20. Float lever
21. Float
22. Float hinge pin
23. Fuel bowl gasket
24. Fuel bowl
25. Gasket
26. Main jet
27. Main jet carrier plug

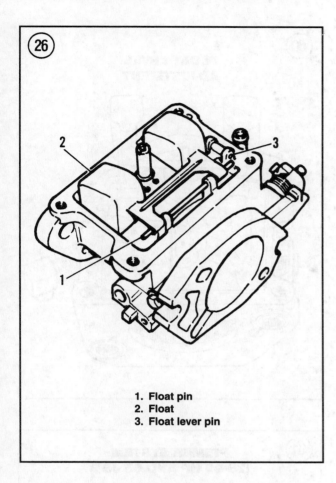

1. Float pin
2. Float
3. Float lever pin

7. Remove the inlet valve needle. Remove the inlet valve seat using an appropriate size wrench. Remove and discard the inlet valve seat gasket.

8. Remove the main nozzle (**Figure 27**) from the carburetor body. Once the nozzle is removed, remove the plastic venturi from the carburetor throat.

9. Remove the vent (back draft) jet from the carburetor body.

NOTE
Further disassembly is not necessary for normal carburetor cleaning and inspection. If the throttle shaft requires removal, proceed to Step 10. If not, proceed directly to Step 13.

10. Remove the 2 screws securing the throttle valve to the throttle shaft. Remove the valve.

11. Remove the throttle lever retaining screw, then slide the throttle lever off the shaft. Remove the return spring and spacer. See **Figure 28**.

6

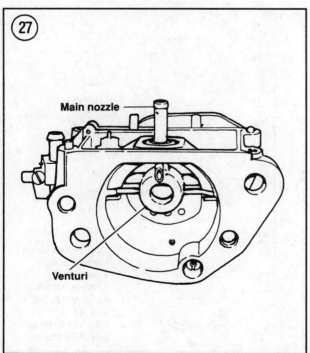

Main nozzle

Venturi

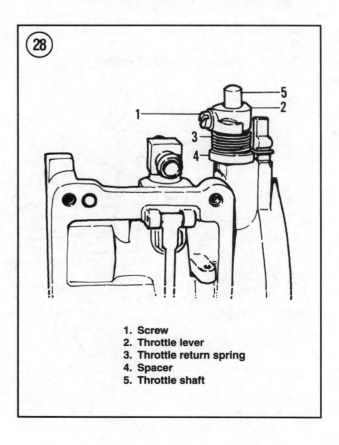

1. Screw
2. Throttle lever
3. Throttle return spring
4. Spacer
5. Throttle shaft

12. Pull the throttle shaft from the carburetor body to complete disassembly.

13. Refer to *Cleaning and Inspection—All Models* in this chapter.

Reassembly

1. If removed, insert the throttle shaft into the carburetor body. Place the plastic spacer over the throttle shaft, then install the return spring, throttle lever and lever retaining screw. Tighten the screw securely. See **Figure 28**.

2. Position the throttle plate in its original orientation in the throttle bore. Apply Loctite 271 threadlocking adhesive to the threads of the throttle valve screws, then install the screws finger-tight.

3. Check the alignment of the throttle plate. Make sure the throttle plate opens and closes fully without binding. Adjust throttle plate posi-

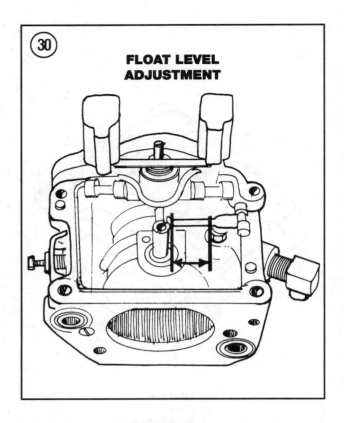

(30) **FLOAT LEVEL ADJUSTMENT**

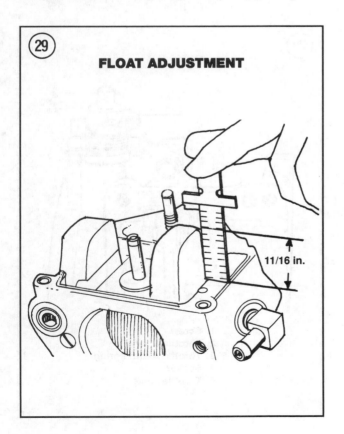

(29) **FLOAT ADJUSTMENT**

11/16 in.

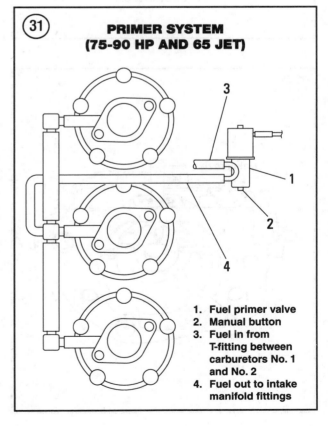

(31) **PRIMER SYSTEM (75-90 HP AND 65 JET)**

3
1
2
4

1. Fuel primer valve
2. Manual button
3. Fuel in from T-fitting between carburetors No. 1 and No. 2
4. Fuel out to intake manifold fittings

tion as necessary and tighten the throttle plate screws to 6 in.-lb. (0.7 N•m).

4. Place the plastic venturi into the carburetor throat, then install the main nozzle. See **Figure 27**.

5. Using a new gasket, install the inlet valve seat into the carburetor body. Tighten the seat securely. Place the inlet needle into the seat.

6. Install the float lever and secure with the lever pin. Push the pin into position until the knurled end is flush with the mount (**Figure 26**).

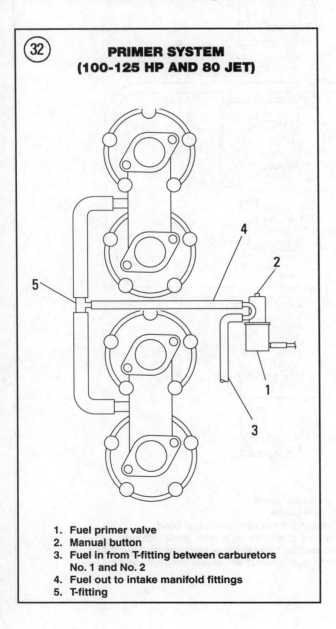

PRIMER SYSTEM (100-125 HP AND 80 JET)

1. Fuel primer valve
2. Manual button
3. Fuel in from T-fitting between carburetors No. 1 and No. 2
4. Fuel out to intake manifold fittings
5. T-fitting

7. Install the float and secure with the float pin (**Figure 26**).

8. Invert the carburetor and measure the float level as shown in **Figure 29**. The measurement should be 11/16 in. (17.5 mm). If adjustment is necessary, carefully bend the float lever in the area shown in **Figure 30**.

9. Recheck the float level. Readjust as necessary.

10. Place a new fuel bowl gasket onto the carburetor body. Install the fuel bowl. Tighten the 4 fuel bowl screws evenly and securely.

11. Install the main jet into the main jet carrier plug. Using a new gasket, install the main jet carrier plug assembly into the fuel bowl. Tighten the carrier plug securely.

12. Install the vent (back draft) jet into the carburetor body.

13. Install the idle jet into the carburetor body. Place a new gasket onto the idle jet access plug and install the access plug. Tighten the access plug securely.

14. Install the top cover with a new gasket. Tighten the 4 screws securely.

FUEL PRIMER VALVE (75-200 HP, 275 HP AND 65-140 JET [REMOTE CONTROL MODELS])

The electrically operated fuel primer valve provides additional fuel for easier cold starts. Fuel is gravity fed from the top carburetor (or pressure fed from the fuel pump) to the fuel primer valve. When the ignition switch is held in the CHOKE or PRIME position, the valve opens and allows fuel to flow to the carburetor(s), intake manifold fitting(s) or balance tube(s), depending on model. The valve can be operated manually by depressing and holding the button located on the valve. Typical fuel primer valve system hose routing is shown in **Figures 31-34**. Refer to Chapter Three for electrical troubleshooting procedures.

6

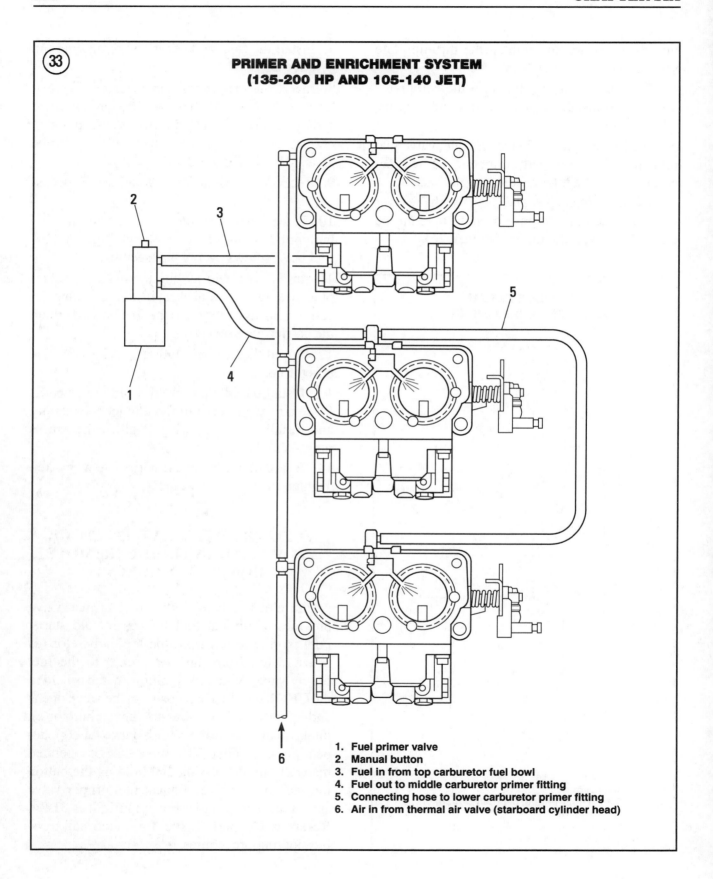

**PRIMER AND ENRICHMENT SYSTEM
(135-200 HP AND 105-140 JET)**

1. Fuel primer valve
2. Manual button
3. Fuel in from top carburetor fuel bowl
4. Fuel out to middle carburetor primer fitting
5. Connecting hose to lower carburetor primer fitting
6. Air in from thermal air valve (starboard cylinder head)

Fuel Primer Valve Replacement

1. Disconnect the fuel primer valve yellow/black lead at the engine wiring harness bullet connector.

2. Disconnect the 2 fuel lines from the valve.

3. Remove the bolt holding the clamp around the valve and the black ground wire. Remove the valve from the clamp.

4. To install the fuel primer valve, position the clamp around the fuel primer valve. Install the bolt through the clamp and ground wire. Secure the clamp, ground wire and valve assembly to the power head. Tighten the bolt securely.

5. Reconnect the 2 fuel lines to the valve. Secure the fuel lines with new tie-straps.

6. Reconnect the fuel primer valve yellow/black leads to the engine wiring harness bullet connector.

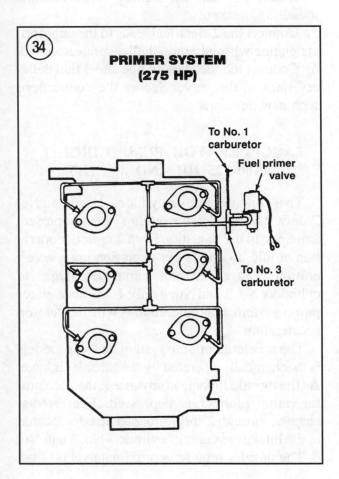

**PRIMER SYSTEM
(275 HP)**

To No. 1 carburetor

Fuel primer valve

To No. 3 carburetor

THERMAL AIR VALVE (135-200 HP CARBURETED MODELS)

The thermal air valve is installed in the starboard cylinder (below the No. 3 spark plug). See **Figure 35**. During cold engine operation (below 100° F), the thermal air valve closes, causing an air restriction to the idle circuits of all three carburetors. This restriction results in a richer mixture, eliminating the need to activate the enrichment circuit periodically to keep the engine running. When the engine warms up, the thermal air valve opens, permitting normal fuel metering. Refer to Chapter Three for troubleshooting procedures.

6

Thermal Air Valve Replacement

NOTE
One port of the thermal air valve is always open to the atmosphere.

1. Disconnect the air line from the thermal air valve.

2. Unscrew the thermal air valve from the cylinder head with a wrench.

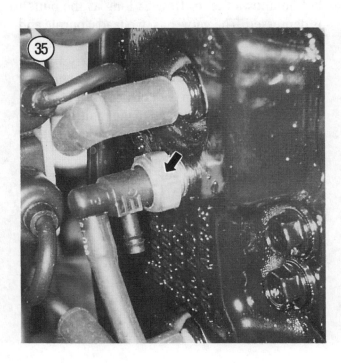

3. Lightly coat the threads of the thermal air valve with Quicksilver Perfect Seal.

4. Install the thermal air valve into the cylinder head and tighten it securely.

5. Reconnect the air line to the thermal air valve outer port as shown in **Figure 35**.

FUEL ENRICHMENT VALVE (225 HP CARBURETED MODELS)

The fuel enrichment valve on the 225 hp carbureted models is controlled by the ignition ECM (electronic control module), based on input from the ECT (engine coolant temperature) sensor. The fuel enrichment valve receives fuel (gravity fed) from the top carburetor float chamber. When activated, the valve delivers fuel to each carburetor's primer fitting (located behind the throttle plates). See **Figure 36**. The throttle plates must be fully closed (to develop the most vacuum) for the system to function correctly.

The fuel enrichment valve is a simple solenoid valve. It can only open and close. A button on the valve allows manual operation should the electrical portion of the valve fail. Depressing the button allows fuel to flow as long as the button is depressed. The valve has two leads, purple and yellow/black. The purple lead is battery positive voltage from the ignition switch. Battery voltage should be present at the purple lead connector any time the ignition switch is ON. The yellow/black lead is connected to the ignition ECM. The ECM grounds the yellow/black lead to activate the valve.

The ECM operates the valve in two modes: ECT temperature below 122° F (50° C) or ECT temperature above 122° F (50° C).

When the ECT indicates temperatures below 122° F (50° C) the ECM will activate the valve for 2-3 seconds each time the ignition is switched on and the engine is not started. If the engine is cranking or running, the ECM will reopen the valve (or keep the valve open) until the ECT indicates 122° F (50° C).

When the ECT indicates temperatures above 122° F (50° C), the ECM will activate the valve for approximately 1/2 second each time the key is turned on, but will not activate the valve when the engine is cranking or running.

Refer to Chapter Three for troubleshooting procedures.

Fuel Enrichment Valve Replacement

Refer to **Figure 36** for this procedure. Note that the large fitting of the valve is always open to the atmosphere.

1. Disconnect the fuel supply line and 3 fuel delivery lines from the valve.

2. Disconnect the 2 electrical leads from the engine wiring harness bullet connectors.

3. Remove the valve from the mounting bracket.

4. Install the fuel enrichment valve into the mounting bracket.

5. Connect the 2 electrical leads to the appropriate engine wiring harness bullet connectors.

6. Connect the fuel supply line and 3 fuel delivery lines to the valve. Secure the connections with new tie-straps.

ACCELERATOR PUMP CIRCUIT (100-125 HP AND 80 JET)

These engines idle on cylinders No. 1 and No. 2 only. The accelerator pump system is present to help with the transition from 2-cylinder operation at idle, to 4-cylinder operation upon acceleration. The accelerator pump discharges to cylinders No. 3 and No. 4 only. If the accelerator pump system fails, the engine will hesitate on acceleration.

The accelerator pump system on these models is mechanically operated by the throttle linkage. As the throttle linkage is advanced, the accelerator pump plunger is depressed. Fuel is discharged through 2 spring-loaded nozzles located in the intake passages of cylinders No. 3 and No. 4. The nozzles require approximately 11-14 psi

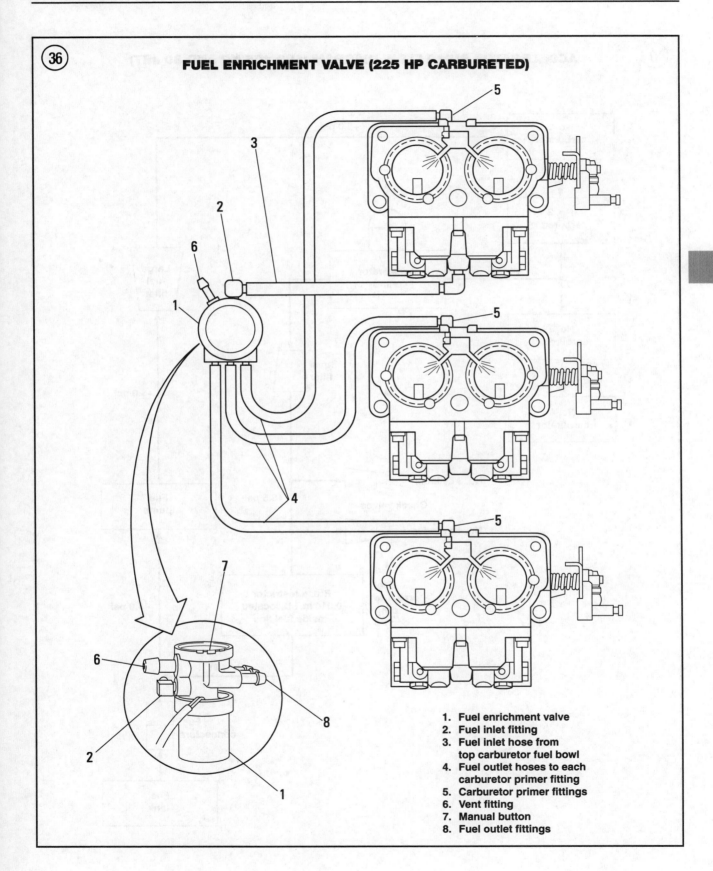

(36) **FUEL ENRICHMENT VALVE (225 HP CARBURETED)**

1. Fuel enrichment valve
2. Fuel inlet fitting
3. Fuel inlet hose from top carburetor fuel bowl
4. Fuel outlet hoses to each carburetor primer fitting
5. Carburetor primer fittings
6. Vent fitting
7. Manual button
8. Fuel outlet fittings

6

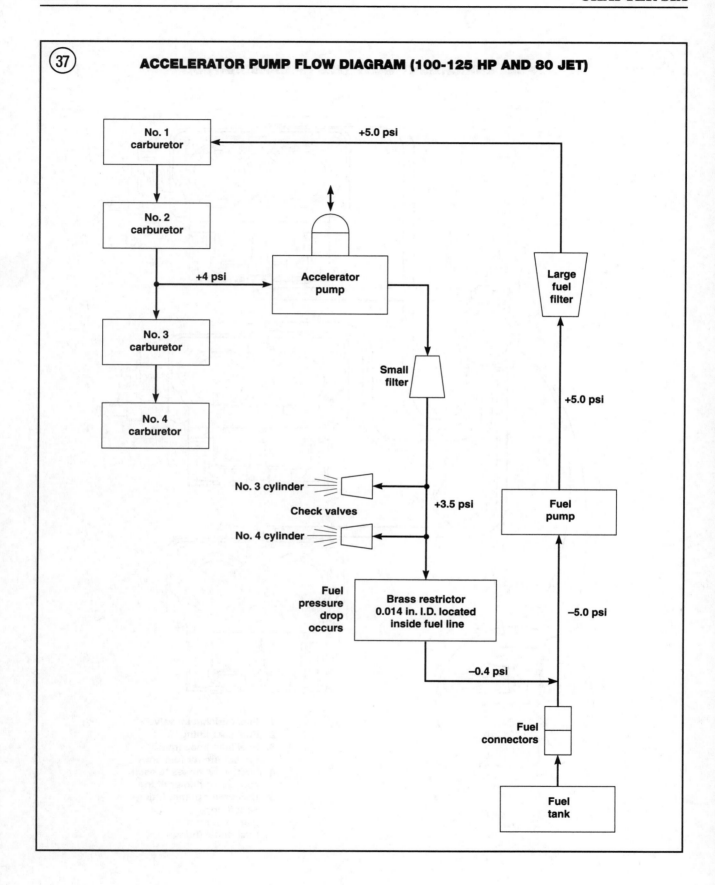

ACCELERATOR PUMP FLOW DIAGRAM (100-125 HP AND 80 JET)

(75.8-96.5 kPa) to unseat. The higher pressure enhances fuel atomization and prevents fuel from being siphoned into the intake manifold.

Refer to **Figure 37** for a block diagram of the complete accelerator pump circuit. Note that the 0.014 in. (0.36 mm) brass restrictor is located inside of the fuel line as shown in **Figure 38**. If the restrictor is missing or the filter becomes obstructed, the system will not function. Refer to Chapter Five for accelerator pump adjustment procedures.

ANTISIPHON DEVICES

In accordance with industry safety standards, late model boats equipped with a built-in fuel tank must have some form of antisiphon device installed between the fuel tank outlet and the outboard fuel inlet. The most common method of compliance is the antisiphon valve. This device is mounted at the outlet of the fuel tank pickup tube and is designed to prevent siphoning of the fuel from the fuel tank (and into the bilge) should the fuel line develop a break or leak between the fuel tank and the engine.

Other methods of compliance are electrical solenoid and manually operated fuel valves. Quite often, the malfunction of an antisiphon device leads to the replacement of a fuel pump in the mistaken belief that it is defective. Antisiphon devices cause running problems when they restrict the fuel flow to the engine. If the antisi-

6

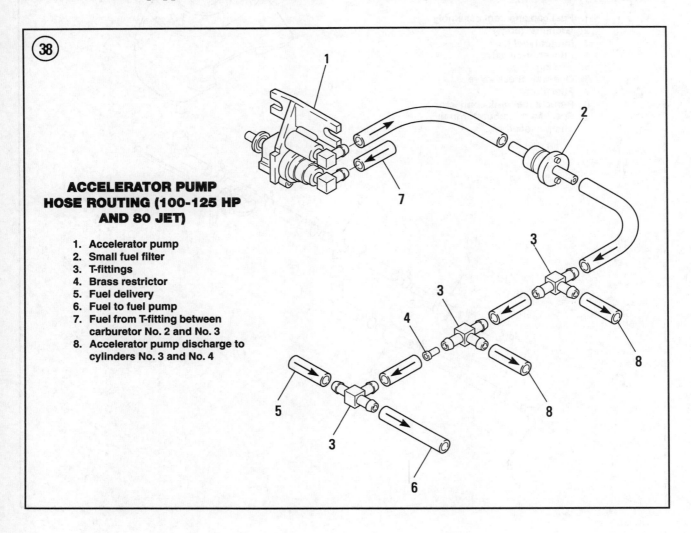

38

ACCELERATOR PUMP HOSE ROUTING (100-125 HP AND 80 JET)

1. Accelerator pump
2. Small fuel filter
3. T-fittings
4. Brass restrictor
5. Fuel delivery
6. Fuel to fuel pump
7. Fuel from T-fitting between carburetor No. 2 and No. 3
8. Accelerator pump discharge to cylinders No. 3 and No. 4

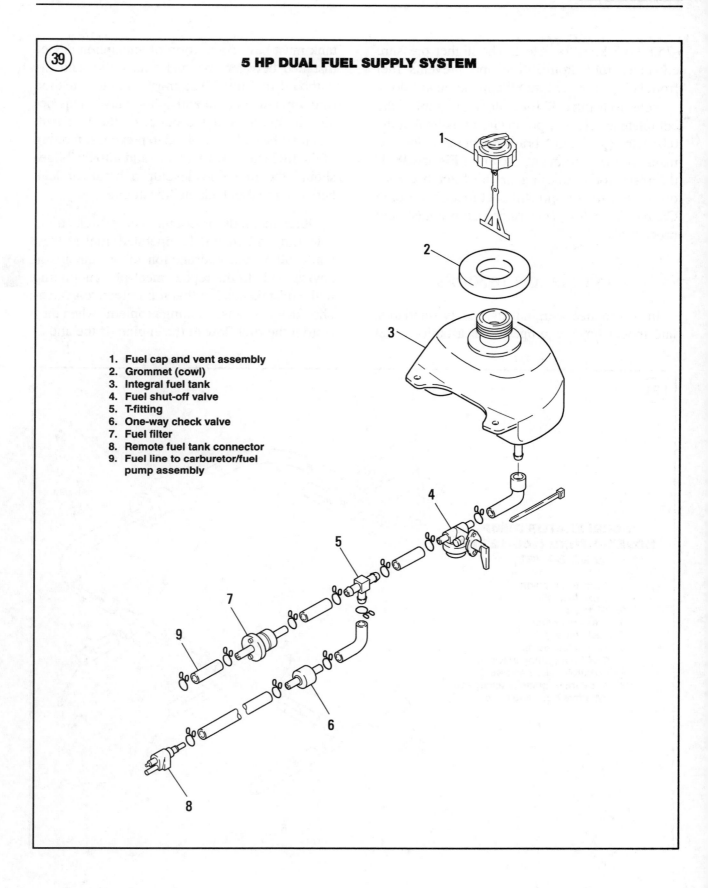

39

5 HP DUAL FUEL SUPPLY SYSTEM

1. Fuel cap and vent assembly
2. Grommet (cowl)
3. Integral fuel tank
4. Fuel shut-off valve
5. T-fitting
6. One-way check valve
7. Fuel filter
8. Remote fuel tank connector
9. Fuel line to carburetor/fuel pump assembly

phon device is suspected of causing a fuel starvation problem:

1. The device can be temporarily bypassed. If the fuel starvation problem disappears, the antisiphon device is known to be the problem and must be replaced. Do not return the boat to service with an inoperative antisiphon device.

2. Connect a vacuum gauge into the fuel delivery line using a T-fitting. The vacuum required to draw fuel from the fuel tank must not exceed 4 in. Hg (13.5 kPa) at any engine speed. See Chapter Three for fuel system troubleshooting procedures.

3. Connect a portable fuel tank to the motor. This is the easiest method to determine if the boat's fuel supply system (and possibly the antisiphon device) is defective. If the motor runs correctly on the portable fuel tank, the problem is known to be in the boat's fuel supply system. Check the easy things first. Check any boat mounted fuel filters for blockage, inspect all fittings, clamps and fuel delivery and vent lines for secure attachment, leaks and routing problems that could cause a restriction. Inspect the fuel pickup tube filter screen for blockage and the antisiphon valve for corrosion, mechanical damage or blockage from debris or contamination. Replace any damaged, deteriorated or corroded parts.

FUEL FILTERS

Refer to Chapter Four for standard fuel filter service procedures on all models *except* the final fuel filter on EFI (electronic fuel injection) and DFI (direct fuel injection) models.

1994-1995 150-200 hp EFI models—Refer to *Final Fuel Filter Service* in this chapter.

1996-1997 150-200 hp EFI models and all 200 DFI and 225-250 hp EFI models—Refer to *Vapor Separator Service* in this chapter.

FUEL TANKS (INTEGRAL AND PORTABLE [REMOTE])

The integral tank (and fuel filter) should be inspected, cleaned and flushed at least once a season and during each tune-up or major repair procedure.

Inspect the integral fuel tank, shutoff valve, lines, fittings, fuel filter and the fill cap and vent assembly for leaks, loose connections, deterioration, corrosion and contamination. Replace any suspect parts. Secure all fuel line connections with the original spring clamps or new tie-straps as shown in **Figure 39**.

Portable (remote) fuel tanks come in 3.2 gal. (12 L) and 6.6 gal. (25 L) sizes. **Figure 40** shows

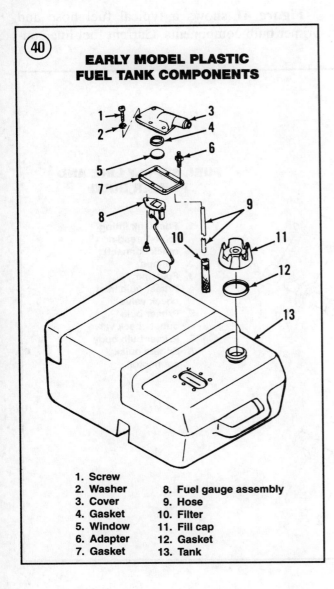

(40)

EARLY MODEL PLASTIC FUEL TANK COMPONENTS

1. Screw
2. Washer
3. Cover
4. Gasket
5. Window
6. Adapter
7. Gasket
8. Fuel gauge assembly
9. Hose
10. Filter
11. Fill cap
12. Gasket
13. Tank

an early model plastic portable fuel tank and components. Late model plastic fuel tanks use a simple threaded pickup tube or threaded retaining nut. The tube or nut is simply unscrewed to remove the pickup tube and clean the filter. Replace the o-ring or seal each time the pickup assembly is removed.

The portable fuel tank (and pickup tube fuel filter) should be inspected (and cleaned if necessary) at least once a season and during each tune-up or major repair procedure.

Inspect the portable fuel tank, pickup assembly, fuel lines, fittings, connectors and the fill cap and vent assembly for leaks, loose connections, deterioration, corrosion and contamination. Re-place any suspect parts, secure all fuel line connections with new tie-straps.

NOTE
All integral and portable fuel tanks contain an air vent to allow air into the tank as the fuel is consumed. A plugged or blocked air vent will create a vacuum in the tank and the engine will eventually starve for fuel. Always inspect the tank vent and make sure that it will allow air to enter the tank.

FUEL HOSE AND PRIMER BULB

Figure 41 shows a typical fuel hose and primer bulb components. Current fuel line con-

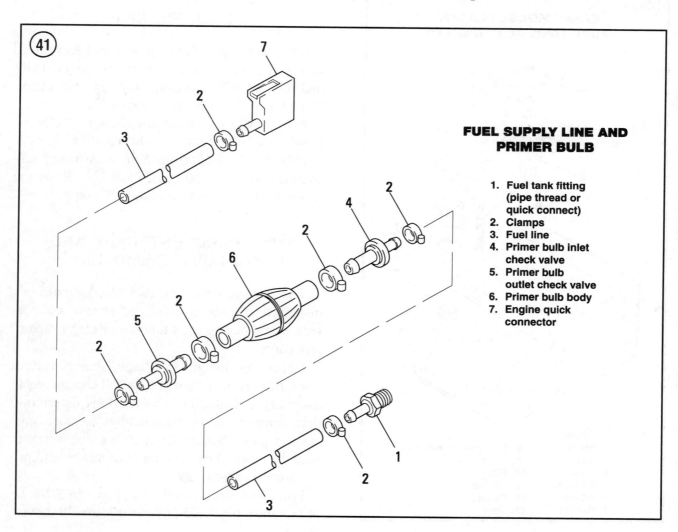

FUEL SUPPLY LINE AND PRIMER BULB

1. Fuel tank fitting (pipe thread or quick connect)
2. Clamps
3. Fuel line
4. Primer bulb inlet check valve
5. Primer bulb outlet check valve
6. Primer bulb body
7. Engine quick connector

nectors are called *Quick Connect* snap lock style connectors. These connectors come in 2 different hose inside diameter sizes—1/4 in. (6.3 mm) for smaller engines and 5/16 in. (7.9 mm) for larger engines. *Quick Connect* connectors are replaced as assemblies, no internal components are available for the engine or fuel tank ends.

On large engines, such as V-6 models, avoid the use of *Quick Connect* connectors as they can cause a fuel flow restriction at high speed. These engines are best supplied fuel from a permanently mounted fuel tank with the fuel supply line connected directly to the fuel pump inlet line (eliminating the quick connectors).

On all engines with permanent mounted fuel tanks, consider connecting the fuel supply line directly to the fuel pump inlet line (eliminating

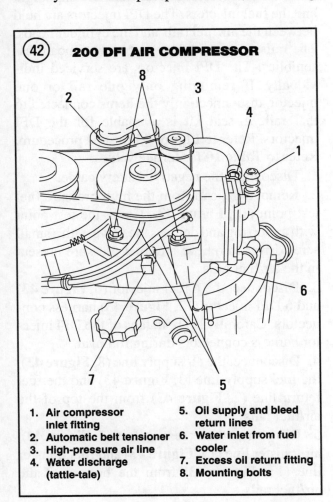

(42) 200 DFI AIR COMPRESSOR

1. Air compressor inlet fitting
2. Automatic belt tensioner
3. High-pressure air line
4. Water discharge (tattle-tale)
5. Oil supply and bleed return lines
6. Water inlet from fuel cooler
7. Excess oil return fitting
8. Mounting bolts

the quick connectors) to minimize all possible fuel restrictions and ensure adequate fuel supply to the engine.

The fuel hose and primer bulb should be inspected periodically for leaks, deterioration, loose clamps, kinked or pinched lines and other damage. Make sure all fuel hose connections are tight and securely clamped. It is usually considered cheap insurance to replace the fuel supply line and primer bulb as an assembly if there are any doubts as to its integrity.

ELECTRONIC FUEL INJECTION (EFI) AND DIRECT FUEL INJECTION (DFI)

This section covers component removal and replacement for the fuel related components on the 150-200 EFI and 225-250 EFI models. This section also covers component removal and replacement for the fuel and air related components on the 200 DFI engine. Refer to Chapter Three for operational descriptions and troubleshooting procedures. Refer to **Table 13** for torque values on these models.

CAUTION
Make sure the ignition switch is in the OFF position and the negative battery cable is disconnected before attempting any service on an EFI or DFI model engine.

Air Compressor Removal/Installation (200 DFI Models)

NOTE
The air compressor inlet line (in the flywheel cover) is equipped with a restrictor that must be installed if the engine is operated below 5000 ft. (1524 m). Remove the restrictor if the engine is operated at high altitude (above 5000 ft. [1524 m]).

Refer to **Figure 42** for this procedure. Refer to **Table 13** for torque values.

1. Disconnect the negative battery cable.

2. Lift the flywheel cover off the air compressor inlet fitting (1 **Figure 42**). Disconnect the vent line from the front of the flywheel cover, near the air filter.

3. Hold the automatic belt tensioner (2, **Figure 42**) in the fully retracted position (away from the belt) and remove the alternator and air compressor serpentine belt.

4. Disconnect the high-pressure air discharge hose (3, **Figure 42**) from the bottom of the air compressor cylinder head.

5. Disconnect the water discharge (tattle-tale) line (4, **Figure 42**) from the top of the cylinder head.

6. Disconnect the small oil supply and bleed return lines (5, **Figure 42**) from the air compressor cylinder block.

7. Disconnect the water supply line (from the fuel cooler) from the cylinder block near the cylinder head (6, **Figure 42**).

8. Disconnect the excess oil return line (7, **Figure 42**) from the bottom of the cylinder block.

9. Remove the 4 air compressor mounting bolts (8, **Figure 42**). Remove the air compressor.

10. Remove the 3 drive pulley mounting screws from the air compressor. Remove the drive pulley.

11. To install the air compressor, begin by installing the drive pulley to the air compressor. Install and tighten the 3 pulley screws to specifications (**Table 13**).

12. Set the air compressor on the power head and install the 4 mounting bolts. Tighten the mounting bolts to specification (**Table 13**).

13. Reconnect the excess oil return line, water supply line, small oil supply and bleed return lines to the air compressor. See **Figure 42**. Secure all connections with new tie-straps.

14. Reconnect water discharge (tattle-tale) to the top of the cylinder head and secure it with a new tie strap.

15. Lubricate the flare fitting of the high-pressure air line with outboard motor oil and install the high-pressure discharge line to the bottom of the cylinder head. Tighten the fitting securely.

16. Hold the automatic belt tensioner in the fully retracted position and install the alternator and air compressor belt. Release the tensioner against the belt.

17. Reinstall the flywheel cover. Reconnect the vent line at the front of the cover and make sure the air compressor inlet line is connected to the inlet fitting (1, **Figure 42**).

18. Reconnect the negative battery cable.

Air/Fuel Rails and DFI Injector Removal/Installation (200 DFI Models)

The air/fuel rails house the fuel pressure regulator, air pressure regulator, tracker diaphragm and the fuel injectors. The DFI injectors are held between the air/fuel rails and the cylinder heads. The rails are serviced as port and starboard assemblies. The DFI injectors are serviced individually. If removing only one rail or one injector, disconnect only the items connected to that rail. A seal kit is available for the DFI injectors. Refer to **Figure 43** for this procedure. Refer to **Table 10** for torque values.

1. Disconnect the negative battery cable.

2. Remove the cap from the high pressure fuel test point (10, **Figure 43**). Cover the test point with a shop rag and depress the valve with a small screwdriver to relieve any fuel pressure present in the air/fuel rails.

3. Disconnect the 6 fuel injector (6, **Figure 43**) and 6 DFI injector (12, **Figure 43**) harness connectors. Carefully lift both tabs of the DFI injector harness connectors during removal.

4. Disconnect the air supply line (8, **Figure 43**), the fuel supply line (3, **Figure 43**) and the fuel return line (2, **Figure 43**) from the top of the air/fuel rails.

5. Disconnect the excess air line (7, **Figure 43**), air transfer line (14, **Figure 43**) and fuel transfer line (13, **Figure 43**) from the bottom of the air/fuel rails.

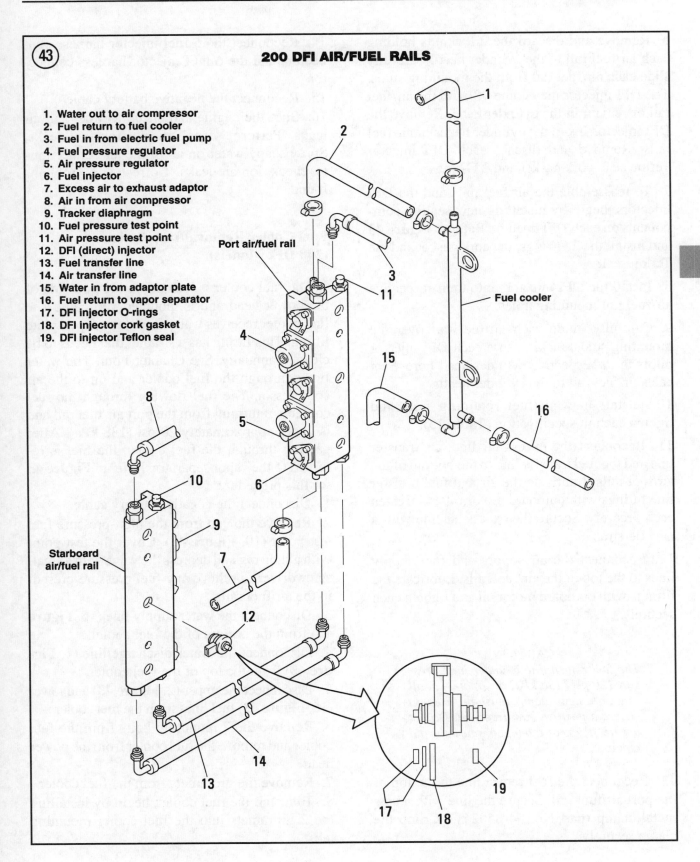

43

200 DFI AIR/FUEL RAILS

1. Water out to air compressor
2. Fuel return to fuel cooler
3. Fuel in from electric fuel pump
4. Fuel pressure regulator
5. Air pressure regulator
6. Fuel injector
7. Excess air to exhaust adaptor
8. Air in from air compressor
9. Tracker diaphragm
10. Fuel pressure test point
11. Air pressure test point
12. DFI (direct) injector
13. Fuel transfer line
14. Air transfer line
15. Water in from adaptor plate
16. Fuel return to vapor separator
17. DFI injector O-rings
18. DFI injector cork gasket
19. DFI injector Teflon seal

Port air/fuel rail

Fuel cooler

Starboard
air/fuel rail

6

6. Remove and discard the 2 locknuts holding each air/fuel rail to the cylinder head. Carefully slide each air/fuel rail from the mounting studs. The DFI injector may come off with the air/fuel rail or remain in the cylinder head. Remove the DFI injectors from the cylinder heads or air/fuel rails. Remove and discard each DFI injector Teflon seal, cork gasket and 2 O-rings.

7. To reassemble the air/fuel rails and the DFI injectors, begin by installing new sealing components on each DFI injector. Refer to **Figure 43** and install the 2 O-rings, the cork gasket and the Teflon seal.

8. Install the DFI injectors into their respective air/fuel rail mounting holes.

9. Carefully guide each air/fuel rail over the mounting studs, making sure each DFI injector pilots in its respective cylinder head bore. Seat each air/fuel rail to the cylinder head.

10. Install new air/fuel retaining nuts and tighten each to specification (**Table 13**).

11. Reconnect the excess air line, air transfer line and the fuel transfer line to the bottom of the air/fuel rails. Lubricate the air and fuel transfer line fittings with outboard motor oil and tighten each securely. Secure the excess air line with a new tie-strap.

12. Reconnect the air supply and fuel supply lines to the top of the air/fuel rails. Lubricate the fittings with outboard motor oil and tighten each securely.

CAUTION
The fuel return line is under high pressure (20 psi [138 kPa] or greater) at all times. A new clamp must be used to ensure a positive leak-free seal. Do not use tie-straps or attempt to reuse the old clamp.

13. Reconnect the fuel return line to the top of the port air/fuel rail. Secure the line with a new metal clamp (part No. 54-850241). Crimp the clamp securely.

14. Reconnect the 6 fuel injector harness connectors and the 6 DFI injector harness connectors.

15. Reconnect the negative battery cable.

16. Start the engine and check for fuel and air leaks. Perform visual checks for fuel leaks. Spray soapy water on all of the air connections to check for air leaks. Correct any problems found.

**Fuel Cooler Removal/Installation
(200 DFI Models)**

The fuel cooler is located on the port side of the power head and is mounted vertically. The fuel cooler receives water from the adapter plate fitting. This fitting has a strainer that needs to be cleaned annually. See Chapter Four. The water flows through the fuel cooler and on to the air compressor. The fuel flowing through the fuel cooler is returning from the port air/fuel rail and is under approximately 20 psi (138 kPa). After passing through the fuel cooler, the fuel is returned to the vapor separator. Refer to **Figure 43** for this procedure.

1. Disconnect the negative battery cable.

2. Remove the cap from the high-pressure fuel test point (10, **Figure 43**). Cover the test point with a shop rag and depress the valve with a small screwdriver to relieve any fuel pressure present in the air/fuel rails.

3. Disconnect the water supply line (15, **Figure 43**) from the bottom of the fuel cooler.

4. Disconnect the water discharge line (1, **Figure 43**) from the top of the fuel cooler.

5. Disconnect the upper (2, **Figure 43**) and lower (16, **Figure 43**) fuel lines from the fuel cooler.

6. Remove the 2 mounting bolts from the fuel cooler and remove the fuel cooler from the power head.

7. Remove the grommets from the fuel cooler.

8. To install the fuel cooler, begin by installing the 2 grommets into the fuel cooler mounting tabs.

9. Position the fuel cooler on the power head, over the engine mounted oil reservoir and install the 2 mounting bolts. Tighten the 2 mounting bolts securely.

CAUTION
The fuel return lines are under high pressure (20 psi [138 kPa] or greater) at all times. The correct (new) clamps must be used to ensure positive leak-free seals. Do not use tie-straps or attempt to reuse the old clamps.

10. Reconnect the upper and lower fuel lines to the fuel cooler. Secure the lines with new metal

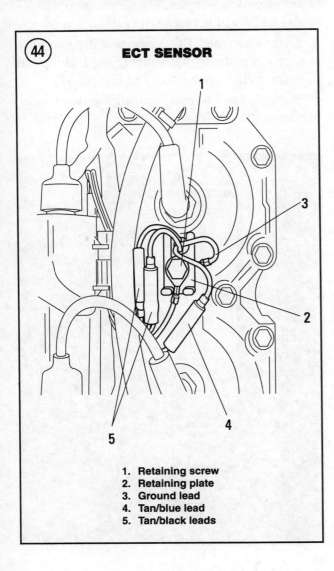

ECT SENSOR

1. Retaining screw
2. Retaining plate
3. Ground lead
4. Tan/blue lead
5. Tan/black leads

clamps (part No. 54-850241). Crimp the clamps securely.

11. Reconnect the upper and lower water lines and secure the connections with new tie-straps.

12. Reconnect the negative battery cable.

13. Start the engine and check for fuel and water leaks. Correct any problems found.

ECT (Engine Coolant Temperature) Sensor Removal/Installation

The ECT sensor is mounted on the port cylinder head on 150-200 hp EFI models and is mounted on the starboard cylinder head on 225-250 hp EFI and 200 DFI models. The sensor is grounded with a ring terminal secured by the sensor mounting bolt. **Figure 44** shows a typical ECT sensor installation.

1. Disconnect the negative battery cable.

2. Remove the screw and retainer (1 and 2, **Figure 44**) securing the sensor to the appropriate cylinder head.

3. Disconnect the 3 sensor leads (2 tan/black and 1 tan/blue) at the engine harness bullet connectors.

4. Remove the sensor from the cylinder head.

5. Thoroughly clean the cylinder head sensor bore.

6. Install the sensor into the cylinder head bore. Seat the sensor in the bore.

7. Place the ground terminal, followed by the retaining plate, over the sensor screw and install the assembly over the ECT sensor and to the cylinder head. Tighten the screw to specifications (**Table 13**). Make sure the retainer is properly positioned and the ground lead terminal is not twisted.

8. Reconnect the 3 sensor leads to the appropriate engine harness bullet connectors.

9. Reconnect the negative battery cable.

6

Electronic Control Module (ECM) Removal/Installation

150-200 hp EFI models

1. Disconnect the negative battery cable.
2. Disconnect the ECM wiring harness connector (A, **Figure 45**).
3. Remove the screws (B, **Figure 45**) and remove the water sensing module (E).
4. Remove the nuts (C, **Figure 45**) and screw (D, **Figure 45**).
5. Lift the ECM upward off the studs. Disconnect the MAP sensor hose at the manifold fitting and remove the ECM.
6. To reinstall, reconnect the MAP sensor hose to the manifold fitting and mount the ECM on the power head.
7. Secure the ECM to the power head with the 2 nuts and 1 screw. Tighten the fasteners to specification (**Table 13**).
8. Install the water sensing module. Make sure the 2 ground wires are installed under the outer module screw. Tighten the mounting screws to specification (**Table 13**).
9. Reconnect the ECM wiring harness connector.
10. Reconnect the negative battery cable.

225 and 250 hp EFI models—fuel ECM

The fuel ECM is the lower of the two ECMs mounted on the rear of the power head. The upper ECM is the ignition ECM. Refer to **Figure 46** for this procedure.
1. Disconnect the negative battery cable.
2. Disconnect the main engine wiring harness ECM connector (B, **Figure 46**) from the bottom of the fuel ECM. Squeeze the rubber boot tab to unlock the connector.
3. Remove the 4 fuel ECM mounting bolts (A, **Figure 46**). Remove the fuel ECM.
4. To install the fuel ECM, begin by positioning the ECM on the power head mounting plate.

5. Install the 4 mounting screws, making sure to connect the ground lead (C, **Figure 46**) to the lower starboard mounting screw. Tighten the 4 mounting screws to specification (**Table 13**).
6. Reconnect the main engine wiring harness to the fuel ECM.
7. Reconnect the negative battery cable.

200 DFI models

Refer to **Figure 47** for this procedure.
1. Disconnect the negative battery cable.
2. Remove the electrical cover from the starboard side of the engine. The cover snaps onto 3 studs and is held in place with rubber grommets.
3. Disconnect the 3 ECM engine wiring harness connectors at the ECM. Squeeze the locking tab to remove each connector. See **Figure 47**.
4. Remove the 2 screws securing the fuse holder bracket to the ECM.

5. Remove the 3 ECM mounting screws/electrical cover studs, 1 upper and 2 lower. Remove the ECM.

6. Remove the 3 metal sleeves from the 3 grommets on the ECM. Remove the 3 grommets from the ECM.

7. To install the ECM, begin by installing the 3 rubber grommets into the ECM. Slide a metal

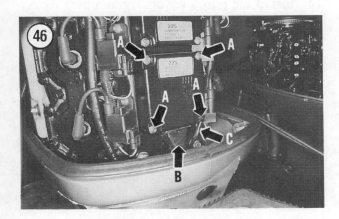

sleeve into each grommet from the back of the ECM.

8. Position the ECM on the power head and install the 3 ECM mounting screws/electrical cover studs. Tighten the fasteners to specifications (**Table 13**).

9. Position the fuse holder bracket on the ECM and install the 2 retaining screws. Tighten the screws to specification (**Table 13**).

10. Reconnect the 3 ECM engine wiring harness connectors to the ECM. Make sure each connector locks in place.

11. Reinstall the electrical cover over the ECM and fuse bracket.

12. Reconnect the negative battery cable.

Electric Fuel Pump Removal/Installation

The electric fuel pump is externally mounted on 1994-1995 150-200 hp EFI models and is internally mounted inside the vapor separator on 200 DFI, 225-250 hp EFI and 1996-1997 150-200 hp EFI models. Refer to *Vapor Separator Service* in this section, for service on the internally mounted electric fuel pump.

> *CAUTION*
> *EFI systems operate under high pressure. Do not remove the crimped stainless steel clamps unless absolutely necessary. Do not disconnect the rubber lines from the electric fuel pump, fuel pressure regulator and fuel management adaptor unless new hoses and clamps are to be installed. Always replace all O-rings and seals when servicing EFI systems.*

Externally mounted (1994-1995 150-200 hp EFI models)

1. Disconnect the negative battery cable.

2. Remove the cap from the high pressure fuel test point on top of the final fuel filter. Cover the test point with a shop rag and depress the valve

with a small screwdriver to relieve any fuel pressure present in the air/fuel rails. Reinstall the cap after the pressure has been relieved.

3. Remove the 4 screws (A, **Figure 48**) securing the fuel pump cover and remove the cover.

> *CAUTION*
> *Make sure the negative battery cable is disconnected before proceeding. Battery voltage is present at both fuel pump terminals at all times. Fuel pump and/or ECM damage can result if the pump terminals are shorted.*

4. Lift the fuel pump lead boot covers away from the terminals. Disconnect the positive and negative pump leads (B, **Figure 48**).

5. Remove the final filter screw (C, **Figure 48**) and separate the filter cover from the filter base.

6. Disconnect the fuel pump inlet hose from the bottom of the pump.

7. To clean the inlet filter inside the inlet line, remove the inlet line from the vapor separator and flush the line with clean solvent in both directions and blow dry. If the filter cannot be satisfactorily cleaned, remove and replace the filter.

8. Reconnect the inlet line to the vapor separator and secure it with a new tie-strap.

9. Remove the final filter base mounting screws (D, **Figure 48**). Remove the electric fuel pump, final filter base and rubber blanket (around the pump) as an assembly.

10. Remove the clamp and disconnect the pump discharge hose from the pump and separate the pump from the final filter base.

> *CAUTION*
> *The output of the electric fuel pump is considered high pressure. Use only the recommended clamps on all high-pressure lines.*

11. To install the fuel pump, start by connecting the pump to the discharge hose and securing it with a new part No. 54-13791 clamp. Crimp the clamp securely.

12. To reinstall the pump, mount the pump and rubber blanket into position.

13. Install the final filter base mounting screws. Tighten the screws securely.

14. Connect the fuel pump inlet hose. Secure the new connection with a new clamp part No. 54-F698772. Tighten the clamp securely.

15. Install the pump cover. Tighten the 4 cover screws evenly to 45 in.-lb. (5.1 N·m).

16. Connect the pump positive and negative leads. Slide the wire boot covers down into position.

17. Reassemble the final filter cover to the final filter base as described in the next section.

18. Reconnect the negative battery cable after the final fuel filter is reassembled.

19. Start the engine and check for fuel leaks. Correct any problems found.

Final Filter Service

This procedure covers 1994-1995, 150-200 hp EFI models with an externally mounted final fuel filter located above the vapor separator and electric fuel pump. The filter cover also contains the high pressure test point (8, **Figure 49**).

To service the final fuel filter on all other EFI and DFI models, refer to *Vapor Separator Service* later in this section.

To service the final fuel filter on 1994-1995, 150-200 hp EFI models, proceed as follows:

CAUTION
The final fuel filter is under high fuel pressure. Replace all O-rings each time the filter is disassembled. Do not disconnect the fuel lines from the filter cover and base unless parts replacement is required. Use only the recommended clamps on high pressure fuel lines.

1. Remove the cap from the high pressure fuel test point (8, **Figure 49**). Cover the test point with a shop rag and depress the valve with a small screwdriver to relieve any fuel pressure present in the air/fuel rails. Reinstall the cap after the pressure has been relieved.

2. Remove the screw and lock washer (7, **Figure 49**).

3. Separate the fuel filter cover (6, **Figure 49**) from the filter base.

4. Remove the filter element (3, **Figure 49**) and the three O-rings (2, 4 and 5, **Figure 49**). Discard the O-rings.

5. Clean the filter element in a mild solvent and blow dry. Replace the element if it can not be satisfactorily cleaned.

6. To reassemble the filter, install new O-rings (4 and 5, **Figure 49**) into the filter cover.

7. Install a new O-ring (2, **Figure 49**) into the filter element.

8. Carefully assemble the filter cover to the base being careful not to displace any of the O-rings. Make sure the high-pressure test point is pointing straight up.

9. Install the screw and lock washer and tighten securely.

10. Reconnect the negative battery cable.

6

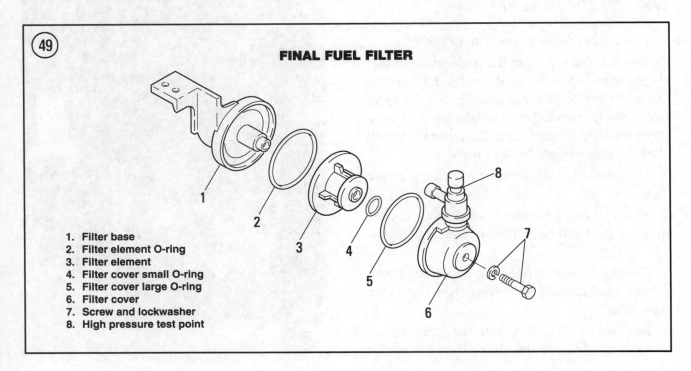

49

FINAL FUEL FILTER

1. Filter base
2. Filter element O-ring
3. Filter element
4. Filter cover small O-ring
5. Filter cover large O-ring
6. Filter cover
7. Screw and lockwasher
8. High pressure test point

11. Start the engine and check for fuel leaks. Correct any problem found.

Fuel Pressure Regulator Removal/Installation (EFI models)

The fuel regulator controls the fuel pressure by dumping excess fuel into the vapor separator when fuel pressure exceeds the regulator's preset value. Fuel pressure will vary with engine load based on the vacuum signal to the pressure regulator.

> *CAUTION*
> *EFI systems operate under high pressure. Do not remove the crimped stainless steel clamps unless absolutely necessary. Do not disconnect the rubber lines from the electric fuel pump, fuel pressure regulator and fuel management adaptor unless new hoses and clamps are to be installed. Always replace all O-rings and seals when servicing EFI systems.*

1994-1995 150-200 hp EFI models

1. Disconnect the negative battery cable.
2. Remove the cap from the high-pressure fuel test point on top of the final fuel filter. Cover the test point with a shop rag and depress the valve with a small screwdriver to relieve any fuel pressure present in the air/fuel rails. Reinstall the cap after the pressure has been relieved.
3. Disconnect the vacuum line from the pressure regulator.
4. Remove the 2 regulator mounting screws. Remove the regulator retaining plate and grommet.
5. Lift the regulator from the vapor separator. Remove and discard the O-ring from the vapor separator.
6. Remove the 2 screws from the regulator elbow fitting. Remove the elbow fitting from the

regulator. Remove and discard the elbow fitting O-ring from the regulator.

7. To reinstall the regulator, begin by installing a new elbow fitting O-ring into the regulator groove. Install the regulator to the elbow and secure it with 2 screws. Tighten the 2 screws to specification (**Table 13**).

8. Install a new O-ring into the vapor separator groove.

9. Install the regulator onto the vapor separator and seat it against the vapor separator.

10. Slide the grommet and regulator retaining plate over the pressure regulator. Secure the plate with the 2 regulator mounting screws. Tighten the screws evenly and securely.

11. Reconnect the vacuum line to the regulator.

12. Reconnect the negative battery cable.

13. Start the engine and check for fuel leaks. Correct any problems found.

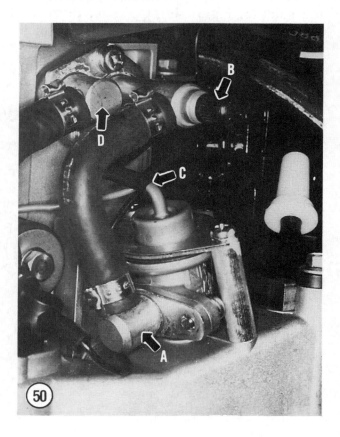

225-250 hp EFI and 1996-1997 150-200 hp EFI models

Refer to **Figure 50** and **Figure 51** for this procedure.

1. Disconnect the negative battery cable.

2. Remove the cap from the high-pressure fuel test point on the fuel pressure regulator elbow fitting (A, **Figure 50**) or on the fuel management adaptor, just above the fuel pressure regulator (B, **Figure 50**). Cover the test point with a shop rag and depress the valve with a small screwdriver to relieve any fuel pressure present in the air/fuel

rails. Reinstall the cap after the pressure has been relieved.

3. Disconnect the vacuum line (C, **Figure 50**) from the pressure regulator.

4. Remove the 2 regulator mounting screws. Remove the regulator retaining plate, grommet and 2 spacer tubes. See **Figure 51**.

5. Lift the regulator from the vapor separator. Remove and discard the O-ring from the vapor separator.

6. Remove the 2 screws from the regulator elbow fitting. Remove the elbow fitting from the regulator. Remove the hat filter from the elbow fitting (**Figure 51**). Remove and discard the elbow fitting O-ring.

7. To reinstall the regulator, begin by cleaning the hat filter. Replace the filter if it cannot be satisfactorily cleaned.

8. Install a new elbow fitting O-ring into the regulator groove. Install the hat filter into the regulator elbow. Install the regulator to the elbow and secure it with 2 screws (**Figure 51**). Tighten the 2 screws to specification (**Table 13**).

9. Install a new O-ring into the vapor separator groove.

10. Install the regulator onto the vapor separator and seat it against the vapor separator.

11. Slide the grommet and regulator retaining plate over the pressure regulator. Secure the plate with the 2 regulator mounting screws and spacers. Tighten the screws evenly to specification (**Table 13**).

12. Reconnect the vacuum line to the regulator.

13. Reconnect the negative battery cable.

14. Start the engine and check for fuel leaks. Correct any problems found.

Induction Manifold Removal/Installation

CAUTION
EFI systems operate under high pressure. Do not remove the crimped stainless steel clamps unless absolutely necessary. Do not disconnect the rubber lines from the electric fuel pump, fuel

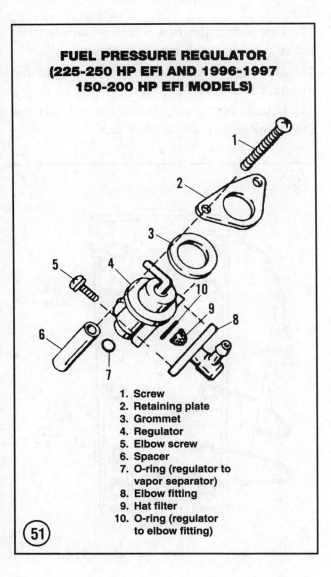

FUEL PRESSURE REGULATOR
(225-250 HP EFI AND 1996-1997
150-200 HP EFI MODELS)

1. Screw
2. Retaining plate
3. Grommet
4. Regulator
5. Elbow screw
6. Spacer
7. O-ring (regulator to vapor separator)
8. Elbow fitting
9. Hat filter
10. O-ring (regulator to elbow fitting)

(51)

6

pressure regulator and fuel management adaptor unless new hoses and clamps are to be installed. Always replace all O-rings and seals when servicing EFI systems.

150-200 hp EFI models

1. Disconnect the negative battery cable.

2A. *1994-1995 models*—Remove the cap from the high pressure fuel test point (8, **Figure 49**). Cover the test point with a shop rag and depress the valve with a small screwdriver to relieve any fuel pressure present in the air/fuel rails. Reinstall the cap after the pressure has been relieved.

2B. *1996-1997 models*—Remove the cap from the high pressure fuel test point on the fuel pressure regulator elbow fitting (A, **Figure 50**). Cover the test point with a shop rag and depress the valve with a small screwdriver to relieve any fuel pressure present in the air/fuel rails. Reinstall the cap after the pressure has been relieved.

3. Remove the ECM assembly as described previously in this section.

4. Remove the oil reservoir as described in Chapter Eleven.

5. Remove the 2 screws securing the water separating fuel filter assembly to the induction manifold. Lay the filter to one side. Do not disconnect the fuel lines.

6. Disconnect the vacuum line from the fuel pressure regulator.

7. Disconnect the vent line from the vapor separator fitting. It is not necessary to disconnect the bleed return line (with the small filter) from the vapor separator at this time.

8. Remove the 2 screws securing the fuel management adaptor (D, **Figure 50**, typical) to the top port side of the induction manifold.

NOTE
It may be necessary to remove the 4 fuel pump cover screws on 1994-1995 models to gain access to all of the vapor separator mounting screws in the next step. It should not be necessary to dis-

connect the electric fuel pump leads or fuel lines from the fuel pump.

9. Remove the 3 screws securing the vapor separator assembly to the induction manifold. Pull the fuel management adaptor and the vapor separator away from the induction manifold and lay the vapor separator and fuel management adaptor to one side. Do not disconnect any additional lines.

10. Disconnect the throttle position sensor from the engine harness 3-pin connector.

11. Disconnect the 2 intake air temperature sensor leads from the engine harness bullet connectors.

12. Disconnect the fuel injector harness from the engine harness 4-pin connector.

13. Disconnect the throttle link rod from the throttle cam.

14. Disconnect the oil injection control rod from the oil injection pump control arm.

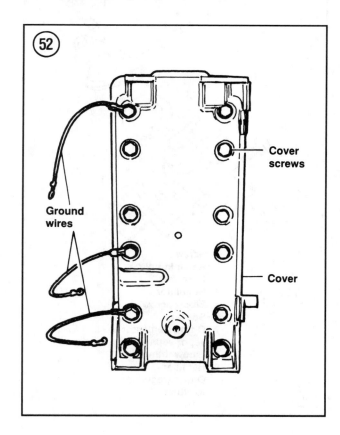

15. Note the location of the ground wires (**Figure 52**) for reference during installation.

NOTE
The manifold cover and the manifold body are held together by the 12 mounting screws. Support the manifold as the last screws are removed.

16. Remove the 12 manifold cover screws and remove the manifold cover (**Figure 52**).

17. *1994-1995 models*—Disconnect the bleed hose from the bleed shutoff valve on the port side of the induction manifold.

18. Pull the manifold away from the power head enough to disconnect the bleed hoses from the fittings at the bottom of the manifold assembly.

19. Remove the induction manifold assembly from the power head.

20. Carefully remove all gasket material from the intake and induction manifolds.

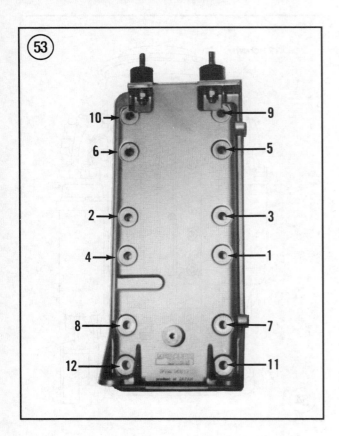

21. To reinstall the induction manifold, first place a new gasket onto the manifold-to-engine mating surface.

22. Hold the manifold in position while connecting the bleed hoses to the bleed fittings at the bottom of the manifold. Install the manifold onto the power head and secure with the 12 screws.

23. Tighten the manifold screws to specification (**Table 13**) in the sequence shown in **Figure 53**. Remove the excess gasket material from the area adjacent to each throttle plate. This is gasket material that is not clamped to the intake manifold or the induction manifold.

24. *1994-1995 models*—Connect the bleed line to the bleed shutoff valve.

25. Rotate the oil injection pump control arm clockwise until the arm is facing aft, then connect the oil pump control rod to the pump arm.

26. Connect the throttle link rod to the throttle cam.

27. Install new O-rings on the fuel management adaptor (D, **Figure 50**). Position the vapor separator and install the fuel management adapter to the induction manifold. Tighten the 2 retaining screws to specification (**Table 13**).

28. Reconnect the vacuum line from the fuel pressure regulator.

29. Reconnect the vent line from the vapor separator fitting.

30. Position the vapor separator and install the 3 screws securing the vapor separator assembly to the induction manifold. Tighten the screws to specification (**Table 13**). If necessary, reinstall the fuel pump cover and secure with 4 screws. Tighten the screws securely.

31. Install the oil reservoir as described in Chapter Eleven.

32. Reconnect the throttle position sensor, intake air temperature sensor and fuel injector wiring harnesses to the appropriate engine wiring harness connectors.

33. Install the water separating filter assembly and the ECM as described in this section.

34. Reconnect the negative battery cable.

35. Start the engine and check for fuel leaks. Correct any problems found.

36. Refer to Chapter Five for synchronization and linkage adjustments.

225-250 hp EFI models

1. Disconnect the negative battery cable.

2. Remove the cap from the high pressure fuel test point on the fuel management adaptor, just above the fuel pressure regulator (B, **Figure 50**). Cover the test point with a shop rag and depress the valve with a small screwdriver to relieve any fuel pressure present in the air/fuel rails. Reinstall the cap after the pressure has been relieved.

3. Remove the 2 screws securing the water separating fuel filter assembly to the induction manifold. Lay the filter to one side. Do not disconnect the fuel lines.

4. Disconnect the throttle position sensor from the engine harness 3-pin connector.

5. Disconnect the 2 intake air temperature sensor leads from the engine harness bullet connectors.

6. Disconnect the fuel injector harness from the engine harness 4-pin connector.

7. Disconnect the throttle link rod from the throttle cam.

8. Disconnect the vacuum line from the MAP (manifold absolute pressure) sensor.

9. Disconnect the vacuum line from the fuel pressure regulator.

10. *1994-1995 models*—Remove the 2 screws securing the final fuel filter base to the induction manifold.

11. Disconnect the vent line from the vapor separator fitting. It is not necessary to disconnect the bleed return line (with the small filter) from the vapor separator at this time.

12. Remove the 2 screws securing the fuel management adaptor (D, **Figure 50**) to the top port side of the induction manifold.

13. Remove the 3 screws securing the vapor separator assembly to the induction manifold.

Pull the fuel manifold and vapor separator away from the induction manifold and lay the vapor separator and fuel manifold assembly to one side. Do not disconnect any additional lines.

NOTE
The manifold cover and the manifold body are held together by the 12 mounting screws. Support the manifold as the last screws are removed.

14. Remove the 12 manifold cover screws (**Figure 54**).

15. Remove the induction manifold assembly from the power head.

16. Carefully remove all gasket material from the intake and induction manifolds.

17. To reinstall the induction manifold, first place 3 new gaskets onto the manifold-to-engine mating surface. It may be necessary to *lightly* glue the gaskets to the intake manifold to prevent

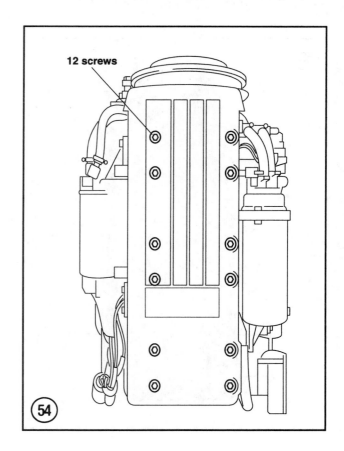

12 screws

(54)

them from falling out of alignment during assembly. Use a dab of contact adhesive, such as Quicksilver Bellows Adhesive.

18. Hold the manifold assembly in position while installing the 12 screws. Make sure all 3 gaskets are in position and correctly aligned.

19. Tighten the manifold screws evenly to specification (**Table 13**). Use a circular sequence starting in the center of the manifold and working outward.

20. Reconnect the throttle link rod to the throttle cam.

21. Install new O-rings of the fuel management adaptor (D, **Figure 50**). Position the vapor separator and install the fuel management adapter to the induction manifold. Tighten the 2 retaining screws to specification (**Table 13**).

22. Reconnect the vacuum line to the MAP (manifold absolute pressure) sensor.

23. Reconnect the vacuum line to the fuel pressure regulator.

24. Reconnect the vent line to the vapor separator fitting.

25. Position the vapor separator and install the 3 screws securing the vapor separator assembly to the induction manifold. Tighten the screws to specification (**Table 13**).

26. *1994-1995 models*—Install the 2 screws securing the final fuel filter base to the induction manifold. Tighten the screws securely.

27. Reconnect the throttle position sensor to the engine harness 3-pin connector.

28. Reconnect the 2 intake air temperature sensor leads to the engine harness bullet connectors.

29. Reconnect the fuel injector harness to the engine harness 4-pin connector.

30. Position the water separating fuel filter assembly on the induction manifold. Install and tighten the screws to specification (**Table 13**).

31. Reconnect the negative battery cable.

32. Start the engine and check for fuel leaks. Correct any problems found.

33. Refer to Chapter Five for synchronization and linkage adjustments.

200 DFI models

1. Disconnect the negative battery cable.

2. Remove the 2 screws securing the water separating fuel filter assembly to the induction manifold. Lay the filter to one side. Do not disconnect the fuel lines.

3. Disconnect both throttle position sensor leads from each sensor body 3-pin connector.

4. Disconnect the 2 intake air temperature sensor leads from the engine harness bullet connectors.

5. Disconnect the throttle link rod from the throttle cam.

6. Disconnect the vacuum line from the MAP (manifold absolute pressure) sensor.

7. Remove the 3 screws securing the vapor separator assembly to the induction manifold. Pull the vapor separator away from the induction manifold and lay the vapor separator assembly to one side. Do not disconnect any additional lines.

> *NOTE*
> *The manifold cover and the manifold body are held together by the 12 mounting screws. Support the manifold as the last screws are removed.*

8. Remove the 12 manifold cover screws (**Figure 54**).

9. Remove the induction manifold assembly from the power head.

10. Carefully remove all gasket material from the intake and induction manifolds.

11. To reinstall the induction manifold, first place 3 new gaskets onto the manifold-to-engine mating surface. It may be necessary to *lightly* glue the gaskets to the intake manifold to prevent them from falling out of alignment during assembly. Use a dab of contact adhesive, such as Quicksilver Bellows Adhesive.

12. Hold the manifold assembly in position while installing the 12 screws. Make sure all 3 gaskets are in position and correctly aligned.

6

13. Tighten the manifold screws evenly to specification (**Table 13**). Use a circular sequence starting in the center of the manifold and working outward.

14. Reconnect the throttle link rod to the throttle cam.

15. Position the vapor separator and install the 3 screws securing the vapor separator assembly to the induction manifold. Tighten the screws to specification (**Table 13**).

16. Reconnect the vacuum line to the MAP (manifold absolute pressure) sensor.

17. Reconnect both throttle position sensor leads to each sensor body 3-pin connector.

18. Reconnect the 2 intake air temperature sensor leads to the engine harness bullet connectors.

19. Position the water separating fuel filter assembly on the induction manifold. Install and tighten the screws to specification (**Table 13**).

20. Reconnect the negative battery cable.

21. Refer to Chapter Five for synchronization and linkage adjustments.

Induction Manifold Disassembly/Reassembly

The induction manifold on the 150-200 hp and 250 hp models always use 4 throttle plates mounted on 2 separate shafts. The 225 hp uses 2 throttle plates mounted on a single shaft. The service procedures between the 150-200 hp and

225-250 hp induction manifolds are very similar, with only minor differences in the number of fasteners and torque values. The following procedure focuses mainly on fuel injector and fuel injector harness replacement.

Replace all O-rings and seals. Seal and O-ring kits are available from Mercury/Mariner Dealerships. Lubricate all O-rings and seals with outboard motor oil. Refer to **Table 13** for torque values.

150-250 hp EFI models

1. Place the induction manifold assembly on a clean work surface.

2. Remove the induction manifold cover seal.

NOTE
Early model 150-200 hp induction manifolds may be equipped with a test port located on the lower corner of the induc-

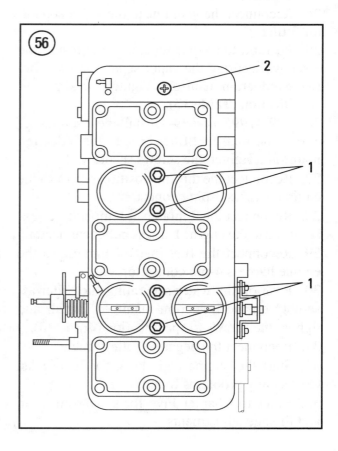

tion manifold on the port side. If so equipped, Steps 3-5 must be performed. If not so equipped, continue at Step 6.

3. Remove the 2 screws (A, **Figure 55**) securing the test port outer plate (C) to the manifold.

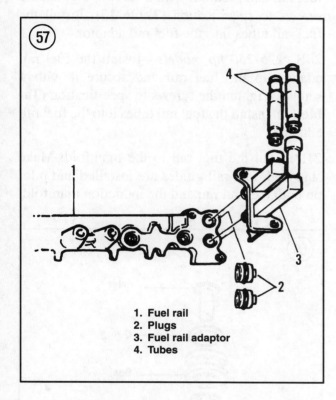

1. Fuel rail
2. Plugs
3. Fuel rail adaptor
4. Tubes

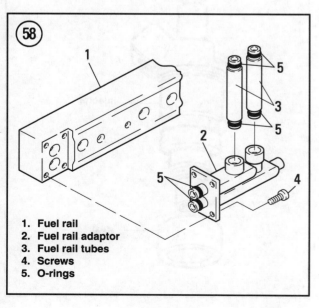

1. Fuel rail
2. Fuel rail adaptor
3. Fuel rail tubes
4. Screws
5. O-rings

4. Remove the screw (B, **Figure 55**) securing the test port inner plate (C) to the fuel rail.

5. Remove the test port assembly from the manifold. Remove and discard the test port O-rings.

6A. *150-200 hp models*—Remove the 4 fuel rail mounting screws (1, **Figure 56**) and remove the fuel rail from the manifold. Do not lose the 2 fuel rail locating guides located in the 2 fuel rail mounting bolt bores.

6B. *225-250 hp models*—Remove the 5 fuel rail mounting screws (1 and 2, **Figure 56**) and remove the fuel rail from the manifold. Do not lose the 2 fuel rail locating guides located in 2 fuel rail mounting bolt bores.

7A. *150-200 hp models*—Remove the 2 fuel rail adaptor screws. Remove the fuel rail adaptor, fuel rail tubes and the fuel rail plugs. Discard all O-rings. See **Figure 57**.

7B. *225-250 hp models*—Remove the 4 fuel rail adaptor screws. Remove the fuel rail adaptor and the fuel rail tubes. Discard all O-rings. See **Figure 58**.

8. Lift the wire clip that secures the injector connectors to the injectors, from its groove. Disconnect the injector connectors. See **Figure 59**.

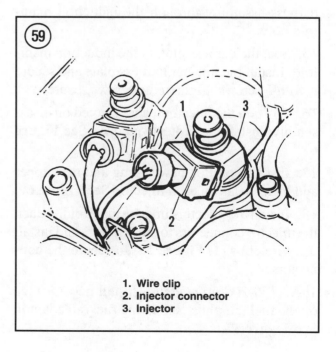

1. Wire clip
2. Injector connector
3. Injector

9. Remove the injectors by lifting straight up from the manifold.

10. Remove the upper and lower seal, the O-ring and the filter from each injector (**Figure 60**). Discard the O-ring and seals. Clean the filter in mild solvent and blow dry. Replace any filter that cannot be satisfactorily cleaned.

NOTE
The following steps deal with injector harness replacement. If injector harness replacement is not required, go directly to Step 17 for reassembly.

11. Note the position of the injector harness and protective casing for reassembly. Remove the protective casing covering the injector harness. See **Figure 61**.

12. Remove the 3 screws securing the injector harness plate. Remove the injector harness plate. See **Figure 61**.

13. Remove the injector harness from the induction manifold. Discard the injector harness plug O-ring.

14. To reassemble, install a new O-ring on the injector harness plug. Insert the injector lead and harness assembly through the induction manifold bore.

15. Seat the harness plug in the induction manifold. Install the injector harness plate and secure it with 3 screws. Tighten the screws securely.

16. Position the injector leads as noted on disassembly. Install the protective cover. See **Figure 61**.

17. Install the filter, new O-ring and new upper and lower seals on each injector. See **Figure 60**.

18. Install the injectors into the manifold. Attach the injector connectors to the injectors and install the wire clips (1, **Figure 59**) to secure the connectors.

19A. *150-200 hp models*—Install new O-rings on the fuel rail plugs, tubes and fuel rail adaptor. See **Figure 57**.

19B. *225-250 hp models*—Install new O-rings on the fuel rail tubes and fuel rail adaptor. See **Figure 58**.

20A. *150-200 hp models*—Install the plugs into the fuel rail. Install the fuel rail adaptor to the fuel rail and secure it with 2 screws. Tighten the screws to specification (**Table 13**). Install the fuel rail tubes into the fuel rail adaptor.

20B. *225-250 hp models*—Install the fuel rail adaptor to the fuel rail and secure it with 4 screws. Tighten the screws to specification (**Table 13**). Install the fuel rail tubes into the fuel rail adaptor.

21. Install the fuel rail to the manifold. Make sure both fuel rail guides are installed and pilot on both the fuel rail and the induction manifold.

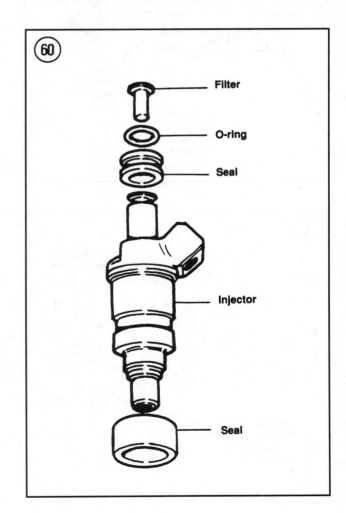

Install the 4 or 5 fuel rail screws and tighten the screws evenly to specification (**Table 13**).

22. If so equipped, install new O-rings on the service port tube, install the tube and inner plate. Install and tighten the inner plate screw securely. Install the outer plate and secure with 2 screws. Tighten the 2 screws securely.

23. Install the induction manifold assembly as described in this chapter.

200 DFI models

The induction manifold contains no serviceable components other than the externally mounted throttle position sensors and the intake air temperature sensor. The induction manifold controls air intake only and contains no fuel passages or components.

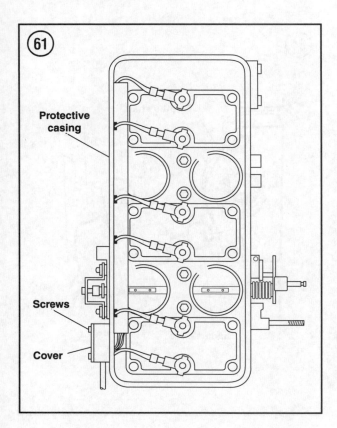

Intake Air Temperature (IAT) Sensor Removal/Installation

1. Disconnect the negative battery cable.

2. *150-200 hp EFI models*—Remove the 2 screws securing the water separating fuel filter bracket to the induction manifold. Lay the filter to one side.

3. Disconnect the 2 sensor leads from the engine harness bullet connectors.

4. Remove the 3 screws securing the sensor (**Figure 62**, typical) to the induction manifold. Remove and discard the O-ring from the inner surface of the sensor.

5. To install the sensor, install a new O-ring to the sensor. Insert the sensor into the induction manifold and seat it with hand pressure.

6. Install the 3 retaining screws. Tighten the screws securely. Do not over-tighten.

7. Reconnect the 2 sensor leads to the engine wiring harness bullet connectors.

8. *150-200 hp EFI models*—Position the fuel filter on the induction manifold. Install the 2 screws securing the water separating fuel filter

bracket to the induction manifold. Tighten the screws to specification (**Table 13**).

9. Reconnect the negative battery cable.

Manifold Absolute Pressure (MAP) Sensor Removal/Installation

150-200 hp EFI models

The MAP sensor is an integral part of the ECM on 150-200 hp EFI models. If the MAP is not functioning correctly, verify that the vacuum line is not damaged or deteriorated and is securely connected to the intake manifold. The line can be repaired up to the point it enters the ECM. If the line is in satisfactory condition and is securely attached to the intake manifold, yet the MAP sensor portion of the ECM is not functioning correctly, the ECM must be replaced.

200 DFI and 225-250 hp EFI models

The map sensor is mounted on top of the vapor separator and is connected to the intake manifold by a vacuum line. Refer to **Figure 63** for this procedure.

1. Disconnect the negative battery cable.

2. Disconnect the MAP sensor 3-pin electrical connector.

3. Disconnect the MAP sensor vacuum line from the sensor.

4. Remove the 2 screws securing the MAP sensor to the vapor separator. Remove the MAP sensor.

5. To install the MAP sensor, position the sensor on the vapor separator and install the 2 retaining screws. Tighten the retaining screws to specification (**Table 13**).

6. Connect the 3-pin electrical connector and the vacuum hose to the MAP sensor. Secure the vacuum hose with a new tie-strap.

7. Reconnect the negative battery cable.

Throttle Position Sensor (TPS) Removal/Installation

The TPS on all EFI models requires readjustment any time it is removed or the mounting screws are turned. Refer to Chapter Five for adjustment procedures.

The 200 DFI uses 2 throttle position sensors. Both sensors are automatically calibrated by the

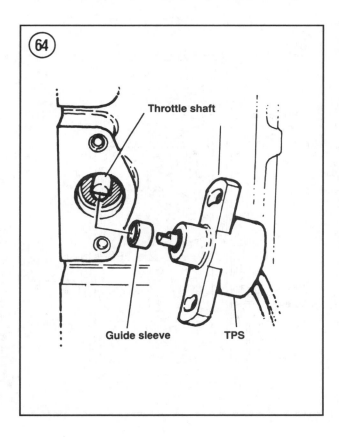

Throttle shaft

Guide sleeve   **TPS**

ECM during start-up. If one sensor fails, the warning panel will illuminate and the warning horn will sound. If both sensors fail, the engine will not run above idle.

150-200 hp EFI models

1. Disconnect the negative battery cable.
2. If the same TPS is going to be reinstalled, place match marks on the TPS base and induction manifold for reference during reinstallation.
3. Disconnect the TPS 3-pin connector from the engine harness.
4. Remove the 2 mounting screws and remove the TPS and guide sleeve (**Figure 64**).

5. To reinstall the TPS, place the guide sleeve onto the TPS shaft.
6. Install the TPS onto the induction manifold, making sure the TPS shaft properly aligns and engages the throttle shaft.
7. If applicable, align the match marks made during removal. Lightly tighten the mounting screws.
8. Reconnect the negative battery cable.
9. Adjust the TPS as described in Chapter Five.

225-250 hp models

Refer to **Figure 65** for this procedure.
1. Disconnect the negative battery cable.
2. If the same TPS is going to be reinstalled, place match marks on the TPS base and induction manifold for reference during reinstallation.
3. Disconnect the TPS 3-pin connector from the engine harness.
4. Remove the 2 mounting screws and remove the TPS. The coupler (guide sleeve) should remain in the induction manifold.
5. To reinstall the TPS, make sure the coupler (guide sleeve) is present in the induction manifold.
6. Install the TPS on the induction manifold, making sure the TPS shaft properly aligns and engages the throttle shaft coupler.
7. If applicable, align the match marks made during removal. Lightly tighten the mounting screws.
8. Reconnect the negative battery cable.
9. Adjust the TPS as described in Chapter Five.

200 DFI models

1. Disconnect the negative battery cable.
2. Disconnect the outer sensor 3-pin connector.
3. Remove the outer sensor mounting screws (A, **Figure 66**) and remove the outer sensor.

NOTE
If the inner sensor does not require replacement, go directly to Step 13.

4. Remove the tie-strap from the upper aft sensor mounting plate screw.

5. Remove the 4 inner sensor mounting plate screws (B, **Figure 66**).

6. Remove the inner sensor and mounting plate assembly.

7. Disconnect the inner sensor 3-pin connector.

8. Remove the 2 inner sensor mounting screws and remove the inner sensor from the mounting plate.

9. To reinstall the inner sensor, position the sensor on the mounting plate with the connector facing down. Install and tighten the 2 screws to specification (**Table 13**).

10. Reconnect the engine harness 3-pin connector to the inner sensor.

11. Carefully slide the inner sensor and mounting plate over the throttle shaft. Make sure the sensor aligns and engages the throttle shaft.

12. Install the 4 mounting plate screws and tighten to specification (**Table 13**).

13. Carefully position the outer sensor on the mounting plate. Make sure the sensor aligns and engages the throttle shaft.

14. Install and tighten the 2 outer sensor screws to specification (**Table 13**).

15. Reconnect the engine harness 3-pin connector to the outer sensor.

16. Reconnect the negative battery cable.

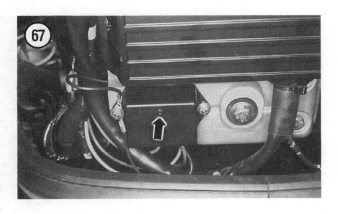

Water Sensing Warning Module Removal/Installation (150-200 hp EFI models)

Refer to **Figure 67** for this procedure.

1. Disconnect the negative battery cable.

2. Disconnect the tan lead from the water separating fuel filter sensor.

3. Disconnect the light blue lead from the engine harness bullet connector and the purple lead from the terminal block or engine harness bullet connector.

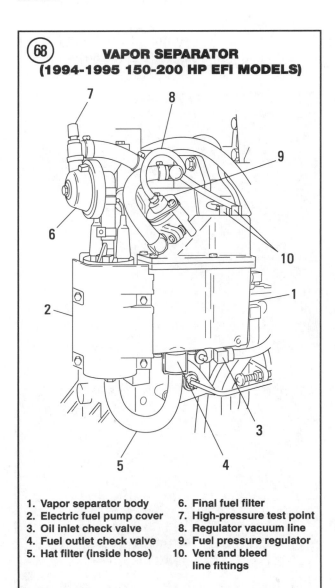

VAPOR SEPARATOR (1994-1995 150-200 HP EFI MODELS)

1. Vapor separator body
2. Electric fuel pump cover
3. Oil inlet check valve
4. Fuel outlet check valve
5. Hat filter (inside hose)
6. Final fuel filter
7. High-pressure test point
8. Regulator vacuum line
9. Fuel pressure regulator
10. Vent and bleed line fittings

4. Remove the 2 mounting screws (**Figure 67**) and remove the module.

5. To install the module, position the engine and module ground wires under the mounting screw as shown in **Figure 67**. Install and tighten both screws to specification (**Table 13**).

6. Reconnect the tan lead to the water separating fuel filter sensor.

7. Reconnect the light blue to the engine harness bullet connector and the purple lead to the terminal block or engine harness bullet connector.

8. Reconnect the negative battery cable.

Water Separating Filter Assembly Removal/Installation

1. Disconnect the negative battery cable.

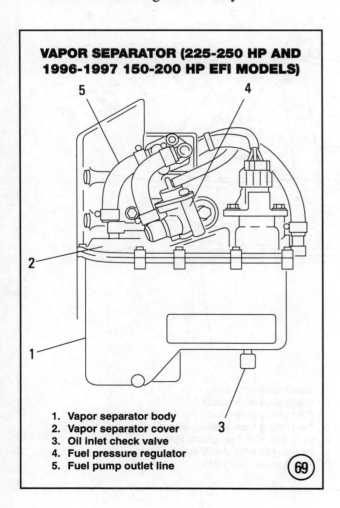

VAPOR SEPARATOR (225-250 HP AND 1996-1997 150-200 HP EFI MODELS)

1. Vapor separator body
2. Vapor separator cover
3. Oil inlet check valve
4. Fuel pressure regulator
5. Fuel pump outlet line

69

2. Remove the 2 fuel lines from the water separator fuel filter bracket. Label each hose for reassembly.

3. Remove the tan lead from the water sensor probe at the bottom of the filter canister.

4. Remove the 2 screws securing the filter bracket to the induction manifold and remove the filter assembly.

5. If necessary, service the filter assembly as described in Chapter Four.

6. To reinstall the filter assembly, position the filter bracket on the induction manifold.

7. Install and tighten the 2 retaining screws to specification (**Table 13**).

8. Reconnect the 2 fuel lines to the appropriate fittings on the filter bracket. Secure the connections with new tie-straps.

9. Reconnect the tan lead to the water sensor probe at the bottom of the filter canister.

10. Reconnect the negative battery cable.

Vapor Separator Service

The vapor separator is a fuel reservoir that ensures that the electric fuel pump always has a raw fuel supply and does not ingest air or vapor. The vapor separator receives fuel from the mechanical fuel pump. An inlet needle and float system control the fuel entering the vapor separator much like the float chamber on a carburetor. The float level is preset and does not require adjustment.

Three distinct versions of the vapor separator are used. The 1994-1995 150-200 hp EFI models are equipped with a vapor separator (**Figure 68**) that features an external electric fuel pump, an external final fuel filter, an external check valve in the fuel outlet and an internal hat-type filter in the fuel outlet line.

The 225-250 hp EFI and 1996-1997 150-200 hp EFI models are equipped with a vapor separator (**Figure 69**) that features an internal fuel pump and internal final filter. The only difference between the 225-250 hp and 150-200 hp models is the location of the high-pressure test point.

The 200 DFI uses a vapor separator (**Figure 70**) with an internal fuel pump (special to 200 DFI models) and an internal final filter, but does not have a fuel pressure regulator mounted on the vapor separator cover.

On EFI models, the fuel pressure regulator is mounted to the vapor separator. Excess fuel is returned from the fuel rail to the vapor separator through the fuel pressure regulator. Oil from the injection pump enters through a 2 psi (13.8 kPa) check valve fitting at the bottom aft corner of the vapor separator. Air and fuel vapors are vented to the induction manifold through a small line and fitting on the top of the vapor separator cover. Fuel return from the bleed (recirculation) system enters the vapor separator after passing through a small inline fuel filter.

On DFI models, the fuel return from the air/fuel rails (and pressure regulator) enters through a fitting where the fuel pressure regulator is mounted on EFI models. A pressure regulation check valve in the return line maintains 20

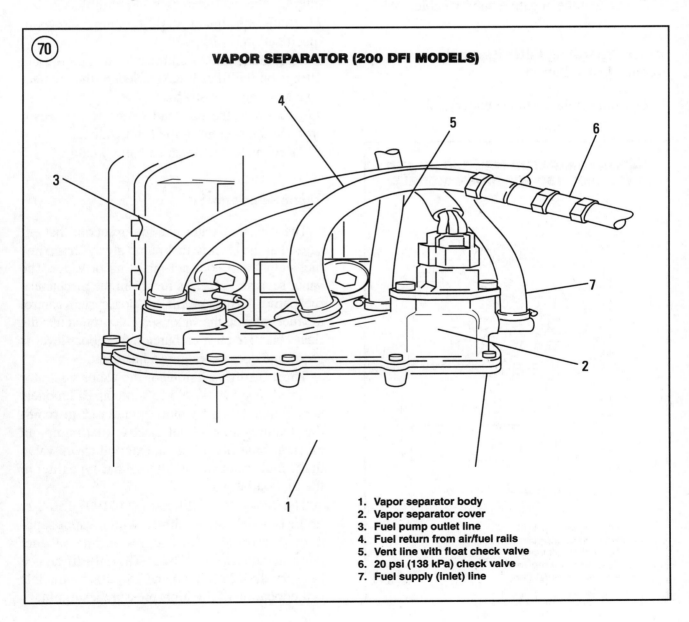

VAPOR SEPARATOR (200 DFI MODELS)

1. Vapor separator body
2. Vapor separator cover
3. Fuel pump outlet line
4. Fuel return from air/fuel rails
5. Vent line with float check valve
6. 20 psi (138 kPa) check valve
7. Fuel supply (inlet) line

psi (138 kPa) in the return line upstream of the check valve. Oil is not injected to the vapor separator on DFI models. Air and fuel vapors are vented to the air compressor filter chamber. A float-type check valve in the vent line allows air and vapor to pass, but not raw fuel.

CAUTION
EFI systems operate under high pressure. Do not remove the crimped stainless steel clamps unless absolutely necessary. Do not disconnect the rubber lines from the electric fuel pump, fuel pressure regulator and fuel management adaptor unless new hoses and clamps are to be installed.

Vapor separator removal/installation (1994-1995 150-200 hp EFI models)

Refer to **Figure 68** for this procedure.
1. Disconnect the negative battery cable.
2. Remove the oil reservoir. See Chapter Eleven.
3. Remove the electric fuel pump as described in this chapter.
4. Remove the 2 screws securing the fuel management adapter to the port aft corner of induction manifold.
5. Disconnect the vacuum hose (8, **Figure 68**) from the fuel pressure regulator.
6. Disconnect the bleed and vent hoses (10, **Figure 68**) from the vapor separator fittings.
7. Disconnect the oil inlet hose (3, **Figure 68**) from the bottom of the vapor separator assembly.
8. Remove the 3 screws securing the vapor separator to the induction manifold. Pull outward on the fuel management adapter and the vapor separator. Remove the vapor separator and fuel management adaptor assembly.
9. Remove and discard the O-rings on the fuel management adaptor.
10. To reinstall the vapor separator, install new O-rings on the fuel management adaptor and position the vapor separator and fuel management adaptor on the induction manifold. Seat the

fuel management adaptor into the induction manifold with hand pressure.
11. Secure the vapor separator with 3 screws. Tighten the screws to specification (**Table 13**).
12. Install and tighten the 2 fuel management adaptor screws to specification (**Table 13**).
13. Reconnect the oil delivery hose to the fitting on the bottom of the separator. Secure the hose with a new tie-strap.
14. Reconnect the bleed and vacuum hoses to the top cover (**Figure 68**).
15. Install the electric fuel pump as described previously in this section.
16. Reinstall the oil tank and bleed the oil system as described in Chapter Eleven.
17. Reconnect the negative battery cable.
18. Start the engine and check for fuel leaks. Correct any problems found.

Vapor separator removal/installation (225-250 hp EFI and 1996-1997 150-200 hp EFI models)

Refer to **Figure 69** for this procedure.
1. Disconnect the negative battery cable.
2. Remove the cap from the high-pressure test point on the fuel management adaptor, just above the fuel pressure regulator or on the fuel pressure regulator elbow fitting. Cover the test point with a shop rag and depress the valve with a small screwdriver to relieve any fuel pressure present in the air/fuel rails. Reinstall the cap after the pressure has been relieved.
3. *150-200 hp models*—Remove the oil reservoir. See Chapter Eleven.
4. *225-250 hp models*—Disconnect the MAP sensor 3-pin connector.
5. Remove the 2 screws securing the fuel management adapter to the port aft corner of induction manifold.
6. Disconnect the vacuum hose from the fuel pressure regulator.
7. Disconnect the bleed and vent hoses from the vapor separator top cover fittings.

8. Disconnect the oil inlet hose (3, **Figure 69**) at the bottom of the vapor separator assembly.

9. Remove the 3 screws securing the vapor separator to the induction manifold. Pull outward on the fuel management adaptor and the vapor separator. Remove the vapor separator and fuel management adaptor assembly.

10. Remove and discard the O-rings on the fuel management adaptor.

11. To reinstall the vapor separator, install new O-rings on the fuel management adaptor and position the vapor separator and fuel management adaptor on the induction manifold. Seat the fuel management adaptor into the induction manifold with hand pressure.

12. Secure the vapor separator with 3 screws. Tighten the screws to specification (**Table 13**).

13. Install and tighten the 2 fuel management adaptor screws to specification (**Table 13**).

14. Reconnect the oil delivery hose to the fitting on the bottom of the separator. Secure the hose with a new tie-strap.

15. Reconnect the bleed and vacuum hoses to the top cover.

16. Reconnect the MAP sensor 3-pin connector.

17. *150-200 hp models*—Reinstall the oil tank and bleed the system as described in Chapter Eleven.

18. Reconnect the negative battery cable.

19. Start the engine and check for fuel leaks. Correct any problems found.

Vapor separator removal/installation (200 DFI models)

Refer to **Figure 70** for this procedure.

> *CAUTION*
> *DFI systems operate under extremely high pressure. Do not remove the crimped stainless steel clamps unless absolutely necessary. Do not disconnect the rubber lines from the electric fuel pump, vapor separator and air/fuel rails unless new clamps are to be installed.*

1. Disconnect the negative battery cable.

2. Remove the cap from the high-pressure test point on top of the starboard air/fuel rail. Cover the test point with a shop rag and depress the valve with a small screwdriver to relieve any fuel pressure present in the air/fuel rails. Reinstall the cap after the pressure has been relieved.

3. Disconnect the MAP sensor 3-pin connector.

4. Disconnect the fuel pump outlet hose (3, **Figure 70**). Discard the clamp.

5. Disconnect the fuel return line (4, **Figure 70**). Discard the clamp.

6. Disconnect the vent line (5, **Figure 70**). Discard the clamp.

7. Disconnect the fuel supply line (7, **Figure 70**). Discard the clamp.

8. Remove the 3 screws securing the vapor separator to the induction manifold. Remove the vapor separator assembly.

9. To reinstall the vapor separator, position the vapor separator and fuel management adaptor on the induction manifold. Secure the vapor separator with 3 screws. Tighten the screws to specification (**Table 13**).

10. Reconnect the fuel supply line and secure the connection with a new clamp. Crimp the clamp securely.

11. Reconnect the vent line and secure with a new tie-strap.

12. Reconnect the fuel return line and secure the connection with a new clamp. Crimp the clamp securely.

13. Reconnect the fuel pump outlet hose and secure the connection with a new clamp. Crimp the clamp securely.

14. Reconnect the MAP sensor 3-pin connector.

15. Reconnect the negative battery cable.

16. Start the engine and check for fuel leaks. Correct any problems found.

Vapor separator disassembly/reassembly (1994-1995 150-200 hp EFI models)

Refer to **Figure 71** for this procedure.

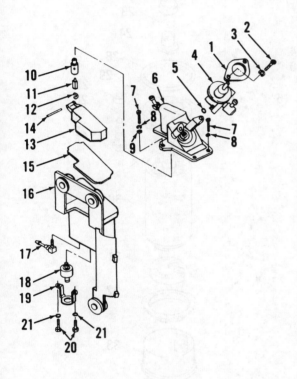

(71)

VAPOR SEPARATOR ASSEMBLY

1. Retainer
2. Screw
3. Lockwasher
4. Fuel pressure
   regulator assembly
5. O-ring
6. Cover assembly
7. Screw
8. Lockwasher
9. Flat washer
10. Inlet valve seat
11. Inlet valve needle
12. Wire clip
13. Float
14. Float pin
15. Seal
16. Bowl and bracket
    assembly
17. Check valve
18. Check valve
19. Bracket
20. Screws
21. Lockwasher

1. Remove the fuel pressure regulator as described previously in this section.

2. Remove the 6 vapor separator cover screws and lock washers. Lift off the cover assembly. Discard the cover seal.

NOTE
The float level is factory adjusted. **Do not** *bend the float's brass tab.*

3. Remove the float hinge pin using needle nose pliers. Remove the float and inlet needle.

4. Clean and inspect all components. Replace any suspect parts.

5. To reassemble, begin attach the inlet needle to the float with the wire clip.

6. Install the float, making sure the inlet needle enters the seat, then install the float hinge pin.

7. Install a new cover seal into the vapor separator body.

8. Install the cover assembly onto the body. Secure the cover with 6 screws and lock washers. Tighten the screws evenly and securely.

9. Install the fuel pressure regulator as described previously in this section.

Vapor separator disassembly/reassembly (200 DFI, 225-250 hp EFI and 1996-1997 150-200 hp EFI models)

Refer to **Figure 72** or **Figure 73** for this procedure. It is possible to service the final filter on some models without removing the vapor separator from the engine. If the 9 cover screws can be accessed, it is not necessary to remove the vapor separator from the engine.

The electric fuel pump is not serviceable. If the pump malfunctions, it must be replaced.

1. *All EFI models*—Remove the fuel pressure regulator as described in this chapter.

2. Remove the 9 vapor separator cover screws and lock washers. Lift off the cover assembly. Discard the cover seal.

3A. *All EFI models*—Grasp the final filter on the end of the fuel pump and pull down, while

6

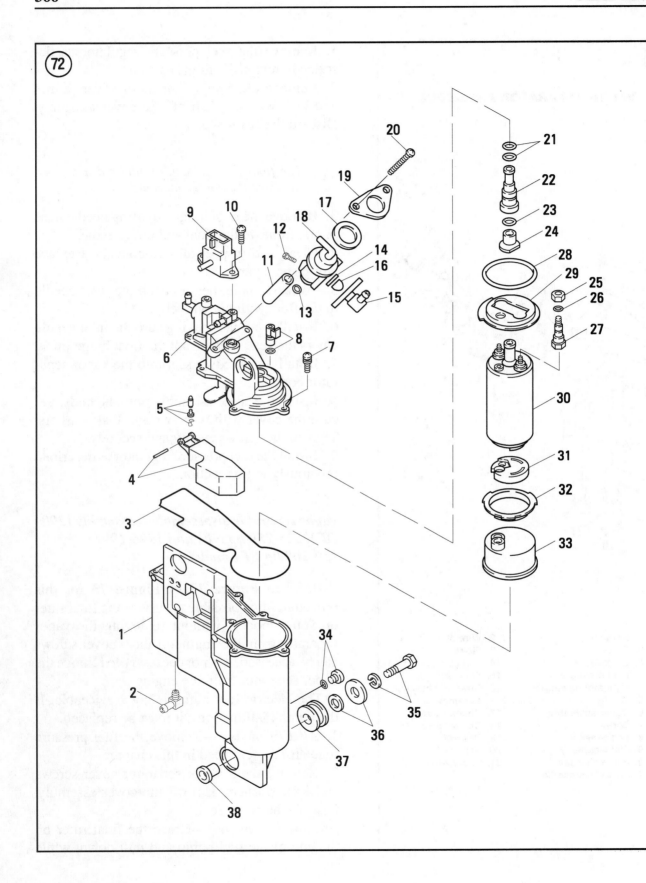

VAPOR SEPARATOR ASSEMBLY
(225-250 HP AND
1996-1997 150-200 HP EFI MODELS)

1. Vapor separator body
2. 2 psi (13.8 kPa) oil inlet check valve
3. Cover seal
4. Float and hinge pin
5. Inlet needle and spring clip
6. Top cover
7. Cover screws
8. Insulator and O-ring
9. MAP sensor (225 and 250 hp)
10. Screw
11. Spacer
12. Screw
13. O-ring
14. O-ring
15. Elbow fitting
16. Hat filter
17. Grommet
18. Fuel pressure regulator
19. Regulator retaining plate
20. Screw
21. O-ring
22. Fuel pump outlet fitting
23. O-ring
24. Fuel pump adapter fitting
25. Terminal nut
26. O-ring
27. Terminal stud
28. O-ring
29. Plate
30. Fuel pump
31. Rubber grommet
32. Stabilizing ring
33. Final fuel filter
34. Drain plug and seal washer
35. Bolt and lockwasher
36. Flat washers
37. Grommet
38. Sleeve collar

rotating the filter counterclockwise. Remove and inspect the final filter. Discard the filter if it is not clean. Remove the stabilizing ring and the rubber grommet.

3B. *200 DFI models*—Depress the 2 lock tabs of the final filter and remove it from the fuel pump. Inspect the final filter. Discard the final filter if it is not clean.

NOTE
*The float level is factory adjusted. **Do not** bend the float arm or the float drop limit bracket.*

4. Remove the float hinge pin using needlenose pliers. Remove the float and inlet needle.

NOTE
If fuel pump replacement is not required, proceed directly to Step 6. If fuel pump replacement is required, proceed with Step 5.

5A. *All EFI models*—To replace the fuel pump, remove the nuts from the negative and positive fuel pump terminal. Pull the pump out of the vapor separator cover. Remove the pump adaptor. Remove both terminal insulators from the pump cover. Discard all O-rings and seals. See **Figure 72**.

5B. *200 DFI models*—To replace the fuel pump, pull the fuel pump out of the vapor separator cover. Disconnect the 2-pin connector from the fuel pump. If necessary, push the fuel pump adaptor cap out of the vapor separator cover. Discard all O-rings and seals. See **Figure 73**.

6. Clean and inspect all components. Replace any suspect parts.

7A. *All EFI models*—Install the fuel pump as shown in **Figure 72**, using all new O-rings and seals. Seat the fuel pump assembly in the top cover. Install the terminal insulators and O-rings into the cover and over the terminal studs. Tighten each terminal stud nut to specification (**Table 10**).

7B. *200 DFI models*—Install the fuel pump as shown in **Figure 73**, using all new O-rings and seals. If the adaptor cap was removed, install a new O-ring on the cap and seat it into the fuel pump cover with hand pressure. Connect the 2-pin connector to the fuel pump and seat the fuel pump into fuel pump adaptor cap.

8. Attach the inlet needle to the float with the wire clip.

9. Install the float, making sure the inlet needle enters the seat, then install the float hinge pin.

10. Install a new cover seal into the vapor separator body.

11A. *All EFI models*—Install the stabilizing ring and rubber grommet to the end of the fuel pump. Install the final filter to the fuel pump. Press the filter onto the fuel pump while rotating the filter clockwise. Make sure the filter has locked in place.

11B. *200 DFI models*—Make sure the O-ring (16, **Figure 73**) and stabilizing and retaining ring (17, **Figure 73**) are installed. Align the final fuel filter with the stabilizing ring notches. Press the final fuel filter on with hand pressure until it locks in place.

> *NOTE*
> *There are 2 sizes of cover screws. Tighten each to the appropriate torque listed in **Table 13**.*

12. Install the cover assembly onto the body. Secure the cover with 9 screws and lock washers. Tighten the screws evenly to specification (**Table 13**).

13. *All EFI models*—Install the fuel pressure regulator as described previously in this section.

REED VALVE SERVICE

All Mercury/Mariner 2-stroke outboard motors are equipped with one set of reed valves per cylinder. The reed valves allow the air/fuel mixture from the carburetor to enter the crankcase, but not exit. They are in essence, one-way check valves.

**VAPOR SEPARATOR ASSEMBLY
(200 DFI MODELS)**

1. Vapor separator body
2. Cover seal
3. Float and hinge pin
4. Inlet needle and spring clip
5. Top cover
6. Cover screws
7. MAP sensor (225 and 250 hp)
8. Screw
9. O-ring
10. Terminal nut
11. Fuel pump adaptor cap
12. O-ring
13. Fuel pump
14. O-ring
15. Terminal studs and connector
16. O-ring
17. Stabilizing and retaining ring
18. Final fuel filter
19. Screw
20. Flat washers
21. Grommet
22. Drain plug and seal washer
23. Sleeve collar

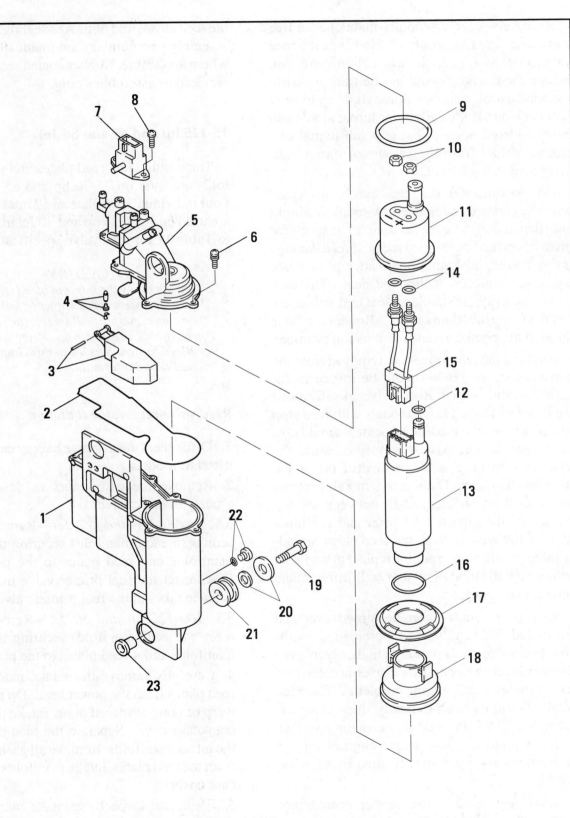

Reed valves are essentially maintenance free and cause very few problems. However, if a reed valve does not seal, the air/fuel mixture will escape the crankcase and not be transported to the combustion chamber. Some slight spitting of fuel back out of the carburetor throat at idle can be considered normal, but any substantial discharge of fuel from the carburetor throat indicates reed valve failure.

On most models, the reeds can be inspected with the carburetor removed. A small flashlight and dental mirror can be used to inspect for broken, cracked or chipped reeds. If reed damage is discovered, it is important to attempt to locate the missing pieces of the reed petal. The reed petals are made of stainless steel and will cause internal engine damage if allowed to pass through the crankcase and combustion chamber.

Anytime the reed valves are removed from the power head, the reeds should be inspected for excessive stand-open. Reed valve specifications are listed in **Table 11**. On models with reed stop specifications, the reed stop opening should also be measured. The easiest way to measure the reed stop opening is to use a drill bit of the specified diameter. The shank (smooth portion) of the drill bit should just fit between the top surface of the closed reed petal and the inner edge of the reed stop. Some reed stops are adjustable, while some require replacement if not within specification. The text will differentiate between such models.

Reed petals must never be turned over and reinstalled. This can lead to a preloaded condition. Preloaded reeds require a higher crankcase vacuum level to open. This causes acceleration and carburetor calibration problems. The reed petals should be flush to nearly flush along the entire length of the reed block mating surface with no preload. Most larger engines have a maximum stand-open specification listed in **Table 11**.

Many new models use rubber coated reed blocks. These reed blocks cushion the impact as the reed closes and improves sealing. Reed block assembly part numbers automatically supersede where applicable. Rubber coated reed blocks are serviced as assemblies only.

75-125 hp and 65 and 80 Jet

Three individual reed plates and intake manifolds are used on 75-90 hp and 65 Jet models. Four individual reed plate and 2 intake manifolds are used on 100-125 hp and 80 Jet models. Refer to **Table 11** for reed valve specifications.

> *CAUTION*
> *Do not allow the internal bleed (recirculation) system check valves to fall out or become misplaced while the intake manifolds are removed. Refer to* **Fuel Bleed System Service** *in this chapter for additional information.*

Reed valve removal/installation

1. Disconnect the negative battery cable on electric start models.

2. Remove the carburetors as described previously in this chapter.

3A. *75-90 hp and 65 Jet*—Remove the 15 screws (5 each manifold) securing the 3 intake manifolds and reed plates to the power head. Disconnect the fuel primer valve line from the balance tubes at the fuel primer valve.

3B. *100-125 hp and 80 Jet*—Remove the 18 screws (9 each manifold) securing the 2 intake manifolds and 4 reed plates to the power head.

4. Carefully remove the intake manifolds and reed plates from the power head. Do not scratch, warp or gouge the reed plate, intake manifold or crankcase cover. Separate the reed plates from the intake manifolds. Remove all gasket material from the reed plates, intake manifolds and crankcase cover.

5. Clean and inspect the intake manifolds and reed plates as described in this chapter. Do not

remove the reed valves from the reed plates unless replacement is necessary.

6. Using new gaskets, install the reed plates and intake manifolds to the power head. Install the retaining screws finger-tight.

8A. *75-90 hp and 65 Jet*—Tighten the 15 screws (5 each manifold) evenly to 18 ft.-lb. (24.4 N•m) in a crossing pattern. Reconnect the fuel primer valve hose from the balance tubes to the fuel primer valve. Secure the connection using a new tie-strap clamp.

8B. *100-125 hp and 80 Jet*—Tighten the 18 screws (9 each manifold) evenly to 18 ft.-lb. (24.4 N•m) in a circular pattern starting with the 2 middle screws in each manifold.

9. Install the carburetors as described in this chapter.

10. Reconnect the negative battery cable.

Cleaning and inspection

NOTE
Do not remove the reed petals from the reed plate unless replacement is necessary. Always replace reed petals in com-

plete sets. Never turn a reed over for reuse or attempt to straighten a damaged reed.

1. Thoroughly clean the reed plates using clean solvent.

2. Check for excessive wear (indentations), cracks or grooves in the seat area of the reed plate. Replace the reed plate if any damaged is noted.

3. Check the reed petals for cracks, chips or evidence of fatigue. Replace the reed petals if any damage is noted.

4. Check the stand-open gap between the reed petals and the reed plate mating surface. See **Figure 74**, typical. Replace the reed petals if they are preloaded (stick tightly to the reed plate) or stand open more than specified (**Table 11**).

5. To replace the reed petals, bend the lock-washer lock tabs away from the screw heads. Remove the screws attaching the reed petals and retaining washer to the reed plate. Discard the lock tab washers. See **Figure 75**, typical.

6. To reinstall, apply Loctite 271 threadlocking adhesive to the threads of the screws. Position the new reed petals, the original retaining washers and new lock tab washers on the intake manifold. Make sure all components are aligned with the alignment pins in the intake manifold.

7. Tighten the screws to 80 in.-lb. (9.0 N•m) and check the alignment of the screw head to the lock tab washer. If necessary, continue to tighten to a maximum of 100 in.-lb. (11.3 N•m) to align the screw head with the lock tab washer.

8. Bend the lock tab washer of each washer against each screw head.

V6 Models (135-275 hp and 105-140 Jet)

The 135-200 hp and 105-140 Jet models (carbureted and EFI) use a one-piece intake manifold with 6 reed valve blocks. Model years 1994 and 1995 use reed blocks with tapered reed petals that are serviceable. The reed petals are secured by 5 screws on each side of the reed block. Since

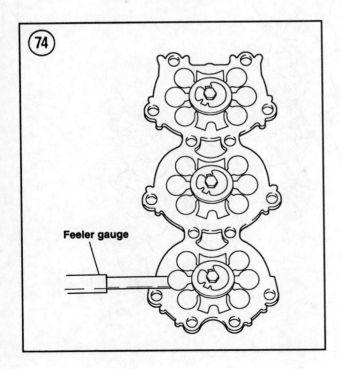

Feeler gauge

1996, all models have been equipped with rubber coated reed blocks and square-tipped reeds. These reed blocks *will* backfit to 1994 and 1995 models.

The 225-250 hp carbureted and EFI models use a one-piece intake manifold with 6 reed valve blocks. Model years 1994-1996 use reed blocks with serviceable tapered reed petals. Early model reed blocks use 4 screws to secure the reed petal to each side of the reed block. Replacement reed blocks for these models use 6 screws to secure

each reed petal and provide more durability. Since 1997, all models have been equipped with rubber coated reed blocks and square-tipped reeds. Rubber coated reed blocks are only serviced as assemblies and will *not* backfit previous model year motors.

The 200 DFI uses the same rubber coated reed blocks and square-tipped reeds that the 1997 225-250 hp models use. The 200 DFI intake manifold is unique in that the electric oil pump is mounted directly to the intake manifold and an

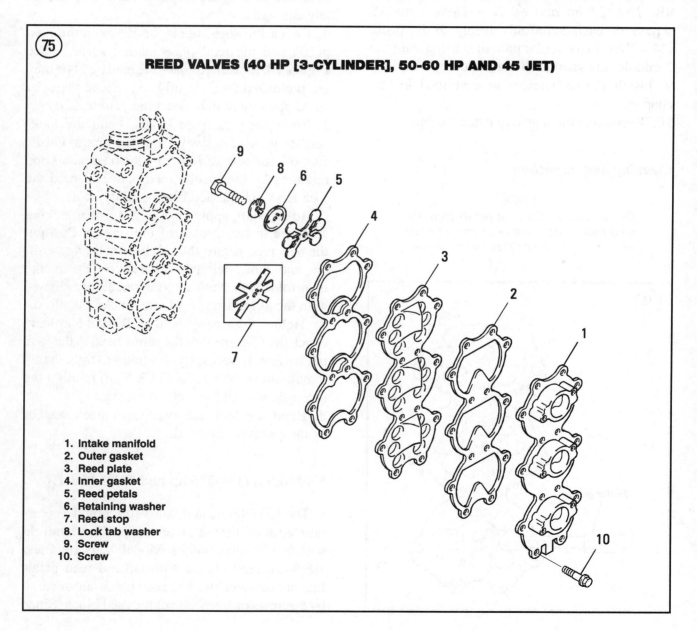

(75)

REED VALVES (40 HP [3-CYLINDER], 50-60 HP AND 45 JET)

1. Intake manifold
2. Outer gasket
3. Reed plate
4. Inner gasket
5. Reed petals
6. Retaining washer
7. Reed stop
8. Lock tab washer
9. Screw
10. Screw

additional spacer (lubrication) plate and gasket are used. The oil pump moves oil through the reed plate's machined channels to each cylinder's reed box area. When removing the intake manifold, remember to disconnect the oil pump electrical connection and external oil supply and air compressor lubrication lines.

The 275 hp models are unique in that they use a separate intake manifold for each cylinder. The intake manifolds and gaskets are different from port to starboard. Each intake manifold contains 2 reed valve block assemblies. The reed valve blocks are only serviced as assemblies.

Removal/installation (135-200 hp and 105-140 Jet models [carbureted and EFI])

1. Disconnect the negative battery cable.

2A. *Carbureted models*—Remove the carburetors as described previously in this chapter.

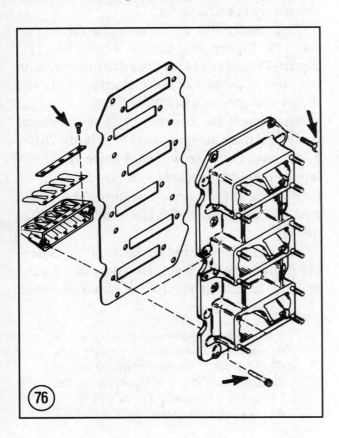

76

2B. *EFI models*—Remove the induction manifold as described previously in this chapter.

NOTE
There are 20 intake manifold screws: 6 of the 12 reed box retaining screws are located in the intake passages and 6 are external, each is in the same horizontal plane as their companion inner screw. Only 8 screws actually secure the intake manifold to the crankcase cover.

3. Remove the 8 screws securing the intake manifold assembly to the power head. See **Figure 76**. If you are unsure which screws to remove, remove all 20 intake manifold screws at this time.

4. Note the position and routing of all bleed (recirculation) lines on the intake manifold. Disconnect all bleed lines from the intake manifold.

5. Carefully remove the intake manifold assembly from the power head. Do not scratch, warp or gouge the intake manifold or crankcase cover.

6. If not already removed, remove the 12 screws (2 each reed box) securing the 6 reed boxes to the intake manifold. Separate the reed boxes from the intake manifold. Remove all gasket material from the reed boxes, intake manifold and crankcase cover.

7. Clean and inspect the reed boxes and intake manifold as described in the next section. On models with serviceable reeds, do not remove the reed petals from the reed plate(s) unless they are going to be replaced.

8. Using a new gasket, install the reed boxes to the intake manifold. Install the 12 retaining screws (2 each reed box) finger-tight.

9. Verify that the gasket is properly positioned and that all holes align correctly. Tighten the 12 reed box retaining screws evenly to 80 in.-lb. (9.0 N•m).

10. Position the intake manifold against the crankcase cover and install the 8 retaining screws. Tighten the retaining screws evenly to 105 in.-lb. (11.9 N•m).

6

11. Reconnect all bleed lines to their original positions.

12A. *Carbureted models*—Install the carburetors as described previously in this chapter.

12B. *EFI models*—Install the induction manifold as described previously in this chapter.

13. Reconnect the negative battery cable on electric start models.

Removal/installation (225-250 hp carbureted and EFI models)

1. Disconnect the negative battery cable.

2A. *Carbureted models*—Remove the carburetors as described previously in this chapter.

2B. *EFI models*—Remove the induction manifold as described previously in this chapter.

3. Remove the 12 screws securing the intake manifold assembly to the power head (10, **Figure 77**).

4. Note the position and routing of all bleed (recirculation) lines on or over the intake manifold. Disconnect all bleed lines that interfere with manifold removal.

5. Carefully remove the intake manifold assembly from the power head. Do not scratch, warp or gouge the intake manifold or crankcase cover.

6. Remove the 12 screws (2 each reed box) securing the 6 reed boxes to the intake manifold (4, **Figure 77**). Separate the reed boxes from the intake manifold. Remove all gasket material from the reed boxes, intake manifold and crankcase cover.

7. Clean and inspect the reed boxes and intake manifold as described in this chapter. On models with serviceable reeds, do not remove the reed petals from the reed plate(s) unless they are going to be replaced. Make sure all machined passages in the intake manifold are clean.

8. Using a new gasket, install the reed boxes to the intake manifold. Coat the threads of the reed box retaining screws with Loctite 271 threadlocking adhesive. Install the 12 retaining screws (2 each reed box) finger-tight.

9. Verify that the gasket is properly positioned and that all holes are aligned. Tighten the 12 reed box retaining screws evenly to 90 in.-lb. (10.2 N•m).

10. Position the intake manifold against the crankcase cover and install the 12 retaining screws. Tighten the retaining screws evenly to 100 in.-lb. (11.3 N•m).

11. Reconnect all bleed lines to their original positions.

12A. *Carbureted models*—Install the carburetors as described previously in this chapter.

12B. *EFI models*—Install the induction manifold as described previously in this chapter.

13. Reconnect the negative battery cable on electric start models.

Removal/installation (200 DFI models)

1. Disconnect the negative battery cable.

2. Remove the induction manifold as described previously in this chapter.

3. Disconnect the air compressor lubrication line (14, **Figure 78**), the oil supply line (13, **Figure 78**) and any bleed lines that interfere with manifold removal. Cap the oil pump supply and the air compressor lubrication lines.

4. Disconnect the electric oil pump electrical connector from the oil pump (11, **Figure 78**).

5. Remove the 2 screws (10, **Figure 78**) securing the oil pump bracket to the power head.

6. Remove the 12 screws securing the intake manifold assembly to the power head (15, **Figure 78**).

7. Carefully remove the intake manifold assembly from the power head. Do not scratch, warp or gouge the intake manifold or crankcase cover.

NOTE
Internal recirculation valves are used on this engine. The 6 valves fit into machined grooves on the mating surface of the crankcase cover to intake manifold. The valves are installed in rubber carriers. Do not lose or misplace the check

INTAKE MANIFOLD AND REED VALVES
(200-225 HP)

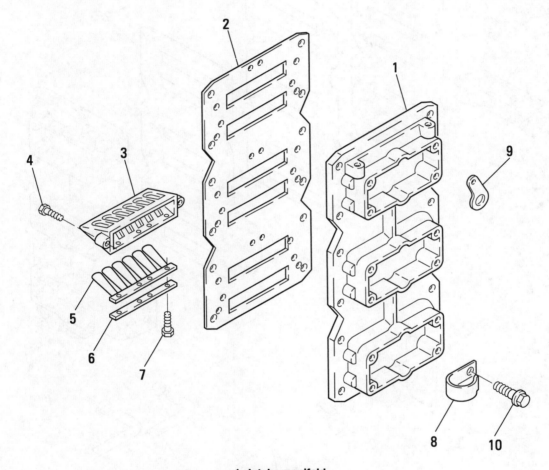

6

1. Intake manifold
2. Gasket
3. Reed box
4. Reed box mounting screw
5. Reed petals
6. Reed clamp plate
7. Reed box screws
8. Clamp (1994-1995 models)
9. Retainer (1996-1997 models)
10. Intake manifold
    mounting screws

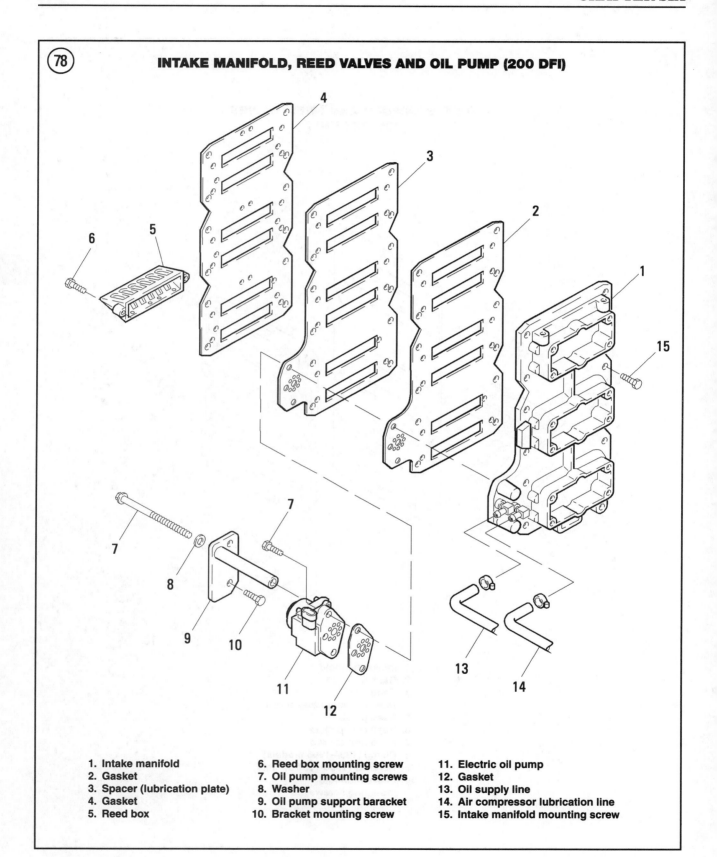

INTAKE MANIFOLD, REED VALVES AND OIL PUMP (200 DFI)

1. Intake manifold
2. Gasket
3. Spacer (lubrication plate)
4. Gasket
5. Reed box
6. Reed box mounting screw
7. Oil pump mounting screws
8. Washer
9. Oil pump support baracket
10. Bracket mounting screw
11. Electric oil pump
12. Gasket
13. Oil supply line
14. Air compressor lubrication line
15. Intake manifold mounting screw

valves and carriers. See Bleed System Service for more information.

8. Remove the 2 screws (7, **Figure 78**) securing the oil pump to the intake manifold. Remove the oil pump from the intake manifold.

9. Remove the 12 screws (2 each reed box) securing the 6 reed boxes to the space plate and intake manifold Separate the reed boxes from the spacer plate. Separate the spacer plate from the intake manifold. Remove all gasket material from the reed boxes, spacer plate, oil pump, intake manifold and crankcase cover.

10. Clean and inspect the reed boxes and intake manifold as described in the next section. The reed boxes are not serviceable. If any defects are noted, replace the suspect reed box. Make sure all machined passages in the intake manifold are clean.

11. Using new gaskets, install the reed boxes to the spacer plate and intake manifold. Coat the threads of the reed box retaining screws with

Loctite 271 threadlocking adhesive. Install the 12 retaining screws (2 each reed box) finger-tight.

12. Verify that the gaskets and spacer plate are properly positioned and that all holes are aligned. Tighten the 12 reed box retaining screws evenly to 90 in.-lb. (10.2 N•m).

13. Using a new gasket, install the oil pump and oil pump bracket to the intake manifold assembly. Install and tighten the 2 screws securely.

14. Position the intake manifold assembly against the crankcase cover and install the 12 retaining screws. Tighten the retaining screws evenly to 100 in.-lb. (11.3 N•m).

15. Install the 2 screws securing the oil pump bracket to the power head. Tighten the screws securely.

16. Reconnect the oil pump electrical connector, oil supply line and air compressor lubrication line. Secure the line connections with new tie-straps.

17. Install the induction manifold as described previously in this chapter.

18. Reconnect the negative battery cable on electric start models.

19. Purge the electric oil pump as described in Chapter Eleven.

Removal/installation (275 hp models)

1. Disconnect the negative battery cable.

2. Remove the carburetors as described previously in this chapter.

3. Remove the 2 screws securing the fuel primer valve bracket to the 2 lower, port intake manifolds. Lay the fuel primer valve and bracket to one side.

4. Note the position and routing of the balance hoses and fuel primer lines to and from each intake manifold. Disconnect the balance hoses, bleed lines and fuel primer lines from the intake manifolds. Refer to **Figures 79-81** for routing diagrams.

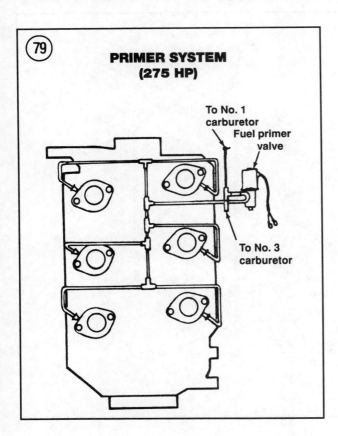

PRIMER SYSTEM (275 HP)

To No. 1 carburetor
Fuel primer valve
To No. 3 carburetor

5. Remove the 4 screws (8, **Figure 82**) securing each intake manifold assembly to the power head. Note the position of the control cable support bracket mounted to the bottom of the port lower intake manifold.

6. Carefully remove each intake manifold assembly from the power head. Do not scratch, warp or gouge any intake manifold or the crankcase cover.

7. Remove the 2 lower screws (9, **Figure 82**) securing the reed mounting block to each intake manifold.

8. Remove the 2 upper reed box screws securing the reed mounting block and upper reed block to each intake manifold. Separate each manifold assembly's reed mounting block (5, **Figure 82**), upper reed box and intake manifold from each other.

9. Remove the 2 screws (11, **Figure 82**) securing the lower reed box to each reed mounting

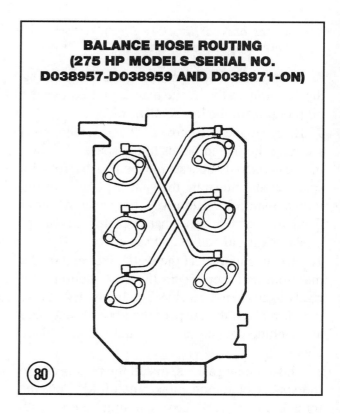

BALANCE HOSE ROUTING (275 HP MODELS—SERIAL NO. D038957-D038959 AND D038971-ON)

⑧⓪

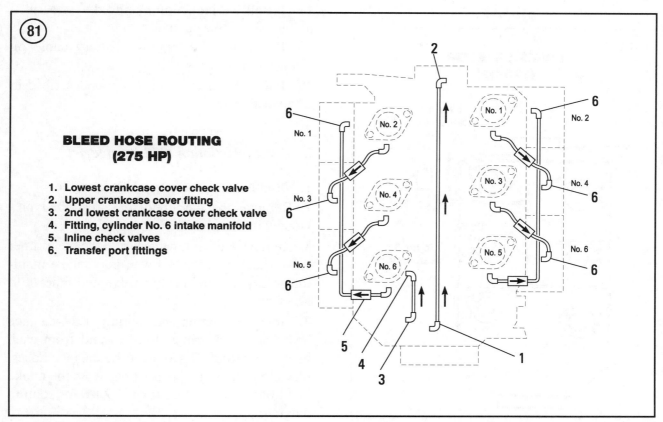

⑧①

BLEED HOSE ROUTING (275 HP)

1. Lowest crankcase cover check valve
2. Upper crankcase cover fitting
3. 2nd lowest crankcase cover check valve
4. Fitting, cylinder No. 6 intake manifold
5. Inline check valves
6. Transfer port fittings

block. Separate each lower reed box from each reed mounting block.

10. Remove all gasket material from the reed boxes, reed mounting blocks, intake manifolds and crankcase cover.

11. Clean and inspect the reed boxes and intake manifolds as described in this chapter. The reed boxes are not serviceable. If any defects are noted, replace the suspect reed box. Make sure all machined passages and fittings in the intake manifold are clean.

12. Using new gaskets, install the lower reed boxes to the reed mounting blocks. Coat the threads of the reed box retaining screws with Loctite 271 threadlocking adhesive. Install and evenly tighten the screws to 60 in.-lb. (6.8 N•m).

13. Using new gaskets install the reed mounting blocks to the intake manifolds. Coat the threads of the reed block lower retaining screws (9, **Figure 82**) with Loctite 271 threadlocking adhesive. Install the screws finger-tight.

14. Using new gaskets install the upper reed boxes to the reed mounting block and intake manifold assemblies. Coat the threads of the reed box retaining screws with Loctite 271 threadlocking adhesive. Install the screws finger-tight.

15. Check the alignment of the reed boxes, reed mounting blocks and intake manifolds. Make sure all holes are aligned. Tighten the 2 upper screws (10, **Figure 82**) and 2 lower screws (9, **Figure 82**) on each intake manifold assembly evenly to 60 in.-lb. (6.8 N•m).

6

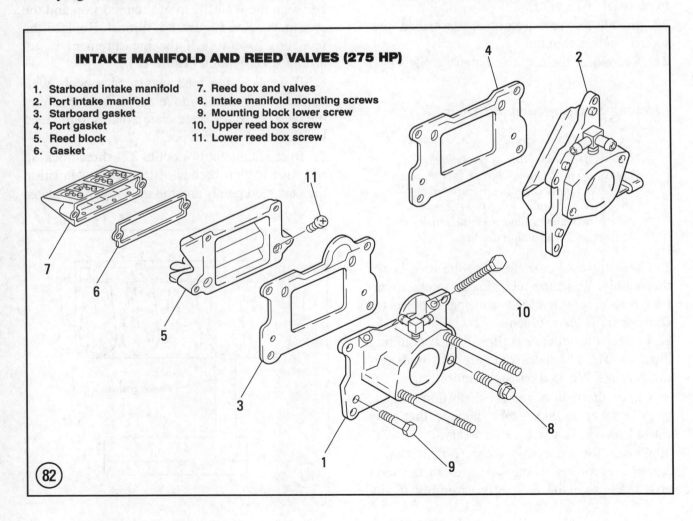

INTAKE MANIFOLD AND REED VALVES (275 HP)

1. Starboard intake manifold
2. Port intake manifold
3. Starboard gasket
4. Port gasket
5. Reed block
6. Gasket
7. Reed box and valves
8. Intake manifold mounting screws
9. Mounting block lower screw
10. Upper reed box screw
11. Lower reed box screw

82

16. Install the intake manifold assemblies to the crankcase cover. Coat the threads of the retaining screws with Loctite 271 threadlocking adhesive. Install the 24 retaining screws (4 each intake manifold) finger-tight.

17. Verify that the intake manifolds are correctly positioned and that control cable bracket is installed on the bottom of the lower port manifold. Tighten each manifold's 4 retaining screws evenly to 150 in.-lb. (16.9 N•m).

18. Reconnect the balance hose, bleed lines and fuel primer lines to the intake manifolds. Refer to **Figures 79-81** for line routing.

19. Position the fuel primer valve bracket on the 2 lower port intake manifolds. Coat the threads of the 2 retaining screws with Loctite 271 threadlocking adhesive. Install and tighten the screws to 60 in.-lb. (6.7 N•m).

20. Install the carburetors as described previously in this chapter.

21. Reconnect the negative battery cable.

Cleaning and inspection (all V-6 models)

NOTE
On reed blocks with serviceable reed petals, do not remove the reeds from the reed block unless replacement is necessary. Always replace reeds in complete sets. Never turn a reed over for reuse or attempt to straighten a damaged reed.

1. Clean the gasket surfaces of the reed boxes thoroughly. Wash the reed boxes, intake manifold, reed mounting blocks and spacer plates (as equipped) in clean solvent.

2. Inspect the intake manifold, reed mounting blocks and spacer plates (as equipped) for distortion, cranks, blocked passages and fittings.

3. Check the reed boxes for distortion, cracks, deep grooves or any other damage that may cause leakage. Replace as necessary.

4. Check for excessive wear (indentations), cracks or grooves in the seat area of the reed boxes. Replace the reed box assembly if any

damage is noted. On rubber coated reed blocks, check for rubber delamination from the reed box casting. Replace any reed box showing rubber delamination.

5. Check the reed petals for cracks, chips or evidence of fatigue. Replace the reed petals or reed box assembly if any damage is noted.

6. Check the stand-open gap between the reed petals and the reed plate mating surface. See **Figure 83**, typical. Replace the reed petals or reed box assembly if any are preloaded (stick tightly to the reed plate) or stand open more than specified (**Table 11**).

7. *275 hp models*—Check the reed stop opening by measuring from the inside edge of the reed stop to the surface of the closed reed petal. A drill bit of the specified dimension should just fit between the widest gap of the reed stop and the reed petal. See **Figure 84**, typical. Replace the reed box assembly if the measurement is not within specification (**Table 11**).

8. To replace the reed petals on models with serviceable reeds, remove the screws attaching the reed petals and reed clamp plates to the reed box. Discard the reed petals.

9. To reinstall, apply Loctite 271 threadlocking adhesive to the threads of the screws. Position the new reed petals and the reed retaining plates

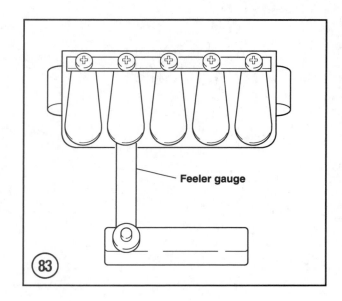

Feeler gauge

83

on the reed box. Install the screws finger-tight. Make sure all components are properly aligned.
10. Tighten the screws evenly to 25 in.-lb. (2.8 N.m).

FUEL BLEED (RECIRCULATION) SYSTEM

Multiple cylinder motors are equipped with a fuel bleed (recirculation) system designed to col-

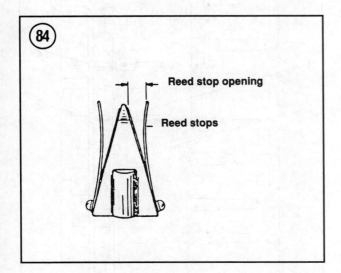

Reed stop opening
Reed stops

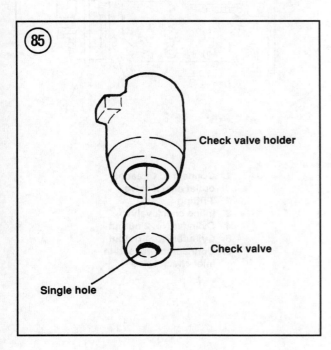

Check valve holder
Check valve
Single hole

lect unburned fuel and oil from the low spots of the individual crankcase areas. Since the intake system used by 2-stroke engines does not completely transfer all of the fuel sent through the crankcase to the combustion chamber (especially during low-speed operation), the recirculation system provides a method of collecting the fuel and oil pooled in the low spots of the crankcase. The bleed system pumps the fuel/oil to the intake ports or intake manifold where it can be transferred to the combustion chamber and burned.

Many recirculation systems also collect the fuel and oil pooled in the lower crankshaft bearing area and pump it to the upper crankshaft bearing to ensure proper upper crankshaft bearing lubrication. These models can suffer an upper crankshaft bearing failure if the system malfunctions and does not pump fuel and oil to the upper bearing carrier.

Correct recirculation system operation is vitally important to efficient engine operation. If the system fails, excessive amounts of fuel and oil will puddle in the crankcase and not reach the combustion chamber during low-speed operation, causing a lean mixture. When the engine is accelerated, the puddles of fuel and oil are quickly drawn into the engine causing a temporary excessively rich mixture. This will result in the following symptoms:
1. Poor low-speed performance.
2. Poor acceleration.
3. Spark plug fouling.
4. Stalling or spitting at idle.
5. Excessive smoke on acceleration.

Recirculation System Service

Refer to the appropriate **Figure 85-99** for this procedure.

All recirculation systems require one-way check valves for operation. External check valves are either mounted directly to the crank-

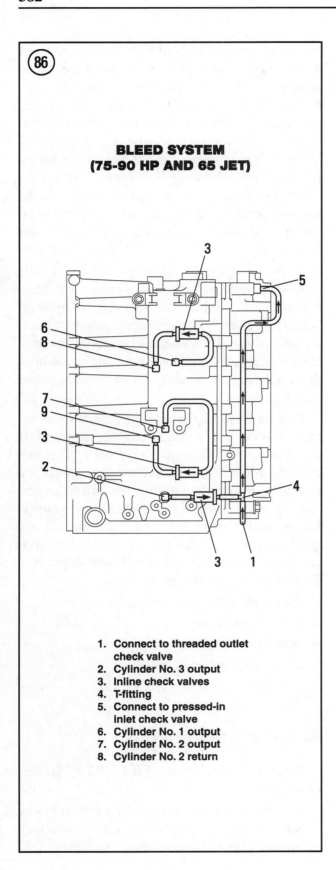

(86)

**BLEED SYSTEM
(75-90 HP AND 65 JET)**

1. Connect to threaded outlet
   check valve
2. Cylinder No. 3 output
3. Inline check valves
4. T-fitting
5. Connect to pressed-in
   inlet check valve
6. Cylinder No. 1 output
7. Cylinder No. 2 output
8. Cylinder No. 2 return

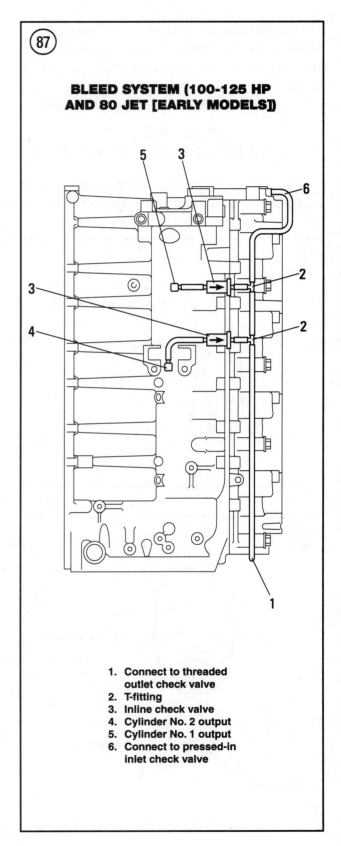

(87)

**BLEED SYSTEM (100-125 HP
AND 80 JET [EARLY MODELS])**

1. Connect to threaded
   outlet check valve
2. T-fitting
3. Inline check valve
4. Cylinder No. 2 output
5. Cylinder No. 1 output
6. Connect to pressed-in
   inlet check valve

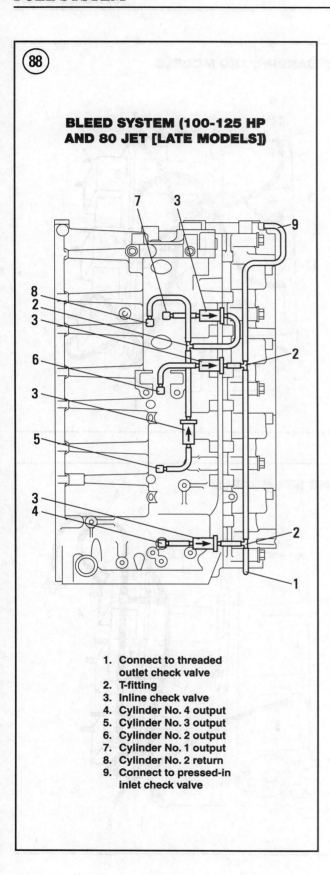

(88)

BLEED SYSTEM (100-125 HP AND 80 JET [LATE MODELS])

1. Connect to threaded outlet check valve
2. T-fitting
3. Inline check valve
4. Cylinder No. 4 output
5. Cylinder No. 3 output
6. Cylinder No. 2 output
7. Cylinder No. 1 output
8. Cylinder No. 2 return
9. Connect to pressed-in inlet check valve

case (or intake manifold) or are mounted in the recirculation lines.

Internal check valves are mounted in the crankcase cover, just behind the intake manifolds. Refer to Chapter Eight for additional power head exploded views.

Inspect the internal check valves by removing them from their holder/carrier and looking into the check valve assembly. If light is visible, the nylon check ball is missing (melted) and the check valve must be replaced. If light is not visible, insert a fine wire into the valve to check for slight movement of the check ball. Replace the check valve if movement is not possible. Replace the check valve holder/carrier if it is burned or damaged.

The end of the check valve with one hole is the inlet side. Fluid show flow into this hole, but not back out. The end of the check valve with 2 (or more) holes is the outlet side. Fluid should exit these holes, but not enter. On inline models, the internal valves are always installed in a manner that allows fluid to flow toward the intake manifold, but not toward the crankshaft.

All check valves should flow in the direction of the arrow on the appropriate diagram, but not flow in the opposite direction. Fittings should flow in both directions. A small syringe and a piece of recirculation line can quickly test the system. Replace or clean any fitting that will not flow in both directions. Replace any check valve that flows in both directions or will not flow in either direction. Push on the syringe plunger to check flow into a fitting or check valve. Pull on the syringe plunger to check flow out of a fitting or check valve. Also, inspect and replace any recirculation lines that are damaged or deteriorated.

When replacing fittings or check valves, coat pipe thread fittings with Loctite PST pipe sealant. Check valves that are press fit should be coated lightly with Loctite 271 threadlocking adhesive prior to installation.

6

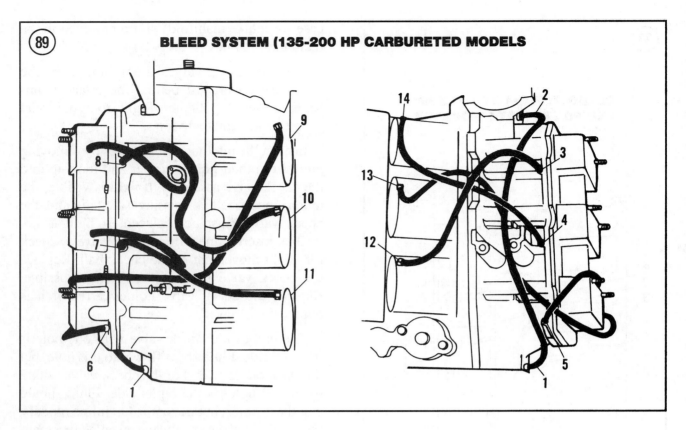

89

BLEED SYSTEM (135-200 HP CARBURETED MODELS

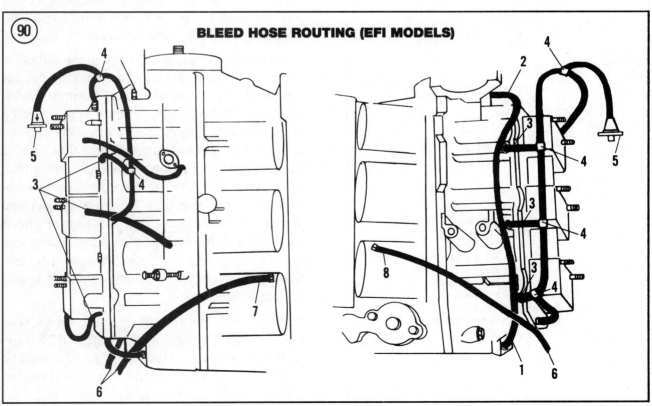

90

BLEED HOSE ROUTING (EFI MODELS)

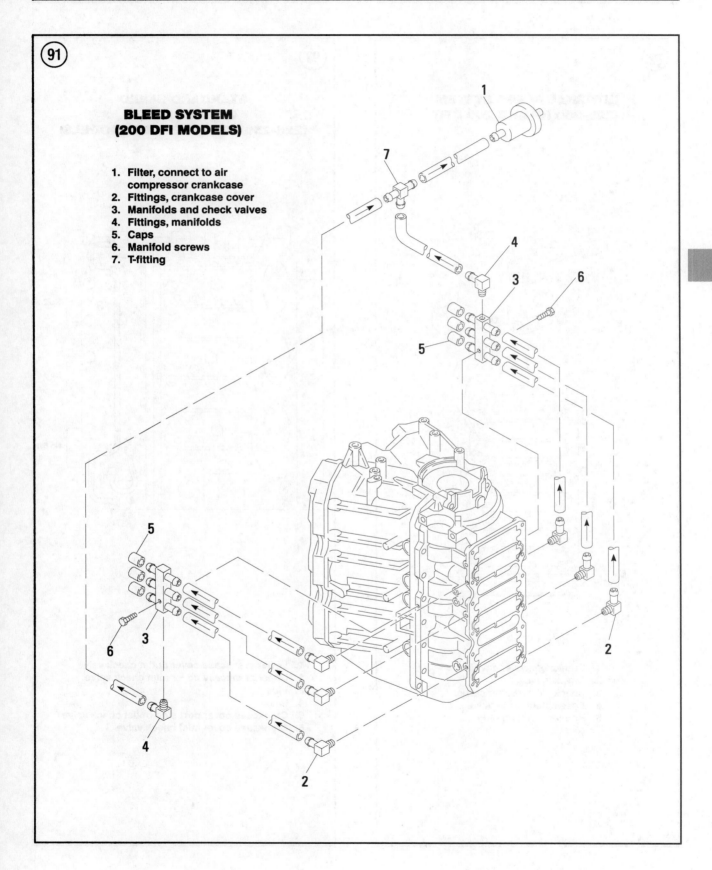

91

**BLEED SYSTEM
(200 DFI MODELS)**

1. Filter, connect to air
   compressor crankcase
2. Fittings, crankcase cover
3. Manifolds and check valves
4. Fittings, manifolds
5. Caps
6. Manifold screws
7. T-fitting

6

**INTERNAL BLEED SYSTEM
(225-250 HP AND 200 DFI)**

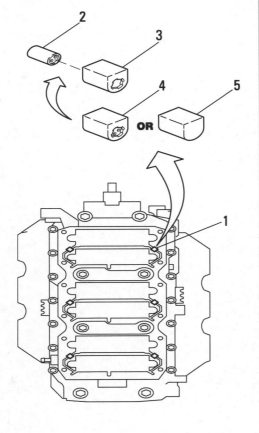

1. Crankcase cover cavities
2. Check valve
3. Check valve rubber carrier
4. Assembled check valve
5. Rubber blocking plug

**STANDARD BLEED
HOSE ROUTING
(225-250 HP AND 200 DFI MODELS)**

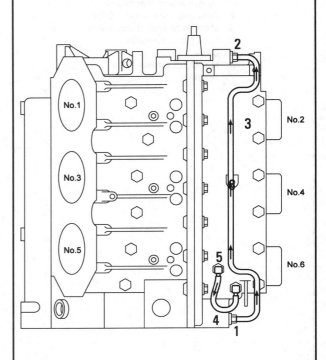

1. Lower crankcase cover outlet check valve
2. Upper crankcase cover inlet check valve
3. Line
4. Line
5. Crankcase cover port side outlet check valve
6. Crankcase cover inlet check valve

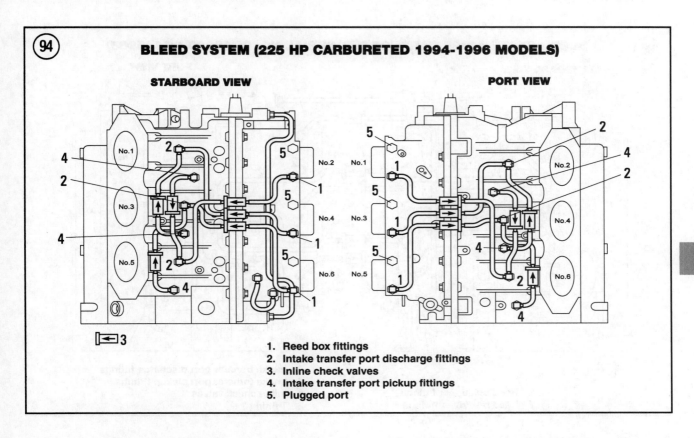

94

BLEED SYSTEM (225 HP CARBURETED 1994-1996 MODELS)

STARBOARD VIEW   PORT VIEW

1. Reed box fittings
2. Intake transfer port discharge fittings
3. Inline check valves
4. Intake transfer port pickup fittings
5. Plugged port

6

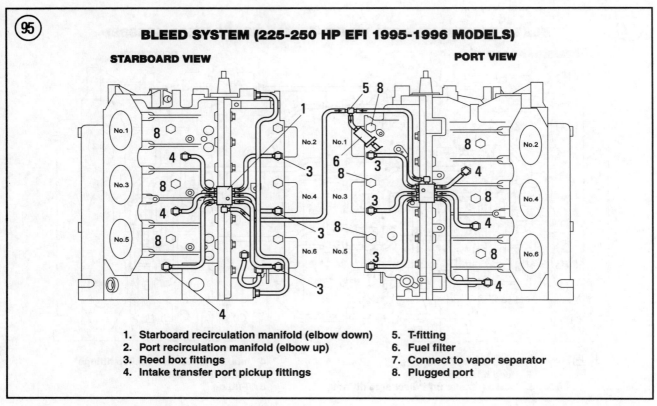

95

BLEED SYSTEM (225-250 HP EFI 1995-1996 MODELS)

STARBOARD VIEW   PORT VIEW

1. Starboard recirculation manifold (elbow down)
2. Port recirculation manifold (elbow up)
3. Reed box fittings
4. Intake transfer port pickup fittings
5. T-fitting
6. Fuel filter
7. Connect to vapor separator
8. Plugged port

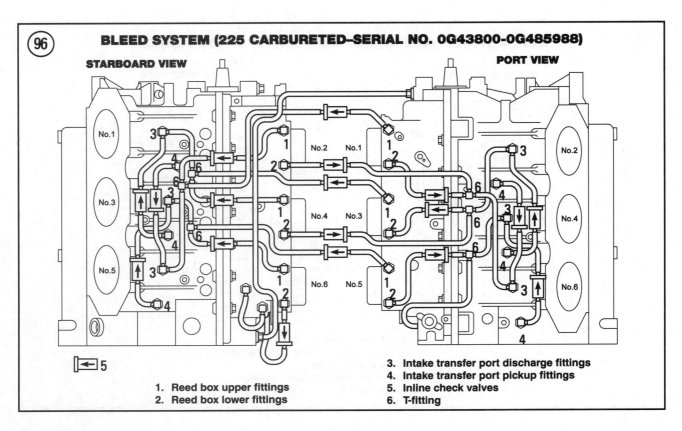

96 **BLEED SYSTEM (225 CARBURETED–SERIAL NO. 0G43800-0G485988)**

1. Reed box upper fittings
2. Reed box lower fittings
3. Intake transfer port discharge fittings
4. Intake transfer port pickup fittings
5. Inline check valves
6. T-fitting

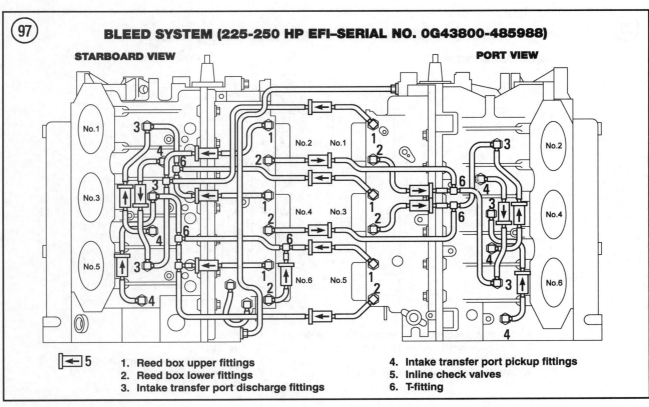

97 **BLEED SYSTEM (225-250 HP EFI–SERIAL NO. 0G43800-485988)**

1. Reed box upper fittings
2. Reed box lower fittings
3. Intake transfer port discharge fittings
4. Intake transfer port pickup fittings
5. Inline check valves
6. T-fitting

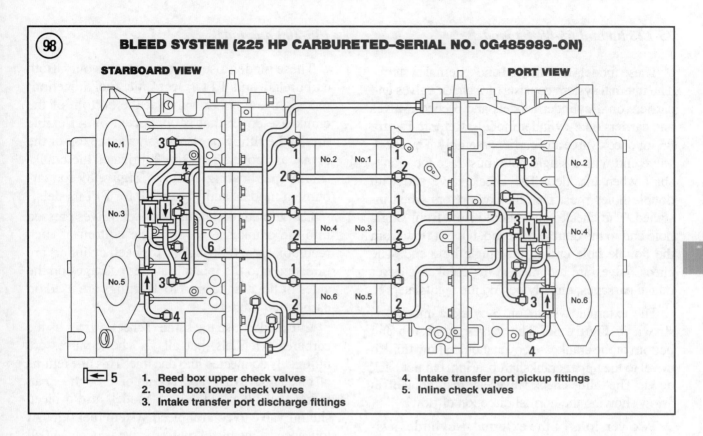

(98) **BLEED SYSTEM (225 HP CARBURETED–SERIAL NO. 0G485989-ON)**

STARBOARD VIEW   PORT VIEW

1. Reed box upper check valves   4. Intake transfer port pickup fittings
2. Reed box lower check valves   5. Inline check valves
3. Intake transfer port discharge fittings

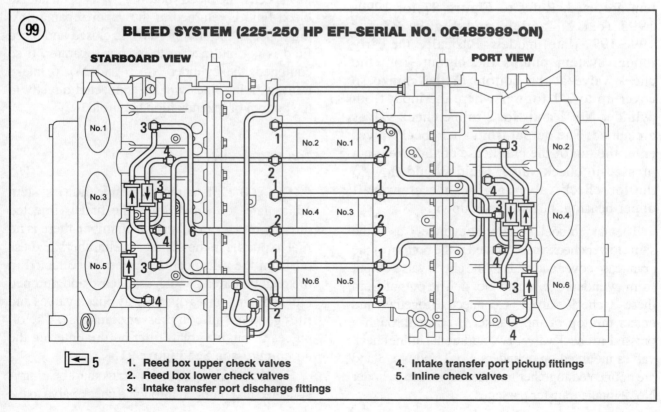

(99) **BLEED SYSTEM (225-250 HP EFI–SERIAL NO. 0G485989-ON)**

STARBOARD VIEW   PORT VIEW

1. Reed box upper check valves   4. Intake transfer port pickup fittings
2. Reed box lower check valves   5. Inline check valves
3. Intake transfer port discharge fittings

75-125 hp and 65-80 Jet models

These models use internal and external systems. The internal system consists of 2 check valves and carriers on 3-cylinder models and 3 check valves and carriers on 4-cylinder models. Refer to **Figure 85** for check valve and carrier assembly. The check valve end with a single hole must face the crankshaft when installed. The check valve end with double holes must face the carburetors when installed. The check valve should flow from single hole end to the double hole end, but not flow from the double hole end to the single hole end. The check valves are mounted in the crankcase cover intake passages, directly behind the reed plate(s).

The external system on 3-cylinder models is shown in **Figure 86**. The valves at the top and bottom of the crankcase cover should allow fluid to travel to the upper crankshaft bearing, but not back down. The inline check valves are marked with an arrow showing the normal direction of flow.

Two versions of the external 4-cylinder system are used. Refer to **Figure 87** for 1994-1995 (early) models and **Figure 88** for 1996-1997 (late) models. Basically, the early model system pumps the output from the check valve at the bottom of the crankcase cover up to 2 T-fittings where the input from cylinder No. 1 and No. 2 inline check valves are added. The output from all 3 check valves enter the top of the crankcase cover through a pressed-in check valve. Fluid should flow to the top check valve and into the crankshaft upper bearing, but not back down.

The late model system (4-cylinder) uses the same lower check valve located at the bottom of the crankcase cover and adds inline check valve output from cylinders No. 2 and No. 4. The output from these 3 check valves is connected together and enters the top of the crankcase cover through a pressed-in check valve. Two additional inline check valves mounted on cylinders No. 1 and No. 3 and are connected together and discharge into cylinder No. 2 intake transfer passages.

135-200 hp models

These models use external systems only. Both carbureted and EFI (electronic fuel injection) models use a check valve at the bottom of the crankcase cover that is connected by a flexible line to the fitting or check valve at the top of the crankcase cover. This line lubricates the crankshaft upper bearing. Refer to **Figure 89** for carbureted models and **Figure 90** for EFI models.

Carbureted models use 6 check valves pressed into the crankcase cover at the bottom of each reed box area. 6 fittings (1 for each cylinder) are threaded into the intake transfer passages on the sides of the crankcase. No T-fittings are used on carbureted models.

EFI models use the same 6 check valves as the carbureted models, but all six check valves are ultimately connected into one line. This line returns all bleed fluid to the vapor separator through a small inline fuel filter. 1994-1995 models use a bleed shutoff valve to control bleed system fuel flow. At low speeds, the bleed shutoff valve is open and all bleed fluid is returned to the vapor separator. At high speeds, the shutoff valve is closed and bleed fluid is not returned to the vapor separator. If so equipped, the cylinder No. 5 and No. 6 intake transfer fitting lines will be connected directly to the bottom of the induction manifold.

200 DFI models

The 200 DFI (direct fuel injection) system recirculates oil only. Since the fuel is injected directly into the combustion chamber, there is no fuel to puddle in the crankcase chambers. Excess oil from the oil injection system is collected in the reed box area of each crankcase and pumped out through a series of one-way check valves and fittings to the air compressor crankcase. The oil passes through a small filter before entering the air compressor. See **Figure 91**.

Excess oil from the lower crankshaft bearing is collected and pumped through a check valve to the upper main bearing. Additionally, 2 check valves are located on the starboard, lower front corner of the crankcase cover. The 2 check valves are connected with a short piece of hose. Refer to *225-250 hp models*, as these check valves and hose routings are the same as 225-250 hp models.

An internal system of 6 check valves, mounted in rubber carriers is also used. The 6 valves are mounted in the grooved cavities on the crankcase cover side of the crankcase cover to intake manifold mating surface. Refer to *225-250 hp models* and **Figure 92** for more information.

225-250 hp models

All 225-250 hp models use external bleed systems. Models equipped with internal systems are accessed by removing the intake manifold. The check valves or blocking plugs are mounted in the grooved cavities on the crankcase cover to the intake manifold mating surface. See **Figure 92**. Internal systems are used as follows:

225 hp carbureted models, prior serial No. 0G129222—These models do not use internal recirculation systems and cannot accept the check valves.

225-250 hp carbureted and EFI models, serial No. 0G129222-0G437999—These models use 6 internal recirculation check valves mounted in rubber carriers in the grooved cavities on the crankcase cover. This group includes the 200 DFI engine.

225-250 hp carbureted and EFI models, serial No. 0G438000-on—These models use 6 rubber plugs to block the grooved cavities on the crankcase cover.

To service the internal valves or rubber plugs, remove the intake manifold as described previously in this chapter under *Reed valve service*. Remove and inspect the check valves or rubber plugs. Replace any valves or plugs that show evidence of heat damage or deterioration. The check valves should flow fluid in one direction only. Replace any check

valve that flows in both directions or is blocked in both directions. Install the check valves so that the end with 2 holes is facing downward.

The external bleed systems used on 225-250 hp carbureted and EFI models have undergone numerous major revisions. It is very important to note the original position of the lines and valves before removal. The use of an instant camera is definitely warranted on these systems. In addition, consider using color-coded tape or tie-straps to identify the lines.

The upper crankshaft bearing lubrication system and port side mounted check valves with 4 in. (102 mm) hose are common to all 225-250 hp models, as well as the 200 DFI. Refer to **Figure 93** for component location and routing on these circuits.

> *CAUTION*
> *If you do not note and mark the external recirculation system before disassembly or disconnection, it will be nearly impossible to reconnect the system properly, even with the aid of diagrams.*

Make sure that both recirculation circuits shown in **Figure 93** are connected and identified before attempting to service the remaining recirculation circuits. Refer to **Figure 94-99** as necessary for the specific system that applies to your motor. EFI models (1995-1996) with the recirculation manifolds mounted on each side of the power head, must be orientated as shown in **Figure 95**. The discharge fitting must face up on the starboard side and face down on the port side.

> *CAUTION*
> *Due to the many systems used in the 1994-1997 model line, replacement power heads will be compatible with all recirculation systems. Make sure all unused ports on 1994-1996 models are plugged with the appropriate pipe plugs and Loctite PST pipe sealant. Any open*

ports will cause a massive air leak into that cylinder, leading to power head failure.

275 hp models

This engine uses an external bleed system only. Routing of the bleed system and balance tubes is relatively straight forward and is covered under *Reed valve service*. Refer to **Figure 80** and **Figure 81** for routing diagrams.

All 6 inline check valve arrows should point away from the intake manifolds and toward the intake transfer fittings. The lower crankcase cover fittings should flow out of the valves to their respective fittings, but not back in.

Table 1 CARBURETOR SPECIFICATIONS (75-225 AND 275 HP AND 65-140 JET)

Float level	
75-125 hp and 65 and 80 Jet	27/64-29/64 in. (10.72-11.51 mm)
135-225 hp and 105 and 140 Jet	Flush with bowl edge (bowl inverted)
275 hp	11/16 in. (17.5 mm)
Float weight	
75-125 hp and 65 and 80 Jet	0.23-0.26 oz. (6.6-7.4 g)
Initial idle mixture screw adjustment	
75 hp	1-1/8 turns out
90 hp and 65 Jet	1-1/4 turns out
100-125 hp and 80 Jet	1-1/2 turns out
135-225 hp and 105 and 140 Jet	1-1/2 turns out
275 hp	Fixed
Vent Jet	
WME-46, 47, 48 and 49 carburetors	0.094 in.
All other carburetors	None

Table 2 STANDARD MAIN JET (75-125 HP AND 65-80 JET)

	Cylinder number			
Standard main jet	**No. 1**	**No. 2**	**No. 3**	**No. 4**
75 hp				
WME-46 carburetor	0.052 in.	0.052 in.	0.052 in.	–
WME-59 carburetor	0.052 in.	0.054 in.	0.052 in.	–
WME-59-3A carburetor	0.052 in.	0.054 in.	0.054 in.	–
90 hp and 65 Jet				
WME-49 carburetor	0.062 in.	0.064 in.	0.062 in.	–
WME-62 carburetor	0.062 in.	0.064 in.	0.062 in.	–
WME62-3A carburetor	0.062 in.	0.064 in.	0.064 in.	–
100 hp				
WME-32 carburetor	0.046 in.	0.048 in.	0.052 in.	0.052 in.
WME-50 carburetor	0.048 in.	0.050 in.	0.048 in.	0.052 in.
WME-50-3A carburetor	0.048 in.	0.050 in.	0.050 in.	0.052 in.
115 hp and 80 Jet				
WME-33 carburetor	0.052 in.	0.056 in.	0.056 in.	0.060 in.
WME-40 carburetor	0.060 in.	0.070 in.	0.070 in.	0.074 in.
WME-51 carburetor	0.062 in.	0.062 in.	0.060 in.	0.064 in.
WME-51-3A carburetor	0.062 in.	0.062 in.	0.062 in.	0.064 in.
(continued)				

Table 2 STANDARD MAIN JET (75-125 HP AND 65-80 JET) (continued)

Standard main jet	Cylinder number			
	No. 1	No. 2	No. 3	No. 4
125 hp				
WME-34 carburetor	0.066 in.	0.068 in.	0.070 in.	0.072 in.
WME-52 carburetor	0.070 in.	0.080 in.	0.078 in.	0.080 in.
WME-52-3A carburetor	0.070 in.	0.080 in.	0.080 in.	0.080 in.

Table 3 STANDARD MAIN AND IDLE AIR JETS
(135-225 HP, 275 HP AND 105-140 JET)

	No.1	No.2	No.3	No.4	No.5	No.6
Standard main jet						
WMH-30	0.066 in.	0.066 in.	0.066 in.	0.066 in.	0.066 in.	0.066 in.
WMH-31	0.062 in.	0.062 in.	0.062 in.	0.062 in.	0.062 in.	0.062 in.
WMH-32	0.062 in.	0.062 in.	0.062 in.	0.062 in.	0.062 in.	0.062 in.
WMH-33	0.064 in.	0.064 in.	0.064 in.	0.064 in.	0.064 in.	0.064 in.
WMH-34/39	0.066 in.	0.066 in.	0.064 in.	0.064 in.	0.064 in.	0.064 in.
WMV-1	0.072 in.	0.072 in.	0.072 in.	0.072 in.	0.072 in.	0.072 in.
WMV-2	0.074 in.	0.074 in.	0.074 in.	0.074 in.	0.074 in.	0.074 in.
WMV-3	0.074 in.	0.074 in.	0.074 in.	0.074 in.	0.074 in.	0.074 in.
WMV-4	0.078 in.	0.078 in.	0.078 in.	0.078 in.	0.078 in.	0.078 in.
WMV-5	0.082 in.	0.082 in.	0.080 in.	0.080 in.	0.080 in.	0.080 in.
WMH-19	0.078 in.	0.078 in.	0.078 in.	0.074 in.	0.080 in.	0.076 in.
WMH-19A	0.074 in.	0.074 in.	0.076 in.	0.074 in.	0.076 in.	0.074 in.
WMH-46	0.074 in.	0.074 in.	0.076 in.	0.074 in.	0.076 in.	0.074 in.
WMH-47	0.074 in.	0.074 in.	0.074 in.	0.076 in.	0.074 in.	0.076 in.
WMV-7	0.086 in.	0.086 in.	0.088 in.	0.088 in.	0.088 in.	0.088 in.
WMV-13	0.084 in.	0.082 in.	0.084 in.	0.86 in.	0.084 in.	0.082 in.
275 hp	0.082 in.	0.082 in.	0.084 in.	0.082 in.	0.088 in.	0.082 in.
Idle air bleed jet						
WMH-30	.054 in.	.054 in.	.054 in.	.054 in.	.054 in.	.054 in.
WMH-31	.052 in.	.054 in.	.054 in.	.054 in.	.054 in.	.054 in.
WMH-32	.058 in.	.058 in.	.058 in.	.058 in.	.058 in.	.058 in.
WMH-33	.048 in.	.048 in.	.048 in.	.048 in.	.048 in.	.048 in.
WMH-34/39	.046 in.	.046 in.	.046 in.	.046 in.	.046 in.	.046 in.
WMV-1	.036 in.	.036 in.	.036 in.	.036 in.	.040 in.	.036 in.
WMV-2	.034 in.	.034 iet.	.034 in.	.034 in.	.038 in.	.034 in.
WMV-3	.044 in.	.044 in.	.044 in.	.044 in.	.048 in.	.044 in.
WMV-4	.030 in.	.030 in.	.030 in.	.030 in.	.034 in.	.030 in.
WMV-5	.052 in.	.052 in.	.028 in.	.028 in.	.032 in.	.028 in.

Table 4 STANDARD OFF-IDLE AIR JET AND
BACK DRAFT VENT JET SIZES (135-225 HP AND 105 AND 140 JET)

Off-idle air jet	
WMH-32	.040 in.
All other WMH models	.050 in.
All WMV models	not applicable

(continued)

Table 4 STANDARD OFF-IDLE AIR JET AND BACK DRAFT VENT JET SIZES (135-200 HP AND 105 AND 140 JET) (continued)

Back draft vent jet	
WMH-30	.084 in.
WMH-31	.086 in.
WMH-32	.090 in.
WMH-33	.084 in.
WMH-34/39	.084 in.
WMV-1	.086 in.
WMV-2	.086 in.
WMV-3	.082 in.
WMV-4	.086 in.
WMV-5	.096 in.

Table 5 CARBURETOR IDENTIFICATION (135-200 HP AND 105 AND 140 JET)

	1994-1995 models	1996-1997 models
135 hp	WMH-30	WMV-1
150 hp and 105 Jet	WMH-31	WMV-2
XR6 and Magnum III	WMH-32	WMV-3
175 hp	WMH-33	WMV-4
200 hp and 140 Jet	WMH-34/39	WMV-5

Table 6 CARBURETOR IDENTIFICATION (225 HP)

Model year	1994	1994-1/2	1995	1996	1997
Carburetor number	WMH-19A	WMH-46	WMH-47	WMV-7	WMV-13

Table 7 WMV AND WMH HIGH ALTITUDE MAIN JET SPECIFICATIONS

Standard jet	5000 ft. (1524 m)	7000 ft. (2134 m)	9000 ft. (2743 m)	11000 ft. (3353 m)
0.060 in.	0.056 in.	0.056 in.	0.056 in.	0.054 in.
0.062 in.	0.058 in.	0.058 in.	0.056 in.	0.054 in.
0.064 in.	0.060 in.	0.060 in.	0.058 in.	0.056 in.
0.066 in.	0.062 in.	0.062 in.	0.060 in.	0.058 in.
0.068 in.	0.064 in.	0.064 in.	0.062 in.	0.060 in.
0.070 in.	0.066 in.	0.064 in.	0.064 in.	0.062 in.
0.072 in.	0.068 in.	0.066 in.	0.066 in.	0.064 in.
0.074 in.	0.070 in.	0.068 in.	0.068 in.	0.066 in.
0.076 in.	0.072 in.	0.070 in.	0.068 in.	0.068 in.
0.078 in.	0.074 in.	0.072 in.	0.070 in.	0.068 in.
0.080 in.	0.076 in.	0.074 in.	0.072 in.	0.070 in.
0.082 in.	0.078 in.	0.076 in.	0.074 in.	0.072 in.
0.084 in.	0.080 in.	0.078 in.	0.076 in.	0.074 in.
0.086 in.	0.082 in.	0.080 in.	0.078 in.	0.076 in.
0.088 in.	0.084 in.	0.082 in.	0.080 in.	0.078 in.
0.090 in.	0.086 in.	0.084 in.	0.082 in.	0.080 in.

Table 8 EFI AND DFI SPECIFICATIONS (150-200 HP)

Injector fuel line pressure	
1994-1995 models	36-39 psi (248.2-268.9 kPa)
1996-1997 models	34-36 psi (234.4-248.2 kPa)
Vapor separator float level	Factory preset
Throttle position sensor specifications	
ECM part No.14632A13 and below	
Throttle position sensor	
Idle position	0.125-0.145 volt
Wide-open throttle position	7.00-7.46 volt
ECM part No.14632A15	
Throttle position sensor	
Idle position	0.24-0.26 volt
Wide-open throttle position	7.00-7.46 VDC
ECM part No.14632A16 or 824003-1-on	
Throttle position sensor	
Idle position	0.20-0.30 volt
Wide-open throttle position	7.00-7.46 volt
Fuel injector resistance	
At individual injectors	2.0-2.4 ohms
At injector harness (pairs)	0.9-1.3 ohms
ECM amperage draw	60-90 milli-amps
Fuel injector fuel line pressure (200 DFI)	87-91 psi (600-627 kPa)
Direct injector air line pressure (200 DFI)	77-81 psi (531-559 kPa)
Vapor separator float level (200 DFI)	Factory preset
Direct injector resistance (200 DFI)	1.0-1.6 ohms (measured at each injector)
Fuel injector resistance (200 DFI)	1.7-1.9 ohms (measured at each injector)
Injector fuel line pressure (225-250 EFI)	34-36 psi (234-248 kPa)
Vapor separator float level (225-250 EFI)	Factory preset
Throttle position sensor voltage	
Carbureted models	
Idle position	0.90-1.00 volts
Wide open throttle position	3.70-3.80 volts
EFI models	
Idle position	0.90-1.00 volts
Wide open throttle position	3.55-4.05 volts
Fuel injector resistance	
At individual injectors	11.0-13.0 ohms
At injector harness (pairs)	5.0-7.0 ohms

Table 9 FUEL PUMP SPECIFICATIONS (MECHANICAL FUEL PUMP)

	psi (kPa) @ idle	psi (kPa) @ wide-open throttle
75-125 hp and 45-80 Jet	2.5-4 (17.2-27.6)	4-7 (27.6-48.3)
135-250 hp and 105-140 Jet	1-3 (6.9-10.3)	6-8 (41.4-55.2)
275 hp (2 pumps)	5 (34.5)	6-8 (41.4-55.2)

Table 10 FUEL PUMP SPECIFICATIONS (ELECTRIC FUEL PUMP)

	psi (kPa)
150-200 hp EFI at fuel rail	
1994-1995 models	36-39 (248.2-268.9)
1996-1997 models	34-36 (234.4-248.2)
225-250 hp EFI at fuel rail	34-36 (234.4-248.2)
200 DFI at air/fuel rail	87-91 (600-627.4), 10 psi (69 kPa) above air rail pressure
Amperage draw	6-9 amps at all speeds

Table 11 REED VALVE SPECIFICATIONS

Model	Maximum stand open	Reed stop opening
75-250 hp and 45-140 Jet	0.020 in. (0.51 mm)	not adjustable
275 hp	0.020 in. (0.51 mm)	0.130 in. (3.30 mm)

Table 12 TORQUE SPECIFICATIONS (CARBURETED MODELS)

Fastener	in.-lbs.	ft.-lbs.	N•m
Carburetor air intake cover			
225 hp (air box plate)	70	–	7.9
Carburetor emulsion tube or plug			
135-225 hp and 105-140 Jet	33	–	3.7
Carburetor fuel bowl screws			
75-125 hp and 60-80 Jet	18	–	2.0
135-200 hp and 105-140 Jet	26	–	2.9
225 hp	26	–	2.9
Carburetor main jet access plug			
75-125 hp and 65-80 Jet	22	–	2.5
135-200 hp and 105-140 Jet	33	–	3.7
225 hp (all float chamber plugs)	33	–	3.7
Carburetor mounting nuts or screws			
75-125 hp and 65-80 Jet	100	–	11.3
135-225 hp and 105-140 Jet	70	–	8.0
275 hp	60	–	6.8
Carburetor top cover			
75-125 hp and 20-80 Jet	18	–	2.0
135-225 hp (WMV models)	18	–	2.0
Carburetor throttle plate screws			
75-125 hp and 20-80 Jet	6	–	0.7
Mechanical fuel pump cover and			
fuel pump mounting screws			
75-125 hp and 65-80 Jet	40	–	4.5
135-200 hp and 105-140 Jet	55	–	6.0
225 hp	60	–	6.8
275 hp	40	–	4.5
Throttle position sensor (TPS)			
225 hp	20	–	2.3

Table 13 TORQUE SPECIFICATIONS (INJECTED MODELS)

Fastener	in.-lbs.	ft.-lbs.	N•m
200 DFI Air compressor pulley	110	–	12.4
200 DFI Air compressor mounting	–	19	25.8
200 DFI Air/fuel rails	–	33	44.7
Electronic control module (ECM)			
150-200 hp EFI models	45	–	5.1
225-250 hp EFI models	80	–	9.0
200 DFI models	70	–	7.9
Fuel holder bracket	83	–	9.4
Engine coolant temperature (ECT) sensor			
All models	204	17	23
Electric fuel pump terminals (150-200 [1996-1997], 200 DFI and 225-250 hp)			
Positive (small) stud	6	–	0.7
Negative (large) stud	8	–	0.9
Fuel management adaptor (from pressure regulator) to induction manifold			
150-250 hp (except 200 DFI)	45	–	5.1
Fuel pressure regulator (EFI models)			
150-200 hp (1994-1995)			
Return line elbow fitting	30	–	3.4
150-200 hp (1996-1997) and 225-250 hp			
Mounting screws	30	–	3.4
Return line elbow fitting	45	–	5.1
Fuel rail adapter to fuel rail			
150-250 hp (except 200 DFI)	18	–	2.0
Fuel rail to induction manifold (EFI models)			
150-200 hp	35	–	4.0
225-250 hp	45	–	5.1
Induction manifold assembly to power head			
150-200 hp (specified sequence)	90	–	10.2
200 DFI	–	18	24.4
225-250 hp	–	19	25.8
Manifold absolute pressure (MAP) sensor			
200 DFI and 225-250 hp	100	–	11.3
Mechanical fuel pump cover and mounting screws			
150-200 hp EFI models	55	–	6.2
200 DFI and 225-250 hp EFI	60	–	6.8
Throttle position sensor (TPS)			
200 DFI			
Sensor to mounting bracket	30	–	3.2
Bracket to induction manifold	45	–	5.1
150-250 hp (EFI models)	20	–	2.3
Vapor separator			
150-200 hp EFI models (1994-1995)			
Mounting screws	45	–	5.1

(continued)

6

Table 13 TORQUE SPECIFICATIONS (INJECTED MODELS) (continued)

Fastener	in.-lbs.	ft.-lbs.	N•m
Vapor separator (continued)			
150-200 hp (1996-1997), 200 DFI			
and 225-250 hp			
Mounting screws	45	–	5.1
Large cover screws	30	–	3.4
Small cover screws	20	–	2.3
Water sensing warning module			
(150-200 hp EFI models)			
Mounting screws	25	–	2.8
Water separating fuel filter bracket			
150-200 hp EFI models	70	–	7.9
225-250 hp EFI and 200 DFI	100	–	11.3

Table 14 STANDARD TORQUE VALUES (U.S. STANDARD FASTENERS)

Screw or Nut Size	in.-lbs.	ft.-lbs.	N•m
6-32	9	–	1.0
8-32	20	–	2.3
10-24	30	–	3.4
10-32	35	–	4.0
12-24	45	–	5.1
1/4-20	70	6	7.9
1/4-28	84	7	9.5
5/16-18	160	13	18.1
5/16-24	168	14	19.0
3/8-16	270	23	30.5
3/8-24	300	25	33.9
7/16-14	–	36	48.8
7/16-20	–	40	54.2
1/2-13	–	50	67.8
1/2-20	–	60	81.3

Table 15 STANDARD TORQUE VALUES (METRIC FASTENERS)

Screw or Nut Size	in.-lbs.	ft.-lbs.	N•m
M5	36	–	4.1
M6	70	6	8.1
M8	156	13	17.6
M10	312	26	35.3
M12	–	35	47.5
M14	–	60	81.3

Chapter Seven

Ignition and Electrical Systems

This chapter provides service procedures for the battery, starter motor, charging system and ignition system used on outboard motors covered in this manual. Wiring diagrams are located at the end of the manual.

Battery charge percentage, wire color codes, battery capacity and battery cable size recommendations are listed in **Tables 1-4**. Fastener torque values are listed in **Tables 5-8**. Ignition and charging system identification are listed in **Tables 9-10**. All tables are at the end of the chapter.

BATTERY

Batteries used in marine applications endure far more rigorous treatment than those used in automotive electrical systems. Marine batteries have a thicker exterior case to cushion the plates during tight turns and rough water operation. Thicker plates are also used, with each one individually fastened within the case to prevent premature failure. Spill-proof caps on the battery cells prevent electrolyte from spilling into the bilge.

Automotive batteries should be used in a boat *only* during an emergency situation when a suitable marine battery is not available.

> *CAUTION*
> *Sealed or maintenance-free batteries are not recommended for use with unregulated charging systems. Excessive charging during continued high-speed operation will cause the electrolyte to boil, resulting in its loss. Since water cannot be added to sealed batteries, prolonged overcharging will destroy the battery. Refer to **Table 9** for charging system identification.*

Battery Rating Methods

The battery industry has developed specifications and performance standards to evaluate batteries and their energy potential. Several rating methods are available to provide meaningful information on battery selection.

Cold cranking amps (CCA)

This figure represents in amps the current flow the battery can deliver for 30 seconds at 0° F (-17.6° C) without dropping below 1.2 volts per cell (7.2 volts on a standard 12 volt battery). The higher the number, the more amps it can deliver to crank the engine. CCA times 1.3 equals MCA.

Marine cranking amps (MCA)

This figure is similar to the CCA test figure except that the test is run at 32° F (0° C) instead of 0° F (-17.6° C). This is more aligned with actual boat operating environments. MCA times 0.77 equals CCA.

Reserve capacity

This figure represents the time (in minutes) that a fully charged battery at 80° F (26.7° C) can deliver 25 amps, without dropping below 1.75 volts per cell (10.5 volts on a standard 12 volt battery). The reserve capacity rating defines the length of time that a typical vehicle can be driven after the charging system fails. The 25 amp figure takes into account the power required by the ignition, lighting and other accessories. The higher the reserve capacity rating, the longer the vehicle could be operated after a charging system failure.

Amp-hour rating

The ampere hour rating method is also called the 20 hour rating method. This rating represents the steady current flow that the battery will deliver for 20 hours while at 80° F (26.7° C) without dropping below 1.75 volts per cell (10.5 volts on a standard 12 volt battery). The rating is actually the steady current flow times the 20

hours. Example: A 60 amp-hour battery will deliver 3 amps continuously for 20 hours. This rating method has been largely discontinued by the battery industry. Cold cranking amps (or MCA) and reserve capacity ratings are now the most common battery rating methods.

Battery Recommendations

75-200 hp (except 200 DFI)

The manufacturer recommends a battery with a *minimum rating* of 465 cold cranking amps (CCA) or 350 marine cranking amps (MCA) and 100 minutes reserve capacity for the 6-60 hp models.

200 DFI

The manufacturer recommends a battery with a *minimum rating* of 1000 cold cranking amps

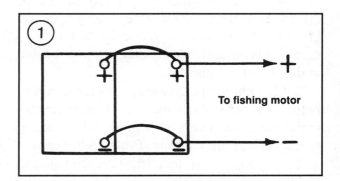

To fishing motor

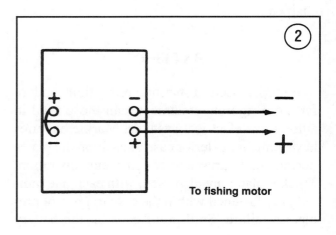

To fishing motor

(CCA) or 750 marine cranking amps (MCA) and 100 minutes reserve capacity for the 200 DFI (direct fuel injection) model.

225-275 hp

The manufacturer recommends a battery with a *minimum rating* of 630 cold cranking amps (CCA) or 490 marine cranking amps (MCA) and 100 minutes reserve capacity for the 225, 250 and 275 hp models.

Battery Installation

Separate batteries may be used to provide power for accessories such as lighting, fish finders and depth finders. To determine the required capacity of such batteries, calculate the acces-

sory current (amperage) draw rate of the accessory and refer to **Table 3**.

Two batteries may be connected in parallel to double the ampere-hour capacity while maintaining the required 12 volts. See **Figure 1**. For accessories which require 24 volts, batteries may be connected in series (**Figure 2**), but only accessories specifically requiring 24 volts should be connected to the system. If charging becomes necessary, batteries connected in a parallel or series circuit should be disconnected and charged individually.

Safety concerns

The battery must be securely fastened in the boat to prevent the battery from shifting or moving in the bilge area. The positive battery terminal (or the entire top of the battery) must also be covered with a nonconductive shield or boot.

If the battery is not properly secured it may contact the hull (or metal fuel tank) in rough water or while being transported. If the battery shorts against the metal hull or fuel tank, the resulting short circuit will cause sparks and an electrical fire. An explosion could follow if the fuel tank or battery case are compromised.

If the battery is not properly grounded and the battery contacts the metal hull, the battery will try to ground through the control cables or the boat's wiring harness. Again, the short circuit will cause sparks and an electrical fire. The control cables and boat wiring harness will be irreparably damaged.

Observe the following preventive steps when installing a battery in any boat, especially a metal boat or a boat with a metal fuel tank.

1. Choose a location as far as practical from the fuel tank while still providing access for maintenance.

2. Secure the battery to the hull with a plastic battery box and tie-down strap (**Figure 3**) *or* a battery tray *with* a nonconductive shield or boot covering the positive battery terminal (**Figure 4**).

7

3. Make sure that all battery cable connections (2 at the battery, 2 at the engine) are clean and tight. Do *not* use wing nuts to secure battery cables. If wing nuts are present, discard them and replace with corrosion resistant hex nuts and lock washers to ensure positive electrical connections. Loose battery connections can cause every symptom imaginable.

4. Periodically inspect the installation to make sure the battery is physically secured to the hull and that the battery cable connections are clean and tight.

Care and Inspection

1. Remove the battery tray top or battery box cover. See **Figure 3** or **Figure 4**.

2. Disconnect the negative battery cable, then the positive battery cable.

> *NOTE*
> *Some batteries have a built-in carry strap (**Figure 5**) for use in Step 3.*

3. Attach a battery carry strap to the terminal posts. Remove the battery from the boat.

4. Inspect the entire battery case for cracks, holes or other damage.

5. Inspect the battery tray or battery box for corrosion or deterioration. Clean as necessary with a solution of baking soda and water.

> *NOTE*
> *Do not allow the baking soda cleaning solution to enter the battery cells in Step 6 or the electrolyte will be severely weakened.*

6. Clean the top of the battery with a stiff bristle brush using the baking soda and water solution (**Figure 6**). Rinse the battery case with clear water and wipe dry with a clean cloth or paper towel.

7. Clean the battery terminal posts with a stiff wire brush or battery terminal cleaning tool (**Figure 7**).

> *NOTE*
> *Do not overfill the battery cells in Step 8. The electrolyte expands due to heat from the charging system and will overflow if the level is more than 3/16 in. (4.8 mm) above the battery plates.*

8. Remove the filler caps and check the electrolyte level. Add distilled water, if necessary, to bring the level up to 3/16 in. (4.8 mm) above the plates in the battery case. See **Figure 8**.

9. Clean the battery cable clamps with a stiff wire brush (**Figure 9**).

10. Place the battery back into the boat and into the battery tray or battery box. If using a battery tray, install and secure the retaining bracket.

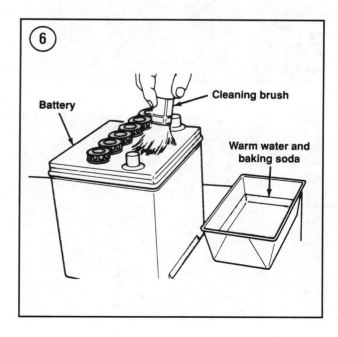

11. Reconnect the positive battery cable first, then the negative cable.

CAUTION
Be sure the battery cables are connected to their proper terminals. Reversing the battery polarity will result in electrical and ignition system damage.

12. Securely tighten the battery connections. Coat the connections with petroleum jelly or a light grease to minimize corrosion. If using a battery box, install the cover and secure the assembly with a tie-down strap.

Battery Testing

Hydrometer testing

On batteries with removable vent caps, checking the specific gravity of the electrolyte using a hydrometer is the best method to check the battery state of charge. Use a hydrometer with numbered graduations from 1.100-1.300 points rather than one with color-coded bands. To use the hydrometer, squeeze the rubber bulb, insert

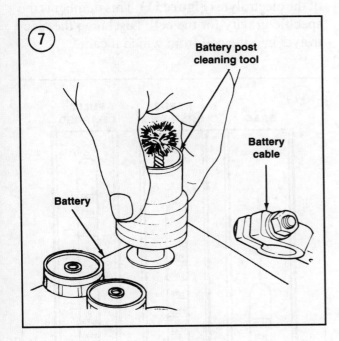

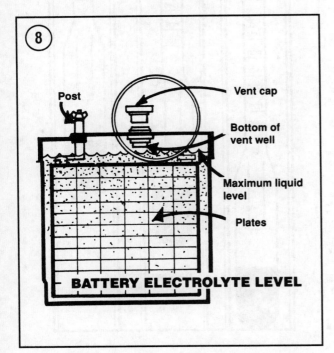

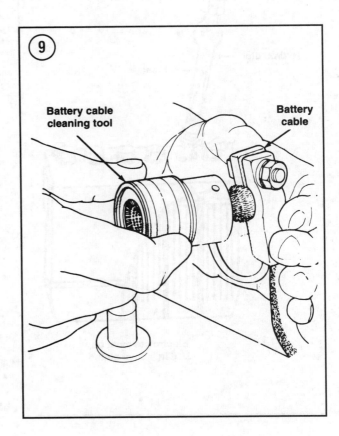

7

the tip into a cell, then release the bulb to fill the hydrometer. See **Figure 10**.

> *NOTE*
> *Do not test specific gravity immediately after adding water to the battery cells, as the water will dilute the electrolyte and lower the specific gravity. To obtain an accurate hydrometer reading, the battery must be charged after adding water and before testing with a hydrometer.*

Draw sufficient electrolyte to raise the float inside the hydrometer. When using a tempera-ture-compensated hydrometer, discharge the electrolyte back into the battery cell and repeat the process several times to adjust the temperature of the hydrometer to that of the electrolyte.

Hold the hydrometer upright and note the number on the float that is even with the surface of the electrolyte (**Figure 11**). This number is the specific gravity for the cell. Discharge the electrolyte into the cell from which it came.

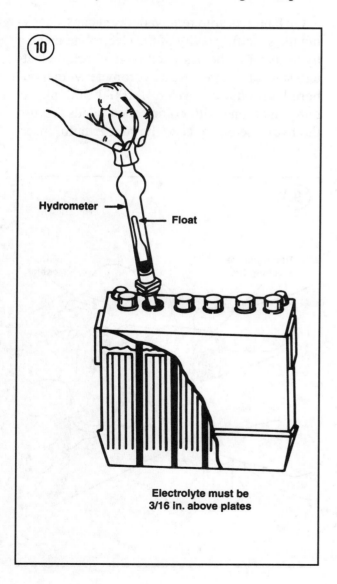

Electrolyte must be
3/16 in. above plates

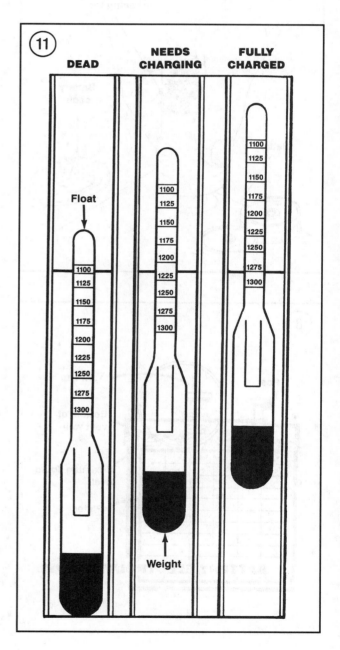

The specific gravity of a cell is the indicator of the cell's state of charge. A fully charged cell will read 1.260 or more at 80°F (26.7°C). A cell that is 75 percent charged will read from 1.220-1.230 while a cell with a 50 percent charge will read from 1.170-1.180. Any cell reading 1.140 or less should be considered discharged. All cells should be within 30 points specific gravity of each other. If over 30 points variation is noted, the battery condition is questionable. Charge the battery and recheck the specific gravity. If 30 points or more variation remains between cells after charging, the battery has failed and should be replaced.

NOTE
*If a temperature-compensated hydrometer is **not** used, add 4 points specific gravity to the actual reading for every 10° above 80°F (26.7°C). Subtract 4 points specific gravity for every 10° below 80°F (26.7°C).*

Open-circuit voltage test

On sealed or maintenance free batteries (vent caps not removable), the state of charge must be checked by measuring the open-circuit (no load) voltage of the battery. Use a digital voltmeter for best results. Forthe most accurate results, allow the battery to set at rest for at least 30 minutes to allow the battery to stabilize. Then, observing the correct polarity, connect the voltmeter to the battery and note the meter reading. if the open-circuit voltage is 12.7 or higher, the battery can be considered fully charged. A reading of 12.4 volts means the battery is approximately 75 percent charged, a reading of 12.2 means the battery is approximately 50 percent charged and a reading of 12.1 volts means that the battery is approximately 25 percent charged.

Load testing

To check the battery's ability to maintain the starting system's minimum required voltage while cranking the engine, proceed as follows:

1. Attach a voltmeter across the battery as shown in **Figure 12**.

2. Remove and ground the spark plug leads to the power head to prevent accidental sparking.

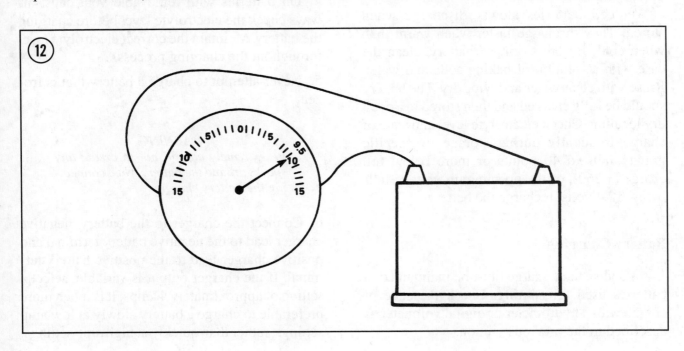

3. Crank the engine for approximately 15 seconds while noting the voltmeter reading.

4A. If the voltage is 9.5 volts or higher at the end of the 15 second period, the battery is sufficiently charged and of sufficient capacity for the outboard motor.

4B. If the voltage is below 9.5 volts at the end of the 15 second period, one of the following conditions is present:

  a. The battery is discharged or defective. Charge the battery and retest.
  b. The battery is of too small capacity for the outboard motor. Refer to *Battery Recommendations* in this chapter.
  c. The starting system is drawing excessive current causing the battery voltage to drop. Refer to Chapter Three for starting system troubleshooting procedures.
  d. A mechanical defect is present in the power head or gearcase creating excessive load (and current draw) on the starting system. Inspect the power head and gearcase for mechanical defects.

Battery Storage

Wet cell batteries slowly discharge when stored. They discharge faster when warm than when cold. Before storing a battery, clean the case with a solution of baking soda and water. Rinse with clear water and wipe dry. The battery should be fully charged and then stored in a cool, dry location. Check electrolyte level and state of charge frequently during storage. If specific gravity falls to 40 points or more below full charge (1.260), or the open circuit voltage falls below 12.4 volts, recharge the battery.

Battery Charging

A good state of charge must be maintained in batteries used for starting. Check the state of charge with a hydrometer or digital voltmeter as described in the previous section.

The battery should be removed from the boat for charging, since a charging battery releases highly explosive hydrogen gas. In many boats, the area around the battery is not well ventilated and the gas may remain in the area for hours after the charging process has been completed. Sparks or flames occurring near the battery can cause it to explode, spraying battery acid over a wide area.

If the battery cannot be removed for charging, make sure the bilge access hatches, doors or vents are fully open to allow adequate ventilation. For this reason, it is important to observe the following precautions when charging batteries:

1. Never smoke in close proximity to any battery.

2. Make sure all accessories are turned off before disconnecting the battery cables. Disconnecting a circuit that is electrically active will create a spark that can ignite explosive gas that may be present.

3. Always disconnect the negative battery cable first, then the positive cable.

4. On batteries with removable vent caps, always check the electrolyte level before charging the battery. Maintain the correct electrolyte level throughout the charging process.

5. Never attempt to charge a battery that is frozen.

WARNING
Be extremely careful not to create any sparks around the battery when connecting the battery charger.

6. Connect the charger to the battery, negative charger lead to the negative battery terminal and positive charger lead to the positive battery terminal. If the charger output is variable, select a setting of approximately 4 amps. It is much more preferable to charge a battery slowly at low amp settings, rather than quickly at high amp settings.

7. If the charger has a dual voltage setting, set the voltage switch to 12 volts, then switch the charger on.

8. If the battery is severely discharged, allow it to charge for at least 8 hours. Check the charging process with a hydrometer. Consider the battery fully charged when the specific gravity of all cells does not increase when checked 3 times at 1 hour intervals, and all cells are gassing freely.

Jump Starting

If the battery becomes severely discharged, it is possible to *jump start* the engine from another battery (in or out of a vehicle). Jump starting can be dangerous if the proper procedure is not followed. Always use caution when jump starting.

Check the electrolyte level of the discharged battery before attempting the jump start. If the electrolyte is not visible or if it appears to be frozen, do not jump start the discharged battery.

WARNING
*Use extreme caution when connecting the booster battery to the discharged battery to avoid personal injury or damage to the system. **Be certain** the jumper cables are connected in the correct polarity.*

1. Connect the jumper cables in the order and sequence shown in **Figure 13**.

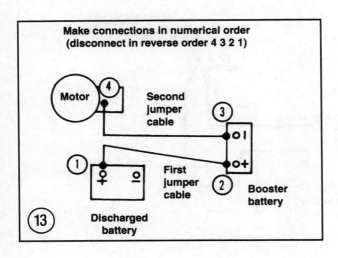

Make connections in numerical order (disconnect in reverse order 4 3 2 1)

Motor
Second jumper cable
First jumper cable
Discharged battery
Booster battery

13

WARNING
An electrical arc may occur when the final connection is made. This could cause an explosion if it occurs near the battery. For this reason, the final connection should be made to a good engine ground, away from the battery and not to the battery itself.

2. Check that all jumper cables are out of the way of moving engine parts.

CAUTION
*Do not run the engine without an adequate water supply and do not exceed 3000 rpm without an adequate load. Refer to **Safety Precautions** in Chapter Three.*

3. Start the engine. Once it starts, run it at a moderate speed (fast idle).

CAUTION
Running the engine at high speed with a discharged battery can damage the charging system.

4. Remove the jumper cables in the exact reverse of the order shown in **Figure 13**. Remove the cable at point 4, then 3, then 2 and finally 1.

BATTERY CHARGING SYSTEM

Description

An alternator charging system is used on all electric start models. The job of the charging system is to keep the battery fully charged and supply current to run accessories. Charging systems can be divided into 3 basic designs: integral unregulated, integral regulated and external (belt-driven) regulated. Refer to **Table 10** for charging system identification.

Integral systems use permanent magnets mounted in the flywheel and a stator coil winding mounted to the power head. As the flywheel rotates, the magnetic fields in the flywheel pass through the stator coil windings, inducing AC (alternating current). Unregulated systems use a rectifier (a series of 4 diodes) to change the AC current to DC (direct current). See **Figure 14**. The output from an unregulated charging system is directly proportional to engine speed. Because an unregulated system has the potential to over-charge the battery during long periods of wide-open throttle operation, maintenance-free batteries are not recommended. Overcharging a battery causes the electrolyte level to drop, lead-ing to premature battery failure. Vented batteries that allow removal of the vent caps and refilling of the electrolyte as needed will provide longer service life.

Integral regulated systems use the same type flywheel magnets and stator coil windings as the unregulated system, with the rectifier being re-placed with a rectifier/regulator. The rectifier portion of the rectifier/regulator changes the AC current to DC current, while the regulator portion monitors system voltage and controls the charg-ing system output accordingly. Batteries that are maintained at 13-15 volts will stay fully charged without excessive venting. The regulator con-

trols the output of the charging system to keep system voltage at approximately 14.5 volts. The large red lead of the rectifier/regulator is DC output. The small red lead is the sense terminal which allows the regulator portion to monitor system voltage. See **Figure 15**.

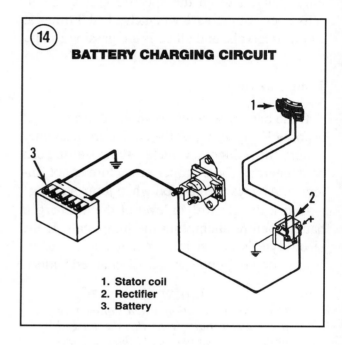

BATTERY CHARGING CIRCUIT

1. Stator coil
2. Rectifier
3. Battery

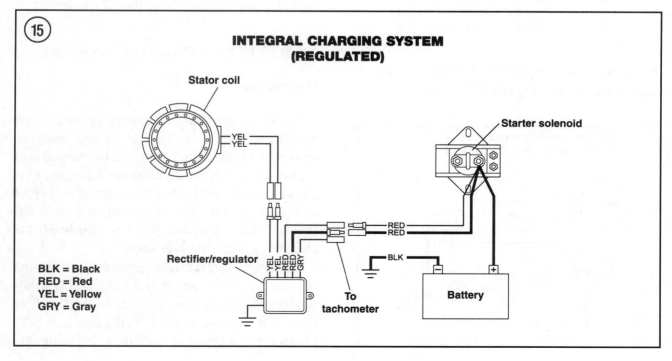

INTEGRAL CHARGING SYSTEM (REGULATED)

Stator coil

Starter solenoid

YEL
YEL

RED
RED

BLK

BLK = Black
RED = Red
YEL = Yellow
GRY = Gray

Rectifier/regulator

YEL
YEL
RED
RED
GRY

To tachometer

Battery

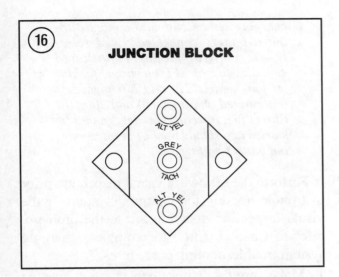

16 JUNCTION BLOCK

ALT YEL
GREY TACH
ALT YEL

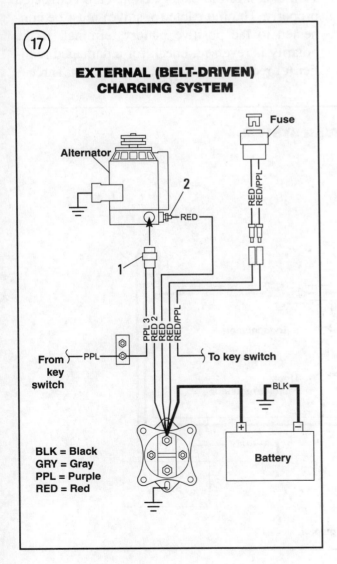

17 EXTERNAL (BELT-DRIVEN) CHARGING SYSTEM

Fuse

Alternator

2

RED

1

RED
RED/PPL

PPL 3
RED 2
RED
RED
RED/PPL

From key switch — PPL

To key switch

BLK

Battery

BLK = Black
GRY = Gray
PPL = Purple
RED = Red

Another function of the integral charging system is to provide the signal for the tachometer. The tachometer simply counts AC voltage pulses coming from the stator before the AC voltage is rectified to DC. Tachometer failure on models with integral charging systems is related to the charging system, not the ignition system. The tachometer connects to one of the stator yellow leads on unregulated systems and connects to the rectifier/regulator gray lead (**Figure 15**) on regulated models.

NOTE
*The 75-125 hp and 65-80 Jet models with the original black stator use a terminal block that looks similar to a standard rectifier, except that it is gray colored. This terminal block has 2 yellow stator leads and the gray tachometer lead connected to it. It contains no electrical components or circuitry. It is simply a junction point. See **Figure 16**.*

External (belt-driven) regulated systems use a belt-driven, excited rotor, internally regulated 60 amp alternator, similar to many automotive designs. See **Figure 17**. The alternator has no permanent magnets. The voltage regulator sends current through the rotor windings to create a magnetic field. By changing the strength of the rotor magnetic field, the output of the alternator can be controlled. The alternator is not serviceable and is sold only as an assembly. This system is used on the 200 DFI, 225 and 250 hp models. The tachometer signal on these models is produced by the ECM (electronic control module).

A malfunction in the charging system generally causes the battery to be undercharged and on integral systems, the tachometer to read erratically or totally fail. The following conditions will result in charging system failure.

a. Reversing the battery leads.

b. Disconnecting the battery leads while the engine is running.

7

c. Loose connections in the charging system circuits, including battery connections and ground circuits.

NOTE
The 40 amp (integral regulated) charging system used on the 135-200 hp, 275 hp and 105-140 Jet is basically 2 separate 20 amp charging systems. Half of the stator windings are connected to the upper regulator/rectifier assembly and the remaining stator windings are connected to the lower regulator/rectifier. Should one regulator/rectifier fail, the charging system will still function, but at only one half of its rated output. See Figure 18.

CAUTION
It is not recommended to attempt to operate external (belt-driven) regulated charging system outboard motors without a battery connected. ECM (electronic control module) equipped engines, such as EFI (electronic fuel injection) models, 225 and 250 hp models (carbureted and injected) and 200 DFI (direct fuel injection) models cannot be started and should not be operated without battery voltage.

Perform the following visual inspection prior to troubleshooting the charging system. If the visual inspection does not locate the problem, refer to Chapter Three for complete charging system troubleshooting procedures.

1. Make sure the battery cables are connected properly. The red cable (positive) must be connected to the positive battery terminal. If the polarity is reversed, check for a damaged rectifier (or rectifier/regulator). See Chapter Three.

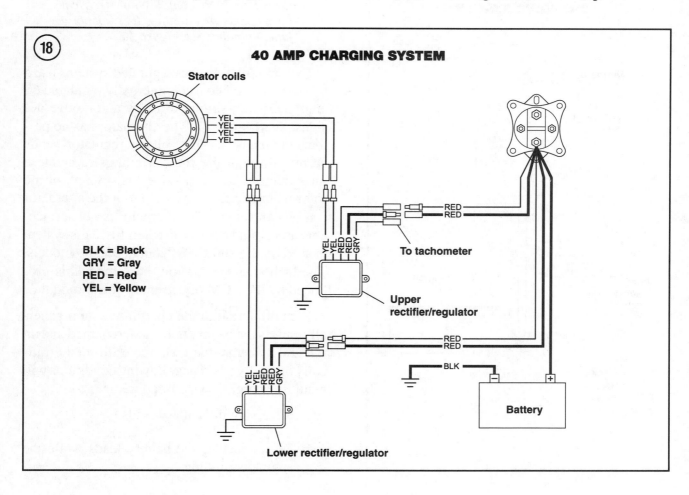

(18)   **40 AMP CHARGING SYSTEM**

Stator coils

YEL
YEL
YEL
YEL

RED
RED

To tachometer

YEL
YEL
RED
RED
GRY

BLK = Black
GRY = Gray
RED = Red
YEL = Yellow

Upper
rectifier/regulator

RED
RED

BLK

YEL
YEL
RED
RED
GRY

Battery

Lower rectifier/regulator

2. Inspect the battery terminals for loose or corroded connections. Tighten or clean as necessary. Replace any wing nuts with corrosion resistant hex nuts and lock washers.

3. Inspect the physical condition of the battery. Look for bulges or cracks in the case, leaking electrolyte and corrosion buildup. Clean, refill or replace the battery as necessary.

4. Carefully check the wiring between the stator coil and battery for damage or deterioration.

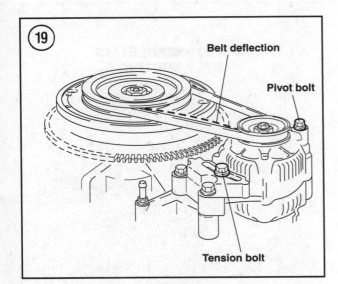

Refer to the back of the manual for wiring diagrams. Repair or replace wires and connectors as necessary.

5. Check all accessory circuits and associated wiring for corroded, loose or disconnected connections. Clean, tighten or reconnect as necessary.

6. Determine if the accessory load on the battery is greater than the charging system's capacity by performing the *Current draw* test. See Chapter Three.

Alternator Removal/Installation (External Belt-Driven Models)

225-250 hp models

The 225 and 250 hp models use a V-belt to drive the alternator off of the crank pulley. The belt is tensioned by rotating the alternator away or toward the flywheel pulley. Belt tension should be 1/4-1/2 in. (6.3-12.7 mm) deflection under moderate thumb pressure at the point shown in **Figure 19**. Always inspect the belt for deterioration, wear and fraying when servicing or replacing the alternator.

To replace the alternator, proceed as follows:

1. Disconnect and ground the spark plug leads to the power head to prevent accidental starting.

2. Disconnect the negative battery cable.

3. Remove the flywheel cover.

4. Loosen the pivot and tension bolts (**Figure 19**). Rotate the alternator toward the flywheel and slip the belt off of both pulleys.

5. Remove the alternator positive output lead (A, **Figure 20**) and disconnect the 2-pin connector (B, **Figure 20**).

6. Remove the pivot and tension bolts. Remove the alternator from the engine.

7. To install the alternator, set the alternator onto the mounting brackets. Install the pivot and tension bolts finger-tight.

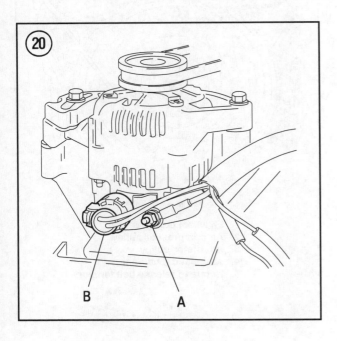

8. Connect the alternator positive output lead and the 2-pin connector. Make sure the protective boot covers the positive output lead terminal.

9. Install the belt over both pulleys. Rotate the alternator away from the flywheel until the belt is properly tensioned (1/4-1/2 in. [6.3-12.7 mm] deflection under moderate thumb pressure). Snug the tension bolt to hold the alternator in place.

10. Recheck belt tension, repeating Step 9 as necessary. When tension is verified, tighten both the pivot bolt and tension bolt to 40 ft.-lb. (54 N•m).

11. Reinstall the flywheel cover.

12. Reconnect the spark plug leads to the spark plugs.

13. Reconnect the negative battery cable.

14. Recheck belt tension and condition after the first 10 hours of new belt operation and every 50 hours thereafter.

200 DFI models

The 200 DFI uses a serpentine belt and automatic tensioner system very similar to current automotive designs. While no adjustments are required with this system, inspect the belt and belt tensioner assembly for deterioration, wear, fraying and any mechanical damage or failure.

To replace the alternator, proceed as follows:

1. Disconnect and ground the spark plug leads to the power head to prevent accidental starting.

2. Disconnect the negative battery cable.

3. Remove the flywheel cover. Be careful to disconnect the air compressor inlet at the rear and the vent line at the front.

4. Manually rotate the tensioner (4, **Figure 21**) away from the belt (5, **Figure 21**) and slip the belt off the pulleys.

5. Remove the alternator positive output lead (A, **Figure 20**) and disconnect the 2-pin connector (B, **Figure 20**).

6. Remove the 2 bolts (A and B, **Figure 22**) securing the alternator to the brackets. Loosen the tensioner bracket bolt (C, **Figure 22**) slightly.

7. Remove the alternator from the engine.

8. To install the alternator, set the alternator onto the mounting brackets. Install the 2 alternator bolts (A and B, **Figure 22**) and tighten to 33 ft.-lb. (44.5 N•m). Tighten the tensioner bracket bolt (C, **Figure 22**) to 16.5 ft.-lb. (22.5 N•m).

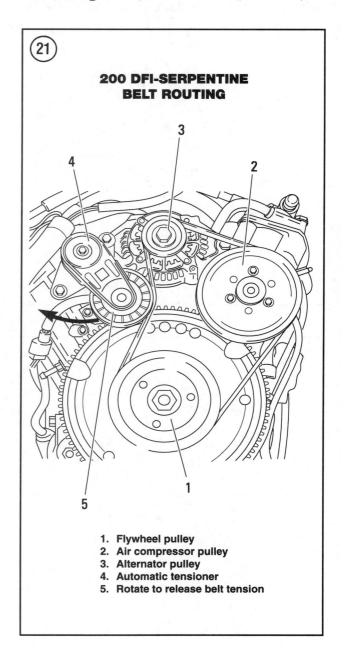

(21)

200 DFI-SERPENTINE BELT ROUTING

1. Flywheel pulley
2. Air compressor pulley
3. Alternator pulley
4. Automatic tensioner
5. Rotate to release belt tension

9. Connect the alternator positive output lead and the 2-pin connector. Make sure the protective boot covers the positive output lead terminal.

10. Install a new belt while holding the tensioner fully open. Route the belt as shown in **Figure 21**.

11. Release the tensioner against the belt. Make sure the belt is tracking on each pulley correctly.

12. Reinstall the flywheel cover. Make sure the air compressor inlet is connected at the rear and the vent line is connected at the front.

13. Reconnect the negative battery cable.

14. Reconnect the spark plug leads to the spark plug.

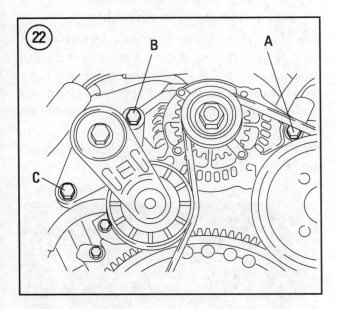

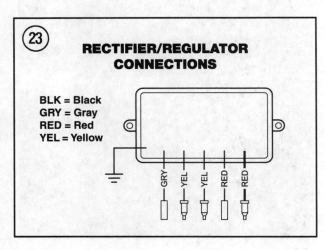

RECTIFIER/REGULATOR CONNECTIONS

BLK = Black
GRY = Gray
RED = Red
YEL = Yellow

Rectifier Removal/Installation (Internal Unregulated Models)

1. Disconnect the negative battery cable.

2. Disconnect and ground the spark plug leads to the power head to prevent accidental starting.

3. Locate the rectifier on the power head. On some models it may be necessary to remove a plastic cover to gain access to the electrical and ignition system components.

4. Note the location and color of the wires attached to the rectifier. Remove the 2 yellow (or 1 yellow and 1 gray) leads and 1 red lead from the rectifier terminal studs.

5. Remove the 2 screws securing the rectifier to the engine or electrical bracket. Remove the rectifier from the engine.

6. To install the rectifier, begin by making sure that the mounting location is clean and free of corrosion or paint. Clean all corrosion and paint from mounting area as necessary.

7. Secure the rectifier to the engine or electrical bracket with 2 screws. Tighten the screws securely.

8. Connect the 2 yellow (or 1 yellow and 1 gray) leads and 1 red lead to the rectifier as noted during removal or refer to **Figure 16**. Tighten the terminal nuts securely.

9. Coat the terminal studs with Quicksilver Liquid Neoprene.

10. Reinstall the electrical and ignition access cover, if so equipped.

11. Reconnect the spark plug leads.

12. Reconnect the negative battery cable.

Rectifier/Regulator Removal/Installation (Internal Regulated Models)

The rectifier/regulators used on all internal models are of the same basic construction and use the exact same electrical connections. See **Figure 23**.

The 40 amp charging system used on 135-200 hp, 275 hp and 105 and 140 Jet models use 2 voltage rectifier/regulators (**Figure 18**).

1. Disconnect and ground the spark plug leads to the power head to prevent accidental starting.

2. Disconnect the negative battery cable.

3. Locate the rectifier/regulator(s) on the power head. On some models it may be necessary to remove a plastic cover to gain access to the electrical and ignition system components. **Figure 24** shows a typical regulator installation.

4. Cut the tie-strap(s) (A, **Figure 24**) and/or loosen the clamps (B, **Figure 24**) securing the electrical leads and bullet connectors of each regulator to the power head or electrical/ignition bracket. Discard the tie-strap(s).

NOTE
On the 135-200 hp and 105-140 Jet, the ignition coil bracket may have to be removed before the lower regulator leads can be accessed and disconnected. This does not apply to the 275 hp.

5. Disconnect the 2 yellow, 2 red and 1 gray lead bullet connectors of each regulator from the engine wiring harness. Be careful not to damage the connector terminals or insulating sleeve.

6A. *75-125 hp, 275 hp and 105 and 140 Jet*—Remove the 2 screws (C, **Figure 24**) (4 screws on 275 hp) securing the rectifier/regulator(s) to the power head or electrical/ignition bracket. Remove the rectifier/regulator(s).

6B. *135-200 hp and 65 and 80 Jet*—Proceed as follows:

   a. Remove the 4 locknuts and washers securing the ignition coil bracket to the power head.

   b. Slide the ignition coil bracket off the studs and position it to one side.

   c. Remove the spacer collar from each of the 4 studs.

   d. Slide the rectifier/regulator off the mounting studs.

7A. *75-125 hp, 275 hp and 65 and 80 Jet*—To install, position the rectifier/regulator(s) on the power head or electrical/ignition bracket and install the mounting screws. Tighten the screws to specification (**Table 5**).

7B. *135-200 hp and 105 and 140 Jet*—Install the rectifier/regulator(s) as follows:

   a. Slide the rectifier/regulator(s) over the mounting studs and against the power head. Make sure the solid metal side of the rectifier/regulator(s) contacts the power head.

   b. Slide a spacer collar over each mounting stud.

   c. Position the ignition coil bracket over the mounting studs.

   d. Install the 4 locknuts and washers. Tighten the nuts to specification (**Table 5**).

8A. *75-125 hp, 275 hp and 65 and 80 Jet*—Connect the rectifier/regulator 2 yellow, 1 red and 1 gray wires to the engine wiring harness. Secure the wires to the power head or electrical/ignition bracket using the original clamps or install new tie-straps.

8B. *135-200 hp and 105 and 140 Jet*—Connect the rectifier/regulator(s) as follows:

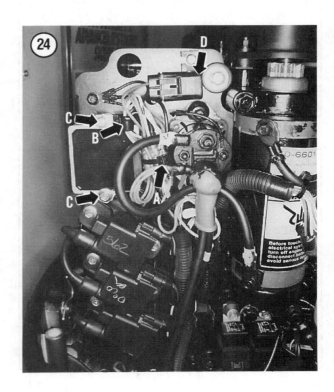

a. Connect the 2 long yellow stator wires and 1 long red wire to the lower rectifier/regulator. The gray lead is normally not used on the lower rectifier/regulator.

b. Connect the 2 short yellow stator wires, 1 short red wire and 1 gray wire to the upper rectifier/regulator. Secure the wires to the power head or ignition coil bracket using original clamps or use new tie-straps.

9. Reinstall the electrical and ignition access cover, if so equipped.

10. Reconnect the spark plug leads.

11. Reconnect the negative battery cable.

Stator Removal/Installation (All Internal Models)

The alternator and ignition windings of the stator are integrated into one assembly on all models.

Removal and installation procedures for all stator windings (charging, ignition and inte-

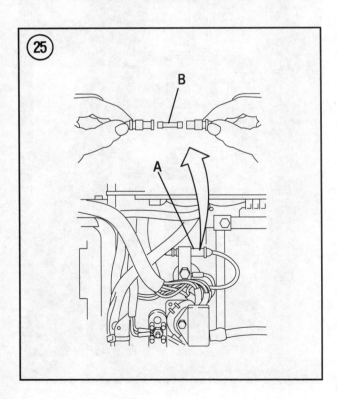

grated models) are covered under *Ignition Systems* located later in this chapter.

FUSES

Fuses are designed to protect wire and electrical components from damage due to excessive current (amp) flow. A fuse that repeatedly blows indicates a problem with the circuit or component that the fuse is protecting.

Do not install a larger fuse in an attempt to remedy the problem. Refer to Chapter Three and locate the defect that is causing excessive current flow in the suspect circuit.

While a visual inspection can quickly tell you if a fuse is *bad*, do not trust a visual inspection alone when trying to determine if a fuse is *good*. Fuses can be quickly and accurately tested using an ohmmeter. A good fuse will indicate a full continuity reading (0 ohms). When testing fuses, be careful not to touch both ohmmeter probes at the same time with your hands. Ohmmeters set to higher scales will typically show a false continuity reading through your body.

Fuse Locations

A 20 amp blade type fuse is located near the voltage rectifier/regulator in a locking-type fuse holder (D, **Figure 24**) on the following models:
  a. 75-125 hp (serial No. OG437800-on).
  b. 65 and 80 Jet (serial No. OG437800-on).

A 20 amp glass cartridge fuse is located in an inline fuse holder (A, **Figure 25**) located near the starter motor, above the starter solenoid on the following models:
  a. 75-125 hp (prior to serial No. OG437800).
  b. 65 and 80 Jet (prior to serial No. OG437800).

To remove the fuse, gently pull and twist the fuse holder from each end to separate the fuse holder and access the fuse (B, **Figure 25**).

A 20 amp blade-type fuse is located either at the top or bottom of the plastic electrical/ignition

7

component access cover on the starboard side of the engine (**Figure 26**) on 225-250 hp models. To remove the fuse, simply pull it straight out of its holder.

Four 20 amp blade-type fuses are located under the access cover on the starboard side of the engine, next to the ECM (electronic control module) on 200 DFI models. All 4 fuses are secured in locking-type fuse holders. Refer to **Figure 27** for each fuse location. Fuse A protects the electric fuel pump, fuse B protects the ECM, fuse C protects the ignition switch and remote control harness and fuse D protects the oil pump and ignition coils.

Fuse Replacement
(Locking-Type Fuse Holder)

1. On 200 DFI models, remove the electrical/ignition component access cover located on the starboard side of the engine.
2. Carefully lift the lock clip and slide the fuse holder out of the protective cover.
3. Pull the defective fuse from the fuse holder.
4. Push a new fuse into the fuse holder.
5. Push the fuse holder into the protective cover until the locking clip snaps into place.
6. On 200 DFI models, reinstall the electrical/ignition component access cover.

STARTING SYSTEMS

Mercury and Mariner outboards can be equipped with electric start only, manual (automatic rewinding rope) start only, or both electric and manual starters. Manual starters are covered in detail in Chapter Twelve.

A typical electric starter system consists of the battery, starter solenoid, neutral safety switch, starter motor, starter (or ignition) switch and the associated wiring. On tiller models, the neutral safety switch is mounted on the engine shift linkage. On remote control models, the neutral safety switch is mounted in the remote control

box. Troubleshooting of the electric starter system is covered in Chapter Three.

Starter Motor Description

Marine starter motors are very similar in design and operation to those found on automotive engines. The starter motors used on outboards covered in this manual have an inertia-type drive

in which external spiral splines on the armature shaft mate with internal splines on the drive (or bendix) assembly.

The starter motor is an intermittent duty electric motor, capable of producing a very high torque, but only for a brief time. The high amperage flow through the starter motor causes the starter motor to overheat very quickly. To prevent overheating, never operate the starter motor continuously for more than 10-15 seconds. Allow the starter motor to cool 2-3 minutes before cranking the engine again.

If the starter motor does not crank the engine, check the battery cables and terminals for loose or corroded connections. Correct any problems found. If this does not solve the starting problem, refer to Chapter Three for starting system troubleshooting procedures.

CAUTION
Mercury and Mariner electric starter motors use permanent magnets glued to THE main housing. Never strike a starter as this will damage the magnets, leading to total starter failure. Inspect the magnets anytime the starter is disassembled. Replace the housing if the magnets are cracked, damaged or loose.

Starter Motor Removal/Installation (75-200 hp and 65-140 Jet)

1. Disconnect the negative battery cable from the battery.
2. Disconnect and ground the spark plug leads to the power head to prevent accidental starting.
3. On 275 hp models, remove the oil reservoir as described in Chapter Eleven. Note that 2 starter motor mounting bolts are removed during oil reservoir removal.
4. Disconnect the black ground cable (B, **Figure 28**, typical) from the starter motor.
5. Remove the positive cable (A, **Figure 28**, typical) from the starter motor terminal stud. This is the cable from the starter solenoid to the starter motor. The cable is normally black with yellow ends (sleeves).
6A. *275 hp models*—Remove the 2 remaining starter motor mounting bolts (C, **Figure 28**, typical). Note the position of any additional ground cables or straps.
6B. *All other models*—Remove the 4 starter motor mounting bolts (C, **Figure 28**, typical). Note the position of any additional ground cables or straps.
7. Remove the starter motor along with the upper and lower mounting clamps.
8. Remove the upper and lower mounting clamps from the starter motor.
9. Remove the rubber collars from each end of the starter motor. If present, remove the spacer from the drive end frame of the starter motor.
10. To install the starter, begin by installing the spacer over the drive end frame, if so equipped.
11. Install the rubber collars over each end of the starter motor.
12. Position the starter motor in the power head brackets. Make sure the starter cable terminal stud and ground cable bolt hole are positioned as shown in **Figure 28**.
13A. *275 hp models*—Position the upper and lower mounting clamps over the starter, one at a time. Secure each bracket with 1 bolt mounted

7

in the rearward hole. Tighten the bolts finger-tight at this time.

13B. *All other models*—Position the upper and lower mounting clamps over the starter, one at a time. Secure each bracket with 2 bolts. Tighten the bolts finger-tight at this time.

NOTE
It is best to install 2 bolts temporarily in place of the oil reservoir mounting bolts during Step 14A. This will help hold the starter mounting clamps aligned while the permanent (rearward) bolts are tightened. Remove the 2 temporary bolts after the rear bolts are properly tightened.

14A. *275 hp models*—Make sure that all ground cables and straps are reconnected to the 2 starter mounting bolts and that the starter motor is correctly orientated in the mounting clamps. Tighten the 2 mounting bolts (1 upper, 1 lower) to specification (**Table 5**).

14B. *All other models*—Make sure all ground cables and straps are reconnected to the starter mounting bolts and that the starter motor is correctly orientated in the mounting clamps. Tighten the mounting bolts to specification (**Table 5**).

15. Connect the positive cable (A, **Figure 28**, typical) and the ground cable (C) to the starter motor. Tighten the fasteners securely.

16. On 275 hp models, reinstall the oil reservoir and bleed the oil injection system as described in Chapter Eleven.

17. Reconnect the spark plug leads and the negative battery cable.

Starter Motor Removal/Installation (200 DFI, 225 and 250 hp)

1. Disconnect the negative battery cable.
2. Disconnect and ground the spark plug leads to the power head to prevent accidental starting.
3. Remove the positive cable (A, **Figure 29**, typical) from the starter motor terminal stud.

This is the cable from the starter solenoid to the starter motor. The cable is normally black with yellow ends (sleeves).

4. Remove the 2 starter motor mounting bolts from the top of the starter (B, **Figure 29**) and the one bolt from the bottom of the starter (C, **Figure 29**).

5. Remove the starter from the power head.

6. To install the starter, begin by positioning the starter motor to the power head brackets. Install the 3 mounting bolts hand tight. If the battery ground cable, other ground cables or ground straps are attached to one or more of the mounting bolts, make sure the ground cable(s) is(are) reconnected at this time.

7. Tighten the 3 starter mounting bolts to specifications (**Table 5**).

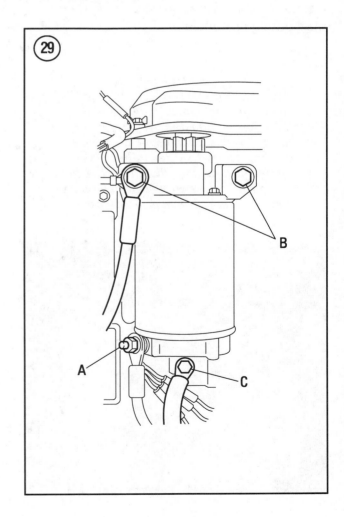

8. Connect the positive cable to the starter motor terminal stud. Tighten the nut to specifications (**Table 5**).

9. Reconnect the spark plug leads.

10. Reconnect the negative battery cable.

Starter Motor Disassembly/Reassembly (75-275 hp and 65-140 Jet)

Fabricate a brush retaining tool from 18-gauge sheet metal to the dimensions shown in **Figure 30**. This tool is necessary to position the brushes properly and prevent damaging them when reassembling the starter end cap to the housing.

Refer to *Cleaning and Inspection (75-275 hp and 65-140 Jet)* before reassembly.

1. Remove the starter motor as described previously in this chapter.

2. Place match marks on the drive end frame, main housing and lower end cap for alignment reference during reassembly.

3. Remove the 2 through-bolts, then lightly tap on the drive end frame and lower end cap with a rubber mallet until they are both loosened.

4. Remove the end cap taking care not to lose the brush springs.

5. Lift the armature and drive end frame assembly from the starter housing.

NOTE
Do not remove the drive assembly in Step 6 and Step 7 unless the drive assembly or end frame requires replacement.

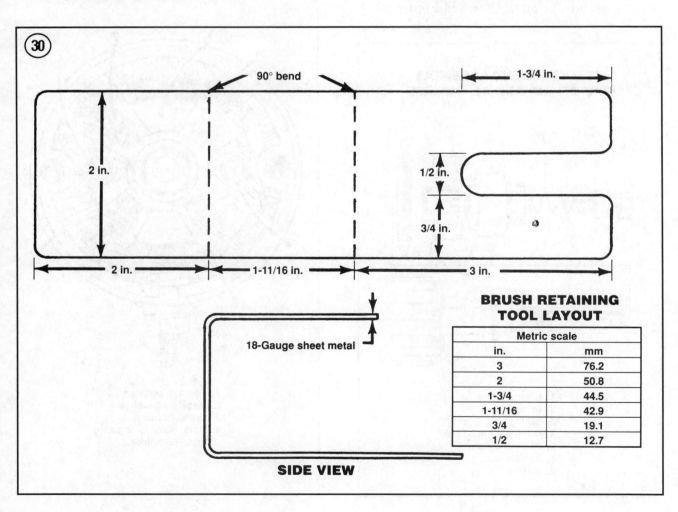

BRUSH RETAINING TOOL LAYOUT

Metric scale	
in.	mm
3	76.2
2	50.8
1-3/4	44.5
1-11/16	42.9
3/4	19.1
1/2	12.7

6. Place an appropriate size wrench on the hex area located on the back side of the drive gear. See **Figure 31**.

7. Remove the drive assembly lock nut and slide the drive components and drive end frame off of the armature shaft.

8. Remove the screws securing the brush holder and negative brushes to the end cap. Lift the brush holder from the end cap. See **Figure 32**.

9. Remove the negative brushes from the brush holder.

10. Remove the hex nut and washers from the positive terminal. Remove the positive terminal and positive brushes from the end cap as an assembly.

11. To reassemble, install new positive brushes and terminal assembly into the end cap. Locate the longest brush lead as shown in **Figure 33**.

12. Install the negative brushes into the brush holder. Install the brush holder into the end cap. Tighten the fasteners securely.

13. Fit the springs and brushes into the brush holder. Hold the brushes in place with the brush retaining tool (**Figure 34**).

14. Lubricate the armature shaft splines and the drive end frame bushing each with one drop of SAE 10W oil.

15. Install the drive components (**Figure 31**) onto the armature shaft. Tighten the locknut se-

---

(31)

STARTER DRIVE ASSEMBLY
(750-275 HP AND 65-140 JET)

1. Locknut
2. Spacer
3. Spring
4. Drive gear assembly
5. Drive end frame
6. Armature
7. Washer

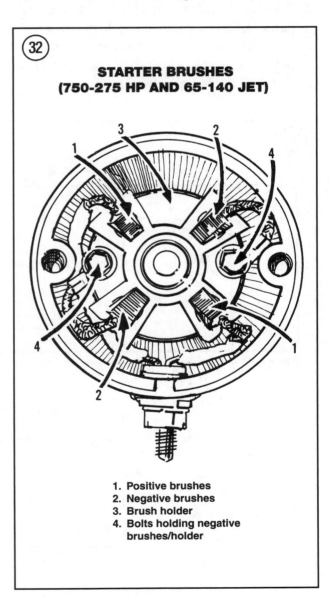

(32)

STARTER BRUSHES
(750-275 HP AND 65-140 JET)

1. Positive brushes
2. Negative brushes
3. Brush holder
4. Bolts holding negative brushes/holder

curely while holding the drive gear with an appropriate size wrench.

16. Place the armature and end frame assembly into the starter housing. Be sure the commutator end of the armature is located at the end of the housing with the magnets recessed 1 in. (25.4 mm). Align the match marks on the housing and end frame.

CAUTION
Do not over-lubricate the starter bushing in Step 17. The starter will not operate properly and can be ruined if oil

contaminates the commutator and brushes.

17. Lubricate the lower end cap bushing with a single drop of SAE 10W motor oil. Do not over-lubricate.

18. With the brushes held in position with the brush retaining tool (**Figure 34**), install the end cap onto the armature and up against the starter housing. Remove the brush retaining tool, align the match marks on the end cap and housing, then install the through-bolts. Tighten the through-bolts to specifications (**Table 5**).

Cleaning and inspection
(75-275 hp and 65-140 Jet)

1. Thoroughly clean all starter motor components with clean solvent, then dry them with compressed air.

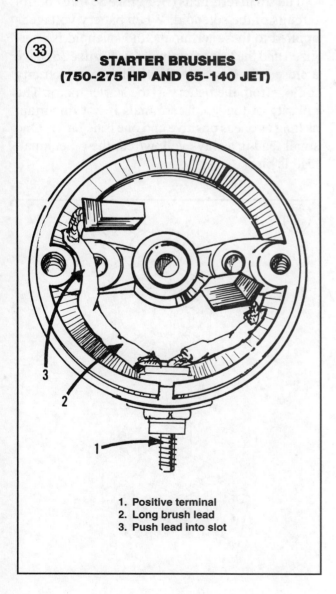

STARTER BRUSHES (750-275 HP AND 65-140 JET)

1. Positive terminal
2. Long brush lead
3. Push lead into slot

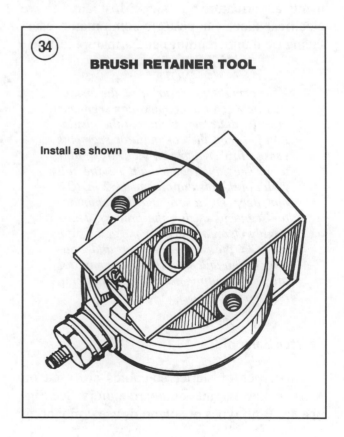

BRUSH RETAINER TOOL

Install as shown

2. Check the starter drive gear for chipped teeth, cracks or excessive wear. Replace drive components as necessary.

3. Inspect the brushes and replace all brushes if any are chipped, pitted, oil soaked or worn to 1/4 in. (6.4 mm) or less.

4. Using an ohmmeter, check for continuity between each commutator segment and the armature shaft (core). Replace the armature if any continuity is noted.

5. Inspect the armature shaft bushings in the drive end frame and lower end cap for excessive wear or other damage. Replace the bushings, end frame or end cap as necessary.

6. Clean the commutator using 00 sandpaper. Clean any copper particles or other contamination from between the commutator segments.

7. If the commutator is pitted, rough or worn unevenly, it can be resurfaced (and undercut) or replaced. If the armature shows water or overheat damage, have it checked for shorted windings using an armature growler. Most automotive electrical shops can perform commutator resurfacing (and undercutting) and armature testing.

NOTE
If the armature is resurfaced, the insulation between the commutator segments must be undercut. Undercut the insulation between the commutator segments using a broken hacksaw blade or similar tool. The undercut should be the full width of the insulation and 1/32 in. (0.8 mm) deep. Do not damage the commutator segments during the process. Thoroughly clean any copper particles from between the segments after undercutting. Clean and smooth the commutator after undercutting using 00 sandpaper to remove all burrs.

Starter Solenoid

Two types of starter solenoids are used on Mercury and Mariner outboard motors. See **Figure 35**. Both types of solenoids use 2 mounting

screws, the same type and quantity of electrical connections and are serviced in the same manner, but are not interchangeable.

The large terminals (A, **Figure 35**) always carry the electrical load from the battery to the starter motor. The large terminals have an open circuit across them when the solenoid is not energized. The large lead from the battery is usually black with red ends (sleeves). The large lead from the solenoid to the starter motor is usually yellow or black with yellow ends (sleeves).

The small terminals (B, **Figure 35**) are control circuits of the solenoid. When battery voltage is applied to these terminals, the solenoid is energized and the large terminals (A, **Figure 35**) have a closed circuit across them allowing electricity to flow from the battery to the starter motor. The polarity of the small terminals is not important as long as one is positive and one is negative. One small lead is always yellow/red, the other small lead is black.

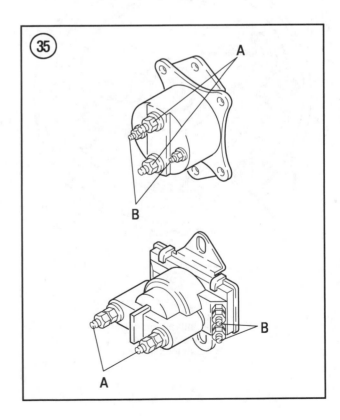

The starter solenoid is always located near the starter motor and depending on model, may or may not be behind an electrical/ignition component access cover. Refer to Chapter Three for troubleshooting procedures.

Starter solenoid removal/installation

To replace the starter solenoid, refer to **Figure 36**, typical and proceed as follows:

1. Disconnect the negative battery cable.

2. Disconnect and ground the spark plug leads to the power head to prevent accidental starting.

3. Locate the starter solenoid on the power head. Remove the electrical/ignition component access cover, if so equipped.

4. Note the location and position of all wires on starter solenoid and mounting screws.

5. Remove the nuts, lock washers and electrical cables from the 2 large solenoid terminals.

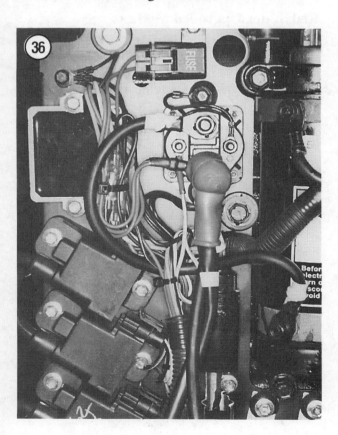

6. Remove the nuts, lock washers and electrical leads from the 2 small solenoid terminals.

7. Remove the 2 solenoid mounting screws, then remove the solenoid from the power head or electrical bracket.

8. To install the solenoid, position the solenoid on the power head or electrical bracket. Make sure any ground leads or ground straps are reconnected to the mounting screws as noted on removal. Tighten both mounting screws securely.

9. Install the small leads, lock washers and nuts. Tighten the nuts securely.

10. Install the large cables, lock washers and nuts. Tighten the nuts securely. Make sure the positive battery cable is covered with a protective boot as shown in **Figure 36** unless the engine is equipped with a plastic electrical/ignition component access cover.

11. Reinstall the electrical/ignition component access cover, if so equipped.

12. Reconnect the spark plug leads.

13. Reconnect the negative battery cable.

Neutral Safety Switch

On tiller models, the neutral safety switch is mounted on the engine shift linkage. On remote control models, the neutral safety switch is mounted in the remote control box. Refer to Chapter 12 for Mercury/Mariner remote control box service procedures. If your boat is equipped with an aftermarket control box, consult with the control box manufacturer for service procedures.

The neutral safety switch is designed to prevent the engine from starting in gear. In other words, the electric starter can only engage when the engine shift linkage is in neutral. A neutral safety switch should have continuity across its two terminals (or leads) any time the shift linkage is in neutral. The switch should indicate no continuity any time the shift linkage is in gear.

IGNITION SYSTEMS

Refer to **Table 9** for ignition system identification. This section deals mainly with operating theory and component removal and replacement. Refer to Chapter Three for ignition system troubleshooting procedures.

ALTERNATOR DRIVEN CAPACITOR DISCHARGE IGNITION (60-275 HP AND 65-140 JET)

This section covers all models quipped with alternator driven capacitor discharge ignition (ADI). Refer to **Table 9** for ignition system identification.

Major components of the ADI system include the flywheel, stator assembly (with low- and high-speed charge coils), trigger coil assembly, switch box(es), ignition coils, spark plugs and related wiring. There is one low- and one high-speed charge coil winding for each switch box. V6 models use 2 switch boxes. All other models are equipped with one switch box. One ignition coil and one spark plug are required for each cylinder.

A series of permanent magnets are located along the inner diameter of the outer rim of the flywheel. As the flywheel rotates, alternating current (AC) is induced into the low- and high-speed charge coil windings. The low-speed windings provide the majority of the voltage required for starting and low-speed operation. The high-speed windings provide the majority of the voltage required for high-speed operation. However, the low- and high-speed winding outputs are combined in the switch box. The switch box contains a rectifier to convert (rectify) the AC voltage into direct current (DC) so it can be stored in the switch box capacitor. The capacitor holds this voltage until it is released by a signal from the trigger coil(s).

Another set of permanent magnets is located along the outer diameter of the flywheel inner hub. As the flywheel rotates, low voltage signals are induced in the trigger coil windings. This low voltage pulse is sent to the switch box where it causes an electronic switch in the switch box called an SCR (silicon controlled rectifier) to close, allowing the stored voltage in the capacitor to discharge to the appropriate ignition coil. The ignition coil amplifies the voltage and discharges it into the spark plug lead.

This sequence of events is duplicated for each cylinder of the engine, and is repeated upon each revolution of the flywheel. One spark occurs for each cylinder for each complete flywheel rotation.

All models are equipped with mechanical spark advance. The spark advance is controlled by rotating the position of the trigger coil assembly in relation to the magnets on the flywheel inner hub. The trigger coil rotation is based on throttle lever position.

Red Stator Upgraded Models

Red stator and adapter module upgrade kits are available for 75-125 hp and 65-80 Jet models. If the stator on your engine is encased in red plastic, the upgrade kit has been installed. If the stator on your engine is encased in black plastic, it is the original stator.

Description

Red stator upgraded models are standard ADI models that have had the black stator removed and a red stator and adapter module installed. The new stator has a single winding around 3 bobbins with 2 ignition leads (white/green and green/white) exiting the stator assembly. There are no separate low and high speed windings. There are 2 different adapter modules available: 1 for the 3-cylinder models and 1 for 4-cylinder models. Voltage regulation is incorporated into both adaptor modules to keep the increased output of the red stator from damaging the switch box internal components.

Manual start models may incorporate a separate stator winding (blue/white and black) for powering the warning circuits and rpm limit modules on models so equipped.

Red stator upgrade kits also incorporate improved charging system stator windings. The output is increased to 9 or 16 amps, depending on model and an upgraded rectifier/regulator is included (where required).

3-cylinder adaptor

The 3-cylinder adapter module uses 4 leads. The green/white and white/green leads are connected to the same colored ignition stator leads. The black lead is connected to ground and the blue lead is connected to the switch box low speed ignition stator terminal or bullet connector. The switch box high speed (red lead) terminal or bullet connector is not used. The adapter module incorporates a full wave rectifier and a shunt voltage regulator. The rectifier changes the ignition stator AC voltage in to DC voltage, the voltage regulator limits the voltage entering the switch box to 300 volts. The regulator and rectifier are necessary because the high speed winding (red lead) is no longer used and the red stator is not grounded to the engine block.

4-cylinder adaptor

The 4-cylinder adapter module uses 5 leads. The green/white and white/green leads are connected to the same colored ignition stator leads. The black lead is connected to ground. The blue and blue/white leads are connected to the switch box low-speed ignition stator terminals or bullet connectors. The switch box high-speed (red and red/white leads) terminals or bullet connectors are not used. The adapter module incorporates 2 shunt voltage regulators. Each voltage regulator limits the voltage entering the switch box (from the green/white or white/green) to 300 volts. Two regulators are necessary because of the 2 (blue and blue/white) leads entering the switch box. One regulator controls the voltage on the green/white lead, the other regulator controls the voltage on the white/green lead. The rectifier is not needed because the switch box rectifier network has a complete current path between the blue and blue/white leads.

Component Wiring

Modern outboard motor electrical systems can be intimidating, especially on the higher output engines. For this reason, electrical wiring is color-coded, and the terminals on the components to which each wire connects are embossed with the correct wire color. When used in conjunction with the correct electrical diagram, incorrect wire connections should be eliminated.

In addition, the routing of the wiring harness and individual leads is very important to prevent possible electrical interference and/or physical damage to the wiring harnesses from moving engine parts or vibration. Mercury outboards are shipped from the factory with all wiring harnesses and leads properly positioned and secured with the appropriate clamps and tie-straps.

Should component replacement become necessary, it is highly recommended that you take the time to either carefully draw a sketch of the area to be serviced, noting the positioning of all wire harnesses involved, or use an instant camera to take several close-up photographs of the area to be serviced. Either method can be invaluable when it comes time to reroute the harnesses for reassembly. Be sure to reinstall all clamps and new tie-straps where necessary to maintain the correct wire routing.

If wiring harness repairs are required, refer to *Electrical Repairs* at the beginning of Chapter Three.

7

Flywheel

Since the flywheel contains permanent magnets, the flywheel must never be struck with a hammer. Striking the flywheel (and magnets) can cause the magnets to lose their charge. Repeatedly striking a flywheel can lead to weak, erratic spark. Crankshafts are made of hardened steel, striking the flywheel (or crankshaft) can also permanently damage the crankshaft. Use only the recommended flywheel puller tools or their equivalents.

Removal/Installation (75-200 hp, 275 hp and 65-140 Jet)

1. Disconnect and ground the spark plug leads to the power head to prevent accidental starting.

2. Disconnect the negative battery cable and remove the flywheel cover.

3. Hold the flywheel using flywheel holder part No. 91-52344 (or equivalent). Remove the flywheel nut and washer. See **Figure 37**.

> *CAUTION*
> *Do not remove the flywheel without using a protector cap (2, **Figure 38**) or crankshaft damage can occur.*

4. Install crankshaft protector cap (part No. 91-24161, or equivalent) on the end of the crankshaft. Use a small amount of cold grease to hold the protector cap in position.

> *CAUTION*
> *Do not apply heat or strike the puller screw with a hammer in Step 5. Heat and/or hammering can damage the ignition components, the crankshaft or flywheel.*

5. Install flywheel puller part No. 91-73687A1 (1, **Figure 38**) into the flywheel. Hold the puller with one wrench and tighten the puller screw until the flywheel is dislodged from the crankshaft taper. See **Figure 39**.

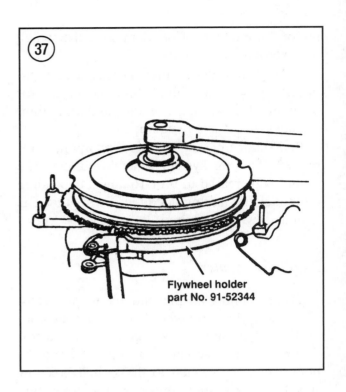

(37)

Flywheel holder
part No. 91-52344

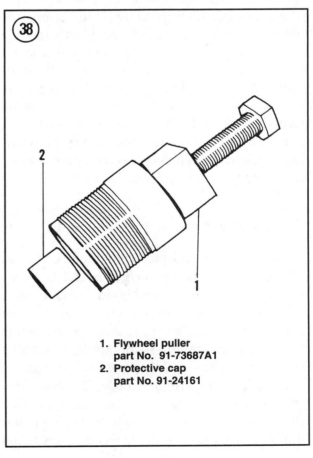

(38)

1. Flywheel puller
   part No. 91-73687A1
2. Protective cap
   part No. 91-24161

6. Lift the flywheel off the crankshaft. Remove the flywheel key from the crankshaft slot.

7. Inspect and clean the flywheel, key and crankshaft as described in this chapter.

8. To reinstall the flywheel, insert the flywheel key into the crankshaft slot.

9. Place the flywheel onto the crankshaft while aligning the key slot in the flywheel with the flywheel key.

10. Install the flywheel nut and washer. Hold the flywheel using the flywheel holder and tighten the flywheel nut to specification (**Table 5**).

11. Install the flywheel cover, reconnect the negative battery cable and reconnect the spark plug leads.

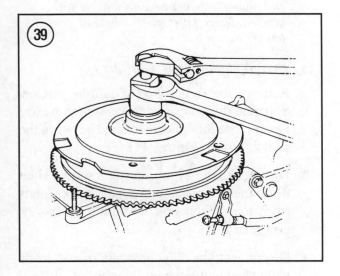

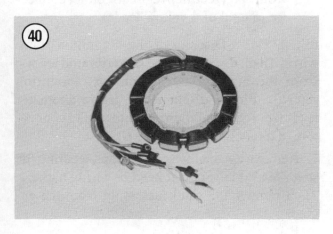

Flywheel inspection

1. Inspect the entire flywheel for cracks, chips, mechanical damage, wear and corrosion.

2. Carefully inspect the flywheel and crankshaft tapers for cracks, wear, corrosion and metal transfer.

3. Inspect the flywheel and crankshaft key slots for wear or damage.

4. Carefully inspect the flywheel key. Replace the key if it is in questionable condition.

5. Inspect the flywheel for loose, cracked or damaged magnets. The flywheel must be replaced if the magnets are loose, cracked or damaged.

> *WARNING*
> *Defective flywheels must be replaced. A defective flywheel may fly apart at high engine speed, throwing fragments over a large area. Do not attempt to use or repair a defective flywheel.*

6. Clean the flywheel and crankshaft tapers with a suitable solvent and blow dry with compressed air. The tapers must be clean, dry and free of oil or other contamination.

Stator Assembly Removal/Installation (75-200 hp and 65-140 Jet)

The stator assembly is a one-piece integrated unit, containing both the ignition stator windings and the alternator coils. **Figure 40** shows a typical 4-cylinder stator. All stator assemblies are mounted under the flywheel. All original equipment stators are encased in black plastic. The black stator contains separate low- and high-speed ignition windings. Black stators used on 4-cylinder engines are not equipped with a separate ground lead and the stator windings are not grounded to the power head. All other engines have a separate ground lead that connects the low- and high-speed windings to the power head ground. Alternator coil leads are always yellow.

7

The 75-125 hp and 65 and 80 Jet models may be equipped with a red (upgraded) stator. If the upgrade is installed, the stator will be encased in red plastic. Models equipped with a red stator are also equipped with an adapter module to allow the red stator to work with the standard switch box. The red stator is not equipped with a separate ground lead and the stator windings are not grounded to the power head. Troubleshooting procedures and test specifications vary between the black (original) and red (upgraded) stators. Refer to Chapter Three for red stator and adapter module operational descriptions, troubleshooting procedures and test specifications.

V6 models use a unique black stator assembly that has 2 sets of ignition stator windings (2 low- and 2 high-speed windings) and 2 sets of alternator coil windings. The ignition windings are separated by a yellow band on one set of ignition stator leads. All the yellow banded leads must be routed to the outer or lower switch box. The alternator coil leads are identified by lead length. The 2 long leads go to the lower rectifier/regulator and the 2 short leads go to the upper rectifier/regulator.

This section covers removal and replacement for black and red stators. Refer to the back of the manual for wiring diagrams.

1. Remove the flywheel as described in this chapter.

2. Note the orientation of the stator assembly and stator leads before proceeding.

3. Remove the stator mounting screws (typically 4 screws).

4. *75-125 hp and 65 and 80 Jet*—Remove the electrical/ignition component access cover.

5. *75-125 hp and 65 and 80 Jet*—Remove the starter motor as described in this chapter.

6A. *75-125 hp and 65 and 80 Jet (black stator)*—Disconnect the 4 ignition stator wires (blue, blue/white, red and red/white) from the switch box terminal studs. Then disconnect the 2 yellow alternator leads from the terminal block or rectifier/regulator bullet connectors.

6B. *75 and 90 hp and 65 Jet (black stator)*—Disconnect the 2 ignition stator wires (blue and red) from the switch box bullet connectors. Then, disconnect the stator ground (black) lead from the solenoid. Finally, disconnect the 2 yellow alternator leads from the terminal strip, rectifier terminals studs or rectifier/regulator bullet connectors.

6C. *75-125 hp and 65 and 80 Jet (red stator)*—Disconnect the green/white and white/green ignition stator leads from the adapter module bullet connectors. Then, disconnect the 2 yellow alternator leads from the terminal strip, rectifier terminal or rectifier/regulator bullet connectors.

NOTE
A yellow band separates the 2 ignition stator windings on V6 models. All yellow banded leads must go to the out (or lower) switch box.

6D. *135-200 hp and 105 and 140 Jet*:

a. Remove the switch box mounting screws. Separate the outer and inner switch boxes. Do not lose the spacers located between the switch boxes (**Figure 41**).

b. Disconnect the 4 ignition stator wires. Then disconnect the stator ground (black) leads from the switch box mounting screws or power head.

c. Disconnect the 2 yellow alternator leads from each rectifier/regulator bullet connector (a total of 4 yellow leads).

6E. *275 hp*—Disconnect the 4 ignition stator wires. Then, disconnect the stator ground lead(s) from the appropriate switch box mounting screw(s). Finally disconnect 2 yellow alternator leads from each rectifier/regulator bullet connectors (a total of 4 yellow leads).

7. Remove any clamps or tie-straps securing the stator leads to the power head or wiring harness. Then remove the stator assembly from the engine.

CAUTION
Stator mounting position is critical on most models. Make sure the stator is positioned in its original position unless instructions or decals included with the replacement stator show otherwise. All stator positions described are referenced by clock position with the front of the engine being 12 o'clock. Also make sure the stator wiring is not pinched between the stator and power head during installation.

8. To install the stator, begin by positioning the stator on the power head as follows:

   a. *75-125 hp and 65 and 80 Jet (red stator)*—Position the stator as shown on the stator's decal. The appropriate arrow must point aft or to the 6 o'clock position. Position the stator wiring harness between the 4 and 5 o'clock position. Route the harness directly through the grommet and into the electrical/ignition components box.

   b. *75-125 hp and 65 and 80 Jet (black stator)*—Depending on stator style, position the wiring harness at the 4 or 5 o'clock position. Make sure the stator seats fully on the power head without the wiring harness or plastic case contacting the power head. Change stator position as necessary to obtain clearance between the power head, the stator case and the stator wiring harness.

   c. *135-200 hp, 275 hp and 105 and 140 Jet*—Position the stator as noted on removal. Make sure none of the stator windings or harnesses are contacting the power head.

9. Clean the stator mounting screws with Locquic Primer and allow to air dry. Apply Loctite 271 threadlocking compound to the threads of the screws.

10. Install the stator screws and tighten evenly to specification (**Table 5**).

11. Route the stator wiring harness as noted during removal. Secure the harness to the power head or other harnesses with clamps and/or new tie-straps.

12. Connect all stator wires to their respective connectors or terminals.

13. *135-200 hp and 105 and 140 Jet*—Install the outer switch box over the inner switch box. Make sure the spacers are properly located and install the 2 mounting screws. Tighten the screws securely. Make sure all ground leads are connected to the switch box(es).

14. 75-125 hp and 65 and 80 Jet—Install the electrical/ignition component access cover. Install the starter motor as described in this chapter.

15. Install the flywheel as described in this chapter.

7

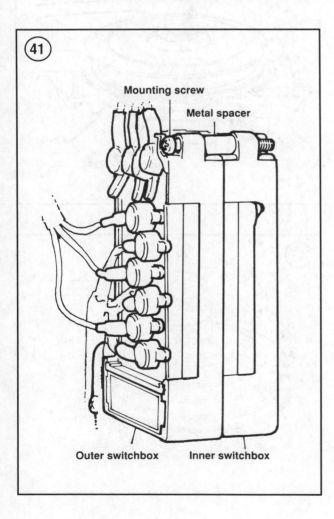

41

Mounting screw

Metal spacer

Outer switchbox   Inner switchbox

Trigger Coil Removal/Installation (75-125 hp and 65 and 80 Jet [prior to serial No. 0G438000])

The trigger coil assembly is mounted under the flywheel. Note the routing of the trigger wiring harness for reference during installation. After trigger coil installation, refer to Chapter Five and perform the synchronization and linkage adjustments procedure.

1. Remove the flywheel nut (**Figure 42**) as then remove the flywheel (**Figure 43**) described in this chapter.

2. Without disconnecting the stator wiring, remove the stator from the power head as described in this chapter. Set the stator to one side.

3. Remove the starter motor as described in this chapter.

4. Disconnect the trigger link rod from the ball and socket connector on the spark control arm (**Figure 44**).

5A. *3-cylinder models*—Disconnect the 4 trigger wires (white, brown, purple and white/black) from the switch box bullet connectors. Remove any clamps or tie-straps securing the wiring harness, then, remove the trigger assembly.

5B. *4-cylinder models*—Disconnect the 4 trigger wires (white, brown, purple and black) from the switch box terminal studs. Remove any clamps or tie-straps securing the trigger wiring harness, then remove the trigger assembly.

6. If necessary, transfer the link rod assembly to the new trigger assembly.

7. To install the trigger, begin by lubricating the trigger bearing surface with 2-4-C Multi-Lube. Then position the trigger assembly on the power head boss.

8. Connect the trigger link to the spark control arm. See **Figure 44**.

9. Route the trigger wires as noted during removal. Install the necessary clamps and/or tie-straps to secure the harness.

NOTE
Make sure the trigger assembly rotates freely with the control linkage after installation is complete.

10. Connect the trigger leads to their respective switch box terminal studs or bullet connectors.

11. Reinstall the stator assembly as described in this chapter. Make sure all stator wires are secured with clamps and/or tie-straps.

12. Install the flywheel as described in this chapter.

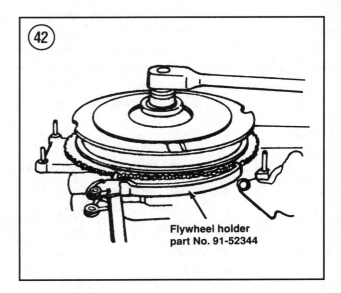
42
Flywheel holder
part No. 91-52344

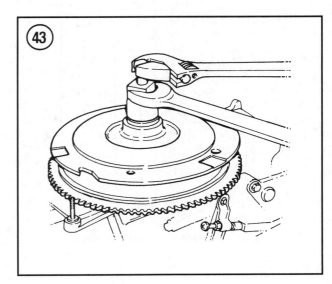
43

13. Perform the synchronization and linkage adjustments as described in Chapter Five.

Trigger Coil Removal/Installation (135-200 hp, 275 hp and 105-140 Jet)

The trigger coil assembly is mounted under the flywheel. Note the trigger wiring harness

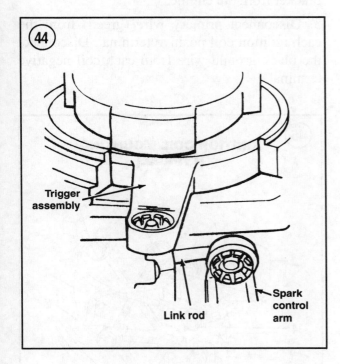

Trigger assembly

Spark control arm

Link rod

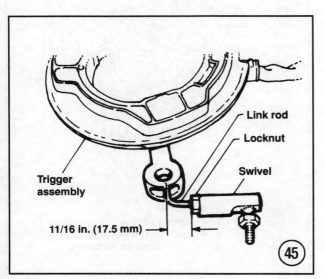

Trigger assembly

Link rod

Locknut

Swivel

11/16 in. (17.5 mm)

routing for reference during installation. After trigger coil installation, refer to Chapter Five and perform the synchronization and linkage adjustments as specified for your engine.

1. Remove the flywheel as described in this chapter.

2. Remove the stator as described in this section, but do not disconnect the stator electrical leads. Lift the stator off of the power head and set it to one side.

3. Remove the lock nut securing the link rod to the spark advance lever, then pull the link rod from the arm.

4. *135-200 hp and 105-140 Jet*—Remove the switch box mounting screws. Separate the outer and inner switch boxes. Do not lose the spacers located between the switch boxes. See **Figure 41**.

5. Disconnect the 3 trigger leads (white, brown and purple) from each switch box. Remove any clamps and tie-straps securing the trigger coil wiring harness. Remove the trigger coil assembly from the power head.

6. If necessary, transfer the link rod and swivel assembly to the new trigger assembly.

7. To install the trigger, begin by lubricating the trigger bearing surfaces with 2-4-C Multi-Lube. Then position the trigger assembly on the power head boss.

8. Verify the link rod dimension as shown in **Figure 45**. Position the swivel to provide 11/16 in. (17.5 mm) between the lock nut and the center of the trigger pivot as shown in **Figure 45**, then tighten the locknut securely.

9. Connect the link rod swivel to the spark advance lever. Install the lock nut and tighten securely.

> *NOTE*
> *A yellow band separates the 2 trigger coil harnesses. All yellow-banded leads must go to the outer (or lower) switch box.*

10. Route both trigger wiring harnesses as noted during removal. Install the necessary clamps and/or tie-straps to secure the harness.

NOTE
Make sure the trigger coil rotates freely with the control linkage after installation is complete.

11. Connect the trigger leads to their respective switch box terminal studs. The trigger leads with the yellow band must be connected to the outer (or lower) switch box.

12. Reinstall the stator assembly as described previously in this section. Make sure all stator wires are clamped and/or tie-strapped in place.

13. *135-200 hp and 105-140 Jet*—Install the outer switch box over the inner switch box. Make sure all the spacers are properly located and install the 2 mounting screws. See **Figure 41**. Tighten the screws securely. Make sure all ground leads are reconnected to the switch box(es).

CAUTION
The switch boxes must be grounded to the power head or switch box damage will result when the engine is cranked or started.

14. Reinstall the flywheel as described previously in this section.

15. Refer to Chapter Five and perform the synchronization and linkage adjustments as specified.

Ignition Coil Removal/Installation (75-200 and 275 hp)

Each ignition coil primary wire is a green wire, with or without a colored stripe. The color of the green primary wire determines the engine firing order. Each switch box primary wire must be connected to the correct ignition coil. Note the primary wire color on all cylinders before disconnecting any wires.

Refer to the back of the manual for wiring diagrams and **Figure 46** for a typical ignition coil installation.

1. Disconnect the spark plug leads from the spark plugs.

2A. *75-125 hp and 65 and 80 Jet*—Remove the electrical/ignition components access cover.

2B. *275 hp*—Remove the rear cowl support bracket from the engine.

3. Disconnect primary wire (green) from the each ignition coil positive terminal. Disconnect the black ground wire from each coil negative terminal.

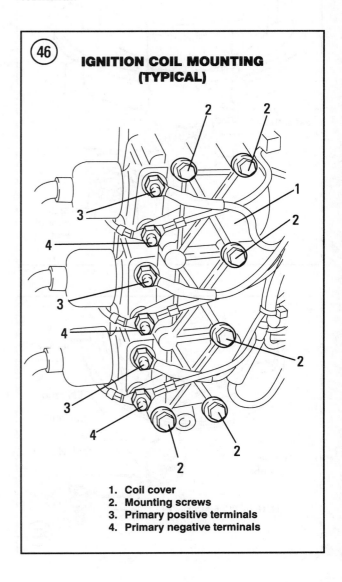

(46)

IGNITION COIL MOUNTING (TYPICAL)

1. Coil cover
2. Mounting screws
3. Primary positive terminals
4. Primary negative terminals

4A. *75-125 hp and 65 and 80 Jet*—Remove the coil cover screws and washers. Then remove the coil cover (with coils) from the engine.

4B. *135-200 hp and 105 and 140 Jet*—Two coil covers are used; each cover contains 3 coils. Remove the 6 screws and washers holding each coil cover in place (**Figure 46**). Remove the coil cover(s) and coils from the engine.

4C. *275 hp*—Three coil covers are used; each cover contains 2 coils. A ground strap is connected to every other coil cover screw. Remove the 4 screws and ground straps holding each coil cover to the power head. Remove the cover(s) and coils from the power head. Remove the coil(s) from the cover(s) as necessary.

5. If necessary, cut the tie-strap securing the spark plug boot to each ignition coil. Remove the spark plug lead from the coil.

6. To install the coils, begin by connecting the spark plug lead to each ignition coil. Apply Quicksilver Ignition Coil Insulating Compound to the boots to create a water-tight seal. Secure each boot to the coil using a new tie-strap.

7A. *75-200 hp and 65-140 Jet*—Install each coil into its cover. Position the coil cover on the power head and secure the cover(s) with the screws and washers. Tighten the cover screws to specification (**Table 5**).

7B. *275 hp*—Install 2 coils into each coil cover. Position the coil cover(s) on the power head and secure with the mounting fasteners. Make sure the ground straps are attached to every other coil cvover screw (2 ground straps per cover). Tighten the screws to specification (**Table 5**).

8. Connect the switch box primary lead (green) to each coil positive terminal. Connect the black ground lead to each coil negative terminal. Tighten the screws to specification (**Table 5**).

9. Coat the coil primary terminal connections with Quicksilver Liquid Neoprene. Reconnect the spark plug leads to the spark plugs.

Switch Box Removal/Installation

All terminal stud style switch boxes have the wire color code for each stud embossed into the switch box body. All bullet connector style switch boxes use leads that are always connected to another lead with the exact same color code. Although these steps have been taken by the manufacturer, it is still a good practice to take special note of the wire routing and terminal connections before disconnecting any leads. Correct wire routing is very important to prevent insulation and wire damage from heat, vibration or interference with moving parts.

The stacked (dual) switch box arrangement on 135-200 hp and 105-140 Jet models can be especially confusing if care and caution are not exercised. All V-6 trigger coils and stator coils use leads that are separated (identified) by yellow bands on one set of leads. The yellow banded leads always attach to the outer (or lower) switch box.

Refer to the back of the manual for wiring diagrams.

75-125 hp and 65 and 80 Jet

The switch box on 3-cylinder models uses bullet connectors while the switch box on 4-cylinder models uses terminal studs. Switch boxes with terminal studs are equipped with rubber boots to protect the terminal connection. Pull the rubber boot away from the switch box to access the terminal nut.

Take special note of all ground wires located under the switch box mounting screws and/or attached to the power head. The switch box will be damaged if not properly grounded. Refer to the back of the manual for wiring diagrams.

1. Disconnect the negative battery cable from the battery.

2. Disconnect and ground the spark plug leads to the power head to prevent accidental starting.

7

3. Remove the electrical/ignition component access cover. Loosen any clamps and cut any tie-straps securing the switch box leads.

4. Proceed as follows:

a. Disconnect the trigger coil leads from the switch box terminals. The brown terminal may also have a separate lead connected to an rpm limit module. Make sure all leads are disconnected from the brown terminal.

b. Disconnect the stator leads and the stop circuit lead from the switch box.

c. Disconnect the ignition coil primary leads from the switch box.

5. Remove the switch box mounting screws. Make sure all black ground leads are disconnected (if so equipped) and remove the switch box from the power head. See **Figure 47**.

6. To install the switch box, position the switch in its mounting bracket. Apply Loctite 242 threadlocking compound to the threads of the mounting screws. Attach any ground wires as required, then install and tighten the mounting screws to specification (**Table 5**).

7. Connect all switch box leads to their respective bullet connectors or terminal studs. Tighten the terminal nuts to specification (**Table 5**).

8. Install all clamps/tie-straps to secure the wiring harnesses.

9. Connect the spark plug leads to the spark plugs. Connect the negative battery cable to the battery.

135-200 hp and 105-140 Jet

These engines use 2 switch boxes with terminal studs. Terminal stud switch boxes use leads with rubber boots to protect the terminal connection. Pull the rubber boot away from the switch box(es) to gain access to the terminal nut.

The stacked (dual) switch box arrangement on these models can be confusing if care and caution are not exercised. These trigger coils and stator coils use leads that are separated (identified) by

yellow bands on one set of leads. The yellow banded leads always go to the outer switch box.

Take special note of all ground wires connected directly to the switch boxes, located under the switch box mounting screws and/or attached to the power head. The switch boxes will be damaged if not properly grounded.

Refer to the back of the manual for wiring diagrams.

1. Disconnect the negative battery cable.

2. Disconnect and ground the spark plug leads to the power head to prevent accidental starting.

3. Remove the 2 switch box mounting screws (**Figure 48**). Separate the inner and outer switch

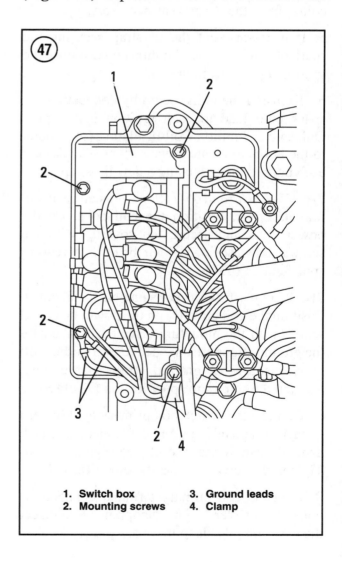

| 1. Switch box | 3. Ground leads |
| 2. Mounting screws | 4. Clamp |

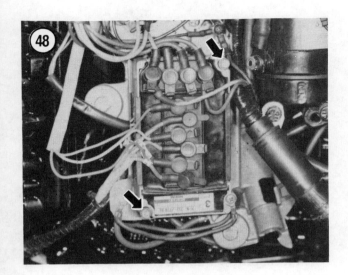

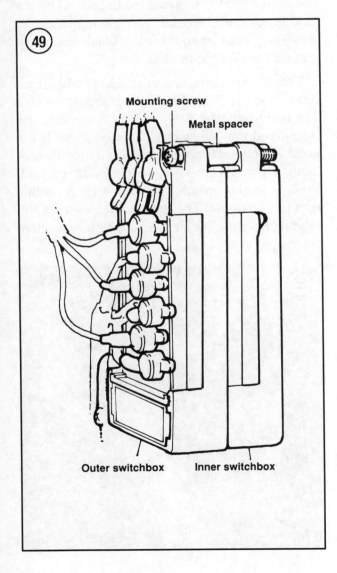

Mounting screw

Metal spacer

Outer switchbox   Inner switchbox

boxes and remove the metal spacers between the switch boxes (**Figure 49**).

4. Note the position and routing of each switch box lead. The color code for each terminal is embossed in the switch box body. The outer switch box stator leads are identified as blue and red even though they are actually red/white and blue/white.

5. Unsnap the neoprene cap on each wire terminal. Pull the caps back and remove the terminal nuts. Disconnect the wires from the terminals and remove the switch boxes.

6. To install the switch boxes, reconnect the wires to the appropriate switch box terminals. The yellow banded leads must be connected to the outer switch box.

7. Connect the ground lead to each switch box. Tighten the ground screws securely.

8. Apply Loctite 242 threadlocking adhesive to the threads of the switch box mounting screws. Install the switch boxes to the power head using the mounting screws and spacers. Make sure that *both* switch boxes are properly grounded to the power head or the switch boxes will be damaged when the engine is cranked or started.

9. Tighten the switch box mounting screws (**Figure 48**) to specifications (**Table 5**).

10. Reconnect the spark plug leads and the negative battery cable.

275 hp models

These engines use 2 switch boxes with terminal studs. Terminal stud switch boxes use leads with rubber boots to protect the terminal connection. Pull the rubber boot away from the switch box(es) to gain access to the terminal nut.

The 2 switch box arrangement on these models can be confusing if care and caution are not exercised. This engine's trigger coils and stator coils use leads that are separated (identified) by yellow bands on one set of leads. The yellow banded leads always go to the lower switch box.

7

Take special note of all ground wires connected directly to the switch box, located under the switch box mounting screws and/or attached to the power head. The switch boxes will be damaged if not properly grounded.

Refer to the back of the manual for wiring diagrams.

1. Disconnect the negative battery cable.

2. Disconnect and ground the spark plug leads to the power head to prevent accidental starting.

3. Note the position and routing of each switch box lead. The color code for each terminal is embossed in the switch box body. The lower switch box stator leads are identified as blue and red even though they are actually red/white and blue/white.

4. Unsnap the neoprene cap on each wire terminal. Pull the caps back and remove the terminal nuts. Disconnect the wires from the terminals and remove the switch boxes.

5. Remove the ground lead(s) from each switch box, then remove the 2 mounting screws from each switch box. Remove the switch boxes from the engine.

6. To install the switch boxes, apply Loctite 242 threadlocking adhesive to the threads of the switch box mounting screws. Position the switch boxes on the power head. Install and tighten the switch box mounting screws to specification (**Table 5**).

7. Connect the ground lead(s) to each switch box, tighten the ground screws securely. Make sure that *both* switch boxes are properly grounded to the power head or the switch boxes will be damaged when the engine is cranked or started.

8. Reconnect the wires to the appropriate switch box terminals. The yellow banded leads must be connected to the lower switch box.

9. Reconnect the spark plug leads and the negative battery cable.

Rpm Limit Module

The 100-125 hp and 65-140 Jet models are equipped with a rpm limit module. The rpm limit module is connected to the switch box stop circuit (black/yellow). When engine speed exceeds the preprogrammed limit, the rpm limit module momentarily shorts the black/yellow lead to ground, limiting engine speed. There are 4 leads on the rpm limit module. The purple lead is power for the module from the key switch. The brown lead is connected to the brown trigger coil lead and is an engine speed signal for the module. The black/yellow lead is connected to the switch box stop circuit and is shorted to ground by the module to control engine speed by switching the ignition system on and off. The black lead is the ground path for the module.

The 275 hp model is also equipped with a rpm limit module. This rpm limit module is also connected to the switch box stop circuits (black/yellow). When engine speed exceeds the preprogrammed limit, the rpm limit module momentarily shorts the black/yellow lead to ground, limiting engine speed. There are 4 leads on this rpm limit module. The red lead is power for the module from the starter solenoid battery positive

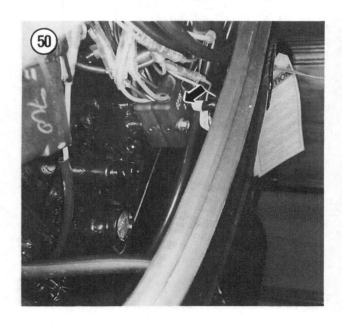

terminal. The gray lead is connected to the gray voltage regulator lead and is an engine speed signal for the module. The black/yellow lead is connected to the switch box stop circuits and is shorted to ground by the module to control engine speed by switching the ignition system on and off. The black lead is the ground path for the module.

The 275 hp also incorporates a diode in the rpm limit module black/yellow circuit to prevent the rpm limit module from shorting out all 6 cylinders (both switch boxes). When the diode is working correctly only the lower switch box (cylinder No. 2, No. 4 and No. 6) is affected by the rpm limit module.

Removal/Installation (100-125 hp and 65-140 Jet)

Locate the rpm limit module on the power head. On 100-125 hp and 65 and 80 Jet models, the module is typically mounted in the lower cowl area on the starboard side of the power head as shown in **Figure 50**. On 105 and 140 Jet, the module is typically mounted on the top or side of the cylinder block port bank. Verify the location by matching the wire colors. On 100-125 hp and 65 and 80 Jet models, it may be necessary to split the lower cowl to access the module.

1. Disconnect the negative battery cable.

2. Disconnect and ground the spark plug leads to the power head to prevent accidental starting.

3. Disconnect the brown, purple and black/yellow leads at the module bullet connectors. If necessary, cut any tie-straps securing the module leads.

4. Remove the screw securing the black ground lead to the power head.

5. Remove the module mounting screws, then remove the module from the power head.

6. To install the module, position the module on the power head and secure it with the appropriate screws. Tighten the screws securely.

7. Connect the module ground lead to the power head. Tighten the ground screw securely.

8. Connect the brown, purple and black/yellow leads to the module bullet connectors. If necessary, secure the leads with a new tie-strap.

9. Reconnect the spark plug leads and the negative battery cable.

Removal/replacement (275 hp)

Locate the rpm limit module on the power head. The rpm limit module is mounted low on the starboard side of the power head, below the engine mounted oil reservoir. Verify that you have located the correct module by matching the color codes of the four wires.

1. Disconnect the negative battery cable.

2. Disconnect and ground the spark plug leads to the power head to prevent accidental starting.

3. Remove any clamps and cut all tie-straps securing the module leads.

4. Disconnect the gray leads from the voltage regulator and engine harness at the rpm limit module bullet connectors.

5. Disconnect the black ground lead from the lower switch box case.

6. Disconnect the black/yellow lead from the lower switch box black/yellow terminal stud.

7. Disconnect the red lead from the starter solenoid battery positive terminal.

8. Remove the 2 module mounting screws, then remove the module from the power head.

9. To install the module, position the module on the power head and secure it with 2 screws. Tighten the screws securely.

10. Connect the module ground lead to the lower switch box. Make sure all ground leads are reconnected to the switch box. Tighten the ground screw securely.

11. Connect the module black/yellow lead to the lower switch box terminal stud. Make sure all black/yellow leads are reconnected to the switch box stud. Tighten the terminal nut to specification (**Table 5**).

7

12. Connect the module red lead to the starter solenoid battery positive terminal. Make sure all red leads are reconnected to the solenoid positive terminal. Tighten the nut securely.

13. Connect the gray voltage regulator and engine harness leads to the module gray lead bullet connectors.

14. Secure the module leads with clamps and/or new tie-straps.

15. Reconnect the spark plug leads and the negative battery cable.

CAPACITOR DISCHARGE MODULE (CDM) IGNITION

CDM ignition systems are unique in that they combine the switch box and ignition coil functions into one module, called the CDM module. There is one CDM module for each cylinder. The rectifier in each CDM transforms the ignition stator AC voltage into DC voltage so it can be stored in the CDM module capacitor. The capacitor holds the voltage until the SCR (silicon controlled rectifier), which is simply an electronic switch, releases the voltage to the integral ignition coil primary windings. Depending on the engine model, the SCR is triggered by either a conventional trigger coil, a TPM (timing and protection module) or an Ignition ECM (electronic control module). The ignition coil transforms the relatively low voltage from the capacitor into voltage high enough (45,000 volts) to jump the spark plug gap and ignite the air/fuel mixture.

There are 2 versions of the CDM module. Early modules (typically through 1995 model year engines) have a 3-pin connector (A, **Figure 51**) and a separate ground lead (B, **Figure 51**). Later modules (typically 1996 and newer model engines) have a 4-pin connector with an integrated ground (**Figure 52**). Ignition test harness part No. 84-825207A1 (3-pin models) or part No. 84-825207A2 (4-pin models) is required to test the CDM system without damaging the wiring harness and connectors.

Refer to Chapter Three for troubleshooting procedures on all CDM ignition systems. Refer to the back of the manual for wiring diagrams.

Spark Plugs

There is one spark plug for each cylinder. Use only the recommended spark plugs or catastrophic engine damage may result. Resistor or suppressor plugs are designed to reduce RFI (radio frequency interference) emissions that can cause interference with electrical accessories. Use the recommended RFI spark plug if RFI interference is suspected of causing interference or malfunction of electrical accessories.

Stop circuit

The stop circuit is connected to one end of the capacitor in each CDM module. Whenever the stop circuit is connected to ground, the capacitor is shorted and cannot store electricity. At this point there is no voltage available to send to the ignition coil windings and the ignition system

ceases producing spark. The stop circuit must have an open circuit (to ground) for the engine to run. The stop circuit leads are always color-coded black/yellow.

The 100-125 hp and 65 and 80 Jet models are equipped with an rpm limit module. The rpm limit module is connected to the CDM module's stop circuit (black/yellow). When engine speed exceeds the preprogrammed limit, the rpm limit module momentarily shorts the black/yellow lead to ground, limiting engine speed.

The 1994 model 225 hp carbureted engine uses a shift interrupt circuit connected to the black/yellow stop circuit of the port bank of cylinders (No. 2, No. 4 and No. 6). A diode is used to separate the stop circuit from the star-board cylinder bank. When shift load exceeds the spring force of the shift interrupt switch, the diode protected black/yellow circuit is shorted to ground, disabling the port bank of cylinders. The resultant drop in engine speed reduces shift ef-fort. As soon as the shift is completed, the shift interrupt switch opens and all cylinders resume normal operation. The shift switch is mounted underneath the shift cable on the PORT side of the engine.

Component Wiring

Modern outboard motor electrical systems can be intimidating, especially on the higher output engines. For this reason, electrical wiring is color coded, and the terminals on the components to which each wire connects are embossed with the correct wire color. When used in conjunction with the correct electrical diagram, incorrect wire connections should be eliminated.

In addition, the routing of the wiring harness and individual leads is very important to prevent possible electrical interference and/or physical damage to the wiring harnesses from moving engine parts or vibration. Mercury/Mariner out-boards are shipped from the factory with all wiring harnesses and leads properly positioned and secured with the appropriate clamps and tie-straps.

Should component replacement become nec-essary, it is highly recommended that you take the time to either carefully draw a sketch of the area to be serviced, noting the positioning of all wire harnesses involved, or use an instant camera to take several close-up photographs of the area to be serviced. Either method can be invaluable when it comes time to reroute the harnesses for reassembly. Be sure to reinstall all clamps and new tie-straps where necessary to maintain the correct wire routing.

If wiring harness repairs are required, refer to *Electrical Repairs* in Chapter Three.

Flywheel

Since the flywheel contains permanent mag-nets, the flywheel must never be struck with a hammer. Striking the flywheel (and magnets) can cause the magnets to lose their magnetism. Repeatedly striking a flywheel can lead to weak, erratic spark. Crankshafts are made of hardened steel; therefore, striking the flywheel (or crank-shaft) can also permanently damage the crankshaft. Use only the recommended flywheel puller tools or their equivalents.

Removal/installation

1. Disconnect and ground the spark plug leads to the power head to prevent accidental starting.

2. On 225 and 250 hp models, remove the timing pointer from the top of the starter motor drive end frame.

3. Hold the flywheel using flywheel holder part No. 91-52344 (or equivalent). See **Figure 53**. If no ring gear teeth are present, hold the flywheel with a strap wrench (part No. 91-24937A-1, or equivalent). See **Figure 54**, typical.

> *CAUTION*
> *To prevent crankshaft damage, do not remove the flywheel without using a crankshaft protector cap (**Figure 55**).*

4. Install the crankshaft protector cap (part No. 91-24161, or equivalent) on the end of the crankshaft. Use cold grease to hold the protector cap in place.

> *CAUTION*
> *Never apply heat or strike the puller screw with a hammer during flywheel removal. Heat and/or hammering can*

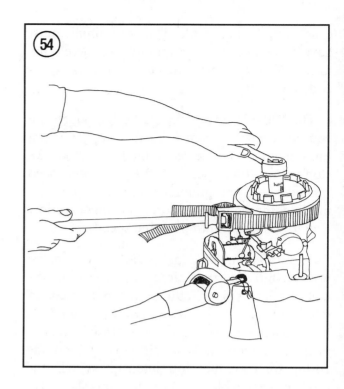

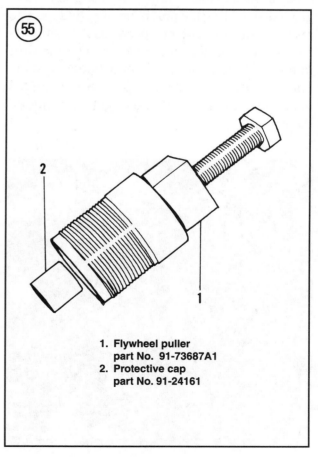

1. Flywheel puller
   part No. 91-73687A1
2. Protective cap
   part No. 91-24161

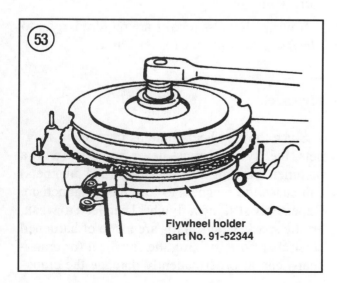

Flywheel holder
part No. 91-52344

damage the ignition components, flywheel and crankshaft.

5. Install flywheel puller part No. 91-73687A1 (or equivalent) into the flywheel. See **Figure 55**. Hold the puller with one wrench and tighten the puller screw until the flywheel is dislodged from the crankshaft taper.

6. Lift the flywheel off the crankshaft. Remove the flywheel key from the crankshaft slot.

7. Inspect and clean the flywheel, key and crankshaft as described in this chapter.

8. To install the flywheel, insert the flywheel key into the slot in the crankshaft.

9. Align the flywheel key slot with the flywheel key and place the flywheel onto the crankshaft.

10. Install the flywheel nut and washer. Hold the flywheel with the strap wrench or the flywheel holder and tighten the flywheel nut to specification (**Table 5**).

11. On 225 and 250 hp models, install the timing pointer. Refer to Chapter Five for timing pointer adjustment.

12. Reconnect the spark plug leads to the spark plugs.

Flywheel inspection

1. Inspect the entire flywheel for cracks, chips, mechanical damage, wear and corrosion.

2. Carefully inspect the flywheel and crankshaft tapers for cracks, wear, corrosion and metal transfer.

3. Inspect the flywheel and crankshaft key slots for wear or damage.

4. Carefully inspect the flywheel key. Replace the key if it is in questionable condition.

5. Inspect the flywheel for loose, cracked or damaged magnets. The flywheel must be replaced if the magnets are loose, cracked or damaged.

WARNING
A defective flywheel must be replaced. A defective flywheel may fly apart at high

engine speed, throwing fragments over a large area. Do not attempt to use or repair a defective flywheel.

6. Clean the flywheel and crankshaft tapers with a suitable solvent and blow dry with compressed air. The tapers must be clean, dry and free of oil or other contamination.

CDM IGNITION (75-125 HP AND 65-80 JET [SERIAL NO. 0G438000-ON])

Description

This CDM ignition is an alternator driven, capacitor discharge module system with mechanical spark advance. It is used on 75-125 hp and 65-80 Jet models (serial No. 0G438000-on).

The major components are the:

1. *Flywheel*—The flywheel inner magnet is for the trigger coil (timing information). The outer magnets are for the ignition stator and battery charging stator. See 1, **Figure 56**.

2. *Ignition stator (charge) coils*—The stator (2, **Figure 56**, typical) consists of one winding around 3 bobbins. The ignition stator windings are not grounded to the power head. The ignition stator provides power to the CDM modules. Stator output is always AC (alternating current) voltage.

NOTE
The ignition stator circuit must be complete from the stator to a CDM module and back to the stator through a different CDM module for the system to function. See Chapter Three.

3. *Trigger coil*—The trigger coil (3, **Figure 56**) tells the CDM modules (4, **Figure 56**) when to fire. The trigger coil is rotated by mechanical linkage to change the trigger's position relative to the flywheel. This movement advances or retards the ignition spark timing.

4. *CDM modules, spark plugs and stop circuit*—All of these components function as described at the beginning of this section.

Flywheel Removal/Installation

Flywheel removal and installation is covered at the beginning of the *Capacitor Discharge Module (CDM) Ignition* section. Refer to Chapter Three for troubleshooting procedures and Chapter Fourteen for wiring diagrams.

Stator Removal/Installation

The stator assembly is a one-piece integrated unit, containing both the ignition stator windings and the alternator coils. The stator assembly is mounted under the flywheel. Alternator coil leads are always yellow. Ignition stator leads are green/white and white/green.

1. Remove the flywheel as described in this chapter.

2. Note the orientation of the stator assembly and all stator leads before proceeding.

3. Remove the 4 stator assembly mounting screws.

4. Disconnect the green/white and white/green ignition stator leads from the wiring harness bullet connectors. Then disconnect the 2 yellow alternator coil leads from the terminal strip, rectifier terminal studs or rectifier/regulator bullet connectors.

5. Remove any clamps or tie-straps securing the stator leads to the power head, electrical bracket or wiring harness. Then remove the stator assembly from the engine.

> *CAUTION*
> *Make sure the stator is repositioned in its original position unless instructions or decals included with the replacement stator show otherwise. The stator windings and wiring harness must not contact (be crushed) between the stator and the power head.*

6. To install the stator, begin by positioning the stator on the power head as noted on removal. Make sure none of the stator windings or harnesses are contacting the power head.

7. Clean the stator mounting screws with Locquic Primer and allow to air dry. Apply Loctite 271 threadlocking adhesive to the threads of the screws.

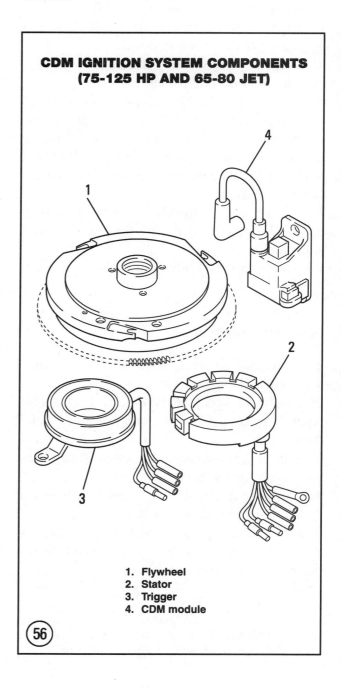

CDM IGNITION SYSTEM COMPONENTS (75-125 HP AND 65-80 JET)

1. Flywheel
2. Stator
3. Trigger
4. CDM module

56

8. Install the stator screws and tighten evenly to specification (**Table 5**).

9. Route the stator wiring harness as noted on removal. Secure the harness to the power head, electrical bracket or other harnesses with clamps and/or new tie-straps.

10. Connect all stator wires disconnected in Step 4 to their respective bullet connectors.

11. Reinstall the flywheel as described previously in this section.

Trigger Coil Removal/Installation

The trigger coil assembly is mounted under the flywheel. Note the trigger wiring harness routing for reference during installation. After trigger coil installation, refer to Chapter Five and perform the synchronization and linkage adjustments as specified for your engine.

1. Remove the flywheel as described previously in this section.

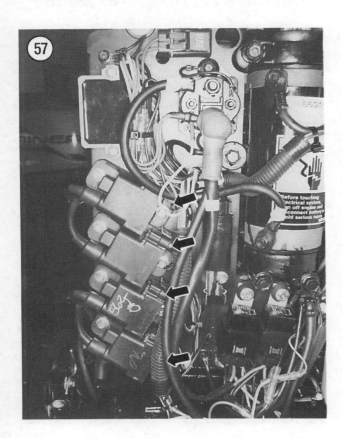

2. Remove the stator as described previously in this section, but do not disconnect the stator electrical leads. Lift the stator off of the power head and set it to one side.

3. Disconnect the trigger link rod ball and socket connector from the spark control arm.

4. Disconnect the trigger leads from the wiring harness bullet connectors. If so equipped, remove the screw securing the trigger coil ground lead to the power head or electrical bracket.

5. If necessary, transfer the link rod assembly to the new trigger coil assembly.

6. To install the trigger, begin by lubricating the trigger bearing surfaces with 2-4-C Multi-Lube. Then position the trigger assembly on the power head boss.

7. Connect the trigger link rod ball and socket connector to the spark control arm.

8. Route the trigger wires as noted during removal. Install the necessary clamps and/or tie-straps to secure the harness.

NOTE
Make sure the trigger coil rotates freely with the control linkage after the installation is complete.

9. Connect the trigger leads to the appropriate wiring harness bullet connectors. If so equipped, secure the trigger coil ground lead to the power head or electrical bracket. Tighten the ground screw securely.

10. Reinstall the stator assembly as described previously in this section. Make sure all stator wires are clamped and/or tie-strapped in place.

11. Reinstall the flywheel as described previously in this section.

12. Refer to Chapter Five and perform the synchronization and linkage adjustments as specified.

CDM Modules Removal/Installation

Refer to **Figure 57** for this procedure.

7

1. Disconnect and ground the spark plug leads to the power head to prevent accidental starting.

2. Disconnect the 4-pin connector from each CDM module to be removed.

3. Remove the 2 CDM module mounting bolts from each module. Then remove the module(s) from the engine.

4. To install the CDM module(s), position each module in its mounted position and secure it with 2 screws. Tighten both mounting screws to specification (**Table 5**).

5. Reconnect the 4 pin connector to each module.

6. Reconnect the spark plug leads.

Rpm Limit Module Removal/Installation

All models are normally equipped with an rpm limit module. The rpm limit module is connected to the switch box stop circuit (black/yellow). When engine speed exceeds the preprogrammed limit, the rpm limit module momentarily shorts the black/yellow lead to ground, limiting engine speed. There are four leads on the rpm limit module. The purple lead is power for the module from the key switch. The brown lead is connected to the brown trigger coil lead and is an engine speed signal for the module. The black/yellow lead is connected to the switch box stop circuit and is shorted to ground by the module to control engine speed by switching the ignition system on and off. The black lead is the ground path for the module.

Locate the rpm limit module on the power head. The module is typically mounted in the lower cowl ara on the starboard side of the engine as shown in **Figure 58**. Verify the location by matching the color of the wires. It may be necessary to split the lower cowl to access the module.

1. Disconnect the negative battery cable.

2. Disconnect and ground the spark plug leads to the power head to prevent accidental starting.

3. Disconnect the brown, purple and black/yellow leads at the module bullet connectors. If necessary, cut any tie-straps securing the module leads.

4. Remove the screw securing the black ground lead to the power head.

5. Remove the 2 module mounting screws, then remove the module from the power head or electrical bracket.

6. To install the module, position the module on the power head or electrical bracket and secure it with 2 screws. Tighten the screws securely.

7. Connect the module ground lead to the power head. Tighten the ground screw securely.

8. Connect the brown, purple and black/yellow leads to the module bullet connectors. If necessary, secure the leads with a new tie-strap.

9. Reconnect the spark plug leads and the negative battery cable.

CDM IGNITION (225 AND 250 HP)

Description

This CDM ignition is an alternator driven, capacitor discharge module system with electronic spark advance. It is used on 1994-1997,

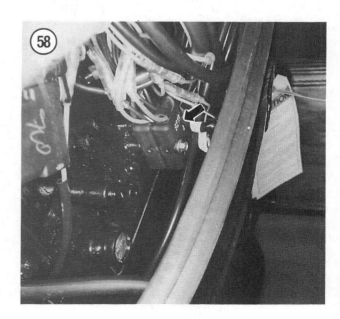

225 hp (carbureted and EFI [electronic fuel injection] models) and 250 hp EFI models. The 1994-1995 model engines use 3-pin CDM modules with a separate ground lead. The 1996-1997 model engines use 4-pin CDM modules with an integrated ground.

This ignition system is designed to be most easily diagnosed with the Quicksilver DDT (digital diagnostic terminal). The DDT is normally found only in Mercury or Mariner dealerships, where the investment can be justified. The DDT displays sensor input values and actuator output values as the ECM (electronic control module) sees them.

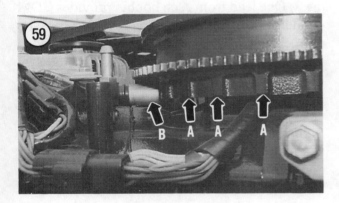

The major components are the:

1. *Flywheel*—The magnets are for the ignition stator. The outer diameter, lower edge of the flywheel contains cast in encoding ribs (A, **Figure 59**) for the crankshaft position sensor (B, **Figure 59**).

2. *Crankshaft position sensor*—The crankshaft position sensor (CPS) detects the presence of the encoding ribs on the flywheel and sends a signal to the electronic control module (ECM). This signal tells the ECM crankshaft position and engine rpm. The air gap between the flywheel encoding ribs and the CPS must be set to 0.020-0.060 in. (0.51-1.52 mm).

3. *Ignition stator (charge) coils*—The stator consists of six windings around 6 bobbins. The ignition stator provides power to the CDM modules. Stator output is always AC (alternating current) voltage.

4. *CDM modules, spark plugs and stop circuit*—These components function as described at the beginning of this section.

5. *Ignition ECM*—The ignition ECM (electronic control module) is the heart of the ignition system. The ignition ECM (**Figure 60**, typical) monitors input from the crankshaft position sensor (CPS), Throttle position sensor (TPS) and Engine coolant temperature sensor (ECT). The ECM then calculates the correct timing for each cylinder. On EFI models, the ignition ECM interfaces with the fuel ECM to coordinate the firing of the fuel injectors. The ignition ECM contains a cold engine start, idle stabilizer, rpm limit, overheat protection, low oil level (carbureted models) and sensor failure warning programs all described in Chapter Three.

Newer models (1995-1997) use a shift interrupt circuit connected to the ignition ECM. When shift load, exceeds the spring force of the shift interrupt switch, the ignition ECM green/yellow lead is shorted to ground. The ignition ECM then retards spark advance to 20° ATDC. The retarded timing reduces engine speed, reducing shift effort. As soon as the shift

7

is completed, the shift interrupt switch opens and the ignition ECM returns spark advance to normal. If for some reason the shift interrupt switch stays closed for more than 2 seconds, the ignition ECM automatically returns spark advance to normal.

> *NOTE*
> *EFI models incorporate the low oil level and the water in fuel warning programs into the Fuel ECM.*

6. *Warning panel*—A multifunction warning panel is recommended for all models. The EFI model has 3 lights that allow easy identification of low oil tank level, engine overheat, engine over-speed, sensor malfunction or water in fuel situations. The carbureted model does not include the water in fuel light. See **Figure 61**.

Component Removal/Installation

Flywheel removal and installation is covered at the beginning of the *Capacitor Discharge Module (CDM) Ignition* section.

Replacement of the ECT (engine coolant temperature) sensor, IAT (intake air temperature) sensor, MAP (manifold absolute pressure) sensor and TPS (throttle position sensor) is covered in Chapter Six under *EFI Fuel Systems*.

Refer to Chapter Three for troubleshooting procedures and the back of the manual for wiring diagrams.

Ignition Stator Removal/Installation

The ignition stator assembly is a one-piece unit containing only ignition stator windings. The stator assembly is mounted under the flywheel. An external, belt-driven alternator is used on these engines.

On 1994 models, the 2 leads from each bobbin (12 total) are individually wired through a single quick-connect connector to the main engine harness. One lead from each bobbin provides CDM module power, the other lead provides a back-up trigger signal. The ignition stator is not grounded to the power head. This stator and ignition system features *Limp home mode*. If the ignition ECM should fail, the timing will be fixed at approximately 9° BTDC by the back-up trigger signal leads.

On 1995 models, one lead from each bobbin (6 total) is connected to engine ground (A, **Figure 62**). The 6 individual bobbin leads are connected to the main engine harness through a quick-disconnect connector (B, **Figure 62**). This stator does not feature *Limp home mode*. If the ignition ECM fails, there will be no spark.

1. Remove the flywheel as described in this chapter.

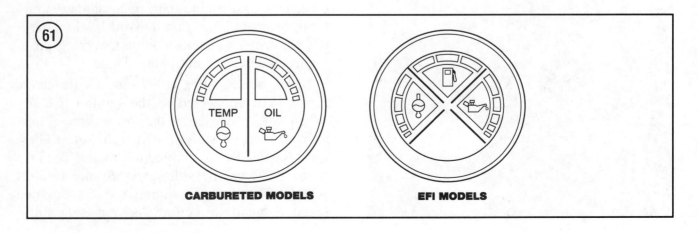

CARBURETED MODELS

TEMP OIL

EFI MODELS

2. Note the orientation of the stator assembly and all stator leads before proceeding.

3. Remove the 4 stator assembly mounting screws.

4A. *1994 models*—Disconnect the 12 lead stator connector from the engine wiring harness connector.

4B. *1995-1997 models*—Disconnect the 6 lead stator connector from the engine wiring harness. Then remove the screw securing the stator ground leads (A, **Figure 62**) to the power head.

5. Remove any clamps or tie-straps securing the stator leads to the power head. Then remove the stator assembly from the engine.

> *CAUTION*
> *Make sure the stator is repositioned in its original position unless instructions or decals included with the replacement stator show otherwise. The stator windings and wiring harness must not contact (be crushed) between the stator and the power head.*

6. To install the stator, begin by positioning the stator on the power head as noted on removal. Make sure none of the stator windings or harnesses are contacting the power head.

7. Clean the stator mounting screws with Locquic Primer and allow to air dry. Apply Loctite 271 threadlocking adhesive to the threads of the screws.

8. Install the stator screws and tighten evenly to specification (**Table 5**).

9. Route the stator wiring harness as noted on removal. Secure the harness to the power head with clamps and/or new tie-straps.

10. Connect all stator leads disconnected in Step 4 to their respective connectors or grounds.

11. Reinstall the flywheel as described previously in this section.

Ignition ECM Removal/Installation

The ignition ECM is the only ECM on the 225 hp carbureted models and mounted above the fuel ECM on 225 and 250 hp EFI models. The ECMs are mounted on the rear of the power head. The lower ECM is the fuel ECM. Refer to **Figure 60** (1995-1997 models) for this procedure.

1. Disconnect the negative battery cable.

2A. *1994 models*—Disconnect the 2 ECM harness leads from the engine harness at the 2 quick-connect connectors.

2B. *1995-1997 models*—Disconnect the main engine wiring harness ECM connector from the top of the ignition ECM. Squeeze the rubber boot tab to unlock the connector.

3. Note the position of any ground leads, then remove the 4 ignition ECM mounting bolts. Remove the ignition ECM.

4. To install the ignition ECM, begin by positioning the ECM on the power head mounting plate.

5. Install the 4 mounting screws, making sure to reconnect any ground leads to the appropriate mounting screws. Tighten the 4 mounting screws to specification (**Table 5**).

6. Reconnect the main engine wiring harness to the ignition ECM.

7. Reconnect the negative battery cable.

Crankshaft Position Sensor Removal/Installation

1. Disconnect and ground the spark plug leads to the power head to prevent accidental starting.

2. Disconnect the negative battery cable.

3. Remove the flywheel cover.

4. Remove the 2 screws securing the crankshaft position sensor to the power head.

5. Disconnect the sensor 2-wire connector from the engine wiring harness.

6. Remove any tie-straps securing the sensor leads to the power head or wiring harness and remove the sensor from the power head.

7. If necessary, transfer the sensor bracket to the new sensor. Tighten the screw that holds the sensor to the bracket to specification (**Table 5**).

8. To install the sensor, begin by positioning the sensor on the power head mounting bosses and securing the sensor with 2 screws. Tighten the 2 screws hand tight at this time.

9. Reconnect the sensor connector to the engine wiring harness.

10. Secure the sensor leads to the power head and/or engine wiring harness with new tie-strap(s).

11. Adjust the sensor air gap as follows:

   a. Slightly rotate the flywheel to align an encoder rib (A, **Figure 63**) with the crankshaft position sensor (B, **Figure 63**).

   b. Measure the gap (C, **Figure 63**) between the flywheel encoder rib and the crankshaft position sensor with a feeler gauge. The gap should be 0.020-0.060 in. (0.51-1.52 mm). If the gap is not within specification, loosen the 2 sensor mounting screws (D, **Figure 63**) slightly and reset the gap to specification.

   c. Tighten the screws to 100 in.-lb. (11.3 N•m) and recheck the sensor air gap.

12. Install the flywheel cover.

13. Reconnect the negative battery cable and the spark plug leads.

CDM Modules Removal/Installation

1. Disconnect and ground the spark plug leads to the power head to prevent accidental starting.

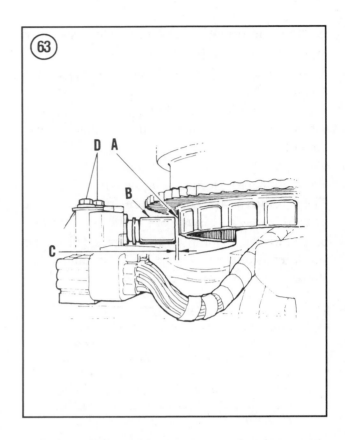

2. Disconnect the 3 or 4-pin connector from each CDM module to be removed.

3. Remove the 2 CDM module mounting bolts from each module. Then remove the module(s) from the engine.

NOTE
On 3-pin CDM modules, the separate ground lead must be installed under one of the CDM module mounting screws. The CDM will not operate correctly unless it is properly grounded.

4. To install the CDM module(s), position each module in its mounted position and secure it with 2 screws. On 3-pin CDM modules, secure the ground lead with one of the mounting screws. Tighten both mounting screws to specification (**Table 5**).

5. Reconnect the 3 or 4 pin connector to each module.

6. Reconnect the spark plug leads.

DIGITAL INDUCTIVE IGNITION (200 DFI)

Description

The digital inductive ignition system is a battery driven, ECM (electronic control module) controlled system with electronic spark advance. Once the engine starts, a 60 amp belt-driven alternator provides all operating voltage for the system. This system is used exclusively on the 1997 model year 200 hp DFI (direct fuel injection).

This ignition system is designed to be diagnosed with the Quicksilver DDT (digital diagnostic terminal). The DDT is normally found only in Mercury or Mariner dealerships, where the investment can be justified. The DDT displays sensor input values and actuator output values as the ECM (electronic control module) sees them.

The major components are the:

1. *Flywheel*—The outer diameter, lower edge of the flywheel (A, **Figure 64**) contains cast in encoding ribs for the crankshaft position sensor (B, **Figure 64**).

2. *Crankshaft position sensor*—The crankshaft position sensor (CPS) detects the presence of the encoding ribs on the flywheel and sends a signal to the electronic control module (ECM). This signal tells the ECM crankshaft position and engine rpm. The air gap between the flywheel encoding ribs and the CPS must be set to 0.030 in. (0.76 mm).

3. *Ignition coils*—There is one ignition coil (**Figure 65**) for each cylinder. The ignition coil transforms the relatively low voltage from the battery into voltage high enough (50,000 volts) to jump the spark plug gap and ignite the air/fuel mixture. The ignition coils positive (+) terminal has battery voltage present any time the ignition switch is on. The ECM opens the ignition coil negative (–) terminal to create spark.

4. *Spark plugs*—There is one spark plug for each cylinder. Use only the recommended spark

7

plugs or engine damage may result. The only recommended spark plug for the 200 DFI is the Champion RC10ECC.

5. *Stop circuit*—The stop circuit is connected to the ECM. Whenever the stop circuit is connected to ground the ECM shuts off the ignition coils. The stop circuit must have an open circuit (to ground) in order for the engine to run.

6. *ECM*—The ECM (electronic control module) is the heart of the electrical, ignition and fuel systems. The ECM (C, **Figure 64**) monitors input from all of the sensors. The ECM then calculates the correct spark timing, fuel injector timing and direct injector timing for each cylinder. The ECM contains a cold engine start, idle stabilizer, rpm limit, overheat protection, water in fuel, low oil level, no oil flow and sensor failure warning programs. The ECM receives power from a main power relay. The main power relay is activated by the ignition switch.

  a. *Cold start program*—The cold engine start program increases the fuel injector pulse width any time the engine is below operating temperature. The amount of fuel injector pulse width increase is proportional to engine temperature.

  b. *Idle stabilizer program*—The idle stabilizer program controls the idle speed by advancing or retarding spark advance to maintain 625-675 rpm anytime the TPS (throttle position sensor) indicates that the throttle control is in the idle position. Idle speed is not adjustable.

  c. *Rpm limit program*—The rpm limit program is activated anytime engine speed exceeds 5800 rpm. If engine speed exceeds 6050 rpm, the ECM shuts the engine systems off until engine speed drops below the preprogrammed speed limit, at which point engine operation returns to normal. The warning horn will sound continuously anytime the rpm limit program is activated.

  d. *Overheat warning program*—The overheat warning program retards ignition timing any time the ECT (engine coolant temperature sensor) indicates 221° Fahrenheit (105° Celsius). Timing is retarded until rpm is reduced (and limited) to approximately 3000 rpm. Timing advance will return to normal when the ECT indicates normal temperature. The overheat lamp will flash and the warning horn will sound continuously any time the overheat warning program is activated.

  e. *Water-in-fuel warning program*—The water-in-fuel warning program sounds the warning horn and illuminates the water in fuel warning light any time the water separating fuel filter accumulates enough water to short the sensor to ground. When the water sensor shorts to ground, the horn will beep 4 times (at 1 second intervals), then shut off for 2-minutes and then begin the warning cycle again. The warning light illuminates continuously until the ignition switch is turned off. This program does not affect ignition system operation.

  f. *Low-oil warning program*—The low oil warning program sounds the warning horn and illuminates the oil warning light any time the switch in the engine mounted oil tank closes. When the oil switch closes, the horn will beep 4 times (at 1 second intervals), then shut off for 2-minutes and then begin the warning cycle again. The warning light illuminates continuously until the ignition switch is turned off. This program does not affect ignition system operation.

  g. *No oil flow warning program*—The no oil flow warning program sounds the warning horn and illuminates the oil light and check engine light. Engine speed will be reduced and limited to 3000 rpm. The ignition switch must be turned off to reset the warning program. If the no oil flow warning program is activated, the motor should be stopped as soon as possible and the defect corrected. Operating the motor without oil flow will result in catastrophic engine failure.

h. *Sensor failure warning program*—The sensor warning program is designed to alert the boat operator to a sensor (such as TPS [throttle position sensor]), ignition coil or injector failure. This is very similar to the check engine light on a modern fuel injected car. If the ECM detects a failure in any of the sensor, ignition coil or injector circuits, the check engine lamp will illuminate. If one of the two TPS sensors has failed, the warning horn will also sound. If both TPS sensors fail, the engine will not run above idle speed. The ignition coils, injectors and the ECT (engine coolant temperature) sensor can be tested with an ohmmeter. All other sensors require the DDT to determine if they are functioning correctly.

NOTE
The MAP (manifold absolute pressure), IAT (intake air temperature) and knock sensor are installed and wired to the ECM, but are not used by 1997 model ECM internal programming.

7. *Warning panel*—A multifunction warning panel is recommended for this model. The warning panel has 4 lights that allow easy identification of low oil tank level, no oil flow, engine overheat, sensor malfunction, ignition coil or injector malfunction and water in fuel situations. See **Figure 66**.

The 200 hp DFI models use a shift interrupt circuit connected to the ECM. When shift load exceeds the spring force of the shift interrupt switch, the ECM black/red lead is shorted to ground. The ECM then reduces engine speed by shutting off fuel to 3 cylinders, reducing shift effort. As soon as the shift is completed, the shift interrupt switch opens and the ECM returns fuel delivery and engine speed to normal.

Component Removal/Installation

Flywheel removal and installation is covered at the beginning of the *Capacitor Discharge Module (CDM) Ignition* section.

Replacement of the ECT (engine coolant temperature) sensor, IAT (intake air temperature) sensor, MAP (manifold absolute pressure) sensor, TPS (throttle position sensor) and the ECM (electronic control module) are covered in Chapter Six under *DFI Air/Fuel Systems*.

Refer to Chapter Three for troubleshooting procedures and Chapter Fourteen for wiring diagrams.

Crankshaft Position Sensor Removal/Installation

1. Disconnect and ground the spark plug leads to the power head to prevent accidental starting.
2. Disconnect the negative battery cable.
3. Remove the flywheel cover.
4. Remove the 2 screws securing the crankshaft position sensor to the power head.

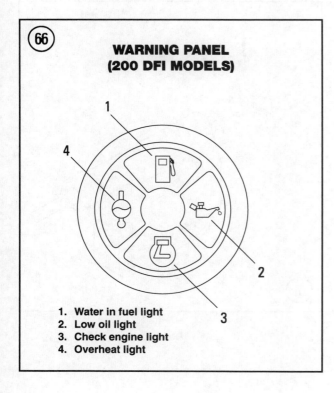

**WARNING PANEL
(200 DFI MODELS)**

1. Water in fuel light
2. Low oil light
3. Check engine light
4. Overheat light

5. Disconnect the sensor 3-wire connector from the engine wiring harness and remove the sensor from the power head.

6. If necessary, transfer the sensor bracket to the new sensor. Tighten the screw that holds the sensor to the bracket to specification (**Table 5**).

7. To install the sensor, begin by positioning the sensor on the power head mounting bosses and securing the sensor with 2 screws. Tighten the 2 screws hand tight at this time.

8. Reconnect the sensor connector to the engine wiring harness.

9. Adjust the sensor air gap as follows:
   a. Slightly rotate the flywheel to align an encoder rib with the crankshaft position sensor.
   b. Measure the gap between the flywheel encoder rib and the crankshaft position sensor with a feeler gauge. The gap should be 0.030 in. (0.76 mm). If the gap is not within specifications, loosen the 2 sensor mounting screws slightly and reset the gap to specifications.
   c. Tighten the screws to 100 in.-lb. (11.3 N·m) and recheck the sensor air gap.

10. Install the flywheel cover.

11. Reconnect the negative battery cable and the spark plug leads.

Coil Removal/Installation

Each coil's primary leads are connected through a 2 pin connector. A yellow/red lead carries battery voltage to each ignition coil positive terminal. A different color coded lead connects each coil's negative terminal to the ECM. The color coding of this lead determines the engine's firing order. Each coil connector must be connected to the correct ignition coil. Note the coil primary negative lead color code of all cylinders before disconnecting any leads.

The coils are held to the coil plate (**Figure 65**) in groups of three. Refer to the back of the manual for wiring diagrams and **Figure 65** for ignition coil removal/installation.

1. Disconnect the spark plug leads from all of the spark plugs.

2. Disconnect the 2-pin primary lead connector from each coil to be removed by pressing down on the wire lock (**Figure 67**), while pulling gently on the connector body.

3. Note the position of any harness clamps and/or ground straps. Remove the 4 screws securing each clamp that holds 3 coils to the coil plate. Remove the clamp(s) and coils from the coil plate.

4. To install the coils, begin by positioning the coils into the coil plate. Secure the coils with the clamp(s) and screws. Make sure that any electrical clamps and/or ground straps are reattached. Tighten the screws securely.

5. Reconnect all spark plug leads.

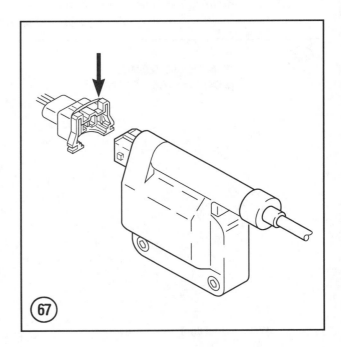

Table 1 BATTERY—STATE OF CHARGE PERCENTAGE

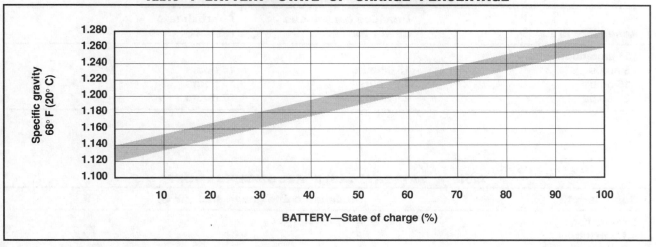

Table 2 BOAT WIRING HARNESS STANDARD COLOR CODES

	Color code
Main harness circuits	
Starter engagement	Yellow/red
Tachometer	Gray
Stop 1 (ignition side)	Black/yellow
Stop 2 (ground side)	Black
Choke or primer	Yellow/black
Overheat warning	Tan/blue
Switched B+	Purple
Protected B+	Red/purple
Temperature gauge	Tan
Fuel sender circuit	Pink
Grounds	Black
Trim/tilt circuits	
Trim motor up	Blue
Trim motor down	Green
Switching circuit up	Blue/white
Switching circuit down	Green/white
Switching circuit B+	Red/white
Trim trailer circuit	Purple/white
Trim sender circuit	Brown/white
Trim system grounds	Black
Ignition coil primary circuit	Green/(stripe)
Stator output (charging circuit)	Yellow

Table 3 BATTERY CAPACITY (HOURS)

Accessory draw	Provides continuous power for:	Approximate recharge time
80 amp-hour battery		
5 amps	13.5 hours	16 hours
15 amps	3.5 hours	13 hours
25 amps	1.8 hours	12 hours
	(continued)	

Table 3 BATTERY CAPACITY (HOURS) (continued)

Accessory draw	Provides continuous power for:	Approximate recharge time
105 amp-hour battery		
5 amps	15.8 hours	16 hours
15 amps	4.2 hours	13 hours
25 amps	2.4 hours	12 hours

Table 4 BATTERY CABLE RECOMMENDATIONS

Cable length	Minimum cable gauge size (AWG)
To 3-1/2 ft.	4
3-1/2 to 6 ft.	2
6 to 7-1/2 ft.	1
7-1/2 to 9-1/2 ft.	0
9-1/2 to 12 ft.	00
12-15 ft.	000
15-19 ft.	0000

Table 5 TORQUE SPECIFICATIONS

Fastener	in.-lbs.	ft.-lbs.	N•m
Alternator mounting hardware			
200 DFI			
M10 X 70	–	40	54.2
M8 X 35	–	16.5	22.3
M10 X 55	–	33	44.7
225-250 hp	–	40	54.2
CDM Module			
75-125 hp and 65-80 Jet	60	–	6.8
225-250 hp	80	–	9.0
Crankshaft position sensor			
Sensor to bracket	50	–	5.6
Bracket to power head	100	–	11.3
ECM (electronic control module)			
200 DFI	70	–	7.9
225-250 hp	80	–	9.0
Idle stabilizer module	30	–	3.4
Ignition coil			
75-200 hp, 275 hp and			
65-140 Jet (AD-CDI ignitions)			
Mounting	20	–	2.5
Terminal nuts	30	–	3.5
200 DFI	35	–	4.0
Spark plugs			
75-250 hp and 65-140 Jet	–	20	27.1
275 hp	–	17	23.0

(continued)

Table 5 TORQUE SPECIFICATIONS (continued)

Fastener	in.-lbs.	ft.-lbs.	N•m
Stator coil			
75-125 hp and 65-80 Jet	60	–	6.8
135-200 hp and 105-140 Jet	50	–	5.6
225-250 hp	105	–	11.9
275 hp	150	12.5	17.0
Starter motor			
Mounting			
75-125 hp and 65-80 Jet	168	14.5	19.0
135-200 hp and 105-140 Jet	210	17.5	23.7
200 DFI, 225-250 hp			
Bottom bolt	–	21	28.5
Top bolts	–	23	31.2
275 hp	150	12.5	16.9
Terminal nut			
75-275 hp and 65-140 Jet	60	–	6.8
Through-bolts			
75-275 hp and 65-140 Jet	70	–	7.9
Switch box			
Mounting screws			
75-125 hp and 65-80 Jet	40	–	4.5
135-200 hp and 105-140 Jet	50	–	5.6
Terminal nuts			
75-200 hp and 65-140 Jet	20	–	2.3
Throttle position sensor			
200 DFI			
Sensors to bracket	30	–	3.4
Bracket to manifold	45	–	5.1
225-250 hp	20	–	2.3
Voltage regulator (rectifier/regulator)			
75-125 hp and 65-80 Jet			
ADI-CD ignition	70	–	7.9
CDM ignition	60	–	6.8
135-200 hp and 105-140 Jet	80	–	9.0

Table 6 FLYWHEEL NUT OR BOLT TORQUE VALUES

Model	in.-lbs.	ft.-lbs.	N•m
75-200 hp and 65-140 Jet	–	120	163
200 DFI, 225 and 250 hp	–	125	169.5
275 hp	–	100	136

Table 7 STANDARD TORQUE VALUES (U.S. STANDARD FASTENERS)

Screw or nut size	in.-lbs.	ft.-lbs.	N•m
6-32	9	–	1.0
8-32	20	–	2.3
10-24	30	–	3.4
10-32	35	–	4.0
12-24	45	–	5.1

7

**Table 7 STANDARD TORQUE VALUES
(U.S. STANDARD FASTENERS) (continued)**

Screw or nut size	in.-lbs.	ft.-lbs.	N•m
1/4-20	70	6	7.9
1/4-28	84	7	9.5
5/16-18	160	13	18.1
5/16-24	168	14	19.0
3/8-16	270	23	30.5
3/8-24	300	25	33.9
7/16-14	–	36	48.8
7/16-20	–	40	54.2
1/2-13	–	50	67.8
1/2-20	–	60	81.3

Table 8 STANDARD TORQUE VALUES (METRIC FASTENERS)

Screw or nut size	in.-lbs.	ft.-lbs.	N•m
M5	36	–	4.1
M6	70	6	8.1
M8	156	13	17.6
M10	312	26	35.3
M12	–	35	47.5
M14	–	60	81.3

Table 9 IGNITION SYSTEM IDENTIFICATION

Model	System	Advance	Features
75-125 hp and 65-80 Jet (serial No. 0D283222-0G437999)			
75-90 hp	ADI-CD	Mechanical	
100-125 hp and 65-80 Jet	ADI-CD	Mechanical	Rpm limit module
75-125 hp and 65-80 Jet (serial No.0G438000-on)			
75-90 hp	CDM	Mechanical	
100-125 hp and 65-80 Jet	CDM	Mechanical	Rpm limit module
105 and 140 Jet	ADI-CD	Mechanical	Idle stabilizer, rpm limit modules
135-200 hp	ADI-CD	Mechanical	Idle stabilizer module
XR6 and Magnum III	ADI-CD	Mechanical	Idle stabilizer module
200 DFI	DI	Electronic	ECM (integrated fuel and ignition)
225 and 250 hp	CDM	Electronic	Ignition ECM
275 hp	ADI-CD	Mechanical	Rpm limit module

Table 10 CHARGING SYSTEM IDENTIFICATION

Model	Maximum output	Regulated amperage @ rpm
75-125 hp, 65 and 80 Jet with AD-CDI ignition (serial No. 0D283222-0G437999)		
16 amp black stator	18.0 @ 4000	yes
15 amp black stator	14.0 @ 4000	yes
75-125 hp, 65 and 80 Jet with CDM ignition (serial No. 438000-on)		
16 amp red stator	16.0 @ 2000	yes
135-200 hp and 105-140 Jet	38-42 @ 5000	yes
200 DFI	33-38 @ 2000	yes
225-250 hp	60 @ 2000	yes
275 hp	38-42 @ 5000	yes
Red stator upgraded models:		
75-125 hp and 65-80 Jet models		
9 amp electric start	9 amps at wide-open throttle	no
16 amp electric start	16 amps by 3000 rpm	yes

7

Chapter Eight

Power Head

This chapter provides power head removal/installation, disassembly/reassembly, and cleaning and inspection procedures for all models. The power head can be removed from the outboard motor without removing the entire outboard from the boat.

Since this chapter covers a large range of models, spanning several model years, the power heads from different model groups will differ in construction and require different service procedures. Whenever possible, engines with similar service procedures have been grouped together.

The components shown in the accompanying illustrations are generally from the most common models. While it is possible that the components shown in the illustrations may not be identical to those being serviced, the step-by-step procedures cover each model in this manual. Exploded illustrations, typical of each power

head model group are located in the appropriate *Disassembly* section and are helpful references for many service procedures.

This chapter is arranged in a normal disassembly/assembly sequence. When only a partial repair is required, follow the procedure(s) to the point where the faulty parts can be replaced, then jump ahead to reassemble the unit. Many procedures require the use of manufacturer recommended special tools, which can be purchased from a Mercury or Mariner outboard dealer.

Power head work stands and holding fixtures are available from specialty shops or marine and industrial product distributors such as Bob Kerr Marine Tool Company, P.O. Box 771135, Winter Garden, Florida 34777.

Make sure that the work bench, work station, engine stand or holding fixture is of sufficient capacity to support the size and weight of the power head. This is especially important when working on larger engines, such as V-6 models.

SERVICE CONSIDERATIONS

Performing internal service procedures on the power head requires considerable mechanical ability. Carefully consider your capabilities before attempting any operation involving major disassembly of the engine.

If, after studying the text and illustrations in this chapter, you decide not to attempt a major power head disassembly or repair, it may be financially beneficial to perform certain preliminary operations yourself. Consider separating the power head from the outboard motor and removing the fuel, ignition and electrical systems and all accessories yourself, taking only the basic power head to the dealership for the actual overhaul or major repair.

Since most marine dealers often have lengthy waiting lists for service (especially during the spring and summer), this practice can reduce the time your unit is in the shop. If you have done much of the preliminary work, your repairs can be scheduled and performed much quicker. Always discuss your options with the dealer before appearing at the dealership with a disassembled engine. Dealers will often want to install, adjust and test run the engine in order to be comfortable providing warranty coverage for the overhaul or repair.

No matter who is doing the work, repair will be quicker and easier if the motor is clean before starting any service procedure. There are many special cleaners (degreasers) available from any automotive supply store. Most of these cleaners are simply sprayed on, then rinsed off with a garden hose after the recommended time period. Always follow all instructions provided by the manufacturer. Cleaning solvent should not be applied to electrical and ignition components

and should never be sprayed into the induction system.

WARNING
Never use gasoline as a cleaning agent. Gasoline presents an extreme fire and explosion hazard. Work in a well-ventilated area when using cleaning solvent. Keep a large fire extinguisher rated for gasoline and oil fires nearby in case of an emergency.

Once you have decided to do the job yourself, thoroughly read this chapter until you understand what is involved in completing the repair satisfactorily. Make arrangements to buy or rent the necessary special tools and obtain a source for replacement parts *before* starting. It is frustrating and time-consuming to start a major repair and then be unable to finish because the necessary tools or parts are not available.

NOTE
A series of at least 5 photographs, taken from the front, rear, top and both sides of the power head (before removal) will be very helpful during reassembly and installation. The photographs are especially useful when trying to route electrical harnesses, fuel, primer and recirculation lines. They will also be helpful during the installation of accessories, control linkages and brackets.

Before beginning the job, review Chapter One and Chapter Two of this manual. You will do a better job with this information fresh in your mind.

Tables 1-6 list torque values, **Table 7** and **Table 8** list all power head service specifications. **Table 9** and **Table 10** list special tools. **Table 11** lists model number codes and **Table 12** provides starting serial numbers for the models covered in this manual. All Tables are located at the end of the chapter.

MERCURY/MARINER MODEL IDENTIFICATION

All 1994 through 1997 Mercury/Mariner outboard models use an individual, unique serial number for the primary means of identification. The serial number plate is located on the midsection (**Figure 1**) of the outboard motor and is usually attached to the swivel bracket or the stern bracket. Serial numbers are never duplicated. If the engine is still equipped with its original power head, the serial number is also stamped on a welch plug affixed to the power head (**Figure 2**, typical).

The serial number plate on late 1995 models and all 1996-1997 models contain a coded model number and model information. See **Figure 3**.

Model number codes are listed in **Table 11**. Shaft length relates to the transom height of the boat. A long shaft (20 in. [50.8 cm]) motor is designed to fit a transom that measures approximately 20 in. (50.8 cm). If no shaft length code is specified, the motor is a standard (15 in. [38.1 cm]) shaft model.

In the example shown in **Figure 3**, the model plate is for a 1997 model year, 40 hp manual start, long shaft, tiller handle outboard motor. The motor was built in the calendar year of 1996.

When ordering replacement parts (or ordering a parts catalog), it is imperative that you provide the serial number to the Mercury/Mariner dealer. On engines equipped with coded model numbers and model information, make sure all of this data is also provided to the dealer.

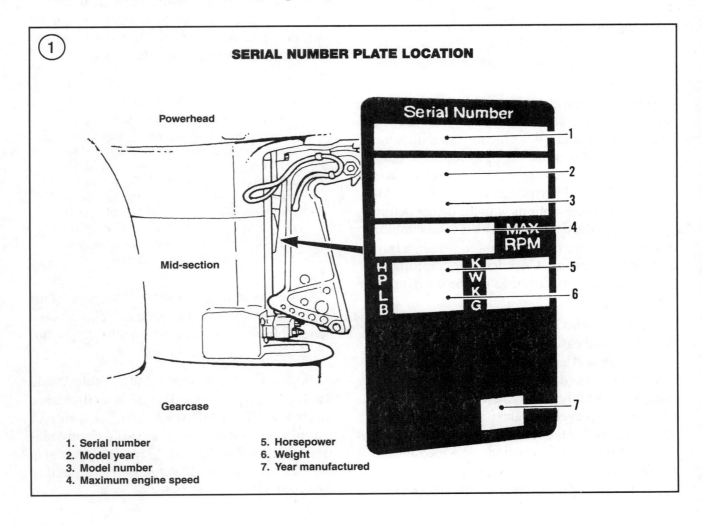

① SERIAL NUMBER PLATE LOCATION

1. Serial number
2. Model year
3. Model number
4. Maximum engine speed
5. Horsepower
6. Weight
7. Year manufactured

POWER HEAD BREAK-IN

Whenever a power head has been rebuilt or replaced, or if *any* new internal parts have been installed, it must be treated as a new engine. The engine must be run on the specified fuel/oil mixture and operated in accordance with the recommended break-in procedure as described in Chapter Four.

CAUTION
Failure to follow the recommended break-in procedure will result in prema-

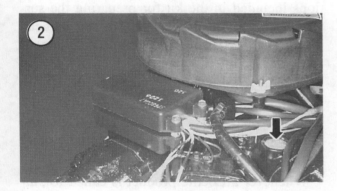

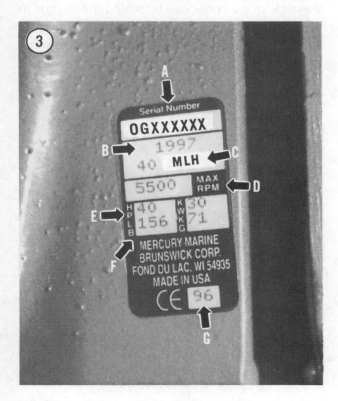

ture and often catastrophic engine failure.

SERVICE RECOMMENDATIONS

If the engine has experienced a catastrophic failure, every attempt must be made to determine the cause of the failure. Refer to the *Engine* section in Chapter Three for troubleshooting procedures.

Many failures are caused simply from using the incorrect (or stale) fuel and lubricating oil. Refer to Chapter Four for all fuel and oil recommendations.

When rebuilding or performing a major repair on the power head, consider performing the following steps to prevent the failure from reoccurring.

1. Service the water pump. Replace the impeller and all seals and gaskets. See Chapter Nine.

2. Replace the thermostat(s) and remove and inspect the poppet valve assembly (on models so equipped) as described in this chapter. Replace any suspect components.

3. Drain the fuel tank(s) and dispose of the old fuel in an approved manner.

4. Fill the fuel tank with fresh fuel and add the recommended oil to the fuel tank at the *break-in* ratio as described in Chapter Four.

5. Replace (or clean) all fuel filters. See Chapter Four.

6. Clean and adjust the carburetors on carbureted models or drain the vapor separator on EFI (electronic fuel injection) models. See Chapter Six.

7. On oil-injected models, drain and clean the oil reservoir(s). Dispose of the old oil in an approved manner. Then refill the oil system with the specified oil (Chapter Four) and bleed the oil system as described in Chapter Eleven.

8. Install new spark plugs. Use only the recommended spark plugs listed in Chapter Four. Make sure the spark plugs are correctly torqued as described in Chapter Four.

9. Perform *all* of the synchronization and linkage adjustments as described in Chapter Five before returning the motor to the operator.

LUBRICANTS, SEALANTS AND ADHESIVES

The part numbers for the lubricants, sealants and adhesives specified in this chapter are all listed in the Quick Reference Data at the front of this manual. Equivalent (after-market) products are acceptable for use, as long as they meet or exceed the original manufacturer's specifications.

During power head assembly, all internal engine components should be lubricated with Quicksilver 2-cycle (TCW-3) outboard motor oil. Do not assemble any components *dry*. Lubricate all seal lips and O-rings with Quicksilver 2-4-C Multi-Lube grease. Lubricate and hold all needle and roller bearings in place with Quicksilver Needle Bearing Assembly Grease.

To efficiently remove the carbon from the pistons and combustion chambers use Quicksilver Power Tune Engine Cleaner. Allow ample time for the cleaner to soak into and soften carbon deposits.

When no other sealant or adhesive is specified, coat all gaskets with Quicksilver Perfect Seal. Coat the threads of all external fasteners (when no other sealant or adhesive is specified) with Quicksilver Perfect Seal to help prevent corrosion and ease future removal.

When sealing the crankcase cover/cylinder block, both mating surfaces must be free of all sealant residue, dirt, oil or other contamination. Locquic Primer, lacquer thinner, acetone or similar solvents work well when used in conjunction with a plastic scraper. Solvents with an oil, wax or petroleum base should not be used.

> *CAUTION*
> *Clean all mating surfaces carefully to avoid nicks and gouges. A plastic scraper can be improvised from a com-*

*mon household electrical outlet cover or a piece of Lucite with one edge ground to a 45° angle. Extreme caution must be used if a metal scraper, such as a putty knife is used. Nicks and gouges will prevent the sealant from curing. The crankcase cover-to-cylinder block surface must **not** be lapped or machined.*

Loctite Master Gasket Sealant is the only recommend sealant used to seal the crankcase cover-to-cylinder block mating surfaces on models without a gasket. The sealant comes in a kit that includes a special primer. Follow the instructions included in the kit for preparing the surfaces and applying the sealant. The sealant bead must be applied to the inside (crankshaft side) of all crankcase cover screw holes.

Apply Loctite 271 threadlocking adhesive to the outer diameter of all seals before pressing the seals into place. Also apply this adhesive to the threads of all internal fasteners (where no other adhesive is called for).

Whenever a Loctite product is called for, always clean the surface to be sealed (or threads to be secured) with Locquic Primer. Locquic Primer cleans and primes the surface and ensures a quick secure bond by leaving a thin film of catalyst on the surface (or threads). The primer

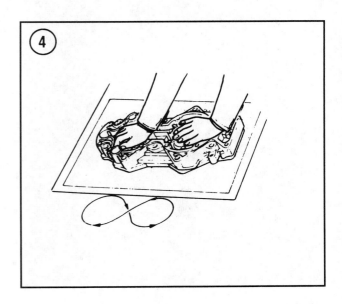

must be allowed to air dry, as blow drying will remove the catalyst.

SEALING SURFACES

Clean all sealing surfaces carefully to prevent nicks and gouges. Often a shop towel soaked in solvent can be used to rub gasket material and/or sealant from a mating surface. If scrapers must be used, try using a plastic scraper (such as a household electrical outlet cover) or a piece of Lucite with one edge ground to a 45° angle to prevent damage to the sealing surfaces. If a metal scraper or putty knife is being used, great skill and patience must be displayed to prevent destroying the component being cleaned.

NOTE
Plate glass (or a machinist's surface plate or straightedge) must be used for surface checking. Ordinary window glass does not have a uniform surface and will give false readings. Plate glass has a very uniform surface flatness.

Once the surfaces are clean, the component can be checked for warpage by placing the component onto a piece of plate glass or a machinist's surface plate. Apply uniform downward pressure and try to insert a selection of feeler gauges between the plate and the component. Specifications for maximum cylinder head warpage are listed in **Table 7** or **Table 8**. On other components, it is up to you to decide if the warpage is minor enough to be removed by lapping, or if the component must be replaced.

CAUTION
The cylinder block-to-crankcase cover must not be lapped (on all models). In addition, the cylinder heads on the 225-275 hp and 200 DFI models must not be lapped or resurfaced.

To remove minor warpage, minor nicks or scratches, or traces of sealant or gasket material, place a large sheet of 320-400 grit wet sandpaper onto the plate glass or surface plate. Apply light downward pressure and move the component in a figure-8 pattern as shown in **Figure 4**. Use a light oil (such as WD-40) to keep the sandpaper from loading up. Remove the component from the sandpaper and recheck the sealing surface. A machinist's straightedge may be used to check areas that cannot be accessed using the glass or surface plate. See **Figure 5**.

It may be necessary to repeat the lapping process several times to achieve the desired results. Never remove any more material than is absolutely necessary. Make sure the component is thoroughly washed to remove all grit before reassembly.

FASTENERS AND TORQUE

Always replace a worn or damaged fastener with one of equal size, type and torque requirement. Power head torque values are listed in **Tables 1-4**. If a specification is not provided for a given fastener, use the standard torque values listed in **Table 5** and **Table 6** according to fastener size.

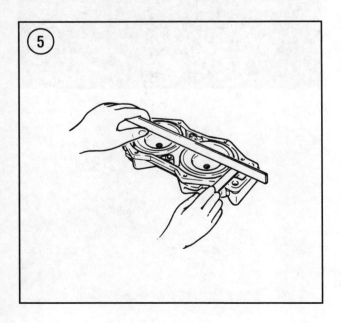

Determine the fastener size by measuring the shank of the screw (or bolt) as shown in **Figure 6**. Determine the thread pitch using the appropriate Metric or American thread pitch gauge as shown in **Figure 7**.

Damaged threads in components and castings may be repaired using a Heli-Coil (or equivalent) stainless steel threaded insert (**Figure 8**, typical). Heli-coil kits are available at automotive or marine and industrial supply stores. Never run a thread tap or thread chaser into a hole equipped with a Heli-coil. Damaged Heli-coils may be replaced (if damaged) by gripping the outermost coil with needlenose pliers and unthreading the coil from the hole. Do not pull the coil straight out or the threads in the hole will be damaged.

CAUTION
*Metric **and** American fasteners are used on these engines. Always match a replacement fastener to the original. Do not run a tap or thread chaser into a hole (or over a bolt) without first verifying the thread size and pitch. Newer model manufacturer's parts catalogs will list every standard fastener by diameter, length and pitch. Always have the engine model and serial numbers when ordering a parts catalog from a dealership.*

Unless otherwise specified, components secured by more than one fastener should be tightened in a *minimum* of 3 steps. Evenly tighten all fasteners hand-tight (snug) as a first step. Then evenly tighten all fasteners to 50% of the specified torque value as the second step. Finally, evenly tighten all fasteners to 100% of the specified torque value as the third step.

Be sure to follow torque patterns (sequences) as directed. If no pattern is specified, start at the center of the component and tighten in a circular pattern, working outward. All torque sequences are listed in the appropriate *Assembly* section of this chapter.

CAUTION
*Many models use a new torque process for the connecting rod bolts, cylinder head bolts and crankcase cover screws. This procedure is called **torque and turn**. Be sure to follow the new procedure as outlined in this chapter to prevent damaging components. Never retorque any fastener secured by the **torque and turn** method. Refer to **Tables 1-2** and **Table 4** to see which models use this process.*

On models *not* equipped with torque and turn fasteners, the cylinder head screws should be retorqued after the engine has reached operating temperature and allowed to cool. To retorque the cylinder head screws (and any other fasteners desired), loosen each fastener approximately one turn, then retighten to the specified torque value. Repeat the process until all of the fasteners are retorqued. Do not retorque any fastener tightened using the *torque and turn* process.

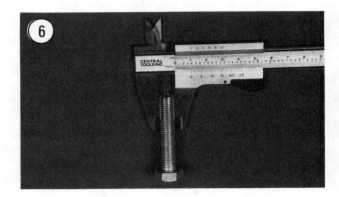

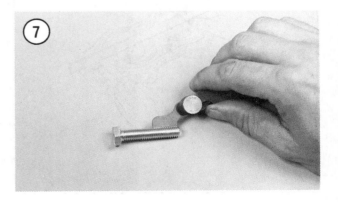

Retorque spark plugs to ensure proper heat transfer and to prevent preignition and detonation (Chapter Three). Retorque spark plugs after the engine has reached operating temperature and allowed to cool. Do not loosen the spark plug, simply retighten the plug to the specified torque value.

When no other sealant or adhesive is specified, coat the threads of all external fasteners with Quicksilver Perfect Seal to help prevent corrosion and ease future removal.

POWER HEAD REMOVAL/INSTALLATION

The removal and installation procedures in this chapter represent the most efficient sequence for removing the power head while preparing for complete disassembly. If complete disassembly is not necessary, stop disassembly at the appropriate point, then begin reassembly where disassembly stopped. Remove the power head as an assembly if major repair must be performed. Power head removal is not required for certain service procedures such as cylinder head removal, intake and exhaust cover removal (if so equipped), ignition component replacement, fuel system component replacement and reed block/intake manifold removal.

Removal/Installation (75-125 hp and 65-80 Jet)

Models with serial No. 0G437999 and below are equipped with the alternator-driven, capacitor discharge ignition (AD-CDI) in which most of the electrical and ignition system components are mounted behind an electrical/ignition component access cover.

Models with serial No. 0G438000-on are equipped with the CDM ignition system (capacitor discharge module) in which all of the electrical/ignition components are mounted openly on a metal plate that is grounded to the power head. There is no access cover.

Models prior to serial No. 0G360003 are equipped with trim/tilt solenoids and a 3-wire trim/tilt motor.

Models with serial No. 0G360003-on will be equipped with trim/tilt relays and a 2-wire trim/tilt motor.

The power head is best removed with most of the accessories and systems left installed. These items are removed after the power head is sepa-

8

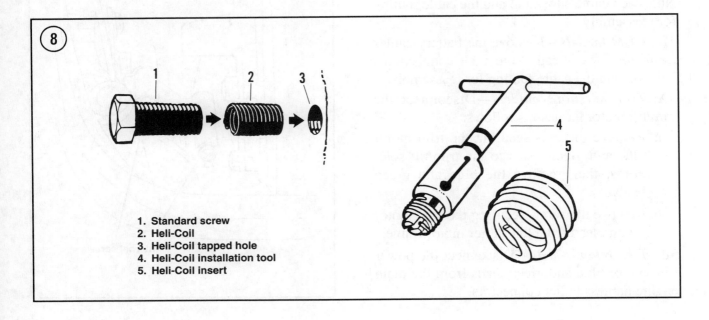

1. Standard screw
2. Heli-Coil
3. Heli-Coil tapped hole
4. Heli-Coil installation tool
5. Heli-Coil insert

rated from the drive shaft housing. Refer to the back of the manual for wiring diagrams. Make sure all cable clamps are reinstalled in their original positions and new tie-straps are installed to replace any that were removed.

1. Disconnect the spark plug leads and remove all spark plugs.

2. Disconnect both battery cables from the battery.

3. Remove the split lower cowls as follows:

   a. Remove the 2 aft internal screws (**Figure 9**) and the 1 front external screw (just above the steering arm). Then, loosen the port nut (**Figure 10**) securing the front latch plate to both lower cowls.

   b. Disconnect the lower cowl mounted trim switch leads at their bullet connectors and the water (tell-tale) discharge hose from the top of the exhaust cover.

   c. Remove the starboard and port lower cowls. Pull the fuel line connector and grommet free from the starboard cowl. Lift the electrical harnesses and control cables (and grommets) from each cowl as it is removed.

4A. *AD-CDI models*—Remove the electrical/ignition component access cover, then remove the battery cables from the power head. Note each cable's location and the cable routing for reassembly.

4B. *CDM models*—Remove the battery cables from the power head. Note each connection's location and the cable routing for reassembly.

5A. *Trim solenoid models*—Disconnect the trim/tilt motor harness as follows:

   a. Remove the nuts securing the trim motor blue and green leads to the trim/tilt solenoids, then remove the blue and green leads.

   b. Remove the screw securing the trim motor ground lead from the starter motor frame.

5B. *Trim relay models*—Disconnect the power trim motor blue and green leads from the main engine harness bullet connectors.

6. Disconnect the remote control harness from the engine harness at the main harness connector. Then disconnect the remote control harness blue/white and green/white power trim/tilt leads at their bullet connectors. If an engine temperature switch or trim indicator gauge are installed, disconnect the remote control harness tan and/or brown/white leads (respectively) at their bullet connectors.

> *NOTE*
> *The 65 and 80 Jet models do not require the shift cable or shift linkage to be disconnected to remove the power head.*

7. Disconnect and remove the remote control throttle and shift cables as described in Chapter Twelve.

8. Remove the locknut securing the shift link arm to the bottom of the shift slide (located on the shift rail). Disengage the link arm from the shift slide. Locate and secure the bushing. If any

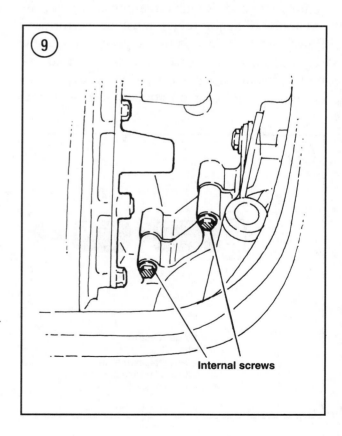

Internal screws

washers are present, note their positioning and secure them for reassembly.

9. Remove the flywheel cover and the plastic protective cap from the center of the flywheel. Install lifting eye (part No. 91-90455) or equivalent into the flywheel a minimum of 5 full turns.

10. Remove the 8 power head mounting nuts and washers. There are 3 nuts on each side (A, **Figure 11**) and 2 nuts across the rear (B, **Figure 11**) of the drive shaft housing.

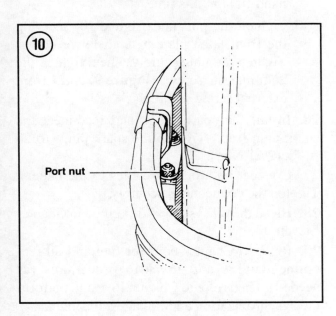

Port nut

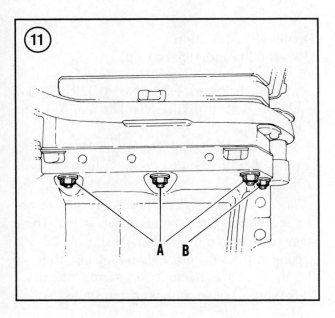

CAUTION
At this point, there should be no hoses, wires or linkage connecting the power head to the drive shaft housing. Make sure that nothing will interfere with power head removal before continuing.

11. Apply upward pressure with a suitable hoist while rocking the power head to break the gasket seal between the drive shaft housing and power head. Then, continue lifting the power head until the mounting studs are free of the drive shaft housing.

12. Place the power head on a clean workbench or onto a power head (crankshaft) stand (part No. 91-812549). The power head stand must be securely clamped in a vise.

13. Thoroughly clean all gasket material from the drive shaft housing and power head mating surfaces.

14. To install the power head, begin by lubricating the drive shaft splines with Quicksilver Special Lubricant 101 or 2-4-C Multi-Lube. Wipe any excess lubricant from the top of the drive shaft.

15. Place a new gasket onto the drive shaft housing.

16. Thread the lifting eye (part No. 91-90455) into the flywheel a minimum of 5 full turns. Support the power head with a suitable hoist.

17. Coat the threads of the 8 power head mounting studs with Loctite 271 threadlocking adhesive. Then, position the power head over the drive shaft housing and lower it into position. Rotate the crankshaft as necessary to align the drive shaft splines.

18. Install the 8 nuts and washers to the power head mounting studs. Evenly tighten the nuts in 3 progressive steps to 45 ft.-lb. (61.0 N·m).

19. Remove the lifting eye and reinstall the flywheel plastic plug and the flywheel cover.

20. Install the shift bushing over the stud on the bottom of the shift slide. Then, engage the shift link arm to the stud (and bushing). If any washers were present on removal, reinstall them as noted.

Secure the link arm with a locknut. Tighten the nut securely, then back it off 1/4 turn to allow free linkage movement.

21. Install and adjust the remote control throttle and shift cables as described in Chapter Twelve.

22. Connect the remote control harness to the engine harness at the main harness connector. Position the connector in its bracket or spring clamp. Then, connect the remote control harness blue/white and green/white power trim/tilt leads to the engine harness bullet connectors. If an engine temperature switch or trim indicator gauge is installed, reconnect the remote control harness tan and/or brown/white leads (respectively) to the appropriate engine harness bullet connectors.

23A. *Trim solenoid models*—Connect the trim/tilt motor harness as follows:

    a. Position the blue and green trim motor leads onto the appropriate trim/tilt solenoid terminal stud. Secure each lead with a nut. Tighten both nuts securely. Coat the terminal stud connections with Quicksilver Liquid Neoprene.

    b. Secure the trim motor black ground lead to the starter motor frame with a screw. Tighten the screw securely.

23B. *Trim relay models*—Connect the power trim motor blue and green leads to the main engine harness bullet connectors.

24A. *ADI-CD models*—Connect the battery cables to the power head (as noted on removal). Tighten the connections securely. Then, install the electrical/ignition component access cover. Tighten the cover screws securely.

24B. *CDM models*—Connect the battery cables to the power head (as noted on removal). Tighten the connection securely.

25. Install the split lower cowls as follows:

    a. Position the starboard and port lower cowls on the power head and drive shaft housing. Push the fuel line connector and grommet into the starboard cowl. Slide the electrical

harnesses and control cables (and grommets) into each cowl as it is installed.

    b. Connect the lower cowl mounted trim switch leads to the engine harness bullet connectors and the tell-tale water discharge hose to the exhaust cover. Secure the hose connection with a new tie-strap.

    c. Install the 2 aft internal screws (**Figure 9**) and the 1 front external screw (just above the steering arm). Tighten these screws hand-tight at this time.

    d. Tighten the port nut (**Figure 10**) securing the front latch plate to both lower cowls. Tighten the nut securely. Then, tighten the 2 aft internal screws (**Figure 9**) and 1 front external screw securely.

26. Install the spark plugs and reconnect the spark plug leads. Tighten the spark plugs to 20 ft.-lb. (27.1 N•m).

27. Connect both battery cables to the battery. Tighten the connections securely.

28. Bleed the oil system as described in Chapter Eleven.

29. Refer to Chapter Four for fuel and oil recommendations and break-in procedures (as needed). Then refer to Chapter Five and perform the synchronization and linkage adjustments.

Removal/Installation (135-200 hp and 105-140 Jet)

Models prior to serial No. 0G201875 are equipped with trim/tilt solenoids and a 3-wire trim/tilt motor.

Models with serial No. 0G201875-on are equipped with trim/tilt relays and a 2-wire trim/tilt motor.

The power head is best removed with most of the accessories and systems left installed. These items can be removed after the power head is separated from the drive shaft housing. Refer to the back of the manual for wiring diagrams. Make sure all cable clamps are reinstalled in their original positions and new tie-straps are installed to replace any that were removed.

Removal

1. Disconnect the spark plug leads and remove all spark plugs.

2. Disconnect both battery cables from the battery, then disconnect the battery cables from the power head. Note each cable's location and the routing for reassembly.

3. Remove the 2 screws securing the split harness clamp (that holds the remote control harness) to the port side (1994-1995 models) or starboard side (1996-1997 models) of the split lower cowl. Remove the upper and lower halves of the clamp from the lower cowl.

4. Disconnect the remote control harness from the engine harness at the main harness connector (located near the starter motor). Then disconnect the remote control harness blue/white and green/white power trim/tilt leads at their bullet connectors. If an engine temperature switch or trim indicator gauge is installed, disconnect the remote control harness tan and/or brown/white leads (respectively) at their bullet connectors.

5A. *Trim solenoid models*—Disconnect the trim/tilt motor harness as follows:

    a. Unclip the plastic cover from the trim up and trim down solenoids (located at the rear of the engine).

    b. Remove the nuts securing the trim motor blue and green leads to the trim/tilt solenoids, then remove the blue and green leads.

    c. Remove the nut securing the trim motor ground lead to the solenoid and ignition coil plate.

5B. *Trim relay models*—Disconnect the power trim motor blue and green leads from the main engine harness bullet connectors.

NOTE
The 105 and 140 Jet models do not require the shift cable or shift linkage to be disconnected in order to remove the power head.

6. Disconnect and remove the remote control throttle and shift cables as described in Chapter Twelve.

7A. *1994-1995 models*—Remove the screw securing the fuel line connector to the port lower cowl. Pull the fuel line connector free from its grommet.

7B. *Carbureted models (1996-1997)*—Disconnect the fuel supply hose from the fitting just before the fuel pump. Plug the line and cap the fitting to prevent contamination and leakage.

7C. *EFI models (1996-1997)*—Disconnect the fuel supply hose from the inline fuel fitting just inside the front of the lower cowl. Plug the line and cap the fitting to prevent contamination and leakage.

8A. *1994-1995 models*—Remove the split lower cowls as follows:

    a. Disconnect the cowl-mounted trim/tilt switch leads from the engine wiring harness bullet connectors.

    b. Disconnect the water (tell-tale) discharge hose from the fitting at the rear of the starboard lower cowl.

    c. Remove the 4 external screws securing the lower cowl halves to each other. The screws are accessed from the starboard side of the motor. There are 2 screws at the rear, 1 at the front and 1 just above the steering arm.

    d. Remove the starboard and port lower cowls.

8B. *1996-1997 models*—Remove the split lower cowls as follows:

    a. Disconnect the cowl-mounted trim/tilt switch leads from the engine wiring harness bullet connectors.

    b. Disconnect the water (tell-tale) discharge hose from the fitting at the rear of the starboard lower cowl.

    c. Remove the screws (3 internal and 1 external) securing the lower cowl halves to each other. The screws are accessed from the port side of the motor. There are 2 internal

8

screws at the rear and 1 internal screw at the front. The external screw is just above the steering arm.

    d. Remove the starboard and port lower cowls.

9. Disconnect the oil line (with blue stripe) from the fitting located just below the engine-mounted oil reservoir. Then, disconnect the vent line from the crankcase fitting on the starboard side, below the starter motor. Plug the lines and cap the fittings to prevent contamination and leakage.

10. Position the outboard shift linkage in the NEUTRAL position. This is the midpoint of the total shift linkage travel. Rotate the propeller when moving the shift linkage to prevent gearcase damage.

11. Remove the locknut holding the shift cable swivel latch assembly to the shift slide rail. Then, remove the washer, swivel latch and nylon wear plate from the control cable anchor bracket. See **Figure 12**.

12. Remove the 10 nuts and washers holding the power head to the adaptor plate and drive shaft housing. See **Figure 13**.

13. Remove the flywheel cover access plug and the plastic cap from the center of the flywheel. Thread the lifting eye (part No. 91-90455 or equivalent) into the flywheel a minimum of 5 full turns.

CAUTION
At this point, there should be no hoses, wires or linkage connecting the power head to the drive shaft housing. Make sure that nothing will interfere with power head removal before continuing.

14. Apply upward pressure with a suitable hoist while rocking the power head to break the gasket seal between the power head and the drive shaft housing. Continue lifting the power head until the studs are free from the drive shaft housing.

CAUTION
*If a power head (crankshaft) stand (part No. 91-30591A-1) is to be used, it must be **securely** clamped in a vise large enough to support the weight of the*

power head. The vise must be fastened to a workbench or support stand that can support the weight of the power head and the stresses of disassembly and reassembly.

15. Place the power head on a clean workbench or onto a power head (crankshaft) stand (part No. 91-30591A-1). The power head stand must be securely clamped in a vise.

16. Thoroughly clean all gasket material from the drive shaft housing and power head mating surfaces. Remove the guide block and spring from the shift linkage arm on the drive shaft housing.

Installation

1. To install the power head, begin by lubricating the drive shaft splines with Quicksilver Special Lubricant 101 or 2-4-C Multi-Lube. Wipe

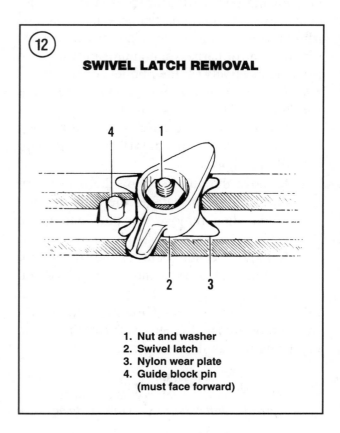

12

SWIVEL LATCH REMOVAL

1. **Nut and washer**
2. **Swivel latch**
3. **Nylon wear plate**
4. **Guide block pin (must face forward)**

any excess lubricant from the top of the drive shaft.

2. Place a new gasket over the power head studs and against the power head mating surface. A *small* amount of contact adhesive may be used to hold the gasket in place.

3. Lubricate the spring and guide block with Quicksilver 2-4-C Multi-Lube. Install the spring and guide block onto the shift linkage arm on the drive shaft housing. Position the guide block with the anchor pin facing forward (**Figure 12**).

4. Thread the lifting eye (part No. 91-90455) into the flywheel a minimum of 5 full turns. Support the power head with a suitable hoist.

5. Coat the shanks and threads of the power head mounting studs with Quicksilver Perfect Seal.

6. Position the power head over the drive shaft housing and carefully lower the power head onto the drive shaft housing. Make sure the shift linkage guide block is piloted in the shift slide rail with the guide block anchor pin facing forward.

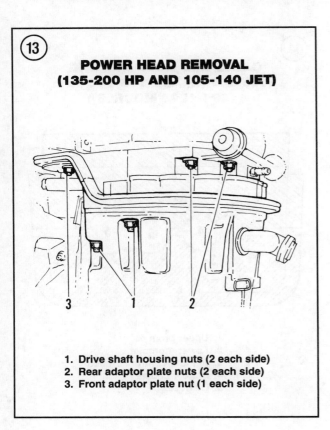

⑬

POWER HEAD REMOVAL (135-200 HP AND 105-140 JET)

1. **Drive shaft housing nuts (2 each side)**
2. **Rear adaptor plate nuts (2 each side)**
3. **Front adaptor plate nut (1 each side)**

Then, rotate the flywheel to align the crankshaft and drive shaft splines and seat the power head to the drive shaft housing.

7. Install the power head mounting nuts and flat washers (**Figure 13**). Evenly tighten the nuts in 3 progressive steps. Tighten the drive shaft housing nuts to 240 in.-lb. (27.1 N•m) and the adaptor plate nuts to 276 in.-lb. (31.2 N•m).

8. Remove the hoist and lifting eye, then reinstall the plastic cap in the center of the flywheel and the access plug in the flywheel cover.

9. Install the nylon wear plate, swivel latch, flat washer and locknut onto the shift linkage arm. Tighten the locknut until 2 or 3 threads are exposed beyond the top of the nut. See **Figure 12**.

10. Connect the oil line (with blue stripe) to the T-fitting located just below the engine-mounted oil reservoir. Then, connect the vent line to the crankcase fitting on the starboard side of the power head, below the starter motor. Secure both connections with new tie-straps.

11. Install the split lower cowls as follows:
   a. Position the starboard and port lower cowls to the power head and the drive shaft housing.
   b. Secure the cowls to each other with 4 external screws (1994-1995 models) or 3 internal screws and 1 external screw (1996-1997 models). Tighten the 4 screws securely.
   c. Connect the cowl-mounted trim/tilt switch leads to the engine wiring harness bullet connectors.
   d. Connect the water (tell-tale) discharge hose to the fitting at the rear of the starboard lower cowl. Secure the connection with a new tie-strap.

12A. *1994-1995 models*—Position the fuel line connector in the port lower cowl and secure it in place with one screw. Tighten the screw securely.

12B. *Carbureted models (1996-1997)*—Connect the fuel supply hose to the fitting just before the fuel pump. Secure the connection with the hose (worm) clamp.

8

12C. *EFI models (1996-1997)*—Connect the fuel supply hose to the inline fuel fitting just inside the front of the lower cowl. Secure the connection with the hose (worm) clamp.

13. Install the remote control throttle and shift cables as described in Chapter Twelve.

14A. *Trim solenoid models*—Connect the trim/tilt motor harness as follows:

 a. Position the green and blue trim motor leads on the appropriate trim solenoid terminal studs. Install a nut on each terminal stud. Tighten both nuts securely.

 b. Install the plastic cover over the trim up and trim down solenoid's terminal studs.

 c. Position the trim motor black ground lead on the solenoid and ignition coil plate mounting stud. Secure the ground lead with a nut. Tighten the nut securely.

14B. *Trim relay models*—Connect the power trim motor blue and green leads to the main engine harness bullet connectors.

15. Connect the remote control harness to the engine harness at the main harness connector. Then, connect the remote control harness blue/white and green/white power trim/tilt leads to the engine harness bullet connectors. If an engine temperature switch or trim indicator gauge is installed, connect the remote control harness tan and/or brown/white leads (respectively) to their bullet connectors.

16. Connect the battery cables to the engine (as noted on removal). Tighten the connections securely.

17A. *1994-1995 models*—Secure all cables, harnesses and hoses to the lower split cowls as follows:

 a. Position the lower halve of the split clamp grommet in the starboard lower cowl. Position the remote control harness, battery cables and oil lines as shown in **Figure 14**.

 b. Install the top half of the split clamp grommet and secure it in place with 2 screws. Make sure that nothing is pinched, then tighten the 2 screws securely.

c. Install the rubber grommet in the port lower cowl. Make sure the grommet is positioned around the fuel line connector, both control cables and is seated into the lower cowl groove. If necessary, remove the fuel line connector screw temporarily to allow easier positioning of the grommet.

17B. *1996-1997 models*—Position the lower half of the split clamp grommet in the port lower cowl. Position the electrical harnesses, oil and fuel lines, battery cables and control cables as shown in **Figure 15**. Install the top half of the split clamp grommet and secure it in place with 2 screws. Make sure that nothing is pinched, then tighten the 2 screws securely.

18. Install the spark plugs and reconnect the spark plug leads. Tighten the spark plugs to 20 ft.-lb. (27.1 N•m).

19. Connect the battery cables to the battery. Tighten the connections securely.

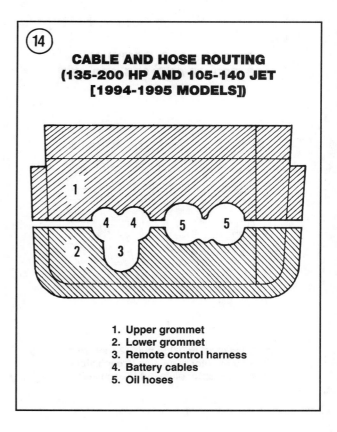

(14)

CABLE AND HOSE ROUTING (135-200 HP AND 105-140 JET [1994-1995 MODELS])

1. Upper grommet
2. Lower grommet
3. Remote control harness
4. Battery cables
5. Oil hoses

20. Bleed the oil injection system as described in Chapter Eleven.

21. Refer to Chapter Four for fuel and oil recommendations and break-in procedures (as needed). Then, refer to Chapter Five and perform synchronization and linkage adjustments.

Removal/Installation (225-250 hp and 200 DFI)

Carbureted 225 hp engines prior to serial No. 0G129222 are equipped with trim/tilt solenoids and a 3-wire trim/tilt motor.

Carbureted 225 hp engines serial No. 0G129222-0G303045 may be equipped with *either* trim/tilt solenoids and a 3-wire motor or trim/tilt relays and a 2-wire motor.

Carbureted 225 hp engines with serial No. 0G303046-on are equipped with trim/tilt relays and a 2-wire trim/tilt motor.

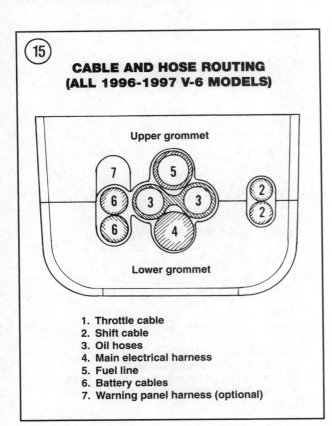

(15)

CABLE AND HOSE ROUTING (ALL 1996-1997 V-6 MODELS)

Upper grommet

Lower grommet

1. Throttle cable
2. Shift cable
3. Oil hoses
4. Main electrical harness
5. Fuel line
6. Battery cables
7. Warning panel harness (optional)

All 200 DFI (direct fuel injection) and 225-250 hp EFI (electronic fuel injection) models are equipped with trim/tilt relays and a 2-wire trim/tilt motor.

The power head is best removed with most of the accessories and systems left installed. These items can be removed after the power head is separated from the drive shaft housing. Refer to the back of the manual for wiring diagrams. Make sure all cable clamps are reinstalled in their original positions and new tie-straps are installed to replace any that were removed.

Removal

1. Disconnect the spark plug leads and remove all spark plugs.
2. Disconnect both battery cables at the battery, then remove the electrical/ignition component access cover (located on the starboard side of the power head). Disconnect the battery cables from the power head after noting each cable's location and the routing for reassembly.
3. Remove the 2 screws securing the split harness clamp (that holds the harnesses, hoses and cables) to the starboard side of the split lower cowl. Remove the upper and lower halves of the clamp from the lower cowl.
4. Disconnect the remote control harness from the engine harness at the main harness connector (located to the rear of the starter motor). Then, disconnect the remote control harness blue/white and green/white power trim/tilt leads at their bullet connectors. If an engine temperature switch or trim indicator gauge are installed, disconnect the remote control harness tan and/or brown/white leads (respectively) at their bullet connectors.
5. If the engine is equipped with the factory warning panel (gauge), disconnect the warning panel harness leads from the appropriate engine wiring harness bullet connectors. Refer to the back of the manual for specific wiring diagrams. The color codes are normally:

8

a. *Carbureted models*—Tan/black and tan/white.

b. *EFI models*—Tan/black, tan/white and pink/light blue.

c. *DFI models*—Tan/black, tan/white, pink/light blue and orange.

6A. *Trim solenoid models*—Disconnect the trim/tilt motor harness as follows:

a. Remove the nuts securing the trim motor blue and green leads to the trim/tilt solenoids, then remove the blue and green leads.

b. Remove the screw securing the trim motor ground lead to the electrical component plate or a solenoid mounting base.

c. Remove any clamps or tie-straps securing the trim motor harness to the power head.

6B. *Trim relay models*—Disconnect the power trim motor blue and green leads from the main engine harness bullet connectors (located on or near the electrical component plate). Remove any clamps or tie-straps securing the trim motor harness to the power head.

7. Disconnect and remove the remote control throttle and shift cables as described in Chapter Twelve.

8. Disconnect the fuel supply hose from the inline fuel fitting just inside the front of the lower cowl. Plug the line and cap the fitting to prevent contamination and leakage.

9. Remove the split lower cowls as follows:

a. Disconnect the cowl-mounted trim/tilt switch leads from the engine wiring harness bullet connectors.

b. Remove the screws (3 internal and 1 external) securing the lower cowl halves to each other. The screws are accessed from the port side of the motor. There are 2 internal screws at the rear and 1 internal screw at the front. The external screw is just above the steering arm.

c. Remove the starboard and port lower cowls.

10. Disconnect the water discharge (tell-tale) and water flushing hoses from the fittings at the rear of the power head. See **Figure 16**.

11. Locate the water bypass hoses that connect each cylinder head's thermostat housing to an adaptor plate fitting. Disconnect the hoses (3 and 4, **Figure 16**) from the adaptor plate fittings.

12. *200 DFI models*—Disconnect the fuel cooler water hose from the fitting on the starboard rear corner of the adapter plate.

13. *200 DFI models*—Locate the air discharge hose that connects the bottom of the port air/fuel rail to the adaptor plate. Disconnect the air discharge hose from the adaptor plate.

14. Disconnect the oil line (with blue stripe) from the T-fitting located just below the engine-mounted oil reservoir. Then, disconnect the vent line from the crankcase fitting on the starboard side, far below the starter motor. Plug the lines and cap the fittings to prevent contamination and leakage.

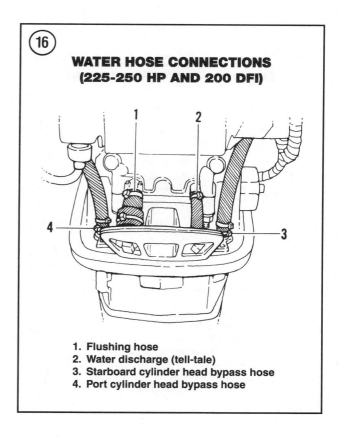

(16)

WATER HOSE CONNECTIONS (225-250 HP AND 200 DFI)

1. Flushing hose
2. Water discharge (tell-tale)
3. Starboard cylinder head bypass hose
4. Port cylinder head bypass hose

15. Remove the 10 nuts and washers holding the power head to the adaptor plate and drive shaft housing. See **Figure 17**.

NOTE
When removing the flywheel cover on 200 DFI models, be careful to disengage the air compressor fitting at the rear and the vent line at the front of the cover.

16. Remove the flywheel cover and the plastic cap from the center of the flywheel. Thread the lifting eye (part No. 91-90455 or equivalent) into the flywheel a minimum of 5 full turns.

CAUTION
At this point, there should be no hoses, wires or linkage connecting the power head to the drive shaft housing. Make sure that nothing will interfere with power head removal before continuing.

17. Apply upward pressure with a suitable hoist while rocking the power head to break the gasket

POWER HEAD MOUNTING (225-250 HP AND 200 DFI)

1. Front adaptor plate nut and washer (1 each side)
2. Rear adaptor plate nut and washer (1 each side)
3. Drive shaft housing nuts and washers (3 each side)

seal between the power head and the drive shaft housing. Rotate the shift linkage slide as necessary to disengage the shift link arm and roller from the slide and anchor bracket. Then, continue lifting the power head until the studs are free from the drive shaft housing.

CAUTION
*If the power head (crankshaft) stand (part No. 91-30591A-1 [8-spline] or part No. 91-812549 [13-spline]) is to be used, it must be **securely** clamped in a vise large enough to support the power head's weight. The vise must be fastened to a workbench or support stand that can support the weight of the power head **and** the stresses of disassembly and reassembly.*

18. Place the power head on a clean workbench or onto the appropriate power head (crankshaft) stand. The power head stand must be securely clamped in a vise.

19. Thoroughly clean all gasket material from the drive shaft housing and power head mating surfaces.

Installation

1. To install the power head, begin by lubricating the drive shaft splines with Quicksilver Special Lubricant 101 or 2-4-C Multi-Lube. Wipe any excess lubricant from the top of the drive shaft.

2. Place a new gasket over the power head studs and against the power head mating surface. A *small* amount of contact adhesive may be used to hold the gasket in place.

3. Thread the lifting eye (part No. 91-90455) into the flywheel a minimum of 5 full turns. Support the power head with a suitable hoist.

4. Coat the shanks and threads of the power head mounting studs with Quicksilver Perfect Seal.

5. Position the power head over the drive shaft housing and carefully lower the power head onto the drive shaft housing. Rotate the shift slide as

8

necessary to allow the shift link arm roller to pilot into the shift slide. Then, rotate the flywheel to align the crankshaft and drive shaft splines and seat the power head to the drive shaft housing.

6. Install the power head mounting nuts and flat washers (**Figure 17**). Evenly tighten the nuts in 3 progressive steps to 50 ft.-lb. (67.8 N•m).

7. Remove the hoist and lifting eye, then reinstall the plastic cap in the center of the flywheel.

8. Connect the oil line (with blue stripe) to the T-fitting located just below the engine-mounted oil reservoir. Then, connect the vent line to the crankcase fitting on the starboard side of the power head, below the starter motor. Secure both connections with new tie-straps.

9. Connect the water (tell-tale) discharge and water flushing hoses to appropriate fittings at the rear of the power head. See **Figure 16**.

10. Connect the water bypass hoses (from each cylinder head's thermostat housing) to the appropriate adaptor plate fittings. See **Figure 16**. Secure each connection with a new tie-strap.

11. *200 DFI models*—Connect the fuel cooler water hose to the fitting on the starboard rear corner of the adapter plate. This fitting has an internal strainer screen that should be cleaned periodically (Chapter Four). Secure the connection with a new tie-strap.

12. *200 DFI models*—Connect the air discharge hose (from the port air/fuel rail) to the adaptor plate fitting. Secure the connection with a new tie-strap.

13. Install the split lower cowls as follows:
   a. Position the starboard and port lower cowls to the power head and the drive shaft housing.
   b. Secure the cowls to each other with 3 internal screws and 1 external screw. Tighten the 4 screws to 65 in.-lb. (7.3 N•m).
   c. Connect the cowl-mounted trim/tilt switch leads to the engine wiring harness bullet connectors.

14. Connect the fuel supply hose to the inline fuel fitting just inside the front of the lower cowl.

Secure the connection with the hose (worm) clamp.

15. Install the remote control throttle and shift cables as described in Chapter Twelve.

16A. *Trim solenoid models*—Connect the trim/tilt motor harness as follows:
   a. Position the green and blue trim motor leads on the appropriate trim solenoid terminal studs. Install a nut on each terminal stud. Tighten both nuts securely.
   b. Connect the trim motor black ground lead to the electrical component plate or a solenoid mounting base. Secure the ground lead with a screw. Tighten the screw securely.

16B. *Trim relay models*—Connect the power trim motor blue and green leads to the main engine harness bullet connectors.

17. If the engine is equipped with the factory recommended warning panel (gauge), connect the warning panel harness leads to the appropriate engine wiring harness bullet connectors. Refer to the back of the manual for specific wiring diagrams. The color codes are normally:
   a. *Carbureted models*—Tan/black and tan/white.
   b. *EFI models*—Tan/black, tan/white and pink/light blue.
   c. *DFI models*—Tan/black, tan/white, pink/light blue and orange.

18. Connect the remote control harness to the engine harness at the main harness connector (located to the rear of the starter motor). Then, connect the remote control harness blue/white and green/white power trim/tilt leads to the engine harness bullet connectors. If an engine temperature switch or trim indicator gauge is installed, connect the remote control harness tan and/or brown/white leads (respectively) to the engine harness bullet connectors.

19. Connect the battery cables to the engine (as noted on removal). Tighten the connections securely. Then install the electrical/ignition component access cover. Tighten the cover screws securely.

20. Position the lower half of the split clamp grommet in the port lower cowl. Position the electrical harnesses, oil and fuel lines, battery cables and control cables as shown in **Figure 15**. Install the top half of the split clamp grommet and secure it in place with 2 screws. Make sure that nothing is pinched, then tighten the 2 screws securely.

21. Install the spark plugs and reconnect the spark plug leads. Tighten the spark plugs to 20 ft.-lb. (27.1 N•m).

22. Connect the battery cables to the battery. Tighten the connections securely.

23. Bleed the oil injection system as described in Chapter Eleven.

24. Refer to Chapter Four for fuel and oil recommendations and break-in procedures (as needed). Then, refer to Chapter Five and perform all synchronization and linkage adjustments.

Removal/Installation (275 hp)

The power head is best removed with most of the accessories and systems left installed. These items can be removed after the power head is

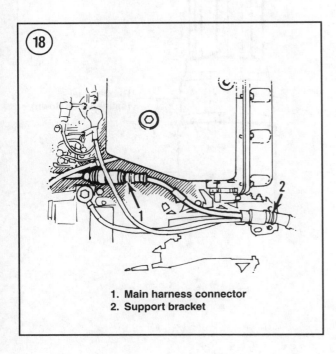

1. Main harness connector
2. Support bracket

separated from the drive shaft housing. Refer to the end of the manual for wiring diagrams. Make sure all cable clamps are reinstalled in their original positions and new tie-straps are installed to replace any that were removed.

The exhaust adaptor plate is removed with the power head and is separated from the power head later. The water pressure relief (poppet) valve is located in the exhaust adapter.

The trim and tilt system on this engine is mounted remotely in the boat. There are no trim or tilt components to deal with during power head removal and installation.

Removal

1. Disconnect the spark plug leads and remove all spark plugs.

2. Disconnect both battery cables from the battery, then disconnect the battery cables from the power head. Note each cable's location and the routing for reassembly.

3. Disconnect and remove the shift and throttle cables as described in Chapter Twelve.

4. Disconnect the oil line (with blue stripe) from the T-fitting located just below the engine-mounted oil reservoir. Then, disconnect the vent line from the crankcase fitting near the base of the power head, behind the throttle cable mounting brackets. Plug the lines and cap the fittings to prevent contamination and leakage.

5. Disconnect the remote control harness from the engine harness at the main harness connector (1, **Figure 18**). Remove the 2 screws, clamp and plate securing the remote control harness and battery cables to the front lower cowl support bracket (2, **Figure 18**), then slide the oil line retainer and oil lines from the support bracket.

6. Remove the oil lines, battery cables and remote control harness from the engine.

7. Disconnect the water discharge (tell-tale) hose from the aft cowl support bracket fitting. Then, remove the 4 nuts and washers securing

the aft cowl support bracket to the power head. Remove the bracket from the power head.

8. Using an appropriate size punch and hammer, drive out the roll pin (**Figure 19**) securing the shift arm to the vertical shift shaft. Then, remove the shift arm from the vertical shaft.

9. Remove 6 nuts, lockwashers and flat washers (3 each side) securing the power head and exhaust adaptor plate to the drive shaft housing. Then, remove the 1 bolt securing the exhaust adaptor plate to the drive shaft housing. This bolt is located at the rear of the adaptor plate.

10. Remove the 4 wing nuts securing the flywheel cover. Then, remove the large washer and small washer from each stud. Remove the flywheel cover. Finally, locate and secure the small and large washer from each stud. The correct stack up on each stud is: large washer, small washer, flywheel cover, small washer, large washer and wing nut.

11. Remove the plastic cap from the center of the flywheel. Thread a lifting eye (part No. 91-90455 or equivalent) into the flywheel a minimum of 5 full turns.

> *CAUTION*
> *At this point, there should be no hoses, wires or linkage connecting the power head to the drive shaft housing. Make sure that nothing will interfere with power head removal before continuing.*

12. Apply upward pressure with a suitable hoist while rocking the power head to break the gasket seal between the power head and the drive shaft housing. Then, continue lifting the power head until the studs are free from the drive shaft housing.

> *WARNING*
> *Due to the weight of this power head, the power head (crankshaft) stand (part No. 91-30591A-1) should not be used to support the entire weight of a fully-assembled power head. A suitable heavy-duty power head fixture, available from a ma-*

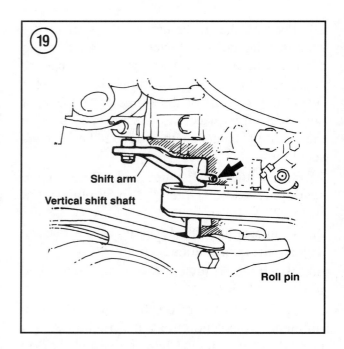

Shift arm

Vertical shift shaft

Roll pin

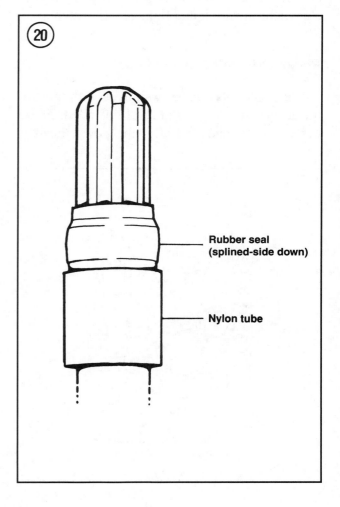

Rubber seal
(splined-side down)

Nylon tube

rine tool manufacturer (such as Bob Kerr Marine Tools) must be used.

13. Place the power head on a clean workbench or mount it in a suitable holding fixture.

14. Thoroughly clean all gasket material from the drive shaft housing and power head mating surfaces. Locate and secure the splined nylon tube and rubber seal from the drive shaft (**Figure 20**).

Installation

1. To install the power head, begin by lubricating the drive shaft splines with Quicksilver Special Lubricant 101 or 2-4-C Multi-Lube. Wipe any excess lubricant from the top of the drive shaft. Install the nylon tube and rubber seal onto the drive shaft. The splined end of the rubber seal must face the nylon tube. See **Figure 20**.

2. Place a new gasket over the power head studs and against the exhaust adaptor mating surface. A *small* amount of contact adhesive may be used to hold the gasket in place.

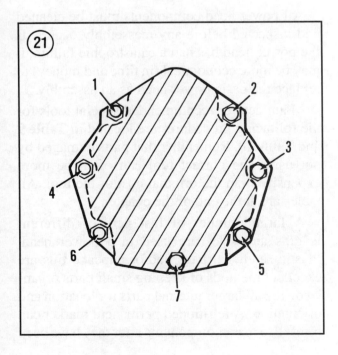

3. Thread the lifting eye (part No. 91-90455) into the flywheel a minimum of 5 full turns. Support the power head with a suitable hoist.

4. Coat the shanks and threads of the power head mounting studs with Quicksilver Perfect Seal.

5. Position the power head over the drive shaft housing and carefully lower the power head onto the drive shaft housing. Make sure the shift shaft pilots into its support bracket at the front of exhaust adaptor. Then, rotate the flywheel to align the crankshaft and drive shaft splines and seat the power head to the drive shaft housing.

> *CAUTION*
> *Water leakage between the power head and drive shaft housing may occur if the power head mounting fasteners are not tightened in the correct sequence as shown in **Figure 21**.*

6. Install the 6 power head mounting nuts, lockwashers and flat washers onto the power head studs, then install the single bolt into the rear of the exhaust adaptor plate. Evenly tighten the nuts and bolt in 3 progressive steps to 30 ft.-lb. (40.7 N•m), following the torque sequence shown in **Figure 21**.

7. Remove the hoist and lifting eye, then reinstall the plastic cap in the center of the flywheel. Install the flywheel cover, making sure that the stack up on each stud is a large washer, small washer, flywheel cover, small washer and large washer. Secure the flywheel cover and washers in place with 4 wing nuts. Tighten the wing nuts securely.

8. Install the shift arm (**Figure 19**) onto the vertical shift shaft so the roll pin hole is pointing straight port and starboard. Align the roll pin holes and secure the shift arm to the shift shaft with a new roll pin. Drive the roll pin in until it is flush with the shift arm.

9. Connect the oil line (with blue stripe) to the T-fitting located just below the engine mounted oil reservoir. Then, connect the vent line to the crankcase fitting near the base of the power head, behind the throttle cable mounting brackets. Se-

8

cure both connections with new tie-straps. Position the oil line retainer (and oil lines) into the notch in the cowl lower support bracket.

10. Route the battery cables to the power head and connect both cables to the power head as noted on disassembly.

11. Connect the remote control harness to the engine harness at the main harness connector (1, **Figure 18**). Verify that the oil lines are correctly installed in the support bracket, then position the battery cables and remote control harness against the support bracket (2, **Figure 18**) and secure them in place with the clamp over the cables and the plate behind them. Secure the clamp and plate with 2 screws. Tighten the screws securely.

12. Connect the water discharge (tell-tale) hose to the aft cowl support bracket fitting. Secure the connection with a new tie-strap. Then position the support bracket onto the 4 cushioned mounts. Secure the bracket with 4 nuts and washers. Tighten the nuts securely.

13. Install the throttle and shift cables as described in Chapter Twelve.

14. Install the spark plugs and reconnect the spark plug leads. Tighten the spark plugs to 20 ft.-lb. (27.1 N•m).

15. Connect the battery cables to the battery. Tighten the connections securely.

16. Bleed the oil injection system as described in Chapter Eleven.

17. Refer to Chapter Four for fuel and oil recommendations and break-in procedures (as needed). Then, refer to Chapter Five and perform synchronization and linkage adjustments.

POWER HEAD DISASSEMBLY

Power head overhaul gasket sets are available for all models. It is often more economical and always simpler to order the gasket set instead of each component individually. It is good mechanical practice to replace *every* gasket, seal and O-ring during a power head reassembly. The piston rings must be replaced if the piston(s) have been taken out of the cylinder bore.

Dowel pins are used to locate the crankcase halves to each other and to locate some crankshaft bearings. The dowel pins do not have to be removed if they are securely seated in a bore on either side of the crankcase halves or in the bearing. However, they must be accounted for during disassembly and reassembly. If a dowel pin can be readily removed from its bore, it should be removed and secured (stored with the other internal components) until reassembly begins.

The connecting rods on all models are of the fractured cap design. This means that the cap is broken from the rod during the manufacturing process, leaving a jagged (fractured) mating surface that will mate perfectly if installed in its original orientation. If the cap is installed reversed and the rod screws are tightened, the rod will be distorted and must be discarded. While alignment marks are provided, always mark the rod and cap with a permanent marker for redundancy. Correct orientation is obvious if the time is taken to examine the mating surfaces of the rod and cap.

All power head components must be cleaned and inspected before any reassembly occurs. If the power head has had a catastrophic failure, it may be more economical (in time and money) to replace the basic power head as an assembly.

Manufacturer recommended special tools for the following procedures are located in **Table 9** and **Table 10**. Remember that parts damaged by not using the correct tool can often be more expensive than the original cost of the tool. All tables are at the end of the chapter.

A large number of fasteners of different lengths and sizes are used in a power head. Plastic sandwich bags and/or cupcake tins are excellent methods of keeping small parts organized. Tag all larger internal parts for location and orientation. A felt-tipped permanent marker can be used to mark components after they have been cleaned. Avoid scribing or stamping internal components as the marking process may damage or weaken the component.

NOTE
A series of at least 6 photographs, taken from the front, rear, top, bottom and both sides of the power head (after removal, before disassembly) is very helpful during reassembly. The photographs are especially useful when trying to route electrical harnesses, fuel, primer and recirculation lines, and installing accessories and control linkages.

Disassembly (75-125 hp and 65-80 Jet)

Refer to **Figure 22** and **Figure 23** for this procedure. Since the power head is removed with most of the accessories installed, it is necessary to first finish removing all accessories and systems from the power head.

Engines prior to serial No. 0G438000 are equipped with the AD-CDI (alternator-driven capacitor discharge ignition) ignition system. These models are referred to as *early models* for this procedure.

Engines with serial No. 0G438000-on are equipped with the CDM (capacitor discharge module) ignition system. These models are referred to as *late models* for this procedure.

Because this section covers 3- and 4-cylinder models, and since the 3-cylinder models are essentially a shortened version of a 4-cylinder model, the exploded illustrations are of the 4-cylinder model. Any procedures specific to one model are called out in the text.

After power head disassembly, refer to the *Cleaning and Inspection* in this chapter and clean and inspect all components before reassembling the power head.

1. Remove the flywheel and electric starter as described in Chapter Seven.
2. Remove the oil reservoir (if not already removed), oil pump, oil warning module and all oil lines as described in Chapter Eleven.

3. Remove the carburetors, fuel pump, fuel filter, fuel primer valve, intake manifold(s) and reed block(s), and all fuel, primer and fuel bleed (recirculation) lines as described in Chapter Six.
4. *4-cylinder models*—Remove the accelerator pump, the 2 check valves, filter and all associated fuel lines. See Chapter Six.
5. Remove the internal fuel bleed (recirculation) valves and carriers from the crankcase cover openings for cylinders No. 2, 3 (and 4). See 8 and 9, **Figure 22**.
6A. *Early models*—Remove the remaining ignition and electrical components as an assembly. This includes the stator assembly, trigger coil, and the electrical/ignition plate (containing the switch box, ignition coils, voltage regulator, starter solenoid and the trim/tilt solenoids [or relays]). If equipped with an rpm limit module, remove it along with the other components. Do not disconnect electrical components from each other unless absolutely necessary; simply remove the mounting screws, cable clamps and tie-straps. See Chapter Seven.
6B. *Late models*—Remove the remaining ignition and electrical components as an assembly. This includes the stator assembly, trigger coil, trim/tilt relays and the electrical/ignition plate (containing the CDM modules, voltage regulator and starter solenoid). If equipped with an rpm limit module, remove it along with the other components. Do not disconnect electrical components from each other unless absolutely necessary; simply remove the mounting screws, cable clamps and tie-straps. See Chapter Seven.
7. Remove the screw at the center of the main throttle and spark control arm (located on the port side of the power head). Then, remove the control arm and any remaining control linkage as an assembly. Position the screw through the control arm, then install a suitable nut to keep the control arm components together.

NOTE
Three cylinder models (serial No. 0G127500-on) have a washer that fits

8

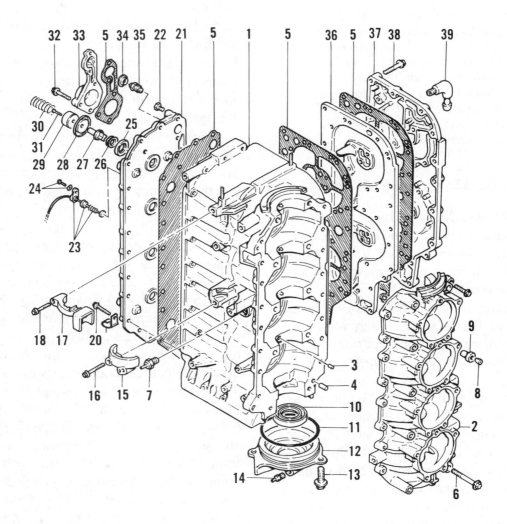

**CYLINDER BLOCK
(75-125 HP AND 65-80 JET [4-CYLINDER SHOWN])**

1. Cylinder block
2. Crankcase cover
3. Bearing locating pin
4. Dowel pin
5. Gaskets
6. Crankcase cover screws
7. Accelerator pump discharge nozzle
8. Check valve
9. Check valve carrier
10. Crankshaft lower seal
11. O-ring
12. Lower end cap
13. Screw
14. Check valve
15. Lower starter bracket
16. Screw
17. Upper starter bracket
18. Screw
19. Clamp
20. Screw
21. Cylinder block cover
22. Brass pipe plug
23. Engine temperature switch
24. Screw and washer
25. Carrier
26. Grommet
27. Poppet
28. Diaphragm
29. Cup
30. Spring
31. Screw
32. Screw
33. Thermostat cover
34. Grommet
35. Thermostat
36. Exhaust manifold
37. Exhaust cover
38. Screw
39. Water discharge (tell-tale) fitting

**CRANKSHAFT ASSEMBLY
(75-125 HP AND 65-80 JET [4-CYLINDER SHOWN])**

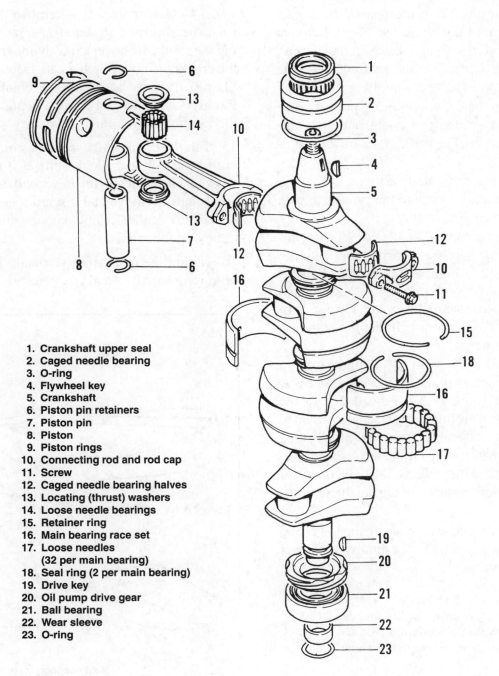

1. Crankshaft upper seal
2. Caged needle bearing
3. O-ring
4. Flywheel key
5. Crankshaft
6. Piston pin retainers
7. Piston pin
8. Piston
9. Piston rings
10. Connecting rod and rod cap
11. Screw
12. Caged needle bearing halves
13. Locating (thrust) washers
14. Loose needle bearings
15. Retainer ring
16. Main bearing race set
17. Loose needles
    (32 per main bearing)
18. Seal ring (2 per main bearing)
19. Drive key
20. Oil pump drive gear
21. Ball bearing
22. Wear sleeve
23. O-ring

8

between the thermostat cover and the thermostat and grommet assembly. Do not misplace the washer.

8. Remove the 5 screws securing the thermostat cover (33, **Figure 22**) to the rear of the power head at the top of the crankcase cover. Remove the thermostat cover and discard the gasket. Then, remove thermostat and grommet, and the poppet valve and spring assembly.

9. Reach into the cylinder block's poppet valve cavity and retrieve the grommet from the grommet carrier. See 26, **Figure 22**. Discard the grommet.

10. Remove the screw and washer securing the engine temperature switch to the cylinder block. Remove the switch assembly.

11. Remove the 14 (3-cylinder) or 18 (4-cylinder) remaining screws securing the cylinder block cover (21, **Figure 22**) to the cylinder block. Carefully pry the cover from the block, then remove and discard the gasket. Do not damage or distort the cover or cylinder block during the removal process.

12. Remove the 24 screws (3-cylinder) or 35 screws (4-cylinder) securing the exhaust cover and manifold (36 and 37, **Figure 22**) to the cylinder block. Carefully pry at the tabs provided to remove the assembly from the block, then separate the manifold from the cover plate. Remove and discard the gaskets. Do not damage or distort the cover or manifold during the removal process.

13. Remove the 3 screws securing the lower end cap to the power head. Do not remove the lower end cap at this time.

CAUTION
The crankcase cover and cylinder block are a matched, align-bored unit. Do not scratch, nick or damage the machined mating surfaces.

14A. *3-cylinder models*—Remove the 8 long (main bearing) and 12 short (outer) screws securing the crankcase cover to the cylinder block. Tap

the crankcase cover with a soft-faced (rubber or plastic) hammer to break the crankcase seal. Remove the crankcase cover. Locate and secure the locating dowel pin as necessary.

14B. *4-cylinder models*—Remove the 10 long (main bearing) and 16 short (outer) screws securing the crankcase cover to the cylinder block. Tap the crankcase cover with a soft-faced (rubber or plastic) hammer to break the crankcase seal. Remove the crankcase cover. Locate and secure the locating dowel pin as necessary.

15. Lift the crankshaft assembly straight up and out of the cylinder block and set it on a clean workbench. Then pull the lower end cap from the crankshaft. Remove and discard the O-ring and crankshaft seal. Do not damage the end cap removing the seal.

16. Mount the crankshaft vertically in a power head (crankshaft) stand (part No. 91-812549 or

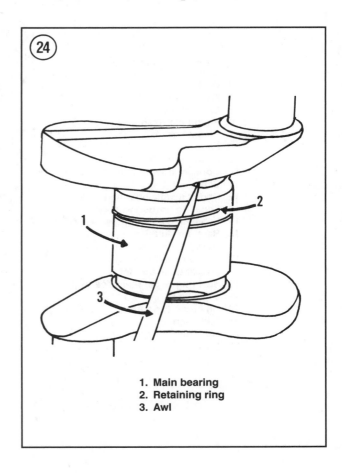

1. Main bearing
2. Retaining ring
3. Awl

equivalent). Make sure the stand is securely clamped in a vise.

17. Locate and secure the crankshaft center main bearing locating pins (3, **Figure 22**) as necessary. There are 3 pins on a 3-cylinder and 4 pins on a 4-cylinder.

18. Slide the upper crankshaft seal and caged roller bearing assembly from the crankshaft. Remove the seal from the bearing, then discard the seal.

NOTE
There are 2 center main bearing assemblies on a 3-cylinder and 3 center main bearing assemblies on a 4-cylinder. Each center main bearing consists of a retainer ring, 2 bearing race halves, 32 loose needle bearings and 2 seal rings (mounted in one groove with the open ends 180° apart).

19. Remove the retaining ring from around a center main bearing. See **Figure 24**. Then, remove the outer race halves, 32 loose rollers and the 2 crankshaft seal rings. Store the bearing

REMOVING PISTON RINGS

components in marked containers to allow reassembly in their original location. Repeat the procedure for the remaining center main bearing(s).

20. Mark the corresponding cylinder number on the pistons and connecting rods with a felt-tipped permanent marker. Mark the connecting rods and rod caps so the rod caps can be reinstalled in their original orientation.

NOTE
*Always store **all** components from each connecting rod and piston assembly together. They must be reinstalled in their original locations.*

CAUTION
Wear suitable eye protection for piston ring and piston pin retainer removal procedures.

21. Remove the piston rings from all of the pistons using a piston ring expander (part No. 91-24697 or equivalent). See **Figure 25**, typical. Retain the rings for cleaning the piston's ring grooves.

22. Remove each connecting rod and piston assembly as follows:

   a. Remove the connecting rod screws from the upper (cylinder No. 1) connecting rod. Alternately loosen each screw a small amount until all tension is off of both screws.

   b. Tap the rod cap with a soft metal (brass) mallet to separate the cap from the rod.

   c. Remove the cap and rod from the crankshaft, then remove the 2 caged roller bearing halves from the crankshaft.

   d. Reinstall the rod cap to the connecting rod in its original orientation. Tighten the rod cap screws finger-tight.

   e. Store the caged roller bearing assemblies in clean, numbered containers, corresponding to the cylinder number.

   f. Repeat this procedure to remove the remaining (cylinders No. 2-4) connecting rods.

8

23. Using lock ring remover (part No. 91-52952A-1) or a suitable awl, remove and discard all piston pin retainers.

24. Place the piston pin tool (part No. 91-76160A-2 or equivalent), into one end of the cylinder No. 1 piston pin bore. Support the bottom of the piston with one hand and drive the pin tool and pin from the piston.

25. Remove the piston from the connecting rod. Remove the locating (thrust) washers and the 29 loose needle bearings (**Figure 26**). Store the components in clean, numbered containers corresponding to the cylinder number.

26. Repeat Steps 24 and 25 to separate the remaining pistons (cylinders No. 2-4) from their connecting rods.

27. If the crankshaft ball bearing and/or the oil pump drive gear requires replacement, proceed as follows:

   a. Support the ball bearing in a knife-edged bearing plate and press against the crankshaft (using the power head stand as a mandrel) until the bearing is free from the crankshaft. See **Figure 27**. Discard the bearing.

   b. If necessary, pull the oil pump gear from the crankshaft and discard it.

   c. Locate and secure the oil pump gear drive key.

28. Remove and discard the O-ring (23, **Figure 23**) inside the splined bore of the crankshaft. Use a dental pick or similar instrument to hook the O-ring and pull it from the bore.

29. If the wear sleeve is damaged, pull it from the crankshaft with a pair of pliers. Be careful not to damage the crankshaft surface during the removal process. Discard the sleeve. If necessary, apply mild heat (with a heat light [part No. 91-63209] or equivalent) to the sleeve to loosen the Loctite bond.

30. Refer to *Cleaning and Inspection* in this chapter before beginning reassembly procedure.

Disassembly (135-200 hp and 105-140 Jet)

Refer to **Figure 28** and **Figure 29** for this procedure. Since the power head is removed with

1. Loose needle bearings
2. Locating (thrust) washers

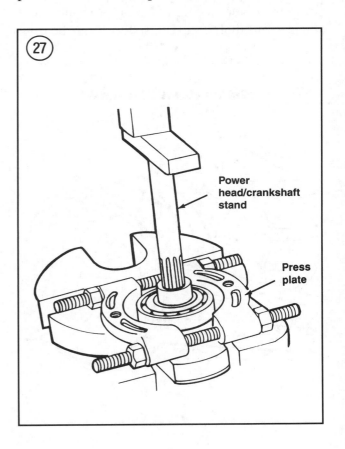

Power head/crankshaft stand

Press plate

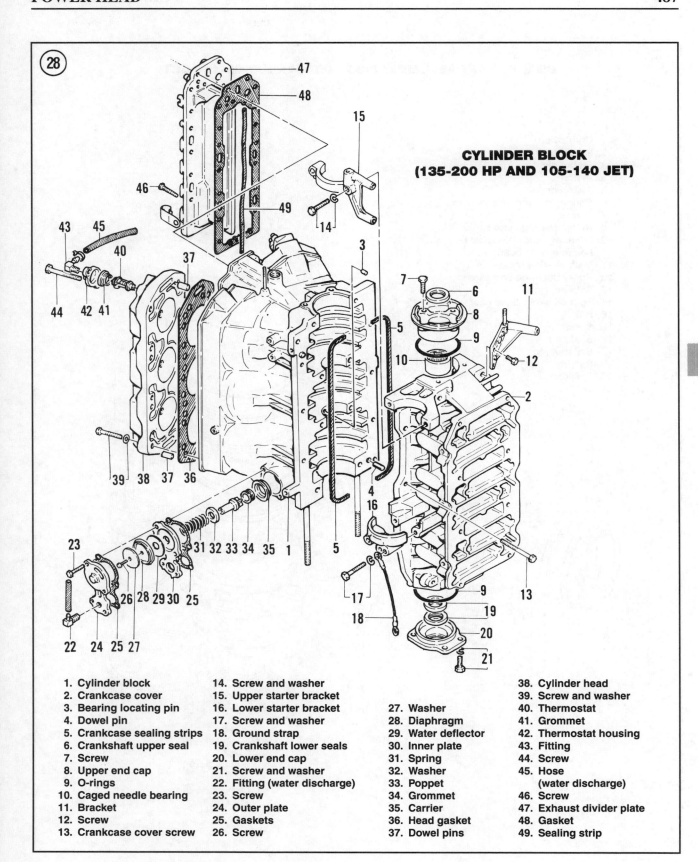

**CYLINDER BLOCK
(135-200 HP AND 105-140 JET)**

1. Cylinder block
2. Crankcase cover
3. Bearing locating pin
4. Dowel pin
5. Crankcase sealing strips
6. Crankshaft upper seal
7. Screw
8. Upper end cap
9. O-rings
10. Caged needle bearing
11. Bracket
12. Screw
13. Crankcase cover screw
14. Screw and washer
15. Upper starter bracket
16. Lower starter bracket
17. Screw and washer
18. Ground strap
19. Crankshaft lower seals
20. Lower end cap
21. Screw and washer
22. Fitting (water discharge)
23. Screw
24. Outer plate
25. Gaskets
26. Screw
27. Washer
28. Diaphragm
29. Water deflector
30. Inner plate
31. Spring
32. Washer
33. Poppet
34. Grommet
35. Carrier
36. Head gasket
37. Dowel pins
38. Cylinder head
39. Screw and washer
40. Thermostat
41. Grommet
42. Thermostat housing
43. Fitting
44. Screw
45. Hose (water discharge)
46. Screw
47. Exhaust divider plate
48. Gasket
49. Sealing strip

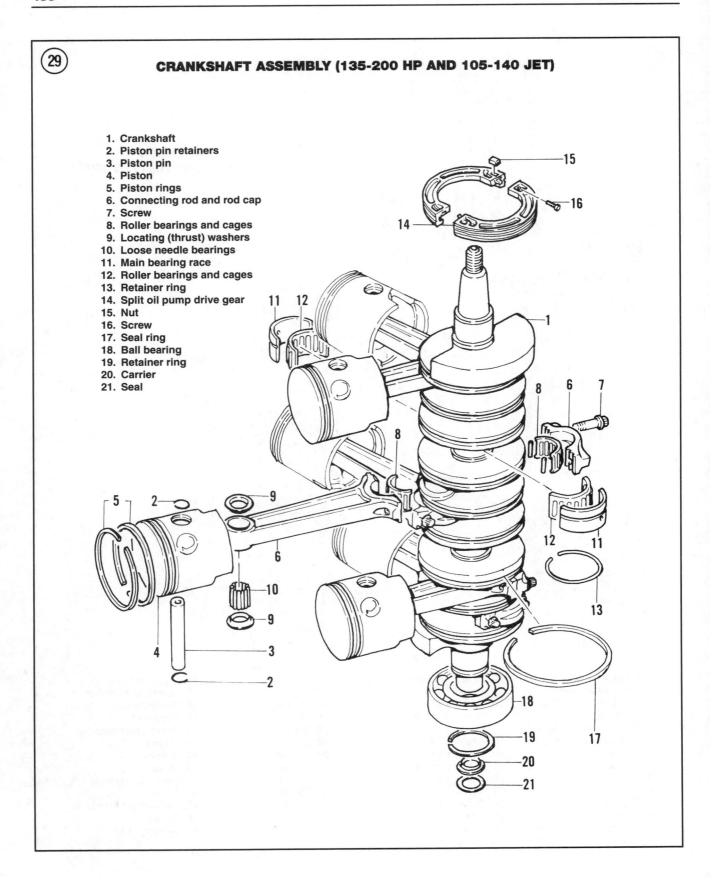

㉙ CRANKSHAFT ASSEMBLY (135-200 HP AND 105-140 JET)

1. Crankshaft
2. Piston pin retainers
3. Piston pin
4. Piston
5. Piston rings
6. Connecting rod and rod cap
7. Screw
8. Roller bearings and cages
9. Locating (thrust) washers
10. Loose needle bearings
11. Main bearing race
12. Roller bearings and cages
13. Retainer ring
14. Split oil pump drive gear
15. Nut
16. Screw
17. Seal ring
18. Ball bearing
19. Retainer ring
20. Carrier
21. Seal

most of the accessories installed, it is necessary to first finish removing all accessories and systems from the power head.

1. Remove the flywheel and electric starter as described in Chapter Seven.

2. Remove the oil reservoir, oil pump, oil warning module and all oil lines as described in Chapter Eleven.

3A. *Carbureted models*—Remove the carburetors, fuel pump, fuel filter, fuel primer valve, intake manifold and reed blocks, and all fuel, primer and fuel bleed (recirculation) lines as described in Chapter Six.

3B. *EFI models*—Remove the induction manifold assembly (and ECM [electronic control module]), mechanical fuel pump, vapor separator assembly, water separating fuel filter, water warning module, intake manifold and reed blocks, and all fuel and fuel bleed (recirculation) lines as described in Chapter Six.

4. *200 hp EFI models*—Remove the detonation sensor and module as described in Chapter Six.

5. On models equipped with an idle speed stabilizing shift switch, such as XR6, Magnum III, 175 hp carbureted, 150 and 175 XRI and Magnum (EFI) models and any engines with this system added as an accessory, disconnect the shift switch leads from the engine harness bullet connector and the ring terminal from engine ground.

6. Remove the remaining ignition and electrical components as an assembly. This includes the stator assembly, trigger coil, both switch boxes, starter solenoid, idle stabilizer module, oil and overheat warning module and the electrical/ignition plate (containing the ignition coils, voltage regulators and trim solenoids [or relays]). If equipped with an rpm limit module, remove it along with the other components. Do not disconnect electrical components from each other unless absolutely necessary, simply remove the mounting screws, cable clamps and tie-straps. See Chapter Seven.

7. Remove the screw from the center of the throttle and spark control arm (located on the port side of the power head). Then remove the control arm and any remaining control linkage as an assembly. Position the screw through the control arm, then install a suitable nut to keep the control arm components together.

8. Remove the shift and throttle cable anchor bracket from the port lower side of the power head.

9. Disconnect the water discharge hose(s) from both thermostat housings. Then remove the 2 screws securing the thermostat cover to the top of each cylinder head. Remove both thermostat covers, grommets and thermostats. Discard both grommets.

10. Remove the water discharge hose from the poppet valve fitting (22, **Figure 28**). Then remove the 4 screws securing the poppet valve assembly to the power head. Remove the valve assembly from the power head. Separate the inner and outer plates, then remove and discard both gaskets.

11. Reach into the cylinder block's poppet valve cavity and retrieve the grommet from the carrier in the cavity. See 34, **Figure 28**. Discard the grommet.

12. Remove the 12 screws securing each cylinder head to the cylinder block. Carefully pull each head from the block, then remove and discard both gaskets. If necessary, tap each cylinder head with a soft-faced (rubber or plastic) hammer to break the gasket seal. Do not damage the sealing surfaces during the removal process.

13. Remove the 20 screws securing the exhaust divider plate to the cylinder block. Carefully pry the divider from the block, then remove and discard the gasket. Do not damage or distort the divider plate, or damage the cylinder block sealing surfaces during the removal process.

14. Remove and discard the strip seal (49, **Figure 28**) from the exhaust cavity.

8

15. Remove the 4 screws securing the lower end cap to the power head (**Figure 30**). Do not remove the lower end cap at this time.

16. Remove the 4 screws securing the upper end cap to the power head (**Figure 31**). Do not remove the upper end cap at this time.

CAUTION
The crankcase cover and cylinder block are a matched, align-bored unit. Do not scratch, nick or damage the machined mating surfaces.

17. Remove the 8 large (main bearing) and 6 small (outer) screws securing the crankcase cover to the cylinder block. Carefully pry the crankcase cover at the points shown in **Figure 32** to break the crankcase seal. Then, remove the crankcase cover. Locate and secure the locating dowel pins as necessary.

18. Mark the corresponding cylinder number on the pistons and connecting rods with a felt-tipped permanent marker. Mark the connecting rods and rod caps so the rod caps can be reinstalled in their original orientation.

NOTE
*Always store **all** components from each connecting rod and piston assembly together. They must be reinstalled in their original locations.*

19. Remove each connecting rod and piston assembly as follows:

a. Manually rotate the crankshaft to position the upper (cylinder No. 1) piston at the bottom of its cylinder bore. This will expose the connecting rod screws (**Figure 33**, typical) for easy removal.

b. Using a 12-point socket, remove the connecting rod screws from the upper (cylinder No. 1) connecting rod. Alternately loosen each screw a small amount until all tension is off of both screws.

c. Tap the rod cap with a soft metal (brass) mallet to separate the cap from the rod.

d. Remove the cap and rod from the crankshaft, then remove the roller bearings and cages from the crankshaft.

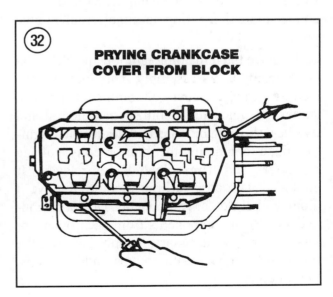

PRYING CRANKCASE COVER FROM BLOCK

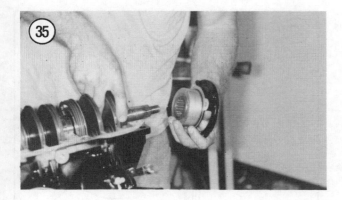

e. Carefully slide the piston and rod assembly from its cylinder bore. Be ready to catch the assembly as it leaves the cylinder bore (**Figure 34**).

CAUTION
Each connecting rod and cap is a matched assembly and must not be mismatched. The cap must be installed in its original orientation.

f. Reinstall the rod cap to the connecting rod in its original orientation. Tighten the rod cap screws finger-tight.

g. Store the roller bearings and cages in clean, numbered containers, corresponding to the cylinder number.

h. Repeat this procedure to remove the remaining (cylinders No. 2-6) connecting rod assemblies.

20. Remove the upper end cap from the crankshaft. See **Figure 35**. Then remove the lower end cap. If the lower end cap sticks, tap it *gently* with a soft-faced (rubber or plastic) hammer to free it from the ball bearing. Rotate the end cap and tap around the entire outer diameter or it will cock (and be damaged).

NOTE
If the caged roller bearing in the upper end cap requires replacement, it is recommended that the end cap be replaced as an assembly.

21. Remove and discard the O-ring from each end cap. Then, drive the seal(s) from each end cap with a suitable punch and hammer. Be careful not to damage either end cap's seal bore during the removal process. Discard all seals.

22. Lift the crankshaft assembly straight up and out of the cylinder block (**Figure 36**) and mount it vertically in a power head (crankshaft) stand (part No. 91-30591A-1 or equivalent). Make sure the stand is securely clamped in a vise.

23. Locate and secure the crankshaft center main bearing locating pins (3, **Figure 28**) as necessary. There are 2 pins on these models.

8

24. Remove the retaining ring from around a center main bearing. See **Figure 37**, typical. Then remove the outer race halves and the roller bearings and cages. Store the bearing components in marked containers to allow reassembly in their original location. Repeat the procedure for the remaining center main bearing.

CAUTION
Wear suitable eye protection for piston ring and piston pin retainer removal procedures.

25. Remove the piston rings from all of the pistons using a piston ring expander (part No. 91-24697 or equivalent). See **Figure 38**, typical. Retain the rings for cleaning the piston ring grooves.

26. Using a lock ring remover (part No. 91-52952A-1) or a suitable awl, remove and discard all piston pin retainers. See **Figure 39**, typical.

27. Place the piston pin tool (part No. 91-76159A-2 or equivalent), into one end of the cylinder No. 1 piston pin bore. Support the bot-

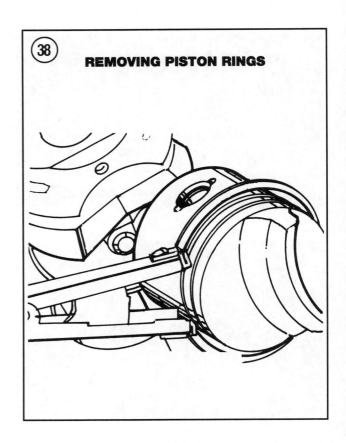

38 **REMOVING PISTON RINGS**

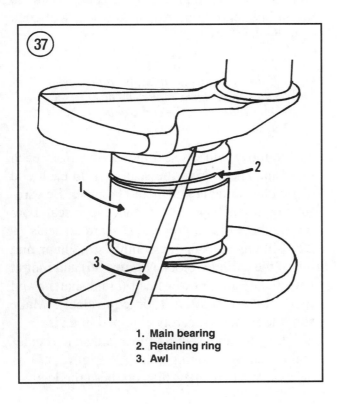

37

1. Main bearing
2. Retaining ring
3. Awl

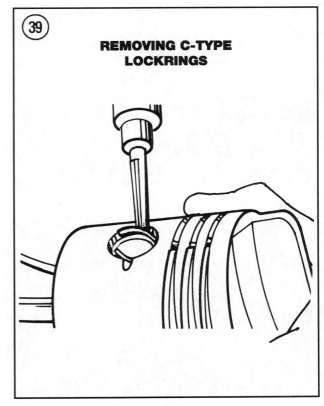

39 **REMOVING C-TYPE LOCKRINGS**

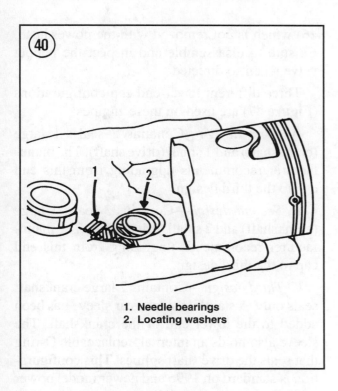

1. Needle bearings
2. Locating washers

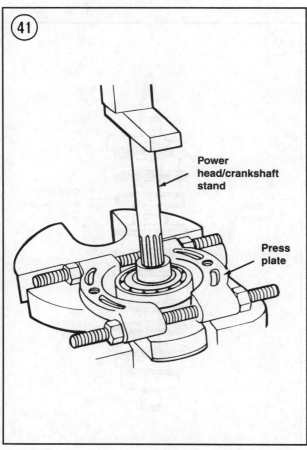

Power head/crankshaft stand

Press plate

tom of the piston with one hand and drive the pin tool and pin from the piston.

28. Remove the piston from the connecting rod. Remove the locating (thrust) washers and the 29 loose needle bearings (**Figure 40**). Store the components in clean, numbered containers corresponding to the cylinder number.

29. Repeat the previous 2 Steps to separate the remaining (cylinders No. 2-6) pistons from their connecting rod.

30. If the crankshaft ball bearing requires replacement, proceed as follows:

   a. Remove the retainer ring with pliers (part No. 91-822778A-3) or Sears Craftsman (part No. 4735).

   b. Support the ball bearing in a knife-edged bearing plate, such as part No. 91-37241.

   c. Press against the crankshaft (using the power head stand as a mandrel) until the bearing is free from the crankshaft. See **Figure 41**.

   d. Discard the bearing.

31. Remove and discard the seal and seal carrier from the drive shaft end of the crankshaft. See **Figure 42**, typical.

8

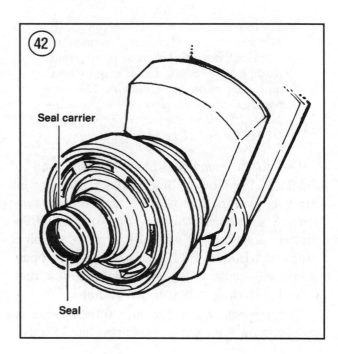

Seal carrier

Seal

32. If the oil pump drive gear (**Figure 43**) requires replacement, remove the 2 screws (16, **Figure 29**) securing the gear. Then remove and discard the drive gear halves and the 2 screws.

> *CAUTION*
> *There are 7 seal rings (**Figure 43**) that seal each crankcase chamber from the adjacent chamber(s). If the rings are damaged or broken, they must be replaced. Do not remove any seal ring unless it is going to be replaced.*

33. If the crankshaft seal ring(s) must be replaced, remove the ring(s) using a piston ring expander (part No. 91-24697 or equivalent).
34. Refer to *Cleaning and Inspection* in this chapter before beginning reassembly procedure.

Disassembly (225-250 hp and 200 DFI)

Refer to **Figure 44** and **Figure 45** for this procedure. Since the power head is removed with most of the accessories installed, it will be necessary to first finish removing all accessories and systems from the power head.

> *CAUTION*
> *These are complex power heads. Take pictures or draw sketches of component locations, hose and harness routing and linkage assemblies. Label components and connections as necessary. The fuel bleed (recirculation) system is particularly difficult to reroute. Refer to Chapter Six for fuel bleed system diagrams.*

Due to the many fuel bleed systems used in the 1994-1997 model line, replacement power heads are compatible with all recirculation systems. Make sure all unused ports on 1994-1996 models are plugged with the appropriate pipe plugs and Loctite PST pipe sealant. Any open ports will cause a massive air leak into that cylinder, leading to power head failure.

The poppet (water pressure relief) valve is mounted on the exhaust adaptor plate (**Figure 46**) which is not removed with the power head. Be sure to disassemble and inspect the poppet valve when so directed.

Three different lower end cap configurations (**Figure 47**) are used on these engines:

A. *First design*—Contains 2 seals: 1 large (crankshaft) and 1 small (drive shaft). The manufacturer recommends upgrading from this end cap to the third design.

B. *Second design*—Contains 3 seals: 1 large (crankshaft) and 2 small (drive shaft). The manufacturer recommends upgrading from this end cap to the third design.

C. *Third design*—Contains 2 large crankshaft seals only. A stainless steel wear sleeve has been added to the lower end of the crankshaft. The sleeve also holds an internal, replaceable O-ring that seals the drive shaft splines. This configuration is standard on 1996 and newer model power

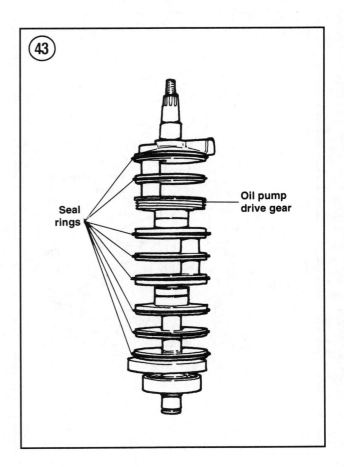

(43)

Seal rings

Oil pump drive gear

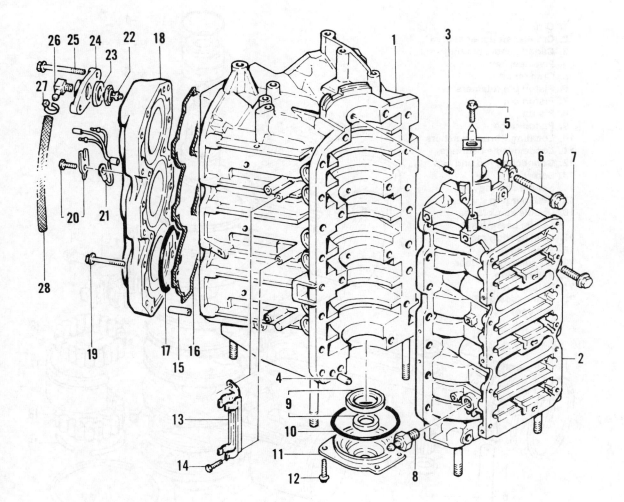

CYLINDER BLOCK (225-250 HP AND 200 DFI)

1. Cylinder block
2. Crankcase cover
3. Bearing locating pin
4. Dowel pin
5. Adjustable timing pointer and screw
6. Main bearing (large) screw
7. Outer (small) screw
8. Pulse fitting (remote oil tank)
9. Crankshaft lower seals
10. O-ring
11. Lower end cap
12. Screw
13. Main harness connector bracket
14. Screw
15. Dowel pin
16. Water jacket seal
17. O-ring
18. Cylinder head
19. Cylinder head screw
20. Retainer plate and screw
21. ECT sensor
22. Thermostat
23. Gasket
24. Thermostat housing
25. Thermostat housing/cylinder head screw
26. Water discharge fitting
27. Tie-strap
28. Water discharge hose

8

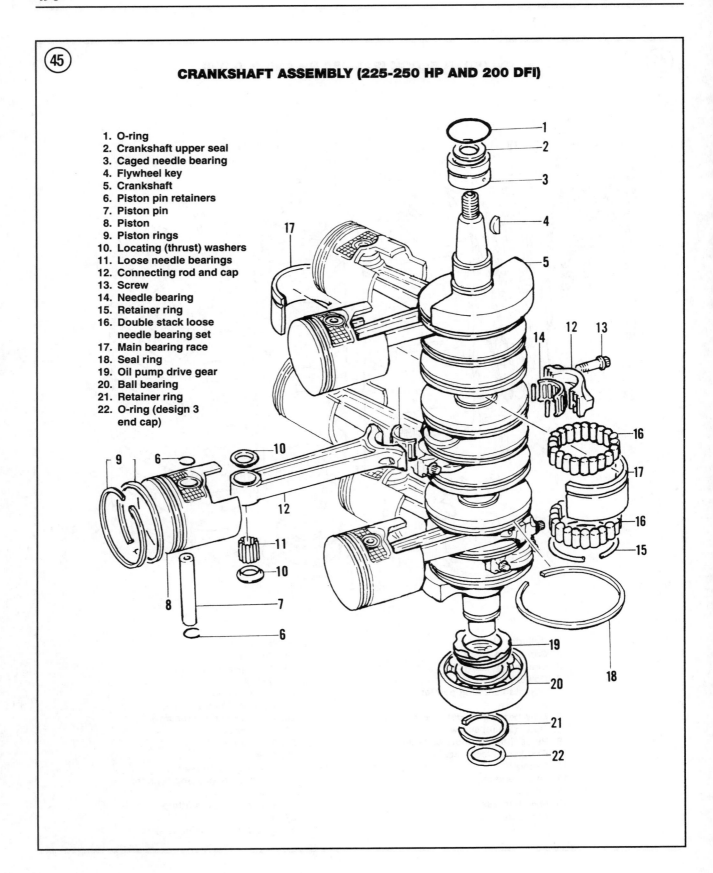

CRANKSHAFT ASSEMBLY (225-250 HP AND 200 DFI)

1. O-ring
2. Crankshaft upper seal
3. Caged needle bearing
4. Flywheel key
5. Crankshaft
6. Piston pin retainers
7. Piston pin
8. Piston
9. Piston rings
10. Locating (thrust) washers
11. Loose needle bearings
12. Connecting rod and cap
13. Screw
14. Needle bearing
15. Retainer ring
16. Double stack loose
    needle bearing set
17. Main bearing race
18. Seal ring
19. Oil pump drive gear
20. Ball bearing
21. Retainer ring
22. O-ring (design 3
    end cap)

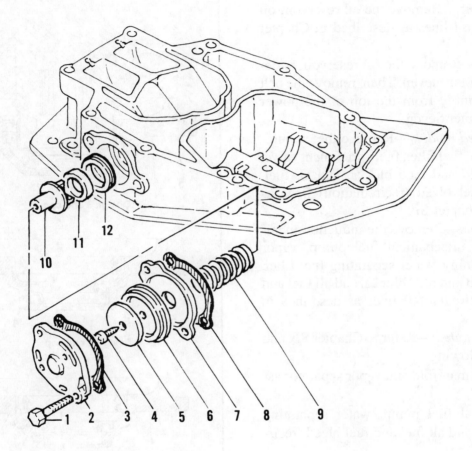

46

**POPPET VALVE ASSEMBLY
(225-275 HP AND 200 DFI)**

1. Screws
2. Outer plate
3. Gasket
4. Screw
5. Washer
6. Diaphragm
7. Inner plate
8. Gasket
9. Spring
10. Poppet
11. Grommet
12. Carrier

8

heads. An upgrade kit (part No. 1171-9787A-5) contains the necessary components to retrofit older engines.

To disassemble the power head, proceed as follows:

1. Remove the alternator, flywheel and electric starter as described in Chapter Seven.

2A. *225-250 hp*—Remove the oil reservoir, oil pump and all oil lines as described in Chapter Eleven.

2B. *200 DFI*—Remove the oil reservoir as described in Chapter Eleven. Then, remove the belt tensioner assembly from the top of the power head. See Chapter Seven.

3A. *Carbureted models*—Remove the carburetors, fuel pump, fuel filter, fuel enrichment valve, intake manifold and reed blocks, and all fuel, primer and fuel bleed (recirculation) lines as described in Chapter Six.

3B. *EFI models*—Remove the induction manifold assembly, mechanical fuel pump, vapor separator assembly, water separating fuel filter, intake manifold and reed blocks, and all fuel and fuel bleed (recirculation) lines as described in Chapter Six.

3C. *200 DFI models*—Refer to Chapter Six and remove the following:

    a. Induction manifold and vapor separator assemblies.

    b. Mechanical fuel pump, water separating fuel filter and all fuel and fuel bleed (recirculation) lines.

    c. Intake manifold and reed blocks (with the electric oil pump and oil line to air compressor).

    d. Air compressor, port and starboard air/fuel rails (with the DFI injectors) and all remaining air, fuel and bleed lines.

NOTE
All models are equipped with a shift interrupt switch mounted on the shift and throttle cable anchor bracket. Disconnect the switch leads from the engine harness bullet connectors and leave the

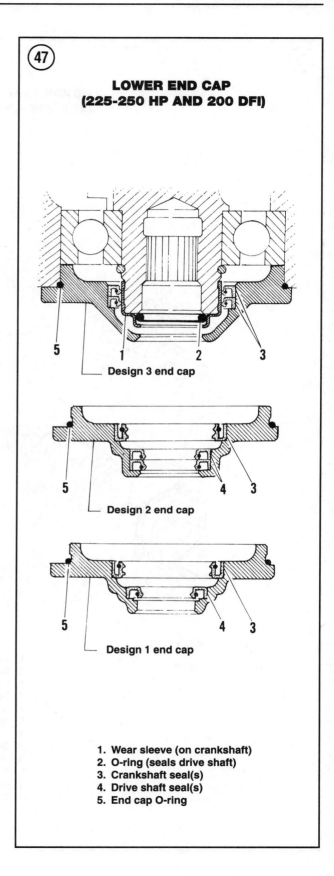

LOWER END CAP (225-250 HP AND 200 DFI)

Design 3 end cap
Design 2 end cap
Design 1 end cap

1. Wear sleeve (on crankshaft)
2. O-ring (seals drive shaft)
3. Crankshaft seal(s)
4. Drive shaft seal(s)
5. End cap O-ring

switch installed on the bracket. All models are also equipped with an ECT (engine coolant temperature) sensor. The sensor may be removed or left in place, depending on the service to be performed. Disconnect the leads and/or remove the sensor before proceeding.

4A. *Carbureted models*—Remove the remaining ignition and electrical components as an assembly. This includes the stator assembly, crankshaft position sensor, the ignition ECM (electronic control module), CDM modules, and the electrical/ignition plate (containing the starter solenoid and the trim/tilt solenoids or relays). Do not disconnect electrical components from each other unless absolutely necessary, simply remove the mounting screws, cable clamps and tie-straps. See Chapter Seven.

4B. *EFI models*—Remove the remaining ignition and electrical components as an assembly. This includes the stator assembly, crankshaft position sensor, the ignition and fuel electronic control modules (and mounting plate), CDM modules, and the electrical plate (containing the starter solenoid, fuse and the trim/tilt solenoids [or relays]). Do not disconnect electrical components from each other unless absolutely necessary, simply remove the mounting screws, cable clamps and tie-straps. Refer to Chapter Six for the Fuel ECM and Chapter Six for all other items.

4C. *DFI models*—Remove the remaining ignition and electrical components as an assembly. This includes the stator assembly, crankshaft position sensor, the ECM (electronic control module), the electrical plate (containing the starter solenoid, fuses and main power and trim/tilt relays) and the ignition plate (containing the ignition coils). Do not disconnect electrical components from each other unless absolutely necessary, simply remove the mounting screws, cable clamps and tie-straps. Refer to Chapter Six and Seven as necessary.

5. Remove the screw at the center of the throttle control arm (located on the port side of the power head). Then remove the control arm and any remaining control linkage as an assembly. Position the screw through the control arm, then install a suitable nut to keep the control arm components together.

6. Remove the shift and throttle cable anchor bracket (and shift interrupt switch) from the port lower side of the power head.

7. Remove the 2 cylinder head screws (25, **Figure 44**) securing the thermostat cover to the top of each cylinder head. Remove both thermostat covers, gaskets and thermostats. Discard both gaskets.

8. Remove the 2 screws (1, **Figure 46**) securing the poppet valve assembly to the exhaust adaptor plate (at the top of the drive shaft housing). Remove the valve assembly from the adaptor plate. Separate the inner and outer plates, then remove and discard both gaskets.

9. Reach into the adaptor plate's poppet valve cavity and retrieve the grommet and grommet carrier from the cavity. See 11 and 12, **Figure 46**. Discard the grommet.

10. Remove the 18 remaining screws (19, **Figure 44**) securing each cylinder head to the cylinder block. Carefully pull each head from the block, then remove and discard the 3 combustion chamber O-ring seals and the water jacket molded seal from each head. If necessary, tap each cylinder head with a soft-faced (rubber or plastic) hammer to break the seals. Do not damage the sealing surfaces during the removal process.

11. Remove the 4 screws (12, **Figure 44**) securing the lower end cap to the power head. Do not remove the lower end cap at this time.

CAUTION
The crankcase cover and cylinder block are a matched, align-bored unit. Do not scratch, nick or damage the machined mating surfaces.

8

12. Remove the 8 large (main bearing) and 14 small (outer) screws securing the crankcase cover to the cylinder block. Carefully tap the cover with a soft-faced (plastic or rubber) hammer to break the crankcase seal. Then, remove the crankcase cover. Locate and secure the locating dowel pin as necessary.

13. Mark the corresponding cylinder number on the pistons and connecting rods with a felt-tipped permanent marker. Mark the connecting rods and rod caps so the rod caps can be reinstalled in their original orientation.

NOTE
*Always store **all** components from each connecting rod and piston assembly together. They must be reinstalled in their original locations.*

14. Remove each connecting rod and piston assembly as follows:
  a. Manually rotate the crankshaft to position the upper (cylinder No. 1) piston at the bottom of its cylinder bore. This will expose the connecting rod screws (**Figure 33**, typical) for easy removal.
  b. Using a 12-point socket, remove the connecting rod screws from the upper (cylinder No. 1) connecting rod. Alternately loosen each screw a small amount until all tension is off of both screws.
  c. Tap the rod cap with a soft metal (brass) mallet to separate the cap from the rod.
  d. Remove the cap and rod from the crankshaft, then remove the roller bearings and cages from the crankshaft.
  e. Carefully slide the piston and rod assembly from its cylinder bore. Be ready to catch the assembly as it leaves the cylinder bore (**Figure 34**, typical).

CAUTION
Each connecting rod and cap is a matched assembly and must not be mismatched. The cap must be installed in its original orientation.

  f. Reinstall the rod cap to the connecting rod in its original orientation. Tighten the rod cap screws finger-tight.
  g. Store the roller bearings and cages in clean, numbered containers, corresponding to the cylinder number.
  h. Repeat this procedure to remove the remaining (cylinders No. 2-6) connecting rod assemblies.

15. Lift the flywheel end of the crankshaft slightly and slide the upper bearing assembly (3, **Figure 45**) from the crankshaft. Remove and discard the O-ring and seal from the bearing case.

16. Remove the lower end cap. Discard the O-ring, then drive the seals from the end cap with a suitable punch and hammer. Be careful not to damage the end cap's seal bore during the removal process. Discard the seals.

17. Lift the crankshaft assembly straight up and out of the cylinder block (**Figure 36**, typical) and mount it vertically in a crankshaft stand (part No. 91-30591A-1 [8-spline] or part No. 91-812549 [13-spline] or equivalent). Make sure the stand is securely clamped in a vise.

18. Locate and secure the crankshaft center main bearing locating pins (3, **Figure 44**) as necessary. There are 3 pins on these models.

19. Remove the retaining ring from around a center main bearing. See **Figure 37**, typical. Then, remove the outer race halves and the double stack of loose roller bearings. Store the bearing components in marked containers to allow reassembly in their original location. Repeat the procedure for the remaining center main bearing.

CAUTION
Wear suitable eye protection for piston ring and piston pin retainer removal procedures.

20. Remove the piston rings from the pistons using piston ring expander (part No. 91-24697 or equivalent). See **Figure 38**, typical. Retain the rings for cleaning the piston's ring grooves.

21. Using lock ring remover (part No. 91-52952A-1) or a suitable awl, remove and discard all piston pin retainers. See **Figure 39**, typical.

22. Place the piston pin tool (part No. 91-92973A-1 or equivalent), into one end of the cylinder No. 1 piston pin bore. Support the bottom of the piston with one hand and drive the pin tool and pin from the piston.

23. Remove the piston from the connecting rod. Remove the locating (thrust) washers and the 34 loose needle bearings (**Figure 40**). Store the components in clean, numbered containers corresponding to the cylinder number.

24. Repeat Steps 22 and 23 to separate the remaining (cylinders No. 2-6) pistons from their connecting rods.

25. If the crankshaft ball bearing and/or oil pump drive gear requires replacement, proceed as follows:

   a. Remove the retainer ring with pliers (part No. 91-822778A-3) or Sears Craftsman (part No. 4735).

   b. Support the ball bearing in a knife-edged bearing plate, such as part No. 91-37241.

   c. Press against the crankshaft (using the power head stand as a mandrel) until the bearing is free from the crankshaft. See **Figure 41**.

   d. Discard the bearing.

   e. Slide the oil pump drive gear off of the crankshaft. Discard the gear.

26. *Design 3 lower end cap*—Remove and discard the O-ring from inside the wear sleeve on the drive shaft end of the crankshaft.

NOTE
In the next step, it may be necessary to heat the wear sleeve with a heat lamp, such as part No. 91-63209 (or equivalent), to loosen the Loctite seal. Do not use an open flame.

27. *Design 3 lower end cap*—If the wear sleeve on the crankshaft lower end is damaged or worn, pull it from the crankshaft with a pair of pliers.

Do not damage the crankshaft surface during the removal process. Discard the wear sleeve.

CAUTION
*There are 7 seal rings (18, **Figure 45**) that seal each crankcase chamber from the adjacent chamber(s). If the rings are damaged or broken, they must be replaced. Do not remove any seal ring unless it is going to be replaced.*

28. If the crankshaft seal ring(s) must be replaced, remove the ring(s) using piston ring expander (part No. 91-24697 or equivalent).

29. Refer to *Cleaning and Inspection* (located later in this chapter) before beginning reassembly procedure.

Disassembly (275 hp)

Refer to **Figures 48-49** for this procedure. Since the power head is removed with most of the accessories installed, it is necessary to first finish removing all accessories and systems from the power head.

The poppet (water pressure relief) valve is mounted on the exhaust adaptor plate (**Figure 46**) which is removed with the power head and must be separated from the power head before the power head can be completely disassembled. Be sure to disassemble and inspect the poppet valve when so directed.

If oil pump drive gear failure is the reason for disassembly, the oil pump drive gear can be accessed by removing only the exhaust adaptor plate and lower end cap. If the lower end cap can be worked free without splitting the crankcase, a great amount of time and effort can be saved. This may not be an easy task. Always replace the end cap O-ring and seal before reassembly.

To disassemble the power head, proceed as follows:

1. Remove the flywheel and electric starter as described in Chapter Seven.

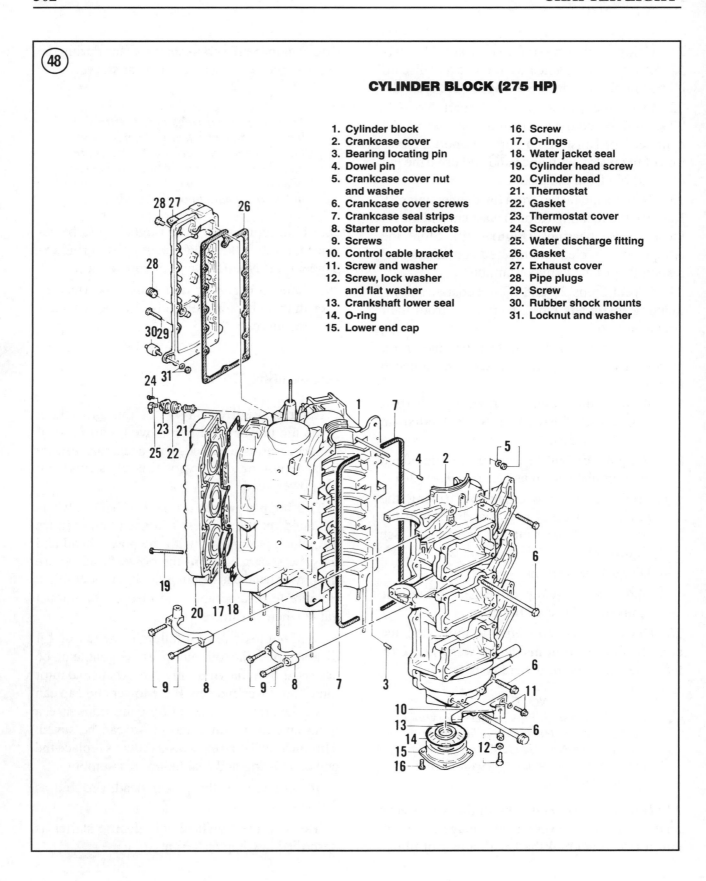

48

CYLINDER BLOCK (275 HP)

1. Cylinder block
2. Crankcase cover
3. Bearing locating pin
4. Dowel pin
5. Crankcase cover nut and washer
6. Crankcase cover screws
7. Crankcase seal strips
8. Starter motor brackets
9. Screws
10. Control cable bracket
11. Screw and washer
12. Screw, lock washer and flat washer
13. Crankshaft lower seal
14. O-ring
15. Lower end cap
16. Screw
17. O-rings
18. Water jacket seal
19. Cylinder head screw
20. Cylinder head
21. Thermostat
22. Gasket
23. Thermostat cover
24. Screw
25. Water discharge fitting
26. Gasket
27. Exhaust cover
28. Pipe plugs
29. Screw
30. Rubber shock mounts
31. Locknut and washer

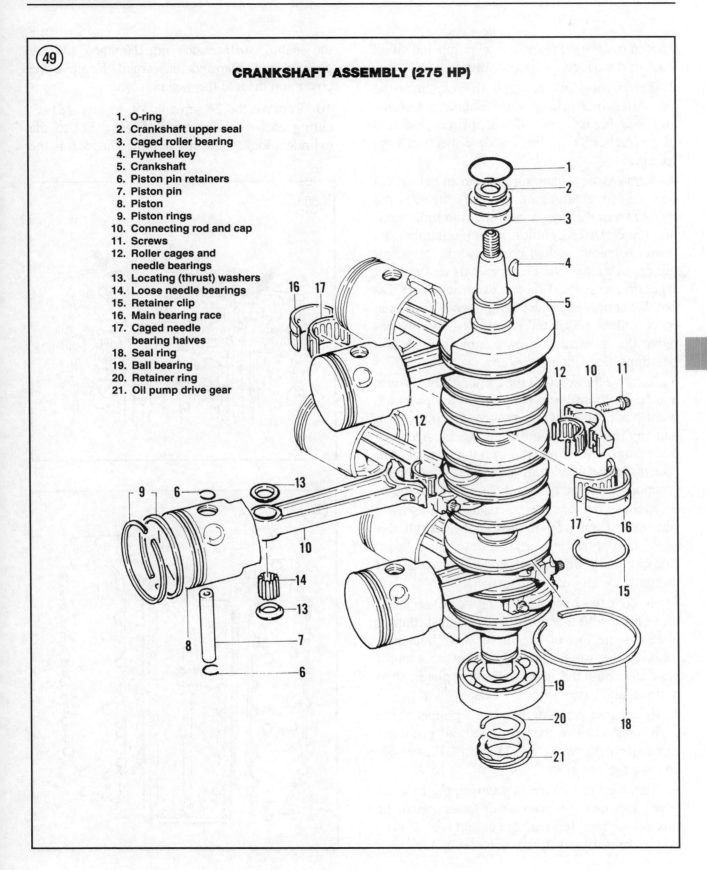

49

CRANKSHAFT ASSEMBLY (275 HP)

1. O-ring
2. Crankshaft upper seal
3. Caged roller bearing
4. Flywheel key
5. Crankshaft
6. Piston pin retainers
7. Piston pin
8. Piston
9. Piston rings
10. Connecting rod and cap
11. Screws
12. Roller cages and needle bearings
13. Locating (thrust) washers
14. Loose needle bearings
15. Retainer clip
16. Main bearing race
17. Caged needle bearing halves
18. Seal ring
19. Ball bearing
20. Retainer ring
21. Oil pump drive gear

8

2. Remove the oil reservoir, oil pump and all oil lines as described in Chapter Eleven.

3. Remove the carburetors, both fuel pumps, the fuel filter, fuel primer valve, intake manifolds and reed blocks, and all fuel, primer and fuel bleed (recirculation) lines as described in Chapter Six.

4. Remove the remaining ignition and electrical components as an assembly. This includes the stator assembly, trigger coil, the rpm limit module, the electrical/ignition plate (containing the starter solenoid, switch boxes and the oil warning module), and the ignition coils and voltage regulators (mounted on the exhaust cover). Do not disconnect electrical components from each other unless absolutely necessary, simply remove the mounting screws, cable clamps and tie-straps. See Chapter Seven.

5. Remove the screw at the center of the throttle and spark control arm (located on the port side of the power head). Then, remove the control arm and any remaining control linkage as an assembly. Position the screw through the control arm, then install a suitable nut to keep the control arm components together.

6. Remove the 2 screws securing each thermostat cover (**Figure 50**) to the top of each cylinder bank, on the exhaust cover side of each head. Remove both thermostat covers, gaskets and thermostats. Discard both gaskets.

7. Remove the 2 screws (1, **Figure 46**) securing the poppet valve assembly to the exhaust adaptor plate (at the top of the drive shaft housing). Remove the valve assembly from the adaptor plate. Separate the inner and outer plates, then remove and discard both gaskets.

8. Reach into the adaptor plate's poppet valve cavity and retrieve the grommet and grommet carrier from the cavity. See 11 and 12, **Figure 46**. Discard the grommet.

9. Remove the 17 screws securing the exhaust cover. Tap the cover with a soft-faced (plastic or rubber) hammer to break the gasket seal. If necessary, carefully pry the cover loose, making sure

the sealing surfaces are not damaged and the cover is not distorted or warped. Remove the cover and discard the gasket.

10. Remove the 24 screws (19, **Figure 48**) securing each cylinder head (**Figure 51**) to the cylinder block. Carefully pull each head from the

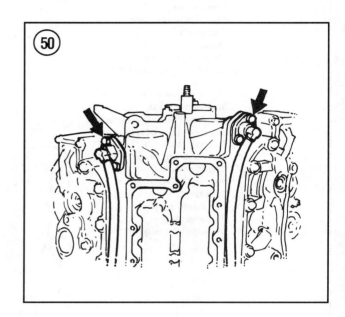

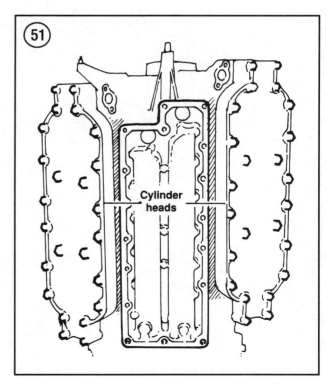

block, then remove and discard the 3 combustion chamber O-ring seals and the water jacket molded seal from each head. If necessary, tap each cylinder head with a soft-faced (rubber or plastic) hammer to break the seals. Do not damage the sealing surfaces during the removal process.

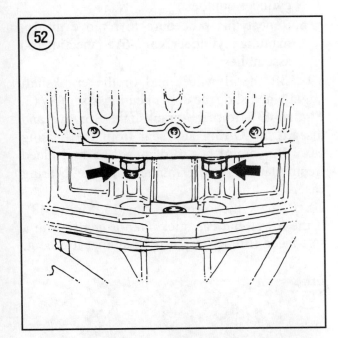

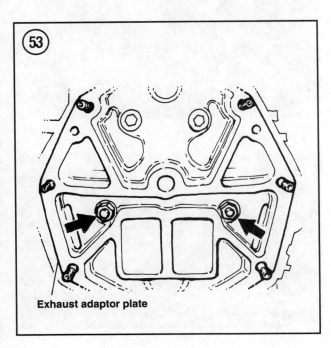

Exhaust adaptor plate

11. Remove the exhaust adaptor plate as follows:

   a. Remove 2 nuts and washers at the rear of the power head, just below the exhaust cover cavity. See **Figure 52**.

   b. Carefully lay the power head on its side and remove the 2 nuts and washers from the bottom of the adaptor plate as shown in **Figure 53**.

   c. Remove the exhaust adaptor plate. Tap the plate with a soft-faced (rubber or plastic) hammer to break it free. Tap from side-to-side in order to walk the adaptor off of the studs. If corroded, apply liberal amounts of penetrating oil to the stud shanks. Do not damage the machined mating surfaces during the removal process.

12. Remove the 4 screws (16, **Figure 48**) securing the lower end cap to the power head. Do not remove the lower end cap at this time.

CAUTION
The crankcase cover and cylinder block are a matched, align-bored unit. Do not scratch, nick or damage the machined mating surfaces. The cylinder cover is secured by many different length screws and one nut. Note the location of each screw as it is removed.

13. Remove the 13 screws and one nut (at the top, port side) securing the crankcase cover to the cylinder block. Four of the screws are in the reed box cavities of the crankcase cover.

14. Remove the screws securing the cable anchor bracket to the bottom of the crankcase cover. Remove the anchor bracket.

15. Carefully tap the cover with a soft-faced (plastic or rubber) hammer to break the crankcase seal. Then, remove the crankcase cover.

16. Locate and secure the locating dowel pins as necessary. Then, remove and discard the crankcase cover seal strips (7, **Figure 48**) from the crankcase cover.

17. Mark the corresponding cylinder number on the pistons and connecting rods with a felt-tipped

permanent marker. Mark the connecting rods and rod caps so the rod caps can be reinstalled in their original orientation.

> *NOTE*
> *Always store **all** components from each connecting rod and piston assembly together. They must be reinstalled in their original locations.*

18. Remove each connecting rod and piston assembly as follows:

   a. Manually rotate the crankshaft to position the upper (cylinder No. 1) piston at the bottom of its cylinder bore. This will expose the connecting rod screws (**Figure 54**, typical) for easy removal.

   b. Using a 12-point socket, remove the connecting rod screws from the upper (cylinder No. 1) connecting rod. Alternately loosen each screw a small amount until all tension is off of both screws.

   c. Tap the rod cap with a soft metal (brass) mallet to separate the cap from the rod.

   d. Remove the cap and rod from the crankshaft, then remove the roller bearings and cages from the crankshaft.

   e. Carefully slide the piston and rod assembly from its cylinder bore. Be ready to catch the assembly as it leaves the cylinder bore (**Figure 55**, typical).

> *CAUTION*
> *Each connecting rod and cap is a matched assembly and must not be mismatched. The cap must be installed in its original orientation.*

   f. Reinstall the rod cap to the connecting rod in its original orientation. Tighten the rod cap screws finger-tight.

   g. Store the roller bearings and cages in clean, numbered containers, corresponding to the cylinder number.

   h. Repeat this procedure to remove the remaining (cylinders No. 2-6) connecting rod assemblies.

19. Lift the flywheel end of the crankshaft slightly and slide the upper bearing assembly (3, **Figure 49**) from the crankshaft. Remove and discard the O-ring and seal from the bearing case. Be careful not to damage the fuel bleed (recirculation) fitting mounted in the bearing case.

20. Remove the lower end cap (15, **Figure 48**). If the lower end cap sticks, tap it *gently* with a soft-faced (rubber or plastic) hammer to free it.

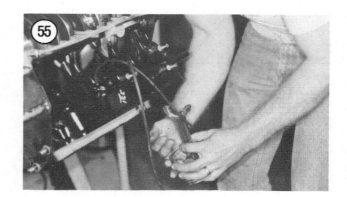

26. Using a lock ring remover (part No. 91-52952A-1) or a suitable awl, remove and discard all piston pin retainers. See **Figure 59**, typical.

27. Place the piston pin tool (part No. 91-92973A-1 or equivalent), into one end of the cylinder No. 1 piston pin bore. Support the bottom of the piston with one hand and drive the pin tool and pin from the piston.

28. Remove the piston from the connecting rod. Remove the locating (thrust) washers and the 34 loose needle bearings (**Figure 60**). Store the components in clean, numbered containers corresponding to the cylinder number.

29. Repeat the preceding 2 steps to separate the remaining (cylinders No. 2-6) pistons from their connecting rods.

30. If the crankshaft ball bearing requires replacement, proceed as follows:

   a. Remove the retainer ring using snap ring pliers (part No. 91-822778A-3) or Sears Craftsman pliers (part No. 4735).

   b. Support the ball bearing in a knife-edged bearing plate, such as part No. 91-37241.

   c. Press against the crankshaft (using the power head stand as a mandrel) until the bearing is free from the crankshaft. See **Figure 61**.

   d. Discard the bearing.

CAUTION
*There are 7 seal rings (18, **Figure 49**) that seal each crankcase chamber from the adjacent chamber(s). If the rings are damaged or broken, they must be replaced. Do not remove any seal ring unless it is going to be replaced.*

31. If the crankshaft seal ring(s) are to be replaced, remove the ring(s) using a piston ring expander (part No. 91-24697 or equivalent).

32. Refer to *Cleaning and Inspection* in this chapter before beginning reassembly procedure.

POWER HEAD CLEANING AND INSPECTION

Refer to Chapter Six and clean and inspect the reed blocks and the fuel bleed (recirculation) system. Test all check valves in the fuel bleed system for correct function as described in Chapter Six.

Review the following sections: *Sealing Surfaces, Fasteners and Torque* and *Sealants, Lubricants and Adhesives* all located at the beginning of this chapter.

The manufacturer recommends replacing all seals, O-rings, gaskets, connecting rod screws, piston pin retainers, piston rings and all bearings any time a power head is disassembled.

Perform the cleaning and inspection procedure in each of the following sections that applies to your engine *before* beginning assembly procedures.

Cylinder Block/Crankcase (All Models)

Mercury outboard cylinder blocks and crankcase covers are matched, align-bored assemblies.

(59)
REMOVING C-TYPE LOCKRINGS

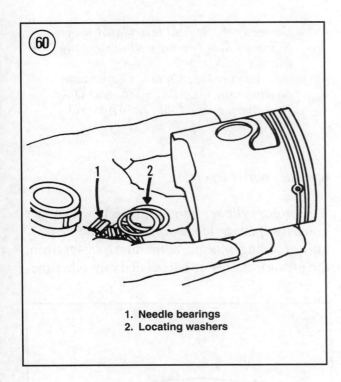

1. Needle bearings
2. Locating washers

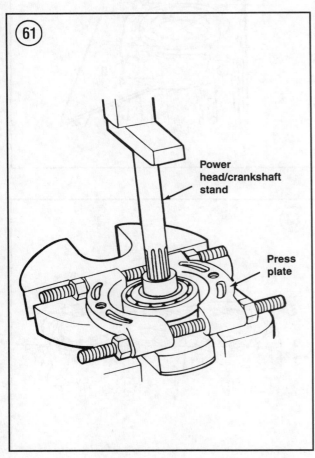

Power
head/crankshaft
stand

Press
plate

For this reason, do not attempt to assemble an engine with parts salvaged from other blocks. If the following inspection procedure indicates that the block or cover requires replacement, replace the cylinder block and crankcase cover as an assembly.

NOTE
All fuel bleed components (hoses, T-fittings, threaded fittings, check valves and check valve carriers) must be removed if it is necessary to submerge the block and/or cover in a strong cleaning solution. See Chapter Six.

1. Clean the cylinder block and crankcase cover thoroughly with clean solvent and a parts washing brush. Carefully remove all gasket and sealant material from mating surfaces.
2. Remove all carbon and varnish deposits from the combustion chambers, exhaust ports and exhaust cavities with a carbon removing solvent, such as Quicksilver Power Tune. A hardwood dowel or plastic scraper can be used to remove stubborn deposits. Do not scratch, nick or gouge the combustion chambers or exhaust ports.

NOTE
Chrome-plated aluminum bores are used on all 275 hp models. All other models use cast-iron bores.

WARNING
Use suitable hand and eye protection when using muriatic acid products. Avoid breathing the vapors. Use only in a well-ventilated area.

CAUTION
Do not allow muriatic acid to come into contact with the aluminum surfaces of the cylinder block.

3. *Chrome and cast-iron cylinder bores*—If the cylinder bore(s) has aluminum transfer from the piston(s), clean loose deposits using a stiff bristle brush. Apply a *small* quantity of diluted muriatic acid to the aluminum deposits. A bubbling action indicates that the aluminum is being dissolved.

8

Wait 1-2 minutes, then thoroughly wash the cylinder with hot water and detergent. Repeat this procedure until the aluminum deposits are removed. Lightly oil the cylinder wall to prevent rust.

4. Check the cylinder block and crankcase cover for cracks, fractures, stripped threads of other damage.

NOTE
*On 135-275 hp and 105-140 Jet models, the crankshaft seal rings will wear grooves in the cylinder block and crankcase cover. The grooves should not be a problem unless the crankshaft is replaced. If the seal rings on a new crankshaft do not perfectly align with the seal grooves in the original cylinder block/crankcase cover assembly, the crankshaft may bind. If this happens, the manufacturer recommends replacing the cylinder block. See **Power Head Assembly**, later in this chapter.*

5. Inspect gasket mating surfaces for nicks, grooves, cracks or distortion. Any of these defects will cause leakage. Check the surfaces for distortion (warpage) as described in *Sealing Surfaces* in this chapter. Distortion of more than 0.004 in. (0.1 mm) is cause for component replacement, unless otherwise specified. Smaller imperfections can be removed by lapping the component as described under *Sealing Surfaces*. **Figures 62-64** show typical directions in which to check for warpage on the cylinder head and exhaust cover/manifold surfaces.

6. Check all water, oil and fuel bleed passages in the block and cover for obstructions. Make sure all pipe plugs are installed tightly. Seal pipe plugs with Loctite 567 PST pipe sealant.

NOTE
Chrome-plated cylinder bores cannot be rebored or honed. No oversize pistons are available for chrome bore models. However, scored or damaged chrome cylinder bores (on 275 hp models) can be replated to standard dimensions.

Currently the bores are replated using Ni-com, which is more environmentally friendly than regular chrome. For details, contact U.S. Chrome Corporation of Wisconsin, P.O. Box 1536, 650 Oak Park Avenue, Fond du Lac, Wisconsin, 54935.

Cylinder bore inspection

1. *Chrome cylinder bores*—Inspect the cylinder bores for flaking (loose or missing chrome plating), grooving, scoring, aluminum transfer (from the piston), cracks or bulges and any other me-

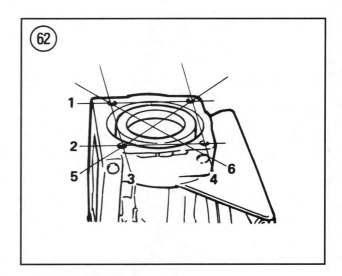

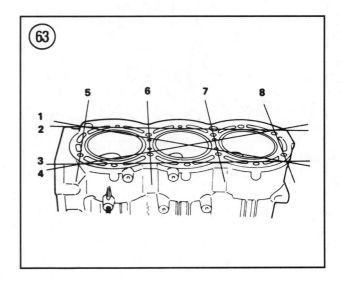

chanical damage. If damage that penetrates through the chrome plating is present, replace the cylinder block and crankcase cover or have the cylinder bores replated (275 hp).

NOTE
Chrome-plated cylinder bores have a porous appearance. See ***Figure 65***. *Do not mistake this for cylinder damage.*

2. *Cast iron cylinder bores*—Inspect the cylinder bores for scoring, scuffing, grooving, cracks or bulging and any other mechanical damage. Inspect the cylinder block (casting) and cast-iron liner for separation or delamination. There must be no gaps or voids between the aluminum casting and the liner. Remove any aluminum deposits (aluminum transfer from the pistons) as described previously in this section. If the cylinders are in a visually acceptable condition, hone the cylinders as described in *Cylinder wall honing*. If the cylinders are in an unacceptable condition, rebore the defective cylinder bore(s) or replace the cylinder block and crankcase cover as an assembly.

NOTE
It is not necessary to rebore all cylinders in a cylinder block. Rebore only the cylinders that are defective. It is acceptable to have a mix of standard and oversize

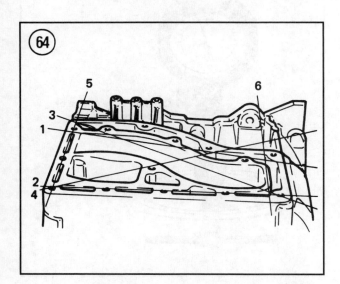

cylinders on a given power head as long as the correct piston (standard or oversize) is used to match each bore. Always check the manufacturer's parts catalog for oversize piston availability and bore sizes, before over-boring the cylinder(s).

Cylinder bore honing (cast-iron or Mercosil bores only)

The manufacturer recommends using only a rigid type cylinder hone to deglaze the bore to aid in the seating of new piston rings. If the cylinder has been bored oversize, the rigid hone will be used in 2 steps, a rough (deburring) hone to remove the machining marks and a finish (final) hone to establish the correct cross-hatch pattern in the cylinder bore.

Flex (ball type) hones and spring-loaded hones are not acceptable as they will not produce a true (straight and perfectly round) bore.

NOTE
If you are not proficient with the correct use of a rigid cylinder hone, It is recommended that cylinder bore honing be performed at a qualified machine shop or dealership. The manufacturer recommends rigid hones from the Sunnen Products Company, 7910 Manchester Ace, St. Louis, Missouri 63143. Sunnen products are often available from tool and industrial suppliers.

If the cylinders are in a visually acceptable condition, prepare the cylinder bore for new piston rings and remove any glazing, light scoring and/or scuffing by lightly honing the cylinders as follows:

1. Follow the rigid hone manufacturer's instructions when using the hone. Make sure the correct stones for your bore (cast-iron or aluminum) are installed on the hone.

2. A continuous flow of honing oil must be pumped into the bore during the honing operation. If an oil pumping system is not available,

8

enlist the aid of assistant (and oil can) to keep the cylinder walls flushed with honing oil.

3. If the hone loads (slows down) at one location in the bore, this indicates the narrowest portion of the bore. Localize the stroking in this location to remove stock until the hone maintains the same speed (and load) throughout the entire bore.

4. Frequently remove the hone from the cylinder bore and inspect the bore. Do not remove any more material than necessary.

5. Attempt to achieve a stroke rate of approximately 30 cycles per minute, adjusting the speed of the hone to achieve a cross-hatch pattern with an intersecting angle of approximately 30°. Do not exceed a cross-hatch of more than 45°.

6. After honing, the cylinder block must be thoroughly cleaned using hot water, detergent and a stiff bristle brush. Make certain all abrasive material from the honing process is removed. After washing and flushing, coat the cylinder walls with a film of outboard motor oil to prevent rust.

7. Proceed to *Cylinder bore measurements* to determine if the cylinder bores are within the manufacturer's specifications for wear, taper and out-of-round.

Cylinder bore measurements

Measure each cylinder bore as follows. Oversize bore specifications are simply the standard bore specification *plus* the oversize dimension (check parts catalog for available oversize dimensions). All standard bore specifications, maximum taper and out-of-round specifications are listed in **Table 7** and **Table 8.** The maximum wear limit on a given cylinder is equal to the standard bore plus the maximum taper specification.

Use a cylinder bore gauge (**Figure 66**), inside micrometer, or a telescoping gauge (**Figure 67**) and a regular micrometer to measure the entire area of ring travel in the cylinder bore. Three sets

of readings must be taken at the top, middle and bottom of the ring travel area (**Figure 68**).

1A. *Cast-iron*—Take the first reading at the top of the ring travel area (approximately 1/2 in. [12.7 mm] from the top of the cylinder bore) with the gauge aligned with the crankshaft centerline. Record your reading. Then, turn the gauge 90° to the crankshaft centerline and record another reading.

1B. *Chrome bores*—Take the first reading at the top of the ring travel area (approximately 1/2 in. [12.7 mm] from the top of the cylinder bore) with

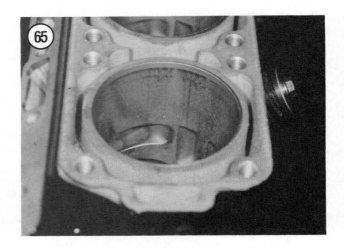

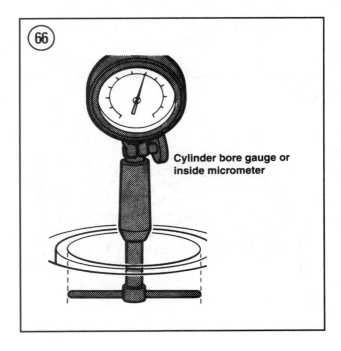

Cylinder bore gauge or inside micrometer

the gauge aligned with the crankshaft centerline. Record your reading. Then, turn the gauge 45° from the first reading and record another reading. Continue this process until 4 readings have been taken at 4 points, 45° from each other.

2. The difference between the 2 (or highest and lowest) readings is the cylinder out-of-round. The reading cannot exceed specification (**Table 7** and **Table 8**).

3. Take a second set of readings at the midpoint of the ring travel area (just above the ports) using the same alignment points described in Step 1. Record the readings. Calculate the cylinder out-of-round by determining the difference between the 2 (or highest and lowest) readings. The read-

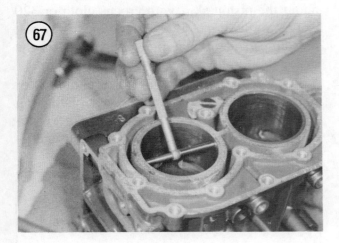

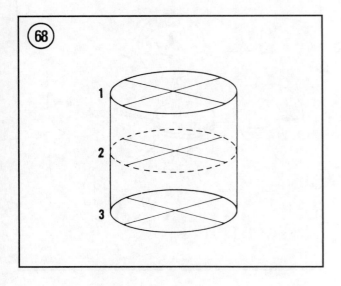

ing cannot exceed specification (**Table 7** and **Table 8**).

4. Take a third set of readings at the bottom of the ring travel area (near the bottom of the cylinder bore) using the same alignment points described in Step 1. Record the readings. Calculate the cylinder out-of-round by determining the difference between the 2 (or highest and lowest) readings. The reading cannot exceed specification (**Table 7** and **Table 8**).

5. To determine the cylinder taper, subtract the readings taken at the top of the cylinder bore (Step 1) from the readings taken at the bottom of the cylinder bore (Step 4). The difference in these readings is the cylinder taper. The reading cannot exceed specification (**Table 7** and **Table 8**).

NOTE
*If the cylinder has already been bored oversize, add the oversize dimension to the standard bore dimension **and** the maximum out-of-round specification in the next step.*

6. To determine if the cylinder is excessively worn, add the maximum taper specification (**Table 7** and **Table 8**) to the standard cylinder bore. If any of the readings taken in Steps 1-4 exceed this figure, the cylinder is excessively worn.

7. Repeat Steps 1-6 for each remaining cylinder.

8. If any cylinder exhibits excessive out-of-round, taper or is excessively worn, the cylinder(s) must be bored oversize or replated (as applicable) or the cylinder block and crankcase cover replaced as an assembly.

Piston

The piston and piston pin are serviced as an assembly. If either is damaged, they must be replaced together. Piston pins must be reinstalled in the pistons that they were removed from.

CAUTION
Do not use an automotive ring groove cleaning tool as it can damage the ring

grooves and loosen the ring locating pins.

1. Clean the piston(s), piston pin(s), thrust (locating) washers and the piston pin needle bearing assemblies thoroughly with clean solvent and a parts washing brush. Do not wire brush the piston as metal from the wire wheel may become imbedded in the piston. This can lead to preignition and detonation.

2. Remove all carbon and varnish deposits from the top of the piston, piston ring groove(s) and under the piston crown with a carbon removing solvent, such as Quicksilver Power Tune. Use a piece of hardwood or a plastic scraper to remove stubborn deposits. Do not scratch, nick or gouge any part of the piston. Do not remove any stamped or cast identification marks.

3. Clean stubborn deposits from the ring groove(s) as follows:

   a. Fashion a ring cleaning tool from the original piston ring(s). Rings are shaped differently for each ring groove. Make sure you are using the correct original ring for each ring groove.

b. Break off approximately 1/3 of the original ring. Grind a beveled edge onto the broken end of the ring.

NOTE
On keystone and semi-keystone rings, it is necessary to grind off enough of the ring taper to allow the inside edge of the broken ring to reach the inside diameter of the ring groove.

   c. Use the ground end of the ring to gently scrape the ring groove clean (**Figure 69**). Be careful to only remove the carbon. Do not gouge the metal and do not damage or loosen the piston ring locating pin(s).

4. Polish any nicks, burrs or sharp edges on and about the piston skirt with crocus cloth or 320 grit carborundum cloth. Do not remove any cast or stamped identification markings. Wash the piston thoroughly to remove all abrasive grit.

5. Inspect the piston(s) overall condition for scoring, cracks, worn or cracked piston pin bosses and any other mechanical damage. Carefully inspect the crown and the top outer diame-

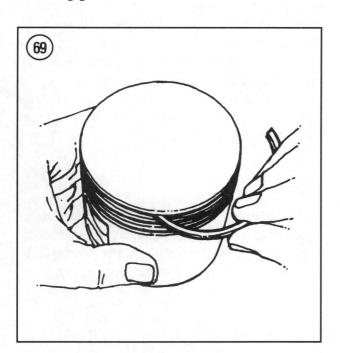

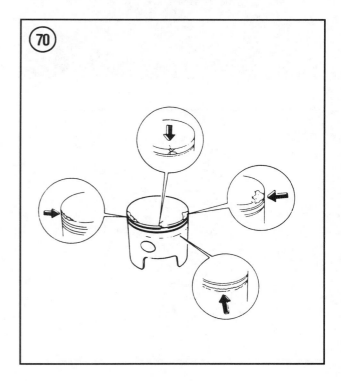

ter for burning, erosion, evidence of ring migration and mechanical damage (**Figure 70**). Replace the piston and pin as necessary.

6. Check piston ring grooves for wear, erosion, distortion and loose ring locating pins.

7. Inspect the piston pin for water etching, pitting, scoring, heat discoloration, excessive wear,

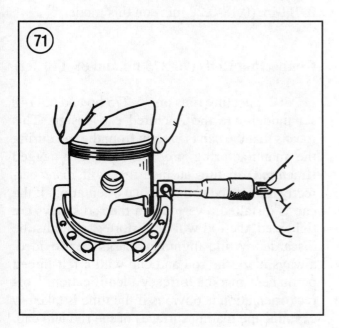

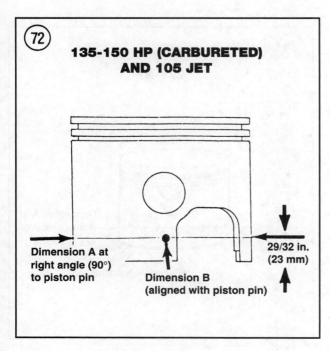

distortion and mechanical damage. Roll the pin across a machinist's surface plate to check the pin for distortion.

8. Inspect the thrust (locating) washers and needle bearings for water damage, pitting, scoring, overheating, wear and mechanical damage.

Piston measurements

Most pistons used in these engines are cam shaped. This means that the piston is built out-of-round on purpose. The piston is engineered to fit the bore perfectly when at operating temperature (and fully expanded), which makes the engine run more quietly and efficiently. The piston must be measured at the specified point(s) or the readings will be inaccurate.

Measure each piston skirt with a micrometer as described in the following text and compare the readings to the specifications listed in **Table 7** and **Table 8**.

To calculate the specified skirt dimension on oversize pistons, simply add the oversize dimension to the standard skirt diameter listed in **Table 7** and **Table 8**.

1. *75-125 hp, 65 and 80 Jet*—Using a micrometer, measure each piston's skirt diameter at a point 0.50 in. (12.7 mm) up from the bottom of the skirt *and* at a 90° angle to the piston pin bore. See **Figure 71**, typical. Record the reading. Compare the reading to the specification in **Table 7**. Each piston's dimension must be within 0.001 in. (0.025 mm) of the listed specification. If not, replace the piston(s).

2. *135-150 hp (carbureted) and 105 Jet*—Using a micrometer, refer to **Figure 72** and measure each piston's skirt diameter at a point 29/32 in. (23 mm) up from the bottom of the skirt at a 90° angle to the piston pin bore. Record the reading. The reading must be within 3.113-3.117 in. (79.07-79.17 mm). If not, replace the piston(s). Then, record a second reading aligned with the pin bore. The second reading must be within

0.008 in. (0.203 mm) of the first reading. If not, replace the piston(s).

3. *150 EFI, XR6, Magnum III, 175-200 hp and 140 Jet*—Using a micrometer, refer to **Figure 73** and measure each piston skirt diameter at a point 0.50 in. (12.7 mm) up from the bottom of the skirt *and* at a 90° angle to the piston pin bore. Record the reading. The reading must be within 3.493-3.495 in. (88.72-88.77 mm). If not, replace the piston(s). Then, take record a second reading *inline* with the pin bore. The second reading must be within 0.008 in. (0.203 mm) of the first reading. If not, replace the piston(s).

4. *225-250 hp and 200 DFI*—Using a micrometer, measure each piston's skirt diameter at a point 1.0 in. (25.4 mm) up from the bottom of the skirt at a 90° angle to the piston pin bore. See **Figure 71**, typical. Record the reading. Each reading must be 3.6205-3.6215 in. (91.961-91.686 mm) on 225-250 hp models and 3.6200-3.6210 in. (91.948-91.973 mm) on 200 DFI models. If not, replace the piston(s).

5. *275 hp*—Using a micrometer, refer to **Figure 74** and measure each piston's skirt diameter at a point 27/32 in. (21.4 mm) up from the bottom of

the skirt at a 90° angle to the piston pin bore. Record the reading. The reading must be within 3.731-3.733 in. (94.77-94.82 mm). If not, replace the piston(s). Then, record a second reading *inline* with the pin bore. The second reading must be within 0.003 in. (0.076 mm) of the first reading. If not, replace the piston(s). The piston-to-cylinder clearance specification is 0.007-0.011 in. (0.18-0.28 mm) on this model.

Connecting Rods (75-275 hp and 65-140 Jet)

All connecting rods on 75-275 hp and 65-140 Jet models are the fractured cap design. This means that the cap is broken from the rod during the manufacturing process, leaving a jagged (fractured) mating surface that will mate perfectly if installed in its original orientation. If the cap is installed reversed and the rod screws are tightened, the rod will be distorted and must be discarded. While alignment marks are provided, always mark the rod and cap with a felt-tipped permanent marker for easy identification. Correct orientation is obvious if the time is taken to examine the mating surfaces of the rod and cap.

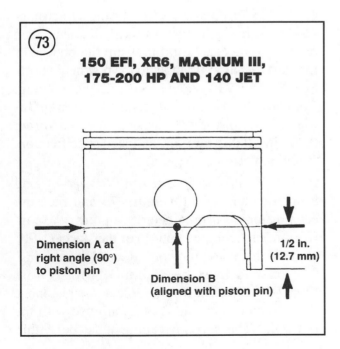

(73)

150 EFI, XR6, MAGNUM III, 175-200 HP AND 140 JET

Dimension A at right angle (90°) to piston pin

Dimension B (aligned with piston pin)

1/2 in. (12.7 mm)

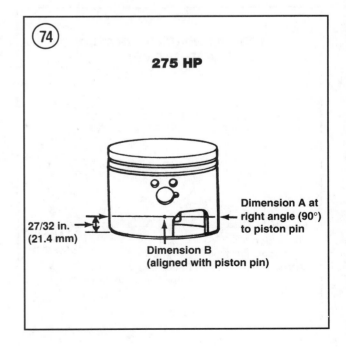

(74)

275 HP

27/32 in. (21.4 mm)

Dimension A at right angle (90°) to piston pin

Dimension B (aligned with piston pin)

The connecting rod cap must be held firmly in position as the screws are installed.

New connecting rod screws must be installed upon final assembly, but the old screws can be used for cleaning and inspection. All connecting rod screw torque specifications are listed in **Table 1**.

All models use a process referred to as *Torque and Turn* to tighten the connecting rod screws properly. In this process, oil is applied to the screw threads and under the screw head. The screws are tightened to an initial torque (**Table 1**), and the alignment of the rod cap is verified. Then, the screws are tightened to a second, higher torque (**Table 1**), and finally, both screws are turned an additional 90°.

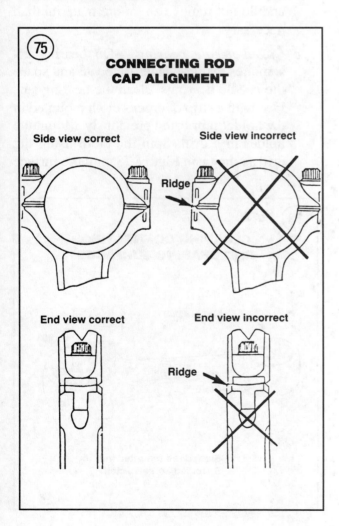

To clean and inspect the connecting rods, proceed as follows.

1. Clean the connecting rods thoroughly with clean solvent and a parts washing brush.

2. Check the connecting rod big and small end bearing surfaces for rust, water damage, pitting, spalling, chatter marks, heat discoloration and excessive or uneven wear. If the defect can be felt by dragging a pencil lead or a fingernail over it, the rod must be discarded. Stains or marks that cannot be felt can be removed by polishing the bearing surface in later steps.

3. Assemble the rod cap to the connecting rod as follows:

   a. Clamp the cylinder No. 1 connecting rod securely in a soft-jawed vise.

   b. Install the matching connecting rod cap to the connecting rod in its original orientation. Carefully observe fracture and alignment marks to ensure correct installation (**Figure 75**).

   c. Lubricate the screw threads and underside of the screw head with outboard lubricant. Then while holding the cap firmly in position, install the connecting rod screws and thread them fully into the rod.

   d. Tighten each screw to 15 in.-lb. (1.69 N•m). Run a fingernail or pencil lead over each edge of the rod to cap joint (**Figure 76**). No

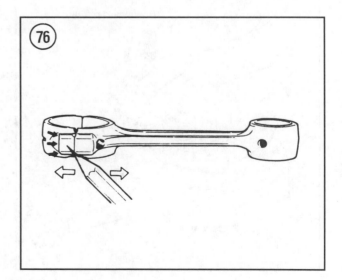

ridge should be seen or felt. Realign and retorque the cap as necessary.

e. Once the alignment has been verified, finish torquing the rod screws as specified in **Table 1**. Make a final check of alignment after the final torque is applied.

f. Repeat this procedure for each remaining rod.

4. Check the connecting rods for straightness. Place each rod/cap assembly on a machinist's surface plate and press downward on the rod beam. The rod should not wobble under pressure. While holding the rod against the plate, attempt to insert a 0.002 in. feeler gauge between the machined surfaces of the rod and the plate (**Figure 77**). If the feeler gauge can be inserted between any machined surface of the rod and the surface plate, the rod is bent and must be discarded.

CAUTION
*Use only crocus cloth **or** 320 carborundum cloth as specified in the following steps. Do not substitute any other abrasive cloth to clean the connecting rod bearing surfaces. Clean both ends of the connecting rod in the following steps.*

5. If the connecting rod has passed all inspections to this point, slight defects in either bearing surface (as noted in Step 2) may be cleaned up as follows:

a. Fabricate a holder by cutting a 1 in. (25.4 mm) notch lengthwise into a 4 in. (102 mm) long, 5/16 in. (8 mm) shank, rod or bolt with a hacksaw.

b. *Loose needle bearings*—On bearing assemblies without bearing cages (only needles), clean the bearing surface with a strip of 320 Carborundum cloth mounted in the holder fabricated previously. Mount the holder in a drill. Spin the cloth using the drill as shown in **Figure 78** until the surface is polished. Maintain a 90° angle as shown and do not remove any more material than necessary.

c. *Caged needle bearings*—On bearing assemblies that use cages to locate and space the needle bearings, clean the bearing surface with a strip of crocus cloth mounted in the holder fabricated previously. Mount the holder in a drill. Spin the cloth using the drill as shown in **Figure 78** until the surface

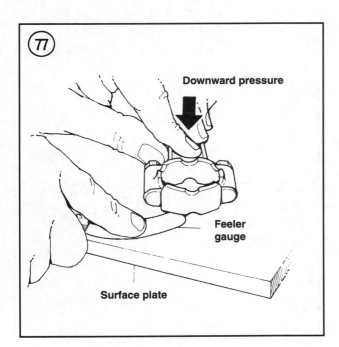

Downward pressure

Feeler gauge

Surface plate

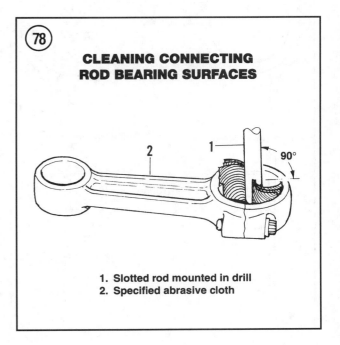

CLEANING CONNECTING ROD BEARING SURFACES

90°

1. Slotted rod mounted in drill
2. Specified abrasive cloth

is polished. Maintain a 90° angle as shown and do not remove any more material than necessary.

d. Wash the connecting rod thoroughly in clean solvent to remove any abrasive grit, then inspect the bearing surfaces. Replace any connecting rod assembly that does not clean up properly.

e. Remove and discard the rod cap screws. Wash the rod and cap again in clean solvent. Retag the rod and cap for identification. Lightly oil the bearing surfaces with outboard lubricant to prevent rust.

f. Repeat this process for each remaining connecting rod.

6. On models with specifications, measure the inside diameters of the bearing surfaces and compare to specifications (**Tables 7-9**). Replace any connecting rod assembly that is excessively worn.

Crankshaft (75-275 hp and 65-140 Jet)

Crankshaft dimensions are listed in **Table 7** and **Table 8**. Measure all surfaces where specifications are given. Replace any crankshaft that is excessively worn.

1. Thoroughly wash the crankshaft and the main and connecting rod bearing assemblies with clean solvent and a parts washing brush.

2. Inspect the drive shaft splines, flywheel taper, flywheel key groove (or splines) and flywheel nut (or bolt hole) threads for corrosion, cracks, excessive wear and mechanical damage.

3. Inspect the upper and lower seal surfaces for excessive grooving, pitting, nicks or burrs. The seal surfaces may be polished with crocus cloth as necessary. If the crankshaft is equipped with a wear sleeve on the drive shaft end, it can be replaced if damaged.

4A. *135-275 hp and 105-140 Jet*—Inspect each of the 7 crankshaft seal rings (**Figure 79**, typical) for broken segments and excessive wear. Replace any seal ring that is damaged or worn.

4B. *All other models*—Inspect the seal ring groove at each center main journal location for wear and mechanical damage.

5. Check the crankshaft bearing surfaces for rust, water damage, pitting, spalling, chatter marks, heat discoloration and excessive or uneven wear. If the defect can be felt by dragging a pencil lead or a fingernail over it, the crankshaft must be discarded. Stains or marks that cannot be felt can be removed by polishing the bearing surface as follows:

a. *Loose needle bearings*—On bearing assemblies without bearing cages (only needles), clean the bearing surface with a strip of 320 carborundum cloth. Work the cloth back and forth evenly over the entire journal

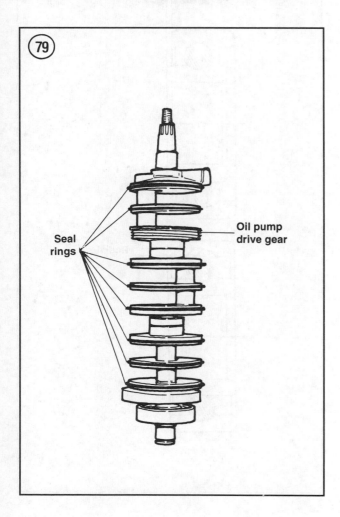

(79)

Seal rings

Oil pump drive gear

8

until the surface is polished. Do not remove any more material than necessary.

   b. *Caged needle bearings*—On bearing assemblies that use cages to locate and space the needle bearings, clean the bearing surface with a strip of crocus cloth. Work the cloth back and forth evenly over the entire journal until the surface is polished. Do not remove any more material than necessary.

6. Thoroughly clean the crankshaft again in clean solvent and recheck the crankshaft surfaces. Replace the crankshaft if it cannot be properly cleaned. If the crankshaft is in a visually acceptable condition, lightly oil the crankshaft to prevent rust.

7. *Oil injected models*—Inspect the oil pump drive gear for worn or chipped teeth, heat damage or any other damage. Replace the oil pump drive gear if it is damaged. On 135-200 hp and 105-140 Jet models, the drive gear is located as shown in **Figure 79**. On all other models, the drive gear is located on the drive shaft end of the crankshaft.

8. Inspect the bearings as follows:

   a. *Ball bearing(s)*—Rotate the bearing(s). Each bearing should rotate smoothly with no rough spots, catches or noise. There should be no discernible end or axial play (**Figure 80**) between the inner and outer races of the bearing. If the bearing shows any visible signs of wear, corrosion or deterioration, it must be replaced.

   b. *Roller/needle bearings*—Inspect the rollers and/or needles for water etching, pitting, chatter marks, heat discoloration and excessive or uneven wear. Inspect the cages for wear and mechanical damage. Replace bearings as an assembly—do not attempt to replace individual rollers or needles.

CAUTION
Some bearing cages are designed to retain the rollers, others are not. All or none of the rollers should be retained. If some rollers fall out of the cage, yet some

are retained, the bearing assembly must be replaced. If any bearing's condition is questionable, replace it.

9. Support the crankshaft assembly at upper and lower main bearing journals as shown in **Figure 81**, typical. Rotate the crankshaft assembly and check the runout at each main journal with a dial indicator. Replace the crankshaft if runout exceeds specifications (**Table 7** and **Table 8**).

10. Replace the crankshaft and all bearings based on the inspection results.

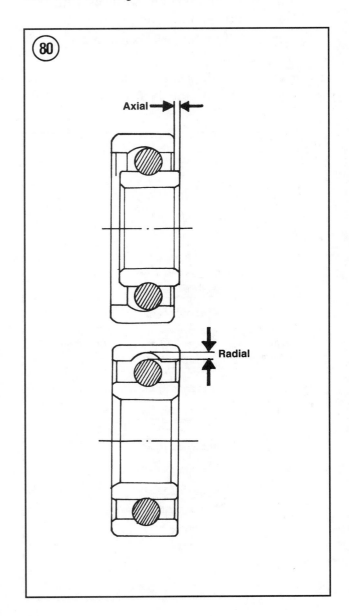

End Cap(s), Cylinder Head(s), Exhaust, Intake and Cylinder Block Cover(s)

If the engine is equipped with any or all of these components, clean and inspect each as described in the following sections.

Cylinder head(s) or cylinder block cover

1. Clean the cylinder head(s) or block cover thoroughly with clean solvent and a parts washing brush. Carefully remove all gasket and sealant material from mating surfaces.

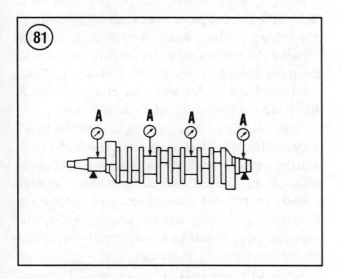

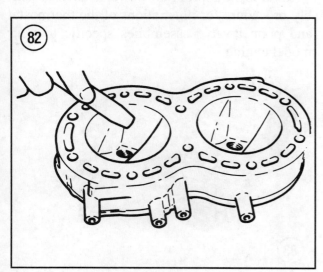

2. *Cylinder heads*—Remove all carbon and varnish deposits from the combustion chambers with a carbon removing solvent, such as Quicksilver Power Tune. A sharpened hardwood dowel or plastic scraper can be used to remove stubborn deposits (**Figure 82**, typical). Do not scratch, nick or gouge the combustion chambers.

> *NOTE*
> *The cylinder head(s) on 135-200 hp and 105-140 Jet can be lapped or resurfaced to remove warpage up to 0.010 in. (0.254 mm). Do not remove more than 0.010 in. (0.254 mm) of material. The cylinder heads on 225-275 hp and 200 DFI models may not be lapped or resurfaced.*

3. Check the cylinder head(s) and block cover for cracks, fractures, distortion or other damage. Check the cylinder head(s) for stripped or damaged threads. Refer to *Sealing surfaces* at the beginning of this chapter and check the cylinder head(s) for warpage. Maximum warpage specifications are listed in **Table 7** and **Table 8**. Minor imperfections can be removed (except 225-275 hp and 200 DFI) by lapping the cylinder head as described in *Sealing Surfaces*.

4. Inspect all gasket surfaces (or O-ring and water seal grooves) for nicks, grooves, cracks, corrosion or distortion. Replace the cylinder head or block cover if the defect is severe enough to cause leakage.

5. Check all water, oil and fuel bleed passages in the head(s) for obstructions. Make sure all pipe plugs are installed tightly. Seal all pipe plugs with Loctite 567 PST pipe sealant.

Exhaust cover/manifold/plate

1. Clean the exhaust cover, manifold (and plate) thoroughly with clean solvent and a parts washing brush. Carefully remove all gasket and sealant material from mating surfaces.

2. Remove all carbon and varnish deposits with a carbon removing solvent, such as Quicksilver Power Tune. A hardwood dowel or plastic

scraper can be used to remove stubborn deposits. Do not scratch, nick or gouge the mating surfaces.

3. Inspect the component and all gasket surfaces for nicks, grooves, cracks, corrosion or distortion. Replace the cover/manifold/plate if the defect is severe enough to cause leakage.

Intake cover(s)

1. Clean the intake cover(s) thoroughly with clean solvent and a parts washing brush. Carefully remove all gasket and sealant material from mating surfaces.

2. Inspect the cover and all gasket surfaces (or O-ring grooves) for nicks, grooves, cracks, corrosion or distortion. Replace the cover if the defect could cause leakage.

End caps

The upper end cap on 135-200 hp and 105-140 Jet models contains a caged roller bearing assembly. If the bearing needs replacement, it is recommended that you replace the upper end cap as an assembly, rather than attempt to remove the bearing from the end cap.

1. Clean the end cap(s) thoroughly with clean solvent and a parts washing brush. Carefully remove all sealant material from mating surfaces.

2. Inspect the seal bore(s) for nicks, gouges or corrosion that would cause the seal to leak around its outer diameter. Replace the end cap if the seal bore is damaged.

3. Inspect the end cap mating surface and O-ring groove for nicks, grooves, cracks, corrosion or distortion. Replace the end cap(s) if the defect could cause leakage.

4. If the end cap contains a bearing, inspect the bearing as described under *Crankshaft (75-275 hp and 65-140 Jet)* under *Cleaning and Inspection* in this chapter.

Thermostat and Poppet Valve Assembly (Models So Equipped)

The thermostat regulates the water leaving the power head. V-6 models will have one thermostat for each cylinder head. Consider replacing the thermostat during any major disassembly or repair. Correct thermostat operation is vital to engine break-in, spark plug life, smooth consistent idling and maximum performance and durability.

The poppet valve assembly (if equipped) is controlled by water pressure in the block. At higher engine speeds, the water pump pressure will be sufficient to force the poppet valve open. When the poppet valve opens, an additional exit for heated cooling water is provided. This increased flow of heated water leaving the cylinder head (in addition to the thermostat flow), allows additional cold inlet water to enter the block, lowering the operating water temperature.

The benefit of this system is that the block stays warm enough at low speeds (under thermostat control) to maintain smooth idle and keep the plugs from fouling, but cools enough at high speeds to prevent preignition and detonation. Consider installing a new poppet valve diaphragm, poppet and grommet (seat) during any major disassembly or repair.

Refer to the appropriate power head disassembly procedure for illustrations of the thermostat and poppet valve assemblies specific to your model engine.

1. Carefully clean all gasket material from the thermostat housing, poppet valve inner and outer plates and their mating surfaces. Most thermostats are sealed by a grommet around the thermostat and/or a gasket between the thermostat and the housing. **Figure 83** shows a typical grommet installation and thermostat cover for a V-6 power head.

2. Check thermostat covers and poppet valve inner and outer plates for cracks, corrosion or distortion and replace as necessary. **Figure 84** shows the poppet valve assembly for the 225-275

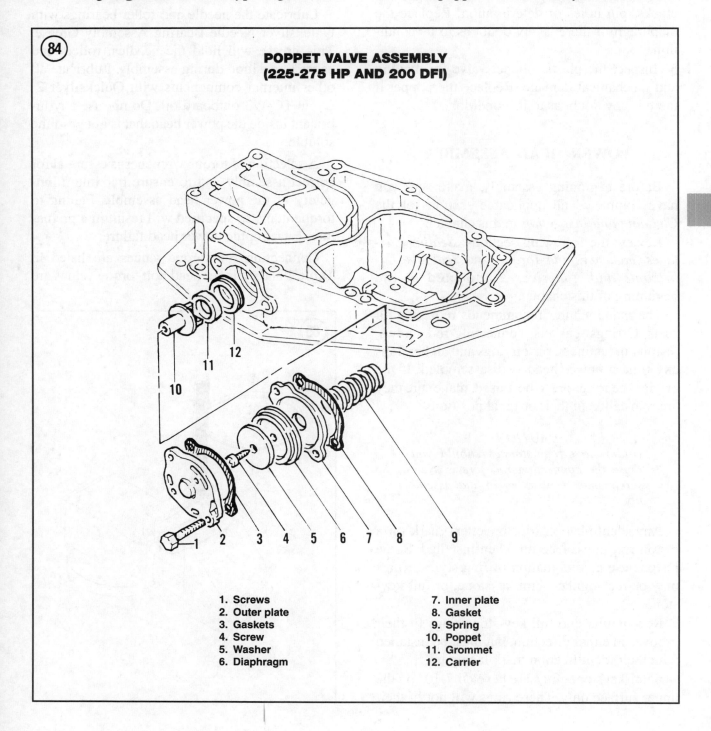

**POPPET VALVE ASSEMBLY
(225-275 HP AND 200 DFI)**

1. Screws
2. Outer plate
3. Gaskets
4. Screw
5. Washer
6. Diaphragm
7. Inner plate
8. Gasket
9. Spring
10. Poppet
11. Grommet
12. Carrier

hp and 200 DFI models. All poppet valves use a similar construction.

3. If the thermostat is to be reused, refer to *Engine Temperature* in Chapter Three for cleaning, inspection and testing procedures.

4. Inspect the poppet valve diaphragm for cracks, pin holes or deterioration. Replace the diaphragm if there is any doubt as to its condition.

5. Inspect the plastic poppet valve for melting and mechanical damage. Replace the poppet if there is any doubt as to its condition.

POWER HEAD ASSEMBLY

Before beginning assembly, make sure you have completed all applicable sections of the *Cleaning and Inspection* in this chapter.

Review the following sections: *Sealing Surfaces, Fasteners and Torque*, and *Sealants, Lubricants and Adhesives* all located at the beginning of this chapter.

The manufacturer recommends replacing all seals, O-rings, gaskets, connecting rod screws, piston pin retainers, piston rings and all bearings any time a power head is disassembled. If the original bearings are to be reused, make sure they are reinstalled in their original positions.

> *CAUTION*
> *Under no circumstances should you reuse the connecting rod screws. New screws must be installed for final assembly.*

Any identification (dot or letter) mark on a piston ring must face up when installed. Some pistons use a combination of ring styles. Rings may be rectangular, semi-keystone, or full-keystone.

Rectangular and full key-stone rings fit their grooves in either direction, but must be installed with their identification mark facing up.

Semi-keystone rings are beveled 7-10° on the upper surface only. These rings will not fit their groove correctly if installed upside down. Carefully examine the construction of the rings and look for identification marks before installation. The beveled side must face up (matching the ring groove) and is identified by the mark (dot or letter) on the upper surface.

Lubricate the needle and roller bearings with Quicksilver Needle Bearing Assembly Grease. This grease will hold the needles, rollers and cages in position during assembly. Lubricate all other internal components with Quicksilver 2-Cycle TC-W3 outboard oil. Do not use any lubricant inside the power head that is not gasoline soluble.

A selection of torque wrenches is essential for correct assembly and to ensure maximum longevity of the power head assembly. Failing to torque items so specified will result in a premature, catastrophic power head failure.

Connecting rod torque values are listed in **Table 1** and cylinder head bolt torque values are

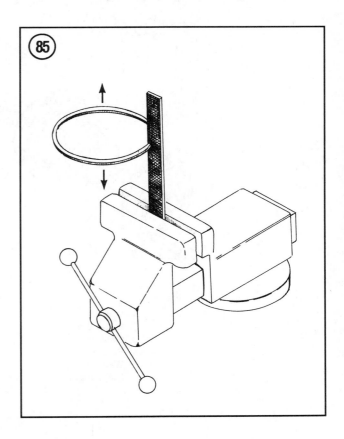

listed in **Table 2**. All other power head torque values are listed in **Table 3** and **Table 4**. Standard torque values are listed in **Table 5** and **Table 6**.

Mating surfaces must be absolutely free of gasket material, sealant residue, dirt, oil, grease or any other contaminant. Lacquer thinner, acetone, isopropyl alcohol and similar solvents are excellent oil, petroleum and wax-free solvents to use for the final preparation of mating surfaces.

All power head specifications are listed in **Table 7** and **Table 8**. All tables are located at the end of the chapter.

Piston Ring End Gap (All Models)

Before assembling the engine the piston ring end gap must be checked (and adjusted if necessary) before installing the piston rings on the pistons.

Insufficient end gap will result in the piston sticking in the cylinder bore when the engine is hot. There must be adequate end gap to allow for heat expansion.

Excessive end gap will result in an excessive amount of combustion gases leaking past the gap

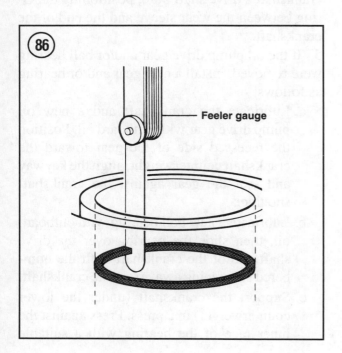

between the ring ends. This will cause a reduction in performance and can lead to excessive carbon buildup in the ring grooves and on the piston skirt.

Once the end gap has been set, the rings must be tagged for correct installation in the bore in which they were checked (and fitted). All models use 2 rings on each piston. Both rings must be checked (and fitted).

Excessive ring end gap can be caused by a worn or oversize bore. Recheck the cylinder bore as described previously in this chapter and/or check that the correct piston rings are being used for the actual bore size.

Insufficient ring end gap can be corrected by carefully filing the ring ends until the correct end gap is achieved. See **Figure 85**. Precision ring end gap grinders are available from: The Eastwood Company, Box 3014, Malvern, PA, 19355-0714.

To check the piston ring end gap, refer to **Figure 86** and proceed as follows.

1. Select a piston ring and place it inside of the cylinder No. 1 bore. Push the ring squarely into the bore using the piston. The ring must be square in the bore.

2. Measure the ring end gap with a feeler gauge as shown in **Figure 86**. If the ring gap is not within specification, repeat the measurement with the same ring in the cylinder No. 2 bore. Repeat the process as necessary until a bore is found that the ring fits correctly in *or* there are no more cylinder bores to check.

3A. *Excessive end gap*—If the measured ring end gap is excessive in every bore, the ring is defective or the cylinder is oversize. Measure the cylinder bore and recheck the piston ring application (part number). If the bore is within specification and the correct ring is being used, the ring being checked is defective and must be replaced with another new ring.

3B. *Insufficient end gap*—If the ring end gap is insufficient in every bore, carefully file the ends of the ring as shown in **Figure 85**. Keep the file

86

Feeler gauge

at a 90° angle to the ring. Do not remove any more material than necessary and do not create any burrs on the ring ends.

4. Once a ring correctly fits in a cylinder or has been fitted to a cylinder, tag the ring with the cylinder number so it can be installed on the correct piston during power head assembly.

5. Repeat this process until all piston rings (top and bottom) are fitted to a specific cylinder bore and properly tagged for identification.

Assembly (75-125 hp and 65-80 Jet)

Engines prior to serial No. 0G438000 are equipped with the AD-CDI (alternator-driven capacitor discharge ignition) system. These models are referred to as *early models* for the following procedures.

Engines with serial No. 0G438000-on are equipped with the CDM (capacitor discharge module) ignition system. These models are referred to as *late models* for the following procedures.

Because this section covers 3- and 4-cylinder models, and since the 3-cylinder models are essentially a shortened version of a 4-cylinder model, the exploded illustrations are of the 4-cylinder model. Any procedures specific to one model is identified in the text.

Refer to **Figure 87** and **Figure 88** for the following procedures.

Crankshaft and pistons

1. Check the end gap of the new piston rings as described under *Piston Ring End Gap* in this chapter. The ring end gap must be 0.010-0.018 in. (0.25-0.46 mm).

2. Assemble the lower end cap as follows:
   a. Coat the outer diameter of a new lower seal with Loctite 271 threadlocking adhesive.
   b. Press the seal into the end cap until the seal is seated in the end cap bore. The lip of the

seal must face up (toward the flywheel) when the end cap is installed.
   c. Grease a new O-ring with Quicksilver 2-4-C Multi-Lube. Install the O-ring into the end cap's groove.

> *CAUTION*
> *The wear sleeve is made of very thin material and is easy to crush or distort during installation.*

3. *Wear sleeve removed*—Install a new wear sleeve on the lower end of the crankshaft as follows:
   a. Coat the wear sleeve contact area of the crankshaft with Loctite 271 threadlocking adhesive.
   b. Pilot the wear sleeve over the lower end of the crankshaft.
   c. Using a suitable block of wood and a hammer, drive the wear sleeve onto the crankshaft until the sleeve seats on the crankshaft shoulder. Make sure the sleeve is driven straight and not crushed.

4. Grease a new O-ring with Quicksilver 2-4-C Multi-Lube. Carefully install the O-ring into the crankshaft's drive shaft bore, positioning the O-ring between the wear sleeve and the end of the crankshaft.

5. If the oil pump drive gear and/or ball bearing were removed, install a new gear and/or bearing as follows:
   a. Lubricate the crankshaft and a new oil pump drive gear with outboard oil. Position the recessed side of the gear toward the crankshaft counterweight, align the keyway and seat the gear against the crankshaft shoulder.
   b. Lubricate a new ball bearing with outboard oil, then slide the bearing over the drive shaft end of the crankshaft with the numbered side facing away from the crankshaft.
   c. Support the crankshaft (under the lower counterweight) in a press. Press against the inner race of the bearing with a suitable

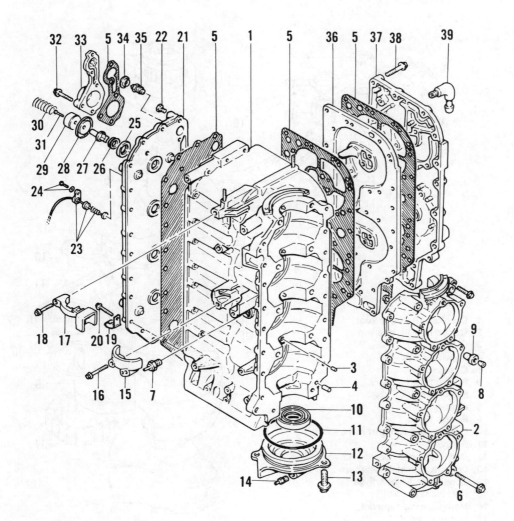

CYLINDER BLOCK
(75-125 HP AND 65-80 JET [4-CYLINDER SHOWN])

1. Cylinder block
2. Crankcase cover
3. Bearing locating pin
4. Dowel pin
5. Gaskets
6. Crankcase cover screws
7. Accelerator pump discharge nozzle (4-cylinder)
8. Check valve
9. Check valve carrier
10. Crankshaft lower seal
11. O-ring
12. Lower end cap
13. Screw
14. Check valve
15. Lower starter bracket
16. Screw
17. Upper starter bracket
18. Screw
19. Clamp
20. Screw
21. Cylinder block cover
22. Brass pipe plug
23. Engine temperature switch
24. Screw and washer
25. Carrier
26. Grommet
27. Poppet
28. Diaphragm
29. Cup
30. Spring
31. Screw
32. Screw
33. Thermostat cover
34. Grommet
35. Thermostat
36. Exhaust manifold
37. Exhaust cover
38. Screw
39. Water discharge (tell-tale) fitting

8

CRANKSHAFT ASSEMBLY
(75-125 HP AND 65-80 JET [4-CYLINDER SHOWN])

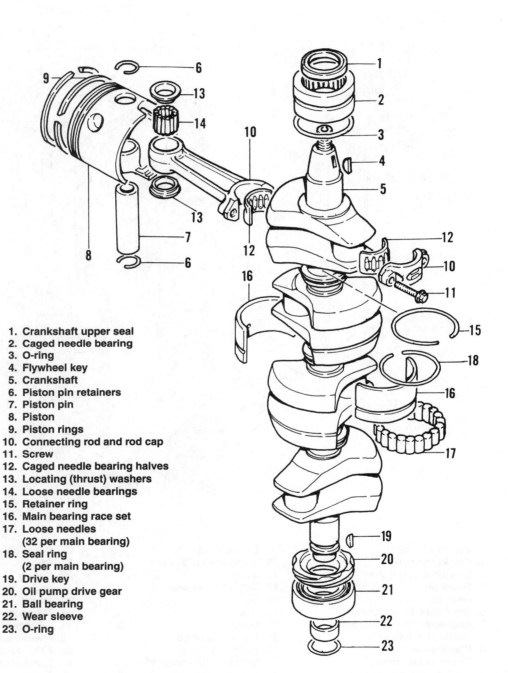

1. Crankshaft upper seal
2. Caged needle bearing
3. O-ring
4. Flywheel key
5. Crankshaft
6. Piston pin retainers
7. Piston pin
8. Piston
9. Piston rings
10. Connecting rod and rod cap
11. Screw
12. Caged needle bearing halves
13. Locating (thrust) washers
14. Loose needle bearings
15. Retainer ring
16. Main bearing race set
17. Loose needles
    (32 per main bearing)
18. Seal ring
    (2 per main bearing)
19. Drive key
20. Oil pump drive gear
21. Ball bearing
22. Wear sleeve
23. O-ring

mandrel until the bearing is seated on the crankshaft.

6. Mount the crankshaft vertically on a power head (crankshaft) stand (part No. 91-812549 or equivalent). The power head stand must be securely clamped in a vise.

CAUTION
If the original bearings are reused, they must be installed in their original locations. Each crankshaft seal ring groove requires 2 seal rings to be installed. The open ends of seal rings must be 180° apart from each other.

7. Assemble the 2 (3-cylinder models) or 3 (4-cylinder models) center main bearings as follows:

  a. Install 2 new seal rings into the upper center main bearing journal's seal groove. Do not expand the rings any further than necessary to install them. Position the open ends of each seal ring 180° apart from each other.

  b. Apply a thick coat of needle bearing assembly grease to the journal's twin bearing surfaces. Then install the 16 loose rollers to each bearing surface (32 rollers for each bearing assembly).

  c. Position the outer race halves over the bearing rollers and seal rings. The retaining ring groove must be positioned up (toward the flywheel).

  d. Carefully align the fracture lines, then install the retainer ring (15, **Figure 88**). Posi-

tion the retainer ring to cover as much of both fracture lines as possible.

  e. Repeat this procedure as necessary to assemble the lower center main bearing on 3-cylinder models or the center *and* lower center main bearings on 4-cylinder models.

8. Coat the outer diameter of a new upper seal with Loctite 271 threadlocking adhesive. Press the seal into the upper main bearing with a suitable mandrel. The lip of the seal must face down (away from the flywheel).

9. Coat a new O-ring with Quicksilver 2-4-C Multi-Lube and install the O-ring into the upper main bearing groove.

10. Lubricate the upper main bearing rollers with outboard oil, then install the bearing onto the crankshaft.

11. Begin assembly of the connecting rods to the pistons by greasing the sleeve portion of the piston pin installation tool (part No. 91-76160A-2) with needle bearing assembly grease.

12. Position the No. 1 cylinder connecting rod in its original orientation, as marked during disassembly.

13. Hold the lower locating (thrust) washer under the connecting rod small end, then insert the greased sleeve into the small end bore.

14. Lubricate the 29 needles with needle bearing assembly grease and insert them into the small end, around the sleeve as shown in **Figure 89**.

15. Position the upper locating (thrust) washer on top of the needles. Carefully slide the No. 1 cylinder piston over the rod (with the stamped UP marking facing up) and align the piston pin bores. Then, insert the main body of piston pin tool (part No. 91-76160A-2) into the piston pin bore and through the connecting rod, pushing the sleeve out the other side of the piston pin bore. Remove the sleeve.

16. Lubricate the piston pin with outboard oil and pilot it into the open end of the piston pin bore. Support the piston (and tool) with one hand and drive the piston pin into the piston with a

8

soft-faced (rubber or plastic) mallet. Allow the pin tool to be pushed out as the piston pin is driven in.

17. Remove the piston pin tool from the bottom of the piston, then insert it into the top of the piston pin bore and gently tap it until the pin is centered in the pin bore.

18. Make sure that no needles or locating washers were displaced, then secure the piston pin with 2 new piston pin retainers (6, **Figure 88**) using a lock ring installation tool (part No. 91-77109A-2) as follows:

   a. Position a new retainer ring into the stepped, open end of the tool's sleeve (**Figure 90**).

   b. Insert the drive handle into the opposite end of the sleeve.

   c. Pilot the stepped end of the sleeve into either end of the cylinder No. 1 piston pin bore.

   d. While holding the sleeve to the pin bore, press the drive handle quickly and firmly to install the ring.

   e. Remove the handle and sleeve. Make sure the retainer is completely seated in its groove in the piston pin bore.

   f. Install the second retainer in the opposite end of the piston pin bore in the same manner.

19. Repeat Steps 11-18 for the remaining pistons and connecting rods.

CAUTION
Install the piston rings onto the pistons that match the cylinder bore for which the rings were fitted.

20. Install the 2 semi-keystone piston rings onto each piston using a ring expander (part No. 91-24697 or equivalent). Install the bottom ring first, then the top ring, expanding each ring just enough to slip over the piston. The identification mark on both rings (dot or letter [**Figure 91**, typical]) must face up.

21. Make sure that each ring can be rotated freely in its groove, then position the end gap of each piston ring to straddle the ring locating pin in its groove.

Power head assembly

1. Lubricate the piston rings, pistons and cylinder bores with outboard oil. Verify that the end gap of each piston ring is still straddling the locating pin in its groove.

NOTE
A ring compressor is not required as the cylinder bores have a tapered entrance.

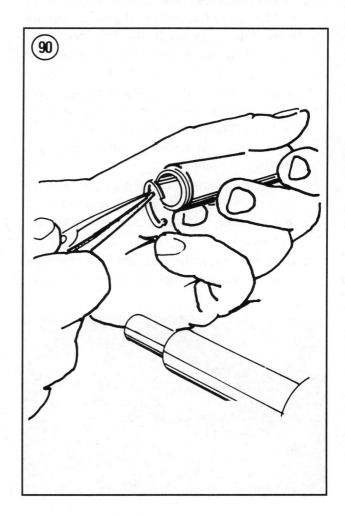

2. Install each piston into its appropriate cylinder bore. Make sure the stamped UP marks are facing the flywheel end of the cylinder block and that the connecting rods are aligned with the crankshaft throws. Rock each piston slightly to help it enter its cylinder bore, making sure the piston rings do not rotate or catch and break while entering the bore. Seat each piston at the bottom of its bore.

3. Insert a thin screwdriver through the exhaust port of each cylinder and depress each piston ring. If the ring does not spring back when the screwdriver is removed, it was probably broken during piston installation. Replace any broken or damaged rings.

4. Verify that the upper and center main bearing locating pins (3, **Figure 87**) are installed in the cylinder block. Then, position the cylinder block so that the block-to-crankcase cover mating surface is pointing upward. Position all connecting rods toward one side on the cylinder block.

5. Slowly lower the crankshaft assembly into the block. Rotate the crankshaft main bearing assemblies as necessary to align the hole in the bearing races with the bearing locating pins (3, **Figure 87**).

CAUTION
Do not strike the end of the crankshaft directly or the wear sleeve will be destroyed.

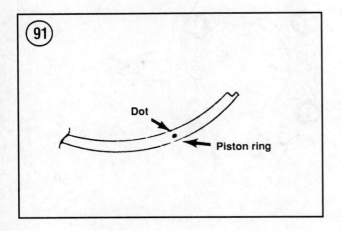

6. Insert the power head (crankshaft) stand into the lower end of the crankshaft. Then, carefully tap the stand (with a soft hammer) to seat the ball bearing in its bore.

7. Install the connecting rods to the crankshaft journals as follows:

  a. Grease the crankpin journals with a thick coat of needle bearing assembly grease. Install the bearing cages and needle bearing to the journals. If the original bearings are reused, they must be installed in their original position.

  b. Pull the No. 1 cylinder rod and piston assembly up to the No. 1 crankpin journal and bearings. Rotate the crankshaft as necessary to allow mating of the rod and journal.

  c. Install the matching connecting rod cap in its original orientation. Carefully observe fracture and alignment marks to ensure correct installation (**Figure 75**, typical).

  d. Lubricate the screw threads and underside of the screw heads of *new* connecting rod screws with outboard lubricant. Then, while holding the cap firmly in position, install the connecting rod screws and thread them fully into the rod.

  e. Tighten each screw to 15 in.-lb. (1.69 N•m). Run a fingernail or pencil lead over each edge of the rod-to-cap joint (**Figure 76**). No ridge should be seen or felt. Realign and retorque the cap as necessary.

  f. Once the alignment is verified, apply a second torque of 30 ft.-lb. (40.7 N•m) in 2 progressive steps. Then, apply the final torque by turning each rod screw an additional 90°. Make a final check of the alignment after the final torque has been applied.

  g. Repeat this procedure to install the remaining connecting rods to their respective crankshaft journals.

8. Using an oil and wax free solvent, such as acetone or lacquer thinner, clean the cylinder block and crankcase cover mating surfaces.

8

9. Install the dowel pin (4, **Figure 87**) into the cylinder block or crankcase cover (if not already installed).

10. Install the lower end cap over the crankshaft. Coat the mating surfaces with Quicksilver Perfect Seal. Align the screw holes in the cylinder block and seat the end cap to the block. Install 2 screws finger-tight to hold the end cap in position.

CAUTION
Loctite Master Gasket Sealant is the only sealant recommended to seal the crankcase cover-to-cylinder block mating surfaces. The sealant comes in a kit that includes a special primer. Follow the instructions included in the kit for preparing the surfaces and applying the sealant. The sealant bead must be applied to the inner (crankshaft side) of all crankcase cover screw holes.

11. Following the instructions supplied with the sealer, apply a continuous bead of Loctite Master Gasket Sealant to the mating surface of the cylinder block. Run the sealant bead along the inside of all bolt holes as shown in **Figure 92**, typical. Make sure the bead is continuous.

12. Install the crankcase cover into position on the cylinder block. Seat the cover to the block with hand pressure.

13. Insert the power head (crankshaft stand) into the lower end of the crankshaft. Tap against the stand with a soft hammer to make sure the ball bearing is seated in its bore.

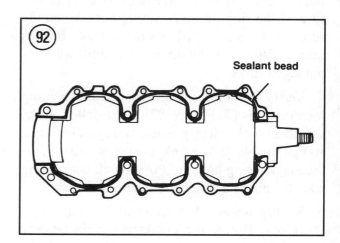

Sealant bead

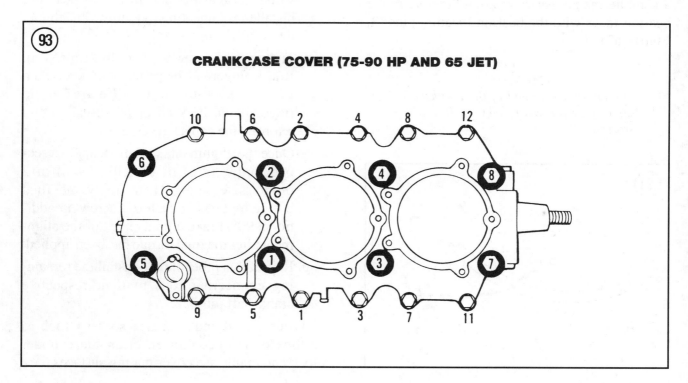

CRANKCASE COVER (75-90 HP AND 65 JET)

14A. *3-cylinder models*—Coat the threads of the 8 large (main bearing) and 12 smaller (outer) crankcase cover screws with Loctite 242 threadlocking adhesive, then install the cover screws. Tighten the large (main bearing) cover screws to 25 ft.-lb. (33.9 N•m) in a minimum of 2 progressive steps, following the pattern shown in **Figure 93**. Then, tighten the smaller (outer) cover screws to 216 in.-lb. (24.4 N•m) in a minimum of 2 progressive steps, following the pattern shown in **Figure 94**.

14B. *4-cylinder models*—Coat the threads of the 10 large (main bearing) and 16 smaller (outer) crankcase cover screws with Loctite 242 threadlocking adhesive, then install the cover screws. Tighten the large (main bearing) cover screws to 25 ft.-lb. (33.9 N•m) in a minimum of 2 progressive steps, following the pattern shown in **Figure 94**. Then, tighten the smaller (outer) cover screws to 216 in.-lb. (24.4 N•m) in a minimum of 2 progressive steps, following the pattern shown in **Figure 94**.

15. Rotate the crankshaft several revolutions to check for binding or unusual noise. If binding or noise is noted, the power head must be disassembled and the cause of the defect located and corrected before proceeding.

16. Remove the end cap screws installed previously. Coat the threads of the 3 end cap screws with Loctite 242 threadlocking adhesive. Install and evenly tighten the screws to 216 in.-lb. (24.4 N•m).

17. Install the cylinder block cover using a new gasket. Do not use any sealer on this gasket. Apply Loctite 242 threadlocking adhesive to the threads of the cover screws. Install the 14 (3-cylinder) or 18 (4-cylinder) screws. Tighten the screws finger-tight at this time.

18. Assemble the thermostat housing as follows:

   a. Install a new grommet around the thermostat and install it into the cylinder block cover with the sensing pellet facing the power head.

   b. Install a new grommet (26, **Figure 87**) into the poppet valve cavity in the cylinder block cover.

   c. Install the poppet valve assembly as shown in **Figure 87**.

   d. Install the cover using a new gasket and secure with 4 screws. Coat the screw threads with Quicksilver Perfect Seal. Tighten the screws finger-tight at this time.

8

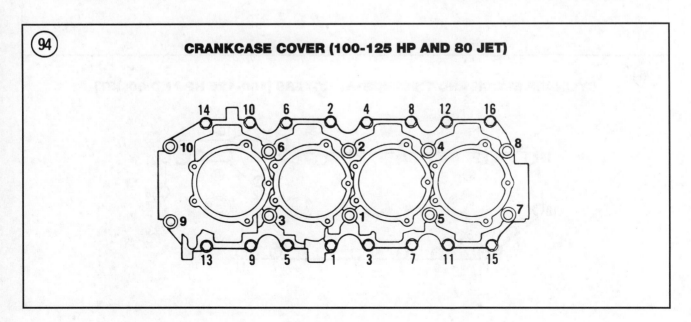

(94) CRANKCASE COVER (100-125 HP AND 80 JET)

19. Tighten the cylinder block cover and thermostat cover screws to 216 in.-lb. (24.4 N·m) in 3 progressive steps, following the pattern shown in **Figure 95** (3-cylinder) or **Figure 96** (4-cylinder).

20. Install the engine temperature switch into the cylinder block cover. Secure the switch with a screw and washer. Tighten the screw securely.

21. Assemble the exhaust manifold and cover with 2 new gaskets. Use no sealer on these gaskets. Sandwich the exhaust plate between the gaskets, then position the cover over the outer gasket (and manifold). Position the assembly on the power head and secure it with 24 (3-cylinder) or 35 (4-cylinder) screws. Coat the screw threads with Loctite 242 threadlocking adhesive and tighten them to 216 in.-lb. (24.4 N·m) in 3 progressive steps, following the pattern shown in **Figure 97** (3-cylinder) or **Figure 98** (4-cylinder).

22. Position the spark and throttle control arm assembly to its power head mounting boss. Install and tighten the arm's center screw securely.

23A. *Early models*—Install the ignition and electrical components as an assembly. This includes the stator assembly, trigger coil, and the

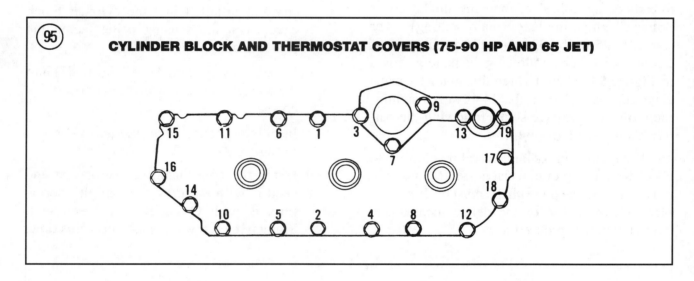

95 CYLINDER BLOCK AND THERMOSTAT COVERS (75-90 HP AND 65 JET)

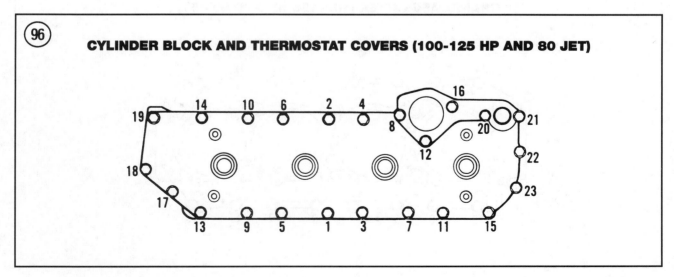

96 CYLINDER BLOCK AND THERMOSTAT COVERS (100-125 HP AND 80 JET)

electrical/ignition plate (containing the switch box, ignition coils, voltage regulator, starter solenoid and the trim/tilt solenoids [or relays]). If equipped with an rpm limit module, install it at this time. Secure all cables and harnesses with the original clamps and/or new tie-straps. See Chapter Seven.

23B. *Late models*—Install the ignition and electrical components as an assembly. This includes the stator assembly, trigger coil, trim/tilt relays and the electrical/ignition plate (containing the CDM modules, voltage regulator and starter solenoid). If equipped with an rpm limit module, install it at this time. Secure all cables and harnesses with the original clamps and/or new tie-straps. See Chapter Seven.

24. Install the internal fuel bleed (recirculation) valves and carriers (8 and 9, **Figure 87**) into the

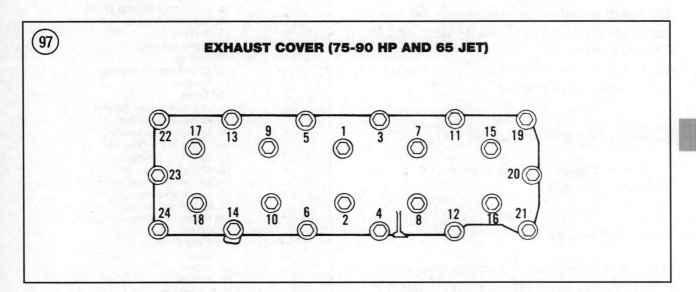

(97) EXHAUST COVER (75-90 HP AND 65 JET)

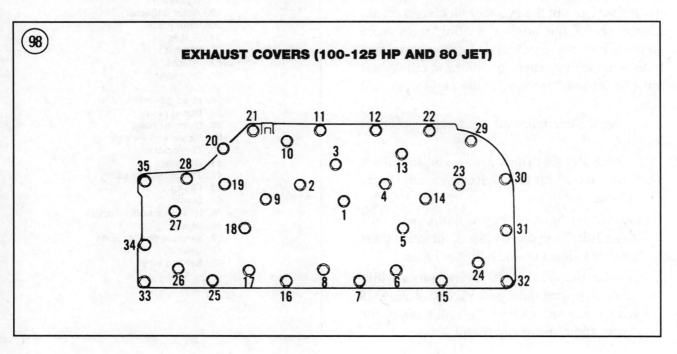

(98) EXHAUST COVERS (100-125 HP AND 80 JET)

crankcase cover openings for cylinders No. 2, 3 (and 4). See Chapter Six for fuel bleed system information.

25. Install the intake manifold(s) and reed blocks, carburetors, fuel pump, fuel filter, fuel primer valve and all fuel, primer and fuel bleed (recirculation) lines as described in Chapter Six.

26. *4-cylinder models*—Install the accelerator pump system and adjust the pump clearance as described in Chapter Six.

27. Install the oil pump, oil reservoir, oil warning module and all oil lines as described in Chapter Eleven.

28. Install the flywheel and electric starter as described in Chapter Seven.

Assembly (135-200 hp and 105-140 Jet)

Refer to **Figures 99** and **Figure 100** for the following procedures.

Crankshaft replacement

If a new crankshaft is installed into a used cylinder block, inspect the crankshaft seal ring mating surfaces in the cylinder block and crankcase cover. If the original sealing rings wore grooves into the block and cover mating surfaces, the sealing rings of the new crankshaft must fit into the grooves or the crankshaft will bind.

To check for crankshaft binding, proceed as follows:

  a. Check the seal rings grooves in the block and cover for burrs. Remove any burrs found.

  b. Lubricate the crankshaft seal rings with outboard oil. Temporarily install the crankshaft and end caps into the cylinder block.

  c. Rotate the crankshaft several turns while checking for binding or excessive drag. If either is noted, recheck the seal grooves for burrs and remove any found.

**CYLINDER BLOCK
(135-200 HP AND 105-140 JET)**

1. Cylinder block
2. Crankcase cover
3. Bearing locating pin
4. Dowel pin
5. Crankcase sealing strips
6. Crankshaft upper seal
7. Screw
8. Upper end cap
9. O-rings
10. Caged needle bearing
11. Bracket
12. Screw
13. Crankcase cover screw
14. Screw and washer
15. Upper starter bracket
16. Lower starter bracket
17. Screw and washer
18. Ground strap
19. Crankshaft lower seals
20. Lower end cap
21. Screw and washer
22. Fitting (water discharge)
23. Screw
24. Outer plate
25. Gaskets
26. Screw
27. Washer
28. Diaphragm
29. Water deflector
30. Inner plate
31. Spring
32. Washer
33. Poppet
34. Grommet
35. Carrier
36. Head gasket
37. Dowel pins
38. Cylinder head
39. Screw and washer
40. Thermostat
41. Grommet
42. Thermostat housing
43. Fitting
44. Screw
45. Hose (water discharge)
46. Screw
47. Exhaust divider plate
48. Gasket
49. Sealing strip

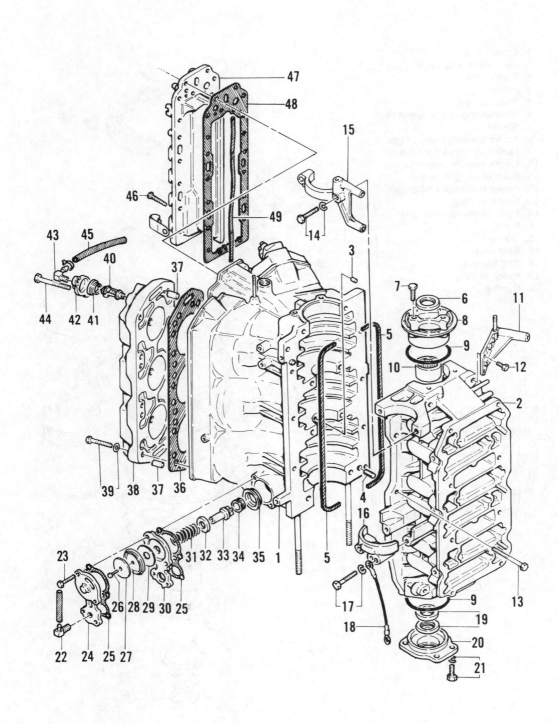

8

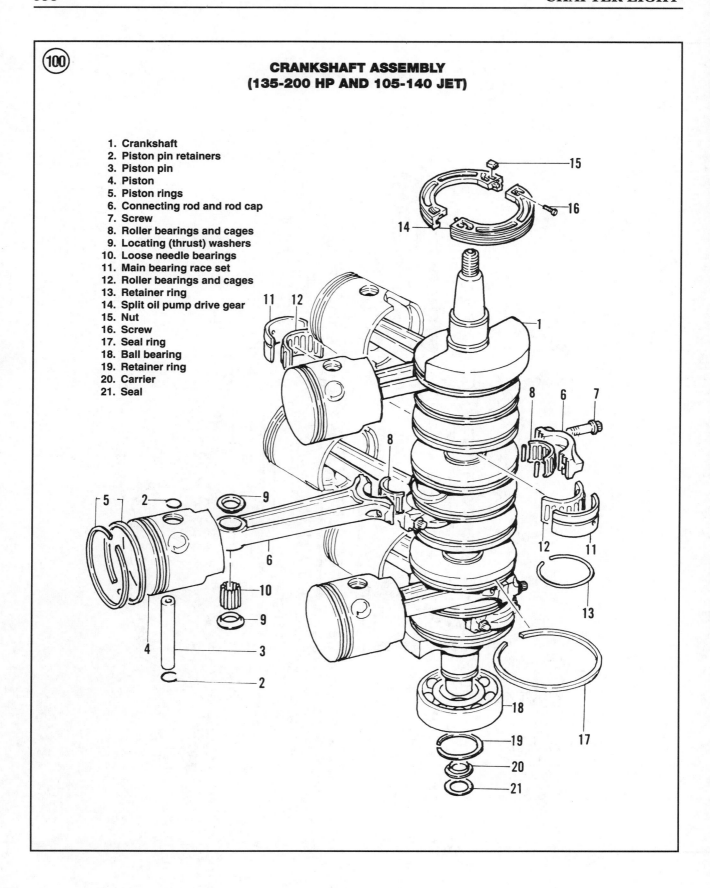

100

CRANKSHAFT ASSEMBLY
(135-200 HP AND 105-140 JET)

1. Crankshaft
2. Piston pin retainers
3. Piston pin
4. Piston
5. Piston rings
6. Connecting rod and rod cap
7. Screw
8. Roller bearings and cages
9. Locating (thrust) washers
10. Loose needle bearings
11. Main bearing race set
12. Roller bearings and cages
13. Retainer ring
14. Split oil pump drive gear
15. Nut
16. Screw
17. Seal ring
18. Ball bearing
19. Retainer ring
20. Carrier
21. Seal

d. If excessive drag or binding is still evident, the cylinder block and crankcase cover must be replaced as an assembly.

Crankshaft and pistons

Each cylinder and piston is identified (numbered) as shown in **Figure 101**. The pistons must be installed with their stamped markings positioned as shown in **Figure 101**.

1. Check the end gap of the new piston rings as described under *Piston Ring End Gap* in this chapter. The ring end gap must be 0.018-0.025 in. (0.46-0.64 mm).

2. To assemble the lower end cap, refer to **Figure 102** and proceed as follows:

 a. Coat the outer diameter of 2 new lower seals with Loctite 271 threadlocking adhesive.

 b. Press the seals into the end cap (one at a time, on top of each other) using driver head (part No. 91-55919 or equivalent), until each seal is seated in the end cap bore. The lip of both seals must face down (toward the drive shaft) when the end cap is installed.

 c. Grease a new O-ring with Quicksilver 2-4-C Multi-Lube. Install the O-ring into the end cap's groove.

3. To assemble the upper end cap, refer to **Figure 103** and proceed as follows:

 a. Coat the outer diameter of a new upper seal with Loctite 271 threadlocking adhesive.

 b. Press the seal into the end cap with a suitable mandrel. The lip of the seal must face down (toward the drive shaft) and must not cover the fuel bleed hole as shown in **Figure 103**.

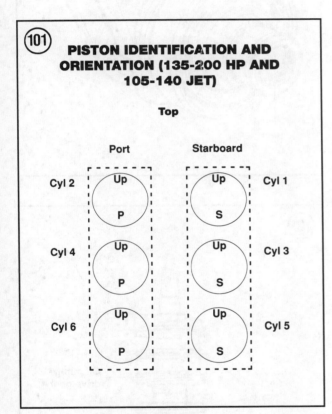

(101)

PISTON IDENTIFICATION AND ORIENTATION (135-200 HP AND 105-140 JET)

Top

Port		Starboard
Cyl 2	Up / P	Up / S	Cyl 1
Cyl 4	Up / P	Up / S	Cyl 3
Cyl 6	Up / P	Up / S	Cyl 5

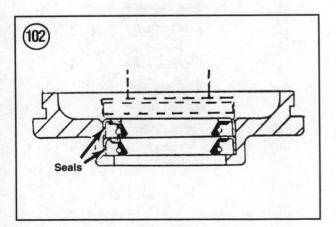

(102)

Seals

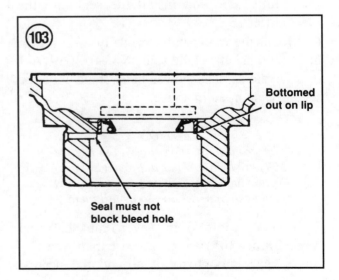

(103)

Bottomed out on lip

Seal must not block bleed hole

8

4. If the ball bearing was removed, install a bearing as follows:

  a. Lubricate a new ball bearing with outboard oil, then slide the bearing over the drive shaft end of the crankshaft with the numbered side facing away from the crankshaft.

  b. Support the crankshaft (under the lower counterweight) in a press. Press against the inner race of the bearing with a suitable mandrel until the bearing is seated on the crankshaft.

  c. Install the retainer ring (19, **Figure 100**) with retainer ring pliers (part No. 91-922778A-3). Make sure the retainer ring is fully seated in the crankshaft groove.

5. Install the seal carrier and seal (**Figure 104**, typical) to the lower end of the crankshaft as follows:

  a. Coat the carrier contact area of the crankshaft with Loctite 271 threadlocking adhesive.

  b. Pilot the carrier into the drive shaft bore at the lower end of the crankshaft.

  c. Using a suitable block of wood and a hammer, drive the carrier onto the crankshaft until the carrier is seated. Make sure the carrier is driven straight.

  d. Grease a new seal with Quicksilver 2-4-C Multi-Lube and install the seal into the carrier.

6. Mount the crankshaft vertically on a power head (crankshaft) stand (part No. 91-30591A-1 or equivalent). The power head stand must be securely clamped in a vise.

> *CAUTION*
> *The crankshaft seal rings (17, **Figure 100**) are brittle. Wear approved eye protection and do not expand the ring(s) any further than necessary to install them.*

7. If one (or more) of the seven crankshaft seal rings (**Figure 105**) was removed, expand the new ring(s) just enough to fit around the nearest

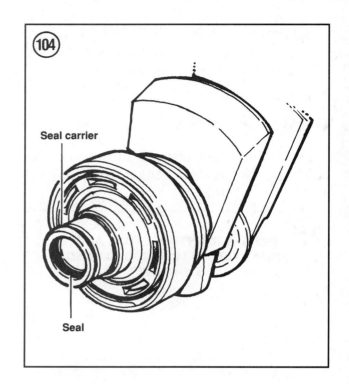

Seal carrier

Seal

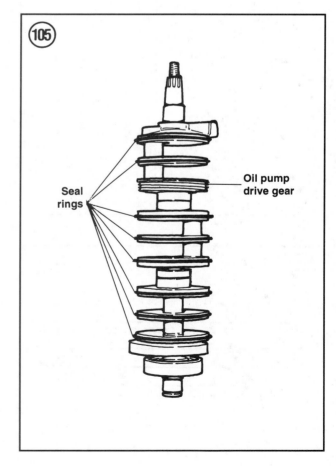

Seal rings

Oil pump drive gear

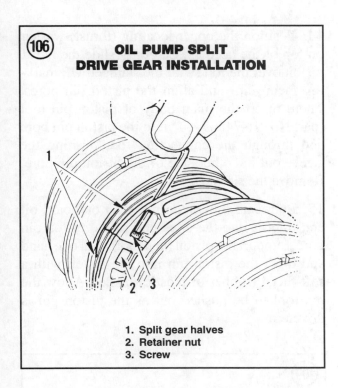

106 OIL PUMP SPLIT DRIVE GEAR INSTALLATION

1. Split gear halves
2. Retainer nut
3. Screw

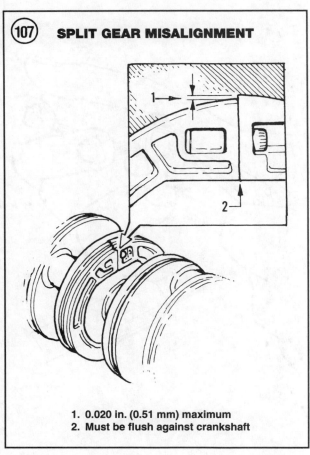

107 SPLIT GEAR MISALIGNMENT

1. 0.020 in. (0.51 mm) maximum
2. Must be flush against crankshaft

crankpin journal. Then, install the ring(s) into the crankshaft groove(s) using piston ring expander part No. 91-24697 (or equivalent).

8. If the oil pump drive gear was removed, install a new drive gear as follows:

    a. Position the oil pump drive gear halves (14, **Figure 100**) around the crankshaft (**Figure 105**) with the screw and nut access holes facing the upper center main bearing (down). Make sure the alignment pins align, then seat the halves to each other.

    b. Coat the threads of the 2 screws with Loctite RC680 retaining compound. Position a retainer nut as shown in **Figure 106**, then install and tighten the screw finger-tight. Install the second screw and nut in the same manner.

    c. Evenly and carefully tighten both screws to 8 in.-lb. (0.9 N·m). Make sure the gears halves pull down tightly and evenly.

    d. Check the gear tooth mismatch at both mating points. See **Figure 107**. The mismatch cannot exceed 0.020 in. (0.51 mm) at either mating point (1, **Figure 107**) or the gear will fail prematurely.

    e. If the misalignment is excessive, remove the gear and repeat the installation procedure. Make sure the gear seats against the crankshaft at the point shown at 2, **Figure 107**. Do not proceed until the misalignment is within specification.

CAUTION
If the original bearings are reused, they must be installed in their original locations.

9. Assemble the 2 center main bearings as follows:

    a. Apply a thick coat of needle bearing assembly grease to the upper center main bearing journal. Then, install the roller bearing halves to the bearing surface.

    b. Position the outer race halves over the bearing rollers and seal rings. The retaining ring

8

groove must be positioned up (toward the flywheel).

c. Carefully align the fractured parting lines, then install the retainer ring (13, **Figure 100**). Position the retainer ring to cover as much of both fracture lines as possible.

d. Repeat this procedure to assemble the lower center main bearing.

10. Begin assembly of the connecting rods to the pistons by greasing the sleeve portion of piston pin installation tool (part No. 91-74607A-1) with needle bearing assembly grease.

11. Position the No. 1 cylinder connecting rod with its part number (in the I-beam) facing up.

12. Hold the lower locating (thrust) washer under the connecting rod small end, then insert the greased sleeve into the small end bore.

13. Lubricate the 29 needles with needle bearing assembly grease and insert them into the small end, around the sleeve as shown in **Figure 108**.

> *NOTE*
> *All pistons are marked (stamped) UP to signify the top of the piston. However, the cylinder No. 1, 3 and 5 pistons are also marked with an S, signifying the starboard cylinder bank of the engine. The cylinder No. 2, 4 and 6 pistons are also marked with a P, signifying the port cylinder bank of the engine. Each piston must be installed in its correct orientation. See Figure 101.*

14. Position the upper locating (thrust) washer on top of the needles. Carefully slide the No. 1 piston over the rod (with the stamped UP marking facing up) and align the piston pin bores. Then, insert the main body of piston pin tool (part No. 91-74607A-1) into the piston pin bore and through the connecting rod, pushing the sleeve out the other side of the piston pin bore. Remove the sleeve.

15. Lubricate the piston pin with outboard oil and pilot it into the open end of the piston pin bore. Support the piston (and tool) with one hand and drive the piston pin into the piston with a soft-faced (rubber or plastic) mallet. Allow the pin tool to be pushed out as the piston pin is driven in.

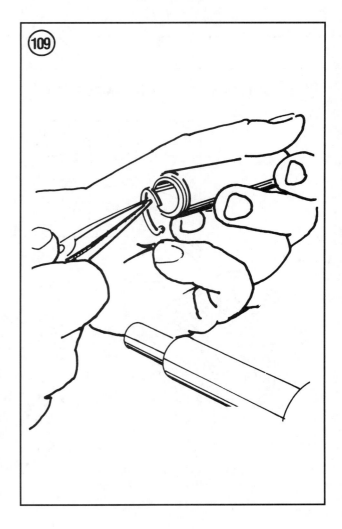

16. Remove the piston pin tool from the bottom of the piston, then insert it into the top of the piston pin bore and gently tap it until the pin is centered in the pin bore.

17. Make sure no needles or locating washers were displaced, then secure the piston pin with 2 new piston pin retainers (2, **Figure 100**) using a lock ring installation tool (part No. 91-77109A-2) as follows:

a. Position a new retainer ring into the stepped, open end of the tool's sleeve (**Figure 109**).

b. Insert the drive handle into the opposite end of the sleeve.

c. Pilot the stepped end of the sleeve into either end of the cylinder No. 1 piston pin bore.

d. While holding the sleeve to the pin bore, press the drive handle quickly and firmly to install the ring.

e. Remove the handle and sleeve. Make sure the retainer is completely seated in its groove in the piston pin bore.

f. Install the second retainer in the opposite end of the piston pin bore in the same manner.

18. Repeat Steps 10-17 for the remaining pistons and connecting rods.

CAUTION
Install the piston rings onto the pistons that match the cylinder bore for which the rings were fitted.

19A. *135-150 hp (carbureted) and 105 Jet—* Refer to **Figure 110** and install the piston rings onto each piston using ring expander (part No. 91-24697 or equivalent). Install the bottom (rectangular) ring first, then the top (full keystone) ring, expanding each ring just enough to slip over the piston. The identification mark on both rings (dot or letter) must face up.

8

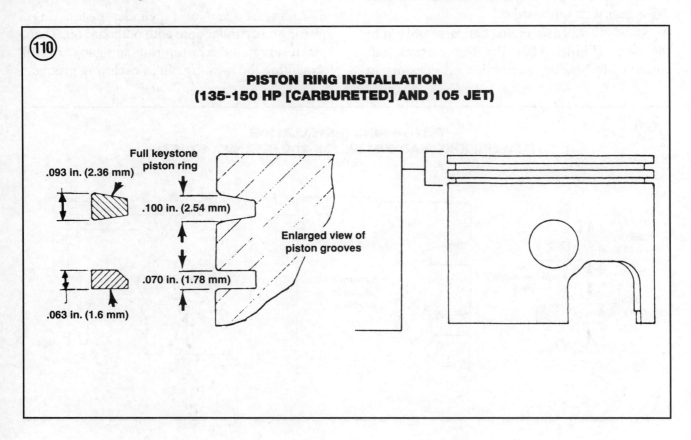

110

**PISTON RING INSTALLATION
(135-150 HP [CARBURETED] AND 105 JET)**

.093 in. (2.36 mm)

Full keystone piston ring

.100 in. (2.54 mm)

Enlarged view of piston grooves

.070 in. (1.78 mm)

.063 in. (1.6 mm)

19B. *150 EFI, XR6, Magnum III, 175-200 hp and 140 Jet*—Refer to **Figure 111** and install the 2 semi-keystone rings onto each piston using a ring expander (part No. 91-24697 or equivalent). Install the bottom ring first, then the top ring, expanding each ring just enough to slip over the piston. The identification mark on both rings (dot or letter) must face up.

20. Make sure that each ring can be rotated freely in its groove, then position the end gap of each piston ring to straddle the ring locating pin in its groove.

Power head assembly

1. Verify that the 2 center main bearing locating pins (3, **Figure 99**) are installed in the cylinder block. Then, position the cylinder block so that the block-to-crankcase cover mating surface is pointing upward.

2. Lubricate all 7 seal rings and the oil pump drive gear with outboard oil.

3. Slowly lower the crankshaft assembly into the block (**Figure 112**). Rotate the crankshaft center main bearing assemblies as necessary to align the hole in the bearing races with the bearing locating pins (3, **Figure 99**). Position each seal ring (17, **Figure 100**) so the ring end gap is pointing straight up.

> *CAUTION*
> *Do not strike the end of the crankshaft directly or the seal carrier may be damaged.*

4. Insert the power head (crankshaft) stand into the lower end of the crankshaft. Carefully tap the stand (with a soft hammer) to seat the ball bearing in its bore.

5. Install the upper (**Figure 113**) and lower end caps over their respective end of the crankshaft. Coat the mating surfaces with Quicksilver Perfect Seal. Align the screw holes of each end cap with the cylinder block and seat the caps against the block. Install 2 screws finger-tight in each end cap to hold it in position.

6. Lubricate the No. 1 cylinder piston rings, piston and cylinder bore with outboard oil. Then, make sure that the piston ring end gaps are still straddling the locating pin in each ring groove.

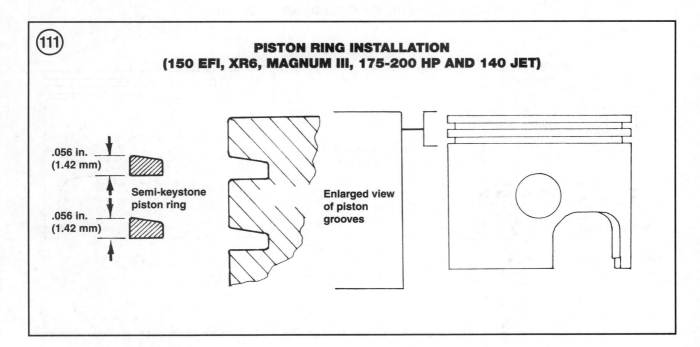

(111) PISTON RING INSTALLATION (150 EFI, XR6, MAGNUM III, 175-200 HP AND 140 JET)

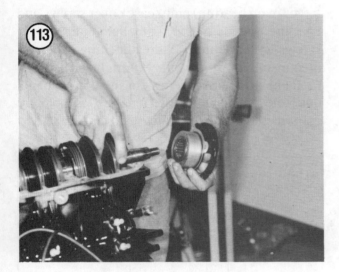

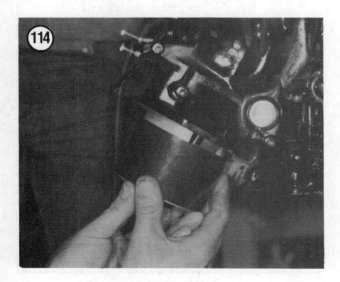

7. Install the cylinder No.1 piston and connecting rod assembly as follows:

   a. Lubricate the cylinder No. 1 piston, piston rings and cylinder bore.

   b. Verify that the end gap of each piston ring is positioned over the ring locating pin in each ring groove.

   c. Using the appropriate tapered sleeve ring compressor (part No. 91-65494 [3.125 in. bore] or part No. 91-818773 [3.501 in. bore]), install the No. 1 piston in to the cylinder bore (**Figure 114**) with the UP mark facing the flywheel and the connecting rod big end aligned with the crankshaft journal. Be careful to keep the rod's big end from damaging the cylinder bore and the crankshaft journal.

   d. Insert a small screwdriver through the exhaust port and depress each piston ring. If the ring does not spring back when the screwdriver is removed, it was probably broken during piston installation. Replace any broken or damaged rings.

8. Install the No. 1 cylinder connecting rod to the crankshaft journal as follows:

   a. Grease the crankpin journals with a thick coat of needle bearing assembly grease. Install the bearing cages and needle bearing to the journals. If the original bearings are reused, they must be installed in their original position.

   b. Pull the No. 1 cylinder rod and piston assembly up to the No. 1 crankpin journal and bearings. Rotate the crankshaft as necessary to allow mating of the rod and journal.

   c. Install the connecting rod cap in its original orientation. Carefully observe fracture and alignment marks to ensure correct installation (**Figure 75**, typical).

   d. Lubricate the screw threads and underside of the screw heads of the *new* connecting rod screws with outboard lubricant. Then, while holding the cap firmly in position, install the connecting rod screws and thread them fully into the rod.

e. Tighten each screw to 15 in.-lb. (1.69 N•m). Run a fingernail or pencil lead over each edge of the rod-to-cap joint (**Figure 76**). No ridge should be seen or felt. Realign and retorque the cap as necessary.

f. Once the alignment is verified, apply a second torque of 30 ft.-lb. (40.7 N•m) in 2 progressive steps. Then apply the final torque by turning each rod screw an additional 90°. Make a final check of alignment after the final torque has been applied.

g. Rotate the crankshaft several revolutions to check for binding or unusual noise. If noted, remove the piston and connecting rod just installed and correct the defect before proceeding.

9. Repeat Steps 6-8 for the remaining piston and connecting rod assemblies. Refer to **Figure 101** for piston location and orientation.

10. Using an oil and wax free solvent, such as acetone or lacquer thinner, clean the cylinder block and crankcase cover mating surfaces.

11. Install the 2 dowel pins (4, **Figure 99**) into the cylinder block or crankcase cover (if not already installed).

CAUTION
Loctite Master Gasket Sealant is the only sealant recommended to seal the crankcase cover-to-cylinder block mating surfaces. The sealant comes in a kit that includes a special primer. Follow the instructions included in the kit for preparing the surfaces and applying the sealant. The sealant bead must be applied to the inner (crankshaft side) of all crankcase cover screw holes.

12. Following the instructions supplied with the sealer, apply a continuous bead of Loctite Master Gasket Sealant to the mating surface of the cylinder block. Run the sealant bead along the inside of all bolt holes and to within 1/16 in. (1.6

mm) of the seal rings and center main bearings. Make sure the bead is continuous.

13. Install new gasket strips (5, **Figure 99**) into the grooves in the crankcase cover. Trim the ends of the strips flush with the end cap bores. Then, install the crankcase cover into position on the cylinder block. Seat the cover to the block as far as possible with hand pressure. The seal rings will prevent seating the cover completely.

14. Insert the power head (crankshaft stand) into the lower end of the crankshaft. Tap against the stand with a soft hammer to make sure the ball bearing is seated in its bore.

15. Oil the threads and under the heads of the 8 large (main bearing) crankcase cover screws and coat the threads of the 6 smaller (outer) cover screws with Loctite 242 threadlocking adhesive, then install the screws. Evenly tighten the large (main bearing) cover screws in small increments until the crankshaft seal rings are completely compressed and the crankcase cover is seated to

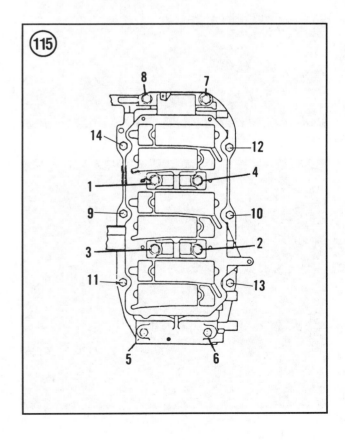

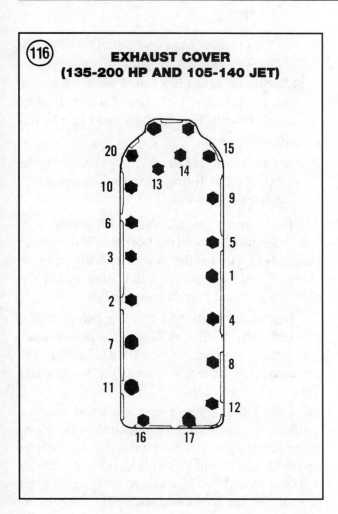

(116) **EXHAUST COVER (135-200 HP AND 105-140 JET)**

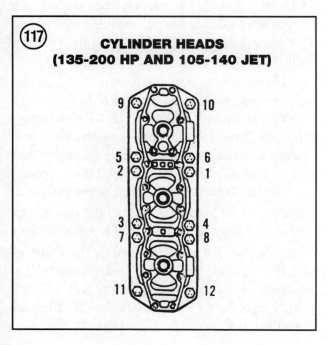

(117) **CYLINDER HEADS (135-200 HP AND 105-140 JET)**

the cylinder block. Then, tighten the 6 outer screws finger-tight.

16. Torque the 8 large (main bearing) screws to 38 ft.-lb. (51.5 N·m) in 3 progressive steps, following the pattern (1-8) shown in **Figure 115**. Then, torque the 6 smaller (outer) screws to 15 ft.-lb. (20.3 N·m) in 3 progressive steps, following the pattern (9-14) shown in **Figure 115**.

17. Rotate the crankshaft several revolutions to check for binding or unusual noise. If binding or noise is noted, the power head must be disassembled and the cause of the defect located and corrected before proceeding.

18. Remove the end cap screws installed previously. Coat the threads of the 3 lower and 4 upper end cap screws with Loctite 242 threadlocking adhesive. Install and evenly tighten the upper screws to 150 in.-lb. (17.0 N·m) and the lower screws to 80 in.-lb. (9.0 N·m).

19. Install a new strip seal (49, **Figure 99**) into the slot in the exhaust cavity.

20. Install the exhaust divider plate using a new gasket. Coat the threads of the 20 screws with Loctite 271 threadlocking adhesive. Install and tighten the screws to 200 in.-lb. (22.6 N·m) in 3 progressive steps, following the pattern shown in **Figure 116**.

21. Install both cylinder heads to the power head using new gaskets. Position the thermostat pockets up (toward the flywheel). Coat the threads and under the screw head of each head's 12 bolts with outboard oil. Install and tighten the bolts as follows:

a. Tighten all 12 screws snugly.

b. Torque the bolts to 30 ft.-lb. in 3 progressive steps following the pattern shown in **Figure 117**.

c. Turn each head bolt an additional 90°, following the pattern shown in **Figure 117**.

d. Do not retorque the head bolts after operation.

22A. *Carbureted models*—Install the engine temperature switch (2-wires) into the port cylinder head, just below the No. 2 spark plug hole.

Secure the switch with the plate and screw. Secure the switch's ground lead under the screw. Coat the screw threads with Loctite 242 threadlocking adhesive. Tighten the screw to 200 in.-lb. (22.6 N•m).

22B. *EFI models*—Install the engine coolant temperature sensor (4-wires) into the port cylinder head, just below the No. 2 spark plug hole. Secure the sensor with the plate and screw. Secure the sensor's ground lead under the screw. Coat the screw threads with Loctite 242 threadlocking adhesive. Tighten the screw to 200 in.-lb. (22.6 N•m).

23. If equipped with an engine temperature gauge, install the temperature sending unit (1-wire) into the starboard cylinder head, just below the No. 1 spark plug hole. Secure the sending unit with the plate and screw. Coat the screw threads with Loctite 242 threadlocking adhesive. Tighten the screw to 200 in.-lb. (22.6 N•m).

24. Install a new grommet around each thermostat. Install a thermostat into each cylinder head with the sensing pellet facing the head. Install a thermostat cover over each thermostat and against each cylinder head. The water fittings on each thermostat cover must face towards each other. Coat the threads of the thermostat cover screws with Quicksilver Perfect Seal. Install and evenly tighten the screws to 200 in.-lb. (22.6 N•m).

25. Connect the water discharge hose(s) to the thermostat cover fittings. Secure each connection with a new tie-strap.

26. Assemble and install the poppet valve as follows:

a. Install a new grommet (34, **Figure 99**) into the poppet valve cavity in the cylinder block.

b. Assemble the poppet valve components as shown in **Figure 99**. Tighten the screw (26, **Figure 99**) to 25 in.-lb. (3.0 N•m).

c. Sandwich a new gasket between the outer and inner plates, then position the assembly to the cylinder head using another new gasket.

d. Secure the assembly with 4 screws. Coat the screw threads with Quicksilver Perfect Seal. Evenly tighten the screws to 150 in.-lb. (17.0 N•m).

e. Connect the water discharge hose to the poppet valve fitting. Secure the connection with a new tie-strap.

27. Position the throttle and spark control arm to its mounting boss on the port side of the power head. Make sure the thrust washer is between the assembly and the power head, then install the center screw and tighten it securely.

28. Install the shift and throttle cable anchor bracket to the port lower side of the power head. Coat the 3 mounting screws with Loctite 271 threadlocking adhesive. Install the screws and tighten them securely.

29. Install the ignition and electrical components as an assembly. This includes the stator assembly, trigger coil, both switch boxes, starter solenoid, idle stabilizer module, oil and overheat warning module and the electrical/ignition plate (containing the ignition coils, voltage regulators and trim solenoids [or relays]). If equipped with an rpm limit module, install it at this time. Secure all cables and harnesses with the original clamps and/or new tie-straps. See Chapter Seven.

30. On models equipped with an idle speed stabilizing shift switch, such as XR6, Magnum III, 175 hp carbureted, 150 and 175 XRI and Magnum [EFI] models and any engines with this system added as an accessory, connect the shift switch leads to the engine harness bullet connector and the ring terminal to the engine ground.

31. *200 hp EFI models*—Install the detonation sensor and module as described in Chapter Six.

32A. *Carbureted models*—Install the carburetors, fuel pump, fuel filter, fuel primer valve, intake manifold and reed blocks, and all fuel, primer and fuel bleed (recirculation) lines as described in Chapter Six.

32B. *EFI models*—Install the induction manifold assembly (and ECM [electronic control module]), mechanical fuel pump, vapor separator assembly, water separating fuel filter, water warning module, intake manifold and reed blocks, and all fuel and fuel bleed (recirculation) lines as described in Chapter Six.

33. Install the oil reservoir, oil pump, oil warning module and all oil lines as described in Chapter Eleven.

34. Install the flywheel and electric starter as described in Chapter Seven.

Assembly (225-250 hp and 200 DFI)

Refer to **Figure 118** and **Figure 119** for the following procedures. Due to the many fuel bleed systems used in the 1994-1997 model line, replacement power heads are compatible with all recirculation systems. Make sure all unused ports on 1994-1996 models are plugged with the appropriate pipe plugs and Loctite PST pipe sealant. Any open ports will cause a massive air leak into that cylinder, leading to power head failure.

The poppet (water pressure relief) valve is mounted on the exhaust adaptor plate, which is not removed with the power head. Be sure to reassemble the poppet valve when so directed.

Three different lower end cap configurations are used on these engines. Refer to **Figure 120** for illustrations of each.

A. *First design*—Contains 2 seals: 1 large (crankshaft) and 1 small (drive shaft). The manufacturer recommends upgrading from this end cap to the third design.

B. *Second design*—Contains 3 seals: 1 large (crankshaft) and 2 small (drive shaft). The manufacturer recommends upgrading from this end cap to the third design.

C. *Third design*—Contains 2 large crankshaft seals only. A stainless steel wear sleeve has been added to the lower end of the crankshaft. The sleeve also holds an internal, replaceable O-ring

that seals the drive shaft splines. This configuration is standard on 1996 and newer model power heads. An upgrade kit (part No. 1171-9787A-5) contains the necessary components to retrofit older engines.

Crankshaft replacement concerns

If a new crankshaft is installed into a used cylinder block, inspect the crankshaft seal ring mating surfaces in the cylinder block and crankcase cover. If the original sealing rings wore grooves into the block and cover mating surfaces, the sealing rings of the new crankshaft must fit into the grooves or the crankshaft will bind.

To check for crankshaft binding, proceed as follows:

a. Check the seal ring's grooves in the block and cover for burrs. Remove any burrs found.

b. Lubricate the crankshaft seal rings with outboard oil. Temporarily install the crankshaft and lower end cap into the cylinder block.

c. Rotate the crankshaft several turns while checking for binding or excessive drag. If either is noted, recheck the seal grooves for burrs and remove any found.

d. If excessive drag or binding is still evident, the cylinder block and crankcase cover must be replaced as an assembly.

Crankshaft and pistons

Each cylinder and piston is identified (numbered) as shown in **Figure 121**. The pistons must be installed with their stamped markings positioned as shown in **Figure 121**.

1. Check the end gap of the new piston rings as described under *Piston Ring End Gap* in this chapter. The ring end gap must be 0.010-0.018 in. (0.25-0.46 mm).

CYLINDER BLOCK (225-250 HP AND 200 DFI)

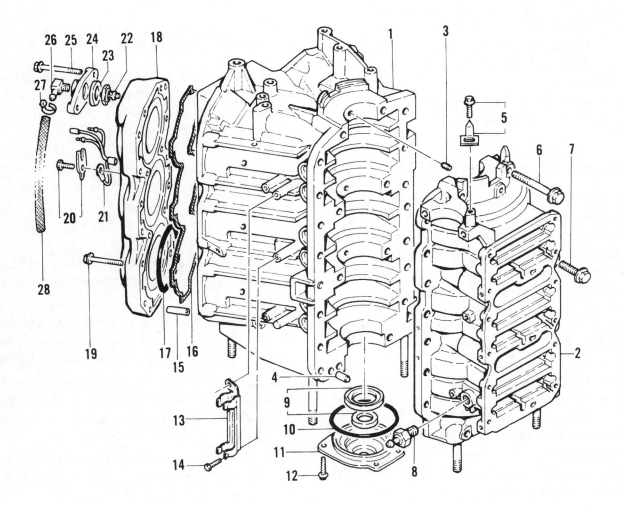

1. Cylinder block
2. Crankcase cover
3. Bearing locating pin
4. Dowel pin
5. Adjustable timing
   pointer and screw
6. Main bearing (large) screw
7. Outer (small) screw
8. Pulse fitting (remote oil tank)
9. Crankshaft lower seals
10. O-ring

11. Lower end cap
12. Screw
13. Main harness
    connector bracket
14. Screw
15. Dowel pin
16. Water jacket seal
17. O-ring
18. Cylinder head
19. Cylinder head screw
20. Retainer plate and screw

21. ECT sensor
22. Thermostat
23. Gasket
24. Thermostat housing
25. Thermostat housing/cylinder
    head screw
26. Water discharge fitting
27. Tie-strap
28. Water discharge hose

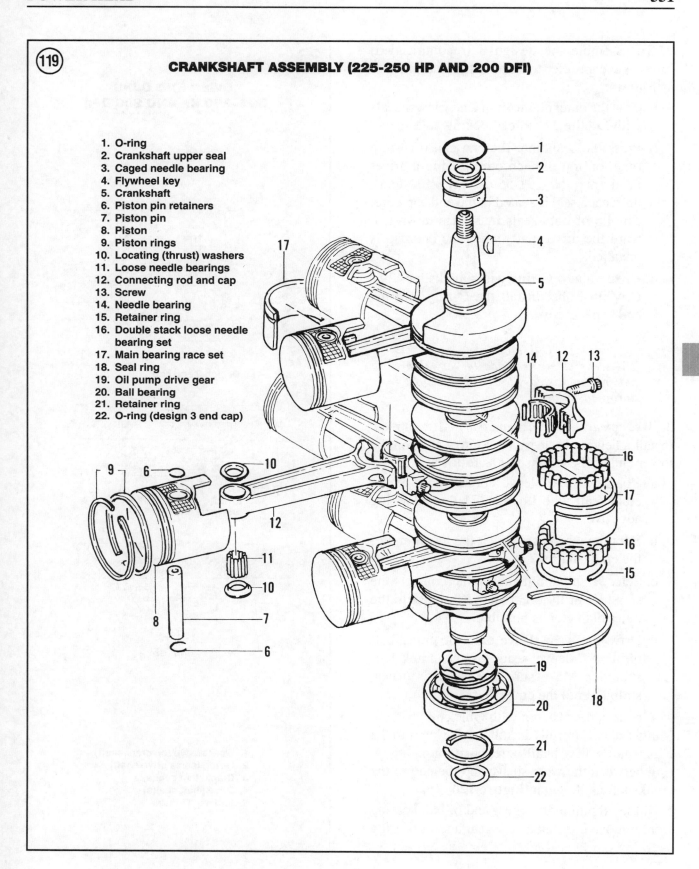

119

CRANKSHAFT ASSEMBLY (225-250 HP AND 200 DFI)

1. O-ring
2. Crankshaft upper seal
3. Caged needle bearing
4. Flywheel key
5. Crankshaft
6. Piston pin retainers
7. Piston pin
8. Piston
9. Piston rings
10. Locating (thrust) washers
11. Loose needle bearings
12. Connecting rod and cap
13. Screw
14. Needle bearing
15. Retainer ring
16. Double stack loose needle bearing set
17. Main bearing race set
18. Seal ring
19. Oil pump drive gear
20. Ball bearing
21. Retainer ring
22. O-ring (design 3 end cap)

8

2. To assemble the design 3 (recommended) lower end cap, refer to **Figure 120** and proceed as follows:

    a. Coat the outer diameter of 2 new lower seals with Loctite 271 threadlocking adhesive.

    b. Press the seals into the end cap (one at a time, on top of each other) using a driver head (part No. 91-55919 or equivalent), until each seal is seated in the end cap bore. The lip of both seals must face down (toward the drive shaft) when the end cap is installed.

    c. Grease a new O-ring with Quicksilver 2-4-C Multi-Lube. Install the O-ring into the end cap's groove.

CAUTION
The wear sleeve is made of very thin material and is easy to crush or distort during installation.

3. *Wear sleeve (design 3 end cap)*—If removed, install a new wear sleeve (1, **Figure 120**) on the lower end of the crankshaft as follows:

    a. Coat the wear sleeve contact area of the crankshaft with Loctite 271 threadlocking adhesive.

    b. Pilot the wear sleeve over the lower end of the crankshaft.

    c. Select a suitable mandrel that contacts the shoulder of the wear sleeve as close to the outer diameter as possible.

    d. Drive the wear sleeve onto the crankshaft until the sleeve seats on the crankshaft shoulder. Make sure the sleeve is driven straight onto the crankshaft.

4. Grease a new O-ring with Quicksilver 2-4-C Multi-Lube. Carefully install the O-ring into the crankshaft's drive shaft bore, positioning the O-ring between the wear sleeve and the end of the crankshaft as shown in **Figure 120**.

5. If the oil pump drive gear and/or ball bearing were removed, install a new gear and/or bearing as follows:

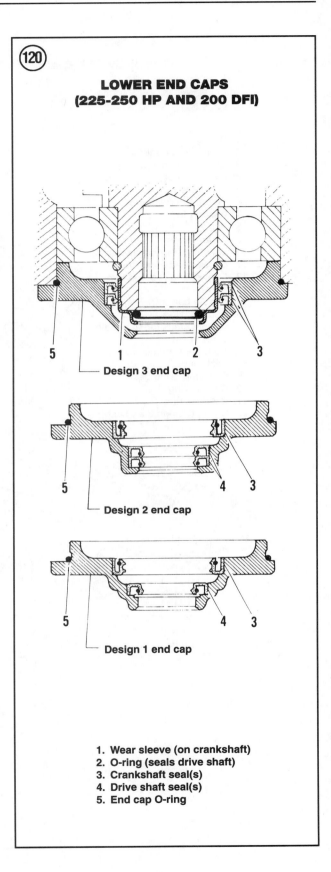

(120)

LOWER END CAPS (225-250 HP AND 200 DFI)

Design 3 end cap

Design 2 end cap

Design 1 end cap

1. Wear sleeve (on crankshaft)
2. O-ring (seals drive shaft)
3. Crankshaft seal(s)
4. Drive shaft seal(s)
5. End cap O-ring

a. Lubricate the crankshaft and a new oil pump drive gear with outboard oil. Position the flanged side of the gear away from the crankshaft, align the keyway and seat the gear against the crankshaft shoulder.

b. Lubricate a new ball bearing with outboard oil, then slide the bearing over the drive shaft end of the crankshaft with the numbered side facing away from the crankshaft.

c. Support the crankshaft (under the lower counterweight) in a press. Press against the inner race of the bearing with a suitable mandrel until the bearing is seated on the crankshaft.

d. Install the retainer ring (21, **Figure 119**) with retainer ring pliers (part No. 91-922778A-3) or Sears Craftsman pliers (part No. 4734). Make sure the retainer ring is fully seated in the crankshaft groove.

6. Mount the crankshaft vertically on a power head (crankshaft) stand (part No. 91-30591A-1 [8-spline], part No. 912549 [13-spline] or equivalent). The power head stand must be securely clamped in a vise.

> *CAUTION*
> *The crankshaft seal rings (18, **Figure 119**) are brittle. Wear approved eye protection and do not expand the ring(s) any further than necessary to install them.*

7. If one (or more) of the seven crankshaft seal rings (**Figure 105**, typical) was removed, expand the new ring(s) just enough to fit around the nearest crankpin journal. Then, install the ring(s) into the crankshaft groove(s) using a piston ring expander part No. 91-24697 (or equivalent).

> *CAUTION*
> *If the original bearings are reused, they must be installed in their original locations.*

8. Assemble the 2 center main bearings as follows:

a. Apply a thick coat of needle bearing assembly grease to the upper center main bearing journal. Then, install the double stack of loose bearing rollers to the bearing surface.

b. Position the outer race halves over the bearing rollers and seal rings. The retaining ring groove must be positioned up (toward the flywheel).

c. Carefully align the fractured parting lines, then install the retainer ring (15, **Figure 119**). Position the retainer ring to cover as much of both fracture lines as possible.

d. Repeat this procedure to assemble the lower center main bearing.

9. Assemble and install the upper main bearing as follows:

a. Coat the outer diameter of a new upper seal with Loctite 271 threadlocking adhesive.

b. Position the seal in the open bore of the upper main bearing with the seal lip facing down.

c. Using a suitable mandrel, press the seal into the bearing until it is seated.

8

(121)

PISTON IDENTIFICATION AND ORIENTATION (225-250 HP AND 200 DFI)

Top

Port	Starboard
Cyl 2 Up / P	Up / S Cyl 1
Cyl 4 Up / P	Up / S Cyl 3
Cyl 6 Up / P	Up / S Cyl 5

d. Coat a new O-ring with Quicksilver 2-4-C Multi-Lube grease and install the O-ring into the bearing's groove.

e. Slide the bearing over the flywheel end of the crankshaft and seat it against the crankshaft shoulder.

10. Begin assembly of the connecting rods to the pistons by greasing the sleeve portion of piston pin installation tool (part No. 91-92973A-1) with needle bearing assembly grease.

11. Position the No. 1 cylinder connecting rod in its original orientation, as marked during disassembly.

12. Hold the lower locating (thrust) washer under the connecting rod small end, then insert the greased sleeve into the small end bore.

13. Lubricate the 34 needles with needle bearing assembly grease and insert them into the small end, around the sleeve as shown in **Figure 108**, typical.

NOTE
All pistons are marked (stamped) UP to signify the top of the piston. However, the cylinder No. 1, 3 and 5 pistons are also marked with an S, signifying the starboard cylinder bank of the engine. The cylinder No. 2, 4 and 6 pistons are also marked with a P, signifying the port cylinder bank of the engine. Each piston must be installed in its correct orientation. See Figure 121.

14. Position the upper locating (thrust) washer on top of the needles. Carefully slide the No. 1 piston over the rod (with the stamped UP marking facing up) and align the piston pin bores. Then insert the main body of piston pin tool (part No. 91-92973A-1) into the piston pin bore and through the connecting rod, pushing the sleeve out the other side of the piston pin bore. Remove the sleeve.

15. Lubricate the piston pin with outboard oil and pilot it into the open end of the piston pin bore. Support the piston (and tool) with one hand and drive the piston pin into the piston with a soft-faced (rubber or plastic) mallet. Allow the pin tool to be pushed out as the piston pin is driven in.

16. Remove the piston pin tool from the bottom of the piston, then insert it into the top of the piston pin bore and gently tap it until the pin is centered in the pin bore.

17. Make sure that no needles or locating washers were displaced, then secure the piston pin with 2 new piston pin retainers (6, **Figure 119**) using a lock ring installation tool (part No. 91-93004A-2) as follows:

a. Position a new retainer ring into the stepped, open end of the tool's sleeve (**Figure 122**).

b. Insert the drive handle into the opposite end of the sleeve.

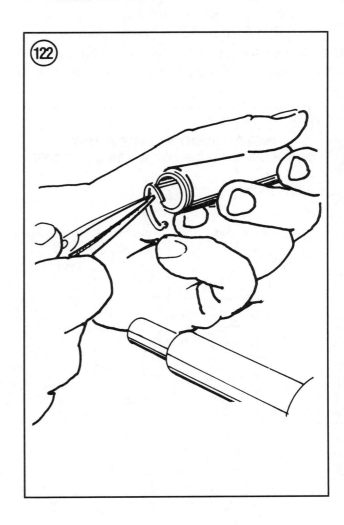

c. Pilot the stepped end of the sleeve into either end of the No. 1 cylinder piston pin bore.

d. While holding the sleeve to the pin bore, press the drive handle quickly and firmly to install the ring.

e. Remove the handle and sleeve. Make sure the retainer is completely seated in its groove in the piston pin bore.

f. Install the second retainer in the opposite end of the piston pin bore in the same manner.

18. Repeat Steps 10-17 for the remaining pistons and connecting rods.

CAUTION
Install the piston rings onto the pistons that match the cylinder bore for which the rings were fitted.

19. Refer to **Figure 123** and install the 2 semi-keystone rings onto each piston using a ring expander (part No. 91-24697 or equivalent). Install the bottom ring first, then the top ring, expanding each ring just enough to slip over the piston. The identification mark on both rings (dot or letter) must face up.

20. Make sure that each ring can be rotated freely in its groove, then position the end gap of each piston ring to straddle the locating pin in its groove.

Power head assembly

1. Verify that the single upper main bearing pin and 2 center main bearing locating pins (3, **Figure 118**) are installed in the cylinder block. Then, position the cylinder block so the block-to-crankcase cover mating surface is pointing upward.

2. Lubricate all 7 seal rings and the oil pump drive gear with outboard oil.

3. Slowly lower the crankshaft assembly into the block (**Figure 112**, typical). Rotate the crankshaft center main bearing assemblies as necessary to align the holes in the bearing races with the bearing locating pins (3, **Figure 118**). Position each seal ring (18, **Figure 119**) so the ring end gap is pointing straight up.

CAUTION
Do not strike the end of the crankshaft directly or the wear sleeve will be damaged.

8

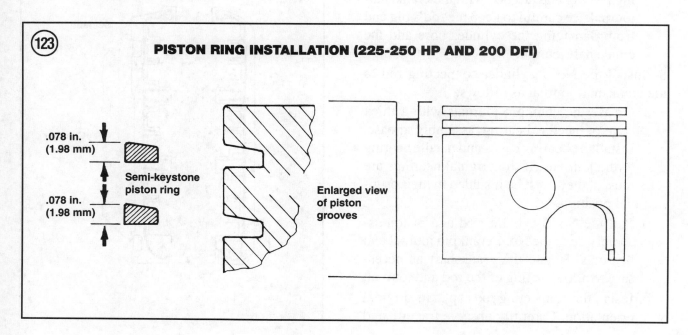

123 **PISTON RING INSTALLATION (225-250 HP AND 200 DFI)**

.078 in. (1.98 mm)

Semi-keystone piston ring

.078 in. (1.98 mm)

Enlarged view of piston grooves

4. Insert the appropriate power head (crankshaft) stand into the lower end of the crankshaft. Carefully tap the stand (with a soft hammer) to seat the ball bearing in its bore.

5. Install the lower end cap over the crankshaft. Coat the mating surfaces with Quicksilver Perfect Seal. Align the screw holes with the cylinder block and seat the end cap to the cylinder block. Install 2 screws finger-tight to hold the end cap in position.

6. Lubricate the No. 1 cylinder piston rings, piston and cylinder bore with outboard oil. Then, make sure that the piston ring end gaps are still straddling the locating pins in their ring grooves.

7. Install the No. 1 cylinder piston and connecting rod assembly as follows:

   a. Lubricate the cylinder No. 1 cylinder bore, piston and piston rings.

   b. Verify that the end gap of each piston ring is positioned over the ring locating pin in its ring groove.

   c. Using the appropriate tapered sleeve ring compressor (part No. 91-823237 or equivalent), install the No. 1 piston into its cylinder bore (**Figure 114**, typical) with the UP mark facing the flywheel and the connecting rod big end aligned with the crankshaft journal. Be careful to keep the rod's big end from damaging the cylinder bore and the crankshaft journal.

8. Install the No. 1 cylinder connecting rod to the crankshaft journal as follows:

   a. Grease the crankpin journals with a thick coat of needle bearing assembly grease. Install the bearing cages and needle bearing to the journals. If the original bearings are reused, they must be installed in their original position.

   b. Pull the No. 1 cylinder rod and piston assembly up to the No. 1 crankpin journal and bearings. Rotate the crankshaft as necessary to allow mating of the rod and journal.

   c. Install the connecting rod cap in its original orientation. Carefully observe fracture and

alignment marks to ensure correct installation (**Figure 75**, typical).

   d. Lubricate the screw threads and underside of the screw heads of *new* connecting rod screws with outboard lubricant. Then, while holding the cap firmly in position, install the connecting rod screws and thread them fully into the rod.

   e. Tighten each screw to 15 in.-lb. (1.69 N•m). Run a fingernail or pencil lead over each edge of the rod-to-cap joint (**Figure 76**). No ridge should be seen or felt. Realign and retorque the cap as necessary.

   f. Once the alignment is verified, apply a second torque of 30 ft.-lb. (40.7 N•m) in 2 progressive steps. Then apply the final torque by turning each rod screw an additional 90°. Make a final check of alignment after the final torque has been applied.

   g. Rotate the crankshaft several revolutions to check for binding or unusual noise. If noted,

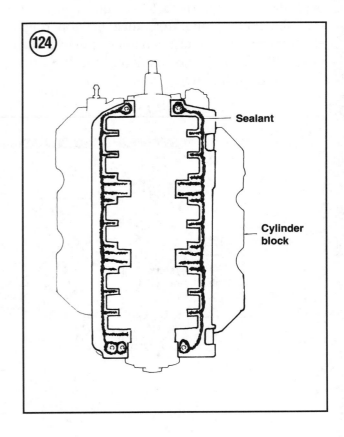

Sealant

Cylinder block

remove the piston and connecting rod just installed and correct the defect before proceeding.

9. Repeat Steps 6-8 for the remaining piston and connecting rod assemblies. Refer to **Figure 121** for piston location and orientation.

10. Using an oil and wax free solvent, such as acetone or lacquer thinner, clean the cylinder block and crankcase cover mating surfaces.

11. Install the dowel pin (4, **Figure 118**) into the cylinder block or crankcase cover (if not already installed).

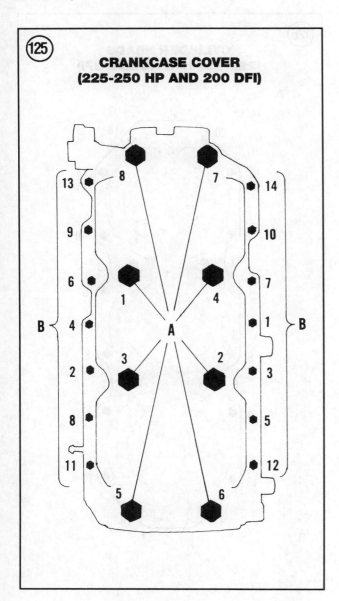

**CRANKCASE COVER
(225-250 HP AND 200 DFI)**

CAUTION
Loctite Master Gasket Sealant is the only sealant recommended to seal the crankcase cover-to-cylinder block mating surfaces. The sealant comes in a kit that includes a special primer. Follow the instructions included in the kit for preparing the surfaces and applying the sealant. The sealant bead must be applied to the inner (crankshaft side) of all crankcase cover screw holes.

12. Following the instructions supplied with the sealer, apply a continuous bead of Loctite Master Gasket Sealant to the mating surface of the cylinder block as shown in **Figure 124**. Run the sealant bead along the inside of all bolt holes and to within 1/16 in. (1.6 mm) of the seal rings and center main bearings. Make sure the bead is continuous.

13. Install the crankcase cover into position on the cylinder block. Seat the cover to the block as far as possible with hand pressure. The seal rings will prevent complete seating of the cover.

14. Insert the power head (crankshaft stand) into the lower end of the crankshaft. Tap against the stand with a soft hammer to make sure the ball bearing is seated in its bore.

15. Oil the threads and under the heads of the 8 large (main bearing) crankcase cover screws and coat the threads of the 14 smaller (outer) cover screws with Loctite 242 threadlocking adhesive, then install the screws. Evenly tighten the large (main bearing) cover screws in small increments until the crankshaft seal rings are completely compressed and the crankcase cover is seated to the cylinder block. Then, tighten the 14 outer screws finger-tight.

16. Torque the 8 large (main bearing) screws as follows:

a. Tighten all 8 screws snugly.

b. Tighten all 8 screws to 30 ft.-lb. in 3 progressive steps, following the pattern shown in A, **Figure 125**.

c. Turn each one of the 8 screws an additional 90°, following the pattern shown in A, **Figure 125**.

17. Torque the 14 smaller (outer) screws to 21 ft.-lb. (28.5 N•m) in 3 progressive steps, following the pattern shown in B, **Figure 125**.

18. Rotate the crankshaft several revolutions to check for binding or unusual noise. If binding or noise is noted, the power head must be disassembled and the cause of the defect located and corrected before proceeding.

19. Remove the end cap screws installed previously. Coat the threads of the 4 lower end cap screws with Loctite 242 threadlocking adhesive. Install and evenly tighten the screws to 85 in.-lb. (9.6 N•m).

20. Install both cylinder heads to the power head as follows:

   a. Grease the O-rings and molded seals (16 and 17, **Figure 118**) with Quicksilver 2-4-C Multi-Lube and position them in each cylinder head's grooves.

   b. Position the heads on the cylinder block with the thermostat pockets facing up (toward the flywheel).

   c. Lubricate the 18 short bolts with clean engine oil. Apply oil to the threads and the bottom of the bolt heads.

   d. Install the bolts in every hole except the 2 used by the thermostat covers. Tighten the 18 screws on each head finger-tight at this time.

21. Install a new grommet around (or a new gasket over) each thermostat and install a thermostat into each cylinder head with the sensing pellet facing the head. Position a thermostat cover over each thermostat with the water fittings facing down and towards each other. Coat the threads and underside of the heads of the thermostat cover/cylinder head bolts with outboard oil. Install the screws finger-tight at this time.

22. Torque all 20 bolts on each cylinder head as follows:

   a. Tighten all 20 bolts on each head snugly.

   b. Torque all 20 bolts to 20 ft.-lb. (27.1 N•m) in 3 progressive steps following the pattern shown in **Figure 126**.

   c. Torque the thermostat cover screws to 30 ft.-lb. (40.7 N•m).

   d. Turn each head (and thermostat cover) bolt an additional 90°, following the pattern shown in **Figure 126**.

   e. Do not retorque the head bolts after operation.

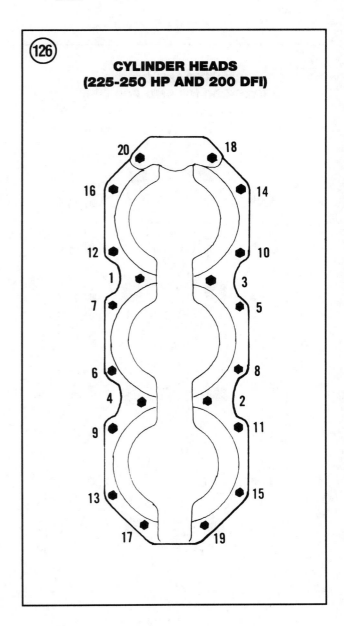

(126)

**CYLINDER HEADS
(225-250 HP AND 200 DFI)**

23. Assemble and install the poppet valve as follows:

 a. Install a new grommet (11, **Figure 127**) into the poppet valve cavity in the exhaust adaptor plate.

 b. Assemble the poppet valve components as shown in **Figure 127**. Tighten the screw (4, **Figure 127**) to 25 in.-lb. (3.0 N·m).

 c. Sandwich a new gasket between the outer and inner plates, then position the assembly

to the cylinder head using another new gasket.

 d. Secure the assembly with 2 screws. Coat the screw threads with Quicksilver Perfect Seal. Evenly tighten the screws to 20 ft.-lb. (27.1 N·m).

24. Position the throttle and spark control arm to its mounting boss on the port side of the power head. Make sure the thrust washer is between the

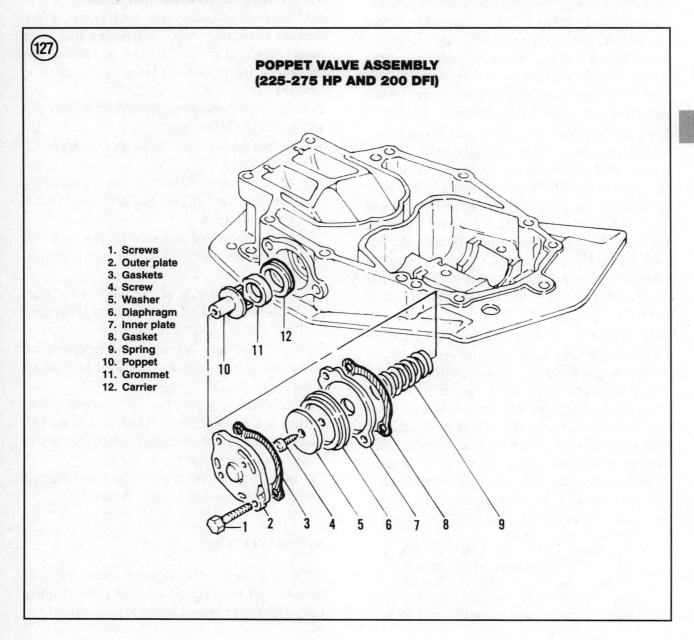

(127)

**POPPET VALVE ASSEMBLY
(225-275 HP AND 200 DFI)**

1. Screws
2. Outer plate
3. Gaskets
4. Screw
5. Washer
6. Diaphragm
7. Inner plate
8. Gasket
9. Spring
10. Poppet
11. Grommet
12. Carrier

8

assembly and the power head, then install the center screw and tighten it securely.

25. Install the shift and throttle cable anchor bracket (and shift interrupt switch) to the port lower side of the power head. Coat the 3 mounting screws with Loctite 271 threadlocking adhesive. Install the screws and tighten them securely.

26A. *Carbureted models*—Install the ignition and electrical components as an assembly. This includes the stator assembly, crankshaft position sensor, the Ignition ECM (electronic control module), CDM modules, and the electrical/ignition plate (containing the starter solenoid and the trim/tilt solenoids or relays). Secure all cables and harnesses with the original clamps and/or new tie-straps. See Chapter Seven.

26B. *EFI models*—Install the ignition and electrical components as an assembly. This includes the stator assembly, crankshaft position sensor, the ignition and fuel electronic control modules (and mounting plate), CDM modules and the electrical plate (containing the starter solenoid, fuse and the trim/tilt solenoids [or relays]). Secure all cables and harnesses with the original clamps and/or new tie-straps. Refer to Chapter Six for the Fuel ECM and Chapter Six all other items.

26C. *DFI models*—Install the ignition and electrical components as an assembly. This includes the stator assembly, crankshaft position sensor, the ECM (electronic control module), the electrical plate (containing the starter solenoid, fuses and main power and trim/tilt relays) and the ignition plate (containing the ignition coils). Secure all cables and harnesses with the original clamps and/or new tie-straps. Refer to Chapter Six and Chapter Seven as necessary.

NOTE
All models are equipped with a shift interrupt switch mounted on the shift and throttle cable anchor bracket. Connect the switch leads to the engine harness bullet connectors at this time. All models

are also equipped with an ECT (engine coolant temperature) sensor. If the sensor was removed, refer to Chapter Six and install it. Install the sensor, or connect the leads before proceeding.

27A. *Carbureted models*—Install the carburetors, fuel pump, fuel filter, fuel enrichment valve, intake manifold and reed blocks, and all fuel, primer and fuel bleed (recirculation) lines as described in Chapter Six.

27B. *EFI models*—Install the induction manifold assembly, mechanical fuel pump, vapor separator assembly, water separating fuel filter, intake manifold and reed blocks, and all fuel and fuel bleed (recirculation) lines as described in Chapter Six.

27C. *200 DFI models*—Refer to Chapter Six and install the following:
   a. Induction manifold and vapor separator assemblies.
   b. Mechanical fuel pump, water separating fuel filter and all fuel and fuel bleed (recirculation) lines.
   c. Intake manifold and reed blocks (with the electric oil pump and oil line to air compressor).
   d. Air compressor, port and starboard air/fuel rails (with the DFI injectors) and all remaining air, fuel and bleed lines.

28A. *225-250 hp*—Install the oil reservoir, oil pump and all oil lines as described in Chapter Eleven.

28B. *200 DFI*—Install the oil reservoir as described in Chapter Eleven. Then, install the belt tensioner assembly from the top of the power head. See Chapter Seven.

29. Install the alternator, flywheel and electric starter as described in Chapter Seven.

Assembly (275 hp)

The poppet (water pressure relief) valve is mounted on the exhaust adaptor plate (**Figure 127**) which is removed with the power head and must be separated from the power head before the power head can be completely disassembled. Be sure to reassemble and install the poppet valve when so directed.

Refer to **Figure 128** and **Figure 129** for the following procedure.

Crankshaft replacement concerns

If a new crankshaft is installed into a used cylinder block, inspect the crankshaft seal ring mating surfaces in the cylinder block and crankcase cover. If the original sealing rings wore grooves into the block and cover mating surfaces, the sealing rings of the new crankshaft must fit into the grooves or the crankshaft will bind.

To check for crankshaft binding, proceed as follows:

a. Check the seal rings' grooves in the block and cover for burrs. Remove any burrs found.

b. Lubricate the crankshaft seal rings with outboard oil. Temporarily install the crankshaft and lower end cap into the cylinder block.

c. Rotate the crankshaft several turns while checking for binding or excessive drag. If either is noted, recheck the seal grooves for burrs and remove any found.

d. If excessive drag or binding is still evident, the cylinder block and crankcase cover must be replaced as an assembly.

Crankshaft and pistons

Each cylinder and piston is identified (numbered) as shown in **Figure 130**. The pistons must be installed with their stamped markings positioned as shown in **Figure 130**.

1. Check the end gap of the new piston rings as described under *Piston Ring End Gap* in this chapter. The ring end gap must be 0.012-0.024 in. (0.31-0.61 mm).

2. To assemble the lower end cap, refer to **Figure 131** and proceed as follows:

a. Coat the outer diameter of a new lower seal with Loctite 271 threadlocking adhesive.

b. Press the seal into the end cap using driver head (part No. 91-55919 or equivalent), until the seal is seated in the end cap bore. The seal lip must face the drive shaft when installed.

c. Grease a new O-ring with Quicksilver 2-4-C Multi-Lube. Install the O-ring into the end cap's groove.

3. If the ball bearing was removed, install a new bearing as follows:

a. Lubricate a new ball bearing with outboard oil, then slide the bearing over the drive shaft end of the crankshaft with the numbered side facing away from the crankshaft.

b. Support the crankshaft (under the lower counterweight) in a press. Press against the inner race of the bearing with a suitable mandrel until the bearing is seated on the crankshaft.

c. Install the retainer ring (20, **Figure 129**) with retainer ring pliers (part No. 91-922778A-3 or Sears Craftsman part No. 4734). Make sure the retainer ring is fully seated in the crankshaft groove.

4. Mount the crankshaft vertically on a power head (crankshaft) stand (part No. 91-30591A-1 or equivalent). The power head stand must be securely clamped in a vise.

CAUTION
The crankshaft seal rings (18, Figure 129) are brittle. Wear approved eye protection and do not expand the ring(s) any further than necessary to install them.

5. If one (or more) of the seven crankshaft seal rings (**Figure 105**, typical) were removed, expand the new ring(s) just enough to fit around the nearest crankpin journal. Then, install the ring(s) into the crankshaft groove(s) using a

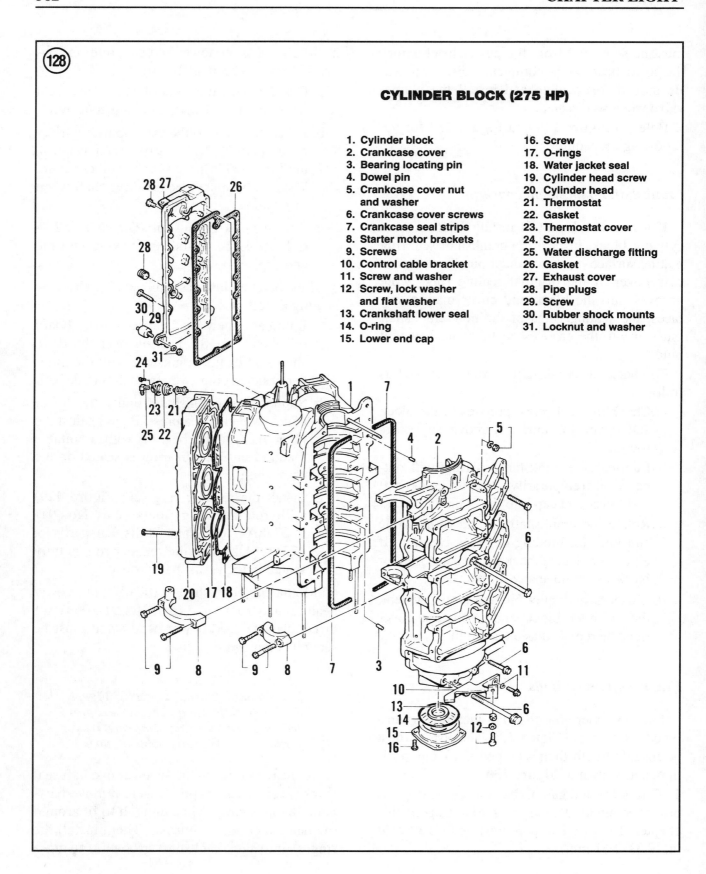

CYLINDER BLOCK (275 HP)

1. Cylinder block
2. Crankcase cover
3. Bearing locating pin
4. Dowel pin
5. Crankcase cover nut
   and washer
6. Crankcase cover screws
7. Crankcase seal strips
8. Starter motor brackets
9. Screws
10. Control cable bracket
11. Screw and washer
12. Screw, lock washer
    and flat washer
13. Crankshaft lower seal
14. O-ring
15. Lower end cap

16. Screw
17. O-rings
18. Water jacket seal
19. Cylinder head screw
20. Cylinder head
21. Thermostat
22. Gasket
23. Thermostat cover
24. Screw
25. Water discharge fitting
26. Gasket
27. Exhaust cover
28. Pipe plugs
29. Screw
30. Rubber shock mounts
31. Locknut and washer

8

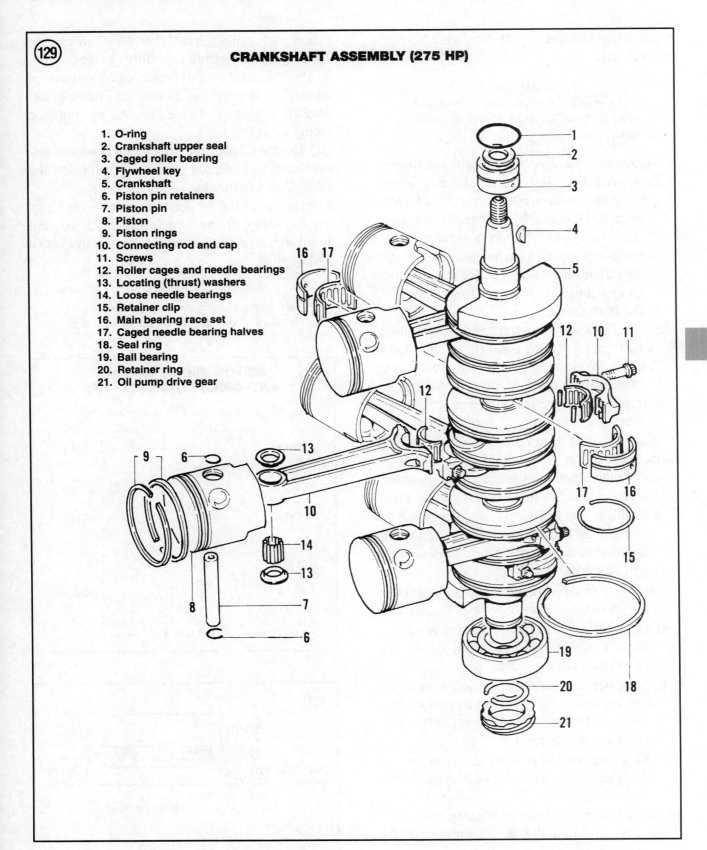

(129) **CRANKSHAFT ASSEMBLY (275 HP)**

1. O-ring
2. Crankshaft upper seal
3. Caged roller bearing
4. Flywheel key
5. Crankshaft
6. Piston pin retainers
7. Piston pin
8. Piston
9. Piston rings
10. Connecting rod and cap
11. Screws
12. Roller cages and needle bearings
13. Locating (thrust) washers
14. Loose needle bearings
15. Retainer clip
16. Main bearing race set
17. Caged needle bearing halves
18. Seal ring
19. Ball bearing
20. Retainer ring
21. Oil pump drive gear

piston ring expander part No. 91-24697 (or equivalent).

CAUTION
If the original bearings are reused, they must be installed in their original locations.

6. Assemble the 2 center main bearings as follows:

   a. Apply a thick coat of needle bearing assembly grease to the upper center main bearing journal. Then, install the caged roller bearing halves onto the bearing surface.

   b. Position the outer race halves over the bearing rollers and seal rings. The retaining ring groove must be positioned down (toward the drive shaft).

   c. Carefully align the fractured parting lines, then install the retainer ring (15, **Figure 129**). Position the retainer ring to cover as much of both fracture lines as possible.

   d. Repeat this procedure to assemble the lower center main bearing.

7. Assemble and install the upper main bearing carrier as follows:

   a. Coat the outer diameter of a new upper seal with Loctite 271 threadlocking adhesive.

   b. Position the seal in the open bore of the upper main bearing carrier with the seal lip facing down. This is the bore closest to the fuel bleed fitting.

   c. Using a suitable mandrel, press the seal into the carrier until it is flush with the carrier.

   d. Coat a new O-ring with Quicksilver 2-4-C Multi-Lube grease and install the O-ring into the carrier's groove.

   e. If the bearing was removed, lubricate a new bearing with outboard oil and press it into the carrier (with a suitable mandrel) until it is flush with the carrier.

   f. Slide the bearing over the flywheel end of the crankshaft and seat it against the crankshaft shoulder.

8. Begin assembly of the connecting rods to the pistons by greasing the sleeve portion of the

piston pin installation tool (part No. 91-92973A-1) with needle bearing assembly grease.

9. Position the No. 1 cylinder connecting rod in its original orientation, as marked during disassembly. The original side that was up, must be facing up at this time.

10. Hold the lower locating (thrust) washer under the connecting rod small end, then insert the greased sleeve into the small end bore.

11. Lubricate the 34 needles with needle bearing assembly grease and insert them into the small end, around the sleeve as shown in **Figure 108**, typical.

NOTE
All pistons are marked (stamped) with an S or P on the top of the piston. The

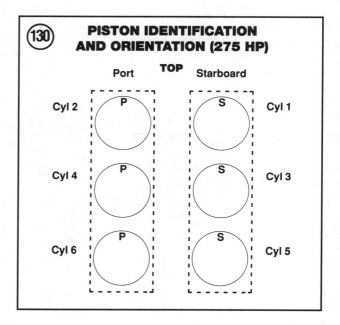

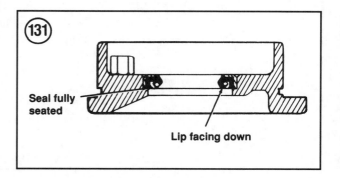

cylinder No. 1, 3 and 5 pistons are marked with an S, signifying the starboard cylinder bank of the engine. The cylinder No. 2, 4 and 6 pistons are marked with a P, signifying the port cylinder bank of the engine. Each piston must be installed in its correct orientation. See Figure 130.

12. Position the upper locating (thrust) washer on top of the needles. Carefully slide the cylinder No. 1 piston over the rod (with the stamped UP marking facing up) and align the piston pin bores. Then, insert the main body of piston pin tool (part No. 91-92973A-1) into the piston pin bore and through the connecting rod, pushing the sleeve out the other side of the piston pin bore. Remove the sleeve.

13. Lubricate the piston pin with outboard oil and pilot it into the open end of the piston pin bore. Support the piston (and tool) with one hand and drive the piston pin into the piston with a soft-faced (rubber or plastic) mallet. Allow the pin tool to be pushed out as the piston pin is driven in.

14. Remove the piston pin tool from the bottom of the piston, then insert it into the top of the piston pin bore and gently tap it until the pin is centered in the pin bore.

15. Make sure no loose needles or locating washers were displaced, then secure the piston

pin with 2 new piston pin retainers (6, **Figure 129**) using lock ring installation tool (part No. 91-93004A-2) as follows:

a. Position a new retainer ring into the stepped, open end of the tool's sleeve (**Figure 122**).

b. Insert the drive handle into the opposite end of the sleeve.

c. Pilot the stepped end of the sleeve into either end of the cylinder No. 1 piston pin bore.

d. While holding the sleeve to the pin bore, press the drive handle quickly and firmly to install the ring.

e. Remove the handle and sleeve. Make sure the retainer is completely seated in its groove in the piston pin bore.

f. Install the second retainer in the opposite end of the piston pin bore in the same manner.

16. Repeat Steps 8-15 for the remaining pistons and connecting rods.

CAUTION
Install the piston rings onto the pistons that match the cylinder bore for which the rings were fitted.

17. Refer to **Figure 132** and install the piston rings onto each piston using a ring expander (part

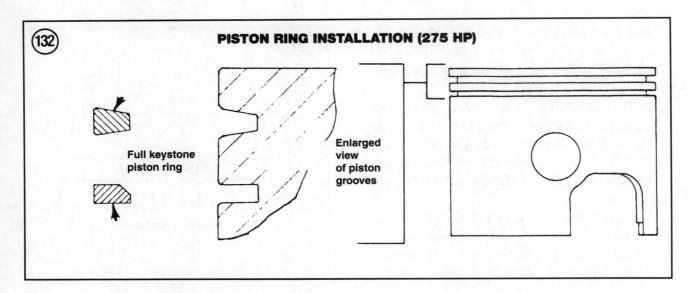

No. 91-24697 or equivalent). Install the bottom (rectangular) ring first, then the top (full keystone) ring, expanding each ring just enough to slip over the piston. The tapered end of the piston ring ends (**Figure 133**) must face up.

18. Make sure that each ring can be rotated freely in its groove, then position the end gap of each piston ring to straddle the ring locating pin in its groove.

Power head assembly

1. Verify that the single upper main bearing pin and 2 center main bearing locating pins (3, **Figure 128**) are installed in the cylinder block. Then, position the cylinder block so the block-to-crankcase cover mating surface is pointing upward.

2. Lubricate all 7 seal rings and the oil pump drive gear with outboard oil.

3. Slowly lower the crankshaft assembly into the block (**Figure 112**, typical). Rotate the crankshaft upper and center main bearing assemblies as necessary to align the hole in the bearing races with the bearing locating pins (3, **Figure 128**). Position each seal ring (18, **Figure 129**) so the ring end gap is pointing straight up.

4. Carefully tap the lower end of the crankshaft (with a soft hammer) to seat the ball bearing in its bore.

5. Install the oil pump drive gear onto the crankshaft with the chamfer on the gear facing the crankshaft ball bearing. Seat the gear against the crankshaft.

6. Install the lower end cap over the crankshaft. Coat the mating surfaces with Quicksilver Perfect Seal. Align the screw holes with the cylinder block and seat the end cap to the cylinder block. Install 2 screws finger-tight to hold the end cap in position.

7. Lubricate the No. 1 cylinder piston rings, piston and cylinder bore with outboard oil.

8. Install the No. 1 cylinder piston and connecting rod assembly as follows:

a. Verify that the end gap of each piston ring is positioned over the locating pin in each ring groove.

b. Using a suitable hose clamp, such as part No. 54-815504348, compress the piston rings. Tighten the hose clamp only enough to compress the rings.

c. Install the No. 1 piston into the cylinder bore with the S mark facing the flywheel and the connecting rod big end aligned with the crankshaft journal. Be careful to keep the rod's big end from damaging the cylinder bore and the crankshaft journal.

9. Install the No. 1 cylinder connecting rod to the crankshaft journal as follows:

a. Grease the crankpin journals with a thick coat of needle bearing assembly grease. Install the bearing cages and needle bearing to the journals. If the original bearings are reused, they must be installed in their original position.

b. Pull or push the No. 1 cylinder rod and piston assembly up to the No. 1 crankpin journal and bearings. Rotate the crankshaft as necessary to allow mating of the rod and journal.

c. Install the connecting rod cap in its original orientation. Carefully observe the fracture

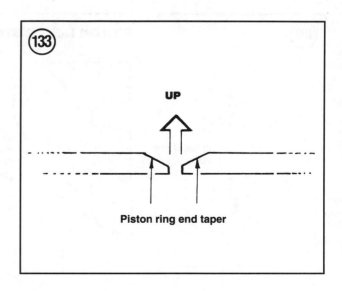

and alignment marks to ensure correct installation (**Figure 75**, typical).

d. Apply a small amount of Loctite 271 threadlocking adhesive to the threads of the *new* connecting rod screws. The screws must be clean and free of any oil before applying the Loctite.

e. While holding the cap firmly in position, install the connecting rod screws and thread them fully into the rod.

f. Tighten each screw to 15 in.-lb. (1.69 N•m). Run a fingernail or pencil lead over each edge of the rod-to-cap joint (**Figure 76**). No ridge should be seen or felt. Realign and retorque the cap as necessary.

g. Once the alignment is verified, apply a second torque of 30 ft.-lb. (40.7 N•m) in 2 progressive steps. Then, apply the final torque by turning each rod screw an additional 90°. Make a final check of alignment after the final torque has been applied.

h. Rotate the crankshaft several revolutions to check for binding or unusual noise. If noted, remove the piston and connecting rod just installed and correct the defect before proceeding.

10. Repeat Steps 7-9 for the remaining piston and connecting rod assemblies. Refer to **Figure 130** for piston location and orientation.

11. Using an oil- and wax-free solvent, such as acetone or lacquer thinner, clean the cylinder block and crankcase cover mating surfaces.

12. Install the dowel pins (4, **Figure 128**) into the cylinder block or crankcase cover (if not already installed).

CAUTION
Loctite Master Gasket Sealant is the only sealant recommended to seal the crankcase cover-to-cylinder block mating surfaces. The sealant comes in a kit that includes a special primer. Follow the instructions included in the kit for preparing the surfaces and applying the sealant. The sealant bead must be applied to the inner (crankshaft side) of all crankcase cover screw holes.

13. Following the instructions supplied with the sealer, apply a continuous bead of Loctite Master Gasket Sealant to the mating surface of the cylinder block as shown in **Figure 124**, typical. Run the sealant bead along the inside of all bolt holes and to within 1/16 in. (1.6 mm) of the seal rings and center main bearings. Make sure the bead is continuous.

14. Install new gasket strips (7, **Figure 128**) into the grooves in the crankcase cover. Trim the ends of the strips flush with the end cap bores. Then, install the crankcase cover into position on the cylinder block. Seat the cover to the block as far as possible with hand pressure. The seal rings will prevent complete seating of the cover.

15. Tap the lower end of the crankshaft with a soft hammer to make sure the ball bearing is seated in its bore.

16. Oil the threads of the 13 crankcase cover screws and the 1 stud. Install the screws (and nut and washer). Tighten screws 1-4, **Figure 134** in small increments until the crankcase cover is seated to the block and the crankshaft seal rings have been compressed. Then tighten the remaining screws (and nut) snugly.

17. Tighten screws 1-4, **Figure 134** in 3 progressive steps to 30 ft.-lb. (40.7 N•m), sequentially following their numbers as shown in **Figure 134**. Then, tighten the remaining screws 5-14, in 3 progressive steps to 30 ft.-lb. (40.7 N•m), sequentially following their numbers as shown in **Figure 134**.

18. Rotate the crankshaft several revolutions to check for binding or unusual noise. If binding or noise is noted, the power head must be disassembled and the cause of the defect located and corrected before proceeding.

19. Remove the end cap screws installed previously. Coat the threads of the 4 lower end cap screws with Loctite 271 threadlocking adhesive. Install and evenly tighten the screws to 150 in.-lb. (17.0 N•m).

8

20. Install both cylinder heads to the power head as follows:

   a. Grease the O-rings and molded seals (17 and 18, **Figure 128**) with Quicksilver 2-4-C Multi-Lube and position them in their groove in each cylinder head.

   b. Coat the threads of each head's 24 screws (19, **Figure 128**) with outboard oil.

   c. Position the heads on the cylinder block. Make sure the O-rings and molded seals are not displaced. Then, install and tighten each head's 24 screws finger-tight at this time.

   d. Tighten the head screws to 180 in.-lb. (20.3 N•m) in 3 progressive steps, following the sequence shown in **Figure 135**.

21. Install a new grommet around (or a new gasket over) each thermostat and install each thermostat into its pocket in the cylinder block with the sensing pellet facing the block. Position a thermostat cover over each thermostat with the water fittings facing down and towards each other. Coat the threads of the thermostat cover screws (24, **Figure 128**) with Loctite 271 thread-locking adhesive. Install and evenly tighten the screws to 150 in.-lb. (17.0 N•m).

22. Install the exhaust cover using a new gasket. Coat the threads of the 17 screws with Loctite 271 threadlocking adhesive. Install and evenly tighten the screws to 150 in.-lb. (17.0 N•m) in 3 progressive steps, following a crossing pattern that starts in the center of the plate and works outward.

23. Carefully lay the power head on its side and install the exhaust adaptor plate as follows:

   a. Coat the shanks of the power head studs with Quicksilver Perfect Seal to help prevent corrosion and ease future disassembly.

   b. Position a new gasket over the power head studs. Slide the exhaust adaptor plate over the studs and seat it against the power head.

   c. Install the 2 nuts and washer at the rear of the power head, just below the exhaust cover cavity. See **Figure 136**.

   d. Install 2 nuts and washers to the bottom of the adaptor plate as shown in **Figure 137**.

   e. Tighten the 4 nuts and washers evenly to 30 ft.-lb. (40.7 N•m) in 3 progressive steps.

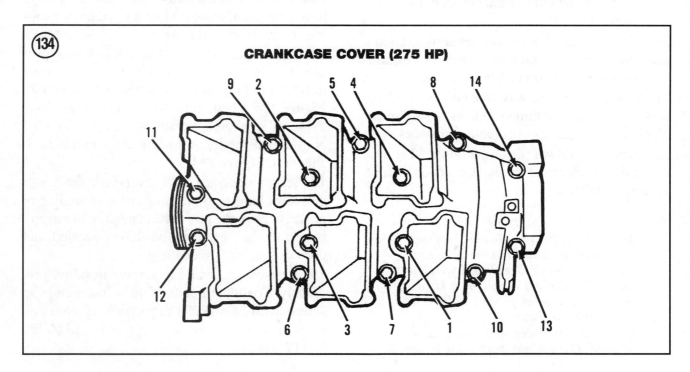

(134)

CRANKCASE COVER (275 HP)

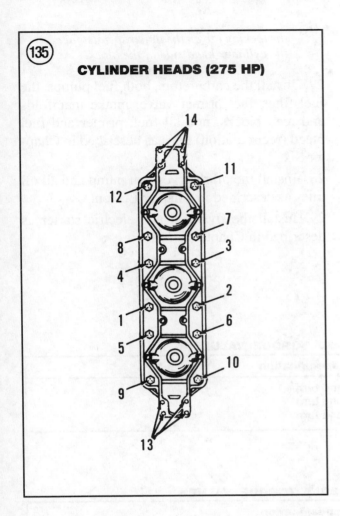

CYLINDER HEADS (275 HP)

24. Assemble and install the poppet valve as follows:

   a. Install a new grommet (11, **Figure 127**) into the poppet valve cavity in the exhaust adaptor plate.

   b. Assemble the poppet valve components as shown in **Figure 127**. Tighten the screw (4, **Figure 127**) to 25 in.-lb. (3.0 N·m).

   c. Sandwich a new gasket between the outer and inner plates, then position the assembly to the cylinder head using another new gasket.

   d. Secure the assembly with 2 screws. Coat the screw threads with Quicksilver Perfect Seal. Evenly tighten the screws to 20 ft.-lb. (27.1 N·m).

25. Position the throttle and spark control arm to its mounting boss on the port side of the power head. Make sure the thrust washer is between the assembly and the power head, then install the center screw and tighten it securely.

26. Install the ignition and electrical components as an assembly. This includes the stator assembly, trigger coil, the rpm limit module, the electrical/ignition plate (containing the starter

8

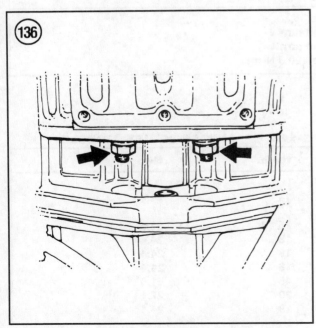

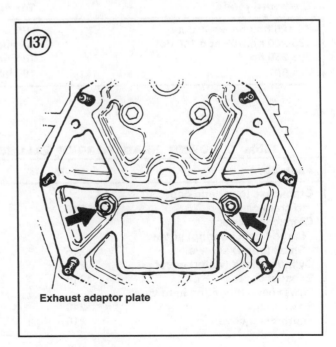

Exhaust adaptor plate

solenoid, switch boxes and the oil warning module), and the ignition coils and voltage regulators (mounted on the exhaust cover). Secure all cables and harnesses with the original clamps and/or new tie-straps. See Chapter Seven.

CAUTION
These models are equipped with an upper main bearing carrier which incorporates a fuel bleed fitting. Clamp the bleed hose to the bleed fitting with a tie-strap. To prevent the tie-strap from interfering with movement of the trigger assembly,

*the locking tab on the tie-strap **must** face the cylinder head side of the block.*

27. Install the carburetors, both fuel pumps, the fuel filter, fuel primer valve, intake manifolds and reed blocks, and all fuel, primer and fuel bleed (recirculation) lines as described in Chapter Six.

28. Install the oil reservoir, oil pump and all oil lines as described in Chapter Eleven.

29. Install the flywheel and electric starter as described in Chapter Seven.

Table 1 CONNECTING ROD TORQUE VALUES

Outboard model	Torque specification
75-125 hp and 65-80 Jet	Torque and turn
135-250 hp and 105-140 Jet	Torque and turn
275 hp	Torque and turn

Table 2 CYLINDER HEAD BOLT TORQUE VALUES

Outboard model	Torque specification
75-125 hp and 60-80 Jet	N/A
135-200 hp, 105 and 140 Jet	Torque and turn
225-250 hp	Torque and turn
275 hp	180 in.-lbs. (20.3 N•m)

Table 3 POWER HEAD TORQUE VALUES (75-125 HP AND 65-80 JET MODELS)

Fastener	in.-lb.	ft.-lb.	N•m
Crankcase lower end cap to crankcase	216	18	24.4
Crankcase cover			
Large (main bearing) screws	–	25	33.9
Small (outer) screws	216	18	24.4
Cylinder block (water) cover	216	18	24.4
Exhaust cover	216	18	24.4
Power head mounting hardware	–	45	61.0
Spark plug	240	20	27.1
Thermostat cover	216	18	24.4

Table 4 POWER HEAD TORQUE VALUES (135-275 HP AND 105-140 JET MODELS)

Fastener	in.-lb.	ft.-lb.	N•m
Crankcase lower end cap			
to crankcase			
135-200 hp and 105-140 Jet	80	–	7.9
225-250 hp and 200 DFI	85	–	9.6
275 hp	150	12.5	17.0
Crankcase upper end cap			
to crankcase			
135-200 hp and 105-140 Jet	150	12.5	17.0
Crankcase cover			
135-200 hp and 105-140 Jet			
3/8 in. (main bearing) screws	–	38	51.5
5/16 in. (outer) screws	180	15	20.3
225-250 hp and 200 DFI			
Large (main bearing) screws	Torque and turn		
Small (outer) screws	–	21	28.5
275 hp	–	30	40.7
Exhaust cover (divider plate)			
135-200 hp and 105-140 Jet	200	16.7	22.6
275 hp	150	12.5	17.0
Oil pump drive gear			
135-200 hp and 105-140 Jet	8	–	0.9
Poppet (relief) valve cover			
135-200, 275 hp and 105-140 Jet	150	12.5	17.0
225-250 hp and 200 DFI	240	20	27.1
Power head mounting hardware			
135-200 hp and 105-140 Jet			
Nuts (drive shaft housing,			
long studs)	240	20	27.1
Nuts (adaptor plate,			
short studs)	276	23	31.2
225-250 hp and 200 DFI	–	50	67.8
275 hp	–	30	40.7
Spark plug			
135-250 hp, 200 DFI			
and 105-140 Jet	240	20	27.1
275 hp	204	17	23.0
Thermostat cover			
135-200 hp and 105-140 Jet	200	16.7	22.6
275 hp	150	12.5	17.0

Table 5 STANDARD TORQUE VALUES (U.S. STANDARD FASTENERS)

Screw or nut size	in.-lbs.	ft.-lbs.	N•m
6-32	9	–	1.0
8-32	20	–	2.3
10-24	30	–	3.4
10-32	35	–	4.0
12-24	45	–	5.1
1/4-20	70	6	7.9
1/4-28	84	7	9.5

(continued)

8

Table 5 STANDARD TORQUE VALUES (U.S. STANDARD FASTENERS) (continued)

Screw or nut size	in.-lbs.	ft.-lbs.	N•m
5/16-18	160	13	18.1
5/16-24	168	14	19.0
3/8-16	270	23	30.5
3/8-24	300	25	33.9
7/16-14	–	36	48.8
7/16-20	–	40	54.2
1/2-13	–	50	67.8
1/2-20	–	60	81.3

Table 6 STANDARD TORQUE VALUES (METRIC FASTENERS)

Screw or nut size	in.-lbs.	ft.-lbs.	N•m
M5	36	–	4.1
M6	70	6	8.1
M8	156	13	17.6
M10	312	26	35.3
M12	–	35	47.5
M14	–	60	81.3

Table 7 POWER HEAD SPECIFICATIONS (75-125 HP AND 65 AND 85 JET)

Component	Specification-in. (mm)
Connecting rod	
Maximum misalignment on surface plate	0.002 (0.051)
Crankshaft	
Crankshaft runout	0.006 (0.152)
Cylinder	
Bore diameter—standard	3.501 (88.93)
Maximum cylinder out-of-round	0.003 (0.076)
Maximum cylinder taper	0.003 (0.076)
Piston	
Skirt diameter	
75-125 hp and 65-80 Jet	3.495 (88.77)
Piston ring end gap	0.010-0.018 (0.25-0.46)

Table 8 POWER HEAD SPECIFICATIONS (V-6 MODELS)

Component	Specification-in. (mm)
Connecting rod	
Maximum misalignment on surface plate	0.002 (0.051)
Piston end inside diameter (275 hp)	1.105 (28.07)
Crankshaft end inside diameter (275 hp)	1.734 (44.04)
Side clearance (275 hp)	0.003-0.009 (0.076-0.229)

(continued)

Table 8 POWER HEAD DIMENSIONAL SPECIFICATIONS (V-6 MODELS) (continued)

Component	Specification-in. (mm)
Crankshaft	
Crankpin diameter	
135-200 hp and 105-140 Jet	1.181 (30.00)
275 hp	2.230 (56.64)
Center main journal diameter	
135-200 hp and 105-140 Jet	1.375 (34.93)
275 hp	2.677 (68.00)
Top main journal diameter	
135-200 hp and 105-140 Jet	1.145 (29.08)
275 hp	1.498 (38.05)
Bottom main journal diameter	
135-200 hp and 105-140 Jet	1.575 (40.01)
275 hp	1.768 (44.91)
Crankshaft runout (at center main journals)	0.002 (0.051)
Oil pump drive gear misalignment	
135-200 hp and 105-140 Jet	0.020 (0.51)
Cylinder	
Bore diameter—standard	
135, 150 hp and 105 Jet (carbureted)	3.125 (79.38)
150 hp EFI (electronic fuel injection)	3.501 (88.93)
175-200 hp, XR6 and Magnum III	3.501 (88.93)
225-250 hp and 200 DFI	3.6265 (92.113)
275 hp	3.740 (95.0)
Maximum cylinder out-of-round	
135-200, 275 hp and 105-140 Jet	0.006 (0.152)
225-250 hp and 200 DFI	0.003 (0.076)
Maximum cylinder taper	
135-200, 275 hp and 105-140 Jet	0.006 (0.152)
225-250 hp and 200 DFI	0.003 (0.076)
Maximum cylinder head warpage	
135-200 hp and 105-140 Jet	0.004 (0.102)
225-275 hp and 200 DFI	0.005 (0.127)
Piston	
Piston-to-cylinder clearance	
275 hp	0.007-0.011 (0.178-0.279)
Skirt diameter	
135-150 hp and 105 Jet (carbureted)	3.113-3.117 (79.07-79.17)
150 EFI (electronic fuel injection)	3.493-3.495 (88.72-88.77)
175-200 hp, XR6 and Magnum III	3.493-3.495 (88.72-88.77)
200 DFI	3.6200-3.6210 (91.948-91.973)
225-250 hp	3.6205-3.6215 (91.961-91.686)
275 hp	3.731-3.733 (94.77-94.82)
Piston ring end gap	
135-200 hp and 105-140 Jet	0.018-0.025 (0.46-0.64)
225-250 hp and 200 DFI	0.010-0.018 (0.25-0.46)
275 hp	0.012-0.024 (0.31-0.61)

Table 9 MANUFACTURER RECOMMENDED SPECIAL TOOLS (75-125 HP AND 65-80 JET)

Description	Part No.	Application
Heat lamp (wear sleeve removal)	91-63209	All
Knife-edged bearing plate	91-37241	All
	(continued)	

Table 9 MANUFACTURER RECOMMENDED SPECIAL TOOLS (75-125 HP AND 65-80 JET) (continued)

Description	Part No.	Application
Lifting eye	91-90455	All
Lock ring installer	91-77109A-3	75-125 hp and 65-80 Jet
Lock ring removal tool	91-52952A-1	All
Piston ring expander	91-24697	All
Power head (crankshaft) stand	91-812549	75-125 hp and 65-80 Jet

Table 10 MANUFACTURER RECOMMENDED SPECIAL TOOLS (V-6 MODELS)

Description	Part No.	Application
Crankshaft stand (8-spline)	91-30591A-1	135-200 and 275 hp, early 225-250 hp
Crankshaft stand (13-spline)	91-812549	Late 225-250 hp, 200 DFI
Driver head (seal installer)	91-55919	All
Heat lamp	91-63209	All
Knife-edged bearing plate	91-37241	All
Lifting eye	91-90455	All
Lock ring removal tool	91-52952A-1	All
Lock ring installer	91-77109A-3	135-200 hp
Lock ring installer	91-93004A-2	225-275hp and 200 DFI
Lock ring pliers	91-822778A-3	All
Piston pin tool	91-74607A-2	135-200 hp
Piston pin tool	91-92973A-1	225-275 hp and 200 DFI
Piston ring compressor	91-65494	3.125 in. (79.38 mm) bore
Piston ring compressor (hose clamp)	54-815504348	3.74 in. (95 mm) bore
Piston ring compressor	91-818773	3.501 in. (88.93 mm) bore
Piston ring compressor	91-823237	3.6265 in. (92.113 mm) bore
Piston ring expander	91-24697	All

Table 11 MODEL NUMBER CODES

Code	Definition
C	Counter rotation
E	Electric start
EFI	Electronic fuel injection
H	Handle (tiller steering handle)
M	Manual start (rope recoil starter)
O	Oil injection
PT	Power trim and tilt
L	Long shaft (20 in.)
XL	Extra long shaft (25 in.)
XXL	Extra, extra long shaft (30 in.)

Table 12 STARTING SERIAL NUMBER LISTING

	1994	1995	1996	1997
Mercury outboard models				
75 hp	0D283222	0G077367	0G301751	0G438000
90 hp	0D283222	0G077369	0G301751	0G438000
100 hp	0D283222	0G090125	0G301751	0G438000
		(continued)		

Table 12 STARTING SERIAL NUMBER LISTING (continued)

	1994	1995	1996	1997
Mercury outboard models (continued)				
115 hp	0D283222	0G127522	0G301751	0G438000
125 hp	0D283222	0G090127	0G301751	0G438000
135 hp	0D284788	0G127861	0G303046	0G438000
150 hp	0D284788	0G129272	0G303046	0G438000
175 hp	0D284788	0G129337	0G303046	0G438000
200 hp	0D284788	0G077376	0G303046	0G438000
200 DFI	–	–	0G386496	0G438000
225 hp	0D280813	0G077384	0G303046	0G438000
250 EFI	–	–	0G303046	0G438000
275 hp	0D280900	–	–	–
Mercury Jet models				
Jet 65 hp	0G052651	0G077369	0G301804	0G438000
Jet 80 hp	0G052652	0G127529	0G302040	0G438000
Jet 105 hp	0G052656	0G129884	0G304512	0G438000
Jet 140 hp	0G052657	0G129601	0G304134	0G438000
Mariner outboard models				
75 hp	0D283222	0G127540	0G301751	0G438000
90 hp	0D283222	0G127561	0G301751	0G438000
100 hp	0D283222	0G127812	0G302262	0G438000
115 hp	0D283222	0G127500	0G301751	0G438000
125 hp	0D283222	0G127766	0G301751	0G438000
135 hp	0D284788	0G129222	0G303046	0G438000
150 hp	0D284788	0G129477	0G303046	0G438000
175 hp	0D284788	0G129394	0G303046	0G438000
200 hp	0D284788	0G129303	0G303046	0G438000
200 DFI	–	–	0G386496	0G438000
225 hp	0D280813	0G106786	0G303046	0G438000
250 EFI	–	–	0G303046	0G438000
275 hp	0D280900	–	–	–
Mariner Jet models				
Jet 65 HP	0G052651	0G127642	0G302037	0G438000
Jet 80 HP	0G052652	0G127629	0G301751	0G438000
Jet 105 HP	0G052656	0G129872	0G325593	0G438000
Jet 140 HP	0G052657	0G129675	0G303046	0G438000

8

Chapter Nine

Lower Gearcase and Jet Drive Units

LOWER GEARCASE

This section provides lower gearcase removal/installation and rebuilding and resealing procedures for all standard rotation models. **Table 1** lists the recommended gear ratios and approximate lubricant capacities, **Tables 2-6** list torque specifications, **Table 7** lists gearcase service specifications, **Tables 8-10** list the recommended special tools and **Table 11** provides torque specifications for jet drive models. **Table 12** provides information to properly use gearcase shimming tools. All Tables are located at the end of the chapter. Jet drive service is covered in a separate section near the end of the chapter.

Exploded illustrations of each lower gearcase are located in the appropriate *Disassembly* section and are helpful references for many service procedures.

The lower gearcase can be removed from the outboard motor without removing the entire outboard from the boat.

The many gearcases covered in this chapter differ in construction and require different service procedures. The chapter is arranged in a normal disassembly/assembly sequence. When only a partial repair is required, follow the procedure(s) to the point where the faulty parts can be replaced, then jump ahead to reassemble the unit.

Since this chapter covers a large range of models, the gearcases shown in the accompanying illustrations are the most common models. While it is possible that the components shown in the pictures may not be identical with those being serviced, the step-by-step procedures will cover each model in this manual.

GEARCASE OPERATION

A drive shaft transfers engine torque from the engine crankshaft to the lower gearcase. A pinion (drive) gear on the drive shaft is in constant mesh with forward and reverse (driven) gears in the lower gearcase housing. These gears are spiral bevel cut to change the vertical power flow into the horizontal flow required by the propeller shaft. The spiral bevel design also provides for smooth, quiet operation.

All models have full shifting capability. A sliding clutch, splined to the propeller shaft, engages the spinning forward or reverse gear. This creates a direct coupling of the drive shaft to the propeller shaft. Since this is a straight mechanical engagement, shifting should only be done at idle speed. Shifting at higher speeds will cause premature gearcase failure.

All lower gearcases incorporate a water pump to supply cooling water to the power head. All models require gearcase removal to service the water pump. Water pump removal and installation procedures are covered in this chapter.

Larger gearcases use precision shimmed gears. This means that the gears are precisely located in the gear housing by the use of very thin metal spacers, called shims. After assembly, correct shimming of the gears is verified by measuring the *gear lash*, also referred to as *backlash*. Gear lash is the measurement of the clearance (or air gap) between a tooth on the pinion gear and 2 teeth on the forward or reverse gear.

Excessive gear lash indicates that the gear teeth are too far apart. This will cause excessive gear noise (whine) and a reduction in gear strength and durability since the gear teeth are not sufficiently overlapping.

Insufficient gear lash indicates that the gear teeth are too close together. This can be catastrophic since there will not be enough clearance to maintain a film of lubricant. Heat expansion will only compound the problem.

GEAR RATIO

The gear ratio refers to the amount of gear reduction between the crankshaft and the propeller provided by the lower gearcase. Gear ratios range from as low as 2.30:1 to as high as 1.64:1. A gear ratio of 2.30:1 means that the crankshaft turns 2.3 times for every 1 turn of the propeller shaft. Higher number ratios are easier for the engine to turn. **Table 1** lists the recommended gear ratio and tooth count for all models.

If the gear ratio is suspected as being incorrect, the gear ratio can be determined by two different methods. The first method does not require removing the gearcase. Mark the flywheel and a propeller blade for counting purposes. Manually shift the gearcase into FORWARD gear. While counting, turn the flywheel in the normal direction of rotation (clockwise as viewed from the top of the flywheel) until the propeller shaft has made exactly 10 turns. Divide the number of flywheel rotations counted by 10 and compare the result with the list of gear ratios in **Table 1**. Round the result to the nearest ratio listed.

The second method of determining gear ratio involves counting the actual number of teeth on the gears. This method requires at least partial disassembly of the gearcase. To determine the gear ratio, divide the driven gear tooth count (forward or reverse gear) by the drive gear (pinion or drive shaft gear) tooth count.

For example, on a gearcase with a 15:28 (drive to driven) tooth count, divide 28 (driven) by 15 (drive) = 1.87 ratio.

It is very important that the engine be operated with the factory recommended gear ratio. Running the engine with an incorrect gear ratio can cause poor performance, poor fuel economy and make it difficult or impossible to obtain the correct wide-open throttle engine speed, which will lead to catastrophic power head failure.

Some horsepower groups of engines that use the same gearcase housing will have several factory ratios, depending on the exact horsepower of the engine within that group. Refer to **Table 1** for gear ratio specifications for each specific engine.

Regardless of which gear ratio is used, it is imperative that the engine operate within the recommended speed range at wide-open throttle. Change propeller pitch and diameter as necessary to adjust engine speed. Increasing pitch or diameter increases the load on the engine and reduces the wide-open throttle speed. Decreasing the pitch or diameter reduces the load on the

9

engine and increases the wide-open throttle speed. Use an accurate shop tachometer for wide-open throttle engine speed verification.

HIGH-ALTITUDE OPERATION

On certain models, a high-altitude gear ratio set is available. The factory recommended gear ratio is adequate for altitudes to 5000 ft. (1524 m). At higher altitudes, it is recommended to change the gear ratio to a higher number ratio (more gear reduction) to compensate for the loss of horsepower caused by the thinner (less dense) air. Refer to **Table 1** for gear ratio recommendations.

The propeller must also be changed to maintain the recommended wide-open-throttle speed range.

If the boat is returned to lower altitudes, it is recommended that the gear ratio be changed back to the factory recommended ratio and the wide-open-throttle speed be adjusted with propeller changes as necessary.

NOTE
If the boat is operated in a high-altitude environment temporarily (such as a vacation trip), it is recommended that only the propeller be changed to achieve the correct wide-open-throttle speed during the stay at high altitude. Change back to the original propeller when the boat is returned to its normal altitude.

Carbureted models

At high altitude, the lower density air also affects the engine's carburetor calibration, causing the engine's air/fuel mixture to become richer. Richer mixtures cause the engine to produce less horsepower and lead to fouled spark plugs, reduced fuel economy and accelerated carbon build-up in the combustion chamber.

All Mercury/Mariner carbureted motors come from the factory calibrated to operate efficiently between sea level and 2500 ft. (762 m). Mercury/Mariner recommends rejetting the carburetor for operation at altitudes of 5000 ft. (1524 m) or higher. Refer to Chapter Six for jetting information.

SERVICE PRECAUTIONS

When working on a gearcase, there are several good procedures to keep in mind that will make your work easier, faster and more accurate.

1. Never use elastic locknuts more than twice. It is a good practice to replace such nuts each time they are removed. Never use an elastic locknut that can be turned by hand (without the aid of a wrench).

2. Use special tools where noted. The use of makeshift tools can damage components and cause serious personal injury.

3. Use the appropriate fixtures to hold the gearcase housing whenever possible. Use a vise with protective jaws to hold smaller housings or individual components. If protective jaws are not available, insert blocks of wood or similar padding on each side of the housing or component before clamping.

4. Remove and install pressed-on parts with an appropriate mandrel, support and press (arbor or hydraulic). Do not attempt to pry or hammer press-fit components on or off.

5. Refer to **Tables 2-6** for torque values. Proper torque is essential to ensure long life and satisfactory service from gearcase components.

6. To help reduce corrosion, especially in saltwater areas, apply Quicksilver Perfect Seal or equivalent to all external surfaces of bearing carriers, housing mating surfaces and fasteners when no other sealant, adhesive or lubricant is recommended. Do not apply sealing compound where it can get into gears or bearings.

7. Discard all O-rings, seals and gaskets during disassembly. Apply Quicksilver 2-4-C Multi-

Lube grease or equivalent to new O-rings and seal lips to provide initial lubrication.

8. Tag all shims with the location and thickness of each shim as it is removed from the gearcase. Shims are reusable as long as they are not damaged or corroded. Follow shimming instructions closely and carefully. Shims control gear location and/or bearing preload. Incorrectly shimming a gearcase can cause catastrophic failure of the gears and/or bearings.

9. Work in an area with good lighting and sufficient space for component storage. Keep an ample number of clean containers available for parts storage. When not being worked on, cover parts and assemblies with clean shop towels or plastic bags.

> *CAUTION*
> *Metric **and** American fasteners are used on Mercury/Mariner gearcases. Always match a replacement fastener to the original. Do not run a tap or thread chaser into a hole (or over a bolt) without first verifying the thread size and pitch. Check all threaded holes for Heli-Coil stainless steel locking thread inserts. Never run a tap or thread chaser into a Heli-Coil equipped hole. Heli-Coil inserts are replaceable, if damaged.*

10. Whenever a threadlocking adhesive is specified, first spray the threads of the threaded hole or nut and the screw with Locquic Primer. Allow the primer to air dry before proceeding. Locquic primer will clean the surfaces and allow better adhesion. Locquic primer also accelerates the cure rate of threadlocking adhesives from an hour or longer, to 15-20 minutes.

CORROSION CONTROL

Sacrificial zinc or aluminum anodes are standard equipment on all models. The anodes must have good electrical continuity to ground or they will not function. Anodes are inspected visually and tested electrically. Anodes must not be painted or coated with any material.

The most common location for the anode is the anodic trim tab, but some newer models use a painted trim tab with an anode mounted at the rear of the gearcase, above the antiventilation plate. On all models, an anode is mounted across the bottom of the stern brackets. Refer to the exploded illustrations of each lower gearcase in the appropriate *Disassembly* section for exact anode location(s) for a specific gearcase.

If the unit is operated exclusively in freshwater, magnesium anodes are available from Quicksilver Parts and Accessories. Magnesium anodes provide better protection in freshwater, but must *not* be used in saltwater. Magnesium anodes will overprotect the unit in saltwater and cause the paint to blister and peel off.

Electronic corrosion control, called the Mer-Cathode system is also available from Quicksilver Parts and Accessories. The controller module is mounted inside the bilge and the reference electrode and anode are mounted on the transom, below the waterline.

Sacrificial Anode Visual Inspection

Check for loose mounting hardware, verify that the anodes are not painted and check the amount of deterioration present. Replace anodes if they are 1/2 their original size (1/2 gone). Test the electrical continuity of each anode after installation as described in the next section.

Sacrificial Anode Electrical Testing

This test requires an ohmmeter.

1. Calibrate the ohmmeter on the lowest scale available.

2. Connect one ohmmeter lead to the anode being tested. Connect the other ohmmeter lead to a good ground point on the gearcase that the anode is mounted to. The meter should indicate

9

a very low reading (zero or very near zero), which indicates electrical continuity.

3. If the reading is not very low, remove the anode and clean the mounting surfaces of the anode, gearcase and mounting hardware. Reinstall the anode and retest continuity.

4. Test the continuity of the gearcase to the engine and negative battery post by connecting one ohmmeter lead to the negative battery cable and the other ohmmeter lead to a good ground point on the lower gearcase. The meter should indicate a very low reading (zero or very near zero), which indicates electrical continuity.

5. If the reading is not very low, check the electrical continuity of the lower gearcase to the driveshaft housing, the upper drive shaft housing to the power head and the power head to the negative battery terminal. Check for loose mounting hardware, broken or missing ground straps, or excessive corrosion. Repair as necessary to establish a good electrical ground path.

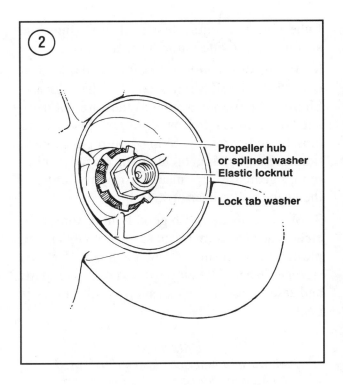

Propeller hub
or splined washer
Elastic locknut

Lock tab washer

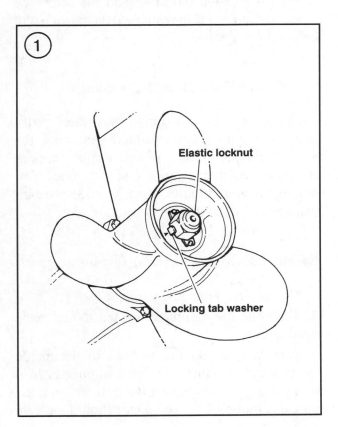

Elastic locknut

Locking tab washer

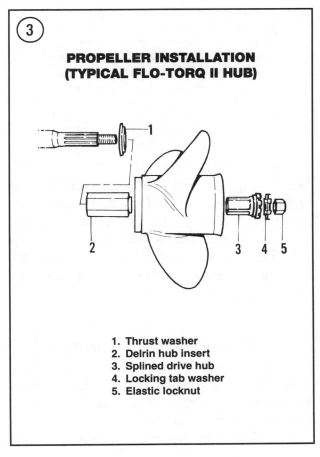

**PROPELLER INSTALLATION
(TYPICAL FLO-TORQ II HUB)**

1. Thrust washer
2. Delrin hub insert
3. Splined drive hub
4. Locking tab washer
5. Elastic locknut

GEARCASE LUBRICATION

To ensure maximum performance and durability, the gearcase requires periodic lubrication. Change the gearcase lubricant every 100 hours of operation or once each season.

The recommended lubricant for all models is Quicksilver Premium Blend Gear Lube. If the gearcase is subjected to severe duty, consider using Quicksilver High Performance Gear Lube.

Refer to Chapter Four to change the lower gearcase lubricant.

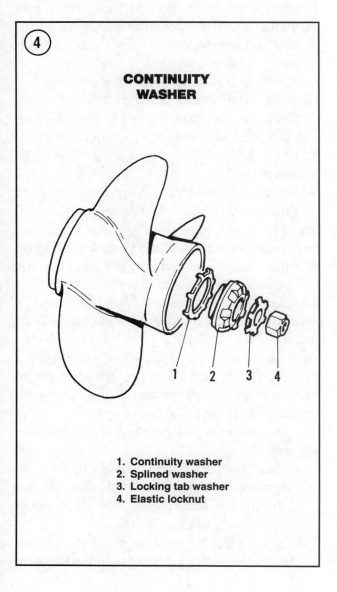

CONTINUITY WASHER

1. Continuity washer
2. Splined washer
3. Locking tab washer
4. Elastic locknut

PROPELLER

The propeller pushes against a thrust washer that rides against a tapered step on the propeller shaft. The propeller is retained by an elastic locknut and a lock tab washer that engages 2 protrusions on the propeller hub *or* by a spline washer (built into propeller on some models), a lock tab washer and an elastic locknut. After the elastic locknut is tightened, the locking tabs are either bent up against the nut (**Figure 1**) or driven down into the propeller hub or spline washer (**Figure 2**).

All propellers use a shock absorbing rubber or *Delrin* hub which is primarily designed to absorb the shock loads produced from shifting the unit into gear. When a hub fails, it will generally slip at higher throttle settings, but still allow the boater to return to port at reduced throttle. The

9

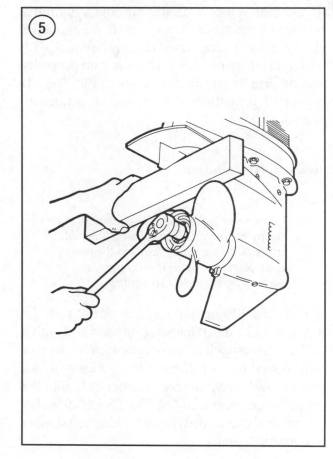

582   **CHAPTER NINE**

defective rubber hub can be removed and a new hub pressed into the propeller using a hydraulic or arbor press (generally by a propeller repair station), or the propeller can be replaced.

Late model Quicksilver or Mercury Marine Propeller Company propellers incorporate the Flo-Torq II square *Delrin* drive hub that can be replaced by the operator, without the use of a hydraulic or arbor press. See **Figure 3**. If the propeller was originally equipped with a *square* rubber hub, it may be possible to upgrade the propeller to the Flo-Torque II style hub. Consult a Mercury/Mariner dealer.

A continuity (toothed) washer is used on 135 hp and larger engines (with the 4-3/4 in. [121 mm] diameter torpedo) equipped with a *rubber* hub to ensure proper grounding of the propeller and mounting components to the gearcase. The continuity washer fits between the rear splined washer and the propeller hub as shown in **Figure 4**. Do not remove or discard the continuity washer on models so equipped. If the propeller shows signs of accelerated corrosion, check with a Mercury/Mariner dealer to see if your propeller should use a continuity washer. Flo-Torq II equipped propellers do not use a continuity washer.

Removal/Installation

WARNING
To prevent accidental engine starting during propeller service, disconnect and ground all spark plug leads to the power head. Remove the ignition key and safety lanyard from models so equipped.

Only the 135 hp and larger models, with the 4-3/4 in. (121 mm) diameter torpedo and with a rubber hub propeller, use the continuity washer and splined rear washer shown in **Figure 4**. All other models have the rear washer built into the propeller or drive hub (on Flo-Torq II models). All models use some type of locking tab washer and elastic locknut.

1. Pry the lock tab(s) up from the propeller (or rear splined washer) or down from the elastic stop nut as required with an appropriate tool.
2. Place a suitable block of wood between a propeller blade and the antiventilation plate to prevent propeller rotation. See **Figure 5**.
3. Remove the propeller elastic stop nut with an appropriate socket. Replace the nut if it can be unthreaded by hand.
4. Slide the propeller and all related hardware from the propeller shaft.
5. Clean the propeller shaft thoroughly. Inspect the propeller shaft for cracks, wear or damage. Rotate the propeller shaft to check for a bent propeller shaft. Inspect the propeller thrust washer and rear washer(s) for wear or damage. Replace any damaged parts.
6. *Flo-Torq II models*—Inspect the *Delrin* hub for wear, deterioration, damage or failure.
7. Lubricate the propeller shaft liberally with 2-4-C Multi-Lube or Special Lubricant 101.
8. Slide the propeller thrust washer onto the propeller shaft.
9A. *Rubber hub models*—Align the splines and seat the propeller against the thrust washer.
9B. *Flo-Torq II models*—Assemble the *Delrin* hub, propeller and drive hub as shown in **Figure 4**. Align the splines and seat the propeller and drive hub against the thrust washer.
10. Install the continuity washer (if equipped), splined washer (if equipped), locking tab washer and the elastic lock nut.
11. Place a suitable block of wood between a propeller blade and the antiventilation plate to prevent propeller rotation and tighten the propeller nut to 55 ft.-lb. (74.6 N•m).
12. Secure the propeller nut in one of the following ways:
   a. Bend both lock tabs securely against the appropriate flats of the elastic stop nut. See **Figure 1**. If necessary, tighten the propeller nut slightly to align the tabs.
   b. Select 3 lock tabs that align with the notches in the propeller hub or rear splined washer.

Drive the lock tabs into the notches with a hammer and punch. See **Figure 2**. If necessary tighten the propeller nut slightly to align the tabs.

TRIM TAB ADJUSTMENT

Adjust the trim tab so the steering wheel will turn with equal ease in each direction at the normal cruising speed and trim angle. The trim tab can only provide neutral steering effort for

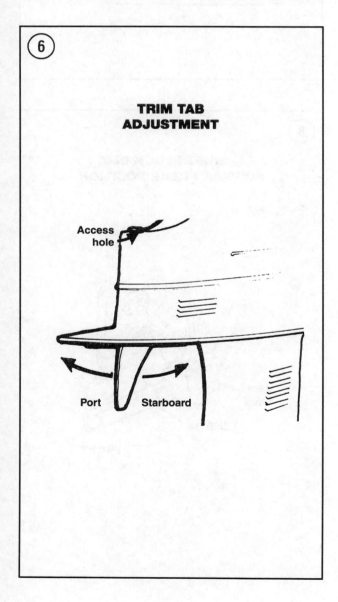

the speed and trim angle for which it was set. Trimming the outboard out (up) or in (down) or changing engine speed will change the torque load on the propeller and the resultant steering effort.

If adjustment is desired, run the boat at the speed and trim angle desired. If the boat turns more easily to starboard than port, loosen the trim tab retaining screw and move the tab trailing edge slightly to starboard. If the boat turns more easily to port, move the tab slightly to port. See **Figure 6**, typical. Tighten the trim tab retaining screw to specification (**Tables 2-6**) after adjustment and before water testing.

On models equipped with an anodic trim tab, deterioration of the anode will reduce the effectiveness of the trim tab. Replace the anodic trim tab as necessary.

GEAR HOUSING

Removal/Installation (75-125 hp)

1. Disconnect and ground the spark plug leads to the power head to prevent accidental starting.
2. Remove the propeller as described in this chapter.
3. Tilt the outboard to the fully UP position and engage the tilt lock.
4. Shift the gearcase into the FORWARD position. Rotate the propeller shaft while shifting to assist full gear engagement.
5. Mark the trim tab position (with a white grease pencil or china marker) and remove the trim tab retaining screw. Remove the trim tab.
6. Remove the 4 screws (2 on each side) and washers and one locknut and washer (in the trim tab cavity) securing the gearcase to the drive shaft housing.
7. Remove the 4 screws or locknuts (2 on each side) and washers and one locknut and washer (in front of the trim tab cavity) securing the gearcase to the drive shaft housing.

8. Pull the gearcase straight down and away from the drive shaft housing.

9. Place the gearcase in a suitable holding fixture or on a clean workbench.

10. If the water tube guide and seal remains on the water tube in the drive shaft housing, remove the water tube guide and seal from the water tube. Inspect the guide and seal and replace it if damaged.

11. To install the gearcase, begin by verifying that the water tube guide and seal are securely attached to the water pump housing. If the guide and seal are loose, glue the guide and seal to the water pump housing with Loctite 405 adhesive. See **Figure 7**.

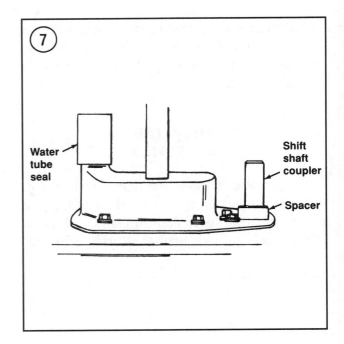

CAUTION
Do not apply lubricant to the top of the drive shaft in the next step. Excess lubricant between the top of the drive shaft and the engine crankshaft can create a hydraulic lock, preventing the drive shaft from fully engaging the crankshaft.

12. Clean the drive shaft splines as necessary, then coat the splines with Quicksilver 2-4-C Multi-Lube grease. Coat the shift shaft splines and inner diameter of the water tube seal (in the water pump housing) with the same grease. See **Figure 7**.

13. Shift the gearcase into FORWARD gear. Rotate the propeller shaft to assist gear engagement. When FORWARD gear is engaged and the propeller shaft is turned clockwise, the sliding clutch will ratchet.

14. Position the shift block on the power head in the full forward position. If the remote control cable is attached, make sure the block is traveling to the full forward position. See **Figure 8**.

15. Position the outboard shift block in the FORWARD gear position. When in the proper position, the shift block will extend 1/8 in. (3.2 mm) past the front of the shift rail. See **Figure 8**.

16. Install the shift shaft spacer and coupler shaft to the gearcase shift shaft. Install the nylon spacer over the shift shaft. Then, install the shift

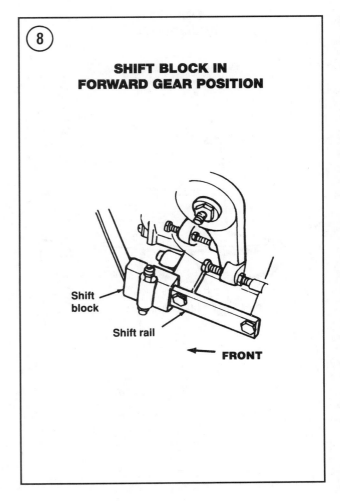

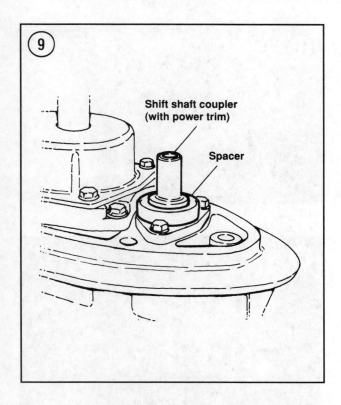

Shift shaft coupler (with power trim)

Spacer

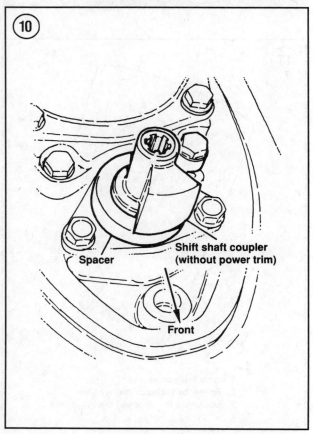

Spacer

Shift shaft coupler (without power trim)

Front

shaft coupler as shown in **Figure 9** (models equipped with power trim) or **Figure 10** (models without power trim).

17. Run a 1/4 in. (6.4 mm) bead of RTV sealant (**Table 17**) along the water dam at the rear of the water pump base.

18. Position the gearcase under the drive shaft housing. Align the water tube in the water pump, the drive shaft with crankshaft splines and the shift shaft with the shift shaft coupler.

CAUTION
Do not rotate the flywheel counterclockwise in the next step or water pump impeller damage can result. It may be necessary to rotate the shift mechanism slightly to engage the shift block splines with the gearcase shift rod splines.

19. Push the gearcase toward the drive shaft housing, rotating the flywheel clockwise as required to align the drive shaft and crankshaft splines. In addition, move the shift block *slightly* on the power head as necessary to align the shift shaft splines.

20. Make sure the water tube is seated in the water pump seal and the shift rod splines are engaged, then push the gearcase against the drive shaft housing.

21. On models equipped with screws to secure the gearcase to the drive shaft housing, apply Loctite 271 threadlocking adhesive to the threads of the 4 mounting screws.

22. Secure the gearcase to the drive shaft housing with the 4 mounting screws and one locknut (and washers) or 5 locknuts (and washers). Tighten the fasteners hand tight at this time.

NOTE
If the gearcase does not shift as described in the next step, the shift shafts are incorrectly indexed. Remove the gearcase and repeat Steps 12-20.

23. Shift the outboard into FORWARD gear—the propeller shaft should ratchet when turned

clockwise. Shift into NEUTRAL—the propeller shaft should turn freely in both directions. Shift into REVERSE gear—the propeller shaft should not turn in either direction. If shift operation is not as specified, remove the gearcase from the drive shaft housing and re-index the upper shift shaft with the lower shift shaft coupler.

24. Once proper shift function is verified, evenly tighten the gearcase mounting screws and/or locknut(s) to 40 ft.-lbs. (54.2 N•m).

25. Install the trim tab and secure it with the screw and washer. Align the marks made during removal and tighten the trim tab screw to 22 ft.-lb. (29.8 N•m).

26. Install the propeller as described in this chapter.

27. Release the tilt lock and return the outboard to the normal operating position.

28. Check the lubricant level or refill the gearcase with the recommended lubricant as described in Chapter Four.

29. If the remote control shift cable adjustment is needed, refer to Chapter Twelve.

30. Reconnect the spark plug leads.

Removal/Installation (135-200 hp and 275 hp)

Factory installed 4-3/4 in. (121 mm) diameter torpedo gearcases on 135-200 hp (prior to serial No. 0G438000) and all 275 hp models are *ratcheting* gearcases. This means that the propeller can overrun the sliding clutch during deceleration. The propeller can be turned clockwise when in FORWARD gear, but not counterclockwise. The propeller can be turned counterclockwise when in REVERSE gear, but not clockwise.

Factory installed 4-3/4 in. (121 mm) diameter torpedo gearcases on 135-200 hp (serial No. 0G438000-on) are *not ratcheting* gearcases. This means that the propeller cannot overrun the sliding clutch during deceleration. The propeller will lock in either FORWARD or REVERSE gear.

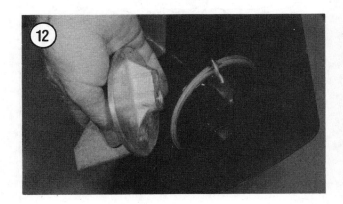

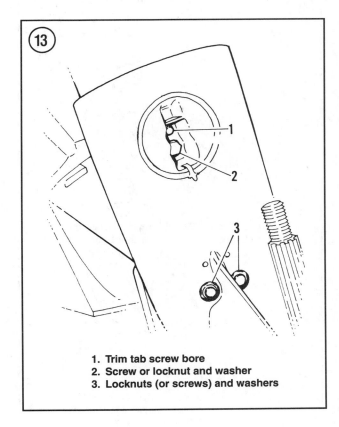

1. Trim tab screw bore
2. Screw or locknut and washer
3. Locknuts (or screws) and washers

The propeller will still spin freely in either direction in NEUTRAL.

Factory installed 4-1/4 in. (108 mm) diameter torpedo gearcases on XR6 and Magnum III models are ratcheting in FORWARD, but not ratcheting in REVERSE. This means that the propeller can overrun the sliding clutch in FORWARD gear during deceleration, but not in REVERSE gear. The propeller will lock in REVERSE gear. The propeller will still spin freely in either direction in NEUTRAL.

Turning the gearcase shift rod clockwise engages the FORWARD gear and turning the shift rod counterclockwise engages the REVERSE gear.

Removal

1. Disconnect and ground the spark plug leads. Remove the spark plugs from the engine.

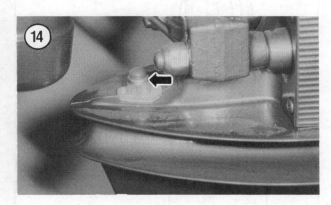

2. Shift the outboard into NEUTRAL. The propeller should rotate freely in both directions.
3. Tilt the outboard to the fully UP position and engage the tilt lock.
4. Remove the propeller as described in this chapter.
5. Mark the trim tab position (with a white grease pencil or china marker).
6A. *135-200 hp*—Pry the plastic access plug (**Figure 11**) from the rear of the drive shaft housing. Insert a suitable socket into the hole and remove the screw securing the trim tab. Remove the trim tab (**Figure 12**).
6B. *275 hp*—Remove the screw securing the trim tab to the gearcase. Remove the trim tab.
7. Remove the locknut and washer (or screw) located inside the trim tab cavity. See 2, **Figure 13**.
8. Remove the 2 locknuts (or screws) from the bottom of the antiventilation plate at the trailing edge of the gearcase strut. See 3, **Figure 13**.
9. Remove the upper lock nut and washer securing the gearcase to the leading edge of the drive shaft housing. See **Figure 14**.

NOTE
On badly corroded units, the gearcase may be frozen to the drive shaft housing. Apply penetrating oil to the mounting studs. Mild heat can be applied (such as a propane torch) and a soft mallet can be used to free the gearcase. In extreme cases, it may be necessary to pry the gearcase from the drive shaft housing. Avoid damaging the gearcase and drive shaft housing mating surfaces.

10A. *135-200 hp*—Loosen the locknut on each side of the gearcase (**Figure 15**) one turn at a time, them move back to the other side. Remove one nut and washer, but leave the other nut threaded on 2-3 turns, to prevent the gearcase from falling free.
10B. *275 hp*—Loosen the 2 locknuts from each side of the gearcase. Loosen each nut 1 turn at a time, then move on to the next nut. Remove 3 of

the nuts and washers, but leave one nut threaded on 2-3 turns, to prevent the gearcase from falling free.

11. If equipped with a gearcase speedometer pickup, disconnect the speedometer line from the connector fitting at the entrance to the swivel tube (near the front of the lower motor mounts).

12. Holding the gearcase firmly, remove the last nut and washer, then pull the gearcase straight down and away from the drive shaft housing.

13. Mount the gearcase into a suitable holding fixture or place the gearcase on a clean workbench.

14. If the water tube guide and water tube seal remained on the water tube in the drive shaft housing, remove the water tube guide and water tube seal from the water tube. If the water tube guide and water tube seal remained in the water pump, remove the water tube guide and the water tube seal from the water pump housing. Discard the water tube seal.

15. *275 hp*—Remove the drive shaft rubber seal and splined nylon support tube from the drive shaft. Discard the rubber seal. See **Figure 16**.

Installation

1. To install the gearcase, begin by installing a new water tube seal into the water pump housing. Then install the water tube guide to the water pump housing.

> *CAUTION*
> *Do not apply lubricant to the top of the drive shaft and shift shaft in the next step. Excess lubricant between the top of the drive shaft and the engine crankshaft can create a hydraulic lock, preventing the drive shaft from fully engaging the crankshaft.*

2. Clean the drive shaft splines as necessary, then coat the splines with Quicksilver 2-4-C Multi-Lube grease. Coat the shift shaft splines and inner diameter of the water tube seal (in the water pump housing) with the same grease.

3. *275 hp*—Install the splined nylon support tube and a new drive shaft rubber seal. Make sure the splined side of the rubber seal faces the nylon tube. See **Figure 16**.

4. Shift the gearcase into FORWARD gear by rotating the shift shaft fully clockwise while rotating the propeller shaft counterclockwise.

5. *135-200 hp*—Run a thin bead of RTV Sealant across the top of the exhaust divider plate and set the trim tab retaining screw into the furthest aft hole on the gearcase deck.

6A. *135-200 hp*—Position the engine shift linkage into the full FORWARD gear position. The engine shift linkage guide block anchor pin should be positioned as shown in **Figure 17**.

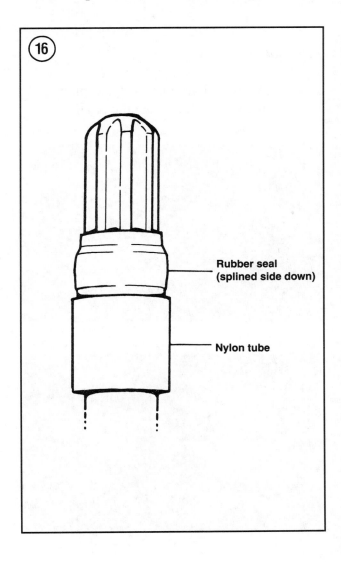

Rubber seal (splined side down)

Nylon tube

6B. *275 hp*—Position the engine shift linkage into the full FORWARD gear position. This should provide a dimension of 4-1/8 in. (104.8 mm) between the shift cable casing guide anchor stud and the closest edge of the shift cable sleeve support bracket.

7. Clean the threads of all gearcase mounting screws with Locquic Primer. Allow the primer to air dry, then apply Loctite 271 threadlocking adhesive to the screw threads.

8. Position the gearcase under the drive shaft housing. Align the water tube in the water pump, the drive shaft with crankshaft splines and the shift shaft with the shift shaft coupler. Insert the speedometer hose through the shift shaft hole in the drive shaft housing and connect the hose to its connector.

CAUTION
Do not rotate the flywheel counterclockwise in the next step or water pump impeller damage can result. It may be necessary to rotate the shift mechanism slightly to engage the shift block splines with the shift rod splines.

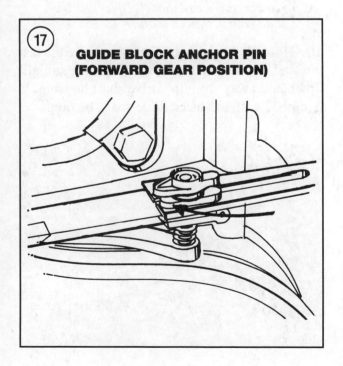

GUIDE BLOCK ANCHOR PIN (FORWARD GEAR POSITION)

9. Push the gearcase toward the drive shaft housing, rotating the flywheel clockwise as required to align the drive shaft and crankshaft splines. In addition, move the shift linkage *slightly* on the power head as necessary to align the shift shaft splines.

10. Make sure the water tube is seated in the water pump seal and the shift rod splines are engaged, then push the gearcase against the drive shaft housing.

11. Install the screw (or locknut and washer) into the trim tab cavity (2, **Figure 13**). Tighten the fastener hand-tight to keep the gearcase from falling from the drive shaft housing.

12. Install the locknuts and flat washers on the sides and the locknut and washer on the front (**Figure 14**) of the gearcase. Tighten the locknuts hand-tight at this time.

13. Install the 2 locknuts (or screws) (3, **Figure 13**) and washers under the antiventilation plate. Tighten the fasteners hand-tight at this time.

14. Verify correct shift rod engagement by first moving the engine shift linkage into full FORWARD gear. Manually rotate the flywheel clockwise (as viewed from top) while observing the propeller shaft—the shaft must turn clockwise. Then move the engine shift linkage to the NEUTRAL position. The propeller shaft must rotate freely in both directions. Finally, move the engine shift linkage to the full REVERSE position. Manually rotate the flywheel clockwise (as viewed from top) while observing the propeller shaft—the shaft must turn counterclockwise. If shift operation is not as specified, remove the gearcase and re-index the shift shaft splines.

15. Once shift shaft indexing is verified, tighten all gearcase mounting hardware to specification.

16A. *135-200 hp*—Install the trim tab and secure it with previously installed screw. Align the marks made during removal and tighten the trim tab screw to specification.

16B. *275 hp*—Apply Loctite 271 Threadlocking adhesive to the trim tab screw threads. Install

9

the trim tab and secure it with the screw and washer. Align the marks made during removal and tighten the trim tab screw to 15 ft.-lb. (20.3 N•m).

17. Install the propeller as described in this chapter.

18. Release the tilt lock and return the outboard to the normal operating position.

19. Check the lubricant level or refill the gearcase with the recommended lubricant as described in Chapter Four.

20. If remote control shift cable adjustment is needed, refer to Chapter Twelve.

21. Install the spark plugs and connect the spark plug leads.

Removal/Installation (200 DFI and 225-250 hp)

Factory-installed gearcases on models prior to serial No. 0G438000 are *ratcheting* gearcases. This means that the propeller can overrun the sliding clutch during deceleration. The propeller can be turned clockwise when in FORWARD gear, but not counterclockwise. The propeller can be turned counterclockwise when in REVERSE gear, but not clockwise.

Factory installed gearcases on serial No. 0G438000-on models are *not ratcheting* gearcases. This means that the propeller cannot overrun the sliding clutch during deceleration. The propeller will lock in either FORWARD or REVERSE gear. The propeller will still spin freely in either direction in NEUTRAL.

Removal

1. Disconnect and ground the spark plug leads. Remove the spark plugs from the engine.

2. Shift the outboard into NEUTRAL. The propeller must rotate freely in both directions.

3. Tilt the outboard to the fully UP position and engage the tilt lock.

4. Remove the propeller as described in this chapter.

5. Mark the trim tab position (with a white grease pencil or china marker).

6. Pry the plastic access plug (**Figure 18**) from the rear of the drive shaft housing. Insert a suitable socket into the hole and remove the screw securing the trim tab. Remove the trim tab (**Figure 19**).

7. Remove the screw located inside the trim tab cavity. See **Figure 20**.

8. Loosen the 2 locknuts on each side of the gearcase. Loosen each nut 1 turn at a time, then move on to the next nut. Remove 3 of the nuts and washers, but leave one nut threaded on 2-3 turns, to prevent the gearcase from falling free.

9. If equipped with a gearcase speedometer pickup, disconnect the speedometer line from the connector fitting at the entrance to the drive shaft housing (near the front of the lower motor mounts).

NOTE
Late model gearcases use a 2-piece drive shaft. A splined coupler connects the upper and lower drive shafts just above the water pump housing. If necessary, replace the early model 1-piece drive shaft with a 2-piece shaft.

10. Holding the gearcase firmly, remove the last nut and washer, then pull the gearcase straight down and away from the drive shaft housing. If equipped with a 2-piece drive shaft, be prepared

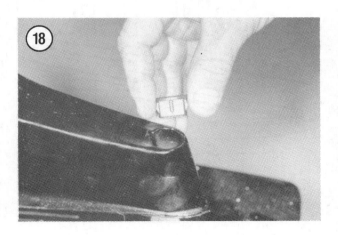

to catch the upper drive shaft and coupler if they separate from the lower drive shaft.

11. Mount the gearcase into a suitable holding fixture or place the gearcase on a clean workbench. Remove and discard the trim tab screw.

12. Remove the water tube guide and seal assembly from the water pump housing. Remove and discard the 2 O-rings from the inner diameter of the guide.

13. *2-piece drive shaft models*—Lift the upper drive shaft and coupler from the lower drive shaft.

Installation

1. To install the gearcase, begin by installing 2 new water tube O-rings into the water tube guide.

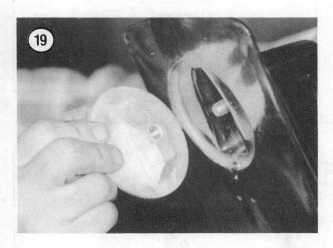

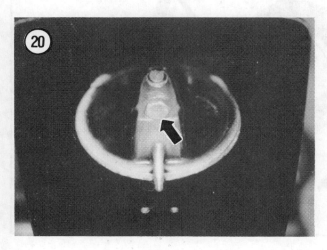

Lubricate the O-rings with Quicksilver 2-4-C Multi-Lube grease. Then, install the water tube guide to the water pump housing.

> *CAUTION*
> *Do not apply lubricant to the top of the drive shaft(s) in the next step. Excess lubricant between the top of the drive shaft and the engine crankshaft can create a hydraulic lock, preventing the drive shaft from fully engaging the crankshaft.*

2. Clean the drive shaft splines as necessary, then coat the splines with Quicksilver 2-4-C Multi-Lube grease. Coat the shift shaft splines with the same grease.

3. *2-piece drive shaft models*—Install the drive shaft coupler and upper drive shaft to the lower drive shaft. Make sure all of the splined areas are lubricated.

4. Shift the gearcase into NEUTRAL gear by rotating the shift shaft until the propeller spins freely in both directions.

5. If the water dam behind the water pump was removed, run a thin bead of RTV Sealant across both sides of the dam and install it into the gear housing.

6. Install a new patch lock trim tab retaining screw into the furthest aft hole on the gearcase deck.

7. Position the engine shift linkage into the NEUTRAL gear position. The shift linkage guide block anchor pin should be positioned in the middle of its total travel as shown in **Figure 21**.

8. Position the gearcase under the drive shaft housing. Align the water tube in the water pump, the drive shaft with crankshaft splines and the shift shaft with the shift shaft coupler. Insert the speedometer hose through its opening in the drive shaft housing and connect the hose to its connector.

> *CAUTION*
> *Do not rotate the flywheel counterclockwise in the next step or water pump impeller damage can result. It may be necessary to rotate the shift mechanism slightly to engage the shift block splines with the shift rod splines.*

9

9. Push the gearcase toward the drive shaft housing, rotating the flywheel clockwise as required to align the drive shaft and crankshaft splines. In addition, move the shift linkage *slightly* on the power head as necessary to align the shift shaft splines.

10. Make sure the water tube is seated in the water pump guide and the shift rod splines are engaged, then push the gearcase against the drive shaft housing.

11. Install the mounting screw located in the trim tab cavity (**Figure 20**). Tighten the fastener

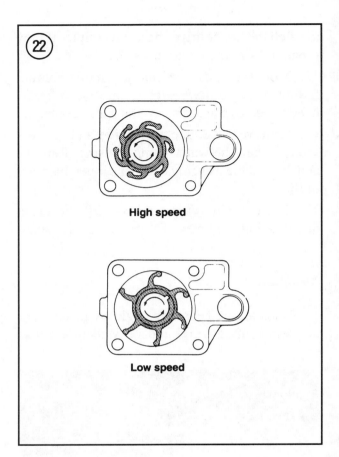

High speed

Low speed

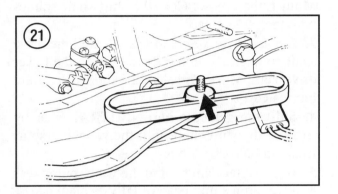

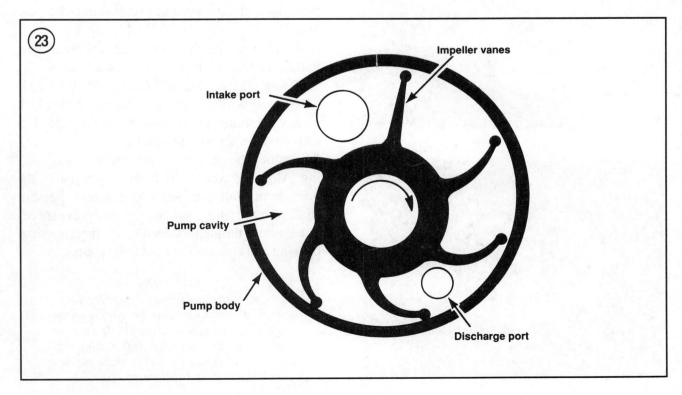

Impeller vanes

Intake port

Pump cavity

Pump body

Discharge port

hand tight to keep the gearcase from falling from the drive shaft housing.

12. Install the locknuts and flat washers (2 on each side). Tighten the locknuts hand-tight at this time.

13. Verify correct shift rod engagement by first moving the shift linkage into full FORWARD gear. Manually rotate the flywheel clockwise (as viewed from top) while observing the propeller shaft—the shaft must turn clockwise. Then, move the engine shift linkage to the NEUTRAL

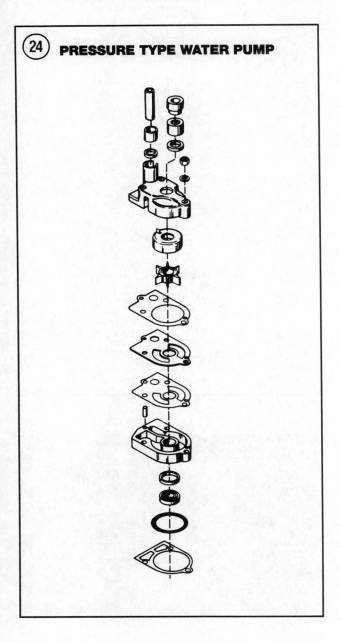

24 PRESSURE TYPE WATER PUMP

position. The propeller shaft must rotate freely in both directions. Finally move the engine shift linkage to the full REVERSE position. Manually rotate the flywheel clockwise (as viewed from top) while observing the propeller shaft—the shaft must turn counterclockwise. If shift operation is not as specified, remove the gearcase and re-index the shift shaft.

14. Once shift shaft indexing is verified, tighten all gearcase mounting hardware to specification.

15. Install the trim tab and secure it with the previously installed screw. Align the marks made during removal and tighten the trim tab screw to 40 ft.-lb. (54.2 N•m). Install the plastic access plug (**Figure 18**).

16. Install the propeller as described in this chapter.

17. Release the tilt lock and return the outboard to the normal operating position.

18. Check the lubricant level or refill the gearcase with the recommended lubricant as described in Chapter Four.

19. If remote control shift cable adjustment is needed, refer to Chapter Twelve.

20. Install the spark plugs and connect the spark plug leads.

WATER PUMP

All outboard motors in this manual use an offset-center pump housing that causes the vanes of the impeller to flex during rotation. At low speed the pump operates as a positive displacement pump. At high speed, water resistance causes the impeller vanes to flex inward, causing the pump to operate as a centrifugal pump. See **Figure 22**.

The pump draws water into the intake port(s) as the vanes expand (flex outward) and pumps water out of the discharge port(s) as the vanes compress (flex inward) as shown in **Figure 23**.

Two basic water pump designs are used: the high-pressure pump (**Figure 24**, typical) and the

9

high-volume pump (**Figure 25**, typical). The high-pressure pump develops more pressure than volume, while the high-volume pump delivers more volume than pressure.

On all models, the pump is located on the gearcase upper deck and is driven by a key in the drive shaft.

The impeller only operates in a clockwise rotation with the drive shaft (or propeller shaft) and is held in a flexed (compressed) position at all times. Over time, this causes the impeller to take a *set* in one direction. Turning an impeller over and attempting to turn it against its natural *set* will cause premature impeller failure and power head damage from overheating. The manufacturer recommends replacing the impeller *every* time the water pump is disassembled. The impeller should only be reused if there is no other option. If the impeller must be reused, reinstall the impeller in its original position.

Overheating and extensive power head damage can result from a faulty water pump. Therefore, the manufacturer recommends replacing the water pump impeller, seals and gaskets as follows:

1. *High-pressure pump*—Once a year or every 100 hours of operation. The 135-200 hp (except 200 DFI), 275 hp and 105-140 Jet models use a high-pressure pump. An exploded view of a typical high-pressure pump is shown in **Figure 24**.

2. *High-volume pump*—Every three years or 300 hours of operation. All models not listed previously under *High-pressure pumps* will use a high-volume pump. An exploded view of a typical high-volume pump is shown in **Figure 25**.

Individual operating conditions may dictate that the pump require service more often. It is also recommended that the water pump be serviced any time the lower gearcase (or Jet pump unit) is removed for any type of service.

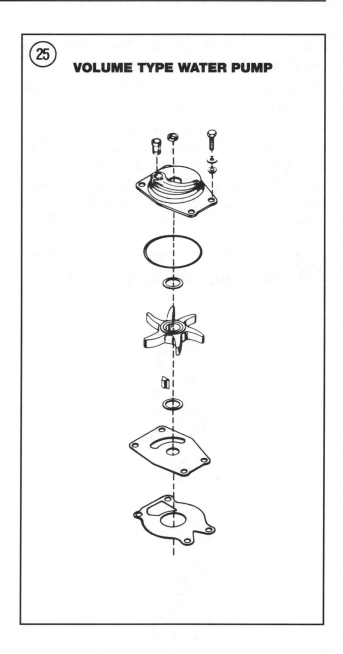

(25) VOLUME TYPE WATER PUMP

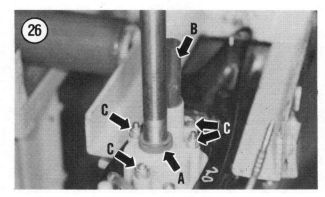

Removal and Disassembly

The manufacturer recommends replacing all seals and gaskets whenever the water pump is disassembled. Since the drive shaft seals operate at crankshaft speed and are under motion any time the engine is running, the water pump base (on models so equipped) should be removed and the drive shaft seals replaced any time the water

pump is disassembled. The manufacturer also recommends replacing the water pump impeller anytime the pump is disassembled.

135-200 hp

1. Remove the gearcase as described previously in this chapter. Secure the gearcase in a suitable holding fixture or a vise with protective jaws. If protective jaws are not available, position the unit upright in a vise with the skeg between wooden blocks.

2. Remove the rubber centrifugal slinger (A, **Figure 26**) from the drive shaft.

3. Remove the water tube guide (B, **Figure 26**) and seal from the top of the pump housing. Discard the seal.

4. Remove the 3 elastic locknuts and washers and the single screw at the rear of the housing (C, **Figure 26**) holding the water pump housing to the gearcase.

5. Carefully insert screwdrivers at the fore and aft ends of the pump housing and pry the housing upward. See **Figure 27**. Lift the housing up and off the drive shaft.

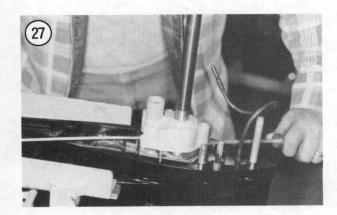

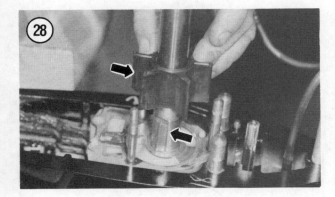

NOTE
In extreme cases, it may be necessary to split the impeller hub with a hammer and chisel to remove it from the drive shaft in Step 6.

6. Remove the impeller and drive key from the drive shaft (**Figure 28**). If necessary, drive the impeller upward on the shaft with a punch and hammer. Do not damage the drive shaft in the process.

7. Remove the impeller plate (**Figure 29**) and the top and bottom gaskets. Discard the gaskets.

8. Insert screwdrivers at the fore and aft ends of the pump base. Pad the pry areas under each screwdriver with clean shop towels and pry the

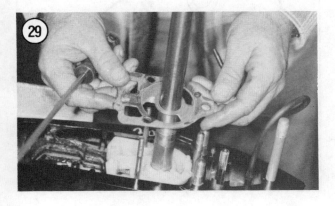

pump base loose. Remove the base from the shaft (**Figure 30**).

9. Remove and discard the pump base-to-gearcase O-ring (A, **Figure 31**).

10. Pry (or drive) the drive shaft seals (B, **Figure 31**) from the pump base from (towards) the gearcase side of the base.

11. *135-200 hp models*—If the housing liner must be replaced, drive the liner from the pump cover with a punch and hammer inserted through the drive shaft bore. If the insert refuses to come out, carefully drill a 3/16 in. (4.8 mm) hole through the top (but not through the insert) on each side of the cover as shown in **Figure 32** and drive the insert out with a hammer and punch.

12. Inspect the water pump components as described under *Water Pump Cleaning and Inspection*, in this chapter.

75-125 hp

Refer to **Figure 33** for this procedure.

1. Remove the gearcase as described in this chapter. Secure the gearcase in a suitable holding fixture or a vise with protective jaws. If protective jaws are not available, position the unit upright in a vise with the skeg between wooden blocks.

2. Remove the water tube guide and seal from the pump housing.

3. Remove 4 pump housing screws. Lift the pump housing up and off the drive shaft. If

necessary, carefully pry at each end with a suitable tool.

4. Remove the impeller from the drive shaft.

5. Remove the impeller drive key from the drive shaft flat.

6. Remove the impeller plate and the upper and lower gaskets. Discard the gaskets.

7. Remove the 6 screws securing the pump base to the gearcase. Dislodge the base from the gearcase by carefully prying at each end using 2 screwdrivers. Lift the base up and off the drive shaft. Remove and discard the base-to-gearcase gasket. Carefully pry the drive shaft seal from the pump base.

8. Inspect the water pump components as described in *Water Pump Cleaning and Inspection*, located later in this chapter.

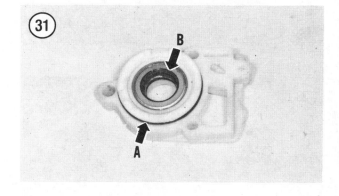

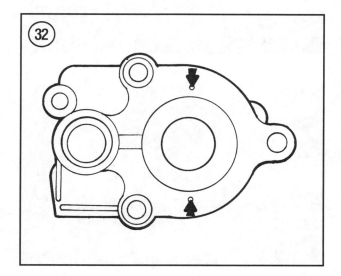

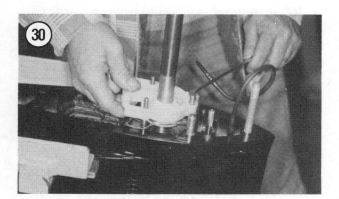

200 DFI (direct fuel injection) and 225-275 hp

Refer to **Figure 34** for 200 DFI and 225 and 250 hp models and **Figure 35** for 275 hp models.

1. Remove the gearcase as described in this chapter. Secure the gearcase in a suitable holding fixture or a vise with protective jaws. If protec-

tive jaws are not available, position the unit upright in a vise with the skeg between wooden blocks.

2A. *200 DFI, 225 and 250 hp*—Remove the water tube guide and seal assembly from the pump housing. Remove and discard the 2 O-rings in the guide.

2B. *275 hp*—Remove the water tube guide and water tube seal from the pump housing. Discard the seal.

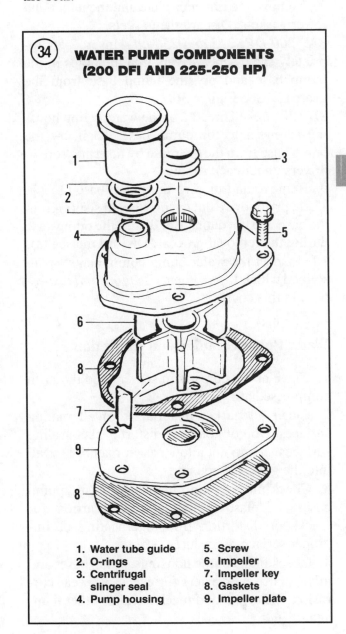

(33) WATER PUMP COMPONENTS (75-125 HP)

1. Water tube guide and seal
2. Pump housing
3. Screw
4. Impeller
5. Impeller key
6. Gaskets
7. Impeller plate
8. Pump base
9. Screw
10. Large drive shaft seal
11. Small drive shaft seal

(34) WATER PUMP COMPONENTS (200 DFI AND 225-250 HP)

1. Water tube guide
2. O-rings
3. Centrifugal slinger seal
4. Pump housing
5. Screw
6. Impeller
7. Impeller key
8. Gaskets
9. Impeller plate

9

3. *200 DFI, 225 and 250 hp*—Remove the centrifugal slinger seal from the drive shaft. Slide the seal up and off of the drive shaft.

4. Remove 4 pump housing screws. Lift the pump housing up and off the drive shaft. If necessary, carefully pry at each end with a suitable tool.

5. Remove the impeller from the drive shaft.

6. Remove the impeller drive key from the drive shaft flat.

7. Remove the impeller plate and the upper and lower gaskets. Discard the gaskets.

8A. *200 DFI 225 and 250 hp*—Insert 2 appropriately sized screwdrivers into the holes in the pump base and pry the pump base from the gearcase. See **Figure 36**.

8B. *275 hp*—Thread 2 of the water pump housing screws into the pump base. Then pry the pump base from the gearcase by inserting screwdrivers under each screw.

9. Remove and discard the pump base O-ring. Then, pry or drive out the drive shaft seal(s) from the base. Do not damage or distort the pump base during the removal process. Discard the seal(s).

10. Inspect the water pump components as described which *Water Pump Cleaning and Inspection*, in this chapter.

Water Pump Cleaning and Inspection

1. Clean all metal parts in solvent and dry with compressed air.

2. Clean all gasket material from all mating surfaces. Do not gouge or distort gasket sealing surfaces and do not allow gasket material to fall into the gearcase housing.

3. Check plastic pump housings, plastic pump bases and plastic drive shaft seal carriers for cracks or distortion from overheating or improper service procedures.

4. Check metal pump housings, pump bases and drive shaft seal carriers for excessive wear corrosion, distortion and mechanical or other damage.

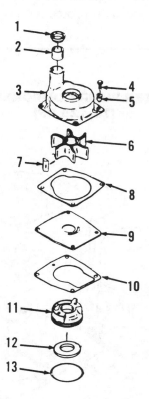

WATER PUMP COMPONENTS (275 HP)

1. Water tube guide
2. Water tube seal
3. Pump housing
4. Screw
5. Insulator
6. Impeller
7. Impeller key
8. Gasket
9. Impeller plate
10. Gasket
11. Pump base
12. Drive shaft seal
13. O-ring

5. Check the lower plate and pump liner (or housing) for grooves, rough surfaces or excessive wear. Replace the pump liner insert (or housing) and lower plate as necessary. Grooves from the impeller sealing rings are not a concern.

> *NOTE*
> *The water pump impeller must be able to float on the drive shaft. Clean the impeller area of the drive shaft thoroughly using emery cloth. Be certain the impeller slides onto the drive shaft easily.*

6. Replace the impeller any time it is removed. If the impeller must be reused, check the bonding of the rubber to the impeller hub for separation. Check the side seal surfaces and blade ends for cracks, tears, excessive wear or a glazed or melted appearance. If any of these defects are noted, do *not* reuse the impeller under any circumstances.

7. Measure the thickness of the pump cover at the discharge slots. Replace the cover if the metal thickness is 0.060 in. (1.52 mm) or less.

8. Inspect the pump housing and impeller plate for grooves or excessive wear. Replace the housing and/or the impeller plate if grooves (except the impeller seal ring grooves) exceed 0.030 in. (0.76 mm) deep.

Assembly and Installation

135-200 hp

1. If the pump housing liner was removed, lightly coat the liner area in the housing with Quicksilver Perfect Seal. Align the insert tab

9

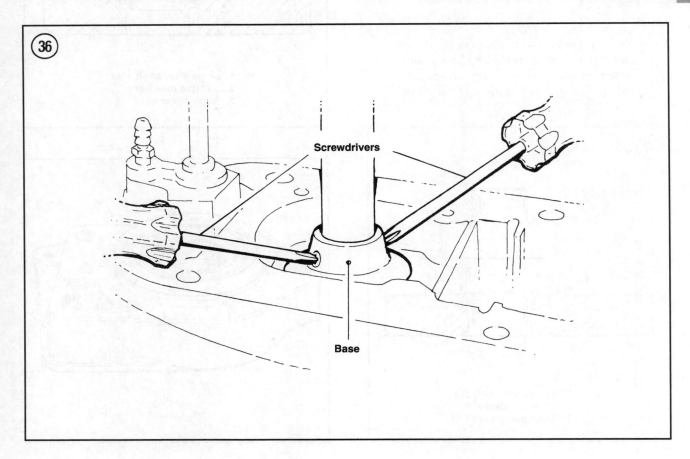

with its respective recess in the housing and press the liner into the housing until it is seated.

> *NOTE*
> *If insert removal required drilling holes into the pump cover, fill the holes with RTV sealant. Allow the sealer to fully cure before operation.*

2. Position the pump base on a press. Apply Loctite 271 Threadlocking adhesive to the outside diameter of 2 new drive shaft seals. Press the smaller diameter seal (with the lip facing the impeller) into the pump base until it is seated as shown in **Figure 37**. Then, press the larger diameter seal (with the lip facing the gearcase) into the pump base until it is also seated as shown in **Figure 38**.

3. Lubricate a new pump base O-ring and the drive shaft seal lips with Quicksilver 2-4-C Multi-Lube grease. Install the O-ring into its groove in the pump base (1, **Figure 39**).

> *NOTE*
> *Be very careful not to damage the drive shaft seals when installing the pump base over the drive shaft and drive shaft spline. Remove any sharp burrs or nicks from the drive shaft and splines with emery cloth. If necessary, wrap tape over the splines.*

4. Install a new pump base gasket (2, **Figure 39**) onto the pump base. Install the pump base over the drive shaft and into position in the housing. See **Figure 40**.

5. Install new lower and upper gaskets on the impeller plate. Install the plate and gaskets onto

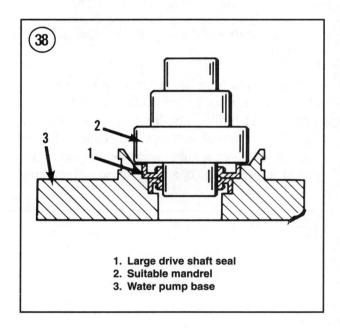

38

1. Large drive shaft seal
2. Suitable mandrel
3. Water pump base

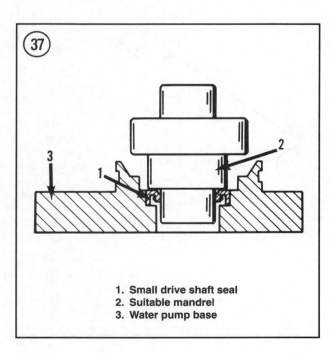

37

1. Small drive shaft seal
2. Suitable mandrel
3. Water pump base

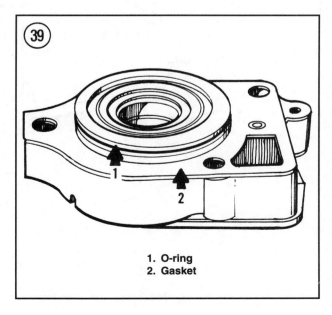

39

1. O-ring
2. Gasket

the pump base. See **Figure 41**. Make sure the dowel pins on the base properly engage the face plate and gaskets.

6. Lubricate the impeller key with Quicksilver 2-4-C Multi-Lube grease. Position the impeller key on the drive shaft flat.

7. Lubricate the impeller with Quicksilver 2-4-C Multi-Lube grease. Slide the impeller over the

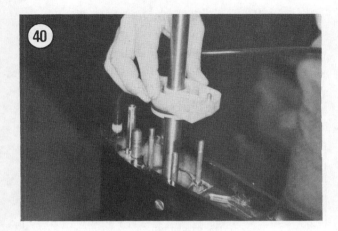

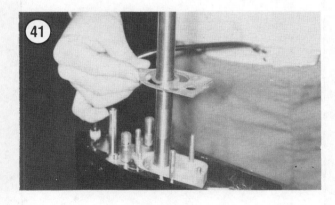

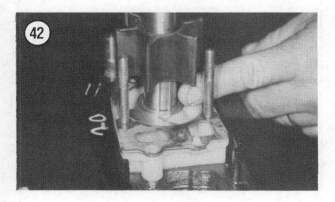

drive shaft and engage the impeller key (**Figure 42**).

8. Install a new water tube seal into the pump housing with the plastic side of the seal facing downward. Then, install the water tube guide to the pump housing.

9. Slide the pump housing assembly over the drive shaft and into position over the impeller and onto the mounting studs. Turn the drive shaft clockwise and press the housing down to feed the impeller into the housing. Seat the pump housing against the plate.

CAUTION
Do not over-tighten the fasteners in the next step or the pump housing may crack during operation.

10. Install the 3 elastic locknuts and washers and the 1 guide (rear) screw. Evenly tighten the nuts and screw to specifications (**Table 5**).

11. Install the rubber centrifugal slinger over the drive shaft and against the pump cover.

12. Install the gearcase to the outboard motor as described previously in this chapter.

9

75-125 hp

Refer to **Figure 33** for this procedure.

1. Apply Loctite 271 Threadlocking adhesive to the outer diameter of 2 new drive shaft seals. Set the water pump base (stepped side facing up) into a press. Install the Teflon coated seal (flat brown/black color) with the spring facing the power head onto the longer stepped side of the seal installer (part No. 91-13949 or equivalent). Press the seal into the water pump base until the tool bottoms. Install the non-Teflon coated seal (glossy black color) with spring facing the gearcase onto the short stepped side of the same installer. Press the seal into the water pump base until the tool bottoms. Coat the seal lips with 2-4-C Multi-Lube grease.

2. Place a new gasket onto the gearcase. Slide the water pump base over the drive shaft and into position on the gasket. Be careful not to cut or damage the seals on the drive shaft splines. Make sure the water pump base is piloted into the gearcase bore and has not pinched the gasket in the gearcase bore.

3. Coat the 6 water pump base screws with Loctite 271 threadlocking adhesive. Install the screws and washers. Evenly tighten the screws to 60 in.-lb. (6.8 N•m).

4. Install a new gasket on top of the water pump base. Slide the impeller plate over the drive shaft and into position on the gasket. Then, install a new housing gasket on the plate.

5. Grease the impeller key with 2-4-C Multi-Lube grease and position it on the drive shaft flat. Slide the impeller onto the drive shaft and engage the key.

6. Slide the pump housing over the drive shaft and into position over the impeller. Turn the drive shaft clockwise and press the housing down to feed the impeller into the body. Seat the pump housing against the plate.

7. Coat the threads of the 4 housing screws with Loctite 271 Threadlocking adhesive. Install and evenly tighten the screws to 60 in.-lb. (6.8 N•m).

8. If the water tube guide and seal were removed, glue the guide and seal to the water pump housing with Loctite 405 adhesive. Then, lubricate the water tube seal with Quicksilver 2-4-C Multi-Lube grease.

9. Install the gearcase to the outboard motor as described previously in this chapter.

200 DFI (direct fuel injection) and 225-275 hp

The water pump base on 275 hp models uses a single case, double lip seal. The water pump base on 1994 and 1995 225 and 250 hp models uses 2 seals of different outer diameters. The water pump base on 1996 and 1997 200 DFI and

225 and 250 hp models uses 2 seals with the same outer diameter.

Refer to **Figure 34** for 200 DFI and 225 and 250 hp models and **Figure 35** for 275 hp models.

1A. *225-250 hp (1994-1995)*—Apply Loctite 271 Threadlocking adhesive to the outer diameter of 2 new drive shaft seals. Then, set the water pump base into a press with the tapered end facing down.

a. Install the small diameter seal with the lip facing the power head onto the longer stepped side of seal installer part No. 91-817569 or equivalent. Press the seal into the water pump base until the tool bottoms as shown in A, **Figure 43**.

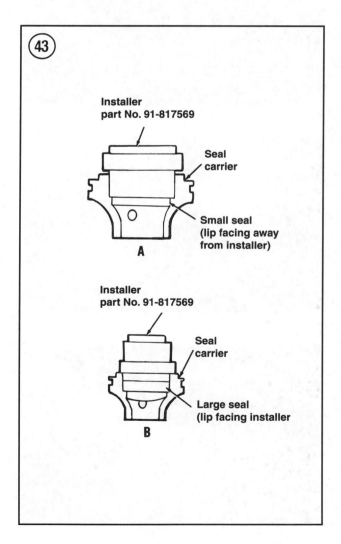

b. Install the large diameter seal with the lip facing the gearcase onto the short stepped side of the same installer. Press the seal into the water pump base until the tool bottoms as shown in B, **Figure 43**.

1B. *200 DFI, 225-250 hp (1996-1997)*—Apply Loctite 271 Threadlocking adhesive to the outer diameter of 2 new drive shaft seals. Then, set the water pump base into a press with the tapered end facing down.

a. Press the first seal into the base with the lip facing down. Press the seal with a suitable mandrel until the seal is seated in the base bore.

b. Press the second seal into the base with the lip facing up. Press the seal with a suitable mandrel until the seal is flush with the base bore.

1C. *275 hp*—Apply Loctite 271 Threadlocking adhesive to the outer diameter of a new drive shaft seal. Press the seal into the water pump base with a suitable mandrel until the seal is flush with the base.

2. Lubricate a new water pump base O-ring with Quicksilver 2-4-C Multi-Lube grease. Install the O-ring into the base groove.

3. Slide the water pump base over the drive shaft and into position in the gearcase bore. Be careful not to cut or damage the seal(s) on the drive shaft splines. Make sure the water pump base is seated in the gearcase bore.

4. *275 hp*—If the exhaust deflector plate was removed, coat both ends of the deflector with RTV sealant and install it into the gearcase recess just behind the pump base.

5. Install a new gasket on top of the water pump base. Slide the impeller plate over the drive shaft and into position on the gasket. Then, install a new housing gasket on the plate. Make sure the gasket and plate holes are aligned with the gearcase holes.

6. Grease the impeller key with 2-4-C Multi-Lube grease and position it on the drive shaft flat.

Slide the impeller onto the drive shaft and engage the key.

7. Install 2 water pump alignment pins into the water pump housing screw holes in the gearcase. Use 2 opposing screw holes.

8. Slide the pump housing over the drive shaft and into position over the impeller. Turn the drive shaft clockwise and press the housing down to feed the impeller into the body. Seat the pump housing over the alignment pins and against the plate.

9. Coat the threads of the 4 housing screws with Loctite 271 Threadlocking adhesive.

10A. *200 DFI, 225-250 hp*—Install 2 screws finger-tight, then remove the alignment pins and install the last 2 screws finger-tight. Finally, tighten all 4 housing screws evenly to 60 in.-lb. (6.8 N•m).

10B. *275 hp*—Install 2 screws and plastic insulators finger-tight, then remove the alignment pins and install the last 2 screws and plastic insulators finger-tight. Make sure the insulators are correctly aligned with the housing, gasket and screw holes. Then, tighten all 4 housing screws evenly to 60 in.-lb. (6.8 N•m).

11A. *200 DFI, 225-250 hp*—Lubricate 2 new water tube guide O-rings with Quicksilver 2-4-C Multi-Lube grease. Install the O-rings into the guide. Then, install the guide assembly to the pump housing.

11B. *275 hp*—Lubricate the water tube seal with Quicksilver 2-4-C Multi-Lube grease. Install the seal into the pump housing with the plastic side of the seal facing downward. Then, install the water tube guide to the pump housing.

12. Install the gearcase to the outboard motor as described previously in this chapter.

GEARCASE DISASSEMBLY/ASSEMBLY

The section covers complete disassembly and reassembly procedures for each lower gearcase covered in this manual. Once the gearcase is

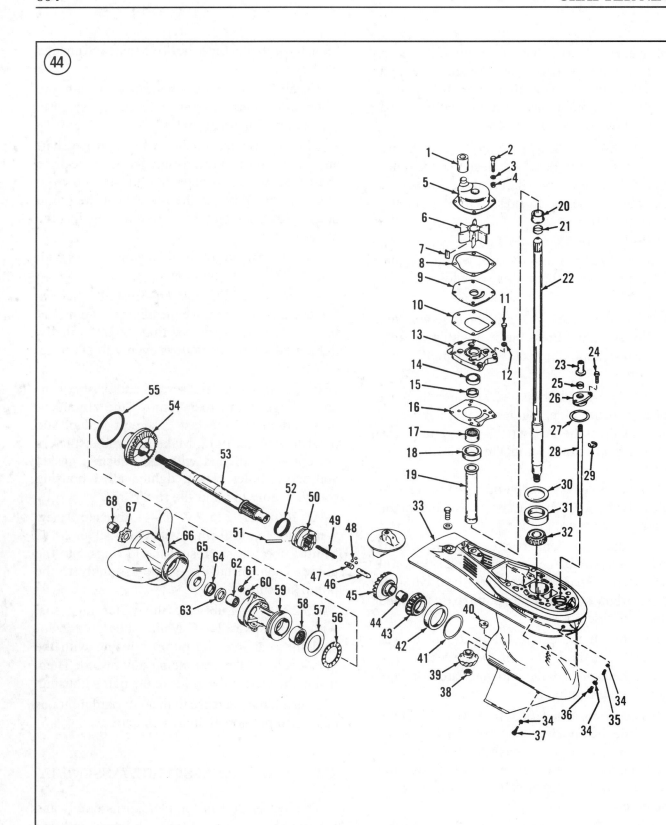

**GEARCASE ASSEMBLY
(60 HP BIGFOOT AND 75-125 HP)**

1. Water tube seal
2. Screw
3. Washer
4. Insulator
5. Water pump cover
6. Impeller
7. Impeller drive key
8. Gasket
9. Face plate
10. Gasket
11. Screw
12. Washer
13. Water pump base
14. Seal
15. Seal
16. Gasket
17. Roller bearing
18. Carrier
19. Sleeve
20. Wear sleeve
21. Seal ring
22. Drive shaft
23. Shift shaft coupler
24. Screw
25. Seal
26. Shift shaft retainer
27. O-ring
28. Shift shaft
29. Retaining ring
30. Shim pack
31. Bearing race
32. Tapered roller
    bearing
33. Gear housing
34. Gasket
35. Plug
36. Plug
37. Plug
38. Pinion gear nut
39. Pinion gear
40. Shift cam
41. Shim pack
42. Bearing race
43. Tapered roller
    bearing
44. Roller bearing
45. Forward gear
46. Shift cam follower
47. Guide
48. Balls
49. Spring
50. Sliding clutch
51. Cross pin
52. Cross pin retainer
53. Propeller shaft
54. Reverse gear
55. O-ring
56. Thrust bearing
57. Thrust washer
58. Roller bearing
59. Bearing carrier
60. Washer
61. Nut
62. Roller bearing
63. Seal
64. Seal
65. Thrust hub
66. Propeller
67. Tab washer
68. Propeller nut

disassembled, refer to *Gearcase Cleaning and Inspection* before assembly.

Larger models require that the gears be shimmed and the gear lash (clearance) between forward gear and the pinion gear verified before continuing with assembly. On V-6 models (135-275 hp models), the gear lash must also be verified between reverse gear and the pinion gear. The assembly procedure will refer you to *Gearcase Shimming* at the proper time.

Disassembly (75-125 hp)

The propeller shaft bearing carrier and propeller shaft can be removed without removing the gearcase from the drive shaft housing, if so desired. Refer to **Figure 44** for this procedure.

Early model gearcase housings use an anodic trim tab and 2 screws and flat washers to secure the propshaft bearing carrier to the gearcase.

Late model housings use a painted trim tab and an anode mounted on each side of the gearcase housing, just above the antiventilation plate, toward the rear of the gearcase. Late models also use 2 locknuts and flat washers to secure the propshaft bearing carrier to the gearcase mounting studs.

There is no specific serial number for the change from early models to late models.

NOTE
If the forward gear or drive shaft roller bearings require replacement, replace the bearing rollers and races as assemblies. Do not remove any pressed in bearing (and/or race) unless replacement is necessary.

1. Remove the gearcase as described in this chapter.

2. Drain the gearcase lubricant as described in Chapter Four.

3. Remove the water pump and pump base as described in this chapter.

9

4. Remove the 2 screws and flat washers (early models) or 2 elastic locknuts and flat washers (late models) securing the propeller shaft bearing carrier to the gearcase.

5. Install puller jaws part No. 91-46086A-1 and puller bolt part No. 91-85716 or equivalent and pull the bearing carrier from the gearcase. If necessary, use a propeller thrust hub (**Figure 45**, typical) to prevent the puller jaws from sliding inward.

NOTE
If the needle bearing inside the bearing carrier must be replaced, the propeller shaft seals must also be removed during the bearing removal process. If needle bearing replacement is not necessary, remove and discard both propshaft seals at this time using a suitable seal puller. Do not damage the seal bore in the process.

6. Remove the reverse gear, thrust bearing and thrust washer from the propeller shaft bearing carrier. Then, remove and discard the O-ring.

7. Pull the propeller shaft assembly from the gearcase. If the shift cam follower (46, **Figure 44**) falls out of the propeller shaft, retrieve it from the gearcase and reinstall it into the propeller shaft.

8. Remove the pinion nut by holding the nut with a suitable socket or wrench, then turn the drive shaft counterclockwise using spline socket part No. 91-817070 or equivalent, until the nut is free from the drive shaft.

9. Pull the drive shaft assembly from gearcase.

10. Remove the pinion gear, pinion gear roller bearing and the forward gear assembly from the propeller shaft bore.

11. Remove the 2 screws securing the shift shaft retainer/bushing (26, **Figure 44**) to the gearcase. Carefully pry the shift shaft retainer from the gearcase. Then, remove the shift shaft assembly from the gearcase.

12. Remove the shift cam from the front of the gearcase bore. See **Figure 46**.

13. Remove the O-ring and seal from the shift shaft bushing. Discard the seal and o-ring.

14. If the bearing carrier needle bearings require replacement, proceed as follows:

   a. Clamp the carrier assembly into a soft-jawed vise or between wooden blocks.

   b. Pull the reverse gear needle bearing from the bearing carrier using a suitable slide hammer, such as part No. 91-34569A-1. Discard the bearing.

   c. Set the carrier in a press with the propeller end facing down.

   d. Assemble mandrel part No. 91-26569 and driver rod part No. 91-37323 or equivalent. Position the mandrel and driver rod in the carrier bore, on top of the needle bearing.

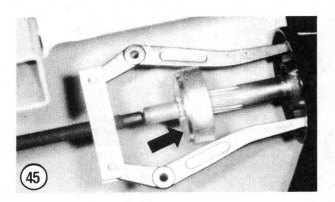

45

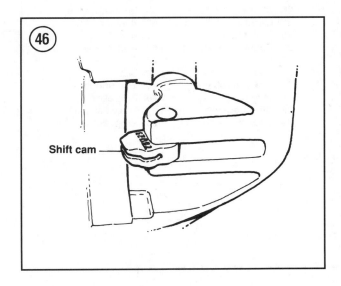

46

Shift cam

e. Press the propeller shaft needle bearing (and seals) from the carrier. Discard the bearing (and seals).

15. To remove the forward gear roller bearing and/or the forward gear internal needle bearing and/or the forward gear bearing race, proceed as follows:

a. Press the roller bearing from the forward gear. Support the bearing with a knife-edged bearing plate, such as part No. 91-37241. Press on the gear hub using a suitable mandrel. Discard the roller bearing.

b. Clamp the gear in a soft-jawed vise with the gear engagement lugs facing up. Drive the internal needle bearing from the gear using a suitable punch and hammer. Discard the bearing.

NOTE
If the forward gear bearing race is removed only for the purpose of changing the shim(s) and forward gear lash, do not discard the bearing race.

c. To remove the forward gear bearing race from the gearcase, pull the race from the front of the propeller shaft bore using a suitable slide hammer, such as part No. 91-34569A-1. See **Figure 47**. Remove the shim(s) from the bearing bore. Measure and record the thickness of the shims for later reference. Discard the race if the roller bearing assembly must be replaced.

16. If the drive shaft wear sleeve and seal require replacement, proceed as follows:

a. Support the drive shaft wear sleeve in a knife-edged bearing plate such as part No.

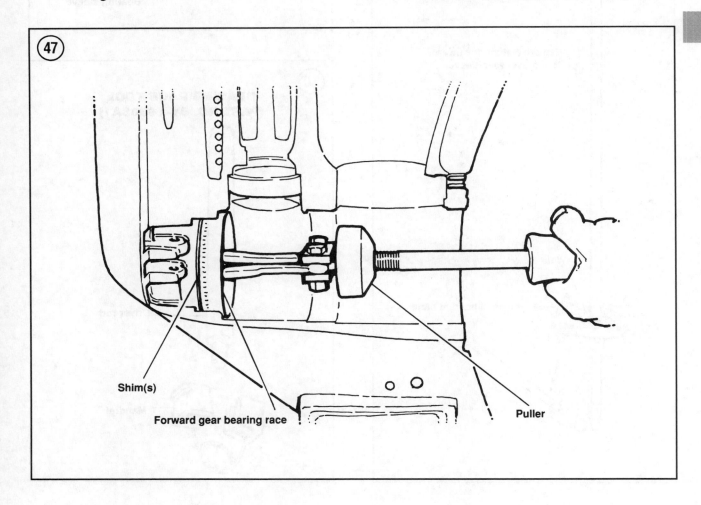

(47)

Shim(s)

Forward gear bearing race

Puller

91-37241. The pinion gear end of the shaft must face down.

b. Press on the crankshaft end of the drive shaft until the sleeve is free. See **Figure 48**. Discard the sleeve and rubber seal.

17. If the drive shaft upper bearing or the lubrication sleeve require replacement, proceed as follows:

a. Remove the bearing by pulling it out of the drive shaft bore using puller part No. 91-83165M or an equivalent 2-jaw puller (**Figure 49**). Discard the bearing.

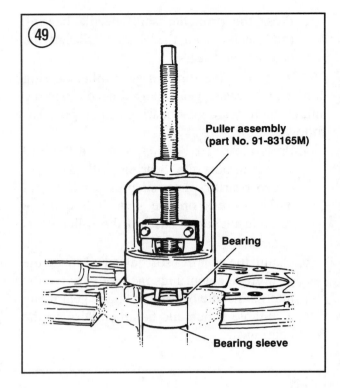

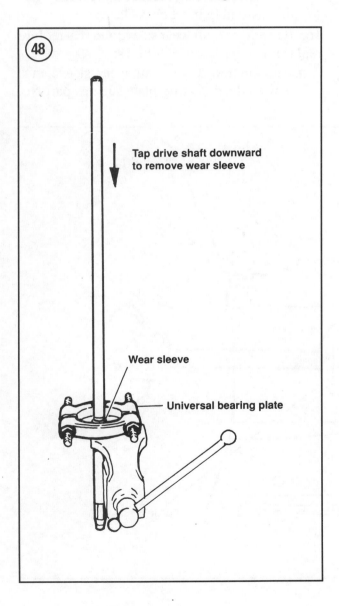

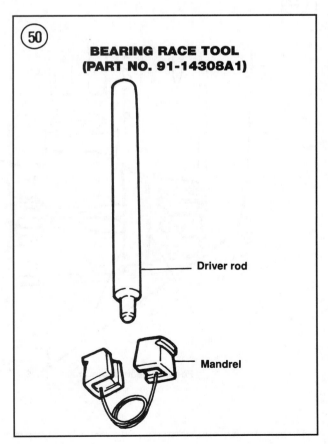

b. Remove the bearing sleeve by also pulling it out of the drive shaft bore using puller part No. 91-83165M or an equivalent 2-jaw puller (**Figure 49**). Discard the sleeve.

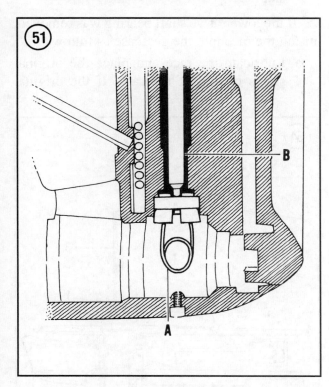

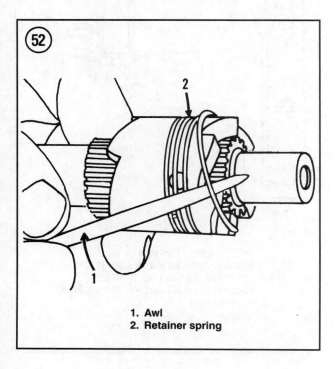

1. Awl
2. Retainer spring

c. Remove the lubrication sleeve by pulling it out of the drive shaft bore using puller part No. 91-83165M or an equivalent 2-jaw puller. Discard the lubrication sleeve.

NOTE
If the drive shaft roller bearing race is removed only for the purpose of changing the shim(s) and the pinion gear depth, do not discard the bearing race. The drive shaft needle bearing and lubrication sleeve do not have to be removed before removing the roller bearing race.

18. If the drive shaft roller bearing race requires removal or replacement, proceed as follows:

a. Remove the bearing race from the gearcase by driving it down into the propeller shaft bore with a bearing remover part No. 91-14308A-1 or equivalent. See **Figure 50**.

b. Insert the puller jaws (A, **Figure 51**) from the propeller shaft bore. Insert the driver (B, **Figure 51**) through the drive shaft bore.

c. Place a shop cloth under the bearing puller. Use a suitable mallet and drive the bearing race out into the propeller shaft bore. Discard the bearing race and matching roller bearing.

19. If the propeller shaft requires disassembly, proceed as follows:

a. Remove and discard the cross pin retainer spring with a small screwdriver or awl. Insert the tool under one end of the spring and rotate the propeller shaft to unwind the spring. See **Figure 52**, typical.

b. Place the shift cam follower against a solid surface and push on the propeller shaft to unload the spring pressure on the sliding clutch cross pin. Remove the pin with a suitable punch. Carefully release the pressure from the cam follower and spring. Remove the cam follower, 3 steel balls, spring guide, spring and sliding clutch from the propeller shaft. See **Figure 53**, typical.

20. Refer to *Gearcase Cleaning and Inspection*. Clean and inspect all components as directed before beginning the reassembly procedure.

Assembly (75-125 hp)

Lubricate all internal components with Quicksilver Premium Blend gear oil or equivalent. Do not assemble components *dry*. Refer to **Table 2** for torque values and **Table 7** for dimensional specifications. Refer to **Figure 44** for this procedure.

1. If the drive shaft wear sleeve and seal (20 and 21, **Figure 44**) were removed, install a new seal and sleeve as follows:

   a. Position a new rubber seal into the drive shaft groove. Coat the outside diameter of the seal with Loctite 271 threadlocking adhesive.

   b. Place a new wear sleeve into the holder from sleeve installation kit part No. 91-14310A-1. Slide the drive shaft into the sleeve and holder.

   c. Place the driver (from sleeve installation kit) over the pinion end of the drive shaft. Place the drive shaft and tool assembly in a

press. Press the driver against the holder until they contact each other.

   d. Wipe any excess Loctite from the drive shaft.

2. If the lower drive shaft bearing was removed, install the race into the gearcase as follows:

   a. Lubricate the race and place the original shims on top of the race. If the original

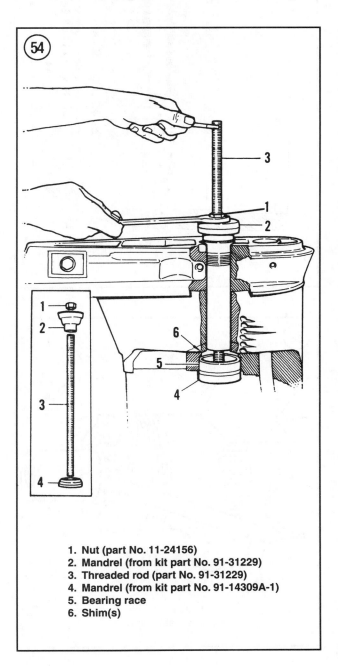

1. Nut (part No. 11-24156)
2. Mandrel (from kit part No. 91-31229)
3. Threaded rod (part No. 91-31229)
4. Mandrel (from kit part No. 91-14309A-1)
5. Bearing race
6. Shim(s)

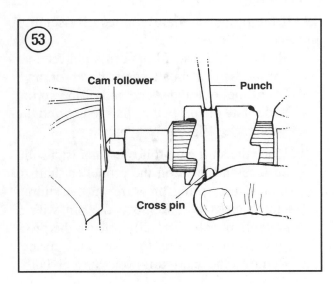

Cam follower   Punch
Cross pin

shims are lost or damaged (beyond meas-urement), install 0.025 in. (0.635 mm) shim(s).

b. Position the race into its bore with the ta-pered side facing down.

c. Assemble the bearing installer components as shown in **Figure 54**.

d. Tighten the nut to seat the race fully in the bearing bore.

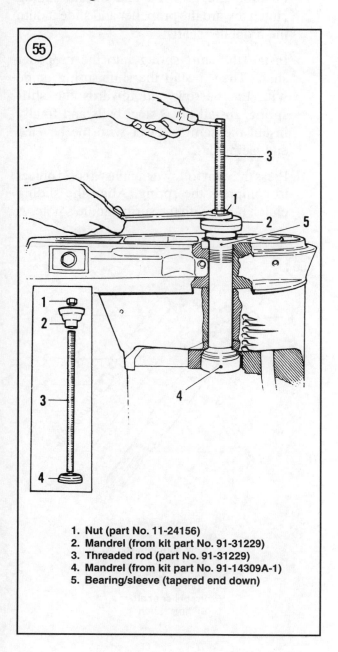

1. Nut (part No. 11-24156)
2. Mandrel (from kit part No. 91-31229)
3. Threaded rod (part No. 91-31229)
4. Mandrel (from kit part No. 91-14309A-1)
5. Bearing/sleeve (tapered end down)

3. If the drive shaft lubrication sleeve was re-moved, lubricate a new sleeve and press the sleeve into the gearcase as far as possible with hand pressure. Make sure the tab at the top of the sleeve points to the rear of the gearcase. The sleeve will be fully seated into the gearcase in the next step.

NOTE
The drive shaft oil sleeve must be in-stalled before proceeding with the next step.

4. If drive shaft needle bearing and sleeve were removed, install a new bearing assembly as fol-lows:

a. If the new bearing is separate from the new bearing sleeve, lubricate both parts with Quicksilver 2-4-C Multi-Lube grease. Set the sleeve (tapered side down) into a press. Position the bearing (numbered side up) into the sleeve and press it into the sleeve with a suitable mandrel until it is flush with the sleeve.

b. Lubricate the outside diameter of a new bearing assembly with Quicksilver 2-4-C Multi-Lube grease.

c. Position the bearing assembly into the drive shaft bore with the tapered (beveled) end facing down.

d. Assemble the installer components as shown in **Figure 55**.

e. Tighten the nut to seat the bearing assembly (and lubrication sleeve) into the drive shaft bore.

5. If the forward gear bearing race was removed, install the race into the gearcase as follows:

a. Position the original shims into the bearing bore. If the original shims were lost, start with 0.010 in. (0.254 mm) shim(s).

b. Lubricate the bearing race and set it into the gearcase bearing bore. Place mandrel part No. 91-31106 or equivalent over the race.

c. Place the propeller shaft into the mandrel hole. Install the propeller shaft bearing carrier into the gearcase (to hold the propeller shaft centered).

d. Thread a scrap propeller nut onto the propeller shaft. Use a mallet and drive the propeller shaft against the mandrel until the bearing race is fully seated in the gearcase bearing bore.

e. Remove the propeller nut, propeller shaft, bearing carrier and mandrel.

6. If the forward gear roller bearing was removed, lubricate a new roller bearing and set it on the gear hub with the rollers facing up. Press the bearing fully onto the gear with mandrel part No. 91-37350 or equivalent. Do not press on the roller cage.

7. If the forward gear internal needle bearing was removed, install a new bearing as follows:

a. Position the forward gear in a press with the gear teeth facing down.

b. Lubricate the new needle bearing and position it in the gear bore with the numbered side facing up.

c. Press the bearing into the gear with a suitable mandrel until the bearing bottoms in the bore. Be careful not to damage the bearing by over-pressing.

8. If the bearing carrier needle bearings were removed, install new bearings as follows:

a. Set the carrier into a press with the propeller end facing down. Lubricate a new reverse gear needle bearing and position it into the carrier bore with its lettered end facing up.

b. Press the bearing into the carrier with bearing installer part No. 91-13945 or equivalent. Press until the tool seats.

c. Set the carrier in a press (propeller end facing up), on bearing installer (part No. 91-13945) or equivalent to protect the carrier and reverse gear needle bearing.

d. Lubricate a new propeller shaft needle bearing and position it into the carrier bore with the lettered end facing up.

e. Press the bearing into the carrier with a suitable mandrel (such as part No. 91-

15755), until the bearing bottoms in its bore.

9. If the propeller shaft was disassembled, refer to **Figure 56** and reassemble it as follows:

a. Lubricate all components Quicksilver 2-4-C Multi-Lube grease.

b. Align the cross pin holes of the sliding clutch with the slot in the propeller shaft. Position the grooved end of the sliding clutch toward the propeller and slide it onto the propeller shaft.

c. Install the shift spring into the propeller shaft. Then, install the shift spring guide with the narrow end towards the shift spring. Install the 3 steel balls and finally install the cam follower with the beveled end facing out.

d. Press the cam follower against a solid object to compress the spring. Align the sliding clutch holes with the spring guide's hole. A

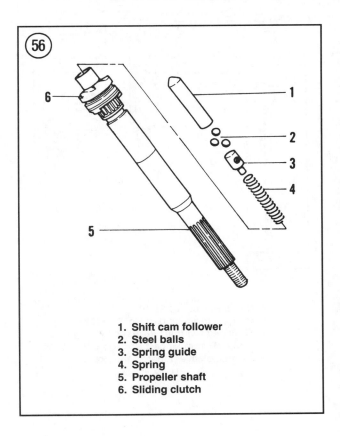

1. Shift cam follower
2. Steel balls
3. Spring guide
4. Spring
5. Propeller shaft
6. Sliding clutch

small punch may be used to ease alignment. See **Figure 53**, typical.

e. Insert the sliding clutch cross-pin into the clutch and through the spring guide's hole. The cross-pin must pass through the spring guide.

NOTE
The sliding clutch retaining spring must lay flat, with no overlapping coils.

f. Secure the pin to the sliding clutch with a new retainer spring. Do not open the spring any more than necessary to install it.

10. Install 2 new propeller shaft seals as follows:

a. Coat the outer diameter of 2 new propeller shaft seals with Loctite 271 threadlocking adhesive.

b. Set the carrier in a press (propeller end facing up), on bearing installer part No. 91-13945 or equivalent to protect the carrier and reverse gear needle bearing.

c. Install the small diameter seal with the spring facing the gearcase. Press the seal in with the large stepped end of mandrel part No. 91-31108 or equivalent until the tool bottoms against the carrier.

d. Install the large diameter seal with the spring facing the propeller. Press the seal in with the small stepped end of mandrel part

No. 91-31108 or equivalent until the tool bottoms against the carrier.

11. Coat a new propeller shaft bearing carrier O-ring and the propeller shaft seal lips with 2-4-C Multi-Lube grease. Then, install the O-ring into the carrier groove.

12. Assemble the propeller shaft bearing carrier, reverse gear and bearings and the propeller shaft assembly as follows:

a. Lubricate the propeller shaft bearing carrier thrust washer with Quicksilver Needle Bearing Assembly Grease. Install the thrust washer onto the propeller shaft carrier.

b. Lubricate the thrust bearing with the same grease and place it on top of the thrust washer.

c. Install the reverse gear into the propeller shaft bearing carrier being careful not to disturb the position of the thrust washer and bearing.

d. Carefully slide the propeller shaft into the carrier assembly. Be careful not to damage the carrier seals.

e. Obtain a piece of 1-1/4 or 1-1/2 in. (31.75 or 38.10 mm) diameter PVC pipe, 6 in. (152.5 mm) long. Install the PVC pipe over the propeller shaft, then install the propeller locking tab washer and propeller nut. Hand tighten the nut to hold the propeller shaft securely into the bearing carrier. See **Figure 57**.

13. Assemble and install the shift components as follows:

a. Coat the outer diameter of a new shift shaft seal with Loctite 271 threadlocking adhesive. Press the seal into the shift shaft retainer/bushing (with a suitable mandrel) until it is flush with the retainer bore.

b. Lubricate the seal lip and a new retainer O-ring with Quicksilver 2-4-C Multi-Lube grease. Install the O-ring into the shift bushing groove.

c. If removed, install the E-ring onto the shift shaft.

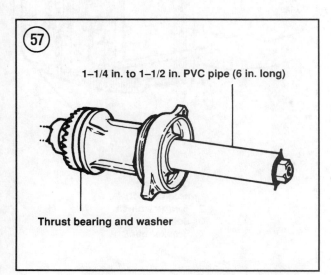

(57)

1–1/4 in. to 1–1/2 in. PVC pipe (6 in. long)

Thrust bearing and washer

9

d. Lubricate the shift shaft with the same grease and carefully insert the shift shaft into the shift shaft retainer and seal.

e. Place the shift cam into the gear housing with the numbered side up as shown in **Figure 46**. Install the shift shaft assembly into the gearcase and engage the shift shaft splines to the shift cam internal splines.

f. Apply Loctite 271 threadlocking adhesive to the threads of the 2 shift shaft retainer screws. Install and tighten the screws to 35 in.-lb. (4.0 N•m).

14. Rotate the gearcase so that the propeller shaft bore is pointing upward. Install the forward gear assembly into the propshaft bore and into the forward gear bearing race.

15. Position the drive shaft roller bearing into the race at the bottom of the drive shaft bore, then place the pinion gear in position over the bearing.

16. Spray the threads of the drive shaft with Locquic primer. Insert the drive shaft into the drive shaft bore while holding the pinion gear and lower bearing in position. Rotate the shaft as necessary and engage the drive shaft splines to the pinion gear splines.

NOTE
*Apply Loctite 271 threadlocking adhesive to a **new** pinion nut **after** the pinion gear depth and forward gear lash have been verified. Install the old pinion nut without sealant to check the gear depth and forward gear lash.*

17. Install the original pinion nut with the recessed side facing *toward* the pinion gear. Tighten the nut finger-tight at this time.

18. Hold the pinion nut with a suitable wrench or socket. Attach spline socket part No. 91-56775 or equivalent to a suitable torque wrench. Tighten the pinion nut to 70 ft.-lb. (94.9 N•m). See **Figure 58**, typical.

19. Refer to *Gearcase Shimming* and set the *Pinion gear depth*. Do not continue until the pinion gear depth has been verified.

20. Once the pinion gear depth has been verified, install the propeller shaft assembly into the gearcase and into the forward gear internal needle bearing. Make sure the shift cam follower does not fall out during assembly.

21. Liberally lubricate the front and rear flanges of the propeller shaft bearing carrier with Quicksilver Special Lubricant 101. Install the carrier over the propeller shaft, being careful not to damage the carrier seals on the propeller shaft

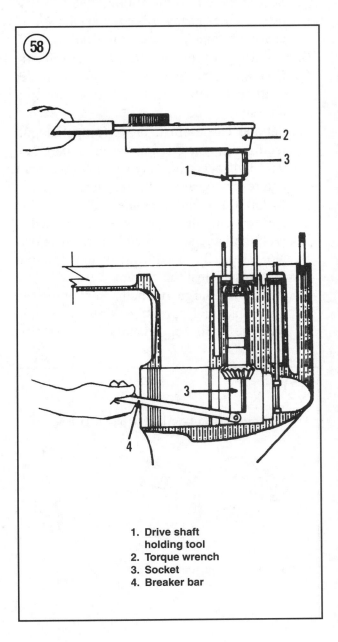

(58)

1. Drive shaft holding tool
2. Torque wrench
3. Socket
4. Breaker bar

splines. Make sure the screw holes are aligned with the gearcase. Rotate the drive shaft to ensure the gear teeth are meshed, then seat the carrier into the gearcase bore.

22. Secure the carrier with 2 screws (or locknuts) and washers. Tighten the fasteners to 25 ft.-lb. (33.9 N•m). Then, remove the propeller nut, washer and PVC pipe.

23. Refer to *Gearcase Shimming* in this chapter and set the *Forward gear lash*. Do not continue until the correct gear lash is verified.

24. Once the gear lash verification procedure is complete, remove the propeller shaft and bearing carrier and install a *new* pinion nut (with Loctite 271 threadlocking adhesive) as described previously in this section. Then, reinstall the propeller shaft and bearing carrier as described previously in this section. Coat the 2 bearing carrier screws (or studs) with Loctite 271 threadlocking adhesive and install the screws (or locknuts) and washers. Tighten the 2 fasteners to 25 ft.-lb. (33.9 N•m).

25. Install the water pump assembly as described in this chapter.

26. Pressure test the gearcase as described in *Gearcase Pressure Testing*.

27. Fill the gearcase with the recommended lubricant as described in Chapter Four.

Disassembly (135-200 hp and 275 hp)

Two basic types of shift mechanisms, 3 different housings and 2 types of sliding clutch engagement lugs are used on the models covered in this section.

XR6 and Magnum III models (prior to serial No. 0G303046) may be equipped with a 4-1/4 in. (108 mm) diameter gearcase. These small diameter gearcases use a shift cam and shift cam follower very similar to the 125 hp and smaller gearcases. Refer to **Figure 59** for an exploded view of the small diameter, cam shift XR6 and Magnum III model gearcase. Service procedures unique to this gearcase are called out in the text;

otherwise, follow all references to *135-200 hp models*. These gearcases are called *cam shift models* for service procedures specific to these models.

All other 135-200 hp and 275 hp models are equipped with an *E-Z Shift* gearcase. This gearcase uses a special shift cam and follower that provides positive sliding clutch engagement into and out of both gears. The housing used on 135-200 hp *E-Z Shift* models are all identical and feature a 4-3/4 in. (121 mm) diameter torpedo. The housing used on the 275 hp is unique to that engine. Refer to **Figure 60** and **Figure 61** for 135-200 hp *E-Z Shift* models and **Figure 62** and **Figure 63** for 275 hp models. These gearcases are called *E-Z Shift models* for service procedures specific to these models.

On cam shift models, the propeller shaft bearing carrier and propeller shaft can be removed without removing the gearcase from the drive shaft housing, if so desired.

On E-Z Shift models, the propeller shaft bearing carrier can be removed from the gearcase without removing the gearcase from the drive shaft housing, but the propeller shaft *cannot* be removed unless the gearcase is removed from the drive shaft housing.

NOTE
If the forward gear or drive shaft roller bearings require replacement, replace the bearing rollers and races as assemblies. Do not remove any pressed in bearing (and/or race) unless replacement is necessary.

To disassemble the gearcase, proceed as follows.

1. Remove the gearcase as described in this chapter.

2. Drain the gearcase lubricant as described in Chapter Four.

3. Remove the water pump and pump base as described in this chapter.

9

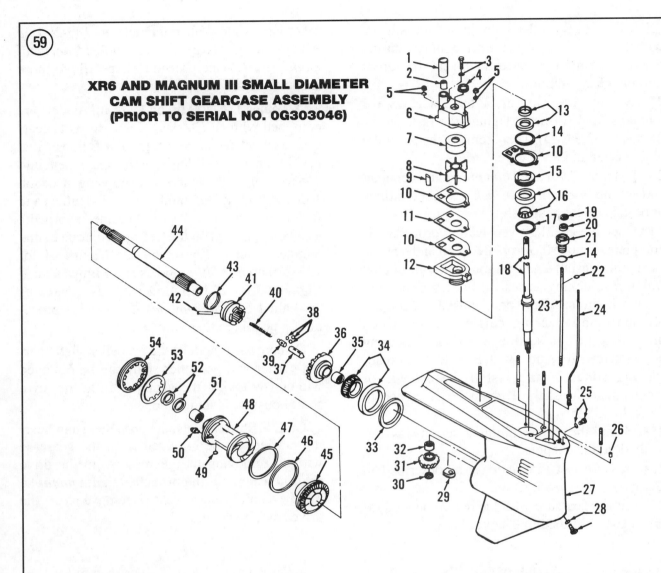

XR6 AND MAGNUM III SMALL DIAMETER CAM SHIFT GEARCASE ASSEMBLY (PRIOR TO SERIAL NO. 0G303046)

1. Water tube guide
2. Water tube seal
3. Screw and washer
4. Rubber centrifugal slinger
5. Locknut and washer
6. Water pump housing
7. Impeller liner
8. Impeller
9. Impeller drive key
10. Gaskets
11. Impeller plate
12. Pump base
13. Drive shaft seals
14. O-rings
15. Drive shaft bearing retainer
16. Roller bearing assembly
17. Shim(s)
18. Drive shaft
19. Washer

20. Shift shaft seal
21. Shift shaft bushing
22. Lock clip
23. Shift shaft
24. Speedometer hose and fitting
25. Vent plug and seal
26. Dowel pin
27. Gearcase housing
28. Drain/fill plug and seal
29. Shift cam
30. Pinion nut
31. Pinion gear
32. Loose needle bearing
33. Shim(s)
34. Roller bearing assembly
35. Needle bearing
36. Forward gear
37. Shift cam follower

38. Steel balls
39. Spring guide block
40. Spring
41. Sliding clutch
42. Cross pin
43. Retainer spring
44. Propeller shaft
45. Reverse gear
46. Thrust washer
47. O-ring
48. Propeller shaft bearing carrier
49. Alignment key
50. Grease fitting
51. Needle bearing
52. Propeller shaft seals
53. Locking tab washer
54. Retaining ring

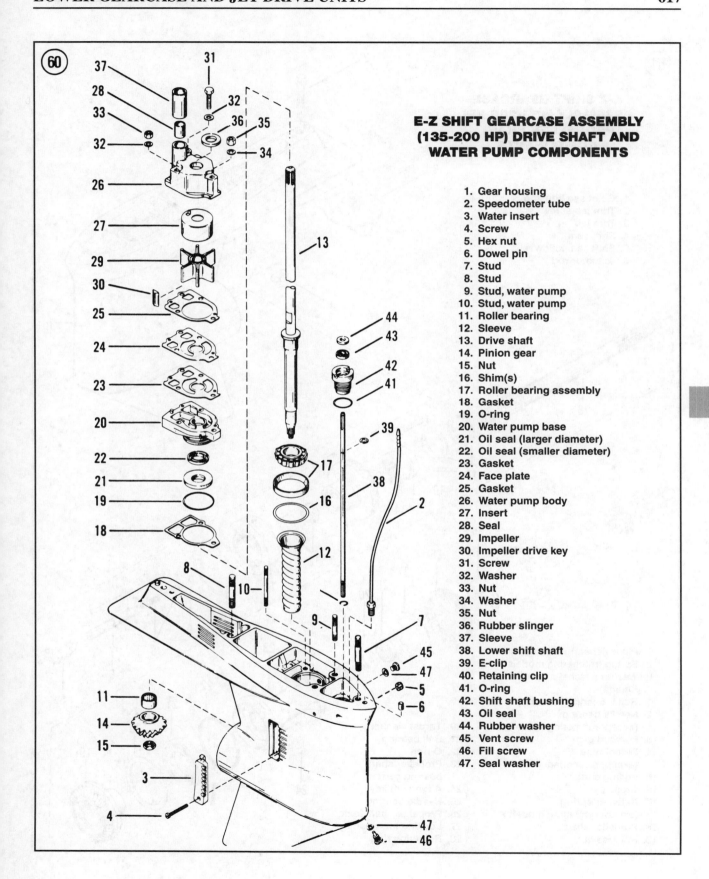

E-Z SHIFT GEARCASE ASSEMBLY (135-200 HP) DRIVE SHAFT AND WATER PUMP COMPONENTS

1. Gear housing
2. Speedometer tube
3. Water insert
4. Screw
5. Hex nut
6. Dowel pin
7. Stud
8. Stud
9. Stud, water pump
10. Stud, water pump
11. Roller bearing
12. Sleeve
13. Drive shaft
14. Pinion gear
15. Nut
16. Shim(s)
17. Roller bearing assembly
18. Gasket
19. O-ring
20. Water pump base
21. Oil seal (larger diameter)
22. Oil seal (smaller diameter)
23. Gasket
24. Face plate
25. Gasket
26. Water pump body
27. Insert
28. Seal
29. Impeller
30. Impeller drive key
31. Screw
32. Washer
33. Nut
34. Washer
35. Nut
36. Rubber slinger
37. Sleeve
38. Lower shift shaft
39. E-clip
40. Retaining clip
41. O-ring
42. Shift shaft bushing
43. Oil seal
44. Rubber washer
45. Vent screw
46. Fill screw
47. Seal washer

9

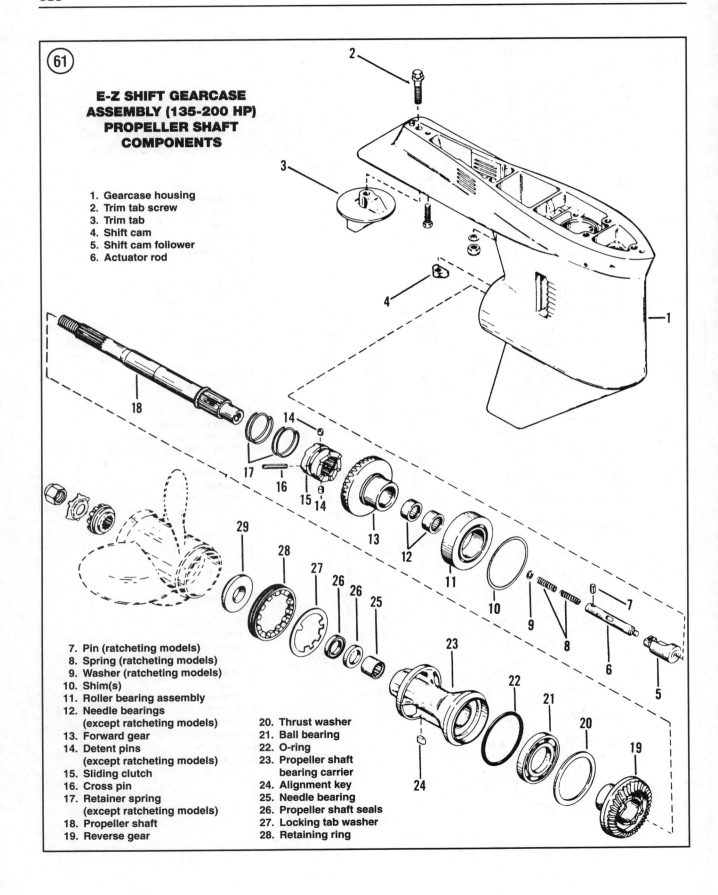

(61)

**E-Z SHIFT GEARCASE
ASSEMBLY (135-200 HP)
PROPELLER SHAFT
COMPONENTS**

1. Gearcase housing
2. Trim tab screw
3. Trim tab
4. Shift cam
5. Shift cam follower
6. Actuator rod

7. Pin (ratcheting models)
8. Spring (ratcheting models)
9. Washer (ratcheting models)
10. Shim(s)
11. Roller bearing assembly
12. Needle bearings
    (except ratcheting models)
13. Forward gear
14. Detent pins
    (except ratcheting models)
15. Sliding clutch
16. Cross pin
17. Retainer spring
    (except ratcheting models)
18. Propeller shaft
19. Reverse gear

20. Thrust washer
21. Ball bearing
22. O-ring
23. Propeller shaft
    bearing carrier
24. Alignment key
25. Needle bearing
26. Propeller shaft seals
27. Locking tab washer
28. Retaining ring

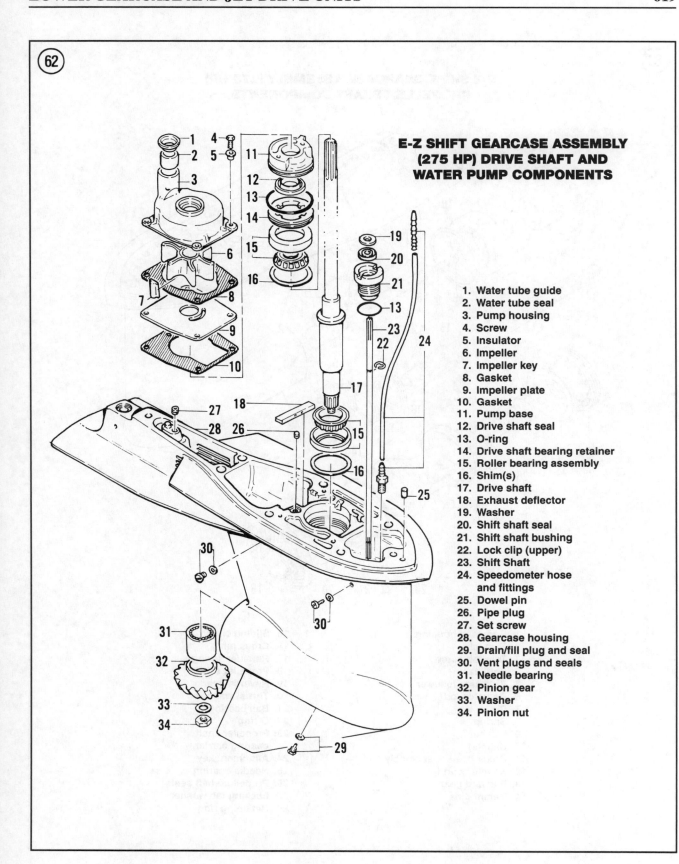

62

**E-Z SHIFT GEARCASE ASSEMBLY
(275 HP) DRIVE SHAFT AND
WATER PUMP COMPONENTS**

1. Water tube guide
2. Water tube seal
3. Pump housing
4. Screw
5. Insulator
6. Impeller
7. Impeller key
8. Gasket
9. Impeller plate
10. Gasket
11. Pump base
12. Drive shaft seal
13. O-ring
14. Drive shaft bearing retainer
15. Roller bearing assembly
16. Shim(s)
17. Drive shaft
18. Exhaust deflector
19. Washer
20. Shift shaft seal
21. Shift shaft bushing
22. Lock clip (upper)
23. Shift Shaft
24. Speedometer hose
    and fittings
25. Dowel pin
26. Pipe plug
27. Set screw
28. Gearcase housing
29. Drain/fill plug and seal
30. Vent plugs and seals
31. Needle bearing
32. Pinion gear
33. Washer
34. Pinion nut

9

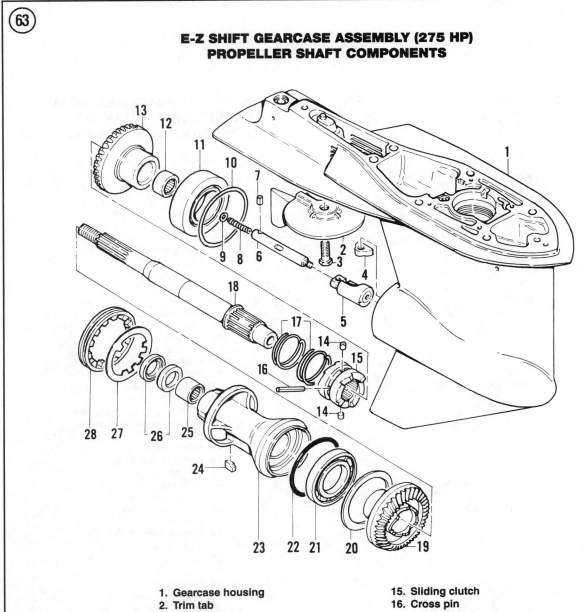

63

**E-Z SHIFT GEARCASE ASSEMBLY (275 HP)
PROPELLER SHAFT COMPONENTS**

1. Gearcase housing
2. Trim tab
3. Trim tab screw
4. Shift cam
5. Shift cam follower
6. Actuator rod
7. Pin
8. Spring
9. Washer
10. Shim(s)
11. Roller bearing assembly
12. Needle bearing
13. Forward gear
14. Detent pins
15. Sliding clutch
16. Cross pin
17. Retainer springs
18. Propeller shaft
19. Reverse gear
20. Thrust washer
21. Ball bearing
22. O-ring
23. Propeller shaft
    bearing carrier
24. Alignment key
25. Needle bearing
26. Propeller shaft seals
27. Locking tab washer
28. Retaining ring

4. Bend the locking tab away from the propshaft bearing carrier retaining ring using a suitable punch and hammer. See **Figure 64**, typical.

NOTE
If the retaining ring is frozen in place and cannot be removed in the next step, apply penetrating oil and mild heat (with an electric heat gun, heat lamp or propane torch). If removal still proves difficult, drill through the ring in several places (parallel to the propshaft) and break the ring into several pieces with a suitable chisel and hammer. Do not drill into the gearcase threads or into the bearing carrier.

5A. *Cam shift models*—Remove the retaining ring using spanner wrench part No. 91-73688. Turn the ring counterclockwise until it is free

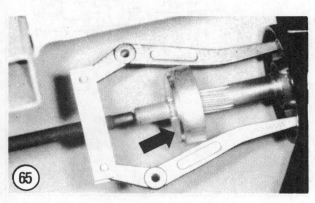

from the gearcase threads. If the ring is corroded or damaged, discard it. Then, remove the locking tab washer.

5B. *E-Z Shift models*—Remove the retaining ring using spanner wrench part No. 91-61069 or equivalent. Turn the ring counterclockwise until it is free from the gearcase. If the ring is corroded or damaged, discard it. Then, remove the locking tab washer.

6. Install puller jaws (part No. 91-46086A-1) and puller bolt (part No. 91-85716) or equivalent and pull the bearing carrier from the gearcase. If necessary, use a propeller thrust hub to prevent the puller jaws from sliding inward. See **Figure 65**, typical.

7. Locate and secure the bearing carrier alignment key, then remove and discard the carrier O-ring.

NOTE
If the needle bearing inside the bearing carrier must be replaced, the propeller shaft seals also must be removed during the bearing removal process. If bearing replacement is not necessary, remove and discard both propshaft seals at this time using a suitable seal puller. Do not damage the seal bore in the process.

8A. *Cam shift models*—Remove the propeller shaft, reverse gear and shift mechanism as follows:

    a. Pull the propeller shaft assembly from the gearcase. If the shift cam follower (37, **Figure 59**) falls out of the propeller shaft, retrieve it from the gearcase and reinstall it into the propeller shaft temporarily.

    b. Slide the reverse gear and thrust washer from the propeller shaft.

    c. Remove the shift shaft bushing with bushing tool part No. 91-31107 or equivalent. Lift the shift shaft bushing and shift shaft assembly from the gearcase. See **Figure 66**, typical.

    d. Slide the bushing off of the shift shaft. Remove the washer from the top of the

9

bushing, then remove and discard the bushing O-ring and internal seal.

e. Reach inside the propeller shaft bore and remove the shift cam (**Figure 67**, typical).

8B. *E-Z Shift models*—Remove the propeller shaft and shift mechanism as follows:

a. Unthread (but do not remove) the shift shaft bushing with bushing tool part No. 91-31107 or equivalent.

b. Shift the gearcase into neutral by placing the shift shaft in the middle of its total rotational travel. The straight edge of the shift cam must be parallel with the shift cam follower as shown in **Figure 68**.

> *NOTE*
> *Do not rotate shift shaft either direction during its removal in the next substep. The shift mechanism must be in NEUTRAL before the shift shaft and prop-shaft can be removed.*

c. Pull the shift shaft assembly from the gearcase (**Figure 66**, typical). If it is necessary to use pliers to remove the shaft, protect the shift shaft splines by wrapping a strip of aluminum or other soft metal, around the splines.

> *CAUTION*
> *At this point, side force must **not** be applied to the propeller shaft or it may break the clutch actuator rod neck.*

d. Pull the propeller shaft, cam follower and shift cam straight out of the gearcase with a single smooth movement. If the shaft jams and cannot easily be removed, push the propeller shaft back into place against the forward gear. Look into the shift shaft hole with a flashlight. If the splined hole in the shift cam is visible, reinstall the shift shaft and rotate it again to the neutral position. Then, remove the shift shaft and remove the propeller shaft, cam follower and shift cam.

e. If propeller shaft still cannot be removed, push the shaft back into place against the forward gear. Reinstall the propeller shaft bearing carrier to support the propeller shaft. Remove the gearcase from the holding fixture and lay it on its PORT side. Strike the upper leading edge of the housing with a rubber mallet to dislodge the shift cam from the cam follower. Remove the bearing carrier and pull the propeller shaft from the housing. Retrieve the shift cam after the forward gear is removed.

9A. *135-200 hp*—Remove the drive shaft upper bearing retainer using retainer tool part No. 91-43506.

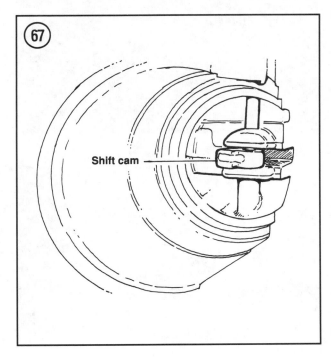
Shift cam

9B. *275 hp*—Remove the drive shaft upper bearing retainer using retainer tool part No. 91-93227.

10A. *135-200 hp*—Install drive shaft spline socket part No. 91-90094 or equivalent, onto the drive shaft splines.

10B. *275 hp*—Install drive shaft spline socket part No. 91-12362 or equivalent, onto the drive shaft splines.

11. Hold the pinion nut using a suitable wrench or socket. Pad the area around the handle with shop towels to prevent housing damage.

12. Loosen and remove the pinion nut by turning the drive shaft counterclockwise. Remove the pinion nut (and washer) from the housing.

13. Clamp the drive shaft into a soft-jawed vise, or between wooden blocks. Clamp as close to the water pump studs as possible.

NOTE
On 135-200 hp models, the lower drive shaft bearing contains 18 loose rollers that may fall out during drive shaft removal. Be sure to retrieve all rollers from the housing.

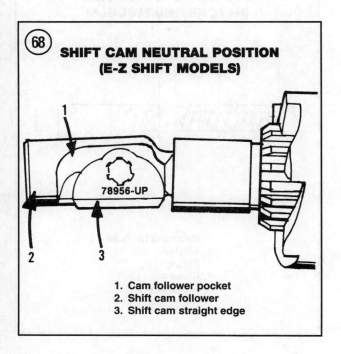

(68)
SHIFT CAM NEUTRAL POSITION (E-Z SHIFT MODELS)

78956-UP

1. Cam follower pocket
2. Shift cam follower
3. Shift cam straight edge

14. Place a wooden block against the gearcase mating surface. With the aid of an assistant, hold the housing securely and tap the wooden block with a mallet until the drive shaft separates from the pinion gear. Then, pull the gearcase housing off of the drive shaft.

15. *135-200 hp models*—Remove the 18 loose bearing rollers from the drive shaft lower bearing race (or propeller shaft bore).

16A. *135-200 hp*—Remove the shim(s) from the drive shaft bearing bore. Measure and record the thickness of the shim(s) for later reference. Tag the shim(s) for identification during reassembly. Discard the race if the roller bearing assembly is being replaced.

CAUTION
The 275 hp gearcase uses a pair of tapered roller bearings to support the upper portion of the drive shaft. The shim(s) under the lower tapered roller bearing race (if present) control drive shaft end play. The shim(s) under the upper tapered roller bearing race controls the pinion gear depth. Do not intermix the upper and lower drive shaft shims. Tag each shim as to its original location.

16B. *275 hp*—Remove (and immediately tag) the shim(s) from under the upper bearing race shim. Then, pull the lower tapered roller bearing race from the drive shaft bore. Remove (and immediately tag) the lower bearing race shim(s) from the drive shaft bore (if present). Measure and record the thickness of the shim(s) for later reference. Discard the race(s) if the roller bearing(s) is being replaced.

Propeller shaft bearing carrier disassembly (cam shift models)

On cam shift models, there is no bearing for the reverse gear. The gear rides directly in the carrier bore and against the carrier face. If the

9

propeller shaft needle bearing requires replacement, proceed as follows.

1. Set the carrier in a press with the propeller end facing down.

2. Press the bearing (and seals) from the carrier with a suitable mandrel.

3. Discard the bearing (and seals).

Propeller shaft bearing carrier disassembly (E-Z shift models)

On E-Z shift models, the reverse gear rides on a ball bearing that is pressed into the carrier. The propeller shaft has a needle bearing located near the propeller shaft seals. The reverse gear must be removed to service the propeller shaft needle bearing. To remove the reverse gear (and bearing) and the propeller shaft needle bearing, proceed as follows.

1. Clamp the carrier in a soft-jawed vise or between 2 blocks of wood.

2. *E-Z Shift models*—Pull the reverse gear assembly from the bearing carrier with a suitable slide hammer, such as part No. 91-34569A-1.

3. If the reverse gear ball bearing requires replacement, proceed as follows:

   a. Support the ball bearing in a suitable knife-edged bearing plate, such as part No. 91-37241.

   b. Press against the gear hub with a suitable mandrel until the bearing is free from the gear.

   c. Remove the thrust washer from the reverse gear or bearing carrier.

   d. Discard the bearing.

4. If the propeller shaft needle bearing requires replacement, proceed as follows:

   a. Set the carrier in a press with the propeller end facing down.

   b. Press the bearing (and seals) from the carrier with a suitable mandrel.

   c. Discard the bearing (and seals).

Propeller shaft disassembly (cam shift models)

If the propeller shaft requires disassembly, proceed as follows:

1. Remove and discard the cross pin retainer spring with a small screwdriver or awl. Insert the tool under one end of the spring and rotate the propeller shaft to unwind the spring.

2. Place the shift cam follower against a solid surface and push on the propeller shaft to unload the spring pressure on the sliding clutch cross pin. Remove the pin with a suitable punch. Carefully release the pressure on the cam follower and spring. Remove the cam follower, 3 steel balls, spring guide, spring and sliding clutch from the propeller shaft.

Propeller shaft disassembly (E-Z shift models)

The ratcheting gearcase will has 2 cross pin retaining springs and two detent pins. The actu-

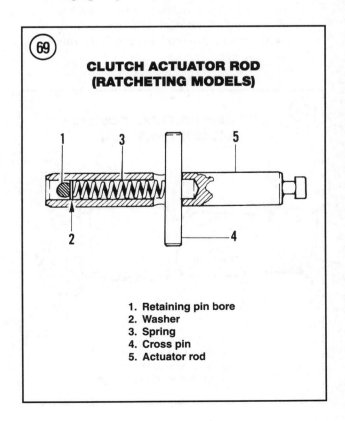

(69)

CLUTCH ACTUATOR ROD (RATCHETING MODELS)

1. Retaining pin bore
2. Washer
3. Spring
4. Cross pin
5. Actuator rod

ating rod is hollow and incorporates a spring, washer and pin.

The non-ratcheting gearcase has 1 cross pin retaining spring and one detent pin. The actuating rod is solid and does not have a spring, washer and pin.

1. Remove the shift cam from the cam follower.

2. Insert a thin-blade screwdriver or similar tool under the retaining spring(s). Lift the coil up and rotate the propeller shaft to unwind the spring from the sliding clutch. Discard the spring.

3. *Ratcheting models*—Repeat Step 2 to remove the remaining cross pin retainer.

4. Remove the single detent pin from the sliding clutch on non-ratcheting models, or the 2 detent pins on ratcheting models.

5. Push the cross pin through the clutch and propeller shaft using a suitable punch. Slide the clutch off the shaft.

6. Pull the cam follower and clutch actuator rod straight out of the propeller shaft. Do not move the cam follower up and down or side-to-side during removal.

7. Separate the clutch actuator rod from the cam follower.

8. *Ratcheting models*—Push the pin (1, **Figure 69**) out of the actuator rod using a suitable punch. Then, remove the spring and washer from the rod.

Forward gear bearing removal

If the forward gear bearing race must be removed to adjust forward gear lash, or the roller bearing assembly or internal needle bearing(s) must be replaced, proceed as follows:

NOTE
If the forward gear bearing race is removed only for the purpose of changing the shim(s) and forward gear lash, do not discard the bearing race.

1. To remove the forward gear bearing race from the gearcase, pull the race from the front of the propeller shaft bore with a suitable slide hammer, such as part No. 91-34569A-1. See **Figure 70**, typical.

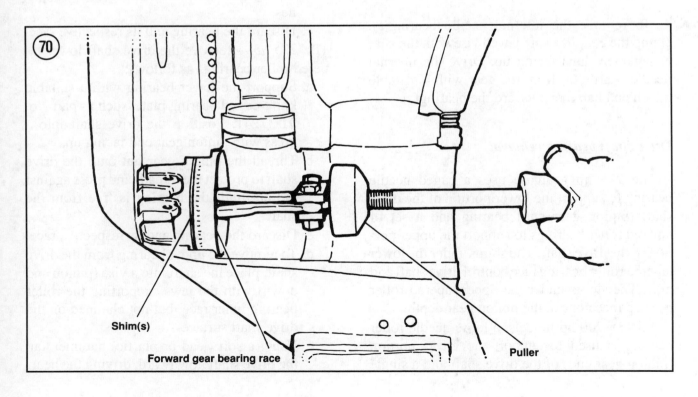

Shim(s)

Forward gear bearing race

Puller

2. Remove the shim(s) from the bearing bore. Measure and record the thickness of the shims for later reference. Tag the shim(s) for identification during reassembly. Discard the race if the roller bearing assembly is being replaced.

NOTE
In Step 3, it may be necessary to cut the roller cage from the bearing and grind a groove in the inner race to provide a lip for the knife-edged puller.

3. To remove the roller bearing from the forward gear, support the bearing with a knife-edged bearing plate, such as part No. 91-37241. Press on the gear hub with a suitable mandrel until the bearing is free from the gear. Discard the roller bearing.

NOTE
The forward gear on 135-200 hp ratcheting style gearcase uses 2 internal needle bearings stacked on top of each other. The forward gear on 275 hp models and 135-200 hp non-ratcheting style gearcase uses a single internal needle bearing.

4. To remove the internal needle bearing(s), clamp the gear in a soft-jawed vise with the gear engagement lugs facing up. Drive the internal needle bearing(s) from the gear with a suitable punch and hammer. Discard the bearing(s).

Drive shaft bearing removal

The 275 hp gearcase uses a caged needle bearing to support the lower portion of the drive shaft (pinion gear end) bearing and a set of tapered roller bearings to support the upper portion of the drive shaft. The shims under the lower tapered roller bearing race control drive shaft end play. The shims under the upper tapered roller bearing race control the pinion gear depth.

On 135-200 hp models, a loose needle roller bearing is used to support the lower portion (pinion gear end) of the drive shaft and a single tapered roller bearing is used to support the upper portion of the drive shaft. The shims under the tapered roller bearing race control the pinion gear depth.

If the drive shaft upper roller bearing(s) and/or lower needle bearing require replacement, proceed as follows:

CAUTION
Do not intermix the upper and lower drive shaft shims on 275 hp models. The lower shims control drive shaft end play and the upper shims control pinion gear depth. Tag each shim to identify its original location.

1A. *135-200 hp*—To remove the drive shaft roller bearing, proceed as follows:
   a. Place the drive shaft (pinion end down) into a vise with the jaws supporting the roller bearing inner race, but not clamped on the drive shaft surface.
   b. Using a soft (lead or plastic) hammer, tap the drive shaft downward, driving the bearing off toward the top of the shaft. Do not damage the drive shaft-to-crankshaft splines.
   c. Discard the bearing and its respective race.

1B. *275 hp*—Remove the drive shaft lower tapered roller bearings as follows:
   a. Support the lower bearing with a suitable knife-edged bearing plate, such as part No. 91-37241. Position the drive shaft into a press with pinion gear end facing up.
   b. Thread the pinion gear nut onto the drive shaft to protect the threads and press against the nut until the bearing is free from the shaft.
   c. Discard the bearing and its respective race.
   d. To remove the upper bearing from the drive shaft, place the shaft into a vise (pinion end down) with the jaws supporting the roller bearing inner race, but not clamped on the drive shaft surface.
   e. Using a soft (lead or plastic) hammer, tap the drive shaft downward, driving the bear-

ing off toward the top of the shaft. Do not damage the drive shaft-to-crankshaft splines.

f. Discard the bearing and its respective race.

NOTE
On 135-200 hp models, the drive shaft lower bearing contains 18 loose bearing rollers that may fall out of the race during drive shaft removal. The loose bearing rollers must be reinstalled in the outer race to provide a contact surface for the removal tool.

2A. *135-200 hp*—To remove the loose needle bearing at the bottom of the drive shaft bore, proceed as follows:

a. Install the 18 loose bearing rollers into the lower bearing race. Use a suitable grease, such as Quicksilver Needle Bearing Assembly Grease to hold the rollers in place.

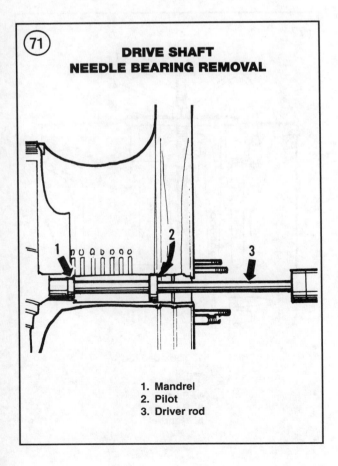

⑦①
**DRIVE SHAFT
NEEDLE BEARING REMOVAL**

1. Mandrel
2. Pilot
3. Driver rod

b. Using mandrel part No. 91-15755, pilot part No. 91-36571 and driver rod part No. 91-37323 or equivalent, assembled as shown in **Figure 71**, drive the bearing into the gear cavity.

c. Remove and discard the bearing making sure all loose bearing rollers are accounted for.

2B. *275 hp*—To remove the caged needle bearing from the bottom of the drive shaft bore, proceed as follows:

a. Using a heat lamp (such as part No. 91-63209), heat both sides of the gearcase in the area of the drive shaft lower bearing.

b. Using mandrel part No. 91-092789, pilot part No. 91-92790 and driver rod part No. 91-37323 (or equivalent), drive the bearing into the gear cavity. See **Figure 71**.

c. Remove and discard the bearing.

CAUTION
If drive shaft lower bearing failure has occurred, causing the bearing outer race to spin inside the housing, the gearcase housing must be replaced. A new bearing installed into a worn bearing bore will result in premature bearing and gearcase failure.

Assembly (135-200 hp and 275 hp)

If the drive shaft bearings, forward gear bearing, reverse gear or propeller shaft bearings were removed, or the propeller shaft was disassembled, install new bearings or reassemble the propeller shaft as described in the following sections. When finished, proceed to *Assembly (Continued [135-200 hp and 275 hp])*.

Lubricate all internal components with Quicksilver Premium Blend gear oil or equivalent. Do not assemble components *dry*. Refer to **Table 3** for torque values and **Table 7** for dimensional specifications. Refer to **Figures 59-63** as appropriate for this procedure.

9

Drive shaft bearing installation

1. To install a new needle bearing or loose roller bearing at the bottom of the drive shaft bore, begin by lubricating a new bearing with Quicksilver Needle Bearing Assembly Grease. On 135-200 hp models, the 18 loose rollers must be installed.

2. Assemble the bearing installer components as shown in **Figure 72**. The numbered side of the bearing must face up the drive shaft bore (away from the pinion gear) when installed.

   a. *Cam shift models*—Use mandrel part No. 91-38628, pilot part No. 91-36571, plate part No. 91-29310 and threaded rod part No. 91-31229 (or equivalent).

   b. *E-Z shift models*—Use mandrel part No. 91-92788, pilot part No. 91-92790, plate part No. 91-29310 and threaded rod part No. 91-31229 (or equivalent).

3. Pull the bearing into the drive shaft bore by turning the nut (2, **Figure 72**) until the bearing is seated in the drive shaft bore. Do not apply excessive force to the bearing.

4. To install the new roller bearing(s) onto the drive shaft, begin by lubricating the bearing(s) and applicable area on the drive shaft with Quicksilver Needle Bearing Assembly Grease.

5A. *135-200 hp*—Slide the bearing over the drive shaft splines. The rollers must face the power head (away from the pinion gear). Support the bearing's inner race with a suitable round mandrel, such as a scrap drive shaft roller bearing inner race. Place the assembly in a press with the mandrel (or scrap bearing race) supported by a knife-edged bearing plate, such as part No. 91-37241. The pinion end of the shaft must face up.

5B. *275 hp*—Slide the upper bearing over the drive shaft splines. The rollers must face the power head (away from the pinion gear). Support the bearing with bearing installer part No. 91-12364 or equivalent. Place the assembly into a press with the installer supported by the press and the pinion end of the shaft facing up.

6. Thread an old pinion nut onto the drive shaft threads (to protect the threads). Press against the pinion nut until the bearing is seated against the drive shaft shoulder.

7. *275 hp*—Install a new drive shaft lower roller bearing as follows:

   a. Slide the lower bearing over the pinion end of the drive shaft. The rollers must face the pinion end of the shaft (away from the power head).

   b. Support the shaft in a press with the pinion end facing up. Use bearing installer part No. 91-12364 (or equivalent) to support and protect the upper bearing installed in Step 5B.

   c. Fabricate a metal pipe of the appropriate inside diameter to fit over the drive shaft, but press only against the bearing's inner race. Make sure the pipe is long enough to

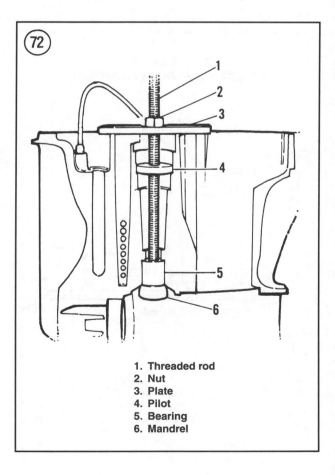

72

1. Threaded rod
2. Nut
3. Plate
4. Pilot
5. Bearing
6. Mandrel

allow seating of the bearing against the drive shaft shoulder.

d. Press against the pipe until the bearing is seated against the shaft's shoulder.

Forward gear bearing installation

1. To install the forward gear roller bearing race into the gearcase housing, begin by positioning the original shim(s) into the housing bearing bore. If the original shims were lost, start with 0.010 in. (0.254 mm) shim(s) on 135-200 hp models or 0.020 in. (0.51 mm) shim(s) on 275 hp models.

2A. *Cam shift models*—Lubricate the bearing race and set it into the gearcase bearing bore on top of the shim(s). Place mandrel part No. 91-31106 or equivalent over the race.

2B. *E-Z shift models*—Lubricate the bearing race and set it into the gearcase bearing bore on top of the shim(s). Place mandrel part No. 91-87120 or equivalent over the race.

3. Place the propeller shaft into the mandrel hole. Install the propeller shaft bearing carrier into the gearcase (to hold the propeller shaft centered).

4. Thread a scrap propeller nut onto the propeller shaft. Use a mallet and drive the propeller shaft against the mandrel until the bearing race is fully seated in the gearcase bearing bore.

5. Remove the propeller nut, propeller shaft, bearing carrier and mandrel.

6. If the forward gear roller bearing was removed, lubricate a new roller bearing and set it on the gear hub with the rollers facing up. Press the bearing fully onto the gear with a suitable mandrel. Do not press on the roller cage.

7A. *Cam shift models*—If the forward gear internal needle bearing was removed, install a new bearing as follows:

a. Position the forward gear in a press with the gear teeth facing down.

b. Lubricate the new needle bearing and position it in the gear bore with the numbered side facing up.

c. Press the bearing into the gear with bearing installer part No. 91-818149 (or equivalent) until the tool seats against the gear hub face.

7B. *E-Z shift (dual bearing) models*—If the forward gear internal needle bearings were removed, install 2 new bearings as follows:

a. Position the forward gear in a press with the gear teeth facing down.

b. Lubricate the new needle bearings. Position the first bearing into the gear bore with the numbered side facing up.

c. Press the bearing into the gear using the long-stepped side of the bearing installer part No. 91-86943 or equivalent until the tool seats against the gear hub face.

d. Position the second bearing into the gear bore with its numbered side facing up.

e. Press the bearing into the gear using the short-stepped side of bearing installer part No. 91-86943 or equivalent until the tool seats against the gear hub face.

7C. *E-Z shift (single bearing) models*—If the forward gear internal bearing was removed, install a new bearing as follows:

a. Position the forward gear in a press with the gear teeth facing down.

b. Lubricate the new needle bearing and position it in the gear bore with the numbered side facing up.

c. Press the bearing into the gear with the short stepped side of bearing installer (part No. 91-86943) or equivalent until the tool seats against the gear hub face.

Propeller shaft bearing carrier assembly

1. Set the carrier in a press with the propeller end facing up.

2. Lubricate a new propeller shaft needle bearing and position it into the carrier bore with the lettered end facing up.

9

3A. *Cam shift models*—Press the bearing into the carrier with a suitable mandrel until the bearing bottoms in its bore. Do not over-press the bearing.

3B. *E-Z shift models*—Press the bearing into the carrier bore with a mandrel (part No. 91-15755) or equivalent. Press the bearing into the carrier until the tool or bearing seats (whichever happens first). Do not over-press the bearing.

4. *E-Z shift models*—If the reverse gear was removed from the bearing carrier and/or if the ball bearing was removed from the reverse gear, proceed as follows:

   a. To install a new bearing to the reverse gear, begin by lubricating the bearing and the reverse gear hub. Then, set the gear into a press with the gear teeth facing down.

   b. Position the thrust washer over the gear hub with the larger diameter side of the washer facing toward the gear.

   c. Set the bearing onto the gear hub with the numbered side facing up. Press the bearing onto the gear with a suitable mandrel until the bearing is fully seated on the gear. Press only on the bearing's inner race.

   d. Lubricate the bearing carrier's reverse gear bearing bore and place the carrier over the reverse gear and ball bearing assembly. Press against the propeller end of the carrier until the ball bearing is seated in the carrier bore.

Propeller shaft assembly (cam shift models)

If the propeller shaft was disassembled, refer to **Figure 73** and reassemble it as follows:

1. Lubricate all components Quicksilver 2-4-C Multi-Lube grease.

2. Align the cross pin holes of the sliding clutch with the slot in the propeller shaft. Position the grooved end of the sliding clutch toward the propeller and slide it onto the propeller shaft.

3. Install the shift spring into the propeller shaft. Then, install the shift spring guide with the nar-

row end toward the shift spring. Install the 3 steel balls and finally install the cam follower with the beveled end facing out. See **Figure 73**.

4. Press the cam follower against a solid object to compress the spring. Align the sliding clutch holes with the spring guide's hole. A small punch may be used ease alignment. See **Figure 53**, typical.

5. Insert the sliding clutch cross-pin into the clutch and through the spring guide's hole. The cross-pin must pass through the spring guide.

NOTE
The sliding clutch retaining spring must lay flat, with no overlapping coils.

6. Secure the pin to the sliding clutch with a new retainer spring. Do not open the spring any more than necessary to install it.

Propeller shaft assembly (E-Z shift models)

Ratcheting gearcases have 2 cross pin retaining springs and 2 detent pins. The actuating rod

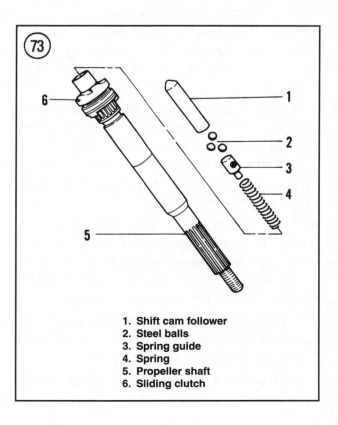

1. Shift cam follower
2. Steel balls
3. Spring guide
4. Spring
5. Propeller shaft
6. Sliding clutch

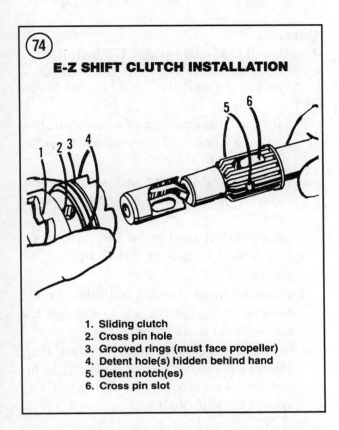

E-Z SHIFT CLUTCH INSTALLATION

1. Sliding clutch
2. Cross pin hole
3. Grooved rings (must face propeller)
4. Detent hole(s) hidden behind hand
5. Detent notch(es)
6. Cross pin slot

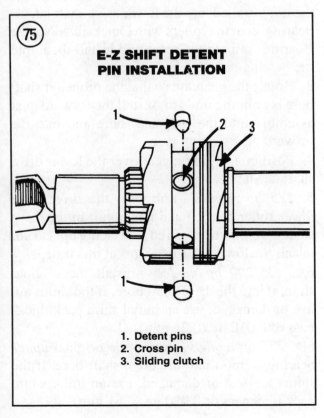

E-Z SHIFT DETENT PIN INSTALLATION

1. Detent pins
2. Cross pin
3. Sliding clutch

is hollow and incorporates a spring, washer and pin. All 275 hp models use a ratcheting gearcase.

Non-ratcheting gearcases use 1 cross pin retaining spring and one detent pin. The actuating rod is solid and does not have a spring, washer and pin.

1. Lubricate all components Quicksilver 2-4-C Multi-Lube grease.

2. Align the cross pin holes of the sliding clutch with the slot in the propeller shaft and the detent pin hole(s) with the detent notch(es) in the propeller shaft splines. Position the grooved end of the sliding clutch towards the propeller and slide it onto the propeller shaft. See **Figure 74**.

3. *Ratcheting models*—Refer to **Figure 69** and assemble the actuator rod as follows:

    a. Insert the spring into the rod bore, followed by the washer.

    b. Compress the spring as necessary with a pin punch, then install the retaining pin into the retaining pin bore (1, **Figure 69**). Drive the pin flush with the outer diameter of the rod.

4. Connect the clutch actuator rod to the shift cam follower. Then, insert actuator rod into the propeller shaft bore.

5A. *Ratcheting models*—Install the cross pin as follows:

    a. Align the actuator rod's cross pin bore with the cross pin holes in the sliding clutch and the slot in the propeller shaft.

    b. Insert an awl or very small tapered punch through a clutch hole, shaft slot and into the actuator rod. Position the awl *behind* the spring (3, **Figure 69**) and push the spring toward the shift cam follower.

    c. Carefully insert the cross pin into the sliding clutch, withdrawing the awl as the cross pin enters the actuator rod bore. The cross pin must pass behind the spring (3, **Figure 69**).

    d. Install the 2 detent pins into the sliding clutch bores. Make sure both detent bores have been aligned with the notches in the shaft splines and that the rounded ends of the detent are facing the propeller shaft as shown in **Figure 75**. Use Quicksilver Nee-

9

dle Bearing Assembly Grease to help hold each detent in position.

NOTE
The sliding clutch cross pin (and detent) retaining springs must lay flat, with no overlapping coils.

e. Install the first new retainer spring by inserting the tang (hooked) end into a detent pin. Wind the retainer spring into the sliding clutch groove. The straight end of the retainer spring should be against one side of the clutch groove.

f. Install the second new retainer spring by inserting the tang (hooked) end into the other detent pin. Wind the retainer spring into the sliding clutch groove in the opposite direction of the first retainer. Position the straight end of the retainer spring against the side of the clutch groove opposite the first spring.

5B. *Except ratcheting models*—Install the cross pin as follows:

a. Align the actuator rod's cross pin bore with the cross pin holes in the sliding clutch and the slot in the propeller shaft. Use a small punch to help with alignment.

b. Insert the cross pin through the sliding clutch *and* actuator rod.

c. Install the detent pin into the sliding clutch bore. Make sure the bore has been aligned with the notch in the shaft splines. Use Quicksilver Needle Bearing Assembly Grease to hold the detent in position.

NOTE
The sliding clutch retaining spring must lay flat, with no overlapping coils.

d. Secure the cross pin and detent pin to the sliding clutch with a new retainer spring. Do not open the spring any more than necessary to install it.

Assembly
(Continued [135-200 hp and 275 hp])

1. Assemble the shift shaft components as follows:

a. Coat the outer diameter of a new shift shaft seal with Loctite 271 threadlocking adhesive.

b. Press the seal into the shift shaft bushing (with the lip side facing up) using a suitable mandrel.

c. Coat the shift shaft and a new bushing O-ring with Quicksilver 2-4-C Multi-Lube grease.

d. Carefully insert the shift shaft through the bushing being careful not to damage the seal with the shaft splines.

e. Install the lock clip into the shift shaft groove (on models so equipped). Then install the washer over the shift shaft and against the shift shaft seal.

2. *135-200 hp models*—If the 18 loose rollers are not installed into the lower drive shaft needle bearing, coat the rollers with Quicksilver Needle Bearing Assembly Grease and install them into the bearing race.

3. Rotate the gearcase so that the propeller shaft bore is pointing upward. Install the forward gear assembly into the propshaft bore and into the forward gear bearing race.

4. Position the pinion gear over the lower drive shaft needle bearing.

5. *275 hp models*—Lubricate the drive shaft *lower* roller bearing and position it in the drive shaft bore with the tapered side facing up. Do *not* install the lower bearing shims at this time.

6A. *135-200 hp models*—Install the original shim(s) into the drive shaft bore. If the shims are lost or damaged, use an initial shim pack thickness of 0.010 in. (0.25 mm).

6B. *275 hp models*—Install the original *upper* bearing shim(s) into the drive shaft bore. If the shims are lost or damaged, use an initial shim pack thickness of 0.020 in. (0.51 mm).

7. Spray the threads of the drive shaft with Locquic primer. Insert the drive shaft into the drive shaft bore while holding the pinion gear in position. Rotate the shaft as necessary and engage the drive shaft splines to the pinion gear splines.

NOTE
*Apply Loctite 271 threadlocking adhesive to a **new** pinion nut **after** the pinion gear depth and forward gear lash have been verified. Install the old pinion nut without sealant to check the gear depth and forward gear lash.*

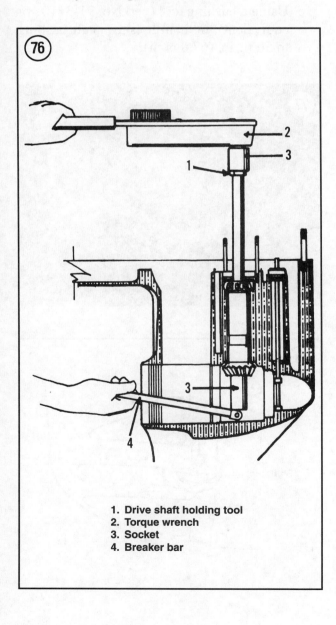

1. **Drive shaft holding tool**
2. **Torque wrench**
3. **Socket**
4. **Breaker bar**

8. Install the pinion nut washer, then install the original pinion nut with its flat side facing *away* from the pinion gear. Tighten the nut finger-tight at this time.

9. Install the drive shaft roller bearing race (upper race on 275 hp models). Lubricate the threads of the drive shaft bearing retainer with Quicksilver Special Lubricant 101, then install the retainer as follows:

  a. *135-200 hp*—The *OFF* marking on the retainer must face up.

  b. *275 hp*—The unthreaded portion of the retainer must face down.

10. Using the appropriate retainer tool (part No. 91-43506 [135-200 hp]) or (part No. 91-93227 [275 hp]), tighten the bearing retainer to 100 ft.-lb. (135.6 N•m).

11. Hold the pinion nut with a suitable wrench or socket. Attach spline socket (part No. 91-90094 [135-200 hp]) or (part No. 91-12362 [275 hp] or equivalent) to a suitable torque wrench. Tighten the pinion nut to specification (**Table 3**). See **Figure 76**, typical.

12. Refer to *Gearcase Shimming* and set the *Pinion gear depth*. Do not continue until the correct pinion gear depth is verified.

NOTE
Do not install the shift shaft assembly and shift cam until the correct gear lash is verified.

13A. *Cam shift models*—Once the correct pinion gear depth is verified, install the propeller shaft assembly into the gearcase and into the forward gear internal needle bearing. Make sure the shift cam follower does not fall out during assembly by liberally greasing the cam with Quicksilver 2-4-C Multi-Lube grease.

13B. *E-Z Shift models*—Once the pinion gear depth has been verified, install the propeller shaft assembly into the gearcase and into the forward gear internal needle bearing(s). Do not install the shift cam at this time.

9

14. *Cam shift models*—Lubricate the reverse gear and install the gear (and thrust washer) into the propeller shaft bearing carrier.

15. Liberally coat both flanges of the propeller shaft bearing carrier with Quicksilver Special Lubricant 101.

16. Align the alignment key slots in the bearing carrier and gearcase, then install the carrier over the propeller shaft. Use care not to damage the propeller shaft seals. Rotate the drive shaft as necessary to ensure the pinion and reverse gears are properly meshed.

17. Push the bearing carrier into the gearcase as far as possible by hand, then install the alignment key into the carrier and gearcase slots. Drive the key in with a suitable punch until it is flush with the carrier. See **Figure 77**.

18. Install a new tab washer into the gearcase bore and against the rear of the bearing carrier.

19. Liberally apply Quicksilver Special Lubricant 101 to the carrier retaining ring. Then, install the retaining ring with the *OFF* marking facing outward. Screw the ring into the gearcase as far as possible by hand.

20. Tighten the retaining ring to 210 ft.-lb. (284.7 N·m) using spanner wrench part No. 91-73688 (cam shift models) or part No. 91-61069 (E-Z shift models).

21. Refer to *Gearcase Shimming* in this chapter and set the *Forward gear lash*. Do not continue until the correct forward gear lash is verified.

22A. *135-200 hp models*—Once the correct forward gear lash is verified, remove the propeller shaft bearing carrier (and propeller shaft) and install a *new* pinion nut (with Loctite 271 thread-locking adhesive) as described previously in this section.

22B. *275 hp models*—Proceed as follows:

   a. Once the correct forward gear lash is verified, refer to *Gearcase Shimming* and set the *Drive shaft end play (275 hp models)*.

   b. Once the correct drive shaft end play is verified, remove the propeller shaft bearing carrier (and propeller shaft) and install a

new pinion nut (with Loctite 271 thread-locking adhesive) as described previously in this section.

23A. *Cam shift models*—Install the shift shaft assembly, shift cam and propeller shaft as follows:

   a. Place the shift cam into the gear housing with its numbered side up as shown in **Figure 78**.

   b. Install the shift shaft assembly into the gearcase and engage the shift shaft splines to the shift cam internal splines.

   c. Using a bushing tool (part No. 91-31107 or equivalent), tighten the shift shaft bushing to 50 ft.-lb. (67.8 N·m).

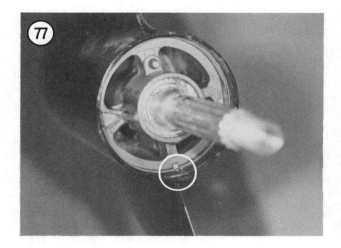

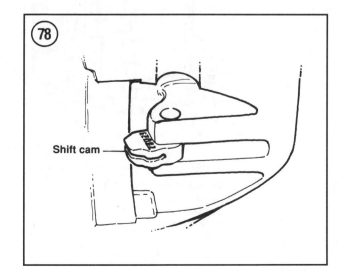

Shift cam

23B. *E-Z Shift models*—Install the shift shaft assembly, shift cam and propeller shaft as follows:

a. Fill the shift cam follower cavity with Quicksilver 2-4-C Multi-Lube grease. See 1, **Figure 79**.

b. Place the shift cam into the cam follower cavity. Be sure the numbered side of the cam is facing up and that the straight edge of the shift cam is parallel to the cam follower as shown in **Figure 79**.

CAUTION
The shift cam must be positioned in the NEUTRAL position as shown in Figure 79 for propeller shaft installation.

c. Install the propeller shaft assembly into the gearcase, inserting the shift cam follower into the forward gear, until the shaft is fully seated. Make sure the shift cam did not fall out of the follower.

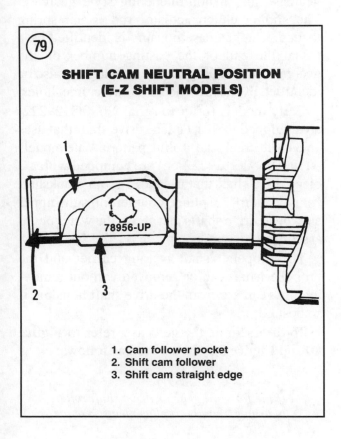

79

SHIFT CAM NEUTRAL POSITION (E-Z SHIFT MODELS)

78956-UP

1. Cam follower pocket
2. Shift cam follower
3. Shift cam straight edge

CAUTION
At this time, use extreme caution not to apply any side (radial) load to the propeller shaft. Until the propeller shaft bearing carrier is installed, the neck of the clutch actuator rod can be easily broken by side-to-side or up-and-down propeller shaft movement.

d. Coat the shift bushing threads with Quicksilver Special Lubricant 101. Install the shift shaft assembly into the gearcase and engage the shift cam splines. If necessary, rotate the shift shaft back and forth slightly to engage the shift cam splines.

e. Tighten the shift shaft bushing finger-tight at this time.

24. Install 2 new propeller shaft seals as follows:

a. Coat the outer diameter of 2 new propeller shaft seals with Loctite 271 threadlocking adhesive.

b. Set the carrier in a press with the propeller end facing up.

c. Install the small diameter seal with the spring facing the gearcase. Press the seal in with the large-stepped end of mandrel part No. 91-31108 (or equivalent) until the tool bottoms against the carrier.

d. Install the large diameter seal with the spring facing the propeller. Press the seal in with the small-stepped end of mandrel part No. 91-31108 (or equivalent) until the tool bottoms against the carrier.

25. Coat the a new propeller shaft bearing carrier O-ring and the propeller shaft seal lips with 2-4-C Multi-Lube grease. Then, install the O-ring between the thrust washer and the carrier beveled edge (cam shift models) or in the carrier groove (E-Z shift models).

26. Liberally coat both flanges of the propeller shaft bearing carrier with Quicksilver Special Lubricant 101.

27. Align the alignment key slots in the bearing carrier and gearcase, then install the carrier over the propeller shaft. Use care not to damage the propeller shaft seals. Rotate the drive shaft as

9

necessary to ensure the pinion and reverse gears are properly meshed.

28. Push the bearing carrier into the gearcase as far as possible by hand, then install the alignment key into the carrier and gearcase slots. Drive the key in with a suitable punch until it is flush with carrier. See **Figure 77**.

29. Install the tab washer into the gearcase bore and against the rear of the bearing carrier.

30. Liberally apply Quicksilver Special Lubricant 101 to the carrier retaining ring. Then, install the retaining ring with the *OFF* marking facing outward. Screw the ring into the gearcase as far as possible by hand.

31. Tighten the retaining ring to 210 ft.-lb. (284.7 N•m) using spanner wrench part No. 91-73688 (cam shift models) or part No. 91-61069 (E-Z shift models).

32. Determine which locking tab is aligned with a slot in retaining ring. Bend the tab over firmly into the retaining ring slot (**Figure 64**, typical). Then, bend all remaining tabs forward.

33. *E-Z Shift models*—Using bushing tool part No. 91-31107 or equivalent, tighten the shift shaft bushing to 50 ft.-lb. (67.8 N•m).

34. Refer to *Gearcase Shimming* in this chapter and verify the *Reverse Gear Lash*, if so desired.

35. Install the water pump base and water pump assembly as described previously in this chapter.

36. Pressure test the gearcase as described in *Gearcase Pressure Testing*.

37. Fill the gearcase with the recommended lubricant as described in Chapter Four.

Disassembly (200 DFI, 225 and 250 hp)

This gearcase is very similar in design and operation to the MerCruiser Alpha One Generation Two lower gearcase. Many of the manufacturer recommended special tools are the same part number. Two types of sliding clutch engagements lugs and 2 types of drive shafts with 2 different spline patterns are used on the models covered in this section.

The gears (forward and reverse) and sliding clutch engagement lugs were originally designed to ratchet. This means that the propeller (and sliding clutch) can overrun the gear engagement lugs during deceleration. When shifted into either gear, the propeller will lock in one direction, but ratchet in the other.

Models prior to serial No. 0G438000 are equipped with ratcheting gearcases. The sliding clutch shift spool assembly is spring-loaded. The gearcase housing is identified by a *C2* at the end of the casting number on the gearcase deck. This gearcase housing also can be identified by the presence of 10 water inlet holes.

Starting with serial No. 0G438000, all engines are equipped with a non-ratcheting gearcase. This means that the propeller will lock in either direction, in either gear.

The forward gear, reverse gear, sliding clutch, shift spool and a few other shift components were changed to convert the ratcheting style gearcase into a non-ratcheting style gearcase. The sliding clutch actuator rod is *not* spring loaded. The gearcase housing is identified by a *C3* at the end of the casting number on the gearcase deck. This gearcase housing can also be identified by the presence of 16 water inlet holes.

Early models (prior to serial No. 0G129222) are equipped with a 1-piece drive shaft that uses an 8 tooth crankshaft spline pattern. Late models (serial No. 0G129222-on) are equipped with a 2 piece drive shaft that uses a 13 tooth crankshaft spline pattern. A splined coupler joins the upper and lower drive shafts just above the water pump assembly.

The propeller shaft bearing carrier and the propeller shaft can be removed without removing the gearcase from the drive shaft housing, if so desired.

To disassemble the gearcase, refer to **Figure 80** and **Figure 81** and proceed as follows:

NOTE
If the forward gear or drive shaft roller bearings require replacement, replace

GEARCASE ASSEMBLY
(200 DFI, 225-250 HP) DRIVE SHAFT
AND WATER PUMP COMPONENTS

1. Water tube guide
2. O-rings
3. Centrifugal slinger seal
4. Pump housing
5. Screw
6. Impeller
7. Impeller key
8. Gaskets
9. Impeller plate
10. Pump base
11. O-ring
12. Small drive shaft seal
13. Large drive shaft seal
14. Drive shaft bearing retainer
15. Roller bearing assembly
16. Shim(s)
17. Drive shaft (or lower drive shaft)
18. Drive shaft coupler (late models)
19. Upper drive shaft (late models)
20. Exhaust block (water dam)
21. Vent plug and seal
22. Screw
23. Anodes
24. Locknut
25. Dowel pins
26. Speedometer tube and fittings
27. Shift shaft
28. Washer
29. Shift shaft seal
30. Shift shaft retainer/bushing
31. O-rings
32. Screw
33. Drain/fill plug and seal
34. Loose needle bearing
35. Pinion gear
36. Washer
37. Pinion nut
38. Pivot pin
39. Gearcase housing

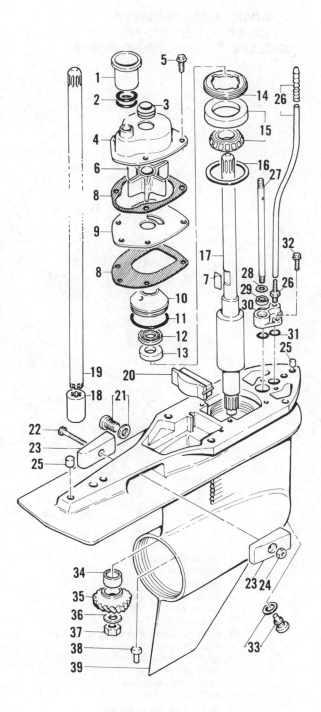

9

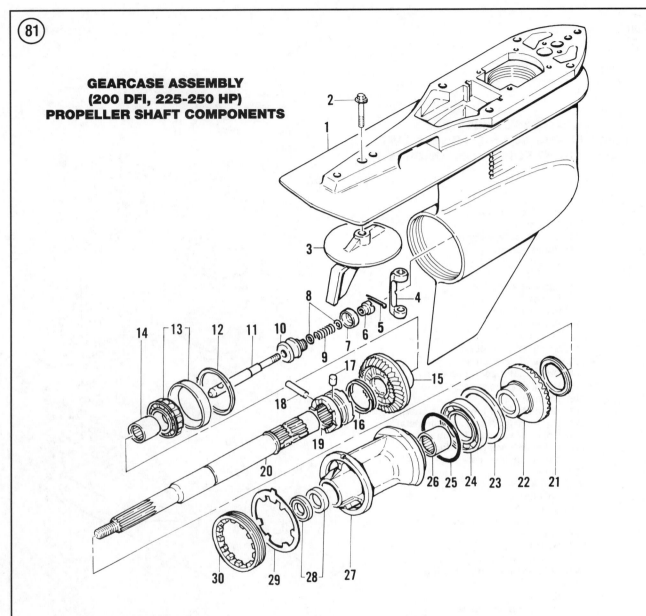

(81)

**GEARCASE ASSEMBLY
(200 DFI, 225-250 HP)
PROPELLER SHAFT COMPONENTS**

1. Gearcase housing
2. Trim tab screw
3. Trim tab
4. Shift crank
5. Cotter pin
6. Castle nut
7. Retainer cup (ratcheting models)
8. Washers (ratcheting models)
9. Spring (ratcheting models)
10. Shift spool
11. Clutch actuator rod
12. Shim(s)
13. Roller bearing assembly
14. Needle bearing assembly
15. Forward gear

16. Retainer spring
17. Shift detent pin
18. Cross pin
19. Sliding clutch
20. Propeller shaft
21. Thrust washer
22. Reverse gear
23. Thrust washer
24. Ball bearing
25. O-ring
26. Needle bearing
27. Propeller shaft bearing carrier
28. Propeller shaft seals
29. Tabbed locking washer
30. Retaining ring

the bearing rollers and races as assemblies. Do not remove any pressed in bearing (and/or race) unless replacement is necessary.

1. Remove the gearcase as described in this chapter.

2. Drain the gearcase lubricant as described in Chapter Four.

3. Remove the water pump and pump base as described in this chapter.

4. Bend the locking tab away from the propshaft bearing carrier retaining ring with a suitable punch and hammer. See **Figure 82**, typical.

NOTE
If the retaining ring is frozen in place and cannot be removed in the next step, apply penetrating oil and mild heat (with an electric heat gun, heat lamp or propane torch). If removal still proves difficult, drill through the ring in several places (parallel to the propshaft) and break the ring into several pieces with a suitable chisel and hammer. Do not drill into the gearcase threads or into the bearing carrier.

5. Remove the retaining ring using spanner wrench part No. 91-61069 or equivalent. See **Figure 83**. Turn the ring counterclockwise until it is free from the gearcase. If the ring is corroded or damaged, discard it. Then, remove the locking tab washer (29, **Figure 81**).

6. Install puller jaws part No. 91-46086A-1 and puller bolt part No. 91-85716 or equivalent and pull the bearing carrier and reverse gear assembly from the gearcase. Position the puller jaws as close to the carrier bosses as possible. Remove and discard the carrier O-ring.

7. Reach into the propeller shaft bore and remove the reverse gear thrust washer (21, **Figure 81**) by sliding it off of the propeller shaft.

NOTE
If the needle bearing inside the bearing carrier requires replacement, the propeller shaft seals will be removed during the bearing removal process. If bearing replacement is not required, remove and discard both propshaft seals at this time with a suitable seal puller. Do not damage the seal bore in the process.

8. Install the drive shaft upper bearing retainer tool (part No. 91-43506) over the drive shaft and

9

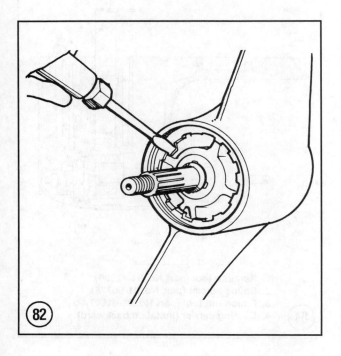

82

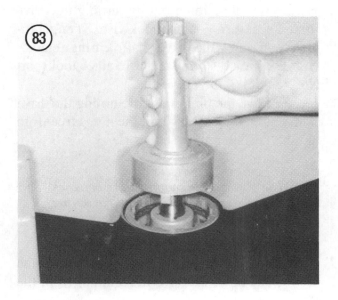

83

engage the retainer lugs, but do not loosen or remove the retainer at this time. See **Figure 84**.

9. Install the drive shaft spline socket (part No. 91-56775) or equivalent onto the drive shaft splines.

10. Insert the pinion nut tool (part No. 91-61067A-2) or equivalent over the propeller shaft and engage the *MR* slot to the pinion nut. If necessary, loosen the drive shaft retainer up to 2 full turns (with part No. 91-43506) to allow the drive shaft to be raised high enough for the tool to engage the pinion nut. See **Figure 84**.

NOTE
If the drive shaft is broken, install the propeller shaft spline socket (part No. 91-61077) which is included with part No. 91-61067A-2 (Figure 85) onto the propeller shaft splines. Shift the gearcase into FORWARD gear and rotate the propeller shaft 1/2 turn counterclockwise to loosen the pinion nut. Remove the drive shaft retaining nut before completely unthreading the pinion nut.

11. Install the propeller shaft bearing carrier *backwards* over the propeller shaft, into the gearcase bore and over the end of the pinion nut tool (to stabilize the tool). Only the rear flange of the carrier will pilot in the gearcase bore. See **Figure 84**.

12. Loosen the pinion nut by turning the drive shaft 1 full turn counterclockwise. Then, completely unscrew the drive shaft bearing retainer with the previously installed retainer tool (part No. 91-43506) or equivalent.

13. Remove the pinion nut by turning the drive shaft counterclockwise until the nut is free from the shaft. Then remove all tools.

NOTE
The lower drive shaft bearing contains 18 loose rollers that may fall out during drive shaft removal. Be sure to retrieve all rollers from the housing.

14. Lift the drive shaft straight up and out of the drive shaft bore. Remove the shim(s) from the drive shaft bearing bore. Measure and record the thickness of the shim(s) for later reference. Tag the shim(s) for identification during reassembly. Discard the race if the roller bearing assembly is being replaced.

15. Remove the pinion nut, washer and pinion gear by moving the rear of the propeller shaft to the lower port area of the propeller shaft bore and allowing the components to fall into the propeller shaft bore from the drive shaft bore. Then, remove the 18 loose bearing rollers from the drive shaft lower bearing race (or propeller shaft bore).

16. Remove the propeller shaft and forward gear assembly by moving the rear of the propeller shaft to the port side of the propeller shaft bore to disengage the shift crank from the shift spool. It may be necessary to rotate the shift shaft

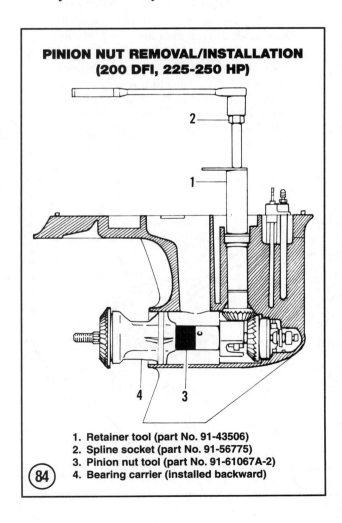

PINION NUT REMOVAL/INSTALLATION (200 DFI, 225-250 HP)

1. Retainer tool (part No. 91-43506)
2. Spline socket (part No. 91-56775)
3. Pinion nut tool (part No. 91-61067A-2)
4. Bearing carrier (installed backward)

(84)

slightly while holding the shaft to port and pulling it rearward.

17. Remove the shift mechanism as follows:

  a. Remove the 2 screws securing the shift shaft retainer/bushing (30, **Figure 80**) to the gearcase. Carefully pry the shift shaft retainer from the gearcase, then remove the shift assembly from the gearcase.

  b. Pull the shift shaft from the shift shaft retainer. Locate and secure the washer (28, **Figure 80**).

  c. Remove and discard the 2 O-rings from the gearcase deck or shift shaft retainer.

  d. Remove and discard the shift shaft seal from the shift shaft retainer.

  e. Remove the shift crank (4, **Figure 81**) from the front of the gearcase bore. Lift the crank

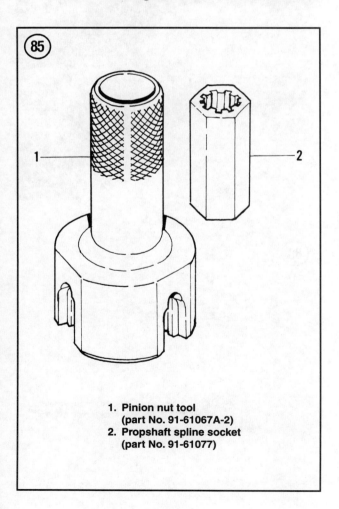

1. Pinion nut tool
(part No. 91-61067A-2)
2. Propshaft spline socket
(part No. 91-61077)

off of the lower pivot pin to free the crank from the gearcase.

Propeller shaft bearing carrier disassembly

The reverse gear rides on a ball bearing that is pressed into the carrier. The propeller shaft has a needle bearing located near the propeller shaft seals. The reverse gear must be removed to service the propeller shaft needle bearing. To remove the reverse gear (and bearing) and the propeller shaft needle bearing (and seals), proceed as follows:

1. Clamp the carrier in a soft-jawed vise or between 2 blocks of wood.

2. Pull the reverse gear assembly from the bearing carrier with a suitable slide hammer, such as part No. 91-34569A-1.

3. If the reverse gear ball bearing requires replacement, proceed as follows:

  a. Support the ball bearing in a suitable knife-edged bearing plate, such as part No. 91-37241.

  b. Press against the gear hub with a suitable mandrel until the bearing is free from the gear.

  c. Remove the thrust washer from the reverse gear or bearing carrier.

  d. Discard the bearing.

4. If the propeller shaft needle bearing requires replacement, proceed as follows:

  a. Set the carrier in a press with the propeller end facing down.

  b. Press the bearing (and seals) from the carrier with mandrel part No. 91-36569 and driver rod part No. 91-37323 or equivalent.

  c. Discard the bearing (and seals).

Propeller shaft disassembly

Ratcheting models—The shift spool is hollow and incorporates a spring, 2 washers and a threaded retainer cup.

9

Except ratcheting models—The shift spool is solid and does not contain a spring or washers.

1. Insert a thin-blade screwdriver or similar tool under the retaining spring. Lift the coil up and rotate the propeller shaft to unwind the spring from the sliding clutch (**Figure 86**). Discard the spring.

2. Remove the single detent pin from the sliding clutch. Then, push the cross pin through the clutch and propeller shaft using a suitable punch. See **Figure 87**.

3. Pull the shift spool and clutch actuator rod straight out of the propeller shaft.

4. Slide the forward gear and bearing assembly off of the propeller shaft.

5. Slide the sliding clutch off of the propeller shaft splines.

6. To disassemble the shift spool and actuator rod, proceed as follows:

   a. Remove the cotter pin from the castle nut.

   b. Unthread the castle nut from the actuator rod.

   c. Slide the shift spool from the rod. See **Figure 88**.

NOTE
On ratcheting models, the shift spool (and internal components), actuator rod and castle nut are serviced as an assembly. If the parts are obviously damaged, replace the assembly.

7. *Ratcheting models*—To disassemble the spring-loaded spool, clamp the spool in a soft-jawed vise and remove the retainer cup by unthreading it with a pair of pliers. Then, remove the spring and 2 washers. See **Figure 89**.

Forward gear bearing removal

If the forward gear bearing race must be removed to adjust forward gear lash, or the roller bearing assembly or internal needle bearing(s) must be replaced, proceed as follows:

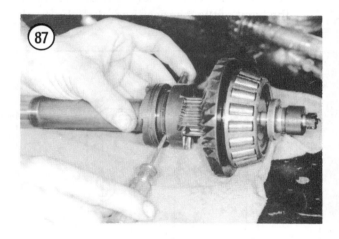

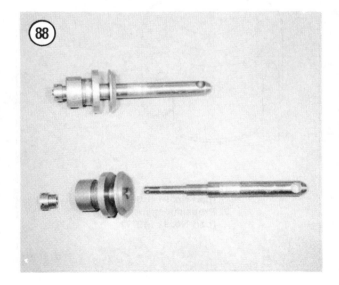

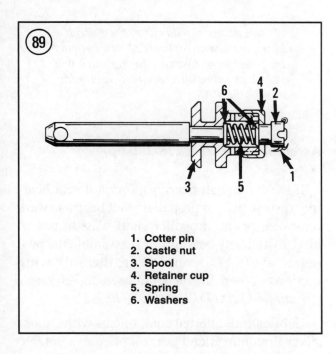

89

1. Cotter pin
2. Castle nut
3. Spool
4. Retainer cup
5. Spring
6. Washers

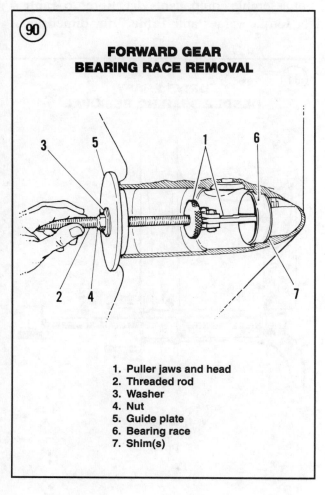

90

**FORWARD GEAR
BEARING RACE REMOVAL**

1. Puller jaws and head
2. Threaded rod
3. Washer
4. Nut
5. Guide plate
6. Bearing race
7. Shim(s)

*NOTE
If the forward gear bearing race is removed only for the purpose of changing
the shim(s) and forward gear lash, do
not discard the bearing race.*

1. To remove the forward gear bearing race from
the gearcase, pull the race from the front of the
propeller shaft bore as shown in **Figure 90**, using
the following tools:

   a. The puller head and jaws from slide hammer part No. 91-34569A-1 (or equivalent).

   b. Puller shaft part No. 91-3229 or a suitable
5/8 in., fine-threaded rod.

   c. Washer part No. 11-24156 or a suitable 5/8
in. flat washer.

   d. Guide plate part No. 91816243 or equivalent.

A suitable slide hammer, such as part No.
91-34569A-1 may be used, but the race must be
pulled straight from its bore.

2. Remove the shim(s) from the bearing bore.
Measure and record the thickness of the shims
for later reference. Tag the shim(s) for identification during reassembly. Discard the race if the
roller bearing assembly is being replaced.

*NOTE
In Step 3, it may be necessary to cut the
roller cage from the bearing and grind a
groove in the inner race to provide a lip
for the knife-edged puller.*

3. To remove the roller bearing from the forward
gear, support the bearing with a knife-edged
bearing plate, such as part No. 91-37241. Press
on the gear hub with a suitable mandrel until the
bearing is free from the gear. Discard the roller
bearing.

4. To remove the internal needle bearing, clamp
the gear in a soft-jawed vise with the gear engagement lugs facing up. Drive the internal needle bearing from the gear with a suitable punch
and hammer. Discard the bearing.

9

Drive shaft bearing removal

A loose needle roller bearing is used to support the lower portion (pinion gear end) of the drive shaft and a single, tapered roller bearing is used to support the upper portion of the drive shaft. The shims under the tapered roller bearing race control the pinion gear depth.

1. Remove the drive shaft tapered roller bearing as follows:

   a. Support the bearing's inner race in a press with a suitable knife-edged bearing plate, such as part No. 91-37241. Position the drive shaft with the crankshaft end facing up.

   b. Press against the crankshaft end of the shaft until the bearing is free from the shaft.

   c. Discard the roller bearing and its race.

NOTE
The drive shaft lower bearing contains 18 loose bearing rollers that may fall out of the race during drive shaft removal. The loose bearing rollers must be reinstalled into the outer race to provide a surface for the removal tool to drive against.

2. To remove the loose needle bearing at the bottom of the drive shaft bore, proceed as follows:

   a. Install the 18 loose bearing rollers into the lower bearing race. Use a suitable grease, such as Quicksilver Needle Bearing Assembly Grease to hold the rollers in place.

   b. Using mandrel part No. 91-36569, pilot part No. 91-36571 and driver rod part No. 91-37323 or equivalent, assembled as shown in **Figure 91**, typical, drive the bearing into the gear cavity.

   c. Remove and discard the bearing making sure all loose bearing rollers are accounted for.

CAUTION
If drive shaft lower bearing failure has occurred, causing the bearing outer race

to spin inside the housing, the gearcase housing must be replaced. A new bearing installed into a worn bearing bore will result in premature bearing and gearcase failure.

Assembly (200 DFI, 225-250 hp)

If the drive shaft bearings, forward gear bearing, reverse gear or propeller shaft bearings were removed, or the propeller shaft was disassembled, install new bearings or reassemble the propeller shaft as described in the following sections. When finished, proceed to *Assembly (Continued [200 DFI, 225-250 hp]).*

Lubricate all internal components with Quicksilver Premium Blend gear oil or equivalent. Do not assemble components *dry*. Refer to **Table 4** for torque values and **Table 7** for dimensional

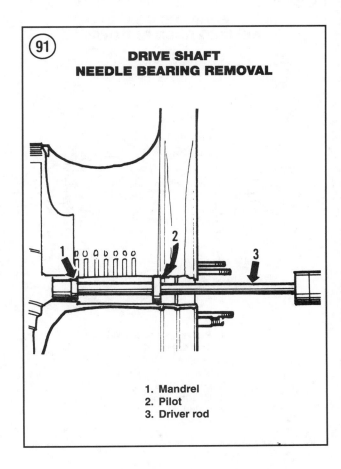

91

DRIVE SHAFT NEEDLE BEARING REMOVAL

1. Mandrel
2. Pilot
3. Driver rod

specifications. Refer to **Figure 80** and **Figure 81** as appropriate for this procedure.

Drive shaft bearing installation

1. To install a new needle bearing at the bottom of the drive shaft bore, begin by lubricating a new bearing with Quicksilver Needle Bearing Assembly Grease. Make sure all 18 loose rollers are installed.

2. Assemble the bearing installer components as shown in **Figure 92**. The numbered side of the bearing must face up (away from the pinion gear) when installed. Use mandrel part No. 91-38628, pilot part No. 91-36571, plate part No. 91-29310 and threaded rod part No. 91-31229 or equivalent.

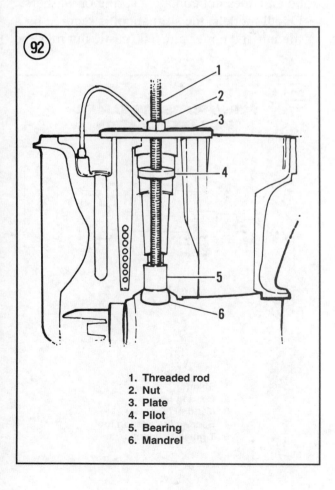

1. Threaded rod
2. Nut
3. Plate
4. Pilot
5. Bearing
6. Mandrel

3. Pull the bearing into the drive shaft bore by turning the nut (2, **Figure 92**) until the bearing is seated in the drive shaft bore. Do not apply excessive force to the bearing.

4. To install the new roller bearing(s) onto the drive shaft, begin by lubricating the bearing(s) and applicable area on the drive shaft with Quicksilver Needle Bearing Assembly Grease.

5. Slide the bearing over the drive shaft splines. The rollers must face the power head (away from the pinion gear). Support the bearing's inner race with a suitable round mandrel, such as a scrap drive shaft roller bearing inner race. Place the assembly in a press with the mandrel (or scrap bearing race) supported by a knife-edged bearing plate, such as part No. 91-37241. The pinion end of the shaft must face up.

6. Thread an old pinion nut onto the drive shaft threads (to protect the threads). Press against the pinion nut until the bearing is seated against the drive shaft shoulder.

Forward gear bearing installation

1. To install the forward gear roller bearing race into the gearcase housing, begin by positioning the original shim(s) into the housing bearing bore. If the original shims were lost or damaged beyond measurement, start with 0.020 in. (0.51 mm) shim(s).

2A. *Ratcheting models*—Lubricate the bearing race and set it into the gearcase bearing bore on top of the shim(s). Place mandrel part No. 91-36577 or equivalent over the race.

2B. *Except ratcheting models*—Lubricate the bearing race and set it into the gearcase bearing bore on top of the shim(s). Place mandrel part No. 91-31106 or equivalent over the race.

NOTE
Take great care to prevent cocking the bearing race in the gearcase bore.

3. Thread the bearing cup installation tool part No. 91-18605A-1 or equivalent, into the propel-

ler shaft bore until its threads are fully engaged in the retaining ring threads as shown in **Figure 93**. Tighten the hex head screw (5, **Figure 93**) to press the bearing into its bore. Make sure the bearing is fully seated.

4. Remove the installation tool and mandrel.

5. If the forward gear roller bearing was removed, lubricate a new roller bearing and set it on the gear hub with the rollers facing up. Press the bearing fully onto the gear using a suitable mandrel. Do not press on the roller cage.

6. If the forward gear internal needle bearing was removed, install a new bearing as follows:

  a. Position the forward gear in a press with the gear teeth facing down.

  b. Lubricate the new needle bearing and position it in the gear bore with the numbered side facing up.

  c. Press the bearing into the gear with a suitable mandrel until the bearing is seated in the gear bore. Do not over-press the bearing.

Propeller shaft bearing carrier assembly

1. Set the carrier in a press with the propeller end facing up.

2. Lubricate a new propeller shaft needle bearing and position it into the carrier bore with the lettered end facing up.

3. Press the bearing into the carrier bore with mandrel part No. 91-15755 or equivalent. Press the bearing into the carrier until the tool seats. Do not over-press the bearing.

4. If the reverse gear was removed from the bearing carrier and/or if the ball bearing was removed from the reverse gear, proceed as follows:

  a. To install a new bearing to the reverse gear, begin by lubricating the bearing and the reverse gear hub. Then, set the gear into a press with the gear teeth facing down.

  b. Position the thrust washer (23, **Figure 81**) over the gear hub.

  c. Set the bearing onto the gear hub with the numbered side facing up. Press the bearing onto the gear with a suitable mandrel until the bearing is fully seated on the gear. Press only on the bearing's inner race.

  d. Lubricate the bearing carrier's reverse gear bearing bore and place the carrier over the reverse gear and ball bearing assembly. Press against the propeller end of the carrier until the ball bearing is seated in the carrier bore.

Propeller shaft assembly

On ratcheting models, the shift spool is hollow and incorporates a spring, 2 washers and a threaded retainer cup.

On non-ratcheting models, the shift spool is solid and does not contain a spring or washers.

On all models, the shift spool is secured by a castle nut and cotter pin. The castle nut must be

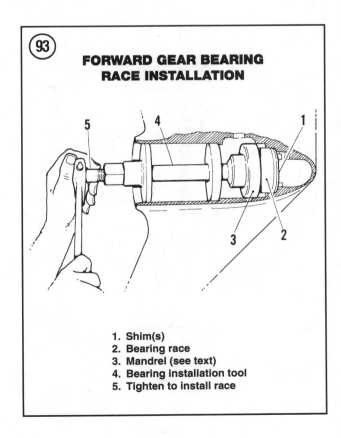

93

FORWARD GEAR BEARING RACE INSTALLATION

1. Shim(s)
2. Bearing race
3. Mandrel (see text)
4. Bearing installation tool
5. Tighten to install race

adjusted to provide 0.002-0.010 in. (0.051-0.254 mm) end play between the shift spool and the actuator rod.

1. Lubricate all components Quicksilver 2-4-C Multi-Lube grease.

2. Align the cross pin holes of the sliding clutch with the slot in the propeller shaft and the detent pin hole(s) with the detent notch(es) in the propeller shaft splines. Position the grooved end of the sliding clutch towards the propeller and slide it onto the propeller shaft.

3A. *Ratcheting models*—Refer to **Figure 94** and assemble the shift spool and actuator rod as follows:

  a. Install the shift spool over the actuator rod with the retainer cup end facing away from the actuator rod. See **Figure 94**.

  b. If the retainer cup, spring and 2 washers were removed, lightly coat the threads of the shift spool with Loctite 271 threadlocking adhesive. Install the washer, spring, washer and retainer cup as shown in **Figure 94**.

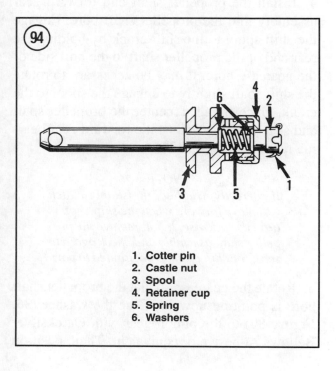

1. Cotter pin
2. Castle nut
3. Spool
4. Retainer cup
5. Spring
6. Washers

  c. Clamp the shift spool in a soft-jawed vise and tighten the retainer cup securely with a suitable pair of pliers.

  d. Install the castle nut and tighten the nut until it is lightly seated.

  e. Back off the castle nut just enough to align a set of slots in the nut with the cotter pin bore.

  f. Measure the spool end play on the actuator shaft. Adjust the nut as necessary. The shift spool must have 0.002-0.010 in. (0.051-0.254 mm) of end play between the shift spool and the actuator rod. If the end play can not be set, replace the shift spool assembly.

  g. Install a new cotter pin. Bend both ends of the cotter pin to provide a secure attachment.

3B. *Except ratcheting models*—Assemble the shift spool and actuator rod as follows:

  a. Install the shift spool over the actuator rod.

  b. Install the castle nut and tighten the nut until it is lightly seated.

  c. Back off the castle nut just enough to align a set of slots in the nut with the cotter pin bore.

  d. Measure the spool end play on the actuator shaft. Adjust the nut as necessary. The shift spool must have 0.002-0.010 in. (0.051-0.254 mm) of end play between the shift spool and the actuator rod.

  e. Install a new cotter pin. Bend both ends of the cotter pin to provide a secure attachment.

4. Slide the forward gear and bearing assembly over the propeller shaft. Then, insert the actuator rod and spool assembly into the propeller shaft bore.

5. Install the cross pin as follows:

  a. Align the actuator rod's cross pin bore with the cross pin holes in the sliding clutch and the slot in the propeller shaft. Use a small punch to help with alignment.

9

b. Insert the cross pin through the sliding clutch *and* actuator rod.

c. Install the detent pin into the sliding clutch bore. Make sure the bore has been aligned with the notch in the shaft splines. Use Quicksilver Needle Bearing Assembly Grease to hold the detent in position.

NOTE
The sliding clutch retaining spring must lay flat, with no overlapping coils.

d. Secure the cross pin and detent pin to the sliding clutch with a new retainer spring. Do not open the spring any more than necessary to install it.

Assembly
(Continued [200 DFI, 225-250 hp])

1. Assemble the shift shaft components as follows:
   a. Coat the outer diameter of a new shift shaft seal with Loctite 271 threadlocking adhesive.
   b. Press the seal into the shift shaft retainer/bushing (with the lip side facing up) using a suitable mandrel.
   c. Coat the shift shaft and 2 new bushing O-rings with Quicksilver 2-4-C Multi-Lube grease. Position the O-rings on the shift shaft retainer.
   d. Carefully insert the shift shaft through the bushing being careful not to damage the seal with the shaft splines.
   e. Install the washer over the shift shaft and against the shift shaft seal.
2. Install the shift crank and shift shaft assembly as follows:
   a. Position the shift crank in the gearcase bore with the splined end facing up and the cranked end facing port. The crank must be piloted on the lower pivot pin.
   b. Install the shift shaft assembly into the gearcase and engage the shift crank splines.

c. Verify that the shift retainer O-rings are still in position, then seat the retainer to the gearcase deck.

d. Install and tighten the 2 retainer screws to 60 in.-lb. (6.8 N•m). Verify that the shift shaft and crank pivot freely and that the shift crank is positioned to the port side of the gearcase.

e. Make sure the washer (28, **Figure 80**) is in position over the shift shaft seal.

3. If the 18 loose rollers are not installed into the lower drive shaft needle bearing, coat the rollers with Quicksilver Needle Bearing Assembly Grease and install them into the bearing race.

NOTE
If setting the pinion gear depth using the universal shim tool (part No. 91-12349A-2), the propeller shaft must not be installed. Go directly to Step 5. After setting pinion gear depth, return to this point and install the propeller shaft assembly. If setting the pinion gear depth using the MerCruiser shim tool (part No. 91-56048), the propeller shaft can be installed at this time.

4. Install the propeller shaft and forward gear assembly into the propeller shaft bore. Engage the shift spool to the shift crank by holding the rear end of the propeller shaft to the port side of the gearcase bore. It may be necessary to rotate the shift shaft slightly to engage the spool to the crank. Once engaged, center the propeller shaft and seat the shaft against the forward gear bearing race.

NOTE
If correctly installed, the sliding clutch will move forward when the shift shaft is turned clockwise. If not, remove the propeller shaft assembly and check again to see if the shift crank is positioned to port.

5. Rotate the gearcase so that the propeller shaft bore is pointing upward. Glue the washer (36, **Figure 80**) to the pinion gear with Quicksilver Bellows Adhesive or equivalent. Then, position

the pinion gear over the lower drive shaft needle bearing.

6. Install the original shim(s) into the drive shaft bore. If the shims are lost or damaged, use an initial shim pack thickness of 0.038 in. (0.97 mm).

7. Spray the threads of the drive shaft with Loc-quic primer. Insert the drive shaft into the drive shaft bore while holding the pinion gear in position. Rotate the shaft as necessary and engage the drive shaft splines to the pinion gear splines.

> *NOTE*
> *Apply Loctite 271 Threadlocking adhesive to a **new** pinion nut **after** the pinion gear depth and forward gear lash have been verified. Install the old pinion nut without threadlocking compound to check the gear depth and forward gear lash.*

8. Position the pinion nut into the *MR* slot in the pinion nut tool (part No. 91-61067A-02). Use a

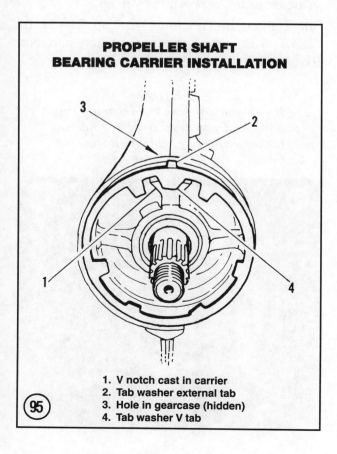

PROPELLER SHAFT BEARING CARRIER INSTALLATION

1. V notch cast in carrier
2. Tab washer external tab
3. Hole in gearcase (hidden)
4. Tab washer V tab

95

small amount of grease to help hold the nut in position. Do not allow grease to get on the threads.

9. Slide the pinion nut tool over the propeller shaft and into position under the pinion gear. It may be necessary to lift the drive shaft and pinion gear slightly to allow the tool to pass under the gear and shaft.

10. Engage the pinion nut to the drive shaft by turning the drive shaft clockwise until the nut is seated finger-tight. Leave the pinion nut tool in position.

11. Install the drive shaft roller bearing race. Lubricate the threads of the drive shaft bearing retainer with Quicksilver Special Lubricant 101, then install the retainer with the *OFF* marking facing up. Thread the retainer in hand-tight at this time.

12. Using retainer tool (part No. 91-43506), tighten the bearing retainer to 100 ft.-lb. (135.6 N•m). See 1, **Figure 84**.

13. Install the propeller shaft bearing carrier *backward* as shown in **Figure 84** to support the pinion nut tool.

14. Attach spline socket part No. 91-56775 or equivalent to a suitable torque wrench. Tighten the pinion nut to 75 ft.-lb. (101.7 N•m). See **Figure 84**. Remove all tools when finished.

15. Refer to *Gearcase Shimming* and set the *Pinion gear depth*. Do not continue until the pinion gear depth has been verified.

16. Once the pinion gear depth has been verified, install the propeller shaft assembly (if not already installed) as described previously in this section.

17. Liberally coat both flanges of the propeller shaft bearing carrier with Quicksilver Special Lubricant 101.

18. Install the carrier over the propeller shaft. Make sure the *V*-shaped notch (casting) in the carrier is facing up, directly under the hole in the propeller shaft bore as shown in **Figure 95**. Then, push the carrier into the gearcase until it is

9

seated. Rotate the drive shaft as necessary to align and mesh the reverse gear teeth.

19. Install a new locking tab washer. Position the external tab into the hole at the top of the propeller shaft bore. Make sure the *V* notch on the tab washer fits into the *V* notch on the bearing carrier. See **Figure 95**.

20. Liberally apply Quicksilver Special Lubricant 101 to the carrier retaining ring. Then, install the retaining ring and screw the ring into the gearcase as far as possible by hand.

21. Tighten the retaining ring to 210 ft.-lb. (284.7 N•m) using spanner wrench part No. 91-61069.

22. Refer to *Gearcase Shimming*, in this chapter, and set the *Forward gear lash*. Do not continue until the correct forward gear lash is verified.

23. Once the correct forward gear lash is verified, remove the propeller shaft bearing carrier and install a *new* pinion nut (with Loctite 271 threadlocking adhesive) as described in this section.

24. Install 2 new propeller shaft seals as follows:

   a. Coat the outer diameter of 2 new propeller shaft seals with Loctite 271 threadlocking adhesive.

   b. Set the carrier in a press with the propeller end facing up.

   c. Install the inner seal with the spring facing the gearcase. Press the seal in with the large stepped end of mandrel part No. 91-31108 or equivalent until the tool bottoms against the carrier.

   d. Install the outer seal with the spring facing the propeller. Press the seal in with the small stepped end of mandrel part No. 91-31108 or equivalent until the tool bottoms against the carrier.

25. Coat a new propeller shaft bearing carrier O-ring and the propeller shaft seal lips with 2-4-C Multi-Lube grease. Then install the O-ring

between the thrust washer and the carrier beveled edge.

26. Liberally coat both flanges of the propeller shaft bearing carrier with Quicksilver Special Lubricant 101.

27. Install the carrier over the propeller shaft. Make sure the *V* shaped notch (casting) in the carrier is facing up, directly under the hole in the propeller shaft bore as shown in **Figure 95**. Then push the carrier into the gearcase until it is seated. Rotate the drive shaft as necessary to align and mesh the gear teeth.

28. Install the locking tab washer. Position the external tab into the hole at the top of the propeller shaft bore. Make sure the *V* notch on the tab washer fits into the *V* notch on the bearing carrier. See **Figure 95**.

29. Liberally apply Quicksilver Special Lubricant 101 to the carrier retaining ring. Then, install the retaining ring and screw the ring into the gearcase as far as possible by hand.

30. Tighten the retaining ring to 210 ft.-lb. (284.7 N•m) using spanner wrench part No. 91-61069.

CAUTION
If necessary, tighten the retaining ring additionally to align a locking tab. Do not loosen the ring to align a locking tab.

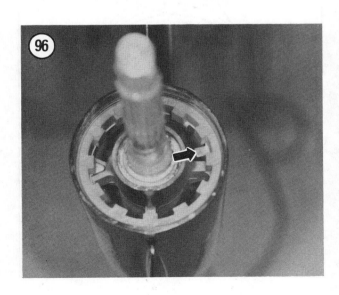

31. Determine which locking tab is aligned with a slot in retaining ring. Bend the tab over firmly into the retaining ring slot (**Figure 96**, typical). Then, bend all remaining tabs forward.

32. Refer to *Gearcase Shimming*, located later in this chapter, and verify the *Reverse Gear Lash*, if so desired.

33. Install the water pump assembly as described in this chapter.

34. Pressure test the gearcase as described in *Gearcase Pressure Testing*.

35. Fill the gearcase with the recommended lubricant as described in Chapter Four.

GEARCASE CLEANING AND INSPECTION

NOTE
Do not remove any pressed-on roller or ball bearing, or pressed-in needle bearing, ball bearing or bushing unless replacement is necessary. A tapered roller bearing consists of the roller assembly and a bearing race. The roller and race are a matched assembly and must be replaced as such.

1. Discard all seals, gaskets and O-rings removed during disassembly.

2. Clean all parts in clean solvent and dry with compressed air. Lightly lubricate all internal components to prevent rusting.

CAUTION
*Metric **and** American fasteners are used on Mercury/Mariner gearcases. Always match a replacement fastener to the original. Do not run a tap or thread chaser into a hole (or over a bolt) without first verifying the thread size and pitch. Check all threaded holes for Heli-Coil stainless steel locking thread inserts. Never run a tap or thread chaser into a Heli-Coil equipped hole. Heli-Coil inserts are replaceable, if damaged.*

3. Inspect all screws, bolts, nuts and other fasteners for damaged, galled or distorted threads. Replace any elastic locknuts that can be installed without the aid of a wrench. Clean all sealing compound, RTV sealant and threadlocking compound from the threaded areas. Minor thread imperfections can be corrected with an appropriate thread chaser.

4. Clean all gasket and sealant material from the gearcase housing. Make certain that all water and lubricant passages are clean and unobstructed. Make sure all threaded holes are free of corrosion, gasket sealant or threadlocking adhesive. Damaged or distorted threads may be repaired with stainless steel threaded inserts (locally available).

5. On models with propshaft bearing carrier retaining rings, remove any corrosion from the gearcase threaded area with a suitable non-corrosive (brass or stainless steel) wire brush. A thread file may be used to repair minor thread defects. If the threads are severely damaged, the gearcase housing must be replaced.

6. Inspect all castings (gearcase, propeller shaft bearing carrier and all other seal or bearing carriers) for cracks, porosity, wear, distortion and mechanical damage. Replace any housing that shows evidence of having a bearing spun in its bore.

7. If the gearcase is equipped with a speedometer pickup, verify that the pickup port is not clogged with debris. Use a very small drill bit mounted in a pin vise to remove any debris from the pickup port. Make sure air can flow freely from the pickup port to the speedometer hose connection.

8. Inspect all anodes as described at the beginning of this chapter. Replace any anode that has deteriorated to 1/2 of its original size.

9. Inspect the water inlet screen(s) for damage or obstructions. Clean or replace the screen(s) as necessary.

9

10. Inspect the drive shaft and propeller shaft for worn, damaged or twisted splines. See A, **Figure 97**, typical. Excessively worn drive shaft splines are usually the result of shaft misalignment caused by a distorted drive shaft housing or lower gearcase housing, due to impact with an underwater object. Distorted housings must be replaced.

11. Inspect the drive shaft and propeller shaft threaded areas for damage. See A, **Figure 97**, typical. If equipped, check the impeller drive pin and propeller drive pin holes for wear, elongation and cracks.

12. Inspect each shaft's bearing and seal surfaces for excessive wear, grooving, metal transfer and discoloration from overheating. See B, **Figure 97**, typical.

13. Check for a bent propeller shaft by supporting the propeller shaft with V-blocks at its bearing surfaces. Mount a dial indicator on the propeller splines. Rotate the propeller shaft while observing the dial indicator. Any noticeable wobble, or a reading mf more than 0.006 in. (0.15 mm) indicates excessive shaft runout. Replace the propeller shaft if excessive runout is evident.

14. Check each gear for excessive wear, corrosion or rust and mechanical damage. Check the teeth for galling, chips, cracks, missing pieces, distortion or discoloration from overheating. Check the sliding clutch and each gear's engagement lugs (**Figure 98**) for chips, cracks and excessive wear.

15. Check the pinion gear and sliding clutch splines for wear, distortion or mechanical damage.

16. Inspect all shift components and shift linkage for excessive wear and mechanical damage. Inspect the shift cam for wear or grooving. Replace the shift cam if it is damaged or worn. On rotary shift shaft models, inspect the shift shaft splines for corrosion, wear, distortion or twisting. Replace the shift shaft if it is corroded, damaged or worn.

17. Inspect all roller, ball and needle bearings for water damage, pitting, discoloration from overheating and metal transfer. Be sure to locate and inspect all internal needle bearings (**Figure 99**, typical). On models with bushings, inspect each bushing for excessive wear. Any bushing that is noticeably out of round or elongated, must be replaced.

18. Check the propeller for nicks, cracks or damaged blades. Minor nicks can be removed with a file, taking care to retain the original shape and contour of the blade. Replace or have the propeller repaired, if any blades are bent, cracked or badly chipped. If the propeller is excessively corroded, it must be replaced.

GEARCASE PRESSURE TESTING

When a gearcase is disassembled, it must be pressure tested after reassembly to ensure that no

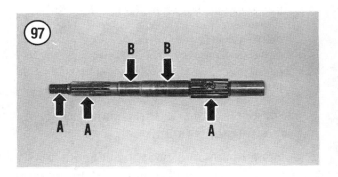

leakage is present. If the gearcase fails the pressure test, the source of the leakage must be found and corrected. Failure to correct any leakage will result in major gearcase damage from water entering the gearcase or lubricant leaking out.

Do not fill the gearcase with lubricant until the pressure test has been satisfactorily completed.

To pressure test the gearcase, proceed as follows.

NOTE
The gearcase lubricant must be drained before pressure testing. Refer to Chapter Four if needed.

1. Verify that the gearcase lubricant is completely drained. Then, make sure the fill/drain plug is installed and properly tightened. Always use a new sealing washer on the fill plug.

2. Remove the vent plug. Install the pressure tester (part No. FT-8950) into the vent hole. Tighten the tester securely. Always use a new sealing washer on the pressure tester.

3. Pressurize the gearcase to 10 psi (69 kPa) for at least 5 minutes. During this time, periodically rotate the propeller and drive shafts and move the shift linkage through its full range of travel.

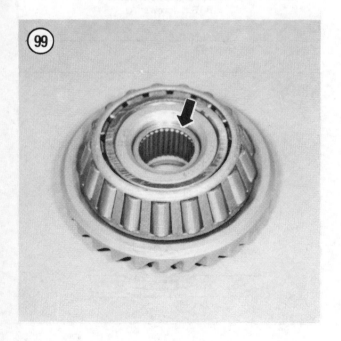

NOTE
Single-lip shift shaft seals may not be able to maintain the full 10 psi (69 kPa) test pressure. This type of seal is used on rotary shift shaft models (75-275 hp). Make sure the shift shaft bushing O-ring is not leaking and that no leakage is present elsewhere on the gearcase before filling the gearcase with lubricant. The replacement shift shaft bushing may be equipped with a 2-lip seal which should be able to maintain the 10 psi (69 kPa) test pressure without leaking.

4. The gearcase must hold pressure for 5 minutes. If not, pressurize the gearcase again and spray soapy water on all sealing surfaces or submerge the gearcase in water to locate the source of the leak.

5. Correct any problems found. When the gearcase will hold pressure for 5 minutes, refer to Chapter Four and fill the gearcase with the recommended lubricant.

GEARCASE SHIMMING

Proper pinion gear to forward/reverse gear engagement and corresponding gear lash are crucial for smooth, quiet operation and long service life. Several shimming procedures must be performed to set up the lower gearcase properly. The pinion gear must be shimmed (positioned vertically) to the correct height (depth) and the forward gear must then be shimmed (positioned horizontally) to the pinion gear for the proper backlash.

On 135-275 hp models, reverse gear backlash is not adjustable, but should be checked to ensure the gearcase is properly assembled.

Refer to **Table 7** for all gearcase service specifications.

75-275 hp

Pinion gear depth

1. Position the gearcase with the drive shaft facing upward.

> *NOTE*
> *Drive shaft bearing preload tool part No. 91-14311A-1 is necessary to check/adjust pinion gear depth and gear backlash properly. The plate (1, **Figure 100**) is not used on 75-200 hp and 275 hp models. However, the engine's original impeller plate must be used on 200 DFI and 225-250 hp models.*

2. Install the bearing preload tool part No. 91-14311A-1 onto the drive shaft in the order shown in **Figure 100**. Do not install the plate (1, **Figure 100**). On 200 DFI and 225-250 hp install the original impeller plate first, (to support the tool) then install the adaptor (2, **Figure 100**).

   a. Make sure the thrust bearing and washer are clean and lightly oiled.

   b. Screw the nut (7, **Figure 100**) completely onto the main body (6), then securely tighten the set screws (8) making sure the holes in the sleeve (9) are aligned with the set screws.

   c. Measure the distance (D, **Figure 101**) between the top of the nut and the bottom of the bolt head. Then, screw the nut downward increasing the distance (D, **Figure 101**) by 1 in. (25.4 mm).

   d. Rotate the drive shaft 10-12 turns to seat the drive shaft bearing(s).

> *NOTE*
> *Pinion gear locating tool (part No. 91-56048 [MerCruiser tool]) may be used on the 200 DFI and 225-250 hp models. This tool requires no setup or adjustments and may be used with the propeller shaft installed, if so desired. Insert the tool into the propeller shaft bore and skip ahead to Step 7.*

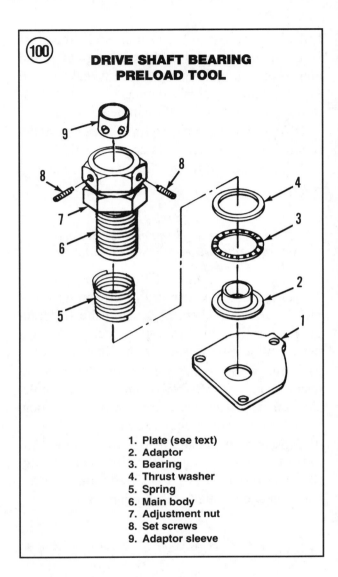

100 DRIVE SHAFT BEARING PRELOAD TOOL

1. Plate (see text)
2. Adaptor
3. Bearing
4. Thrust washer
5. Spring
6. Main body
7. Adjustment nut
8. Set screws
9. Adaptor sleeve

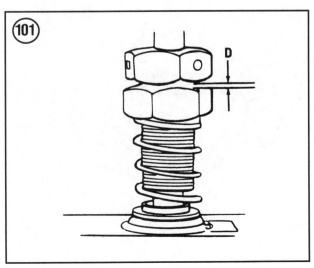

101

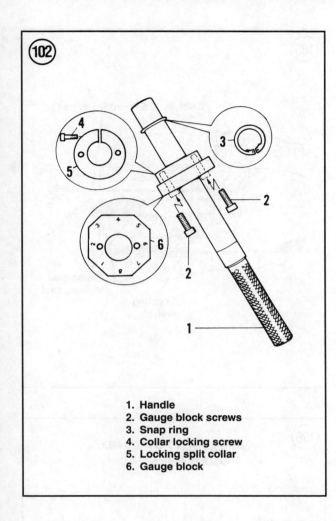

1. Handle
2. Gauge block screws
3. Snap ring
4. Collar locking screw
5. Locking split collar
6. Gauge block

3. Assemble the pinion gear locating tool (part No. 91-12349A-2) as shown in **Figure 102**. Face the numbered side of the gauge block out so the numbers can be seen as the tool is being used. Tighten the split collar retaining screw to the point where the collar can still slide back and forth on the handle with moderate hand pressure.

4. Insert the tool into the gearcase, making sure the tool pilots in the forward gear needle bearing. Slide the gauge block back and forth as necessary to position the gauge block directly under the pinion gear teeth as shown in **Figure 103**.

5. Without disturbing the position of the gauging block, remove the tool and tighten the collar screw securely.

6. Reinsert the pinion gear locating tool into the forward gear. Position the specified gauge block flat (**Table 12**) under the pinion gear, then install the specified locating disc (**Table 12**) over the tool's handle as shown in **Figure 104**. Make sure the locating disc is fully seated against the bear-

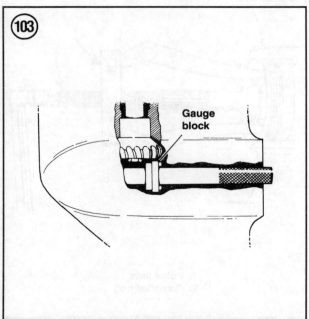

Gauge block

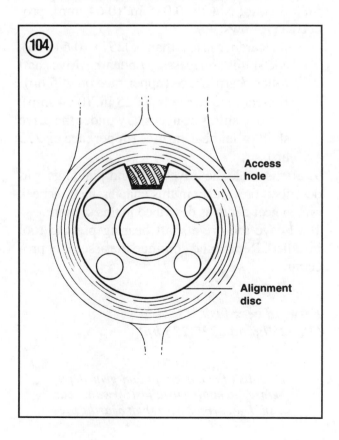

Access hole

Alignment disc

ing carrier shoulder inside the gear cavity and the disc access hole is aligned with the pinion gear.

> *NOTE*
> *Rotate the drive shaft and take several readings in Step 7. Then, average the feeler gauge readings.*

7. Insert a 0.025 in. (0.64 mm) flat feeler gauge between the gauging block and pinion gear. See **Figure 105**. The average clearance between the gear and gauging block must be 0.025 in. (0.64 mm).

8A. *75-125 hp*—If the average clearance in Step 6 is not exactly 0.025 in. (0.64 mm), proceed as follows:
   a. If clearance is less than 0.025 in. (0.64 mm), remove shims as necessary from under the drive shaft roller bearing race.
   b. If clearance exceeds 0.025 in. (0.64 mm), add shims as necessary under the drive shaft roller bearing race.

8B. *135-275 hp*—If the average clearance in Step 6 is not exactly 0.025 in. (0.64 mm), proceed as follows:
   a. If clearance is less than 0.025 in. (0.64 mm), add shims as necessary under the drive shaft roller bearing race (upper race on 275 hp).
   b. If clearance exceeds 0.025 in. (0.64 mm), remove shims as necessary under the drive shaft roller bearing race (upper race on 275 hp).

9. Reassemble the drive shaft and pinion gear as described previously in this chapter, then recheck pinion gear depth as described in this section.

10. Leave the drive shaft bearing preload tool installed. Return and continue the assembly procedure.

Forward gear lash
(75-125 hp and 225-275 hp)

> *NOTE*
> *Establish the correct pinion gear depth **before** attempting to adjust forward gear lash. The correct drive shaft bearing pre-*

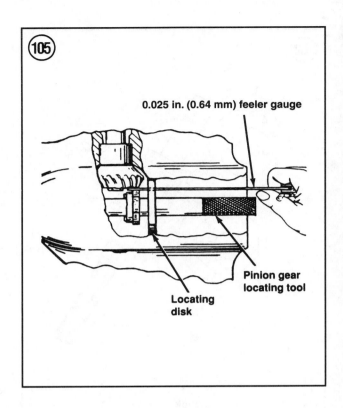

105

0.025 in. (0.64 mm) feeler gauge

Pinion gear locating tool

Locating disk

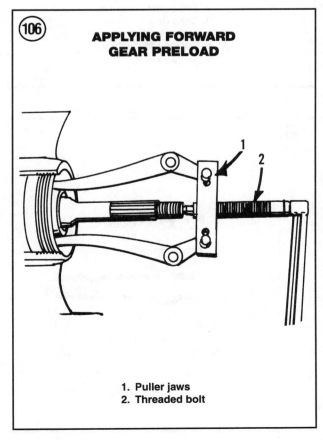

106

APPLYING FORWARD GEAR PRELOAD

1. Puller jaws
2. Threaded bolt

*load tool (part No. 91-14311A-1) must be installed for this procedure. Refer to the previous section as necessary **before** attempting this procedure.*

1. Assemble puller jaws (part No. 91-46086A1) and threaded bolt (part No. 91-85716) or equivalent. Install the assembly to the propeller shaft and bearing carrier as shown in **Figure 106**.

2A. *75-125 hp, 200 DFI, 225 and 250 hp models*—Tighten the puller bolt to 45 in.-lb. (5.1 N•m), then turn the drive shaft 5-10 revolutions to seat the forward gear bearing and race. This will preload the forward gear assembly in its bearing race. Recheck the torque after the 5-10 turns.

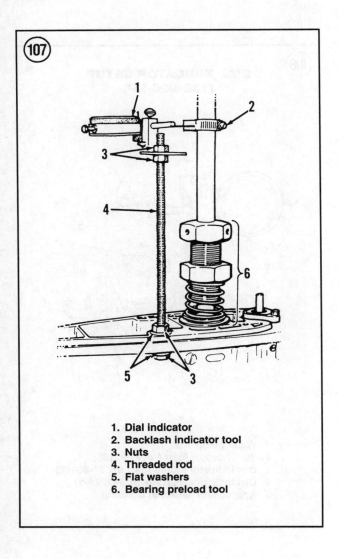

1. Dial indicator
2. Backlash indicator tool
3. Nuts
4. Threaded rod
5. Flat washers
6. Bearing preload tool

2B. *275 hp models*—Tighten the puller bolt to 80 in.-lb. (9.0 N•m), then turn the drive shaft 5-10 revolutions to seat the forward gear bearing and race. This will preload the forward gear assembly in its bearing race. Recheck the torque after the 5-10 turns.

3. Fasten a suitable threaded rod to the gearcase using flat washers and nuts. Then, install a dial indicator to the threaded rod. See **Figure 107**.

4A. *75-125 hp*—Install backlash indicator tool part No. 91-19660-1 onto the drive shaft, align the tool with the indicator plunger and tighten the tool securely on the drive shaft. See **Figure 107**.

4B. *200 DFI, 225 and 250 hp*—Install the correct backlash indicator tool as follows:

  a. On models with gear ratios of 1.64:1, 1.75:1 or 1.62:1, install backlash indicator tool part No. 91-53459 onto the drive shaft. Align the indicator tool with the dial indicator plunger and securely tighten the indicator tool on the drive shaft. See **Figure 107**.

  b. On models with a gear ratio of 1.87:1, install backlash indicator tool part No. 91-78743 onto the drive shaft. align the tool with the indicator plunger and tighten the indicator tool securely on the drive shaft. See **Figure 107**.

4C. *275 hp models*—Place backlash indicator tool part No. 91-53459 onto the drive shaft. Align the indicator tool with the dial indicator plunger, then tighten the tool securely on the drive shaft. See **Figure 107**.

5. Adjust the dial indicator mounting so the plunger is aligned with the specified line (**Table 12**) on the backlash indicator tool. Then, zero the dial gauge.

NOTE
The propeller shaft must not move during gear lash measurement. Rotate the drive shaft just enough to contact a gear tooth in one direction, then rotate the drive shaft just enough in the opposite

direction to contact the opposing gear tooth.

6A. *200 DFI, 225 and 250 hp*:

　a. Lightly rotate the drive shaft back and forth while noting the dial indicator. Record the indicator reading.

　b. Lift the indicator, then rotate the drive shaft 90° and reset the indicator.

　c. Take a new reading at the new drive shaft position. Repeat the process until 4 readings taken 90° to each other are taken.

　d. Average the readings by adding the 4 readings together, then dividing the sum by 4.

　e. The average indicator reading must be within the specification in **Table 7**.

6B. *All other models*—Lightly rotate the drive shaft back and forth while noting the dial indicator. The indicator. The lash must be as specified in **Table 7**.

7. If gear lash is excessive, add shims behind the forward gear bearing race as necessary. If gear lash is insufficient, subtract shims from behind the forward gear bearing race as necessary.

> *CAUTION*
> *Once the correct backlash is verified, the gearcase can be completely assembled. However, a new pinion nut secured with Loctite 271 threadlocking compound must be used. On 75-125 hp models, the propeller shaft bearing carrier screws must also be secured with Loctite 271.*

8. Complete the remaining assembly procedure.

Forward gear lash (135-200 hp)

> *NOTE*
> *Establish the correct pinion gear depth **before** attempting to adjust the forward gear lash. The drive shaft bearing preload tool (part No.91-14311A-2) must be installed for this procedure. Refer to the **Pinion gear depth** section as necessary **before** attempting this procedure.*

1. Assemble puller jaws part No. 91-46086A1 and threaded bolt part No. 91-85716 or equivalent. Install the assembly to the propeller shaft and bearing carrier as shown in **Figure 106**.

2. Tighten the puller bolt to 45 in.-lb. (5.1 N•m), then turn the drive shaft 5-10 revolutions to seat the forward gear bearing and race. This will preload the forward gear assembly into its bearing race. Recheck the torque after 5-10 revolutions.

3. Thread the dial indicator adapter part No. 91-83155 onto one water pump stud, then install a dial indicator holder part No. 91-89897 onto the adaptor. Then, install the dial indicator (part No. 91-58222A-1) onto the adapter. See **Figure 108**.

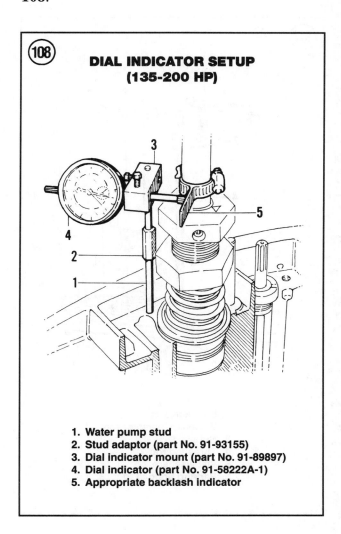

DIAL INDICATOR SETUP (135-200 HP)

1. Water pump stud
2. Stud adaptor (part No. 91-93155)
3. Dial indicator mount (part No. 91-89897)
4. Dial indicator (part No. 91-58222A-1)
5. Appropriate backlash indicator

4A. *Cam shift models*—Place backlash indicator tool part No. 91-19660 onto the drive shaft, align the indicator tool with the dial indicator plunger, then tighten the tool securely on the drive shaft. See **Figure 108**.

4B. *E-Z Shift models*—Place the appropriate backlash indicator tool (listed below) onto the drive shaft, align the indicator tool with the dial indicator plunger, then tighten the tool securely to the drive shaft. See **Figure 108**.

   a. *2.30:1 high-altitude gear sets*—Use backlash indicator tool part No. 91-19660 on serial No. 0G437999 and below. Use indicator tool part No. 91-78743 on serial No. 0G438000-on.

   b. *All other gear sets*—Use backlash indicator tool part No. 91-78743.

5. Adjust the dial indicator mounting so the plunger is aligned with specified line (**Table 7**) on the backlash indicator tool. Then, zero the indicator gauge.

NOTE
The propeller shaft must not move during gear lash readings. Rotate the drive shaft just enough to contact a gear tooth in one direction, then rotate the drive shaft just enough in the opposite direction to contact the opposing gear tooth.

6. Lightly rotate the drive shaft back and forth while noting the dial indicator reading. The indicator must read within the specified (**Table 7**) gear lash range.

NOTE
A 0.001 in. (.025 mm) change in forward gear bearing shim thickness will change forward gear backlash by approximately 0.00125 in. (0.032 mm).

7. If gear lash is excessive, add shim(s) behind the forward gear bearing race as necessary. If gear lash is insufficient, subtract shim(s) from behind the forward gear bearing race as necessary.

CAUTION
Once the correct gear backlash is verified, the gearcase can be completely assembled. However, a new pinion nut, secured with Loctite 271 threadlocking adhesive must be installed before completing assembly. Also, the propeller shaft bearing carrier's retaining ring must be secured by bending the locking tab washer when assembly is complete.

8. Complete the assembly procedure.

Drive Shaft End Play (275 hp Models)

This procedure determines the shim(s) required to control the vertical movement (end play) of the drive shaft. The shims will be placed under the lower tapered roller bearing race at the top of the drive shaft bore. End play must be between 0.002-0.006 in. (0.05-0.15 mm). There can be no preload on the bearings.

1. Install the drive shaft bearing preload tool (part No. 91-14311A-1) as described previously under *Pinion gear depth*.

2. Fasten a suitable threaded rod to the gearcase using flat washers and nuts. Then, install a dial indicator to the threaded rod. See **Figure 109**.

3. Adjust the dial indicator mounting so the plunger rests on the top nut of the bearing preload tool as shown in **Figure 109**. The plunger must be parallel to the drive shaft.

4. Zero the dial indicator gauge.

5. Move the drive shaft straight up and down while noting the indicator reading. Subtract the measured end play from the desired end play (0.004 in. [0.102 mm]). Record your result.

6. Remove the drive shaft and the lower tapered roller bearing race as described previously in this chapter. Add the resulting amount of shims under the *lower* tapered roller bearing race. Do *not* change the shims under the upper tapered roller bearing race.

7. Recheck the drive shaft end play. Do not proceed until the end play is between 0.002-0.006 in. (0.05-0.15 mm).

9

8. Complete the assembly procedure.

Reverse Gear Lash

Reverse gear backlash is not adjustable; however, it should be checked to ensure the gearcase is properly assembled.

135-200 hp and 275 hp Models

Check the reverse gear lash after setting the forward gear lash and after installation of the shift shaft and the shift cam.

1. Install the bearing preload tool as described under *Pinion gear depth.* Then, install the dial indicator and backlash indicator tool as described under *Forward gear lash.*

2A. *Cam shift models*—Proceed as follows:

   a. Shift the gearcase into REVERSE gear while carefully positioning the propeller shaft to ensure that the clutch engagement lugs push against (on top of) the reverse gear lugs.

   b. The lugs must not engage and the shift linkage will not move to its full travel when *lug-on-lug* positioning is achieved.

   c. Maintain a moderate amount of pressure on the shift linkage to hold the reverse gear against the propeller shaft bearing carrier.

2B. *E-Z Shift models*—Shift the gearcase into the full REVERSE gear position while rotating the propeller to ensure full clutch engagement.

3. *E-Z Shift models*—Install a piece of PVC pipe 6 in. (152.4 mm) long and 1-1/2 in. (38.1 mm) in diameter over the propeller shaft and against the bearing carrier. Tighten the pipe against the bearing carrier using the propeller nut and tap washer. Tighten only to the point that the propeller shaft is pulled securely against the propeller shaft bearing carrier. Do not over-tighten.

4. Gently turn the drive shaft back and forth (propeller shaft must not move), while noting the dial indicator reading. The amount of drive shaft

travel indicates reverse gear lash, which must be within specification (**Table 7**).

5. If the lash is not within specifications (**Table 7**), the gearcase is incorrectly assembled, or contains excessively worn components. Disassemble the gearcase, determine and repair the problem before returning the gearcase to service.

6. If the lash is within specification, complete the assembly procedure.

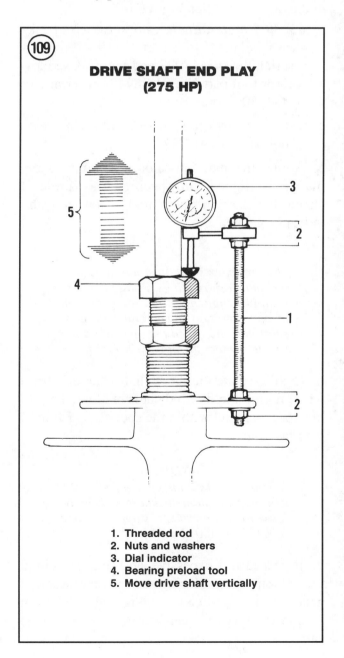

(109)

DRIVE SHAFT END PLAY (275 HP)

1. **Threaded rod**
2. **Nuts and washers**
3. **Dial indicator**
4. **Bearing preload tool**
5. **Move drive shaft vertically**

200 DFI and 225-250 hp models

Check the reverse gear lash after setting the forward gear lash. The propeller shaft assembly must be installed for this procedure.

1. Install the bearing preload tool as described under *Pinion gear depth*. Then, install the dial indicator and backlash indicator tool as described under *Forward gear lash*.

2. Install pinion nut tool part No. 91-61067A-2 over the propeller shaft and against the propeller shaft bearing carrier. See **Figure 110**.

3. Install a flat washer, such as part No. 12-54048 over the propeller shaft and against the pinion nut tool. See **Figure 110**.

4. Install the propeller nut and tighten the nut to 45 in.-lb. (5.1 N•m). Rotate the drive shaft at least 3 full turns (to seat the bearings), then retighten the propeller nut to 45 in.-lb. (5.1 N•m).

5. Gently turn the drive shaft back and forth (propeller shaft must not move), while noting the

APPLYING REVERSE GEAR PRELOAD (225-250 HP MODELS)

1. Pinion nut tool (part No. 91-616067A-2)
2. Flat washer (part No. 12-54048)
3. Propeller nut

dial indicator reading. The amount of drive shaft travel indicates reverse gear lash, which must be within specification (**Table 7**).

6. If the lash is not within specification (**Table 7**), the gearcase is incorrectly assembled, or contains excessively worn components. Disassemble the gearcase, determine and repair the problem before returning the gearcase to service. Make sure the reverse gear thrust washer (21, **Figure 81**) has been installed.

7. If the lash is within specification, complete the assembly procedure.

JET DRIVE MODELS

Jet drive models are based on the following basic outboard models. The standard lower gearcase has been removed and a jet pump unit installed.

a. *65 Jet*—90 hp power head (3-cylinder).
b. *80 Jet*—115 hp power head (4-cylinder).
c. *105 Jet*—150 hp power head (V-6).
d. *140 Jet*—200 hp power head (V-6).

All Jet drive models are carbureted engines. Service to the power head, ignition, electrical, fuel and power trim and tilt systems is the same as on propeller-driven outboard models. Refer to the appropriate chapter and service section for the engine models or component serviced. Only service on the jet drive assembly is covered in this chapter. Refer to **Table 11** for all special torque values and **Table 5** and **Table 6** for standard torque values.

JET PUMP UNIT MAINTENANCE

Outboard Mounting Height

A jet drive outboard must be mounted higher on the transom plate than an equivalent propeller-driven outboard motor. However, if the jet drive is mounted too high, air will be allowed to enter the jet drive resulting in cavitation and power loss. If the jet drive is mounted too low,

9

excessive drag, water spray and loss in speed will result.

Water intake fin kits are available to reduce cavitation when running with the wind in rough water. The 65-140 Jet water fin kits are available from Specialty Manufacturing Company, 2035 Edison Avenue, San Leandro, California 94577.

To set the initial height of the outboard motor, proceed as follows:

1. Place a straightedge against the boat bottom (not keel) and abut the end of the straightedge with the jet drive intake.

2. The fore edge of the water intake housing should align with the top edge of the straightedge (**Figure 111**).

3. Secure the outboard motor at this setting, then test run the boat.

4. If cavitation occurs (over-revving and/or loss of thrust), the outboard motor must be lowered in 1/4 in. (6.35 mm) increments until uniform operation is noted.

> *NOTE*
> *A slight amount of cavitation in rough water and during sharp turns is normal. However, excessive cavitation will damage the impeller and can cause power head overheating.*

5. If uniform operation is noted with the initial setting, the outboard motor should be raised in 1/4 in. (6.35 mm) increments until cavitation is noted. Then, lower the motor to the last uniform setting.

> *NOTE*
> *The outboard motor should be in a vertical position when the boat is on plane. Adjust the motor trim setting as needed. If the outboard trim setting is altered, the outboard motor height must be checked and adjusted, if needed, as previously outlined.*

Steering Torque

A minor adjustment to the trailing edge of the drive outlet nozzle may be made if the boat tends to pull in one direction when the boat and outboard are pointed in a straight-ahead direction. Should the boat tend to pull to the starboard side, bend the top and bottom trailing edge of the jet drive outlet nozzle 1/16 in. (1.6 mm) toward the starboard side of the jet drive. See **Figure 112**.

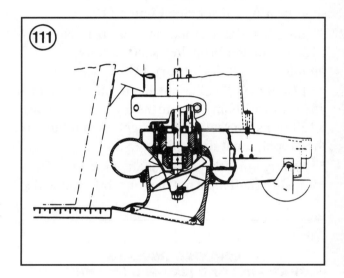

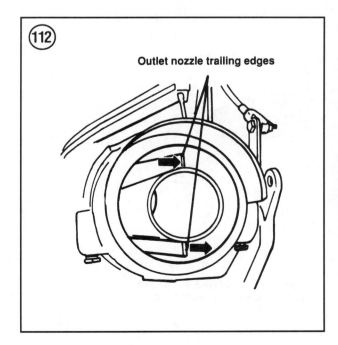

Outlet nozzle trailing edges

Bearing Lubrication

The jet pump bearing(s) should be lubricated after *each* operating period, after every 10 hours of operation and prior to storage. In addition, after every 30 hours of operation, additional grease should be pumped into the bearing(s) to purge any moisture. The bearing(s) is lubricated by first removing the vent hose on the side of the jet pump housing to expose the grease fitting. See

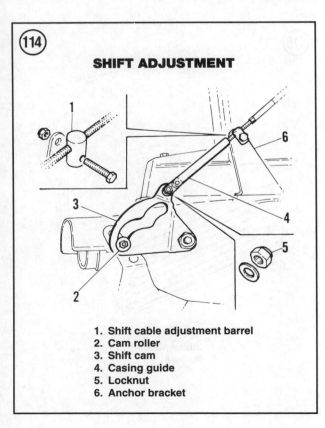

SHIFT ADJUSTMENT

1. Shift cable adjustment barrel
2. Cam roller
3. Shift cam
4. Casing guide
5. Locknut
6. Anchor bracket

Figure 113. Use a grease gun and inject Quicksilver 2-4-C Multi-Lube grease into the fitting until grease exits the end of the hose. After every 30 hours, pump fresh grease into the fitting until all dirty grease is expelled and fresh (clean) grease exits from the end of the hose.

Directional Control

The boat's operational direction is controlled by a thrust gate. The thrust gate is controlled by a remote control shaft cable. When the directional control lever is placed in the full forward position, the thrust gate should completely uncover the jet drive housing's outlet nozzle opening and seat securely against the rubber pad on the jet drive pump housing. When the directional control lever is placed in full reverse position, the thrust gate should completely close off the pump housing's outlet nozzle opening. Neutral position is located midway between complete forward and complete reverse position.

Shift Cable Adjustment

The directional control cable is properly adjusted if after placing the remote control lever in the full FORWARD position, the thrust gate *cannot* be moved into the NEUTRAL position by hand.

WARNING
Shift cable adjustment must be correct or water pressure from the boat's forward movement can engage the thrust gate, causing REVERSE to engage unexpectedly.

To adjust the remote control shift cable, refer to **Figure 114** and proceed as follows:

1. Place the remote control shift lever into the full FORWARD position. Remove the screw and locknut securing the shift cable barrel (1, **Figure 114**) to the shift cable anchor bracket.

2. Adjust the shift cable barrel to position the cam roller (2, **Figure 114**) at the end of the shift cam slot. Secure the cable barrel to the anchor bracket with the screw and locknut. Tighten the locknut securely.

3. Shift the remote control to NEUTRAL, then back to the full FORWARD position.

4. Attempt to move the thrust gate upward (towards REVERSE). If the thrust gate can be moved upward, toward the REVERSE position, readjust the cable barrel as necessary to prevent the gate from moving toward REVERSE.

5. After the correct adjustment is obtained, securely tighten the screw and locknut securing the cable barrel to the anchor bracket.

6. Tighten the cable casing guide retaining nut (5, **Figure 114**) until it bottoms, then back the nut off 1/8 to 1/4 turn.

Impeller Clearance Adjustment and Impeller Removal/Installation

If a loss of high speed performance and/or a higher than normal full throttle engine speed (not boat speed) is evident, check the clearance between the edge of the impeller and the water intake casing liner. Also, check the leading edge(s) of the impeller for wear or damage. If worn or damaged, refer to *Worn (dull) impeller* immediately following this procedure.

NOTE
Impeller wear can occur quickly when operated in water with excessive silt, sand or gravel.

1. Disconnect the spark plug leads to prevent accidental starting.

2. Using a feeler gauge set, determine the clearance between the impeller blades and the intake liner. See **Figure 115**.

3. The impeller-to-liner clearance should be approximately 0.030 in. (0.8 mm).

4. If the clearance is not as specified, remove the 6 water intake housing mounting screws. Remove the intake housing. See **Figure 116**, typical.

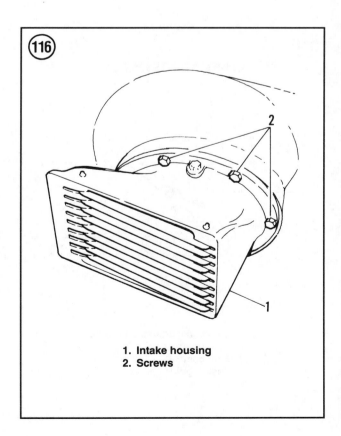

116

1. Intake housing
2. Screws

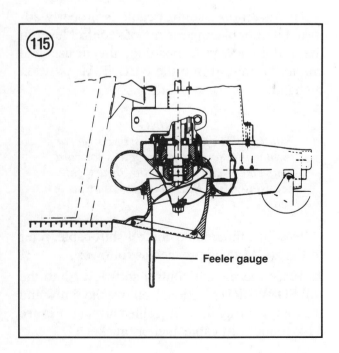

115

Feeler gauge

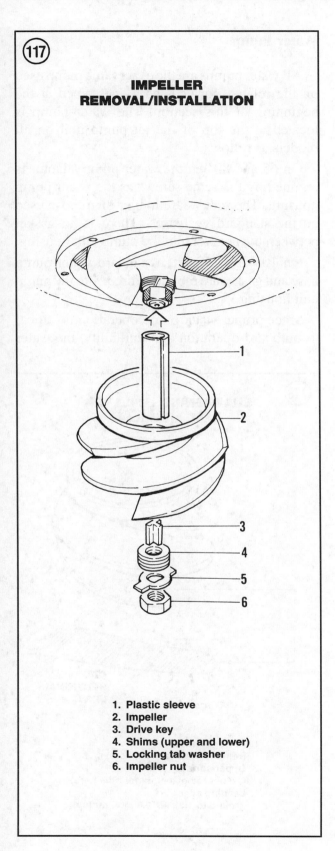

(117)

**IMPELLER
REMOVAL/INSTALLATION**

1. Plastic sleeve
2. Impeller
3. Drive key
4. Shims (upper and lower)
5. Locking tab washer
6. Impeller nut

5. Bend the tabs on the tab washer retaining the impeller nut to allow a suitable tool to be installed on the impeller nut. Remove the nut, tab washer, lower shims impeller, drive key, plastic sleeve and upper shims. Note the number of lower and upper shims. See **Figure 117**.

NOTE
If the impeller is stuck to the drive shaft, use a suitable block of wood (and hammer) to rotate the impeller in the opposite direction of normal rotation. Rotate the impeller just enough to free the drive key and allow impeller removal.

6. If clearance is excessive, remove shims as needed from below the impeller (lower shims) and position them above the impeller (nut side).

NOTE
Lubricate the impeller shaft, impeller sleeve and drive key with Quicksilver 2-4-C Multi-Lube grease or Quicksilver Special Lubricant 101, prior to reassembly.

7. Install the impeller with the selected number of shims. Hold the upper shims to the drive shaft with grease. Then, position the plastic sleeve in the impeller and install the impeller, drive key and lower shims.

8. Install a new tab washer and impeller retaining nut on the drive shaft. Tighten the nut snugly (securely). Do not bend the tabs on the tab washer at this time.

9. Apply Quicksilver Perfect Seal to the threads of the intake housing retaining screws. Install the housing and screws. Tighten the screws finger-tight.

NOTE
The intake housing can be moved slightly on its mounting to center the liner over the impeller.

10. Rotate the impeller to check for rubbing or binding. Make sure the housing is centered over the impeller.

9

11. Repeat Steps 2 and 3 to recheck impeller clearance. Readjust clearance as necessary.

12. After the correct clearance is obtained, remove the intake housing screws and housing. Make sure the impeller nut is tightened snugly (securely), then lock the nut in place with the tab washer. Make sure the tabs are bent up securely against the nut.

13. Reinstall the intake housing, again making sure the housing is centered on the impeller. Tighten the housing screws in a crossing pattern to specification (**Table 11**).

Worn (dull) impeller

The leading edge(s) of the impeller can become worn due to ingestion of gravel, silt and other debris. If a noticeable performance loss, increased wide-open throttle speed, or difficulty in getting the boat on plane is noted, check the leading edge(s) of the impeller for wear or damage.

1. If the leading edge(s) is(are) damaged, remove the impeller as described in the previous section.

2. Then, sharpen the impeller by removing material (with a flat file) from the lower surface of the leading edge(s) as shown in **Figure 118**. Do not remove material from the upper surface or alter the top side lifting angle of the impeller.

3. When finished, file or sand a 1/32 in. (0.8 mm) radius on the leading edge(s) as shown in **Figure 118**.

4. Reinstall the impeller and recheck the impeller clearance as described in the previous section.

Cooling System Flushing

The cooling system can become plugged by sand and salt deposits if it is not flushed occasionally. Clean the cooling system after each use in salt, brackish or silt-laden water. Refer to Chapter Four for cooling system flushing procedures.

Water Pump

All water pumps are the exact same pump used on the related power head as described at the beginning of this section. The water pump is located at the top of the jet pump unit on all models as follows.

On 65 and 80 Jet, the water pump adaptor is retained by the same screws as the water pump housing. The screws are longer than those used on the standard gearcases. There is no gasket between the adaptor and the pump unit housing.

On 105 and 140 Jet, a standard water pump base and gasket are mounted directly to the pump unit housing.

Since proper water pump operation is critical to outboard operation and durability, the water

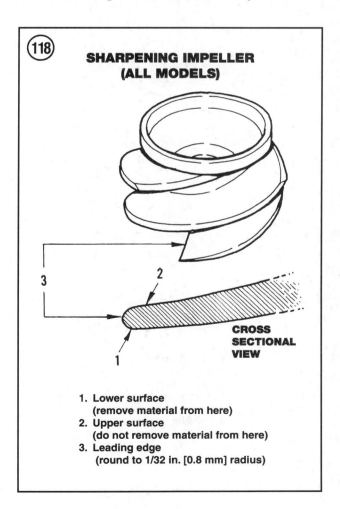

SHARPENING IMPELLER (ALL MODELS)

CROSS SECTIONAL VIEW

1. Lower surface (remove material from here)
2. Upper surface (do not remove material from here)
3. Leading edge (round to 1/32 in. [0.8 mm] radius)

pump should be serviced anytime the jet pump unit is removed from the outboard. To service the water pump, remove the jet drive assembly as described in this chapter and refer to the appropriate water pump service section in this chapter for the related power head.

JET PUMP UNIT SERVICE

When removing the jet drive mounting fasteners, it is not uncommon to find that they are

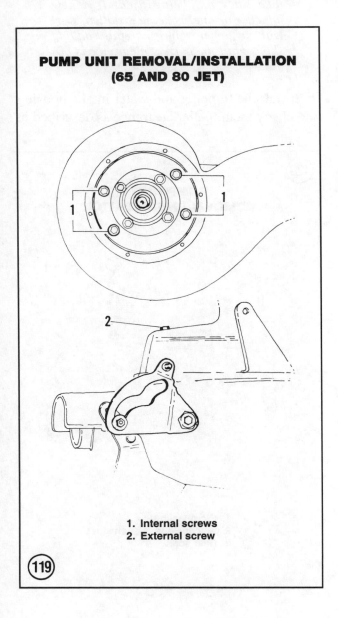

PUMP UNIT REMOVAL/INSTALLATION (65 AND 80 JET)

1. Internal screws
2. External screw

(119)

corroded. Such fasteners should be discarded and new ones installed. Apply Quicksilver Perfect Seal to the threads of the mounting screws during installation.

Pump Unit Removal/Installation

Removal (65 and 80 Jet)

1. Disconnect and ground the spark plug leads to the power head to prevent accidental starting.
2. Tilt the outboard to the fully UP position and engage the tilt lock lever, securely block the drive shaft housing or support the drive shaft housing with a suitable hoist.
3. Remove the shift cable adjustment barrel from the anchor bracket and the casing guide from the shift cam stud. See **Figure 114**.
4. Remove the 6 water intake housing mounting screws. Remove the intake housing. See **Figure 116**, typical.
5. Bend the tabs on the impeller nut tab washer away from the impeller nut. Remove the impeller nut and tab washer. Discard the tab washer. See **Figure 117**.

> *NOTE*
> *Note the number and location of impeller adjustment shims for reference during reassembly.*

6. Remove the shims located below the impeller and note the number. Remove the impeller and the shims located above the impeller and note the number.
7. Slide the impeller sleeve and drive key off the drive shaft.
8. Remove the 4 screws (1, **Figure 119**) located inside of the impeller cavity. Then, remove the screw (2, **Figure 119**) at the rear of the drive shaft housing. Support the pump unit as the last screw is removed.
9. Remove the jet pump unit by pulling it straight down and away from the drive shaft housing until the drive shaft is free from the

9

housing. Place the pump unit on a clean workbench.

10. Locate and secure the fore and aft dowel pins that align the jet pump unit to the drive shaft housing.

Installation (65 and 80 Jet)

1. To install the pump unit, begin by verifying that the water tube guide and seal are securely attached to the water pump housing. If the guide and seal is loose, glue the guide and seal to the water pump housing with Loctite 405 adhesive.

> *CAUTION*
> *Do not apply lubricant to the top of the drive shaft in the next step. Excess lubricant between the top of the drive shaft and the engine crankshaft can create a hydraulic lock, preventing the drive shaft from fully engaging the crankshaft.*

2. Clean the drive shaft splines as necessary, then coat the splines with Quicksilver 2-4-C Multi-Lube grease. Coat the inner diameter of the water tube seal (in the water pump housing) with the same grease.

3. Verify that the fore and aft dowel pins are installed in either the drive shaft housing or the jet pump unit housing.

4. Position the pump unit under the drive shaft housing. Align the water tube in the water pump and the drive shaft with crankshaft splines.

> *CAUTION*
> *Do not rotate the flywheel counterclockwise in the next step or water pump impeller damage can result. It may be necessary to rotate the shift mechanism slightly to engage the shift block splines with the gearcase shift rod splines.*

5. Push the pump unit toward the drive shaft housing, rotating the flywheel clockwise as required to align the drive shaft and crankshaft splines.

6. Make sure the water tube is seated in the water pump seal, then push the gearcase against the drive shaft housing.

7. Coat the threads of the mounting screws with Loctite 271 threadlocking adhesive.

8. Secure the pump unit to the drive shaft housing. See **Figure 120**. Tighten the screws securely.

> *NOTE*
> *Install the original amount of upper and lower impeller shims (as noted on disassembly) if the original impeller and intake liner are being used. If a new impeller or liner is being installed, start with no upper shims, carefully adding shims until the correct clearance is obtained.*

9. Install the impeller and water intake housing and check the impeller clearance as described in

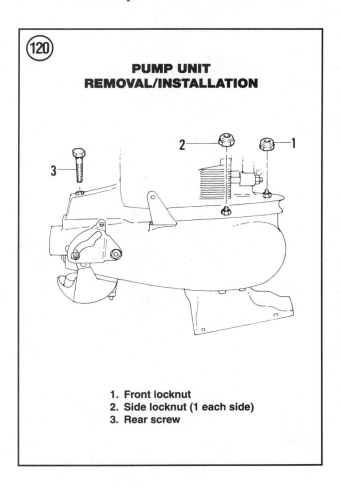

(120)

**PUMP UNIT
REMOVAL/INSTALLATION**

1. **Front locknut**
2. **Side locknut (1 each side)**
3. **Rear screw**

Impeller Clearance Adjustment and Impeller Removal/Installation.

10. Connect and adjust the shift link rod (20 Jet) or remote control shift cable (45-80 Jet) as described previously in this section.

11. Reconnect the spark plug leads.

Removal (105 and 140 Jet)

1. Disconnect and ground the spark plug leads to the power head to prevent accidental starting.

2. Tilt the outboard to the fully UP position and engage the tilt lock lever, securely block the drive shaft housing or support the drive shaft housing with a suitable hoist.

3. Remove the shift cable adjustment barrel from the anchor bracket and the casing guide from the shift cam stud. See **Figure 114**.

> *NOTE*
> *It is not necessary to remove the impeller before removing the Jet pump unit on these models.*

4. Remove the front locknut (1, **Figure 120**) and 2 side locknuts (2, **Figure 120**). Then, remove the screw (3, **Figure 120**) at the rear of the drive shaft housing. Support the pump unit as the last screw is removed.

5. Remove the jet pump unit by pulling it straight down and away from the drive shaft housing until the drive shaft is free from the housing. Place the pump unit on a clean workbench.

6. Locate and secure the fore and aft dowel pins that locate the jet pump unit to the drive shaft housing.

Installation (105 and 140 Jet)

1. To install the pump unit, begin by verifying that the water tube guide and seal are securely attached to the water pump housing.

> *CAUTION*
> *Do not apply lubricant to the top of the drive shaft in the next step. Excess lubricant between the top of the drive shaft and the engine crankshaft can create a hydraulic lock, preventing the drive shaft from fully engaging the crankshaft.*

2. Clean the drive shaft splines as necessary, then coat the splines with Quicksilver 2-4-C Multi-Lube grease. Coat the inner diameter of the water tube seal (in the water pump housing) with the same grease.

3. Verify that the fore and aft dowel pins are installed in either the drive shaft housing or the jet pump unit housing.

4. Position the pump unit under the drive shaft housing. Align the water tube in the water pump and the drive shaft with crankshaft splines.

> *CAUTION*
> *Do not rotate the flywheel counterclockwise in the next step or water pump impeller damage can result. It may be necessary to rotate the shift mechanism slightly to engage the shift block splines with the gearcase shift rod splines.*

5. Push the pump unit toward the drive shaft housing, rotating the flywheel clockwise as required to align the drive shaft and crankshaft splines.

6. Make sure the water tube is seated in the water pump seal, then push the gearcase against the drive shaft housing.

7. Coat the threads of the rear mounting screw (not the locknuts) with Loctite 271 threadlocking adhesive.

8. Secure the pump unit to the drive shaft housing with the 3 locknuts and 1 screw (**Figure 120**). Tighten the fasteners as follows:

   a. Locknuts to 50 ft.-lb. (67.8 N•m).

   b. Rear screw to 23 ft.-lb. (31.2 N•m).

9. Connect and adjust the remote control shift cable as described previously in this section.

10. Reconnect the spark plug leads.

9

BEARING HOUSING

Quicksilver part and accessories only sells the bearing housing and drive shaft as an assembly. Therefore, only removal and installation of the bearing housing and drive shaft assembly is covered.

Removal

1. Remove the pump unit as described previously in this section.

2. Remove the water pump assembly. Refer to the appropriate water pump servicing section at the beginning of this chapter.

3A. *105-140 Jet*—Remove the water pump base and gasket from the pump unit housing if not already removed.

3B. *65 and 80 Jet*—Remove the water pump base adaptor from the top of the pump unit housing.

4. *30 and 45 Jet*—Remove the 4 screws securing the bearing housing and drive shaft assembly to the pump unit housing. See **Figure 121**. Withdraw the bearing housing and drive shaft assembly for the pump unit housing and place it on a clean work bench.

5. Locate and secure the 3 O-rings from bearing housing-to-drive shaft housing mating surface. See **Figure 122**.

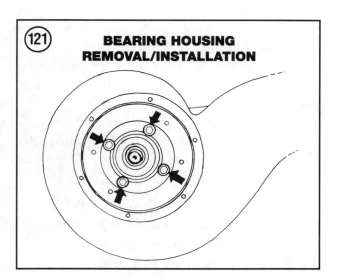

(121)
**BEARING HOUSING
REMOVAL/INSTALLATION**

Installation

1. Lubricate the 3 O-rings with Quicksilver 2-4-C Multi-Lube grease. Position the O-rings into the recesses on the mating surface of the bearing housing as shown in **Figure 122**.

2. Install the housing and drive shaft assembly into the pump unit housing. Make sure the retainer screw holes are aligned and that the O-rings are not displaced during installation.

3. Apply Loctite 271 threadlocking adhesive to the threads of the bearing housing screws.

4. Install the 4 housing retaining screws (**Figure 121**). Evenly tighten the screws to 70 in.-lbs. (7.9 N.m).

5A. *65 and 80 Jet*—Install the water pump base adaptor to the top of the pump unit housing.

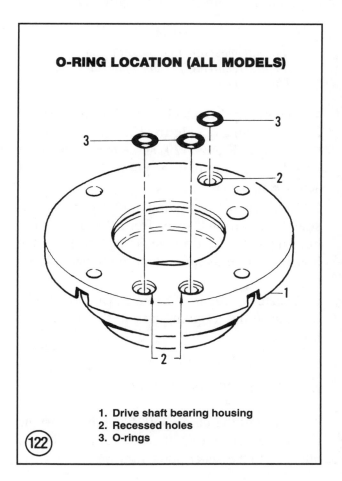

O-RING LOCATION (ALL MODELS)

1. **Drive shaft bearing housing**
2. **Recessed holes**
3. **O-rings**

(122)

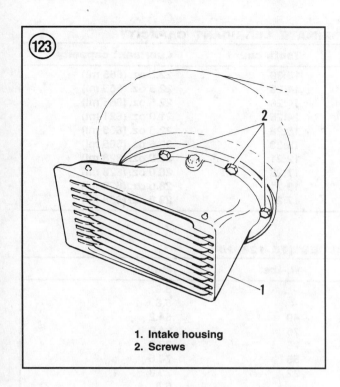

1. Intake housing
2. Screws

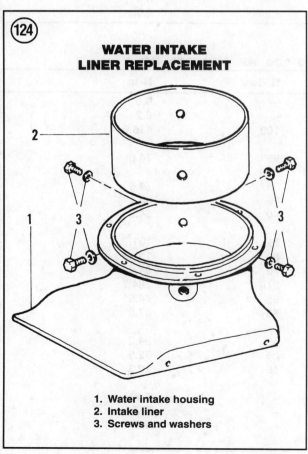

**WATER INTAKE
LINER REPLACEMENT**

1. Water intake housing
2. Intake liner
3. Screws and washers

Coat the mating surfaces with Quicksilver Perfect Seal.

5B. *105-140 Jet*—Install the water pump base to the pump unit housing using a new gasket.

6. Install the water pump assembly as described in the appropriate water pump servicing section in this chapter.

7. Install the jet pump unit as described in this section. Lubricate the jet pump unit bearings before operation as described in this chapter.

WATER INTAKE HOUSING LINER

Replacement

1. Remove the 6 water intake housing mounting screws. See **Figure 123**. Then, pull the water intake housing down and away from the pump unit housing.

2. Mark or tag the liner screws for reassembly in the same location, then remove the screws and washers. See **Figure 124**.

3. Tap the liner loose by inserting a long drift punch through the intake housing grate. Place the punch on the edge of the liner and tap with a hammer.

4. Withdraw the liner from the liner housing.

5. Install the new liner into the intake housing. See **Figure 124**.

6. Align the liner screw holes with their respective intake housing holes. Gently tap the liner into place with a soft hammer if necessary.

7. Apply Quicksilver Perfect Seal to the threads of the liner retaining screws.

8. Install the liner retaining screws (and washers). Evenly tighten the screws to 100 in.-lb. (11.3 N·m).

9. Remove any burrs from the inner diameter of the liner and grind the end of the screws as necessary to ensure a flush inner surface.

10. Install the intake housing and set the impeller clearance as described under *Impeller Clearance Adjustment and Impeller Removal/Installation.*

9

Table 1 GEAR RATIO AND APPROXIMATE LUBRICANT CAPACITY

Model	Gear ratio	Tooth count	Lubricant capacity
75 and 90 hp	2.3:1	13:30	22.5 oz. (665 ml)
100, 115 and 125 hp	2.07:1	14:29	22.5 oz. (665 ml)
135 and 150 hp	2.00:1	14:28	22.5 oz. (665 ml)
XR6 and Magnum III (small gearcase)	1.78:1	14:25	21.0 oz. (621 ml)
XR6 and Magnum III (large gearcase)	1.87:1	15:28	22.5 oz. (665 ml)
150-200 XRI, 175-200 hp	1.87:1	15:28	22.5 oz. (665 ml)
200 DFI (direct fuel injected)	1.75:1	12:21	28.0 oz. (828 ml)
225-250 hp (1994)	1.64:1	17:28	28.0 oz. (828 ml)
225-250 hp (1995-1997)	1.75:1	12:21	28.0 oz. (828 ml)
275 hp	1.64:1	17:28	29.0 oz. (858 ml)

Table 2 TORQUE VALUES (75-125 HP)

Component	in.-lbs.	ft.-lbs.	N•m
Anode (not trim tab)	60	–	6.8
Drain and vent plugs	60	–	6.8
Gearcase mounting	–	40	54.2
Pinion nut	–	70	94.9
Propshaft bearing carrier	–	25	33.9
Propeller nut	–	55	74.6
Trim tab	–	22	29.8
Water pump and base	60	–	6.8
Shift shaft housing	35	–	4.0

Table 3 TORQUE VALUES (135-200 HP AND 275 HP)

Component	in.-lbs.	ft.-lbs.	N•m
Anode (not trim tab)	60	–	6.8
Drain and vent plugs	55	–	6.2
Drive shaft bearing retainer	–	100	135.6
Gearcase mounting			
135-200 hp	–	55	74.6
XR6 and Magnum III			
Nuts	–	55	74.6
Bolts	–	65	88.1
275 hp	–	40	54.2
Pinion nut			
135-200 hp	–	75	101.7
XR6 and Magnum III	–	80	108.5
275 hp	–	70	94.9
Propshaft bearing carrier	–	210	284.7
Propeller nut (minimum)	–	55	74.6
Shift shaft bushing	–	50	67.8
Trim tab			
135-200 hp	–	40	54.2
XR6 and Magnum III	–	24	32.5
275 hp	–	15	20.3
Water pump housing			
135-200 hp	50	–	5.7
XR6 and Magnum III	50	–	5.7
275 hp	60	–	6.8

(continued)

Table 3 TORQUE VALUES (135-200 HP AND 275 HP) (continued)

Component	in.-lbs.	ft.-lbs.	N•m
Water pump guide screw			
135-200 hp prior to			
serial No. 0G437999	50	–	6.8
135-200 hp serial No.			
0G438000-on	35	–	4.0
XR6 and Magnum III	35	–	4.0

Table 4 TORQUE VALUES (200 DFI, 225 AND 250 HP)

Component	in.-lbs.	ft.-lbs.	N•m
Anode (not trim tab)	60	–	6.8
Drain and vent plugs	60	–	6.8
Drive shaft retainer	–	100	135.6
Gearcase mounting			
Nuts	–	55	74.6
Bolt	–	45	61.0
Pinion nut	–	75	101.7
Propshaft bearing carrier	–	210	284.7
Propeller nut (minimum)	–	55	74.6
Trim tab	–	40	54.2
Water pump	60	–	6.8
Shift shaft housing	60	–	6.8

Table 5 STANDARD TORQUE VALUES (U.S. STANDARD FASTENERS)

Screw or nut size	in.-lbs.	ft.-lbs.	N•m
6-32	9	–	1.0
8-32	20	–	2.3
10-24	30	–	3.4
10-32	35	–	4.0
12-24	45	–	5.1
1/4-20	70	6	7.9
1/4-28	84	7	9.5
5/16-18	160	13	18.1
5/16-24	168	14	19.0
3/8-16	270	23	30.5
3/8-24	300	25	33.9
7/16-14	–	36	48.8
7/16-20	–	40	54.2
1/2-13	–	50	67.8
1/2-20	–	60	81.3

Table 6 STANDARD TORQUE VALUES (METRIC FASTENERS)

Screw or nut size	in.-lbs.	ft.-lbs.	N•m
M5	36	–	4.1
M6	70	6	8.1
M8	156	13	17.6
M10	312	26	35.3
M12	–	35	47.5
M14	–	60	81.3

9

Table 7 GEARCASE DIMENSIONAL SPECIFICATIONS

Component	Specification–in. (mm)
Drive shaft vertical movement (end play)	
275 hp	0.002-0.006 (0.05-0.15)
Forward gear lash	
75-90 hp	0.012-0.019 (0.30-0.48)
100-125 hp	0.015-0.022 (0.38-0.56)
XR6 and Magnum III	0.016-0.019 (0.41-0.48
135-200 hp	
1.87:1 ratio	0.018-0.027 (0.46-0.69)
2.00:1 ratio	0.015-0.022 (0.38-0.56)
2.30:1 ratio	0.018-0.023 (0.46-0.58)
225-250 hp	0.017-0.028 (0.43-0.71)
275 hp	0.019-0.027 (0.48-0.69)
Propeller shaft straightness (runout)	0.006 in. (0.152 mm) maximum
Pinion gear height	
75 -90 hp	0.025 (0.64)
100-125 hp	0.025 (0.64)
XR6 and Magnum III	0.025 (0.64)
135-200 hp	0.025 (0.64)
225-250 hp	0.025 (0.64)
275 hp	0.025 (0.64)
Reverse gear lash	
XR6 and Magnum III	0.030-0.048 (0.76-1.21)
135-200 hp	
1.87:1 ratio	0.030-0.050 (0.76-1.27)
2.00:1 ratio	0.030-0.050 (0.76-1.27)
2.30:1 ratio	0.030-0.050 (0.76-1.27)
225-275 hp	0.030-0.050 (0.76-1.27)
Shift spool end play	
200 DFI, 225-250 hp	0.002-0.010 (0.051-0.254)

Table 8 SPECIAL TOOLS (75-125 HP)

Description	Part No.	Models
Pressure tester	FT-8950	All
Nut	11-24156	All
Pinion gear shim tool	91-12349A-2	All
Bearing installer	91-13945	All
Seal installer	91-13949	All
Bearing race tool	91-14308A-1	All
Bearing installer	91-14309A-1	All
Wear sleeve installer	91-14310A-1	All
Bearing preload tool	91-14311A-2	All
Mandrel	91-15755	All
Backlash indicator	91-19660–1	100-125 hp
Mandrel	91-31106	All
Seal installer	91-31108	All
Threaded rod	91-31229	All
Slide hammer	91-34569A-1	All
Puller plate (knife edge)	91-37241	All
Mandrel	91-36569	All
Mandrel	91-37350	All
Driver rod	91-37323	All
Puller jaws	91-46086A-1	All
	(continued)	

Table 8 SPECIAL TOOLS (75-125 HP) (continued)

Description	Part No.	Models
Drive shaft holding tool	91-56775	All
Dial indicator	91-58222A-1	All
Backlash indicator	91-78473	75-90 hp
Dial indicator adaptor kit	91-83155	All
Bearing puller assembly	91-83165M	All
Puller bolt	91-85716	All

Table 9 SPECIAL TOOLS (135-200 HP AND 275 HP)

Description	Part No.	Models
Pressure tester	FT8950	All
Nut	11-24156	All
Water pump alignment pin	17-92786	275
Universal shim tool	91-12349A-2	All
Drive shaft spline socket	91-12362	275
Forward gear needle bearing tool	91-12363	275
Drive shaft bearing installer	91-12364	275
Bearing preload tool	91-14311A-2	135-200 hp
Mandrel	91-15755	135-200 hp, 275 hp
Backlash indicator	91-19660-1	XR6, Magnum III
Plate	91-29310	All
Bearing installer	91-31106	
Shift shaft bushing tool	91-31107	All
Seal installer	91-31108	All
Threaded rod	91-31229	All
Bearing installer	91-34379	275
Slide hammer	91-34569A-1	All
Pilot	91-36571	135-200 hp
Puller plate (knife edge)	91-37241	All
Drive rod	91-37323	135-200 hp
Mandrel	91-38628	135-200 hp
Drive shaft bearing retainer tool	91-43506	135-200 hp
Puller jaws	91-46086A-1	All
Backlash indicator	91-53459	275
Dial indicator	91-58222A-1	All
Spanner wrench	91-61069	135-200 hp, 275 hp
Heat lamp	91-63209	275
Spanner wrench	91-73688	XR6 and Magnum III
Shim tool (alternate)	91-74776	All
Backlash indicator	91-78473	135-200 hp
Seal installer	91-816292	135-200 hp
Seal installer	91-816294	135-200 hp
Dial indicator adaptor kit	91-83155	All
Puller bolt	91-85716	All
Cross pin tool	91-86642	135-200 hp, 275 hp
Bearing installer	91-87120	275 hp
Forward gear needle bearing tool	91-86943	135-200 hp, 275 hp
Dial indicator holder	91-89897	135-200 hp
Drive shaft spline socket	91-90094	135-200 hp
Drive shaft remover	91-92785A-1	275
Bearing installer	91-92788	135-200 hp, 275 hp
Bearing remover	91-92789	275
Pilot plate	91-92790	275
Collar	91-93227	275

9

Table 10 SPECIAL TOOLS (225 AND 250 HP)

Description	Part No.	Models
Pressure tester	FT8950	All
Nut	11-24156	All
Washer	12-34961	All
Belleville washer	12-54048	All
Universal shim tool	91-12349A-2	All
Bearing preload tool	91-14311A-2	All
Mandrel	91-15755	All
Plate	91-29310	All
Collar	91-30366A-1	All
Bearing installer	91-31106	All
Seal installer	91-31108	All
Threaded rod	91-31229	All
Bearing service kit	91-31229A-7	All
Puller head	91-32325	All
Driver head	91-32336	All
Bearing installer	91-33491	All
Puller head	91-36379	All
Driver head	91-36569	All
Pilot washer	91-36571	All
Bearing installer	91-36577	All
Pilot	91-36571	All
Puller plate (knife edge)	91-37241	All
Bearing adaptor	91-37263	All
Bearing remover/installer	91-37292	All
Driver head	91-37311	All
Driver head	91-37312	All
Drive rod	91-37323	All
Mandrel	91-38628	All
Drive shaft bearing retainer tool	91-43506	All
Driver head	91-52393	All
Puller rod	91-52394	All
Backlash indicator	91-53459	All
Drive shaft spline socket	91-56775	All
Dial indicator	91-58222A-1	All
Spanner wrench	91-61069	All
Backlash indicator	91-78473	All
Seal installer	91-817569	All
Water pump alignment pin	91-821571A-1	All
Dial indicator adaptor kit	91-83155	All

Table 11 TORQUE VALUES (JET DRIVES)

Component	in.-lbs.	ft.-lbs.	N•m
65-80 Jet			
Bearing housing	70	–	7.9
Impeller liner	100	–	11.3
Intake housing	144	–	16.3
Jet pump mounting			
Internal screws	–	25	33.9
External screw	–	23	31.2
Water pump	60	–	6.8

(continued)

Table 11 TORQUE VALUES (JET DRIVES) (continued)

Component	in.-lbs.	ft.-lbs.	N•m
105-140 Jet			
Bearing housing	70	–	7.9
Impeller liner	100	–	11.3
Intake housing	144	–	16.3
Jet pump mounting			
Locknuts	–	50	67.8
Rear screw	–	23	31.2
Water pump			
Locknuts and front screw	50	–	5.7
Rear screw	35	–	4.0

Table 12 SHIMMING TOOL SETUP

Pinion gear height (pinion gear locating tool part No. 91-12349A-2 or 91-56048)	
75-90 hp	Gauge block flat No. 8, disc No. 3
100-125 hp	Gauge block flat No. 2, disc No. 3
XR6 and Magnum III	
Prior to serial No. 0G303046	Gauge block flat No. 1, disc No. 1
Serial No. 0G303046-on	Gauge block flat No. 7, disc No. 2
135-200 hp	Gauge block flat No. 7, disc No. 2
225-250 hp	Gauge block flat No. 4, disc No. 2
275 hp	Gauge block flat No. 2, disc No. 2
Forward gear lash (backlash indicator tool)	
75-90 hp	line 4
100-125 hp	line 1
XR6 and Magnum III (prior to serial No. 0G303046)	line 1
XR6 and Magnum III (serial No. 0G303046-on) and 135-200 hp	
1.87:1 ratio	line 1
2.00:1 ratio	line 2
2.30:1 ratio	
Prior to serial No. 0G438000	line 1
Serial No. 0G438000-on	line 4
225-275 hp	line 1
Reverse gear lash (backlash indicator tool)	
XR6 and Magnum III (prior to serial No. 0G303046)	line 1
XR6 and Magnum III (serial No. 0G303046-on) and 135-200 hp	
1.87:1 ratio	line 1
2.00:1 ratio	line 2
2.30:1 ratio	
Prior to serial No. 0G438000	line 1
Serial No. 0G438000-on	line 4

9

Chapter Ten

Power Trim and Tilt Systems and Power Steering System

TRIM AND TILT SYSTEMS

On models without any form of power trim and tilt, the raising and lowering of the motor is a mechanical process. The reverse lock must be released and the motor lifted manually. To change the running position of the gearcase thrust line to the boat (trim angle), the trim pin must be moved to another one of the different positions available in the stern brackets. Different operating conditions and changes to the boat load will require frequent changes to the trim pin position to maximize boat performance and efficiency.

Power trim and tilt was developed to provide an easy and convenient way to change the trim angle while under way and allow hands free tilting of the motor for trailer loading or beaching.

The term *integral* refers to components located between the stern brackets, while the term *external* refers to components located outside of the stern brackets or inside of the boat.

Mercury Marine uses both manual (charged accumulator) tilt systems and power (electro-hydraulic) trim and tilt systems.

This section includes maintenance, component replacement and troubleshooting procedures for manual and power trim and tilt systems. **Table 1** lists recommended test equipment and tools, **Table 2** lists specifications and **Tables 3-5** lists torque specifications. All tables are located at the end of the chapter.

POWER TRIM AND TILT SYSTEMS

Power Trim and Tilt System Description

The typical system consists of:

1. A reversible electric motor controlled from the remote control or dash.

2. A hydraulic pump and fluid reservoir assembly.

3. A single hydraulic trim and tilt cylinder on 75-125 hp, 275 hp, 65 and 80 Jet models or a

separate tilt cylinder and 2 integral trim rams on 135-225 hp, 105 and 140 Jet.

4. Electrical wiring, a fuse and 2 relays or 2 solenoids.

5. *275 hp*—Hydraulic hoses, fittings and a trim limit switch.

6. A sacrificial anode mounted at the bottom of the stern brackets to control corrosion.

A power trim/tilt system is standard equipment on large outboards and Jets and optional equipment on midsize models.

Power trim/tilt systems incorporate several special hydraulic functions:

1. *Impact*—This circuit is designed to absorb and dissipate the energy of an impact with an underwater object, while in forward motion. It does NOT protect the unit from impact damage when backing up. The circuit allows the hydraulic system to act as a shock absorber. High-pressure springs and check balls in the tilt cylinder piston vent hydraulic fluid to the opposite side of the piston when the pressure (caused by the impact) reaches a predetermined value. When fluid is vented, the engine is allowed to tilt up as necessary, dissipating the energy of the impact.

2. *Memory piston*—The memory piston works in conjunction with the impact circuit to return the engine to the trim angle it was at before the impact occurred. The memory piston stays in place during an impact as the tilt cylinder's piston pulls away during impact. After the impact has passed, propeller thrust will push against the tilt cylinder piston. A valve in the tilt piston allows venting of the fluid between the tilt piston and memory piston. This allows the tilt piston to move downward until it seats against the memory piston, restoring the original trim angle. Memory pistons contain no valves.

3. *Reverse lock*—Reverse lock is a function of multiple circuits in the system. Its function is to hold the gearcase in the water during reverse thrust. Reverse thrust occurs during deceleration and when operating in reverse gear. If the gearcase is not held in the water during deceleration

and reverse gear operation, the operator will not have control of the boat.

4. *Manual release*—The manual release valve allows the operator to raise or lower the engine should the electric motor or hydraulic system not function. The valve can be opened and the engine positioned as desired. After positioning the engine, the manual release valve must be closed in order for the engine to hold position and for the impact and reverse lock circuits to function. Manual release valves must never be totally unscrewed (except during disassembly).

WARNING
Do not operate a boat with the manual release valve opened.

5. *Hydraulic trim limit (except 275 hp)*—All trim and tilt systems (except the 275 hp) use hydraulic valving to limit the maximum amount of positive trim the unit can achieve while under way. The trim range is limited to approximately 20° positive trim. The engine can be tilted higher than this when operating below planing speeds (shallow water drive) or when trailering the boat. If the unit is tilted above 20° positive trim and the operator attempts to plane out or accelerate the boat, propeller thrust will overcome the tilt relief valve(s) and the unit will trim down to the maximum trim out (approximately 20° positive) position. If the operator tries to exceed the maximum trim out (up) limit while under way, the electric motor and pump will run, but the unit can trim no higher as the internal valving will bypass the pump's output to prevent additional trimming out.

Power Trim and Tilt System Identification

Power trim/tilt systems can be divided into the following basic designs.

75-125 hp and 65-80 Jet—These models use an integral single ram system of the same hydraulic design described in the previous paragraph, but with additional hydraulic strength to handle the larger engines. There are two versions. Early models use a 3-wire (square) electric motor controlled by solenoids, while late models use a 2-wire (round) motor controlled by relays. The hydraulic systems are different, depending on which electric motor is used. Early model hydraulic systems are also identified by a black reservoir fill plug. Late model hydraulic systems are identified by a yellow reservoir fill plug. An optional trim indicator gauge sending unit is available from Quicksilver parts and accessories.

135-225 hp and 105-140 Jet—These models use an integral 3 ram system. There is one tilt cylinder and 2 trim rams. The trim rams are cast into the manifold assembly. The trim rams push against replaceable striker (wear) plates. The complete system is mounted between the stern brackets. There are 2 versions. Early models use a 3-wire (square) electric motor controlled by solenoids, while late models use a 2-wire (round) motor controlled by relays. The hydraulic systems are the same, regardless of which electric motor is used. A trim indicator gauge sending unit is standard equipment.

275 hp models—This model uses a single integral trim/tilt ram with an external hydraulic pump assembly. A 3-wire electric motor (controlled by solenoids) powers the system. An adjustable trim limit switch electrically controls the maximum trim out (up) the system can achieve. There is no hydraulic trim limi, and there are no tilt relief valves. A *trailer* or *tilt* switch on the remote control (or dash) allows the unit to be tilted beyond the trim limit setting. This unit also comes standard with a trim indicator gauge sending unit.

Electric Motor Operation

All models will use one of 2 basic designs of electric motor, either permanent magnet or field wound.

If the electric motor has 2 leads, it is a permanent magnet motor. There are no field windings

and electricity flows only through the rotating armature. Strong permanent magnets are glued to the main housing. Permanent magnet motors should never be struck with a hammer as this will crack the magnets and destroy the motor. The 2 motor leads are blue and green. When the blue wire is connected to positive and the green wire is grounded, the motor runs in the *up* direction. When the green wire is connected to positive and the blue wire is grounded, the motor runs in the *down* direction. Two relays take care of switching the polarity of the green and blue leads to change the motor direction.

If the electric motor has 3 leads, it is a field wound motor. Electricity flows through the rotating armature and the main housing field windings. The 3 leads are blue (or blue/white), green (or green/white) and black. The black wire is permanently hooked to ground. When the blue wire is hooked to positive, the motor runs in the *up* direction. When the green wire is hooked to positive the motor runs in the *down* direction. The black provides the ground in both directions.

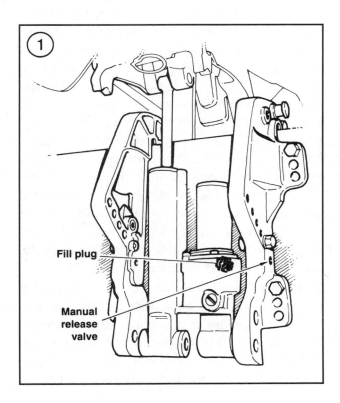

Fill plug

Manual release valve

The green and blue leads must never be hooked to positive at the same time. Two solenoids provide for the switching of the blue and green leads to positive.

On 275 hp models, the trim motor has a large blue/white lead, a large green/white lead and a small black lead. This is a field wound motor as described previously, but the ground for the motor is through the motor frame. The small black lead is connected to a thermal switch inside the electric motor. The tilt up and trim down solenoids are grounded through the thermal switch and motor frame. If the electric trim/tilt motor should overheat for any reason, the thermal switch will open, causing the solenoid(s) to open, stopping the trim motor.

Manual Release Valve Operation

All models incorporate a manual release valve. On 1-piece integral models the valve is located at the lower outside corner of the starboard stern bracket. The valve may be accessed through a hole in the stern bracket or accessed directly depending on model. See **Figure 1**, typical. On 275 hp models the valve is located on the boat-mounted hydraulic pump and motor unit and is positioned between the hydraulic lines as shown in **Figure 2**. The manual release valve allows the motor to be raised or lowered to any position if the electric motor has failed for any reason.

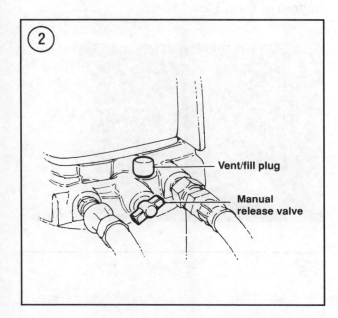

WARNING
Do not operate the engine with the manual release valve in the open position. Reverse lock protection will be disabled. There would be nothing to prevent the engine from tilting out of the water when backing up in reverse gear and when decelerating in forward gear. This will cause a loss of directional control. Retighten the manual release valve securely once the motor has been positioned as desired.

1A. *75-125 hp and 80 Jet (round motor)*—To raise or lower the motor manually, open the manual release valve (**Figure 2**) 3-4 full turns. Do not open the valve further than recommended.

1B. *75-125 hp and 80 Jet (square motor)*—To raise or lower the motor manually, open the manual release valve (A, **Figure 3**, typical) no

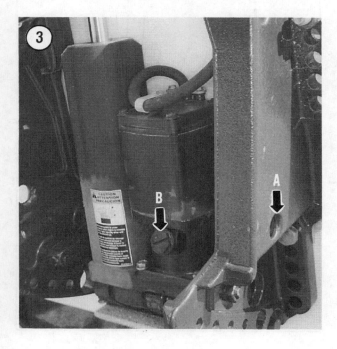

10

more than 3 full turns. Do not open the valve further than recommended.

1C. *135-250 hp and 105 and 140 Jet*—To raise or lower the motor manually, open the manual release valve (**Figure 4**) 3-4 turns. Do not open the valve further than recommended.

1D. *275 hp*—To raise or lower the motor manually, open the manual release valve (**Figure 2**) as necessary to position the engine at the desired tilt or trim position. Avoid opening the valve further than necessary or fluid leakage will occur.

2. Position the engine at the desired tilt or trim position.

3. Retighten the manual valve securely.

Maintenance

Periodically check the wiring system for corrosion and loose or damaged connections. Tighten any loose connections, replace damaged components and clean corroded terminals as necessary. Coat the terminals and connections with anticorrosion grease or liquid neoprene. Check the reservoir fluid level as outlined in the following procedures.

Inspect the anode for loose mounting hardware, loose or damaged ground straps (if equipped) and excessive deterioration. The anode must be replaced if it is reduced to one-half of its original size. Make sure the anode is not painted or coated with any substance. If paint or any other coating covers the anode, the anode must be removed and the coating stripped or the anode replaced.

Reservoir fluid check (all 1-piece integral systems)

The fill plug (B, **Figure 3**, typical) is located just below the electric motor on all 75-125 hp and 65 and 80 Jet models. On 135-250 hp and 105-140 Jet models the fill plug is located on the port side of the manifold assembly as shown in **Figure 5**.

1. Trim the outboard to the full UP position. Clean the area around the fill plug. Carefully remove the fill plug while holding a shop cloth over the plug to block any oil spray.

2. The fluid level should be even with the bottom of the fill plug hole. If necessary, add Quicksilver Power Trim Fluid or automatic transmission fluid to bring the level up to the bottom of the oil level hole.

3. Install the fill plug. Cycle the outboard fully down and up several times to bleed any air that might be in the system.

4. Recheck the fluid level as described in Steps 1 and 2. Make sure the fill plug is tightened securely when finished.

Reservoir fluid check
(275 hp with remote pump)

1. Trim the outboard to the full *DOWN* position. Clean the area around the fill/vent plug (**Figure 2**). Carefully remove the fill/vent plug while holding a shop cloth over the plug to block any oil spray.

2. Check the oil level on the dipstick portion of the plug. The fluid level should be at the full mark (**Figure 6**) on the dipstick.

3. If necessary, add SAE 10W-30 or 10W-40 engine oil as required to bring oil level to the full mark. Do not overfill the system.

> CAUTION
> *The fill/vent plug must be backed out 1-1/2 turns from a seated position to allow the reservoir to vent properly.*

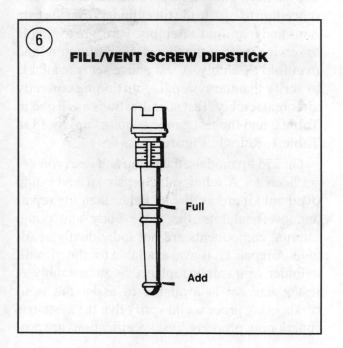

6

FILL/VENT SCREW DIPSTICK

Full

Add

4. Reinstall the fill/vent plug. Tighten the plug lightly, then back out 1-1/2 turns. Cycle the outboard fully up and down 3-5 times to bleed any air that might be in the system.

5. Recheck the fluid level as described in Steps 1 and 2. Make sure the fill/vent plug is backed out 1-1/2 turns from the lightly seated position when finished.

Bleeding air from hydraulic system

All trim and tilt systems are considered self-bleeding. Simply cycle the unit fully up and down a total of 3-5 times to bleed all air from the system. Make sure the fluid level in the reservoir is maintained as described previously in this section. If the fluid appears foamy, allow the unit to sit for a minimum of 30 minutes to allow the air to separate from the fluid.

Maximum Trim In Limit Adjustment

To limit the total amount of negative (down/in) trim an outboard can obtain, an adjustable trim limit rod is used. All models use a single long bolt (**Figure 7**) that passes

10

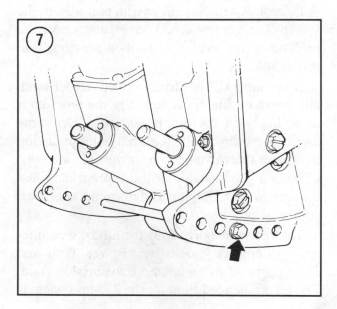

7

through both stern brackets and is secured with a locknut.

> *CAUTION*
> *Do not over-tighten the trim angle adjustment bolt on 275 hp models or the stern brackets may be pinched together, binding the swivel bracket from being able to tilt and trim. Component damage will result from over-tightening. Tighten the elastic locknut just enough to remove all play.*

Hydraulic Troubleshooting

If a problem develops in the trim/tilt system, the initial step is to determine whether the problem is located in the electrical system or in the hydraulic system. If the electric motor runs normally, the problem is hydraulic in nature. If the electric motor does not run or runs slowly, go to *Electric system testing* in this chapter. It is possible for an internal hydraulic component problem to cause the pump to turn slowly or lock up completely, but not likely.

If the electric motor seems to run abnormally fast in both directions (up and down), remove the electric motor and check for a sheared pump drive shaft (or coupler).

If the unit will only tilt or trim partially, or the system's movement is *jerky* or *erratic*, check the reservoir fluid level as described previously in this chapter.

If the unit will not trim out (up) under load, but otherwise functions normally, the problem is most likely in the pump assembly. On some units, the pump can be replaced without having to replace the valve body or manifold assembly. Consult a parts catalog or the appropriate illustrations in this chapter to determine your best course of action.

The recommended fluid for all 1-piece integral systems is Quicksilver Power Trim and Steering Fluid or automatic transmission fluid. The recommended fluid for the 275 hp system is

10W-40 or 10W-30 motor oil. Lubricate all seals and O-rings with the recommended fluid during assembly. Apply Loctite 271 threadlocking adhesive to all threaded fasteners. If removed, lubricate the manual release valve with Quicksilver Special Lubricant 101.

> *NOTE*
> *Always replace all O-rings, seals and gaskets that are removed. Clean the outside of the component before disassembly. Always use a lint-free cloth when handling trim/tilt components. Dirt or lint can block passages causing valves to stick and preventing O-rings from sealing.*

One-piece, single-ram integral units (75-125 hp, 65 and 80 Jet) are removed and installed as an assembly. No specific troubleshooting procedure to isolate the trim/tilt cylinder from the pump and manifold is available. Parts are available to service most of the cylinder and pump/valve body components. Refer to **Figure 8** and **Figure 9** as appropriate.

One-piece, triple-ram integral units (135-250 hp 105 and 140 Jet) are removed and installed as an assembly. There is no specific troubleshooting procedure to isolate the tilt cylinder from the trim rams and manifold assembly. Parts are available to service most of the tilt cylinder, trim rams and manifold assembly. A test gauge set is available to verify that the system is functioning correctly after reassembly. Test specifications are listed in **Table 2** and the test gauge adaptors are listed in **Table 1**. Refer to **Figure 10**.

On 275 hp models, the pump and reservoir are serviceable. A relief valve repair kit and pump overhaul kit are available. Other than the repair and overhaul kits, the valve body and pump internal components are not individually available. A repair kit is also available for the trim/tilt cylinder, or it can be replaced as an assembly. A test gauge set is available to assist the troubleshooting process and verify that the system is functioning properly. Test specifications are pro-

EARLY MODEL ONE-PIECE INTEGRAL TRIM/TILT SYSTEM—BLACK FILL PLUG (75-125 HP AND 65-80 JET)

1. Cylinder rod
2. End cap
3. O-rings and seals
4. Memory piston
5. Trim/tilt cylinder
6. Dowel pins
7. Screw
8. Pilot valve seat, spool and spring
9. Screw
10. Rocker arm
11. Drive shaft (coupler)
12. Pump and valve body assembly
13. Fill plug
14. Manual release valve and lock clip
15. Pump and motor O-rings and seals
16. Screw and washer
17. Reservoir and motor base
18. Armature and thrust washers
19. Motor frame (field)
20. Brush plate assembly
21. Brushes and springs
22. End cap and harness (serviced with frame)
23. Seal and flat washer
24. Screw
25. Pivot shafts
26. Trilobe or dowel pin

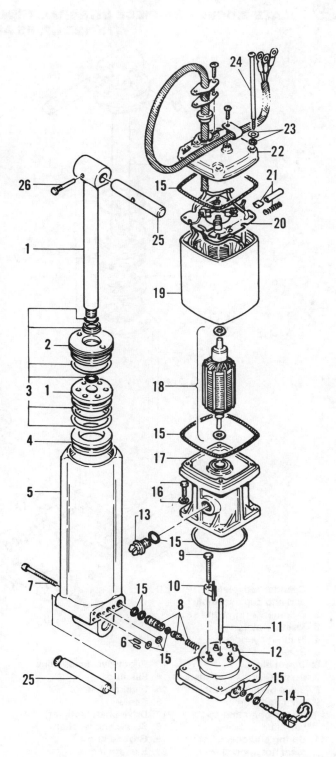

10

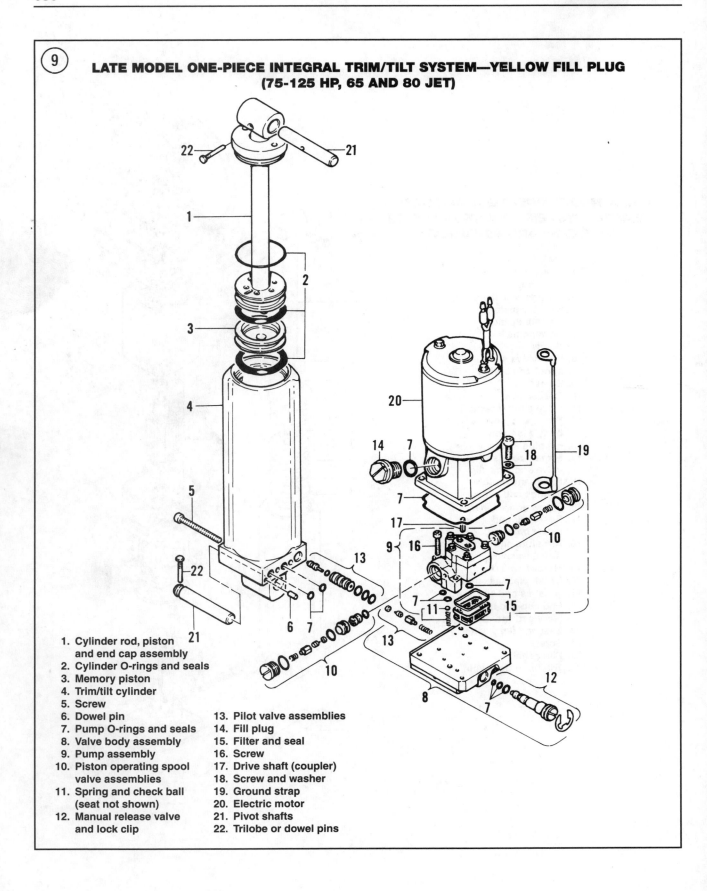

⑨ **LATE MODEL ONE-PIECE INTEGRAL TRIM/TILT SYSTEM—YELLOW FILL PLUG
(75-125 HP, 65 AND 80 JET)**

1. Cylinder rod, piston
   and end cap assembly
2. Cylinder O-rings and seals
3. Memory piston
4. Trim/tilt cylinder
5. Screw
6. Dowel pin
7. Pump O-rings and seals
8. Valve body assembly
9. Pump assembly
10. Piston operating spool
    valve assemblies
11. Spring and check ball
    (seat not shown)
12. Manual release valve
    and lock clip
13. Pilot valve assemblies
14. Fill plug
15. Filter and seal
16. Screw
17. Drive shaft (coupler)
18. Screw and washer
19. Ground strap
20. Electric motor
21. Pivot shafts
22. Trilobe or dowel pins

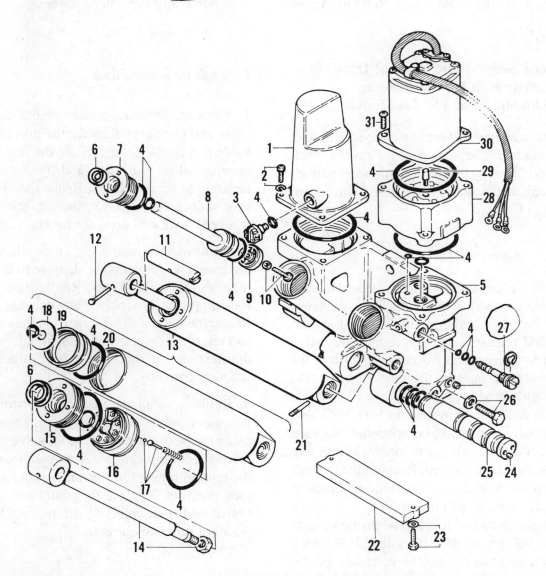

**ONE-PIECE, THREE RAM, INTEGRAL TRIM/TILT SYSTEM
(135-250 HP AND 105-140 JET)**

1. Reservoir
2. Screw and washer
3. Fill plug
4. O-rings
5. Manifold
6. Wiper
7. Trim rod end cap
8. Trim rod
9. Trim rod filter (port rod)
10. Screw and washer (port rod)
11. Upper pivot shaft
12. Trilobe or dowel pin

13. Tilt cylinder assembly
14. Tilt cylinder rod and nut
15. Tilt cylinder end cap
16. Tilt cylinder piston
17. Spring, spring seat
     and check ball
18. Retaining washer
19. Memory piston
20. Tilt cylinder
21. Retaining pin
22. Anode
23. Screw and washer

24. Pipe plug(s)
25. Lower pivot shaft
26. Screw and washer
27. Manual release valve
     and lock clip
28. Pump and valve
     body assembly
29. Drive shaft (coupler)
30. Electric motor
     (3-wire shown)
31. Screw (2 short, 2 long)

10

vided in **Table 2** and the test gauge is listed in **Table 1**. The cylinder simply has 2 connections; the lower connection is for the UP line and thte top fitting is for the DOWN line. Refer to **Figure 11**.

One-Piece, Single-Ram, Integral Trim/Tilt System Hydraulic Troubleshooting (75-125 hp and 65 and 80 Jet Models)

Additional troubleshooting is divided into 2 failure modes: The unit has no reverse lock (kicks up in reverse or trails out on deceleration) or the unit leaks down (will not hold a trim position in forward gear).

Unit leaks down

1. Remove, clean and inspect the manual release valve and O-ring(s). Replace the manual release valve if it or the O-ring(s) are damaged. Install the manual release valve and tighten the valve securely to prevent leaks. Retest the system for leak-down. Continue to the next step if leak-down is still noted.
2. Remove, clean and inspect the tilt relief valve (or pilot valve assembly) components. Replace all of the tilt relief valve components if it or any of the O-rings are damaged. Reassemble the unit and retest for leak-down. Continue to the next step if leak-down is still noted.
3. Remove, clean and inspect the piston operating spool valve assembly (if equipped). Replace the piston operating spool valve if any of the components are damaged. Reassemble the unit and retest for leak-down. Continue to the next step if leak-down is still noted.
4. Remove, clean and inspect the memory piston and the cylinder rod piston (and impact relief valves). If the O-rings are undamaged and the cylinder wall is not scored, replace the memory piston and cylinder rod and piston assembly.
   a. If the cylinder wall is scored or damaged, replace the cylinder assembly.

b. Reassemble the unit with new seals and O-rings. Retest the system for leak-down. If leak-down is still evident, replace the pump and valve body assembly.

Unit has no reverse lock

1. Remove, clean and inspect the manual release valve and O-ring(s). Replace the manual release valve if it or the O-ring(s) are damaged. Install the manual release valve and tighten the valve securely to prevent leaks. Retest the system for reverse lock function. Continue to the next step if reverse lock still does not function correctly.
2. Remove, clean and inspect the cylinder piston rod assembly for debris or damage to the impact relief (shock rod) valves. Replace the cylinder rod and piston assembly if any damage is noted. Reassemble the unit with new O-rings and seals and retest for reverse lock function. Continue to the next step if the reverse lock still does not function correctly.
3. Remove, clean and inspect the piston operating spool valve assemblies (if equipped). Replace the piston operating spool valves if any of the valve components are damaged. Reassemble the unit with new O-rings and retest for reverse lock function. Replace the pump and manifold (valve body) assembly if the reverse lock still does not function correctly.

One-Piece, Triple Ram, Integral Trim/Tilt System Hydraulic Troubleshooting (135-250 Hp and 105-140 Jet Models)

Additional troubleshooting is divided into 2 failure modes: The unit has no reverse lock (kicks up in reverse or trails out on deceleration) or the unit leaks down (will not hold a trim position in forward gear).

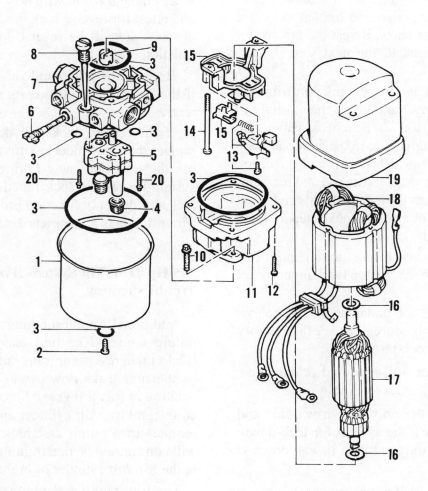

275 HP TRIM/TILT HYDRAULIC PUMP ASSEMBLY

1. Reservoir
2. Screw
3. O-rings
4. Hat filter
5. Pump assembly
6. Manual release
   valve assembly
7. Valve body
8. Fill/vent plug/dipstick
9. Coupler
10. Screw
11. End cap and bearing
12. Screw
13. Brush, holder and spring
14. Screw
15. Brush holder assembly
16. Thrust washers
17. Armature
18. Field winding and
    thermal switch
19. Main motor housing
    and bearing
20. Pump screws

10

Unit leaks down

1. Remove, clean and inspect the manual release valve and O-ring(s). Replace the manual release valve if it or the O-ring(s) are damaged. Install the manual release valve and tighten the valve securely to prevent leaks. Retest the system for leak-down. Continue to the next step if leak-down is still noted.

2. Remove, clean and inspect the port trim ram rod. Inspect the upper and lower check valves in the trim rod's piston. If no check valves are found, the check valves are in the starboard trim ram rod. If no dirt or debris is found the check valves, replace the suspect trim rod and reassemble the unit with new O-rings and seals and retest leak-down. Continue to the next step if leak-down is still noted.

3. Remove, clean and inspect the memory piston and the cylinder rod piston (and impact relief valves).

   a. If the O-rings are undamaged and the cylinder wall is not scored, replace the memory piston and shock piston.

   b. If the cylinder wall is scored or damaged, replace the cylinder assembly.

   c. Reassemble the unit with new seals and O-rings. Retest the system for leak-down. Continue to the next step if leak-down is still noted.

4. If leak-down is still noted, replace the pump and valve body assembly.

Unit has no reverse lock

1. Remove, clean and inspect the manual release valve and O-ring(s). Replace the manual release valve if it or the O-ring(s) are damaged. Install the manual release valve and tighten the valve securely to prevent leaks. Retest the system for reverse lock function. Continue to the next step if the reverse lock still does not function correctly.

2. Remove, clean and inspect the cylinder piston rod assembly for debris or damage to the impact relief (shock rod) valves. Replace the cylinder rod and piston assembly if any damage is noted. Reassemble the unit with new O-rings and seals and retest for reverse lock function. Continue to the next step if the reverse lock still does not function correctly.

3. Replace the pump and valve body assembly if the reverse lock still does not function correctly.

4. If the reverse lock still does not function, replace the tilt cylinder as an assembly. Reassemble the unit with new O-rings and retest the system for reverse lock function. If the reverse lock still does not function properly, replace the trim/tilt unit as a complete assembly.

275 Hp Trim/Tilt System Hydraulic Troubleshooting

Additional troubleshooting is divided into 2 failure modes: The unit has no reverse lock (kicks up in reverse or trails out on deceleration) or the unit leaks down (will not hold a trim position in forward gear). Since this system has an integral trim/tilt cylinder and an external (or remote) trim pump assembly, troubleshooting will concentrate on determining if the leakage is in the trim/tilt cylinder or in the pump.

The trim pump assembly can be tested with the pressure gauge listed in **Table 1** and compared against the specifications listed in **Table 2**, but the following procedure will quickly determine where leakage is occurring.

Isolating cylinder from pump

1A. *No reverse lock*—Trim the unit to the full trim in (down) position.

1B. *Unit leaks down*—Trim the unit to the full trim out (up) position. Securely block the gearcase or support the gear with a hoist.

WARNING
The gearcase must be securely blocked or supported in Step 1B or the engine will tilt down in Step 2, possibly causing serious personal injury.

2. Open the manual release valve several turns. Make sure the reservoir fill/vent plug is open 1-1/2 turns from a lightly seated (closed) position.

3. Remove both trim lines from the trim pump assembly. Cap the lines and plug the pump ports with the appropriate flare fittings. Most automotive supply stores carry hydraulic flare fittings for automotive brake systems.

4A. *No reverse lock*—Perform one of the following:

    a. With the boat in the water, operate the engine in reverse gear and note if the unit holds position or not.

    b. With the aid of a suitable hoist or an assistant, attempt to tilt the engine up and note whether or not the unit holds position.

4B. *Unit leaks down*—Remove the blocks or hoist supporting the gearcase and note if the unit holds position or not.

5. If the unit still will not hold position in Step 4A or 4B, the trim/tilt cylinder is leaking internally and must be resealed or replaced. If the unit will now hold position in Steps 4A or 4B, the trim pump assembly is leaking internally and must be repaired or replaced.

6. When finished, reconnect the trim lines and close the manual release valve. Then, bleed the system and check the reservoir fluid level as described previously in this chapter.

Electrical System Troubleshooting

Electrical system troubleshooting is divided into 3 major procedures, depending on the unit being tested. Refer to the appropriate section heading when troubleshooting a trim/tilt electrical system problem.

1. Testing models with trim relays (2-wire electric motors).

2. Testing models with trim solenoids (3-wire electric motors [except 275 hp]).

3. Testing the 275 hp system (with thermal and trim limit switches).

Green-colored leads are primarily used for the up circuits. Blue-colored leads are primarily used for the down circuits. The switching circuits for the trim/tilt system are normally protected by the main 20 amp fuse. Electrical testing is performed most accurately using a multimeter (**Table 1**). However, a 12-volt test lamp and a self-powered continuity meter may be used if a multimeter is unavailable. Before beginning any troubleshooting with a test lamp, connect the test lamp directly to the battery and observe the brightness of the bulb. You must reference the rest of your readings against this test. If the bulb does not glow as brightly as when it was hooked directly to the battery, a problem (low voltage) is indicated. If a multimeter is used, take a battery voltage reading to reference all of your readings against. If the voltmeter reads 1 or more volts less than battery voltage, a definite problem is indicated. When checking continuity with an ohmmeter, a zero reading is good. The higher the ohmmeter reads above zero, the worse the condition is for that circuit.

Before attempting to troubleshoot any electrical circuit:

1. Make sure that all connectors are properly engaged and that all terminals and leads are free of corrosion. Clean and tighten all connections as required.

2. Make sure the battery is fully charged. Charge or replace the battery as required.

Models with relays (2-wire motor)

Refer to **Figure 12** for a typical relay-controlled system wiring diagram. Refer to the back of the manual for specific wiring diagrams for each

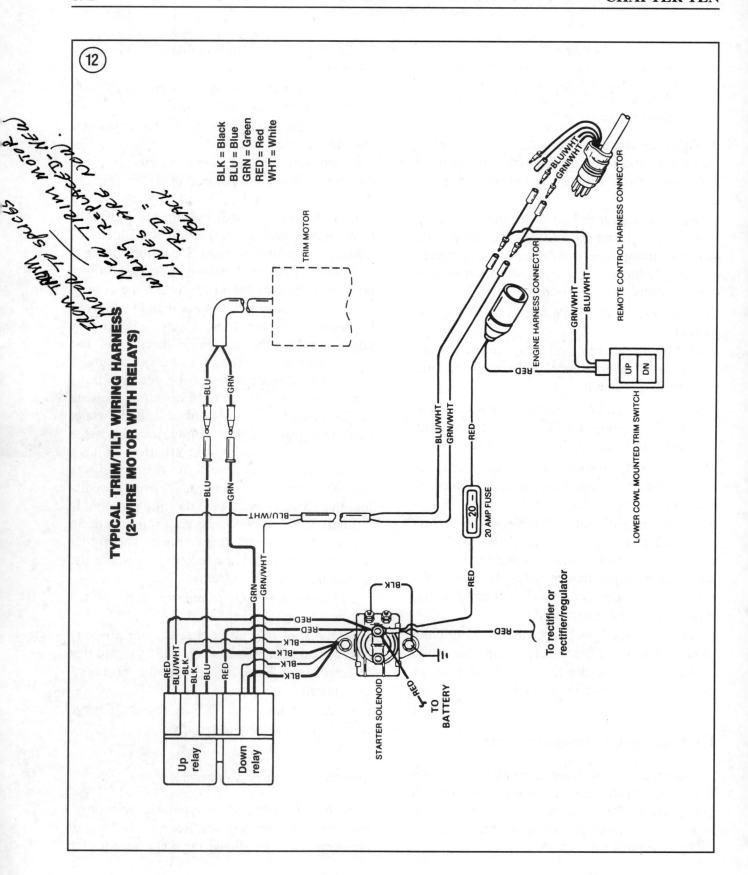

**TYPICAL TRIM/TILT WIRING HARNESS
(2-WIRE MOTOR WITH RELAYS)**

model. Some trim/tilt system wiring diagrams are separate and others are integrated into the main wiring harness.

The 2-wire motor is reversed by switching the polarity of the trim motor blue and green leads. There are 2 relays, one for each trim motor lead. Both relays hold their trim motor lead (blue or green) to ground when they are not activated. When the UP relay is activated, it takes the blue trim motor lead off of ground and connects it to positive. The DOWN relay is inactive and holds the green lead to ground. Current can then flow from the positive terminal to the UP relay to the trim motor and back to ground through the down relay causing the motor to run in the UP direction. When the DOWN relay is activated, it takes the green trim motor lead off of ground and connects it to positive. The UP relay is inactive and holds the blue lead to ground. Current can then flow from the positive terminal to the DOWN relay to the trim motor and back to ground through the UP relay causing the motor to run in the DOWN direction. If the motor runs in one direction, but not the other, the problem *cannot* be the trim motor.

1. Connect the test lamp lead to the *positive* terminal of the battery and touch the test lamp probe to metal anywhere on the engine block. The test lamp should light. If the lamp does not light or is dim, the battery ground cable connections are loose or corroded, or there is an open circuit in the battery ground cable. Check connections on both ends of the ground cable.

2. Connect test lamp lead to a good engine ground.

3. Connect the test lamp probe to the starter solenoid input terminal (Test point A). The test lamp should light. If the lamp does not light or is very dim, the battery cable connections are loose or corroded, or there is an open in the cable between the battery and the solenoid. Clean and tighten connections or replace the battery cable as required.

4. Remove the 20 amp fuse and connect the test lamp probe to the input side of the 20 amp fuse (Test point B). The test lamp should light. If not, repair or replace the wire between the starter solenoid and the fuse holder.

5. Reinstall the fuse and connect the test lamp probe to the output side of the fuse (Test point C). The test lamp should light. If not, replace the fuse.

6. Disconnect the trim/tilt relays from their connector bodies.

7. Connect the test lamp probe to the input side of each relay (red lead terminal). The test lamp should light at each point. If not, repair or replace the wire from the starter solenoid to each relay.

8. Connect the test lamp lead to the *positive* terminal of the battery and touch the test lamp probe to each of the 2 black leads at each relay connector. The test lamp should light at each point (a total of 4 leads). If not, repair or replace each wire (from the relay connector body to the ground) that failed the test.

NOTE
*Refer to **Key (Ignition) Switch Test** in Chapter Three for more information on testing the ignition switch and the wire connections to the switch. Refer to the back of the manual for remote control harness wiring diagrams.*

9. Connect the test lamp lead to a clean engine ground. Connect the test lamp probe to the red or red/purple lead (B, B+ or BAT terminal) at the ignition switch. If the lamp does not light, repair or replace the wire, or the main engine harness connector terminals between the starter solenoid positive terminal and the ignition switch terminal.

10. Connect the test lamp probe to the center terminal (red or red/purple wire) of each trim/tilt switch. The test lamp should light. If not, repair or replace the wire from the ignition switch red or red/purple lead (B, B+ or BAT terminal) connection to the defective trim/tilt switch center terminal.

10

11. Connect the test lamp probe to the blue/white terminal in the UP relay connector body. Hold each trim switch in the UP position and observe the test lamp. The test lamp should light as each switch is activated. If not, connect the test lamp probe to the blue/white wire at each trim switch. Hold each trim switch in the UP position and observe the test lamp. The test lamp should light when each trim switch is activated. If not, replace the defective trim/tilt switch. If the test lamp lights at the trim switch, but not at the UP relay blue/white terminal, repair or replace the blue/white wire from the suspect trim/tilt switch to the UP relay connector.

12. Connect the test lamp probe to green/white terminal in the DOWN relay connector body. Hold each trim switch in the DOWN position and observe the test lamp. The test lamp should light as each switch is activated. If not, connect the test lamp probe to the green/white wire at each trim switch. Hold each trim switch in the DOWN position and observe the test lamp. The test lamp should light when each trim switch is activated. If not, replace the defective trim/tilt switch. If the test lamp lights at the trim switch, but not at down relay green/white terminal, repair or replace the green/white wire from the suspect trim/tilt switch to the relay connector.

13. Reconnect the trim/tilt relays to the wiring harness connectors. Probing from the rear of the relay connector body, connect the test lamp probe to the big blue lead terminal in the UP relay connector body. Hold the trim switch in the UP position and observe the test lamp. The test lamp should light. If not, replace the UP trim relay.

14. Probing from the rear of the relay connector body, connect the test lamp probe to the big green lead terminal in the DOWN relay connector body. Hold the trim switch in the DOWN position and observe the test lamp. The test lamp should light. If not, replace the down trim relay.

NOTE
Each relay grounds its respective blue or green trim motor lead when not acti-

vated. Step 15 is checking that the relays are providing the required ground path.

15. Connect the test lamp lead to the *positive* terminal of the battery. Probing from the rear of each relay connector body, alternately touch the test lamp probe to the big blue lead terminal of the UP relay and the big green terminal of the DOWN relay. The test lamp should light at each test point. If not, replace the defective relay(s).

16. If all previous tests are satisfactory and the electric motor still does not operate correctly, repair or replace the electric motor.

Models with solenoids (3-wire motor [except 275 hp])

Refer to **Figure 13** for a typical solenoid-controlled system wiring diagram. Refer to the back of the manual for specific wiring diagrams for each model. Some trim/tilt system wiring diagrams are separate and others are integrated into the main wiring harness.

The 3-wire motor is reversed by switching the power on to only one of the blue or green leads at a time. The black lead is direct wired to ground. There are 2 solenoids, one for each trim motor positive lead. Both solenoids hold the (blue or green) lead open from battery power when they are not activated. When the UP solenoid is activated, it connects the blue trim motor lead to positive. The black lead is already hooked to ground. Current can then flow from the positive terminal through the UP solenoid to the trim motor and back to the ground through the black lead, causing the motor to run in the UP direction. When the DOWN solenoid is activated, it connects the green trim motor lead to positive. The black lead is already hooked to the ground. Current can then flow from the positive terminal through the DOWN solenoid to the trim motor and back to the ground through the black lead causing the motor to run in the DOWN direction.

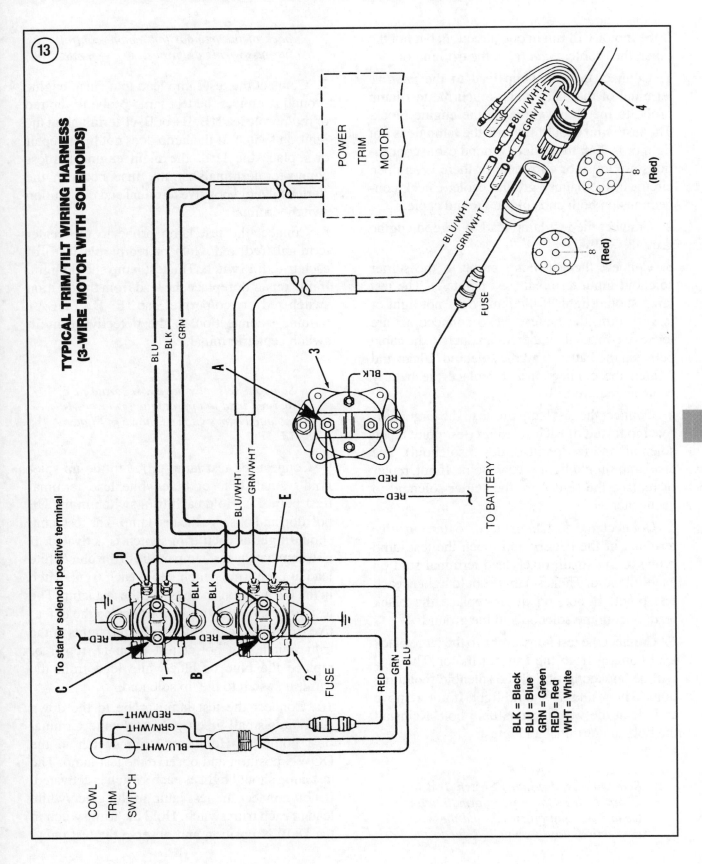

TYPICAL TRIM/TILT WIRING HARNESS
(3-WIRE MOTOR WITH SOLENOIDS)

POWER
TRIM
MOTOR

(Red)

(Red)

FUSE

BLU/WHT
GRN/WHT

BLK

A

3

BLU/WHT
GRN/WHT

RED

RED

TO BATTERY

BLU
BLK
GRN

D

E

C   To starter solenoid positive terminal

RED

1

B

RED

2

FUSE

RED
GRN
BLU

RED/WHT
GRN/WHT
BLU/WHT

COWL
TRIM
SWITCH

BLK = Black
BLU = Blue
GRN = Green
RED = Red
WHT = White

10

If the motor will run in one direction, but not the other, the problem *can* be in the trim motor.

1. Connect the test lamp lead to the *positive* terminal of the battery and touch the test lamp probe to metal anywhere on the engine block. The test lamp should light. If the lamp does not light or is dim, the battery ground cable connections are loose or corroded, or there is an open circuit in the battery ground cable. Check connections on both ends of the ground cable.

2. Connect the test lamp lead to a good engine ground.

3. Connect the test lamp probe to the starter solenoid input terminal (test point A). The test lamp should light. If the lamp does not light or is very dim, the battery cable connections are loose or corroded, or there is an open in the cable between the battery and the solenoid. Clean and tighten the connections or replace the battery cable as required.

4. Connect the test lamp probe to the large positive input stud of each solenoid (test point C, up solenoid and test point B, down solenoid). The test lamp should light at each point. If not, repair or replace the lead from the starter solenoid to each solenoid.

5. Connect the test lamp lead to the *positive* terminal of the battery and touch the test lamp probe to the small, black lead terminal stud on each solenoid. The test lamp should light at each test point. If not, repair or replace the black lead(s) from the solenoids to the ground.

6. Connect the test lamp probe to the large black lead coming from the trim/tilt motor. The lead will be hooked to one of the solenoid mounting bolts. The test lamp should light. If not, remove and clean the wire terminal and bolt. Reinstall the bolt and terminal and retest.

NOTE
*Refer to **Key (Ignition) Switch Test** in Chapter Three for more information on testing the ignition switch and the wire connections to the switch. Refer to the back of the manual for remote control harness wiring diagrams.*

7. Connect the test lamp lead to a clean engine ground. Connect the test lamp probe to the red or red/purple lead (B, B+ or BAT terminal) at the ignition switch. If the lamp does not light, repair or replace the lead, the main engine harness connector terminals or the fuse between the starter solenoid positive terminal and the ignition switch terminal.

8. Connect the test lamp probe to the center terminal (red, red/white or red/purple lead) of each trim/tilt switch. The test lamp should light. If not, repair or replace the lead from the ignition switch red or red/purple lead (B, B+ or BAT terminal) connection to the defective trim/tilt switch center terminal.

NOTE
*Some models may have a separate fuse and red lead to operate the lower cowl-mounted trim switch as shown in **Figure 13**.*

9. Connect the test lamp probe to the up solenoid's small blue or blue/white lead terminal (test point D). Hold each trim switch in the UP position and observe the test lamp. The test lamp should light as each trim switch is activated. If not, connect the test lamp probe to the blue/white lead at each trim switch. Hold each trim switch in the UP position and observe the test lamp. The test lamp should light. If not, replace the defective trim/tilt switch. If the test lamp lights at the trim switch, but not at test point D, repair or replace the blue or blue/white lead from the trim/tilt switch to the up solenoid.

10. Connect the test lamp probe to the down solenoid's small green or green/white terminal (test point E). Hold each trim switch in the DOWN position and observe the test lamp. The test lamp should light as each switch is activated. If not, connect the test lamp to the green/white lead at each trim switch. Hold the trim switch in the DOWN position and observe the test lamp.

The test lamp should light. If not, replace the defective trim/tilt switch. If the test lamp lights at the trim switch, but not at test point E, repair or replace the green/white lead from the trim/tilt switch to the down solenoid.

11. Connect the test lamp probe to the up solenoid large blue lead stud. Hold the trim switch in the UP position and observe the test lamp. The test lamp should light. If not, replace the up solenoid.

12. Connect the test lamp probe to the down solenoid large green lead stud. Hold the trim switch in the DOWN position and observe the test lamp. The test lamp should light. If not, replace the down solenoid.

13. If all previous tests are satisfactory and the electric motor still does not operate correctly, repair or replace the electric motor.

275 hp models

Refer to **Figure 14** for the 275 hp trim/tilt system wiring diagram and **Figure 15** for the remote control trim/tilt and trailer circuits. Refer to the back of the manual for complete engine wiring.

This 3-wire motor is reversed by switching the power on to only one of the blue/white or green/white leads at a time. The motor is grounded through its frame and mounting hardware and a separate black lead back to the battery. The motor small black lead is internally connected to the thermal switch in the trim/tilt motor and externally connected to both solenoid's ground terminals. If the thermal switch opens, the solenoids cannot operate. There are 2 solenoids, one for each trim motor positive lead. Both solenoids hold the (blue/white or green/white) lead open from battery power when they are not activated. When the UP solenoid is activated, it connects the blue/white trim motor lead to positive. Since the motor is permanently grounded, current can then flow from the positive terminal through the UP solenoid to the trim

motor and back to ground, causing the motor to run in the UP direction. When the DOWN solenoid is activated, it connects the green/white trim motor lead to positive. Again, since the motor is permanently grounded, current can then flow from the positive terminal through the DOWN solenoid to the trim motor and back to ground causing the motor to run in the DOWN direction. If the motor will run in one direction, but not the other, the problem *can* be in the trim motor.

1. Connect the test lamp lead to the *positive* terminal of the battery and touch the test lamp probe to metal anywhere on the valve body. The test lamp should light. If the lamp does not light or is dim, the trim pump battery ground cable connections are loose or corroded, or there is an open circuit in the trim pump battery ground cable. Check connections on both ends of the ground cable.

2. Connect the test lamp lead to a good engine ground.

3. Connect the test lamp probe to the 90 amp fuse input terminal. The test lamp should light. If the lamp does not light or is very dim, the battery cable connections are loose or corroded, or there is an open in the cable between the battery and the 90 amp fuse. Clean and tighten the connections or replace the battery cable as required.

4. Connect the test lamp probe to the large positive input stud of each solenoid (connected by the bus bar). The test lamp should light at each point. If not, replace the 90 amp fuse and retest.

5. Connect the test lamp lead to the *positive* terminal of the battery and touch the test lamp probe to the small black lead terminal stud on each solenoid. The test lamp should light at each test point. If not, either the small black leads have an open circuit to the trim motor, or the thermal switch in the electric motor has failed. Repair or replace the black lead(s) from the solenoids to the trim motor, or replace the electric motor (or the motor field windings).

10

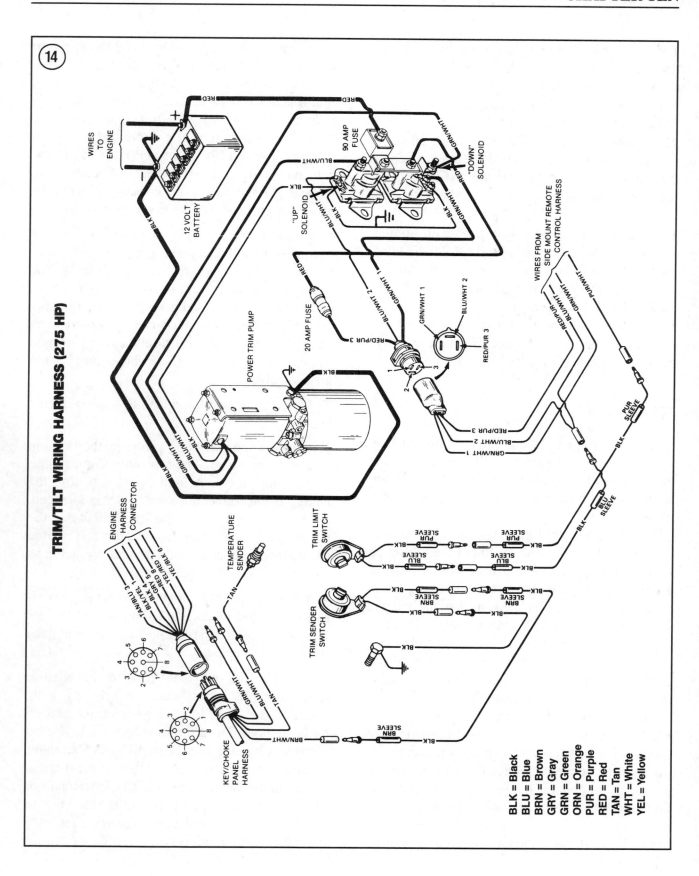

TRIM/TILT WIRING HARNESS (275 HP)

⑭

WIRES TO ENGINE

12 VOLT BATTERY

90 AMP FUSE

"DOWN" SOLENOID

"UP" SOLENOID

POWER TRIM PUMP

20 AMP FUSE

GRN/WHT 1
BLU/WHT 2
RED/PUR 3

WIRES FROM SIDE MOUNT REMOTE CONTROL HARNESS

PUR SLEEVE

BLU SLEEVE

ENGINE HARNESS CONNECTOR

TEMPERATURE SENDER

TAN/BLU 3
BLK/YEL 1
BLK 4
GRY 5
RED 7
YEL/BLK 6

KEY/CHOKE PANEL HARNESS

TRIM LIMIT SWITCH

TRIM SENDER SWITCH

PUR SLEEVE
BLU SLEEVE
BRN SLEEVE
BRN SLEEVE

BLK = Black
BLU = Blue
BRN = Brown
GRY = Gray
GRN = Green
ORN = Orange
PUR = Purple
RED = Red
TAN = Tan
WHT = White
YEL = Yellow

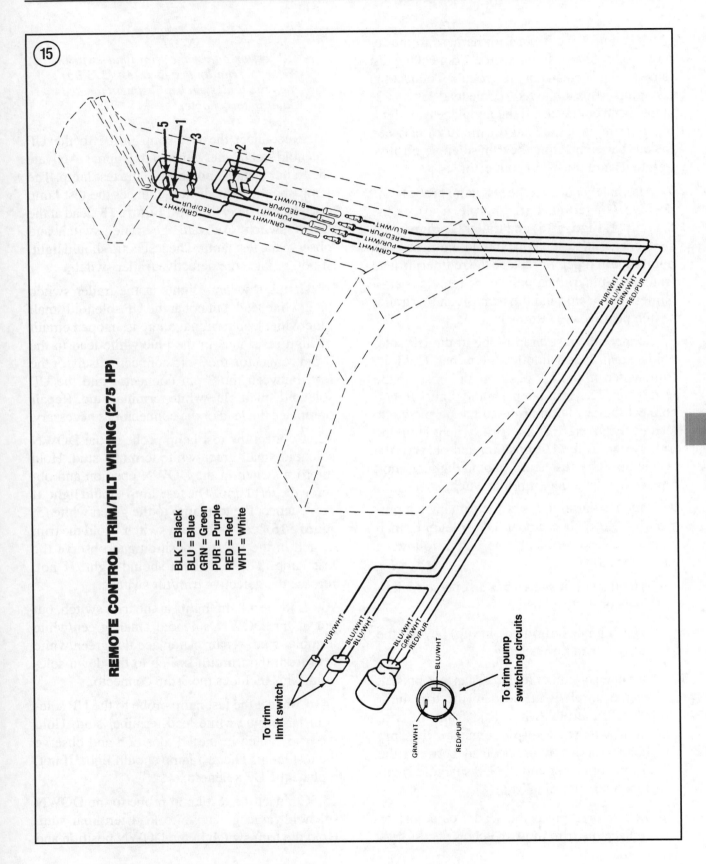

15

REMOTE CONTROL TRIM/TILT WIRING (275 HP)

BLK = Black
BLU = Blue
GRN = Green
PUR = Purple
RED = Red
WHT = White

To trim
limit switch

To trim pump
switching circuits

10

6. Disconnect the 3-pin trim harness to the remote control harness connector. Connect the test lamp lead to a clean engine ground. Connect the test lamp probe to the red/purple lead (pin No.3) at the 3-pin connector. If the lamp does not light, repair or replace the lead (or the fuse) between the bus bar connecting the trim solenoid positive terminals and the 3-pin connector.

7. Alternately connect the test lamp probe to the positive (+) terminal (red/purple lead) of the trim/tilt (1, **Figure 15**) and trailer (2, **Figure 15**) switches. The test lamp should light at each point. If not, repair or replace the red/purple lead from the 3-pin trim harness to the remote control harness connector and the trim/tilt and/or trailer switch positive (+) terminals.

8. Connect the test lamp probe to the UP solenoid's small blue/white lead terminal. Hold the trim switch in the UP position and observe the test lamp. The test lamp should light. If not, connect the test lamp probe to the purple/white lead (3, **Figure 15**) at the trim switch. Hold the trim switch in the UP position and observe the test lamp. The test lamp should light. If not, replace the defective trim/tilt switch.

9. If the test lamp lights at the trim switch purple/white lead, but not at UP solenoid small blue/white lead terminal, one of the following has occurred:

   a. The trim limit switch has an open circuit or is incorrectly adjusted.

   b. The engine is trimmed out (up) beyond the correct trim limit setting.

   c. An open circuit or high resistance is present in the purple/white lead to the trim limit switch, the blue/white lead from the trim limit switch to the 3-pin connector, the 3 pin connector itself, or the lead between the 3-pin connector and the UP solenoid small blue/white terminal stud.

   d. Repair or replace the leads, or adjust or replace the trim limit switch as necessary.

NOTE
*To test or adjust the trim limit switch, refer to **Trim limit switch test (275 hp)** or **Trim limit switch adjustment** located later in this chapter.*

10. Reconnect the test lamp probe to the UP solenoid small blue/white lead terminal. Activate the trailer switch and observe the test lamp. The lamp should light. If not, connect the test lamp probe to the blue/white (4, **Figure 15**) lead at the trailer switch. Activate the trailer switch and observe the test lamp. The test lamp should light. If not, replace the defective trailer switch.

11. If the test lamp lights at the trailer switch blue/white lead, but not at the UP solenoid small blue/white lead terminal, there is an open circuit or high resistance in the blue/white lead to the 3-pin connector, the 3-pin connector itself, or the lead between the 3-pin connector and the UP solenoid small blue/white terminal stud. Repair or replace the lead or the connector as necessary.

12. Connect the test lamp probe to the DOWN solenoid small green/white terminal stud. Hold the trim switch in the DOWN position and observe the test lamp. The test lamp should light. If not, connect the test lamp to the green/white (5, **Figure 15**) lead at the trim switch. Hold the trim switch in the DOWN position and observe the test lamp. The test lamp should light. If not, replace the defective trim/tilt switch.

13. If the test lamp lights at the trim switch, but not at the DOWN solenoid small green/white terminal stud, repair or replace the green/white lead from the trim/tilt switch to the down solenoid. This includes the 3-pin connector.

14. Connect the test lamp probe to the UP solenoid large blue/white lead terminal stud. Hold the trim switch in the UP position and observe the test lamp. The test lamp should light. If not, replace the UP solenoid.

15. Connect the test lamp probe to the DOWN solenoid large green/white lead terminal stud. Hold the trim switch in the DOWN position and

observe the test lamp. The test lamp should light. If not, replace the DOWN solenoid.

16. If all previous tests are satisfactory and the electric motor still does not operate correctly, repair or replace the electric motor.

Trim Limit Switch Test (275 hp Models)

Refer to **Figure 14** for this procedure.

1. Trim the outboard to the fully in (down) position.

2. Disconnect the trim limit switch leads at the following connectors:

    a. Black lead with purple sleeve from the purple/white lead bullet connector.

    b. Black lead with blue sleeve from the blue/white lead bullet connector.

3. Calibrate an ohmmeter on the R × 1 scale. Connect the ohmmeter between the trim limit switch leads. The meter should read continuity (very low reading). If not, the switch is defective

or out of adjustment. Attempt adjustment and repeat Steps 1-3. If the meter still does not read correctly, replace the trim limit switch.

4. Using the trailer switch, trim the outboard out (up) while noting the meter reading, the meter must jump to a no continuity reading (very high reading) *before* the swivel bracket has less than 1.5 in. (38.1 mm) overlap with the stern brackets as shown in **Figure 16**. If not, the switch is defective or out of adjustment. Attempt adjustment and repeat Steps 1-4. If the meter still does not read correctly, replace the trim limit switch.

Trim/Tilt Solenoid Bench Tests

NOTE
All engine wiring harness leads must be disconnected from both trim/tilt solenoids for this test.

Solenoid style varies from engine to engine, but all solenoids have 2 large terminal studs and 2 small terminal studs.

1. Disconnect the negative battery cable from the battery.

2. Disconnect all leads from both solenoid's terminal studs. If necessary, remove the solenoids from the engine.

3. Connect an ohmmeter (calibrated on the R × 1 scale) to the 2 large terminal studs. The ohmmeter must indicate no continuity. Replace the solenoid if any other reading is noted.

4. Attach a 12-volt battery (with suitable jumper leads) to the 2 small terminal studs. Polarity is not important. An audible click will be heard as (if) the solenoid engages. The ohmmeter must now indicate continuity. Replace the solenoid if any other reading is noted.

5. Repeat the test for the other trim/tilt solenoid.

6. Reconnect all leads when finished. Connect the negative battery cable last.

10

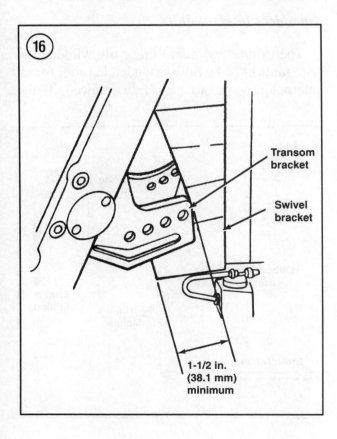

(16)

Transom bracket

Swivel bracket

1-1/2 in. (38.1 mm) minimum

Trim Sending Unit Test

The trim sender is standard equipment on 135-275 hp and 105 and 140 Jet models. If so equipped, test trim sender operation as follows:

1. Make sure the black trim sender lead has a good ground connection. Clean and tighten the connection as necessary.

2. Trim the outboard to its fully in (down) position. Make sure the ignition switch is turned OFF.

3A. *75-250 hp and 65-140 Jet*—Connect an ohmmeter (calibrated on the R × 1 scale) between a good engine ground and test point 1, **Figure 17**, typical.

3B. *275 hp models*—Refer to **Figure 14** and disconnect the black and black with brown sleeve trim sender leads at their bullet connectors. Connect an ohmmeter (calibrated on the R × 1 scale) between the 2 trim sender leads.

4. Trim the outboard out (up) while noting the meter reading. It will be necessary to use the trailer switch on 275 hp models.

5. The resistance must smoothly increase as the outboard trims out (up) and smoothly decrease when the unit is trimmed in (down). If not, the trim sender is defective and must be replaced.

6. Reconnect all leads when finished.

POWER TRIM AND TILT SYSTEM SERVICE

CAUTION
*Metric **and** American fasteners may be found on trim/tilt units, stern brackets and swivel brackets. Always match a replacement fastener to the original. Do not run a tap or thread chaser into a hole (or over a bolt) without first verifying the thread size and pitch.*

The recommended fluid for all 1-piece integral systems is Quicksilver Power Trim and Steering Fluid or automatic transmission fluid. The recommended fluid for the 275 hp system is 10W-40 or 10W-30 motor oil. Lubricate all seals and O-rings with the recommended fluid during assembly. Apply Loctite 271 threadlocking adhesive to all threaded fasteners. If removed, lubricate the manual release valve with Quicksilver Special Lubricant 101. Refer to **Tables 3-5** for torque values.

NOTE
Always replace all O-rings, seals and gaskets. Clean the outside of the component before disassembly. Always use a lint-free cloth when handling trim/tilt components. Dirt or lint can cause blocked passages, sticking valves and prevent O-rings from sealing.

Relieving System Pressure

CAUTION
*Before **disassembling** any trim/tilt system, the internal pressure must be relieved.*

One-piece integral units

The trim/tilt cylinder ram or tilt cylinder and trim rams must be fully extended in order for all internal pressure to be safely relieved. If the

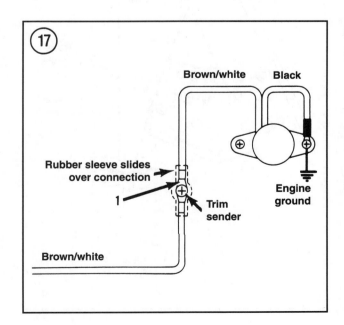

trim/tilt unit has already been removed from the outboard motor, simply reconnect the electric motor leads to the solenoids (or relays) and run the unit out (up) until the ram(s) is (are) fully extended.

1. Trim the outboard to the full out (up) position.

2. Engage the tilt lock, securely block the outboard or support the outboard with a suitable hoist. Refer to your owner's manual if you are not sure how the tilt lock works on your engine.

3. Open the manual release valve as described previously in this chapter and allow the outboard to settle onto the tilt lock, blocks or hoist.

4. Carefully remove the fill plug while covering the plug with a shop towel.

5. All internal pressure should be relieved at this point.

6. The fill plug may be reinstalled and the manual release valve closed to minimize fluid leakage, if so desired.

275 hp models

The system uses a vented reservoir. If the outboard is fully trimmed in (down), the fill/vent plug is open 1-1/2 turns from a lightly seated position and the manual release valve is opened as described previously in this chapter, no pressure will be present in the system.

If the pressure must be relieved with the outboard fully tilted (up), proceed as follows:

1. Using the trailer switch, trim the outboard to the full out (up) position.

2. Engage the tilt lock, securely block the outboard or support the outboard with a suitable hoist. Refer to your owner's manual if you are not sure how the tilt lock works on your engine.

3. Open the manual release valve as described previously in this chapter and allow the outboard to settle onto the tilt lock, blocks or hoist.

4. Carefully remove the fill plug while covering the plug with a shop towel.

5. All internal pressure should be relieved at this point.

6. Reinstall the fill/vent plug and back it out 1-1/2 turns from a lightly seated position. The manual release valve may be closed to minimize fluid leakage, if so desired.

75-125 hp and 65-80 Jet Models

On early models (black fill plug), the electric motor is serviceable and all major components are individually replaceable. However, the hydraulic pump is only available as an assembly with valve body.

On late models (yellow fill plug), the electric motor is not serviceable and must be replaced as an assembly with the reservoir. However, the hydraulic pump can be replaced without replacing the valve body.

System removal/installation

1. Tilt the outboard to the full tilt position and engage the tilt lock, or block the outboard securely or secure the outboard with a suitable hoist. If it is necessary to use the manual release valve to tilt the outboard, do not open the manual release valve more than 3 full turns on black fill plug models or 4 full turns on yellow fill plug models.

2. Disconnect the negative battery cable.

3A. To remove the starboard split lower cowl and disconnect the trim motor leads from the engine, proceed as follows:

    a. Remove the 2 aft internal screws and the 1 front external screw (just above the steering arm). Loosen the port nut securing the front latch plate to both lower cowls.

    b. Disconnect the lower cowl mounted trim switch leads at their bullet connectors and the tell-tale water discharge hose from the exhaust cover. Then, remove the starboard lower cowl.

10

c. Remove the 4 screws securing the electrical/ignition component access cover. Remove the cover.

d. Remove the 2 screws and clamps securing the trim motor harness to the starboard stern bracket. See **Figure 18**.

e. Remove the nuts securing the trim motor blue and green leads to the trim/tilt solenoids, then remove the blue and green leads. Remove the screw securing the trim motor ground lead from the starter motor frame.

f. Remove any remaining clamps or tie-straps securing the trim motor harness. Then, push the motor harness grommet up and out of the lower cowl support plate and remove it from the trim motor harness. Pull the trim motor harness free from the lower cowl support plate.

g. Pull the trim motor harness through and free from the starboard stern bracket.

NOTE
If the trilobe pin proves difficult to remove in Step 4, the upper pivot shaft may be driven forcefully from its bore, shear-ing the trilobe pin. Make sure all trilobe pin remnants are removed and the pivot shaft and trilobe pin bores are cleaned and inspected for damage.

4. Using a diagonal cutters, pull the trilobe pin from the swivel bracket as shown in **Figure 19**. Remove and inspect the trilobe pin, replace the pin if it is damaged. Then, drive the upper pivot shaft laterally from the bracket using a punch and hammer.

5. Using a suitable punch, drive the dowel pin securing the lower pivot shaft upward. Remove and inspect the dowel pin. Replace the dowel pin if it is damaged. See **Figure 20**.

6. Remove the lower pivot shaft from the trim/tilt unit and the stern brackets by driving it laterally with a suitable punch and hammer.

7. Note the position and routing of the trim motor ground strap. Then, remove the anode at the bottom of the stern brackets to free the trim motor ground strap.

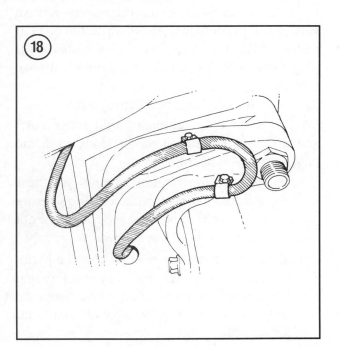

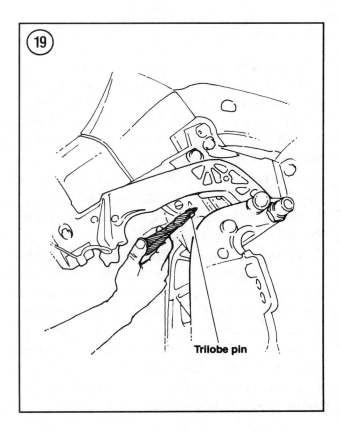

Trilobe pin

8. Remove the trim/tilt system by pivoting the top of the trim/tilt cylinder out and away from the stern brackets.

9. To install the system, begin by liberally applying Quicksilver 2-4-C Multi-Lube grease to the upper and lower pivot shafts, pivot shaft bores, dowel pin and trilobe pin bores and the dowel pin and trilobe pin.

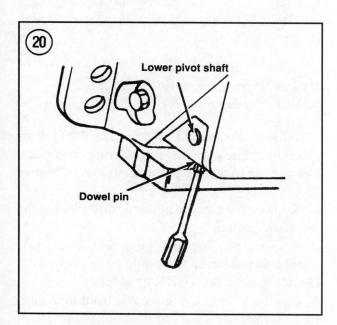

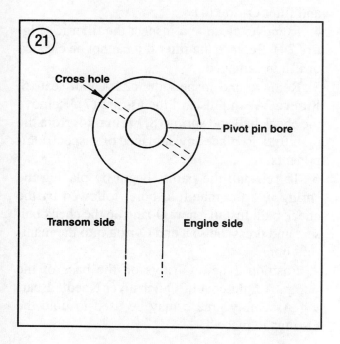

NOTE
Make sure the grooved end of each pivot shaft is positioned on the same side of the engine as the retaining pin bore.

10. Start the lower pivot shaft (with the grooved end facing the dowel pin bore) into its bore from the port side stern bracket, then start the lower dowel pin from the *top* of its bore, but do not drive either pin far enough to interfere with tilt unit installation.

11. Install the trim/tilt system, inserting the bottom into the stern brackets first, then rotating the trim/tilt cylinder towards the transom and into position. Route the motor harness out through the hole in the starboard stern bracket.

12. Drive the lower pivot shaft flush with the stern bracket (or mounting bracket) outer surfaces. Then, using a suitable punch, drive the dowel pin in from the top until it is fully seated.

13. Align the upper pivot shaft bore with the trim/tilt cylinder rod eye. The cylinder rod eye must be facing as shown in **Figure 21**.

14. Install the upper pivot shaft into the swivel bracket bore and through the trim/tilt cylinder rod eye. The shaft should be flush with the swivel bracket outer surfaces. Verify that the bores align, then drive the dowel pin (or trilobe) pin into its bore until fully seated.

15. Install the anode and connect the trim motor ground strap as noted on removal. Tighten the anode screws to specification.

16A. To reconnect the trim motor leads to the engine and install the starboard split lower cowl, proceed as follows:

　a. Route the trim motor harness through the lower cowl support plate. Install the grommet and seat the grommet in the lower support plate.

　b. Install the 2 screws and clamps to secure the trim motor harness to the starboard stern bracket as shown in **Figure 18**.

　c. Install the trim motor blue and green leads to the trim/tilt solenoids and tighten the nuts securely. Secure the trim motor ground lead

10

to the starter motor frame. Tighten the screw securely.

d. Install any remaining clamps or tie-straps to the trim motor harness.

e. Install the electrical/ignition component access cover and secure it with 4 screws. Tighten the screws securely.

f. Install the starboard lower split cowl. Reattach the tell-tale water discharge hose to the exhaust cover fitting and secure it with a new tie-strap. Reconnect the trim/tilt switch leads to the engine harness bullet connectors.

g. Install the 2 aft internal screws and the 1 front external screw (just above the steering arm) and tighten them securely. Tighten the port nut securing the front latch plate to both lower cowls.

Electric motor removal/installation

Remove and install the electric motor and reservoir as an assembly. On early models (black fill plug) the electric motor can be further disassembled (if so desired) after removal. Refer to **Figures 22** and **Figure 23** as appropriate for this procedure.

1. Remove the trim/tilt system as described in the previous section.

2. Make sure the internal pressure has been relieved as described in this chapter. Then, drain the reservoir into a suitable container.

3. Secure the system in a soft-jawed vise or between 2 suitable blocks of wood.

4. Note the position of the motor ground strap, then remove the 4 screws and washers securing the electric motor to the manifold assembly.

5. Remove the electric motor. Locate and secure the pump coupler (drive shaft) to prevent its loss.

6. Remove and discard the motor O-ring or molded seal.

7. To install the motor, begin by positioning the pump coupler (drive shaft) onto the hydraulic pump.

8. Install a new O-ring or molded seal on the electric motor. Carefully align the motor armature shaft with the pump coupler (drive shaft) and install the motor to the manifold. Be careful not to pinch the O-ring.

9. Install and evenly tighten the 4 screws and washers to specification (**Table 4**). Make sure the ground strap is reinstalled under the starboard rear screw as noted on disassembly.

10. Reinstall the trim/tilt system as described in the previous section.

Hydraulic pump removal/installation (yellow fill plug models)

Refer to **Figure 23** and **Figure 24** for this procedure. The filter and filter O-ring are located beneath the hydraulic pump as shown in **Figure 25**.

1. Remove the electric motor as described in the previous section.

2. Remove the 3 pump mounting screws (1, **Figure 24**) securing the pump to the manifold. Do not remove the TORX head screws.

3. Lift the pump (2, **Figure 24**) from the manifold. Remove and discard the pump O-rings (3) and filter O-ring (4).

4. Remove, clean and inspect the filter (5, **Figure 24**). Replace the filter if it cannot be cleaned or if it is damaged.

5. Remove and inspect the check ball seat (6, **Figure 24**) and discard the O-ring (7). Remove the check ball and spring (8, **Figure 24**) from the manifold. Replace any damaged or suspect components.

6. To reinstall the pump, begin by placing the spring into the manifold bore, followed by the check ball. Install a new O-ring on the check ball seat and press the seat and O-ring into the manifold bore.

7. Position 2 new O-rings on the base of the pump. A light coat of Quicksilver Needle Bearing Assembly grease may be used to hold the O-rings in place.

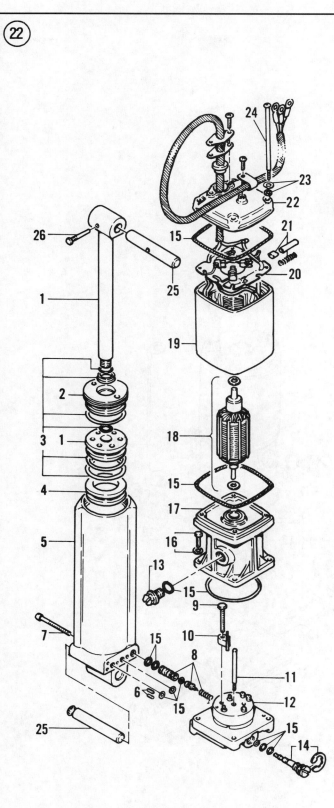

EARLY MODEL ONE-PIECE INTEGRAL TRIM/TILT SYSTEM—BLACK FILL PLUG (75-125 HP AND 65-80 JET)

1. Cylinder rod
2. End cap
3. O-rings and seals
4. Memory piston
5. Trim/tilt cylinder
6. Dowel pins
7. Screw
8. Pilot valve seat, spool and spring
9. Screw
10. Rocker arm
11. Drive shaft (coupler)
12. Pump and valve body assembly
13. Fill plug
14. Manual release valve and lock clip
15. Pump and motor O-rings and seals
16. Screw and washer
17. Reservoir and motor base
18. Armature and thrust washers
19. Motor frame (field)
20. Brush plate assembly
21. Brushes and springs
22. End cap and harness (serviced with frame)
23. Seal and flat washer
24. Screw
25. Pivot shafts
26. Trilobe or dowel pin

10

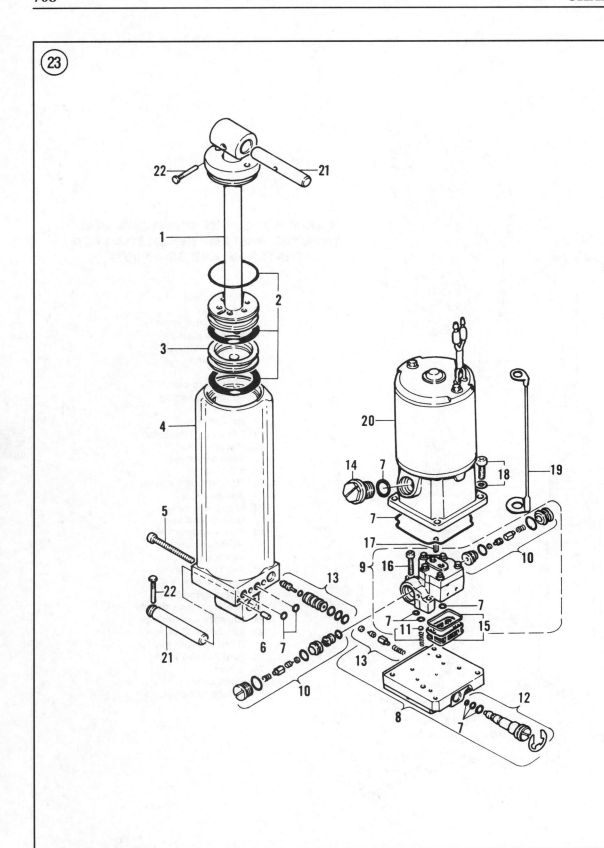

LATE MODEL ONE-PIECE INTEGRAL TRIM/TILT SYSTEM—YELLOW FILL PLUG (75-125 HP AND 65-80 JET)

1. Cylinder rod, piston and end cap assembly
2. Cylinder O-rings and seals
3. Memory piston
4. Trim/tilt cylinder
5. Screw
6. Dowel pin
7. Pump O-rings and seals
8. Valve body assembly
9. Pump assembly
10. Piston operating spool valve assemblies
11. Spring and check ball (seat not shown)
12. Manual release valve and lock clip
13. Pilot valve assemblies
14. Fill plug
15. Filter and seal
16. Screw
17. Drive shaft (coupler)
18. Screw and washer
19. Ground strap
20. Electric motor
21. Pivot shafts
22. Trilobe or dowel pins

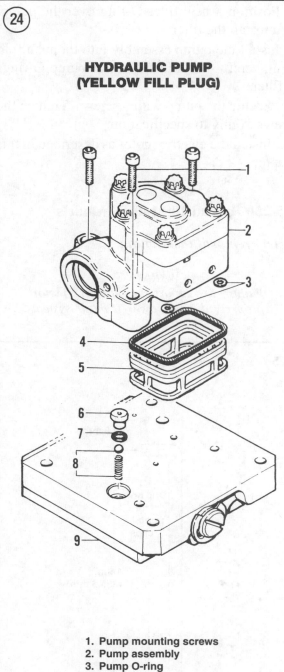

(24)

HYDRAULIC PUMP (YELLOW FILL PLUG)

1. Pump mounting screws
2. Pump assembly
3. Pump O-ring
4. Filter O-ring
5. Filter
6. Check ball seat
7. O-ring
8. Check ball and spring
9. Valve body

10

8. Position a new filter O-ring over the pump, then install the filter.

9. Install the pump assembly into the manifold being careful not to displace the pump O-rings or filter.

10. Secure the pump with 3 screws. Tighten the screws evenly to specification.

11. Install the electric motor as described in this chapter.

135-250 Hp and 105-140 Jet Models

System removal/installation

WARNING
Failure to support the outboard motor properly during power trim/tilt system removal/installation can result in severe personal injury and/or damage to the boat or motor.

This procedure requires the use of a suitable hoist, or the fabrication of a support tool made from a used shift shaft or other 3/8 in. (9.53 mm) diameter rod as shown in **Figure 25**. Use the hoist or the support tool to prevent the outboard motor from falling during power trim assembly removal/installation procedures.

1. Tilt the outboard to the full tilt position and engage the tilt lock *and* secure the outboard with a suitable hoist or install the support tool as shown in **Figure 26**. If it is necessary to use the manual release valve to tilt the outboard, do not

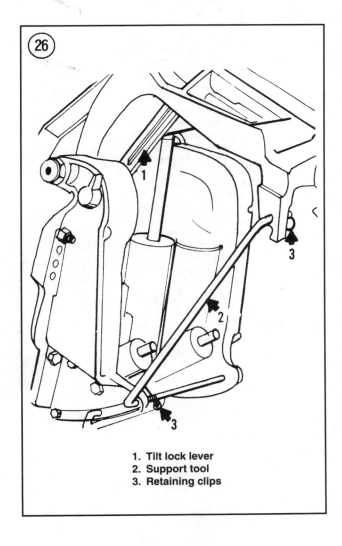

1. **Tilt lock lever**
2. **Support tool**
3. **Retaining clips**

open the manual release valve more than 4 full turns.

2. Disconnect the negative battery cable.

3. Remove the 2 screws and clamps (**Figure 27**) securing the trim harness to the starboard stern bracket.

4A. *2-wire motors*—Disconnect the blue and green trim motor leads from the engine harness bullet connectors. Remove any tie-straps or clamps and pull the trim motor harness through the lower cowl.

4B. *3-wire motors*—Remove the starboard split lower cowl (135-200 hp and 105-140 Jet models

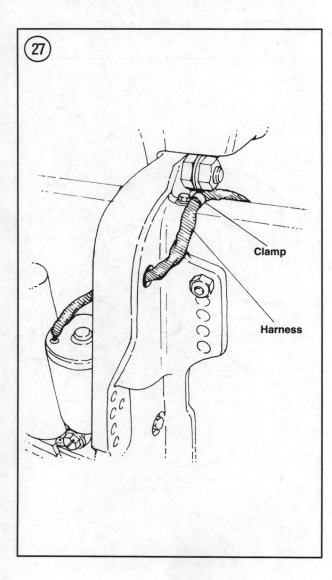

(27)

Clamp

Harness

only) and disconnect the trim motor harness (all models) as follows:

  a. *135-200 hp and 105-140 Jet*—Remove the 4 screws securing the starboard side split lower cowl.

  b. *Early 135-200 hp and 105-140 Jet*—Disconnect the tell-tale water discharge hose from the lower cowl.

  c. *135-200 hp and 105-140 Jet*—Disconnect the lower cowl mounted trim switch leads at their bullet connectors. Then remove the starboard lower cowl.

  d. *All 3-wire motors*—Remove the nuts securing the trim motor blue and green leads to the trim/tilt solenoids, then remove the blue and green leads. Remove the black trim motor lead from the mounting screw of one of the solenoids. Remove any tie-straps or clamps and pull the trim motor harness through the lower cowl.

  e. *All 3-wire motors*—Pull the trim motor harness through and free from the starboard stern bracket.

5. Remove the anode at the bottom of the stern brackets.

6. Remove the trim-in limit adjustment bolt from the stern brackets (if present).

7. Attach a suitable wooden block under the engine swivel bracket with a large C-clamp to support the starboard side of the outboard. See **Figure 28**. The purpose of the block and C-clamp is to keep the engine from rotating away from the transom when the starboard stern bracket is removed.

8. If equipped with a standard tilt tube steering cable, remove the cable retaining nut from the end of the tilt tube. It is not necessary to totally remove the steering cable from the motor.

9. On the starboard side of the outboard, remove the 2 transom bracket mounting bolts, nuts and washers. Remove the tilt tube nut (3, **Figure 28**) and the wave washer behind it.

10

10. Remove the 3 bolts and washers holding the starboard stern bracket to the power trim/tilt system.

11. Move the starboard stern bracket away from the power trim assembly far enough to allow the manual release valve to clear the bracket and allow the system to be removed.

NOTE
*Do not reuse the cross pin that secures the tilt cylinder pivot shaft (**Figure 29**) once it has been removed.*

12. Drive out the cross pin securing the tilt cylinder pivot shaft with a suitable punch and hammer. Discard the cross pin. Then, drive the pivot shaft laterally from the swivel bracket bore with a suitable punch and hammer. See **Figure 29**.

13. Remove the 3 bolts and washers holding the power trim/tilt system to the port transom bracket. Then remove the power trim assembly.

14. To reinstall the power trim assembly, apply Loctite 271 threadlocking adhesive to the threads of the 3 port side trim/tilt system mounting bolts. Install the system into the port transom bracket. Install the 3 bolts and washers and tighten them finger-tight.

15. Lubricate the wave washer and the steering tube with Quicksilver 2-4-C Multi-Lube grease. Then, install the wave washer onto the tilt tube.

16. Route the power trim wiring harness through the hole in the top of the starboard stern bracket.

17. Apply Loctite 271 threadlocking adhesive to the threads of the 3 trim system mounting bolts that secure the system to the starboard stern bracket. Install the starboard stern bracket, then fasten the bracket to the trim/tilt system with the 3 bolts and washers. Use caution not to damage the power trim manual release valve. Tighten the 3 port and 3 starboard bolts to specification.

18. Coat the shanks (not threads) of the outboard mounting bolts with a suitable marine sealer, then reattach the starboard transom bracket to the boat transom with the bolts, flat

washers and locknuts. The installation *must* be watertight. Tighten the bolts securely.

19. Install the tilt tube nut and tighten securely.

20. Remove the C-clamp and wooden block (**Figure 28**).

21. If equipped with standard tilt tube steering cable, reinstall the cable retaining nut onto the tilt tube and tighten it securely.

22. Make sure the chamfered hole in the tilt cylinder rod eye faces the rear of engine. Rotate the rod eye as necessary. See **Figure 30**.

NOTE
If the tilt ram overextends in Step 23A, retract it by reversing the battery con-

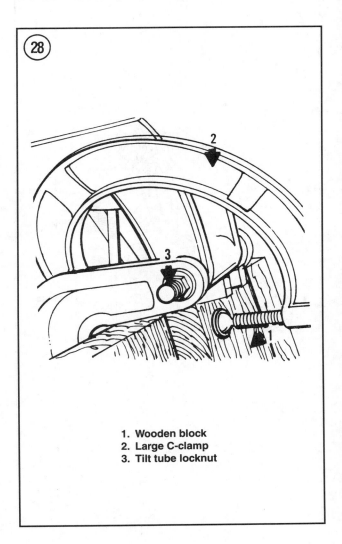

1. Wooden block
2. Large C-clamp
3. Tilt tube locknut

nections (green to positive and blue to negative).

23A. *2-wire motor*—Connect the trim motor to a 12-volt battery to extend the tilt ram enough to install the pivot shaft. Use a pair of suitable jumper leads and connect the trim motor blue lead to the positive battery terminal and the green lead to the negative battery terminal. When the end of the tilt ram is aligned with the swivel bracket bore, disconnect the jumper leads.

NOTE
If the tilt ram overextends in Step 23B, retract it by connecting the green wire to the positive battery terminal.

23B. *3-wire motor*—Connect the trim motor to a 12-volt battery to extend the tilt ram enough to install the pivot shaft. Use a suitable pair of jumper leads and connect the trim motor blue lead to the positive battery terminal and the black lead to the negative battery cable. When the end of the tilt ram is aligned with the swivel bracket bore, disconnect the jumper leads.

24. Align the tilt cylinder rod eye with the swivel bracket bore. Coat the pivot shaft with Quicksilver 2-4-C Multi-Lube grease and install the pivot shaft into its bore with the slotted end of the shaft facing the port side of the engine.

25. Rotate the pivot shaft by engaging a large screwdriver in the slotted end. Align the cross pin holes as shown in **Figure 30** and **Figure 31**. A

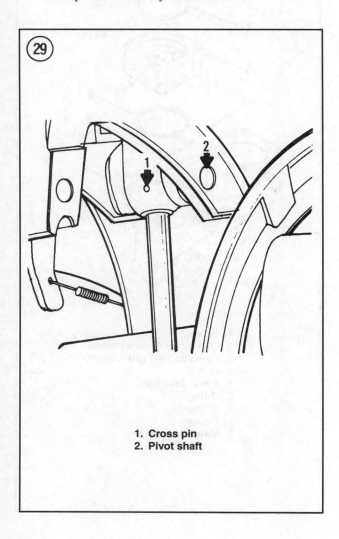

1. Cross pin
2. Pivot shaft

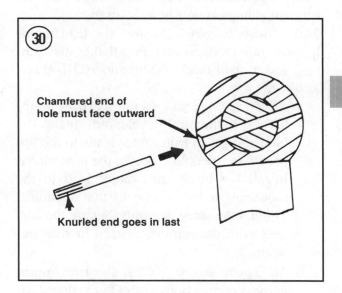

Chamfered end of hole must face outward

Knurled end goes in last

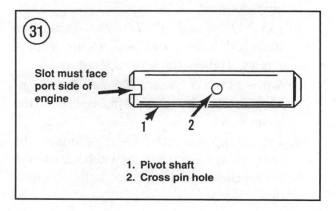

Slot must face port side of engine

1. Pivot shaft
2. Cross pin hole

10

small tapered punch can be used to speed the alignment process.

26. Once the holes are aligned, remove the punch and install a new cross pin as shown in **Figure 30**. Tap the cross pin in until it is flush with the tilt ram surface.

27. Install the anode to the bottom of the stern brackets. Tighten the screws to specification.

28. Install the trim-in limit adjustment bolt into its original position in the stern brackets (if bolt was present during disassembly).

29. Secure the trim harness to the starboard stern bracket with the 2 screws and clamps as shown in **Figure 27**.

30A. *2-wire motors*—Connect the blue and green trim motor leads to the engine harness bullet connectors. Secure the harness with the original clamps and/or new tie-straps.

30B. *3-wire motors*—Connect the trim motor harness (all models) and install the starboard split lower cowl (135-200 hp and 105-140 Jet) as follows:

   a. *All 3-wire motors*—Route the trim motor harness to the trim/tilt solenoids. Install the blue and green trim motor leads to the appropriate solenoid. Tighten the nuts surely. Install the black trim motor lead to the mounting screw of one of the solenoids. Tighten the screw securely. Secure the harness with the original clamps or new tie-straps.

   b. *All 3-wire motors*—Coat the trim motor harness connections with Quicksilver Liquid Neoprene.

   c. *135-200 hp and 105-140 Jet*—Install the starboard lower cowl and secure with 4 screws. Tighten the screws securely.

   d. *Early 135-200 hp and 105-140 Jet*—Connect the tell-tale water discharge hose to the lower cowl.

   e. *135-200 hp and 105-140 Jet*—Connect the lower cowl mounted trim switch leads to the appropriate engine harness bullet connectors.

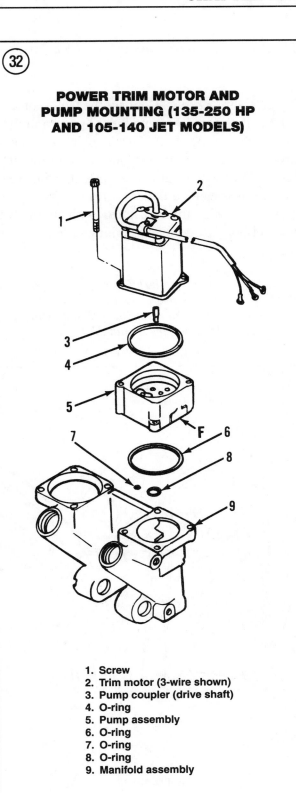

32

POWER TRIM MOTOR AND PUMP MOUNTING (135-250 HP AND 105-140 JET MODELS)

1. Screw
2. Trim motor (3-wire shown)
3. Pump coupler (drive shaft)
4. O-ring
5. Pump assembly
6. O-ring
7. O-ring
8. O-ring
9. Manifold assembly

31. Reconnect the negative battery cable and disengage the tilt lock or remove the support tool or hoist. Check the reservoir oil level as described previously in this chapter.

Electric motor removal/installation

Depending on the serial number, two types of electric motors are used. Models prior to serial No. 0G201875 use a 3-wire, field wound electric motor. Models with serial No. 0G201875-on use a 2-wire, permanent magnet electric motor. Both motors are serviceable and most major internal components are individually available.

NOTE
The pump and electric motor can be removed and installed without removing the power trim assembly from the outboard motor.

1. Make sure the internal pressure has been relieved as described under *Relieving System Pressure* in this chapter.

2. *System removed from engine*—Drain the reservoir into a suitable container and secure the system in a soft-jawed vise or between 2 suitable blocks of wood.

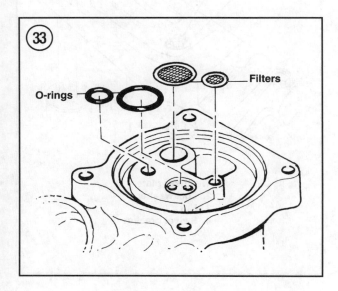

3. *System installed on engine*—Place a suitable drain pan under the stern brackets and trim/tilt system.

4. *System installed on engine*—Disconnect the trim motor harness from the engine and remove the starboard stern bracket as described in Steps 2-11 under *System removal/installation* in this chapter.

5. Remove the 2 socket head screws (1, **Figure 32**) securing the base of the electric motor to the trim pump and manifold assembly. Then, remove the motor.

6. Locate and secure the pump coupler (3, **Figure 32**) to prevent its loss. Then, discard the motor O-ring (4, **Figure 32**).

7. To install the motor, begin by positioning the pump coupler (drive shaft) onto the hydraulic pump.

8. Install a new O-ring or molded seal on the electric motor. Carefully align the motor armature shaft with the pump coupler (drive shaft) and install the motor to the manifold. Be careful not to pinch the O-ring.

9. Install and evenly tighten the 2 socket head screws to specification (**Table 3**).

10. Reinstall the trim/tilt system or reinstall the starboard stern bracket and reconnect the trim motor harness as described in the previous section.

Hydraulic pump removal/installation

The hydraulic pump is serviced only as an assembly.

1. Remove the electric motor as described in the previous section.

2. Remove the 2 socket head screws securing the pump to the manifold.

3. Lift the pump (5, **Figure 32**) from the manifold. Remove and discard the pump O-rings (6, 7 and 8, **Figure 32**).

4. If present, remove, clean and inspect the filters (**Figure 33**). Replace the filters if they cannot be cleaned or if they are damaged.

10

5. To reinstall the pump, begin by positioning the filters into the manifold recesses.

6. Position 3 new O-rings on the base of the pump or in the manifold bore. A light coat of Quicksilver Needle Bearing Assembly grease may be used to hold the O-rings in place.

7. Install the pump assembly into the manifold being careful not to displace the pump O-rings or filters. The cast in the flat of the pump (F, **Figure 32**) must face the starboard stern bracket.

8. Secure the pump with 2 screws. Tighten the screws evenly to specification (**Table 3**).

9. Install the electric motor as described previously in the previous section.

Striker plate removal/installation

The striker plates (**Figure 34**) are the plates in the swivel bracket that the trim rods push against to trim the motor throughout the approximately 20° positive trim angle range. The striker plates should be replaced when damaged or worn.

Simply remove the nut and lockwasher, then remove the striker plate. Replace the lockwasher if is damaged or defective. To install the striker plate, position the plate in the swivel bracket bore and secure it in place with the lockwasher and nut. Tighten the nut to 80 in.-lb. (9.0 N•m).

Trim sender removal/installation

Refer to **Figure 35** for this procedure.

1. Tilt the outboard to its fully UP position and engage the tilt lock lever, block the outboard securely or secure the outboard with a hoist.

2. Disconnect the trim sender leads.

3. Remove the sender attaching screws. Then, remove the sender.

4. To install the sender, position the sender in the swivel bracket and install the 2 screws finger-tight.

5. Connect the trim sender leads to the wiring harness.

6. Adjust the trim sender as described in the next section.

Trim indicator gauge adjustment

Refer to **Figure 35** for this procedure.

1. With the outboard in the fully DOWN position, the trim indicator needle should point to the full DOWN position on the gauge. If not, trim the engine to its fully UP position and engage the tilt lock lever, block the outboard securely or secure the outboard with a hoist.

2. Loosen the trim sender attaching screws just enough to allow sender rotation. Rotate the sender unit slightly counterclockwise to raise or slightly clockwise to lower the trim indicator needle.

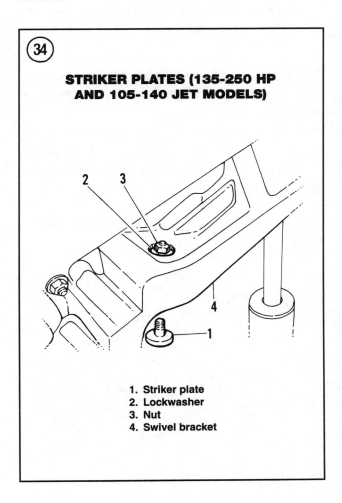

STRIKER PLATES (135-250 HP AND 105-140 JET MODELS)

1. Striker plate
2. Lockwasher
3. Nut
4. Swivel bracket

3. Repeat Steps 1 and 2 until the correct needle position is obtained. Then, securely tighten the attaching screws and make a final check of the needle position.

275 Hp Models

Trim cylinder removal/installation

The trim cylinder rod eye and trim cylinder pivot pin bores have bushings that can be replaced if they are damaged or worn. The cylinder can be resealed or replaced. No internal components (other than a seal and O-ring kit) are available.

WARNING
Failure to support the outboard motor properly during trim/tilt cylinder or pump removal/installation can result in

severe personal injury and/or damage to the boat or motor.

1. Trim the outboard to the full out (up) position and engage the tilt lock lever, block the outboard securely or secure the outboard with a suitable hoist. If it is necessary to use the manual release valve to tilt the outboard, do not open the manual release valve more than necessary to allow manual tilting.

2. Disconnect the negative battery cable.

3. Make sure the internal pressure has been relieved as described previously in *Relieving System Pressure*.

4. Remove the trim IN angle adjustment bolt from both stern brackets. See **Figure 36**.

5. Place a suitable container under the trim/tilt cylinder, then remove the upper and lower hydraulic hoses from the cylinder. Plug the hoses

10

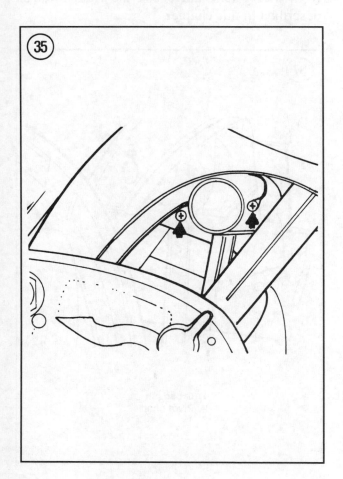

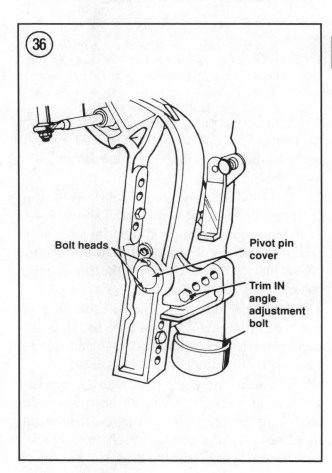

and cap the cylinder fittings to prevent leakage and contamination.

6. Remove 2 bolts and washers securing the pivot pin cover plates (**Figure 36**) to the side of each stern bracket. Remove both cover plates.

7. Thread a 5/16 × 18 bolt into the pivot pin on each side of the clamp bracket. Using the bolts, remove each pivot pin and spring from each stern bracket. Then remove the thrust washer from between each stern bracket and the trim cylinder. If necessary, adapt a suitable slide hammer to pull the pivot pins.

8. Remove the 4 screws and 2 metal straps securing the trim sender and the trim limit switch to the swivel bracket.

9. Using a suitable punch and hammer, drive out the cross pin that secures the trim cylinder pivot shaft into the trim cylinder rod eye. See **Figure 37**, typical. Discard the cross pin.

CAUTION
Do not damage the slotted ends of the pivot shaft in Step 10. Use a soft metal (brass or aluminum) or very blunt punch.

10. While supporting the trim cylinder, drive out the trim cylinder pivot shaft (**Figure 37**, typical) using a suitable punch. Remove the trim cylinder assembly.

11. To install the trim cylinder, lubricate the trim cylinder pivot shaft with Quicksilver 2-4-C Multi-Lube grease. Support the trim cylinder in position, then install the pivot shaft through the swivel bracket bore and through the trim cylinder rod eye.

12. Align the pivot shaft hole with the retaining pin hole in the cylinder rod eye. Install a new cross pin into the cylinder rod eye and drive it flush with the cylinder rod eye.

13. Lubricate the pivot pins with Quicksilver 2-4-C Multi-Lube grease. Align the trim cylinder and clamp bracket pivot pin holes, then install the thrust washers between each stern bracket and the trim cylinder. Install the springs into each

pivot pin bore, then install the pivot pins into the stern bracket and trim cylinder.

14. Install the pivot pin cover plates and secure each with 2 screws and washers. Tighten the cover screws securely.

15. Install the trim sender and trim limit switch as described in this chapter.

16. Connect the hydraulic hoses to the trim cylinder. Tighten both fittings securely.

17. Install the trim IN angle adjustment bolt and locknut. Tighten the locknut just enough to remove all end play. Do not over-tighten the nut.

18. Remove the hoist and/or blocks securing the outboard.

19. Reconnect the negative battery cable.

20. Fill the hydraulic reservoir, bleed the air from the system and check the fluid level as described in this chapter.

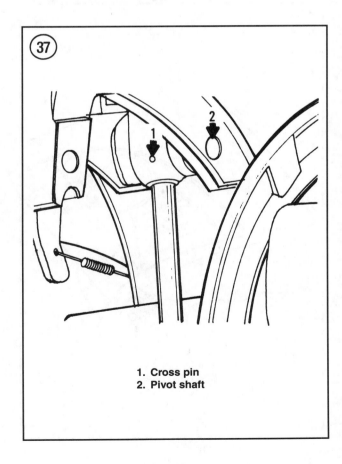

1. Cross pin
2. Pivot shaft

Trim pump assembly removal/installation

1. Trim the outboard to the full in (down) position.

2. Disconnect the trim pump red and black leads from the battery.

3. Open the manual release valve as described previously in this chapter.

4. Carefully remove the fill plug while covering the plug with a shop towel. Then, reinstall the fill plug and back it out 1-1/2 turns from a lightly seated position.

5. Disconnect the switching circuits 3-pin connector from the trim pump.

6. Remove the hydraulic hoses from the pump assembly. Plug the pump ports and cap or plug the hoses to prevent leakage and contamination.

7. Remove the single bolt and lockwasher securing the pump to the pump mounting bracket and slide the pump assembly from the pump mounting bracket.

8. To install the trim pump assembly, slide the pump assembly into its mounting bracket and secure it with one bolt and lockwasher. Tighten the bolt securely.

9. Connect the hydraulic hoses to the pump. Tighten the line fittings securely.

10. Reconnect the switching circuits 3-pin connector to the trim pump.

11. Close the manual release valve (clockwise till seated).

12. Connect the trim pump red and black leads to the battery.

13. Check the reservoir fluid level and bleed air from the system as described in this chapter.

Electric motor removal/installation

Remove and install the electric motor as an assembly. The motor may be disassembled after removal. Most of the major internal components are available for replacement. Refer to **Figure 38** for this procedure.

1. Remove the power trim pump assembly from the outboard motor as described in the previous section.

2. Verify that the trim pump red and black leads are disconnected from the battery.

3. Disconnect the trim motor blue/white, green/white and small black leads from the trim solenoids. Remove the 2 screws securing the top of the solenoid mounting plate to the top of the motor, then remove the screw securing the bottom of the solenoid mounting plate to the valve body. Remove the solenoid plate assembly from the pump and motor assembly.

4. Remove the 4 screws (10, **Figure 38**) securing the trim motor lower flange to the valve body.

5. Lift the motor from the valve body. Remove and discard the motor O-ring.

6. Locate and secure the pump coupler (9, **Figure 38**) to prevent its loss.

7. To install the motor, install a new O-ring onto the motor mounting base.

8. Position the pump coupler (drive shaft) into the hydraulic pump.

9. Install the motor onto the valve body, making sure the motor shaft is aligned with the pump coupling and the O-ring is not displaced. The motor will sit flush on the valve body when the shaft and coupling are properly aligned.

10. Secure the motor to the pump with 4 screws. Tighten the screws evenly and securely.

11. Install the solenoid mounting plate and attach the trim motor leads to the appropriate solenoid terminals.

12. If removed, install the trim pump assembly onto its mounting bracket in the boat, as described previously in this chapter.

13. Reconnect the trim pump red and black leads to the battery.

Hydraulic pump assembly removal/installation

The pump assembly (pump and valve body) may be replaced as an assembly, or the pump (5,

10

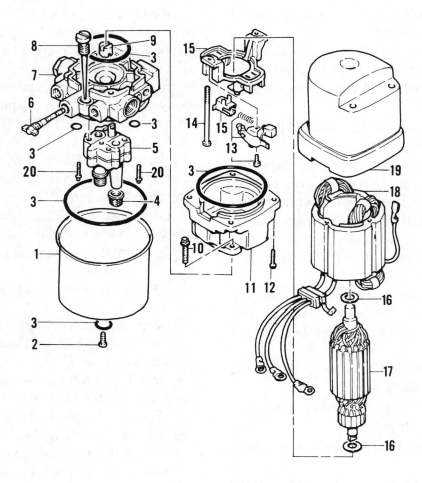

(38)

275 HP TRIM/TILT HYDRAULIC PUMP ASSEMBLY

1. Reservoir
2. Screw
3. O-rings
4. Hat filter
5. Pump assembly
6. Manual release
   valve assembly
7. Valve body
8. Fill/vent plug/dipstick
9. Coupler
10. Screw
11. End cap and bearing
12. Screw
13. Brush, holder and spring
14. Screw
15. Brush holder assembly
16. Thrust washers
17. Armature
18. Field winding and
    thermal switch
19. Main motor housing
    and bearing
20. Pump screws

Figure 38) and valve body (7, **Figure 38**) may be replaced separately. Overhaul repair kit and a relief valve repair kits are also available. This procedure covers replacement of the pump and valve body. Refer to **Figure 38** for this procedure.

1. Remove the power trim pump assembly from the boat as described in this chapter.

2. Remove the fill/vent plug and drain the reservoir into a suitable container.

3. Remove the electric motor as described in the previous section.

4. Remove the screw (2, **Figure 38**) securing the reservoir to the valve body. Remove the reservoir.

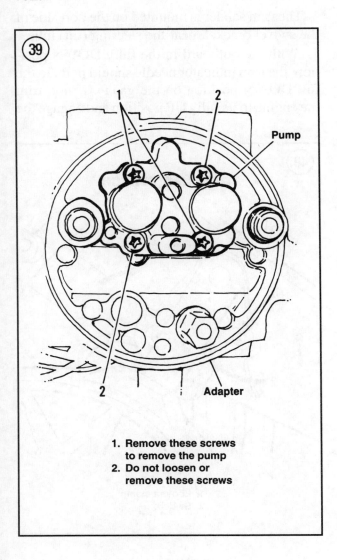

39

Pump

2

Adapter

1. **Remove these screws to remove the pump**
2. **Do not loosen or remove these screws**

5. Remove and discard the reservoir O-ring(s).

6. Remove, clean and inspect the filters (4, **Figure 38**) on each relief valve tower. Replace the filters if they are damaged or cannot be cleaned.

7. To separate the pump from the valve body, use an appropriate external Torx socket and remove the pump mounting screws (1, **Figure 39**). Do not loosen or remove the screws (2, **Figure 39**). Remove the pump from the adapter. Remove and discard the pump O-rings.

8. To install the pump to the adaptor, position 2 new O-rings on the pump body. A light coat of Quicksilver Needle Bearing Assembly grease may be used to hold the O-rings in place.

9. Position the pump to the valve body and secure it with 2 screws. Tighten the screws to specification (**Table 3**).

10. Install a filter over each relief valve tower.

11. Install the reservoir to the valve body using a new O-ring. Secure the reservoir with the screw (2, **Figure 38**) using a new O-ring.

12. Install the electric motor as described in the previous section.

13. Install the pump assembly into the boat as described previously in this chapter.

14. Fill the reservoir and bleed air from the system as described in this chapter.

10

Trim limit switch removal/installation

The trim limit switch is mounted on the starboard side of the swivel bracket, near the steering (tilt) tube. Refer to the back of the manual for wiring diagrams.

1. Trim the outboard to the full out (up) position and engage the tilt lock lever, block the outboard securely or secure the outboard with a hoist.

2. Disconnect the trim limit switch leads from the engine wiring harness.

3. Remove the 2 screws securing the clamp plate over the switch. Remove the plate and trim limit switch. See **Figure 40**.

4. To install the switch, position the trim limit switch into its recess on the starboard side of the swivel bracket. Route the sender leads into the lower cowl. Connect the leads to the appropriate wiring harness bullet connectors.

5. Install the clamp plate and 2 screws. Tighten the screws finger-tight at this time.

6. Adjust the switch as described in the next section.

Trim limit switch adjustment

Always water test the boat after making a trim angle adjustment. If handling characteristics are undesirable, readjust the trim angle to reduce the trim OUT (UP) limit.

> *WARNING*
> *NEVER adjust the OUT angle so that less than 1-1/2 in. (38.1 mm) of the swivel bracket is engaged (overlapped) inside the stern brackets with the outboard trimmed out to the trim switch electrical limit. See **Figure 42**. Readjust the OUT angle as necessary to obtain at least 1-1/2 in. (38.1 mm) engagement.*

1. Trim the outboard to the full out (up) position and either engage the tilt lock lever, block the outboard securely or secure the outboard with a hoist.

2. To adjust the OUT angle, loosen the clamp plate screws (1, **Figure 40**). Rotate the trim limit switch (2) slightly clockwise to reduce the trim out angle or slightly counterclockwise to increase the trim out angle.

3. Tighten the trim limit switch clamp screws securely. Remove the blocks or hoist.

> *NOTE*
> *Do not use the TRAILER switch in Step 4. Use the trim UP button only.*

4. Trim the outboard fully IN (down), then trim the outboard OUT (up), using the trim UP button, until the trim limit switch stops the trim motor. Measure the overlap of the swivel bracket to the stern brackets as shown in **Figure 41**. If the overlap is less than 1-1/2 in. (38.1 mm), adjust the limit switch clockwise until at least 1-1/2 in. (38.1 mm) of overlap is present.

5. Water test the boat with the outboard trimmed out to the trim limit. If undesirable handling characteristics are noted, reduce the trim out angle and retest.

Trim indicator gauge adjustment

The trim sender is mounted on the port side of the swivel bracket, near the steering (tilt) tube.

1. With the outboard in the fully DOWN position, the trim indicator needle should point to the full DOWN position on the gauge. If not, trim the engine to its fully UP position and engage the

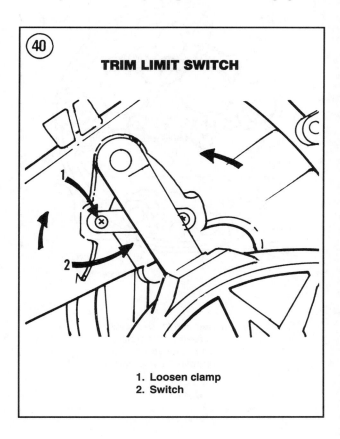

TRIM LIMIT SWITCH

1. Loosen clamp
2. Switch

tilt lock lever, block the outboard securely or secure the outboard with a hoist.

2. Loosen the trim sender clamp plate screws just enough to allow sender rotation. Rotate the sender unit slightly counterclockwise to raise or slightly clockwise to lower the trim indicator needle.

3. Repeat Steps 1 and 2 until the correct needle position is obtained. Then, securely tighten the attaching screws and make a final check of the needle position.

POWER STEERING SYSTEM

A Quicksilver Ride Guide Power Steering system is available for 75-250 hp model engines. The system is an electro-hydraulic system, powered by the battery. A relay connected to the ignition switch turns the system off and on. An internal pressure switch shuts the electric motor off when the accumulator is sufficiently charged.

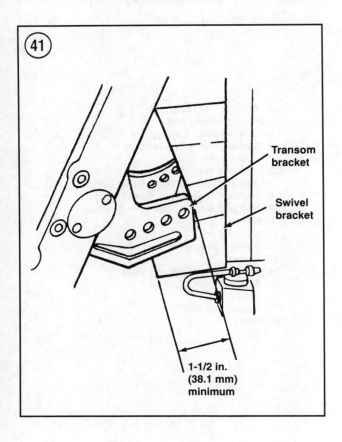

41

Transom bracket

Swivel bracket

1-1/2 in. (38.1 mm) minimum

The system is considered a *run on demand* system since the pump will only run when the accumulator pressure falls below a predetermined level. The accumulator can be transom-mounted or remote-mounted in the boat. **Figure 42** shows the components of a transom-mounted power steering system.

Operation

The system consists of the following components:

1. Accumulator assembly.
2. Steering cylinder assembly.
3. 2 hydraulic lines.
4. Relay and wiring harness.
5. Steering link.
6. Necessary brackets and fasteners.

The accumulator assembly (1, **Figure 42**) incorporates the electric motor, controller unit, hydraulic pump, fluid reservoir and the accumulator into one component. An accumulator is simply a reservoir or storage tank for hydraulic pressure. The controller unit runs the electric motor as necessary to maintain pressure in the accumulator. When the boat is being operated in a straight line, the pump will not run for long periods of time. When the boat is being steered continuously (such as docking), the pump will operate almost continuously.

A magnetically-controlled switch is opened and closed by a magnet riding in the accumulator piston. This switch tells the controller if accumulator pressure is acceptable or too low. The controller unit then turns the electric motor on and off as necessary.

The steering cylinder (4, **Figure 42**) consists of a unique actuator valve that is integrated into the cylinder piston and cylinder rod. The actuator valve detects operator effort being applied to the steering cable and opens internal valving to supply fluid pressure to the appropriate side of the cylinder, providing power assist. This power assist greatly reduces the effort required to steer the

10

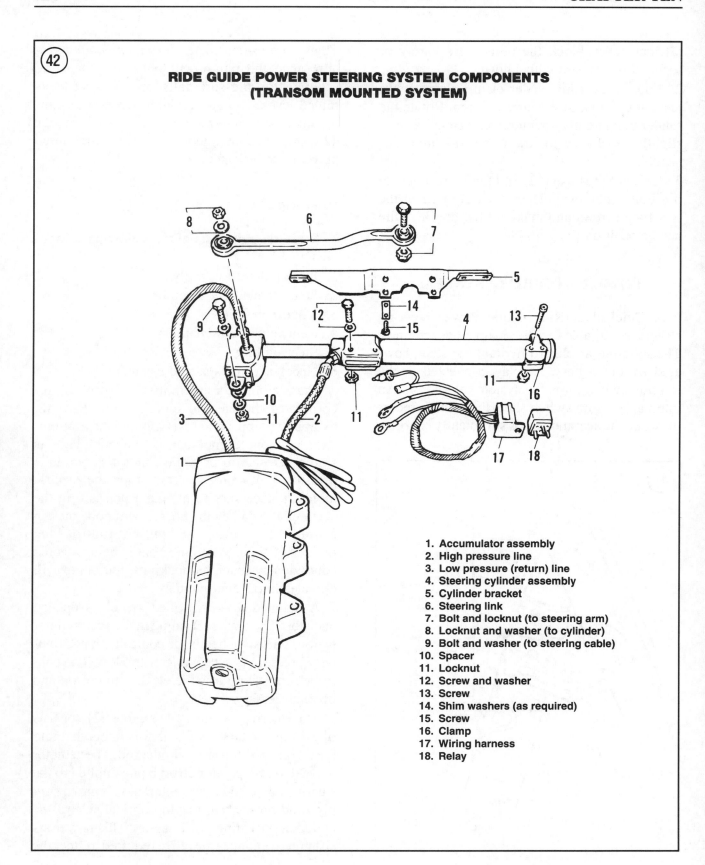

42

**RIDE GUIDE POWER STEERING SYSTEM COMPONENTS
(TRANSOM MOUNTED SYSTEM)**

1. Accumulator assembly
2. High pressure line
3. Low pressure (return) line
4. Steering cylinder assembly
5. Cylinder bracket
6. Steering link
7. Bolt and locknut (to steering arm)
8. Locknut and washer (to cylinder)
9. Bolt and washer (to steering cable)
10. Spacer
11. Locknut
12. Screw and washer
13. Screw
14. Shim washers (as required)
15. Screw
16. Clamp
17. Wiring harness
18. Relay

motor and reduces feedback (steering torque) to the operator.

When the unit is being operated in a fixed input mode (no steering wheel movement), hydraulic pressure is balanced on both sides of the steering piston (by the actuator valve). This provides full hydraulic pressure to hold the engine in position, with nominal steering effort required of the operator.

The steering link connects the steering cylinder output to the outboard steering arm. A bracket holds the steering cylinder to the swivel bracket of the outboard.

A pressure gauge is available to test the accumulator assembly's pressure. The gauge is listed in **Table 1** and the pressure specifications are listed in **Table 2**.

Fluid Level Check

The recommended fluid is Quicksilver Power Trim and Steering Fluid or automatic transmission fluid. To check the fluid level, refer to **Figure 43** and proceed as follows:

> *CAUTION*
> *Accumulator pressure must be relieved before removing the fill plug.*

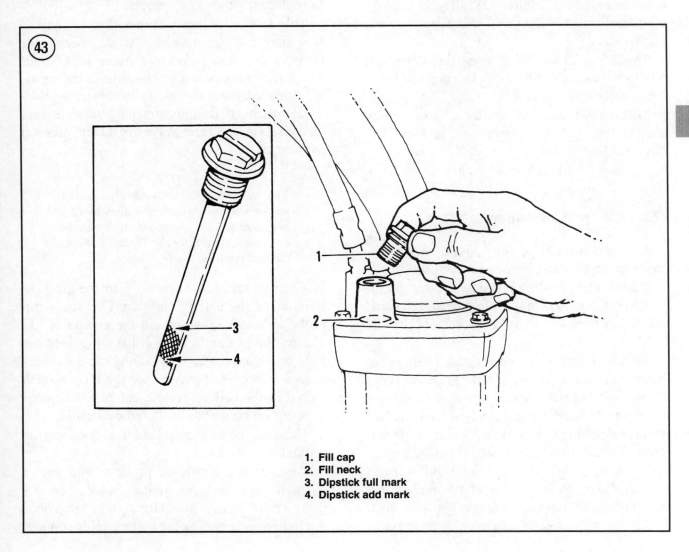

1. Fill cap
2. Fill neck
3. Dipstick full mark
4. Dipstick add mark

1. Relieve accumulator pressure by turning the ignition switch to the OFF position and steering the system lock to lock (full travel) at least 3 times. Leave the steering cylinder fully extended when finished (full right hand turn).

2. Carefully loosen the fill cap (or dipstick) while holding a shop towel over the fill cap (or dipstick). Allow all pressure and/or power steering fluid to vent. Then, remove the fill cap (or dipstick). Inspect the O-ring on the fill cap (or dipstick). Replace the O-ring if it is damaged.

3A. *Fill cap models*—The fluid level should be level with the bottom of the fill neck (2, **Figure 43**). Add fluid as necessary.

3B. *Dipstick models*—The fluid level should be between the full (3, **Figure 43**) and add (4) marks with the dipstick resting on its threads. Add fluid as necessary.

4. Install the fill cap (or dipstick) and thread it 2 full turns into the fill neck. Do not tighten it completely at this time.

5. Bleed any remaining air from the system by turning the steering system lock to lock (full travel) at least 3 times.

6. Tighten the fill cap to 30 in.-lb. (3.4 N•m).

Electrical Troubleshooting

A relay controlled by the ignition switch purple lead, sends battery voltage from the starter solenoid battery positive terminal to the accumulator assembly. The relay should be closed (activated) any time the ignition switch is in the ON or RUN position.

Electrical testing is performed most accurately with a multimeter (**Table 1**). However, a 12-volt test lamp and a self-powered continuity meter may be used if a multimeter is unavailable. Before beginning any troubleshooting with a test lamp, connect the test lamp directly to the battery and observe the brightness of the bulb. You must reference the rest of your readings against this test. If the bulb does not glow as brightly as when it was connected to the battery, a problem is

indicated. If a multimeter is to be used, take a battery voltage reading to reference all of your readings against. If the voltmeter reads 1 or more volts less than battery voltage, a definite problem is indicated. When checking continuity with an ohmmeter, a zero reading is good. The higher the ohmmeter reads above zero, the worse the condition of that circuit.

Before attempting to troubleshoot any electrical circuit:

1. Make sure that all connectors are properly engaged and that all terminals and leads are free of corrosion. Clean and tighten all connections as required.

2. Make sure the battery is fully charged. Charge or replace the battery as required.

This test procedure assumes that the engine will start and run normally. If any starting or running problem is present, refer to Chapter Three for troubleshooting procedures before attempting to troubleshoot the power steering electrical system. To troubleshoot the power steering electrical system, refer to **Figure 44** and proceed as follows:

> *NOTE*
> *The accumulator assembly's electric motor will only run when accumulator pressure is low. The motor will not run continuously unless the system is being steered continuously.*

1. Connect the test lamp lead to the *positive* terminal of the battery and touch the test lamp probe to metal anywhere on the engine block. The test lamp should light. If the lamp does not light or is dim, the battery ground cable connections are loose or corroded, or there is an open circuit in the battery ground cable. Check connections on both ends of the ground cable.

2. Connect the test lamp lead to a good engine ground.

3. Connect the test lamp probe to the starter solenoid input terminal (battery cable connection). The test lamp should light. If the lamp does not light or is very dim, the battery cable connec-

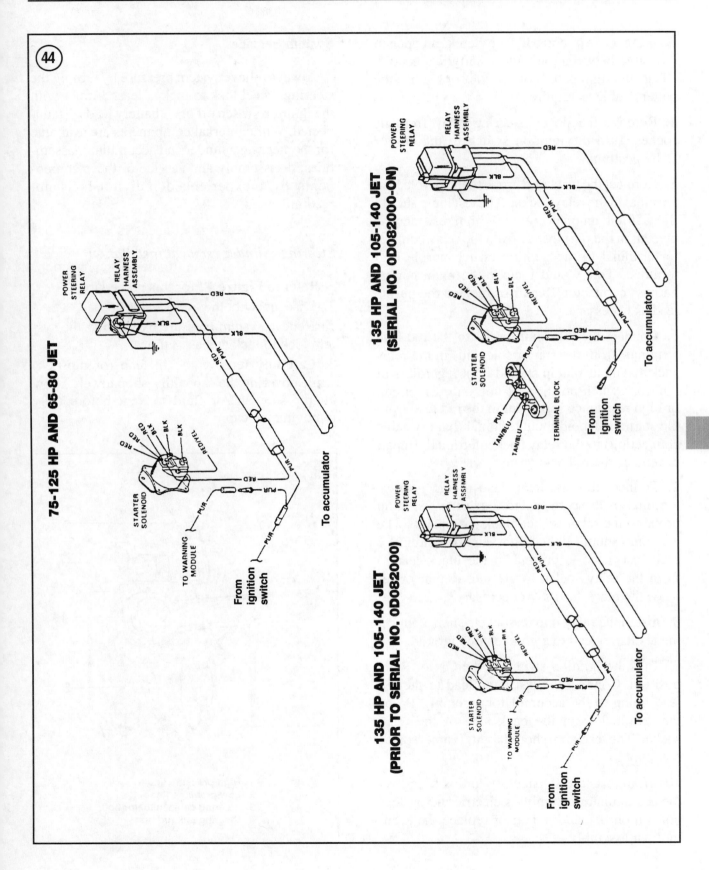

44

75-125 HP AND 65-80 JET

POWER STEERING RELAY
RELAY HARNESS ASSEMBLY
RED
BLK
RED
BLK
STARTER SOLENOID
RED RED BLK BLK RED/YEL
RED
PUR
PUR
TO WARNING MODULE
PUR
From ignition switch
To accumulator

135 HP AND 105-140 JET (SERIAL NO. 0D082000-ON)

POWER STEERING RELAY
RELAY HARNESS ASSEMBLY
RED
BLK
RED
STARTER SOLENOID
RED RED BLK BLK RED/YEL
RED
PUR
PUR
PUR
TAN/BLU
TAN/BLU
TERMINAL BLOCK
From ignition switch
To accumulator

135 HP AND 105-140 JET (PRIOR TO SERIAL NO. 0D082000)

POWER STEERING RELAY
RELAY HARNESS ASSEMBLY
RED
BLK
RED
STARTER SOLENOID
RED RED BLK BLK RED/YEL
RED
PUR
PUR
TO WARNING MODULE
From ignition switch
To accumulator

10

tions are loose or corroded, or there is an open in the cable between the battery and the solenoid. Clean and tighten the connections or replace the battery cable as required.

4. Remove the power steering relay from its socket. Turn the ignition switch to the ON or RUN position.

5. Connect the test lamp probe to the purple lead terminal in the relay socket. The test lamp should light. If not, an open circuit or high resistance is present in the purple lead from the relay connector terminal to the ignition switch purple lead terminal. This would include the main engine harness connector. Repair or replace the purple lead as necessary.

6. Connect the test lamp probe to the red lead terminal (from the starter solenoid) in the relay socket. The test lamp should light regardless of ignition switch position. If not, an open circuit or high resistance is present in the red lead from the starter solenoid input terminal (battery cable connection) to the relay socket terminal. Repair or replace the red lead as necessary.

7. Connect the test lamp lead to the *positive* terminal of the battery and touch the test lamp probe to the relay socket black terminal(s). The test lamp should light. If not, an open circuit or high resistance is present in the black lead(s) from the relay socket to ground. Repair or replace the black lead(s) as necessary.

8. Install the relay into its socket. Then, connect the test lamp lead to a good engine ground.

9. Turn the ignition switch to the ON or RUN position. Connect the test lamp lead to the red lead going to the accumulator assembly. Probe the terminal from the back side of the relay socket. The test lamp should light. If not, replace the relay.

10. If all tests are satisfactory to this point, yet the accumulator assembly's electric motor does not run on demand, repair or replace the accumulator assembly.

System Service

Always relieve system pressure by turning the steering wheel lock to lock at least 3 times with the ignition switch off or all battery leads disconnected. While internal components are available for the steering cylinder and accumulator assemblies, disassembly and service of these components by inexperienced individuals is not recommended.

Steering cylinder removal/installation

Refer to **Figure 42** for this procedure.
1. Disconnect both battery cables.
2. Relieve system pressure by steering the system lock to lock at least 3 times.
3. Carefully remove the fill cap (or dipstick) while covering the cap with a shop towel. Allow all pressure and/or fluid to vent before fully removing the cap.

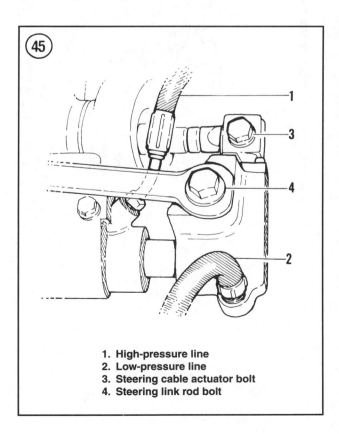

1. High-pressure line
2. Low-pressure line
3. Steering cable actuator bolt
4. Steering link rod bolt

4. Disconnect the high-pressure (1, **Figure 45**) and low-pressure (2) lines from the steering cylinder assembly. Cap or plug the lines and fittings to prevent leakage and contamination.

5. Remove the steering cable actuator bolt (3, **Figure 45**), washer, spacer and locknut.

6. Remove the steering link rod bolt (4, **Figure 45**), upper and lower washers and locknut.

7. Remove the 2 port steering cylinder mounting screws and washers (12, **Figure 42**) and locknuts. Then, remove the 2 clamp screws (13, **Figure 42**) and washers. Then, slide the clamp (16, **Figure 42**) from the cylinder.

8. Remove the cylinder from its mounting bracket.

9. To install the cylinder, begin by positioning the cylinder to its mounting bracket and securing it to the port end with 2 screws, washers and locknuts as shown in **Figure 42**. Tighten the screws finger-tight at this time.

10. Secure the starboard end of the cylinder with the clamp and 2 screws and locknuts. Tighten the port and starboard screws to specification (**Table 3**).

11. Secure the link arm to the cylinder with the bolt, upper and lower washers and locknut. Tighten the bolt and nut to specification (**Table 3**).

12. Secure the steering cable to the actuator with the bolt, upper washer, lower spacer and locknut. Tighten the bolt and nut to specification (**Table 3**).

13. Connect the high and low pressure lines to the cylinder. Apply a small amount of Loctite 567 PST pipe sealant to the fittings before installation. Tighten both line fittings securely.

14. Reconnect the battery leads.

15. Check the fluid level and bleed air from the system as described previously in this section.

Accumulator removal/installation

1. Disconnect both battery cables.

2. Relieve system pressure by steering the system lock to lock at least 3 times.

3. Carefully remove the fill cap (or dipstick) while covering the cap with a shop towel. Allow all pressure and/or fluid to vent before fully removing the cap.

4. Disconnect the high-pressure (1, **Figure 45**) line from the steering cylinder (or extension line fitting on remote models). Disconnect the low pressure line from the top of the accumulator assembly. Cap or plug the lines and fittings to prevent leakage and contamination.

5. Disconnect the accumulator red and black leads from the wiring harness. Then, remove the 3 mounting nuts and washers (transom mounts) or 2 mounting bolts, 4 washers and 2 nuts (remote mounts) securing the accumulator and remove the accumulator.

6. To install the accumulator, position the accumulator on its mounting studs or against its mounting bracket and secure it with the 3 nuts and washers or 2 bolts, 4 washers and 2 nuts. Tighten the hardware to specification (**Table 3**).

7. Connect the accumulator red and black leads to the wiring harness.

8. Connect the high- and low-pressure lines. Apply a small amount of Loctite 567 PST pipe sealant to the fittings before installation. Tighten both line fittings securely.

9. Reconnect the battery leads.

10. Check the fluid level and bleed air from the system as described in this section.

10

Tables 1-5 are on the following pages.

Table 1 RECOMMENDED TEST EQUIPMENT AND TOOLS

Description	Part No.	Models
Multimeter	91-99750	All
Heat lamp	91-63209	All
Lock ring pliers	91-822778A-3	All
Spanner wrench	91-74951	1-piece integral units
Alignment tool	91-11230	135-250 hp/105-140 Jet
Trim rod remover	91-44486A-1	135-250 hp/105-140 Jet
Trim rod end cap remover	91-44487A-1	135-250 hp/105-140 Jet
Test gauge set	91-52915A-6	135-275 hp/105-140 Jet
Test gauge adaptor (up)	91-822778-2	135-250 hp/105-140 Jet
Test gauge adaptor (down)	91-822778-3	135-250 hp/105-140 Jet
Pressure test gauge	91-38053A-4	Ride Guide power steering

Table 2 TEST SPECIFICATIONS

135-250 hp and 105-140 Jet models	
Full tilt out (up) stall[1]	1300 psi (8964 kPa) minimum
Full trim in (down) stall[1]	500 psi (3448 kPa) minimum
275 hp models	
Full tilt out (up) stall[1]	3100-3500 psi (21375-24133 kPa)
Full tilt out (up) holding pressure[2]	1500 psi minimum
Full trim in (down) stall[1]	1500-1900 psi
Full trim in (down) holding pressure[2]	750 psi minimum
Ride Guide power steering	
Shut off pressure	1150-1250 psi (7929-8619 kPa)
Start up pressure	800-1000 psi (5516-6895 kPa)
Motor amperage draw hot (cold)	38 (36)

[1] Taken at the end of full travel with the electric motor running.
[2] Taken with electric motor not running, but after a stall reading.

Table 3 TORQUE VALUES

Fastener	in.-lb.	ft.-lb.	N•m
Power trim/tilt systems			
1-piece, single ram (75-125 hp and 65-80 Jet models)			
Anode	60	–	6.8
Cylinder end cap	–	45	61.0
Cylinder piston valve screws	35	–	4.0
Piston operating spool valves	120	–	13.6
Pump to valve body	70	–	7.9
Manifold to cylinder screws	100	–	11.3
Reservoir to pump body	70	–	7.9
Reservoir to pump body	80	–	9.0
Motor top end cap	13	–	1.5
135-250 hp and 105-140 Jet			
Anode	70	–	7.9
Electric motor	60	–	6.8
Manifold to stern brackets	–	40	54.2
Pump to manifold	80	–	9.0
Striker plates	80	–	9.0
(continued)			

Table 3 TORQUE VALUES (continued)

Fastener	in.-lb.	ft.-lb.	N•m
Power trim/tilt systems (continued)			
275 hp			
Pump to valve body	75	–	8.5
Quicksilver Ride Guide Power Steering			
Cylinder bracket to motor	100	–	11.3
Cylinder to cylinder bracket screws			
Hex head (starboard)	80	–	9.0
Socket head (port)	45	–	5.1
Fill cap/dipstick	30	–	3.4
Link rod to cylinder	–	30	40.7
Link rod to motor			
Pivot bolt	–	30	40.7
Locknut and bracket screws	–	20	27.1
Motor through-bolts	30	–	3.4
Accumulator mounting hardware	–	20	27.1
Steering cable bolt	–	20	27.1

Table 4 STANDARD TORQUE VALUES (U.S. STANDARD FASTENERS)

Screw or nut size	in.-lbs.	ft.-lbs.	N•m
6-32	9	–	1.0
8-32	20	–	2.3
10-24	30	–	3.4
10-32	35	–	4.0
12-24	45	–	5.1
1/4-20	70	6	7.9
1/4-28	84	7	9.5
5/16-18	160	13	18.1
5/16-24	168	14	19.0
3/8-16	270	23	30.5
3/8-24	300	25	33.9
7/16-14	–	36	48.8
7/16-20	–	40	54.2
1/2-13	–	50	67.8
1/2-20	–	60	81.3

10

Table 5 STANDARD TORQUE VALUES (METRIC FASTENERS)

Screw or nut size	in.-lbs.	ft.-lbs.	N•m
M5	36	–	4.1
M6	70	6	8.1
M8	156	13	17.6
M10	312	26	35.3
M12	–	35	47.5
M14	–	60	81.3

Chapter Eleven

Oil Injection System

All models except the 200 DFI (direct fuel injection) are lubricated by mixing oil with the gasoline. On models that are not oil-injected, the oil and gasoline are premixed in the fuel tank(s) by the boat operator. The recommended fuel/oil mixture for normal operation in all models without oil injection is 50 parts of fuel to 1 part of oil (50:1). This is the standard 6 gal. (22.7 L) of fuel to one pint (16 fl. oz. [473 mL]) of oil.

On oil-injected models, the oil is automatically mixed with the gasoline. An engine-mounted oil pump injects oil into the fuel pump inlet line on carbureted models or into the vapor separator on EFI (electronic fuel injection) models. On models equipped with a variable-ratio oil injection system, the fuel/oil ratio is changed based on throttle position. At wide-open throttle the fuel/oil ratio is approximately 50-60:1, while at idle speeds the ratio will be approximately 80-100:1.

The various engine components are lubricated as the fuel and oil mixture passes through the crankcases and into the combustion chambers. The fuel/oil ratio required by the engine varies with engine load and speed. Oil demands are always highest at wide-open throttle.

The advantages of oil injection are that the operator only has to keep the oil reservoir(s) filled. No calculations must be made as to how much oil to add when refueling. Over-oiling (and under-oiling) from operator miscalculations are eliminated, along with the associated engine problems caused by under- or over-oiling.

Variable-ratio oil injection offers the additional benefits of reduced smoke and spark plug fouling (at idle and low speeds), due to the reduced oil consumption.

The 200 DFI (direct fuel injection) uses an ECM (electronic control module) controlled, electric oil pump that is mounted directly to the intake manifold. Oil is not mixed with the fuel. Straight oil flows from the oil pump directly into machined passages in the intake manifold and is discharged in front of each reed block. A single external line delivers oil to the belt-driven air compressor.

Four different oil injection systems are used on models covered in this chapter.

1. Variable-ratio injection—75-125 hp and 65-80 Jet models.
2. Variable-ratio injection—135-200 hp, 275 hp and 105-140 Jet models.
3. Variable-ratio injection—225-250 hp models.
4. Variable-ratio electronically controlled injection—200 DFI (direct fuel injection) models.

Refer to Chapter Four for fuel and oil requirements, engine break-in procedures and oil tank filling procedures. Refer to Chapter Five for synchronizing the oil pump and throttle linkages on variable ratio models.

Table 1 lists oil injection system specifications, **Table 2** lists special torque values, **Table 3** and **Table 4** list standard torque values. All tables are at the end of the chapter.

VARIABLE RATIO OIL INJECTION (75-125 HP AND 65-80 JET MODELS)

CAUTION
While it should not normally be necessary, if a boat-mounted electric fuel supply pump is used, fuel pressure must not exceed 2 psi (13.8 kPa) at the engine fuel line connector. If necessary, install a fuel pressure regulator between the electric fuel pump and engine fuel line connector. Adjust the fuel pressure regulator to a maximum of 2 psi (13.8 kPa) fuel pressure. The electric fuel pump should also conform to all applicable Coast Guard safety standards for permanently-installed fuel systems.

A variable-ratio crankshaft driven oil injection pump is used on these models. The oil pump injects oil into the fuel line just prior to the fuel pump. The oil pump delivers oil relative to throttle lever position and engine speed. A linkage rod connects the oil pump control lever to the throttle linkage and varies the oil pump stroke according to throttle lever position. The fuel/oil ratio varies from approximately 80:1 at idle to approximately 50:1 at wide-open throttle.

Operation

The 75-125 hp and 65-80 Jet models are equipped with the oil injection system shown in **Figure 1**.

On 1994-1995 models, the engine-mounted oil reservoir capacity is 1 gal. (3.78 L) on 75-90 hp and 65 Jet models and 1.4 gal. (5.3 L) on 100-125 hp and 80 Jet models. This capacity provides sufficient oil for approximately 6 hours of operation at wide-open throttle. The reservoir is equipped with an oil level sight gauge, visible through an opening in the engine cowl.

On 1996-1997 models, the engine-mounted oil reservoir capacity is 3.2 qt. (3.0 L) on 75-90 hp and 65 Jet models and 5.13 qt. (4.9 L) on 100-125 hp and 80 Jet models. This capacity provides sufficient oil for approximately 5 hours of operation at wide-open throttle. The reservoir on 1996-1997 models is equipped with a dipstick to determine the oil level.

A check-valve vent at the top of the oil tank provides for atmospheric venting of the reservoir and prevents oil leakage when the outboard motor is tilted.

A low oil level switch contained within the oil reservoir activates a warning module and warning horn when the oil level drops to 1 qt (0.95 L). When the low-oil warning horn sounds, enough oil for approximately 50-60 minutes of wide-open throttle operation remains. The warning module incorporates a self-test that should sound briefly each time the ignition switch is turned to the ON or RUN position to indicate the warning system is functioning. The warning horn will also sound if the engine temperature switch (located in the cylinder block) closes to ground.

A 2 psi (13.8 kPa) check valve is installed in the fuel line between the fuel line T-fitting and the oil pump discharge line. See **Figure 2**. The check valve is used to prevent gasoline from entering the oil pump discharge line.

11

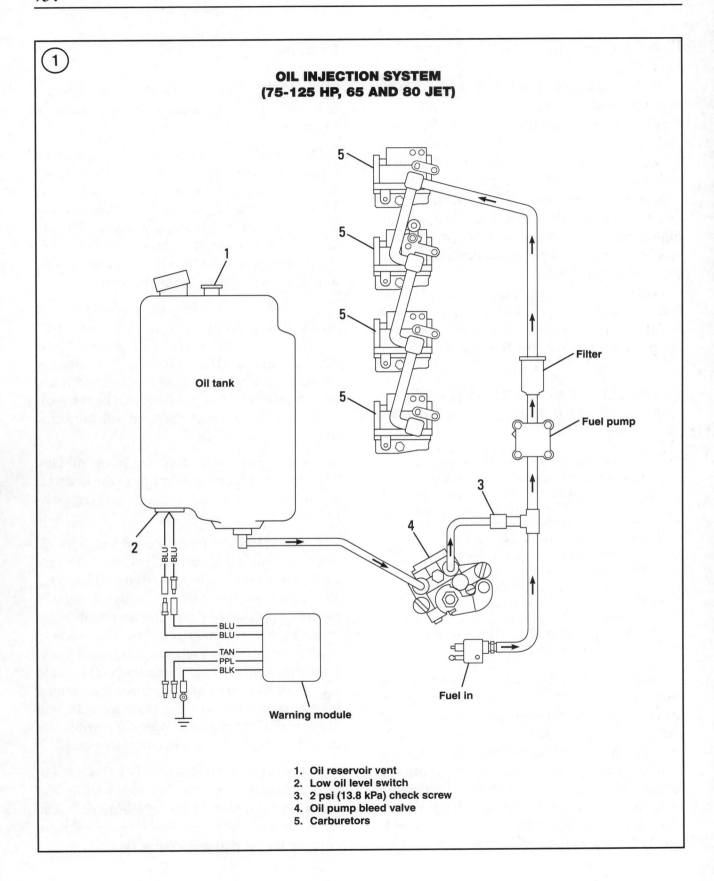

① **OIL INJECTION SYSTEM
(75-125 HP, 65 AND 80 JET)**

Oil tank

Filter

Fuel pump

BLU
BLU

BLU
BLU

TAN
PPL
BLK

Warning module

Fuel in

1. **Oil reservoir vent**
2. **Low oil level switch**
3. **2 psi (13.8 kPa) check screw**
4. **Oil pump bleed valve**
5. **Carburetors**

Warning System Troubleshooting

If a malfunction is suspected in the oil injection system (warning horn sounds), immediately stop the engine and check the oil level in the engine-mounted reservoir. If the oil is low, fill the reservoir with a recommended oil (Chapter Four). Refer to the back of the manual for wiring diagrams and **Figure 1** for this procedure.

> *CAUTION*
> *If an oil injection system malfunction is suspected, do not operate the outboard on straight gasoline. Operate the motor on a remote fuel tank containing a 50:1 fuel/oil mixture until the* **Oil Pump Output Test** *can be performed.*

> *NOTE*
> *The warning module will beep (pulse) the warning horn off and on when it detects low oil level in the reservoir. If the engine is overheating, the warning horn will sound continuously as long as the key is on and the engine is overheating.*

Warning system does not self-test

1. Check the warning module black lead for a clean, tight connection to ground. Clean and tighten the connection as necessary.
2. Turn the ignition switch to the ON or RUN position. Check the warning module purple lead for battery voltage. If voltage is not present, an open circuit or high resistance is present in the purple lead from the warning module bullet connector to the ignition switch. This includes the main harness connector and the ignition switch. Repair or replace the lead, connections or ignition switch as necessary.
3. Disconnect the warning module tan or tan/blue lead from the engine temperature switch located in the cylinder cover.
4. Turn the ignition switch to the ON or RUN position. Ground the warning module lead to the engine using a suitable jumper wire. The warning horn should activate when the wire is grounded. If the warning horn now sounds, replace the warning module and recheck the self-test function.
5. If the warning horn does not activate, check the tan or tan/blue lead between the warning horn and the engine temperature switch bullet connector for an open circuit. Repair or replace the lead as necessary.
6. If the tan or tan/blue lead tests satisfactorily in Step 5, verify that the warning horn is receiving battery voltage through its purple lead. If the horn is receiving battery voltage, but does not sound when the tan or tan/blue lead is grounded in Step 4, replace the warning horn.

Warning system sounds continuously (all models)

1. Turn the ignition switch to the ON or RUN position.
2. Disconnect the engine temperature switch tan or tan/blue lead at its bullet connector or terminal strip. If the warning horn stops when the lead is disconnected, the engine temperature switch is defective or the engine is overheating. Replace the defective switch or correct the cause of the engine overheat.
3. If the warning horn continues to sound after the temperature switch lead is disconnected, disconnect the warning module tan (or tan/blue) lead at the warning module bullet connector or

11

terminal strip. If the warning horn stops when the lead is disconnected, the warning module is defective and must be replaced.

4. If the warning horn continues to sound after the temperature switch and warning module tan (or tan/blue) leads have been disconnected, the tan (or tan/blue) lead is shorted to ground somewhere between the warning horn and the engine temperature switch/warning module bullet connectors. Repair or replace the lead as necessary.

Warning system sounds erratically

> *CAUTION*
> *Do not run the engine without an adequate water supply and do not exceed 3000 rpm without an adequate load. Refer to* **Safety Precautions** *at the beginning of Chapter Three or Chapter Five.*

1. Verify that the oil tank is full. Then, disconnect the 2 oil level switch blue (or light blue) leads at the warning module bullet connectors.

2. Run the engine and check if the warning horn still sounds erratically. If the horn no longer sounds, replace the low oil level switch in the oil tank.

3. If the horn still sounds in Step 2, disconnect the engine temperature switch tan or tan/blue lead at its bullet connector.

4. Run the engine and check if the warning horn still sounds erratically. If the horn no longer sounds, the engine temperature switch is defective or the engine is overheating. Refer to Chapter Three for troubleshooting procedures.

5. If the horn still sounds in Step 4, replace the warning module.

Oil level switch tests

1. Verify that the oil tank is full. Then, disconnect the 2 oil level switch blue leads at the warning module bullet connectors.

2. Connect an ohmmeter, calibrated on an appropriate scale to check continuity, between the 2 oil level switch blue wires. The meter should indicate no continuity when the oil tank is full. If continuity is noted, the oil level switch is defective and must be replaced.

Oil Pump Output Test

> *CAUTION*
> *Do not run the engine without an adequate water supply and do not exceed 3000 rpm without an adequate load. Refer to* **Safety Precautions** *in Chapter Three or Chapter Five.*

Obtain a graduated container, capable of accurately measuring up to 50 cc, before continuing.

1. Connect a remote fuel tank containing a 50:1 fuel/oil mixture to the engine.

2. Disconnect the oil pump discharge line from the check valve fitting (**Figure 2**). Securely cap or plug the check valve fitting to prevent leakage.

3. Connect an accurate shop tachometer to the engine following its manufacturer's instructions.

4. Insert the disconnected end of the oil pump discharge line into the graduated container.

5. Disconnect the oil pump link rod from the oil pump control arm. Rotate the pump arm fully against the spring (counter clockwise) until the arm is against the pump casting. Hold the arm in this position.

6. Start the outboard motor and run at 700 rpm for exactly 15 minutes.

> *NOTE*
> *Injection pump output specifications are based on tests performed at 70° F (21° C). If ambient temperature is more or less, actual pump output may vary from that specified.*

7. Stop the engine and check the quantity of oil in the graduated container. Oil pump output should be 22 cc (minimum) on 75-90 hp and 65 Jet models and 29 cc (minimum) on 100-125 hp and 80 Jet models.

8. If injection pump output is less than specified, replace the pump assembly as described in this chapter.

9. Reconnect the pump discharge line to the check valve fitting. Secure the connection with a new tie-strap. Then, bleed the injection system as described in this chapter.

10. Reconnect the oil pump link rod to the control arm. Adjust the link rod as specified in Chapter Five.

Oil Injection System Service

Oil pump synchronization

Refer to Chapter Five for throttle linkage to oil pump linkage adjustment and synchronization procedures.

Bleeding oil pump

If the pump has been removed, any of the lines replaced, or if air is present in the oil pump lines, proceed as follows to bleed air from the oil injection pump and lines:

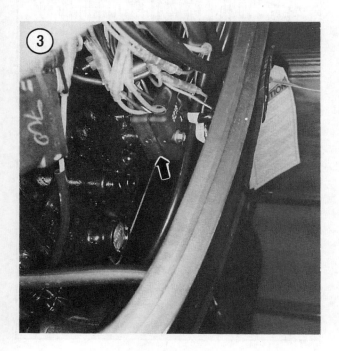

1. Place a shop towel beneath the oil pump.

2. Loosen the oil pump bleed screw (4, **Figure 1**) 3-4 turns.

3. Allow oil to flow from the bleed screw until no air bubbles are noted in the inlet hose.

4. Tighten the bleed screw to 25 in.-lb. (2.8 N•m).

> *CAUTION*
> *Do not run the engine without an adequate water supply and do not exceed 3000 rpm without an adequate load. Refer to* **Safety Precautions** *at the beginning of Chapter Three or Chapter Five.*

5. If air is present in the pump discharge line, connect a remote tank containing a 50:1 fuel/oil mixture to the engine. Start the engine and run at idle until no air bubbles are noted in the discharge hose. To speed the bleeding process, disconnect the pump link rod and rotate the pump arm to the full output position.

Warning module removal/installation

The warning module is mounted in the lower cowl area on the starboard side of the engine. On engines equipped with RPM limit modules, the warning module is mounted side by side with the RPM limit module as shown in **Figure 3**. It may be necessary to split the lower cowl to gain access to the warning module.

1. Disconnect the negative battery cable.

2. Disconnect and ground the spark plug leads to the power head to prevent accidental starting.

3. Disconnect the warning module purple, tan (or tan/blue) and 2 blue leads at their bullet connectors.

4. Remove the 2 warning module mounting screws. Disconnect the module ground (black) lead (under one module mounting screw or connected directly to the power head) and remove the module.

5. To install the module, begin by positioning the module on the power head. Secure the mod-

11

ule to the power head with 2 screws. Tighten both screws securely. Connect the ground lead as it was removed (either to a mounting screw or directly to the power head). The module must be grounded in order to operate.

6. Connect the purple, tan (or tan/blue) and 2 blue leads to the module bullet connectors.

7. Reconnect the negative battery cable and the spark plug leads.

Oil tank removal/installation

1. Disconnect the negative battery cable.

2. Disconnect and ground the spark plug leads to the power head to prevent accidental starting.

3A. *1994-1995 models*—Remove the screw securing the oil tank to the bracket near the fill cap.

3B. *1996-1997 models*—Remove the 2 small screws securing the top oil tank bracket and the 1 larger screw securing the bottom rear corner of the oil tank to the power head.

4. Disconnect the oil level switch blue leads at the switch's bullet connectors.

5. Lift the oil tank sufficiently to access the bottom of the tank. Cut the tie-strap securing the oil outlet hose to the oil tank, then disconnect the hose from the tank.

6. Remove the oil tank from the power head.

7. Remove the screw securing the oil level switch to the bottom of the tank. Remove the switch.

8. To install the oil tank, begin by installing the oil level switch into the oil tank. Secure the switch with one screw. Tighten the screw securely.

9. Position the oil tank assembly to the power head. Then, attach the oil outlet hose to the oil tank. Secure the hose with a new tie-strap.

10. Secure the oil tank with 1 screw (1994-1995 models) or 3 screws (1996-1997 models). Tighten the screws to specification (**Table 2**).

11. Connect the oil level switch leads to the wiring harness bullet connectors.

12. Fill the oil tank with the recommended oil (Chapter Four), then bleed the oil pump as described in this chapter.

13. Reconnect the negative battery cable and the spark plug leads.

Oil pump removal/installation

Refer to Chapter Eight for oil pump drive gear removal/installation procedures. Refer to **Figure 4** for this procedure.

1. Disconnect the oil inlet and discharge lines from the pump.

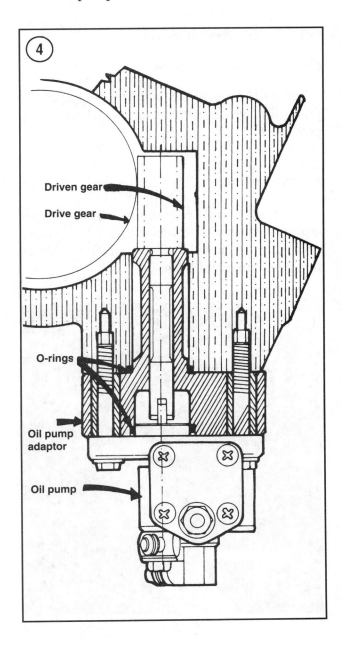

2. Disconnect the link rod from the pump control arm, then remove the pump mounting screws.

3. Remove the pump assembly from the power head. If the pump adaptor and/or driven gear remains in the engine block, retrieve them using needle nose pliers.

4. Remove and inspect the bushings from the adaptor. Replace all worn or damaged components.

5. To install the pump, thoroughly lubricate the adaptor and 2 bushings with Quicksilver Needle Bearing Assembly Grease. Install the bushings into the sleeve. Make sure the flanged bushing faces the oil pump driven gear.

6. Thoroughly lubricate the driven gear shaft with Quicksilver Needle Bearing Assembly Grease. Insert the driven gear into the bearing assembly, making sure the gear properly engages the pump shaft.

7. Install new O-rings onto the pump. Lubricate the O-rings with Quicksilver Needle Bearing Assembly Grease.

8. Install the pump assembly onto the power head. Apply Loctite 271 threadlocking adhesive to the threads of the pump mounting screws. Install the screws and tighten to 60 in.-lb. (6.8 N·m).

9. Reconnect the oil inlet and discharge hoses to the pump. Securely clamp the hoses to the pump using new tie-straps.

10. Reconnect the link rod to the pump control arm. Refer to Chapter Five for oil pump adjustment and synchronization procedures.

11. Perform the oil pump bleeding procedure as described in this chapter.

VARIABLE-RATIO OIL INJECTION (135-200, 275 HP AND 105-140 JET MODELS)

CAUTION
While it should not normally be necessary, if a boat-mounted electric fuel supply pump is used, fuel pressure must not exceed 4 psi (27.6 kPa) at the engine fuel line connector. If necessary, install a fuel pressure regulator between the electric fuel pump and engine fuel line connector. Adjust the fuel pressure regulator to a maximum of 4 psi (27.6 kPa) fuel pressure. The electric fuel pump must also conform to all applicable Coast Guard safety standards for permanently installed fuel systems.

A variable-ratio crankshaft driven oil injection pump is used on these models. The oil pump injects oil into the fuel line just prior to the fuel pump on carbureted models or into the bottom of the vapor separator on EFI (electronic fuel injection) models. The oil pump delivers oil relative to throttle lever position and engine speed. A linkage rod connects the oil pump control lever to the throttle linkage and varies the oil pump stroke according to throttle lever position. The fuel/oil ratio varies from approximately 100:1 (80:1 on the 275 hp) at idle to approximately 50:1 at wide-open throttle.

11

Operation

A 3 gallon (11.4 L) remote oil tank supplies oil to the reservoir mounted under the engine cowl (**Figure 5**, typical). The reservoir oil capacity is 2.75 qt. (2.6 L) on 275 hp models and 0.94 qt. (0.89 L) on all other models. The engine-mounted reservoir provides enough oil for approximately 1 hour (275 hp models) or 30 minutes (all other models) of wide-open throttle operation after the remote oil tank is empty. Refer to **Figure 6** for 135-200 hp and 105-140 Jet models or **Figure 7** for 275 hp models.

NOTE
The vent valve for the engine-mounted reservoir may be a 4 psi (27.6 kPa) or 2 psi (13.8 kPa) check valve. New models use the higher pressure valve to prevent air from being drawn into the system if the remote oil tank is mounted low in the bilge.

The remote oil tank is pressurized by crankcase pressure through a one-way check valve, causing oil to flow from the remote tank to the engine-mounted reservoir. Should the oil line between the remote tank and engine-mounted reservoir become restricted, the 2 or 4 psi (13.8 or 27.6 kPa) check valve will unseat, allowing air to vent through the hose, allowing the injection pump to consume the oil in the engine-mounted reservoir.

The oil pickup tube in the remote tank is equipped with a filter screen to prevent dirt or other contamination from entering the injection system.

The injection pump is mounted to the engine block and is driven by a gear on the crankshaft. On carbureted models, the oil pump injects the oil into the fuel stream prior to the mechanical fuel pump. On EFI (electronic fuel injection) models, the oil is injected into the fuel at the bottom of the vapor separator assembly.

A low-oil level switch (**Figure 8**, typical) attached to the reservoir fill cap activates the warning module and warning horn if the oil level in the reservoir becomes low. If this occurs, the engine must be stopped immediately and both oil reservoirs refilled; otherwise, permanent power head damage will occur once the oil reservoir is empty.

On 135-200 hp and 105-140 Jet models a motion sensor (6, **Figure 6**) is used that detects movement of the oil pump shaft via a magnet inside the pump coupler. The warning module also receives a tachometer signal from the outer switch box, No.2 cylinder (primary ignition coil lead). If the motor is running and the motion sensor detects no oil pump shaft movement, the warning module will pulse the warning horn intermittently. If this occurs, the engine must be stopped immediately and the cause of the failure determined and corrected; otherwise, permanent power head damage will occur.

The warning module incorporates a self test feature that should sound the warning horn briefly each time the ignition switch is turned to the ON or RUN position. This indicates that the warning module is functioning. If the self test does not occur, or if the horn sounds intermittently or continuously after the ignition is switched ON, do not attempt to start the engine. The warning horn will also sound if the engine temperature switch (located in the cylinder head[s]) closes to ground.

A 2 psi (13.8 kPa) check valve (13, **Figure 6** or 6, **Figure 7**) is used to prevent gasoline from being forced into the oil lines.

Warning System Troubleshooting

If a malfunction is suspected in the oil injection system (warning horn sounds), immediately stop the engine and check the oil levels in the remote oil tank and the engine-mounted reservoir. If the oil is low, fill the oil tank and reservoir with a recommended oil (Chapter Four).

CAUTION
*If an oil injection system malfunction is suspected, do not operate the outboard on straight gasoline. Operate the motor on a remote fuel tank containing a 50:1 fuel/oil mixture until the **Oil Pump Output Test** can be performed.*

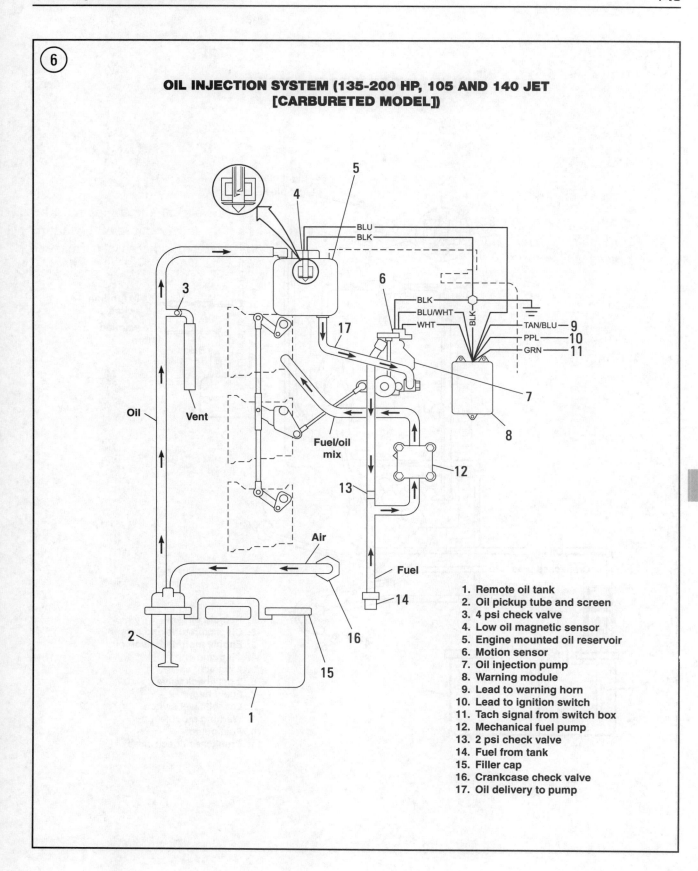

6

OIL INJECTION SYSTEM (135-200 HP, 105 AND 140 JET [CARBURETED MODEL])

BLU
BLK

BLK
BLU/WHT
WHT
BLK
TAN/BLU — 9
PPL — 10
GRN — 11

Oil

Vent

Fuel/oil mix

Air

Fuel

1. Remote oil tank
2. Oil pickup tube and screen
3. 4 psi check valve
4. Low oil magnetic sensor
5. Engine mounted oil reservoir
6. Motion sensor
7. Oil injection pump
8. Warning module
9. Lead to warning horn
10. Lead to ignition switch
11. Tach signal from switch box
12. Mechanical fuel pump
13. 2 psi check valve
14. Fuel from tank
15. Filler cap
16. Crankcase check valve
17. Oil delivery to pump

11

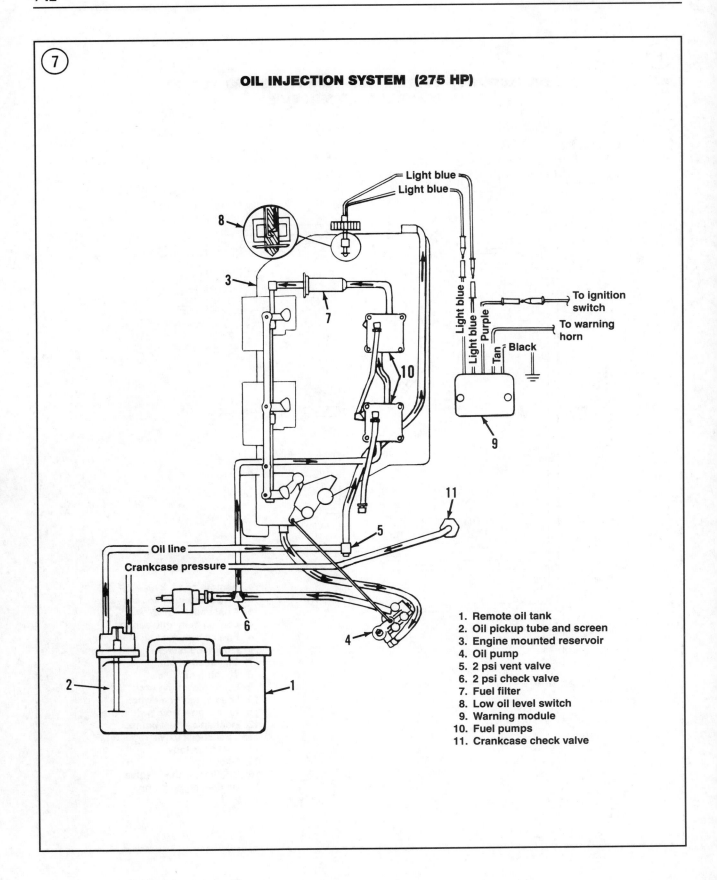

OIL INJECTION SYSTEM (275 HP)

Light blue
Light blue
Light blue
Light blue
Purple
Tan
Black
To ignition switch
To warning horn

Oil line
Crankcase pressure

1. Remote oil tank
2. Oil pickup tube and screen
3. Engine mounted reservoir
4. Oil pump
5. 2 psi vent valve
6. 2 psi check valve
7. Fuel filter
8. Low oil level switch
9. Warning module
10. Fuel pumps
11. Crankcase check valve

Each time the ignition switch is turned to the ON or RUN position from the OFF position, the warning module should briefly activate the warning horn to indicate the warning system is functioning. If an oil injection malfunction occurs, the warning module will trigger a pulsing (on and off) tone from the warning horn. If the power head overheats, the engine temperature switch will trigger a continuous tone from the horn.

NOTE
Remember that the 135-200 hp and 105-140 Jet models use an oil pump motion sensor. If the warning horn is pulsing, yet both oil tanks (reservoirs) are full, it is possible that the oil pump drive gear has failed. Operate the motor on a remote fuel tank containing a 50:1 fuel/oil mixture until the oil injection system can be inspected.

If the warning horn activates during operation, immediately shut down the engine and check the oil level in the engine-mounted reservoir. If necessary, fill the remote tank with a recommended

oil. If the reservoir oil level is low, but the remote tank is full, proceed as follows:

1. Check the O-rings or gaskets in the reservoir fill cap for cracking, deterioration or other damage. Replace the O-rings or gaskets as necessary. Make sure the fill caps are screwed tightly on the reservoir and remote tank. Air leakage at the remote tank will prevent the movement of oil from the tank to the reservoir. Leakage at the reservoir will result in oil spillage.

2. Check the oil line between the remote tank and reservoir for kinks, restrictions or leakage. Repair or replace the line as required.

3. Check the crankcase pressure line between the crankcase check valve and remote tank for kinks, restrictions or leakage. Make sure the crankcase one-way check valve is functioning properly.

4. Check the oil pickup tube and filter for restrictions. Clean or replace the tube or filter as necessary.

5. Check all oil lines for kinks, cracks, deterioration, leakage or other damage. Make sure all connections are tightly clamped.

Warning system does not self test

Refer to the back of the manual for wiring diagrams.

1. Check the warning module black lead for a clean, tight connection to ground. Clean and tighten the connection as necessary.

2. Turn the ignition switch to the ON or RUN position. Check the warning module purple lead for battery voltage. If voltage is not present, an open circuit or high resistance is present in the purple lead from the warning module bullet connector to the ignition switch. This includes the main harness connector and the ignition switch. Repair or replace the lead, connections or ignition switch as necessary.

3. Disconnect the warning module tan or tan/blue lead from the engine temperature switch's terminal strip.

11

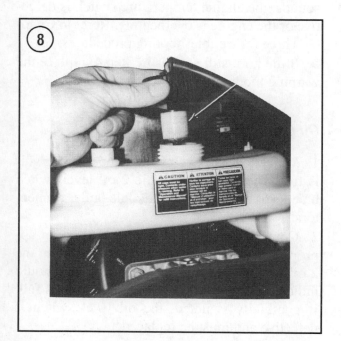

8

4. Turn the ignition switch to the ON or RUN position. Ground the warning module lead to the engine. The warning horn should activate when the wire is grounded. If the warning horn now sounds, replace the warning module and recheck the self-test function.

5. If the warning horn does not activate, check the tan or tan/blue lead between the warning horn and the engine temperature switch's terminal strip for an open circuit. Repair or replace the lead as necessary.

6. If the tan or tan/blue lead tests satisfactorily in Step 5, verify that the warning horn is receiving battery voltage through its purple lead. If the horn is receiving battery voltage, but does not sound when the tan or tan/blue lead is grounded in Step 4, replace the warning horn.

Warning system sounds continuously

Refer to the back of the manual for wiring diagrams.

1. Turn the ignition switch to the ON or RUN position.

2. Disconnect the engine temperature switch black lead from the terminal strip where it junctions with the warning module tan or tan/blue lead. If the warning horn stops when the lead is disconnected, the engine temperature switch is defective or the engine is overheating. Replace the defective switch or correct the cause of the engine overheat.

3. If the warning horn continues to sound after the temperature switch lead is disconnected, disconnect the warning module tan (or tan/blue) lead from the warning module bullet connector or terminal strip. If the warning horn stops when the lead is disconnected, the warning module is defective and must be replaced.

4. If the warning horn continues to sound after the temperature switch and warning module tan (or tan/blue) leads are disconnected, the tan (or tan/blue) lead is shorted to ground between the warning horn and the engine temperature

switch/warning module bullet connectors. Repair or replace the lead as necessary.

Warning system sounds erratically

Refer to the back of the manual for wiring diagrams.

> *CAUTION*
> *Do not run the engine without an adequate water supply and do not exceed 3000 rpm without an adequate load. Refer to **Safety Precautions** in Chapter Three or Chapter Five.*

1. Verify that both oil tanks are full. Then, disconnect the 2 oil level switch blue (or light blue) leads at the warning module bullet connectors.

2. Run the engine and see if the warning horn still sounds erratically. If the horn no longer sounds, replace the low oil level switch in the oil tank.

3. If the horn still sounds in Step 2, disconnect the engine temperature switch black lead at the terminal strip where it junctions with the warning module tan or tan/blue lead.

4. Run the engine and see if the warning horn still sounds erratically. If the horn no longer sounds, the engine temperature switch is defective or the engine is overheating. Refer to Chapter Three for troubleshooting procedures.

5. If the horn still sounds in Step 4, replace the warning module.

Oil level switch tests

1. Verify that the engine-mounted oil reservoir is full. Then, disconnect the 2 oil level switch blue leads at the warning module bullet connectors.

2. Connect an ohmmeter, calibrated on an appropriate scale to check continuity, between the 2 oil level switch blue wires. The meter should indicate no continuity when the oil tank is full. If continuity is noted, the oil level switch is defective and must be replaced.

Motion sensor tests
(135-200 hp, 105 and 140 Jet)

The following tests are intended to diagnose a problem in the warning system that produces a pulsing horn only when the engine is being cranked or running. For this procedure, the low oil level switch should have already been tested as described in the previous section. Refer to the back of the manual for wiring diagrams.

1. Disconnect and ground the spark plug leads to the power head to prevent accidental starting.

2. Inspect the green lead from the warning module to the outer switch box No. 2 cylinder primary lead terminal for loose connections, open circuits or high resistance. Correct any problems found.

3. Test the ignition system with an air gap tester as described in Chapter Three to make sure that the No. 2 cylinder has adequate spark. If the primary voltage is incorrect, it can cause the warning module to malfunction, which can create false warning signals.

4. Disconnect the warning module white lead at its bullet connector between the module and the

motion sensor. Connect a voltmeter between a good engine ground and the white wire from the module. Turn the ignition switch to the ON position and note the voltmeter. The voltage should be within 1 volt of battery voltage.

5. Reconnect the white lead to the module. Insert a suitable probe into the blue/white lead bullet connection between the motion sensor and warning module. A paper clip or piece of wire is sufficient.

6. Connect a voltmeter between the engine ground and the blue/white wire. Place the ignition switch in the ON position.

7. Using the emergency starting rope, rotate the flywheel while noting the voltmeter.

The voltage should peak at 4-6 volts, then drop to less than 1.0 volt during every 2 revolutions of the flywheel.

8. If no voltage is noted, the motion sensor is defective or the oil pump drive gear is not turning. Check the oil pump output as described in this chapter. If pump output is acceptable, replace the motion sensor as described later in this section, then recheck the voltage.

9. Reconnect the spark plug leads when finished.

11

Oil Pump Output Test
(135-200 hp, 105 and 140 Jet)

CAUTION
Do not run the engine without an adequate water supply and do not exceed 3000 rpm without an adequate load. Refer to Safety Precautions in Chapter Three or Chapter Five.

Obtain a graduated container, capable of accurately measuring up to 50 cc, before continuing.

1. Connect a remote fuel tank containing a 50:1 fuel/oil mixture to the engine.

2. Disconnect the oil pump discharge line from the check valve fitting near the fuel pump on carbureted models (**Figure 9**) or from the bottom of the vapor separator on EFI (electronic fuel

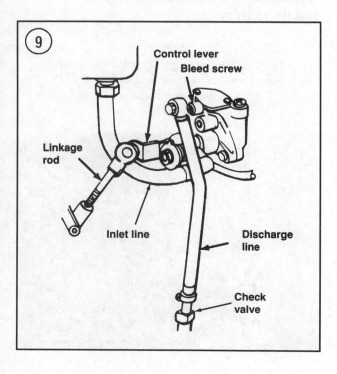

(9)

Control lever
Bleed screw

Linkage rod

Inlet line

Discharge line

Check valve

injection) models (**Figure 10**). Securely cap or plug the check valve fitting to prevent leakage.

3. Connect an accurate shop tachometer to the engine following its manufacturer's instructions.

4. Insert the disconnected end of the oil pump discharge line into the graduated container.

5. Start the outboard motor and run at 1500 rpm for exactly 3 minutes.

NOTE
Injection pump output specifications are based on tests performed at 70° F (21° C). If ambient temperature is more or less, actual pump output may vary from that specified.

6. Stop the engine and check the quantity of oil in the graduated container. Oil pump output should be 6.1-7.5 cc on 135-150 hp and 105 Jet models and 7.4-9 cc on XR6, Magnum III, 175-200 hp and 140 Jet models.

7. If the injection pump output is less than specified, replace the pump assembly as described in this chapter.

8. Empty the container. Disconnect the linkage rod from the injection pump control lever. See **Figure 9**. Rotate the control lever to the wide-open throttle position, then repeat Steps 4 and 5.

9. Stop the engine and again check the quantity of oil in the graduated container. Oil pump output should now be 15.3-18.7 cc on 135-150 hp and 105 Jet models and 17.3-21.1 cc on XR6, Magnum III, 175-200 hp and 140 Jet models.

10. If injection pump output is less than specified, replace the pump assembly as described in this chapter.

11. Reconnect the pump discharge line to the check valve fitting. Secure the connection with a new tie-strap. Then, bleed the injection system as described in this chapter.

12. Reconnect oil pump link rod to the control arm. Adjust the link rod as specified in Chapter Five.

Oil Pump Output Test (275 hp)

CAUTION
*Do not run the engine without an adequate water supply and do not exceed 3000 rpm without an adequate load. Refer to **Safety Precautions** in Chapter Three or Chapter Five.*

Obtain a graduated container, capable of accurately measuring up to 100 cc, before continuing.

1. Connect a remote fuel tank containing a 50:1 fuel/oil mixture to the power head.

2. Disconnect the oil pump discharge line (**Figure 9**) from the check valve T-fitting near the engine fuel tank connector. Securely cap or plug the check valve T-fitting.

3. Connect an accurate shop tachometer to the engine following its manufacturer's instructions.

4. Remove the oil pump linkage rod from the pump control lever. See **Figure 9**.

5. Rotate the pump control lever to the wide-open throttle position (fully counterclockwise).

6. Insert the disconnected end of the pump discharge line into the graduated container.

7. Start the motor and run it at 700 rpm for exactly 15 minutes.

NOTE
Injection pump output specifications are based on tests performed at 70° F (21° C). If ambient temperature is more or

less, actual pump output will vary from that specified.

8. Stop the engine and check the graduated container. The minimum injection pump output is 61.25 cc.

9. If injection pump output is less than specified, replace the pump assembly as described later in this section.

10. Reconnect the pump discharge line to the check valve T-fitting. Secure the connection with a new tie-strap. Then, bleed the injection system as described in this chapter.

11. Reconnect oil pump link rod to the control arm. Adjust the link rod as specified in Chapter Five.

Oil Injection System Service

Oil pump synchronization

Refer to Chapter Five for throttle linkage to oil pump linkage adjustment and synchronization procedures.

Bleeding oil pump

If the pump has been removed, any of the lines replaced, or if air is present in the oil pump lines, proceed as follows to bleed air from the oil injection pump and lines.

1. Place a shop towel beneath the oil pump.

2. Loosen the oil pump bleed screw 3-4 turns (**Figure 9**).

3. Allow oil to flow from the bleed screw until no air bubbles are noted in the inlet hose.

4. Tighten the bleed screw to 25 in.-lb. (2.8 N•m).

> *CAUTION*
> *Do not run the engine without an adequate water supply and do not exceed 3000 rpm without an adequate load. Refer to **Safety Precautions** in Chapter Three or Chapter Five.*

5. If air is present in the pump discharge line, connect a remote tank containing a 50:1 fuel/oil mixture to the engine. Start the engine and run at idle until no air bubbles are noted in the discharge hose. The pump link rod may be disconnected and the pump arm rotated to the full output position to speed the process.

6. *Carbureted models*—If necessary, gently pinch the fuel pump inlet hose between the injection pump T-fitting and remote fuel tank connector, causing the fuel pump to create a slight vacuum in the hose. This will quicken the purging process.

7. Continue running the outboard until all air is purged, then stop the engine and reconnect the linkage rod to the control lever (if disconnected).

Warning module removal/installation (135-200 hp and 105-140 Jet)

1. Disconnect the negative battery cable.

> *NOTE*
> *The warning module is mounted on the port cylinder bank as shown in **Figure 11**. Note the warning module wire routing for reference during installation.*

2. Disconnect the warning module purple and tan leads from the terminal block located on top of the engine. It may be necessary to remove the flywheel cover to gain access to the terminal strip.

3. Disconnect the module blue, blue/white and white leads at the module's bullet connectors.

> *NOTE*
> *While normally connected to the outer switch box, the green wire from the warning module may be connected to either switch box. If connected to the inner switch box, separate the switch boxes as described in Chapter Seven.*

4. Disconnect the green module wire from the appropriate switch box.

11

5. Remove the 3 module mounting screws and remove the module (**Figure 11**).

6. If the module ground (black) lead was not under a mounting screw, remove the ground lead from the power head.

7. To install the module, apply Loctite 242 threadlocking adhesive to the threads of the mounting screws. Install the module and tighten the 3 screws to 25 in.-lb. (2.8 N•m). If the ground lead was under a mounting screw, reinstall the ground lead at this time. The module must be grounded to operate.

8. Connect the module wires at their respective locations. Route the module wires as noted during removal.

9. Reconnect the negative battery cable.

Warning module removal/installation (275 hp)

1. Disconnect the negative battery cable.

> *NOTE*
> *The warning module is mounted on the starboard side of the engine, beneath the starter motor. Note the routing of the warning module wires for reference during installation.*

2. Disconnect the light blue module leads from the engine-mounted reservoir fill cap bullet connectors.

3. Disconnect the tan and black module leads from the terminal block located adjacent to the starter motor solenoid.

4. Disconnect the module purple lead at its bullet connector.

5. Remove the 2 module mounting screws and remove the module.

6. To install the module, apply Loctite 242 threadlocking adhesive to the threads of the mounting screws. Install the module and tighten the screws to 25 in.-lb. (2.8 N•m).

7. Connect the module wires. Route the wires as noted during removal.

8. Reconnect the negative battery cable.

Engine-mounted oil reservoir removal/installation

1. Disconnect the reservoir to oil pump line at the oil pump. If the reservoir contains oil, cap or plug the line to prevent leakage.

2. Disconnect the remote oil tank to engine reservoir input line from the top of the reservoir.

3. Disconnect the low-oil level switch leads at their bullet connectors or remove the fill cap from the reservoir.

4. Remove the 3 reservoir mounting screws and remove the reservoir.

5. To install the reservoir, begin positioning the reservoir to the power head. Secure the reservoir with 3 screws. Apply Loctite 242 threadlocking adhesive to the threads of the mounting screws. Tighten the screws to 25 in.-lb. (2.8 N•m) on 135-200 hp and 105-140 Jet models or 150 in.-lb. (16.9 N•m) on 275 hp models.

6. Install the reservoir inlet and outlet lines. Securely clamp the oil lines using new tie-straps.

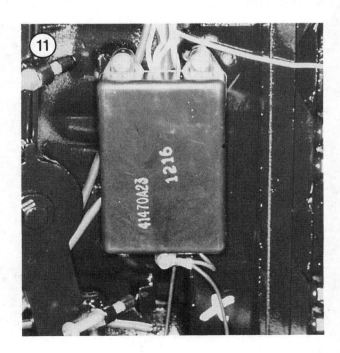

7. Reconnect the low-oil level switch leads or reinstall the fill cap to the reservoir.

8. Bleed the injection system as described in this chapter.

Oil pump removal/installation

Refer to Chapter Eight for oil pump drive gear removal/installation procedures. Refer to **Figure 9** for this procedure.

1. Disconnect the inlet and outlet oil lines from the injection pump. Cap or plug the lines to prevent leakage or contamination.

2. Disconnect the link rod from the pump control lever.

3. Remove the 2 screws securing the pump to the cylinder block, then remove the pump assembly.

4. *135-200 hp and 105-140 Jet models*—Grasp the driven gear shaft with needlenose pliers and pull the driven gear shaft and bearing assembly from the power head.

5A. *135-200 hp and 105-140 Jet models*—Remove the bushing and seal assembly (**Figure 12**) from the pump. If the worm gear is removed with the bushing, be sure to retrieve the thrust washer located between the pump and worm gear. Remove and discard the O-rings from the bushing. If the seal inside the bushing is defective, the bushing assembly must be replaced.

5B. *275 hp models*—If necessary, remove the pump adapter and driven gear from engine cylinder block. See **Figure 13**. Remove and discard the O-rings (2 and 5, **Figure 13**).

6. Inspect all components for excessive wear or other damage. Replace all suspect components. If the teeth on the driven gear are damaged, the pump drive gear on the crankshaft must be replaced. See Chapter Eight.

7. Install new O-rings prior to installing the pump. Lubricate the O-rings and all components with Quicksilver Needle Bearing Assembly Grease.

8. *135-200 hp and 105-140 Jet models*—Install the driven gear shaft and bearing assembly into the power head bore. Seat the assembly in the bore.

11

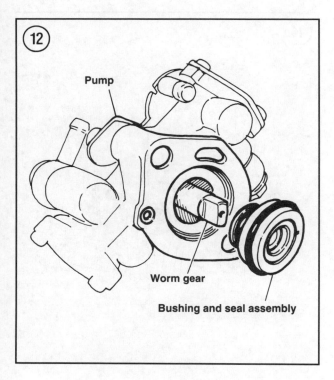

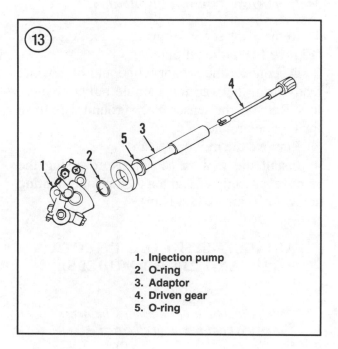

1. Injection pump
2. O-ring
3. Adaptor
4. Driven gear
5. O-ring

9A. *135-200 hp and 105-140 Jet models*—Install the worm gear into the pump assembly. Be certain the thrust washer is properly positioned at the bottom of the oil pump bore, between the pump body and worm gear.

9B. *275 hp models*—If removed, install the pump driven gear and adapter into the power head bore. Seat the assembly into power head bore.

10. Apply Loctite 271 threadlocking adhesive to the threads of the pump mounting screws. Install the pump and tighten the screws to 25 in.-lb. (2.8 N•m) on 135-200 hp and 105-140 Jet models or 60 in.-lb. (6.8 N•m) on 275 hp models.

11. Reconnect the oil inlet and outlet lines to the pump. Securely clamp the lines using new tie-straps.

12. Reconnect the link rod to the pump control arm. Refer to Chapter Five for oil pump adjustment and synchronization procedures.

13. Perform the oil pump bleeding procedure as described in this chapter.

Motion sensor removal/installation

1. Remove the screw securing the motion sensor (**Figure 14**) to the oil pump.
2. Disconnect the sensor white and blue/white leads from the warning module bullet connectors. Remove the sensor black ground wire from the engine ground.
3. Remove the motion sensor.
4. Install the motion sensor by reversing the removal procedure. Tighten the sensor mounting screw to 30 in.-lb. (3.4 N•m).

VARIABLE-RATIO OIL INJECTION (225 AND 250 HP MODELS)

CAUTION
While it should not normally be necessary, if a boat-mounted electric fuel sup-

ply pump is used, fuel pressure must not exceed 4 psi (27.6 kPa) at the engine fuel line connector. If necessary, install a fuel pressure regulator between the electric fuel pump and engine fuel line connector. Adjust the fuel pressure regulator to a maximum of 4 psi (27.6 kPa) fuel pressure. The electric fuel pump must also conform to all applicable Coast Guard safety standards for permanently installed fuel systems.

A variable-ratio crankshaft driven oil injection pump is used on these models. The oil pump injects oil into the fuel line just prior to the fuel pump on carbureted models or into the bottom of the vapor separator on EFI (electronic fuel injection) models. The oil pump delivers oil relative to throttle lever position and engine speed.

A linkage rod connects the oil pump control lever to the throttle linkage and varies the oil pump stroke according to throttle lever position. The fuel/oil ratio varies from approximately 100:1 at idle to approximately 50:1 at wide-open throttle.

Operation

A 3 gallon (11.4 L) remote oil tank supplies oil to the reservoir-mounted under the engine cowl (**Figure 15**). The reservoir oil capacity is approximately 50 fl. oz. (1.5 L) and is sufficient for approximately 30 minutes of wide-open throttle operation after the low oil level warning has sounded. Refer to **Figure 16** for the following description.

NOTE
*The vent valve for the engine-mounted reservoir (3, **Figure 16**) may be a 4 psi (27.6 kPa) or 2 psi (13.8 kPa) check valve. New models use the higher pressure valve to prevent air from being drawn into the system if the remote oil tank is mounted low in the bilge.*

The remote oil tank is pressurized by crankcase pressure through a one-way check valve, causing oil to flow from the remote tank to the engine-mounted reservoir. Should the oil line between the remote tank and engine-mounted reservoir become restricted, the 2 or 4 psi (13.8 or 27.6 kPa) check valve will unseat, allowing air to vent through the hose, allowing the injection pump to consume the oil in the engine-mounted reservoir.

The oil pickup tube in the remote tank is equipped with a filter screen to prevent dirt or other contamination from entering the injection system.

The injection pump is mounted to the engine block and is driven by a gear on the crankshaft. On carbureted models, the oil pump injects the oil into the fuel stream prior to the mechanical fuel pump. On EFI (electronic fuel injection) models, the oil is injected into the fuel at the bottom of the vapor separator assembly. A 2 psi (13.8 kPa) check valve is used at the injection point to prevent gasoline from being forced into the oil lines.

A low-oil level switch (4, **Figure 16**) attached to the engine-mounted reservoir activates the warning program in the ignition ECM (electronic control module), which triggers the warning horn and illuminates the warning panel if the oil level in the reservoir becomes low. If this occurs, the engine must be stopped immediately and both oil reservoirs refilled; otherwise, permanent power head damage will occur once the oil reservoir is empty.

The ECM warning program incorporates a self test feature that should sound the warning horn briefly each time the ignition switch is turned to the ON or RUN position. This indicates that the warning system is functioning. If the self test does not occur, or if the horn sounds after the ignition is switched ON, do not attempt to start the engine.

11

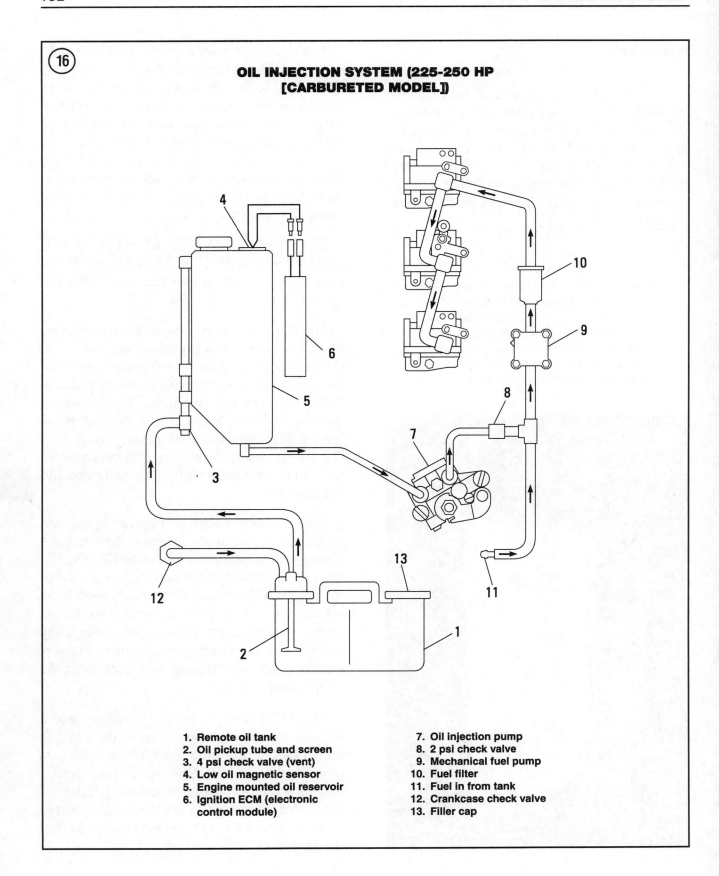

⑯

OIL INJECTION SYSTEM (225-250 HP [CARBURETED MODEL])

1. Remote oil tank
2. Oil pickup tube and screen
3. 4 psi check valve (vent)
4. Low oil magnetic sensor
5. Engine mounted oil reservoir
6. Ignition ECM (electronic control module)
7. Oil injection pump
8. 2 psi check valve
9. Mechanical fuel pump
10. Fuel filter
11. Fuel in from tank
12. Crankcase check valve
13. Filler cap

Warning System Troubleshooting

These models incorporate a warning panel (**Figure 17**) and a warning horn. When the ignition switch is first turned to the ON or RUN position, the warning horn will beep momentarily as part of the warning system's self-test. The warning horn and warning panel are controlled by the ignition ECM on carbureted models and by the ignition and fuel ECMs on EFI models. Refer to Chapter Three for full explanation of the warning system. These systems are intended to be diagnosed with the Quicksilver DDT (digital diagnostic terminal). If the following procedure does not determine the cause of the problem, a DDT must be obtained or the motor taken to a Mercury/Mariner dealership for diagnosis.

If a malfunction is suspected in the oil injection system (warning horn sounds and warning panel low oil level light illuminates), immediately stop the engine and check the oil levels in the remote oil tank and the engine-mounted reservoir. If the oil is low, fill the oil tank and reservoir with a recommended oil (Chapter Four).

CAUTION
*If an oil injection system malfunction is suspected, do not operate the outboard on straight gasoline. Operate the motor on a remote fuel tank containing a 50:1 fuel/oil mixture until the **Oil Pump Output Test** can be performed.*

If the reservoir oil level is low, but the remote tank is full, proceed as follows:

1. Check the O-rings or gaskets in the reservoir fill cap for cracking, deterioration or other damage. Replace the O-rings or gaskets as necessary. Make sure the fill caps are screwed tightly on the reservoir and remote tank. Air leakage at the remote tank will prevent the movement of oil from the tank to the reservoir. Leakage at the reservoir will result in oil spillage.

2. Check the oil line between the remote tank and reservoir for kinks, restrictions or leakage. Repair or replace the line as required.

3. Check the crankcase pressure line between the crankcase check valve and remote tank for kinks, restrictions or leakage. Make sure the crankcase one-way check valve is functioning properly.

4. Check the oil pickup tube and filter for restrictions. Clean or replace the tube or filter as necessary.

5. Check all oil lines for kinks, cracks, deterioration, leakage or other damage. Make sure all connections are tightly clamped.

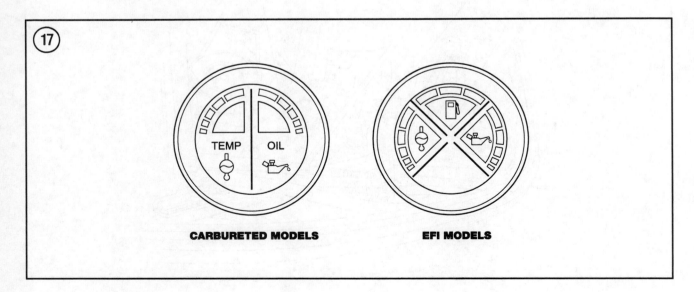

CARBURETED MODELS   EFI MODELS

Warning system does not self test

Refer to the back of the manual for wiring diagrams.

1. Turn the ignition switch to the ON or RUN position. Check the purple lead at the warning horn for battery voltage. The purple lead should show within 1 volt of battery voltage anytime the ignition switch is in the ON or RUN position. Repair or replace the lead as necessary.

2. With the ignition switch still in the ON or RUN position, ground the tan or tan/blue lead at the warning horn. The horn should sound. If not, replace the warning horn.

3. Check the tan or tan/blue lead from the ignition ECM to the warning horn for continuity. Repair or replace the lead as necessary.

4. If all tests to this point are satisfactory, the ignition ECM may be defective. Check all ECM connections and ground leads for secure attachment.

Warning system sounds continuously

If the warning horn sounds continuously, check if any of the warning panel lights are illuminated. If the engine temperature light is illuminated, either the ECT sensor has failed or the engine is overheating. Refer to Chapter Three for troubleshooting procedures. If no lights are illuminated, yet the horn is sounding continuously when the ignition switch is in the ON or RUN position, refer to the appropriate wiring diagram at the back of the manual, then proceed as follows:

1. Check the tan/blue lead from the ignition ECM to the warning horn for shorts to ground and damaged or missing insulation. Repair or replace the lead as necessary.

2. If the tan/blue lead is not shorted to ground or if it does not have damaged or missing insulation, the ignition ECM may be defective. Check all ECM connections and ground leads for secure attachment.

Oil level switch tests

1. Verify that the engine-mounted oil reservoir is full. Then, disconnect the 2 oil level switch blue leads at the warning module bullet connectors.

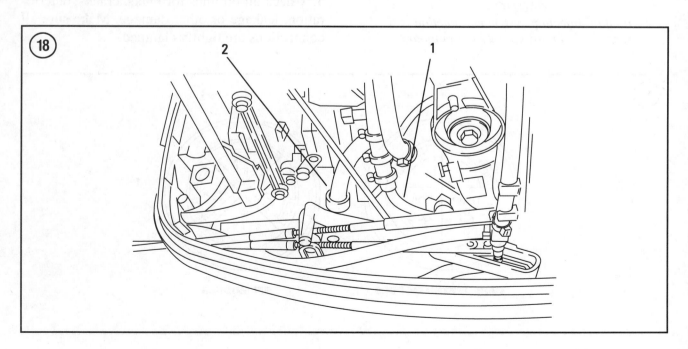

2. Connect an ohmmeter, calibrated on an appropriate scale to check continuity, between the 2 oil level switch blue wires. The meter should indicate no continuity when the oil tank is full. If continuity is noted, the oil level switch is defective and must be replaced.

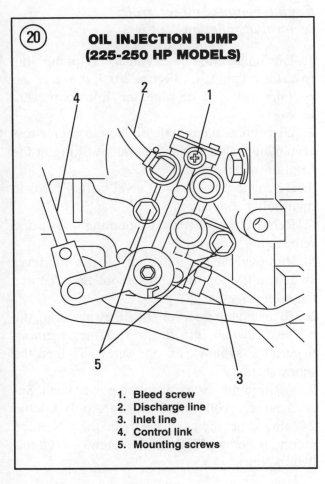

OIL INJECTION PUMP (225-250 HP MODELS)

1. Bleed screw
2. Discharge line
3. Inlet line
4. Control link
5. Mounting screws

Oil Pump Output Test

CAUTION
*Do not run the engine without an adequate water supply and do not exceed 3000 rpm without an adequate load. Refer to **Safety Precautions** in Chapter Three or Chapter Five.*

Obtain a graduated container, capable of accurately measuring up to 50 cc, before continuing.

1. Connect a remote fuel tank containing a 50:1 fuel/oil mixture to the engine.

2. Disconnect the oil pump discharge (1, **Figure 18**) line from the check valve fitting below the Y-fitting which is just below the fuel pump on carbureted models or at the bottom of the vapor separator (**Figure 19**, typical) on EFI (electronic fuel injection) models. Securely cap or plug the check valve fitting to prevent leakage.

3. Connect an accurate shop tachometer to the engine following its manufacturer's instructions.

4. Insert the disconnected end of the oil pump discharge line into the graduated container.

5. Start the outboard motor and run at 1500 rpm for exactly 3 minutes.

NOTE
Injection pump output specifications are based on tests performed at 70° F (21° C). If ambient temperature is more or less, actual pump output may vary from that specified.

6. Stop the engine and check the quantity of oil in the graduated container. Oil pump output should be 6.1-7.5 cc.

7. If injection pump output is less than specified, replace the pump assembly as described in this chapter.

8. Empty the container. Disconnect the linkage rod from the injection pump control lever. See **Figure 20**. Rotate the control lever to the wide-open throttle position, then repeat Steps 4 and 5.

9. Stop the engine and again check the quantity of oil in the graduated container. Oil pump output should now be 28.4-34.7 cc.

11

10. If injection pump output is less than specified, replace the pump assembly as described in this chapter.

11. Reconnect the pump discharge line to the check valve fitting. Secure the connection with a new tie-strap. Then, bleed the injection system as described in this chapter.

12. Reconnect the oil pump link rod to the control arm. Adjust the link rod as specified in Chapter Five.

Oil Injection System Service

Oil pump synchronization

Refer to Chapter Five for throttle linkage to oil pump linkage adjustment and synchronization procedures.

Bleeding oil pump

If the pump has been removed, any of the lines replaced or if air is present in the oil pump lines, proceed as follows to bleed air from the oil injection pump and lines:

1. Place a shop towel beneath the oil pump.

2. Loosen the oil pump bleed screw 3-4 turns (1, **Figure 20**).

3. Allow oil to flow from the bleed screw until no air bubbles are noted in the inlet hose.

4. Tighten the bleed screw to 25 in.-lb. (2.8 N•m).

> *CAUTION*
> *Do not run the engine without an adequate water supply and do not exceed 3000 rpm without an adequate load. Refer to **Safety Precautions** in Chapter Three or Chapter Five.*

5. If air is present in the pump discharge line, connect a remote tank containing a 50:1 fuel/oil mixture to the engine. Start the engine and run at idle until no air bubbles are noted in the discharge hose. Disconnect the pump link rod and rotate

the pump arm to the full output position to speed the bleeding process.

6. *Carbureted models*—If necessary, gently pinch the fuel pump inlet hose (2, **Figure 18**) between the injection pump Y-fitting and remote fuel tank connector, causing the fuel pump to create a slight vacuum in the hose. This will quicken the purging process.

7. Continue running the outboard until all air is purged, then stop the engine and reconnect the linkage rod to the control lever (if disconnected).

Ignition ECM (electronic control module) removal/installation

Refer to Chapter Seven for ignition ECM removal/installation procedures.

Engine-mounted oil reservoir removal/installation

1. Disconnect the reservoir-to-oil pump line from the oil pump (3, **Figure 20**). If the reservoir contains oil, cap or plug the line to prevent leakage.

2. Disconnect the remote oil tank to engine reservoir input line at the vent valve fitting at the front of the reservoir.

3. Disconnect the low-oil level switch leads at their bullet connectors.

4. Remove the 3 reservoir mounting screws and remove the reservoir.

5. Remove the screw securing the oil level switch to the top of the reservoir, then remove the oil level switch.

6. To install the reservoir, begin by installing the oil level switch into the top of the reservoir. Secure the switch with one screw. Tighten the screw securely.

7. Position the reservoir to the power head. Secure the reservoir with 3 screws. Apply Loctite 242 threadlocking adhesive to the threads of the mounting screws. Tighten the screws to 168 in.-lb. (19 N•m).

8. Install the reservoir inlet and outlet lines. Securely clamp the oil lines using new tie-straps.

9. Reconnect the low-oil level switch leads or reinstall the fill cap to the reservoir.

10. Bleed the injection system as described in this chapter.

Oil pump removal/installation

Refer to Chapter Eight for oil pump drive gear removal/installation procedures. Refer to **Figure 20** for this procedure.

1. Disconnect the inlet and outlet oil lines from the injection pump. Cap or plug the lines to prevent leakage or contamination.

2. Disconnect the link rod from the pump control lever.

3. Remove the 2 screws securing the pump to the cylinder block, then remove the pump assembly. Grasp the driven gear shaft with needlenose pliers and pull the driven gear and bearing assembly from the power head. Make sure the thrust bushing (6, **Figure 21**) is present in the end of the driven gear.

4. Inspect all components for excessive wear or other damage. Replace all suspect parts. If the teeth on the driven gear are damaged, the pump drive gear on the crankshaft must be replaced. See Chapter Eight.

5. Install new O-rings prior to installing the pump. Lubricate the O-rings and all components with Quicksilver Needle Bearing Assembly Grease.

6. Assemble the driven gear, bearing and thrust washer as shown in **Figure 21**. Use Quicksilver Needle Bearing Assembly Grease to keep the thrust bushing (6, **Figure 21**) in place. Insert the gear and bearing assembly into the power head and seat it in its bore.

7. Apply Loctite 271 threadlocking adhesive to the threads of the pump mounting screws. Install the pump, being careful to align the shaft and coupler. Tighten the screws to 55 in.-lb. (6.2 N·m).

11

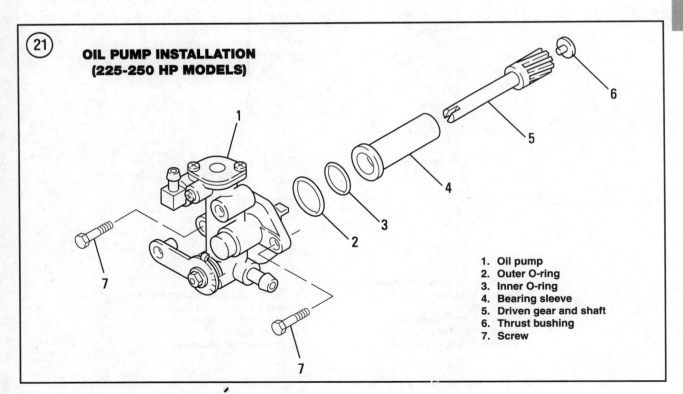

OIL PUMP INSTALLATION (225-250 HP MODELS)

1. Oil pump
2. Outer O-ring
3. Inner O-ring
4. Bearing sleeve
5. Driven gear and shaft
6. Thrust bushing
7. Screw

8. Reconnect the oil inlet and outlet lines to the pump. Securely clamp the lines using new tie-straps.

9. Reconnect the link rod to the pump control arm. Refer to Chapter Five for oil pump adjustment and synchronization procedures.

10. Perform the oil pump bleeding procedure as described in this chapter.

VARIABLE-RATIO ELECTRONICALLY CONTROLLED OIL INJECTION (200 DFI MODELS)

CAUTION
While it should not normally be necessary, if a boat-mounted electric fuel supply pump is used, fuel pressure must not exceed 4 psi (27.6 kPa) at the engine fuel

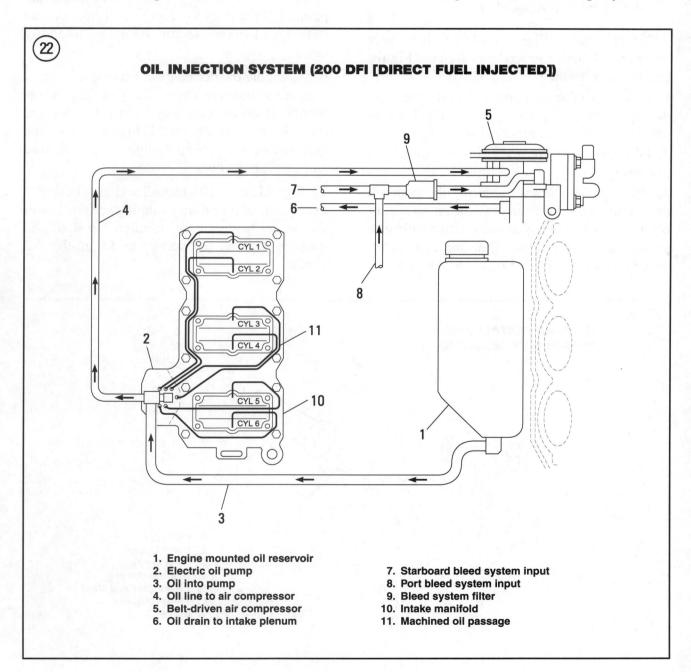

OIL INJECTION SYSTEM (200 DFI [DIRECT FUEL INJECTED])

1. Engine mounted oil reservoir
2. Electric oil pump
3. Oil into pump
4. Oil line to air compressor
5. Belt-driven air compressor
6. Oil drain to intake plenum
7. Starboard bleed system input
8. Port bleed system input
9. Bleed system filter
10. Intake manifold
11. Machined oil passage

line connector. If necessary, install a fuel pressure regulator between the electric fuel pump and engine fuel line connector. Adjust the fuel pressure regulator to a maximum of 4 psi (27.6 kPa) fuel pressure. The electric fuel pump must also conform to all applicable Coast Guard safety standards for permanently installed fuel systems.

Operation

The 200 DFI uses the same 3 gal. (11.4 L) remote oil tank, engine-mounted reservoir (and low oil level switch), 4 psi check valve (vent) and crankcase check valve as the 225-250 hp models described in the previous section. Oil travels from the remote tank to the engine-mounted reservoir in the exact same manner.

The 200 DFI oil injection system differs in how the oil is delivered to the engine. Oil is injected by an ECM (electronic control module) controlled, electric oil pump that is mounted directly to the intake manifold. Oil is not mixed with the fuel. Straight oil flows from the oil pump directly into machined passages in the intake manifold and is discharged in front of each reed block. A single external line delivers oil to the belt-driven air compressor. See **Figure 22**.

The bleed system returns any excess oil from each crankcase to the air compressor (5, **Figure 22**). A filter prior to the air compressor prevents any contaminates from entering the compressor.

The ECM constantly changes the output of the pump based on engine operating conditions. While fuel and oil are not mixed, the ratio of fuel to oil consumed varies from 300:1 at idle, to 60:1 at wide-open throttle. The ECM also pulses the pump on each start up to purge any air from the compressor line and intake passageways.

The ECM monitors oil pump operation and the engine-mounted reservoir oil level at all times. If the ECM detects that the oil pump is malfunctioning or is not receiving oil from the engine-mounted reservoir, the ECM will illuminate the oil and check engine lights on the warning panel, sound the warning horn and reduce (and limit) engine speed to 3000 rpm. The engine should be stopped immediately and the cause of the warning located and repaired. Continued operation without oil flow will cause permanent power head damage.

If the ECM detects that the engine-mounted oil tank level is low, the ECM will illuminate the warning panel oil light (**Figure 23**) and sound 4 short beeps from the warning horn every 2 minutes. When this occurs, the engine should be stopped and both oil tanks refilled as soon as possible.

During the first 90 minutes of new engine operation, the ECM effectively double oils the engine to assist with break-in. After 90 minutes of run time (per the ECM internal clock), oil pump operation returns to normal.

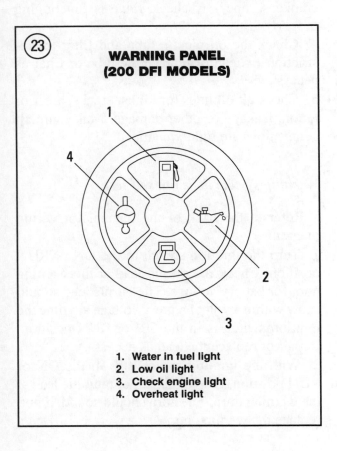

(23)

WARNING PANEL (200 DFI MODELS)

1. Water in fuel light
2. Low oil light
3. Check engine light
4. Overheat light

11

Warning System Troubleshooting

These models incorporate a warning panel (**Figure 23**) and a warning horn. When the ignition switch is first turned to the ON or RUN position, the warning horn will beep momentarily as part of the warning system's self-test. The warning horn and warning panel are controlled by the ECM (electronic control module). Refer to Chapter Three under ignition system and fuel system troubleshooting for a full explanation of the warning system. This system is intended to be diagnosed with the Quicksilver DDT (digital diagnostic terminal). If the following procedures do not determine the cause of the problem, a DDT must be obtained or the motor will have to be taken to a Mercury/Mariner dealership for diagnosis.

If a malfunction is detected in the oil injection system, there are 2 possible warnings.

1. *Low oil level*—Warning horn sounds and warning panel low oil level light illuminates. Stop the engine as soon as possible and check the oil levels in the remote oil tank and the engine-mounted reservoir. If the oil level is low, fill the oil tank and reservoir with the recommended oil (Chapter Four). If the warning continues, the engine may be operated, but the problem should be diagnosed as soon as possible.

2. *No oil flow*—Warning horn sounds and the check engine *and* low oil level lights illuminate. Immediately stop the engine and check the oil levels in the remote oil tank and the engine-mounted reservoir. If the oil is low, fill the oil tank and reservoir with a recommended oil (Chapter Four). If the warning continues, do *not* operate the outboard, as this warning means that the electric pump is not pumping oil. Serious engine damage will result from continued operation.

> *CAUTION*
> *If an oil injection system malfunction is suspected, do not operate the outboard. This engine cannot be run on a remote*

tank with a 50:1 fuel/oil mix. The DFI system does not pass any fuel through the crankcase. The oil can only be injected into the crankcase through the electric oil pump system.

If the reservoir oil level is low, but the remote tank is full, proceed as follows:

1. Check the O-rings or gaskets in the reservoir fill cap for cracking, deterioration or other damage. Replace the O-rings or gaskets as necessary. Make sure the fill caps are screwed tightly on the reservoir and remote tank. Air leakage at the remote tank will prevent the movement of oil from the tank to the reservoir. Leakage at the reservoir will result in oil spillage.

2. Check the oil line between the remote tank and reservoir for kinks, restrictions or leakage. Repair or replace the line as required.

3. Check the crankcase pressure line between the crankcase check valve and remote tank for kinks, restrictions or leakage. Make sure the crankcase one-way check valve is functioning properly.

4. Check the oil pickup tube and filter for restrictions. Clean or replace the tube or filter as necessary.

5. Check all oil lines for kinks, cracks, deterioration, leakage or other damage. Make sure all connections are tightly clamped.

Warning system does not self test

Refer to the back of the manual for wiring diagrams.

1. Turn the ignition switch to the ON or RUN position. Check the purple lead at the warning horn for battery voltage. The purple lead should show within 1 volt of battery voltage anytime the ignition switch is in the ON or RUN position. Repair or replace the lead as necessary.

2. With the ignition switch still in the ON or RUN position, ground the tan or tan/blue lead at the warning horn. The horn should sound, if not, replace the warning horn.

3. Check the tan or tan/blue lead from the ECM to the warning horn for continuity. Repair or replace the lead as necessary.

4. If all tests to this point are satisfactory, the ECM may be defective. Check all ECM connections and ground leads for secure attachment.

Warning system sounds continuously

If the warning horn sounds continuously, check if any of the warning panel lights are illuminated. If the engine temperature light is illuminated, either the ECT sensor has failed or the engine is overheating. Refer to Chapter Three for troubleshooting procedures. If no lights are illuminated, yet the horn is sounding continuously when the ignition switch is in the ON or RUN position, refer to the appropriate wiring diagram at the back of the book, then proceed as follows:

1. Check the tan/blue lead from the ignition ECM to the warning horn for shorts to ground and damaged or missing insulation. Repair or replace the lead as necessary.

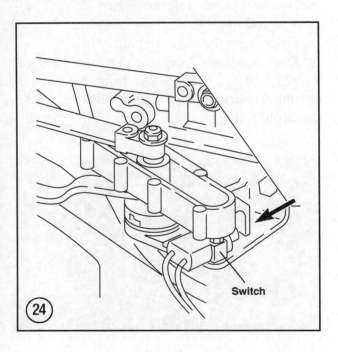

(24)

Switch

2. If the tan/blue lead is not shorted to ground or have damaged or missing insulation, the ECM may be defective. Check all ECM connections and ground leads for secure attachment.

Oil level switch tests

1. Verify that the engine-mounted oil reservoir is full. Then, disconnect the 2 oil level switch blue leads at the warning module bullet connectors.

2. Connect an ohmmeter, calibrated on an appropriate scale to check continuity between the 2 oil level switch blue wires. The meter should indicate no continuity when the oil tank is full. If continuity is noted, the oil level switch is defective and must be replaced.

Oil Pump Purging (Bleeding) Procedure

If the pump has been removed, any of the lines replaced, or if air is present in the oil pump lines, proceed as follows to bleed air from the electric oil injection pump and lines:

1. Make sure that the remote oil tank and engine-mounted reservoir are filled with the recommended oil (Chapter Four).

2. Put the remote control box in the neutral position.

3. Turn the ignition switch to the ON or RUN position.

4. Within 10 seconds, quickly activate the shift interrupt switch 5 times. This is done by pushing the shift linkage against the switch and releasing the linkage. See **Figure 24**. The pump should start clicking and oil movement will be visible in the clear supply hose.

> *NOTE*
> *The purging process can take up to 1 minute.*

5. When the pump ceases clicking, turn the ignition switch to the OFF position.

11

6. If air is still present, repeat Steps 3-5.

CAUTION
*Do not run the engine without an adequate water supply and do not exceed 3000 rpm without an adequate load. Refer to **Safety Precautions** in Chapter Three or Chapter Five.*

7. To purge the last bit of air from the engine-mounted reservoir, loosen the reservoir cap slightly and run the engine at idle speed until oil begins to overflow the reservoir. Then, tighten the cap firmly.

Oil Injection System Service

If the oil pump machined oil distribution lines in the intake manifold are suspected of being blocked or restricted, refer to Chapter Six for intake manifold removal/installation procedures.

ECM removal/installation

ECM (electronic control module) removal/installation is covered in Chapter Six.

Engine-mounted reservoir removal/installation

1. Disconnect the reservoir-to-oil pump line from the electric oil pump. If the reservoir contains oil, cap or plug the line to prevent leakage.
2. Disconnect the remote oil tank-to-engine reservoir input line from the vent valve fitting at the front of the reservoir.
3. Disconnect the low-oil level switch leads at their bullet connectors.
4. Remove the 3 reservoir mounting screws. Pull the fuel cooler slightly away from the engine and remove the reservoir.
5. Remove the screw securing the oil level switch to the top of the reservoir, then remove the oil level switch.

6. To install the reservoir, begin by installing the oil level switch into the top of the reservoir. Secure the switch with one screw. Tighten the screw securely.
7. Position the reservoir to the power head and behind the fuel cooler. Secure the reservoir with 3 screws. Apply Loctite 242 threadlocking adhesive to the threads of the mounting screws. Tighten the screws to 168 in.-lb. (19 N•m).
8. Install the reservoir inlet and outlet lines. Securely clamp the oil lines using new tie-straps.
9. Reconnect the low-oil level switch leads or reinstall the fill cap to the reservoir.
10. Bleed the injection system as described in this chapter.

Electric oil pump removal/installation

If the machined oil distribution lines in the intake manifold are suspected of being blocked or restricted, refer to Chapter Six and remove the oil pump and intake manifold as an assembly.

The electric oil pump is located on the starboard side of the engine, beneath the starter motor. See **Figure 25**. To remove and install the electric fuel pump, refer to **Figure 25** and proceed as follows:
1. Disconnect the negative battery cable.
2. Disconnect and plug (or cap) the clear oil supply line (A, **Figure 25**) from the engine-mounted reservoir to the electric oil pump intake manifold fitting.

3. Disconnect the oil pump 4-pin electrical connector (B, **Figure 25**).

4. Remove the 2 screws securing the oil pump bracket to the power head.

5. Remove the long screw (C, **Figure 25**) securing the bracket and oil pump to the intake manifold and remove the bracket.

6. Remove the short screw securing the oil pump to the intake manifold. Remove the oil pump.

7. Clean all gasket material from the oil pump and intake manifold mating surfaces. Be careful not to scratch the mating surfaces. Do NOT allow any debris to fall into the oil passages of the intake manifold and oil pump.

8. To install the oil pump, place the oil pump against the intake manifold using a new gasket. Install the lower screw and tighten it hand tight.

9. Position the oil pump bracket and secure it to the oil pump and intake manifold with the long screw. Tighten the long screw hand tight.

10. Secure the bracket to the power head with 2 screws. Tighten the screws to 16.5 ft.-lb. (22.5 N•m). Then, tighten the oil pump to intake manifold screws (long and short) to 16.5 ft.-lb. (22.5 N•m).

11. Reconnect the clear oil supply line to the intake manifold fitting. Secure the connection with a new tie-strap.

12. Reconnect the oil pump 4-pin electrical connector to the oil pump.

13. Reconnect the negative battery cable and purge the oil system as described in this section.

11

Table 1 OIL INJECTION SYSTEM SPECIFICATIONS

	Fl. oz. (L)	Run time
Oil tank capacity		
75-90 hp and 65 Jet (1994-1995)	128 (3.8 L)	6 hours
75-90 hp and 65 Jet (1996-1997)	102 (3.2)	6 hours
100-125 hp and 80 Jet (1994-1995)	179 (5.3 L)	6 hours
100-125 hp and 80 Jet (1996-1997)	164 (4.9 L)	6 hours
Remote mounted main tank	3 gal. (11.4)	
135-150 hp and 105 Jet	8.7 hours	
175-200 hp and 140 Jet	6.6 hours	
200 DFI (direct fuel injection)	not available	
225-250 hp	6.5 hours	
275 hp	6.0 hours	
Reserve capacity	**Fl. oz. (L)**	**Run time**
75-90 hp and 65 Jet	32 (0.95)	50 minutes
100-125 hp and 80 Jet	32 (0.95)	60 minutes
150-200 hp and 105-140 Jet	30 (0.89)	30-35 minutes
200 DFI (direct fuel injection)	50 (1.5)	50 minutes
225-250 hp	50 (1.5)	30 minutes
275 hp	88 (2.6)	60 minutes

Table 2 TORQUE VALUES

Fastener	in.-lbs.	ft.-lbs.	N•m
Oil pump to power head			
75-125 hp and 65-80 Jet	60	–	6.8
135-200 hp and 105-140 Jet	25	–	2.8
200 DFI (direct fuel injection)	–	16.5	22.5
225-250 hp	55	–	6.2
275 hp	60	–	6.8
Oil tank			
75-125 hp and 65-80 Jet			
Lower mount	–	15	20.5
Upper mount (1994-1995)	50	–	5.6
Upper mount (1996-1997)	65	–	7.3
135-200 hp/105-140 Jet	25	–	2.8
200 DFI (direct fuel injection)	168	14	19
225-250 hp	168	14	19
275 hp	150	12.5	16.9

Table 3 STANDARD TORQUE VALUES (U.S. STANDARD FASTENERS)

Screw or nut size	in.-lbs.	ft.-lbs.	N•m
6-32	9	–	1.0
8-32	20	–	2.3
10-24	30	–	3.4
10-32	35	–	4.0
12-24	45	–	5.1
1/4-20	70	6	7.9
1/4-28	84	7	9.5
5/16-18	160	13	18.1
5/16-24	168	14	19.0
3/8-16	270	23	30.5
3/8-24	300	25	33.9
7/16-14	–	36	48.8
7/16-20	–	40	54.2
1/2-13	–	50	67.8
1/2-20	–	60	81.3

Table 4 STANDARD TORQUE VALUES (METRIC FASTENERS)

Screw or nut size	in.-lbs.	ft.-lbs.	N•m
M5	36	–	4.1
M6	70	6	8.1
M8	156	13	17.6
M10	312	26	35.3
M12	–	35	47.5
M14	–	60	81.3

Chapter Twelve

Remote Control

The 1994-1997 model year Mercury/Mariner outboard motors primarily use the Quicksilver Commander 2000 or Commander 3000 series remote control boxes. Both the 2000 and 3000 series control boxes come in side-mount and flush-mount configurations.

These control boxes and engines use standard Quicksilver Mercury Marine style control cables. Mercury Marine control cables do not require any adjustments in the control box, only at the engine.

Pre-wired control boxes will include the ignition switch, primer switch, emergency lanyard switch and the trim/tilt switch (on models so equipped). The main harness connector on these pre-wired control boxes is the standard Mercury Marine 8-pin connector. There are typically additional connectors at both ends of the main engine harness for accessory gauges and warning systems. Control box wiring diagrams are located in Chapter Fourteen.

This section primarily covers throttle and shift cable removal, installation and adjustment at the engine.

Control Box Service

When servicing Mercury control boxes, lubricate all internal friction points with Quicksilver 2-4-C Multi-Lube grease or equivalent. Apply Loctite 242 threadlocking adhesive to all internal threaded fasteners. Refer to **Table 1** for torque specifications on Commander 3000 series control boxes. All fasteners on Commander 2000 series control boxes should be tightened securely.

Refer to **Figure 1** for an exploded view of the Commander 3000 series control box internal components and **Figure 2** for an exploded view of the Commander 2000 series control box internal components.

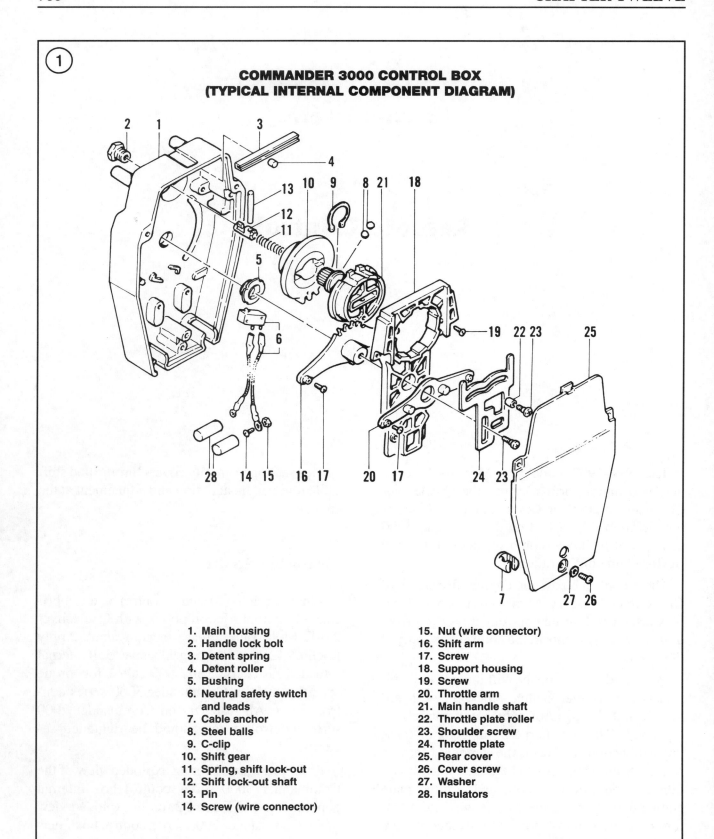

COMMANDER 3000 CONTROL BOX
(TYPICAL INTERNAL COMPONENT DIAGRAM)

1. Main housing
2. Handle lock bolt
3. Detent spring
4. Detent roller
5. Bushing
6. Neutral safety switch
   and leads
7. Cable anchor
8. Steel balls
9. C-clip
10. Shift gear
11. Spring, shift lock-out
12. Shift lock-out shaft
13. Pin
14. Screw (wire connector)
15. Nut (wire connector)
16. Shift arm
17. Screw
18. Support housing
19. Screw
20. Throttle arm
21. Main handle shaft
22. Throttle plate roller
23. Shoulder screw
24. Throttle plate
25. Rear cover
26. Cover screw
27. Washer
28. Insulators

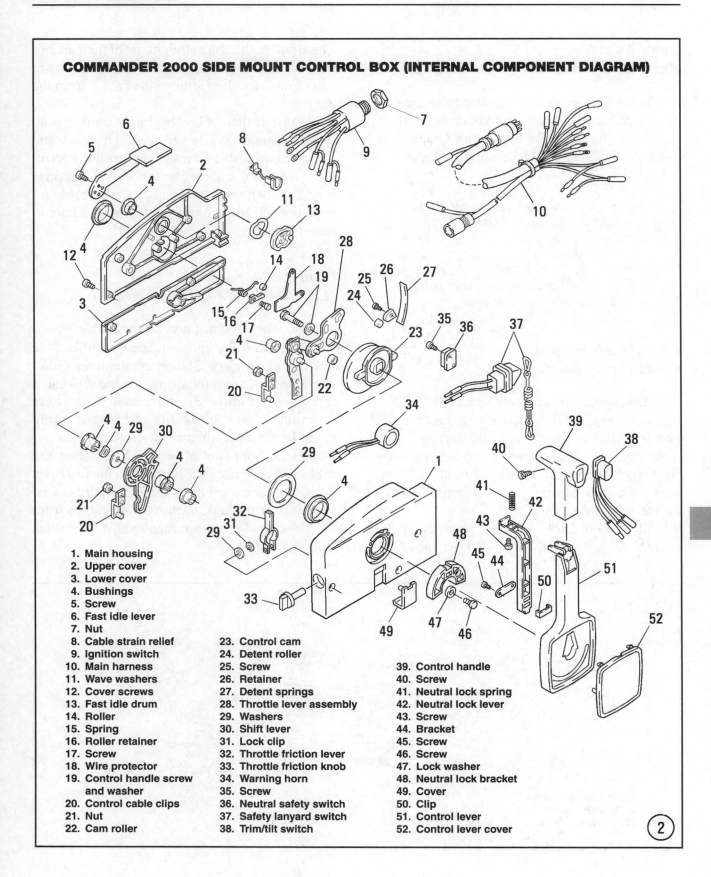

COMMANDER 2000 SIDE MOUNT CONTROL BOX (INTERNAL COMPONENT DIAGRAM)

1. Main housing
2. Upper cover
3. Lower cover
4. Bushings
5. Screw
6. Fast idle lever
7. Nut
8. Cable strain relief
9. Ignition switch
10. Main harness
11. Wave washers
12. Cover screws
13. Fast idle drum
14. Roller
15. Spring
16. Roller retainer
17. Screw
18. Wire protector
19. Control handle screw and washer
20. Control cable clips
21. Nut
22. Cam roller

23. Control cam
24. Detent roller
25. Screw
26. Retainer
27. Detent springs
28. Throttle lever assembly
29. Washers
30. Shift lever
31. Lock clip
32. Throttle friction lever
33. Throttle friction knob
34. Warning horn
35. Screw
36. Neutral safety switch
37. Safety lanyard switch
38. Trim/tilt switch

39. Control handle
40. Screw
41. Neutral lock spring
42. Neutral lock lever
43. Screw
44. Bracket
45. Screw
46. Screw
47. Lock washer
48. Neutral lock bracket
49. Cover
50. Clip
51. Control lever
52. Control lever cover

12

②

Control Cable
Removal/Installation/Adjustment (Engine)

The control cable moveable casing guides, moveable barrel threads and attachment points should be liberally lubricated with Quicksilver 2-4-C Multi-Lube grease before installation.

NOTE
The control cables must be installed into the control box before installation and adjustment at the engine.

CAUTION
Always install and adjust the shift cable first and the throttle cable last.

Control cable removal
(75-125 hp, 65 and 80 Jet)

1. Disconnect the negative battery cable. Disconnect and ground the spark plug leads to the power head to prevent accidental starting.
2. Remove the elastic stop nut and nylon washer from each control arm attachment stud. Then, pull the cables' casing guides from the control arm attachment studs.
3. Unlock both cables' barrels by rotating the cable retainer plate to the full open position.

Then, pull both cables straight out of their anchor pockets. Remove both cables from the lower cowl grommet, then remove the cables from the engine.
4. To install the cables, begin by routing both cables through the lower cowl grommet and position each cable near the appropriate control arm stud and cable anchor barrel retainer bracket. Then refer to the appropriate cable installation/adjustment procedure, located later in this section.

Control cable removal
(135-200 hp and 105-140 Jet models)

1. Disconnect the negative battery cable.
2. Pull out on the spring-loaded throttle cable retainer (1, **Figure 3**) and rotate it in either direction. Lift up on the spring-loaded shift cable retainer (2, **Figure 3**) and rotate it in either direction. Then, pull or lift each cable casing guide from its control arm attachment stud.
3. Unlock both cables' barrels by rotating the cable retainer plate (3, **Figure 3**) to the full open position. Then, pull both cables straight out of their anchor pockets. Remove both cables from the lower cowl grommet, then remove the cables from the engine.

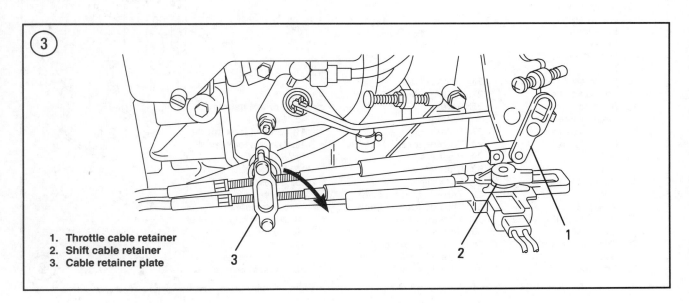

③
1. **Throttle cable retainer**
2. **Shift cable retainer**
3. **Cable retainer plate**

4. To install the cables, begin by routing both cables through the lower cowl grommet and position each cable near the appropriate control arm pin and cable anchor barrel retainer bracket. Then refer to the appropriate cable installation/adjustment procedure, located later in this section.

Control cable removal
(200 DFI and 225-250 hp models)

Refer to **Figure 4** for cable and hose routing through the lower cowl split grommet. The grommet is molded in 2 pieces (upper and lower) that are secured together with 2 screws. It is important that each cable and hose fits in its appropriate molded recess or fuel and oil flow

may be restricted. Also, control cable movement may be restricted.

1. Disconnect the negative battery cable.
2. Remove the elastic stop nut and nylon washer (3, **Figure 5**) from each control arm attachment stud. Then pull the cables' casing guides (1 and 2, **Figure 5**) from the control arm attachment studs.

3. Unlock both cable's barrels by rotating the cable retainer plate (4, **Figure 5**) to the full open position. Then, pull both cables straight out of their anchor pockets. Remove both cables from the lower cowl split grommet by removing the 2 grommet screws, then remove the cables from the engine.

4. To install the cables, begin by routing both cables through the lower cowl grommet and position each cable near the appropriate control arm pin and cable anchor barrel retainer bracket. Then, refer to the appropriate cable installation/adjustment procedure, located later in this section. Refer to **Figure 4** for cable and hose routing through the lower cowl split grommet.

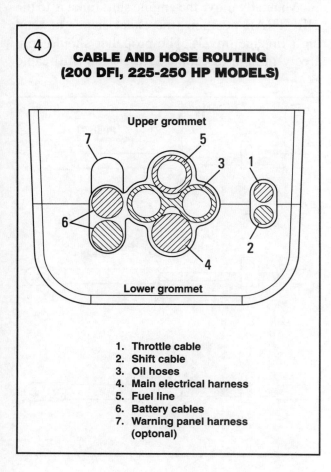

CABLE AND HOSE ROUTING (200 DFI, 225-250 HP MODELS)

1. Throttle cable
2. Shift cable
3. Oil hoses
4. Main electrical harness
5. Fuel line
6. Battery cables
7. Warning panel harness (optonal)

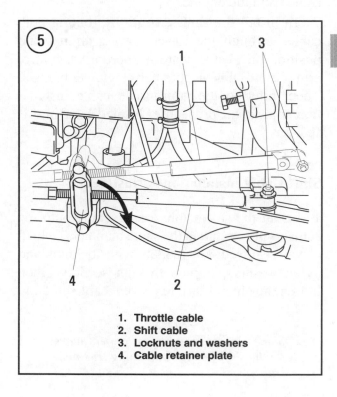

1. Throttle cable
2. Shift cable
3. Locknuts and washers
4. Cable retainer plate

12

Control cable removal (275 hp models)

1. Disconnect the negative battery cable.

2. Remove the elastic stop nut and upper wave washer from the shift cable control arm stud. Lift the shift cable casing guide from the stud and remove the lower wave washer.

3. Remove the through-bolt, flat washer and locknut securing the shift cable barrel to the engine shift bracket.

4. Remove the clamp securing the shift cable to the port cowl bracket. Slide the shift cable casing guide out of the shift cable support bracket and pull the cable sleeve through the slot in the support bracket. Then, remove the shift cable from the engine.

5. Pull out on the spring-loaded throttle cable retainer (1, **Figure 3**, similar) and rotate it in either direction. Then, pull the throttle cable casing guide from the control arm pin.

6. Remove the through-bolt, flat washer and locknut securing the throttle cable barrel to the throttle cable bracket. Then, remove the shift cable from the engine.

7. To install the cables, begin by routing both cables through the lower cowl grommet and position each cable near the appropriate control arm pin and cable anchor barrel retainer bracket. Then, refer to the appropriate cable installation/adjustment procedure, located later in this section.

Shift Cable Installation/Adjustment

1. Install the shift cable casing guide onto the actuator pin or stud in the same manner as which it was removed. On models with locknuts and nylon washers, tighten the nut securely, then loosen the nut 1/4 turn to prevent cable binding.

NOTE
Some models may have a cast-in mark on the shift linkage indicating true neutral.

2. Shift the remote control into the NEUTRAL position. Center the free play in the shift cable by moving the casing guide back and forth and positioning it in the middle of its free play.

   a. Push in on the casing guide as shown in A, **Figure 6** and make a mark on the cable sleeve as shown.

   b. Pull out on the casing guide as shown in B, **Figure 6** and make a mark on the cable sleeve as shown.

   c. Make a third mark on the cable sleeve in the exact middle of the *A* and *B* marks as shown in C, **Figure 6**. The third mark is true neutral of the remote control system.

NOTE
Rotate the propeller when shifting the gearcase in Step 3 to prevent shift linkage and gearcase damage.

3. Manually move the engine shift linkage to the NEUTRAL position (the exact center of total shift linkage travel). The propeller should spin freely in both directions. Adjust the shift cable

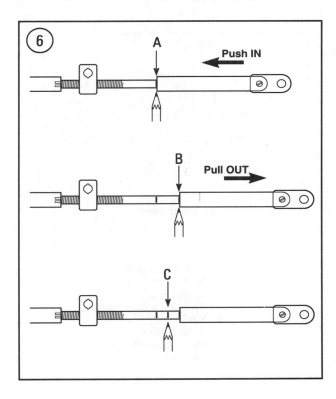

barrel to fit into its anchor when the center mark (C, **Figure 6**) is aligned with the casing guide or slightly pre-loaded toward the reverse gear.

4. Install the shift cable barrel into its anchor in the same manner as it was removed.

5. Shift the remote control into FORWARD gear while rotating the propeller and verify gear engagement in forward. Return the remote control to NEUTRAL and make sure the propeller spins freely in each direction. Shift the control box into REVERSE gear while rotating the propeller and make sure the gear engages in reverse. Adjust the shift cable barrel as necessary if gear engagements are not satisfactory.

NOTE
The best shift verification is done with the boat in the water. Both FORWARD and REVERSE gear engagements should each require the same amount of control box travel from the neutral detent. Both gears should fully engage before any throttle cable movement occurs. If one gear requires more control handle travel than the other gear, the shift cable barrel must be adjusted to take gear engagement from the gear that engages soon and give the gear engagement to the gear that engages late.

Throttle Cable Installation/Adjustment (60-275 hp and 65-140 Jet Models)

Refer to Chapter Five for identification of the idle stop screw. The shift cable must be installed and properly adjusted before attempting throttle cable installation and adjustment.

1. Install the throttle cable casing guide onto the actuator pin or stud in the same manner as which it was removed. On models with locknuts and nylon washers, tighten the nut securely, then loosen the nut 1/4 turn to prevent cable binding.

2. Shift the remote control into the NEUTRAL position. Hold the throttle linkage on the engine against the idle stop screw. Adjust the throttle cable barrel to provide a slight preload of the throttle lever against the idle stop screw. This slight preload will ensure that the throttle returns to the idle stop without binding the control system.

3. Install the throttle cable barrel in the same manner as which it was removed.

4. Shift the remote control into the FORWARD gear, full throttle position while rotating the propeller to ensure full gear engagement. Return the remote control to the NEUTRAL position. 5. Insert a thin piece of paper between the power head and the idle stop screw. Throttle cable preload is correct when the paper can be removed without tearing, but a noticeable drag can be felt. Adjust the throttle cable barrel and repeat Steps 4 and 5 as necessary.

NOTE
The throttle cable must positively return the throttle linkage and position the idle stop screw against the idle stop (power head).

6. Verify that the throttle cable and shift cable barrels are both secured in the appropriate manner in which they were removed.

7. Reconnect the negative battery cable and the spark plug leads (if disconnected).

Table 1 STANDARD TORQUE VALUES (U.S. STANDARD FASTENERS)

Screw or nut size	in.-lbs.	ft.-lbs.	N•m
6-32	9	–	1.0
8-32	20	–	2.3
10-24	30	–	3.4
10-32	35	–	4.0
	(continued)		

Table 1 STANDARD TORQUE VALUES (U.S. STANDARD FASTENERS) (continued)

Screw or nut size	in.-lbs.	ft.-lbs.	N•m
12-24	45	–	5.1
1/4-20	70	6	7.9
1/4-28	84	7	9.5
5/16-18	160	13	18.1
5/16-24	168	14	19.0
3/8-16	270	23	30.5
3/8-24	300	25	33.9
7/16-14	–	36	48.8
7/16-20	–	40	54.2
1/2-13	–	50	67.8
1/2-20	–	60	81.3

Table 2 STANDARD TORQUE VALUES (METRIC FASTENERS)

Screw or nut size	in.-lbs.	ft.-lbs.	N•m
M5	36	–	4.1
M6	70	6	8.1
M8	156	13	17.6
M10	312	26	35.3
M12	–	35	47.5
M14	–	60	81.3

Index

13

13

75-90 HP AND 65 JET (1994-1995)
REMOTE CONTROL MODELS

BLK = Black
BLU = Blue
BRN = Brown
GRN = Green
PUR = Purple
RED = Red
TAN = Tan
WHT = White
YEL = Yellow

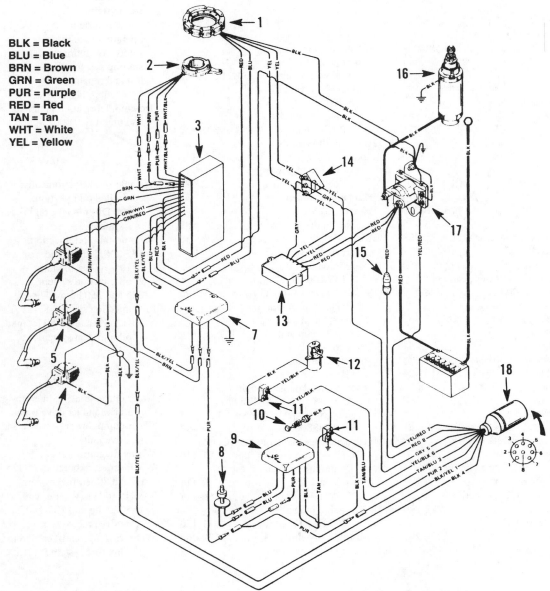

1. Stator assembly
2. Trigger coil
3. Switch box
4. Ignition coil No. 1
5. Ignition coil No. 2
6. Ignition coil No. 3
7. RPM limit module
   (Jet models)
8. Oil level switch
9. Warning module
10. Engine temperature switch
11. Terminal strip
12. Fuel primer valve
13. Rectifier/regulator
14. Terminal block
15. Fuse (20 amp)
16. Starter motor
17. Starter solenoid
18. Main harness connector

75-90 HP AND 65 JET (1996)
REMOTE CONTROL MODELS

BLK = Black
BLU = Blue
BRN = Brown
GRN = Green
PUR = Purple
RED = Red
TAN = Tan
WHT = White
YEL = Yellow

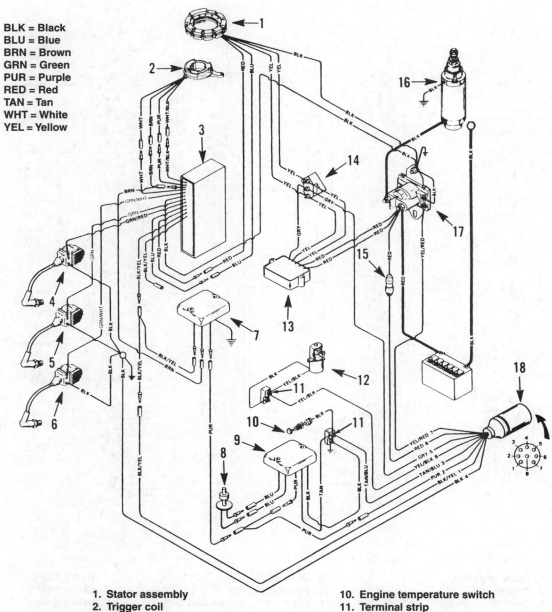

1. Stator assembly
2. Trigger coil
3. Switch box
4. Ignition coil No. 1
5. Ignition coil No. 2
6. Ignition coil No. 3
7. RPM limit module
   (Jet models)
8. Oil level switch
9. Warning module
10. Engine temperature switch
11. Terminal strip
12. Fuel primer valve
13. Rectifier/regulator
14. Terminal block
15. Fuse (20 amp)
16. Starter motor
17. Starter solenoid
18. Main harness connector

14

75-90 HP AND 65 JET (1997 [CDM IGNITION]) REMOTE CONTROL MODELS

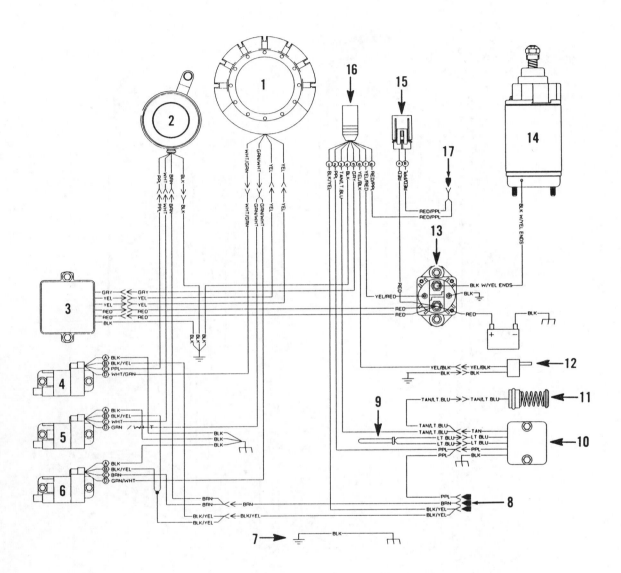

1. Stator assembly
2. Trigger coil
3. Rectifier/regulator
4. CDM No. 1
5. CDM No. 2
6. CDM No. 3
7. Ignition plate ground lead
8. RPM limit module connectors (Jet models)

9. Oil level switch
10. Warning module
11. Engine temperature switch
12. Fuel primer valve
13. Starter solenoid
14. Starter motor
15. Fuse (20 amp)
16. Main harness connector
17. To power trim system

BLK = Black
BLU = Blue
BRN = Brown
GRN = Green
PPL = Purple
RED = Red
TAN = Tan
WHT = White
YEL = Yellow
LT. = Light

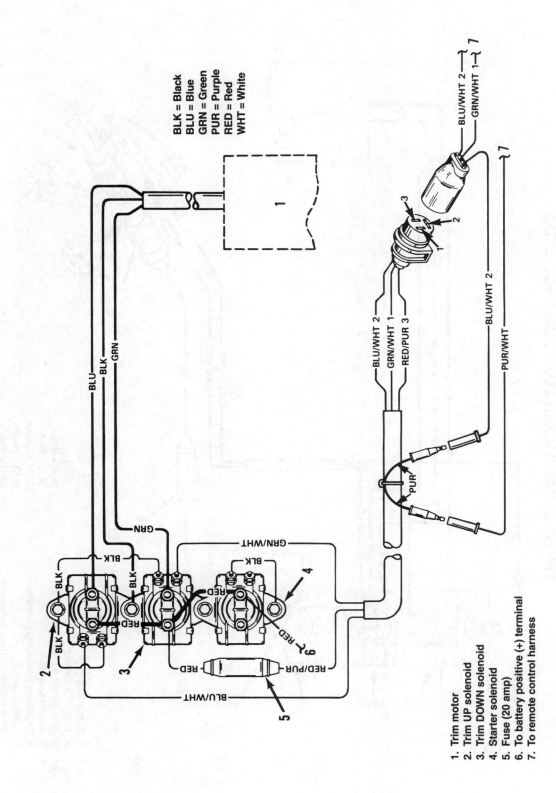

**TRIM/TILT SYSTEM HARNESS 75-90 HP AND 65 JET
(WITH COMMANDER CONTROL BOX)**

BLK = Black
BLU = Blue
GRN = Green
PUR = Purple
RED = Red
WHT = White

1. Trim motor
2. Trim UP solenoid
3. Trim DOWN solenoid
4. Starter solenoid
5. Fuse (20 amp)
6. To battery positive (+) terminal
7. To remote control harness

14

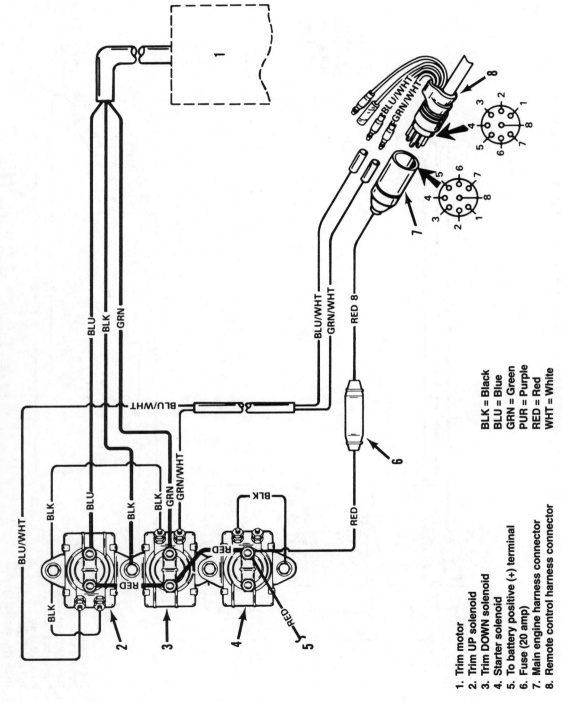

TRIM/TILT SYSTEM HARNESS 75-90 HP AND 65 JET (WITH COMMANDER 2000 CONTROL BOX)

BLK = Black
BLU = Blue
GRN = Green
PUR = Purple
RED = Red
WHT = White

1. Trim motor
2. Trim UP solenoid
3. Trim DOWN solenoid
4. Starter solenoid
5. To battery positive (+) terminal
6. Fuse (20 amp)
7. Main engine harness connector
8. Remote control harness connector

100-125 HP AND 80 JET (1994-1996)
REMOTE CONTROL MODELS

BLK = Black
BLU = Blue
BRN = Brown
GRN = Green
PUR = Purple
RED = Red
TAN = Tan
WHT = White
YEL = Yellow

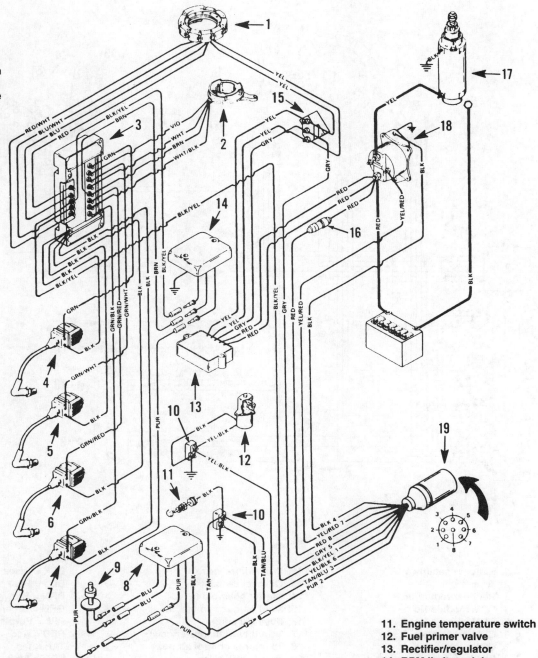

1. Stator assembly
2. Trigger coil
3. Switch box
4. Ignition coil No. 1
5. Ignition coil No. 2
6. Ignition coil No. 3
7. Ignition coil No. 4
8. Warning module
9. Oil level switch
10. Terminal strip
11. Engine temperature switch
12. Fuel primer valve
13. Rectifier/regulator
14. RPM limit module
15. Terminal block
16. Fuse (20 amp)
17. Starter motor
18. Starter solenoid
19. Main harness connector

14

100-125 HP AND 80 JET (1997 [CDM IGNITION]) REMOTE CONTROL MODELS

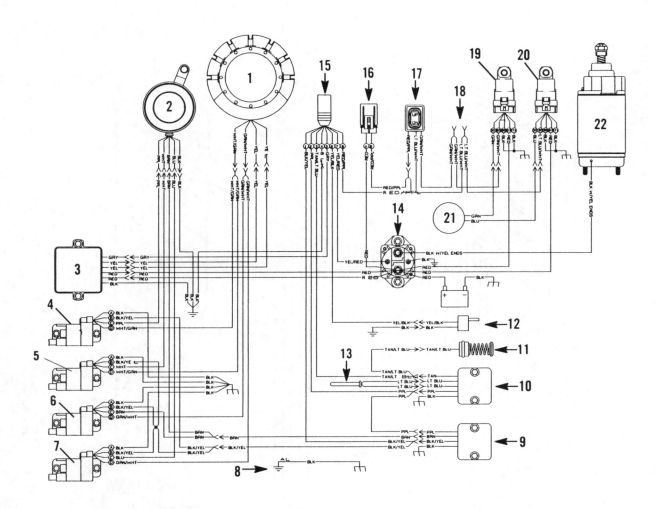

1. Stator assembly
2. Trigger coil
3. Rectifier/regulator
4. CDM module No. 1
5. CDM module No. 2
6. CDM module No. 3
7. CDM module No. 4
8. Ignition plate ground lead
9. RPM limit module
10. Warning module
11. Engine temperature switch

12. Fuel primer valve
13. Oil level switch
14. Starter solenoid
15. Main harness connector
16. Fuse (20 amp)
17. Trim/tilt switch (lower cowl)
18. To remote control harness
19. Trim DOWN relay
20. Trim UP relay
21. Trim motor
22. Starter solenoid

BLK = Black
BLU = Blue
BRN = Brown
GRN = Green
PPL = Purple
RED = Red
TAN = Tan
WHT = White
YEL = Yellow
LT. = Light

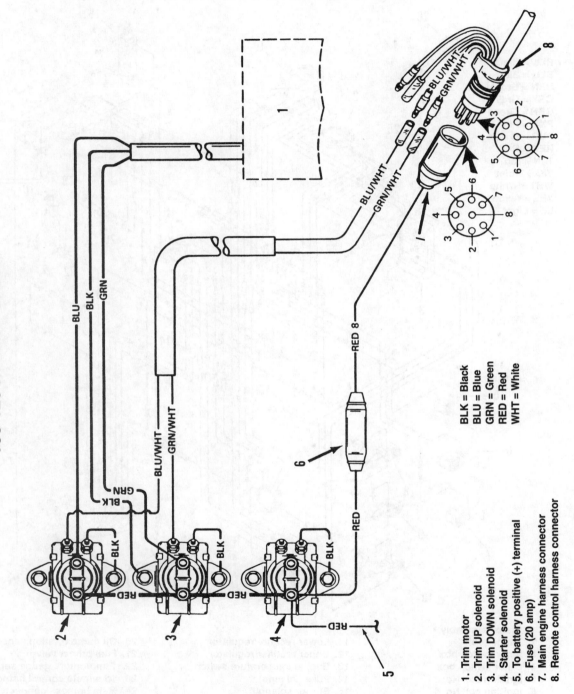

**TRIM/TILT SYSTEM HARNESS
100-125 HP AND 80 JET**

BLK = Black
BLU = Blue
GRN = Green
RED = Red
WHT = White

1. Trim motor
2. Trim UP solenoid
3. Trim DOWN solenoid
4. Starter solenoid
5. To battery positive (+) terminal
6. Fuse (20 amp)
7. Main engine harness connector
8. Remote control harness connector

14

135-200 HP, 150 XR6 AND 150 MAGNUM III
(CARBURETED MODELS)

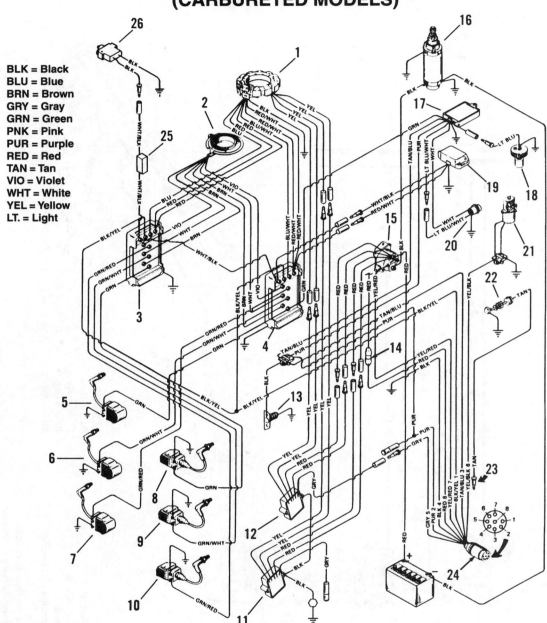

BLK = Black
BLU = Blue
BRN = Brown
GRY = Gray
GRN = Green
PNK = Pink
PUR = Purple
RED = Red
TAN = Tan
VIO = Violet
WHT = White
YEL = Yellow
LT. = Light

1. Stator assembly
2. Trigger coil
3. Inner switch box
4. Outer switch box
5. Ignition coil No. 2
6. Ignition coil No. 4
7. Ignition coil No. 6
8. Ignition coil No. 1
9. Ignition coil No. 3
10. Ignition coil No. 5
11. Lower rectifier/regulator
12. Upper rectifier/regulator
13. Engine temperature switch
14. Fuse (20 amp)
15. Starter solenoid
16. Starter motor
17. Warning module
18. Oil level switch
19. Idle stabilizer module
20. Oil pump rotation sensor
21. Fuel primer valve
22. Temperature gauge sender
23. To remote control harness
24. Main harness connector
25. Resistor (175 hp, XR6 and Magnum III)
26. Shift switch (175 hp, XR6 and Magnum III)

105-140 JET MODELS

BLK = Black
BLU = Blue
BRN = Brown
GRY = Gray
GRN = Green
PNK = Pink
PUR = Purple
RED = Red
TAN = Tan
VIO = Violet
WHT = White
YEL = Yellow
LT. = Light

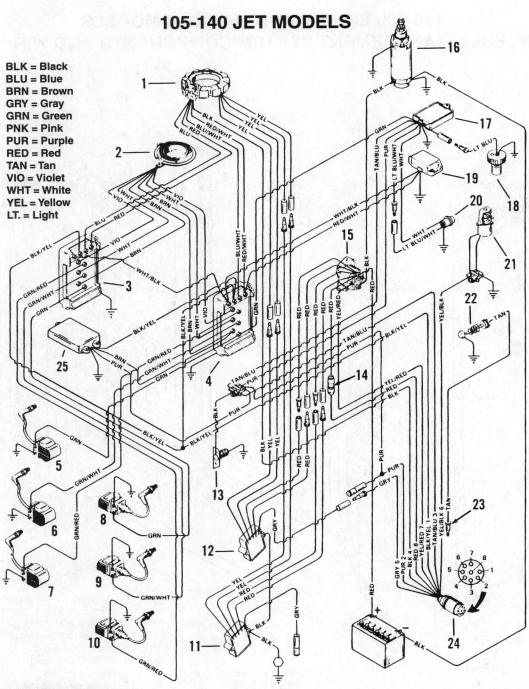

1. Stator assembly
2. Trigger coil
3. Inner switch box
4. Outer switch box
5. Ignition coil No. 2
6. Ignition coil No. 4
7. Ignition coil No. 6
8. Ignition coil No. 1
9. Ignition coil No. 3

10. Ignition coil No. 5
11. Lower rectifier/regulator
12. Upper rectifier/regulator
13. Engine temperature switch
14. Fuse (20 amp)
15. Starter solenoid
16. Starter motor
17. Warning module

18. Oil level switch
19. Idle stabilizer module
20. Oil pump rotation sensor
21. Fuel primer valve
22. Temperature gauge sender
23. To remote control harness
24. Main harness connector
25. RPM limit module

14

150-200 EFI (XRI AND MAGNUM MODELS)
EFI FUEL MANAGEMENT SYSTEM COMPONENTS AND WIRING

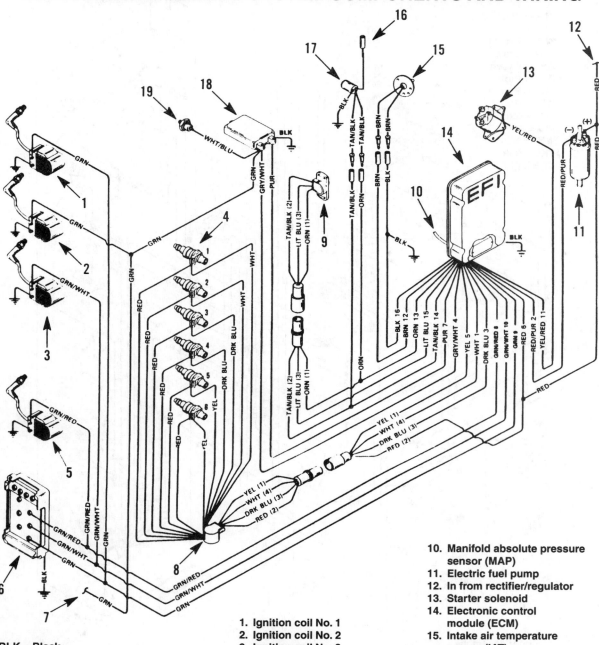

1. Ignition coil No. 1
2. Ignition coil No. 2
3. Ignition coil No. 3
4. Fuel injectors
5. Ignition coil No. 5
6. Inner switch box
7. To outer switch box
8. Injector harness
9. Throttle position sensor (TPS)

10. Manifold absolute pressure sensor (MAP)
11. Electric fuel pump
12. In from rectifier/regulator
13. Starter solenoid
14. Electronic control module (ECM)
15. Intake air temperature sensor (IAT)
16. To temperature gauge
17. Engine coolant temperature sensor (ECT)
18. Detonation module (200 XRI and Magnum models)
19. Detonation (knock) sensor (200 XRI and Magnum models)

BLK = Black
BLU = Blue
BRN = Brown
GRY = Gray
GRN = Green
ORN = Orange
PNK = Pink
PUR = Purple

RED = Red
TAN = Tan
VIO = Violet
WHT = White
YEL = Yellow
LIT = Light
DRK = Dark

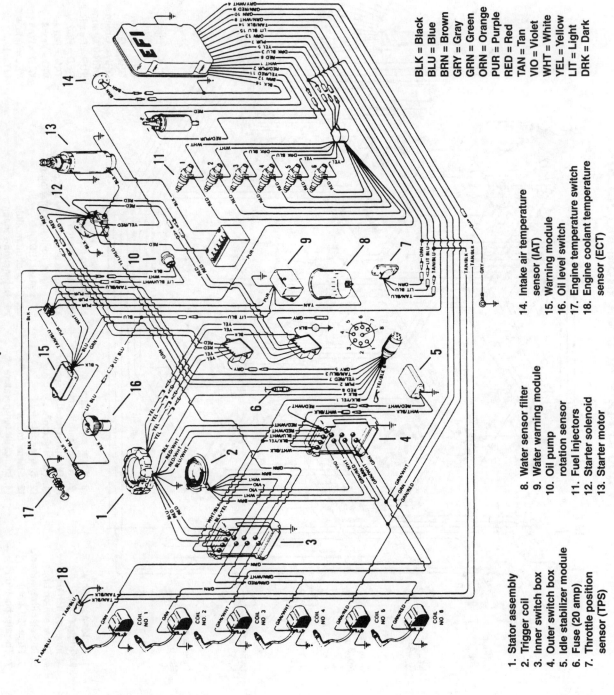

150-175 EFI MODELS (XRI AND MAGNUM MODELS)

BLK = Black
BLU = Blue
BRN = Brown
GRY = Gray
GRN = Green
ORN = Orange
PUR = Purple
RED = Red
TAN = Tan
VIO = Violet
WHT = White
YEL = Yellow
LIT = Light
DRK = Dark

1. Stator assembly
2. Trigger coil
3. Inner switch box
4. Outer switch box
5. Idle stabilizer module
6. Fuse (20 amp)
7. Throttle position sensor (TPS)

8. Water sensor filter
9. Water warning module
10. Oil pump rotation sensor
11. Fuel injectors
12. Starter solenoid
13. Starter motor

14. Intake air temperature sensor (IAT)
15. Warning module
16. Oil level switch
17. Engine temperature switch
18. Engine coolant temperature sensor (ECT)

14

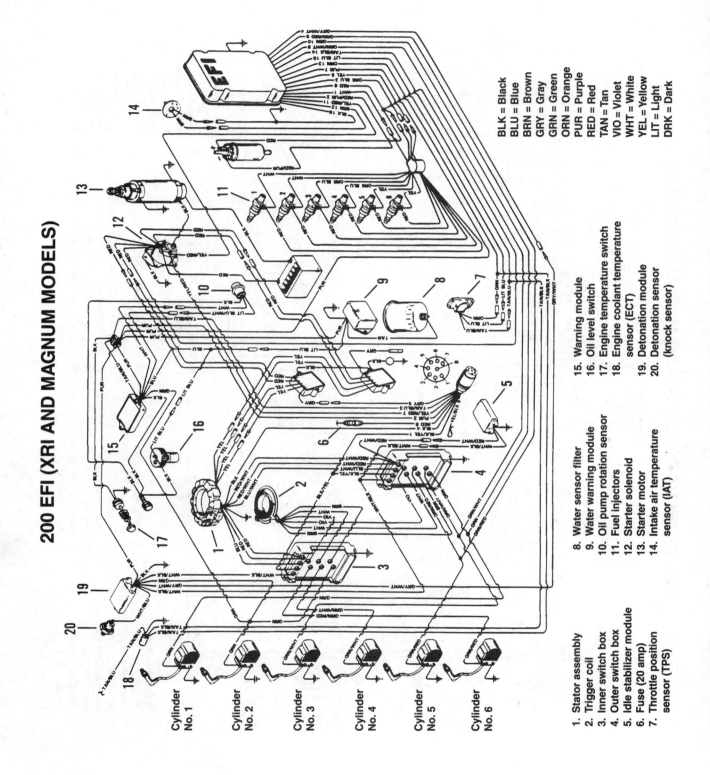

200 EFI (XRI AND MAGNUM MODELS)

BLK = Black
BLU = Blue
BRN = Brown
GRY = Gray
GRN = Green
ORN = Orange
PUR = Purple
RED = Red
TAN = Tan
VIO = Violet
WHT = White
YEL = Yellow
LIT = Light
DRK = Dark

1. Stator assembly
2. Trigger coil
3. Inner switch box
4. Outer switch box
5. Idle stabilizer module
6. Fuse (20 amp)
7. Throttle position sensor (TPS)

8. Water sensor filter
9. Water warning module
10. Oil pump rotation sensor
11. Fuel injectors
12. Starter solenoid
13. Starter motor
14. Intake air temperature sensor (IAT)

15. Warning module
16. Oil level switch
17. Engine temperature switch
18. Engine coolant temperature sensor (ECT)
19. Detonation module
20. Detonation sensor (knock sensor)

Cylinder No. 1
Cylinder No. 2
Cylinder No. 3
Cylinder No. 4
Cylinder No. 5
Cylinder No. 6

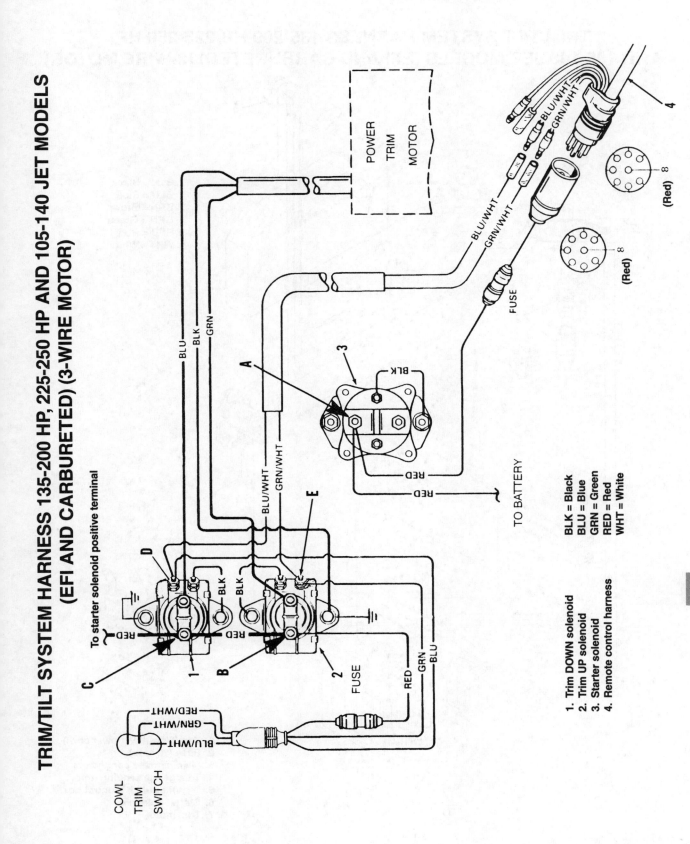

TRIM/TILT SYSTEM HARNESS 135-200 HP, 225-250 HP AND 105-140 JET MODELS (EFI AND CARBURETED) (3-WIRE MOTOR)

POWER TRIM MOTOR

COWL TRIM SWITCH

BLK = Black
BLU = Blue
GRN = Green
RED = Red
WHT = White

1. Trim DOWN solenoid
2. Trim UP solenoid
3. Starter solenoid
4. Remote control harness

14

TRIM/TILT SYSTEM HARNESS 135-200 HP, 225-250 HP AND 105-140 JET MODELS (EFI AND CARBURETED) (2-WIRE MOTOR)

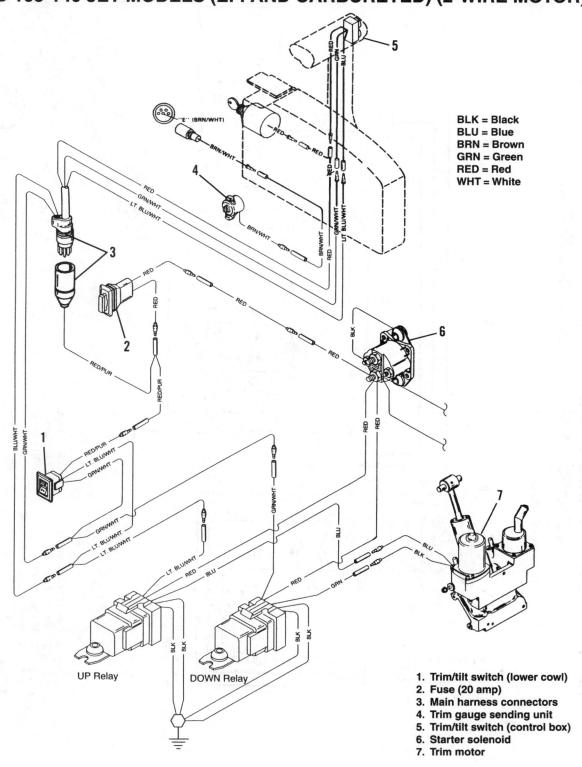

BLK = Black
BLU = Blue
BRN = Brown
GRN = Green
RED = Red
WHT = White

1. Trim/tilt switch (lower cowl)
2. Fuse (20 amp)
3. Main harness connectors
4. Trim gauge sending unit
5. Trim/tilt switch (control box)
6. Starter solenoid
7. Trim motor

225 HP CARBURETED MODELS (1994)

1. Ignition stator
2. Alternator
3. Crankshaft position sensor (CPS)
4. Throttle position sensor (TPS)
5. Engine coolant temperature (ECT) sensor
6. Oil level switch
7. Electronic control module (ECM)
8. Fuel enrichment valve
9. Terminal strip
10. Fuse (20 amp)
11. Trim/tilt switch (lower cowl)
12. To trim/tilt solenoids
13. To remote control harness
14. Main harness connector
15. Starter solenoid
16. Shift interrupt switch
17. Starter motor

BLK = Black
BLU = Blue
BRN = Brown
GRY = Gray
GRN = Green
ORN = Orange
PUR = Purple
RED = Red
TAN = Tan
VIO = Violet
WHT = White
YEL = Yellow
LT. = Light

14

200 DFI (DIRECT FUEL INJECTION) MODELS

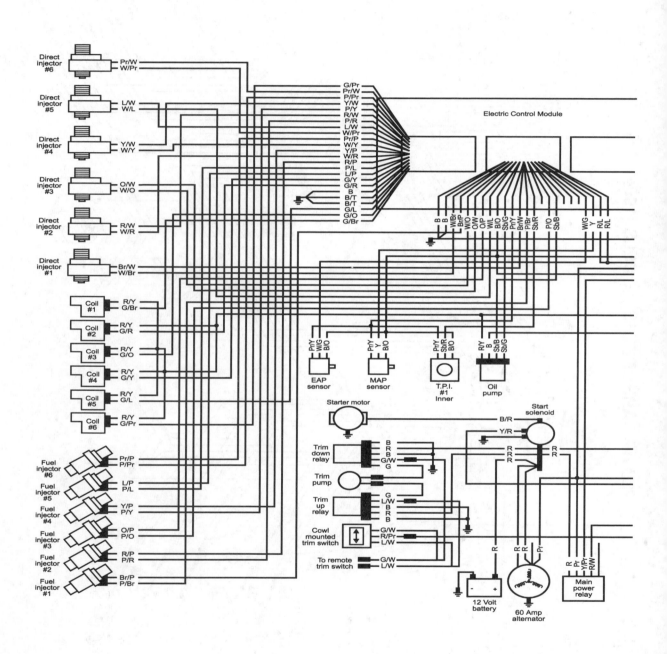

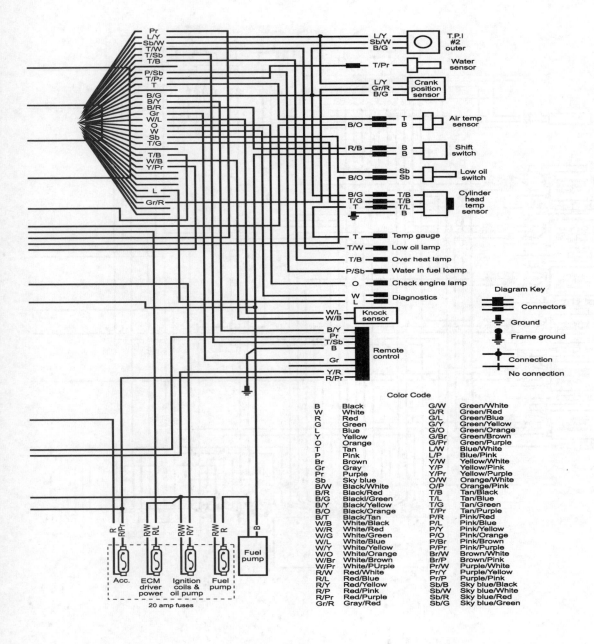

Pr
L/Y
Sb/W
T/W
T/Sb
T/B
P/Sb
T/Pr
T
B/G
B/Y
B/R
Gr
W/L
O
W
Sb
T/G
T/B
W/B
Y/Pr
L
Gr/R

L/Y
Sb/W
B/G — T.P.I #2 outer

T/Pr — Water sensor

L/Y
Gr/R
B/G — Crank position sensor

B/O — T / B — Air temp sensor

R/B — B / B — Shift switch

B/O — Sb / Sb — Low oil switch

B/G — T/B
T/G — T/B
T — T/L
B — Cylinder head temp sensor

T — Temp gauge
T/W — Low oil lamp
T/B — Over heat lamp
P/Sb — Water in fuel loamp
O — Check engine lamp
W — Diagnostics
L

W/L
W/B — Knock sensor

B/Y
Pr
T/Sb
B
Gr
Y/R
R/Pr — Remote control

Diagram Key

Connectors
Ground
Frame ground
Connection
No connection

Color Code

B	Black	G/W	Green/White
W	White	G/R	Green/Red
R	Red	G/L	Green/Blue
G	Green	G/Y	Green/Yellow
L	Blue	G/O	Green/Orange
Y	Yellow	G/Br	Green/Brown
O	Orange	G/Pr	Green/Purple
T	Tan	L/W	Blue/White
P	Pink	L/P	Blue/Pink
Br	Brown	Y/W	Yellow/White
Gr	Gray	Y/P	Yellow/Pink
Pr	Purple	Y/Pr	Yellow/Purple
Sb	Sky blue	O/W	Orange/White
B/W	Black/White	O/P	Orange/Pink
B/R	Black/Red	T/B	Tan/Black
B/G	Blackl/Green	T/L	Tan/Blue
B/Y	Black/Yellow	T/G	Tan/Green
B/O	Black/Orange	T/Pr	Tan/Purple
B/T	Black/Tan	P/R	Pink/Red
W/B	White/Black	P/L	Pink/Blue
W/R	White/Red	P/Y	Pink/Yellow
W/G	White/Green	P/O	Pink/Orange
W/L	White/Blue	P/Br	Pink/Brown
W/Y	White/Yellow	P/Pr	Pink/Purple
W/O	White/Orange	Br/W	Brown/White
W/Br	White/Brown	Br/P	Brown/Pink
W/Pr	White/PUrple	Pr/W	Purple/White
R/W	Red/White	Pr/Y	Purple/Yellow
R/L	Red/Blue	Pr/P	Purple/Pink
R/Y	Red/Yellow	Sb/B	Sky blue/Black
R/P	Red/Pink	Sb/W	Sky blue/White
R/Pr	Red/Purple	Sb/R	Sky blue/Red
Gr/R	Gray/Red	Sb/G	Sky blue/Green

R R/Pr — Acc.
R/W R/L — ECM driver power
R/W R/Y — Ignition coils & oil pump
R/W R — Fuel pump
B — Fuel pump

20 amp fuses

14

225 HP CARBURETED MODELS (1995)

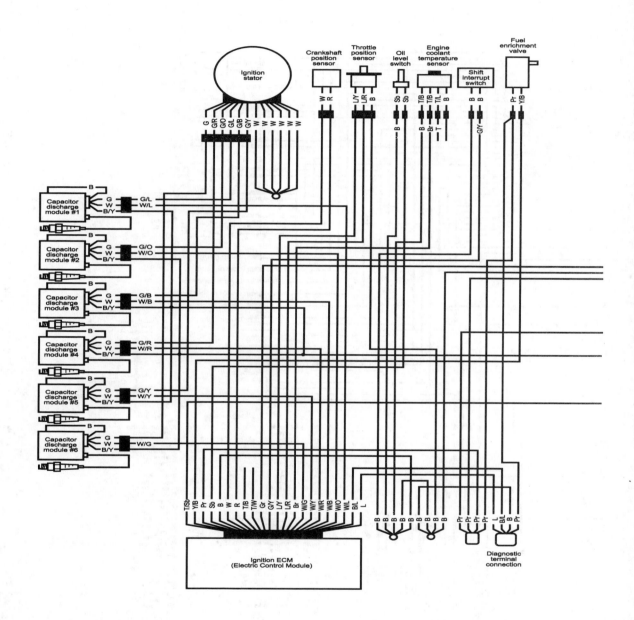

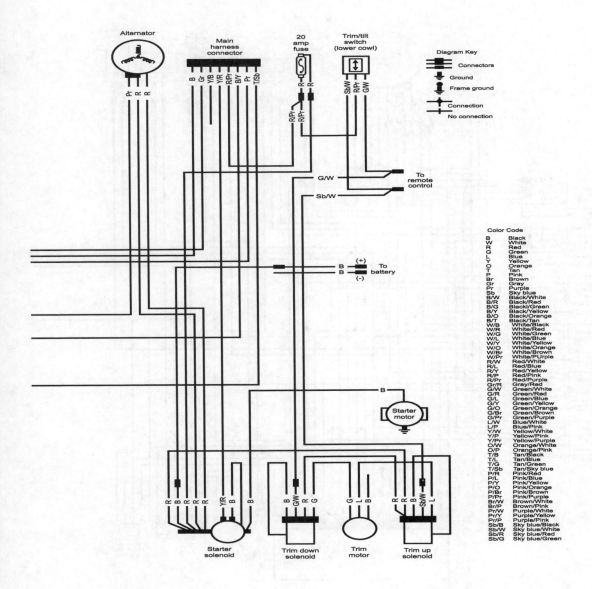

225 HP CARBURETED MODELS (1996-1997)

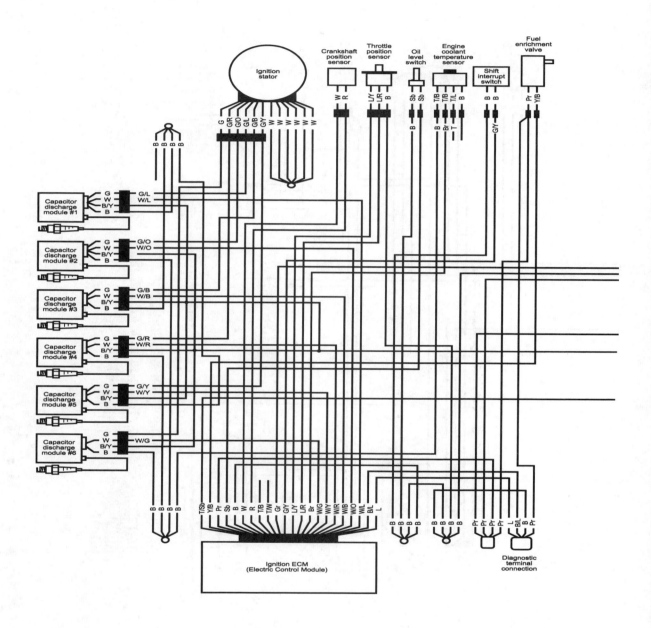

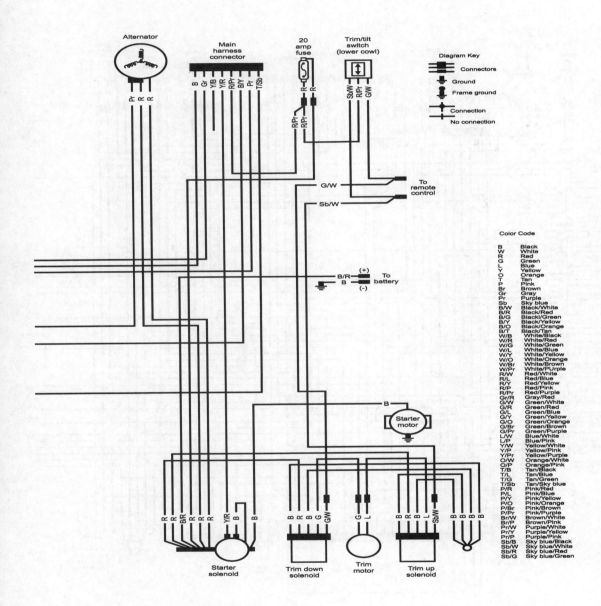

225 HP EFI (ELECTRONIC FUEL INJECTION) MODELS (1995)

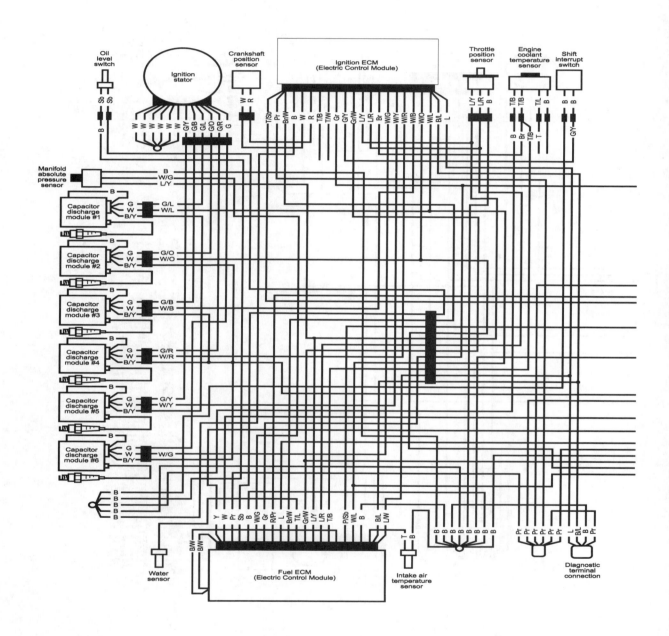

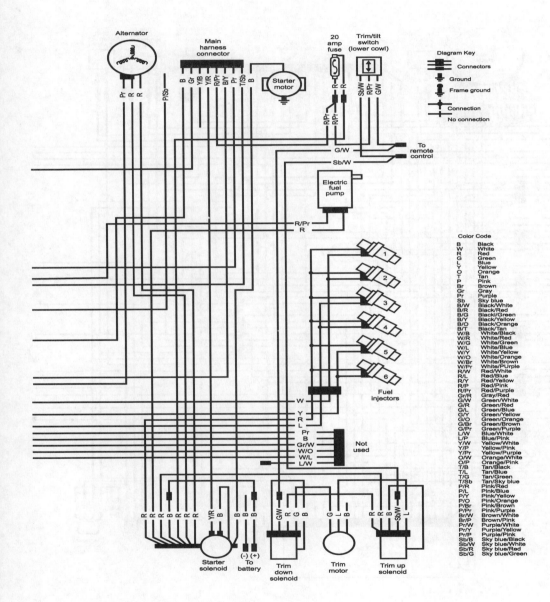

Alternator

Main harness connector

20 amp fuse

Trim/tilt switch (lower cowl)

Diagram Key
- Connectors
- Ground
- Frame ground
- Connection
- No connection

Starter motor

To remote control

Electric fuel pump

Fuel injectors

Not used

Starter solenoid

To battery (-) (+)

Trim down solenoid

Trim motor

Trim up solenoid

Color Code

B	Black
W	White
R	Red
G	Green
L	Blue
Y	Yellow
O	Orange
T	Tan
P	Pink
Br	Brown
Gr	Gray
Pr	Purple
Sb	Sky blue
B/W	Black/White
B/R	Black/Red
B/G	Black/Green
B/Y	Black/Yellow
B/O	Black/Orange
B/T	Black/Tan
W/B	White/Black
W/R	White/Red
W/G	White/Green
W/L	White/Blue
W/Y	White/Yellow
W/O	White/Orange
W/Br	White/Brown
W/Pr	White/PUrple
R/W	Red/White
R/L	Red/Blue
R/Y	Red/Yellow
R/P	Red/Pink
R/Pr	Red/Purple
Gr/R	Gray/Red
G/W	Green/White
G/R	Green/Red
G/L	Green/Blue
G/Y	Green/Yellow
G/O	Green/Orange
G/Br	Green/Brown
G/Pr	Green/Purple
L/W	Blue/White
L/P	Blue/Pink
Y/W	Yellow/White
Y/P	Yellow/Pink
Y/Pr	Yellow/Purple
O/W	Orange/White
O/P	Orange/Pink
T/B	Tan/Black
T/L	Tan/Blue
T/G	Tan/Green
T/Sb	Tan/Sky blue
P/R	Pink/Red
P/L	Pink/Blue
P/Y	Pink/Yellow
P/O	Pink/Orange
P/Br	Pink/Brown
P/Pr	Pink/Purple
Br/W	Brown/White
Br/P	Brown/Pink
Pr/W	Purple/White
Pr/Y	Purple/Yellow
Pr/P	Purple/Pink
Sb/B	Sky blue/Black
Sb/W	Sky blue/White
Sb/R	Sky blue/Red
Sb/G	Sky blue/Green

14

225-250 HP EFI (ELECTRONIC FUEL INJECTION) MODELS (1996-1997)

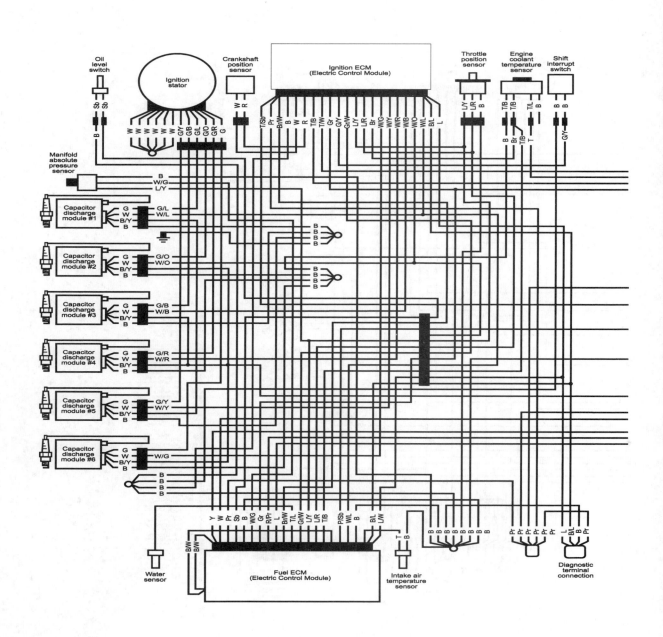

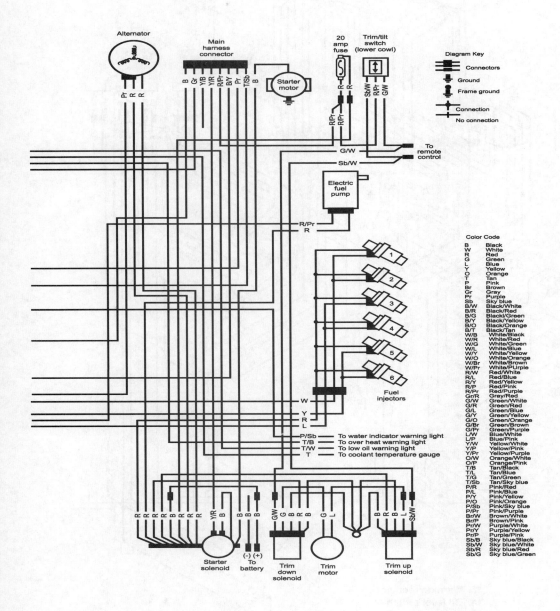

275 HP MODELS

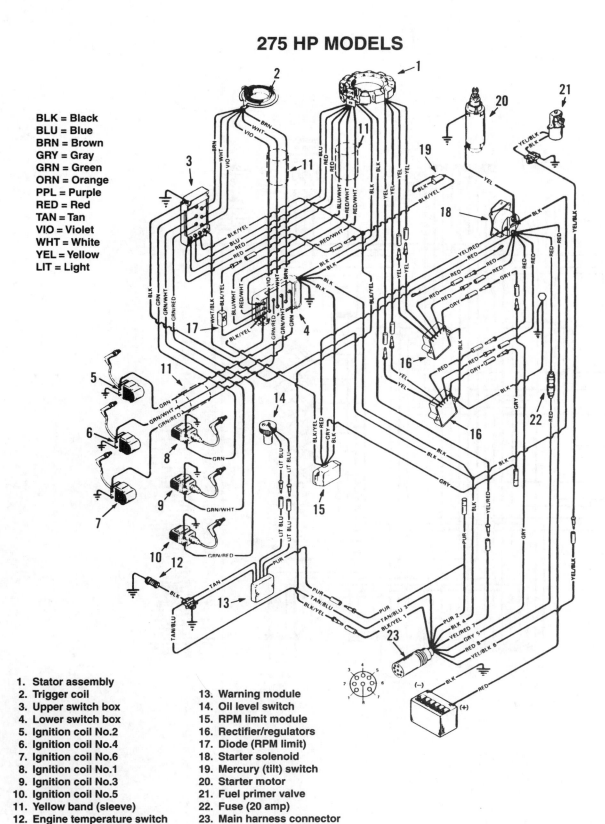

BLK = Black
BLU = Blue
BRN = Brown
GRY = Gray
GRN = Green
ORN = Orange
PPL = Purple
RED = Red
TAN = Tan
VIO = Violet
WHT = White
YEL = Yellow
LIT = Light

1. Stator assembly
2. Trigger coil
3. Upper switch box
4. Lower switch box
5. Ignition coil No.2
6. Ignition coil No.4
7. Ignition coil No.6
8. Ignition coil No.1
9. Ignition coil No.3
10. Ignition coil No.5
11. Yellow band (sleeve)
12. Engine temperature switch
13. Warning module
14. Oil level switch
15. RPM limit module
16. Rectifier/regulators
17. Diode (RPM limit)
18. Starter solenoid
19. Mercury (tilt) switch
20. Starter motor
21. Fuel primer valve
22. Fuse (20 amp)
23. Main harness connector

TRIM/TILT SYSTEM HARNESS 275 HP MODELS

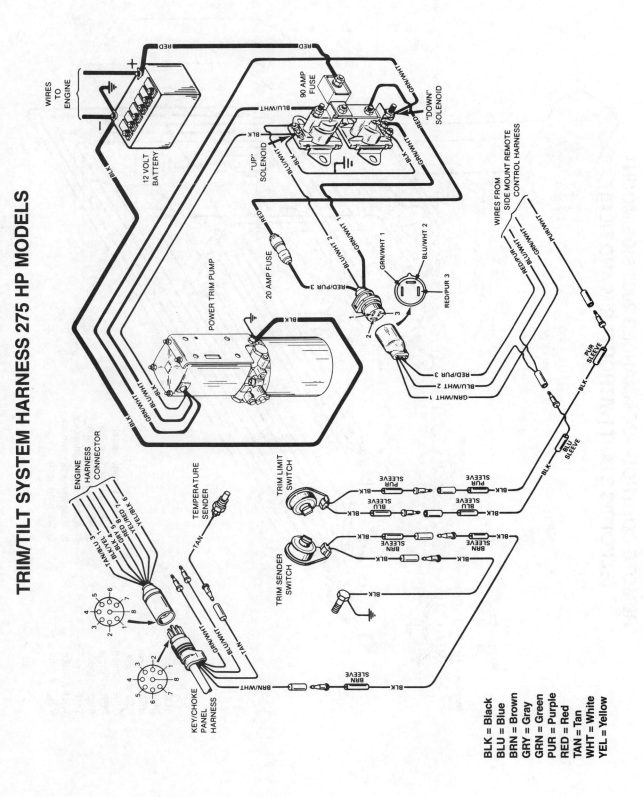

BLK = Black
BLU = Blue
BRN = Brown
GRY = Gray
GRN = Green
PUR = Purple
RED = Red
TAN = Tan
WHT = White
YEL = Yellow

14

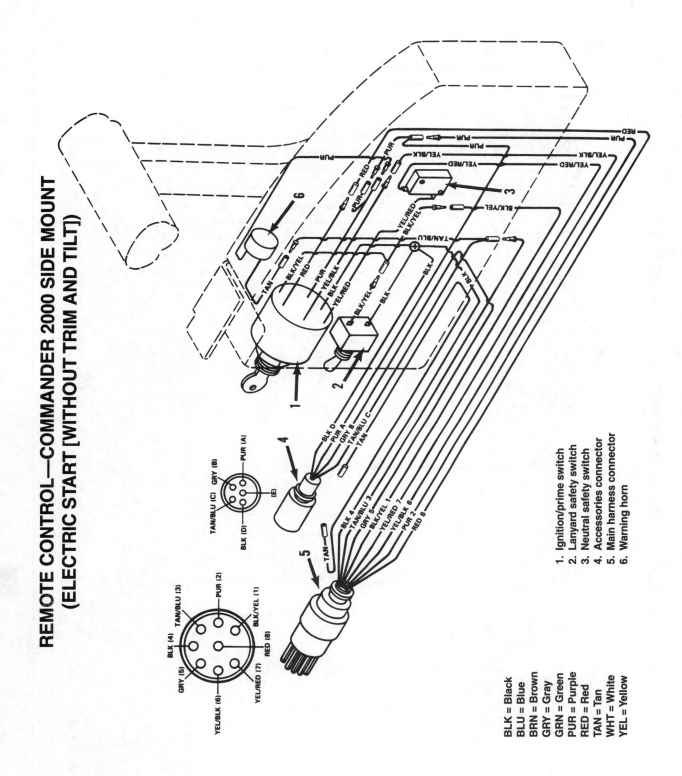

REMOTE CONTROL—COMMANDER 2000 SIDE MOUNT (ELECTRIC START [WITHOUT TRIM AND TILT])

1. Ignition/prime switch
2. Lanyard safety switch
3. Neutral safety switch
4. Accessories connector
5. Main harness connector
6. Warning horn

BLK = Black
BLU = Blue
BRN = Brown
GRY = Gray
GRN = Green
PUR = Purple
RED = Red
TAN = Tan
WHT = White
YEL = Yellow

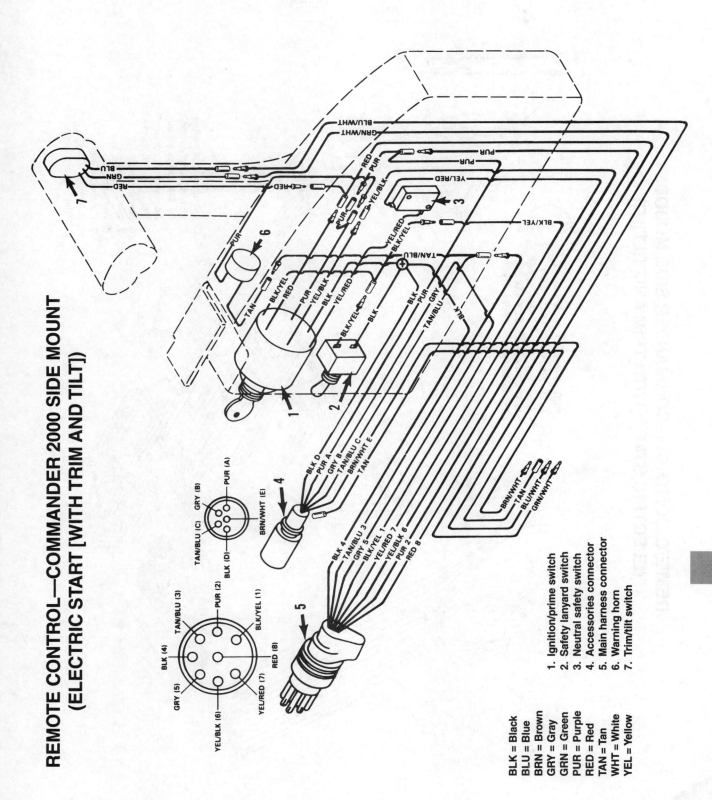

REMOTE CONTROL—COMMANDER 2000 SIDE MOUNT (ELECTRIC START [WITH TRIM AND TILT])

1. Ignition/prime switch
2. Safety lanyard switch
3. Neutral safety switch
4. Accessories connector
5. Main harness connector
6. Warning horn
7. Trim/tilt switch

BLK = Black
BLU = Blue
BRN = Brown
GRY = Gray
GRN = Green
PUR = Purple
RED = Red
TAN = Tan
WHT = White
YEL = Yellow

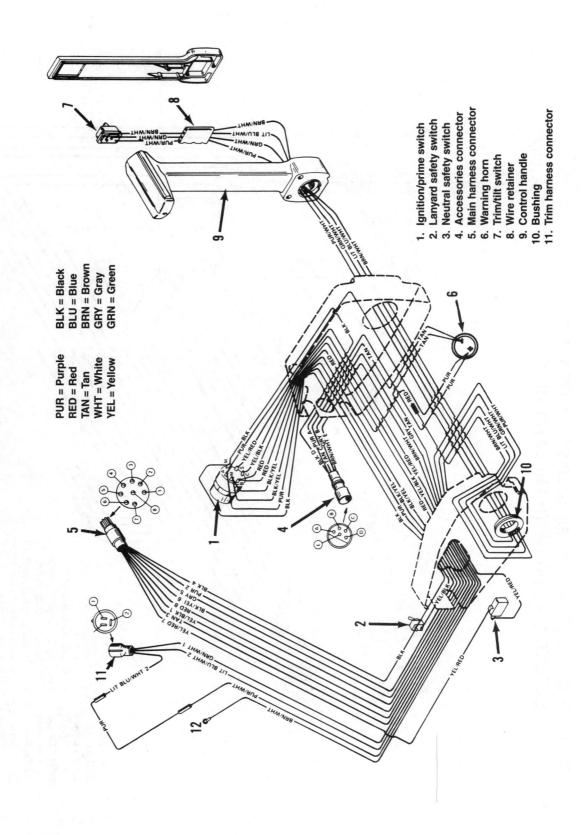

REMOTE CONTROL—COMMANDER SIDE MOUNT (ELECTRIC START [WITH TRIM AND TILT])

PUR = Purple   BLK = Black
RED = Red   BLU = Blue
TAN = Tan   BRN = Brown
WHT = White   GRY = Gray
YEL = Yellow   GRN = Green

1. Ignition/prime switch
2. Lanyard safety switch
3. Neutral safety switch
4. Accessories connector
5. Main harness connector
6. Warning horn
7. Trim/tilt switch
8. Wire retainer
9. Control handle
10. Bushing
11. Trim harness connector

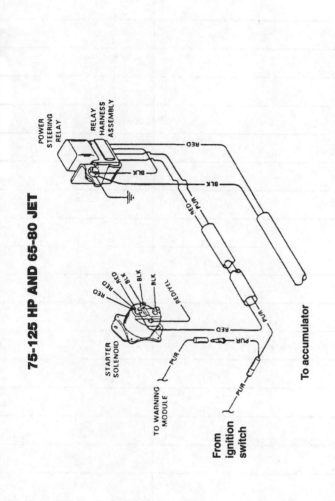

75-125 HP AND 65-80 JET

POWER STEERING RELAY

RELAY HARNESS ASSEMBLY

RED

BLK

PUR/RED

STARTER SOLENOID

RED
RED
BLK
BLK
RED/YEL

RED

PUR

PUR

TO WARNING MODULE

PUR

From ignition switch

To accumulator

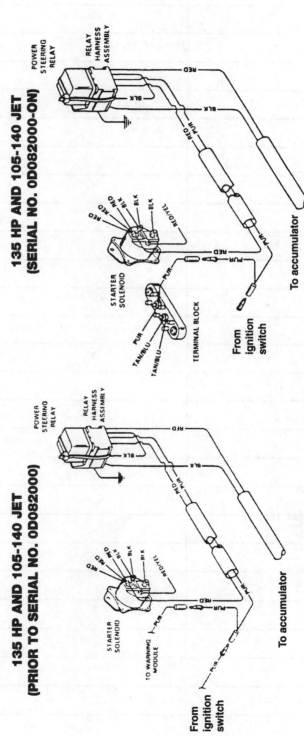

135 HP AND 105-140 JET (SERIAL NO. 0D082000-ON)

POWER STEERING RELAY

RELAY HARNESS ASSEMBLY

RED

BLK

RED
PUR

STARTER SOLENOID

RED
RED
BLK
BLK
RED/YEL

RED

PUR

PUR

PUR

PUR

TAN/BLU

TAN/BLU

TERMINAL BLOCK

From ignition switch

To accumulator

135 HP AND 105-140 JET (PRIOR TO SERIAL NO. 0D082000)

POWER STEERING RELAY

RELAY HARNESS ASSEMBLY

RED

BLK

RED
PUR

STARTER SOLENOID

RED
RED
BLK
BLK
RED/YEL

RED

PUR

PUR

PUR

TO WARNING MODULE

From ignition switch

To accumulator

14

MANUAL
PAGE 687 RELEASE

MAINTENANCE LOG

Date	Maintenance performed	Engine hours
BLEEDING 683		
WIRING 652 (RED)		
FUSE 30 AMP		
WIRING HARNESS 790		